increasingly taking action on the sustainable development goals, and how they can do so. It is eloquently written, yet academically rigorous."

Prof. Klaus Schwab, *President and founder of the World Economic Forum*

"This book is a must read for anyone who craves for inspiration on how to turn companies into a force for positive change. Reaching the Sustainable Development Goals is a matter of commitment, of owning a strong moral compass and of 21st Century Leadership. And books like this is fuel for these visionary leadership skills. But the book is more than that. It brings clarity in the alphabet soup. And, more importantly, it takes key international concepts, standards (such as my own organization the Global Reporting Initiative and the GRI standards) and tools in the arena of sustainability, responsible business and ESG, analyses them critically and scientifically in their potential and shortcomings and then boldly and innovatively improves, enriches and even transforms them into a next level. Take the example of 'materiality', which is turned into the concept of 'reversed materiality', to capture a more forward-looking angle. This is a book that deserves a spot on your desk where you can read it time and again. You will find yourself turning to it when you need to revisit a certain idea. It will help all of us sharpen our mind, and focus on what needs to be done by each of us to build a better world through the Sustainable Development Goals."

Teresa C. Fogelberg, *Former Climate Change Director, Women's Rights Director, Research Director at the Netherlands Ministries of Foreign Affairs and Environment, Co-Founder and Deputy Chief Executive of the Global Reporting Initiative*

"In Africa, we place a high premium on the private sector as a critical engine of growth for the continent. This outstanding book offers excellent insight into how the corporate world can impact positive change – change for the Africa we want and more broadly at a global level, as we strive to bring the SDGs to fruition."

Dr. Akinwumi Adesina, *President African Development Bank and World Food Prize Laureate*

"The Decade of Action needs serious acceleration. The intentions are still there, but the realization requires sophisticated approaches of governments, civil society and companies alike. The frameworks offered by this all-encompassing book provide the badly needed road map for the coming years. A truly amazing achievement!"

Prof. dr. Jan Peter Balkenende, *former Prime Minister of the Netherlands, chair Dutch Sustainable Growth Coalition*

"Sustainability is easy to talk about, but we all know it is much harder to deliver. As this comprehensive guide makes clear, addressing our most pressing societal and environmental issues will require deep organizational transformation. That change must be led from the top. CEOs and boards now face an unprecedented opportunity to embed sustainability across strategy, operations, and leadership cultures. We welcome this timely roadmap to making this transition."

Constantine Alexandrakis, *CEO Russell Reynolds Associates*

"*Principles of Sustainable Business* of Rob van Tulder and Eveline van Mil describes in depth why and how businesses should and can be purposeful by creating economic, societal and ecological value at the same time. The authors recognize the importance of how frontrunner companies in the past have been able to break through a number of the critical tipping points to uplift sustainability and contribute to systems change. Sustainability should be anchored in the core of the business and the SDGs could provide a very relevant framework for companies to define where to contribute. The frameworks developed in this book make it possible for (aspiring) leaders to 'walk the talk'."

Feike Sijbesma, *former CEO DSM, Chair Supervisory Board Philips, member Supervisory Board Unilever*

"*Principles of Sustainable Business* stands out for its breadth, mastery of detail, and its bridging of scientific evidence with actionable tools for making positive real-world impact. The book explains why companies are critical for attaining the SDGs and outlines how they can contribute to these global goals. At Robeco we are dedicated to this ambition: we are a research-driven investment firm that is pioneering SDG investment strategies in fixed income and listed equity. This relevant book confirms and inspires our SDG-investing journey."

Karin van Baardwijk, *CEO Robeco*

"There is no way to keep climate change from surpassing the critical 1.5 degrees Celsius level without the strong engagement of the private sector. Delivering fully on the Paris Agreement and the SDGs is in fact a pipe dream absent the active collaboration of business. This insightful book provides a valuable guide to strategic investment decisions that align with core international priorities in sustainability that can benefit us all."

President Mohamed Nasheed, *Speaker of the Maldives People's Majlis and founding Chair of the Climate Vulnerable Forum*

"The scientific community has argued for a long time that the transformation to sustainable business is necessary for the world to have a chance of delivering the SDGs within a safe operating space on Earth. Rob van Tulder and Eveline van Mil reinforce the urgency of solving the planetary crisis we face, while adding a crucial additional dimension – the new narrative for the future; that sustainable business is not only the path to planetary responsibility, it is also the path to prosperity and equity, i.e., it is not only our common future on Earth that is at stake, it is also a choice between modernity and regress."

Prof. dr. Johan Rockström, *Director of the Potsdam Institute for Climate Impact Research and Professor at the Institute of Earth and Environmental Science at Potsdam University*

"This book speaks to the new world of work. The sustainable future that we all want and the resilience that must be developed by businesses to make it possible for us to arrive at a better quality of life for all. Excellent insights on three broad sets of principles: systemic, societal and dynamic as well as strategic and operational."

Douglas Opio, *Executive Director, Federation of Uganda Employers (FUE)*

"*Principles of Sustainable Business* presents the clear and defining frameworks needed in order to turn our social, ecological and climate problems into business opportunities. Translating the SDG agenda into pro-active business models and cross-sectoral partnership strategies will help business leaders bridge the gap between intention and realization."

Paul Hawken, *creator, author, editor of* 'Drawdown', 'Natural Capitalism', 'The Ecology of Commerce', *and* 'Re-Generation. Ending the climate crisis in one generation'

"From its inception in the form of the 'Millennium Declaration' at the change of the millennium, to the status of the SDGs, and in the midst of the Covid pandemic the world is struggling through different and difficult challenges. Rules, techniques, approaches, and past and newly created systems are simply insufficient to address the complexity of the challenge.

This book is a brave attempt to break the conundrum by elevating our mindset to address it from the 'Principles' level, providing well thought out ideas at the macro, meso and micro level of analysis and action steps. The SDGs tagline: Global Goals National Targets, and its 232 indicators is just a start to appreciate the complexity across the wide spectrum of developments that the world is living in. With the business and corporate world playing a major role in both the economic development and management knowledge fronts, if we are serious about hitting the goals, this book is a must read to elevate our approaches beyond strategy and policy. After all, strategy may change, Principles remain."

Prof. Kuntoro Mangkusubroto, *Head of President of Indonesia's Delivery Unit (2010–2014), and co-founder of School of Business and Management – Institut Teknologi Bandung (SBM-ITB)*

"The 2030 Sustainable Development Agenda, and the 17 SDGs that underpin it, recognize that the natural world and its life-giving services must be urgently protected if we are to fulfil the needs of nine billion people by 2050. The SDGs are premised on the notion that we cannot solve problems in isolation. Protecting these ecosystems will require strong institutions, governance and cooperation from the local to the international level (SDGs 16 and 17). Nature-based Solutions (NbS) are thereby increasingly recognized as a key part of the response to the climate crisis by governments, businesses and communities. It is crucial that these interventions are credible, measurable and inclusive. *Principles of Sustainable Business* fills the intellectual and practical gap for private organizations willing to work on Nature-based approaches in a profound, fundamental as well as thought-provoking manner. For public organizations and communities, the book provides relevant tools, resources and (cross-sector) partnering techniques to help companies move beyond a reactive to a proactive approach in support of Nature-based Solutions."

Angela Andrade, *Chair, IUCN Commission on Ecosystem Management and IUCN's Global Standard for Nature-based Solutions*

"*Principles of Sustainable Business* is a milestone for all executives, academics and students keen to dwell deeper into the SDGs. The book aptly shows the extreme importance of purpose-driven organizations. We like the solid treatment of the opportunities and threats surrounding the 'hybridization' of many organizations that try to combine profits and societal purpose, not as a compromise but as an innovative novel business model that presents a resilient approach to many of today's sustainability challenges. We are, of course, thrilled to see the SDG Action Manager being mentioned as one of the practical tools that can be used by large and small companies to implement the SDGs."

Marcello Palazzi and Leen Zevenbergen, *Co-founders, B Lab Europe*

"This book is essential reading for anyone partnering in or with the corporate sector. The authors are clear – collaboration across and beyond the usual boundaries is fundamental to sustainable and transformative development. Partnering is not only enshrined in SDG 17 – Partnerships for the Goals – but forms the basis of the collaborative approach of all SDGs: People, Planet, Prosperity, Peace and Partnering. The question is no longer 'why?' but 'how?' Those involved in initiating, nurturing and supporting the partnering process have a subtle but vital task to assist partners in navigating what is complicated and penetrating to the heart of what is complex. The concepts so thoroughly articulated here give those in the brokering role the solid ground on which to build their work."

Ros Tennyson, *Founder & Strategic Advisor, Partnership Brokers Association*

"This innovative, state-of-the-art book approaches the SDGs as both wicked problems and wicked opportunities. Its complexity-based approach will challenge leaders (and future leaders) to think and act in new ways to transform their organizations to negotiate the VUCA world that the authors well document."

Sandra Waddock, *Galligan Chair of Strategy, Carroll School Scholar of Corporate Responsibility, Professor of Management, Boston College*

"This is a unique and outstanding textbook and a practitioner treasure. It provides a clear understanding of the Sustainable Development Goals and their relevance to business. It offers insightful, distinctive, and constructive guidance on how to achieve more societally impactful sustainability strategies and operations, including essential cross-sector partnering. The book is rigorous and highly readable. Each chapter starts with guiding Principles and ends with crisp takeaways. Supplemental Web-related sources provide additional resources to deepen and broaden the learning. A timely and valuable contribution."

James E. Austin, *Eliot I. Snider and Family Professor of Business Administration, Emeritus, Co-Founder Social Enterprise Initiative, Harvard Business School*

"FLAME University's core values include ecological balance and an inclusive society, which implies that we often challenge what is known and believed about higher education. For this aim we are collaborating with the Wage Indicator Foundation to learn how students can engage in action research, blended learning and investigative journalism by collecting robust data on Living Wages around the world. *Principles of Sustainable Business*, not only supports us in this effort, but presents the scientific basis to found our research and teaching in the broader agenda of the Sustainable Development Goals. A must-apply approach for all universities."

Dr. Santosh Kumar Kudtarkar, *Dean, Faculty of Liberal Education, FLAME University, India*

"The Sustainable Development Goals (SDGs) are 'wicked problems' (systemic, ambiguous, complex and conflictual problems), where politics trumps evidence, and solutions are never first best or permanent. Wicked problems cannot be solved, only managed or resolved over and over again. However, as Van Tulder and Van Mil argue, the SDGs are not only wicked problems but also provide wicked opportunities for firms that want to become sustainable businesses that add value to society. The core question that motivates the book is how can companies become sustainable businesses? The answer provided by the authors is a principles-based road map for corporate action on the SDGs, organized around three levels of analysis: systemic, societal and dynamic, and strategic and operational principles. Drawing on multiple frameworks, examples and illustrations, Principles of Sustainable Development pulls together the newest thinking in academia, consulting, and government policymaking. The book is a 'one stop shop' – that rare book which provides an over-arching, principle-based approach to understanding sustainable business in the 21st century. Everyone – from instructors looking for a textbook for their course on the SDGs to business executives who want to better link their CSR strategies to the SDGs to policy makers hoping to attract foreign multinationals that will foster sustainable development – will find what they are looking for here. *Principles of Sustainable Business* is a 'must read' for students, corporate executives, and policymakers who want to think intelligently and effectively about the SDGs and how firms can and should develop strategies that are SDG relevant."

Lorraine Eden, *Professor Emerita of Management and Research Professor of Law, Texas A&M University, 2020–2023 Dean of Academy of International Business (AIB) Fellows*

"In a global economy that can only be guided by principles rather than rules, multinational enterprises face many challenges to compete while at the same time sustaining and gaining a license to operate. It is important that companies subscribe to the Sustainable Development Goals as a set of unifying principles and get the frameworks and tools to 'walk the talk'. Dealing with the SDGs has not only been a challenge for firms, but also for International Business (IB) scholars around the world: how can we make sure that companies become a 'force for positive change'. This groundbreaking book by highly acclaimed IB professor Rob van Tulder and his co-author Eveline van Mil provides the intellectual foundation for corporations to base their contributions to the SDGs on intentions and solid academic knowledge to change preferences into realizations. And the teaching material will be very helpful in academia."

Maria Tereza Fleury, *President of the Academy of International Business (AIB), Full Professor at Fundação Getulio Vargas (FGV) and the University of São Paulo*

"*Principles of Sustainable Business* is a gift to the world – and not a moment too soon. If we humans are to survive and thrive into the distant future, we must embrace the SDGs and see them realized in practice. But how? Rob van Tulder and Eveline van Mil provide just the kind of cross-level, cross-sector, substantive and process-oriented approach the world needs at this crucial time. They imagine why and how key actors, and especially businesses, might achieve an idea embodied in an English word that dates from the 15th century – commonwealth – which meant common well-being. These authors show us how well-being can become far more common and far more long lasting."

John M. Bryson, *McKnight Presidential Professor Emeritus, Hubert H. Humphrey School of Public Affairs, University of Minnesota*

"*Principles of Sustainable Business* is extremely valuable for its advocacy and operationalization of a paradigm shift from maximizing shareholder wealth to generating additional societal value by contributing to the achievement of the SDGs. It surfaces the challenges businesses face in an uncertain and disruptive world and provides concrete cases from the literature and the authors' intimate knowledge of sustainable business practices on the ground. The authors' discussion of resilience is a convenient handle for unpredictable situations. At the same time, the chapter on collaboration underscores the importance of carving spaces for cross-sector partnerships as a means to address complex and seemingly insurmountable challenges."

Maria Cynthia Rose Banzon-Bautista, Ph.D., *Vice President for Academic Affairs, University of the Philippines*

PRINCIPLES OF SUSTAINABLE BUSINESS

The basic function of companies is to add value to society. Profits are a means to an end, not an end in itself. The ability of companies to innovate, scale and invest provides them with a powerful base for positive change. But companies are also criticized for not contributing sufficiently to society's grand challenges. An increasingly **VUCA (Volatile, Uncertain, Complex and Ambiguous) world** creates serious governance gaps that not only require new ways of regulation, but also new ways of doing business. Can companies effectively contribute to sustainable development and confront society's systemic challenges?

Arguably the most important frame to drive this ambition was introduced and unanimously adopted in 2015: the **Sustainable Development Goals (SDGs)**. The SDG-agenda not only defines a holistic set of global goals and targets, but also foundational principles to guide meaningful action to their achievement by 2030. Multinational companies have signed up to the SDGs as the world's long-term business plan. Realizing the SDGs provides a yearly $12 trillion investment and growth opportunity, while creating hundreds of millions of jobs in the process. But **progress is too slow** – witnessing society's inability to deal with pressing human, ecological, economic and health crises – whilst the vast potential for societal value creation remains underutilized. This book provides a timely account of the systemic, strategic and operational challenges that need to be addressed to enhance the effectiveness of corporate involvement in society, by using the SDGs as leading principles-based framework for actionable, powerful and transformative change.

Principles of Sustainable Business is written for graduate and postgraduate (executive) students, policymakers and business professionals who want to understand the complex challenges of global sustainability. It shows how companies can design and implement SDG-relevant strategies at three levels: the macro level, to assess whether the SDGs present **wicked problems** or **opportunities**; the micro level, to develop and operationalize innovative **business models,** design new **business cases** and navigate organizational **transition trajectories**; and the meso level, to develop fit-for-purpose **cross-sector partnering strategies**. *Principles of Sustainable Business* presents innovative tools embedded in a coherent sequence of analytical frameworks that can be applied in courses for students, be put into practice by business professionals and used by action researchers to help companies contribute to the **Decade of Action.**

Rob van Tulder is full professor of International Business at RSM Erasmus University, co-founder of the Department of Business-Society Management (one of the world's leading capacity groups on teaching and research in sustainable business). He is academic director of the Partnerships Resource Centre, acclaimed author of more than 20 books on Sustainable Development and Multinational Enterprises, and advisor to many companies, governments, international organizations and NGOs.

Eveline van Mil is strategic advisor to (semi-)public, private and non-profit organizations on societal interface management. Her practical experience and research projects range from 'wicked problems', societal governance, transition theory and issue and stakeholder management to the 'resource curse', sustainable production and consumption, and regulation of controversial sectors.

THE PRINCIPLES FOR RESPONSIBLE MANAGEMENT EDUCATION SERIES

Since the inception of the UN-supported Principles for Responsible Management Education (PRME) in 2007, there has been increased debate over how to adapt management education to best meet the demands of the 21st-century business environment. While consensus has been reached by the majority of globally focused management education institutions that sustainability must be incorporated into management education curricula, the relevant question is no longer why management education should change, but how.

Volumes within the Routledge/PRME book series aim to cultivate and inspire actively engaged participants by offering practical examples and case studies to support the implementation of the Six Principles of Responsible Management Education. Books in the series aim to enable participants to transition from a global learning community to an action community.

Books in the series:

Unmasking Irresponsible Leadership: Curriculum Development in 21st Century Management Education
By Lola-Peach Martins and Maria Lazzarin

Struggles and Successes in the Pursuit of Sustainable Development
Edited by Tay Keong Tan, Milenko Gúdic, and Patricia M. Flynn

The Sustainability Mindset Principles: A Guide to Develop a Mindset for a Better World
Isabel Rimanoczy

Business Transformation for a Sustainable Future
Edited by Samuel Petros Sebhatu, Bo Enquist and Bo Edvardsson

Revolutionizing Sustainability Education: Stories and Tools of Mindset Transformation
Edited by Ekaterina Ivanova and Isabel Rimanoczy

Responsible Management Education: The PRME Global Movement
Edited by Mette Morsing

Principles of Sustainable Business: Frameworks for Corporate Action on the SDGs
Rob van Tulder and Eveline van Mil

PRINCIPLES OF SUSTAINABLE BUSINESS
Frameworks for Corporate Action on the SDGs

Rob van Tulder and Eveline van Mil

Routledge
Taylor & Francis Group

LONDON AND NEW YORK

Cover image: Getty Images / Grant Faint

First published 2023
by Routledge
4 Park Square, Milton Park, Abingdon, Oxon OX14 4RN

and by Routledge
605 Third Avenue, New York, NY 10158

Routledge is an imprint of the Taylor & Francis Group, an informa business

British Library Cataloguing-in-Publication Data
A catalogue record for this book is available from the British Library

Library of Congress Cataloging-in-Publication Data
A catalog record has been requested for this book

ISBN: 978-0-367-56558-9 (hbk)
ISBN: 978-0-367-56559-6 (pbk)
ISBN: 978-1-003-09835-5 (ebk)

DOI: 10.4324/9781003098355

Typeset in Berthold Akzidenz Grotesk
by Apex CoVantage, LLC

This book is printed on FSC or PEFC sustainable papers.

CONTENTS

CONTENTS

FIGURES

TABLES

BOXES

TOOLS

- Scoreboard #1 Assessing levels of complexity and wickedness (section 4.4)
- Scoreboard #2 Defining an intervention logic for the issue (section 5.6)
- Tool #4.1 Applying the 'wisdom of the crowd method' – assessing the wickedness of the SDGs
- Tool #9.1 Better Business Scan
- Tool #9.2 The CANVAS+ model for sustainable business
- Tool #10.1 Making SDGs actionable at target level
- Key Value Indicators (KVIs) map: from triggering event to business model: Table 9.5
- Key Decision-making Indicators (KDIs) maps: Tables 10.2, 10.3, 10.5
- Mapping the SDG alignment challenge – building a Sustainable Corporate Story: Table 10.8
- Key Practice and Performance Indicators (KPIs) mapping frameworks: Tables 11.1–11.7
- Functional-level SDG alignment fiches: sections 11.10.1–11.10.7
- Partnership Portfolio Management (PPM) mapping: Figure 12.4

FOREWORD

In 2016, I became co-chair – together with former UN Deputy Secretary-General Mark Malloch-Brown – of the Business & Sustainable Development Commission. We officially launched at the World Economic Forum (WEF). Our simple objective was to create more awareness of the SDGs among the business community. It was clear to us that most of the goals depended on active ownership and involvement of the business community who, after all, account for the bulk of our economies, financial flow and job creation and has a main role to play in innovation, resources and financing. Business needs the SDGs as much as the SDGs need business. In less than two years' time, we were able to make a compelling business case for sustainable development in general and the SDGs in particular. We showed that private sector involvement in the realization of the SDGs could unlock an estimated annual $12 trillion in business opportunities by 2030, while creating hundreds of millions of much-needed jobs in the process. The corporate community received the SDG-agenda as a compelling growth strategy. It was particularly clear at that time that the SDGs were badly needed to provide an integrated and universal agenda to address the many wicked problems that the world is facing. Business leaders started to reiterate that companies cannot succeed in societies that fail. Nor could we, as business leaders, remain bystanders in a system that gave our companies life in the first place. We well exceeded our objectives, reaching over 2,000 CEOs and helped them integrate the SDGs in the core of their strategy. Subsequently, we are driving the SDGs even harder amongst the 15,000 members of the UN Global Compact, most of which have adopted them in their own business strategies. I continue to share my insights with other corporate leaders to encourage their involvement in the SDGs. The book *Net Positive* adds another dimension. I do that not only as former CEO of one of the largest global and publicly traded multinationals, but also as an active participant in relevant international platforms, committees, think tanks and in my frequent interactions with key governments.

In our book *Net Positive,* I argue – together with my co-author Andrew Winston – that the SDGs are vital as a means to reframe the social contract, rethink the role of business in society, and redesign the policies we need. The SDGs push us to go deeper and seek a planet and society in balance. The SDGs are also timely, as more and more we are aware of the price we pay for social exclusion and the devastating effects of our current linear and extractive economic system on our planetary boundaries. We have never been so forewarned about what is going to happen, but also never been so forearmed with tools to do something about it. Given the enormous costs of failure, as Covid-19 has shown, we are rapidly moving from risk mitigation to seizing enormous opportunities. This is one of the main reasons, I believe, why we start to see the financial sector move as well.

When I started as CEO of Unilever and introduced the *Sustainable Living Plan* as a framework and philosophy for the corporate sustainability strategy, I had already referred to the phenomenon of the VUCA world – the increasingly Volatile, Uncertain, Complex, and Ambiguous context in which companies have to develop resilient strategies. Since then, the world has proved far from immune for crises. The Covid-19 crisis is definitely not the last systems crisis we will face. A direct result of our destruction of biodiversity, it has reminded us once more that we can not have healthy people on an unhealthy planet. The SDGs provide the most relevant positive agenda and antidote to the negative fallout of a VUCA world. In a unique confluence of circumstances in 2015, the SDGs were embraced by all governments, major businesses, leading NGOs, all relevant international organizations and many knowledge institutes. But successive progress reports show that progress still goes too slow. In fact, Covid-19 pushed us backwards on many fronts and showed once more that the disadvantaged or minority groups again pay a disproportionate price. As this book diligently documents, this is not because of a lack of intentions or relevant support, but because organizations face considerable challenges in addressing the root causes of societal problems and in converting sustainability challenges into opportunities. Companies have experienced external and internal barriers to translating societal objectives into their core business models and value networks, and to developing proactive strategies – alone or together with partners. Most importantly, many are trying to optimise in a system that is not designed to deliver anymore. The broader partnerships across society to drive the needed systems changes will be key. I call it working 'on' the forest versus 'in' the forest.

For the latter ambition, I consider *Principles of Sustainable Business: Frameworks for Corporate Action on the SDGs* a seminal book. Not only because it starts from the same premise as I did – focusing on the VUCA world and how to deal with the challenge in a purposeful manner – but also because it takes the multidisciplinary and multilevelled approach that is so much needed and so often missing in business studies on corporate sustainability strategies. Or, for that matter, in the development of government policies in support of corporate sustainability strategies. The principles contained in every chapter of this book provide a fundamental take on the role business needs to play in a VUCA world. Companies have to move beyond 'rules' and 'regulation' and consider responsibilities and principles. The layered principles elaborated throughout the twelve chapters neatly complement, reinforce and further underline the five principles that separate the 'net positive companies' from the merely 'well-run' and 'well-meaning' businesses: (1) ownership of all impacts and consequences, or not; (2) operating for the long-term benefit of business and society; (3) creating positive returns for all stakeholders; (4) driving shareholder value as a *result*, not a goal; (5) partnering to drive systemic change.

It is amazing how this book shows how a science-based approach and insights from a rich variety of disciplines not only confirms our own five principles, but actually adds a large number of frameworks, tools, checklists and scorecards to our own approach. One of the many actionable frameworks presented in this book is, for instance, Partnership Portfolio Management. As mentioned, to succeed, all companies have to engage in meaningful partnerships with societal stakeholders, governments and even competitors. In my own experience, I have encountered partnering as a necessary condition for progress and trust-building. But this is never easy and requires impact-driven leadership and sophisticated management skills from all participants. All the insights, as diligently documented in this groundbreaking book by Rob van Tulder and Eveline van Mil, are truly valuable and will help students and executives alike, in considerable detail, to contribute to the Decade of Action. This book presents the perfect scientific foundation for future efforts of companies around the world. Enjoy the read, but above all the fun and reward that comes from putting it in practice.

Paul Polman
Former CEO Unilever, Co-chair and founder IMAGINE,
Vice Chair UN Global Compact, former SDG Advocate,
member High Level UN Panel that developed the SDGs

PREFACE

STEPPING UP
THE PACE

*Why acceleration is needed . . .
and feasible. The post-2020
agenda*

September 2015: **a moment of optimism.** The Sustainable Development Goals (SDGs) were adopted. All 193 United Nations member countries unanimously committed to achieving 17 ambitious Global Goals by 2030 – ranging from ending poverty in all its forms and providing access to health and education for all to adequately addressing climate change and creating peace and justice. These goals were established following a massive, almost three-year process of global multi-stakeholder consultation in which hundreds of big and small corporations, governments, civil society groups, knowledge institutes and other organizations participated. To date, the SDGs arguably are the most all-encompassing, ambitious as well as much needed action-oriented agenda for progress on a global scale ever agreed upon by humankind.

In order to realize the SDGs, the active participation of corporations is considered vital. This new reasoning signals a notable shift away from traditional ways of thinking about sustainable development issues that considered this area to be predominantly 'government territory'. Companies – big and small, local and multinational, in all sectors of society – have a crucial role to play, according to the UN: "We acknowledge the role of the diverse private sector, ranging from micro-enterprises to cooperatives to multinationals . . . in the implementation of the new Agenda" (UN, 2015: 10). Then UN Secretary-General Ban Ki-moon even designated companies the most dynamic role in the SDG endeavour: "Governments must take the lead in living up to their pledges.

At the same time, I am counting on the private sector to drive success" (UN News Centre, 2015).[1]

The business logic to engage and contribute was clear: achieving the SDGs was assessed to unlock an estimated annual $12 trillion in business opportunities (Business and Sustainable Development Commission, 2017) for companies able to come up with innovative sustainable solutions and inclusive business models. Many companies consequently embraced the Global Goals. In 2016, 87% of CEOs believed that the SDGs provide an opportunity to rethink approaches to sustainable value creation, while 78% already recognized opportunities to contribute through integrating the SDGs into their core business (UN Global Compact and Accenture Strategy, 2016). International guideline organizations like the Global Reporting Initiative and UN Global Compact developed tools to support companies to integrate SDGs into their strategies and reporting activities. International organizations like the World Business Council for Sustainable Development and the World Economic Forum unequivocally embraced the SDGs as well and encouraged their members to become active and engage more deeply as a strong and positive influence on society.

September 2018–2019: **moments of realism.** UN Secretary-General António Guterres warns that the world is 'not on track' as the implementation of the SDGs is going too slowly to meet the 2030 deadline. His call intends to 'inject a sense of urgency' for immediate, accelerated action by all countries and stakeholders at all levels. According to the annual check-up report on the SDGs – released in June 2018 – progress on the SDGs proved uneven and was not moving fast enough on almost all accounts (UN, 2018). The 2019 SDG progress report repeated this message in even stronger wording (UN, 2019). Inequality is widening, hunger is on the rise, biodiversity is eroding at an alarming rate, climate change threatens all SDGs. It proves particularly difficult to deal with contradictory developments in the world economy at a very critical moment in time. The lower GDP growth, conflict, climate change and growing inequalities add more challenges to the rise in world hunger and the forced displacement of millions of people. Progress – ambitioned to be inclusive to 'leave no one behind' – has not been reaching the people who need it most. Perhaps the Global Goals were too optimistic? Perhaps they require more time to implement? Surely additional, more specific, timely and better data and indicators are needed to track and steer on developments? Vital in all considerations remains the question of why companies are relatively slow in actively adopting the SDGs and how their performance can be improved. This question is all the more important because of the leading role ascribed to the private sector – representing 75% of global

---

1 https://news.un.org/en/story/2015/09/509862-un-forum-highlights-fundamental-role-private-sector-advancing-new-global-goals.

GDP – in achieving the SDGs. As developments are not materializing at the required scale and speed, profound change is needed that goes "beyond business as usual" (UN, 2018: 3).

January 2020: **a rude awakening**. The Covid-19 pandemic hits the world. 'Business as usual' is not even possible anymore. Countries around the world are in a complete lockdown, global trade collapses and governments are caught ill-prepared. The global health crisis triggers a profound economic crisis, with a decline in global economic activity on a scale not seen since the Great Depression or World War II. To most observers, the Covid-19 pandemic reveals a number of systems failures, systemic hazards and fragilities closely related to the organization of global political, financial, social and economic systems, and the increased rivalry between different models of development. The 2020 SDG progress report, issued by the UN secretariat in May 2020, concludes that:

> "what began as a health crisis has quickly become the worst human and economic crisis of our lifetime. (. . .) Had we been further advanced in meeting the SDGs, we could better face this challenge – with stronger health systems, fewer people living in extreme poverty, less gender inequality, a healthier natural environment, and more resilient societies" (UN, 2020: 2, 11).

More than ever, the SDG-agenda seems to serve as a necessary, timely, coordinated, and positive way out of present and future crises. How to accelerate its implementation during challenging times, in which many countries are inclined to retreat behind closed borders? By September 2020, the UN decided to 'relaunch' the SDG venture, for which now – more than ever – vigorous private sector support is needed.

NEVER WASTE A GOOD CRISIS

When we focus on the role of business, the current status is that business ambitions, efforts and execution are not (yet) measuring up to the size, scale and complexity of the challenge, despite growing commitment of the global business community. The UN Global Compact Progress Report 2020, for instance, found that whereas 84% of signatories report taking specific action to advance the SDGs, only 46% are implementing the SDGs into their core operations while just 37% are designing business models that contribute to the SDGs. "Corporate goals are generally not sufficiently ambitious" (ibid: 18). The UN Global Compact/ Accenture CEO survey of 2019 found that 71% of CEOs recognize the critical role that business could play in contributing to the delivery of the Global Goals, but a mere 21% agreed that business is actually playing that role. In 2018, the

World Business Council for Sustainable Development conducted a global survey to explore trends in the way business has been working to align their activities with the SDGs (WBCSD and DNV GL, 2018). The WBCSD found that companies embrace the SDGs particularly as an opportunity to innovate, gain a reputation and create a better focus on sustainability strategies. Yet progress is slow and gradual, partly because the SDGs are adopted at an overly general level, and often without clear priorities.

The post-2020 agenda. The first results of corporate involvement around the world hint at several gaps in the theoretical and practical knowledge on how companies can substantially increase their contribution to societal challenges – in particular, grand challenges like the SDGs. Companies are faced with five inter-related challenges:

1   **Materiality challenge:** how to make the SDGs part of core business and integrate them into long-term and short-term corporate strategies. Areas of attention: shared/societal/sustainable value creation, social entrepreneurship, and leadership;

2   **Risk avoidance orientation:** how to go beyond relatively 'easy' SDG-targets as part of a risk mitigation and reactive stance in support of the SDGs, to a more proactive approach: from 'avoid doing harm' to pursuing 'doing good'. Areas of attention: business model innovation strategies; internal alignment between functional areas of management and transition management, in particular in supply chain, natural resources and operations management, finance, marketing, human resource management, innovation and communication;

3   **Nexus challenge:** how to translate the SDG-agenda at the target level into a meaningful and actionable combination of corporate interventions to leverage beneficial impact. Area of attention: business model innovation and social *intra*preneurship;

4   **Partnering challenge:** how to include other societal actors in the effort, thereby creating the conditions under which proactive strategies can materialize. Area of attention: cross-sector partnership portfolio management;

5   **Legitimacy challenge:** how to overcome the sizable trust gap that companies face when formulating and implementing their intentions to 'do good'; early adopters of the SDGs have to deal with the inclination for SDG-washing (superficially embracing the SDGs without actually aiming for transformative change). Areas of attention: business community involvement, corporate citizenship, and stakeholder relations.

Dealing with these five challenges requires a more robust understanding of at least four basic questions:

- **Why** are the SDGs so important for companies (as threat mitigation or as an opportunity)?

- **What** concrete topics and issues should be involved when thinking about their implementation in an integrated, aligned and societal value-creating way?

- **Who** is or should be held responsible, and who is to take responsibility for specific SDGs (responsible governance)?

- **How** can companies more effectively contribute to the SDGs?

WHY *PRINCIPLES* OF SUSTAINABLE BUSINESS?

This book emphasizes 'principles' of sustainable business. Principle-based approaches, rather than rule-based approaches derived from laws and legislation, are increasingly relevant for the behaviour of businesses. The sustainability challenge confronts companies with strategic concerns that go beyond mere 'legal', 'moral' or even 'responsibility' considerations. *Principles of Sustainable Business* deals with those 'propositions' and 'values' that create guidance for the behaviour of companies and the evaluation of their performance in the – often quite confusing and multi-dimensional – discourse on sustainable development.

Rules and laws create a predominantly *formal* environment to guide and evaluate behaviour. Juridical laws and rules implement solidified principles in a coercive way, for instance through lawsuits in which liabilities are determined. Moral laws and rules prescribe and evaluate good behaviour in accordance with particular moral ideals. Scientific laws and rules enable knowledge validation and peer review. 'Propositions' and 'values', on the other hand, create a more *informal* and *dynamic* environment which encourages participants to adopt certain actions or behaviours, yet often without precise evaluation mechanisms (and sanctions) in place. Principles, with their underlying values, function as shaping, organizing and normalizing forces that in time can develop into 'systems'. The justice system, countries, alliances, companies and other systems are all founded on organizational and governance principles that build upon a composed set of particular values, such as 'fairness', 'accountability', 'stewardship', 'equality' or 'transparency', often set by groups of like-minded people. Companies – in particular those that operate in many countries and (legal/cultural) systems – have to address formal and informal dimensions of sustainability principles at the same time. Amongst others, they have to deal with:

- *Universal principles*, such as the Universal Declaration of Human Rights (which are nevertheless interpreted differently around the world) and the 'No one left behind' principle underlying the SDGs;

- *Moral principles,* with regard to 'do no harm', 'don't be evil', 'do good';
- *Management principles,* like 'stewardship', 'accountability' or 'transparency';
- *Good governance principles,* like 'comply or explain', 'materiality' or 'fiduciary duty';
- *Constitutional principles,* like 'separation of powers', 'national sovereignty';
- *Religious and cultural principles,* such as wealth-sharing principles – *zakat* – in Islamic countries; subsidiarity and solidarity principles in Christian countries; benevolence principles in Confucian countries;
- *Behaviouristic principles,* like 'honesty', 'integrity', 'mutuality', 'ownership' and 'trust';
- *Sector-specific principles,* like the Principles of Responsible Investment (for the finance sector);
- *Principles introduced by international organizations,* like the OECD, the International Standards Organisation (ISO26000), or the United Nations (Global Compact) that provide guidance on a voluntary basis;
- *Collaborative principles,* developed by involved parties to guide a particular partnership in the right direction.

In a rapidly changing world, formal rules and laws lose part of their norm-setting and guiding value for addressing 'grand challenges', which tend to be transboundary in nature (across countries, across sectors, across actors). Instead, principles – in all sorts and shapes – fill part of the voids that appear at relevant levels of society: global, national, local, personal. On the global scale, no formal laws ever existed. Consequently, a global 'governance gap' exists in which there are no formal laws and rules, only standards and principles (and international treaties to recognize and confirm them). On a national scale, laws are losing part of their relevance because they were founded on past principles, practices and realities. On a local scale, organizations have to move beyond (local) laws and integrate all relevant contexts and dimensions (economic, ecological and social) to become sustainable. To fill the void and raise the bar, frontrunner companies are defining their own principles for creating value for themselves and for society. The business logic and basic principle here is: 'business cannot thrive in a society that fails'. On a personal scale, principled behaviour is considered a virtue, and unprincipled behaviour a character defect. But what this entails in practice, is rather context-sensitive and often far from clear.

Principal, the *adjective*, means 'most important'. Principle, the *noun*, however, has many connotations. Principles guide the behaviour of companies in a variety of ways: as a correction and disciplinary mechanism, as a communication strategy, as a channelling or steering mechanism, or as a means to select and govern collaborative ventures for common goals (like the Sustainable Development Goals). Selecting principles that are 'most important' proves difficult and is situation- and time-bound. The linguistic *combination* of principle and principal as *noun and adjective* defines the ultimate challenge of this book: **how can aspiring sustainable businesses deal with a large number of – sometimes conflicting – principles and still decide what they would prioritize (i.e. consider most important).** Entitling the book as *the* principles of sustainable business would wrongfully suggest that we can distinguish several well-defined principles that apply to all companies, in all local contexts, and under all circumstances. There are indeed several principles that *prevent* companies from becoming *un*sustainable. But for the higher end of this discourse – how to support companies to become *more sustainable* – we have to **explore** all relevant principles. This book will show that principles can originate in the global context, in shared goals, in governance approaches, in a comparable way of looking at issues (wicked opportunities), in the way stakeholders can be involved, and in managerial practices. The SDGs thereby present both an inspiring and challenging general framework for exploring the kind of **goal-oriented principles** needed to create transformational change.

Principles materialize at three basic levels:

■ **Systemic principles:** related to fundamental and even existential 'why' questions'; in Part I, we will specifically address whether the principles on which the SDGs are founded can be considered a new 'paradigm' for sustainable development, and why they are badly needed in today's Volatile, Uncertain, Complex and Ambiguous (VUCA) world;

■ **Societal and dynamic principles:** related to fundamental analytical, participatory and procedural 'what' and 'who' questions; in Part II, we specifically consider what the conditions are for an effective cross-sectoral organization of the SDG-agenda, and what type of thinking is needed to enable progress;

■ **Strategic and operational principles:** related to a translation of societal and dynamic principles in a practical setting; how to 'make this work'. Part III will especially zoom in on sustainable business models, organizational power (resource base, positioning, sphere of influence) as 'assets of potential change', and consider how corporations can realize ambition and 'intent' (based on the systemic, societal and dynamic principles of Part I and II).

THIS BOOK'S FORMULA

This book is organized around four leading questions related to the SDGs – why, what, who, how – in order to present a coherent framework for speeding up corporate strategies in support of the SDGs. The aim is to make corporate strategies more effective for sustainable development and thus more effective for business as well (the business case). This framework is a condensed result of a variety of interdisciplinary research and teaching projects, organized with colleagues in academia, practitioners at companies, civil society organizations and government, and with PhD and Master's students.

Over the course of a considerable number of years, these collaborations have allowed us to develop a more integrated vision on the way corporations could effectively contribute to very complex societal problems through new business models and cross-sector partnerships. This includes new thinking on sustainable development, linking macro-challenges to micro-approaches, positive change trajectories, and a variety of management techniques that are needed to (pro)actively take up complex societal challenges (rather than staying passive or shifting responsibility to others).

The book is, therefore, also closely linked to the creation – 20 years ago – of the department of Business-Society Management at the Rotterdam School of Management. This department focuses on the mainstreaming of sustainable business in management science and practice (B-SM, 2018). It also runs parallel to the adoption of the SDGs by RSM Erasmus University – one of the first business schools in the world to do so – as the leading ambition in its research and teaching programmes.

HOW TO USE THIS TEXTBOOK

Anyone who is interested in a full treatment of 'principles' of 'sustainable business' is faced with a level-of-analysis challenge: Where to start? At the **macro level**, where the full aggregate impact of sustainable or unsustainable business materializes? At the **micro level**, where business models are operationalized and implemented? At the **meso level**, where networks, communities and value chains are organized? Most business books start with the micro angle for obvious reasons. They run the risk, however, of treating the societal level only indirectly – as a context variable. Business scholars often refer to general ethical principles to partly cover for this deficiency. Policy-oriented books, on the other hand, start with a macro angle on sustainability issues. They face the problem of never really reaching the micro level of corporate approaches. Policy scholars (including macro-economists) commonly address this problem by using general theories of companies and other meso-level actors (communities, organizations, sectors), which seriously limits the practical application of their insights to interventions that can (and should) be undertaken by individual companies.

Both approaches have obvious shortcomings. Both nevertheless are quite popular as they provide a definite starting point for study and reading. They also tend to build on mono-disciplinary research, and hence fit more easily into existing curricula at universities. In this book, we have chosen to give all levels of analysis significant attention. Principles of sustainable business should be founded in societal, sectoral as well as organizational levels. Principles also involve a solid understanding of the ambiguities in the system, for which we have introduced 'wicked problems' theory.

HOW TO NAVIGATE THROUGH THIS BOOK?

The choice for a multilevel approach led us to organize the text at three levels in a logical sequence: macro (societal, global) → meso (cross-sectoral, governance, network) → micro (corporate, organizational). This design – with substantial elaborations at each level – might not be equally relevant for all target audiences of this book. Hence, we have come up with a didactical solution to accommodate different needs and preferences, by enabling various audiences to start at different entries and use the parts of the book **in a different sequence** – depending on the available time and individual ambitions:

- ■ **Corporate executives** can immediately jump to Part III. They are advised to start with the strategic Chapters (7, 8, 9, 10) and follow-up on more operational and functional-level challenges (Chapters 11 and 12). After that, a 'backwards' read will provide a deeper understanding of the nature of problems and opportunities that corporate executives face (Part II), to become better equipped to frame corporate strategies in the SDG paradigm, without underestimating the voids and remaining challenges of the SDG framework that still need to be settled.

- ■ **Business students** can start with Part II, to get acquainted with the SDGs and apply wicked problems theory to the 'grand challenges' that companies face (Chapter 4), after which Chapters 5 and 6 help to 'contextualize' the organizational and governance configuration that influences possible approaches. Part III is then required reading, with case studies, frameworks, important concepts and illustrations of leading (standard-setting) initiatives that any business professional should master. If time allows, Part I will help to understand the relevance of long-wave structural change processes in view of the fourth industrial revolution, and to gain deeper insights into the bigger story and the turbulence that companies face, related to the clash of different societal models and the consequential problems that a VUCA world creates.

- ■ **Policy students, policymakers and economists** could start with Part I, to consider the geopolitical context in which the SDG-agenda can be understood as a 'paradigm' change, and then selectively go through Parts II and III to check who should be taking initiative and under what conditions (Part II). Part III supports policymakers and regulators in increasing their ability to distinguish between companies that are more or less serious about the SDGs (Part III). The index can be helpful in skimming through the material.

■ **The aspiring 'SDG professional'** should, of course, consider the whole book as required reading, including the supportive material of MOOCs, clips, case studies. A basic understanding of the SDG paradigm is helpful, so it is best to start in Chapter 1 and to focus on the last part of that chapter. After that, you can zoom in on specific chapters that have your intuitive preference. Whatever sequence you choose, a final benchmark of your professional abilities will be the extent to which you are able to use *Scoreboard #1* (Chapter 4), *Scoreboard #2* (Chapter 5) and the various frameworks, tools and checklists that are included in Part III. These scoreboards and practice mapping exercises form key checks for an understanding of the problems and opportunities that the SDG trajectory poses. The ultimate impact aim of any SDG professional is to help accelerate the implementation of the SDG-agenda, in whatever form, yet in an integrated, meaningful and genuinely contributive manner. One way of achieving that is to become a *partnership broker* (explained in Chapter 12).

Principles of Sustainable Business starts each chapter with an overview of 'principles' addressed, and ends with the main 'takeaways' and supportive materials (a selection of key resources, leading initiatives, hubs, databases). The SDGs have triggered statistical bureaus, standard-setting organizations, consultancies, business alliances and research institutes around the world to collect relevant information at global, regional, national and local levels. As a result of the popularity and relevance of the SDG frame, companies, governments and civil society organizations (NGOs) have started to document and communicate where they are in their approach towards the SDGs and sustainable development in general. These societal efforts provide a rich basis for comparison and further research, both for business professionals and in an educational setting. The *open access* to many of these sources enables easy entry to trend, sector, industry and issue analyses, which in turn makes it relatively easy to consider the (multilevel) context in which particular SDGs are to materialize.

TEACHING FORMULA: PROVEN AND NOVEL CONCEPTS OF ENGAGEMENT

A textbook that documents in any meaningful, systematic and pedagogical manner why, to what extent, how, and with whom companies can effectively contribute to achieving the SDGs has not yet been published. This represents the ambition of this book. It brings together the latest insights on dealing with complex societal problems and translating them into relevant business strategies. The frame of the SDGs was chosen not only because it is the most relevant agenda for the world community or because it is embraced by so many (multinational) companies, but also because it provides an excellent basis to study the impact of corporate behaviour on sustainability issues and to discuss all relevant principles of sustainability.

The book benefits from years of experimenting with integrating the SDG-agenda in teaching programmes at bachelor, graduate and postgraduate (executive) level. We were able to develop several innovative teaching tools that facilitated a structured discussion and learning effort around the SDGs at three important levels of analysis:

(1) **The macro level,** relevant because it defines the 'degree of complexity' of the societal challenges of the SDG-agenda and the approach needed to address them: as wicked problems or wicked opportunity;

(2) **The micro level**, vital because it defines the strategic repertoire that needs to be adopted by individual companies: making SDGs core requires internal alignment and a solid understanding of the business case for sustainability;

(3) **The meso level**, equally vital because none of the SDGs can be achieved by companies alone: implementing the SDGs requires external alignment with societal stakeholders.

At each of these levels, tools needed to be developed to enable strategists and researchers to define approaches to effectively address the SDG challenge. They include scanning techniques to understand the wickedness of societal challenges; creating a safe space for developing innovative solutions ('Wicked Problems Plaza'); a web-based tool to map the gap between intention and realization (the 'Better Business Scan'); upgraded CANVAS models to include richer value propositions of companies; poster presentations that can be used to communicate, share and discuss research results; partnership portfolio mapping exercises and tipping point analyses.

This book showcases some of these techniques. They aim to help tutors to include the SDGs in their learning curriculum. The book consequently provides an accessible textbook for graduate and executive students in economics and business studies that are interested in enhancing the involvement of companies in effective approaches towards sustainability challenges in general, and speeding up progress on the SDGs in particular.

SUPPORTIVE MATERIAL

The teaching formula adopted in the book is already applied at RSM Erasmus University. This has resulted in the development of a large number of direct teaching aids (**didactical concepts, modules, posters, SDG cases, mapping and quick-scan techniques**) and in the creation of long-distance supportive material, such as **clips** on all SDGs (embodied in RSM's 'Positive Change' agenda website).

In 2019, the Rotterdam School of Management launched a **MOOC (Massive Open Online Course)** specifically dedicated to the SDGs. The course **Driving business towards the Sustainable Development Goals** introduces all 17 SDGs and includes video statements and cases from business, academia, policymakers and students on how to deal with the SDGs. Learning objectives of this course:

■ Know what the SDGs are, why they are important and how each individual can be an agent for positive change in the world;

■ Develop a positive, critical, aware and courageous attitude towards the SDGs;

■ Be able to identify interconnectedness of the SDGs and the challenges behind solving them;

■ Understand the role of business in the transition to sustainable development to create a prosperous future for all.

The MOOC was granted the 'excellence' award by the UN Sustainable Development and Solutions Network. For more information, visit: https://www.coursera.org/learn/sdgbusiness.

SDG cases: for every SDG, a number of cases (and teaching notes) were written that take a business perspective and involve one or more functional areas of management (strategy, marketing, supply chain management, human resource management, finance). All cases place the presented managerial challenges in the context of sustainable development. Video learning materials and other resources are available at RSM's SDG website: https://www.rsm.nl/positive-change/sdg-cases/

In 2020, we launched the **Better Business Scan**. This online tool enables managers to map the sustainability transition phase they are in, the challenges this position entails, and to gain insight into how to take sustainability ambitions further. The scan takes 15 minutes and provides immediate personal feedback. It measures the size of the gap between sustainability intentions (business case) and realization (business model). Based on this position, the most important tipping points the organization is faced with can be analysed, as well as the type of leadership skills needed. In Chapters 9 and 11, we elaborate on the 'intention-realization' gap. The (free) scan and background materials are available at: https://www.betterbusinessscan.org/

Poster presentations have proven a fruitful didactical approach to challenge (groups of) students to come to grips with complexity, get to the point, apply a number of analytical and info-graphical techniques, and engage in interrater reliability and peer-review processes that, until recently, were primarily used in scientific conferences (see two examples at varying levels of education).

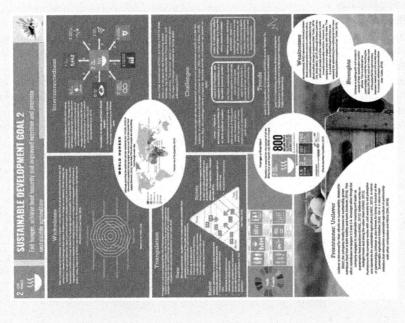

Example of student poster

Example of student poster

Posters, tools, resources and cases on companies' approaches to the SDGs are released and regularly upgraded on the book's accompanying website: https://www.principlesofsustainablebusiness.nl/

Rob van Tulder and Eveline van Mil, January 2022

REFERENCES

B-SM (2018). *Mainstreaming sustainable business. 20 years Business-Society Management, 20 years impact*? SMO and Department of Business-Society Management, SMO-2018/3. Rotterdam: SMO.

Business & Sustainable Development Commission (2017). *Better Business, Better World*.

UN (2020). *Shared Responsibility, Global Solidarity: Responding to the socio-economic impacts of COVID-19*, March. New York: United Nations.

UN (2019). *The Report of the Secretary General: The Special Edition of the Sustainable Development Goals Progress Report*. New York: United Nations.

UN (2018). *The Sustainable Development Goals Report 2018*. New York: United Nations.

UN (2015). *Transforming Our World: The 2050 Agenda for Sustainable Development*. New York: United Nations.

UN Global Compact & Accenture Strategy (2019). *The Decade to Deliver. A Call to Business Action. The United Nations Global Compact – Accenture Strategy CEO Study on Sustainability 2019*, September.

UN Global Compact & Accenture Strategy (2016). *The United Nations Global Compact – Accenture Strategy CEO Study 2016. Agenda 2030: A Window of Opportunity*, June.

WBCSD & DNV GL (2018). *Business and the SDGs: A survey of WBCSD members and Global Network partners*. World Business Council for Sustainable Development, July.

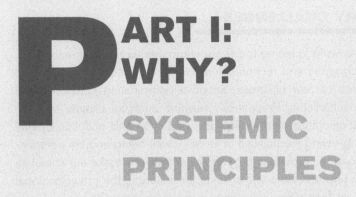

PART I: WHY?

SYSTEMIC PRINCIPLES

The creation of the SDGs – a new paradigm for progress?

We are living in uncertain, turbulent times. The term 'VUCA' is nowadays commonly used to characterize the kind of turbulence that society faces. This acronym – introduced by the US Military College towards the end of the 'cold war' (1987–1991) – stands for the intensified Volatility, Uncertainty, Complexity and Ambiguity that technological, political and economic processes are currently creating. The world has become increasingly multipolar – witness the rapid economic development of China, Russia's foreign interferences, the partial withdrawal from the global stage of the United States and the recurrent fragmentation and indecisiveness of the European Union. The unpredictable movements in our VUCA world are considered 'the new normal', yet seriously hamper the way corporations, organizations and people are able to make decisions, plan ahead, manage risks and foster change. This situation becomes even worse if they want to adopt a longer-term perspective, as is required for most of today's societal challenges.

A VUCA world creates tough and pressing challenges, even for those who manage to come to grips with its dynamics, openings and opportunities. Business scholars address these near intractable issues as 'grand challenges' and strategic 'leadership paradoxes' that require cross-sectoral, collaborative and multi-levelled coordinated efforts. Dealing with rapidly amplifying complexity and uncertainty also calls for business model innovations, new forms of decision-making that are fit to cope with the levels of complexity at hand and, ultimately, for rather different mind-sets, values, norms and standards.

DOI: 10.4324/9781003098355-1

21ST CENTURY CHALLENGES . . .

The challenges the world is facing today are enormous. Ecological, economic, geopolitical, demographic and technological forces are shaping an unsettled landscape in search of new balances, adaptive coordinating structures and resilient coping mechanisms. Present-day realities such as climate change, global warming, accelerated biodiversity loss, depletion and pollution of vital natural resources, growing inequalities in income, well-being and life perspective, stagnated economic growth and geopolitical tensions make our societies vulnerable in quite unpredictable ways. Take, for instance, the growing global population, which, at face value, may seem a relatively easy-to-assess demographic factor with clear, foreseeable consequences. But is it? By the year 2050, the earth will probably have to feed around 9.7 billion people. This implies that the demand for food will be an estimated 60% higher than today. If not dealt with effectively, malnutrition, hunger and conflict are likely to arise. If not dealt with responsibly, ecological degradation, biodiversity loss and natural resource depletion will be the result. A growing world population also implies a growing demand for healthcare, education, housing, energy, transport, connectivity and decent income-generating jobs. The hotspot for many of these developments will be Africa, where the highest increase in population (relative to other areas of the world) is expected over the next decades – from one billion to three billion people.

In parallel, developments in digital technology will continue to influence our ability to cope with these entangled societal challenges. The internet has significantly changed the way we live, work, organize and govern society, thereby affecting or redefining values such as security, privacy, economic value, accountability, fairness and inclusivity. However, the effects of the massive introduction of social media and instant interconnectedness on (social) skills development, productivity and our mental, emotional and physical health are still largely unclear. Digital developments enhance problem-solving capabilities, for instance by producing better data, fit-for-purpose intelligence and smarter coordination. Nevertheless, digital developments may also amplify power concentration, inequality ('digital divides'), erosion of civil rights and disruption of governance, thereby exacerbating societal tensions and vicious dynamics.

Amidst these rapid developments, the gender gap in such crucial domains as access to health, education, earning potential and political power is only decreasing slowly, despite the recognition that gender equality makes perfect economic sense. It has been calculated that at current rates, it will take another 118 years to close the economic gender gap entirely. These challenges, and many concurrently related developments, are highly interlinked, global in scale and complex in nature. How to approach them effectively is open for debate and dependent on emerging insights. The example above is just one of the profoundly interrelated effects that global change processes trigger.

ENTER THE SUSTAINABLE DEVELOPMENT GOALS (SDGs) . . .

On 25 September 2015, the United Nation's Sustainable Development Goals (SDGs) were released as part of the *2030 Agenda for Sustainable Development*. On that date, all 193 member countries of the United Nations unanimously committed to achieving 17 ambitious and interrelated Global Goals by 2030 (UN, 2015). These goals were established following a massive almost three-year global multi-stakeholder consultation process in which hundreds of big and small corporations, governments, civil society groups, knowledge institutes and other organizations participated. In fact, the SDGs represent the most extensive public consultation in the history of the United Nations. The United Nations' survey 'MyWorld2015' asked 9.7 million citizens what they would like to see included in the new goals that were to supersede the preceding Millennium Development Goals as established in the year 2000. The 17 goals and 169 targets resulting from this global consultation process range from eradicating poverty and hunger, improving access to health and education and ensuring human rights, to climate action, protecting ecosystems and safeguarding biodiversity (Figure I.1).

The SDGs are aimed at advancing a diverse range of crucial sustainable development themes simultaneously, with universal coverage, involving all societal stakeholders and through an inclusive approach. But they have also encountered criticism for either being too ambitious and too complex or not being ambitious enough, especially with regard to the modalities of their execution and the omission of addressing crucial financial considerations like *who is going to pay?* Notwithstanding this highly relevant and critical discourse, the SDGs are generally considered to constitute the leading frame of the global sustainable development

Figure I.1 The Sustainable Development Goals

agenda until 2030, in particular for governments around the world. Under which conditions will they also be the leading agenda for corporations? **Part I** of this book will examine three 'why' questions related to the ambition of 'Transforming Our World' (UN, 2015): (1) Why now? (2) Why not? and (3) Why slow?

WHY NOW?

Chapter 1 discusses why the introduction of the Sustainable Development Goals as a global agenda is not only a challenging 'outcome' ambition, but also signals an urgently needed and timely 'paradigm shift' in the thinking on the conditions for global sustainable development and the role(s) to be played by societal actors – such as companies. The SDGs are a novel way of addressing the systemic ecological, economic and social crises of our VUCA world: they are explicitly inclusive, based on positive frames for change, defined as universal challenges, complexity-sensitive, principles-based and collective action-oriented, and based on joint investments (rather than on subsidies, philanthropy or aid-assistance only). Chapter 1 clarifies why this global comprehensive effort can be considered a new paradigm for governments, citizens and corporations alike, and why the SDGs can be appraised to signal the dawn of a new era.

WHY NOT?

The paradigm status of the SDGs as a leading reference framework critically depends on its theoretical and practical elaborations, as well as on how gaps in its original (2015) set-up are tackled. The SDG approach was designed as 'work in (and on) progress', requiring permanent scrutiny in its indicators, strategies and implementation experiences. The SDG-agenda supports a 'learning by doing' approach – not in the least because of the inherent complexity/wickedness of the sustainability problems that are to be addressed under VUCA conditions. **Chapter 2** scrutinizes in more detail the SDG approach from a variety of directions: its (general) design, its (broad) ambitions, its (dashboard) measurement approach, and its adoption of a (multi-stakeholder) process to upgrade and learn during implementation. Implementing the new paradigm faces a considerable number of challenges. Understanding these key challenges – and the logic of the approach chosen – forms the main objective of this chapter.

WHY SLOW?

The effectiveness of the SDG-agenda is as much influenced by dealing with criticisms as by adequately addressing the identified challenges and embracing the opportunities these can entail. Success of the SDGs hinges on their reception in society and the degree of ownership by different societal stakeholders. **Chapter 3** takes stock of the first four-year cycle of SDG implementation, which ended in September 2019. The assessment of this first phase tells two stories: how the SDG-framework has been further developed and fine-tuned, and the extent to which specific flaws in its set-up could be resolved with the involvement of multiple agencies and stakeholders. We will see that the SDG-agenda presents an encouraging and promising 'hybrid governance' approach, but not without flaws, intellectual voids, coordination bottlenecks and significant empirical gaps (for instance, in accumulating all relevant data to track progress). The chapter will, therefore, also explain why progress has been slow on almost all accounts and identify entry points for addressing that state. Chapter 3 lists the conditions under which approaches to the SDGs can be considered successful, while also signifying a 'paradigm change' in the thinking of and way of organizing sustainable development. These conditions serve as the agenda for the remainder of the book and for corporate action on the SDGs in the post-2020 period: **Part II** (What and Who) and **Part III** (How).

REFERENCE

UN (2015). *Transforming Our World: The 2050 Agenda for Sustainable Development*. New York: United Nations.

1 WHY NOW?
A NECESSARY FRAME FOR GRAND SOCIETAL CHALLENGES

DOI: 10.4324/9781003098355-2

P R I N C I P L E S

- **Analytical principle:** always take a long-term ('wave') perspective to contextualize present-day processes. There is no single frame to understand the world. Complex problems require holistic approaches.

- **Safe space principle:** exploring and experimenting with innovative approaches to address societal challenges requires a safe space – analytically, and in practice.

- **Accumulation principle:** acknowledges the importance of continuous enhancement that builds on previous knowledge, moving from 1.0, via 2.0, to 3.0 insights. In dynamic transition processes, accumulation of a series of small steps can ultimately culminate in a tipping point – the point at which change becomes significant enough to cause larger (exponential) change.

- **Openness principle:** open systems are a necessary but not sufficient condition for sustainable development. Balancing democracy, globalization and national sovereignty represents a trilemma. Openness and closedness complement each other.

- **Inclusiveness principle:** inclusion is a necessary but not sufficient condition for sustainable development. In balanced societies, inclusion and exclusion complement each other.

- **Positive change principle:** when faced with complex challenges, doom scenarios and negative frames easily lead to paralysis and denial. Positive frames are more effective in initiating and enabling collaborative action.

- **Balanced society principle:** opposes the idea that a single societal sector (market, civil society and communities, state) should prevail in socio-economic development models. Balanced and more resilient societies thrive on four complementary values: public, private, social and common values.

- **Principles of sustainable development** integrate the People, Planet and Prosperity dimensions of sustainability in ways that strengthen peace and expand freedom – leaving no one behind (inclusiveness). Equality, non-discrimination, better standards of life, and the social and economic advancement of all people lie at the heart of sustainable development.

1.1   INTRODUCTION: WHY NOW?

> "It was the best of times, it was the worst of times,
> it was the age of wisdom, it was the age of foolishness,
> it was the epoch of belief, it was the epoch of incredulity,
> it was the season of Light, it was the season of Darkness,
> it was the spring of hope, it was the winter of despair . . ."
>
> **Charles Dickens (*A Tale of Two Cities*, 1859)**

The 21st century is – by many accounts – the era in which immense technological progress has been made. At the same time, the world is facing many systemic societal problems or 'grand challenges', both causing and driving considerable turbulence and uncertainty. It is quite challenging to assess the exact nature, scale and importance of specific developments, how these affect related fields, and with what likelihood and under what conditions. It is perhaps even more difficult to extrapolate the consequences of present 'trends' to tomorrow's world and decide on how to act on it. This chapter nevertheless aims to define the most important trends as well as delineate relevant approaches to address them. A proper understanding of 'what is at stake' in the global economy at the moment helps to appreciate the importance of a global, goal-oriented, multi-stakeholder initiative like the Sustainable Development Goals (SDGs).

One starting point for a quick impression of major societal challenges for the decade(s) to come are the ten key global challenges as defined in 2016 by the World Economic Forum (WEF), just a few months after the SDGs were launched. The WEF constitutes an influential gathering of global leaders from governments, business, civil society and knowledge institutes. WEF reports try to capture relevant global trends, in particular those related to 'Globalization 4.0' and the so-called 'Fourth Industrial Revolution' (Schwab, 2016). These trends are supposed to fundamentally change the way we live, work and relate to each other. The broad basis on which the WEF accumulates these trends and predictions provides a relevant frame for defining many of the 'grand challenges' of our time (Box 1.1).

TEN KEY CHALLENGES FOR THE WORLD (2016)

(1)   ***Food security:*** by the year 2050, the world will probably have to feed around 9.7 billion people. As a result, the global demand for food will rise by 60%. Agricultural sectors will need to become more productive, and simultaneously more sustainable and resource efficient and less polluting. If not dealt with effectively, malnutrition, hunger and conflicts are likely to arise.

B
O
X

1.1

BOX 1.1

(2) *Inclusive growth:* current political, social and economic systems are exacerbating inequalities. This has tremendous effects on the stability of the system and people's willingness and ability to contribute to (inclusive) growth.

(3) *Employment:* to keep pace with the increasing population (the rising number of young people in particular) and decreased employment in existing industries, hundreds of millions of new jobs will need to be created. This requires vast investments in education, skills development, new industries, trade relations, and financial and physical infrastructure.

(4) *Global warming:* the climate is changing to the extent that insurers have estimated that since the 1980s, weather-related economic loss events have tripled.

(5) *Global finance:* an interconnected global market comes with vulnerabilities in the financial system. The financial system will need to become more resilient to withstand shocks, re-establish public trust in financial institutions, and provide access to finance for all.

(6) *The internet* is considerably changing the way we live, work and organize society. While digital technologies may help to manage resources more efficiently and sustainably, the effects of instant and constant connectedness on our mental and physical health are not easy to assess or influence.

(7) *Gender equality:* the gender gap is only slowly decreasing, despite the recognition that gender equality makes perfect economic sense and is fundamental in making societies thrive. At current rates, it is estimated to take another 118 years to close the economic gender gap entirely.

(8) *International trade and investment:* there is growing unease on topics related to globalization. The global trade framework needs reforms as international treaties are insufficiently capable of dealing with critical questions on the power of corporations, the adequacy of regulations governing employment, environmental issues and taxation.

(9) *Long-term investing:* lack of long-term investment, for instance, in infrastructure, has serious implications for global growth, economic development, the functioning of basic systems and services of countries, and social well-being. Insufficient access to affordable credit and savings hampers the battle against global poverty.

(10) *The global health system:* Major advancements in healthcare have only partly been capable of keeping pace with demographic developments (e.g. population growth, ageing), pandemics and the rise of non-communicable diseases, especially in developing countries. Adjustments require an adequate balance between prevention and treatment and resilient organization of the global healthcare system.

Source: WEF (2016), https://www.weforum.org/agenda/2016/01/what-are-the-10-biggest-global-challenges/

The WEF top ten lists important trends and delineates vital challenges, but there are always additional and equally pressing developments to be considered. For instance, issues around safety, education, production and consumption, biodiversity, water and food security, energy, urbanization, migration, human rights, corruption or violent conflicts. The challenges as ranked by the WEF are relatively undisputed. Some of these have already materialized in the years since this account appeared, and their consequences can be confirmed as 'real'. How these challenges should be interpreted and handled gives rise to serious controversy however. Do they pose opportunities or threats? Should immediate action be taken or can we wait? What action would be effective, in what areas and undertaken by whom?

This chapter contextualizes why the 2015 introduction of the SDGs was not incidental. It explains that the present era represents a *significant and decisive transformation period* that creates increased uncertainty and rivalry, which – without concerted action – may very well lead to negative outcomes for a sustainable future (section 1.2). We define key areas of contention in the debate between a short-term approach towards sustainable development and medium-term and longer-term approaches, by taking some of the most relevant insights from scientific research in a wide variety of disciplines into account (sections 1.3 and 1.4). These insights also explain why the SDGs can be considered not only timely but also pressingly necessary (section 1.5). That does not imply, however, that it will be an easy 'sell'. The SDG-agenda delineates a logical, but nevertheless difficult, road towards addressing many of the systemic issues that require serious attention. This chapter assesses the critical juncture of the present era, and why the SDG-agenda might be society's best shot at embracing ambitious, inclusive and concerted action in creating a 'new economy', and to manage the disruptive dimensions of the so-called fourth industrial revolution.

1.2 THE APPEARANCE OF A VUCA WORLD

Most agree on the existence of a set of powerful and parallel driving forces that are (re)shaping our world. The effects of these drivers are trends that are technological, political, economic and social at the same time.

■ **Technology: revolutionary societal change** under the influence of rapid technological change. Some call the present stage of transition the 'third industrial revolution' (Rifkin, 2011), others refer to it as the 'fourth industrial revolution', 'Industry 4.0', the 'digital economy', the 'new economy' (Schwab, 2016; WEF, 2020b), or the 'Digital Revolution' (TWI2050, 2019). What remains nearly undisputed, however, is the fundamental, even 'disruptive' nature of present transformations. Parallel developments reinforce each other: the spread and integration of ICT, biotechnology, materials and nano-technology are generating applications that have the potential to alter entire systems of production, management, organization and the structure of society. In particular, the coming of age of the internet has proven the most pervasive trend in which other technological revolutions (material, artificial intelligence, biomedical and the like) are diffused at an unprecedented pace, scope and scale. The impacts range from labour market restructuring to new forms of warfare.

■ **Political: growing institutional and regulatory uncertainty** is influenced by the new wave of technological innovations; the rules of the competitive game are changing. New regulatory challenges have arisen, requiring a new or more advanced take on what constitutes effective policies and strategies for sustainable development. Many of the new organizational forms that shape the digital economy have benefited from regulatory frameworks that lack the agility and scope needed to accommodate the pace of technolog-ical developments and their transboundary and cross-jurisdictional implica-tions. Forms of hybrid, or altogether absent, regulation have facilitated a much more rapid spread of the internet than had been thought possible. *The Economist* (12 July 2017) talks about an 'era of digital exceptionalism', in which online platforms in America, and to some extent in Europe, "have been inhabiting a parallel legal universe . . . in which they are not legally responsible, either for what their users do or for the harm that their services can cause in the real world".

■ **Economic: growing dominance of a limited number of (platform) companies concentrated in a few countries** that shape the 'new economy'. A few giant firms dominate the platform economy: Facebook, Amazon, Apple, Microsoft and (Alphabet's) Google from the United States; Alibaba, Tencent and Baidu from China. Arguments are gaining momentum that these new organizational forms have become too dominant – because they are concentrated in the hands of a few multinationals – or are under-mining local regulatory regimes and social contracts (see Chapters 4 and 6). In response, regulatory agencies are enacting antitrust laws to push back on their market dominance. Take, for instance, the €4.3 billion fine the European Commission imposed on Google in July 2018 for abusing its dominant (network) position to discriminate against rivals (and thus in the long run lowering the innovative potential of the internet). This fine was the biggest antitrust penalty ever – and is reminiscent of comparable antitrust cases against earlier carriers of the information age, like Microsoft in the 1990s. Airbnb and Uber are centralized platforms that are increasingly criticized for undermining local safety regulations (on hotels) or minimum wage conventions (for taxi drivers). China's use of the internet as a way to monitor citizens ('social scoring'), and the role played by leading multinationals like Alibaba, Tencent and Huawei, has triggered additional concerns over the 'neutrality of the net' – which, in the original set-up of the internet, had been one of the favourable conditions of its rapid proliferation. In a 2018 UK parliamentary committee report, Facebook and Twitter were accused of 'undermining democracy' through systematic manipulation of information and using their subscribers' private information for commercial goals. Zuboff (2019) described the latter practice as being part of a new, parasitic economic order ('surveillance capitalism') that thrives on the massive capturing of behavioural data of users of free digital services as free raw material for hidden commercial practices of extraction, prediction and sales.

■ **Social: ambiguity arises** when we assess to what extent these trends contribute to positive or negative transition processes and outcomes. What societal problems do these new technological developments actually address, and what frictions and new problems do they create? *The Economist* (30 June 2018) argues that while "the internet was meant to make the world a less centralized place . . . the opposite has happened". Tim Berners-Lee, the inventor of the world wide web (www), stated that the internet "has failed to deliver the positive, constructive society many of us had hoped for".[1] Without appropriate normative frameworks, regulatory standards and capable governance mechanisms, digitalization could eventuate in eroding social cohesion, notably by magnifying fragmentation and inequality, enhancing political and economic power concentration, undercutting civil rights by exploiting and oppressing people, and undermining governance capabilities of public organizations (TWI2050: 2019).

1.2.1 Long waves explain major patterns

What can be asserted from this short coverage of recent events? Technological change never appears in isolation. The consequences are never neutral and require a longer-term lens to assess their influences. To serve this need, political economists and transition scholars delineate so-called 'long waves' (also known as 'Kondratieffs') to contextualize developments. They look at stages of economic development and the appearance of dominant (hegemonic) systems that create a certain level of stability in the global system. Remarkably regular historical patterns were found by studying the development of so-called 'techno-economic paradigms'

---

1 *The Economist*, 30 June 2018 special report: 'How to fix what has gone wrong with the internet'.

(Freeman and Perez, 1988; Perez, 2002) and how these influence the competitive position of countries and leading firms within these countries. Countries appear able to achieve an 'edge' over other countries, in four stages (Kennedy, 1989):

1   First, a **productive edge**, based on efficiency in production systems that lead to high productivity and/or lower wages;

2   Next, based on this competitive advantage, a **commercial edge**, which enables leading companies in the country to expand and grow, also abroad;

3   Then, a **financial edge**, which results in a robust stock exchange (financial centre), but also in investments in new technologies that require longer-term investments;

4   Finally, on the basis of all edges combined, a **military edge** that enables a country to safeguard its political, technological and economic interests around the world.

Combined, these edges can create a *hegemonic position* for one national economic system (Figure 1.1). The appearance of an undisputed and clear hegemon has been found to create relative stability throughout the world. This happened, for instance, in the 19th century, due to the leading position of the British Empire as a result of the first and second industrial revolutions that materialized in that country.[2] The UK not only developed a highly competitive and innovative industry based on their smart use of steam, coal and electricity, it also made London the financial centre of the world and enabled the British Empire to include large parts of the world (the Commonwealth) through its military supremacy. This period is also known as *Pax Brittanica*.

Another hegemonic cycle started with the growth of the US economy in the 20th century, as a result of efficient mass production methods (Fordism) applied in cars and food, the use of new energy sources (electricity, oil), pharmaceutics and telecommunication technologies. Many have qualified the post-war period of the 20th century as *Pax Americana*, with the US dollar as the world currency, New York as the financial centre of the world, and the military strength of the United States as unparalleled. The main contender in this period has been the Soviet Union, but only on the basis of its military strength. Ultimately, the communist alternative societal model to the American model collapsed, because of poor performance on all three other edges (productive, financial and commercial). The end of the cold war by

---

2   There is a vivid discussion on the exact periodization and qualification of 'industrial revolutions' and the outlook and length of long waves of technological, economic and political change. The UK has been attributed either one or two cycles of hegemonic power. For the sake of simplicity, we abstract from this discussion and define three relevant periods in which a hegemonic power appeared and receded and which consequently resulted in (two) major transition periods.

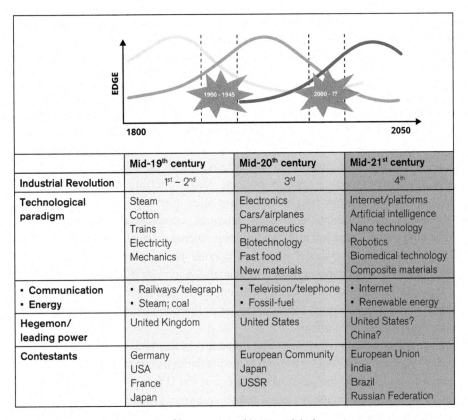

	Mid-19th century	Mid-20th century	Mid-21st century
Industrial Revolution	1st – 2nd	3rd	4th
Technological paradigm	Steam Cotton Trains Electricity Mechanics	Electronics Cars/airplanes Pharmaceutics Biotechnology Fast food New materials	Internet/platforms Artificial intelligence Nano technology Robotics Biomedical technology Composite materials
• Communication • Energy	• Railways/telegraph • Steam; coal	• Television/telephone • Fossil-fuel	• Internet • Renewable energy
Hegemon/ leading power	United Kingdom	United States	United States? China?
Contestants	Germany USA France Japan	European Community Japan USSR	European Union India Brazil Russian Federation

Figure 1.1 Long waves: periods of hegemony and increased rivalry

1989, according to some, signalled the 'end of history' (Fukuyama, 1992) and the victory of Western liberal democracy as championed by the United States.

Focusing on the role of technology and societal organization, economist and social theorist thinker Jeremy Rifkin observed that the great economic revolutions in history occur when new communication technologies converge with new energy systems. In his words: "new energy regimes make possible the creation of more interdependent economic activity and expanded commercial exchange as well as facilitate more dense and inclusive social relationships. The accompanying communication revolutions become the means to organize and manage the new temporal and spatial dynamics that arise from new energy systems" (Rifkin, 2011: 2).

1.2.2 The rise and decline of major powers

But every hegemonic cycle also comes to an end. With the maturing of a new technological paradigm – often combined with a restructuring of society and changes in the set of leading companies – the sources of what constitutes a competitive edge change. The literature on the 'rise and fall/decline of nations' (Olson, 1982; Kennedy, 1989; Sharma, 2016) shows that every cycle of ascendance ultimately leads to a cycle of decline of a leading economic system and country. First because of internal erosion processes, but also through the maturing of strong contenders, often spearheaded by strong companies that try to 'invade' other countries. This process results in major and often turbulent *transition periods* in which the position of the former 'hegemon' or leading economy is challenged by a few powerful and innovative newcomers that represent a more recent technological paradigm.

Historians have pointed to the occurrence of so-called 'systemic wars' precisely during these transition periods. Major conflicts between countries appear when the former hegemonic power finds itself in a downward slope on vital edges (productivity, technology, financial, competitive) and only has its remaining military edge left to defend its international political and economic position. Historically, long-range transition periods have, therefore, always been accompanied by growing conflict and ultimately even war (Kennedy, 1989). The war can be military but often starts as an economic and technology-related battle that involves the economic representatives of the contesting systems, in particular, multinational enterprises.

In more recent history since the beginning of the 19th century, this cyclical pattern was first observed for the end of the first industrial revolution. The declining power of the UK and the upcoming powers of the United States, Germany and Japan resulted in a distinctly violent transition period (World Wars I and II). The victory of the US model of mass production (Fordism), laid the foundation for American hegemony throughout most of the 20th century. At the turn of the century (2000) the cycle repeats itself. Sizable contenders have appeared at the world stage disputing the leadership of the US. To many, the present trade conflicts, geopolitical tensions and rivalry between China and the United States (also) embody a fight for (global) hegemony.[3]

1.2.3 Assessing the characteristics of the present transition period

In any case, the present transition period creates considerable ambiguity on the direction in which the international system is heading. The following features

---

3   Relevant illustration of the military side of the present transition period: the *Stockholm International Peace Research Institute (SIPRI)* keeps track of the size and nature of military expenditures around the world. Global military spending amounted to $1822 billion in 2018. It has been gradually rising, following a post-2009 dip in 2014. In 2018, military expenditure was 76% higher than in the post-cold war low in 1998. Expenditures also create sales for military equipment producers. The sales of the 100 largest weapon producers in the world amounted to $380 billion in 2018. Compared to 2002, this represents a 50% increase (SIPRI database: https://www.sipri.org/databases/milex).

illustrate some of the developments that come with shifting power balances and global systemic transitions:

■ *From hegemony to multipolarity:* without an undisputed 'hegemon', the advent of a multipolar policy system is looming. Current polar relations in the world have become unclear, tense and fickle, and medium-sized powers are gaining in geopolitical and economic influence. Concurrently, regional arrangements have come under pressure: the European Union is challenged by the exit of the UK (Brexit) and anti-European sentiments in some of its member countries; the North American Free Trade Agreement (NAFTA) has been renegotiated under pressure from the United States, with the redrafted trade terms under the United States-Mexico-Canada Agreement (USMCA) now providing for possible tariffs by the United States against Canada, in addition to the possibility of separate bilateral deals.

■ *From globalization frenzy to disillusionment:* there is growing animosity around the fallouts of the 'era of globalization' (Stiglitz, 2018). The extraordinary economic growth observed in the last decades – $87 trillion in global GDP in 2018, up from $11 trillion in 1980 (IMF, 2019) – has failed to close the deep divides within and across countries. According to the UN's *World Economic Situation Prospects 2020*, one in five countries will see per capita incomes stagnate or decline (UN DESA, 2020). At the same time, more than two-thirds (71%) of the world population live in countries where inequality has grown (UN DESA, 2020a). Globally, the wealthiest 1% has been increasing their share of income, whereas the bottom 40% earned less than a quarter of the income in all countries. Oxfam International (2018) assessed that 82% of all wealth created in 2017 went to the richest 1%. In 2019, it found that the world's 2,153 billionaires had accumulated more wealth than the 4.6 billion people who make up 60% of the global population (Oxfam International, 2020). An estimated $7 trillion in private wealth – equal to 8% of global GDP – is hidden in offshore financial centres (IMF, 2019). Meanwhile, the labour income share (as opposed to the share of national income going to the holders of capital) declined at the global level, from 54% in 2004, to 51% in 2017 (ILO, 2020b). These trends in wealth concentration and deepening inequalities have triggered the rise of populism, nationalism, violent conflict, loss of values and the (s)election of authoritarian leaders. Spiralling disparities tend to affect people across several generations.

■ *From stable regulation to growing regulatory ambiguity:* this applies in particular with regard to the appropriateness and effects of privatization, the liberalization of markets, and the way in which the internet, digitalization and platform companies should be regulated. Especially transboundary and global governance problems – climate change, biodiversity loss, migration, pollution, taxation – are progressively difficult to address when (geo)politics, (geo)economics, technological advancement and social structures are highly interlinked, and normative frameworks diverge.

■ *The end of multilateralism*? Trade disputes, global economic slowdown and geopolitical uncertainties deepen political polarization, while scepticism over the benefits of multilateralism increases (UN DESA, 2020). A stalling multilateral regime unfolds. The World Trade Organization (WTO) for instance – one of the clearest supranational organizations, initiated in 1995 – lost most of its appeal after 2000. Instead, bilateral trade and investment deals grow in importance. Increasing unilateral and protectionist sentiments are observed around the world, further nurtured by a synchronized slowdown of the global economy – the emerging markets included (IMF, 2019). In 2019, world Gross Domestic Product growth and world trade growth fell to their lowest level in a decade, while high levels of debt increased the risks of financial instability (UN DESA, 2020). In its World Economic Outlook of April 2021, the IMF projected the global economy – already fragile, indebted and slow-growing before the Covid-19 pandemic hit – to contract sharply in response to the pandemic, with an expected world output loss of 3% by 2024 (see section 7.4). The recession turns out to be more harmful for developing countries than for developed countries.

■ *A protestocracy is developing*, as a result of collapsing levels of trust in societal elites (political and business establishments in particular) to actively handle today's grand challenges. A growing cynicism around capitalism and the fairness of current economic systems can be witnessed, as well as deep-seated fears about the future. Climate marches of young generations (Generation Z and Millennials) appear, accompanied by growing protests in developed and developing countries alike, demanding more democracy, transparency and equality (e.g. the Black Lives Matter marches). In the 2010–2020 period, major protests on these grievances appeared for instance in Sudan, Algeria, Chili, Bolivia, Iran, Ecuador, Colombia, Brazil, Haiti, Egypt, Lebanon, Indonesia, the United States and Hong Kong. To some, these manifestations signal the dawning of an assertive 'commons movement' (Rotmans, 2017) that tries to create countervailing, bottom-up approaches in response to the systemic failures of present societal arrangements. For others, these manifestations signal the rise of populism.

These tendencies have been accompanied by the emergence of new players (including those from post-communist transition countries); the unprecedented acceleration of international commerce and communication by virtue of rapid technological advances and reduced trade and investments barriers; the continued rise of outsourcing; and the profound restructuring of corporate governance and alliance structures. Collectively and individually, these processes continue to reshape the relation and power balance between sovereign states and markets, and thereby the future of (international) business. The consequences will undoubtedly resonate for many decades to come.

The signals for the present transition period are clear: systems failure, rising tensions and distrust, parallel (ecological, financial, economic, social) crises, an unsettled geopolitical landscape, resulting in a growing number of increasingly intertwined societal issues at local, national, regional and global levels. The WEF's *Global Risks Report* gives an account of an increased number of interrelated risks (Figure 1.2) that follow from the present "fog of geopolitical and geo-economic uncertainty" (WEF, 2020a). Likewise, companies have started to identify ever longer lists of risks in their annual reports in order to navigate and manage the inherent threats of increased uncertainty, as well as the opportunities that are opening up (Van Tulder and Roman, 2019). In its *Sustainable Development Outlook 2019*, the United Nations delineates compounding global challenges that have developed against the backdrop of weakening global growth, geopolitical uncertainties and rapid technological change. Growing debt burdens, trade conflicts, rising income inequality within and between countries, aggravating climate change, protracted and escalating violent conflicts and growing migration pressures are identified as 'gathering storms' that are decidedly shaping society's prospects for a sustainable future (UN DESA, 2019a). Many of the present transition phenomena can be related to shifting powers and the rivalrous nature of the global system. The stakes of the 21st century transition period are thus not only technological but also political and profoundly developmental. Today's quest for progress is, therefore: What defines the most *resilient* development model?

1.2.4 Addressing present transition dynamics

In transition periods, it becomes vital but increasingly challenging to get a sense of how the complex interaction of developments will play out. Correspondingly, trend, foresight and scenario analyses have been growing in importance and sophistication. Dynamic modelling approaches (e.g. complex adaptive systems

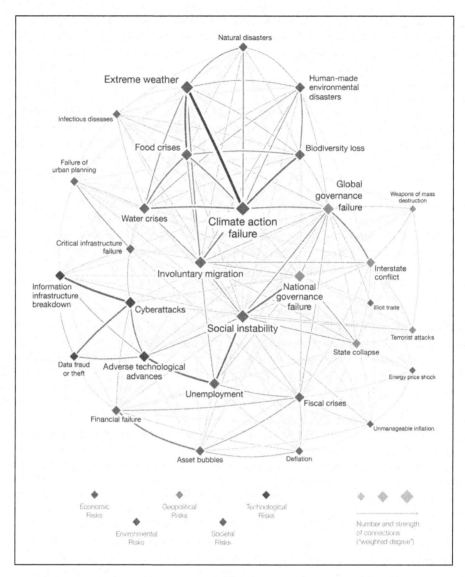

Figure 1.2 The Global Risks Interconnection Map, 2020

Source: WEF (2020a), licensed under CCPL

analyses, integrated assessment modelling) and 'big data' gathering methods that distinguish patterns of interaction, are increasingly being used to help identify critical (policy) interventions and define pathways or roadmaps to a preferred future. Given the myriad complexities of the system dynamics involved, such efforts are more and more organized as collaborative approaches, in which various experts and knowledge centres cooperate (Box 1.2).

PATHWAYS TOWARDS A SUSTAINABLE FUTURE

B O X 1.2

In 2018, three cooperating knowledge centres issued an influential report on trans-formations towards a sustainable future: The International Institute for Applied Systems Analysis (IIASA), the Sustainable Development Solutions Network (SDSN) and the Stockholm Resilience Centre (SRC). They used the pooled knowledge and resources of scientists from over 20 institutes and 100 independent experts from academia, business, government, intergovernmental and non-governmental organiza-tions. Successful identification of pathways towards a sustainable future requires a comprehensive, robust approach that can deal with non-linearity and that spans across disciplines and methodologies. The consortium would thus need to reflect necessary competencies in integrated assessment modelling, earth system model-ling, scenario development, theories of governance, and large-scale dynamics of social change.

Based on studies of current trends and dynamics and a 'back-casting' narrative – with quantitative and qualitative (multidimensional, science-based) targets and indicators of desirable end-states – the consortium's *The World in 2050* report identified six 'exemplary transformations' relevant for achieving long-term sustaina-bility in the coming decades: (1) Human capacity and demography; (2) Consumption and production; (3) Decarbonisation and energy; (4) Food, biosphere and water; (5) Smart cities; and (6) Digital revolution (TWI2050, 2018).

The study aspired to delineate a roadmap along integrated pathways, as well as approaches for governing these transformations to inform and provide guidance for policymakers. The exploration of pathways hence included qualitative and quanti-tative analysis of governance mechanisms and dynamics of social change needed to implement them (the quantification of timing, technologies and costs of the transfor-mations, and the identification of measures such as public awareness, public delib-eration, social activism and democratic oversight of science and technology to overcome obstacles to change). The integrated pathways that resulted from this effort describe "a multidimensional trajectory of economic, social, and demographic change, together with a detailed description of the economic, political, and social instruments to support the trajectory towards the desired goal" (TWI2050, 2018: 9).

A consecutive TWI2050 report (TWI2050, 2019) focused on the opportunities and challenges of *digitalization* in the light of sustainable development for all. It outlines the necessary preconditions for a successful digital transformation, including prosperity, social inclusion, environmental sustainability and governance aspects, and some of the far-reaching social implications associated with an increasingly digital future.

Scientific findings on the *direction* in which societal dynamics need to be guided, converge and are increasingly clear.[4] However, robust predictions on the exact outcome of many transformational aspects are still illusive. Such forecasts would require a fully integrated perspective on and understanding of the interplay, pace and magnitude of all societal dynamics that are presently restructuring our world – a capacity that is yet to be developed. The portrayal by many of the present period as one of *radical* transformation is not accidental. The systemic nature of the changes, but also the relative obscurity of the societal response to the huge transformations that the world is facing, has prompted many to adopt the (neutral) 'VUCA' acronym as a short-hand characterization for the present state of the world. The acronym was first introduced towards the end of the cold war (1987–1991) and has been used by the United States Army War College to describe the Volatility, Uncertainty, Complexity and Ambiguity associated with the new dynamics in technology and society.

A VUCA world has profound implications for the way we look at the world, both in science and in practice. Predictive forecasting methods – which all to a greater or lesser extent assume that the empirical world can be known – no longer suffice. Predictions can only suggest a certain, limited set of possibilities. As has been colourfully asserted, "foresight is to the future what rain dances are to the weather, a belief in untestable causality" (McDermott, 1996: 192). Tipping points, cross-linkages, and actions that prompt whole new branches of unanticipated side effects with unknown consequences, considerably hamper our anticipating policy and planning capacities. Table 1.1 lists a number of typical questions to bear in mind when addressing societal challenges in a 'VUCA' world.

Table 1.1 Critical questions in a VUCA world

Volatility	• Can we extrapolate trends?
	• Is volatility the same as turbulence?
	• Can volatility also be a sign of positive change and transition?
	Economic example:
	- *How to interpret, anticipate and deal with currency fluctuations and volatile equity markets.*

---

4   Several studies have emerged that identify transformational pathways for achieving sustainable development related to the SDGs. Although based on different research approaches with different purposes, the studies converge towards comparable transformational paths that stress similar key themes, entries, levers and types of governance measures. See, for instance, the *Global Sustainable Development Report 2019: The Future is Now: Science for Achieving Sustainable Development*, by the UN Independent Group of Scientists (2019), and 'Six Transformations to Achieve the Sustainable Development Goals (SDGs)' by Sachs et al. (2019).

Uncertainty	• How and when can we take action in addressing problems? • Is it possible to define positive action plans under uncertainty? • How to foresee and mitigate major risks? *Economic examples:* - *How to deal with calculations of key economic indicators like inflation or GDP growth?* - *For pension funds: how to index future income and expenditures?*
Complexity	• To what extent can we simplify grand challenges? • How to understand trends that both shape and are an outcome of developments? • How should we deal with one-sided approaches; what to do with unintended outcomes? • Can technology solve complex societal problems? *Economic example:* - *What to do with the growing complexity of financial instruments, markets and technologies? How to regulate?*
Ambiguity	• Who should be held responsible? • Who can take responsibility? • How to deal with trade-offs? *Economic examples:* - *How to deal with trade-offs in a variety of markets: bonds versus equity; public or private funding of facilities; housing investments?* - *Can 'disruptive' or 'radical' technological change be guided in the 'right' direction?*

1.3   DEALING WITH FUNDAMENTAL TRADE-OFFS IN A VUCA WORLD

How to approach these sources of contention and transformation? Since the start of the 21st century, the thinking on sustainable growth and development has undergone substantive changes, not only under the influence of the VUCA world but also because of major breakthroughs in scientific thinking. Some relevant areas of scientific dispute include the following fundamental debates:

1   Open or closed societies?

2   Inclusive or exclusive ambitions related to growth?

3   How balanced should societies be, and does one size fit all?

4   The degree of common goods provision?

5   How to deal with institutional voids, related complexities and trust issues?

6   What type of science and thinking is needed to deal with present complexity?

7   Focusing on collaborative or competitive pathways, embedded in positive or negative change frames?

1.3.1 Open or closed societies?

Firstly, it has been successfully argued that 'open societies' are important for progress. But because of the nature and stretch of parallel systemic crises that put economic and political systems under pressure, the initial optimism about 'globalization' has been eroding into disillusionment among considerable parts of society. The realization took hold that the way globalization was being organized also comes with fragilities, growing risks and negative side effects. This recognition developed from a worry about the 'millennium bug', via unequal trade deals, ecological crises, refugee crises and civil wars over scarce resources, to the disgruntled responses to the 'Arab Spring' (commenced in 2011) and the related menace of global terrorism. Especially the global financial crisis that started in 2007 in the United States revealed the sizable vulnerabilities related to the set-up of the global financial system. All these crises show a pattern of systemic failure that requires a new – more equitable and smarter – configuration of international relations and institutions, notably those related to the economic and financial interactions between countries.

The alternative – retreating behind national borders – that is considered by a growing number of governments is understandable, but has historically proven to be risky. The scientific consensus amongst institutional economists proceeds towards acceptance that there are many ways to deal with the challenges of systemic failure, although the prevalence of the 'Western' type of policies (privatization, open borders, neoliberalism) contains considerable risks and puts the burden of development mostly on to weaker countries and actors in society. Full free trade and more globalization do not provide an adequate answer to the various global crises either. If not adequately addressed, the political consequences of borderless laissez-faire will create many victims, and a backlash that supports populist and protectionist movements.

A more subtle mix of policy measures is needed. Trade economist Dani Rodrik (2011) refers to this as the inescapable *trilemma* of the world economy. In short, this implies that democracy, national sovereignty and global economic integration are mutually incompatible. The global system can combine any two of the three, but can never have all three simultaneously and in full. This is also one of the reasons why, for instance, a less democratic system like China's – which puts much emphasis on national political and economic sovereignty – seems to profit more from global economic integration than the United States or Europe, who aspire to focus on all three dimensions at the same time.

Currently, the approach on a global scale leans towards re-regulation rather than deregulation, and probably also towards less globalization. In Rodrik's trilemma, many trade-offs exist: "If we want more globalization, we must either give up some democracy or some national sovereignty." Or, conversely, if we seek national sovereignty, globalization has its limits. So, mixed and more balanced models will not only appear but are probably the best way forward to reap the benefits of international interdependence (globalization), while preventing negative effects from taking over.

1.3.2 Inclusive or exclusive societies?

Secondly and closely related to the above realization, evidence is mounting that sustainable progress can only be achieved if countries adopt *inclusive* growth policies and inclusive development strategies. Inequalities represent economic power imbalances that not only undermine economic performance, but also run the risk of becoming politically entrenched. Inequality and exclusion are, therefore, indicators of impending social unrest, crumbling social cohesion and instability. A study by the International Monetary Fund (Dabla-Norris et al., 2015) of 159 economies for the 1980–2012 period, found three trends that are pivotal in this light: (1) growing income inequality had a *negative* effect on economic growth; (2) increasing the income share of the poor and middle class had actually increased economic growth; and (3) a rising income share of the top 20% resulted in lower growth. In other words, when the rich get richer, the poor do not automatically profit. Wealth does not trickle down.

Inclusiveness and reducing income inequality are thus a necessary precondition for sustained progress. They provide the crucial conditions for enhancing human capabilities and agency – through education, health, living standards, dignity and acknowledgement of human rights – that are vital drivers for enhancing productivity and prosperity. Inclusive growth – as a concept – advances equitable opportunities for economic participants and benefits *every* part of society, in monetary and non-monetary terms. This definition implies that there is a direct link between the macro and micro determinants of progress. According to the World Bank (2008), the micro dimension captures the importance of structural transformation for economic diversification and competition. In this regard, the definition of inclusive growth differs from so-called 'pro-poor' growth policies, as the pro-poor approach is mainly interested in the welfare of the deprived. Inclusive growth is concerned with opportunities for the majority of the labour force, poor and middle class alike (OECD, 2014a).

1.3.3 One-sided or balanced societies?

Thirdly, inclusive and sustainable growth is increasingly based on the idea of 'balanced' development. Since the 1980s, the dominant model introduced in most societies was one of neoliberal economics. Welfare states in Western democracies, it was argued, had turned out to be too expensive. In contrast, central planning in communist countries was associated with great inefficiencies and suppression of civil society. A largely one-sided emphasis on markets developed as a leading organizational principle of societies. Privatization and liberalization of markets prevailed, accompanied by the view that governments should also be managed as companies – as embodied in the 'new public management' discourse. In the early decades of the 21st century, however, these organizing principles were seriously challenged, not only by the failure of many liberal economies to serve the needs of *all* groups of the population but also by the recognition that not every aspect of society could be left to the operation of markets.

The basic idea, amongst others advanced by management scholar Henry Mintzberg (2015), was that three institutional spheres of society – state, civil society and markets – actually complement each other and hold (joint) responsibility for inclusiveness and sustainability (Van Tulder and Pfisterer, 2014). Where this interaction is constructive and based on complementary logics and capacities, societies become more resilient and agile and thrive. Balanced societies consequently require 'concerted leadership' on the part of both public and private sectors (Nelson et al., 2009), and acknowledge the role and function of cross-sector partnerships, for instance between civil society organizations (CSOs) and the corporate sector. As the institutional configuration of economies has a strong impact on growth (Rodrik et al., 2004), the concept of a balanced society reiterates the importance of so-called 'inclusive institutions' in support of inclusive growth (Acemoglu et al., 2014; Rajan, 2019). Thinking about the institutional set-up of societies is the realm of welfare economics and public-good theory.

Every challenge of sustainable and balanced development has at least three *value dimensions* that define its nature and delineate possible directions to address it:

■ **Public value:** to what extent can it be classified as an insufficient implementation of the primary roles of governments, in particular regulation and public goods provision on a non-discriminatory basis?

■ **Private value:** to what extent can it be resolved by market-based approaches, in which companies compete and provide private goods on an exclusive and profit-oriented basis?

■ **Social value:** to what extent can it be efficiently addressed by (organized) citizens without interference of governments and/or firms? Social goods provision is often provided on a partly exclusive but non-rival basis, in which the group profits from sharing resources, mainly by virtue of trusted relationships.

Based on these values, a balanced society delivers public, private *and* social goods in sufficient propositions. It profits from the resilience of various mechanisms and capacities that operate in a complementary way. One can distinguish in that between the *degree of rivalry* and the *degree of exclusion.* Goods and values are called 'rival' if their consumption or usage prevents simultaneous consumption or usage by others, as is the case with most consumption goods. Because of their rival nature, consumer goods are easier to produce in an efficient and profitable manner. Non-rival goods do not prevent others from simultaneous consumption. If this involves an unlimited number of users, we talk about 'public goods'.

Economist Paul Samuelson (1954) was the first to draw attention to the essential role of governments (and regulation) in the effective and sufficient production of public goods, which are non-rivalrous (i.e. the consumption by an individual of those goods does not lead to a reduction in any other individual's consumption) and non-excludable. These two characteristics can be positive, but can also have negative effects. Pollution, for instance, does not discriminate against populations and so creates 'public *bads*' for all. If the number of users needs to be limited in order to enable a good or value to be delivered, we speak of 'club goods' or 'social goods'. Table 1.2 provides characteristics and examples of these various goods and values. From this overview, it becomes clear that well-functioning societies require a minimum level of provision of each type of goods.

In balanced societies, three values are generally well represented by three societal spheres, organized around governments, companies and communities or civil societies. Each of these societal sectors has developed 'value propositions' that potentially make it an important part of society, and even a condition for

Table 1.2 Four components of a balanced society: insights from public-good theory

| | | Degree of exclusiveness | |
		Excludable	Non-excludable
Degree of rivalry	Rivalrous	**Private goods:** Food, clothing, cars, parking spaces	**Common goods (common pool resources):** Fish stock, timber, coal, water
		Private values: For-profit; competition; reward; entitlement; innovation; scaling	**Common values:** Common heritage; well-being; responsibility; collaboration; territorial integrity
	Non-rivalrous	**Club/social goods:** Cinemas, private parks, satellite television, ground	**Public goods:** Television, fresh air, national defence, flood control systems
		Club values: Non-profit; belonging; trust; family; tribe; group interests; mutual support; community	**Public values:** Non-profit; justice; safety; security; non-discrimination; public health; public interest

Source: based on Cornes and Sandler (1986); Van Tulder with Van der Zwart (2006)

progress. Companies, for instance, can use the profits they accumulate to inno-vate and scale products and services that respond to people's needs. Ill-functioning sectors, however, create imbalances that contribute to societal problems (Part II will develop this argument further). Figure 1.3 portrays the three sectors as a triangle, each with a clear and complementary 'logic'.

Balanced development, however, does not imply a 'one-size-fits-all' approach. Societies have different starting positions and are embedded differ-ently in international relations. Sustainable development is built on an intricate combination of various coordination and control mechanisms: market-based, network-based and hierarchy-based (Van Tulder and Pfisterer, 2014). 'Rival' or 'divergent' varieties of capitalism (Whitley, 1999) exist that, in principle, can all have a positive impact on national progress and competitiveness (Witt and Jackson, 2016). Various configurations of societies are thus possible in which state and society (civil and corporate) interact, balance each other's powers, and thereby reinforce each other (Acemoglu and Robinson, 2017).

1.3.4 Sufficient common goods provision?

Arguably the biggest challenge for balanced societies lies in the societal middle: how to supply and create sufficient 'common pool' resources and values? Common

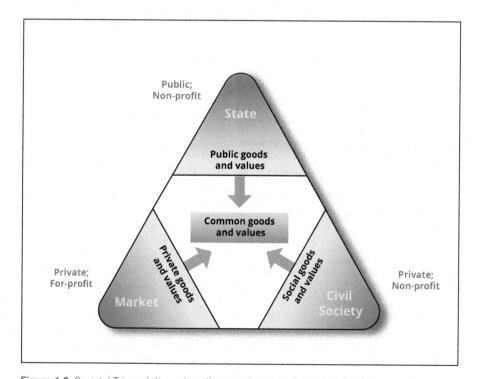

Figure 1.3 Societal Triangulation – how three sectors complement each other

pool resources typically represent natural resource systems – like forests, water or fishing grounds – from which it is difficult to exclude potential beneficiaries. In the literature, common pool problems are also referred to as 'tragedy of the commons'. This term was popularized in 1968 by American biologist Garrett Hardin to point out that individual users that act independently and in their self-interest can behave contrary to the social good by depleting or spoiling the resource through their rival-rous action. A common pasture that is used by herders in a rivalrous manner can lead to overgrazing. Each individual herder receives the full benefit of increased use, whereas the costs are spread among all users. The tragic result is the ruin of the common pasture, which in the end will make all herders suffer. If water gets depleted in a water-scarce region – for instance, because of exploitation by one major rose-growing company or by citizens that use it to water their green lawns – everybody will suffer. If governments cannot or will not regulate negative externalities – such as air, water, soil, thermal and radioactive pollution, ecological degradation or biodiversity loss – that result from rivalrous and irresponsible use of common resources, local, national or even global society will suffer.

There are no simple solutions to 'tragedy of the commons' problems. Three organizational disciplines have evolved from each of the angles of the societal triangle to take ascending levels of complexity into account: public management (state), general management (business) and social movement theory or sociology (communities). All have been moving towards acknowledging and increasingly applying societal complexity. Public management theory, for instance, has been advancing from a 'traditional' public administration approach (1.0), via a 'new' public management approach (2.0) with a focus on efficiency and accountability, to a more recent 'collaborative governance' and 'public value' management approach (3.0). The latter accommodates for defining common 'goal systems' and partnerships that share collaborative advantages by pooling resources, with a positive bearing on the whole of society (Bryson et al., 2015).

Similarly, general management approaches have been developing from a classic 1.0 (profit-maximizing) approach, via a 2.0 approach (decreasing negative effects on society), to a 3.0 approach aimed at maximizing collective or societal value. Theories of needs have been introduced (notably the 'bottom of the pyramid' in marketing and internationalization literature), along with concepts like 'shared-value creation' (in strategic management), 'co-creation', 'open innovation' and 'frugal innovation' (in innovation literature). In these approaches, companies are expected to include the interests of the other societal sectors in order to thrive and to develop new business propositions that help solve (latent) societal needs. Management theory, in general, is increasingly directed to so-called 'purpose-driven' modes of organizing that include, create and produce societal value.

In the organization and management of communities, a comparable devel-opment can be witnessed: from a 1.0 approach primarily aimed at 'mutual support' and the efficient organization of so-called 'club goods', via a 2.0 approach aimed at external advocacy and internal efficiency, to a 3.0 approach in which the 'effectiveness' and 'impact' of the chosen strategies on issues beyond the direct realm of local communities is key. When confronted with common pool problems, the community faces self-governance problems. Institutional political economist and Nobel Prize laureate Elinor Ostrom (2015) studied these issues from the community perspective and identified eight 'design principles' of stable local common-pool resource management. The first principle was one of demarcation: to clearly define the content of the common-pool resource and an effective exclusion of external untitled parties. For more systemic, wicked and common-pool problems that geographically go beyond the direct influence of communities, however, Ostrom's approach has its limitations. Consecutive research has advanced Ostrom's design principles into more expanded (2.0) 'social ecological systems' (SES) frameworks, which include wider communities. In all societal angles, the '3.0 approach' requires *cross-sector partnerships* or *hybrid organizations*. Chapters 5, 6 and 12 further elaborate on this notion.

1.3.5 Dealing with the institutional void and inherent complexity

The societal centre of the triangle with its related common-pool problems is also known as the 'institutional void'. In many developing countries, as well as between countries at the international level, formal institutions do not exist or are only weakly enforced. Emerging economies are typically characterized by institutional voids as markets and economic growth in these economies tend to advance faster than social and institutional (e.g. regulatory and normative) structures do. Without appropriate institutional capacity and governance arrangements in place, overexploitation of natural resources and other types of negative externalities are likely to emerge. Institutional voids thus mirror the absence of 'societal checks and balances', and the lack of 'inclusive institutions' that can support companies and communities in living up to their full potential of contributing to inclusiveness and the common good.

Institutional voids also create 'trust gaps' in societies, which adversely affect the effectiveness of societal actors to contribute to positive change. For new initiatives that seek to go beyond conventional practices, however, institutional voids may also create so-called 'opportunity room' to come up with novel solutions. The void can only be advantageously filled through concerted actions of each of the societal sectors, through which new arrangements can be created to develop the common goods that are needed for the whole of society to thrive (Van Tulder with Van der Zwart, 2006). Successful companies can reshape the institutional void into an 'opportunity' space (Mair and Marti, 2009).

Leading authors thereby emphasize the importance of a 'new social contract' for the creation of a common good at the local, national and global level (Sachs,

2015; Mazzucato, 2018; Reich, 2018). Faced with the present approach of economists to contemporary grand challenges, economic thinker and Nobel Prize laureate Jean Tirole (2017) asked himself "Whatever happened to the common good in economic thinking?" He offers a strongly worded warning about the dominance of one sector in society (markets) and the related "disintegration of the social contract and the loss of human dignity, the decline of politics and public service and the environmental unsustainability of the present economic model" (ibid: 1). A (new) social contract would have to be based on the involve-ment of multiple stakeholders and inspired by the complexity of common-pool problems, and not be simplified into 'either/or' – that is, public *or* private, for-profit *or* non-profit – solutions.

It is increasingly recognized that understanding societal complexity lies at the very core of sustainable development. Development economist and Special Advisor to the UN Secretary General Jeffrey Sachs, for instance, stresses the importance of understanding (societal) complexity as follows: "unless we combine economic growth with social inclusion and environmental sustainability, the economic gains are likely to be short-lived, as they will be followed by social insta-bility and a rising frequency of environmental catastrophes" (Sachs, 2015: 27). Hence, sustainable development can only be addressed in a collaborative manner through the involvement of various stakeholders from all three societal spheres (Figure 1.3): state (public/non-profit), market (private/for-profit) and civil society (public/non-profit). The politics, processes and dynamics that come with that add an additional layer of complexity to the adequate implementation of sustainable development ambitions.

1.3.6   Hard (quantitative, conventional) versus soft (qualitative, emerging) approaches?

The complexity of societal challenges has repercussions for the research approach to be taken by students, practitioners and scholars alike. Whereas so-called 'hard sciences' tend to focus on quantitative 'facts' in a rather linear way, it is not easy to capture social reality through this type of thinking. American astrophysicist Neil deGrasse Tyson framed this as follows: "In science, when human behaviour enters the equation, things go nonlinear. That is why physics is easy and sociology is hard."[5] Placing people and organizations at the centre of attention requires a higher level of 'tolerance for ambiguity' and critical thinking, which involves reasoned and thought-out judgement based on careful analytical and reflexive evaluation, conceptual creativity and contextual consideration. Critical and triangular thinking on wicked problems defines an act of so-called

---

5   Tweet, 5 February 2016, @neiltyson.

sense-making. In this context, Christian Madsbjerg – a strong advocate of using human intelligence to solve problems as opposed to relying on big data only – argues that the feeling of overwhelming complexity of today's world is actually reinforced by people's "obsession with organizing [the world] as an assembly of facts . . . rather than taking responsibility for interpreting" these phenomena (Madsbjerg, 2017: 22).

What constitutes a correct interpretation, however, is not without controversy, nor pitfalls. In his thought-provoking book *Factfulness* (2018), Swedish statistician and international health scholar Hans Rosling, for instance, presents a much more positive world view than is usually adopted by development experts. By taking a long-term perspective on global trends, Rosling found that the world is in a much better state than many observers would argue. Cognitive and evolutionary psychologist Steven Pinker also advances this conclusion (2018), based on accounts on many fields of progress (e.g. health, wealth, inequality, democracy, safety, peace, quality of life) in the human condition since the 17th and 18th centuries. Even experts, Rosling contends, systematically tend to wrongly assess such basic trends like the number of people living in poverty or the percentage of girls finishing school. He identified several dysfunctional 'instincts' that tend to blur our observations and, therefore, our judgement. The most relevant distorting tendencies can be clustered around three dimensions: (1) an instinctive inclination towards 'negativity' and 'fear'; (2) an instinctive preference for simplicity, 'single-perspective' and 'straight-line' judgement; and (3) an instinctive 'urgency' and 'blame' impulse. Each of these inclinations obstructs scholars, policymakers and managers in interpreting trends correctly and in designing appropriate action.

Kate Raworth (2017) takes a comparable stance to critically 'think again'. In her influential *Doughnut Economics*, Raworth pleads for a fundamental rethinking of mainstream economics in order to better understand and more aptly respond to the complex challenges of the 21st century. The conventional economic paradigm, with a fixed focus on GDP growth as the single leading measure of societal success, has led to an untenable yet dominant steering principle in which "economies have to grow, whether or not they make us thrive". What we need instead, Raworth argues, are "economies that make us thrive, whether or not they grow" (ibid: 26). The aspiration of '21st-century economists' should, therefore, be to steer societies into operating within a 'safe and just space for humanity', portrayed by a doughnut in which the inner ring is defined by society's social foundations of well-being, and the upper ring by the ecological ceiling of what earth can sustain (Figure 1.4). This calls for a new narrative on prosperity, fundamentally new ways of thinking about rather antiqued economic assumptions, and new principles to create economies that are distributive and regenerative by design. '21st-century economics' would need to be founded on thinking of the economy as embedded systems that operate within the 'safe and just space', occupied by 'social

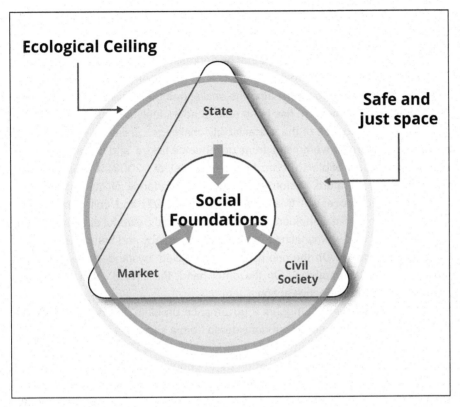

Figure 1.4 Doughnut Triangulation
Source: based on Raworth (2017)

adaptable humans' and interlinked by dynamic complexity. Raworth outlines seven ways to rethink economics, yet also acknowledges that she has no immediate solutions for solving today's complex challenges: "It would be completely unbelievable if I would give solutions, because they would all fall in the old paradigm [of thinking]."[6]

The notion that there is no single correct way of perceiving the world and that there are no evident, undisputed solutions but only more and less effective *approaches* to addressing societal problems, forms the basis of so-called complexity thinking (Part II). Decision-making and goal-setting under VUCA conditions require new techniques of negotiation (collective vision-based), impact measurement (developmental evaluation) and responsibility attribution among societal actors.

---

6   Interview with Kate Raworth by M. Laterveer, published in the Dutch newspaper *de Volkskrant*, 9 December 2017.

1.3.7 The importance of positive change and collaborative solutions

Institutional voids and trust gaps cannot be addressed through rivalry; they call for collective action that can create a 'safe space' for experimenting with new and innovative approaches to addressing the challenges that society presents. None of the three societal sectors has been able to adequately address the complexities and interrelatedness of the sustainability challenges unilaterally. Firms suffer from 'market failure', governments from 'governance failure' and civil society organizations are susceptible to 'civic failure' (Kolk et al., 2008). Complexity and systems theory literature, therefore, stress the importance of multi-stakeholder decision-making processes (Maani and Cavana, 2007) and collaborative joint action of all relevant stakeholders. The existence of two powerful effects at play in the institutional void – emanating from human psychology and behaviour – further supports this finding. On the one hand, the so-called 'bystander effect' and the problem of 'choice paralysis'. On the other hand, the limited value of negative frames in motivating effective action.

The bystander effect triggers a governance problem that is comparable to the 'tragedy of the commons', but considered from a social psychological point of view (Hudson and Bruckman, 2004). Individuals are less likely to offer help – for instance to a person drowning – when other people are present. They become inactive bystanders, even when they are perfectly capable of helping. This mechanism also applies to societal problems. The more 'bystanders' are present in the face of a problem, the less likely they are to take responsibility, step forward and actually act. Bystander effects are related to the distribution of responsibilities in larger groups with rival interests. Confronted with more complex problems, the bystander effect is reinforced by another social psychological effect: 'choice paralysis' (Schwartz, 2004). The concept of choice paralysis implies that people and organizations, when confronted with complex problems, tend to get stuck in negative sentiments, denial and passivity. They do not act, or they look the other way. Social psychological and behavioural research by leading thinkers, including Nobel Prize laureates Richard Thaler (2016) and Daniel Kahneman (2012), suggests that the very nature and complexity of grand challenges tends to feed into reactive, avoidant and negative attitudes.

So, the more complex a problem is, the higher the number of bystanders becomes, and the more people tend to become indecisive and reactive. In the face of global systemic crises like climate change, famine or rising income inequality, this inhibiting effect on the motivation of people to act poses a particularly intricate challenge. Presenting these phenomena as a 'disaster' or a doom-scenario as a means to mobilize action and enact measures often has limited effect. It tends to further feed into paralysis, distancing and denial, even when the overwhelming evidence points towards doom and gloom. Psychologist and economist Per Espen Stoknes (2015) applied these insights to the issue of global warming and concluded that this daunting challenge suffers from 'apocalypse fatigue'. The negative frame of the discourse around flooding coastlines, destructive storms and extinction of species, triggers evasive reactions, even with well-intentioned people. Apparently, 'hell doesn't sell'. The problem is probably widespread as 80% of news concerning sustainability issues is packaged in negative frames.

There is growing consensus among social scientists that the more effective approach to weak engagement and apocalypse fatigue is to reframe the narrative and formulate positive, meaningful and doable actions that can even be supported by deniers. Activating involvement requires a smarter approach of working *with* the peculiarities of human behaviour rather than against it, Espen Stoknes argues, notably by: (1) making the issue feel nearer and more personally relevant by spreading social norms that are positive to solutions; (2) a positive reframing of the issue by associating it with opportunities that relate to ourselves, our families and our social groups (e.g. jobs, human health, safety); and (3) applying 'nudges' that encourage small yet gradual behavioural changes and actions conducive to the cause, while providing information on progress made, impact realized and examples that inspire. These frames and empowering mechanisms create a sense of 'collective efficacy' and 'capability' to do something about the issue. Consequently, it breaks through the bystander effect, choice paralysis or apocalypse fatigue. The conviction that addressing global challenges requires concerted action and cooperation from the public and private sectors, based on positive rather than negative frames, has increasingly taken hold. This is a challenge in itself as searching for collective visions, positive change trajectories and collective action is packed with myriad cross-sectoral, multilevel and multi-stake governance issues that make it far from a naive activity.

1.4 RECONCILING DIVERGENCE AND CONVERGENCE

The previous overview of major societal trends and ways to address them (sections 1.2 and 1.3) essentially shows two dimensions of the present discourse. Both should be considered. On the one hand, we find an emergent and quite dominant response to the VUCA world that feeds into short-term, defensive and reactive sentiments. It largely ignores the consequences of global societal interdependencies in the longer run, yet strongly reacts to the dividing forces that higher levels of risk and uncertainty create, thereby reinforcing them. On the other hand – and partly as an intellectual antidote – we outlined vital insights in scientific thinking on how to understand and address today's interlinked societal challenges. These insights point to the need for convergence and mobilization, collaborative and cross-sector approaches, coherent coordination and a balancing of interests. In general, this discourse suggests that a very different – in certain aspects even radically novel – approach needs to be adopted in order to achieve longer-term positive, more resilient and sustainable outcomes for society as a whole (Figure 1.5).

The world today is complex, and many of the characteristics as depicted in Figure 1.5 can be simultaneously observed to various degrees. Extrapolating the consequences of the two extreme ways of understanding and thinking about the world can help in delineating the ultimate outcome of these frames if they would prevail (Table 1.3). What world do you want to live in?

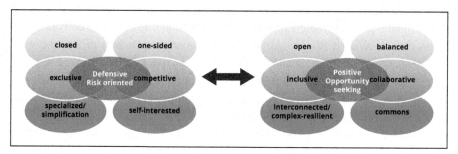

Figure 1.5 Juxtaposed approaches to a VUCA world

Table 1.3 Extrapolating consequences . . .

In a largely VUCA-driven world . . .	In a more collaborative world . . .
• A zero-sum philosophy prevails	• A positive-sum philosophy prevails
• Based on short-term orientations	• Based on medium- to long-term orientations
• Triggering rivalry and a 'race to the bottom' (beggar-thy-neighbour)	• Triggering cooperation and a 'race to the top'
• Sustained crises and systemic failure appear regularly	• Preventing crises from appearing; systemic failure is addressed
• Increased risk (awareness) appears	• Risk is addressed proactively (prevention trumps reaction)
• Linear and partial (narrow) thinking prevails	• Complexity thinking (and seeing the bigger picture) is embraced and accepted
• Market-based, growth-oriented scenarios prevail	• Societal-based, welfare-oriented scenarios prevail
• Divergence	• Convergence
• Debate-orientated	• Dialogue-orientated
• Means-orientated	• Goals-orientated
• Risk aversion drives action	• Risk taking drives action
• Value extraction and consolidation	• Value creation and distribution
• Technology drives society	• Society drives technology
• Doom scenarios prevail (risk mitigation)	• Positive scenarios prevail (opportunity seeking)
• Low-trust society	• High-trust society
• Animosity between countries increases	• Collaboration between countries increases
• Threat of war increases	• Peace through cooperation

1.4.1 Evolving insights on what defines sustainable development

All these (sometimes juxtaposed) insights and (geo)political sentiments have strongly influenced the thinking on how to organize a global agenda on sustainable development that effectively addresses global challenges while reconciling the extremes. As a concept, sustainable development has been thoroughly described by Sachs (2015) as: "both a way of looking at the world, with a focus on the interlinkages of economic, social, and environmental change, and a way of describing our shared aspirations for a decent life, combining economic development, social inclusion, and environmental sustainability" (ibid: xiii). Sustainable development is, therefore, both a science of complex systems, as well as a normative outlook of what goals would constitute the global greater good (Sachs, 2015: 3; UN Independent Group of Scientists, 2019: xx).

Since the 1970s, the appreciation of what defines sustainable development has been gradually evolving. It started with the notion that a 'global equilibrium' needed to be found between the earth's finite supply of resources and exponential economic and population growth. Over the years, the concept came to include a more integrated and richer understanding of the interdependencies involved between the world economy, global society, and the physical environment of our planet.

■ *Limits to growth; overshooting comes with collapse*

The first explicit warning pointing to the possibility of *un*sustainable development was voiced in the early 1970s, by the Club of Rome with its influential publication *Limits to Growth* (Meadows et al., 1972). It was the outcome of an ambitious 'Project on the Predicament of Mankind', which aspired to examine "the complex of problems troubling men of all nations: poverty in the midst of plenty; degradation of the environment; loss of faith in institutions; uncontrolled urban spread; insecurity of employment; alienation of youth; rejection of traditional values; and inflation and other monetary and economic disruptions" (ibid: 10).

According to the Club of Rome, the world's problems all shared three characteristics: (1) they occur to some degree in *all* societies; (2) they contain technical, social, economic and political elements; and (3) they interact. Five basic factors were examined that were assumed to determine and – in their interactions – ultimately limit 'growth on this planet': population increase, agricultural production, non-renewable resource depletion, industrial output and pollution generation. Based on computer simulations, the research team concluded that "the earth's interlocking resources – the global system of nature in which we all live – probably cannot support present rates of economic and population growth much beyond the year 2100, if that long, even with advanced technology. . . . Man can create a society in which he can live indefinitely on earth if he imposes limits on himself and his production of material goods to achieve a state of global equilibrium with population and production in carefully selected balance." Such an effort would call for a "joint endeavour by all peoples, whatever their culture, economic system, or level of development" (ibid: 194). Sustainable development, therefore, was to be understood as the prevention of an 'overshoot-collapse' effect, by curbing economic growth through a collective commitment aimed at achieving global equilibrium.

▤ *Our Common Future; intergenerational reconciliation of needs*

In 1987, the World Commission on Environment and Development – more widely known as the Brundtland Commission – published *Our Common Future*. It was to provide a 'global agenda for change', amidst a decade marked by the growing awareness of "urgent but complex problems bearing on our very survival: a warming globe, threats to the Earth's ozone layer, deserts consuming agricultural land" (UN World Commission on Environment and Development, 1987: 6), as well as the African famines, the leaks at the pesticide factory in Bhopal, India, and the nuclear disaster in Chernobyl that took place during the mid-1980s. In its report, the Brundtland Commission explicitly linked issues of human development (notably inequality, poverty, quality of life) to environmental degradation resulting from growing pressures on natural resources from lands, waters and forests. It stressed the urgent need – but even more so the powerful potential – of reconciling human affairs with natural laws while thriving in the process. The envisioned way forward was a new era of forceful economic growth that simultaneously would have to be socially and environmentally sustainable. Humanity had that possibility, under the condition of greater international willingness and cooperation to combat international poverty, to maintain peace and enhance security worldwide, and to manage the global commons. The goals of economic and social development, therefore, needed to be defined in terms of sustainability in *all* countries – developed or developing, market-oriented or centrally planned. Moreover, the Brundtland Commission stressed that physical sustainability could not be secured unless development policies paid attention to such crucial considerations as access to resources, the distribution of costs and benefits, and social equity between and within generations. The Brundtland Commission therefore defined sustainable development as: "*development that meets the needs of the present without compromising the ability of future generations to meet their own needs*" (ibid: 41).

The Brundtland definition of sustainable development has proven influential and resilient. It is still embraced by many policymakers and scholars, notwithstanding criticism that it is too conservative and optimistic about the influence of technological change. The Brundtland report contrasts with the *Limits to Growth* report, in that it does not regard the natural resource base to be finite, but rather to be imposed by the state of technology, the social organization of environmental

resources, and by the ability of the biosphere to absorb the effects of human activities. Technology and social organization, the report stated, can be both managed
and improved, *if* one could succeed in "furthering the common understanding and
common spirit of responsibility so clearly needed in a divided world" (ibid: 9).

■ *Triple Bottom Line; a 'new capitalism' through unifying People,*
Planet, Profit

In the 1990s, business author John Elkington felt that the language of the global
sustainable development agenda would have to resonate with business if more
substantial progress was to be made. To provoke more profound thinking about
capitalism and its future – and the role of business in it – he introduced the concept
of the 'Triple Bottom Line' (TBL) to delineate 'the sustainable corporation' (Elkington,
1994). The TBL concept reflected a so-called 'triple helix' for value creation by
companies to spur the regeneration of economies, societies and the biosphere.
The management framework introduced aimed at examining the social ('people'),
environmental ('planet') and economic ('profit') performance of companies over a
period of time in order to encourage businesses to both track and manage
economic, social and environmental value added, or destroyed. The concept saw a
rapid uptake in the business terminology on sustainability, accompanied by the
growing relevance of corporate social responsibility (CSR). It inspired consecutive
frameworks on the measuring of – and reporting on – corporate sustainability
performance, such as 'social return on investment' (SROI), 'integrated reporting',
'impact investing' and the ESG framework that is widely used by investors and
financial analysts to assess environmental, social and governance factors of doing
business. In 2018, however, Elkington concluded that the TBL concept had been
poorly understood as a 'balancing act' or false trade-off, being captured and diluted
by accountants and reporting consultants. It was never supposed to be just an
accounting system; the stated goal from the outset was system change by pushing
toward the transformation of capitalism (Elkington, 2018; Henriques and
Richardson, 2004). It led him to recall the TBL concept.

Influenced by the wide uptake of 'People, Planet, Profit' thinking, the
concept of sustainable development evolved into a more practical approach of
linking social inclusion, environmental sustainability and economic development
in an integrative way. In addition, sustainable development was no longer the
exclusive realm of governments as business was increasingly recognized as a
relevant agent for advancing societal progress as well.

■ *The Future We Want; integrated, equitable and inclusive*
development for all

In 2012, the Rio+ 20 UN Conference on Sustainable Development resulted in
the declaration, *The Future We Want* (UN, 2012). The outcome document set

out the direction for sustainable development and a global green economy, accompanied by several strategies and follow-up measures for coordinating and implementing this ambition. In 20 years, the document notes, progress on sustainable development and poverty eradication had been uneven, whereas insufficient progress had been made in the integration of the three dimensions of sustainable development: economic, ecologic and social. The declaration hence underscored the need and reaffirmed commitment "to further mainstream sustainable development at all levels, integrating economic, social and environmental aspects and recognizing their interlinkages, so as to achieve sustainable development in all its dimensions" (ibid: para. 3). Sustainable development was thereby delineated as an integral package of

"promoting sustained, inclusive and equitable economic growth, creating greater opportunities for all, reducing inequalities, raising basic standards of living, fostering equitable social development and inclusion, and promoting integrated and sustainable management of natural resources and ecosystems that supports, inter alia, economic, social and human development while facilitating ecosystem conservation, regeneration and restoration and resilience in the face of new and emerging challenges" (ibid: para. 4).

As part of the process of developing a 'post-2015' agenda, the Rio+ 20 declaration called for the negotiation and adoption of internationally agreed Sustainable Development Goals by the end of 2014 that would build upon the Millennium Development Goals – initiated in 2000 and ending in 2015. These goals would have to "address and incorporate in a balanced way all three dimensions of sustainable development and their interlinkages" (ibid: para. 246), in addition to being "action-oriented, concise and easy to communicate, limited in number, aspirational, global in nature and universally applicable to all countries, while taking into account different national realities, capacities and levels of development and respecting national policies and priorities" (ibid: para. 247). Governments would be given the lead in driving implementation, albeit with the appropriate, active involvement of all relevant actors and stakeholders engaged in the pursuit of sustainable development.

■ *Transforming Our World; People, Planet, Prosperity and Peace through Partnering*

In 2015, the 17 Sustainable Development Goals (SDGs) were successfully adopted as part of the 2030 Agenda for Sustainable Development, titled *Transforming Our World* (UN, 2015). The 2030 Agenda was positioned as "a plan of action for people, planet and prosperity", that concurrently "seeks to strengthen universal peace in larger freedom". It aimed to do so in collaborative partnership with all countries and all stakeholders, by taking "bold and transformative steps which are urgently needed to shift the world onto a sustainable and resilient path". The pledge thereby was to leave no one behind (ibid). (Section 1.5 elaborates further on the SDGs).

1.4.2 Reconciling extremes

This overview of key moments in the discussion on sustainable development shows considerable continuity, as well as a constant challenge to link analysis, ambition, intentions and action together in feasible strategies. In the past, international agreements on sustainable development – notably on climate change and financing for development – had been strongly influenced by defensive motives. Gaps between developed and developing countries persisted as a result of a lack of sufficient international cooperation in such critical areas as finance, debt, trade and technology transfer, innovation, entrepreneurship, capacity-building, transparency and accountability. Many of the statements stressed the consequences of inaction and the destructive scenarios that would follow from that.

The SDGs were framed in a more positive, collaborative and opportunity-seeking mode, with the aspiration of providing a framework for collective global action that could reconcile the extremes of a VUCA world (Figure 1.5; Table 1.3). The SDGs can, therefore, be interpreted as an ambitious endeavour to advance the integration, implementation and coherence of sustainable development efforts in order to address the grand (VUCA) challenges of our time. It is important to recognize that the exact elaboration of the SDGs and their underlying 169 targets has been strongly influenced by political considerations, the process of multi-stakeholder engagement and even 'chance'. The latter realization should help observers to treat the SDG-agenda as a 'work in progress', rather than the definitive answer to all theoretical questions and practical conundrums. Chapters 2 and 3 present analytical lenses to assess the effectiveness of this approach, helped by the first four years of experience with implementing the SDGs.

1.5 CREATION OF A NEW PARADIGM: FROM MDGs TO SDGs

The adoption of the SDGs in 2015 followed the finalization of the Millennium Development Goals (MDGs) (Figure 1.6). The MDGs were initiated in the year 2000 with considerably less ambitious aims, focusing on eight priorities (and 21 targets) such as child survival, basic education, promoting women's rights, and halving world poverty and hunger by the year 2015. These goals were consequently criticized, notably: (1) for not being ambitious enough to be effective levers for progress; (2) for lacking solid analytical reasons to choose these particular objectives and leave others out (Deneulin and Shahani, 2009); and (3) for being 'goals without means'. The MDGs were relatively vague, without precise indicators for in-country issues like income disparities (Kabeer, 2010), while excluding important dimensions of sustainable development such as environmental sustainability related to consumption and production flows. Most of the MDGs were donor-driven – implying that the goals related to government policies only – and had a strong Southern bias, based on the illusion that sustainability issues are primarily located in so-called 'developing' countries. Societal stakeholders were not included in the consultation process. Moreover, the MDGs adopted a simplified concept of development as 'meeting basic needs', stripped of the challenges of inclusion and sustainable growth and development. Neither did the MDGs mention the need to reform institutions.

Critical observers of the MDG experience warned that the "negotiations around the post-2015 development agenda should go beyond just re-writing goals and targets that adhere to 'sustaining' the same old economic and social models" (Moore, 2015: 801). In addition, they should not shy away from including politically sensitive issues on the global agenda – issues such as inequality and income differences or gender equality. Governments had previously explicitly excluded these topics in return for their support for the MDGs.

In the end, the final score on the MDGs remained ambiguous. For some, the glass was half full, for others, the glass remained half empty – or worse. For instance, MDG1 – 'halving poverty' – was reached by 2015, with more than

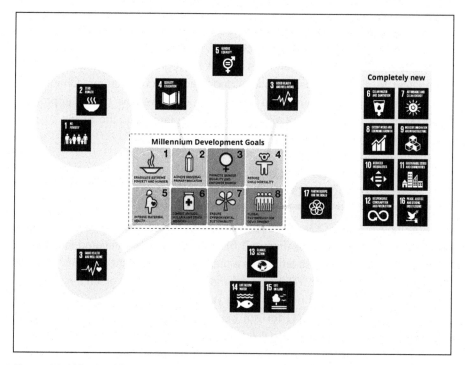

Figure 1.6 Millennium Development Goals and Sustainable Development Goals compared

1 billion out of 1.9 billion people lifted out of extreme poverty (i.e. living on less than $1.25 a day[7]) since 1990. However, this was primarily attributable to Chinese and Indian efforts; the poverty rate in sub-Saharan Africa did not change much, and in other regions, it even increased. By 2015, more than 40% of the sub-Saharan population continued to live in extreme poverty. The goals related to access to improved sanitation, maternal mortality ratios, and prevalence of under-nourishment as a percentage of populations were particularly off-target. In the final report on the achievements of the MDG effort (UN, 2015), then-Secretary General Ban Ki-moon noted that the MDGs had

> "helped to lift more than one billion people out of extreme poverty, to make inroads against hunger, to enable more girls to attend school than ever before and to protect our planet. They generated new and innovative part-nerships, galvanized public opinion and showed the immense value of setting ambitious goals. . . . But I am keenly aware that inequalities persist and that progress has been uneven. The world's poor remain overwhelm-ingly concentrated in some parts of the world. . . . Too many women continue to die during pregnancy or from childbirth-related complications. Progress tends to bypass women and those who are lowest on the economic ladder or are disadvantaged because of their age, disability or ethnicity. Disparities between rural and urban areas remain pronounced. . . . Further progress will require an unswerving political will, and collective, long-term effort. We need to tackle root causes and do more to integrate the economic, social and environmental dimensions of sustainable development."

1.5.1   Institutional ownership

The MDGs' mixed record can be partly explained by limited consideration for the growing insights on crucial preconditions for sustainable development. The major limitation of the MDGs by 2015 was "the lack of political will to implement due to the lack of ownership of the MDGs by the most affected constituencies" (International Planning Committee, 2013). So, even before the MDGs were properly evaluated, the UN proposed to set new goals for the 2015–2030 period. These subsequent goals, the SDGs, actually mirror a number of funda-mental changes in the thinking around sustainable development: from a tradi-tional development assistance rationale to universal goals; from limited in scope and reach to more comprehensive; from a top-down process to a multi-stakeholder bottom-up process in which quantitative indicators are comple-mented by qualitative indicators – even when this implies that not all of these

---

7   According to the World Bank's per capita international poverty line (IPL), the global abso-lute minimum as of 2008 was set on $1,25 per day. In October 2015, the IPL was set on $1.90 a day.

indicators can be measured yet; and from a focus on development aid to a much broader set of financial sources.

The number of goals consequently more than doubled (from 8 to 17 goals). The universal addition of 169 sub-targets added essential complexity, to 'developing' and 'developed' countries alike. The SDGs encompass more diverse global issues, such as supply chains, urbanization, inequality, innovation and infrastructure, migration and the elderly, with the ambition to cover the complexity of interrelations that shape the sustainable whole. Further, the SDGs were created on a multi-stakeholder basis, with contributions from a great variety of people and organizations. The 17 SDGs can, therefore, be considered the outcome of an inclusive process in which many people and organizations added their vision and priorities to the global goals. The SDGs also deal more explicitly with politically sensitive issues, such as reducing inequality (SDG10) – which addresses income differences within and between countries – and responsible consumption (SDG12), which draws into question the very economic model that wealthy developed countries have followed for years (cf. Fukuda-Parr, 2016).

1.5.2   Interrelated ambitions based on pragmatic reasoning

The goal-creation process resulted in the creation of 17 interrelated goals, linked to more clear problem statements. Table 1.4 summarises the ultimate goal of each SDG, as well as some of the stated reasons that explain why addressing the goal is deemed vital in creating sufficient common goods and, ultimately, the conditions for sustainable development. Hardly any of these conditions are 'moral'; they are pragmatic and based on insights gained over the past decades. There is a consequential and a causal side to each reason. *Not* addressing the issue has major implications for everyone in the system, while the causes of the issue are created by the way the system is organized. Causes, (non)actions and consequences are strongly related. Take, for instance, the reasons why ending hunger and reducing malnutrition are considered critical. *Not* adequately addressing the basic need for sufficient food not only creates unhealthy populations, but also severely affects education, equality and ultimately economic and societal development. The 'why' question hence represents, in many respects, economic, political and social 'no-brainers', but with strong reference to the systemic nature of these challenges and their consequential impacts.

Table 1.4 Why are the 17 SDGs important for sustainable development (2015)?

End poverty in all its forms everywhere

- Poverty involves lack of income and resources, including limited opportunities and capabilities.
- Nearly half of the world's population lives in poverty, with >1 billion people living at or below $1.25 a day.
- Poverty negatively impacts economies, social cohesion, deepens political and social tensions, may drive instability and conflict.
- Leading causes: unemployment, social exclusion, vulnerability to disasters and diseases.

End hunger, achieve food security and improved nutrition, promote sustainable agriculture

- It is time to rethink how we grow, share and consume our food (global food and agriculture system).
- Hunger is the leading cause of death, with more than 800 million people suffering worldwide.
- Hunger negatively impacts health, economies, education, equality and social development.
- Leading causes of hunger: poor agricultural practices, food wastage, wars.
- Obesity affects more than 1 billion people.
- Challenge to feed an additional 2 billion people expected by 2050.

Ensure healthy lives and promote well-being for all at all ages

- Each year, more than 6 million children die before age 5; only 50% of women in developing countries have access to adequate health care.
- Without universal health coverage, healthcare costs will remain a main cause of poverty.
- Leading causes: access to medicine and reproductive healthcare, undernourishment, conflict, fear and discrimination contribute to epidemics (HIV/AIDS).

Ensure inclusive and quality education for all and promote lifelong learning

- 103 million young people worldwide lack basic literacy skills.
- Education reduces inequality, intolerance and conflict, and allows for healthier, more sustainable lives and better jobs.
- Education is a key goal to achieve other SDGs, such as combating climate change and responsible production and consumption.

Achieve gender equality and empower all women and girls

- Women and girls constitute 50% of the world's population and hence potential. Gender inequality obstructs this potential.
- Globally, women earn 24% less than men and may have less access to healthcare and education.
- 35% of women have experienced physical and/or sexual intimate partner violence or non-partner sexual violence.
- Every dollar spent on programs that improve education of girls and increase age of marriage can return $5.

(continued)

Table 1.4 (continued)

 **Ensure access to water and sanitation for all**	• Clean water, sanitation and hygiene are a human right. • 1.8 billion use water contaminated with faeces, 2.4 billion lack access to sanitation, water scarcity affects 40% of people worldwide. • This results in almost 2 million deaths per year (mostly children) due to diarrheal diseases. Food, energy production and economic growth are also adversely affected.
Ensure access to affordable, reliable, sustainable and modern energy for all	• Human and economic development requires energy. • Fossil fuels contribute massively to global warming. • 20% of people worldwide lack access to electricity. • Clean energy would save 4+ million people a year dying from indoor air pollution; children can do homework at night, clinics can store vaccines.
 **Promote inclusive and sustainable economic growth, employment and decent work for all**	• In 2012, 200+ million people were unemployed. • 2.2 billion people living on less than $2 per day need well-paid jobs. • Decent, productive work for all promotes peace, harmony, fair globalization, and gender equality. • Result: fair incomes, job security, social protection of families, higher social integration and personal development. • A continued lack of decent work opportunities, insufficient investments and under-consumption leads to an erosion of the basic social contract underlying democratic societies: that all must share in progress.
Build resilient infrastructure, promote sustainable industrialization and foster innovation	• Economic growth, social development and climate action require infrastructure, sustainable industrial development and technological progress. • 1+ billion people have no access to reliable phone services; hardly 30% of food is industrially processed. • Sustainable industry improves living standards and benefits the environment; every job in manufacturing creates 2.2 jobs in other sectors.

Reduce inequality within and among countries

- Unequal distribution of income negatively affects economic growth.
- Inequality based on income, gender, age, disability, sexual orientation, race, class, ethnicity, religion and opportunity persists.
- In various developing countries income inequality is higher now than back in 1990.
- Growing consensus that economic growth is not sufficient to reduce poverty if it is not inclusive and does not involve the three dimensions of sustainable development – economic, social and environmental.
- Result: negative impact on poverty, social and economic development, people's self-fulfilment and self-worth, which breeds crime, disease, environmental degradation.

Make cities inclusive, safe, resilient and sustainable

- Soon, the majority of humanity will live in cities.
- Safe, inclusive, resilient, sustainable cities are key to solving many of today's problems.
- 828 million people live in slums, and this number is growing.
- Globally, cities occupy 3% of land, but emit 60–80% of greenhouse gases and use 75% of energy.
- Urban planning can foster shared prosperity and social stability without harming the environment.
- The size and impact of urban poverty has surpassed that of rural poverty.

Ensure sustainable consumption and production patterns

- With 9.7 billion people in 2050, sustaining current lifestyles will require 3 earths.
- One-third of all food produced is wasted, water is polluted faster than nature can purify.
- Waste that is dumped rather than recycled contaminates soil and groundwater, and may spontaneously combust.
- Not reducing our ecological footprint would cause irreparable environmental damage.

Take urgent action to combat climate change and its impact

- Average global temperature increased by 0.85 °C from 1885 to 2012; without action, the increase this century will be > 3°C.
- Every 1°C rise in temperature reduces grain yields by 5%; sea levels have risen 19 cm from 1901 to 2012.
- Severe weather will impact all, and is already intensifying food and water scarcity; natural disasters are more likely to occur.
- Climate change is disrupting national economies and affecting lives, costing people, communities and countries dearly today and even more tomorrow.
- Climate change is a global challenge that does not respect national borders.

(continued)

Table 1.4 (continued)

 **Conserve and sustainably use the oceans, seas and marine resources**	• Seas ultimately regulate our water, weather, climate, coastlines, oxygen and much of our food. • More than 3 billion people depend on the oceans as their primary source of protein. • Oceans are threatened by marine and nutrient pollution ('plastic soup'), resource depletion and climate change, all caused primarily by human actions. • Adverse effects on marine ecosystems and biodiversity will create global socio-economic problems. • Throughout history, oceans and seas have been vital conduits for trade and transportation.
 **Sustainably manage forests, combat desertification, halt and reverse land degradation, halt biodiversity loss**	• Forests cover 30% of the earth's surface and, in addition to providing food security and shelter, forests are key to combating climate change, protecting biodiversity and the homes of indigenous populations. • Agriculture requires arable land; forests mitigate climate change and are home to > 80% of terrestrial species. • 52% of agricultural land is affected by soil degradation; every year, a forest area the size of Greece is lost. • Of all 8,300 known animal breeds, 8% are extinct, and 22% risk extinction. • For their livelihood, 1.6 billion people depend on forests; land degradation has affected 1.5 billion people as of 2008.
 **Promote just, peaceful and inclusive societies**	• People need to feel free, safe, and included in their everyday lives, necessitating just, accountable, effective institutions. • Developing countries lose $1.26 trillion a year to corruption, bribery, theft and tax evasion (>1.5% of the world's GDP). • The judiciary and police are among the institutions most affected by corruption. • Institutions are essential to the SDGs to deliver quality education, healthcare, just economic policies and protect the environment.
 **Revitalize the global partnership for sustainable development**	• Successfully implementing the Sustainable Development Agenda by 2030 requires integrated partnerships at all levels. • Business, government and civil society need to cooperate based on shared values, principles, and vision. • Partnerships are necessary at the local, regional, national and global level, including developed and developing countries.

Sources: http://www.un.org/sustainabledevelopment/wp-content/uploads/2016/08/1; UN (2015)

1.5.3 Recognition of the new paradigm

The timely importance attributed to the SDGs as a leading global frame, with a shared vision, goal-oriented focus and integrated procedure, immediately became evident. An overwhelming number of organizations from all parts of society embraced them:

■ *National governments and international organizations:* all UN member countries adopted the SDGs as a universal and inclusive ambition (UN, 2015). The SDGs additionally received support from a wide variety of international organizations, including the World Bank, the International Monetary Fund (IMF), the Organization for Economic Cooperation and Development (OECD), the World Resources Institute (WRI), the World Business Council for Sustainable Development (WBCSD) and the World Economic Forum (WEF). The WBCSD described the SDGs as "an effective way for companies to communicate their contribution to sustainable development" (WBCSD, 2015: 8).

■ *Individual companies:* responded supportively: 71% of globally operating companies immediately claimed that they were already planning on how to engage with the SDGs, with 41% stating that they would embed the SDGs in their strategies within five years (PwC, 2015). Additionally, 87% of a representative sample of CEOs worldwide believed that the SDGs would provide an opportunity to rethink approaches to sustainable value creation, while 70% of them saw the SDGs as providing a clear framework to structure sustainability efforts (UN Global Compact and Accenture, 2016). There was a clear business logic to these responses since it was assessed that contributing to the SDGs could unlock at least $12 trillion in business opportunities (Business & Sustainable Development Commission, 2017). The support for the SDGs from influential global corporate platforms was even more unequivocal. In particular, the World Business Council for Sustainable Development, which encompasses more than 80 global companies (e.g. DuPont, 3M, Nestlé, BP, Danone, Royal Dutch Shell) had been involved in the formulation of the SDGs.

■ *International civil society organizations* (NGOs) were markedly supportive of the SDGs as well. World Wide Fund for Nature (WWF), for instance, one of the most prominent environmental NGOs, classified the SDGs as "different from anything that came before them – they're fairer, smarter, and more inclusive". WWF was closely involved in the drafting of the SDGs, as were many other international NGOs. The SDGs include many aspects that the organization deeply cares about. However, like any other NGO, WWF also acknowledged that this was only the start of the 'hard work': "It's now up to us all – governments, charities, businesses, and most of all citizens – to work together to ensure that these commitments become a reality."[8]

1.6 CONCLUSION, TOOLS AND RESOURCES

In addressing the grand global challenges that are associated with major societal transformations of the fourth industrial revolution and the 21st century, various approaches can be adopted. Effective approaches depend on the interests, values, mindsets, envisioned outcomes, means and capabilities of the actors involved. Approaches may range from idealistic to pragmatic, from optimistic to fatalistic, from conservative to progressive, from compromising to transformational, from process-orientated to impact- and goal-orientated. This chapter has introduced significant themes that need to be addressed when considering the complex issue of sustainable development and the (complementary) roles that societal actors from state, market and civil society can – and need to – play. The chapter has made clear that the world is in a state of rapid transition and transformation, which can simultaneously feed into both negative and positive sentiments of countries, firms and citizens. The perspective of a VUCA world was introduced as short-hand for sketching some of the characteristics of this transition period, but also as a warning that a VUCA-driven perspective might lead to societal disruption, increased tensions on a global scale and even to war. There are clear historical precedents for this observation.

Partly as an antidote, we summarized some vital insights from recent research that comes to alternative conclusions on how to conceive and deal with present-day societal challenges. Although this knowledge seems undisputed, the influence of the dominant (defensive) thinking and actions that are triggered and reinforced by VUCA dynamics nonetheless remains relevant. And increasingly so. There is only a limited need to prolong the debate on any of these dimensions. The more relevant debate is how to move from the negative, short-term perspective of a VUCA-driven society in which competition, exclusivity and zero-sum outcomes prevail, to a more positive, longer-term prospect in which sustainable progress for all can be achieved.

The introduction of the Sustainable Development Goals in 2015 actually created the momentum and path to make that transition in a more or less concerted way. This chapter explained why we can consider the SDGs as a smart integration of many of the insights gained over the past few decades in various debates around sustainable development. The potential of the SDG-agenda is to move the

---

8   https://www.wwf.org.uk/what-we-do/projects/transforming-our-world-through-sustainable-development-goals.

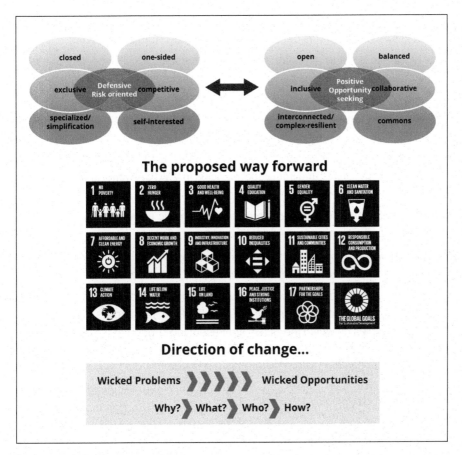

Figure 1.7 From problem to opportunity?

perspective: from one in which the complexity materializes as a 'wicked problem' to one in which the outlook becomes one of 'wicked opportunities'. This challenge involves more critical thinking on what the SDGs actually represent and the extent to which they create the best possible agenda for change in the right direction. Chapters 2 and 3 will deal with these questions in more detail, by addressing the 'why' and 'how' rationales of the SDGs.

T
A
K
E
A
W
A
Y
S

- A VUCA world creates opportunities and threats at the same time;

- The present stage of global development presents an intermediary phase of increased rivalry between upcoming and decreasing hegemonic powers – with dangerous consequences (war, rivalry, divergence);

- In a VUCA world, the choice for one particular (one-size-fits-all) approach is neither necessary nor sufficient;

- Increasingly, scientific insights have been developing on how to better understand the dynamics and interdependencies in a VUCA world, and how to deal with the basic trade-offs that appear;

- The SDGs provide a goal-oriented and pragmatic universal way to reconcile the tensions inherent to the VUCA world;

- The new development paradigm entails an approach rather than a solution, and accommodates a diverse set of positive change pathways;

- On paradigms and principles: to qualify the SDG-approach as a paradigm requires it to become a dominant way of thinking; this applies in particular to the principles on which the SDGs are based; the support of the SDGs by wide and diverse groups of stakeholders around the world reinforces the potential paradigm status of the SDGs;

- On principles and values: values help form principles; values are 'qualities or standards of behaviour'; principles are 'rules or beliefs governing one's behaviour'; the paradigm status of the SDGs, therefore, depends on the values that participants share. This chapter distinguished four types of values: public, private, social, common values.

- **Our World in Data:** Research and data to make progress against the world's biggest problems and to make the knowledge on the big problems accessible and understandable. Provides open-access, open-source historical data and research on long-lasting, forceful changes that reshape our world. Includes 3,294 charts across 297 topics, ranging from poverty, disease, hunger and climate change, to war, trust, existential risks and inequality. https://ourworldindata.org/

- **WEF Strategic Intelligence:** Strategic insights and contextual intelligence from the World Economic Forum. Explores and monitors the issues and forces driving transformational change across economies, industries, and global issues by means of *Dynamic Global Transformation Maps*. Covers over 80 global strategic topics, ranging from artificial intelligence, biodiversity and human rights, to internet governance, values and international security. https://intelligence.weforum.org/topics?type=Global+Issues

- **Gapminder:** "Almost nobody knows the basic global facts". Gapminder promotes a fact-based worldview by fighting devastating misconceptions about global development. It produces free (teaching) resources that make the world easy to understand, based on reliable statistics. Topics covered range from gender equality and vaccination to causes of child death and urban poverty. Gapminder collaborates with universities, UN, public agencies and non-governmental organizations. https://www.gapminder.org/

- **International Institute for Applied Systems Analysis (IIASA):** Conducts independent policy-oriented research into problems of a global nature that are too large or too complex to be solved by a single country or academic discipline. Research topics relate to pressing concerns that affect the future of all of humanity, such as climate change, energy security, population ageing, and sustainable development. Provides access to research publications, policy briefs, models, tools and data. https://iiasa.ac.at/web/home/about/whatisiiasa/what_is_iiasa.html

- **World Poverty Clock:** Every second, some escape while others fall into poverty. Developed by World Data Lab, the clock computes the speed of poverty reduction in each country and region, compared to the average speed needed to end poverty by 2030. It shows the real time poverty forecasts of the number of people living in extreme poverty worldwide, disaggregated by age, gender, and rural/urban location. https://worldpoverty.io/headline

- **World Development Indicators:** a compilation of relevant, high-quality, and internationally comparable statistics about global development by the World Bank. The database contains 1,600 time series indicators for 217 economies and more than 40 country groups, with data for many indicators going back more than 50 years. http://datatopics.worldbank.org/world-development-indicators/

REFERENCES

Acemoglu, D. & Robinson, J.A. (2017). *The Emergence of Weak, Despotic and Inclusive States* (No. w23657), National Bureau of Economic Research.

Acemoglu, D., Gallego, F.A. & Robinson, J.A. (2014). 'Institutions, Human Capital, and Development', *Annual Review of Economics* 6(1):875–912.

Bryson, J.M., Crosby, B.C. & Bloomberg, L. (Eds.) (2015). *Creating Public Value in Practice. Advancing the Common Good in a Multi-sector, Shared-Power, No-One-Wholly-in-Charge World*. CRC Press: Taylor and Francis Group.

Business & Sustainable Development Commission (2017). *Better Business, Better World*.

Cornes, R. & Sandler, T. (1986). *The Theory of Externalities, Public Goods and Club Goods*, Cambridge University Press.

Dabla-Norris, E., Kochhar, K., Suphaphiphat, N., Ricka, F. & Tsounta, E. (2015). *Causes and Consequences of Income Inequality: A Global Perspective*, IMF Staff Discussion Note, Strategy, Policy, and Review Department, SDN/15/13, 15 June.

Deneulin, S. & Shahani, L. (Eds.) (2009). *An Introduction to the Human Development and Capability Approach: Freedom and Agency*. London, Sterling, VA: Earthscan, International Development Research Centre.

Elkington, J. (2018). '25 Years Ago I Coined the Phrase "Triple Bottom Line." Here's Why It's Time to Rethink It', *Harvard Business Review*, 25 June.

Elkington, J. (1994). 'Towards the Sustainable Corporation: Win–Win–Win Business Strategies for Sustainable Development', *California Management Review*, 36(2):90–100.

Espen Stoknes, P. (2015). *What We Think About When We Try Not To Think About Global Warming: Toward a New Psychology of Climate Action*. Chelsea Green Publishing.

Freeman, C. & Perez, C. (1988). 'Structural crises of adjustment, business cycles and investment behaviour.' In: Dosi G., Freeman, C., Nelson, R.R., Silverberg, G. & Soete, L. *Technical Change and Economic Theory*, (pp. 38–66). London, New York: Pinter Publishers.

Fukuda-Parr, S. (2016). 'From the Millennium Development Goals to the Sustainable Development Goals: shift in purpose, concept, and politics of global goal setting for development', *Gender & Development*, 24(1):43–52.

Fukuyama, F. (1992). *The End of History and the Last Man*. New York: Free Press.

Hardin, G. (1968). 'The Tragedy of the Commons', *Science*, New Series, 162(3859):1243–1248.

Henriques, A. & Richardson, E. (Eds.) (2004). *The Triple Bottom Line: Does it All Add Up. Assessing the Sustainability of Business and CSR*. Abingdon: Earthscan.

Hudson, J.M. & Bruckman, A.S. (2004). 'The Bystander Effect: A Lens for Understanding Patterns of Participation', *Journal of the Learning Sciences*, 13(2):165–195.

ILO (2020b). *World Employment and Social Outlook. Trends 2020*. Geneva: International Labour Organization.

IMF (2021). *World Economic Outlook. Managing Divergent Recoveries*. Washington DC: International Monetary Fund, April.

IMF (2019). *World Economic Outlook. Global Manufacturing Downturn, Rising Trade Barriers*. Washington DC: International Monetary Fund, October.

International Planning Committee on Food Sovereignty (2013). 'Informal Thematic Consultation Hunger, Food and Nutrition Post 2015'. Retrieved: 7 October 2013.

Kabeer, N. (2010). *Can the MDGs provide a pathway to social justice?: The challenge of inter-secting inequalities*. Institute of Development Studies. New York: United Nations Development Programme.

Kahneman, D. (2012). *Thinking, Fast and Slow*. New York: Farrer, Strauss and Giroux Inc.

Kennedy, P. (1989). *Rise and Fall of the Great Powers. Economic Change and Military Conflict from 1500 to 2000*. Random House.

Kolk, A., Van Tulder, R. & Kostwinder, E. (2008). 'Business and partnerships for development', *European Management Journal*, 26(4):262–273.

Maani, K.E. & Cavana, R.Y. (2007). *Systems Thinking, System Dynamics: Managing Change and Complexity*. Prentice Hall.

Madsbjerg, C. (2017). *Sensemaking: The Power of the Humanities in the Age of the Algorithm*. Hachette Books.

Mair, J. & Marti, I. (2009). 'Entrepreneurship in and around institutional voids: A case study from Bangladesh', *Journal of Business Venturing*, 24(5):419–435.

Mazzucato, M. (2018). *The Value of Everything. Making and Taking in the Global Economy*. Allen Lane.

McDermott, W.B. (1996). 'Foresight is an illusion', *Long Range Planning*, 29(2):190–194.

Meadows, D.H., Meadows, D.L., Randers, J. & Behrens, W.W. (1972). *The Limits to Growth. A Report for The Club of Rome's Project on the Predicament of Mankind*. New York: Universe Books.

Mintzberg, H. (2015). *Rebalancing Society. Radical Renewal Beyond Left, Right and Centre*. Oakland, CA: Berrett-Koehler Publishers.

Moore, H.L. (2015). 'Global Prosperity and Sustainable Development Goals', *Journal of International Development*, 27(6):801–815.

Nelson, J., Ishikawa, E. & Geaneotes, A. (2009). *Developing inclusive business models: a review of Coca-Cola's Manual Distribution Centers in Ethiopia and Tanzania*. Washington DC: World Bank Group.

OECD (2014a). *All On Board. Making Inclusive Growth Happen*. OECD Initiative on Inclusive Growth. Paris: OECD Publishing.

Olson, M. (1982). *The Rise and Decline of Nations: Economic Growth, Stagflation, and Social Rigidities*. Yale University Press.

Ostrom, E. (2015). *Governing The Commons. The Evolution of Institutions for Collective Action*. Cambridge: Cambridge University Press.

Oxfam International (2020). *Time to care. Unpaid and underpaid care work and the global inequality crisis*. Oxfam Briefing Paper, 20 January.

Oxfam International (2018). *Reward Work, Not Wealth*. Oxfam Briefing Paper, January.

Perez, C. (2002). *Technological Revolutions and Financial Capital. The Dynamics of Bubbles and Golden Ages*. Cheltenham: Edward Elgar.

Pinker, S. (2018). *Enlightment Now. The Case for Reason, Science, Humanism and Progress*. Allan Lane.

PwC (2015). *Make it your business: Engaging with the Sustainable Development Goals*.

Rajan, R.G. (2019). *The Third Pillar: How Markets and the State Leave the Community Behind*. Penguin Press.

Raworth, K. (2017). *Doughnut Economics. Seven Ways to Think Like a 21st-Century Economist*. Cornerstone.

Reich, R.B. (2018). *The Common Good*. New York: Vintage Books.

Rifkin, J. (2011). *The Third Industrial Revolution. How Lateral Power is Transforming Energy, the Economy, and the World*. New York: Palgrave Macmillan.

Rodrik, D. (2011). *The Globalization Paradox: Democracy and the Future of the World Economy*. New York and London: W.W. Norton.

Rodrik, D., Subramanian, A. & Trebbi, F. (2004). 'Institutions Rule: The Primacy of Institutions Over Geography and Integration in Economic Development', *Journal of Economic Growth*, 9(2):131–165.

Rosling, H., with Rosling, O. & Rosling Rönnlund, A. (2018). *Factfulness: Ten Reasons We're Wrong About the World – and Why Things Are Better Than You Think*. Flariton Books.

Rotmans, J. (2017). *Change of Era. Our World in Transition*. Amsterdam: Boom Uitgevers.

Sachs, J.D. (2015). *The Age of Sustainable Development*. Columbia University Press.

Sachs, J.D., Schmidt-Traub, G., Mazzucato, M., Messner, D., Nakicenovic, N. & Rockström, J. (2019). 'Six Transformations to Achieve the Sustainable Development Goals', *Nature Sustainability*, 2(9):805–814.

Samuelson, P.A. (1954). 'The Pure Theory of Public Expenditure', *The Review of Economics and Statistics*, 36(4):387–389.

Schwab, K. (2016). *The Fourth Industrial Revolution*. New York: Crown Business.

Schwartz, B. (2004). *The Paradox of Choice. Why More is Less*. HarperCollins Publishers.

Sharma, R. (2016). *The Rise and Fall of Nations. Forces of Change in the Post-Crisis World*. W.W. Norton & Company.

Stiglitz, J.E. (2018). *Globalization and its Discontents Revisited – Anti-Globalization in the Era of Trump*. New York: Norton.

Thaler, R.H. (2016). *Behavioral Economics. Past, Present and Future*. University of Chicago.

Tirole, J. (2017). *Economics for the Common Good*. Oxfordshire: Princeton University Press.

TWI2050 (2019). *The Digital Revolution and Sustainable Development: Opportunities and Challenges*. Report prepared by The World In 2050 Initiative. Laxenburg, Austria: International Institute for Applied Systems Analysis (IIASA).

TWI2050 (2018). *Transformations to Achieve the Sustainable Development Goals*. Report prepared by The World In 2050 Initiative. Laxenburg, Austria: International Institute for Applied Systems Analysis (IIASA).

UN (2015). *Transforming Our World: The 2050 Agenda for Sustainable Development*. New York: United Nations.

UN (2012). *The Future We Want*. Outcome document of the United Nations Conference on Sustainable Development, Rio de Janeiro, Brazil, 20–22 June 2012. A/RES/66/288. New York: United Nations.

UN DESA (2020). *World Economic Situation and Prospects 2020*. New York: United Nations.

UN DESA (2020a). *World Social Report 2020. Inequality In A Rapidly Changing World*. New York: United Nations.

UN DESA (2019a). *Sustainable Development Outlook 2019. Gathering storms and silver linings. An overview of SDG challenges*. United Nations Department of Economic and Social Affairs.

UN Global Compact & Accenture Strategy (2016). *The United Nations Global Compact – Accenture Strategy CEO Study 2016. Agenda 2030: A Window of Opportunity*, June.

UN Independent Group of Scientists (2019). *Global Sustainable Development Report 2019: The Future is Now – Science for Achieving Sustainable Development*. New York: United Nations.

UN World Commission on Environment and Development (1987). *Our Common Future: Report of the World Commission on Environment and Development*. Oxford: Oxford University Press.

Van Tulder, R. & Roman, M. (2019). 'Re-assessing risk in international markets: a strategic, operational, and sustainability taxonomy'. In: Leonidou, L.C., Katsikeas, C.S., Samiee, S. & Leonidou, C.N. (Eds.), *Socially Responsible International Business: Critical Issues and the Way Forward* (pp. 158–183). Cheltenham UK: Edward Elgar.

Van Tulder, R. & Pfisterer, S. (2014). 'Creating partnering space: exploring the right fit for sustainable development partnerships'. In: Seitanidi, M.M. & Crane, A. (Eds.), *Social Partnerships and Responsible Business. A research handbook*, (pp. 105–125). London: Routledge.

Van Tulder, R. with Van der Zwart, A. (2006). *International Business-Society Management. Linking Corporate Responsibility and Globalization*. London: Routledge.

WBCSD (2015). *Reporting matters. Redefining performance and disclosure. WBCSD 2015 Report*. Geneva: World Business Council for Sustainable Development.

WEF (2020a). *The Global Risks Report 2020*. Insight Report, 15th Edition. Geneva: World Economic Forum.

WEF (2020b). *Taking the Pulse of the New Economy. Chief Economists Outlook*, REF 080120. Geneva: World Economic Forum, January.

WEF (2016). *The Global Risks Report 2016.* Insight Report, 11th Edition, REF: 080116. Geneva: World Economic Forum.

Whitley, R. (1999). *Divergent Capitalisms. The Social Structuring and change of Business Systems.* Oxford: Oxford University Press.

Witt, M.A. & Jackson, G. (2016). 'Varieties of Capitalism and institutional comparative advantage: A test and reinterpretation', *Journal of International Business Studies*, 47(7):778–806.

World Bank (2008). *The Growth Report: Strategies for Sustained Growth and Inclusive Development*, Commission on Growth and Development. Washington, DC: World Bank.

Zuboff, S. (2019). *The Age of Surveillance Capitalism: The Fight for a Human Future at the New Frontier of Power.* London: Profile Books.

2 WHY NOT?
UNDERSTANDING THE POTENTIAL OF THE SDGs

DOI: 10.4324/9781003098355-3

P
R
I
N
C
I
P
L
E
S

- **A principles-based approach:** seeks to set principles that specify intentions and values, rather than set rules detailing requirements. A principles-based approach to sustainability includes 5 Ps: *People, Planet, Prosperity, Peace, Partnering*.

- **Ethics-based principles:** in practice are mutually overlapping and include (a) utilitarian, (b) deontological, (c) (political) rights, (d) virtues, (e) capabilities, and (f) participatory principles.

- **'Leave no one behind' principle:** is the overarching principle of the SDGs. It represents the unequivocal commitment to eradicate poverty in all its forms, end discrimination and exclusion, and reduce the inequalities and vulnerabilities that leave people behind and undermine the potential of individuals, and of humanity as a whole. Sustainable development is possible only if everyone is included in a whole-of-society approach.

- **Multi-stakeholder principle:** engagement of diverse stakeholders in dialogue and decision-making – based on 'participatory ethics' – contributes to a joint understanding of (perceived) problems, which improves the quality of chosen approaches and facilitates implementation processes.

- **Data ecosystem principle:** the creation and governance of 'new data ecosystems' is elemental to developing and tracking all SDG-indicators at the required levels of disaggregation.

- **Opportunities principle:** the potential value of investing in sustainable development-related activities trumps the costs of *not* taking action.

- **Decoupling principle:** decouple growth from environmental impact, including through circularity, dematerialization and the re-use of (natural) resources. GDP growth is an outdated measure of prosperity and well-being. For a sustainable future, goals of human progress and a healthy environment need to be recoupled.

- **Nexus principle:** takes the interrelatedness and interdependencies of an entire system into consideration, to develop insights on opportunities for reducing trade-offs and for leveraging synergies. A nexus approach supports more integrative and coherent decision-making through which more than one goal can be advanced simultaneously – at reduced costs or with greater impact across a larger scale.

- **Layered dashboard principle:** not all dimensions of an issue can be entirely known. Defining a variety of relevant indicators – linked to coverage of interventions – helps reduce selection biases, overly simplistic responses to complex and dynamic problems, and better informed decision-making. A dashboard approach allows to assess progress, monitor developments and identify strengths, weaknesses and priorities for action.

2.1 INTRODUCTION: WHY NOT?

In 2015, the Sustainable Development Goals (SDGs) were introduced at a critical juncture in the history of the world. Chapter 1 explained what was at stake and argued that the SDGs *potentially* present a much-needed way out of a negative frame that has been precipitated by the appearance of a VUCA world. The overall pledge of the 2030 Agenda for Sustainable Development thereby was to 'leave no one behind', an ambition related to all three interlinked dimensions of sustainable development: social, ecological and economic. In addition to formulating several very ambitious goals for the medium term – a time span of 15 years – the SDGs also specified ways and principles to involve important groups of stakeholders in a process of continuous improvement of goal formulation, indicator development and implementation means. Chapter 1 described the SDGs as a paradigm change in the societal approach towards the sustainability challenges of the world.

Whether the ambitions will be achieved, however, depends on the actual translation of the SDG-agenda into substantive strategies and implementation trajectories of major societal stakeholders. Presenting a frame of ambitious goals is not enough to trigger positive change in the right direction. The goal-setting approach hence was a "bet as much as a promise: the bet of a comfortable delivery and the promise that goal-setting could prompt the action that had been inconsistently avoided" by major initiatives before them (Hege et al., 2019: 6).

A CRITICAL REVIEW IS NEEDED

The SDG approach was designed as 'a work in (and on) progress' that requires permanent scrutiny on its indicators, strategies and implementation experiences. The SDG-agenda supported a 'learning by doing' approach, not in the least because of the inherent complexity/wickedness of the problems to be addressed (see Part II for further elaboration). To facilitate this process, a large number of multi-stakeholder initiatives around the world had to be set up at the global, national, regional and local levels by government agencies, stakeholder communities and research organizations, to help fine-tune every dimension of the SDG-agenda and fill in the knowledge gaps. The effectiveness of the SDG approach in accomplishing global sustainable development by the year 2030 should be closely scrutinized from a variety of angles: its (general) design, its (broad) ambitions, its (vague) measurement and its adoption of a (multi-stakeholder, 'hybrid governance') process to assess, learn, adjust and upgrade during implementation.

Understanding the bold chosen approach and its inherent intellectual challenges is the main objective of this chapter. It presents a critical review of the present stage of the SDG initiative by examining the analytical, theoretical and practical challenges that the SDG-agenda poses, in order to understand the conditions for successful implementation and proliferation. How intellectual and practical gaps are approached defines the conditions under which the implementation of the SDG-agenda can be accelerated in the period between now and 2030. Key analytical challenges related to the SDG-framework can be summarized along two lines:

1   **Conceptual clarity:** an understanding of the *key theoretical challenges* that the selection of SDG goals and targets present, including an understanding of negative and positive interactions – the so-called nexus challenge (section 2.2).

2   **Measurement development:** an understanding of *key empirical challenges* in developing the 'right' metrics for measuring relevant aspects of sustainable development (section 2.3).

The exercise of this chapter is aimed at gaining better insights into the potential of the SDG-agenda as an integrative, principles-based and common goal-oriented approach to sustainable development. The chapter identifies several weak points that need addressing to allow the approach to live up to its full potential. What gaps require further attention in terms of theory and conceptual clarity and the development of relevant progress measurement (section 2.4)? Chapter 3 subsequently addresses the process-related challenges for realizing the SDGs and takes stock of the governance dimensions on how gaps have been addressed in the first four-year cycle of the SDG trajectory (2015–2019).

2.2   KEY THEORETICAL CHALLENGES: CAN CONCEPTUAL CLARITY BE CREATED?

Chapter 1 covered relevant parts of the 'sustainable development' discourse, related these to the transition challenges of the 21st century, and delineated why the SDG-framework can be considered the next stage in thinking on (sustainable) development. That does not imply, however, that the SDG-framework is perfect and without flaws. The Millennium Development Goals (MDGs) initiative adopted 8 goals, elaborated through 21 targets and 60 relatively simple indicators. The SDGs consist of 17 goals, further elaborated through 169 targets and 232 indicators, which are more complex to measure compared to the MDGs. The SDGs present a balanced compromise between the aspirations, concerns and experiences of a large and diverse number of actors who, in over two years of multi-stakeholder processes, came up with a particular design. Balanced compromise that seeks to do justice to all voiced concerns carries the risk of bias in the ultimate selection and formulation of goals and targets. Why not more or fewer goals and targets? Shouldn't some SDGs have gotten more priority (weight and attention) than others? Does the SDG-framework constitute a 'general theory of sustainable development', and – if not – how can flaws in its set-up be effectively dealt with?[1] Three *areas of contention* are particularly relevant in this discourse:

■   The very selection of the 17 goals (section 2.2.1);

■   The selection of the 169 SDG-targets and 232 indicators (section 2.2.2);

■   The so-called 'nexus challenge': positive and negative interactions between the SDGs (section 2.2.3).

2.2.1   Why 17 SDGs, and not more or fewer goals?

In the course of the adoption of the SDGs, significant criticism was expressed on the actual choice for 17 main goals and their 169 targets, as being too ambitious or not ambitious enough.

THE SDGs ARE TOO AMBITIOUS

While the MDGs aimed to reduce poverty by half, the SDGs aim to eradicate extreme poverty in *all its variants* by the year 2030. Even for many optimists, this goal is deemed unrealistic and may lead to discouragement once participants realize that targets will not, not fully or not evenly be achieved. The 17 SDGs have also been considered too broad.[2] This line of critique was formulated in particular by the Copenhagen Consensus Centre and its director Bjørn Lomborg. The articulated concern is that the SDGs lack focus – which might get the world 'stuck in transition' – not least because the ambitions require immense financial, human and intellectual contributions. Matters of execution – in particular financial considerations – have been left open in the process, which

---

1   The selection process over the 2010–2015 period has been covered by political scientists and international political economists who examined how international multi-stakeholder processes around the SDGs have materialized, and the kind of 'meta-governance' challenges that were created (cf. Dodds et al., 2016; Kamau et al., 2018). Chapter 3 considers the chosen governance approach.

2   In its 28 March 2015 edition, *The Economist* referred to the SDGs as 'Stupid Development Goals', contending that "Moses brought ten commandments down from Mount Sinai. If only the UN's proposed list of SDGs were as concise."

leaves the goals without dedicated means and priorities. Not making choices may create further stagnation. Lomborg argued that from the appearance of the extensive set of goals and targets, the UN "simply threw everything they had heard into the document".[3] The SDG-agenda fed into a political inclination to "promise all good things to everyone" (Lomborg, 2018: 501). The targets are, therefore, asserted to be misguided and not based on sound research of what is feasible. Even worse, collecting data on the 169 targets could cost almost two years of development aid. These critics hence argued that the 2030 Agenda will probably leave the world's poorest worse off than they could be without it (Box 2.1).

BOX 2.1

WHAT TO FOCUS ON ACCORDING TO THE COPENHAGEN CONSENSUS

The Copenhagen Consensus Centre makes a case for prioritizing the most 'effective development investment', given the available budget. Based on cost-benefit analyses of the 169 SDG-targets, it proposes to focus on only 19 'phenomenal' development targets that it deems more achievable and cost-effective in the shorter run, as these specific targets could achieve as much as quadrupling the global aid budget.

The 19 targets were defined by a group of leading scholars – including a number of Nobel Laureates in economics – who applied a critical eye to how the SDGs will affect the flow of approximately $2.5 trillion in development aid (as well as countless trillions in national budgets) until 2030. The methods used aimed to decipher what pursuing different targets will cost, and what they will deliver in terms of social, economic and environmental benefits. Their analyses point to an emphasis on social and economic targets over environmental ones, with a focus on developing economies in sub-Saharan Africa. The conclusion of the 2018 book suggests that if the UN would concentrate on these particular targets, it "could achieve $20 to $40 in social benefits per dollar spent. In contrast, allocating it evenly across all 169 targets would reduce the figure to less than $10" (ibid: 501). The proposed 19 targets are listed below. Note that these include rather controversial policy measures, like facilitating family planning, circumcision, and a further reduction of trade restrictions.

---

3   https://www.project-syndicate.org/commentary/unsustainable-development-goals-by-bjrn-lomborg-2015-09.

PEOPLE	PLANET	PROSPERITY
• Lower chronic child malnutrition by 40%	• Phase out fossil fuel subsidies	• Reduce trade restrictions (full Doha)
• Halve malaria infections	• Halve coral reef loss	• Improve gender equality in ownership, business, and politics
• Reduce tuberculosis death by 90%	• Tax pollution damage from energy	• Boost agricultural yield growth by 40%
• Cut early death from chronic disease by one-third	• Cut indoor air pollution by 20%	• Increase girls' education by two years
• Avoid 1.1 million HIV infections through circumcision		• Achieve universal primary education in sub-Saharan Africa
• Reduce newborn mortality by 70%		• Triple pre-school in sub-Saharan Africa
• Increase immunization to reduce child deaths by 25%		
• Make family planning available to everyone		
• Eliminate violence against women and girls		

Source: Lomborg (2018)

BOX 2.1

NOT AMBITIOUS ENOUGH?

Several scholars suggested that the SDGs do not actually present a paradigm change. They deemed the new agenda too conservative to be a real transformational swing, as it set goals to address global challenges without tackling either their causes or power dynamics (Koehler, 2016; 2015). The SDG-framework had skirted the question of viable policies – leaving the establishment of implementation plans to national governments. The SDG-framework had also avoided contentious subjects and commitments in order to be able to reach a global 'weak consensus', with essentially non-binding agreements. Consequently, the SDGs have been criticized for being insufficiently radical in their analysis of systemic crises, and insufficiently sophisticated in their approach towards the negative tendencies in a VUCA society. According to Gupta and Vegelin (2016), for instance, real economic transformation is still undermined in the basic SDG-framework, because of the idea that economic growth and its trickle-down effects will be sufficient to get people out of poverty. Furthermore, the involvement of existing and influential stakeholders, such as big companies and other vested interest groups, would make it highly unlikely that the SDGs will create real change. These critics focus in particular on indicators and prioritized nexus relations that might evoke a more defensive reaction to sustainability challenges, and in the end, will not create transition at the required pace and intensity.

2.2.2   Why 169 SDG-targets and 232 indicators?

Just like the choice for 17 Global Goals, the choice for 169 specific targets and 232 indicators may also constitute a selection bias. Even more so, it represents the consequence of choosing between two alternative approaches for monitoring and driving progress, each with their advantages and disadvantages:

1   **Indexation:** which sublimates all relevant aspects of an issue into one quantifiable indicator (like Gross Domestic Product, Dow Jones Index, Human Development Index, Gini coefficient; Price index);

2   **Dashboard:** which compiles a list of various dimensions of a particular issue that interact with each other, to ensure that information collected is linked to coverage of interventions and can inform decisions (even when one does not know exactly how the interaction functions, nor whether all indicators are actually or evenly important).

Policymakers and strategists often prefer to strive for one specific definition of a target – linked with a single outcome indicator or index – because it simplifies the issue, makes it easier to check on progress and enables benchmarking (for instance between countries or companies). It also represents a classic scientific ambition: a quest for the 'one brilliant indicator that explains everything'. However, such an indicator always mediates between different values, perceptions and interests. Accumulating or mediating between different indicators requires weighting what is important and what is not. In many areas of policy and science, this is not (yet) possible. A composite index is also limitedly informative because it obscures insights in interesting, perhaps essential, developments with and between some of the constituting elements (either positive or negative). A single index, in practice, is almost by definition quantitative and thus provides limited insights in the more qualitative aspects of an issue. Taken together, these considerations explain why an index itself – as an oversimplified yardstick for measuring development – can become part of the problem.

A dashboard approach, on the other hand, allows for a variety of indicators to assess progress, monitor developments and identify strengths, weaknesses and priorities for action. As a dashboard is composed of a set of separate relevant indicators, it provides a more diversified picture of parallel developments and, therefore, richer information for policymakers to steer and adjust. The approach reckons that not all dimensions of an issue are (yet) entirely known and that the exact interplay between dimensions may also be unclear – for instance, when taking different contextual circumstances into account – and need to be studied further.

The SDG-framework is constructed as a three-layered dashboard: 17 goals – intended as an integrated, indivisible set – to indicate progress on the 2030 Agenda; 169 targets – about 10 targets per goal – to monitor developments towards each goal; and 232 indicators – frequently more than one per target – to keep track of advancements at the target level. However, even a three-layered dashboard approach does not capture all relevant dimensions of such complex phenomena like poverty, inequality or the resilience of cities. Neither does it imply that the choice for a particular target creates, or is the result of, sufficient clarity. Take, for instance, SDG-target 17.13 – part of the 'partnerships for the goals' ambition – which aims to enhance 'global macroeconomic stability'. There is no consensus on what this objective actually entails, neither conceptually, nor in terms of appropriate metrics. Even at this sub-level, it has been agreed that SDG-target 17.13 will be measured by a dashboard of indicators to develop more insights over time. As noted by MacFeely: "the composition of this dashboard will effectively determine whether the 2030 Agenda adopts an orthodox or heterodox view of the global economy" (2019: 8).

Concerning the choice of the specific 169 targets, critics have stated that the SDGs represent a 'reductionist' (quantitative) agenda for measuring societal progress. In general, a goal-setting approach is susceptible to favouring 'easy-to-measure' indicators of progress over more complex issues that may be of greater importance, but require a more extensive set of indicators (Young, 2017). Others have argued that the 169 targets are still highly diverse – as compared to other efforts to measure progress on sustainable development – and for the moment difficult to prioritize. Either way, the set of targets continues to require elaboration: by December 2019, half of the 232 indicators still faced measurement difficulties (Box 2.2), which is nevertheless an improvement compared to the statistical challenges in two-thirds of the indicators in 2016.

Indicator development around the world not only represents a complex technical effort of getting the definitions right, deciding on adequate metrics and methodologies, and specifying criteria for robust, disaggregated and comparable data collection. The process itself is also susceptible to policy influences, interest battles and different ambitions of scientists – on top of financing requirements, harmonization issues and governance matters. This is a typical VUCA challenge that cuts across all layers of the SDG-agenda. Indicator selection and sophistication are decisive elements in the steering mechanism that not only define what constitutes progress, but also determine to what extent progress will materialize. Only what is measured tends to get done. Adopting meaningful indicators hence requires some tolerance for complexity and the search for better insights, rather than the introduction of one metric for a single-sided dimension (see section 2.3).

'TIERS AND FEARS' OF UN INDICATOR DEVELOPMENT

The UN agreed upon a system of 232 indicators that should keep track of the 169 targets of the SDG-agenda. However, many of these indicators have yet to be developed or made comparable across countries and sectors. In order to deal with the resulting levels of ambiguity and uncertainty in indicator development, the UN classified three indicator tiers:

- **Tier I:** Indicator is conceptually clear, has an internationally established methodology and standards are available, and data are regularly produced by countries for at least 50% of countries and of the population in every region where the indicator is relevant.

- **Tier II:** Indicator is conceptually clear, has an internationally established methodology and standards are available, but data are not regularly produced by countries.

- **Tier III:** No internationally established methodology or standards are yet available for the indicator, but methodology/standards are being (or will be) developed or tested.

The tier classification for many indicators changes periodically, as methodologies are developed and data availability increases. In December 2019, the following scores existed for the 'measurability' of the 232 indicators: Tier I (available and clear): 50% of the indicators; Tier II (clear, but not regularly produced by countries): 39%; Tier III (not yet clear or measured): 9%; Multiple tiers apply to 2% of the indicators. As of December 2020, the classification contained 130 Tier I indicators (56%), 97 Tier II indicators (42%) and 4 indicators (2%) that have multiple tiers.

Indicators usually move up in the tier classification as a result of increased clarity or data availability. Indicators may also be placed back in a lower tier when data availability, after review, proves insufficient. As of October 2018, 5 indicators have been placed back, from Tier I to Tier II.

Source: https://unstats.un.org/sdgs/iaeg-sdgs/tier-classification/

2.2.3 The nexus challenge

All SDGs are interlinked by design. The SDG-framework was intentionally developed as an integrated, indivisible global agenda for achieving balanced progress across the economic, social and environmental dimensions of sustainable development (UN, 2015). The framework itself does not prioritize specific goals and targets over others, in the interest of preventing fragmented approaches and siloed implementation. It is difficult to identify the most relevant policy areas for targeted, cost-efficient investments upfront. How potential spill-over effects will unfold across economic sectors, across societal actors, and between and across countries is hard to predict in a VUCA world. Also, choices for specific actions in the present have anticipated but also *unintended* conse-quences over time. By integrating economic, social and environmental themes into one interlinked framework, the SDGs seek to ensure that "the short-term achievement of improved human well-being does not occur at the cost of under-mining well-being in the long term by damaging the underpinning social and environmental capital on which our global life support system depends" (Stafford-Smith et al., 2017: 912). The SDGs hence present 17 areas of closely connected challenges.

The extent to which each SDG can be effectively addressed separately criti-cally depends on how well governments, companies and other societal actors are able to understand, manage and make use of the interrelations between it and the other SDGs. Success in achieving results in one problem area is thus conditioned by actions, policies and progression in other areas. This phenomenon is also known as the 'nexus challenge'. A nexus approach focuses on the positive synergies and potential negative trade-offs that arise when working to achieve the SDG-agenda. One can adopt four basic positions in this intellectually challenging discourse:

1 *A political systems approach:* which looks at the actual biophysical, economic, social and political connections between the SDGs and their targets that were established in the negotiations around the SDGs;

2 *A top-down theoretical approach:* which classifies the SDGs as part of a systems approach and tries to define which clusters of SDGs are interrelated;

3 *A principles-based approach:* which considers the basic principles that are at the core of all SDGs and takes a more research-oriented approach;

4 *A pragmatic approach:* that takes a bottom-up angle to create scientific insights into what linkages actually exist and reinforce each other.

POLITICAL SYSTEMS APPROACH

This approach was elaborated by David Le Blanc (2015) who identified the various connections between the SDGs as the result of the political process through which the SDGs were formed. His analysis showed that some thematic areas covered by the SDGs are well connected, whereas other parts of the SDG network have weaker connections with the rest of the system (Figure 2.1a). Le Blanc found that the political framework which the SDGs provide does not adequately reflect the array of actual interrelations known to exist from a scientific point of view. The range of links identified – for instance, related to biophysical, social and economic systems – is far greater than the political ones that were recognized, agreed upon and adopted in the 2030 Agenda (ICSU and ISSC, 2015). For instance, missing from the 2030 Agenda is the well-recognized link between energy use and industrialization and its subsequent effects on climate change and ecosystems. Also missing are the links between oceans and climate change, and energy and climate change (Le Blanc, 2015). Especially where missing links are known to be of a strong systemic nature, it is important to integrate recognized insights into subsequent policymaking. Considering that the interconnections between the SDGs are complex and manifold, however, the political framework cannot possibly accommodate all relevant interconnections (ibid). This approach hence provides limited guidance in how to address these interconnections.

TOP-DOWN (DEDUCTIVE) THEORETICAL APPROACH

A second approach – which can be described as a 'top-down scientific approach' – has developed that tries to fill this hole. It uses systems theory to predefine expected interactions, define levels of analysis, and link these to systems outcomes – like climate change and economic growth at a global scale. An example of this approach is the one embraced by the Stockholm Resilience Centre (SRC) in 2016. They developed a hierarchy of SDGs, in which the biosphere presents the general context in which all other goals should be positioned (Figure 2.1b). Economies and societies are seen as embedded parts of the biosphere. The centre defines the planetary boundaries as the ultimate context within which humanity can continue to develop for generations to come while 'societies' represent human-made institutional conditions, and 'economy' more or less how change can be organized efficiently. 'Partnerships for the goals' (SDG17) are portrayed as the linchpin between all levels of interaction. The SRC argues that food as a resource, and the way we produce and organize society around it, actually connects all the SDGs. This approach shows a strong resemblance to Kate Raworth's 'doughnut economics' (2017), as introduced in Chapter 1.

PRINCIPLES-BASED APPROACH

A principles-based approach was adopted at the launch of the SDGs. It resembles a synthesis of principles that had been discussed in the global arena: from universal human rights principles and the OECD guidelines on multinational enterprises, to principles as defined by the UN Global Compact. The Triple-P (People, Planet, Profit) concept, widely used in the business sector, was embraced albeit with a distinctive adjustment: 'profit' – as a guiding principle for business –

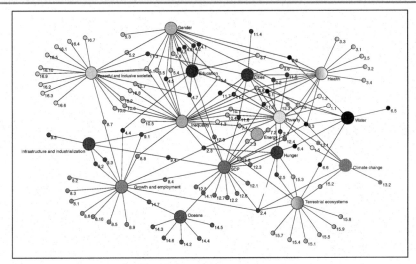

Source: courtesy of Le Blanc (2015), p. 4.

[b] Systemic hierarchy of SDGs according to the Stockholm Resilience Centre

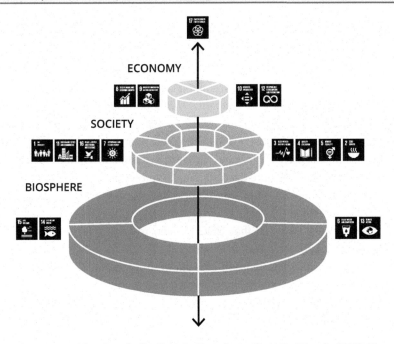

Source: adapted from Azote for Stockholm Resilience Centre, Stockholm University, CC BY 4.0.

[c] Five basic Principles of all SDGs

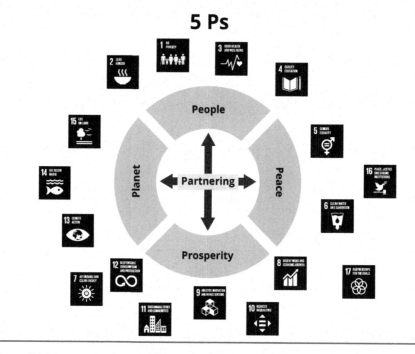

Figure 2.1 Three approaches to defining the nexus between SDGs

was replaced by 'Prosperity', which is more strongly and explicitly related to global common-pool ambitions. Governments and civil society representatives introduced an additional element: the principles of 'justice' and 'dignity'. In the final version of the SDGs, these were summarized as 'Peace'. All actors supported the introduction of a vital fifth element: 'Partnering'. The resulting framework defines the 5 Ps as the foundation for all 17 SDGs. All five principles are of equal weight and apply basic ethical frames like consequences, duties, rights, virtues and capabilities (Box 2.3). 'Partnering' can be interpreted as a means for achieving the other four principles (Figure 2.1c). It can, therefore, be considered of a slightly different order than the four other principles, stressing participatory and discourse-based ethical principles.

Somewhat confusing is that SDG17 also refers to 'Partnerships for the Goals'. Many practitioners mistakenly refer to SDG17 when they intend to stress the importance of collaboration and partnering in general. SDG17, however, is primarily aimed at cross-country government collaboration in pursuit of all the goals. SDG17 aims to strengthen and streamline cooperation between *nation-states*, both developed and developing, using the SDGs as a shared framework and vision. SDG17-targets consequently relate to policy areas like finance (through development assistance), trade, technological cooperation, capacity

SIX ETHICAL FRAMEWORKS

Ethical frameworks help in developing and applying principles of appropriate behaviour and decision-making under challenging situations. Six basic positions can be taken that in practice are mutually overlapping and reinforcing when applied correctly:

1 **Consequence-based ethics** (utilitarian principles introduced by Jeremy Bentham) – this perspective considers the consequences and results of action and the pursuit of the common good (defined as maximized happiness and minimized suffering).

2 **Duty-based ethics** (deontological principles, introduced by Immanuel Kant) – focuses on binding rules for assessing one's motivations (categorical imperative), leading to obligations and duties to others (family, country, group).

3 **(Social) contract-based ethics** (rights, rules and enforcement, inspired by 'social contract theory' or 'principles of political right' as introduced by Jean-Jacques Rousseau) – focuses on rights and agreements, based on formal and informal rules (institutions), to come to a collective understanding and govern actions in the interest of all.

4 **Character-based ethics** (virtue, as introduced by Aristotle) – is aimed at 'doing things right' and practising good habits.

5 **Capabilities-based ethics** (introduced by Amartya Sen and Martha Nussbaum) – an alternative to economic thinking in welfare economics, that stresses the capabilities needed to exert freedom of choice, in order to achieve human well-being. A central notion in this approach is that of human dignity, acknowledging individual heterogeneity and the multidimensional nature of welfare.

6 **Discourse-based ethics** (introduced by Jürgen Habermas) – also known as 'participatory ethics', advancing Kant's categorical imperative to include a collective imperative. It stresses the importance of multi-stakeholder participation in the argumentation and establishment of a norm.

building for policies (in particular in the global South) and the creation of policy coherence. As a principle, the fifth P in the 5 Ps framework applies to *all* SDGs. It recognizes that each of the SDGs can only be achieved on the basis of effective multi-stakeholder and multi-sector collaboration between governments, companies and civil society organizations. Hence, the partnering *principle* can never be implemented in isolation merely by embracing SDG17.

BOTTOM-UP (INDUCTIVE) APPROACH

Each of the former three approaches has advantages and disadvantages, but as systemic analysis in research and policy analysis on SDG interactions had been lacking, progress was slow. Hence, a more pragmatic bottom-up scientific approach materialized to guide actions towards achieving the SDGs and support a better understanding of the nature, dynamics and range of positive and negative interactions between the goals. The approach aims for a science-informed analysis of interactions across SDG domains that "can support more coherent and effective decision making, and better facilitate follow-up and monitoring of progress" (ICSU, 2017: 7). Nilsson, Griggs and Visbeck (2016) proposed a seven-point scale to rate interactions, as a conceptual framework to help identify priorities for policymaking. Three general types of interactions between SDG-targets can be discerned: positive (virtuous), neutral and negative (vicious) dynamics. Positive interactions among SDGs occur when SDGs are enabling, when they are reinforcing or when they are indivisible. Neutral, or consistent, interactions describe a situation in which contributions towards one goal do not yield significant positive or negative interactions with another goal. Negative interactions arise when goals are constraining, counteracting or cancelling (Nilsson et al., 2016). Systematic assessment of the nature, direction and dynamics of the many interactions among the SDGs should improve understanding of the possibilities to leverage interventions for positive impact and to identify concrete focal points. In 2018, a team of specialists further extended and tested their interactions framework, and stressed the importance of particular contextual factors, such as (a) geographical context, (b) resource endowments, (c) time horizon and (d) governance (Nilsson et al., 2018).

2.3 KEY EMPIRICAL CHALLENGES: CAN CLAIMS AND PROGRESS BE QUANTIFIED?

The SDG-agenda has been asserted to usher in a new era in global development through its goal-setting and 'governance-by-indicators' approach (Davis et al., 2012). Hence, the success of the SDG endeavour heavily depends on the extent to which legitimate measurement of relevant progress can be established. The SDG-indicators include economic, social, political, institutional and environmental aspects – often defined as an aggregation of various sub-indicators – which are further disaggregated by income, sex, age, race, ethnicity, migratory status, disability and geographic location, as part of the overarching pledge to 'leave no one behind'. This refinement effort followed from the criticism that the data used in the MDG process were too general, not properly aligned or simply unavailable. Based on the MDG experience, an *Independent Expert Advisory Group* stressed the need to better align data availability and decision-making cycles – more data, better data and, above all, faster data (IEAG, 2014). The group also raised the idea that "in a data-driven world, the inability to access data should be a measure of inequality" (MacFeely, 2019: 7).

THE SCIENTIFIC DISCOURSE – TWO POSITIONS

The empirical challenge of the SDGs takes a particular twist in a VUCA world, where manipulated data, 'alternative facts' and 'fake news' spread rapidly. As an antidote, experts claim that the SDG monitoring and progress tracking process must be based on "sound evidence and science, taking advantage of contemporary approaches from the sustainability sciences, including systems thinking and analysis and quantitative modelling" (Allen et al., 2018: 1454). The urge for *evidence-based* knowledge is mounting, yet this ambition also presents several tough challenges, including: (1) the question of whether robust quantitative evidence can be established for multifaceted or systemic problems, as indicators can be reductionist for the phenomena they try to measure (Ordaz, 2019); (2) whether relevant data are available that are also comparative, reliable and recent; (3) whether new metrics can be developed to fill in the knowledge gaps that the SDG-framework still faces. Evidence-informed benchmarking is vital for governments, companies and civil society organizations to determine whether their efforts are bringing them closer to, or further away from, the SDGs over time. If not established according to accurate definitions and a solid understanding of the complexities involved, however, it can also lead to misleading comparisons based on skewed indicators that may not be relevant for a specific context (be it national or sectoral).

An alternative approach is to look at the entire process of collecting, developing and comparing data as a *circular process* (Davies, 2012). Agenda-setting, monitoring, evaluation and implementation processes are then part of an iterative process that involves stakeholders who help in the upgrading of existing data, and in defining areas of new data gathering. In the development discourse, this approach is also known as 'developmental evaluation' (Patton et al., 2016). These techniques enable a more systemic approach to the SDG-agenda and a process-oriented view on dealing with the large number of interrelated practical challenges, such as measurement, benchmarking and the development of new indicators. Serious concerns on this approach have been voiced too, in particular related to the "politicization of science whereby policymakers bury, misuse, manipulate or cherry-pick evidence to support and promote their own policy preferences" (Eden and Wagstaff, 2021: 42). Fukuda-Parr and McNeill (2019), for instance, asserted that whereas the development of SDG-indicators is purported to be an objective and technical matter, the politicization of international agenda-setting has been moving to the selection of indicators. To prevent such selection biases from happening, sophisticated governance approaches are required on how to select and solicit relevant indicators that help the evidence-based ambition, rather than reinforcing specific political and scientific biases (e.g. Parkhurst, 2017).

Both approaches face important areas of contention in the process of defining, collecting, comparing and developing relevant data. This section inventories relevant areas in this discourse. It describes how the SDG community strives to find practical (empirical) pathways towards apt evidence-based approaches, by identifying and addressing gaps that still require further attention. Part II will further argue that many of the practical and theoretical gaps related to the SDG effort are part and parcel of the 'wicked' nature of any approach that looks at systemic issues (Chapter 4). Wicked problems require *channelling*, rather than 'resolving' approaches as a basic principle for developing evidence-*informed* policies. That involves a more developmental governance approach, as will be elaborated in Chapter 5 and 6.

Following the first years of the SDG journey, several empirical challenges have risen to the surface. They can be summarized in 4 Cs:

- **Claims:** what claims on costs and benefits related to the SDGs can be substantiated? (section 2.3.1);

- **Concerns:** what general concerns have been voiced around the operationalization of the SDG-targets? (section 2.3.2);

- **Conceptualizations:** what major conceptual discussions are still to be addressed? (section 2.3.3);

- **Complexity:** what about mapping and measuring nexus interactions? (section 2.3.4).

2.3.1   Claims of costs and benefits: can they be substantiated?

The positive reception of the SDGs was not only influenced by a growing sense of urgency on parallel global crises (climate, inequality, financial) and the costs of *not* taking action. Equally important were several positive assessments of the *benefits* of acting on (parts of) the SDG-agenda as drivers for resilient growth. In the course of the 2013–2019 period, a large variety of cost-benefit statements were issued, with different angles:

- *Focusing primarily on the net-benefits for companies.* In 2017, the Business & Sustainable Development Commission argued in its *Better Business Better World* report that the SDGs could unlock at least $12 trillion a year in market opportunities (business savings and revenue) by 2030, provided that companies made sustainable development the core of their business strategy. The Commission based its expectations on the potential in four economic systems that together represent around 60% of the real economy: food and agriculture, cities, energy and materials, and health and well-being (see Box 2.4). Achieving the Global Goals in these four systems was estimated to create around 380 million new jobs by 2030 (covering more than 10% of the forecast labour force in 2030), 90% of them in developing countries. Over 50% of identified market opportunities would arise from market 'hotspots' located in developing countries. Contributing to additional

MACRO OPPORTUNITIES DRIVING GROWTH: FOUR ECONOMIC SYSTEMS

BOX 2.4

FOOD AND AGRICULTURE

Food waste in the value chain (US$155 billion to US$405 billion a year)

- Today 20%–30% of food is wasted, most of it in postharvest losses that are easy to prevent.
- Aligned to SDG12

Forest ecosystem services (US$140 billion to US$365 billion a year)

- Deforestation and forest degradation account for 17% of global emissions (more than transport). There are major opportunities for business in sustainable forest services, such as climate change mitigation, watershed services and biodiversity conservation.
- Aligned to SDG15

Low income food markets (US$155 billion to US$265 billion)

- Undernutrition and malnutrition are widespread in the world's poorest populations. Business can address the challenge by investing in supply chains and food innovation to give those on very low incomes access to more nutritious food.
- Aligned to SDG2

ENERGY AND MATERIALS

Circular models in the automotive sector (US$475 billion to US$810 billion)

- More efficient remanufacturing, replacement of weakest link components and refurbishment present opportunities not realized by scrapping cars.
- Aligned to SDG12

Expansion of renewables (US$165 billion to US$605 billion)

- IRENA forecasts that renewables share of energy generation worldwide could increase to 45% by 2030 (from 23% in 2014) presenting opportunities for renewable energy generators and equipment manufacturers.
- Aligned to SDG7

Circular models for the appliances and machinery sectors (US$305 billion to US$525 billion)

- Domestic appliances and industrial machinery in particular present significant remanufacturing opportunities.
- Aligned to SDG12

CITIES

Affordable housing (US$650 billion to US$1,080 billion)

- As well as construction spending to add capacity and replace inadequate housing, innovation is required to unlock new land and make better use of space for development.
- Aligned to SDG11

Energy efficiency in buildings (US$555 billion to US$770 billion)

- Innovations such as retrofitting existing buildings with more efficient heating/cooling technologies and switching to efficient lighting/appliances could shrink energy demand.
- Aligned to SDG7 and SDG11

HEALTH AND WELL-BEING

Risk pooling (US$350 billion to US$500 billion)

- Increasing the penetration of private, public-private and community insurance schemes could address disproportionately high health costs.

Remote patient monitoring (US$300 billion to US$440 billion)

- Emerging technologies that enable remote monitoring of patients could reduce the cost of treating chronic diseases in health systems by 10%-20% by 2025.
- Aligned to SDG3

Telehealth (US$130 billion to US$320 billion)

- Mobile internet technologies could extend access for consultations and diagnosis to remote patients around the world.
- Aligned to SDG3

Source: UNPRI 'SDGs: Macro Opportunities, Driving Growth', 12 October 2017 https://www.unpri.org/sdgs/the-sdgs-will-drive-global-economic-growth/307.article

sectors critical to sustainable development (e.g. information communication technologies, education and consumer goods), indicated a further potential of $8 trillion per year of value created from business opportunities (Business & Sustainable Development Commission, 2017: 26). The Commission presented these opportunities not only as a private sector 'prize', but also as an effort to *regain trust* and a *license to operate* for companies.

- ■ *Focusing primarily on the systemic benefits* of an accelerated, short-term transition to a low-carbon economy. In *Unlocking the Inclusive Growth Story of the 21st Century* (2018) for instance, the Global Commission on the Economy and Climate made a "conservative estimate" (their words) on the global benefits of a decisive shift to a low-carbon economy, compared to a business-as-usual scenario. They assessed this at $26 trillion in economic benefits up to 2030. Provided it is well-managed and implemented within three years, shifting to a climate-smart growth path could avoid over 700,000 premature deaths from air pollution; raise $2.8 trillion annually in government revenues through subsidy reform and carbon pricing; generate over 65 million additional low-carbon jobs; increase female employment and labour participation; and trigger global GDP growth. Mechanisms pointed out for delivering this new growth approach include, for instance, sustainable agriculture and forest protection, which together could deliver over $2 trillion annually in economic benefits. For every $1 spent on restoring degraded forests, as much as an estimated $30 could be earned in economic benefit (ibid: 21); restoring 160 million hectares of degraded land could constitute an $84 billion boost per year. Coordinated, compact and connected cities could result in $17 trillion in economic savings by 2050. Explicit attention is also paid to the costs associated with *not*, or too slowly, taking action and the mixed signals hereof to the market – a typical VUCA challenge. This type of ambiguity and uncertainty could create 'hedging costs' and an estimated $12 trillion of so-called 'stranded assets' in fossil fuel by 2035 (ibid: 12).

- ***Performing cost-benefit analyses to specific issues.*** The *Lifelines* report by the World Bank found that disruption to vital infrastructure costs households and firms in low and middle-income countries at least $390 billion a year, with indirect effects placing a further toll on households, businesses and communities (Hallegatte et al., 2019). The overall net benefit of investing in the resilience of four infrastructure systems in developing countries (power, water and sanitation, transport and telecommunications) was assessed at $4.2 trillion over the lifetime of new infrastructure, a $4 benefit for each dollar invested in resilience. According to the Carbon Disclosure Project (2019) – surveying with the Global500 largest companies – climate-related risk to business (impaired assets, market changes and physical damage, among others) was valued at $1 trillion within five years. The potential value of climate-related opportunities (e.g. electric cars, low carbon products and services) however, far outweighs the costs of investing in the low-carbon transition, by almost seven times ($311bn in costs, $2.1 trillion in opportunities). Regarding gender equality, McKinsey Global Institute (2015) assessed that advancing equality of women can add $12 trillion to global growth. Or reversely formulated: the OECD (2016) calculated that the current level of discrimination is estimated to induce a loss of up to $12 trillion or 16% of global income.

Many of these and related scenarios are based on perceptions and expectations of experts or opinion leaders. Whether any of these will materialize depends not only on a correct understanding of their basic premises (in particular related to the nexus challenge), but also on the reception and adequate implementation of combinations of SDGs by actors around the world. Positive perceptions influence transition processes to the extent that the claim becomes a *self-fulfilling prophecy*, for instance by pooling actors around a common (SDG) agenda. The same applies, however, for negative perceptions, as argued in Chapter 1.

2.3.2 Concerns: operationalization challenges

'What gets measured, gets managed'. Also in the SDG approach, performance indicators have become important steering mechanisms in achieving priority objectives. But what *can* actually be measured? If the set of indicators to cover an issue is limited, policy measures and interventions are probably also limited (Stiglitz et al., 2009). From the start, it was clear that many of the 169 SDG-targets could have been better defined and would be difficult to achieve in all countries and at all envisioned levels. Although presented as 'a work in progress', the gap between the ambition and operationalization could risk to "undercut the overall credibility of the package" (Bhattacharya and Kharas, 2015). The formulation of 169 targets and 232 indicators accordingly triggered several concerns, in particular related to:

1 *The operationalization of indicators:* are these meaningful and substantive enough to uphold a steering mechanism of 'governance-by-indicators';[4]
2 *The availability* of relevant, reliable, comparable and timely data;
3 *The costs* of organizing the production of relevant data.

OPERATIONALIZATION OF INDICATORS

Counting four times more indicators than in the MDG era, many of the 232 SDG-indicators were completely new or were produced outside of the national statistical systems. The subsequent conceptualization and operationalization of the SDG-framework has been described as an unprecedented intellectual and statistical challenge. A considerable number of the proposed indicators are still 'under construction', with methodologies or standards yet to be developed or tested (Tier III indicators, see Box 2.2).

Also, the indicator framework itself is part of a continuous improvement and alignment process. Proposals have been made for replacing, revising or deleting existing indicators, and for adding others that would better cover dimensions that are still lacking. These review and adjustment processes run in parallel to existing indicator-monitoring systems that are being implemented by countries around the world. Many countries and regions are in the process of aligning their statistical indicators with the global SDG-indicators, yet have also been found to systematically use their own methods and to replace the global SDG-indicators with different national proxy indicators. A similar development has been noted with regional statistical organizations, whose SDG-adjusted indicator frameworks have been claimed to compete with, more than complement, the global SDG-indicator framework (Gennari and Navarro, 2020). In practice, the lack of harmonization in indicator frameworks, methods and data collection thus makes it quite difficult to compare findings over countries, and to establish a global benchmark for keeping track on progress.

---

4   In the *Global Policy* special issue (January 2019) on Knowledge and Politics in Setting and Measuring SDGs, the concern was raised that "measurement methods interpret and reinterpret norms, carry value judgements, theoretical assumptions, and implicit political agendas. As social scientists have long pointed out, reliance on indicators can distort social norms, frame hegemonic discourses, and reinforce power hierarchies" (Fukuda-Parr and McNeill, 2019).

Related to this is the concern that many SDG data requirements – associated, for instance, with water resource management, labour rights, financial market regulation, investment promotion, corporate sustainability reporting, coastal conservation, marine litter, fish stocks or corruption – go beyond the scope, expertise and mandate of national statistics offices (MacFeely, 2019). Tracking on *all* SDG-indicators at the required levels of disaggregation hence points to the need for the creation and governance of so-called 'new data ecosystems', in which the expertise from data scientists, experts and national statisticians in all fields relevant to the SDG-framework is pooled, coordinated and validated. Cross-border matters also require cooperation and alignment. Concerns still remain about how to operationalize more than half of the SDG-targets that are transboundary in nature and hence require transboundary efforts. For 97 of the SDG-targets, achieving them in one country is likely to have spill-over effects outside the national borders, affecting neighbouring countries, other countries or global public goods. Many of the transboundary SDG-targets are concentrated in the planet-related SDGs. In 2019, the OECD found that indicators were available for only 31 of the 97 transboundary SDG-targets, leaving considerable gaps in understanding "the global and interconnected aspects of the 2030 Agenda and its implementation" (ibid, 2019: 16).

A final concern relates to changes in the classification of particular target groups over time. For instance, the SDG-targets specify between the least developed (LDCs) and developed countries. Over the years, many LDCs are likely to change classification and become middle-income countries. This raises the question of how this development will translate in the SDG-targets and indicator framework, and whether the original composition of the LDC group of countries will be sustained over the years in order to keep track of relevant changes and be able to adjust policies over time.

DATA QUALITY AND AVAILABILITY

A substantial gap exists between the reliance of the SDG-framework on relevant, validated, comparable and timely data, and the actual capacity of countries to generate, collect and process these. For SDG-indicators without an established methodology (Tier III), no data can be collected. Tier II indicators do have an established methodology, but data are not yet generally collected by countries. This implies that even highly developed countries with well-equipped national statistical offices are only able to track progress on around 50% of the SDG-indicators. At the target level, the OECD in 2019 noted that more than one-third of SDG-targets cannot yet be assessed in OECD countries. Available data allowed assessing 105 of the 169 targets, while "only for 87 of these it had been possible to assess whether indicators have been moving towards target levels, rather than away from them" (OECD, 2019).[5] Data coverage is best on SDG3 and SDG4 ('good health and well-being' and 'quality education') and has been poorest on environment-related SDGs, notably SDG12 and SDG14 ('sustainable consumption and production' and 'life below water'). Many developing countries still struggle to compile basic social and economic statistics. Countries in Africa and Asia have been reported to, on average, have data available on 20% of SDG-indicators, with just 35% of sub-Saharan African countries being able to report on poverty data since 2015 (SDSN-TReNDS, 2019: 7). Many people in the world, including 26 million refugees, around half of whom are under the age of 18 (UNHCR, 2020), do not appear in statistics at all, while coverage of census data remains challenging in countries that cope with low administrative capacity or with large numbers of internally displaced people (estimated in 2020 at 45.7 million worldwide). It has been persistently difficult to collect relevant data on marginalized populations in developing countries and remote areas.

Global environment data is presently also limited. For 68% of the environment-related SDGs, there is insufficient data to formally assess their status as yet. This applies amongst others to such vital policy domains as water efficiency (SDG-target 6.4), management and generation of waste, hazardous waste and food waste (SDG-targets 11.6, 12.4 and 12.3); recycling (SDG-target 12.5); corporate sustainability reporting (SDG-target 12.6); and research and promotion of sustainable lifestyles (UNEP, 2019). Specially disaggregated and geospatial data are essential for a better understanding of ecosystem challenges and the relationship between the environment and human activity.

New (digital) technologies for capturing novel sources of (big) data are emerging that may fill in important blanks in the near future. Developments in artificial and machine intelligence, robotics, remote sensing, drones and geospatial technology offer promising prospects. Novel data compiled from satellite and aerial imagery, mobile phone data, smart meters, road sensors, public transport usage data, ship identification data, social media, scanner data, health records, patent data, criminal record data, Google alerts, and credit card data (MacFeely, 2019a), for instance, could all be part of a 'data revolution' supported by interoperable, 'joined-up' modern data systems for achieving sustainable development (SDSN-TReNDS, 2019). Ways are being examined of how, and under which conditions, such non-official data could augment survey methods and official statistics. The collection, validation and dissemination of these data not only comes with promising opportunities, but presents legal, ethical, governance, technical and reputational challenges as well.

---

5   The indicators used in the 'Measuring Distance to the SDG Targets' studies of the OECD, are closely aligned with those in the UN Global Indicator List agreed by the Inter-Agency and Expert Group on SDG-indicators.

THE COSTS OF ORGANIZING

The implementation of the SDG-indicator framework comes with investment needs, costs and funding requirements. Particularly in developing countries, statistical and administrative systems have been underfunded for years, and implementation of the SDG-framework hence calls for additional effort and support in capacity building. Various estimates have pointed out that the costs of implementing the SDG-framework for low and middle-income countries exceed existing funding. Assessments of the financing gap range between $400–$600 million per annum, which would require an estimated doubling of the current level of official development assistance for statistics and data development, from its current 0.33% share to about 0.7% of ODA (Official Development Assistance).[6] Financing commitments by developed economies to contribute 0.7% of their gross national incomes to ODA have systemically fallen short however. This raises serious concerns on whether sufficient statistical and administrative capacity can be developed within the developing parts of the world to match the data requirements.

Summarizing, there are still considerable operationalization challenges to be addressed, in particular related to the further advancement of the SDG-indicator framework, establishing sufficient levels of harmonization, data coverage, and statistical and administrative capacity-building. New technologies for generating novel data and joined-up data approaches to augment official statistics may offer promising prospects to overcome persistent data gaps. This would further enable evidence-informed policies and could catalyse effective actions. Such novel technologies and networked approaches need time to materialize, however, and also create myriad governance, funding and implementation challenges. The feasibility of an integrated and transformational SDG-agenda depends on the process with which these challenges are tackled. Part II and Part III of this book develop further insights in how to deal with these concerns in more managerial directions.

2.3.3 Conceptualizations: contested definitions

The development discourse is a contentious (mine)field of competing ideas on what constitutes development and sustainability, and varying theories on how best to achieve this. The global adoption of the 17 SDGs hence presented a significant effort in reconciling competing approaches (Chapter 1). Nevertheless, the formulation of the 17 SDGs and their 169 targets left considerable room for interpretation: many lacked clear definition and consistent use of terminology. Discussions

---

6   For an account of costs and financing needs, see for instance MacFeely (2019: 11), Rogerson with Calleja (2019: 8–9) and SDSN-TReNDS (2019: 39).

on the further conceptualization were delegated to the level of SDG-indicators and platforms of researchers and policymakers.

The selection of indicators arguably still only covers part of the conceptual and definition problems that surround the SDGs. The wording of particular SDGs already leads to interesting discussions. For instance, what defines 'zero hunger' (SDG2)? Does that mean the same for people in food-abundant and food-poor regions? What is 'quality education' (SDG4) when weighed against both individual and national needs? What exactly does 'clean' water (SDG6) entail, and is that a consistent given over time, with clear norms equal for all countries? What is 'decent work' (SDG8), for instance, in a flex society with the majority of the population working on short-term contracts? What does 'responsible consumption' (SDG12) imply in different cultural, religious and economic realities? And what constitutes 'peace' (SDG16) in various countries around the world: the absence of war, or the absence of violence? Fundamentally, the SDGs do not always take sides in this discourse, and with good reason. On some of these issues, international consensus exists, leading to a number of global standards. In many more of these issues no consensus on norms and standards exists, however, which leads to often competing standards, for instance with regard to 'human rights'.

To navigate this discourse, each of these SDGs contains a dashboard of five to ten targets that are supposed to channel measurement on progress and enable participants in the discourse to disagree on selected indicators and the relevance of supportive data. Because of continued contention on the extent to which selected indicators can cover all relevant dimensions, it has been argued that progress tracking on the implementation of the SDGs should be accompanied by qualitative analysis, and not on the indicator framework alone. This is to counterbalance a potential over-reliance on numeric indicators which, when "used as policy tools in governance, have specific properties that have distinctive effects on knowledge (how things are conceptualized) and on governance (behaviour of actors, policy choices)" (Fukuda-Parr and McNeill, 2019). A dominant reliance on numeric indicators tends to create selection biases in 'what can be measured', 'what can be achieved', 'what is relevant' and 'what can be proven'. This could induce a watered-down, relatively narrow picture of relevant dimensions of sustainable development. Part II further elaborates on how to deal with this kind of knowledge ambiguity. Here, the effects of a *narrow* and *broad* conceptualization of two key dimensions of the SDG-framework are illustrated: 'sustainability' and 'development'.

WHAT DEFINES 'SUSTAINABLE'

Chapter 1 already referred to the various components that have been introduced over time to delineate the concept of 'sustainability'. In five decades, the definition of sustainable development has matured and broadened to include planet (resources and nature), people (social), profit/prosperity (economy) and peace (and justice). In popular discourse, however, sustainability has primarily been associated with ecological sustainability. The urgency felt in addressing the existential threat of climate change and biodiversity has created a 'perception bias' in favour of ecological sustainability.[7] To some extent, this ecology bias undercuts the legitimacy and understanding of the SDGs as an indivisible, integrated approach, both with policymakers and interest groups. For example, corporations particularly invest in ecological sustainability, while claiming to support all dimensions of sustainability (see Part III). From a practical perspective, this ecology bias is understandable: there is already considerable evidence of a positive 'return on investment' (ROI). The 'business case' and the ROI for more social dimensions of sustainability are often less obvious and, therefore, more difficult to prioritize from a business perspective.

WHAT DEFINES 'ECONOMIC GROWTH' AND 'DEVELOPMENT'?

The tension between a narrow or broader conceptualization of 'development' is relevant for all SDGs, but as a measurement challenge most prominently relates to SDG8 ('decent work and economic growth'). SDG8 aims to promote sustained, inclusive and sustainable economic growth, full and productive employment, and decent work for all. A basic yet narrow indicator for economic growth that is still universally applied is the annual growth rate of 'real GDP per capita'. The adoption of supplementary indicators for SDG8-targets already hints at GDP growth itself representing a very rough and often deceptive yardstick for progress. For instance, GDP does not inform on the level of diversification or the resilience of an economy. Neither does it take 'negative externalities' into account related to the production of goods and services, nor the spill-over effects thereof across borders. Additional measures for SDG8-targets, like average hourly earnings, unemployment rates, informal employment, material footprint, the proportion of youth *not* in education, employment or training, and numbers of jobs in specific sectors like tourism[8], hence present a more nuanced picture of the state and growth potential of an economy.

---

7   The popular definition of sustainable development by the Brundtland Commission (1987) as "development that meets the needs of the present without compromising the ability of future generations to meet their own needs" is mostly used as a benchmark to measure progress on ecological sustainability (section 1.4.1).

8   Picking out tourism – and not other sectors – presents an interesting selection bias for SDG8 and reveals a focus on a particular type of developing countries.

SEARCHING FOR A BETTER INDEX OF NATIONAL PROGRESS

Over time, a number of initiatives have developed to deal with the limitations of the GDP as a single index of national (economic) progress. Three strands of ideas can be distinguished: corrective approaches that try to adjust for some negative elements; active approaches that include different metrics; and novel, broadening approaches that take a different (dashboard) approach.

[1] Corrective approaches have tried to adjust the classical GDP metrics for some of its negative effects and conditions. The 'Net Domestic Product' (NDP) presents such an effort. Based on a comparable logic, indices for a 'green GDP' or a 'Sustainable National Income' were introduced.

- ■ *The green GDP* is a relatively loose concept for an environmentally adjusted domestic product that takes into account the consumption of natural capital (Stiglitz et al., 2009: 66).

- ■ *Sustainable National Income (SNI)* was developed in the Netherlands by the National Institute for Public Health and the Environment (RIVM). SNI measures what a 'green GDP' would involve by deducting the costs involved in recovering damages to the environment, instead of accounting the economic activities necessary to 'clean up' as a positive contribution to GDP. The SNI has been heavily debated, but has not yet been applied by any government.

- ■ The *Genuine Progress Indicator (GPI)* was developed in 1995 by the Californian think-tank 'Redefining Progress'. For the USA, the think-tank calculated that in the 1995–2000 period, wealth – as defined by GPI – did not progress, despite a considerable growth of GDP. Nova Scotia in Canada applied a moderate version of the GPI to assess its own progress.

- ■ The *index of sustainable economic welfare* deducts some of the costs of the present production system (water depletion, air and noise pollution, loss of land and other natural resource depletion). Costs are measured, for instance, by the investment necessary to either compensate for or recover the damage inflicted on the natural system.

[2] Active approaches search for indicators that cover the preferred condition of societies. This often involves a normative theory of what equitable aims are deemed worthwhile to strive for, such as 'quality of life' or other non-income dimensions of well-being.

- ■ The best-known index in this area was developed by economic philosopher and Nobel laureate Armatya Sen who developed the *Human Development Index (HDI)* for the United Nations Development Programme. Since 1980, this index has been annually published in the Human Development Report.

HDI uses measures such as life expectancy and capabilities development (schooling). There has been some debate as to the limitations of the indicators and the weight attributed to each domain, as well as on how to interpret the resulting single HDI-indicator and how to interpret changes. For developed countries in particular, the correlation between HDI growth and GDP growth has been shown to be very high. For developing countries, however, GDP growth and HDI growth are much less linked. It is thus possible to record only moderate economic growth, but much higher HDI growth (Stiglitz et al., 2009: 209). Many statistical bureaus around the world accumulate information on 'quality of life' indicators, but policy is hardly ever made based on these statistics.

■   There is one exception: ***Gross National Happiness (GNH)***. This concept was introduced by the state of Bhutan – one of the countries scoring extremely poorly in international GDP comparisons. Next to economic development, GNH covers cultural, ecological and good governance factors. The GNH places high value on countries having rich and diverse cultural traditions, high biodiversity and no overt expressions of blatant poverty.

[3] The global financial crisis of 2007/2008 has influenced **recent efforts to replace GDP**. In 2008, the French president established a committee consisting of three top economists, Stiglitz, Sen and Fitoussi (2009), following his dissatisfaction with the current state of statistical information about the economy and society. The aim of the committee was to identify the limits of GDP as an indicator of economic performance and social progress and to assess alternative measurement tools.

■   The committee proposed a multidimensional and multilevel ***approach to 'well-being'*** that includes both objective and subjective measures in market as well as non-market activities. They refer to this as the ***Extended Wealth Index.*** The committee also introduced a sustainability benchmark: an assessment of how high overconsumption is or, in individual terms, how big under-investment in sustainability targets is.

The committee presented its findings not as yet another benchmark, but as the opening of an international *multi-stakeholder engagement process*. They sketched the steps to be taken, for instance by establishing roundtables to involve stakeholders to identify and prioritize indicators "that carry the potential for a shared view of how social progress is happening and how it can be sustained over time" (ibid: 18). In other words, the committee proposed a strategic stakeholder dialogue for the development and implementation of new measures of sustainable growth.

■   This French effort clearly applied the basics of 'discourse ethics' (Box 2.3) and many countries followed suit with initiatives to also develop new metrics to cover relevant dimensions of 'well-being'. In 2018, for instance, Iceland, New Zealand and Scotland, three developed countries headed by female prime ministers, organized themselves in the so-called **WE-Go** (Wellbeing Economy Governments) club. They are all trying to develop new economic models that concentrate on well-being, instead of growth through consumption and production.

■ A practical effort materialized in 2011. The OECD developed the **Better Life Index**, which includes such measures as work–life balance, the quality of the social support network, and citizen's involvement in democracy. Criticism was voiced on the methodology for its vagueness, its missing values (like religion) or the use of relative, instead of absolute scores. In 2017, Norway, Australia and Iceland ranked in the top three in this index.

The SDG approach can be considered a continuation of particularly the last type of initiatives: adopting both a broad dashboard and a process-oriented approach, aimed at continuous identification and upgrading of relevant indicators, organized through a multi-stakeholder engagement process.

Over time, many scholars have questioned the value of a single metric for (economic) development, and many alternative measures have been introduced over the years (Box 2.5). Especially after the financial crisis that started in 2007, the discussion on adopting a broader definition of progress – 'well-being' and 'welfare growth', rather than economic growth alone – took flight. The concept of 'broad welfare' still takes classic indicators of economic development (like GDP, consumption and employment) into account, but also includes dimensions of welfare and sustainability, such as education, (public) health and the environment (with spill-over effects across borders increasingly being considered). Generally, it can be concluded that the measurement of national progress has moved beyond the narrow GDP yardstick, to include ever broader dimensions of welfare and well-being.

2.3.4 Complexity: prioritizing nexus challenges

The 'nexus' concept refers to the value of an integrated approach to policy and decision-making that not only focuses on individual components, but takes the interrelatedness and interdependencies of the entire system (or relevant parts of it) into consideration. In doing so, insights are developed about actions that may create opportunities for reducing trade-offs (in case of adverse interactions) and for leveraging synergies (in case of beneficial interactions) to support more coherent and effective decision-making. By identifying nodes for leverage, more than one goal can be advanced simultaneously at reduced cost or with more substantial impact across a larger scale. A nexus approach also informs on policy areas that need mitigation in order to restrain vicious interactions that generate perverse outcomes and make investments evaporate. Furthermore, applying a nexus approach can aid in identifying 'winners and losers' of particular transformations – with accelerating or impairing effects on proposed pathways – and in identifying relevant societal stakeholders that are critical in advancing developments further (Nilsson et al., 2018). Scientific evidence on the nature, scale and scope of various nexus challenges related to the SDG-agenda is still relatively scant. The scientific literature addresses only a limited number of interactions between SDG-targets. Insights into these particular workings of linkages are key in successfully achieving the SDGs, by ensuring that progress in some areas does not come at the expense of other areas.

The nexus assessment challenge essentially involves three questions: [9]

1   How are different dimensions of the SDG-agenda related through *linkages* (for deciding which of the SDG-targets needs to receive priority – if any);

2   To what extent do these linkages create *positive feedback loops* (also known as accelerator, spill-over, leverage, co-benefit, multiplier, ripple effect or in short: 'positive externalities');

3   To what extent do these linkages generate *negative feedback loops* that might diminish or adversely affect positive effects (also known as unintended consequences, crowding out effects, or 'negative externalities').

Progress in dealing with the complexity of the nexus challenge has in particular been made through a bottom-up scientific effort that linked various SDGs to see whether their interaction is positive, negative or neutral. Nilsson and colleagues (2016; 2018) identified seven types of SDG interactions, depicted by a seven-point scale that indicates both the nature and strength of the interaction:

---

9   The answers to these questions are context-specific and depend on the aggregation level addressed. A further contextualization can include such dimensions as the directionality of the interactions (e.g. unilateral, mutual, circular); geographic location and scale; and time frame and pace aspects (e.g. short-term, long-term, temporality, irreversibility, emergence, acceleration). Assessing and addressing complexity along ten characterizing dimensions and dynamics of 'wickedness' is elaborated in Chapter 4.

+3 *Indivisible*	Progress on one target automatically delivers progress on another
+2 *Reinforcing*	Progress on one target makes it easier to make progress on another
+1 *Enabling*	Progress on one target creates conditions that enable progress on another
±0 *Consistent*	There is no significant link between two targets' progress
−1 *Constraining*	Progress on one target constrains the options for how to deliver on another
−2 *Counteracting*	Progress on one target makes it more difficult to make progress on another
−3 *Cancelling*	Progress on one target automatically leads to a negative impact on another

In a first effort to check on the usefulness of this technique, the International Council for Science applied the framework to key interactions for a selected number of SDGs (SDG2, SDG3, SDG7 and SDG14) and their associated targets. This selection – not intended to show any form of prioritization (ICSU, 2017) – was based on the choice for a mixture of key SDGs aimed at human well-being, ecosystem services and natural resources. The study revealed the existence of close interactions between the studied SDGs: 316 target-level interactions, of which 238 (76%) were positive, 66 (21%) were negative and 12 (3%) were neutral. Equally important, the analysis did not find fundamental incompatibilities between the studied goals,[10] though it did identify potential constraints and conditionalities that require aligned policy interventions. The study concluded that the selected goals are to a large extent synergistic with each other, which implies that aiming for one target would not make it impossible to achieve another target. However, an important conclusion of the research was that "there is clearly no one-size-fits-all approach to understanding target interactions, and building on this work will require a commitment to continuous iteration and improvement" (ICSU, 2017: 8).

In another effort to acquire policy-relevant insights, the 2018 *High-Level Political Forum* (HLPF) of the UN prioritized SDGs 6, 7, 11, 12 and 15 as a

---

10 In a review of the ICSU study, it was found that around 80% of the 316 interactions examined were positive, around 20% negative, whereas the '*-3 cancelling*' type of interaction only appeared once. As the ICSU study focused on key interactions between selected SDGs as identified by an expert-based assessment, neutral interactions were mostly filtered out by design (Nilsson et al., 2018: 1494).

prima facie challenge for governing linkages amongst the SDGs. A TWI2050 report (2018) explored these linkages by using scenario literature. They considered synergies and trade-offs between each of these SDGs in order to define policies that maximize synergies and minimize trade-offs. They concluded that this is a promising approach, but also noted that the question on how to achieve the full set of SDGs still requires "further accounting for the interlink-ages across various domains". Modelling methods for providing more inte-grated perspectives would need to "be further developed to widen their applicability, in terms of sectors, spatial coverage and detail", and towards a more dynamic integration of SDG-indictors to include feedback effects (TWI2050, 2018: 100).

In the 2015–2020 period, several (supposed and expected) nexus interac-tions have received particular prominence in the SDG discourse:

■ *Nexus in global agreements: the nexus between the Paris Agreement and the SDGs*
In December 2015, the Paris Climate Agreement was settled, a few months after the adoption of the SDGs. The Paris Agreement addressed part of the SDG-agenda but was aimed at more binding agreements as covered by so-called National Determined Contributions (NDCs) to achieve net-zero greenhouse gas emissions by 2050.[11] The political question was posed on the extent to which both agendas are mutually reinforcing. The *Stockholm Environment Institute* explored the connections between the Paris Agreement and the SDG-agenda and found evidence for several strong interaction effects between the NDCs and SDGs. The strongest links can be found in the areas of water, energy and food (the 'W-E-F' nexus), although not all environmental SDGs are equally reflected in the NDC-commitments (e.g. activities related to SDG14 'life below water' were mentioned four times fewer than those related to SDG15 'life on land'). Social SDGs were found to be highly under-represented in the NDC-commitments (Dzebo et al., 2017).

The *Sustainable Development Solutions Network* (SDSN) engaged in a systemic policy approach to help understand how 'deeper' strategies around the many linkages and trade-offs between the Paris Climate

---

11 Nationally Determined Contributions under the Paris Agreement embody post-2020 climate actions outlined by each country to reduce national emissions and adapt to the impacts of climate change. Many of these statements of action indicate priorities and ambitions that contribute to broader sustainable development.

Agreement and the SDG-agenda could be organized. SDGs and Paris Agreement outcomes are interdependent with complex coupling between human, technical and natural systems. Sachs et al. (2019a) assessed the extent to which key interventions necessary to achieve the SDG outcomes can contribute to several goals, and how their implementation could be organized in a limited set of six transformations[12] that each describe a major change in societal structure (economic, political, social, technological). Trade-offs were addressed through (a) system-based approaches that combine potentially adverse interventions inside a transformation; (b) key interventions designed in line with the 'leave no one behind' principle to ensure that investments in services, infrastructure and technologies promote equity; and (c) natural resource trade-offs were addressed through the principle of 'circularity and decoupling' (ibid: 5).

■ *Nexus in policy priorities: inclusive (green) growth (SDGs 8, 10, 13 and 15)*

To address the myriad downsides of inequalities on prosperity, many countries adopted an 'inclusive growth' agenda to simultaneously pursue broad-based economic growth, equity and poverty reduction. Implementing an inclusive growth agenda is directly related to actions within the realm of SDGs 1, 5, 8, 9 and 10 ('no poverty'; 'gender equality'; 'decent work and economic growth'; 'industry innovation and infrastructure'; 'reduced inequalities'), and indirectly also involves SDGs 2, 3 and 16 ('zero hunger'; 'good health and well-being'; 'peace, justice and strong institutions'). Furthermore, inclusive growth is facilitated by collective action in the domains of SDGs 4, 6, 7 and 11 ('quality education'; 'clean water and sanitation'; 'affordable and clean energy'; 'sustainable cities and communities'). More recently, several developed countries have started to introduce even more integrated growth targets with an ambition for 'inclusive *green* growth' (cf. World Bank, 2012) or a *Green New Deal* (by the EU Commission). This requires that SDGs 13, 14 and 15 ('climate action'; 'life below water'; 'life on land') are also addressed concurrently, and in an integrated way.

---

12 The six SDG transformations formulated are: (1) Education, Gender & Inequality; (2) Health, Well-being & Demography; (3) Energy decarbonization and Sustainable industry; (4) Sustainable food, Land, Water & Oceans; (5) Sustainable cities and Communities, and (6) Digital revolution for sustainable development. Note, that these six SDG transformations build on the earlier TWI2050 report (2018) *Transformations to Achieve the Sustainable Development Goals*, yet diverge from the six transition pathways described therein.

An entry point to address such an intricate agenda can be found in the intensification of efforts related to responsible consumption and production (SDG12). Recent studies indicate that responsible consumption and production "will lead to many co-benefits with other SDGs without significant trade-offs . . . Reducing resource demand may not only positively affect SDGs related to human needs such as energy, water and food and environmental SDGs on climate, land, oceans, but may also facilitate achieving several of the SDGs related to human capacity, such as health and poverty" (TWI2050, 2019: 71). Reduction of air pollution (SDG13) has been associated with a positive effect on health (SDG3) and sustainable cities (SDG11). Trade-offs can occur if, for instance, climate mitigation efforts increase the energy cost for the poor (SDG7; SDG1). The trade-off can be limited by specific national policies, but also by corporate strategies that contribute to the transformation of production systems (see Part III).

■ *Nexus in sequencing: timing the economy-ecology development trade-off*

Thinking in terms of a nexus also helps in defining what targets to prioritize, in what sequence, and at what time. The Copenhagen Consensus (section 2.2), for example, prioritized economic and social SDG-targets over ecological ones on the grounds that a lack of priorities significantly diminishes the impact of international development investment. This type of argument has many arrangements, but perhaps one of the most popular ones – embraced, for instance, by the Chinese government – has been based on the so-called *Ecological Kuznets Curve*. This theory prioritizes establishing economic growth (SDG8) through gaining competitive power in an international economy, even when this happens at the expense of living conditions and the natural environment (SDGs 13–15). Competitive economic power can be achieved by investing in the general conditions for economic growth – infrastructure, energy, labour conditions and the like (SDGs 7–12) – facilitated by good education, gender equality, living wages, decent health provisions. The capital accumulated in a competitive economy can, later on, be invested in ecological goals (SDGs 13, 14 and 15), without diminishing the country's competitive position.

This *sequential* development model defies the idea of *integrated* inclusive green growth. It nevertheless presents a dominant development frame for many developing countries, founded on the historical argument that in the past, most developed countries also followed a sequential (non-inclusive, non-ecological) development path to gain economic hegemony. The 'inclusive green growth' argument is considered to create a barrier for the growth models of developing economies.[13] Successful post-war late-comer countries like Japan and South Korea used the Ecological Kuznets Curve logic to their (economic) advantage; China has applied a comparable logic. However, such a sequencing strategy can only be successful under specific circumstances. If other (developing) countries adopt the same sequencing strategy at the same time, this can lead to a 'race to the bottom' in, for instance, labour laws, environmental laws and emission standards. Competition as the premise of sequenced progress then induces negative nexus interactions that lock countries into perverse development paths and outcomes, with devastating consequences for the global common good. The IPBES (2019) report on biodiversity and ecosystems, for instance, tried to link various SDGs to the extreme negative trends in biodiversity and ecosystems that mark the 'unprecedented' decline of nature. They conclude "that current negative trends . . . will undermine progress towards 80% (35 out of 44) of the assessed targets of the Sustainable Development Goals, related to poverty, hunger, health, water, cities, climate, oceans and land (SDGs 1, 2, 3, 6, 11, 13, 14 and 15). Loss of biodiversity is therefore shown to be not only an environmental issue, but also a developmental, economic, security, social and moral issue as well."[14] Note, however, that the committee does not refer to SDGs 7–10 and SDG12, which are the SDGs most directly and positively related to economic growth. The sequencing discussion, therefore, will continue.

■ *Context nexus: conducive or constraining conditions; SDGs 16 and 17*

SDG16 ('peace, justice and strong institutions') and SDG17 ('partnerships for the goals') play a particular role in the nexus challenge. These goals essentially cut across all other SDGs and provide the enabling (or constraining) conditions for reaping the potential of synergies and minimising adverse outcomes. The nature, strength and potential impact of all interactions between the SDGs depend on the extent to which

---

13 Institutional economist Ha-Joon Chang (2002) collected historical evidence for this assertion, which he refers to as 'kicking away the ladder': countries that applied a different, less sustainable sequence in climbing the development ladder now demand that late-comer countries apply a different logic, thereby preventing them from adopting policies and institutions that they themselves have used. A similar argument had been advanced earlier by economic historian André Gunder Frank (1966) known under the concept of 'the development of underdevelopment', which described dependency dynamics between developing and developed countries related to world systems theory, partly as the result of regulatory capture of local elites by internationally operating companies.

14 IPBES website, visited 31 January 2020.

effective governance systems, institutions, partnerships, and intellectual and financial resources are in place. Together, they provide pivotal conditions for an effective, efficient and coherent approach to implementation (ICSU, 2017:7).

Nevertheless, in spite of their importance to overall SDG implementation, the complementarities between SDG16 and SDG17 at the target level have received relatively little attention in research and policy analysis produced on SDG nexuses, arguably because of their transversal nature (Blind, 2019). Stafford-Smith et al. (2016), for instance, noted that the 'means of implementation' themselves could be activated in more or less integrated ways, thereby affecting what potential can be harnessed from other SDG interactions. Means of implementation refer to the 43 alphabetic SDG-targets under each of the SDGs and all 19 SDG17-targets.[15] They include finance, technology, capacity-building, trade, policy coherence, partnerships, data, monitoring and accountability.[16] Systematically focusing the 'means of implementation' on SDG interactions could result in more integrated decision-making and coherent policy approaches (Nilsson et al., 2018).

In addition, Blind (2019) performed a content analysis on indicators of the 'Addis Ababa Action Agenda on Financing for Development', and the SDG17 and SDG16 targets. Four groups of target-level connections between SDG17 and SDG16 were identified as relevant to 'focus areas' in public administration: (1) national legislation and regulatory framework, with linkages to domestic public resource mobilization; (2) global governance and international cooperation, with linkages to ODA, technology transfer, capacity-building, policy coherence and partnerships; (3) governance elements (transparency, accountability, inclusiveness and effectiveness), with linkages to all SDG17-targets; and (4) governance challenges of crime and corruption, with indirect linkages to SDG17 on domestic public resources. Blind (2019) argued not to have attempted to posit 'operational' linkages between the Addis Ababa Agenda and the 2030 Agenda, but rather "breaking the usual practice of leaving either SDG16 or SDG17 outside the SDG nexus analysis" (ibid: 16).

---

15 See also 'Global indicator framework for the Sustainable Development Goals and targets of the 2030 Agenda for Sustainable Development', E/CN.3/2019/2, version of 11 December 2019.

16 Means of implementation relate to "domestic public resources, domestic and international private business and finance, international development cooperation, international trade as an engine for development, debt and debt sustainability, addressing systemic issues and science, technology, innovation and capacity-building, and data, monitoring and follow-up" (UN, 2015: para. 62).

2.4 CONCLUSION, TOOLS AND RESOURCES

This chapter aimed to gain better insights into the potential of the SDG-agenda in developing an integrative, principles-based and goal-oriented approach to sustainable development. The chapter addressed the relevance and potential of the SDG approach primarily as an intellectual and analytical challenge to operationalize the SDG-framework in an integrated and transformative way. It focused on the SDGs at the goal, target and indicator levels, and identified both impressive progress in indicator development and nexus thinking, and remaining analytical and empirical challenges that actively need to be addressed.

We described the chosen 'dashboard' approach in the SDG-agenda that can be considered a breach with traditional 'economic growth' thinking. We documented the potential of the SDG-agenda as a fundamental paradigm shift in approaching sustainable development from a variety of relevant angles: social ('People'), ecological ('Planet'), economic ('Prosperity'), institutional ('Peace') and procedural ('Partnerships'). On many accounts, the SDGs can be considered a promising point of departure and an interesting breach with past practice. However, addressing them is not proving straightforward. The SDGs best present a global *agenda* and a *frame*, not a fixed and spelt-out blueprint. The SDG approach still represents 'a work in and on progress'.

We noted key theoretical challenges that require more conceptual clarity. We also pointed out significant gaps in the empirical set-up of targets and indicators that presently limit the degree to which progress can be measured. Challenges remain with regard to substantiating claims on the costs and benefits of the SDGs, the operationalization of SDG-targets and indicators, and identification and prioritization of key nexus interactions. Gaps in data coverage – related to data quality, data availability and the need for new types of data – were identified as an important inhibiting factor to evidence-*informed* policymaking and the design of effective interventions to implement the SDGs. We also noted that the chosen dashboard approach to track sustainable development progress provides the potential for creating an 'ecosystem' in which relevant theoretical and data gaps can be overcome.

The gaps and challenges identified in this chapter require approaches that go beyond mere 'evidence-based' policies. They call for active multi-stakeholder engagement to enhance crucial capacities in effective progress measurement and the development of better concepts and intervention strategies. Whether the ambitions of the SDGs will be achieved depends on the strategies adopted by societal stakeholders. This, in turn, depends on whether those same stakeholders can effectively address the theoretical and empirical challenges. The next chapter will take further stock of the extent to which the SDG-framework has triggered adequate action in order to define the preconditions for its success in the years between now and 2030.

- The SDG-agenda presents a broad platform for the development of relevant change trajectories towards sustainable development.

- The SDG paradigm is based on 'governing through goals' and 'governing through indicators'.

- The SDG-agenda represents a 'dashboard' that includes many dimensions of sustainable development; the exact weight and relevance of these dimensions in relation to each other cannot be known upfront; the dashboard approach allows for adjustment along the way ('work in and on progress').

- The SDG approach is not without flaws; there are still major theoretical, conceptual and empirical challenges to be tackled and gaps to be filled.

- When effectively implemented, the SDGs promise significant opportunities for companies and countries; even if assessments on the exact outcome vary widely.

- The multi-stakeholder approach adopted for the SDG-agenda is vital for progress.

- Important areas for progress include the further development of proper indicators and a better understanding of all possible nexus interactions between the SDGs (preferably at the target level).

- Policymakers favour 'evidence-based' research; however, in complex settings a circular approach to research of continuous learning and adjustment – involving joined-up approaches of multiple stakeholders – seems equally appropriate.

TAKEAWAYS

- **UN Sustainable Development Goals:** The SDGs are a universal call to action to end poverty, protect the planet and improve the lives and prospects of everyone, everywhere. By clicking on any specific goal, one can learn more about 'facts and figures', 'goal targets', infographics summarizing trends per SDG and relevant links. https://www.un.org/sustainabledevelopment/sustainable-development-goals/

- **SDG Academy:** The SDG Academy is an education initiative of the *Sustainable Development Solutions Network* (SDSN). It brings together the world's experts to create and deliver educational content on critical issues for the future of people and planet, including health, education, climate change, agriculture and food systems, and sustainable investment. Its materials are free, global in nature, based on science, taught by experts in their fields, accessible online and created in partnership with organizations from around the world. https://www.unsdsn.org/sdg-academy. To access free online educational resources and courses on SDGs: https://sdgacademy.org/courses/

- **UN SDG:Learn:** A UN initiative that aims to offer relevant and curated learning solutions on sustainable development topics to individuals and organizations. Its platform enables smart navigation through the growing wealth of various learning solutions including courses, tutorials, podcasts, analytical and other tools, and the expertise on topics related to SDG achievement. https://www.unsdglearn.org/courses/ and https://www.unsdglearn.org/microlearning/

- **SDG Country Profiles:** Provides a profile for each country, based on (1) population and migration, (2) national accounts and labour market, (3) trade and balance of payments; (4) environment. And, most importantly, a country's profile on all 17 SDGs (several indicators per SDG) using time series, graphs and percentages. https://country-profiles.unstatshub.org/afg#

- **SDG Tracker:** SDG Tracker presents data across all available indicators from the *Our World in Data* database, using official statistics from the UN and other international organizations. It is a free, open-access publication (with downloadable data) that tracks global progress towards the SDGs at the global, regional and country level. Where global maps are provided, clicking on a given country will show a time series of how a given metric (for example, childhood stunting) has changed over time. Countries can be added to this chart to compare progress across neighbours, regions and worldwide. https://sdg-tracker.org/

- **E-Handbook on SDG Indicators:** This online handbook, prepared by the UN Statistics Division, is targeted towards statisticians to enable monitoring of the implementation of the SDGs based on data produced by national statistical systems. It focuses on key aspects – such as concepts, definition, sources, calculations – that are essential for measuring indicators. It also provides additional links and references to more detailed information to delve into detailed references when needed. https://unstats.un.org/wiki/display/SDGeHandbook/Home

■ ***Global SDG Indicators Database:*** UN Statistics dissemination platform that provides access to data compiled through the UN System in preparation for the annual SDG progress reports. The database can be searched by goal, target or indicator. It provides data series (year 2000 – recent) that can be specified by geographical areas (world, regional, per country) and groupings (least developed countries, land-locked developing countries, small island developing states, developed regions). https://unstats.un.org/sdgs/indicators/database/

SELECTED WEB RESOURCES

REFERENCES

Allen, C., Metternicht, G., & Wiedmann, T. (2018). 'Initial progress in implementing the Sustainable Development Goals (SDGs): A review of evidence from countries', *Sustainability Science*, 13(5):1453–1467.

Bhattacharya, A. & Kharas, H. (2015). 'Worthy of support', *The Economist*, 8 April.

Blind, P.K. (2019). *How relevant is governance to financing for development and partnerships? Interlinking SDG16 and SDG17 at the target level.* United Nations, DESA Working Paper No. 162, ST/ESA/2019/DWP/162, October.

Business & Sustainable Development Commission (2017). *Better Business, Better World.*

Carbon Disclosure Project (2019). *Major Risk or Rosy Opportunity. Are companies ready for climate change*', CDP Climate Change Report 2018, Global edition.

Chang, H.J. (2002). *Kicking Away the Ladder. Development Strategy in Historical Perspective.* Anthem Press.

Davies, P. (2012). 'The State of Evidence-Based Policy Evaluation and its Role in Policy Formation', *National Institute Economic Review*, 219(1):R41–R52.

Davis, K., Fisher, A., Kingsbury, B. & Engle Merry, S. (Eds.) (2012). *Governance by Indicators. Global Power through Quantification and Rankings.* Oxford: Oxford University Press.

Dodds, F., Donoghue, D. & Leiva Roesch, J. (2016). *Negotiating the Sustainable Development Goals: A transformational agenda for an insecure world.* London: Routledge.

Dzebo, A., Brandi, C., Janetschek, H., Savvidou, G., Adams, K. & Chan, S. (2017). 'Exploring connections between the Paris Agreement and the 2030 Agenda for Sustainable Development, *SEI Policy Brief*, Stockholm Environment Institute.

Eden, L. & Wagstaff, F.M. (2021). 'Evidence-based policymaking and the wicked problem of SDG5 Gender Equality', *Journal of International Business Policy*, 4(1): 28–57.

Frank, A.G. (1966). 'The Development of Underdevelopment', *Monthly Review Press*, 18(4):17–31.

Fukuda-Parr, S. & McNeill, D. (2019). 'Knowledge and Politics in Setting and Measuring the SDGs: Introduction to Special Issue', *Global Policy*, 10(s1):5–15.

Gennari, P. & Navarro, D.K. (2020). 'Are We Serious About Achieving the SDGs? A Statistician's Perspective', IISD SDG Knowledge Hub, 14 January. Retrieved from: https://sdg.iisd.org/commentary/guest-articles/are-we-serious-about-achieving-the-sdgs-a-statisticians-perspective/.

Global Commission on the Economy and Climate (2018). *Unlocking the Inclusive Growth Story of the 21st Century: Accelerating Climate Action in Urgent Times*, The New Climate Economy.

Gupta, J. & Vegelin, C. (2016). 'Sustainable development goals and inclusive development', *International Environmental Agreements: Politics, Law and Economics*, 16(3): 433–448.

Hallegatte, S., Rentschler, J. & Rozenberg, J. (2019). *Lifelines: The Resilient Infrastructure Opportunity*, Sustainable Infrastructure Series. Washington DC: World Bank.

Hege, E., Barchiche, D., Rochette, J., Chabason, L. & Barthélemy, P. (2019). *Initial assessment and conditions for success of the 2030 Agenda for Sustainable Development*, IDDRI study, No. 7, October.

ICSU (2017). *A Guide to SDG Interactions: From Science to Implementation*. Paris: International Council for Science.

ICSU & ISSC (2015). *Review of Targets for the Sustainable Development Goals: The Science Perspective*. Paris: International Council for Science.

IEAG (2014). *A World That Counts: Mobilising The Data Revolution for Sustainable Development*, The United Nations Secretary-General's Independent Expert Advisory Group on a Data Revolution for Sustainable Development.

IPBES (2019). *Summary for policymakers of the global assessment report on biodiversity and ecosystem services of the Intergovernmental Science-Policy Platform on Biodiversity and Ecosystem Services*, approved by the IPBES Plenary, May 2019 (IPBES-7). Bonn, Germany: IPBES.

Kamau, M., Chasek, P.S. & O'Connor, D. (2018). *Transforming Multilateral Diplomacy. The Inside Story of the Sustainable Development Goals*. Routledge.

Koehler, G. (2016). 'Assessing the SDGs from the standpoint of eco-social policy. Using the SDGs subversively', *Journal of International and Comparative Social Policy*, 32(2):149–164.

Koehler, G. (2015). 'Seven Decades of "Development", and Now What?', *Journal of International Development*, 27(6):733–751.

Le Blanc, D. (2015). *Towards integration at last? The Sustainable Development Goals as a network of targets*. DESA Working Paper No. 141, United Nations Department of Economic and Social Affairs, ST/ESA/2015/DWP/141, March.

Lomborg, B. (Ed.) (2018). *Prioritizing Development: A Cost Benefit Analysis of the United Nations' Sustainable Development Goals*. Cambridge University Press.

MacFeely, S. (2019). *The Political Economy of Measuring the Sustainable Development Goals*, UNCTAD Research Paper No. 32, UNCTAD/SER.RP/2019/4, June.

MacFeely, S. (2019a). 'The Big (data) Bang: Opportunities and Challenges for Compiling SDG Indicators', *Global Policy*, 10(s1):121–133.

McKinsey Global Institute (2015). *The Power of Parity: How Advancing Women's Equality Can Add $12 Trillion to Global Growth*, September.

Nilsson, M., Chisholm, E., Griggs, D., Howden-Chapman, P., McCollum, D., Messerli, P., Neumann, B., Stevance, A., Visbeck, M. & Stafford-Smith, M. (2018). 'Mapping interactions between the sustainable development goals: lessons learned and ways forward', *Sustainability Science*, 13(6):1489–1503.

Nilsson, M., Griggs, D. & Visbeck, M. (2016). 'Map the interactions between Sustainable Development Goals', *Nature*, 534(7607):320–322.

OECD (2019). *Measuring distance to the SDG Targets 2019. An Assessment of Where OECD Countries Stand.* Paris: OECD Publishing.

OECD (2016). *Better Policies for Sustainable Development 2016: A New Framework for Policy Coherence.* Paris: OECD Publishing.

Ordaz, E. (2019). 'The SDGs Indicators: A Challenging Task for the International Statistical Community', *Global Policy*, 10(s1):141–143.

Parkhurst, J. (2017). *The Politics of Evidence: From evidence-based policy to the good governance of evidence.* Routledge Studies in Governance and Public Policy. London: Routledge.

Patton, M.Q., McKegg, K. & Wehipeihana, N. (Eds.) (2016). *Developmental Evaluation Exemplars. Principles in Practice.* New York: The Guilford Press.

Rogerson, A., with Calleja, R. (2019). *Mobilising Data for the SDGs: How could Data Acceleration Facility help, and how might it work?* Paris 21 Discussion Paper No. 15, January.

Sachs, J.D., Schmidt-Traub, G., Kroll, C., Lafortune, G. & Fuller, G. (2019). *Sustainable Development Report 2019.* New York: Bertelsmann Stiftung and Sustainable Development Solutions Network (SDSN), June.

Sachs, J.D., Schmidt-Traub, G., Mazzucato, M., Messner, D., Nakicenovic, N. & Rockström, J. (2019a). 'Six Transformations to Achieve the Sustainable Development Goals', *Nature Sustainability*, 2(9):805–814.

SDSN-TReNDS (2019). *Counting on The World to Act. A Roadmap for Governments to Achieve Modern Data Systems for Sustainable Development.* Report by the Sustainable Development Solutions Network's Thematic Research Network on Data and Statistics (SDSN TReNDS).

Stafford-Smith, M., Griggs, D., Gaffney, O., Ullah, F., Reyers, B., Kanie, N., Stigson, B., Shrivastava, P., Leach, M. & O'Connell, D. (2017). 'Integration: the key to implementing the Sustainable Development Goals', *Sustainability Science*, 12(6):911–919.

Stiglitz, J.E., Sen, A. & Fitoussi J.P. (2009). *Mismeasuring Our Lives: Why GDP Doesn't Add Up.* The report by the commission on the measurement of economic performance and social progress. New York: The New York Press.

TWI2050 (2019). *The Digital Revolution and Sustainable Development: Opportunities and Challenges.* Report prepared by The World In 2050 Initiative. Laxenburg, Austria: International Institute for Applied Systems Analysis (IIASA).

TWI2050 (2018). *Transformations to Achieve the Sustainable Development Goals.* Report prepared by The World In 2050 Initiative. Laxenburg, Austria: International Institute for Applied Systems Analysis (IIASA).

UN (2015). *Transforming Our World: The 2050 Agenda for Sustainable Development.* New York: United Nations.

UNEP (2019). *Measuring Progress: Towards Achieving the Environmental Dimension of the SDGs.* Nairobi: United Nations Environment Programme.

UNHCR (2020). *Global Trends Forced Displacement in 2019.* Copenhagen: United Nations High Commissioner for Refugees.

World Bank (2012). *Inclusive Green Growth: The Pathway to Sustainable Development.* Washington, DC.: World Bank Group.

Young, O.R. (2017). 'Conceptualization: Goal Setting as a Strategy for Earth System Governance'. In: Kanie, N. & Biermann, F. (Eds.), *Governing through Goals: Sustainable Development Goals as Governance Innovation*, (pp. 31–52). Cambridge, Massachusetts: The MIT Press.

3 WHY SLOW? CONDITIONS FOR REALIZING THE SDGs

CONTENT

DOI: 10.4324/9781003098355-4

- **'Governing through goals' principle:** a steering principle for driving progress towards sustainable development, based on shaping, inspiring and directing. Aspirational goal-setting (accompanied by measurable indicators) is to channel multi-stakeholder engagement in the direction of implementing basic norms, universal principles and common values as the foundation for longer-term commitment and meaningful action.

- **Participatory principle:** multi-stakeholder engagement is not a luxury but a necessity for: (1) creating ownership, (2) filling the blanks, (3) exchanging experience for continuous learning, (4) 'collaborative analysis', and (5) striving for both 'procedural justice' and 'distributive justice'.

- **'Purposive coalition' principle:** 'coalitions of the willing' are a necessary but often insufficient condition to work towards transformative change. The real challenge is to trigger the active participation of coalitions of *needed* stakeholders.

- **Diversity principle:** denounce a one-size-fits-all approach to context-specific realities and societal challenges. Trigger a diversity of initiatives and insights from all spheres of society to ensure diversity of thought, diversity of stakeholders, diversity of methods and diversity of competencies, organizational logics and strategies.

- **Coherence principle:** the effectiveness of hybrid governance is conditional on the degree of coherence (in agendas, actions, policies) that can be established at multiple levels, across multiple sectors and among multiple stakeholders.

- **'Open source' principle:** the effective mobilization of communities of change depends on channelling efforts that inspire and enable progress through open, networked platforms aimed at exchange and co-creation of knowledge. 'Open source', 'open innovation' and 'open access' constitute related propositions that are based on principles of collaboration, inclusive meritocracy, accessibility and transparency in support of the common good.

- **Principled prioritization:** a notion introduced by Global Reporting Initiative (GRI) and UN Global Compact to encourage organizations to simultaneously map their most salient negative impacts on people and the planet, while also exploring ways to drive SDG progress. Reporting on negative impacts and SDG contributions should be aligned with all applicable universal principles of corporate behaviour (see Chapter 8).

3.1   INTRODUCTION: WHY SLOW AND WHAT TO DO?

The foundational document for the Sustainable Development Goals (SDGs) – *Transforming Our World* – positioned the 2030 Agenda for Sustainable Development both as a 'plan of action' for people, planet and prosperity, and as a 'call for action' to all stakeholders to mobilize and engage with the Global Goals (UN, 2015). "All countries and all stakeholders, acting in collaborative partnership, will implement this plan", the preamble stated, while also acknowledging the voluntary nature of contributing efforts. To mirror these two sides of the action-oriented agenda, a new (hybrid) type of governance mechanism was embraced to guide the sizeable conceptual, measurement and implementation challenges of the SDGs in a participatory manner. By engaging stakeholders in the process, identified knowledge gaps could be filled, action could be tested, and efforts and means pooled to reach higher degrees of impact. This particular approach of shaping, inspiring and directing is also known as 'governing through goals' (Young, 2017); its further operationalization as 'governance by indicators' (Davis et al., 2012). The parallel organizing challenge to encourage engagement, commitment and ownership is one of *multilevel, multi-stakeholder, networked* and *hybrid governance.*

To turn ambition into realization, the SDG effort faced two general governance challenges: (1) how to translate the SDG-agenda into strong commitments and trigger an effective bottom-up approach that would activate countries and societal actors to contribute, and (2) how to channel, coordinate and support implementation efforts – at all required levels – in such a way that they would actually result in robust progress towards the intended direction, in an integrated and inclusive way. The idea that participants could define their own pathways of change towards an internationally accepted (and hence relatively vague operationalized) set of goals, marked a break with the primarily top-down approach adopted for the Millennial Development Goals (MDGs). The success of the SDG endeavour would now critically rely on the creation of coalitions of (willing) actors that actively participate while advocating change towards as yet reluctant actors to organize the required 'coalitions of the needed'. The effectiveness of this approach is to be measured by the extent to which the SDGs are coherently translated into national policies, budgeting, institutions and regulatory frameworks, and by the way public and private organizations meaningfully integrate the goals in their own strategies.

MULTILEVEL HYBRID GOVERNANCE: STRUCTURING COHERENCE

To channel ambitions, ownership and commitment to the SDGs, a multilevel hybrid kind of governance structure was designed to coordinate the follow-up and review of SDG implementation at the national, regional and global level. The governance structure clarifies roles and institutional responsibilities while allowing for the autonomy of countries and other participants to decide upon their own implementation strategies (UNGA, 2016). Primary responsibility for implementation of the SDGs lies at the national level. The governance structure is hence oriented towards supporting national implementation, with facilitating and coordinating roles for the UN system and specialized intergovernmental organizations and forums related to the UN in order to reinforce knowledge sharing and mutual learning at all relevant levels (Box 3.1).

BOX 3.1

A HYBRID, MULTILEVEL GOVERNANCE APPROACH

■ **Global coordination: overseeing a network of review mechanisms**

The *High-Level Political Forum on Sustainable Development (HLPF)* is the leading UN platform on sustainable development with an intergovernmental character. It has a central role in overseeing the network of follow-up and review processes on the implementation of the SDGs and is tasked with: (1) assessing overall progress, achievements, gaps and challenges; (2) providing political leadership, guidance and recommendations; (3) enhancing integration of the three dimensions of sustainable development in a holistic and cross-sectoral manner, including through coordination and coherence across the UN system and at all levels of governance; (4) ensuring the continued relevance of the 2030 Agenda through consideration of new and emerging issues relevant to sustainable development; (5) enhancing civil society participation and evidence-based decision-making; (6) providing a platform for multi-stakeholder partnerships and peer learning towards achieving the SDGs.

The HLPF is to address: (a) reviews at the *global level* related to the SDG-agenda, including the means of implementation; (b) *national reviews* (based on National Voluntary Reports); (c) *regional reviews*, related to major policy issues in each region; (d) *thematic reviews* on cross-cutting issues; (e) themes that relate to countries and groups in special situations. Based on the reviews, the HLPF annually formulates an inter-governmentally negotiated declaration that captures the essence of the vision and policy recommendations of the multiple platforms, parts, discussions and lessons learned, and translates these into political guidance on further action. The declaration feeds into the General Assembly, which – as the chief deliberative and policymaking organ of the UN – is the main platform for reviewing the UN system's contributions to the implementation of the SDG-agenda. The *UN Sustainable Development Group*, under the General Assembly, is tasked with, amongst others, advancing the implementation of the 2030 Agenda "by bringing the UN development system together" (Strategic results group 1, UNDP and DESA).

■ International organizations: supporting conceptualization, knowledge and data gathering

Intergovernmental bodies, forums, functional commissions and specialized agencies within the UN system and network, develop and disseminate knowledge and data on specific areas of the SDGs. Many act as custodian agencies on global indicator conceptualization and data gathering, convene on specific themes related to the SDGs, coordinate, channel, monitor or report on developments and processes in their field. These intergovernmental organizations and specialized bodies include: UNEP, UNDP, UNCTAD, IMF, FAO, ILO, World Bank, WHO, UN DESA, Inter-Agency and Expert Group on SDG-indicators, and numerous assemblies and treaty bodies that address SDG-related areas, such as the UN Environmental Assembly, the World Education Forum, the World Health Assembly, the International Labour Conference, the Conference of the Food and Agriculture Organization of the United Nations, the UN Conference on Trade and Development, the UN Industrial Development Organization, the Committee on World Food Security, the Human Rights Council.

■ National coordination: country-led and country-driven voluntary national reports

As part of its follow-up and review mechanisms, the 2030 Agenda encourages all member states to "conduct regular and inclusive reviews of progress at the national and sub-national levels, which are country-led and country-driven" (UN, 2015: para. 79). These national reviews are to serve as a basis for the regular reviews by the HLPF, meeting annually under the auspices of ECOSOC (the Council that is tasked with providing coordination and guidance to the UN system to ensure that key policies for development cooperation and country-level modalities are implemented). Reviews by the HLPF – based on *Voluntary National Reports (VNR)* – are voluntary, state-led, undertaken by both developed and developing countries, and should involve multiple stakeholders. Frequency and timing are not stipulated. VNRs aim to facilitate the sharing of experiences, to strengthen policies and institutions of governments, and to mobilize multi-stakeholder support and partnerships for accelerated implementation of the SDGs. To support and advance the set-up of institutional and coordination mechanisms for national and sub-national implementation of the SDGs, guidelines have been developed with regard to institutional structures, integrated cross-sectoral approaches and VNR reporting (cf. UNDP, 2017; UN DESA, 2019). UN resident coordinators and UN country teams also provide support on national SDG implementation.

■ Regional coordination

The 2030 Agenda recognizes the importance of dialogue and review at the regional and sub-regional levels. Regional (intergovernmental) bodies, forums and commissions are well-positioned to: support learning about and assessments of SDG progress and policies; boost regional cooperation and partnerships; coordinate peer review mechanisms; and allow for discussions on overall trends, gaps, lessons learned, best practices, and issues and dynamics specific to the region and its sub-regions. The outcome of regional reviews conducted in regional forums can be provided to the HLPF to contribute to global follow-up and review.

■ Major groups and stakeholder platforms

The 2030 Agenda envisages strong participation of major groups and other stakeholders throughout the follow-up and review process, including at the national and sub-national level. Governments should ensure inclusiveness and participation through appropriate mechanisms. Non-governmental stakeholders – e.g. business, scientists, academia, parliamentarians, local governments, youth representatives – are encouraged to participate in UN intergovernmental forums and bodies. Their input is to be actively solicited through calls for evidence and invitations to be present at the HLPF and official meetings. Stakeholders should be able to access documentation, provide input and comments through multi-stakeholder dialogue and online engagement. Also, major groups and stakeholders – business (e.g. through Global Compact), non-governmental organizations, partnerships and alliances, large cities – are encouraged to announce their voluntary commitments to achieving the SDGs, with measurable milestones and deliverables, and to (voluntarily) report on their contributions to SDG implementation. The UN facilitates visibility, exchange of successful examples in SDG implementation and accountability, for instance through the *Partnerships for Sustainable Development Goals* online platform.

Based on: UNGA (2016) A/70/684, 15 January; UNGA (2016a) A/Res/70/299, 18 August. UNGA (2018) A/res/72/279, 1 June.

The 'common agenda' of the SDGs aimed to create both vertical and horizontal coherence: across all levels (from global to local), across participants (state and non-state actors), across existing governance systems and institutional structures ("taking into account different national realities, capabilities and levels of development and respecting national policies and priorities"), and across policy silos (integrated approaches). For successful implementation of the SDGs, the

OECD (2016) distinguished *five levels of coherence* that need to be organized to create a conducive setting for progress (Figure 3.1):

1   Coherence between the SDGs and national policies (consistency of actions across multiple levels of governance, the sub-national and local levels included);

2   Coherence among international agendas and processes (e.g. G20, Agenda 2063 of the African Union; global frameworks such as the Paris Agreement and Addis Ababa Action Agenda; and global tax, trading, financial, patent and investment systems);

3   Coherence between economic, social and environmental policies (synergistic and integrated approaches to sustainability across policy silos);

4   Coherence between different sources of finance (public, private, domestic, international, blended forms of finance and investments);

5   Coherence between diverse actions of multiple actors and stakeholders (e.g. governments, international organizations, business, civil society, cross-sector platforms or alliances).

If not properly aligned, these five levels of coherence will ultimately limit the effectiveness of the SDGs as a 'universal' and 'holistic' agenda. Non-aligned policy agendas, notably at the national and international level, will lead to inadequate sources of finance and limited actor engagement. The SDG approach hence comprises an immense, intricate governance and process challenge.

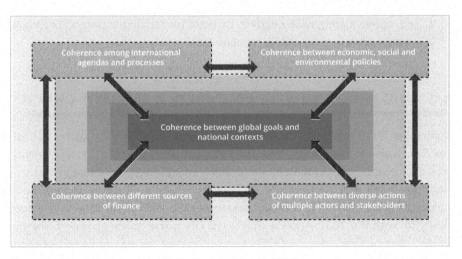

Figure 3.1 Five levels of coherence for implementing the SDGs
Source: based on OECD (2015)

From the start, it had been recognized that major gaps in the selection and definition of goals, targets and indicators existed. All actors involved also recognized the need for continuous improvement and fine-tuning (Chapter 2 documented key conceptual and measurement challenges). In many areas, the UN, national governments and a wide variety of interested stakeholders had to set up 'communities' and platforms in order to trigger mutual exchange and a focused 'learning by doing' process. Such an approach can only succeed if in the process of proliferation and further fine-tuning, important progress is made. Progress stalls, however, in the event of two parallel processes: (a) continued difficulties in identifying and addressing the conceptual and measurement voids related to the integrated realization of the SDGs (Chapter 2); and (b) insufficient recognition, pursuit or use by state and non-state actors of the opportunities that the SDG-agenda offers. How remaining intellectual and practical gaps are approached, thus defines the conditions under which beneficial implementation of the SDG-agenda can be anticipated up to 2030. This chapter consequently considers four key questions to assess the fruits and remaining gaps of this multilevel, hybrid governance process:

1   Intermediate stock-taking: what has been the state of progress in the first four-year cycle of SDG implementation (section 3.2)?

2   What does this state-of-affairs reveal about the governance set-up and the way barriers to progress have been handled by communities of stakeholders (section 3.3)?

3   What have been the consequences for action undertaken by relevant stakeholders (section 3.4)?

4   And, consequently, what needs to be done to step up the pace of progress towards achieving the SDGs (section 3.5)?

3.2   THE FIRST FOUR-YEAR CYCLE: A REALITY CHECK

September 2019 marked the end of the first four-year cycle of the global SDGs' ambition. It also marked the first moment for a reality check on the chosen (hybrid) governance approach. In the course of 2018 and 2019, the realization that the world is 'not on track' had gradually been taking hold. Progress reports from various angles indicated that implementation of the SDGs was progressing too slowly to meet the 2030 Agenda. The 2018 UN global check-up report already warned that progress on the SDGs proved uneven "across regions, between sexes and among people of different ages, wealth and locales, including urban and rural dwellers", and was not moving fast enough on almost all accounts (UN, 2018). Conflict, war and violence were identified as significant barriers to poverty eradication and sustainability, while progress had not yet reached the people who need it most. The 2019 SDG progress report reiterated the need for urgency, more ambition and intensified commitment to collective action in even stronger wording. It concluded that "the shift in development pathways to generate the transformation required to meet the Sustainable Development Goals by 2030 is not yet advancing at the speed or scale required" (UN, 2019: i), and that it was "abundantly clear that a much deeper, faster and more ambitious response is needed to unleash the social and economic transformation needed to achieve our 2030 goals" (UN DESA, 2019: 2).

STATUS OF PROGRESS PER SDG, IN THE FOURTH YEAR OF IMPLEMENTATION (2019)

BOX 3.2

"The decline of global extreme poverty continues, but has slowed. The deceleration indicates that the world is not on track to achieve the target of less than 3 per cent of the world living in extreme poverty by 2030. People who continue to live in extreme poverty face deep, entrenched deprivation often exacerbated by violent conflicts and vulnerability to disasters. Strong social protection systems and government spending on key services often help those left behind get back on their feet and escape poverty, but these services need to be brought to scale."

"Hunger is on the rise again globally and undernutrition continues to affect millions of children. Public investment in agriculture globally is declining, small-scale food producers and family farmers require much greater support and increased investment in infrastructure and technology for sustainable agriculture is urgently needed."

"Major progress has been made in improving the health of millions of people, increasing life expectancy, reducing maternal and child mortality and fighting against leading communicable diseases. However, progress has stalled or is not happening fast enough with regard to addressing major diseases, such as malaria and tuberculosis, while at least half the global population does not have access to essential health services and many of those who do suffer undue financial hardship, potentially pushing them into extreme poverty. Concerted efforts are required to achieve universal health coverage and sustainable financing for health, to address the growing burden of non-communicable diseases, including mental health, and to tackle antimicrobial resistance and determinants of health such as air pollution and inadequate water and sanitation."

"Despite the considerable progress on education access and participation over the past years, 262 million children and youth aged 6 to 17 were still out of school in 2017, and more than half of children and adolescents are not meeting minimum proficiency standards in reading and mathematics. Rapid technological changes present opportunities and challenges, but the learning environment, the capacities of teachers and the quality of education have not kept pace. Refocused efforts are needed to improve learning outcomes for the full life cycle, especially for women, girls and marginalized people in vulnerable settings."

"While some indicators of gender equality are progressing, such as a significant decline in the prevalence of female genital mutilation and early marriage, the overall numbers continue to be high. Moreover, insufficient progress on structural issues at the root of gender inequality, such as legal discrimination, unfair social norms and attitudes, decision-making on sexual and reproductive issues and low levels of political participation, are undermining the ability to achieve SDG 5."

"Despite progress, billions of people still lack safe water, sanitation and handwashing facilities. Data suggests that achieving universal access to even basic sanitation service by 2030 would require doubling the current annual rate of progress. More efficient use and management of water are critical to addressing the growing demand for water, threats to water security and the increasing frequency and severity of droughts and floods resulting from climate change. As of the time of writing, most countries are unlikely to reach full implementation of integrated water resources management by 2030."

"Access to electricity in the poorest countries has begun to accelerate, energy efficiency continues to improve and renewable energy is making gains in the electricity sector. Despite this progress, some 800 million people remain without electricity while access to clean cooking fuels and technologies needs dedicated attention. In addition, if SDGs 7, 13 and related Goals are to be met, much higher levels of ambition are required with regard to renewable energy, including transportation and heating."

"Inclusive and sustainable economic growth can drive progress and generate the means to implement the SDGs. Globally, labour productivity has increased and unemployment is back to pre-financial crisis levels. However, the global economy is growing at a slower rate. More progress is needed to increase employment opportunities, particularly for young people, reduce informal employment and the gender pay gap and promote safe and secure working environments to create decent work for all."

"Aspects of the prevailing global economic environment have not been conducive to rapid progress on SDG 9. While financing for economic infrastructure has increased in developing countries and impressive progress has been made in mobile connectivity, countries that are lagging behind, such as least developed countries, face serious challenges in doubling the manufacturing industry's share of GDP by 2030, and investment in scientific research and innovation remains below the global average."

"Inequality within and among nations continues to be a significant concern despite progress in and efforts at narrowing disparities of opportunity, income and power. Income inequality continues to rise in many parts of the world, even as the bottom 40 per cent of the population in many countries has experienced positive growth rates. Greater emphasis will need to be placed on reducing inequalities in income as well as those based on other factors. Additional efforts are needed to increase zero-tariff access for exports from least developed countries and developing countries, and assistance to least developed countries and small island developing States."

"Substantial progress has been made in reducing the proportion of the global urban population living in slums, though more than 1 billion people continue to live in such situations. Urgent action is needed to reverse the current situation, which sees the vast majority of urban residents breathing poor-quality air and having limited access to transport and open public spaces. With the areas occupied by cities growing faster than their populations, there are profound repercussions for sustainability."

"Worldwide material consumption has expanded rapidly, as has material footprint per capita, seriously jeopardizing the achievement of SDG12 and the Goals more broadly. Urgent action is needed to ensure that current material needs do not lead to the over-extraction of resources or to the degradation of environmental resources, and should include policies that improve resource efficiency, reduce waste and mainstream sustainability practices across all sectors of the economy."

"With rising greenhouse gas emissions, climate change is occurring at rates much faster than anticipated and its effects are clearly felt worldwide. While there are positive steps in terms of the climate finance flows and the development of nationally determined contributions, far more ambitious plans and accelerated action are needed on mitigation and adaptation. Access to finance and strengthened capacities need to be scaled up at a much faster rate, particularly for least developed countries and small island developing States."

"The expansion of protected areas for marine biodiversity and existing policies and treaties that encourage responsible use of ocean resources are still insufficient to combat the adverse effects of overfishing, growing ocean acidification due to climate change and worsening coastal eutrophication. As billions of people depend on oceans for their livelihood and food source and on the transboundary nature of oceans, increased efforts and interventions are needed to conserve and sustainably use ocean resources at all levels."

"There are some encouraging global trends in protecting terrestrial ecosystems and biodiversity. Forest loss is slowing down, more key biodiversity areas are protected and more financial assistance is flowing towards biodiversity protection. Yet, the 2020 targets of SDG15 are unlikely to be met, land degradation continues, biodiversity loss is occurring at an alarming rate, and invasive species and the illicit poaching and trafficking of wildlife continue to thwart efforts to protect and restore vital ecosystems and species."

"Advances in ending violence, promoting the rule of law, strengthening institutions and increasing access to justice are uneven and continue to deprive millions of their security, rights and opportunities and undermine the delivery of public services and broader economic development. Attacks on civil society are also holding back development progress. Renewed efforts are essential to move towards the achievement of SDG 16."

B
O
X

3.2

"Progress on some means of implementation targets is moving rapidly: personal remittances are at an all-time high, an increasing proportion of the global population has access to the Internet and the Technology Bank for the Least Developed Countries has been established. Yet, significant challenges remain: ODA is declining, private investment flows are not well aligned with sustainable development, there continues to be a significant digital divide and there are ongoing trade tensions. Enhanced international cooperation is needed to ensure that sufficient means of implementation exist to provide countries the opportunity to achieve the Sustainable Development Goals."

Source: United Nations (2019) *Special edition: Progress towards the Sustainable Development Goals, Report of the Secretary-General*, E/2019/68, 8 May.

The 2019 message of an urgent "need of a trajectory shift" to "kick-start a decade of delivery and action" was not only stressed by the Secretary-General and Deputy Secretary-General of the UN, but was reiterated by almost all international organizations that had been involved in the first four years of the SDGs. The conclusion was also corroborated by the findings of the first scientific report covering the first implementation cycle of the SDG effort, *The Future is Now. Science for Achieving Sustainable Development. Global Sustainable Development Report 2019*. The group of independent scientists that wrote this 'assessment of assessments' expressed strong and alarming concern on slow progress. The report drew a sobering picture, stating that

> "adding to the concern is the fact that recent trends along several dimensions with cross-cutting impacts across the entire 2030 Agenda are not even moving in the right direction. . . . Just over 10 years remain to achieve the 2030 Agenda, but no country is yet convincingly able to meet a set of basic human needs at a globally sustainable level of resource use. . . . The success of the 2030 Agenda thus depends on the cooperation of governments, institutions, agencies, the private sector and civil society across various sectors, locations, borders and levels" (UN Independent Group of Scientists, 2019: xx, xxi).

This conclusion resonates with parallel reports, issued, for instance, by the Sustainable Development Solutions Network (SDSN) and the Bertelsmann Stiftung that since 2016 have been publishing annual reports in the form of an *SDG Index* and *SDG dashboards*. They had repeatedly been pointing at the problem of 'not walking the talk': "While the global community talks a lot about sustainability goals, it does not invest enough in implementing them. . . . What began as a historic summit could end up as mere lip service. . . . The SDG Report shows that no country is currently on track to meet all targets by 2030" (Kroll, 2019). Similar conclusions were drawn on the involvement of corporations, generally deemed crucial for successfully filling the roughly $5–7 trillion in annual investments required across sectors and industries to achieve the SDGs.[1] The *UN Global Compact Progress Report 2019,* for instance, found that whereas 67% of their corporate signatories are committing to sustainability at the CEO level, only 48% are implementing sustainability into operations. While 71% of the CEOs recognize the critical role that business could play in contributing to the delivery of the SDGs, a mere 21% believe that business is actually playing that role. Box 3.3 gives further illustrations of shared critical assessments on progress made by most of the prime supporters of the SDG-agenda.

SELECTED STATEMENTS IN THE FOURTH YEAR OF SDG IMPLEMENTATION (2019)

B O X 3.3

■ **UN General Assembly, Secretary-General António Guterres** (September 2019): "Our world as we know it and the future we want are at risk. Despite considerable efforts these past four years, we are not on track to achieve the Sustainable Development Goals by 2030. We must dramatically step up the pace of Implementation" (quoted in UN, 2019).

■ **High-Level Political Forum, Secretary-General António Guterres** (24 September 2019): "We must regain the trust of the people and respond to perceptions and experiences of alienation and instability generated by the current model of globalization. We have the best solution in the Agenda 2030, our blueprint for a fair globalization. . . . We must boost the development prospects of the world's most vulnerable countries and most marginalized people. And we must look at the 2030 Agenda not through the prism of the economy of the last decade, but the economy of the next decade . . . . That is why today . . . I am issuing a global call for a decade of action to deliver the Sustainable Development Goals by 2030. . . . As we look forward, we know the great task before us. We need all hands on deck. We need to move together, leaving no one behind."

■ **UN Deputy Secretary-General Amina Mahammed** (25 September 2019): "Global hunger has risen for the third successive year. No country is on track to

---

1   Estimate based on basic infrastructure (roads, rail and ports; power stations; water and sanitation), food security (agriculture and rural development), climate change mitigation and adaptation, health, and education. World Investment Report 2014, UNCTAD.

B
O
X

3.3

achieve the goals on gender equality. Biodiversity is being lost at an alarming rate. And with greenhouse-gas emissions still rising, we are moving closer and closer to a 3 to 5° C temperature increase, with all the devastation that science keeps warning us about. In short, we are not doing enough to bring dignity, opportunity and justice to all, and we are at risk of irreversibly degrading the natural systems that sustain us."

▪ **UN Economic and Social Council (ECOSOC) President Inga Rhonda King** (July 2019): reports that discussions at the High-Level Political Forum revealed that the world is not on track to achieve the SDGs by 2030. To correct current trends, she emphasizes that the international community must "move out of its comfort zones" and pursue new ways of collective action "at a much swifter pace".

▪ **ECOSOC Commission** (May 2019): insufficient progress on the 2030 Agenda, due partly to "silo thinking" and a lack of resources, skills and awareness of the SDGs.

▪ **FAO** (August 2019): "The world is off-track to meet most of the Sustainable Development Goal (SDG) targets linked to hunger, food security and nutrition." (. . .) "Four years into the 2030 Agenda for Sustainable Development, regression is the norm when it comes to ending hunger and rendering agriculture and the management of natural resources – be that on land or in our oceans – sustainable". Hunger is on the rise. "More than 820 million people are still hungry today. The number of hungry people in the world has been on the rise for three years in a row, and is back to levels seen in 2010–2011" (Publication: 'Tracking Progress on Food and Agriculture-related SDG Indicators').

▪ **Africa SDG-index** (June 2019): The second annual report on the progress of African countries found that "the most frequently-observed trend is stagnation," particularly for SDGs 1, 2, 3, 4, 6, 7, 9 and 16. The prime reason: a lack of understanding among governments on what it will take to achieve the SDGs [including] a lack of funding and resources as "the single most significant challenge" in both SDG implementation and monitoring.

▪ **OECD** (May 2019): Advanced economies need to accelerate SDG implementation. More than half of the SDG-targets require a transboundary effort [involving in particular multinational corporations from the corporate side], meaning that achieving these 97 targets in one country will have an impact on neighbouring countries, other countries or on global goods, such as climate change and sustainable fishing (Publication: 'Measuring Distance to the SDG Targets 2019).

▪ **Inter-agency Task Force on Financing for Development** (April 2019): Over 60 international organizations, led by the United Nations and including the International Monetary Fund, the World Bank Group and World Trade Organization, jointly sounded the alarm in a new report. They warned that unless national and international financial systems are revamped, the world's governments will fail to keep their promises on such critical issues as combatting climate change and eradicating poverty by 2030. "The Sustainable Development Goals remain underfunded. Interest in sustainable financing is growing, but the sustainability transition in the financial system is not happening at the required pace."

■   **ILO** (February 2019): The ILO's *World Employment and Social Outlook for 2019* warns that the world is off-track to achieve many SDG8 targets.

■   **World Bank Group President, Jim Yong Kim** (2019): "We can achieve this ambitious Agenda, but it will take much more urgency and focus than we have delivered so far. We all have an obligation to take decisive action on a broad swath of deliverables for the SDGs – and to do it smartly" (World Bank Group, 2019, p. 7). "2030 may seem like a distant future, but there is urgent work that must be done now" (ibid: 136).

■   **WBCSD Director of SDGs James Gomme** (June, 2019): "As we approach four years since the launch of the Sustainable Development Goals, we find ourselves confronted by a world characterized by escalating levels of volatility and uncertainty; a world in which the SDGs' vision of long-term prosperity for people and planet is perhaps more relevant and more urgent than ever before. . . . As an engine of economic growth and employment, responsible for 84% of GDP and 90% of jobs in developing countries, the private sector is ideally placed to improve the lives of the poor and deliver on the promise of sustainable and socially inclusive economic development. . . . Put simply, the SDGs need business. However, this dependence is entirely mutual – ultimately long-term business success also very much hinges on the SDGs being realized. Business cannot thrive in societies that fail" (in: Sachs et al., 2019).

BOX 3.3

3.3 HYBRID GOVERNANCE IN PRACTICE: NAVIGATING PROGRESS, COMMUNITIES OF CHANGE

So, progress has been slow in the first four years of the SDG journey. Was that not to be expected anyway from such a complex, networked, multilevel and multi-stakeholder approach, in which active participation and voluntary commitments were to be triggered by relatively loose governance structures? The hybrid governance structure of the SDG approach was intended to channel progress in a number of concrete areas by means of *goal priorities*, improved *narratives* to facilitate broad awareness and commitment, *better data* development, and instilling *active participation* in, for instance, joint research or the creation of new platforms and partnerships around the implementation of the common agenda. The 2015–2019 implementation period can, therefore, also be interpreted as the *formation period* in which a form of hybrid governance developed that showed some of its potential (and its limitations) in practice.

Over the 2015–2019 period, a multi-layered structure for shaping and tracking on progress indeed materialized with the participation of multiple stakeholders. At the global level, in particular international organizations had been contributing. The annual SDG progress reports, for instance, draw from the assessment efforts of over 50 international and regional organizations and offices, specialized agencies, funds and programmes of the UN system and network. At the national level, national governments and national statistics offices (NSOs) got involved. By 2019, 142 countries had presented voluntary national reviews of their implementation efforts at the High-Level Political Forum – of which 15 states already for a second time. Since governments had responded well to the VNR-reporting arrangements, suggestions for an improved, 'second generation' kind of VNR emerged. These would go beyond a more static representation of the present state of affairs to showcase the entire story of SDG implementation in a country, with a focus on processes and not merely on situations (Surasky, 2019). Non-governmental organizations and private actors have identified entry points to align with the SDGs through platforms and a wide range of initiatives, and have started to collect information and relevant data as well. Scientists have sought to orient their work behind the SDGs, conducting research on vital issues and (transformative) approaches, and on developing solutions and technologies to meet sustainability challenges.

This multi-stakeholder approach potentially provides a richer basis for under-standing and addressing the multiple dimensions of the issues at stake. However, a relatively loose bottom-up approach also poses coordination and coherence problems, for instance when trying to assess overall progress over time, compare efforts and results between countries, or reach consensus on specific valuations. To illustrate some typical efforts that developed in the 2015–2019 period as part of the hybrid governance approach, we explore three kinds of 'communities of change' that materialized around challenges at the goal level (section 3.3.1), the target level (section 3.3.2) and the nexus level (section 3.3.3).

3.3.1 Channelling goal priorities and learning

At the global level, the overarching governance challenge has revolved around how to trigger vital contributions to the implementation of the SDG-agenda that (1) are "robust, voluntary, effective, participatory, transparent and integrated", (2) that also "promote accountability to citizens, support active international coopera-tion" and "foster exchange of best practices and mutual learning", (3) in a coherent, efficient and inclusive way (UNGA, 2016). The approach chosen would have to navigate, energize, support and guide commitments and ownership of many actors, while addressing knowledge gaps and implementation challenges along the way.

In the first four years, an infrastructure indeed materialized to operationalize these requirements and to channel the breadth of initiatives and commitments in the intended direction. In 2012, the United Nations had already established a High-Level Political Forum on Sustainable Development (HLPF) as an effort in collective learning (Hege et al., 2019). The Forum became the core global platform for monitoring and reviewing progress of the SDGs, with annual meetings on VNRs, and four-year cycled thematic reviews on (sets of) SDGs (see Box 3.1).

The UN also established infrastructure for various online platforms aimed at increasing public awareness; inspiring stakeholder engagement; enabling, documenting and mainstreaming implementation modalities; supporting partnerships, action networks and mutual exchange of experiences; and the joint development and broad dissemination of knowledge. Central to all these purposes are the online platforms that have developed around progress tracking, trend analyses, and the collection and exchange of robust data. These draw their information from many international organizations and specialized agencies in the UN system and network (see Table 3.1).

The trends, countertrends and conditions that can be distilled from the combined data are made accessible to a broad public in a vivid way, for instance in the form of so-called *narratives* on each of the 17 SDGs. As a communication technique, narrative development is increasingly used in social-scientific approaches to ambiguous and multidimensional events that are difficult to define, but important to discuss.[2] Narratives offer an explanatory framework that supports a relatively quick understanding of the key relations between various contextual dimensions (Box 3.4). All platforms created within this global 'pooling and channelling' infrastructure invite interested organizations and stakeholders to participate in evaluating progress, speeding up change and supporting capacity development. The open-source character, the up-to-date information on available official data and the explicated link with the SDGs provide a relatively easy starting position for any informed discussion on global trends in sustainable development.

---

2   See, for instance, the theory of *Bayesian Narratives* as developed by Peter Abell (2009). A Bayesian approach suggests that the human mind gets a grip on the overwhelming complexity of our natural and cultural environments through its probability calculus. Learning processes thereby rely on incremental improvements of our sense of the probabilities that are updated based on new observations. The *Bayesian Narrative* theory conceives a narrative as a directed graph comprising multiple causal links, contexts and actions (including assessment of *not* taking action). In Chapter 4, we use a comparable approach to define degrees of wickedness for each of the SDGs.

B
O
X

3.4

EXAMPLES OF CHANNELLING INITIATIVES BY THE UN

■ **United Nations SDG 'Hub':** the UN established a platform, aimed at all audiences, which covers and discusses all the 17 SDGs in terms of trends, facts and figures, targets, and links to key international organizations. It also covers related news, reports and videos. Each SDG is translated into a narrative to include the many dimensions and causes related to it. Take, for instance, the statement on poverty (SDG1). The narrative identifies major dimensions of the challenge and some of the consequences of not addressing the issue, but does not specify which dimensions predominate, nor which causes need to be prioritized:

"More than 700 million people, or 10% of the world population, still live in extreme poverty, struggling to fulfil the most basic needs like health, education, and access to water and sanitation, to name a few. The majority of people living on less than $1.90 a day live in sub-Saharan Africa. Worldwide, the poverty rate in rural areas is 17.2 per cent – more than three times higher than in urban areas. Having a job does not guarantee a decent living. In fact, 8 per cent of employed workers and their families worldwide lived in extreme poverty in 2018. Poverty affects children disproportionately. One out of five children live in extreme poverty. Ensuring social protection for all children and other vulnerable groups is critical to reduce poverty. Poverty has many dimensions, but its causes include unemployment, social exclusion, and high vulnerability of certain populations to disasters, diseases and other phenomena which prevent them from being productive. Growing inequality is detrimental to economic growth and undermines social cohesion, increasing political and social tensions and, in some circumstances, driving instability and conflicts" (https://www.un.org/sustainabledevelopment/poverty/, visited 26 January 2020).

■ **SDGs Knowledge Platform:** the Division for Sustainable Development Goals (DSDG) of UN DESA provides substantive support and capacity-building for the Global Goals and their related thematic issues, including water, energy, climate, oceans, urbanization, transport, science and technology. DSDG plays a key role in the evaluation of UN system-wide implementation of the 2030 Agenda and on advocacy and outreach activities relating to the SDGs. It provides studies and analytical inputs for intergovernmental deliberations and the review of major conferences related to sustainable development. For this purpose, it undertakes reviews of assessments of sustainable development challenges. DSDG serves member states, major groups, stakeholders and the general public by providing wide access to information and knowledge for sustainable development through its online Sustainable Development Knowledge Platform and social media outlets. The platform provides information on, amongst others, SDG databases and analytical tools, partnerships and registered voluntary commitments, SDG Acceleration Actions, and the activities and proceedings of the HLPF https://sdgs.un.org/

■ **Fast-tracking:** other UN organizations aim to fast-track specific goals by providing an active platform for discussion, benchmarking, guidance and experience exchange. The UNDP, for instance, notices that the pledge to 'Leave No One Behind' implies that priority is to be given to those who are furthest behind, which translates into achieving – what the UNDP calls – life-changing 'zeros': zero poverty, zero hunger, zero AIDS, zero discrimination against women and girls. The UNDP's focus explicitly lies with supporting 'integrated solutions' to the SDGs. "Today's development challenges – from climate crisis, to rising inequalities and protracted conflict – cannot be dealt with in isolation. The way countries work and the solutions they develop must be integrated." The UNDP and its fellow UN agencies in 2018 supported 97 projects in 38 countries through integrated MAPS engagements (Mainstreaming, Acceleration, and Policy Support) to help countries align on planning and budgeting processes in order to shift the Global Goals from commitments to action (https://sdgintegration.undp.org/).

■ **Sustainable Stock Exchanges (SSE):** SSE was initiated in 2009 by UNCTAD, UN Global Compact, UN Environment Finance Initiative, and the UN-supported Principles for Responsible Investment (PRI). Its mission is to provide a global platform for exploring how exchanges, in collaboration with investors, companies (issuers), regulators, policymakers and relevant international organizations, can enhance performance on environmental, social and corporate governance (ESG) investment (see also section 11.5). Since 2015, the SSE initiative has also provided a platform to explore how the SDGs can be financed. The SSE "seeks to achieve this mission through an integrated programme of conducting evidence-based policy analysis, facilitating a network and forum for multi-stakeholder consensus-building and providing technical assistance and advisory services". The SSE focuses on SDG-target 17.16 ('enhance the Global Partnership for Sustainable Development, complemented by multi-stakeholder partnerships that mobilize and share knowledge, expertise, technology and financial resources, to support the achievement of the Sustainable Development Goals in all countries, in particular developing countries') and had organized 94 'Partner Exchanges' by January 2020. (https://sseinitiative.org/)

In the same period, groupings of countries initiated participative approaches and supportive techniques on specific SDG-related topics. In 2017, the OECD, for instance, initiated the SDG Financing Lab and SDG tracker[3] to inform decision makers and policy leaders on how to ensure the resources needed to achieve the SDG-agenda. The OECD's Financing Lab addresses vital issues on

---

3   The OECD 'SDG tracker' is not to be confused with the 'SDG-Tracker', which is part of the *Our World in Data* project, developed as a joint collaborative effort between researchers at the University of Oxford and the Global Change Data Lab (Box 3.6).

development finance in support of realizing the SDGs through data collection and reporting, establishing statistical measurement frameworks, and analysis on various development finance topics. These range from assessing progress in the implementation of the SDGs and the Addis Ababa Action Agenda on Financing for Development to the monitoring of new trends (e.g. blended finance, leveraging ODA financing to maximize SDG impact, innovative risk mitigation instruments) that are shaping the international development finance landscape. The OECD takes an open-source approach to increase its accessibility and "to strengthen reporting by statisticians, avoid duplication of efforts, and offer new tools for policy research for the development community" (Box 3.5).

At the country level, the OECD has also been developing methodologies and tools to strengthen public institutions and governance practices to catalyse integrated implementation of the SDGs. From the angle of governance coherence – with an emphasis on 'whole-of-government' coordination, policy coherence, stakeholder engagement, and the strategic use of budgeting, procurement and regulatory tools – the OECD has been sharing good practice, knowledge, tools and country experiences to assist national governments in tackling the multifaceted and interlinked SDG challenges by: (a) 'updating their governance toolbox', (b) informing 'peer-to-peer dialogue', and (c) measuring OECD countries' distance to realization of the SDGs.[4]

BOX 3.5

FILLING THE FINANCE GAP: THE SDG TRACKER OF OECD'S SDG FINANCING LAB

The OECD realized that there are no global statistics available on financing the SDGs. In 2017, it created the **SDG Financing Lab** after issuing a 'wake-up call' to address the need for better indicators and tools related to the alignment of financial flows to the SDGs. The SDG Financing Lab provides estimates of aid allocation per SDG. Its first product was the **SDG tracker,** which allows a mapping of the financial contributions – of bilateral providers, multilateral organizations, or philanthropies that report to the OECD – in visualized flows, either from the providers' or the recipients' perspective. The tracker draws from the OECD CRS database that lists more than 250,000 projects per

---

4 Relevant OECD publications on these themes include: *Measuring Distance to the SDG Targets 2019. An Assessment of Where OECD Countries Stand* (2019); *Governance as an SDG Accelerator. Country Experiences and Tools* (2019a); and *Policy Coherence for Sustainable Development. Empowering People and Ensuring Inclusiveness and Equality* (2019b).

year that contribute to sustainable development. It uses artificial intelligence to link official development flows (ODF) spending to the SDGs. In the words of the website:

> "The tracker offers an answer to one of the most pressing development policy
> issues: which are the SDG darlings? The orphans? What is the SDG portfolio of a
> particular provider in Africa? In Asia? Because its technology allows linking multiple
> SDGs to a single aid project, it is possible to better understand different ways to
> address the SDGs: is gender equality supported through better justice? Through
> education? The tracker offers new perspectives on providers' portfolios and the
> interlinkages with the SDGs. By linking aid to the SDGs, it is possible to identify
> underfunded zones, increase transparency and improve the impact of aid."[5]

The SDG tracker does not provide figures at the target level. Development outcomes
can contribute to a very large number of SDG-targets simultaneously, making it difficult to track at the target level.

Sources: https://sdg-financing-lab.oecd.org/about/ and https://sdg-financing-lab.oecd.org/
explore

BOX 3.5

A considerable number of non-state initiatives matured as well, partly as a
spin-off of UN action. Most of these are aimed at assisting a broad audience in
following progress on each of the SDGs in a user-friendly, engaging, and often
interactive or visualized way. They provide a hub for accessing enriched and
combined data derived from primary sources across a variety of organizations by
bundling, building and sharing knowledge to facilitate broad awareness, capacity
development and informed participation. The SDG-Tracker of the *Our World in
Data* initiative, for instance, has been developed as a free, open-access and
appealing format in the recognition that "engagement with the SDGs and their
potential requires us to tell stories: the narratives of lives across the world. . . . To
explore where we are now, and how far we have to go by 2030, we need interactive and engaging data. Metrics must be specific to the SDG indicators, but
presented in such a way that everyone can engage." Platforms that monitor and
report on country performance towards the SDGs – or lack thereof – have been
providing vital information to identify performance gaps and to hold governments
accountable, thereby spurring a bottom-up 'advocacy function' in support of calls
for accelerated action and initiatives for local implementation. A number of

---

5   Visited 20 February 2020.

relevant knowledge hubs and SDG-mapping and tracking initiatives are described in Box 3.6. Some explicitly position themselves as a 'public good' for advancing collective action on achieving the SDGs.

B
O
X

3.6

SDG KNOWLEDGE HUBS AND INITIATIVES

■ **Sustainable Development Solutions Network (SDSN)**

Under the auspices of the UN Secretary-General, the UN Sustainable Development Solutions Network was created to "mobilize global scientific and technological expertise to promote practical solutions for sustainable development". SDNS works closely with UN agencies, but also with multilateral financing institutions, the private sector and civil society. It brings together 'global sustainable development leaders' to inspire and share progress. The SDSN network spans 6 continents, comprises over 1,100 member institutions (most of which are universities) and is organized in 33 national and regional networks. The SDG Academy is part of the SDSN and leads the education work of SDSN. It provides access to many free online courses on SDG-related topics and a searchable repository of sustainable development resources that draw from its University Partnership Programme. Since 2016, the SDSN secretariat and the SDG Academy have been hosted by the SDSN Association, a non-profit organization with offices in New York and Paris. https://www.unsdsn.org/

■ **SDG Index and Dashboard**

Since 2016, SDNS and Bertelsmann Stiftung have been monitoring national and local governments' performance on the SDGs. Assessments are published through the SDG Index and Dashboards, which map and benchmark country performance to track progress and ensure accountability. The SDG Index ranks countries based on their performance across the 17 SDGs. The Dashboard uses a traffic light chart to assess where a country stands on each of the 17 SDGs. Both official and unofficial metrics are used to measure the distance to targets for each of the SDGs "to identify priorities for action, understand key implementation challenges, track progress, ensure accountability, and identify gaps that must be closed in order to achieve the SDGs by 2030". The assessments aim to provide information on how country leaders can deliver on their promise and not lose momentum for important reforms, and to spur initiatives that develop localized assessment of SDG progress.

The SDG Index exercise resulted in *Sustainable Development Reports*, published since 2018, which list the SDG Index and Dashboards for all UN member states. The interactive SDG Dashboards provide a visual representation of countries' performance on the SDGs "to identify priorities for action". The initiative also developed reports for US and European cities and specific regions, such as the African and Arab regions, the United States and the European Union. https://sdgindex.org/ and https://dashboards.sdgindex.org/#/

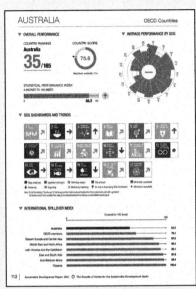

Source: Sachs et al. (2021), licensed under CC BY-NC-ND 4.0

■ IISD 'SDG Knowledge Hub' and 'Earth Negotiation Bulletin'

In 2016, the SDG Knowledge Hub was created as an independent online resource centre for news and commentary regarding the implementation of the SDGs. It is managed by the International Institute for Sustainable Development (IISD) and contains regular updates and news, policy briefs, commentary from thematic experts, guest articles from key actors, and a calendar of upcoming international events related to the 2030 Agenda (the *SDG Update*). The SDG Knowledge Hub provides a rich resource for anyone interested in the SDGs, searchable by regions, actors, events, issues, actions, publications and global partnerships. IISD Reporting Services also provided open-access, neutral, up-to-the-minute records, video coverage and summary reports of ongoing United Nations multilateral negotiations on environment and sustainable development through its *Earth Negotiation Bulletin* (ENB), and of conferences, workshops, symposiums and regional meetings through its ENB+ service. IISD, a non-profit organization based in Canada, is finan-cially supported by UN DESA and a variety of public sponsors, in particular from developed countries (Switzerland, Norway, France, Germany, European Commission, United Arab Emirates). IISD receives information from almost all relevant actors in the evolving SDG community. https://sdg.iisd.org/sdgs/ and https://enb.iisd.org/

BOX
3.6

▪ SDG-Tracker, Our World in Data

SDG-Tracker is a joint collaboration effort between researchers from the University of Oxford and the Global Change Data Lab. It is a free, open-access resource where users can track and explore global and country-level progress towards each of the 17 SDGs, through interactive data visualizations. The SDG-Tracker presents up-to-date data across all available indicators derived from the Our World in Data database, which uses official statistics from the UN and other international organizations. Clicking on a given country in the global map shows moving time series of how a given metric has changed over time, with the chart also allowing for comparing progress across neighbours, regions and worldwide. Across each of the 17 SDGs, specific entries or resources are provided that link back to the extensive *Our World in Data* (OWID) website, where research publications and longer-term data on all aspects of development can be found. The rationale for building the SDG-Tracker was the recognition that

> "to inspire participation and concerted effort towards the SDGs, it's essential that people understand how the world has changed, as it stands today, and the progress we must make to achieve our targets. Without data, it's impossible to assess any of these elements. We will walk blindly through the next 10–15 years with no sense of our progress. Without interactive and engaging presentation of this data, we will not get the level of global participation and inclusivity we need to make it happen".

Our World in Data is a non-profit organization that positions itself as a 'public good' aimed "to build the infrastructure that allows everyone in the world to understand how we make progress against our most pressing problems". It is funded by donations and grants, and is supported by various foundations. https://sdg-tracker.org/about and https://ourworldindata.org/about

▪ SDGs Dashboard

iTechMission – a social enterprise – developed an open-source interactive global SDGs Dashboard that supports tracking and monitoring of the SDGs. It emphasizes the importance given in the 2030 Agenda to 'high-quality, timely, easily accessible, reliable and disaggregated data'. The SDG Dashboard could be considered a response to that call. This data-driven initiative is aimed at enabling governments, policy decision makers, researchers and others to perform easy analysis through visualizations and tools for exploring data from global data sources. It provides a rich variety of graphs, maps, and interactive visualizations that can be assessed at the global and country level. http://www.sdgsdashboard.org/

3.3.2 Channelling target priorities and indicator development

To make informed decisions on the implementation of the SDGs, both the avail-ability of open, disaggregated data and statistics and the capacity to use them are of vital importance to governments, international organizations, the private sector and civil society at large. Without accurate ways of measuring progress, a lack of priorities may lead to misappropriated financial flows. The process of defining and measuring the SDGs has, therefore, also been described in terms of a 'political-economic' process of dynamic negotiations between a multitude of global stake-holders with particular interests. How targets and indicators are defined directs, to a large extent, the success of decisions related to priorities, policy measures and the (re)direction of resources. Consequently, an inaccurate, unbalanced or incomplete definition of progress measures may result in unanticipated conse-quences that arise from the mechanisms put in place. Thinking of indicator devel-opment as a technical procedure would underestimate its relevance as an area of serious political, economic and scientific contention in a VUCA world (see Box 3.7). The logic and fairness of this process and its outcome hence require a participatory approach and careful monitoring and documentation. The SDG metrics can, therefore, be understood as in-between points of reference and convergence in an ongoing intellectual and political discourse, with still sizable gaps that need further addressing (see section 2.3.2).

At the target and indicator level in particular, global communities of researchers and statistical offices have been organized around the SDG-agenda to tackle the measurement gaps and the indicators still 'under construction'. A network of specialized international *custodian agencies* and *partner agencies*

Table 3.1 Who guards the integrity and progress of the SDG-indicators?[6]

Champion custodians (>20 indicators)	OECD (21); World bank (22); FAO (22); UNESCO (22); UNEP (31); WHO (35);
Big custodians (10–20 indicators)	UNICEF (17); UN-Habitat (11); UNDRR (11); UNSD (11); UNODC (16); ILO (15);
Medium-sized custodians (6–10 indicators)	UNDP (6); UN Women (6); WTO (8); UNCTAD (8);
Topical custodians (<6 indicators)	IMF (4); IUCN (5); IRENA (2); IEA (4); UN DESA (5); CITES (2); UNFPA (4); CBD Secretariat (2); PARIS21 (3); UNWTO (3); OHCHR (5); ITC (4); ITU (5); IPU (2);
Focused custodians (1 indicator)	UNAIDs; national government; UNECE; IOM; ICAO; CIDS; Samoa Pathway; UNCCD; UN Ocean Agencies; Ramsar.

---

6   The custodian and partner agencies per indicator were derived from the 'Global SDG indi-cators Tier Classification List', 11 December 2019.

developed – coordinated through UN ECOSOC – to advance methodologies and guard the correct collection and coherence of data. By the end of 2019, most of the 232 indicators – with the exception of several Tier III indicators – had one or more custodian agencies, while 130 indicators had been adopted by partner agencies. Together, the custodian and partnering organizations provide the networked governance structure through which the coherence between the SDGs is to be safeguarded (see Table 3.1).

PROCESSES OF REFRESHMENT AND REVIEW

The political-economic dimensions of indicator development, the analytical complexity involved, and the participatory principle overarching the SDG-agenda imply that indicator advancement needs to be addressed through a process of constant 'refreshment' and periodic review. Since the adoption of the global indicator framework in 2017, many indicators have been subject to this refinement and refreshment process (Box 3.7).

**B
O
X

3.7**

NAVIGATING SDG-INDICATOR DEVELOPMENT

Comprehensive review – technical process

Throughout 2019, the Inter-Agency and Expert Group on Sustainable Development Goal Indicators (IAEG-SDGs) conducted a 'Comprehensive Review' of the global indicator framework, the findings of which were submitted to the UN Statistical Commission. The review comprised work plan updates of Tier III indicators by custodian agencies, and an open call for proposals for replacements, refinements, adjustments and additional indicators to countries, international and regional organizations, civil society, academia and the private sector. Out of the 200 proposals and comments received, a preliminary list was compiled for open consultation. On this, over 600 inputs were received from organizations, countries and individuals.

After weighing them against predetermined criteria, the IAEG-SDGs in December 2019 agreed upon 36 major changes to the present indicator framework adopted in 2017: 14 proposals for the *replacement* of existing indicators, 8 proposals for *revisions* of existing indicators; 8 proposals for *additional* indicators, 6 proposals for the *deletion* of existing indicators. Also, 20 proposals for *minor refinements* were taken on board. The IAEG-SDGs kept its proposed changes as limited as possible in order "to avoid disrupting existing monitoring systems or overburdening national statistical systems".

As part of the continuous updating and tier reclassification process, the IAEG-SDGs also reviewed the status of Tier III indicators. It concluded that significant progress had been made in the methodological development of many Tier III indicators. SDG-indicator 4.7.1 ('mainstreaming sustainability education'), for instance, could be reclassified from Tier III to Tier II, which allowed its custodian agency UNESCO to begin collecting data from countries in 2020. IAEG-SDGs also reported that 17 Tier III indicators remained that had seen their methodological progress stall or still awaited a custodian agency. The areas that these indicators aimed to cover were clearly more complex, given the fact that by December 2019, no work plans had been developed for SDG-indicators 1.a.1, 1.a.3, 1.b.1; 8.9.2; 12.a.1; or 17.18.1. (*Further information:* https://unstats.un.org/sdgs/iaeg-sdgs/2020-comprev/UNSC-proposal/ and https://unstats.un.org/sdgs/tierIII-indicators/)

BOX 3.7

Indicator framework refreshment in a global Bargaining Society – political process

The process of (re)defining SDG-indicators in a 'hybrid governance' regime presents a process of 'dynamic negotiations'. From 3–6 March 2020, the UN Statistical Commission (UNSC) convened in New York for its 51st session to discuss and approve the proposed set of changes to the SDGs global indicator framework.

Country representatives expressed concerns about the proposed deletion of indicator 8.9.2 ('proportion of jobs in sustainable tourism out of total tourism jobs'), in particular by countries that rely on tourism. Some voiced concern about the proposed addition of the 'total greenhouse gas emissions per year' (indicator 13.2.2), which they felt mirrors how the global response to climate change inhibits countries' equal right to development. The proposed 'refinement' of indicator 3.8.1 on 'coverage of essential health services' was brought back to its previous status. Some suggested cancelling all Tier III indicators, as with just ten years to go until 2030, there would probably not be sufficient time left to implement these indicators.

A working group was established to broaden the measurement of Official Development Assistance to 'total official support for sustainable development' (relevant to SDG 17). Although similar discussions on ODA had been going on for decades within the OECD, the working group's deadline was set for 2022. Data disaggregation to ensure adequate measurement of the 'leave no one behind' ambition, was defined as major area of work, as was the aim to focus on the interlinkages (nexus) between the goals and targets, both statistically and 'through a policy and legislation lens'.

The director of the UN Statistical Division, Stefan Schweinfest, recalled that the review process had been lengthy, "very complex", work in progress, but also "a package deal". This would make reconsidering the decision on individual indicators "a dangerous path", he said, urging delegations to accept the premise of a compromise.

Sources: UN ECOSOC (2019), E/CN.3/2020/2, 20 December; IISD News, 10 March 2020; Meeting webcast, 3–6 March 2020 (http://webtv.un.org/search/8th-meeting-51st-statistical-commission-3-6-march-2020/6139190526001/?term=statistical&sort=date)

Gaps and challenges remain, however, and include the development and validation of new kinds of data – 'citizen-generated' (big) data, for instance – as traditional survey data and statistics do not suffice to cover many of the (new) SDG-targets. Also, prioritizing what statistics need to be generated, by whom (at the global or at the national level) and the financing of it, are issues that are still in the process of discussion. An additional problem is that the SDG-indicators only present 'performance metrics' that indicate whether a target is being achieved or not. This approach risks relegating statistics to the downstream role of monitoring and evaluation, whereas a key role of statistics should be to inform policy decisions (MacFeely, 2019).

3.3.3 Channelling nexus priorities: creating insight into what matters

The Global Goals can only be achieved if they are pursued in an integrated manner. This requires actions that build on synergies among the SDGs, generate enablers of development, and address trade-offs between targets and policy areas. "Understanding the range of positive and negative interactions among SDGs is key to unlocking their potential at any scale" (ICSU, 2017: 7). Research on SDG-related nexus challenges is emerging, yet the translation thereof into aligned and coherent governance and policy approaches is still in its infancy. To trigger advancements in both knowledge development and action-oriented policy frameworks, initiatives in the form of communities, conferences, platforms, tools and approaches have developed in several (specialized) areas. Knowledge and tool development are yet to be validated and, therefore, mostly present valuable 'work in, and on progress' (Box 3.8).

BOX 3.8

THE CREATION OF NEXUS COMMUNITIES

A Nexus community

In 2018, a nexus community of researchers, academics, NGOs, policymakers and the private sector convened to further develop ideas and insights on the interconnections between the SDGs and Water, Energy, Food (W-E-F) and Climate.[7] The conference considered the nexus-style of analysis – i.e. focusing on optimizing positive synergies while minimizing negative trade-offs – a vital approach to help develop more practical solutions for addressing key sustainability issues, and "helping global communities in their collective efforts to deliver the SDGs, end poverty, and create more equitable and peaceful societies".

The conference urged all concerned with the advancement of the SDG-agenda to consider adopting a 'nexus-style' of analysis and action, to identify the strongest interconnections between various goals and targets and to generate

---

7   https://council.science/events/nexus-conference-2018/

integrated approaches and policies for them. In addition to the policy-relevant implications of the W-E-F-nexus, it was stressed that "the time has come to consider
applying the approach more widely as it can help to enhance the understanding of
connections among other issues such as health, gender, human mobility, population
growth and other matters pertaining to the 2030 Agenda". The conference also
recommended that:

1   **The governance dimension** should from the outset be factored into any new
     nexus analysis and policy recommendations that emerge;

2   A nexus-style analysis be built into public and private **financial appraisal
     systems** to ensure that investments support key integration objectives and
     appropriate cooperation between different levels of governance, and between
     public and private sectors;

3   Nexus research on interlinkages be linked to **policy formulation** and the poli-
     cymaking community;

4   Nexus thinking be used when implementing **capacity-building for SDG
     delivering**, and thus equip communities with tools to better address SDG
     challenges.

Identifying relevant Nexus Tools

The nexus community identified seven **Nexus Tools** as useful for the W-E-F-
challenge. Many of these tools are intended to channel research, for instance by
getting scientists and policymakers to engage in a structured exchange of information in scenario-building and decision-making:

■   **Wastewater Reuse Effectiveness Index** (WREI): a monitoring tool that
     aggregates bio-physical, institutional and socio-economic data to track coun-
     tries' effective responses to risks that arise from inaction and rebound effects
     of cross-sector developmental interactions; developed at the United Nations
     University (Mathew Kurian).

■   **Long-range Energy Alternatives Planning System** (LEAP): an integrated soft-
     ware modelling tool that can be used to track energy consumption,
     production and resource extraction in all sectors of an economy,
     developed by the Stockholm Environment Institute (SEI).https://openei.org/
     wiki/Long_range_Energy_Alternatives_Planning_(LEAP)_System.

■   **Water Evaluation and Planning System** (WEAP): a software tool that takes
     an integrated approach to water resources planning, developed by the
     Stockholm Environment Institute's US Center. https://www.sei.org/projects-
     and-tools/tools/weap/

■ *Energy Portfolio Assessment Tool* (EPAT): presented as a scenario-based holistic nexus tool that enables energy stakeholders and policymakers to create and evaluate the sustainability of various scenarios based on the W-E-F nexus approach. It identifies the links between energy and other systems (water, land, environment, finance, etc.), and measures the impact of energy portfolios, to offer a foundation for sustainable decision-making in energy planning; developed at Texas A&M University;

■ *WEAP-LEAP Tool:* a tool that provides a 'wizard' for connecting the WEAP and LEAP tools. By using both systems together, planners can explore how individual water or energy management choices ripple through both the water and energy systems, understanding trade-offs that might not be apparent when looking at either system alone.

■ *Water-Energy-Food Nexus Tool 2.0* (WEF 2.0): A scenario-based tool for quantifying interconnections that serves as a platform for scientists and policymakers to identify bottlenecks in resource allocation, while highlighting possible trade-offs and opportunities to overcome resource stress challenges; developed at Texas A&M University. https://www.water-energy-food.org/resources/resources-detail/water-energy-and-food-nexus-tool-2-0/

■ *Water-Energy-Transportation* (WET): an interactive planning tool for assessing the diverse interrelations between water, energy and transportations and their impact under different scenarios; developed at Texas A&M University. http://www.wefnexustool.org/wef/background

SDG Interaction Knowledge Platform

The research team of Nilsson and colleagues (2018) stressed the importance of contextual factors when mapping and assessing interactions across the SDGs, such as (a) geographical context, (b) resource endowments, (c) time horizon, and (d) governance. To navigate further studies along these lines, they proposed to create a global *SDG Interaction Knowledge Platform* as a "key mechanism for assembling, systematizing and aggregating knowledge on interactions".

The proposed web-based knowledge platform should process knowledge development and its use in both science and policy spheres, to search for relevant correlations by coded case studies in "a way that they can be searched, matched and synthesized, and thereby inform stakeholder dialogue and learning in a developing community" (ibid: 1497). The SDG Interactions Knowledge Platform would have to be aimed at globally pooling scientific knowledge, then gradually grow into an interactive learning and collaboration site, and eventually develop into a platform for a global community of practice about SDG interactions. It awaits realization.

B
O
X

3.8

SDG synergies approach: organizing 'collaborative analysis'

To support policymaking and planning, researchers from the *Stockholm Environment Institute (SEI)* developed a practical approach for prioritizing action and identifying collaborations for integrated SDG implementation. The approach is based on an understanding of real-world interactions between SDG-targets in a given context, and intended to offer decision makers a "systemic view of the SDGs, highlighting how interactions between different targets can shape the outcome of policy choices". It builds on the work of Nilsson, Griggs and Visbeck (2016) and Weitz et al. (2018), and involves a three-step process of 'collaborative analysis' between a variety of stakeholders. This not only supports building bridges and partnerships between actors and sectors, but also generates a shared understanding of the challenges and opportunities, highlights common interests, and builds ownership among stakeholders.

■ **Step (1)** of the approach comprises a process of customization, in which the scope of all possible interactions between the 169 SDG-targets is narrowed down to a relevant subset.

■ In **step (2)**, a 'cross-impact matrix' is composed that maps the subset of selected targets, which are then scored in a consistent way – facilitated by the use of the '–3 to +3' scale of different types or strengths of interactions (see section 2.3.4) – along a guiding question, for instance: 'If progress is made towards Target A (on a vertical axis), how does this influence progress towards Target B (on the horizontal axis)?'

■ **Step (3)** involves going beyond the first impression of all direct interactions to identify patterns, clusters of interacting targets and other network effects. Identification of clusters of *positively interacting targets,* for instance, can inform a discussion on how these might interact with other such clusters – which subsequently could provide a basis for creating cross-sectoral working groups. https://www.sei.org/publications/sdg-synergies-factsheet/

3.4 HYBRID GOVERNANCE RESULTS: KEY PROCESS CHALLENGES

The first four-year experience with the implementation of the SDGs shows that some goals and targets are more easily embraced than others, while the potential of synergistic and coherent approaches in support of an integrated implementation has been rather underutilized. General implementation problems inherent to trans-formative, universal goals in an increasingly challenging multilateral setting to a large extent explain this finding. The Global Goals are ambitious, the challenges involved intricate. However, no or slow progress might also partly hint at deficiencies in the governance approach chosen by the United Nations, as a primarily *coordinating* body, in: (a) stimulating voluntary commitments, initiatives and (national) reporting; (b) coordinating a network of international organizations for the advancement of indicators and essential statistics to guidelines of action; and (c) providing a networked infrastructure for mutual learning and sharing experiences.

In an initial assessment of conditions for success, Hege et al. (2019) explored qualitative sources for the observed delays in delivering on the 2030 Agenda and provided four basic explanations. First, actors embracing the SDGs rarely question standing practices or initiate projects with real transformative potential. Second, governments are not yet doing enough to implement the agenda, which notably relates to the translation of the SDGs into national policies and budgetary processes. Third, the participatory approach of the SDGs has created a watered-down vision of what does and does not contribute; everyone can join, without questioning the real impact of their actions. And fourth, the SDG-agenda was based on a 'weak consensus', which undervalues trade-offs and the importance of developing transformative pathways to address fundamental crises in the present system. Additional explanations for slow progress can be further specified at three levels:

1   Technical-related processes: data and measurement gaps (section 3.4.1);

2   Policy coherence and how governments have embraced the SDGs at the national and international level (section 3.4.2);

3   Societal engagement: patterns in the early adoption of the SDGs by the private sector (section 3.4.3).

3.4.1   Technical: progress in data development is slow and arduous

Building on Chapter 2, which identified key *analytical and empirical* challenges related to the SDG-agenda, this chapter documented the arduous *process* through which the ambition to gather and harmonize robust data in support of the SDG-agenda has been executed.

■   **Serious measurement gaps persist.** A critical upfront condition for the successful implementation of the SDG project was the development of high-quality, sufficiently disaggregated, open and timely data needed to measure progress. Tier I type of data – for which the indicator is conceptually clear, with an internationally established methodology, and for which data are regularly produced by at least 50% of countries and of the population in every region where the indicator is relevant – still represent just 56% of the SDG-indicators in the global framework (see Box 2.2). This gap in data coverage thwarts adequate reporting and consequently also limits countries' accountability. OECD research aimed at measuring 'the distance' to achieving the SDG-targets observed that measurement is still difficult, even for developed country members of the OECD, because insufficient data availability creates analytical uncertainty (OECD, 2019).

■ **Relatively weak commitment to harmonization.** Critical observers have argued that global measuring gaps persist because countries, regional and international organizations do not take global SDG monitoring seriously enough and hence have been slow in their commitment to it (Gennari and Navarro, 2020). Many countries would "still view it as an imposition by inter-national organizations", despite the country-led approach taken to the establishment of the global indicator framework. The use of national proxies to replace global SDG-indicators makes it difficult to create a common benchmark to assess progress and come to effective action. The gaps in data development and the implicit resistance to data harmonization lead to fragmented efforts.

■ **Relatively weak accounting standards prevail.** At the start of the SDG-agenda, Pogge and Sengupta (2015) voiced the concern that without detailing specific responsibilities and accountability, the SDGs would "remain a mere list with little moral force" (ibid: 573). Without proper accounting, the risk of embracing the SDGs as a PR activity looms large. It may therefore come as no surprise that – after 'whitewashing' (tax evasion), 'greenwashing' and 'bluewashing' – *SDG-washing* has been introduced as a new marking for state and non-state organizations that claim to embrace the SDGs without really trying to implement them.

■ **Skewed statistics persist.** National statistical agencies encounter partic-ular difficulties in capturing socio-demographic statistics on marginalized populations such as the homeless, refugees, migrants, minorities and the underground economy. Limited resources exacerbate this statistics gap for developing countries. This reality affects one of the foundational corner-stones of the SDG-agenda: the pledge of the international community to 'leave no one behind'. To assess and monitor the extent of readiness of countries to meet this commitment – in terms of systems, policies and prac-tice – the Overseas Development Institute (ODI) developed the *'leave no one behind' index*. With a coverage of 159 countries, the index in 2019 indicated that 81 countries were 'ready' to meet this commitment, with most of them high- and middle-income countries. Many of the low-income countries were assessed as 'partially ready' (Chattopadhyay and Manea, 2019).[8]

3.4.2 Policy and governance: channelling involvement remains fragmented

Proper management and channelling would greatly enhance the coherence of the SDG-agenda (OECD, 2014). National agendas and Global Goals could become sufficiently aligned and – even with the great diversity of initiatives and organizations involved – the net results would be positive. The experience of the 2015–2019 period shows that at both the global and national governance level, a mixed picture has developed.

AT THE GLOBAL LEVEL

▪ **Success in creating platforms:** an infrastructure of many knowledge, tool and data gathering platforms has indeed developed. The boxes throughout this chapter identify some of the key initiatives. In particular, communities of pioneering 'frontrunners' and 'advocates' were established. These initiatives successfully solicited voluntary commitments and 'best practice' cases in a diversity of relevant areas, but also induced the creation of relatively loose coalitions of 'willing' stakeholders.

▪ **Global public support:** the SDG-agenda has been relatively successful at the global level. G7, G8 and G20 Summits regularly refer to the SDG-agenda; the African Union has linked the SDGs to its Agenda 2063; the European Union has been aligning its internal and external policies with the SDG-agenda. The World Bank integrated the SDGs into the planning and monitoring of its activities. Since 2017, the World Bank has published an SDG Atlas based on its World Development Indicators.[9] The IMF, on the other hand, took a rather narrow approach to the SDGs by primarily looking

---

8   54 out of the 159 countries observed were 'partially ready', 12 were 'not ready' and 12 lacked sufficient data to make an assessment. Where comparisons could be made, ODI found that the status of 12 countries had worsened and only six had improved. Most improvements were observed in the 'data dimension' of the index, while most regression (in 23 countries) occurred in the policy dimension of the index. The level of readiness is the lowest in the financing criterion, which particularly affects the most vulnerable groups in society.

9   Also presented as an interactive SDG dashboard, see: http://datatopics.worldbank.org/sdgs/

at accounting measures, the strengthening of national tax and budgeting systems, and how to reduce corruption in the more vulnerable countries it supports. The WTO has not really integrated the SDG-agenda, which reinforces its position as a 'free trade' rather than a 'fair trade' organization. The OECD has already been mentioned as an active supporter of the SDG track. Regional development banks – like the Inter-American Development Bank – can be included as committed as well. They initiated 'SDG bonds' as a new financial tool for supporting SDG-relevant projects for example (see section 11.7 on sustainable corporate finance).

■ **Collective learning, political leadership and guidance trail behind.** A review of the work of the HLPF, at the end of its first four-year cycle, pointed to room for improvement to enhance the effectiveness of the HLPF as the central platform for follow-up and review of the implementation of the SDGs. Key areas identified included ways to strengthen its role related to thematic reviews, interlinkages, voluntary national reviews, preparatory processes, the engagement of stakeholders and political guidance (Expert Group Meeting, 2019).[10] Critical observers pointed out the need for better evaluation of data to inform effective lines of action, notably on context-specific implementation of the SDGs. Beisheim and Bernstein (2020), for instance, noted that preparations for the HLPF had not been including the analysis and evaluation of statistical reports from UN bodies, the data in VNRs or data produced by regional fora. The need to articulate integrated approaches to SDG implementation – in line with available knowledge on nexus-related challenges, policy coherence and transformative pathways – was also stressed. The HLPF has been grappling with encouraging countries to take a more holistic approach to implementation challenges. An acceleration in progress would hence suggest that the HLPF strengthens its political leadership, by providing targeted guidance and action-oriented recommendations. Lastly, the role of the HLPF in coordinating VNRs (a key element of countries' accountability on SDG implementation), has been qualified as 'not convincing' and "a long way from peer review exercises, such as those implemented by the OECD" (Hege et al., 2019: 14). Critics argue that this has contributed to the paradoxical reality that "while VNRs suggest that countries have invested considerable energy and effort to achieve the SDGs, global and regional assessments of progress tell a different story" (Beisheim and Bernstein, 2020).

10 See https://sustainabledevelopment.un.org/hlpf for background documents on the review process that started mid-2019, expert group meeting recommendations and 'lessons learned'.

AT THE NATIONAL LEVEL

■ **Cherry-picking persists.** The 17 SDGs can easily be cherry-picked and tackled in silos. The agenda does not specify who commits to what, while defining targets without assigning clear responsibility. Universal goals like the SDGs risk not being 'owned' by anyone in particular. The experience of national efforts shows that some SDG-targets and goals are clearly more popular than others. Partly because they can be better documented based on available metrics, partly because they are easier to address. The scientist evaluation as covered in the GSDR report consequently warns against the persistent danger of a 'silo approach' to implementing several of the more complex SDGs that involve major trade-offs between the goals due to complex nexus interactions (UN Independent Group of Scientists, 2019). The selection bias portrayed in the present adoption of the goals and targets feeds into possible 'SDG-washing' practices, leaving the broader and trans-formative part of the SDG-agenda essentially without real owners and advo-cates. This inclination also affects the process of data gathering and peer review.

■ **Mixed ownership.** How governments embrace the SDGs is country-led and country-driven and based on voluntary commitments. Many national and regional governments have integrated the SDG-agenda in already existing long-term visions and strategies, like the African Union's Agenda 2063. Such integration may revive interest in sustainable development strategies and accordingly enhance SDG implementation, but can also result in a 'rebranding' of already planned lines of activities and limited addi-tional effort and ownership. By 2019, no country was yet on track to meeting all the goals. SDSN's Sustainable Development Report 2019, for instance, found that "Out of 43 countries surveyed on SDG implementation efforts, including all G20 countries and countries with a population greater than 100 million, 33 countries have endorsed the SDGs in official statements since January 1st, 2018. Yet in only 18 of them do central budget docu-ments mention the SDGs. This gap between rhetoric and action must be closed" (Sachs et al., 2019: x). Responses to the SDG-agenda in the 2015–2019 period show a mixed picture:

   o   In the African region, 34 of the 54 African countries had presented national reports by 2019; 12 additional countries planned to present their VNRs for the first time in 2020. 17 of the 20 least active coun-tries in delivering the SDGs are African (Sachs et al., 2019).

   o   In the Latin American region, many initiatives have been taken and most countries – 29 out of 33, according to an ECLAC (2019) prog-ress report – created formal institutional mechanisms to coordinate

SDG implementation. Colombia and Guatemala had already been a driving force behind the creation of the 2030 Agenda.

o   In Europe, many countries have tried to coordinate their SDG efforts, but real integration into budgeting processes and a solid involvement of stakeholders remains fragmented (Hege et al., 2019). Despite commitments to act differently, the European Commission had not developed an SDG implementation strategy by early 2019, nor fulfilled its intention to mainstream the SDGs in all policies. The European Parliament (DG for External Policies) concluded that "it is time for a frontrunner approach from coalitions of the willing that turn into coalitions of the winning" (European Parliament, 2019: 7). The newly appointed European Commission initiated a *European Green Deal* and formulated renewed commitment to delivering on the SDGs in every relevant policy area, but remained relatively vague on how to achieve this.

o   For Asia and the Middle East, the picture of SDG adoption is mixed, although interesting initiatives have been taken. For instance, the *Belt and Road Initiative* (BRI) that was initiated by China to establish infrastructural connections between 136 countries in Asia and Europe, has embraced the SDGs. It puts the 2030 Agenda at the heart of China's 'Globalization 2.0' project.

o   In North America, the Canadian and Mexican governments have been integrating the SDG-agenda in their national policy frameworks, while the Trump administration in the US in many areas either terminated multilateral agreements (in particular the Paris Agreement), or reduced its efforts to support voluntary agreements like the SDGs.

■   **The role of governments in leveraging sufficient finance remains limited:** from the start of the SDG effort, it had been clear that a considerable finance gap needed to be bridged to achieve the SDG ambitions. UNCTAD (2014) estimated the world's total annual SDG investment needs at roughly $5–7 trillion a year, and total annual investments needs in SDG-relevant sectors in developing countries at between $3.3–4.5 trillion. The financing gap for delivering on the SDGs in developing countries has been assessed at $2.5–3 trillion annually (UN, 2019a), with the lowest-income countries facing the largest SDG financing gaps (Kharas and McArthur, 2019). Official Development Aid (ODA) can only fill a small part of the financing gap. Net ODA flows totalled $149 billion in 2018, down by 2.7% in real terms from 2017. Bilateral ODA to least developed countries fell by 3% in real terms as compared to 2017 (UN, 2019: 29). Only six ODA-providing countries met the internationally agreed upon target to keep ODA at or above 0.7 percent of GDP.

The contribution of the private sector to meeting finance and investment needs is hence considered crucial, but also requires effective regulation by national frameworks to prevent market and coordinating failures "that may cause SDG challenges to persist" (Kharas and McArthur, 2019: 2). The 2019 Financing for Sustainable Development Report – which organizes more than 60 international organizations like the UN, IMF and WTO – emphasized that 75% of individual investors are showing interest in investing in sustainable development (UN IATFD, 2019). This, however, needs to be matched by supportive financial systems and conducive, predictable and transparent national policy environments, in order to reduce investment risk and direct investments to prioritized sustainable development targets. Private financing depends on the availability of investable projects. The UN SDG progress report 2019 found that private investment flows were not well-aligned with sustainable development, although vast differences between countries exist.

▪ **Relatively low levels of coherence persist.** A result of the above processes has been that the level of coherence between national and global efforts is still relatively weak. Although the integrated nature of the SDGs requires governments to take an interlinked approach to environ-mental, social and economic goals and to work across policy silos and sectors, most progress tracking reports find a more or lesser skewed state of affairs. The *Measuring Distance to the SDG Targets* study of the OECD found that OECD countries are, on average, closest to achieving goals on energy, cities and climate (SDGs 7, 11, 13) and goals relating to the planet (SDGs 6, 12, 13, 14, 15). However, they are furthest from reaching goals related to inclusiveness and inequalities (SDGs 5 and 10) and food and institutions (SDGs 2 and 16). Based on 162 countries, SDSN and Bertelsmann Stiftung found that, on average, countries score worst on 'climate action' (SDG13), 'life below water' (SDG14) and 'life on land' (SDG15). Trends on threatened species and greenhouse gas emissions even show adverse development (Sachs et al., 2019). The report also points to the high socio-economic and environmental spill-over effects generated by high-income countries, for instance by their tolerance of poor labour standards and human rights violations in interna-tional supply chains, by importing commodities that trigger deforestation, or by tax evasion practices that undermine the ability of developing coun-tries, in particular, to raise public revenues (ibid: xi). As yet, the policy coherence of countries is difficult to determine and compare, as "there is no one-size-fits-all approach" that covers the breadth of national contexts (OECD, 2019b). By December 2019, the indicator for SDG-target 17.14

('enhance policy coherence for sustainable development') was still classified as Tier III.[11]

3.4.3 Societal: private sector and NGO involvement positive, but shallow

From the outset, the active involvement of stakeholders to implement the SDGs
at all levels was identified as a crucial condition for realizing the SDGs ambitions.
Only through a 'whole-of-society approach', in which societal actors align their
activities with the SDG-agenda, can efforts be scaled up. Societal involvement
showed great enthusiasm, both in the creation of the SDGs and in subsequent
initiatives in general – in particular from 'big business'. As yet, the results appear
relatively modest however. The following areas provide some key explanations as
to why, as a prelude to Part III.

■ **Regulation and market pull are lacking:** a UN Global Compact and
Accenture Strategy CEO Study on Sustainability (September 2019), based
on the responses of 1,000 CEOs across 21 industries and 99 countries,
suggests a number of key barriers that restrain corporate progress on the
SDGs: weak market forces, the lack of global regulatory frameworks and
structured policy and incentives to overcome them, and a lack of market
pull. Pressure to operate with extreme cost-consciousness against investing
in longer-term strategic objectives presents a key trade-off that companies
are facing.

■ **Limited link to core activities:** in 2018, the World Business Council for
Sustainable Development (WBCSD) conducted a global survey to explore
trends in how business has been working to align their activities with the
SDGs (WBCSD & DNV GL, 2018). The survey drew responses from
around 250 companies across 43 countries and 4 continents. Among the
survey's six key findings were the following: (1) there is plenty of support for
the SDGs by companies, (2) but efforts are not related to their core business, and (3) are generally aimed at a small number of relatively easy-to-
achieve SDGs, without attention to leverage and linkages with achieving
other SDG goals (the nexus). This can be partly explained by (4) a lack of
thorough understanding of the business case, and (5) a lack of clear and

---

11 As of March 2021, SDG-target 17.14 has a Tier II classification, being measured as "the
number of countries with mechanisms in place to enhance policy coherence of sustainable
development".

predictable government policies. Finally (6), SDG activities tend to be organized in communication and CSR departments, instead of being mainstreamed throughout all operations. The WBCSD found that companies embrace the SDGs particularly as an opportunity to innovate, gain reputation and create a better focus on sustainability strategies.

■ **Reactive approaches prevail:** management science research on how companies deal with the SDGs is still relatively scant (Van Tulder et al., 2021). Early overviews of a more detailed (target) level of ambition, strategy and execution show that companies embrace particularly those parts of the SDG-agenda that aim at relatively reactive motives – 'avoid doing harm' – rather than more proactive motives – aimed at 'doing good' – that serve the main ambition of the SDG-agenda (Van Zanten and Van Tulder, 2018). This provides an ethical, institutional and strategic explanation for early patterns of (slow) adoption. Many companies seem to treat the SDGs as a risk-mitigation strategy to deal with present reputational issues, rather than as future-oriented investment opportunities. The risk of SDG-washing is apparent and looms large if companies engage in 'cherry-picking' easy targets. In 2018, Global Compact asked companies to stop cherry-picking the SDGs in their reports, and to start prioritizing SDGs in an integrated manner by taking major trade-offs into account as well (the nexus challenge at the micro level).

■ **Effective reporting is only just starting:** the level of sophistication of corporate reporting as a licence to operate and source for stakeholder engagement and collective learning is a vital element for catalysing progress. More aligned, transformative and scaled-up implementation of the SDGs requires cross-sector partnerships. Many companies have started to report on their SDG-related activities, albeit in a rather skewed manner. A 2019 WBCSD follow-up study on sustainability reporting that included 159 companies from 34 countries, found that 95% of these companies recognized the SDGs in some way. However, reporting has been heavily focused on a limited number of SDGs: SDG8 ('decent work and economic growth'), SDG12 ('responsible consumption and production') and SDG13 ('climate action'). Least covered are SDG14 ('life below water'), SDG1 ('no poverty'), SDG10 ('reduced inequalities') and SDG16 ('peace, justice and strong institutions'). There seems to be a 'surge in ambitions' around cross-sector initiatives that address systemic issues, in particular around ecological issues such as food and land, nature, biodiversity and plastic waste.

■ **Limited benchmarking possible:** one way to stimulate progress is by benchmarking the results of companies. It enables scrutiny on performance claims and the risk of SDG-washing, thereby enhancing efforts to deliver on the SDGs. In general, progress by companies on contributing to the SDGs so far has been slow as many have not yet embraced the SDGs at a strategic level, have not targeted clear priorities, or have only marginally integrated these into activities in a fragmented way. Several new benchmarking initiatives have materialized to address this reality. The *World Benchmarking Alliance* (WBA), for instance, pursues a transformative ambition. It targets the SDG performance of 2,000 companies in 74 countries, identified to have the most impact across seven key 'transformation areas': Decarbonization and Energy; Food Systems; Circular; Digital; Financial; Urban; and Social. This 'SDG2000' benchmark intends to promote 'a race to the top' in which corporate leaders are motivated to do more, and laggards are held to account.

■ **NGOs remain ambiguous:** despite strong support by several leading environmental NGOs (like WWF and IUCN) for the SDG-agenda, many NGOs around the world have retained an ambiguous attitude towards SDG roll-out. The emphasis on the role of the private sector in achieving the SDGs heralded a breach with traditional thinking on sustainable development, in which leading roles were attributed to governments and NGOs. In a general 'low-trust' societal atmosphere (Chapter 1), even NGOs that acknowledge the importance of business in working towards sustainability are suspicious of how serious companies are in integrating the SDGs throughout their operations and (international) value chains. Still, various global ecological NGOs (WWF, IUCN) and social NGOs (in particular trade unions) have been actively participating in various initiatives and platforms around the world. It has been more difficult to organize greater institutional representation however. In the HLPF, for instance, NGOs have been marginally included (Hege et al., 2019: 23). Many individual NGOs have started to develop extensive portfolios of partnerships with targeted companies in which the SDG-agenda figures prominently. The early experience of these cross-sector partnerships is that they are difficult to manage and often rely on sponsoring, which, on average, makes them less transformational than envisioned (PrC, 2015).[12] In general, it proves difficult to organize effective partnerships. Chapters 5, 6 and 12 address the related governance challenges.

---

12 The Partnerships Resource Centre (PrC) at the Rotterdam School of Management, Erasmus University, conducts action research on increasing the transformational potential of in particular NGO–Company partnerships for the SDGs: https://www.rsm.nl/faculty-research/centres/partnerships-resource-centre/

3.5 CONCLUSION, TOOLS AND RESOURCES: A DECADE OF DELIVERY

September 2019 marked the end of the first four-year cycle of the SDG trajectory. Clearly, significant *formational* progress has been made: institutions and platforms were installed, there has been strong support from all parts of society, and many countries have taken up the challenge to various degrees. Review on the progress on *implementation and realization*, however, led to a 'wake-up call'. The world is not on track to meet the SDGs by 2030, progress has been too slow, and it has become clear that gradual or half-hearted approaches will not suffice. Accelerated action, raised ambitions, better integrated and more coherent approaches are needed to establish the required transformative change trajectories, and scale up impact. The UN declared the remaining ten years to achieve the 2030 Agenda as the *Decade of Action* so as to stress the urgent need for stepped-up efforts across sectors, borders and governance levels, by all state and non-state actors involved. This call for action appealed to the joint responsibility of the international community to seize the short window of opportunity that the SDGs provide amidst increasing geostrategic tensions. It also appealed to the responsibilities of country governments, companies, and all other societal stakeholders to contribute to collective action and deliver on their commitments. The call for a 'Decade of Action' also reiterates the joined-up, multilevel hybrid kind of governance approach documented in this chapter – with its strengths and obvious shortcomings. Stepped-up ambitions without major changes in the governance (and financing) structure might not create the decisive trajectory change that is direly needed. The prioritization of the nexus ambition, in particular, requires not only intellectual progress, but foremost also sophisticated translation into smart, actionable and scalable nexus projects, and therefore a much greater understanding on how to make that work.

Building upon the analytical and empirical challenges of the SDGs that were identified in Chapter 2, this chapter has documented the breadth of an impressive infrastructure of platforms and multi-stakeholder initiatives that developed to further shape and implement the SDGs. It also documented the reasons why progress is far from self-evident, uneven and too slow. Should we, therefore, turn around and 'skip the whole exercise', as some of the early critics would argue? Or should we try to more ambitiously address the voids, repair the gaps, deal with the governance flaws and accelerate the pace of initiatives? This book takes the latter approach. So far, efforts have resulted in a large number of pooled, collaborative, largely transparent and open (source/access) initiatives around data-gathering, case study coverage, indicator development, and exchange of information, knowledge and experiences. This in-between result should be considered an invaluable public good. The SDG-agenda can still be considered a real opportunity for the world to establish positive change towards a more sustainable future.

Whether ambitions will be achieved and a *Decade of Delivery* will materialize, depends on the level of cooperation between governments, international institutions, the private sector and civil society, as well as on the strategies adopted at the global, national and local levels. These should effectively address the many challenges and causes of stagnation that were identified in Part I (Chapters 1, 2 and 3). The SDGs can be considered a promising point of departure and an interesting breach with the 'old paradigm'. The open, joined-up, navigating and channelling approach taken represents a new, sensible and much-needed way of understanding and dealing with the challenges of our time. The SDGs can hence be considered a new 'paradigm'. A paradigm 'shift', however, is still awaited. The challenges underlying the SDGs are not straightforward to address, let alone resolve. The SDGs present a global *agenda* and a *frame*, not a fixed, spelt-out blueprint. The grand challenges of society as framed by the SDGs, require new approaches that go beyond the prevailing yet rather simplistic paradigms regarding the roles and responsibilities attributed to governments, companies and citizens in enhancing sustainable development. We will further elaborate this in Part II.

CRITICS OF THE SDGs WILL BE PROVEN RIGHT IF:

■ Complexity and systems thinking indeed lead to choice stress and a lack of priorities;

■ The finance gap for all these ambitions is not bridged with complementary action by societal stakeholders, including companies and civil society;

■ Companies and societal parties are unable to effectively fill the institutional void or partnering space that is required to overcome the tragedy of the commons and the bystander effect in order to develop more common goods;

■ Stakeholders look at the SDGs from a defensive point of view, rather than perceiving them as an opportunity;

■ Negative frames prevail, partly because positive adjustment strategies are not really implemented;

■ The dynamics of the transition remain poorly understood; for instance, that inclusiveness also requires some form of 'exclusiveness' and that sequencing of efforts is important;

■ There is limited 'fit' between the efforts of companies – often in partnerships – and the issue at hand;

■ Policymakers and strategists favour one-size-fits-all models; there are actually many models and solutions possible and needed, depending on contextual circumstances and the complexity of the challenge. Creative solutions require diverse approaches.

- The SDG-agenda introduced a novel multilevel hybrid governance mechanism to facilitate the double aim of its approach: a plan *of* action and a call *for* action for multiple global stakeholders.

- Hybrid governance is foremost aimed at *navigating* progress through establishing and scaling communities of change.

- The first cycle of implementation (2015–2019) of this hybrid governance system can be considered as a formation period; it has energized many (communities of) stakeholders to start contributing to the Global Goals.

- A major challenge is the degree of (horizontal and vertical) coherence that can be established through this hybrid governance system.

- To tackle relevant measurement gaps, international 'custodian' and 'partnering' agencies function as part of the networked governance structure of the SDGs; they also enable continuous indicator review and refreshment.

- Progress on implementing the SDG-agenda has been slow for at least five governance-related reasons: (1) the process of filling theoretical and empirical gaps is laborious; (2) effective (peer) learning is daunting, capacities are limited and diverging interests need to be aligned; (3) key stakeholders are not yet seizing the opportunities of the SDG approach; (4) 'coalitions of willing' actors participate, rather than coalitions of 'needed' actors; (5) modest development of 'nexus' communities (and of related tools); higher levels of coherence need to be established.

- Gradual approaches alone are not enough; there is growing consensus that accelerated action is direly needed and feasible; this needs to be based on better aligned and more profound cooperation between governments, agencies, companies and civil society across the world; insights into conducive conditions for action are growing.

- Critical reflection remains imperative: implementation of specific SDGs is not progressing fast enough, given the (geo)strategic challenges of a VUCA world.

- A critical attitude is needed to overcome the promise–performance gap ('walk the talk') and create legitimate participation of actors in the SDG effort; the risk of 'SDG-washing' is real.

- Companies that want to clinch the opportunities occasioned by the SDG approach need to respect critical implementation and strategizing conditions: make it core, become pro-active, search the nexus, innovate, create a strategic partnership portfolio, start reporting.

Throughout this chapter, several boxes already highlighted relevant databases, knowledge hubs and applications as part of the networked infrastructure that developed in the first cycle of implementation of the SDG-agenda. Here, we have selected several web resources that we consider useful entries for quick access to 'SDG essentials' on SDG progress data, key documents and processes, country efforts and news.

- **UN SDG Knowledge Platform:** Knowledge hub of the UN Division for Sustainable Development Goals that provides wide access to information and knowledge for sustainable development. It contains databases, analytical tools and resources, and access to the Voluntary National Review Database (VNRs), inputs to the High-level Political Forum (HLPF), the Partnerships Platform, SDG-related Topics. https://sustainabledevelopment.un.org/

- **UN Open SDG Data Hub:** To fully implement and monitor progress on the SDGs, decision makers everywhere need data and statistics that are accurate, timely, sufficiently disaggregated, relevant, accessible and easy to use. The Open SDG Data Hub promotes the exploration, analysis, and use of authoritative SDG data sources for evidence-based decision-making and advocacy. Its goal is to enable data providers, managers and users to discover, understand, and communicate patterns and interrelationships in the wealth of SDG data and statistics that are now available. Also provides access to the UN Sustainable Development Goals Reports. http://www.sdg.org/

- **UN System SDG Implementation database:** the UN family's repository of actions, initiatives and plans on implementation of the 2030 Agenda and SDGs. It contains information made available by UN system entities. It is searchable, regularly updated and serves as a useful reference tool for learning about what UN system entities have been doing in support of the implementation of the SDGs. https://sustainabledevelopment.un.org/content/unsurvey/index.html

- **UN Acceleration Actions:** A recently created database of voluntarily undertaken initiatives by national governments and any other non-state actors – individually or in partnership – to accelerate SDG implementation. Examples include: announcement of a new or enhanced policy, programme or project related to the achievement of one or more of the 17 SDGs or addressing the interlinked nature of the 2030 Agenda. https://sustainabledevelopment.un.org/sdgactions

- **UN Voluntary National Reviews database:** This online review platform is dedicated to compiling information from countries participating in the voluntary national reviews of the High-level Political Forum on Sustainable Development. Each country page includes, if available, VNRs, statements and UN webcast from the sessions at HLPF. Can be filtered by year and keyword. Also provides key preparation documents, guidelines, handbooks and synthesis reports. https://hlpf.un.org/vnrs

SELECTED WEB RESOURCES

S
E
L
E
C
T
E
D

W
E
B

R
E
S
O
U
R
C
E
S

■ ***Sustainable Development Report:*** annual progress reports on transformations to achieve the SDGs compiled by Sustainable Development Solutions Network and Bertelsmann Stiftung. Provides access to online interactive dashboards, country rankings and scores, country profiles and indicator profiles. https://www.sdgindex.org/

■ ***IISD SDG Knowledge Hub:*** For daily and free SDG news, expert commentary; includes a searchable database that can be filtered by SDG, issue, global partnership, actor, action and region. https://sdg.iisd.org/news/

REFERENCES

Abell, P. (2009). 'History, Case Studies, Statistics, and Causal Inference', *European Sociological Review* 25(5):561–567.

Beisheim, M. & Bernstein, S. (2020). 'Matching the HLPF's Ambition to Performance: Prospects for the Review', Guest article *IISD SDG Knowledge Hub*, 13 February.

Chattopadhyay, S. & Manea, S. (2019). *'Leave no one behind' index 2019*. Briefing note, September. London: Overseas Development Institute.

Davis, K., Fisher, A., Kingsbury, B. & Engle Merry, S. (Eds.) (2012). *Governance by Indicators. Global Power through Quantification and Rankings*. Oxford: Oxford University Press.

ECLAC (2019). *Quadrennial report on regional progress and challenges in relation to the 2030 Agenda for Sustainable Development in Latin America and the Caribbean*. Santiago: United Nations Economic Commission for Latin America and the Caribbean.

European Parliament (2019). *Europe's approach to implementing the Sustainable Development Goals: good practices and the way forward*, Directorate-General for External Policies, EP/EXPO/B/DEVE/2018/01.

Expert Group Meeting (2019). 'The Way Forward – Strengthening ECOSOC and the High-level Political Forum on Sustainable Development', 3–4 December 2019.

Gennari, P. & Navarro, D.K. (2020). 'Are We Serious About Achieving the SDGs? A Statistician's Perspective', *IISD SDG Knowledge Hub*, 14 January.

Gomme, J. (2019). 'Lead, transform, succeed: Translating global needs and ambitions into business solutions on the path to 2030'. In: Sachs, J., Schmidt-Traub, G., Kroll, C., Lafortune, G., Fuller, G. *Sustainable Development Report 2019*. New York: Bertelsmann Stiftung and Sustainable Development and Solutions Network (SDSN).

Hege, E., Barchiche, D., Rochette, J., Chabason, L. & Barthélemy, P. (2019). *Initial assessment and conditions for success of the 2030 Agenda for Sustainable Development*, IDDRI study, No. 7, October.

ICSU (2017). *A Guide to SDG Interactions: From Science to Implementation*. Paris: International Council for Science.

Kharas, H. & McArthur, J. (2019). *Building the SDG economy. Needs, spending, and financing for universal achievement of the Sustainable Development Goals*, Global Economy & Development, Brookings Working paper 131, 21 October.

Kroll, C. (2019). 'Long in words but short on action: UN sustainability goals are threatened to fail', press release 19 June 2019, Bertelsmann Stiftung.

MacFeely, S. (2019). *The Political Economy of Measuring the Sustainable Development Goals*, UNCTAD Research Paper No. 32, UNCTAD/SER.RP/2019/4, June.

Nilsson, M., Chisholm, E., Griggs, D., Howden-Chapman, P., McCollum, D., Messerli, P., Neumann, B., Stevance, A., Visbeck, M. & Stafford-Smith, M. (2018). 'Mapping interactions between the sustainable development goals: lessons learned and ways forward', *Sustainability Science*, 13(6):1489–1503.

Nilsson, M., Griggs, D. & Visbeck, M. (2016). 'Map the interactions between Sustainable Development Goals', *Nature*, 534(7607):320–322.

OECD (2019). *Measuring distance to the SDG Targets 2019. An Assessment of Where OECD Countries Stand*. Paris: OECD Publishing.

OECD (2019a). *Governance as an SDG Accelerator. Country Experiences and Tools*. Paris: OECD Publishing.

OECD (2019b). *Policy Coherence for Sustainable Development 2019: Empowering People and Ensuring Inclusiveness and Equality*. Paris: OECD Publishing.

OECD (2015). *Better Policies for Development 2015: Policy Coherence and Green Growth*, Paris: OECD Publishing.

OECD (2014). *All On Board. Making Inclusive Growth Happen*. OECD Initiative on Inclusive Growth. Paris: OECD Publishing

Pogge, T. & Sengupta, M. (2015). 'The Sustainable Development Goals (SDGs) as Drafted: Nice Idea, Poor Execution', *Washington International Law Journal*, 24(3):571–587.

PrC (2015). *The State of Partnerships Report – 2015. Civil Society Organisations (CSOs) Under Siege – can partnerships provide new venues?* Rotterdam: Partnerships Resource Centre at RSM-Erasmus University.

Sachs, J.D, Kroll, C., Lafortune, G., Fuller, G. & Woelm, F. (2021). *Sustainable Development Report 2021. The Decade of Action for the Sustainable Development Goals*. Cambridge: Cambridge University Press. DOI 10.1017/9781009106559.

Sachs, J.D., Schmidt Traub, G., Kroll, C., Lafortune, G. & Fuller, G. (2019). *Sustainable Development Report 2019*. New York: Bertelsmann Stiftung and Sustainable Development Solutions Network (SDSN), June.

Surasky, J. (2019). 'Towards Second-Generation Voluntary National Reviews', *IISD SDG Knowledge Hub*, 17 October. Retrieved from: http://sdg.iisd.org/commentary/guest-articles/towards-second-generation-voluntary-national-reports/.

UN (2019). *The Report of the Secretary General: The Special Edition of the Sustainable Development Goals Progress Report*. New York: United Nations.

UN (2019a). *United Nations Secretary-General's Roadmap for Financing the 2030 Agenda for Sustainable Development 2019–2021*, July. New York: United Nations.

UN (2018). *The Sustainable Development Goals Report 2018*. New York: United Nations.

UN (2015). *Transforming Our World: The 2050 Agenda for Sustainable Development*. New York: United Nations.

UN DESA (2019). *The Sustainable Development Goals Report 2019*. New York: United Nations.

UN ECOSOC (2019). *Report of the Inter-Agency and Expert Group on Sustainable Development Goal Indicators*, UN Statistical Commission 51st Session, E/CN.3/2020/2, 20 December 2019.

UN Global Compact & Accenture Strategy (2019). *The Decade to Deliver. A Call to Business Action. The United Nations Global Compact – Accenture Strategy CEO Study on Sustainability 2019*, September.

UN Independent Group of Scientists (2019). *Global Sustainable Development Report 2019: The Future is Now – Science for Achieving Sustainable Development*. New York: United Nations.

UN Inter-agency Task Force on Financing for Development (2019). *Financing for Sustainable Development Report 2019*. New York: United Nations.

UNCTAD (2014). *World Investment Report 2014. Investing in the SDGs: An Action Plan*. Geneva: United Nations Conference on Trade and Development.

UNDP (2017). *Institutional and Coordination Mechanisms. Guidance Note on Facilitating Integration and Coherence for SDG Implementation*. New York: United Nations Development Programme.

UNGA (2018). *Repositioning the United Nations development system in the context of the quadrennial comprehensive policy review of operational activities for development of the United Nations system*, Seventy-second session, A/RES/72/279, 1 June 2018.

UNGA (2016). *Critical milestones towards coherent, efficient and inclusive follow-up and review at the global level – Report of the Secretary-General*, seventieth session, A/70/684, 15 January 2016.

UNGA (2016a). *Follow-up and review of the 2030 Agenda for Sustainable Development at the global level*, seventieth session, A/RES/70/299, 18 August 2016.

Van Tulder, R., Rodrigues, S.B., Mirza, H. & Sexsmith, K. (2021). 'The UN's Sustainable Development Goals: Can multinational enterprises lead the Decade of Action?', *Journal of International Business Policy*, 4(1):1–21.

Van Zanten, J.A. & Van Tulder, R. (2018). 'Multinational enterprises and the Sustainable Development Goals: An institutional approach to corporate engagement', *Journal of International Business Policy*, (1):208–233.

WBCSD & DNV GL (2018). *Business and the SDGs: A survey of WBCSD members and Global Network partners*. World Business Council for Sustainable Development, July.

Weitz, N., Carlsen, H., Nilsson, M. & Skånberg, K. (2018). 'Towards systemic and contextual priority setting for implementing the 2030 Agenda', *Sustainability Science*, 13(2):531–48.

World Bank Group (2019). *Implementing the 2030 Agenda. 2018 Update*. Washington DC: World Bank Group.

Young, O.R. (2017). 'Conceptualization: Goal Setting as a Strategy for Earth System Governance'. In: Kanie, N. & Biermann, F. (Eds.), *Governing through Goals: Sustainable Development Goals as Governance Innovation*, (pp. 31–52). Cambridge, Massachusetts: The MIT Press.

PART II: WHAT AND WHO?

SOCIETAL AND DYNAMIC PRINCIPLES

The SDGs as wicked problems or wicked opportunities: Who should address what?

In Part I, we argued that the Sustainable Development Goals (SDGs) highlight a paradigm shift in the thinking on and approaches to the 'grand' and 'systemic' challenges of the present. The 2030 Agenda, an ambitious effort of multilateralism that is simultaneously networked with corporate actors, national governments and civil society stakeholders, is probably the only feasible approach to cope with systemic challenges. But we live in a so-called 'VUCA world' (Chapter 1). A Volatile, Uncertain, Complex and Ambiguous world generates *divergence* and rivalry with highly uncertain outcomes. This uncertainty and rivalry is not incidental but systemic, and needs to be understood as the expression of longer-term change generated by the rise and decline of techno-economic paradigms and related societal models. The stakes are consequently high. The 2030 Agenda, with its SDGs, presented a timely venturous strategy to create *convergence* around common goals. It introduced a framework of common principles through coordinated processes of multi-stakeholder engagement (Chapter 2), which should help organizations to consider the conditions under which they need to develop transformative sustainable development strategies.

Key principles on fundamental 'why' questions introduced in Part I include:

- **Holistic:** a holistic and integrated view is needed because of paralleled systemic failures and increased rivalry;
- **Inclusive:** the principle of 'no one left behind' applies as a minimum benchmark for successful approaches;

DOI: 10.4324/9781003098355-5

- **Partnering** is important to create 'procedural justice' in working towards the four other principles: People, Planet, Prosperity and Peace;

- **Legitimacy** is at stake; all actors need to address the increased trust gap that is associated with major transitions, in order to support positive change (race to the top) and depress negative change sentiments;

- **Common purpose-driven change** creates opportunities, but requires constant feedback and learning on what works and what does not work;

- **Core**: companies, governments and civil society organizations should embrace the SDGs as part of their core strategy and responsibility, not as add-on philanthropic activity;

- **Divergent roads** are not necessarily a problem; they drive and shape the required change dynamics, but should be 'channelled' in order to address voids, fill remaining gaps and develop better approaches through the engagement of multiple stakeholders.

The experience of the first four-year cycle of the SDG journey shows that the process is not progressing at the required pace and scale for a variety of reasons. Stepped-up efforts at all levels of society, across all sectors and by all parties involved are required (Chapter 3). But *who* is going to address *what*, and based on what principles?

Part II considers the next steps in delineating *Principles of Sustainable Business* regarding 'what' and 'who' questions. Who should address what issues? *What* does a systemic and principled approach to grand challenges entail, and what does an inappropriately aligned approach imply ('what if')? The SDG-agenda represents complex challenges that are quickly denounced as 'too complex' to deal with. 'Wicked problems theory' shows that the latter question, in particular, reflects the challenge of linking what and who questions. *Who* is going to address what challenges (and when)? Part II uses systems, complexity, ethical and governance (agency) theory to clarify and define principles of taking, assigning and having responsibility for addressing each of the SDGs. In three chapters, Part II develops a consistently built up, step-by-step *framework of societal triangulation*. It introduces methods that enable the analysis of relevant dimensions of complexity and main societal sources of wickedness while taking into account hybrid forms of organizations and governance. Part II also delineates relevant approaches to societal challenges, in terms of appropriate intervention levels and partnership configurations that can be considered best fit to trigger the kind of change processes required.

WHAT IF?

Chapter 4 explains the implications of looking at the nature of the challenges posed by the SDGs in terms of *wicked problems*. Wicked problems are complexly dynamic and systemic and do not have (clear) solutions – only solution-oriented approaches that require multi-stakeholder action. The chapter inquires how 'wicked' the various challenges as specified by the SDGs are, and what type of ambiguities they represent. The chapter defines a wickedness scale consisting of *ten complexity dimensions* to delineate the *degree of wickedness* of a societal problem. Assessing the various degrees of the complexities involved can indicate the extent to which collective action is needed. Chapter 4 illustrates how these scales can be applied to various SDGs and what techniques can be used – even by non-experts – to assess the 'wickedness' of targeted parts of the SDG-agenda.

WHAT AND WHO?

Chapter 5 changes the perspective drastically by looking at the SDGs as *wicked opportunities*: through the creation of 'synergistic value' and 'collaborative advantage'. It considers the question of *who* should be involved in addressing specific societal challenges. The chapter introduces a 'societal triangulation' technique. By defining the societal origins of the problem, it becomes possible to understand who is best positioned to take responsibility for addressing the problem effectively. The chapter distinguishes *four intervention levels* at which societal issues occur and change processes can be initiated. These are based on a more detailed understanding of the primary (or fiduciary) duties of actors within three distinct yet complementary societal sectors (state, market, civil society), and the extent to which they can be held responsible for the consequences of their action – or inaction. The more complex the sustainability challenge, the more collective action is needed. Consequently, Chapter 5 defines the 'partnering space' as the logical 'arena' in which to address the most transformative ambitions of the SDG-agenda. We will argue that many partnerships have been created as 'coalitions of the willing' that do not necessarily align with the wicked nature of the problem. The final part of this chapter hence introduces a supportive step-by-step approach to consider whether the *partnership configuration* adopted can be considered to match the level of societal complexity involved, and what improvements are needed to make the partnership set-up 'fit for purpose'.

WHO?

Chapter 6 considers the *governance challenge* posed by the SDG-agenda in more detail: how to move from a primarily rules-based governance model and a narrow view on 'fiduciary duty' to a more principles-based governance model that includes a broader take on fiduciary responsibilities. Throughout the years, a large variety of organizational forms has developed in response to societal challenges that necessitated a different take on organizing. Chapter 6 further fine-tunes our understanding of the rich variety of *hybrid* organizational forms and consequent approaches to societal challenges. It first defines the kind of *societal interfaces* that different organizational forms have been designed to manage. To some extent, hybrids may be better able to deal with certain types of sustainability challenges. But hybridization also poses additional *responsible governance* challenges. The higher the degree of complexity involved, the more difficult it is to create hybrid organizations that can deal with all governance challenges effectively. At the international level, hybridity takes the form of simultaneously dealing with distinct governance contexts. Organizations that internationalize their upstream and downstream activities across national borders have to deal with different CSR/sustainability regimes. Whereas international treaties between countries provide for some extent of governance, a largely unmitigated and unregulated space exists at the global scale. This global governance gap is the space where the SDG-agenda aims to facilitate positive change that stimulates a 'race to the top' rather than a 'race to the bottom'.

4 WHAT IF?
THE SDGs AS WICKED PROBLEMS

DOI: 10.4324/9781003098355-6

- **Wickedness principle:** wicked problems cannot be solved, only addressed. There are no optimal ('best') or moral ('right' or 'wrong') solutions to wicked problems, only solution-oriented *approaches* with unknown outcomes.

- **Intellectual principle:** develop a high 'tolerance for ambiguity' to resist thinking in false/misleading contradictions, tensions or trade-offs. Practice paradoxical thinking.

- **Ethical principles:** in particular 'consequential ethics' and 'participatory ethics' principles need to be applied when addressing wicked problems. Wicked problems have no stopping rule; they require constant feedback, contextualization, fine-tuning and involvement of stakeholders to adjust for unforeseen effects and continuously improve interventions.

- **Multidimensionality and pluralism principle:** definitional ambiguity increases with higher degrees of wickedness. Identifying a multitude of definitions, diversity of views and stands – rather than a single approach, theory or method – helps in assessing relevant dimensions of the problem.

- **Participatory principle:** the involvement of multiple stakeholders is not only a way to collect useful information and insights, but also allows to experiment and learn what works and what does not (applying principles of developmental evaluation).

- **Integrative assessment principle:** develop an analytical and reflective attitude that takes all five complexity categories into account: (1) structural, (2) generative, (3) dynamic, (4) communicative and (5) societal complexities.

- **'Wisdom of the crowd' principle:** the combination of multiple, independent judgements of diverse (and relatively uninformed) groups is often more accurate than the professional judgement, prediction or forecast of individual experts. Decisions resulting from the aggregation of information in diverse groups reduces cognitive biases. Harnessing collective intelligence is especially suitable for analyzing wicked problems, provided that sufficient diversity is guaranteed: variance in approach, diversity in thoughts, backgrounds and interests, and across rational and information 'bubbles'.

- **Peer review principle:** create the highest possible consensus on the quality of an assessment.

- **Sociocratic principles:** reaching agreement and group decisions on the basis of equal participation and joint assessment. Principles include equivalence, consent (rather than consensus), effectiveness, intentionality, empiricism, distributive leadership and transparency.

4.1   INTRODUCTION: THE SDGs AS 'WICKED PROBLEMS'

"The best path to addressing wicked problems is
that collaborative, dialogic, and inherently democratic process
which brings the relevant actors together in dialogue"
Sandra Waddock

When confronted with problems, we generally think of them as either simple or complex. Simple or 'tame' problems are (relatively) easy to solve: the problem can be unambiguously defined, approaches and principles for working towards the desired outcome are known and clear, and solutions are either correct or incorrect. Complicated or complex problems, on the other hand, resist solution: the exact nature of the problem, solution and cause–effect relations are unclear but can be known over time. Coming up with adequate solutions then often requires other ways of thinking, or a rethinking of dominant mental models, theoretical insights, values and convictions.

Some problems go *beyond* being complex, however: so-called 'wicked problems'. Wicked problems even *resist definition*: each problem appears to be a symptom of other problems and cannot be properly understood without a proposed solution in mind. The nature and extent of the problem, cause–effect relations and solutions are mostly unclear, unknown, ambiguous and unstable. Moreover, since there is no credible way of structuring, fully understanding and defining the problem, it is impossible to know when it has been satisfactorily resolved. Consequently, wicked problems have no 'stopping rule' that signifies the problem's end. Wicked problems require not only new and different ways and frames of thinking, but also need the involvement of a variety of interested parties to address them (Table 4.1).

Most of today's pervasive problems created by a VUCA world (Chapter 1) are increasingly wicked. They are systemic, complexly interrelated and materialize at the interface between public–private and profit/non-profit interests. They are wicked both by nature and by design (Nie, 2003), the latter referring to the 'politicization' of problems by interest groups and various societal stakeholders through 'manufactured conflict'. Wicked problems pose analytical, conceptual and myriad governance and administrative challenges (Head and Alford, 2015; Daviter, 2017; 2017a; McConnell, 2018), as "one cannot understand the problem without knowing about its context; one cannot meaningfully search for information without the orientation of a solution concept; one cannot first understand, then solve" (Rittel and Webber, 1973: 162). Hence, wicked problems are intellectually challenging and tough to address – let alone to 'resolve'. Addressing wicked problems often requires a significant systems change, which involves profound shifts in the dynamics of multiple, interactive yet independent institutions organized around the problem domain, in desired directions over time (Waddock et al., 2015). This entanglement of challenges creates tenacious barriers that cannot be tackled unilaterally by either firms, governments or civil society organizations.

This chapter applies wicked problems thinking to the SDG-agenda. Wicked problems theory builds on chaos theory and 'complex systems theory', which observe that people and their environment are part of a complicated network or

Table 4.1 Simple, complex and wicked problems compared

SIMPLE – TAME	COMPLICATED – COMPLEX	WICKED
RELATIVELY EASY TO SOLVE	**RESISTS SOLUTION**	**RESISTS DEFINITION**
Clear problem with a clear solution	The problem and solution are not clear, but can be understood with time	Boundaries of the problem and its workings are ill-structured and unclear; problem and solution are not understood and keep shifting when we try to define them
Single-loop learning required: incremental, transfer of existing knowledge and solutions	Double-loop learning required: restructuring and reform; reflection and critical analysis needed	Triple-loop learning required: transformational mindsets searching for new realities; taking action in order to discover the workings of cause–effect dynamics; *de*-learning, *re*learning and breakthrough thinking needed
Leading question: 'Are we doing things right?'	Leading question: 'Are we doing the right things?'	Leading question: 'Are we doing the right things right?'
• Predictable • Straightforward • Obvious • Quantifiable	• Many elements, but the elements themselves are familiar • Hidden root causes • Non-linear • Inter-operating parts affect each other	• Many elements, of which many are hidden / disguised / hitherto unknown • Cognitive, strategic and institutional uncertainty • Complex and multi-layered relations and interdependencies • Chaotic, with (largely) unpredictable dynamics; open-ended • Many stakeholders with conflicting perspectives and spheres of influence; fragmentation • Strong social aspects • Involves changes in belief, behaviour and/or identity • No right or wrong solution • Vital intangible, non-quantifiable elements • No precedent
Technical / Technological Focus	Organizational Focus	Societal Focus

Sources: based on Rittel and Webber (1973); mofox.com; Olsson et al. (2010); Strijker-van Asperen and Van Tulder (2016); Waddock et al. (2015); Alford and Head (2017).

system of interactions. Action and reaction are thereby interlinked in a rather unpredictable manner, which makes it difficult to develop effective strategies. The original wicked problems approach was introduced in 1973 by urban design scientists Horst Rittel and Melvin Webber, who were dealing with complex urban planning challenges for which they could not define adequate rational planning approaches. Since Rittel and Webber, thinking in terms of wicked problems to address complex challenges of all kinds has proven appealing. Research in many scientific areas – including management sciences, policy studies, environmental sciences, educational research and urban studies – has created many insights. However, the concept has also become inflated, overstretched and used (or misused) as a 'buzzword' or an excuse to essentially state that a more precise conceptualization of a problem, or distinguishing between different degrees of 'wickedness', is not possible. Critical assessments of the present state of wicked problems research conclude that "there is extensive literature on complexity and wicked problems, but limited efforts to link sets of ideas in thinking about their implications for systems" (Waddock et al., 2015: 996). In particular, when used in policy practice, the concept "tends to provoke either paralysis or an overestimation of what policy can do about wicked problems" (Termeer et al., 2019: 1). Chapter 1 identified paralysis as a typical characteristic of a VUCA world.

We therefore face the challenge of applying *second-generation* wicked problems thinking (Head, 2019), which should aim for a better framing of problems and the further development of analytically more precise tools to define dimensions of wicked problems – such as conflict, complexity and uncertainty (Termeer et al., 2019). This chapter and the next use the SDG-agenda to delineate a second-generation approach that stresses not only problems (Chapter 4), but also the potential for opportunities (Chapter 5). This chapter first elaborates on what generic dimensions of wickedness can be distinguished and how these, in general, apply to the SDG-agenda (section 4.2). Next, we specify distinct sources of ambiguity in addressing the SDGs (section 4.3) in order to define ten basic dimensions of complexity that can help in assessing the nature and degree of wickedness of specific SDGs and SDG-targets (section 4.4). Techniques will be introduced to delineate both the nature and degrees of wickedness and to come to a shared understanding of the challenge posed by each SDG, even if not all information is available. Section 4.5 synthesizes, by relating the ten complexity dimensions to VUCA dynamics and providing supportive tools.

4.2 DIMENSIONS OF WICKEDNESS

Wicked problems are characterized by dynamic, interlinked issues that both drive and shape complex systems consisting of diverse stakeholders with varying world views and interests. As such, wicked problems demand systemic, emergent and participatory approaches that include a wide range of societal actors. This is challenging, as the boundary-spanning and ambiguous nature of wicked problems tends to generate conflict among multiple stakeholders who attempt to frame, analyse and act on them in line with their own perceptions, needs and interests. These conflicts themselves often create misleading frames that complicate matters more, and so increase the level of wickedness. Wicked problems are prone to creating ideological battles. Paradoxically, however, wicked problems can probably only be resolved by collective action and engaging a considerable diversity of stakeholders in creating and implementing progress. A more inclusive and comprehensive approach to addressing wicked problems is increasingly considered "not to be a curse, but the cure" (Daviter, 2017a: 574).

WICKED VERSUS TAME

A 'tame problem' on the other hand, is one for which more traditional, linear thinking and decision-making is sufficient to produce a workable solution within an acceptable time frame. A tame problem:

- Has a well-defined and stable *problem statement* (very often on a technical level);

- Has a definite *stopping point*: the moment at which the solution is found (which solves the problem);

- Has a solution which can be evaluated as either *right or wrong*;

- Belongs to a *class of similar problems* that can be solved in a similar way (and for which scientific knowledge in a more traditional sense is applicable);

- Has solutions which can quickly be tried and abandoned, '*trial and error*' (which makes it easier to evaluate and monitor progress during implementation);

- Comes with a *limited set of alternatives* (making it relatively easy to define what works best).

The distinction between 'tame' and 'wicked' should not be confused with 'easy' and 'hard' problems. Many tame problems are indeed quite hard, yet can surely be solved when given sufficient time. To illustrate, putting a man on the moon was a problem which initially looked extremely daunting. As soon as the political will and the funding were there to enable the project, however, the 'giant leap for mankind' appeared to contain surprisingly many tame elements. The problem definition – putting a man on the moon and returning him safely – did not change over time. There was a clear point of accomplishment (successfully putting the man on the moon), and the various solutions that were experimented with could be clearly evaluated as having either succeeded or failed. Most of the problems were technical in nature and could be addressed through accumulated and established knowledge in other scientific areas. Alternatives were not too diverse to pose a very complex selection environment. The objective of putting a man on the moon could not have been achieved one century earlier however. It required a certain level of technological progress and favourable contextual conditions. It has also become clear, afterwards, that putting a man on the moon did not solve the more complex, even wicked problems for which the endeavour was also intended: US rivalry with the Soviet Union, American economic decline and global leadership, changes in technology, or any other problems in the US economy. Consequently, ambitions withered in the space programme as soon as the hegemonic rivalry with the Soviet Union was (temporarily) settled with the end of the cold war in 1989 (Chapter 1).

TECHNICAL OR SOCIETAL

The more 'societal' and the less 'technical' a challenge is, the greater its potential to become wicked. The original thinkers behind the wicked problems idea in 1973 already argued that we increasingly live in a time where most problems cannot be solved by planning, as both the observed conditions of societal issues and the desired conditions have become almost indeterminable. As Rittel and Webber put it (1973: 155, 159, 162, 168):

■ "The classical systems approach . . . is based on the assumption that a planning project can be organized into distinct phases: 'understand the problems or the mission', 'gather information', 'analyze information', 'synthesize information and wait for the creative leap', 'work out solution' or the like. For wicked problems, however, this type of scheme does not work."

■ "As we seek to improve the effectiveness of actions in pursuit of valued outcomes, as system boundaries get stretched, and as we become more sophisticated about the complex workings of open societal systems, it becomes ever more difficult to make the planning idea operational."

■ "In a pluralistic society there is nothing like the undisputable public good. . . . In a setting in which a plurality of publics is politically pursuing a diversity of goals, how is the larger society to deal with its wicked problems in a planful way?"

They recognized that a rational-technical policy design for complex (societal) problems generates mere compartmentalized, artificial 'would-be' solutions that may well suppress some of the symptoms temporarily ('taming the problem'), but will eventually lead to even greater undesired consequences. Mis-fitting the level of societal complexity at hand inevitably results in governance failure.

Since Rittel and Webber's seminal paper, many others have followed through on this theme by arguing that wicked problems particularly require leadership, other manners of diagnosis and thinking, other ways of governance and organizing, perhaps even other types of science and research (Grint, 2008). Rittel and Webber themselves had neither an answer nor a theory on how to dispel wickedness, but effectively called for *awareness* on dealing more wisely with these kinds of intractable problems. It has inspired scholars and practitioners to come up with collective, more solid and discursive ways of dealing with wicked problems. This section will further explain what this line of thinking implies for a correct understanding of the SDGs.

WHY NO 'WICKED' SOLUTIONS?

The originators of the wicked problems theory were very clear about the potential for wicked problems to be solved. They concluded that "social problems are never solved. At best, they are only *resolved* – over and over again" (Rittel and Webber, 1973: 160). They specifically distinguished wicked problems from tame problems based on this insolvability. Wicked problems are characterized by high degrees of complexity, erratic dynamics and ambiguity. According to Laurence Peter, "you have to be highly intelligent and well informed just to be undecided about them". Various scholars have described wicked problems as being so 'messy', 'intractable', 'uncontrollable', 'contested' and 'recalcitrant' (Fischer, 1993; Crowley and Head, 2017) that, at best, they can only be "alleviated, superseded, transformed, and otherwise dropped from view" (Wildavsky, 1979; in Daviter, 2017a: 571). Bardi (2015) even asserted that "in a complex system, there are neither problems, nor solutions. There is only change and adaptation." Xiang (2013), who performed a literature overview of wicked problems theory, does not even mention the verb 'to solve' as part of wicked problems thinking.

Nevertheless, thinking in terms of solutions instead of problems is not only tempting, but also preferred by many management scholars and consultants. Policymakers demand solutions as well. Thinking in terms of 'best practice', 'reduction of random events' and the controlling of 'disequilibria' and 'imbalances' still prevails in management thinking. Uncertainty and complexity are usually thought of as conditions that should be contained, managed and preferably eliminated. For wicked problems, however, there are no optimal ('best') or moral ('right' or 'wrong') solutions, only *solution-oriented approaches* with unknown outcomes. Nor are wicked problems amenable to resolution by employing contemporary tools for strategy analysis and decision-making. Conventional strategic management models are generally rendered impotent in the face of wicked problems (Fahey, 2016: 29). (Chapter 5 considers whether 'wicked opportunities' is a better frame than 'solutions' for wicked problems.)

WICKED EQUALS CLUMSY

In order to get out of this predicament, some authors have suggested character-izing solution-oriented approaches to wicked problems as the search for 'poly-rational' or, more provocatively, 'clumsy' solutions. This idea originates from cultural theory (Verweij et al., 2006), a conceptual framework that distinguishes types of rationalities in explaining societal conflict over risk. The concept of 'clumsy solutions' advises against pursuing 'perfect' solutions for uncertain, complex and normative problems, but instead searching for just-viable solutions.[1] The idea is to mix all possible ways of thinking, perceiving and organizing as a technique to 'reduce the unexpected' (Hartmann, 2012). The design method for generating clumsy solutions is based on the recognition that policy efforts need to be as diverse as contemporary sustainability problems are (Ney and Verweij, 2015). It also reflects the importance of dialogue-based problem-solving approaches that combine a variety of perspectives on society's wicked problems and possible ways to resolve them. A clumsy solution, consequently, is one that everyone can more or less agree with. It is not as perfect – and might look a little inept, even 'messy', being patched together from different frames – yet is respon-sive to different rationalities (ibid). IIASA research suggests that clumsy solutions tend to be the more successful ones (Verweij et al., 2011). Clumsy policies – those that involve all voices to reach a negotiated compromise – were found to be the more robust ones; others encountered so much opposition that they were often not implemented, or did not last.

SO, WHAT ABOUT THE SDGs?

The SDG approach, as discussed in Chapters 2 and 3, can be considered well aligned with the basics of wicked problems thinking (Table 4.2). But not all wicked problems are equally intractable, and not all SDGs are equally wicked. Where problems are conceptually complex and sources of knowledge frag-mented and disputed, uncertainty and ambiguity thrive. Entangled complexity creates various sources of ambiguity in assessing the SDGs (section 4.3), which in turn poses an analytical challenge as not all problems are necessarily equally wicked (section 4.4).

---

1   Cybernetics research uses different adjectives, such as 'messy' (Metlay and Sarewitz, 2012) or 'fragmented' (Conklin, 2006). Management research also refers to the iterative process of strategy formulation and implementation as 'tinkering' (Mintzberg, 1980), 'muddling through' (Crilly et al., 2012) or comparable synonyms, all referring to the fact that even successful strategies never evolve as perfect planning exercises.

Table 4.2 The SDGs mirror generic aspects of wickedness

Generic aspects of wickedness	The SDGs are...
Wicked versus tame?	... *wicked*; all elements from Table 4.1 apply. Problem definitions are rather broad and inescapably vague to various degrees; no clear stopping point (except from the 'achievement' ambition set by 2030); no right or wrong solutions as many different yet interdependent (national) realities exist, context-specificity is key; potentially unlimited alternatives and nexuses apply that can either enhance or frustrate interventions (unintended, unforeseen or unexpected consequences).
Technical or societal?	... *societal*: multilevel and cross-sectoral organizational, governance and policy approaches prevail; significant gaps remain in the understanding of what makes approaches successful and scalable; intentionally, no choice is made for any specific technical solution (not *against* one either).
Solutions or approaches?	... *approaches* oriented: the SDG-agenda does not define one-size-fits-all solutions, but delineates a variety of approaches, pathways and entry points, and applies participation principles and actionable solutions-*oriented* directions (no concrete solutions) towards agreed goals and targets for 2030.
Wicked equals clumsy?	... *basically 'clumsy'*: multi-stakeholder, dialogue-based and consensus-oriented approaches prevail; based on 'examining, empowering and enacting change', learning by doing, mutual exchange and continuous review; coalitions of willing parties develop approaches and stepping stones along the way and engage in bottom-up dialogue and action agendas, rather than top-down planning exercises.

4.3 SOURCES OF COMPLEXITY AND AMBIGUITY IN ASSESSING THE SDGs

Wicked problems are called 'wicked' for a reason: there are limits to a profound and detailed understanding of their exact nature, their workings and the likely effects of interventions. Nevertheless, we should not treat wicked problems as black holes of indivisible and massive uncertainty, ambiguity and chaos. To quote former US Secretary of Defence Donald Rumsfeld in a television interview: "There are known knowns. These are things we know that we know. There are known unknowns. That is to say, there are things that we know we don't know. But there are also unknown unknowns. There are things we don't know we don't know." Complexity comes in degrees. Certain dimensions of complexity can be reduced as we gradually become more knowledgeable about them in empirical, analytical and conceptual terms. With regard to the more abstract and unquantifiable dimensions of complexity, concepts like memes, sense-making and narratives are used to capture more tacit and intuitive ways of 'knowing' and the deeper structures of 'meaning'.

Part I already provided evidence of the considerable degree of complexity related to the SDGs, due to the existence of both known and unknown 'knowns' and 'unknowns'. The dynamics of a VUCA world tend to exacerbate these complexities, often reinforcing uncertainty and ambivalence on such vital matters as what knowledge to rely on, what sources of information to trust, how to know whether actions will have the intended outcomes, and how to prevent negative side-effects from occurring. In this section, we distinguish three sources of ambiguity that, to varying extents, are part of the wicked nature of many of the SDGs:

1   Knowledge ambiguities: Do/can we know? (sections 4.3.1 and 4.3.2)

2   Predictive ambiguities: Can we predict? (section 4.3.3)

3   Intervention ambiguities: Can we intervene to reach the intended effect(s)? (section 4.3.4)

4.3.1   Knowledge ambiguities: definition disputes

The knowledge base of each of the SDGs requires a considerable amount of basic data and sophisticated information. Relevant information on achieving the SDGs – particularly in poorly governed or unstable regions of the world – is often incomplete, hidden, disguised or intangible. Also, definitions of the problem may change over time, may not capture the whole of the phenomenon or are considered inconvenient, impractical, conflicting or irrelevant, and thus politically contested. Key disputes include those related to definitions of 'poverty', 'health and well-being', and 'biodiversity.

WHAT DEFINES 'POVERTY' (SDG1)?

SDG1 aims to 'eradicate extreme poverty for all people everywhere' by the year 2030. Extreme poverty is thereby defined as 'people living on less than $1.25 a day' (SDG-target 1.1), with reference to the international poverty line as an absolute global minimum. Although in 2008, this line had indeed been established at $1.25 per day, it was updated to $1.90 per day in 2015. The poverty line measure has been an important yardstick for progress in the global agenda. The degree of success of the Millennium Development Goals, for instance, had been illustrated by a decrease in people living in absolute poverty. According to this yardstick, extreme poverty decreased by more than a billion people, from 36% of the world population in 1990 to 10% (736 million people) in 2015. However, most of the gains were achieved in one country: China. In sub-Saharan Africa, the trend was less favourable, with more than 40% of people still living in extreme poverty by 2015; in absolute numbers, sub-Saharan Africa has more extremely poor people than in the rest of the world combined (World Bank, 2018).

With an increasingly wealthier world, the realization has grown that this global absolute yardstick is probably too low and not sufficiently specific to allow for (between and within) regional differences. The relevance of the poverty line depends on the context in which people earn an income. According to the World Bank (2018), the threshold of extreme poverty in lower-middle income countries hence is more appropriately set at $3.20 a day, for higher-middle income countries at $5.50 a day, whereas in high-income countries living on $5.50 a day is impossible. If adjusted for these figures, the actual SDG1 ambition would thus become more challenging than currently defined in official metrics: with a quarter of the world's population earning less than $3.20, and half of the world's population earning less than $5.50 a day.

In 2018, the World Bank introduced the *societal poverty line* to mirror the costs of 'basic needs' related to the typical level of consumption and income in every country. The societal poverty line measure combines extreme poverty, which is fixed, with relative dimensions of well-being that are country-specific. By this yardstick, in 2015, 2.1 billion people were poor relative to their societies, which is three times the number of people living in extreme poverty (ibid). It is even more challenging to apply the definition of 'extreme' or 'absolute' poverty as formulated in the UN Copenhagen Declaration (1995): "a condition characterized by severe deprivation of basic human needs, including food, safe drinking water, sanitation facilities, health, shelter, education and information. It depends not only on income but also on access to services." To meet this broader view on poverty, the World Bank developed the *multidimensional poverty measure*, which recognizes that poverty is a much more entrenched problem that not only relates to income but also to consumption, education and access to basic utilities and services such as healthcare and security.

One positive development from a justice point of view (**SDG16**) has been that many countries have adopted a 'minimum wage'. However, the metric attached to this principle regularly obscures the discussion since it is often set at a level below subsistence. In the context of the supply chain (**SDG12**), the concept of 'living wage' is considered more appropriate. From a macro-economic perspective, poverty is related to income 'inequalities' (**SDG10**) as an indicator of 'relative poverty'. Research into the origins of happiness and criminality has found that it is not so much absolute levels of income that define happiness (high income) or criminality (low income), but rather the degree of income inequality: **SDG10** (inequality) and **SDG1** are thus closely related (Peterson, 2018). This linkage was found relevant to national economies, but has also been relevant for the internal management of companies and towards their suppliers (**SDG12**). Companies that source from developing countries are faced with a more advanced discussion on what actually defines a 'living income' and a 'fair wage', for which the metrics of SDG1 do not yet provide benchmarks.

WHAT DEFINES HEALTH AND WELL-BEING (SDG3)?

Issues such as 'health' are equally ambiguous. **SDG3** aims to 'ensure healthy lives and promote well-being for all at all ages'. Its underlying targets focus on health-related issues like reducing maternal mortality rates, eradicating preventable deaths of newborns, ending epidemics of AIDs, tuberculosis and neglected or non-communicable diseases, and strengthening the prevention of substance abuse related to drugs and alcohol. It also targets universal access to healthcare services, and preventing deaths and illness from hazardous chemicals and air, water and soil pollution. Health can be defined as the absence of death or disease but is also related to a sense of well-being. It has a curative and a preventive side, a mental and a physical side. But how can we understand the relationship between individual appraisal of 'health' and 'well-being', 'public health', 'basic health', and their related responsibilities, costs and benefits?

Since 2000, major advancements have been made in individual healthcare: the number of children who die before the age of five has fallen by half, and the average life expectancy of the global population has reached 72 years – a gain of 5.5 years between 2000 and 2016, the fastest increase since the 1960s (WHO, GHO-data). The average life expectancy in the African region even increased by 10.3 years in the same period, to 61.2 years. Malaria, tuberculosis and HIV/AIDs are in retreat. The costs of healthcare, however, have skyrocketed in many countries. Many people still have no access to adequate healthcare, health insurance, or medication at affordable prices. In many countries, the healthcare system is considered to be inefficient and skewed towards rich people, which in turn has negative effects on economic growth (**SDG8**), income inequality (**SDG10**) and poverty (**SDG1**). Epidemic virus outbreaks (e.g. Sars, Mers, Ebola, the Covid-19 pandemic) confront countries with the state and vulnerabilities of their healthcare systems, and with how this affects deprived and wealthy people in rather different ways. Conceptual and theoretical problems persist as to what constitutes 'public health' and what should be considered 'basic health', for which governments might provide 'universal basic health' coverage.

Measuring well-being is even more challenging, both in absolute and relative terms. Well-being reflects both material living conditions and the quality of life in a broad sense. The latter ultimately involves a very personal assessment of life conditions. These may include a wide range of *absence from* and *freedom to* dimensions, of which both the score and weight assigned to each will most likely change over time. In 2008, Bhutan adopted a 'gross national happiness' (GNH) index to measure the collective happiness and well-being of their population. The index has been modestly emulated by others – in particular by cities in developed countries – but has never become accepted as a universal yardstick. On an individual level, a measure of the *absence* of well-being might be the number of suicides. Although globally decreasing (from 12.9 per 100,000 in 2000 to 10.6 per 100,000 in 2016), suicide remains the second-highest cause of death among people aged 15 to 29 globally, with 79% of suicides occurring in low- and middle-income countries in 2016 (UN, 2019).

WHAT DEFINES LIFE ON LAND AND BIODIVERSITY (SDG15)?

SDG15 defines life on land as the effort to sustain and restore the use of terrestrial ecosystems like forests and wetlands, combat desertification, halt the loss of biodiversity, and protect and prevent the extinction of threatened specifies. In 2019, the Intergovernmental Science-Policy Platform on Biodiversity and Ecosystem Services alarmingly reported that around one million animal and plant species are presently threatened with extinction, many within decades; more than ever before in human history (IPBES, 2019). The platform even argued that the loss of biodiversity presents a more immediate and urgent danger to the world than climate change (**SDG13**). But how can we demarcate and measure biodiversity or the relevant and related set-up of integrated ecosystems? Should the extinction of each and every species on earth be defined as a loss of biodiversity, and with what direct and indirect impact? How can we take the regular discovery of 'new species' into account? Linguistic confusion about core concepts – biodiversity, natural capital and ecosystems – adds to the ambiguity. In a limited definition, biodiversity is the number of different living organisms. In a broader definition, it refers to the spatial organization of ecosystems (UN, 1992: Article 2).[2]

Related to this is the discussion as to whether one should attach a monetary value to 'nature' in order to prevent it from being destroyed, or to make it possible to calculate 'trade-offs' between economic and ecological interests. Nature and biodiversity represent global public goods for which it is always challenging to translate the collective (macro) problem into actual (micro) economic strategies. As Pavan Sukhdev (2012) put it: "We use nature because it's valuable, but we lose it because it's free." In the policy discussion around biodiversity and life on land, the concepts of *natural capital* and *ecosystem services* have been introduced as an attempt to translate the ecological component into an economic one. Natural capital is then defined as a form of capital that includes all

---

2   More technically, ecosystems can be described as the result of a combination of biotic and abiotic factors in a geographically defined area. The size of this area can vary from very small (a pond) to very large (the earth).

the resources that we can take from nature worldwide. Several countries have adopted so-called *natural capital accounts* (NCAs), for instance, to relate national sustainability objectives with identified nature conservation 'hotspots' in locations with contrary economic and ecological interests (such as tourism, water usage and forests). Companies are confronted with all the (interconnected) challenges related to ecology and ecological resilience, especially those in sectors that heavily depend upon natural resources such as agriculture (**SDG2**), construction (**SDG9**), water (**SDG6**) and energy (**SDG7**).

4.3.2 Knowledge ambiguities (continued): the importance of framing and perceptions

Definitional ambiguities may appear to apply less to issues like 'access to education', which can be measured in terms of children going to school (**SDG4**); 'access to energy', measured as people with access to electricity (**SDG7**); to output-oriented targets related to climate action (**SDG13**), measured in CO_2 emissions; or on 'life below water' (**SDG14**), measured in terms of species and the size of the 'plastic soup' that fills the oceans. In those cases, trend analyses are easier to make, provided that the financial and organizational means are available to measure the phenomenon over longer periods. However, these seemingly straightforward SDGs often also comprise multiple and complex variables and, therefore, require an understanding of many causal links. This problem is aggravated when the available knowledge is *fragmented* amongst multiple stakeholders.

Another source of ambiguity is related to *knowledge-framing*, in which some of the knowledge receives either too much or too little attention because of how it is framed and presented. Chapter 1 already referred to famous statistician Hans Rosling, who argued that a neutral look at the statistics of development (covered, for instance, by general poverty statistics) should provide people with a much more optimistic frame than they inherently have (Rosling et al., 2018). He argued that humans tend to attach more value to bad news than to good news; that we tend to focus on danger; anticipate scarcity; look at what needs to be done now, rather than focus on what can be done later. As a consequence, positive change is difficult to establish because of the *negative frames* that persist in the media, in particular with respect to grand challenges. Knowledge-framing may also take a more malicious form when information is actively moulded to accommodate the interests of some. Justin Parkhurst (2016), for instance, points to the deliberate creation of 'evidentiary bias' that may further drive intractability, by distinguishing between *evidence-based policymaking* and *policy-based evidence-making*. There are fundamental questions to be raised about which bodies of information and evidence can be considered relevant and trustworthy, and how to prioritize between these bodies. Knowledge ambiguity is hence highly related to processes of *creation*, *selection* and *interpretation* of evidence, both in a technical sense (is the information scientifically valid?) and a political sense (what is the interest behind the information and why?).

'WEAPONS OF MASS DECEPTION' AND POLITICAL CULTURE WARS

Ambiguity in the discourse on wicked problems exists for obvious reasons. But ambiguity can also be created. There is growing concern that in a VUCA world, where world views collide, misleading frames and information increase controversy. A particularly illustrative case of this phenomenon starts with the US claim that Iraq owned 'weapons of mass destruction'. This legitimized a highly controversial invasion of the country in 2003 by an international coalition of countries following the American claim. The weapons were never found, but the intervention could not be reversed. Weapons of *'mass deception'* became the communicative synonym to this phenomenon. It was the title of a famous film released in 1997 on the fight between two media moguls but has since been a constant worry about the role of specific media in the creation of misleading knowledge.

Companies have played a particular role in crafting ambiguity as well. For instance, by sponsoring specific research and lobby organizations. Not necessarily to support different insights – which can form part of an intelligent discourse – but to frustrate consensus-building around common issues. Examples of this mechanism can be found, in particular, in those industries that have come under increased societal scrutiny over time like the tobacco industry, the pharmaceutical industry and the oil industry. Oil major Shell, for instance, produced a public film as early as 1991 in which they acknowledged the 'general consensus' that climate change was human-made and created severe problems. At the same time, and for a prolonged period of around 25 years, the company sponsored sceptical scientists and lobby groups that actively denied the adverse effects of CO_2 and the responsibility of companies. In 2018, the company finally ceased denying responsibility and began searching for a less ambiguous strategy. One measure taken in 2020 was to leave a powerful climate denial lobby group – the American Fuel & Petrochemical Manufacturers lobbying group.

In political sciences, this phenomenon is also known as 'political culture wars' in which active reframing of information is used to influence the debate on the problem, and consequently hamper the ability to come up with solutions. What seems logical or profound, actually might not be. A statement of philosopher Friedrich Nietzsche applies here: "They muddy the water to make it seem deep."

Four steps can be distinguished in the active creation of ambiguity around wicked problems: (1) aggressiveness in statements and dismissal of critics; (2) smokescreens around the seriousness and urgency of specific issues like climate

B
O
X

4.1

change, migration, health, ageing, not aimed at being right, but at creating confusion among well-intended audiences; (3) a continuous raising of doubt about the institutions that support a well-functioning democracy – from judges to scientists; (4) by also releasing 'conspiracy' theories on the issues, which feeds into polarization among people, and consequently increases ambiguity.[3]

Ambiguity in the *perception* of the factual status of a problem, feeds into the wickedness of the issue. It creates a framing challenge, which itself is influenced by the very definition of the problem. The nature and extent attributed to a problem depend on who has been asked; different stakeholders have different versions of what they think the problem is and how much weight it should be given. Often, each version of a policy problem has an element of truth; no version is complete or verifiably right or wrong in absolute terms. The debate concerning the causes, the extent and the solutions to climate change **(SDG13)** provides an example. In this area, knowledge ambiguity is generated as both the symptoms and assumed causes of global warming (the extent to which climate change is 'human-made') are drawn into question by an important group of stakeholders (like governments in the US, Brazil and Australia, and many major oil companies). The wickedness of the problem increases, even in the face of almost full consensus among global experts on the relevance and impact of the phenomenon.

B
O
X

4.2

THE WICKEDNESS OF KEY PERFORMANCE *ILLUSIONS*

A popular saying amongst managers is: 'What I can't measure, I cannot manage'. A famous saying amongst scientists, however, is: 'What I want to know I can't measure, what I can measure I don't want to know'.

The discussion on measuring growth and progress on a national and global scale has been covered in Chapter 2 as the contest between a 'narrow' (single indicator) and a 'broad' (dashboard) approach to monitoring relevant change. The management equivalent of this discourse is the use of so-called 'Key Performance Indicators' (KPIs). Management scholars have introduced KPIs with appealing names like 'Net Promotor Score', 'Cost-Income Ratio' or 'Operational Cash-Flow'. Yet Coen de Bruijn (2018), a management scholar, denominates KPIs as 'Key Performance *Illusions*'. Why?

---

3   Four steps based on a column by Sheila Sitalsing (*de Volkskrant*, 22 February 2020).

His most important argument is that KPIs are often narrowly defined, which makes them irrelevant for identifying real problems. Consequently, KPIs are misused, or even worse: incentivize the wrong kind of behaviour. 'Lying with KPIs' then becomes the management equivalent of 'lying with statistics', whereby KPIs become the means in power battles.

That does not imply, however, that KPIs are useless – on the contrary. But their use, or that of any other type of 'performance' indicator, should be treated with great care and be critically assessed continuously. One important way out of this predicament is to use the SDG dashboard as a trigger to define performance in terms of reaching *societal* goals. Chapters 9 and 10 further elaborate on how this technique can create a broader measure of progress: *'Key Value Indicators (KVIs)* and *Key Decision-Making Indicators (KDIs)*. Chapter 11 introduces a bridging technique to overcome the gap between KVIs, KDIs and KPIs: the formulation of Key Performance Questions (KPQs).

As regards the 'know-ability' of the issues addressed by the SDGs, considerable progress has been made on defining the variables on which to measure and track progress. The UN and various related organizations have developed databases to take stock of developments in all of the SDGs, while all countries have promised to develop statistical capacity to measure and monitor progress. These databases provide a good starting point for a discussion on general trends in each of the SDGs. Nevertheless, as illustrated in Chapters 2 and 3, properly using these databases is shrouded in considerable ambiguity: first, because of missing statistics; second, because not all countries are able (or willing) to contribute all relevant information; third, because of missing indicators; and fourth, because of specific selection biases.

4.3.3 Predictive ambiguities

The SDGs in general are aimed at large and transformative changes at a global scale. Nevertheless, complex dynamics seldom bring about predetermined or predicted outcomes. Small changes can unfold nearly unforeseeable system dynamics, leaving 'traces' and creating path dependencies for which there is no ultimate correct answer, but – given the high stakes – 'no right to be wrong' either. The more wicked the problem is, the more every single intervention can have irreversible consequences. This makes an intervention – in the words of Rittel and Webber (1973) – a 'one-shot operation'. These wickedness characteristics apply to all SDGs to a greater or lesser extent, yet appear especially relevant in the context of institutional change (in particular **SDGs 11, 16** and **17**). Policy measures in this area not only define the very legal and institutional conditions under which change can be organized at the meso (community/city) or macro (country/globe) level. They typically also involve a longer-term horizon which inherently comes with higher levels of uncertainty.

Knowledge ambiguity further incites predictive ambiguity. In Chapter 2, knowledge ambiguity was related to the 'nexus challenge': how are SDGs inter-linked, and how do they influence each other positively or negatively. One cannot build predictions on what is insufficiently understood, nor can one extrapolate developments under highly uncertain, unstable and contested conditions. That would involve making assumptions about how unmeasurable things affect other unmeasurable things (Krugman, 2013). Almost *all* SDGs represent a 'moving target', evolving at the same time that multiple stakeholders are trying to address the problem with a variety of efforts, from different angles, at different scales and with quite different impacts. The prognoses underlying many of the SDG-targets are by necessity marked by assumptions – many *ifs* – based on aggregate (growth) trends and extrapolations of current developments under *ceteris paribus* conditions. These do not (and cannot) reckon with, for instance, sudden geopolitical or institutional shifts in power, conflict or new coalitions that may impede or accelerate momentum, financial, economic or ecological 'booms or dooms', breakthrough technological innovations and the speed of their practical uptake, and how these interacting developments add up and affect the SDG-targets. As a consequence, prognoses, in general, provide little guidance as to 'what to do' and 'how to do it'; they are too vague to be of much practical use. They can be considered more as "a measure of our ignorance" (Abramovitz, quoted in *The Economist*, 14 April 2018).

Also, policies related to achieving the SDGs are not excluded from what has become generally known as the *law of unintended consequences*. Unanticipated and unintended consequences of purposeful action can be positive, but also negative or 'perverse' (Merton, 1936). They can vary in their scale of impact (local, national, regional, global) and the stakeholders affected. We can denominate these phenomena as 'generative' and 'dynamic' complexities that are shaped by, and further feed into, societal, communicative and structural complexity dimensions in rather unpredictable, not always overt and often whimsical ways. This makes it impossible to make credible predictions on the assumed effects of policy interventions. The sheer number of known variables is simply too large, the number of unknown variables possibly even larger.

Take, for instance, the issue of hunger (**SDG2**). The wickedness in terms of the sufficient production of nutritious food depends on how the food system is organized. Achieving food security and improved nutrition is strongly influenced by actions on **SDG8** (e.g. jobs), **SDG12** ('responsible production and consumption'), and **SDG15** ('life on land'). However, the workings of these causal relationships also depend on contextual conditions, in particular climatological (**SDG13**) and institutional (**SDG16**) circumstances, in which government policies – such as protectionism or land policies – can undermine or facilitate the activities of companies or citizens in ways that may benefit some or benefit all. Measures introduced 'here and now' to address the problem, may lead to unforeseen consequences 'elsewhere and later'. Some of these consequences may be detrimental and create vicious dependencies, others might create unforeseen momentum and windows of opportunity.

Clarity about what would happen if *no action* is taken would reduce the level of predictive ambiguity. The more urgent an issue is, the higher the likelihood of interventions. That does not guarantee effectiveness, however.[4] Faced with immediate famines in parts of Africa, the global community came 'to the rescue' many times. An unintended side effect, however, was the 'crowding out' of local food producers. This turned out to have longer-term harmful effects on the local capacity to grow and process food, which subsequently formed the basis for yet another food and hunger crisis. At the other extreme, the more slow-moving an issue is, the less likely societal actors are to take immediate action; even if this would result in far-reaching negative effects in the longer run. The urgency dimension presents a particular challenge in managing crisis-sensitive SDGs like **SDG2** (famines), **SDG3** (dying children), **SDG6** (death from water contamination), **SDG7** (death due to indoor air pollution) and **SDG12** (irreparable damage due to waste). Taking action on these immediate disasters may divert attention for the more structural and long-term pervasive aspects of the wicked problem. How short-term action and long-term consequences relate is markedly difficult to predict. Problems of inertia – e.g. the tragedy of the commons, bystander effects – tend to affect particularly those SDGs that do not trigger urgent disasters in the short term, such as **SDG13** ('climate action'), **SDG14** ('life below water') and **SDG15** ('life on land').

4.3.4 Intervention ambiguities

Wicked problems surface particularly when and where there is a dysfunctional distribution of power among societal stakeholders with interests (or values) that are substantially in conflict with those of others. Divergence in interests, values and power bases reflect fragmentation. It leads to an over-stressing of contradictions, trade-offs or win–lose frames that further feed into the divergent tendencies of a VUCA society (Box 4.3). To trigger some level of

---

4   The Chinese word for 'crisis' (危机) has a double meaning: danger *and* opportunity. A popular saying in management circles is 'never waste a good crisis'. Both statements point to the experience that change is easier to trigger under a joint sense of urgency. This mechanism can also be used for change in 'the wrong' direction. In her book *Shock Doctrine* (2007), publicist Naomi Klein documents how crises can be created to push certain 'solutions' that would normally not be supported. This theme will be further used in Chapter 7 to explain the importance of 'triggering events' for the direction of change.

WICKEDNESS AND DEALING WITH FALSE CONTRADICTIONS

The present time faces more 'wicked' problems than ever (Roberts, 2000). A typical approach to the three dimensions of ambiguity in the popular discourse is to frame issues in terms of sharp tensions, contradictions, trade-offs, and 'right' or 'wrong' solutions. As actors attempt to make sense of an increasingly intricate, ambiguous and ever-changing world, they simplify reality into polarized either/or distinctions that conceal complex interrelationships (Lewis, 2000). How one frames the problem also determines how a person or organization will be able to address the problem. Four frames or 'thinking hats' are often used when defining an intervention challenge: dilemma, trade-off, puzzle and paradox. Aligning the level of complexity with the proper thinking frame is vital in delineating effective ways to address a problem.

Complexity level	'Simple'	'Complicated – Complex'		'Wicked'
Thinking frame	Dilemma	Trade-off	Puzzle	Paradox
Nature and scope of problem	Causalities known; Starting position known; Consequences (partly) known	Causalities known; Consequences partly known; Preferred end goal known	Causalities and nexus are known; End goal known	Multi-causal; Unclear how end goals should be achieved
Scope of solutions	Two solutions ('either/or')	One optimal solution direction ('and/or')	One optimal solution	Many innovative approaches ('both/and')
Strategy	'Make a choice'	'Find the right balance'	'Search the optimum'; 'Create a focal point'	'Make the best of both worlds'; 'Involve stakeholders'
	'Inside-the-box thinking'		'Outside-the-box thinking'	

Simple problems can be approached with available solutions and ways of thinking. But the more a problem can be identified as 'wicked', the more alternative approaches are needed. In management theory, this mindset is known as *tolerance for ambiguity* (Whetten et al., 2000) – a construct first introduced in 1949 to define and measure how well people respond when presented with an event that results in ambiguous stimuli or situations (Frenkel-Brunswik, 1949). A higher tolerance for ambiguity separates the (political) 'leader' from the 'manager'. Many wicked problems are nevertheless wrongly characterized as simple trade-offs or tensions: Economy *versus* Ecology, State *versus* Market, Rich *versus* Poor, Public *versus* Private; Shareholder *versus* Stakeholder, Technical *versus* Societal. The discussion on juxtaposed positions consequently becomes polarized and diverging trails of a VUCA society reinforced.

Dealing with complexity

For simple problems – and to a certain extent even for more complex problems – thinking in terms of dilemmas or trade-off can be revealing. This mode of framing and thinking is also popular in scientific reasoning and consequently regularly becomes part of a societal debate, in which one is supposed to take sides. However, in case of complex problems, an 'either/or' frame creates 'false contradictions' that induce intellectual myopia. For more complex and wicked problems, with multiple causes and unclear approaches to what might work and what does not work, a different analytical, decision-making and intervention frame is needed.

Game theory insights can help. Game theory distinguishes between two types of games: non-cooperative and cooperative games. They relate to two types of thinking: inside- and outside-the-box thinking.

1 **Inside-the-box thinking** applies to short-term, interest-based decision-making challenges. The prime challenge of decision-making is how to deal with non-cooperative games, in which *values are distributed* and actors do not want or do not have to cooperate. The results of such games are either negative-sum or zero-sum: one may win, but the other loses. These kinds of competitive strategies for dealing with wicked problems are still evident when two countries fight over the responsibility for a problem in a war (Roberts, 2000).

2 **Outside-the-box thinking** requires developing longer-term visions. It considers the prime challenge of decision-making in how to deal with cooperative games that are aimed at *creating (shared) value*. These games result in positive-sum outcomes that are not focused on an immediate short-term 'win' for some, but on a longer-term 'win-win' for all. If players can collaboratively think of one optimal solution, it is possible to collaborate on 'cracking' the puzzle. This type of thinking requires that collaboration leads to a common understanding of causes and consequences and the formulation of common end goals. However, in the case of multiple causes, there is no clear understanding of how they are interrelated. A wide variety of parallel goals are to be served, and so a different type of approach is needed: paradoxical thinking.

Paradoxical thinking

George Bernard Shaw formulated an anecdote on how to understand the basics of paradoxical thinking: "If you have an apple and I have an apple and we exchange apples, then you and I will still each have one apple. But if you have an idea and I have an idea and we exchange these ideas, then each of us will have two ideas."

The 'apple' statement represents the trade-off argument, whilst the 'ideas' statement gives a perfect illustration of a positive-sum paradox. However, we can add one more dimension to this statement: *when two people get together with their two apples and decide to bake an apple pie, the equation might turn out to be even more positive.* The latter is an example of outside-the-box thinking and of how 'wicked problems' – like those posed by the SDGs – can be reframed into 'wicked opportunities'. It also illustrates a so-called 'collective action' approach.

Framing opposites as paradoxes opens up possibilities that were previously unimaginable. A paradox is the simultaneous existence of two contradictory states, such as innovation and efficiency, collaboration and competition, or new and old. Rather than compromising between the two, one explores ways of reconciliation by searching for another dimension that simultaneously holds the two states. Managing a paradox is about exploring the tension creatively. This is not easy, because by nature we tend to favour less complex representations of reality. Paradoxes become visible when we interact with others and encounter their ideas and perspectives. The more diverse the (groups of) people and perspectives, interests and values are, the more elements of a wicked problem we can discover. We call this pluralism. Pluralism in ideas, among people, within organizations and across industries is a crucial driver of change (Eisenhardt, 2000).

These insights can be applied for the SDG-agenda in three complementary ways:

- **Nexus thinking:** focus not only on reducing negative trade-offs but also on leveraging positive trade-offs and the net effect of both (mixed-sum games);

- **Management thinking:** develop a high tolerance for ambiguity; identify the wickedness of problems, without assuming that there are 'best' solutions;

- **Paradoxical thinking:** develop leadership skills that can address two (seeming) opposites and tensions in a creative way; explore tensions by capturing all pluralism within the duality; 'the grey area'. Disregard false contradictions.

convergence and coherence again, the most purposeful intervention on wicked problems involves *coordinated action* by a range of stakeholders, including public organizations (government agencies at the federal, state and local levels), non-profit organizations, private businesses and individuals. This requires, however, that all parties feel engaged in the problem and challenges ahead, that all feel and take appropriate responsibility, and that all are willing and capable to take action by aligning current practices and changing behaviour accordingly.

A coordinated intervention is difficult to achieve. A shared vision on the exact nature, scope and scale of the problem, or on a definitive, stable and well-defined solution, is often lacking. Problem-solving under such circumstances then typically ends because of pragmatic reasons – parties have run out of time, money or patience – rather than as the result of having found the ultimate solution (Hanson, 2019). To pursue approaches based on 'solving' or 'fixing' may cause policymakers to act on unwarranted and unsafe assumptions that create unrealistic expectations (Australian Public Service Commission, 2012). In the scientific literature on so-called 'intervention logics', it has been found that simple approaches to complex problems often lead to even greater problems. It may hence be more useful to consider how problem-solving efforts can best be guided and managed, in the knowledge that wicked problems call for solution-based *approaches*, innovative *governance arrangements*, and different monitoring and evaluation frameworks.

All nexus challenges of the SDGs present major intervention ambiguities. One of the key insights generated by wicked problems theory is that the more wicked a problem appears to be, the more integrative and 'holistic' approaches are needed. Narrow approaches will not suffice as they may result in the misleading impression of 'fixing' the problem while disregarding unforeseen side effects. But how can we define all relevant linkages, keep track of them, and improve the intervention if and where needed? Scientific research (partly) denotes how the system is intertwined (Box 4.4), but not necessarily how to deal with the various interests, the different institutional logics, values and the different means of power, control and resources of the parties involved or affected. Neither is it clear who should initiate change efforts related to specific SDG-targets (government, business, civil society organizations?), nor what kind of collaborative constellations are suited for addressing a specific issue, and under what contextual conditions. So, intervention ambiguity exists on at least three levels: (1) identification of effective *points of intervention*; (2) *who* should initiate action; and (3) *what collaborative constellation* best fits the complexity of the challenges at hand.

Furthermore, nexus challenges typically present a 'level of analysis' problem. Reducing ambiguity on where and how to intervene requires a proper understanding of how sustainable development dynamics interact at three levels of analysis: the micro level (individual actors, organizations, companies), the meso level (networks and regions) and the macro level (countries and the world). Most nexus challenges related to the SDGs have been addressed at the national and global level, partly because the data-gathering community consists of economists, ecologists and systems scholars who are often organized around (inter)national statistics bodies. Most progress has, therefore, been achieved at the macro level. However, for gaining *practical* insights, a search for concrete linkages at the micro and meso levels of analysis is crucial. The challenge then becomes how relevant nexuses between SDG-targets materialize around the activities of firms and other private organizations (addressed in Part III).

B
O
X

4.4

POINTS OF INTERVENTION: THREE NEXUS CHALLENGES

The W-E-F (climate) nexus

The water-energy-food (W-E-F) nexus is one of the better-documented nexus mechanisms. Research on this nexus shows how specific SDG areas are interdependent (Weitz et al., 2014). Food production (**SDG2**) requires water, land and energy (involving **SDGs 6, 7, 12** and **15**), but also leads to trade-offs and conflicts (protecting forests vs. increasing agricultural land) involving **SDG13** and **SDG15**. Smartly combining these elements could enable beneficial reinforcement. Water and energy efficiency, for instance, positively reinforce renewable energy targets (OECD, 2016). The World Economic Forum took the W-E-F nexus one step further by referring to the food-water-energy-climate nexus. Positive trade-offs can be anticipated if diets become less meat-intensive and by reducing food waste (**SDG12,** combined with **SDG2**), which can also mitigate land pressure (**SDG15**) and lower CO_2 and methane emissions (**SDG13**).

The inclusion nexus

Another example relates to the 'inclusion nexus'. Inclusion is a guiding principle of the SDGs, as stated in the preamble of the goals: 'no one left behind'. Almost all SDGs end their formulation with the provision 'for all' (Partos, 2016: 25). The inclusion of specific vulnerable groups is regularly mentioned across many SDGs (women, children, people with disabilities, the elderly, small-scale farmers, fishers, Indigenous people, migrants and refugees). The same applies for the related ambition to achieve equality, in gender (**SDG5**), within and among countries (**SDG10**), in general (**SDG10**), in cities (**SDG11**) in value chains (**SDG12**), or as precondition for legal inclusion (**SDG16**). **SDG9** ('industry, innovation and infrastructure') acknowledges that every job in manufacturing creates 2.2 jobs in other sectors – which suggests that these types of jobs have great potential to include people in the formal economy through spill-over effects.

The gender-climate-economic development nexus

There is good reason why in many development plans – whether at the national, local or company level – particular focus in the inclusion nexus is given to improving the position of women in general, and girls specifically **(SDG5).** Gender equality involves not only equal treatment of women and men in the workplace, but more generally also relates to the fostering of women's voice and agency, which are fundamental inputs for economic development.

The nexus effects of interventions in this realm are far-reaching. McKinsey's Global Institute (2015), for instance, assessed that advancing *Women's Equality* could add $12 trillion to global growth. **SDG5** is central to this ambition. There is an unrealized contribution of women in general due to the falling number of women in the labour force in countries like Saudi Arabia, but also in India. The IMF calculated that female employment rates in India dropped from 35% in 2005, to 26% in 2018 (*The Economist*, 7 July 2018). It argued that if India rebalanced the gender neutrality of its workforce, it would be 27% wealthier (**SDG5** linked to **SDG8**).

The positive interaction also works for ecological SDGs. A group of scientists in *Project Drawdown* (Hawken, 2017) took an interesting approach in the discussion on global warming in this respect: linking SDG5 with **SDGs 4, 13, 14, 15**. They aimed to develop "the most comprehensive plan . . . to reverse global warming". This group considered quantifiable results representing the total impact of 80 proposed solutions, modelled over a 30-year period – using so-called 'plausible' scenarios. Their top ten solutions include six technological approaches that can be related to ecological SDGs (refrigeration, wind turbines, solar, silvopasture) and two food system-related solutions (reduced waste and plant-rich diets). Interestingly, it also listed two social dimensions in its top ten, of which *'educating girls'* arguably has the greatest longer-term positive effect on climate change. *Why?* Because – as the authors argue – climate change is not gender-neutral. Not only are women and girls disproportionately vulnerable to the impacts of climate change, they also prove pivotal to successfully addressing global warming. *How?* Girls educated through secondary school (1) have fewer and healthier children, (2) actively manage their reproductive health, (3) realize higher wages and greater upward mobility, and (4) contribute to economic growth. This is just one example of the positive reinforcing nexus effects that can be triggered by sending more girls to school (Hawken, 2017: 81).

In conclusion, the nexus challenge comes with substantial intervention ambiguities. How to trigger and leverage potentially positive nexus interactions in practice, is often far from clear and highly context-dependent. A wicked problems approach argues that the actual nexus benefits can probably only be discovered through concrete experimentation, continuous learning and appropriate adjustment of the intervention strategy along the way. Wicked problems require stakeholder engagement and learning-by-doing exercises. This is not an easy task and requires different types of monitoring and evaluation techniques, also referred to as *developmental evaluation*. One element of this technique is that the various stakeholders who work together agree to share knowledge, practical experience and dilemmas, in order to improve both the effectiveness of the intervention and the working of the solution-oriented partnership (Van Tulder and Keen, 2018).

4.4 DIMENSIONS OF COMPLEXITY: ASSESSING THE INTENSITY OF WICKEDNESS

All sources of ambiguity create accumulating degrees of wickedness and thus uncertainty in developing effective approaches to the SDGs. Analytical, contextual, institutional and distributional aspects become entangled, making it exceedingly hard to draw out resilient strategies. An assessment of what to prioritize, what kind of approaches to pursue and under what conditions, hence starts with a more refined analysis of the problem's *various dimensions* of wickedness and the *degrees of complexity* involved. In the words of Schneider et al. (2017), the analytical challenge here is to 'reduce complexity by creating complexity'. Such an analysis should prevent oversimplified approaches to inherently complex problem domains, and overly complicated approaches to relatively simple aspects of it. Effective management and leadership approaches always involve the proper 'management of uncertainty' (Whetten and Cameron, 2008).

Not all dimensions of a wicked problem are equally intractable and not all aspects of the SDGs are equally wicked. Societal problems vary in their degree of wickedness, depending on several conditions that together define the level of complexity. The literature on wicked problems and systems change distinguishes a large number of relevant dimensions that denote sources of complexity (Alford and Head, 2017; Waddock et al., 2015; McConnell, 2018; Australian Public Service Commission, 2012). Relevant insights that shed further light on the nature of linkages and the dynamics at play can be clustered into five general classifications of complexity.

■ *Structural complexity:* is created in the case of a massive number of identifiable elements involved; the more dimensions come into play (political, economic, social, legal, technological and environmental aspects) at different levels (micro, meso, macro), the more 'systemic' a problem is, and the more elements one should take into account to better grasp the problem.

■ *Generative complexity:* increases when the interconnectedness between elements of the phenomenon intensifies; interacting elements can unfold in unpredictable ways; (root) cause and effect are not easy to distinguish (typical 'chicken-or-egg' issues), and tend to sprawl different effects across time ('now' versus 'later') and across boundaries ('here' versus 'elsewhere').

■ *Dynamic complexity:* involves the variety in pace and direction in the evolvement of – and between – different elements or parts of the phenomenon; this includes, for example, non-linearity; non-synchronicity; non-continuity; divergent, convergent, iterative or erratic patterns; urgency, momentum and inertia can exist simultaneously, as has become clear in, for instance, the discussion on climate action.

■ *Communicative complexity:* is created if information is (a) actively moulded to accommodate the interests of some, (b) influenced by people's perception, behaviour, preferences and emotional connectivity and

receptivity, (c) in ways and by means that are not transparent, cannot be verified or are not fully understood, (d) which lowers trust in the messenger as
well as in the information itself ('fake news', 'alternative facts', 'post-truths'),
which (e) may lead to further fragmentation, individualism and polarization.

■ *Societal complexity:* exists when the number and diversity of stakeholders
involved or affected is extensive; this factor is mirrored by the variety of and
differentiation in 'logics', interests, perceptions, behaviours and identities,
and by diffused responsibilities related to roles, loci of power, control,
means and spheres of influence.

For the sake of further nuance, two dimensions of *multiplicity* can be attributed to each of these five categories, resulting in 'ten dimensions of complexity'
as denoted in Table 4.3. This analytical exercise of disentanglement intends to
support a more focused consideration of vital complexity dimensions, in order to
foster greater insight into what aspects of the problem are – or could be – better
understood than the rather totalizing wickedness status of a problem suggests.
Table 4.3 lists navigating questions and exemplary ambiguities to provide entry
points for the further exploration of all ten dimensions. Such exploration subsequently facilitates an assessment of the *degree of complexity* of each of the ten
dimensions (see Scoreboard #1). This can help to improve understanding of the
problem's *level of wickedness*.

Table 4.3 Navigating ten dimensions of complexity

STRUCTURAL COMPLEXITY
1. Multi-dimensional
The extent to which the problem is systemic • The more each of the PESTEL dimensions (Political, Economic, Social, Technological, Environmental, Legal) has to be considered, the more the problem is a sign of 'systemic failure' rather than an incident; • Relevant dimensions are also situational: every specific situation creates a distinct context in which dimensions play out (cf. Remington-Doucette, 2013); • <u>Knowledge ambiguity prevails</u>: reductionist/overly narrow definitions preclude relevant dimensions; multiple definitions of the problem encompass different (sets of) dimensions; alternative measures introduced over the years stress alternative (sets of) dimensions.
2. Multi-level
The extent and scale to which the impact of the problem manifests itself at different levels (micro/meso/macro) • The nature of the nexus between micro and macro developments defines the complexity of the problem;

- Knowledge ambiguity prevails: most databases focus on the macro level, making it difficult to consider the nexus between macro and micro and to assess micro strategies within a 'dynamic system';
- Predictive ambiguity: increasing volatility of and uncertainty about the institutional set-up of the global economy can be observed at the global and regional level, with uncertain consequences at country/city or organizational (micro) level. To what extent can unintended (positive/ negative) consequences at all levels be identified or anticipated?
- Intervention ambiguity: at what level should action be undertaken and in what sequence ('bottom-up'/'top-down')?

GENERATIVE COMPLEXITY

3. Multi-cause

The number of identifiable/assumed root causes that underlie the problem

- The higher the number of root causes underlying a problem, the higher the level of complexity;
- Is it possible to identify specific nexus dimensions (interrelated root causes)? Can differences in strength /dominance between (root)causes be identified?
- Knowledge ambiguity: internally conflicting interdependencies and multiple causes make many of the topics covered by the SDGs difficult to define and measure unambiguously;
- Predictive ambiguity: What would happen if no action is taken? Can we know what (root) causes will have the strongest effect on shaping and driving future events?
- Intervention ambiguity: many responses to sustainable development problems have irreversible consequences and create path dependencies. To what extent can the proposed change be undone? Is it possible to learn by trial and error and create feedback loops?

4. Multi-effect

The number and scale of symptoms that can be attributed to the problem

- Make a mind map: every symptom is an effect of something else. Wicked problems create unpredictable consequences and side effects. Define the extent to which ripple effects have to be taken into account.
- Knowledge ambiguity: relates to linking specific symptoms with assumed causes (for instance, the discussion on the extent to which global warming is 'human-made'); how 'hard' is the linkage (causalities, correlations, the influence of unknown intermediate variables).
- Knowledge ambiguity: ripple effects and unstable 'end states' (definitive resolution) make it difficult to define benchmarks for success; index indicators prevail, whereas a dashboard approach for monitoring is more sophisticated; the more indicators are unknown or insufficiently developed, the greater the generative uncertainty, the more complex the issue becomes.
- Predictive ambiguity: the degree to which unintended consequences can appear (where and when); positive or negative feedback loops; dampened or reinforced effects.
- Intervention ambiguity: how short-term action and long-term consequences relate is difficult to predict. Where to intervene in the cause–effect chain/loop of events to (1) stop the sprawling of further negative effects, (2) leverage beneficial effects to scale positive impact?

(continued)

Table 4.3 (continued)

DYNAMIC COMPLEXITY

5. Multi-directional

Extent of variety in the nature of interactions and interdependencies between elements

- Parts within a system can show different dynamics headed in different directions. To what extent can divergent, convergent, erratic, iterative patterns be identified?
- <u>Predictive ambiguity</u>: To what extent can we anticipate convergence, fragmentation, critical mass or tipping points?
- <u>Intervention ambiguity</u>: complexity theory scholars consider systems as dynamic, complex and adaptive: the conditions for sustainable development continuously change over time and targets constantly morph and move.

6. Multi-paced

The dynamics of the problem that result from differences in pace (e.g. non-linearity; non-synchronicity, non-continuity)

- The higher the variety in dynamics, the higher the level of complexity;
- To what extent can momentum and acceleration (sense of urgency), or inertia (paralysis, denial) be identified, and how does this affect the dynamics of the problem?
- <u>Knowledge ambiguity</u>: Should some goals and targets be prioritized over others over time to leverage overall impact? How exactly does inequality (as a form of non-synchronicity) between regions, countries, stakeholder groups affect the overall pace of progress?
- <u>Predictive ambiguity</u>: How immediate is the sense of urgency? The more slow-moving an issue, the less likely it is that societal actors will take immediate action. How do incidents or immediate crises deviate attention from slow-moving, yet potentially more disastrous developments?
- <u>Intervention ambiguity</u>: What are effective (institutional) enablers of accelerating synchronized, concerted action? The pace of approaches is heavily influenced by the context and strength of interest groups. "A solution that is good enough for one place and time might not be good enough for another. . . . Consequently, the pace with which even the same approaches can be implemented can differ substantially" (Remington-Doucette, 2013).

COMMUNICATIVE COMPLEXITY

7. Multi-frames

The number of competing explanations and understandings (alternative truths)

- What alternative narratives exist, to what extent do these diverge or overlap and to what extent do they represent different world views, values, norms?
- Can the challenge be framed as a positive or negative frame? What prevails in the popular discourse: doom scenarios or opportunity-driven frames?

- Knowledge ambiguity: disagreement among stakeholders on what frame to adopt often reflects the different emphasis they place on the various causal factors (# 3) and anticipated consequences (# 4);
- Knowledge ambiguity in the perception of a problem's factual status feeds into the wickedness of the issue. It adds further complexity to the other nine dimensions;
- Intervention ambiguity: the extent to which the issue is framed in terms of trade-offs and either/or approaches often leads to unproductive and polarized debates;
- Knowledge and intervention ambiguity: experts and stakeholders often see the issue from different world views and problem definitions.[5] Can both be right? Can a synthesis be found between different world views, values and approaches to the challenges (paradox thinking)?
- Intervention ambiguity: sizable definition problems arise for concepts like 'poverty', 'biodiversity', 'fair' and 'inclusiveness' – concepts that are all part and parcel of the language surrounding the SDGs. Disagreement among stakeholders (# 9) often reflects the different emphasis they place on the various causal factors (# 3). Successfully addressing wicked problems usually involves a range of coordinated and interrelated responses, given their multi-causal nature; it often also involves trade-offs between conflicting goals (# 1).

8. Multi-source

Level at which information and sources of the message can be unambiguously verified

- The extent to which reliable, transparent and verifiable sources of knowledge and information are developed and robust, relevant data can be distinguished;
- Knowledge ambiguity: disagreement among stakeholders on what can be considered relevant and reliable sources increases the wickedness of the issue;
- Knowledge and intervention ambiguity: algorithms are affecting the kind of information that is presented to us in intransparant ways, creating filter bubbles and online 'echo chambers' that reinforce ideological silos and societal divides that drive polarization;

(continued)

---

5 Charles Mann documented a famous clash in his book *The Wizard and the Prophet* (2018), in which he portrays two radically opposing world views on four grand challenges the world faces: food, water, energy and climate change. The Prophet takes the environmental point of view and believes that if we don't completely change our way of living, our 'prosperity will bring us to ruin'. The Wizard, on the other hand, believes that science will rise to the four challenges and will come up with science-based solutions. The Wizard is the pioneer in modern high-yield crops. The Prophet is the intellectual forefather of the environmental movement. Various regions in the world and various stakeholders have embraced both frames.

Table 4.3 (continued)

	• <u>Knowledge and intervention ambiguity</u>: digitalization provides new ways of manipulating facts ('fake news', 'fake footage') that instantly spread around the world, thereby distorting perceptions, diverting attention, thwarting decision-making, and undermining collective action and democratic processes; • <u>Intervention ambiguity</u>: How significant is the challenge of 'infobesitas' (selecting relevant information over abundant information)?

SOCIETAL COMPLEXITY

9. Multi-stakeholder

Number of involved or affected parties; heterogeneity in logics, stakes, expectations, behaviours and identities

• The higher the number of stakeholders involved with conflicting logics, expectations, stakes, ways of behaviour and identities, the higher the level of complexity;
• What is the strength of alignment between multiple stakeholders: bound together through a level playing field, minimum rules, (moral) norms, principles, cultures, ideologies?
• <u>Knowledge ambiguity</u>: relevant knowledge and capacities generally reside with multiple parties. Joined-up knowledge as a condition for developing more resilient strategies in coping with wickedness;
• <u>Knowledge and intervention ambiguity</u>: political conflict over the definition of the problem, the values at stake, the appropriateness of policy measures and rules;
• <u>Intervention ambiguity</u>: coordination, collaboration and alignment of relationships. Can dynamic complexities (#5 and #6) be sufficiently mediated through the involvement of the most important stakeholders ('coalitions of the willing' to mobilize 'coalitions of the needed'), to create smarter interventions along the way?

10. Multi-responsibility

Sources of responsibility related to roles, loci of power, control, agency, means and spheres of influence

• The higher the fragmentation of responsibilities, sources of power, agency and control, the higher the level of complexity;
• <u>Intervention ambiguity</u>: allocation of responsibilities is unclear in the case of institutional voids and lacking governance mechanisms (structures, processes) needed to align agency and coordinate action;
• <u>Intervention ambiguity</u>: many of the differences in growth records between states can be explained by political decisions to adopt *looser or tighter regimes* of state control over economic activity, and the institutional and governance arrangements resulting from that.

SCORING SDGs ALONG TEN DIMENSIONS OF COMPLEXITY

There is no need to wait until all dimensions of complexity are fully covered by further research and/or experiential knowledge. The ten complexity dimensions can be used to create first impressions, to share and discuss them with others, and to come to joint initial conclusions on the degree of wickedness of the SDG (-target) that one wants to assess or address. This is the practical aim of Scoreboard #1. Even at the start of an evolving issue, the scoreboard can be used as an immediate assessment tool. Each SDG(-target) can be scored along the ten dimensions of complexity. Scoreboard #1 introduces a 7-point scale to distinguish between 'simple-complex-wicked' problems. By taking all ten of the complexity dimensions into account, each distinct SDG(-target) will likely represent different scores along each of these indicators. Every SDG(-target)'s wickedness score will be influenced by the national or sectoral context in which it is considered; each assessment will be context- and time-dependent.

If, on all accounts, the SDG(-target) scores below 20, it can be considered a relatively simple problem that can probably be addressed with technical

SCOREBOARD #1 Assessing levels of complexity and wickedness

Dimension of complexity	Degree of complexity depends on. . . .	Score Simple Complex Wicked []----[]----[]----[]----[]----[]----[] 1 2 3 4 5 6 7
STRUCTURAL COMPLEXITY		
1. **Multi-dimensional**	The systemic nature of the problem (including Political, Economic, Social, Technological, Environmental and Legal aspects)	Low High []----[]----[]----[]----[]----[]----[] 1 2 3 4 5 6 7
2. **Multi-level**	The extent and scale to which the impact of the problem manifests itself at different levels (micro/meso/macro)	Limited High []----[]----[]----[]----[]----[]----[] 1 2 3 4 5 6 7
GENERATIVE COMPLEXITY		
3. **Multi-cause**	Number of identifiable/ assumed root causes that underlie the problem	Low High []----[]----[]----[]----[]----[]----[] 1 2 3 4 5 6 7
4. **Multi-effect**	Number and scale of symptoms that can be attributed to the problem	Limited High []----[]----[]----[]----[]----[]----[] 1 2 3 4 5 6 7

(continued)

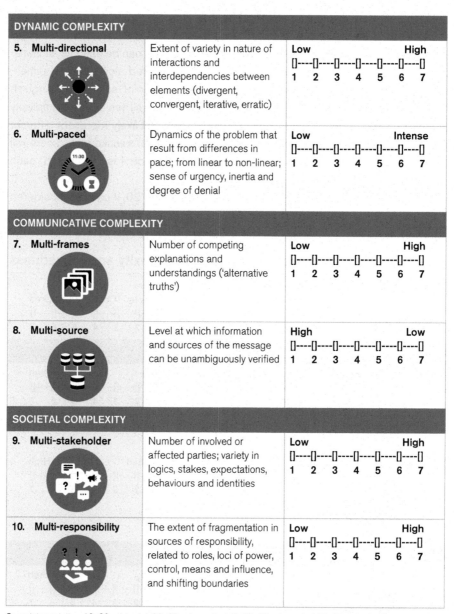

DYNAMIC COMPLEXITY		
5. Multi-directional	Extent of variety in nature of interactions and interdependencies between elements (divergent, convergent, iterative, erratic)	Low High []----[]----[]----[]----[]----[]----[] 1 2 3 4 5 6 7
6. Multi-paced	Dynamics of the problem that result from differences in pace; from linear to non-linear; sense of urgency, inertia and degree of denial	Low Intense []----[]----[]----[]----[]----[]----[] 1 2 3 4 5 6 7
COMMUNICATIVE COMPLEXITY		
7. Multi-frames	Number of competing explanations and understandings ('alternative truths')	Low High []----[]----[]----[]----[]----[]----[] 1 2 3 4 5 6 7
8. Multi-source	Level at which information and sources of the message can be unambiguously verified	High Low []----[]----[]----[]----[]----[]----[] 1 2 3 4 5 6 7
SOCIETAL COMPLEXITY		
9. Multi-stakeholder	Number of involved or affected parties; variety in logics, stakes, expectations, behaviours and identities	Low High []----[]----[]----[]----[]----[]----[] 1 2 3 4 5 6 7
10. Multi-responsibility	The extent of fragmentation in sources of responsibility, related to roles, loci of power, control, means and influence, and shifting boundaries	Low High []----[]----[]----[]----[]----[]----[] 1 2 3 4 5 6 7

Score interpretation: 10–20 = 'simple'; 20–35 = 'complicated'; 35–50 = 'complex'; 50–70 = 'wicked'

solutions (see Table 4.1). If the scores on each dimension are more divergent and total between 20 and 50, the score indicates that the problem is 'complicated' or even outright 'complex', which often requires novel organizational approaches. On specific sub-categories, the problem can still score high on complexity and the problem can still be denominated as 'wicked', depending on the *weight* attributed to that dimension. If accumulated scores reach the level of 50 and above, the problem can be considered 'wicked' on practically all accounts. Effectively addressing the problem then requires not only new organizational forms or approaches, but probably also new societal arrangements.

CREATING COMMON KNOWLEDGE

By intuitively attributing general scores to each of the complexity characteristics, a first rough impression of the degree of wickedness can be obtained by accumulating the scores. Value and reliability can be added to the technique by moving from an individual (intuitive) to a more collective (shared) assessment. The many tend to know more than the few, and a collective can be more intelligent than its smartest member, provided that diversity and independence are embraced. Sharing knowledge, exchanging experiences and collaboratively accumulating information in order to come to more precise assessments are part of dealing with wicked problems. In general, three types of techniques can be applied to work towards a more accurate assessment of the problem:

■   **Wisdom of the crowd, sociocracy and inter-rater reliability tests:** practitioners, (groups of) students or relatively uninformed participants can fill out the checklist individually and subsequently compare results. This leads to a substantive discussion (it is not about persuasion) on possible outliers and potential adjustment based on informed *consent*. If two or more groups arrive at different assessments, this might be an indication of the wickedness of the problem. This method is also known as the 'wisdom of the crowd' method, which is based on the notion that a *diverse collection of independently deciding individuals* is likely to make better predictions than an individual. It is claimed to produce better results than methods involving only experts when addressing wicked problems (Watkins and Stratenus, 2016). The approach can be complemented with 'sociocratic principles', in which each group member has the responsibility to contribute to effective group decision-making based on *equal participation*. Sociocratic deliberation and decision-making are founded on *consent* – rather than achieving consensus as a goal in itself – meaning that no member has a remaining argued or paramount objection to a proposed assessment. In addition to equivalence and consent, sociocratic participative decision-making includes principles of empiricism, intentionality, distributive leadership, transparency and effectiveness.[6]

---

6   Applied to larger groups, sociocratic decision-making can be organized in 'circles' (semi-autonomous working groups that are self-correcting and self-regulating), and 'double links' (feedback loops between these groups that reinforce self-correcting forces).

- **Multiple-stakeholder discussions:** the same 'inter-rater reliability' type of test can be conducted between stakeholders around the issue. Provided that they represent relevant dimensions of the issue, their complementary assessments can create a richer description of the problem. A well-considered selection of the stakeholders on the basis of societal triangulation principles provides better results in defining a problem. Chapter 5 will discuss this further.

- **Expert assessments:** this is the usual technique applied to more complex problems. The UN website provides assessments of trends on each of the SDGs made by experts and international organizations (such as the World Bank, the International Monetary Fund, the World Business Council for Sustainable Development and UN organizations). However, expert assessments must be used critically and prudently. Given the relative specialization of many scientific disciplines, finding expertise that covers all dimensions of a wicked problem and experts able and willing to engage in actionable research, will prove difficult.

The dominant approach in general discussions on the SDGs is often to organize a multi-stakeholder engagement formula and try to get as many experts in the room as possible. In general, this *landscaping* or *scoping* method tends to take a relatively indiscriminate approach towards the ten complexity dimensions. The stakeholders present create a shared problem definition (based on a shared concern), and facilitate projects in which stakeholders try to collaborate. The risk this essentially mobilizing approach runs is that it abstracts from the exact content of the wicked problem (see Chapter 5).

In case of immediate crises, the necessity of a swift yet well-considered and effective response is obvious. Some authors refer to this as 'inescapable wickedity' (Jordan et al., 2014). In such instances, approaches are applied that concentrate on so-called 'coalitions of the willing': those stakeholders ready to act on the wicked problem, for which they will attempt to optimize their involvement. Although effective stakeholder participation is crucial for addressing wicked problems, a coalition of the willing might not represent the 'coalition of the *needed*': all stakeholders that are *relevant* and, therefore, indispensable in any effort to tackle the problem (Chapter 12). Addressing the SDGs through the engagement of multiple stakeholders hence requires a sufficient understanding of the societal complexities involved: Who are part of the problem and hence need to be part of working towards solutions? Societal complexity (dimensions 9 and 10) deserves further elaboration in the next chapter, where we will address 'societal triangulation'.

THE IMPORTANCE OF AN OPEN DISCUSSION

APPLYING THE 'WISDOM OF THE CROWD METHOD': ASSESSING THE WICKEDNESS OF THE SDGs

In the academic years 2018–2021, groups of bachelor's and master's students at the Rotterdam School of Management were asked to assess the wickedness of a specific SDG as part of several courses around leadership, sustainability and governance issues. They were asked to generate a 'poster' that presented the results of their collective effort, which they had to 'defend' in front of their colleagues. They had one week of preparation time. Each group consisted of four students on average, aged between 19 and 22 years. Most groups were diverse with students from all over the world. Not being an expert in any of the topics, they were assigned an SDG and a group. Each group applied the 'wisdom of the crowd' method through six steps:

1   **Quick reading:** They started by reading a booklet that explained the general background of the SDG-agenda, its ambitions and some of its major characteristics, including some general framing exercises on how to deal with 'wicked problems' (Van Tulder, 2018). The booklet also contained information on key UN websites (Chapters 2 and 3) where they could find relevant statistics and information on each of the SDGs.

TOOL 4.1

2   **Sourcing:** Next, they were invited to either take the general SDG or an SDG-target and check whether they could find any appropriate databases to get a first impression on relevant analytical dimensions and trends: is 'the problem' increasing or decreasing, and why? Students could inform each other on useful databases and share first impressions on trends (or identify the lack of clear patterns or information). More advanced students sometimes chose to focus their analysis on one particular sector, region or country.

3   **Application of scoreboard:** Students were then asked to apply the 'wicked-ness' scoreboard on an individual basis, and to give a 'level of complexity' score (1–7) to each of the ten dimensions specified in the scoreboard.

4   **Inter-rater reliability and sociocracy:** This follow-up step focused on inter-rater reliability and peer review within the group: the four students compared each other's 'scores' on the scoreboard and were asked to discuss those complexity dimensions where they had more or less similar scores (-1; +1 difference). Did they have more or less overlapping reasons and arguments to converge on this? If yes, continue. If no, they were asked to discuss those scales where significant differences in scoring appeared: (1) what explained these differences, and (2) whether they could agree on an 'upgraded' score for which they could reach consent. Each of these steps had to be explained in a short supportive statement.

5   **Poster compilation:** Then, they were invited to make an informative and synthesizing poster of their findings, presenting: (a) the general problem of the SDG(-target) that had been considered, (b) significant trends on that, (c) how the issue scored on the total scale (scores from 10–70), (d) how they could explain this in a general narrative (on the poster), and (e) what these findings would imply for any type of approach to the SDGs. The students were also asked to look at possible opportunities and solution-oriented directions, and consider frontrunner examples that could be aligned to the wickedness of the problem.

6   **Poster sharing:** the final step consisted of the groups presenting their posters to their fellow students. Some student groups had been assigned the same SDG, which enabled them to engage in an intergroup inter-rater reliability discussion on findings and further argumentation. Other groups assigned a distinct SDG engaged by giving feedback, in particular on the solid and persua-sive power of the argument and on how it was presented.

The result: in almost all cases, students were able to accumulate, present and discuss wicked SDG problems in an academic and skilful manner. Business students were able and open to exploring the systemic nature of specific problems and learned that 'simple solutions' (or certain business models) were not very 'cool' and would require more sophisticated thinking, also at the micro-level of analysis – the next step of their assignments. The posters based on 'wisdom of the crowd' insights validated the technique of the scoreboard. The poster presentations also offered a stepping stone to further studies and discussion.

The poster presentation form illustrates how rather complex issues can be communicated quite effectively in an informative and attractive manner, along the outcomes of the assessment technique applied. A repository of posters is available for each of the SDGs. Consult https://www.principlesofsustainablebusiness.nl/sdg-posters/.

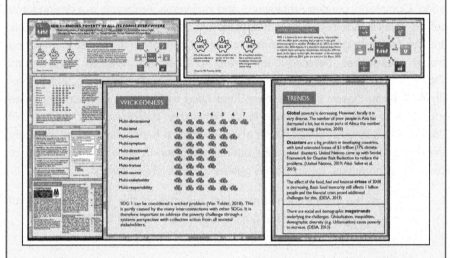

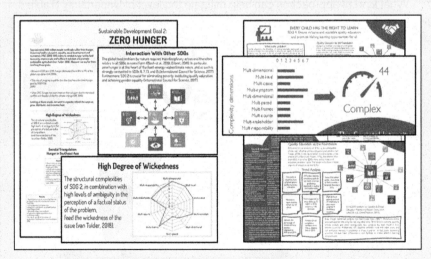

Examples of student SDG posters: applying the wickedness scoreboard

4.5 CONCLUSION, TOOLS AND RESOURCES

It can be argued that we tend to know more about the structural and generative complexities surrounding the SDGs than about their dynamic, communicative and societal complexities. How interdependencies, varying paces of development and diverse frames are linked and affect other complexity dimensions is still largely obscure. Often, this can only be explored and experienced through actual interventions. But what a 'relevant' intervention is depends on the nature of the problem, which in turn hinges on the levels of complexity and ambiguities involved. In a VUCA world, Complexity creates Ambiguity – and vice versa. Ambiguity is a driving force behind Volatility and hence affects both the direction and pattern of developments (trends). Volatility generates further Uncertainty, notably with regard to choosing proper approaches deemed best suited for reaching selected SDG-targets (Figure 4.1). This 'CAVU' interaction is circular, can be self-reinforcing, and eventually defines the 'levels of intervention' that need to be taken into account when addressing the SDGs as an opportunity, rather than a problem only (the topic of Chapter 5). Acting on the SDGs in a VUCA context hence implies that sufficient analytical, conceptual and empirical attention is given to each of the elements of this CAVU interaction. Basically, this relates to iteratively exploring:

1   What is the nature of the problem (navigating the ten dimensions of Complexity and related Ambiguities, see Table 4.3 and Scoreboard #1);

2   What are trends that delineate the Volatility of the issue;

3   What kind of approaches can help mitigate the level of Uncertainty (Table 4.4).

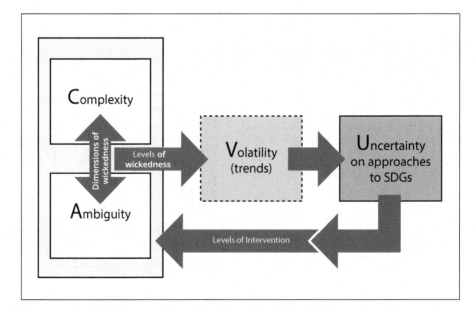

Figure 4.1 VUCA and the SDGs: What explains levels of wickedness?

Table 4.4 Navigating questions to assess the wickedness of an SDG(-target)

1. **What is the nature of the problem?**	**C**	What type of **Complexity** needs to be addressed: is the problem a sign of an (urgent) incident, a temporary (short-term) problem, or of systemic (longer-term) failure?
	A	What type of **Ambiguity** prevails and why: knowledge, predictive and/or intervention ambiguity? Is there sufficient knowledge and definitional clarity? Can we distinguish causalities, correlations, know the likelihood of events (reliable/probable, less reliable/less probable predictions) and account for unintended consequences? What degree of intervention ambiguity exists and why?
2. **What are trends?**	**V**	What are trends that define the **Volatility** of the issue: has the problem been growing or declining over the 2000–recent period? What is the shape of identifiable trends: linear, circular, U-shaped, S-shaped, erratic, exponential? Are interests converging or diverging around the issue? Are effective governance measures in place to channel the problem?
3. **What uncertainties need to be addressed?**	**U**	What type of **Uncertainty** needs to be addressed and by whom? Is it clear who bears primary responsibility and who is willing and able to take up responsibility?

- Most societal problems go beyond being complex: they classify as wicked;

- Wicked problems are systemic, ill-structured, have *no definite solutions* and require the involvement of interested parties to work towards *solution-oriented approaches*;

- The SDGs are generally wicked: they require systemic approaches and multi-stakeholder engagement to understand and address them;

- Societal problems vary in their degree of wickedness: not all problems are equally intractable, not all SDGs are equally wicked. Addressing wicked problems requires an effort of analytical disentanglement by recognizing the structural, generative, dynamic, communicative and societal complexities involved;

- Sources of wickedness can be found in the nature of the VUCA world: Complexity and Ambiguities feed into Volatility (and trends) that create Uncertainty about the 'right' way to approach grand challenges like the SDGs;

- Three types of ambiguity complicate matters in analytical, empirical and conceptual terms: knowledge ambiguity, predictive ambiguity and intervention ambiguity;

- Ten dimensions of complexity were identified that together indicate the degree of wickedness; ten scales facilitate an assessment on the extent to which a multitude of factors contribute to the problem, to develop insights into possible openings;

- Out-of-the-box, creative and paradoxical thinking techniques are necessary to effectively address the kind of complexity that is linked to most (not all) SDGs;

- Wicked problems require stakeholder engagement, developmental evaluation and 'wisdom of the crowd' techniques.

- **WEF Strategic Intelligence:** a navigating tool developed by the World Economic Forum to support strategic insights and contextual intelligence on interrelated societal issues. Facilitates exploration of the themes and forces that drive change across economies, industries and global issues by means of *Dynamic Global Transformation Maps*: a three-layered, attractively visualized tool to discover and zoom in on interlinked issues. Covers over 80 global strategic topics, ranging from artificial intelligence, biodiversity and human rights to internet governance, values, and international security. Provides an entry of interrelated topics via each of the 17 SDGs. https://intelligence.weforum.org/topics?tab=publications&type=Sustainable+Development+Goals

- **Fragile States Index (FSI):** in a highly interconnected world, pressures on one (fragile) state can have serious repercussions, also for neighbouring states and countries halfway across the globe. Fault lines can emerge between identity groups (language, religion, race, ethnicity, nationality, class, caste, clan or area of origin); tensions can deteriorate into conflict through, for instance, competition over resources, predatory or fractured leadership, corruption, or unresolved group grievances. "The reasons for state fragility are complex, but not unpredictable." Produced by The Fund for Peace, FSI is a critical tool in highlighting not only the normal pressures that all states experience but also in identifying when those pressures outweigh a state's capacity to manage those pressures. The index contains dashboards of indicator-level and trend data for 178 countries. https://fragilestatesindex.org/

- **UN SDG Knowledge Platform:** knowledge hub of the UN Division for Sustainable Development Goals that provides wide access to information and knowledge for sustainable development. It contains databases, analytical tools and resources, and access to the Voluntary National Review Database (VNRs), inputs to the High-level Political Forum (HLPF), the Partnerships Platform, SDG-related Topics. https://sustainabledevelopment.un.org/

- **Future Earth:** a global network of scientists and innovators that develops knowledge and tools that government, communities and companies need to meet the 17 SDGs. By understanding connections between environmental, social and economic systems, Future Earth works to facilitate research and innovation, build and mobilize networks, and shape the narrative, turning knowledge into action. Its Knowledge-Action Networks focus on key societal challenges and cross-cutting topics to generate interdisciplinary and actionable scientific knowledge. Topics range from 'emergent risk and extreme events' and 'finance and economics', to 'systems of sustainable consumption and production' and 'urban' development: https://futureearth.org/about/our-work/

- **Sociocracy for all:** a non-profit social enterprise providing easy access to resources (introduction videos, introduction articles, graphics, case studies and models), training and implementation of sociocracy (also known as 'dynamic governance') as a group decision-making method and way of organizing based on principles of equivalence, consent, intentionality, distributive leadership transparency, empiricism and effectiveness. https://www.sociocracyforall.org/start-here/

SELECTED WEB RESOURCES

■ *First Draft:* an independent non-profit coalition and network of international news-rooms, universities, platforms and civil society organizations directed towards empow-ering societies with accurate information at critical moments. It aims to ensure the integrity of the world's information ecosystem, developing and delivering techniques, tools and training for how information is discovered, shared and presented to the public. For tools and guides to recognize and fight misinformation, disinformation, mal-infor-mation, fake news and other information disorders: https://firstdraftnews.org/training/

■ *UN Sustainable Development News:* daily news coverage, special reports, feature pieces (text, audio, video, graphics) from the newsroom of the UN, related to sustain-able development and the 17SDGs. https://www.un.org/sustainabledevelopment/news/

REFERENCES

Alford, J. & Head, B.W. (2017). 'Wicked and less wicked problems: a typology and a contin-gency framework', *Policy and Society*, 36(3):397–413.

Australian Public Service Commission (2012). *Tackling wicked problems: A public policy perspective*, March.

Bardi, U. (2015). 'Wicked problems and wicked solutions: the case of the world's food supply', blogpost on resilience.org, 15 July.

Conklin, J. (2006). *Dialogue Mapping: Building Shared Understanding of Wicked Problems*. Chichester, UK: Wiley and Sons.

Crilly, D., Zollo, M. & Hansen, M.T. (2012). 'Faking It or Muddling Through? Understanding Decoupling in Response to Stakeholder Pressures', *Academy of Management Journal*, 55(6):1429–1448.

Crowley, K. & Head, B.W. (2017). 'The enduring challenge of "wicked problems": revisiting Rittel and Webber', *Policy Sciences*, (50):539–547.

Daviter, F. (2017). 'Coping, taming or solving: alternative approaches to the governance of wicked problems', *Policy Studies*, 38(6):571–588.

Daviter, F. (2017a). 'Policy analysis in the face of complexity: What kind of knowledge to tackle wicked problems?', *Public Policy and Administration*, 34(1):62–83.

De Bruijn, C. (2018). *Key Performance Illusions*: pitfalls and loopholes in performance measure-ment, Van Duuren Management.

Eisenhardt, K.M. (2000). 'Paradox, Spirals, Ambivalence: The New Language of Change and Pluralism', *Academy of Management Review*, 25(4):703–705.

Fahey, L. (2016). 'John C. Camillus: discovering opportunities by exploring wicked problems, *Strategy & Leadership*, 44(5):29–35.

Fischer, F. (1993). 'Citizen participation and the democratization of policy expertise: From theoretical inquiry to practical cases', *Policy sciences*, 26(3):165–187.

Frenkel-Brunswik, E. (1949). 'Intolerance of ambiguity as an emotional and perceptual personality variable', *Journal of Personality*, 18(1):108–143.

Grint, K. (2008). 'Wicked Problems and Clumsy Solutions: The Role of Leadership', *Clinical Leader*, 1(2):54–68.

Hanson, L.L. (2019). 'Wicked Problems and Sustainable Development'. In: Leal Filho, W. (Ed.) *Encyclopedia of Sustainability in Higher Education*, (pp. 2091–2098). Switzerland: Springer Nature.

Hartmann, T. (2012). 'Wicked problems and clumsy solutions: Planning as expectation management, *Planning Theory*, 11(3):242–256.

Hawken, P. (2017). *Drawdown. The Most Comprehensive Plan Ever Proposed to Reverse Global Warming*, Penguin Books.

Head, B.W. (2019). 'Forty years of wicked problems literature: forging closer links to policy studies', *Policy and Society*, 38(2):180–197.

Head, B.W. & Alford, J. (2015). 'Wicked problems: the implications for public policy and management', *Administration & Society*, 47(6):711–739.

IPBES (2019). *Summary for policymakers of the global assessment report on biodiversity and ecosystem services of the Intergovernmental Science-Policy Platform on Biodiversity and Ecosystem Services*, approved by the IPBES Plenary, May 2019 (IPBES-7). Bonn, Germany: IPBES.

Jordan, M.E., Kleinsasser, R.C. & Roe, M.F. (2014). 'Wicked problems: inescapable wickedity', *Journal of Education for Teaching*, 40(4):415–430.

Klein, N. (2007). *The Shock Doctrine. The Rise of Disaster Capitalism*. Allen Lane / Penguin Books.

Krugman, P. (2013). 'The New Growth Fizzle', *The New York Times*, 18 August. Retrieved from: https://krugman.blogs.nytimes.com/2013/08/18/the-new-growth-fizzle/.

Lewis, M. (2000). 'Exploring Paradox: Toward a More Comprehensive Guide, *The Academy of Management Review*, 25(4):760–776.

Mann, C. (2018). *The Wizard and the Prophet. Science and the Future of Our Planet*. New York: Alfred Knopf.

McConnell, A. (2018). 'Rethinking wicked problems as political problems and policy problems', *Policy & Politics*, 46(1):165–180.

McKinsey Global Institute (2015). *The Power of Parity: How Advancing Women's Equality Can Add $12 Trillion to Global Growth*, September.

Merton, R.K. (1936). 'The Unanticipated Consequences of Purposive Social Action', *American Sociological Review*, 1(6):894–904.

Metlay, D. & Sarewitz, D. (2012). 'Decision Strategies for Addressing Complex, "Messy" Problems', *The Bridge*, 42(3):6–16.

Mintzberg, H. (1980). 'Structure in 5's: A Synthesis of the Research on Organization Design', *Management Science*, 26(3):322–341.

Ney, S. & Verweij, M. (2015). 'Messy institutions for wicked problems: How to generate clumsy solutions?', *Environment and Planning C: Politics and Space*, 33(6): 1679–1696.

Nie, M. (2003). 'Drivers of natural resource-based political conflict', *Policy Sciences*, 36(3/4):307–341.

OECD (2016). *Better Policies for Sustainable Development 2016: A New Framework for Policy Coherence*. Paris: OECD Publishing.

Olsson, A., Wadell, C., Odenrick, P. & Bergendahl, M.N. (2010). 'An action learning method for increased innovation capacity in organisations,' *Action Learning: Research and Practice* 7(2):167–179.

Parkhust, J. (2016). 'Appeals to evidence for the resolution of wicked problems: the origins and mechanisms of evidentiary bias", *Policy Sciences*, (49):373–393.

Partos (2016). *Ready for Change? Global Goals at home and abroad*, 19 May. The Hague: Partos.

Peterson, J.B. (2018). *12 Rules for Life. An Antidote to Chaos*. Random House Canada.

Remington-Doucette, S. (2013). *Sustainable World: Approaches to Analyzing and Resolving Wicked Problems*. Kendall Hunt Publishing.

Rittel, H.W.J. & Webber, M.M. (1973). 'Dilemmas in a general theory of planning', *Policy Sciences*, 4(2):155–169.

Roberts, N.C. (2000). 'Wicked Problems and Network Approaches to Resolution', *The International Public Management Review*, 1(1):1–19.

Rosling, H., with Rosling, O. & Rosling Rönnlund, A. (2018). *Factfulness: Ten Reasons We're Wrong About the World – and Why Things Are Better Than You Think*. Flariton Books.

Schneider, A., Wickert, C. & Marti, E. (2017). 'Reducing Complexity by Creating Complexity: A Systems Theory Perspective on How Organizations Respond to Their Environments', *Journal of Management Studies*, 54(2):182–208.

Strijker-van Asperen, Z.M. & Van Tulder, R. (2016). *Wicked Problems Plaza. Principles and Practices for Effective Multi-Stakeholder Dialogue*. Rotterdam: The Partnerships Resource Centre (PrC), RSM-Erasmus University.

Sukhdev, P. (2012). *Corporation 2020. Transforming Business for Tomorrow's World*. Washington: Island Press.

Termeer, C.J.A.M., Dewulf, A. & Biesbroek, R. (2019). 'A critical assessment of the wicked problem concept: relevance and usefulness for policy science and practice', *Policy and Society*, 38(2):167–179.

The Economist (2018). 'The missing 235m. Why India needs women to work', 7 July.

The Economist (2018). 'Economists understand little about the causes of growth', 14 April.

UN (2019). *The Report of the Secretary General: The Special Edition of the Sustainable Development Goals Progress Report*. New York: United Nations.

UN (1992). *Convention on Biological Diversity*, New York: United Nations. Retrieved from: https://www.cbd.int/doc/legal/cbd-en.pdf.

Van Tulder, R. (2018). *Business & The Sustainable Development Goals: A Framework for Effective Corporate Involvement*. Rotterdam: Rotterdam School of Management, Erasmus University.

Van Tulder, R. & Keen, N. (2018). 'Capturing Collaborative Challenges: Designing Complexity-Sensitive Theories of Change for Cross-Sector Partnerships', *Journal of Business Ethics*, 150(2):315–332.

Verweij, M., Ney, S. & Thompson, M. (2011). 'Clumsy solutions for a wicked world'. In: Verweij, M. (2011). *Clumsy Solutions for a Wicked World: How to Improve Global Governance*. Basingstoke: Palgrave Macmillan.

Verweij, M., Douglas, M., Ellis, R., Engel, C., Hendriks, F., Lohmann, S. Ney, S. Rayner, S. & Thompson, M. (2006). 'Clumsy Solutions for a Complex World: The Case of Climate Change', *Public Administration*, 84(4):817–843.

Waddock, S., Meszoely, G.M., Waddell, S. & Dentoni, D. (2015). 'The complexity of wicked problems in large scale change', *Journal of Organizational Change Management*, 28(6):993–1012.

Watkins, A. & Stratenus, I. (2016). *Crowdocracy: The End of Politics?* Wicked & Wise Series. Kent: Urbane Publications.

Weitz, N., Nilsson, M. & Davis, M. (2014). 'A Nexus Approach to the Post-2015 Agenda: Formulating Integrated Water, Energy, and Food SDGs', *SAIS Review of International Affairs*, 34(2):37–50.

Whetten, D.A. & Cameron, K.S. (2008). *Developing Management Skills*, 7th Edition. Upper Saddle River: Prentice Hall.

Whetten, D.A., Cameron, K.S. & Woods, M. (2000). *Developing Management Skills for Europe*, Second Edition. Pearson Education.

Wildavsky, A. (1979). *Speaking Truth to Power. The Art and Craft of Policy Analysis*. New Brunswick: Transaction.

World Bank (2018). *Poverty and Shared Prosperity 2018: Piecing Together the Poverty Puzzle*. Washington, DC: World Bank Group.

Xiang, W.N. (2013). 'Working with wicked problems in socio-ecological systems: Awareness, acceptance, and adaptation', *Landscape and Urban Planning*, 110(1):1–4.

5 WHAT AND WHO?
THE SDGs AS WICKED OPPORTUNITIES

DOI: 10.4324/9781003098355-7

- **Fiduciary duty principle:** applied in corporate ethics to denote primary responsibility for not acting against the benefit of others in the execution of core roles, functions and activities.

- **'Do no harm' principle:** negative duty approach to ethical challenges, meaning that the actions of actors should enclose preventing, reducing and controlling the risk of harm to others (related to trade-off and dilemma thinking).

- **'Doing good' principle:** positive duty approach to ethical challenges, meaning that the actions of actors should contribute to the creation, distribution and maximization of beneficial outcomes for others (related to ethical puzzles and paradoxical thinking).

- **Win-win principle:** a notion that conveys reciprocity and mutually beneficial outcomes. If merely used as a frame that disregards short-term losses or friction problems, it runs the risk of overly optimistic decision-making and engagement that underestimates vital trade-offs in longer-term change processes.

- **Negotiation principles:** traditional approaches to negotiating are either 'interest-based' (win-win compromises) or 'position-based' (win-lose outcomes). 'Collective vision-based' negotiations are directed towards synthesizing interests and positive-sum outcomes that are grounded in agreed upon goals.

- **Principle of conditional morality:** refers to the moral conduct that materializes in the interaction between actors. Moral duties are conceived as conditional on the extent to which others fulfil their moral duties, leaving a margin for 'agency'. Takes into account behavioural concepts such as 'social contract', utilitarian decision-making, free-riding, shirking.

- **Categorical imperative:** a form of unconditional morality that prescribes duties and norms irrespective of contextual conditions and the conduct of others. Unconditional morality may crowd out the moral duties of primary responsible 'issue owners' if actors who reasonably do not hold responsibility for an issue, nevertheless take responsibility (also known as the 'sucker principle').

- **Societal triangulation principle:** always consider the complementary logics, roles, functions, values, means and competences of all three societal spheres (state, market, civil society) when analysing a wicked problem and considering solution-oriented opportunities.

- **Partnering principle:** collaborating can create additional value (collaborative advantage, synergistic value, 'wicked opportunity') for those issues that individual actors cannot effectively deal with on their own. The principle comprises mutually reinforcing arrangements (not compromise), based on goal alignment and complementary logics and competences.

■ **Coalition principles:** to be effective in addressing the envisaged goal, partnerships should strive to represent 'coalitions of the needed' rather than
'coalitions of the willing'.

■ **'Fit' principles**: to seize opportunities from collaborative advantage in
addressing societal problems, various 'fit' dimensions must be reckoned with:
'complexity fit', 'issue-partnering fit', 'partner fit', 'culture fit', 'dynamic fit'.

■ **'Developmental evaluation' principle:** relates to continuous feedback
loops and ongoing review of interventions, to timely adjust to dynamic realities in complex environments. The pursuit of establishing a 'dynamic issue-
partnering fit' is grounded in the learning-by-doing experience of participants,
which should lead to improved intervention logics and the fine-tuning of the
Theory of Change, along various phases of the partnership.

**P
R
I
N
C
I
P
L
E
S**

5.1 INTRODUCTION: FRAMING APPROACHES –
SOLUTIONS OR OPPORTUNITIES?

"In the middle of difficulty lies opportunity"
(attributed to) Albert Einstein

"A pessimist sees the difficulty in every opportunity;
an optimist sees the opportunity in every difficulty"
Winston S. Churchill

A VUCA world creates threats, but also opportunities. Where societal boundaries
shift, blur or dissolve altogether, uncertainty and ambiguity thrive (Chapter 4). The
resulting voids and transition frictions not only generate new complexities
conceived of as 'problems', but also create new 'space', and hence opportunities,
to address societal problems in innovative ways. Driven by developments in digitalization, connectivity, and new modes of collaboration and organization, some
authors have even argued that in the present era the 'art of the possible' is
expanding (Kelly, 2015), enabling fundamentally new approaches to societal
challenges. For those capable of seeing the world through different eyes and
mental frames, complexity may be explored and leveraged as a means to drive
breakthroughs. From that angle, wicked problems could probably be *reframed* as
'wicked opportunities'. Foresight and innovation strategist Frank Spencer coined
this concept to point out the importance of developing a mentality that preserves

a positive relationship with volatile change, by continuing to see 'the big picture' and the convergence in *patterns* amidst accelerating complexity and unpredictability. Instead of operating out of fear, leaders would need to consider complexity as "a catalyst for new ideas that can solve age-old problems" in order to "intentionally seize the opportunities that emerge from the fertile environment of increasing complexity". He hence called for an upsurge of aspirational "wicked organizations, wicked innovators and wicked entrepreneurs" to resolve long-standing societal problems (Spencer, 2013).

OVERCOMING SIMPLIFICATION TENDENCIES

As mentioned in Chapter 4, the general reflex in response to increased complexity is to eliminate it. Narrowed thinking in the search for (quick) fixes and 'solutions' is cognitively determined and, therefore, understandable, but contentious. When faced with difficult challenges, most people rarely ask clarifying questions about the nature, scope, scale, (root) causes or the main dynamics of a problem.[1] Within a narrowed-down scope of reality and a limited set of explanations and options, they quickly get stuck on a certain 'solution' while ignoring possible alternatives with potentially more beneficial overall outcomes in the longer run. Matters get worse if that particular solution pathway is voiced by an authoritative person or influential stakeholder group, and backed by considerable energy spent on forming like-minded *coalitions of the willing*. When these coalitions fall prey to oversimplified 'win-win' framed prospects and group-thinking dynamics, they may actually add complexity to the initial problem and contribute to its wickedness by creating path dependencies. Addressing wicked problems hence calls for counterbalancing through diversity.

The original thinkers behind wicked problems theory – Rittel and Webber (1973) – not only postulated that wicked problems cannot be solved, but also that there is no template to follow when tackling them. Four decades later, second-generation wicked problems scholars have started to acknowledge that it could well be within humanity's reach to effectively address wicked problems. But society needs different arrangements, other (proactive and ambiguity tolerant) mindsets, and renewed joined-up vigour that organizes and benefits from *solution ecosystems*. Unprecedented networks of NGOs, social entrepreneurs, health professionals, governments and businesses are coalescing around societal problems to recast them as opportunities. The SDG approach might define such a

---

1   Daniel Kahneman (2012) noticed the strong psychological roots hereof, pointing to the inclination of people to ask 'heuristic questions': people reformulate a complex question into a simpler one that they find easier to answer. Consequently, heuristic questions not only encourage misleading simplifications, but in the case of more complex problems also lead to inappropriate actions based on wrong and often negatively framed premises. This praxis is adamant in a VUCA society and triggers 'either/or' thinking, rather than 'paradoxical' thinking (see Box 4.3).

uniting and reigniting ecosystem. However, a mere reframing of wicked problems as wicked opportunities to entice a different mindset will hardly suffice in practice. Coming to grips with societal challenges requires a far more comprehensive approach. This chapter delineates ways to get out of the paralysis that wicked problems tend to create and examines what this implies for the SDG trajectory. We consider *two complementary approaches* for exploring how to change wicked problems into opportunities: (1) a more procedural, *inside-out* approach, and (2) a more analytical, *outside-in* approach.

INSIDE-OUT: PROCEDURAL

A procedural approach is often adopted in so-called *multi-stakeholder engagement* strategies that appeal to the willingness of stakeholders to stand against a societal problem and join forces in becoming part of a solution. Although many of these approaches are highly diverse in scope and purpose, most typically seek to mobilize as many stakeholders as possible to express a shared aspiration, come to a common problem definition (based on a shared concern), manage expectations, and basically facilitate those processes in which parties feel they should collaborate to make change happen. This type of response often abstracts from the essence of the wicked problem. It typically adopts an *inside-out* perspective that draws on a search for common denominators and general process characteristics that actors should consider in their efforts to address the problem. The approaches introduced then primarily reflect the *internal dynamics* of the multi-stakeholder configuration (*strategy follows structure*), such as power dynamics, managing compromise and procedures for dealing with conflict, learning and communication. This kind of process orientation has been applied in networked governance approaches to wicked problems (Ferlie et al., 2011), to leadership questions in general and in approaches for corporate leaders on how to deal with wicked problems (Brown et al., 2010).

Chapter 3 documented that a networked, multi-stakeholder, hybrid governance approach was also embraced in the set-up of the SDG-agenda. It concluded that this governance architecture might account for part of the trailing progress in the first four years of implementation. The practice of loosely organized, bottom-up, multi-stakeholder approaches displays several procedural flaws that explain the relatively modest performance of many engagement processes. Multi-stakeholder projects aimed at seizing the opportunities of the SDG-agenda rarely start with a full exploration of the nature of the problem. Neither do they define what they consider the systemic context of the problem, nor what stakeholders' own (direct or indirect) contributions to the cause or continuation of system failures may have been. Partly, this is due to the inherent complexities involved; partly, it also reflects the reticence of (prospective) partners to what might be expected of them in more compelling terms when acknowledging some form of responsibility. Most current multi-stakeholder initiatives within the SDG realm concentrate on voluntary coalitions (of willing actors). However, the more wicked the problem is, the less sufficient an approach of solely voluntary coalition-building tends to be. Voluntary engagement strategies generally focus on optimizing the involvement of the present selection of participants in addressing the problem, rather than enhancing the impact of their collective action by involving *needed* stakeholders – those stakeholders who are presently part of the problem and, therefore, should be considered crucial in working towards scalable, solution-oriented opportunities. Even so, active stakeholder participation is and remains an indispensable requirement for addressing wicked problems, although its effectiveness requires close monitoring.

OUTSIDE-IN: ANALYTICAL

An analytical approach is hence additionally required. Analysis adds an *outside-in* perspective to the process dynamics that allows for consideration of contextual factors. Wicked problems always originate at the societal level, beyond the grasp of individual organizations. An analytical approach defines which societal actors are part of the problem, before considering the configuration and dynamics of any type of stakeholder engagement (*structure follows strategy*). In scientific literature, taking stock of a problem from various angles is also called 'triangulation'. Societal triangulation implies that we take the various societal positions of actors into account when defining the societal sources of wickedness, as well as the appropriate levels of intervention suited to address the problem.

The potential of the SDGs as an opportunity lies in a proper understanding of the societal complexities involved and the complementary logics required for balanced societies. Abstract problems defined at the macro level can only be resolved, however, if they can be reframed into organizational and leadership challenges. This chapter applies institutional and welfare theory (as explained in Chapter 1) to define the *societal sources of wickedness* ('what is needed') and *societal sources of success* ('what gets adopted, by whom, and under what conditions') in section 5.2. The chapter reasons that effectively addressing the SDGs requires a more solid understanding of 'who' and 'what' questions: who is to be engaged, in addressing what type of wicked problem, and at what *level of intervention* (section 5.3). We will see that seizing opportunities while addressing wicked problems almost always involves a collaborative challenge. This consequently raises the question of how to address the institutional void and overcome accompanying trust gaps to create a proper partnering space (section 5.4). Section 5.5 then considers the importance of creating cross-sector partnerships that '*fit*' the complexity level involved and the type of change envisaged. We will argue that *collaborative advantage,* in any event, requires *partnership configurations* that include coalitions of needed partners, rather than coalitions of willing partners. Synergistic value ('wicked opportunity') comes from sameness in goal alignment and uniqueness in complementary 'assets'. Finally, section 5.6 wraps up and supports by mapping the kind of *partnering approach* and the steps required to create opportunities from effectively addressing problems (Scoreboard #2).

5.2 ADDRESSING SOURCES OF WICKEDNESS THROUGH SOCIETAL TRIANGULATION

Arguably the most wicked part of the SDG challenge relates to societal complexities. Stakeholders and interest groups are needed to address the issue. They also steer, shape and affect how issues are framed and perceived, how information is gathered and created, and how decisions are made. *Agency* hence creates additional complexity and may substantially add to the degree of wickedness involved. Chapter 1 already elaborated on the societal argument in terms of public-good theory ('common-pool' problems) and the various value propositions of societal actors (private value, public value, social value) required to deal with grand challenges (section 1.3.3; Figure 1.3). Accordingly, the societal sources of wickedness can best be linked to the three most important 'societal sectors' or 'institutional spheres' that surround and define societal issues: *governments* (state), *firms* (market), and *citizens* (communities/civil society). Each societal sector adds a distinct and complementary logic to the issue, as their primary responsibilities, main competencies and main duties differ markedly from each other. The principle of *societal triangulation* boils down to questions of (1) whether, and to what extent, each of the societal sectors 'have' and actively 'take' responsibilities in addressing a particular societal challenge, and (2) what this entails in a world that is increasingly characterized by shifting, blurring and dissolving (institutional) boundaries.

BALANCED AND COMPLEMENTARY LOGICS

Sustainable development basically requires balanced development (cf. Mintzberg, 2015). Wicked problems appear in particular when and where this balance is disturbed, for instance when one of the societal sectors underperforms in fulfilling its primary responsibilities. State, market and civil society each generate particular complementary goods and services, and thereby add value to society. The three societal sectors each employ a logic, rationality and ideology of their own and essentially also occupy a different role and position in society. Through legislation, the government (state) provides the legal framework that structures society, which answers the need of society for reduced uncertainty. Firms (market) primarily create value and welfare for society by converting inputs into outputs within the bounds of the legal framework. In this way, business satisfies the needs of society through market transactions in pursuit of profit. Civil society or communities represent the sum of social relations among citizens that structures society outside politics and business. It includes family, voluntary organizations, societal groupings, churches and trade unions. As an organized network of citizens, civil society fulfils the need for relationships, mutual support and socialization through the development and sharing of norms (Wartick and Wood, 1999).

Societal and human relations shape a more, or a less, sustainable society. Processes of interaction do, however, require mechanisms for coordination and regulation. The market regulates through competition, profit and rewards; the state through legislation, regulation and enforcement; civil society through shared values and norms, participation and collective action. The sources of income within the three societal spheres also differ fundamentally: governments levy taxes; companies generate profits; (non-profit) civil organizations depend on donations and other voluntary contributions (like membership fees). Furthermore, the three societal sectors 'produce' different goods, services and values. The state specifically tends to those goods and services that would not be readily produced otherwise, given that their (marginal) returns cannot be easily distributed. This applies to so-called 'public goods' such as defence and infrastructure, which are generally funded by taxes. In the case of public goods, it is not always possible to distinguish who pays and who benefits. Private goods can be sold much more easily as singular (discrete) products, rendering turnover and profits. Their distribution via markets is easier to organize. There are also many goods and services that are particularly important to some groups, but which are insufficiently provided for by the market and the state. The provision of these so-called 'club goods' is the territory of civil society. In the case of club goods, it is impossible to price the discrete units of benefit they generate, whereas some of the benefits are exclusive and accessible only by club (family, city) members. Through donations, sponsoring, contributions from members and assistance of unpaid volunteers, non-profit organizations make their contribution to the smooth functioning of this societal sector.

COMPLEMENTARY COORDINATION MECHANISMS

Table 5.1 summarizes the most important characteristics and coordinating mechanisms of the three societal spheres. Each of the three societal sectors has a primary function and related (fiduciary) responsibility: to either produce public, private or social goods, services and value. In case of failure to efficiently produce these, the sector loses legitimacy, and a basic responsible governance challenge is generated. Figure 1.3 (section 1.3.3) showed that a fourth area of responsibility exists, which is not covered by any of these three societal sectors: the creation of *common* goods and value – the infamous *tragedy of the commons* type of problem. These problems represent the most wicked among the wicked problems, especially at the global level (*global commons*), because none of the societal sectors bears primary responsibility here. The bigger the uncoordinated and unregulated space is between each of the three sectors, the greater the 'institutional void' and related 'trust gaps' (section 1.3.5).

Table 5.1 Characteristic coordination and governance mechanisms

	STATE	MARKET	CIVIL SOCIETY
Primary importance	Political	Economic	Social
Principal (*de jure* primary control)	Voters, political parties	Owners, Supervisory Board	Society, members
Agency (de facto/ informal control)	Officials, civil servants	Managers, Board of Directors	Managers, techno-crats, volunteers
Goods/value orientation (fiduciary responsibility)	Public goods/services and values	Private goods/ services and values	Social/club goods/ services and values
Core responsibilities	Enforcement of national standards and norms	Production of goods and services	Mutual support
Primary resource	Legislation; regulation; police; armed forces; monopoly on violence	Financial capital, labour, natural resources	Energy of volunteers
Financed by	Taxes and levies	Profits	Donations, contributions
Dominant organizational form	Public; departments, ministries, local councils, provinces/ federal states	For profit; Plc, Ltd, AG, SA	Non-profit; voluntary organization; foundation; association
Parameters	Coercion; Codification	Competition	Cooperation; co-optation
Primary weaknesses	Rigidity and bureaucratization	Monopoly and other forms of 'market failures'	Fragmentation
Ideologies	Anarchy/ Democracy/ Liberalism/ Totalitarianism	Market capitalism/ Mixed economy	Individualism/ Collectivism

Source: based on Waddell (2000: 113); Wartick & Wood (1999: 26ff); World Bank (1997); Van Tulder with Van der Zwart, 2006.

Applied to delineate wicked problems-opportunities, societal triangulation has to match two perspectives:

■ *Outside-in:* in which the societal nature of the problem defines the layers of complexity (section 5.2.1);

■ *Inside-out:* in which the roles of societal sectors and the distribution of responsibilities among them define various approaches towards the problem (section 5.2.2)

By subsequently bringing these two perspectives together, four levels of intervention can be distinguished at which societal challenges can be addressed (the topic of section 5.3).

5.2.1 Outside-in: societal sources (layers) of wickedness

The degree of wickedness of a problem can be defined in terms of the degree to which each societal sector can be expected to take up responsibility for the problem. The more an issue is beyond the grasp of the primary responsibilities and core capabilities of governments, firms and civil society organizations, the more wicked it will be to come to effective solution-oriented approaches. The most wicked problems are positioned in the societal centre, where institutional voids and trust gaps are the biggest (Figure 5.1).

[4+4+4] SYSTEMIC CHALLENGES

So-called 'common pool' problems are nobody's prime responsibility, although they affect everyone in the longer run. They are also referred to as 'tragedy of the commons' and can be considered the most wicked on the scale of societal complexities (scoring 50–70 in Scoreboard #1). Powerful bystander effects appear in which everybody acknowledges the problem, but nobody is able or willing to act. There is no obvious coalition of the willing, nor of the needed. Such systemic problems are also called 'collective action' problems, as they require the joint, coordinated and simultaneous action of the state, market and civil society.

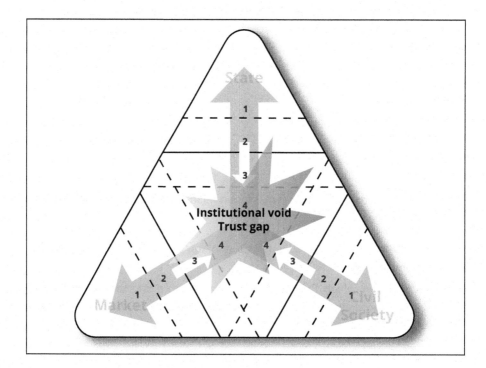

Figure 5.1 The societal intensity of wickedness

[3+3+3] INSUFFICIENT CREATION OF POSITIVE EXTERNALITIES

Some problems can be addressed by either the state, market or civil society, but such efforts run the risk of underperforming if left to the initiating sector itself. This relates to so-called *merit goods*. According to the original economic definition of the concept (Musgrave, 1959), a merit good presents a commodity that a society or individual should have on the basis of some concept of need, rather than the ability and willingness to pay. Insufficient creation of merit goods can be interpreted as an insufficient provision of 'positive externalities'. A positive externality (also called 'external benefit' or 'beneficial externality') is the positive effect that an activity imposes on unrelated others. These can be produced by any sector that is willing and able to invest beyond their own direct interest, thereby creating net benefits to society. Examples of positive externalities include education, vaccination, pollination, job creation effects, open-source software, or investments in enabling public products and services. Individual sectors can take action to fill an identified institutional void, but by doing so may run the risk of taking away the incentive for other sectors to contribute as well. This effect is also known as 'crowding out' (Score: 30–50 in Scoreboard #1).

[2+2+2] LACKING RESPONSIBILITIES TO TAKE CARE OF NEGATIVE EXTERNALITIES

If governments, firms or civil society organizations create adverse effects for society, they impose costs on society. Examples of these so-called 'negative externalities' or 'external costs' are water, soil or air pollution, tax competition ('race to the bottom'), citizens who do not clean up their waste (creating public health issues), and corrupt or inadequate governments. In principle, the sector causing the problem should actively take responsibility and initiate action to solve the issue. Frequently, however, no action is initiated unless those affected *assign responsibility* to those creating the harm (Young, 2006). This can take the form of, for instance, governments regulating against pollution, or citizens and civil society organizations holding governments or firms responsible by protesting against the harmful effects of inaction and neglect (Score: 20–30 in Scoreboard #1).

[1+1+1] SECTORAL FAILURE

Governments, markets and civil society falter in their capabilities to produce sufficient goods, services and values, even when this is their primary responsibility. Market failure exists if firms do not supply goods that people want or can afford; governance failure exists if governments fail to create the laws and provide sufficient regulation to make societies safe and prosperous; civic failure exists if communities do not organize sufficient mutual support and trust to make them secure and stable (Score: 10–20 in Scoreboard #1).

5.2.2 Inside-out: societal sources of success

The various societal sources, or layers, of wickedness show that it is difficult for each societal sector to take up responsibility for any issue that lies beyond their primary role and capacities, even if there is a (longer-term) interest in doing so. Well-functioning societies are 'balanced' societies in which state, market and civil society play constructive and *complementary roles* (Table 5.1). The better each societal sector functions in all its roles at all levels of responsibility, the less intricate it generally becomes to address wicked problems.

COMPLEMENTARY ROLES

Well-functioning sectors take sufficient care of the primary roles or *fiduciary duties* for which they were created: companies effectively compete; governments regulate through laws (mandating); and civil society creates vibrant communities through mutual support. Secondary roles are those roles that are within the sphere of influence of the sector, but which require the involvement of other parties to effectively execute them. Companies can outsource, governments can facilitate (for instance, through policies that create enabling conditions or subsidies), and civil societies can advocate (convince others to do things differently). Tertiary roles relate to those issue domains that societal sectors can only indirectly influence. Companies can delegate means and activities to their corporate foundation in support of a societal cause or community engagement; civil society organizations that adopt 'service-orientation' can enter into the market sphere to ensure that desired, lacking or alternatively produced products and services are provided; governments can endorse activities of companies or others, but will find it difficult to do this in a non-discriminatory manner. The least clear is the exact role that each of the sectors can play in addressing collective action issues. Some form of partnership is needed, but what this entails in terms of collaborative formations, collaborative actions and attribution of joint responsibilities, is highly dependent on the context and issue (see Table 5.2).

HAVING AND TAKING RESPONSIBILITY

In the organization of all these roles, problems can arise. Even in well-functioning societies, the adequate provision of 'common-pool' goods presents a great and continuous challenge. Within the realm of societal complexity, we can define the degree of wickedness as the extent to which societal sectors 'have' and actively 'take' individual or collective responsibilities (Figure 5.2).

Organizations can be held responsible for the issues over which they have direct influence. Most of the thinking in this realm is based on ethical theory (Rawls, 1971) and the normative practice of many professions, such as doctors or civil servants, that pursue a 'do no harm' ethos. In ethical theory, preventing

Table 5.2 Complementary roles of societal sectors

Roles and intervention levels	MARKET: Companies	STATE: Governments	CIVIL SOCIETY: Communities
1. Primary role Fiduciary duty to create value	**Competing** Efficiency, scaling and innovation	**Mandating** Regulation through legislation	**Mutual support** Through communities
2. Secondary role *(within sphere of influence)* Duty not to destroy value	**Outsourcing** Upstream and downstream responsibility to avoid doing harm	**Facilitating** Providing subsidies and other enabling means of (financial) support to sectors	**Advocacy** Within and towards other sectors: advocate the interests of communities
3. Tertiary role *(indirect influence)* Duty to optimize positive value	**Delegating** (through corporate spin-offs, foundations) Beneficial spill-over and networking effects	**Endorsing** Defining level-playing field: through support of minimum standards and identifying 'best-in-class' projects	**Service-orientation** Producing private goods and services that scale club goods and compete with market-based organizations
4. Addressing collective action Duty to create collective value	**Partnering** Support collective action to enhance common good and the role played by companies	**Partnering** Support collective action to enhance common good and the role played by governments	**Partnering** Support collective action to enhance common good and the role played by civil society organizations

negative impacts on others (*avoid doing harm*) is referred to as a 'negative duty' approach. This angle on the breadth of responsibilities one reasonably has, mirrors a strong focus on compliance with established legal and normative frames, practices and standards that prescribe what kind of responsibilities are expected, and under what conditions. The more wicked the nature of the problem, however, the less established regulation and practice to fall back on are in place. Increased levels of wickedness require that the societal sectors 'take' responsibilities beyond their direct influence, by embracing a 'positive duty' approach ('*doing good*'). Activities that aim to avoid harm are expected of any good citizen (Davis, 1973; Lin-Hi and Müller, 2013). In contrast, actions that seek to do good very often exceed social expectations. Actions that seek to do good beyond the sectoral boundaries engage in an even more difficult organizational and ethical pathway: one that requires collective action (ibid.).

Avoiding negative impacts from occurring is generally considered a stronger norm than actively pursuing positive change. In ethical theory, actors who do not actually hold responsibility for an issue but take responsibility nonetheless, act according to the so-called 'categorical imperative' (as 'good citizens', for instance). From a skeptical perspective, they can also be considered

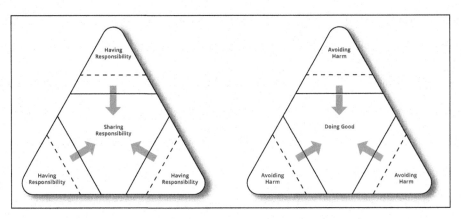

Figure 5.2 'Avoiding harm' versus 'doing good': Having and sharing responsibility

'suckers' (cf. Streeten, 2001), as their engagement in positive action crowds out incentives for others to take up responsibility for issues that they should consider (partly) of their own making. For instance, a government that subsidizes the production of medicine into which the industry itself could (or should) have invested takes away the incentive to innovate with a view to helping the next generation of sick people.

When applying the wicked problems logic of Chapter 4 to fundamental moral questions related to responsibilities, two behaviourist challenges rise to the surface: (1) how to deal with *denial*, and (2) how to deal with *partial* responsibilities. Several *denial mechanisms* influence the wickedness of an issue: (a) actors deny that the issue exists (as is still the case with climate change); (b) they deny the importance of the issue and its consequences (as is the case, for instance, with failing public health systems and increased income inequalities); or (c) deny that they themselves are actually part of the problem, and thus feel less inclined to act (as is the case with the Covid-19 pandemic). Furthermore, wicked problems always create a *blended challenge* regarding taking or having responsibility: actors have *partial* responsibility and may, therefore, be inclined to adopt wait-and-see or free-rider strategies. Partial responsibility for the problem suggests partial responsibility for the solution. However, a wicked problem always involves multiple 'issue owners' and hence can only be resolved by combined or collective action in which actors take full responsibility for the (collective) outcome of their efforts. The collective action arena represents the natural space for tripartite partnering where none of the societal actors holds primary responsibility, but nevertheless all can take responsibility as long as others are taking theirs. This position requires so-called 'conditional morality', a concept in ethical theory that refers to reciprocity in negotiations on the conditions for collaborating and partnering (Box 5.1 and section 5.4).

CONDITIONAL MORALITY: DON'T BE A SUCKER!

Some actors take responsibility for solving a problem while they do not hold responsibility. Others hold responsibility for a problem but are inactive or reactive when it comes to pursuing adequate solutions. In collaborative processes, the natural position in terms of responsibilities is portrayed by the diagonal: holding responsibility (or not) then directly relates to taking responsibility (or not). Actors who choose to take responsibility only if others do the same (in alliance or through a partnership), apply what Basu (2001) has called 'conditional morality'. Partnering is about managing this conditional morality.

		HOLDS RESPONSIBILITY FOR THE ISSUE?		
		Yes (Full)	Somewhat/shared	No
TAKES RESPONSIBILITY?	Yes (Full)	1. Unconditional morality	2. Skewed partnership	3. Categorical imperative; sucker
	Some-what	4. Skewed partnership; diffusion of responsibility	5. Equal partnership	6. Philanthropic partnership
	No	7. Prisoner's dilemma	8. Free-rider in partnership	9. Unconditional immorality

The yes/yes and no/no combinations in the table represent the case of *unconditional (im)morality*. Full acceptance (holding and taking responsibility) by involved actors presents perfect alignment or 'fit' of the partnering effort (position 1); the case of full immorality presents the opposite (9). Actors who hold partial responsibility for an issue but do not take it, are the archetypical 'free-riders' (8). If actors are primarily responsible, but none of them initiates taking responsibility, actions reflect a typical prisoner's dilemma (7) or, in the case of half-hearted initiatives, diffused responsibilities (4). In these instances, sanctions by other actors in society (or by their own constituency) are required to hold actors accountable. Actors who do not hold any responsibility for an issue but take responsibility, act according to the so-called *categorical imperative* (and can be considered 'suckers', according to Streeten, 2001). These actors tend to crowd out the incentive for other actors to take up their fair share of responsibility for issues that can reasonably be considered (partly) theirs.

If actors hold no responsibility but do take some responsibility, they engage in a 'philanthropic' partnership that still holds the risk of crowding out the incentive for directly involved actors to engage with a sufficient level of responsibility – albeit to a lower extent than is the case with the categorical imperative (6). In the case of shared responsibilities for the issue, but with one actor taking full responsibility, the partnership is skewed towards the lead partner's framing and solutions (2). This opens the door to possible opportunistic and strategic behaviour of the other partners.

5.3 FOUR LEVELS OF INTERVENTION

Addressing societal sources of failure (section 5.2.1) requires suitable societal intervention arrangements (section 5.2.2) that match the degree of wickedness involved. By bringing together the outside-in and inside-out perspectives discussed in section 5.2, we can now distinguish four levels of sectoral intervention that reflect the distinct degrees to which actors bear primary, secondary, tertiary and collective responsibilities (Figures 5.3 and 5.4): failure (in meeting fiduciary duties), negative externalities, positive externalities and collective action. This section considers each intervention level in more detail.

LEVEL 1 INTERVENTIONS – ADDRESSING FAILURE

The first layer of societal complexity [1+1+1] finds its source in the societal sectors themselves. 'Failure' does not necessarily refer to illegal activities of organizations, but applies foremost to more structural deficiencies in the operation of each sector, resulting in failure to efficiently deliver its primary value to society. This dimension is also referred to as the *fiduciary duty* in a narrow sense and relates to an organization's duty to its primary stakeholders (customers, members, employees) that follows from its primary role (Table 5.1). Governments can fail to live up to their fiduciary duty due to overly bureaucratic procedures, unaccountable governance or concentration of political power. Deficient and corrupt governments limit the state's ability to develop proper laws and regulate society in an equitable manner. Market failure occurs in the case of monopoly positions (creating information asymmetry), concentration of wealth, collusion, credit rationing, producing harmful or defective products or services, or shortages in the production of relevant goods and services. Market failure also occurs if the market does not provide the right incentives to innovate and improve products and

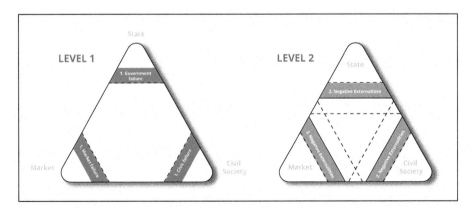

Figure 5.3 'Avoiding harm' and 'having responsibility'

processes to meet latent or future societal needs. Civic failure occurs when special interest groups predominate in defining the 'common good', when communities are not effective in efficiently creating mutual support, or when communities are ineffective in organizing themselves (in civil society organizations, CSOs) around a common concern, value or theme due to paternalism, amateurism, lack of trust or otherwise. Table 5.3 lists several related sources of failure for each societal sector.

If problems of failure within a sector are not addressed adequately, they affect other parts of society. Some of the sources of failure are regulated, but not all. A particularly vicious source of failure is the recurrent plea of many companies to deregulate their sector, even in the face of apparent failures to implement effective self-regulation. But even when regulation exists, it does not necessarily guarantee that it is sufficiently enforced or that it is adjusted in good time to reflect enhanced sustainability requirements. Governments can fail because their regulatory frameworks create unintended outcomes for citizens and consumers. Take, for instance, antitrust laws and competition policy. In general, these are supposed to protect consumers against abuse of power by companies. But in most countries, the rules have a rather narrow definition of what is in the consumer's interest: low prices. Strict regulation then implies that companies are not allowed to collaborate on sustainability issues if that would result in higher consumer prices. Protecting the (narrowly defined) interest of current consumers then comes at the expense of the interests of future generations of consumers.

Addressing *intra-sectoral* failure first and foremost involves coordinated efforts among actors within the same sector to restore public 'trust'. Deficiencies

Table 5.3 Selected sources of 'level 1' failure

State Failure	Market Failure	Civic Failure
• Nepotism	• Monopoly	• Inadequate provision of club
• Corruption	• Inefficient production and	goods & mutual support
• Excessive bureaucracy	insufficient scaling	• Amateurism
• Regulatory capture/	• Collusion	• Corruption
clientelism	• Corruption	• Paternalism
• Authoritarian rule	• Bonus culture	• Power-abusing patriarch
• Inadequate separation of	• Insider trading	• Snitching/defecting
powers	• Rogue trading	• Loneliness/social isolation
• Kleptocracy	• Non-marketable diseases	• Privacy violations
• Military aggression	• Not addressing latent needs	• Group-thinking
• Lack of accountability/	• Unjustified intellectual property	• Human rights violations
transparency	rights protection	• Distrust
• Power concentration	• Short-term innovation	
• Legal inequality/inequity	• Wealth concentration	
	• Deficient self-regulation	
	• Usury prices/profits/interest	
	rates	

in the ability or willingness within each sector to live up to its fiduciary duty can have substantial consequences for the level of public trust bestowed on them. 'Low-trust' societies have greater difficulty in creating social contracts than higher-trust societies.[2] Institutional voids that result from sectoral failures are linked to sizable 'trust gaps', which in turn are linked to the level of wickedness involved when addressing an issue (see section 5.4).

LEVEL 2 INTERVENTIONS – TAKING RESPONSIBILITY FOR NEGATIVE EXTERNALITIES

The second layer of societal complexity [2+2+2] is more difficult to address. It relates to the unwillingness or inability of organizations within a sector to extend their influence beyond a narrowly defined fiduciary duty to also include *secondary stakeholders*. This applies, for instance, to companies that pollute, overuse or extract, but do not pay for the costs imposed on communities surrounding the sites. It applies to consumers not willing to pay a fair price for the products and services they use that better reflects the true costs of production. True costs relate to fair wages and safe working conditions for workers throughout the value chain, to the internalization of the environmental and ecological costs of production, or to improved levels of animal welfare. Governments that fail to develop effective regulation create negative externalities, because they are not able to protect their citizens from *public bads* occurring. Communities can create negative externalities through criminality, intolerance, inequality or pollution, for which others bear the costs.

Negative externalities are often difficult to attribute to the action of individual actors, which may make them difficult to tackle. Consequently, actors who intend to take up more responsibility for dealing with negative externalities oftentimes need to complement their own action and capabilities with those of actors from other societal sectors to actually address the challenge. The more actors operate in this on a conditional basis – 'I will if you will' – the more their strategy becomes reactive, and the more they can dodge their responsibility.

Negative externalities can arise as the *unintended side effects* of a product or service, but can also be intentionally *created*. The mafia and crime gangs seem to be particularly capable of organizing mutual support within their own community, but simultaneously create immense negative costs for society. Famous

---

2   The 2020 Edelman Trust Barometer shows that 51% of respondents around the world trust business leaders to address (sustainability) challenges correctly (with ethical drivers deemed three times more important to company trust than competence). Only 42% of respondents trust government leaders to successfully deal with country challenges. Just 40% of respondents trust NGOs to serve the interests of everyone equally and fairly, while this percentage was only 30% for governments.

Table 5.4 Selected sources of negative externalities

State	Market	Civil Society
• Insufficient provision of public goods • Lacking separation of powers • Debt financing (loan dependency) • Insufficient safety provision (e.g. police, fire brigades, social safety, social security) • Wars • Torture • Protectionism • Backing 'losers', selecting 'winners' (selective industrial policies) • Socialization of losses	• Abuse of power through cartels • Fear-based marketing (e.g. related to health, insurance, financial products) • Pollution • Addiction (e.g. 'sin goods', gambling, gaming, tobacco, alcohol, fast food, social media, medicines) • Negative lock-in effects (e.g. incompatible products; standardization battles) • Built-in deterioration • Dumping • Exploitative value chains • Human rights violations • Child labour • Lobbying for deregulation on negative externalities • Transfer price manipulation • Tax evasion	• Racism and other sources of exclusion • Group supremacy • Mafia • Pyramid games • Crime gangs • Slavery • Torture • Child labour • Gated communities • Gentrification • Populism and victimizing • Hoarding • Weaponization

examples of equally severe externalities relate to so-called 'sin goods' with created addictions as a 'calculated side effect' of the goods and services produced. Tobacco, gaming, gambling and social media industries are known for adding features to their products that are intended to make 'customers' hooked on their products. By doing so, such businesses not only create a product that has negative and disguised attributes for their consumers (with positive effects for their shareholders because of high revenues), but also negative externalities for the families and communities around these people, as well as societal costs in the form of reduced productivity, healthcare costs and the like. Forms of dependency and addiction can arise anywhere in society, even at the level of organizations, branches and entire economies. Citizens, companies and non-profit organizations alike can suffer from a 'subsidy addiction', which may negatively affect their capacity to stand on their own feet. Entire economies have boomed and then busted, for instance because of addiction to subsidized food or oil prices, foreign institutional loans, or overreliance on resource richness that clouded the need to diversify economic activities.

LEVEL 3 INTERVENTIONS – CREATING POSITIVE EXTERNALITIES
The third layer of societal complexity [3+3+3] relates to unmet societal needs that can be addressed through the creation of *external benefits* with *positive spill-over*

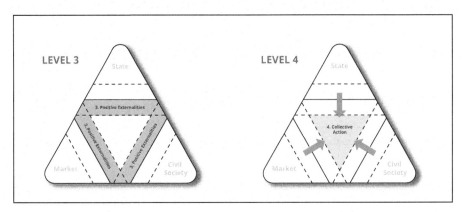

Figure 5.4 'Doing good' and 'sharing responsibility'

effects (see Table 5.5). Firms can extend their positive influence on society by targeting latent societal demands, desires and needs, for instance by providing access to education and healthcare for workers and their families in their production chains. Civil society organizations can take up responsibilities beyond their own community or club, which may take the shape of 'social enterprises' that address societal voids and unmet needs with innovative concepts and business models. It may also take the form of doing volunteering work, or engagement in (solidarity) actions that, for instance, call for the universal application of fundamental human rights, states' upholding of the climate agreements, the restoration of coral reefs or the revitalization of desert grounds. For governments, extending their responsibility to trigger positive externalities involves engaging in 'facilitating' or 'endorsing' activities. This can be done through subsidies, taxation rate differentials, facilitating conducive environments that enhance innovation or social resilience, or other incentivizing measures through which society can be influenced, stimulated, nudged and guided in other ways than through laws (mandating).

The complexities linked to these 'external benefit' problems are often related to the (in)action of other societal sectors in taking up responsibilities. Actors in one sector may feel an urgent need to fill in (part of the) responsibilities that other sectors have left unattended. Businesses and civil society organizations, for instance, have been taking on governance duties to address societal ills, because of regulatory voids left by a retreating or failing state. The risk of *crowding out* primary responsibilities always lies in wait. When citizens or governments clean up the waste produced by companies, they provide a perverse incentive for companies not to live up to responsibilities related to their fiduciary duty of clean and safe production that prevents adverse effects from occurring. One way to approach such boundary-spanning problems is to form coalitions or modes of partnership between the two sectors involved, in order to prevent crowding out from occurring (sections 5.4 and 5.5).

Table 5.5 Complementary sources of positive externalities

State	Market	Civil Society
• Creating enabling conditions (e.g. knowledge diffusion, transparency, outcome benchmarks) • Research into new technologies • Socialization of rewards[3] • Endorsing initiatives • Education • Public health provisions • Immunization campaigns • Preserving cultural heritage (e.g. museums) • Democracy and participation • Public libraries • National parks	• Sponsoring and community engagement • Investing in needs, rather than markets • Investment in new technologies • Open source/open access innovation • Spill-over effects of investment (job creation; spin-off start-ups) • Network effects (e.g. telecom, the internet, mobile money) • Support of national tax base	• Advocacy for public and common goods provision • Creating social resilience/ social cohesion • Donating to NGOs • International solidarity • Greening of the neighbourhood • Vigilantes • Volunteering • Alternative/community currencies • Quality labels and food labelling (e.g. fair trade) • Creative commons

LEVEL 4 INTERVENTIONS – STIMULATING COLLECTIVE ACTION AND JOINT RISK-TAKING

The final layer of societal complexity [4+4+4] is the most difficult to address. It represents that part of the societal set-up that requires the participation of all societal actors, who however may not feel a responsibility and primarily see the risk of getting involved. This is the case for almost all climate issues, the plastic soup in the middle of our oceans where no single government rules, and concerns related to rapid biodiversity loss. It also applies to most economic growth and sustainability topics that require common and collective actions beyond individual responsibilities to establish a minimum level of social, economic and ecological governance. Collective action should provide 'common goods' that go beyond private, public or social goods, by combining private, public and social value. Examples include pension schemes, unemployment programs, or inclusive and green growth policies (see Table 5.6).

In the areas of common goods creation, risk-taking requires risk-sharing. The dimensions and degrees of complexities involved may deter parties from taking action because they cannot oversee all dimensions, consequences and possible outcomes, and may find the risk too high to address on their own. They choose to 'wait and see', and as a result create inertia or a deadlock as to which party – at what level of society – will risk their neck and initiate action first. It is

---

3   Mariana Mazzucato (2018) in this realm argues that a 'market shaping' role of public policy that allows risks *and rewards* to be socialized, can better enable growth to be both 'smart' (innovation-led) and more inclusive.

not easy to define a 'right' approach to 'common good' issues as the impact of interventions will not be clear-cut upfront (Chapter 4). Consequently, it is far from easy to develop straightforward strategies at the scale and scope required. Common goods voids cannot be addressed by one single party alone; these types of problems necessitate a collective effort – in coalition with other societal actors – and call for innovative governance and partnering arrangements that match the degree of wickedness at hand. Tragedy of the commons problems such as climate change that not only involve and affect all societal sectors (state, market, civil society), but also all levels of society (global, regional, national, local, personal), are also characterized as *super-wicked* (Levin et al., 2012).

Table 5.6 Objectives of collective action

State	Market	Civil Society
Joint poverty programmes; climate action; protection of biodiversity, nature, life; societal equity; collective pensions; clean energy; competitiveness; justice; savings; equal income distribution; unemployment programmes; trust-building; public health and education provision; productivity coalitions; sustainable development (SDGs); social contracts		

5.4 CREATING AN ECOSYSTEM FOR COLLABORATION: TRUST GAPS AND PARTNERING SPACE

In many countries, sizable institutional voids persist (Figure 5.1), partly as the result of market failure, governance failure and/or civic failure. Institutions can be understood as 'rules of the game' that govern social behaviour and facilitate market transactions by reducing transaction and informational costs (North, 1990). Institutions can comprise formal as well as informal rules of the game; both are equally important. There is a large and expanding body of knowledge on the importance of informal institutions like trust, social capital and reciprocity to explain a wide range of phenomena that we have summarized under the heading of 'wicked problems' and the VUCA society. A notable outcome of growing ambiguity in societal arrangements is the increasingly common phenomenon of a progressive *trust gap* or *trust deficit* between the societal sectors. Trust gaps cause lowered confidence in governments and their legitimacy as the primary responsible entity for formal institutions (e.g. legislation and regulatory frameworks). The corporate sector – often perceived as too self-interested – also faces low levels of trust, but is nevertheless deemed to have a positive role to play in global governance and, therefore, a necessary force for progress. Civil society organizations are confronted with similarly low levels of trust, with ambiguity on the extent to which they equally and fairly represent the interests of everyone.

None of the societal sectors is sufficiently trusted, although trust attitudes and the resulting trust gaps tend to be cross-country heterogeneous and context, industry and issue dependent. The Edelman Trust Barometer provides survey scores on the trust put in representatives of each of the sectors in a variety of countries around the world. Their collected data enable a rough assessment of the nature and size of the trust gap in several relevant countries at the very start of the SDG-agenda (Figure 5.5). In 2015, the Edelman Trust Barometer showed an 'all-time-low' of just 22% so-called 'truster' countries, referring to countries with an average trust level of 60% and higher in its institutions of government, business, media and NGOs.[4] Nearly two-thirds of surveyed countries were qualified as 'distrusters', which can be considered one of the characteristics of a VUCA world. Faced with rapid technological, economic and political changes that are perceived to be beyond direct control, people feel 'left behind' and lose confidence, and countries accordingly develop into 'low trust' societies.

5.4.1 Overcoming the trust gap

The resulting trust gap defines a significant challenge for actors from all three societal sectors that consider the SDG-agenda an opportunity to address societal problems. On the one hand, there are serious trust and legitimacy gaps to overcome. On the other hand, embracing the SDGs and effectively acting on them might help to regain some of the trust and legitimacy lost, for instance as the result of malpractice or not delivering at level 1 (primary role, fiduciary duty) or shirking at level 2 (not taking responsibility for negative externalities).

Based on the survey scores of the Edelman Trust Barometer, the societal trust gap can be observed as serious problems plotted within the societal triangle, as depicted in Figure 5.5.[5] The trust gap overlaps with the space where institutional voids exist and where suitable societal arrangements and partnerships are most needed to address them. If the level of trust in a societal sector is high – and their legitimacy can be considered high as well – the possibility for that sector to expand its sphere of influence (e.g. to come up with solutions for societal problems) is strong. The flip side, however, is that the inclination to strike partnerships with the two other societal sectors may diminish. Only when these sectors share

---

4   Edelman Trust Barometer surveys have a selection bias in favour of developed countries. It can be assumed that the actual percentage of 'low trust' societies is probably higher. In economic studies, a negative relationship between economic inequality and trust has been suggested, as well as a positive relationship between economic development (measured as gross domestic product per capita) and trust.
5   Note that the Edelman Trust Barometer also includes 'trust in the media' as an indicator. In general, the level of trust in the media is lower than the average trust in the three basic societal institutions and even more prone to volatility and public sentiments. For the countries in Figure 5.5, trust in the media was: Global (51%), China (77%), India (76%), Netherlands (62%), Russia (44%), USA (43%), Brazil (56%), Germany (45%) Japan (31%).

comparable degrees of societal trust (and legitimacy), can we expect *balanced partnerships* to happen.

Trust gaps of varying seizes exist all over the world. Of the largest developing countries (the BRIC-economies), Russia and Brazil show relatively large gaps, with the trust gap in Brazil skewed towards government and in Russia skewed towards NGOs. In India and China, there are no major trust gaps, though the picture for China over longer periods appears to be much more stable than India's. Trust in most developing countries – with the seeming exception of China, India, Singapore, the UAE and Indonesia – tends to be volatile and can alter from one year to the next. Japan shows comparatively low trust levels, in particular towards NGOs. In Anglo-Saxon countries like the UK and the USA, governments are the least trusted, while business and NGOs score only slightly higher. The Netherlands as a neo-corporatist country, comparable to Norway, Sweden and Austria, shows an interesting balance in trust levels: trust levels for each societal sector are not particularly high or low. In these countries, trust levels show relatively stable images over longer periods: fragile, yet more or less balanced.

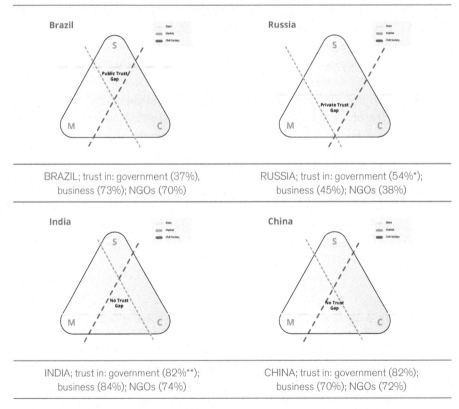

BRAZIL; trust in: government (37%), business (73%); NGOs (70%)

RUSSIA; trust in: government (54%*); business (45%); NGOs (38%)

INDIA; trust in: government (82%**); business (84%); NGOs (74%)

CHINA; trust in: government (82%); business (70%); NGOs (72%)

Figure 5.5 Trust gaps in selected countries at the start of the SDG-agenda (2015)

*Very high increase compared to 2014 (27%), probably caused by the international boycott of Russia after the Ukraine invasion; **High increase compared to 2014 (53%), caused by a change in government (Modi government). Source: Edelman 15th Annual Trust Barometer (2015).

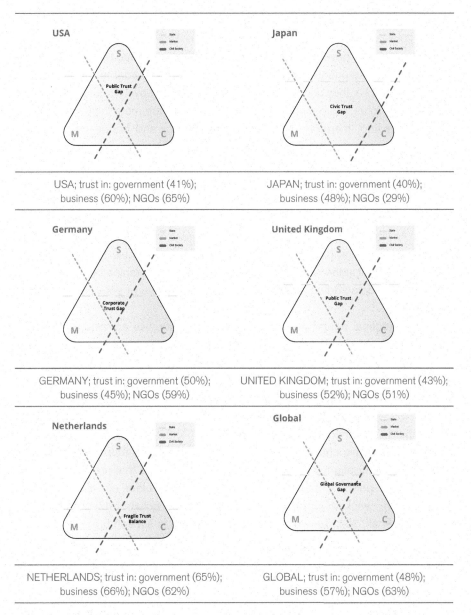

USA; trust in: government (41%);
business (60%); NGOs (65%)

JAPAN; trust in: government (40%);
business (48%); NGOs (29%)

GERMANY; trust in: government (50%);
business (45%); NGOs (59%)

UNITED KINGDOM; trust in: government (43%);
business (52%); NGOs (51%)

NETHERLANDS; trust in: government (65%);
business (66%); NGOs (62%)

GLOBAL; trust in: government (48%);
business (57%); NGOs (63%)

Figure 5.5 (Continued)

CREATING COLLABORATIVE ADVANTAGE – CROSS-SECTOR PARTNERSHIPS

Cross-sector partnerships can be instrumental in addressing trust gaps and establishing novel institutions that more effectively address societal challenges. Partnerships are an alternative to the introduction of hybrid organizational forms that strike a compromise between public and private and for-profit and non-profit ways of organizing (see Chapter 6). Cross-sector partnerships are societal arrangements that *combine complementary* organizational logics, rationalities, roles, values and societal positions (Table 5.1). They provide the potential to create new ways to govern and manage relations in society and to form new kinds of goal- or purpose-oriented institutional configurations to address societal challenges. In doing so, they contribute to the emergence of novel kinds of institutions (also referred to as 'proto-institutions') that potentially are more inclusive (Bryson et al., 2015) and, therefore, may improve legitimacy and bridge existing trust gaps.[6] Cross-sector partnering is geared towards creating *collaborative solutions* (Hart and Sharma, 2004) through 'collaborative advantages' (Huxham and Vangen, 2004) in which new sources of trust can be built between governmental, business and civil society organizations. Trust-building through partnerships may initially be relatively modest because of the inherent differences between the sectors. At later stages, however, these collaborative efforts can develop into deeper trust relations (Austin, 2000) and create effective new types of (proto-) institutions that fill in the existing institutional voids. Partnerships can thus offer a platform for understanding and shaping the mechanisms of emergent systemic change.

The practical relevance of the idea of 'collaborative advantage' critically depends on the appropriateness of the cross-sector collaboration, on the extent to which systemic goals and pressing societal issues are actually embraced, and on incremental and adaptive change that 'leaves no one behind'. This should not be approached naively. Cross-sector collaborations with transformational power are not formed overnight, but involve insightful and strategic consideration. Contemporary partnership practice has been criticized for not adequately addressing systemic change, for instance due to unfit or suboptimal partnering configurations, misaligned issue-partnership fit, ambitions that are too limited or private sector partners that are too dominant (Van Tulder and Keen, 2018). Hence, with 'wicked opportunity' also comes 'collaborative complexity' (Schneider et al., 2017) – which we further address in section 5.5.

5.4.2 The partnering space

In the partnering space (see Figure 5.6), societal actors can take up and share responsibilities for societal issues. In social philosophy, this mechanism is also known as the 'social connection model' of responsibility (Young, 2006). It states that "all agents who contribute to the structural processes that produce injustice have responsibilities to work to remedy these injustices" (ibid: 103). At the first

---

6   Proto-institutions refer to "new practices, rules, and technologies that transcend a particular collaborative relationship and may become new institutions if they diffuse sufficiently" (Lawrence et al., 2002).

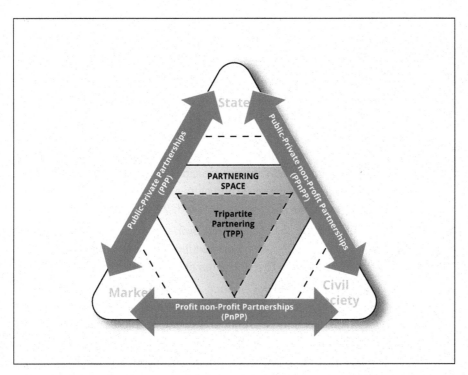

Figure 5.6 Four ways to fill partnering space

two layers of wickedness (section 5.2.1), such 'injustice' is relatively easy to define and to attribute to those liable for causing or prolonging it. However, at level 3 (insufficient creation of positive externalities) and level 4 (systemic challenges), attributing liabilities and responsibilities is ambiguous and, therefore, far more difficult. The question that then begs an answer is on what grounds actors from different societal spheres take responsibility themselves and assign (joint, partial, most) responsibility to others. The partnering space can hence be considered as an 'arena' in which parties with distinct yet complementary logics, values and interests get together to negotiate on the frames, goals and conditions for collaborating, with the purpose of jointly creating solution-oriented opportunities for societal challenges.

Studies on the dynamics of cross-sector partnerships for development have adopted a variety of perspectives on the nature of the partnering space as the arena in which the actual process of partnering takes place. The concept of 'partnering space' can be considered in more idealistic or more realistic terms.

In more **idealistic** terms, the partnering space represents . . .

■ . . . an area for *collaborative solutions* to wicked problems (Hart and Sharma, 2004) in which new sources of trust can be built up. The higher the trust, the lower the transaction costs. The arena can also be considered a 'value creation spectrum' (Austin and Seitanidi, 2014) in which 'collaborative value' or 'shared value' (Kramer and Porter, 2006) can be created.

■ . . . an *area of growing interdependencies* as the result of globalization and the related ideologies of privatization, deregulation, liberalization and decentralization (Biermann et al., 2007: 288).

■ . . . a *new institutional space* in which to advance the common good. New institutional arrangements that are experimented with in the partnering space can distribute values and resources, or can act as "sources of power to the extent that they are effective, and arenas for power-based conflicts on the distribution of values and resources" (ibid: 298).

■ . . . a means to *bridge the institutional divide*, particularly in case of the co-existence of potentially conflicting institutions, by including multiple partners from multiple sectors (Rivera-Santos et al., 2012).

■ . . . a *novel approach to governance and decision-making* needed to address the 'institutional void' that appears in the middle of society. The governance approach that is sought is also referred to as inclusive, meta, transition or hybrid governance, but with recurring problems of legitimacy and accountability (Utting and Zammit, 2009; Glasbergen, 2011).

■ . . . a *discursive space* in which actors collaborate to frame and reframe issues that can be considered of mutual interest. The move into the partnering space forces actors to move out of the existing frames of reference, interest-based positions or comfort zones (mindsets) or homogenous institutional backgrounds. The power of framing by each actor is brought into the partnership and can lead to constructive discourse.

In more **realistic** terms, the partnering space represents . . .

■ . . . a contested *political arena*. Partnerships for sustainable development have been negotiated, endorsed and implemented in a contested political arena (Pattberg et al., 2012: 21).

■ . . . a *bargaining arena* (Van Tulder with Van der Zwart, 2006) in which conflict and power struggles are exercised (Gray, 2007).

■ . . . a *network*, multiple layers of relational structures and the positions therein of actors. "Understanding differences in the structural position of partners is to understand power" (Ellersiek, 2011: 36).

■ . . . as a *new opportunity* for the private sector to "exercise power and influence over domains that were the preserve of public-sector organizations" (Buse and Harmer, 2004: 50), or as an action primarily for self-interest and secondarily for social good.

■ . . . an *idealized tool and discourse*, initiated in particular by multilateral agencies, that diverts "attention from asymmetrical power relations, the struggle for hegemony, participation deficits and trade-off between diverging partnership goals to questions of effectiveness and efficiency" (Bäckstrand, 2012: 169). Partnerships can also crowd out existing roles, functions and responsibilities of actors. Pattberg et al. (2012) argue that international development partnerships are often active in issue areas that "are already densely populated by international law and agreements" (ibid: 240).

It is easy to consider the idealist perspective on partnerships as naive, or the realist angle as overly sceptical. Both perspectives can and should be given fair consideration if one aims to create a 'balanced', 'inclusive' and 'sustainable' society – which in itself implies a process laden with trade-offs and conflicts. How to deal with the trade-offs inherent to different world views has been identified as one of the most important challenges of the SDG-agenda (Chapters 3 and 4). Hence, the type of negotiation required to transform the 'trust gap' into a 'partnering' and 'opportunity' space has to be closely scrutinized. The bigger the trust gap between actors in society is, the more 'position-based' negotiation tends to prevail. Position-based negotiation applied to wicked problems often has limited value, however, and may well bring about dynamics that result in exactly the opposite (e.g. fragmentation, increased conflict, war) of what is considered to be in the common interest. The most common negotiation practice used is that of *compromise-oriented* negotiation, based on the (short-term, concrete and directly attributable) interests of actors (*interest-based negotiation*). The SDG-agenda, by contrast, aims to get actors to work together on longer-term (shared) interests and common goals. This requires that actors apply the principles of *collective vision-based* negotiation (Box 5.2).

APPLYING NEGOTIATION THEORY: FROM 'POSITION-BASED' TO 'COLLECTIVE VISION-BASED'

BOX 5.2

Change that is driven or dominated by the interest of one sector (either state-driven, market-driven or civic-driven change) is not likely to create the right preconditions for a sustainable resolution of a wicked problem. It is prone to several distinctive 'failures' related to each sector, and with it decreased legitimacy of these sectors. When brought together in collaborative or partnering initiatives, fundamental institutional differences and interests are a root cause of conflicting goals (Stadtler and Probst, 2011) and mutual distrust. These differences can clash, but they can also converge or complement each other. But how can they actually be combined and made to cooperate?

Wicked problems cannot be resolved through compromise. Although 'debate' and (multi-)stakeholder 'dialogue' are an indispensable part of the conversation, they do not suffice. New ways of negotiation and structured thinking are necessary. Modern thinking on negotiation has already progressed from 'position-based' to 'interest-based' negotiation practices. With traditional negotiation practice, stalemate situations arise when focusing on one's developed position according to one's pre-set goals for the negotiation, which is also known as 'positional bargaining' or **'position-based negotiating' (PBN)**. The outcome of a PBN approach can only be the realization of one of the parties' positions, which thus creates the problem that if the position of one side (the winner) is adopted, the other side 'loses'. The outcome of traditional PBN generally entails a *win-lose situation* for participants.

Interest-based negotiations (IBN) aim to create more satisfactory situations by refocusing on the interests of both parties. The 'Harvard Negotiation Project' is the clearest protagonist of this line of thinking – with the famous book *Getting to Yes* by Roger Fisher and William Ury (1981) as the classic source of IBN – in which trade-offs and compromises are considered as well. IBN is supposed to build a collaborative spirit and trust amongst the negotiating parties as a basis on which to explore more creative solutions (Katz and Pattarini, 2008). The larger number of potential solutions should then include options that better accommodate the *interests of both sides*, which explains the added value of IBN compared with PBN (Rahwan et al., 2009). An exchange of interests and searching for shared interests are considered more critical (yet still not sufficient) conditions for effective partnerships than just trust or values.

Typical statements of representatives of PBN and IBN can illustrate the differences of each approach. Both can be found around the world. The IBN quote is taken from the Dutch (neo-corporatist) context.

1.0: Position-based negotiations (PBN)	2.0: Interest-based negotiations (IBN)
"It starts with trying to understand your own position and your own interests. Next, you try to represent these to your best abilities in negotiations with your opponent. Then you start searching for common points, where you can define compromises. Which you are going to work towards. If you get stuck, a mediator can help."	*"It starts with trying to understand the interests of your opponent. What does he want, what drives him, what position does he take? Next, you search for points of common understanding. You are going to work towards that. And if you get stuck, humour can be an immense help."*
Typical statement of a conflict mediator	Real statement, chair, corporatist negotiation platform

The problem with IBN is that it may well lead to compromise, but not necessarily to creative solutions needed to escape from *false contradictions* (Box 4.3). Hence, wicked problems require a different type of negotiation: *collective vision-based*. This approach takes the *'problem' as the point of departure* and should facilitate paradoxical decision-making processes and 'out of the box' thinking aimed towards negotiating a clear goal, with realistic resolutions, based on efficient and pragmatic models that nevertheless consider the *interests of all players* involved. How these interests are defined and channelled in a constructive negotiation and deliberation process, is context- and topic-specific.

3.0: Collective vision-based negotiations (CVBN)

"It starts with trying to understand the nature of the problem and the identification of involved stakeholders. In principle, there are no opponents nor supporters, but problem owners and parties with diverse interests and insights. Short-term and long-term interests are made explicit. You try to come to a joint or shared problem analysis and develop a common vision, on the basis of which you design a realistic implementation trajectory. And if you get stuck, joint investment in learning and knowledge exchange – next to a sensible dose of humour – can help tremendously."

Typical statement, partnership broker

Collective vision-based negotiations (CVBN) are first based on understanding the different positions: by juxtaposing idealists (equity) and pragmatists (efficiency). Since a vision is a mental concept, its detailed articulation can be difficult, especially when interacting with partners from different sectors. This reiterates the job of a 'partnership broker' to translate between the parties into a common language, but also to protect against the temptation to slip up with a perceived (superficial) shared vision that actually still entails great differences in its exact interpretation. It is not necessary to try to mediate between all interests. The strength of a partnership for wicked problems lies not so much in compromising parties, but in the creation of novel combinations for *synthesizing interests*. While interests can – and at times need to – diverge, partners are still able to collaborate. *Goal alignment* is a necessary condition for partnerships, whereas interest alignment is not. "All participants must agree … on the primary goals of the collaborative impact initiative as a whole" (Kania and Kramer, 2011: 39); this is what unites the parties to collaborate.

A collective vision-based approach aims to *enable a long-term partnership*. In contrast, the principles of IBN aim *to reach agreement* while maintaining and improving a relation as a base for the long term. CVBN aims to create *positive-sum outcomes* for the negotiating parties while also achieving greater societal benefits. A shared vision is the motivational factor for collaboration, which can reach a transformational (as opposed to a transactional) result. A shared vision is grounded in a common understanding of the problem, less so in a common understanding of the situation.

An agreement on a problem-solving approach alone, however, is fragile; it lacks a unifying reason for its selection and thus can quickly dissolve. It is, therefore, best to sequence the process: (1) first to come to a shared vision founded on a common goal; (2) followed by a shared understanding and definition of the problem, and (3) finally, a joint assessment and understanding of the situational context.

Source: Van Tulder (2018b).

THE MATCHING CHALLENGE: PARTNERSHIP CONFIGURATIONS

Cross-sector partnerships (CPSs), if organized well, should strengthen societal sectors by combining distinct logics, means and ways of organizing, and so enable society to profit from the full potential of 'collaborative advantage' (Huxham and Vangen, 2004). The partnering space consists of four distinct types of partnering configurations that create different types of 'organizational fit' to address wicked problems (Figure 5.6).

■ The classical *public-private partnerships (PPPs)* are predominantly directed towards the underinvestment in public goods. On their own, neither the state nor companies invest sufficiently in general provisions that are conducive for sustainable development. Key issues taken on by this type of bipartite cross-sector partnership often relate to physical infrastructure, including roads, rails, water and energy facilities, and telecommunication.

■ *Public-private non-profit partnerships (PPnPPs)* – bipartite partnerships between the state and civil society – aimed at increasing the effectiveness of public policies and adequate provision of public goods. Key issues in this domain relate to public health (e.g. sanitation, disease control), education, and forms of social safety and security.

■ *Profit non-profit partnerships (PnPPs)* – bipartite partnerships between market and civil society – address the under-provision of relevant private goods, services and values, such as empowerment (e.g. access to finance, access to insurance, 'living wages'), private health and well-being (e.g. access to medicine for rare conditions), nutrition (adequate distribution of food), and sustainable (non-exploitative) sourcing of raw materials.

■ *Tripartite partnerships (TPPs)* address the institutional voids emerging from weak governance structures at all sides of society and the insufficient production of 'common goods'.

Cross-sector partnerships are increasingly considered to constitute a viable, much needed and constructive approach to address interrelated problems that originate in the failure of individual organizations and societal sectors. CSPs transcend the scope of influence of individual organizations across sectoral boundaries to create innovative approaches, synergistic value, and to generate positive effects – on an adequate scale and with adequate impact. According to the theory, cross-sector partnering embodies promising potential to address wicked problems by reaping the fruits of collaborative advantage that comes from the pooling of thoughts, ideas, means and methods of organizing. It is therefore not surprising that SDG-targets 17.16 and 17.17 articulate the critical importance of multi-stakeholder partnerships, and highlight the need to promote effective public, public-private and civil society partnerships.

Presently, a multitude of partnership shapes can be witnessed, with varying numbers of participants that range from two to dozens of partners. Partnerships can be simple or complex, focused or unfocused, bi-sectoral or tripartite, goal-oriented or means-oriented, opportunity- or issue-driven. Despite immense support of the SDG partnering ambition and thousands of cross-sector partnerships around the world, it is also acknowledged that "we are still only scratching the surface in terms of the number, and quality, of partnerships required to deliver the SDGs".[7] The question is thus not so much *whether* cross-sector partnerships are relevant, but rather *how* they should be formed, organized, governed, intensified and enhanced to effectively create the change they were designed to address.

5.5 THE 'FIT' CHALLENGE: CREATING THE RIGHT CONFIGURATION

Entering the 'partnering space' is not noncommittal and partnering in itself no panacea. Partnering presents both opportunities and risks that are directly related to several strategic and tactical alignment questions that require careful consideration. Many partnerships have failed or underperformed due to a misaligned 'configuration'. Such misfitting affects both the internal dynamics of the cross-sector partnership (the degree to which collaborative advantage can be generated for all partners), and its effectiveness in addressing the problem (the impact that can be achieved).

5.5.1 The complexity fit

There is considerable knowledge from organization and strategy studies (notably in the field of business joint ventures) on the compatibility and complementarity of inter-organizational alliances and partnerships. A consistent finding from research on joint ventures and mergers is that, on average, two out of three business partnerships fail (cf. Schenk, 2005). Cross-sector partnerships research has also yielded relevant insights into organizational alignment and formation issues and the search for a suitable *organizational fit* between

---

7 This statement was issued in September 2019, at the launch of the *2030 Agenda Partnership Accelerator*. This is a project by the Division for Sustainable Development Goals (DSDG) of the United Nations Department of Economic and Social Affairs (UN DESA), in collaboration with United Nations Office for Sustainable Development (UNOSD), United Nations Office for Partnerships (UNOP), UN Global Compact, and UN Development Coordination Office. Chapter 12 elaborates further.

prospective partners. But even if the partnership itself portrays sufficient 'fit', it can still fail when it is not *fit for purpose* – that is, when the partnership configuration does not match the complexity of the societal problem it aims to address. Cross-sector partnering literature acknowledges that complex problems need more complex interventions (Austin and Seitanidi, 2014). Partnership practice has been criticized for not addressing systemic change (at levels 3 and 4) adequately, notably because of its inherent 'collaborative complexities'; many multi-stakeholder engagement processes do not address the real complexity of the problem (Pattberg and Widerberg, 2016). Ill-conceived partnerships can undermine the legitimacy of the whole phenomenon, for instance as a result of overly optimistic or superficial claims, lacking responsibilities or poor governance structures. The practical relevance of the idea of 'collaborative advantage' ('wicked opportunity') hence critically depends on: (1) cross-sector partnerships that actually embrace the systemic and transformative goals for which they were designed; (2) on the validity of the proposed (levels of) intervention; and (3) on appropriate monitoring and evaluation techniques to keep track of evolving insights on progress (Patton et al., 2016) in order to learn and adjust along the way.

Many CSPs have started to use so-called *Theories of Change* (ToCs) as an explication of the assumptions underlying their intervention strategy to help resolve the issue. A ToC provides the rationale as to *why* certain outcomes can be expected and what might undermine causal relations. It thus allows for systems thinking on relevant *factors and forces* linked to the issue, rather than taking the partnering intention between engaged actors as the point of departure. ToCs facilitate alignment on *problem-definition* and *intervention logic* during the formation phase of CSPs. By explicitly addressing the complexity level of the societal issue, ToCs can be an appropriate tool to enhance the transformative capacity of CSPs by deliberating the potential effectiveness and impact of interventions.

ToCs also facilitate partnerships in finding out how internal processes, systems and capabilities can be best developed and adapted to the complexity level of the challenge. The so-called 'logic framework' generally used to visualise and formulate ToCs presents the sequence of inputs and intended outputs and outcomes of the partnership (see Figure 5.7). ToC elaborations specify the underlying hypothesised links between inputs, outputs and contextual dependencies as the basis on which to develop a rigorous monitoring and learning plan for adjustment and improvement (James, 2011). ToCs are thus both *theories* of how change can be realised, and *approaches* to making these theories better informed by testing them in practice.

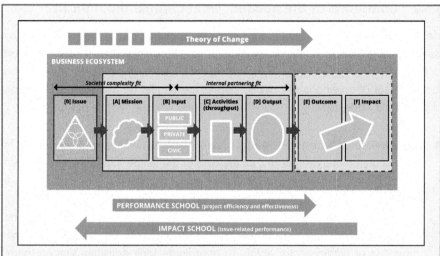

Figure 5.7 In search of the optimal fit – a Theory of Change approach

This *upgraded* 'logic framework' defines the main components of a Theory of Change. The starting point in this version is an *analysis of the nature of the issue* [position 0] so as to grasp: (1) the degree of complexities involved, (2) their societal sources, and (3) the complementary roles, responsibilities and societal functions that are needed to address the problem adequately.

From here, a shared problem definition is linked to a purpose-oriented and goal-aligned mission [A] and the formation of a partnership configuration, aligned around 'complementary inputs' [B] brought into the partnership by each partner. The partnership engages in activities and projects [C], that are supposed to have an 'output' [D], which lead to wider effects in terms of 'outcomes' [E] and ultimately should lead to the intended 'impact' [F].

A logic framework suggests that joined action can be planned and progress monitored. As the potential of collaborative advantage ('wicked opportunity') in reality still tends to be considerably underutilized, however, the question rises whether collaborative complexities can be sufficiently captured *before* the start of a partnership project. The 'complexity fit' challenge hence first considers the type of change required to purposefully address the issue. It accordingly questions whether the present partnership represents a 'coalition of the willing' or a 'coalition of the needed'. The real fit develops when the 'needed' partners are also 'willing' partners, and vice versa.

5.5.2 Coalitions of the needed: what creates the right fit?

Ideally, partnerships configurations – and the specific type of interventions they can bring about by pooling their complementary competences – should be linked to the *type of change* required. An appropriate partnership configuration – one that consists of coalitions of *needed* partners – should be aligned with the type of problem it addresses.

- **Simple: level 1 change needed:** level 1 type issues are relatively simple in terms of societal complexity, as they mirror the failure within the sector itself to efficiently deliver its principal value (fiduciary duty) to society. This is a common and universal phenomenon that is nevertheless often poorly recognized as a source of sustainability problems and opportunities. The complexity of this type of problem primarily relates to the inability or unwillingness of *within-sector actors* to coordinate their activities among themselves and restore trust in the public perception of this sector. Change, then, can be established through *intra-sectoral partnerships*, for instance directed towards self-regulation, standardization, innovation and mutual exchange of information, procedures, knowledge and technology.

- **Complicated: level 2 change needed:** level 2 type change is still largely focused on within-sector improvement processes within the realm of having (direct or indirect) responsibility for negative externalities. Here, opportunities appear for those actors who are willing to extend their primary responsibility and who are able to strike coalitions with *other societal sectors* to address the negative effects. *Bi-sectoral partnerships* are a prime vehicle for level 2 type of change, generally reflecting initiatives directed towards prevention, mitigation, reduction or the internalization of external costs. Triggered by societal advocacy, companies often engage in 'roundtables' or 'labelling' initiatives together with civil society organizations. For instance, trade unions have sought partnerships with frontrunner companies to raise wages to a decent or 'living' income level, to abolish child labour throughout the production chain, to establish safer working conditions and deal with other forms of negative externalities.

- **Complex: level 3 change needed:** level 3 type societal issues relate to the reticence or inability of actors to optimize the positive effects of their actions. Opportunities arise for those actors who are willing and able to strike coalitions with other societal sectors to seize this underutilised potential for society. Change efforts then tend to be aimed at scaling, distribution, social innovation and access to targeted networks. *Bi-sectoral partnerships* represent the most obvious partnering configuration, although additional involvement of actors from a third societal sector may be necessary in the execution of initiatives. To illustrate: Global Goals that primarily relate to the well-functioning of markets and value chains (e.g. SDG2 on food security; SDG12 on responsible production and consumption) foremost require well-aligned private sectors (business and civil society) and limited government involvement, provided, however, that governments do not fail in their primary role of providing a proper legal environment. Global Goals that require infrastructure (e.g. SDG9 on innovation and infrastructure) foremost concern the (partly) private provision of public goods. Bilateral partnerships between governments and firms (classic PPPs) are then the obvious partnering configuration. Active involvement of civil society is primarily necessary in the careful and just execution of these initiatives.

■ **Wicked: level 4 change challenges:** the fourth layer of societal issues is the most complex to address. This is where *systemic change* processes are needed. Systemic change is usually defined as change that pervades all parts of a system, taking into account the interrelationships and interdependencies between those parts. By default, therefore, systemic change is 'complex', 'grand' and 'wicked', and affects all parts of society. Partnerships directed towards level 4 type of change challenges should thus reflect the societal set-up, and, accordingly, require the participation of actors from all three societal sectors *(tri-sectoral partnerships)*. As no sector or formal organization bears prime responsibility for coordinating level 4 type of challenges, the institutional void is substantial. This is the case for almost all global public good issues. Change efforts then require collective action, directed towards the provision of 'common goods' that go beyond what mere private, public or social goods can provide for. Extended responsibility and risk-taking in these areas require *extended responsibility and risk-sharing*. Note, however, that level 4 (and level 3) type of change should not be harnessed to compensate for failure or malperformance at levels 1 and 2. Doing so would constitute an overshooting of efforts and a crowding out of primary and secondary responsibilities.

Table 5.7 lists some examples of (the types of) partnerships that have been initiated around the world to deal with societal challenges at different levels of wickedness. A partnership can be initiated by any sector. The nature of the partnership is strongly influenced by the initiator and the degree to which the partnership configuration represents equal, voluntary and *needed* partners.

5.5.3 Dynamic fit: how to improve coalitions of the willing

Partnerships are rarely formed on the basis of 'necessity'. 'Coalitions of the willing' rather than 'coalitions of the needed' prevail in the partnering landscape. Most partnerships initially have a limited number of participants – mostly for practical reasons – who do not necessarily match the issue complexity and type of change

Table 5.7 Examples of partnership configurations at four levels of intervention

		LEVEL 1 Failure addressing partnerships	LEVEL 2 Negative externalities addressing partnerships	LEVEL 3 Positive externalities creating partnerships	LEVEL 4 Collective action partnerships
PRIME INITIATOR OF PARTNERSHIP	Dominant configuration of partnership	**Intra-sectoral**	**Intra-sectoral and bipartite cross-sector**	**Bipartite and tripartite cross-sector**	**Tripartite cross-sector**
	Markets (firms) Private-for profit	Bottom of the Pyramid; Access to medicine; Product development partnerships (PdPs)	Roundtable on Sustainable Palm Oil/Soy; Marine Stewardship Council;	Food and nutrition security partnerships; Innovation coalitions; Open-access coalitions	Climate coalitions; Globalization 4.0 (WEF); Green growth coalitions
	State (governments) Public-non-profit	Donor coordination partnerships (OECD DAC); NATO and other military alliances; United Nations; G20	Water Operator Partnerships; Education, health, infrastructure, internet safety partnerships; Fair taxation coalitions (OECD)	Healthy food partnerships; Local sourcing partnerships; Education; Water and sanitation; Access to energy; Access to justice	Biodiversity partnerships; The Global Fund; GAVI (the Vaccine Alliance); Global Partnership for Effective Development Co-operation (GPEDC); BEPS-initiative (OECD/G20)[8]
	Civil society (NGOs) Private-non-profit	Human rights coalitions; Urban development partnerships; International Federation of Journalists	Advocacy partnerships; Food security, diversity partnerships; Trade union rights	International sports partnerships (IOC); Girl empowerment coalitions	Poverty, economic growth coalitions; Public health partnerships

Source: based on Van Tulder and Keen, 2018

---

8   The OECD/G20 Inclusive Framework on Base Erosion and Profit Shifting (BEPS) brings together over 135 countries and jurisdictions to collaborate on the implementation of 15 actions. These equip governments with domestic and international instruments to tackle tax avoidance, with the purpose of ensuring that profits are taxed where economic activities generating the profits are performed and where value is created. In October 2021, 136 countries signed a historic deal to ensure that multinationals pay a fairer share of tax. Countries agreed to enforce a corporate tax rate of at least 15% as of the year 2023, and a fairer system of taxing profits where they are earned. According to OECD estimates, the deal could bring in an extra $150 billion of tax a year.

required. Partnerships are often formed under uncertain or incident-, opportunity- or event-driven circumstances that call for immediate and/or visible action. In order to be effective, new parties with vital complementary logics, values, resources and methods should then be involved in later stages of the partnership. But even if a partnership engages many willing stakeholders from the outset, it may still run into organizational problems. Adverse selection of partners, crowding-out effects, gaps in complementarity, redundancy in competences and contributions, or deficient counterbalancing can all impede the partnership's effectiveness. Large incumbents, for instance, are rarely eager to fundamentally change the system that they helped create. In general, the most suitable configurational fit is hardly ever achieved at the start of a partnership.

Figure 5.8 considers all possible combinations between the complexity level of the problem and the partnering approach chosen. Only if the approach is aligned with the problem, can a good complexity *fit* be expected. The central oblique line represents the various types of partnerships that create 'coalitions of the needed'. These can be considered a 'fit-for-purpose' partnership configuration, although how partners organize their activities in practice can, of course, still prove insufficient. Coalitions of the willing, on the other hand, often present either

		Nature of the problem			
		Simple	Complicated	Complex	Wicked
Available approaches:	Simple	Intra-sectoral: technical		Significant 'undershooting'	
Create opportunities by effectively addressing the problem	Complicated		Intra-/bi-sectoral: negative ext.		
	Complex			Bi-sectoral: positive ext.	
	Wicked	Significant 'overshooting'			Tri-sectoral: collective action

	'Coalitions of the needed': Good complexity/dynamic partnering fit
	Overshooting /undershooting 'coalitions of the willing': Limited fit that requires learning and improvement
	Significant overshooting: Overly complex approaches for far less intricate problems
	Significant undershooting: Overly simple approaches for far more intricate problems

Figure 5.8 The alignment challenge

too simple or too complex approaches to a problem, thus creating a suboptimal fit with the issue at stake. These coalitions run the risk of 'undershooting' or 'over-shooting' the problem.

DEALING WITH THE RISK OF UNDERSHOOTING

'Undershooting' rises to the surface when the set-up of a coalition does not resemble the complexity level of the problem or the type of change needed. Because not all vital 'logics' and distinct value-creating capacities are then included, the coalition is prone to introducing overly simple solutions to more complex prob-lems. A famous quote by Einstein applies here: "Everything should be made as simple as possible, but not simpler." Cases of serious 'undershooting' tend to occur when the partnership searches for merely technical solutions (e.g. block-chain, an app, a drone, an algorithm) for far more intricate (e.g. behavioural, organi-zational, societal) problems that are difficult to anticipate, model and control. Organizational research shows that this type of 'poor-fit' partnerships tends to create several problems (cf. Van Tulder, 2018a): (1) a false sense of 'doing some-thing' about a problem, based on the philosophy that 'doing something is better than doing nothing'– this lowers the incentive for others to take up appropriate responsibility (see Box 5.1, conditional morality); (2) during implementation, mounting disappointment in the effectiveness of the partnership (because of limited results), culminating in a diminished sense of 'ownership' of the partnership and the issue and, ultimately, failure; (3) the appearance of unintended consequences (for instance, as a result of overlooking behavioural aspects, ignoring context speci-ficity, or neglecting societal complexity) that might jeopardize the entire project.

DEALING WITH THE RISK OF OVERSHOOTING

Cases of serious 'overshooting' occur when the partnership set-up is overly represented or too complex for the level of complexity and change it aims to address. This mechanism has been observed with coalitions in which 'unwilling' partners participated. Unwilling partners stall progress by (intentionally) creating a multitude of procedural and/or analytical barriers. 'Choice paralysis' and adverse selection effects arise in such coalitions. The first effect has been found in psychological research as the result of choice processes with too many options. The second effect has been noted for coalitions aimed at engaging as many as possible or 'high-profile' coalition partners, without considering their motivation to actually address the issue. These members may become a 'hindrance power' within the coalition, which can be even more destructive than if they remained outside of the coalition. Willing, but essentially unneeded, part-ners can also stall progress, for instance by defining the problem differently (as more complex) or applying more strict evaluation criteria than their partners (because of low trust).

TWO SCHOOLS

So, what happens when the partnership largely consists of willing partners who, as a coalition, initially constitute a suboptimal fit with the change required, but who are motivated to address the issue nevertheless? Two schools of thought present two different approaches to this challenge (see Figure 5.7):

- The **performance-based school** of thinking on partnering, which tries to *optimize the outcomes* of an already existing partnership in terms of efficiency and effectiveness, yet without much reference to the complexity of the issue that the partnership intends to address. This discourse adopts a process perspective of *the partnership as a project* that often includes appropriate governance, timelines and accountability provisions;
- The **impact-based school**, which takes the societal issue (for instance an SDG) as the point of departure, considers its complexity and the kind of change needed over time. This discourse foremost monitors *the impact of the partnership on the issue*, including the partnership configuration itself and the extent to which it is fit for purpose or requires adjustment, to better fill the institutional gaps it was designed to address.

In both instances, *partnership brokers* have been struggling with the design of the partnership configuration and the level of 'sophistication' of the ToC. At the start of a partnership project, funders often expect (a linear type of) action plans to hold the managers of the partnership accountable for the efficient and effective realization of prospected outcomes. This leaves little room for fast learning and quick adaptation to new insights. Performance-based contracts are frequently used for partnering projects, but are prone to 'key performance illusions' (Box 4.2) and difficult to govern, especially in case of extensive partnerships that address complex issues (at levels 3 and 4). Donor organizations (e.g. the UK Department for International Development (DFID), the IMF) hence have gradually started to pay more attention to the complexity of systems and to the need for more *adaptive approaches to change*. ToCs then function not so much as a 'planning' and 'accountability' framework, but rather as a 'navigation' and 'learning' tool (Ramalingam et al., 2014). This line of thinking has been advanced in the strategic management literature at the individual level of organizations when faced with systemic and responsive processes that require adaptive capacity and flexibility (Stacey and Mowles, 2015).

CREATING THE RIGHT FIT

What does this imply for an effective 'complexity fit' for cross-sector partnerships? Many CSPs fall short of designing a sufficiently sophisticated intervention strategy, construct partnership configurations that do not include key actors, or fail to define partnership goals that can be appropriately monitored, governed and enhanced. These CPSs risk underutilizing the transformational potential of collaborative advantage (the 'wicked opportunity'). A poorly defined and applied ToC might even become part of the problem, rather than part of the (intended) solution, by creating path dependencies, sunk costs and lock-ins that may forestall more effective partnering trajectories. Complex partnering initiatives consequently require a more *complexity-sensitive approach* to elaborating their ToC (Van Tulder and Keen, 2018), starting in the initiation phase of the partnering effort. A complexity-sensitive ToC is holistic as well as dynamic: it leaves room for an evolved understanding of how change happens. It supports partnerships in aligning the level of complexity, the aspired change and the partnership configuration. It also facilitates a richer understanding of the issue, adjusted strategy formulation and fine-tuning of the partnership configuration during the trajectory. Critical factors for a complexity-sensitive approach include:

- **Collective vision development:** partners can only fully exploit the synergies of working together if they agree on a common vision, mission and objectives (Clarke and Fuller, 2010). If partners fail to converge towards a shared purpose and a common analysis of the problem, it will be very difficult to agree on a plan of action, mission, vision and goals (see Box 5.2).

- **Scope of change:** the scope of societal change that a CSP can achieve has been referred to as the *transformative capacity* of the partnership (Austin and Seitanidi, 2014). Transformative capacity is determined by the motivation and ambition of the partners, the issue addressed and the level of benefit a partnership can achieve for its partners. It is also dependent on the dynamics of the partnering *formation process* and the complexity fit of the chosen *partnering configuration*. The degree to which partners are able to build consensus on goals and shorter and longer-term effects (first, second and third-order intervention effects) particularly affects the vigour and transformative capacity of the CSP.

- **Problem definition:** developing joint problem definitions and sharing dilemmas during the formation phase constitute vital requirements for partners to successively come to appropriate intervention objectives. Complexity-addressing partnerships will find it necessary to adjust the problem definition during partnership execution. Wicked problems are constantly evolving – partly in response to interventions – and, therefore, moving targets. A *learning by doing* approach through a continuous reviewing, revising and improvement process hence should be part of any complexity-addressing partnership. A 'complexity-sensitive ToC' approach facilitates partners in learning how internal processes, systems and capabilities can be best developed and adapted to match the required complexity level of the change process.

- **Partner fit:** in cross-sector partnerships, organizations from different societal spheres are essentially complementary in their distinct roles, functions, logics, means and capabilities. Each partner should take on the role in the partnership that relates to its core complementary competences in creating value for society. It is foremost in the *pooling of these distinct competences and capacities* that the complementary strengths of each sector can be maximized and leveraged. Synergistic value ('wicked opportunity') comes from sameness in goal alignment, and uniqueness in complementary 'assets' (Tables 5.1 and 5.2). Partner diversity (in experience, vision and opinion) thus constitutes a vital attribute in complexity-addressing partnerships that should be valued and respected, provided that it is (1) adequately balanced (e.g. in view of dimensions of power and representation; ownership and commitment; active participation; willingness to contribute; voice and decision-making), and (2) 'fit for purpose' (functional for the type of change aspired to).

- **Cultural fit:** in addition to distinct complementarities of the partners (to be) involved, complexity-addressing partnerships require a suitable level of compatibility as well. The cultural fit in this realm refers to the *commonality in attitudes towards the partnership* (vital to ensure that the contributions of distinct partners are equally valued), and *organizational practices* between the partners that smoothen cooperation and enhance the vigour of collaborative efforts. Differences in working style and culture can partly be levelled out through (the development of) a set of working practices and procedures, compatible operating cultures, operating philosophies, management styles, teamwork, compatible core values and compatible mechanisms to address incompatibilities (Brinkerhoff, 2002). For instance, where firms are especially interested in their societal license to operate, civil society organizations are particularly interested in the scaling of their operations to increase efficiency and impact. Governments have shown considerable interest in learning from management practices of companies, as can be witnessed from the popularity of 'new public management' thinking.

- **Relational capital:** refers to how the interaction between partners develops over time in terms of relations, trust, reputation and process dynamics (Bryson et al., 2015; 2016). To seize the advantage of collaborating, CSPs need to transcend transaction-based exchange, invest in mutual engagement and develop long-term relationships. Relational capital reflects the degree of trust, commitment and knowledge transfer that has been *built up* between the partners. The partners' commitment can be measured by the degree to which they feel that they cannot achieve the partnership objective(s) alone (especially in later stages of the partnership). The very process of working towards an agreed collective ToC can be considered a first litmus test for the capacity of the partnership to build trust among cross-sector partners, enhance legitimacy and to lay the foundation for constructively managing conflict within the partnership. Similarities in values and joint goals create a *social glue* that increases the level of tolerance for differences in opinion.

BOX 5.3

PRINCIPLES OF EFFECTIVE PARTNERING

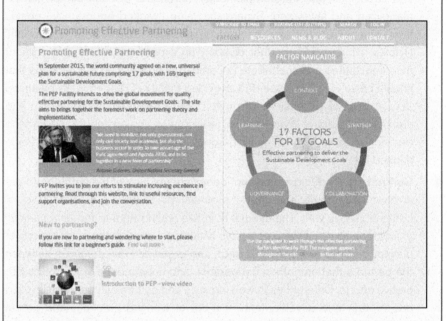

The PEP-platform – a collaborative effort of five international partnering organizations to 'Promote Effective Partnering' – created an online resource to enhance partnering processes for the Sustainable Development Goals. Inspired by the question: 'What will it take to unleash the partnering potential for the SDGs?', the website brings together proven partnering knowledge and expertise, techniques and tools for cross-sector partnering processes. Rather than presenting 'best practice' or benchmarks of success, it uses a 'navigating' approach to guide interested practitioners through a set of leading questions to improve present partnering practices. The initiative is based on the following premises:

- Partnerships are not a luxury but a *necessity*, in particular when addressing 'wicked', systemic or complex challenges that exceed the capabilities and responsibilities of organizations within a single sector;

- Partnerships can create novel kinds of solutions to existing problems, rather than seek (interest-based) compromises;

- Partnerships should build upon the *pooled* and *complementary* strengths of each sector ...

- ... which requires that each sector keeps investing in its *own strength* and the further enhancement of core capabilities;

■   Although partnerships obviously are a means to a goal, they can initially be considered a goal in themselves. By allying parties, partnering can establish a common understanding of a problem and achieve goal alignment, a premise for *directing energy* effectively and productively;

■   Partnerships *are not a panacea* for all sustainable development problems; a continuum of 'multi-stakeholder' approaches exists that relates to various degrees of complexity; change processes require 'fit-for-purpose' types and forms of coalitions; there is no 'one size fits all;

■   The risk of *crowding out* other crucial stakeholders looms large; continuous impact assessments hence are a vital part of any partnership dynamic;

■   You don't partner because you trust each other, *you trust each other because you partner*;

■   Trust is not a necessary, nor a sufficient condition for effective partnering; *mutual respect* (for each other's activities) is; *trust-building*, based on respect, is crucial for the longer-term success of a partnership.

Source: http://www.effectivepartnering.org/; https://www.rsm.nl/faculty-research/centres/partnerships-resource-centre/

5.6 CONCLUSION, TOOLS AND RESOURCES – SCOREBOARD #2

This chapter has argued that the potential of the SDGs as an opportunity is founded in a sound understanding of the societal complexities involved (the 'outside-in' perspective) and the complementary logics of the three societal sectors required for balanced societies (the 'inside-out' perspective). The wicked problems approach, developed in Chapter 4 to define the most salient character-istics of complexity of societal problems, was further elaborated to demarcate the societal origins of wicked problems. Wicked problems appear because solutions cannot be found in any of the traditional societal sectors (state, market, civil society). They require the engagement of actors from multiple sectors.

By bringing the outside-in and inside-out perspectives together, four levels of sectoral intervention were distinguished that reflect the degrees to which soci-etal actors can be expected to bear primary, secondary, tertiary or collective responsibilities. These four levels of intervention relate to responses aimed at 'avoiding harm' or 'doing good', and address: (1) failure in meeting primary responsibilities (fiduciary duty); (2) negative externalities (duty not to destroy value); (3) positive externalities (duty to optimize value); and (4) collective action (shared responsibility). We argued that wicked problems can entail wicked opportunities if: (a) taken seriously (*no denial*); (b) addressed at the reasonably required level(s) of intervention (*no shirking*); (c) there is a proper balance

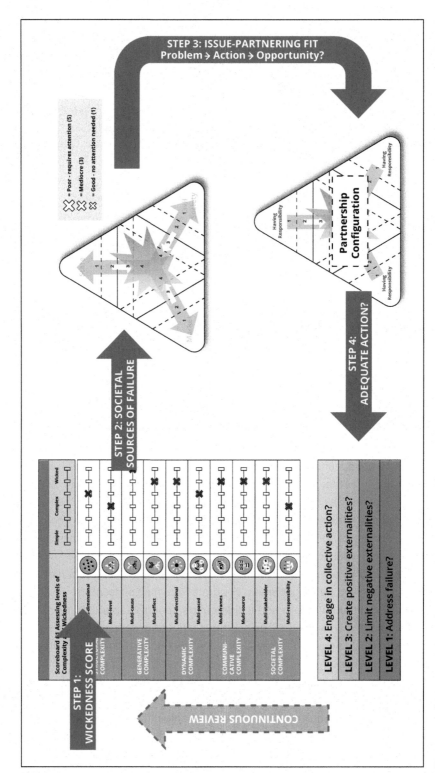

Figure 5.9 Creating a dynamic 'issue complexity-partnering' fit

between having and taking responsibilities (*no crowding out*); (d) they involve actors from complementary sectors (*no institutional void*).

Cross-sector partnerships (CSPs) were highlighted as an increasingly important phenomenon in addressing the institutional voids and in overcoming the trust gaps that extend in a VUCA world. CSPs constitute a vital, constructive, goal-oriented and opportunity-seeking approach to addressing societal problems, provided that the partnership configuration is fit for purpose to face up to the level of complexity and type of change (level 1, 2, 3 or 4) envisaged. Synergistic value ('wicked opportunities') lies in actively seizing the collaborative advantage of CSPs that pursue *partnership impact on the issue*. Complexity fit implies that the partnership can draw from a coalition of *needed* partners – which may evolve from adjusting and enhancing coalitions of *willing* partners accordingly.

The SDG-agenda urges actors from all spheres of society to contribute to their achievement. But not all actors are equally well-positioned to contribute to all sustainable development themes. Certain topics foremost demand dedicated governmental action, while others primarily need the private sector to provide market-based solutions, or civil society organizations to mobilize or tap into the relevant local social networks. The SDGs and their 169 SDG-targets are highly diverse, as are the varied national contexts in which the SDG-agenda is to be implemented. The degree of (direct and indirect) control and the (direct and indirect) responsibilities that different societal actors have in working towards realization, may vary considerably across targets and national realities. Furthermore, many SDG-targets are so complex that they require action at *all* levels of intervention (that is, address sectoral failure *and* negative externalities *and* sufficient positive externalities creation *and* common goods). These SDGs can only be achieved through a 'partnership of partnerships' that includes both intra-sectoral collaborative approaches (to address failure) and combined efforts of governments, companies and civil society organizations in bi- or tripartite type of partnerships, of varying scopes and sizes and across national boundaries.

MAKING IT PRACTICAL – A STEP-BY-STEP ANALYSIS

Badly aligned intervention strategies result in either overly complex interventions for relatively simple problems, or overly simple interventions for reasonably complex problems (Figure 5.8). Where to start, then, in considering: (a) what level of intervention is needed to address the problem, (b) who should be involved in what way, and (c) what degree of 'fit' is required to effectively address the issue? The analytical challenge here is to link the problem's degree of wickedness (Scoreboard #1) to its societal origins, in order to create a match between 'having' and 'taking' responsibility for a specific intervention. This challenge requires a step-by-step approach; one that supports in navigating from a general analysis of the problem to an exploration of 'fit-for-purpose' partnering approaches that have the highest potential to create synergistic opportunities by adequately addressing the problem (Figure 5.9).

Step 1 - wickedness analysis
Wickedness analysis defines the level of wickedness that the issue portrays (while differentiating between ten dimensions of complexity that may display a dispersed range of complexity scores).

▸ Apply **scoreboard #1** (Chapter 4). This exercise helps to delineate the general level at which an issue primarily needs to be addressed. Level 1 issues (failure) probably show a totalled 'wickedness score' of below 20. Level 2 issues, often related to an inadequate approach to negative externalities, score approximately 20–35. Level 3 issues score between 35–50 and involve insufficient creation of positive externalities. Level 4 issues score highest in terms of wickedness, and also show the least direct commitment of actors to take responsibility (low degree of having responsibility).

Step 2 - societal gap and resilience analysis
Societal gap and resilience analysis zooms in on scale 9 and 10 of the wickedness framework ('societal complexity'). It delineates the societal sources of failure (section 5.2.1) that explain the institutional origins of the challenge and the type of organizations that need to get involved (section 5.2.2). The societal triangulation technique requires consideration of the four complementary roles (see Table 5.2) that constitute the basic repertoire of each of the three societal spheres (state, market, civil society). How does each sector 'score' on the issue at hand, at each of the four intervention levels? (See section 5.3).

▸ **Scoreboard #2** helps to identify the sources of failure per societal sector (*the horizontal arrow*), and at each intervention level (*the vertical arrow*). For each of the three societal sectors, one can (intuitively) score their performance on the defined issue, for each of the four levels at which they could create value for society. The five-point Likert-scale facilitates an approximate assessment of the extent to which each sector can be considered to have a poor to a fairly good performance (poor[1] – mediocre[3] – good[5]).

It is worth noticing that this gap assessment is exploratory, in a comparable fashion as with scoreboard #1. Depending on the breadth and level of expertise involved, the effort and time spent on context-specific analysis, and the degree of inter-rater reliability that can be achieved through collaborative analysis, the assessment may prove more intuitive or more robust. The assessment is foremost intended to help *navigate* change by providing guiding questions. It can be executed by experts, practitioners, participants, students or others. It is designed as an exercise that can be done based on desk research, by a consultant or the managers of a partnership, or following 'wisdom-of-the-crowd' rules. The principles of sociocracy and peer review – as explained in Chapter 4 – apply here as well.

SCOREBOARD #2 Defining an intervention logic for the issue

1. Needed? (degree of wickedness)	LEVEL 1 Address failure	LEVEL 2: Deal with negative externalities	LEVEL 3: Create positive externalities	LEVEL 4: Engage in collective action	Societal gap analysis:
	Sources of Societal Failure and/or Success:				
2. Description: Whether organizations	. . . take up their primary role	. . . deal with negative externalities	. . . try to create positive externalities	. . . engage in collective action to resolve systemic problem	Total scores per sector
A. State: Public value creation through . . .	Mandating: laws and regulation	Facilitating: subsidies and regulation against public *bads*	Endorsing and facilitating other organizations to create positive effects	Trilateral partnering for systems change	
	Poor[1] Good[5] 〇—〇—〇—〇—〇	Poor[1] Good[5] 〇—〇—〇—〇—〇	Poor[1] Good[5] 〇—〇—〇—〇—〇	Poor[1] Good[5] 〇—〇—〇—〇—〇	4 10 15 20 〇—〇—〇—〇—〇
B. Market: Private value creation through . . .	Competitive production of goods and services	Minimize negative effects (e.g. pollution)	Optimize positive effects through innovation and scaling	Trilateral partnering to create systems change	
	Poor[1] Good[5] 〇—〇—〇—〇—〇	Poor[1] Good[5] 〇—〇—〇—〇—〇	Poor[1] Good[5] 〇—〇—〇—〇—〇	Poor[1] Good[5] 〇—〇—〇—〇—〇	4 10 15 20 〇—〇—〇—〇—〇
C. Communities: Civic value creation through . . .	Creating social value through mutual support	Advocacy within, towards other sectors	Service delivery to create positive effects	Trilateral partnering to create systems change	
	Poor[1] Good[5] 〇—〇—〇—〇—〇	Poor[1] Good[5] 〇—〇—〇—〇—〇	Poor[1] Good[5] 〇—〇—〇—〇—〇	Poor[1] Good[5] 〇—〇—〇—〇—〇	4 10 15 20 〇—〇—〇—〇—〇
Societal gap analysis: Scores per intervention level					Alignment challenge

[a] The vertical combination of the scores indicates the degree of *resilience* or – in case of poor scores – the *vulnerability* of the whole society (as demarcated for the issue) on that specific intervention level. Chapter 1 already defined a 'resilient' society as one in which all three sectors of society are 'in balance'. We can now make that observation more concrete. For example, if in a given country all three sectors have a good score (5) at level 1 (that is: no failure in fiduciary duty), it is easier to take up a wicked challenge than in the case where one or two of the three sectors score poorly on fulfilling their primary responsibilities. A 'failed government'[9] (score 1), for instance, seriously affects the ability of the market and civil society sectors to fulfil their roles, at all levels of intervention, either within their own sector or in cross-sector partnerships. The more weakly balanced a society is – particularly at levels 1 and 2 – the greater the societal trust gap becomes, and the more vulnerable the society will be to external shocks. Such conditions also imply a more significant challenge to create a dynamic fit for any type of partnership.

[b] The horizontal combination of the scores of one societal sector indicates the overall 'resilience' of that sector (on each intervention level). Very often, this exercise will show a 'mixed' score on many accounts. In case the sectors score poorly on level 1 (fiduciary duty and primary responsibilities), we can also expect them to score poorly on most other levels. However, other patterns have been found as well. For instance, companies with a poor score at levels 1 and 2 as a result of extremely polluting activities may have an incentive to use their philanthropy activities (at level 3) to compensate for the negative externalities they create. It can be a means of seducing or influencing communities and governments to develop activities that (partially) take over the company's primary responsibility. Most probably, this will not create a lasting effect and reiterate vulnerabilities in later stages. Governments that score poorly on level 1 (for instance, because of corruption, nepotism or a lack of separation of powers), will try to influence society by subsidizing activities (intervention levels 2 and 3). But this type of activity will probably not provide them with the legitimacy and trust needed to engage in effective partnerships with other governments or the other sectors. A sufficient score at level 1 can be considered a *hygiene factor* ('license to exist/operate') for effective bi-sectoral or tri-sectoral collaboration at the higher levels of intervention.

---

9   The US Fund for Peace introduced a 'fragile state' index (previously 'failed state' index) to identify states where the government is not able to exercise its primary role of 'mandating', and consequently weak and ineffective in providing public goods, preventing corruption, and creating safety. In 2019, the top five fragile states were: Yemen, Somalia, South-Sudan, Syria and the Democratic Republic of Congo.

As a first rough estimate of the *sectoral* resilience/vulnerability, the following scores apply:

■ 4 = very poor on all accounts: vulnerable sectors make unreliable partners; due diligence and trust-building is needed;

■ 5–10 = poor on most accounts; probably stronger on level 1 and less so on other levels;

■ 10–15 = probably strong on levels 1 and 2, with more moderate scores on levels 3 and 4;

■ 15–20 = strong on all accounts; strong potential partner with a good record.

It is worth noting that sectors normally score better at lower levels of intervention. If this appears the other way around, it is worth examining more closely what might explain this.

Step 3 - issue–partnering fit

Issue–partnering fit delineates the type of (cross-sector) partnership configuration that would best match the level of complexity of the problem. This analysis links the required level(s) of intervention (section 5.3) and the type of change required with actors from those societal sectors that have (and/or are able to take up) primary, secondary, tertiary or collective responsibility for resolution of the problem (Figure 5.6 and section 5.5.2). Parties that are part of the problem preferably should be engaged in addressing the sources of failure.

■ *Level 1 type of problems* should lead to individual action and/or intra-sectoral partnerships by those actors who are mainly responsible for the issue;

■ *Level 2 type of problems* require bi-sectoral partnership configurations (preferably in addition to intra-sectoral initiatives among those that bear primary responsibility for the issue);

■ *Level 3 type of problems* require bi- or tri-sectoral partnerships; their effectiveness strongly depends on the proven strength of each involved sector in having their level 1 and 2 type of responsibilities effectively straightened out;

■ *Level 4 type of problems* require tri-sectoral partnerships (collective action) that can only be effective if the involved partnering organizations do not contribute to major sources of failure at the lower levels of intervention.

Step 4 - dynamic fit

Dynamic fit provides a 'reality check'. It is directed towards improving the actual partnering set-up that is adopted in practice to effectively impact the issue. Considering all the provisos and conditions under which partnerships are created, it can be expected that the initial partnership configuration constitutes a 'coalition of the willing' that is not immediately 'fit for purpose'. The 'dynamic fit' analysis considers to what extent the adopted partnership approach matches a 'coalition of the needed' as required for the level of change and impact it envisages (section 5.5.3). The challenge for later stages of the partnership can then be formulated along the relevant levels of intervention, for instance:

- *Level 1:* what next steps should each of the partners take to integrate the project into their core activities (the 'internalization challenge') to enhance the effectiveness of the partnership;

- *Level 2:* should new (cross-sector) partners be approached – or present partners released – to enhance the effectiveness of the partnership and impact on the issue? Key to this consideration is the ability of existing partnering parties to activate their constituencies in controlling for negative externalities;

- *Level 3:* should new (cross-sector) partners be approached who can expand the effects of the existing partnership to other sectors to scale impact;

- *Level 4:* should the intervention logic (Theory of Change) be enhanced, what potential collaborative advantage has been underutilized, does the partnership reflect the right 'balance' in partners, what value-creating competences are additionally required?

How this can work in practice as an analytical tool for assessing both the action of parties and the effectiveness of partnerships, will be further elaborated in Part III – in Chapter 7 ('making it resilient') and Chapter 12 ('making it collaborative').

BOX 5.4

A HYPOTHETICAL CASE: SDG1 – 'ALLEVIATING POVERTY IN ALL ITS FORMS'

The context: consider the case of SDG1 (poverty alleviation) in country Y. Companies in this country are strongly efficiency-driven, reap monopoly profits and are not concerned with the negative externalities of their actions, let alone about creating welfare for all. The government is functioning but small, partly because of neoliberal principles. It focuses on law-making and law enforcement, and nothing else. Civil society is well-organized and takes good care of its own communities, but is not overly interested in common pool goods.

The partnering case: In country Y, a 'coalition of the willing' has been formed between an international donor organization (government), a local NGO and the corporate foundation of a local company (a bank). They have formulated ambitious goals: to come up with micro-finance schemes to create social enterprises that are aimed at providing employment and services for people living at the 'bottom of the pyramid'. They have agreed on an ambitious budget as well: $10 million for three years. What can we expect from this partnership?

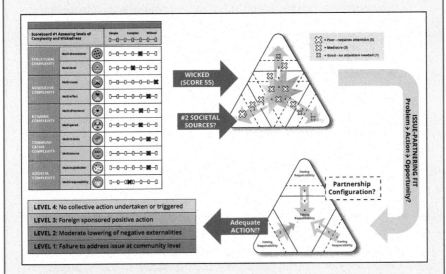

A general analysis: a first assessment of whether the hypothesized partnership potentially creates a 'fit-for-purpose' configuration.

- ■ *Step 1:* SDG1 is a wicked problem in country Y (Score: 55 on Scoreboard#1). There is enormous ambiguity around the issue of poverty, its definition, how to approach it, and who is primarily responsible for addressing it. For instance, the culture of the country considers 'poverty' the result of 'fate' rather than of a poorly functioning economic system.

- ■ *Step 2:* this can also be explained by more carefully considering the societal sources of the problem (zooming in on scales 9 and 10). An assessment points to significant sources of failure within the market sector, which scores poorly in comparison with the other sectors on all levels of intervention (total score 20 on Scoreboard#2). The government's intervention repertoire is limited. Civil society appears the strongest and more resilient sector with higher scores at levels 1 and 2, but is not very 'entrepreneurial' (level 3).

- ■ *Step 3:* the wickedness score suggests the need for level 4 type of interventions in tri-sectoral partnerships (collective action through the pooling of complementary logics and competences from all three societal sectors). A well-aligned issue-partnering fit seems difficult to establish, nevertheless. Major gaps in society appear at levels 2, 3 and 4, with the market sector being the weakest link on all levels (with serious fiduciary duty issues at level 1).

- ■ *Step 4:* it can be seriously doubted whether the proposed partnership addresses these complexity-configuration alignment issues. This 'coalition of

B
O
X

5.4

willing' partners aims to 'solve' poverty through subsidies (level 3 and 4 interventions from a foreign donor, not the country's own government) and sponsoring from foreign and local NGOs. The company participates at level 2 through its corporate foundation, but is not overly interested in 'internalizing' the partnership by integrating the project's goals in its core business activities and improving its business model. It considers contributing to micro-finance a philanthropic activity. Its commitment to the partnership is not strategic and might be terminated if the company changes its sponsoring policy.

This exploratory analysis of a hypothesized case indicates – based on several general characteristics – that the partnership does not appear 'fit for purpose' in at least two ways. First, it is not well-aligned with the nature and complexity of the problem (level 4). Second, the configuration itself ('partner fit') rests on an unequal and unbalanced fit between 'willing' partners who have rather different motivations, ambitions, risk and responsibility appetites, legitimacy positions, competences and time horizons.

Can it be improved? Probably not, because the formulated transformational ambition and the chosen intervention logic (philanthropy, subsidies, voluntary collaboration) do not appear to be aligned. If the partners consider this first step as 'a pilot' to actively grow into a more effective partnership, the NGO participant should be well aware of the weak performance of both the government and the market partner to address the sources of failure on their side of society. The partnership might even be an excuse for not addressing the multi-faceted nature of poverty in the country, and precious time might be lost due to unfounded hopes put on this project to contribute to SDG1.

The Societal Triangle...

- Wicked problems cannot be reframed as 'wicked solutions', but they can be reframed as 'wicked opportunities'. Whether wicked opportunities can be seized, depends on the extent of 'collaborative advantage' that can be created in addressing the problem.

- Wicked opportunities require 'space'; what some consider as an institutional void and a trust gap, for others represents an 'opportunity space' that can be further operationalized as 'partnering space'.

- Trust gaps occur in many countries; they are related to institutional voids (unregulated areas of society resulting from deficient or lacking formal and informal institutions), but not all countries face the same trust gaps.

- Four societal sources of wickedness exist: systemic, positive externalities, negative externalities, failure.

- Four levels of intervention accordingly exist: they represent the 'outside-in'/'inside-out' approach on the issue, from each side of the societal triangle.

- 'Market failure' does not refer to illegal or fraudulent action of companies; it refers foremost to structural deficiencies in the operation of markets to entice companies to deliver sufficient value to society; the same applies to 'civic failure' and 'government failure'.

- Negative externalities are difficult to regulate; 'avoid doing harm' to others is within the realm of influence and, therefore, part of the responsibility (negative duties, duty not to destroy value) of sectors; negative externalities are difficult to organize through solely intra-sectoral coalitions of willing or self-regulation. Generally, they require bi-sectoral efforts.

- Seizing the opportunities of positive externalities (positive duties; duty to optimize positive value) at the least requires coalitions of willing partners and a common goal; scaling and optimizing positive externalities may require coalitions of *needed* partners.

- Collective action requires tripartite cross-sector partnerships representing all three societal sectors; collective action also calls for innovative goal- and solution-oriented approaches, and an ability to think 'outside-the-box' in terms of paradoxes.

- The type of negotiations necessary for implementing most SDGs deviates from position-based or interest-based negotiations; 'collective vision'-based negotiations go beyond 'win-win' and compromise, to seek ways of *synthesizing* interests to bring about collaborative and synergistic value.

- Issue-partnership complexity fit: the 'right' type of partnership depends on a correct assessment of the societal origins of the issue, its complexity level and the kind of change required; to be effective, cross-sector partnership configurations need to 'fit their purpose'.

■ Coalitions of willing partners can evolve to include coalitions of *needed* partners; an impact-oriented perspective on partnering that takes the effect on the issue as a litmus test, enables a dynamic issue-partnering fit.

■ The 'sucker syndrome': taking on too much responsibility, to the extent that it stretches beyond the reasonable sphere of influence. Although sympathetic, this mechanism is likely to undermine the overall impact of a partnership, as it will probably crowd out the responsibility-taking of other parties that do have a (more) crucial part to play in addressing the issue – and thus are needed to create more lasting and more effective impact.

■ There are two schools on cross-sector partnerships: the performance and the impact school. The former considers what it takes to improve the performance of an existing partnership; the latter considers whether the partnership is 'fit for purpose' and can be expected to have the best impact with the right partners.

- ***The Story of Stuff Project:*** Societal change. Transformational goal-setting. 'Growing Solutions'. "Together, we can build a world focused on *better* instead of *more*." Nine award-winning animated movies that have inspired and encouraged global civic engagement in collective action towards sustainability. Community-minded, solutions-focused and action-oriented. The movies (and other media) focus on the big, exciting innovations driving the environmental and social change we need, as well as the little things individuals and communities can do to make a difference. https://www.story ofstuff.org/movies/the-story-of-solutions/; https://www.storyofstuff.org/movies/story-of-change/

- ***The Partnerships Resource Centre:*** An international research and knowledge centre for public-private collaboration for sustainable and inclusive development. Bridges science and practice by creating, connecting and sharing knowledge on: (1) how cross-sector partnerships work, (2) how they can contribute to sustainable transformations, and (3) how to enhance the transformative capacity of partnerships. Embedded within Rotterdam School of Management (RSM), Erasmus University (EUR). Shares tools and publications to guide navigation and the strategization of partnering and mutual learning processes. https://www.rsm.nl/faculty-research/centres/partnerships-resource-centre/

- ***Cross-sector Interactions:*** The CSSI Community is an umbrella organization of academic and practitioner organizations and individuals in the field of cross-sector social interactions. It is aimed at inspiring global collaboration for the social good, by promoting values-based collaborative value creation in theory and practice. CSSI publishes through its Annual Review of Social Partnerships (ARSP) journal, convenes through a bi-annual conference, and serves the community through the website: http://www.cssicommunity.org/

- ***Theory of Change – Learning for sustainability:*** By developing a ToC based on sound theory, managers can be better assured that their programmes are delivering the right activities for the desired outcomes. Programmes are easier to sustain, bring to scale and evaluate, since each step – from the ideas behind it, to the outcomes it hopes to provide, to the resources needed – is clearly defined within the theory. The website provides an annotated guide to a range of online resources providing papers, handbooks, tips, theory and techniques on ToCs and related fields, linked to sustainable development, natural resource management, urban development, public health and agricultural sectors. https://learningforsustainability.net/theory-of-change/

- ***UN SDG Partnerships Platform:*** The achievement of the SDGs will require all hands on deck: different sectors and actors working together in an integrated manner by pooling financial resources, knowledge and expertise. The Partnerships for SDGs online platform is the United Nations' searchable global registry of voluntary commitments and multi-stakeholder partnerships made in support of sustainable development and the 17 SDGs. The platform also facilitates sharing knowledge and expertise among multi-stakeholder SDG-related partnerships, as well as providing periodic updates on their progress. https://sdgs.un.org/partnerships; https://sustainablede-velopment.un.org/partnerships/about

■ *The International Association for the Study of the Commons (IASC):* brings together multidisciplinary researchers, practitioners and policymakers for the purpose of improving governance and management, advancing understanding and creating sustainable solutions for commons, common-pool resources or any other form of shared resources. Aimed at the exchange of knowledge among diverse disciplines, areas and resource types and appropriate institutional design. Accessible resources include open-access journal articles; a digital library; online introductory education material; databases; and methods. https://iasc-commons.org/resources/

■ *Civic-driven change projects:* are developing around the world to create 'common goods' and enhance the social 'fabric' of society by brokering social relationships. Two examples: (1) 'The Broker' is an information platform that collects and shares informa-tion on civic-driven change, particularly in the fields of Human Security, Inclusive Economy and Sustainable Governance: https://www.thebrokeronline.eu/civic-driven-change-d94; (2) the Aspen Institute – a global non-profit organization committed to realizing a free, just and equitable society – initiated 'Weave' as a social fabric project. The project is aimed at 'weaving inclusive communities' to repair the social fabric by putting 'relationalism' at the centre, to counter hyper-individualism: https://www.aspeninstitute.org/programs/weave-the-social-fabric-initiative/

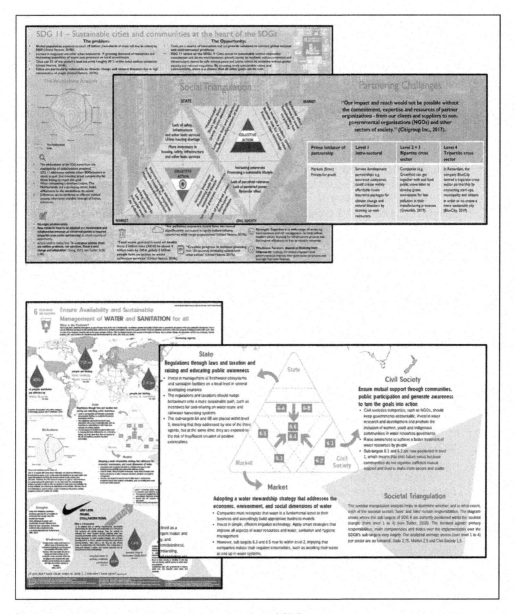

Student posters applying societal triangulation to selected SDGs

REFERENCES

Austin, J.E. (2000). 'Strategic Collaboration between Nonprofits and Businesses', *Nonprofit and Voluntary Sector Quarterly*, 29(1):69–97.

Austin, J.E. & Seitanidi, M.M. (2014). *Creating Value in Nonprofit-Business Collaborations. New Thinking and Practice*. San Fransisco, CA: Jossey-Bass.

Bäckstrand, K. (2012). 'Are partnerships for sustainable development democratic and legitimate?'. In Pattberg, P., Biermann, F., Chan, S. & Mert, A. (Eds.) (2012) *Public-Private Partnerships for Sustainable Development. Emergence, Influence and Legitimacy*, (pp. 165–183). Cheltenham: Edward Elgar Publishing.

Basu, K. (2001). 'On the goals of development'. In: Meier, G.M. & Stiglitz, J.E. (Eds.) *Frontiers of development economics: The future in perspective*. Washington/New York: World Bank/OUP, pp. 61–86.

Biermann, F., Mol, A.P.J. & Glasbergen, P. (2007). 'Conclusion: partnerships for sustainability – reflections on a future research agenda'. In Glasbergen, P., Biermann, F. & Mol, A.P.J. (Eds.), *Partnerships, Governance and Sustainable Development. Reflections on Theory and Practice*, (pp. 288–300). Cheltenham: Edward Elgar.

Brinkerhoff, J.M. (2002). 'Government–nonprofit partnership: a defining framework', *Public Administration and Development*, 22(1):19–30.

Brown, V.A., Harris, J.A. & Russel, J.V. (Eds.) (2010). *Tackling Wicked Problems: Through the Transdisciplinary Imagination*. London: Earthscan.

Bryson, J.M., Crosby, B.C. & Bloomberg, L. (Eds.) (2015). *Creating Public Value in Practice. Advancing the Common Good in a Multi-sector, Shared-Power, No-One-Wholly-in-Charge World*. CRC Press: Taylor and Francis Group.

Bryson, J.M., Crosby, B.C. & Stone, M.M. (2006). 'The Design and Implementation of Cross-Sector Collaborations: Propositions from the Literature', *Public Administration Review*, 66(s1):44–55.

Buse, K. & Harmer, A. (2004). 'Power to the partners? The politics of public-private health partnerships', *Development*, 47(2):49–56.

Clarke, A. & Fuller, M. (2010). 'Collaborative Strategic Management: Strategy Formulation and Implementation by Multi-Organizational Cross-Sector Social Partnerships', *Journal of Business Ethics*, 94(1):85–101.

Davis, K. (1973). 'The Case for and against Business Assumption of Social Responsibilities', *Academy of Management Journal*, (16):312–323.

Ellersiek, A. (2011). *Same Same but Different. Power in Partnerships: An Analysis of Origins, Effects and* Governance, published doctoral dissertation. Tilburg: Tilburg University.

Ferlie, E., Fitzgerald, L., McGivern, G. & Bennet, C. (2011). 'Public policy networks and "wicked problems": A nascent solution?', *Public Administration,* 89(2):307–324.

Fisher, R. & Ury, W. (1981). *Getting to Yes: Negotiating Agreement Without Giving In*. New York: Penguin Books.

Glasbergen, P. (2011). 'Understanding partnerships for sustainable development analytically: The ladder of partnership activity as a methodological tool', *Environmental Policy and Governance,* 21(1):1–13.

Gray, B. (2007). 'The process of partnership construction: anticipating obstacles and enhancing the likelihood of successful partnerships for sustainable development'. In Glasbergen, P., Biermann, F. & Mol, A.P. (2007). *Partnerships, governance and sustainable development. Reflections on Theory and Practice* (pp. 29–48). Glos: Edward Elgar Publishing.

Hart, S.L. & Sharma, S. (2004). 'Engaging fringe stakeholders for competitive imagination', *Academy of Management*, 18(1):7–18.

Huxham, C. & Vangen, S. (2004). 'Doing Things Collaboratively: Realizing the Advantage or Succumbing to Inertia?', *Organizational Dynamics*, 33(2):190–201.

James, C. (2011). *Theory of Change Review: A report commissioned by Comic Relief.* Retrieved from: https://www.dmeforpeace.org/wp-content/uploads/2017/06/James_ToC.pdf.

Kahneman, D. (2012). *Thinking, Fast and Slow.* New York: Farrer, Strauss and Giroux Inc.

Kania, J. & Kramer, M. (2011). 'Collective Impact', *Stanford Social Innovation Review*, 9(1):36–41.

Katz, N. & Pattarini, N.M. (2008). 'Interest-based negotiation: An essential business and communications tool for the public relations counselor', *Journal of Communication Management*, 12(1):88–97.

Kelly, E. (2015). 'Business ecosystems come of age'. In: Deloitte (2015). *Business ecosystems come of age*, Business Trend Report (pp. 3–15), Deloitte University Press.

Kramer, M.R. & Porter, M.E. (2006). 'Strategy and society: The link between competitive advantage and corporate social responsibility', *Harvard Business Review*, 84(12):78–92.

Lawrence, T.B., Hardy, C. & Phillips, N.W. (2002). 'Institutional Effects of Interorganizational Collaboration: The Emergence of Proto-Institutions', *The Academy of Management Journal*, 45(1):281–290.

Levin, K., Cashore, B., Bernstein, S. & Auld, G. (2012). 'Overcoming the tragedy of super wicked problems: constraining our future selves to ameliorate climate change', *Policy Sciences*, 45(2):123–152.

Lin-Hi, N. & Müller, K. (2013). 'The CSR bottom line. Preventing corporate social irresponsibility', *Journal of Business Research*, 66(10):1928–1936.

Mazzucato, M. (2018a). 'The entrepreneurial state: socializing both risks and rewards', *Real-World Economics Review*, (84):201–217.

Mintzberg, H. (2015). *Rebalancing Society. Radical Renewal Beyond Left, Right and Centre.* Oakland, CA: Berrett-Koehler Publishers.

Musgrave, R.A. (1959). 'Taxes and the Budget', *Challenge*, 8(2):18–22.

North, D.C. (1990). *Institutions, Institutional Change and Economic Performance.* Cambridge: Cambridge University Press.

Pattberg, P. & Widerberg, O. (2016). 'Transnational multistakeholder partnerships for sustainable development: Conditions for success', *Ambio*, (45):42–51.

Pattberg, P., Biermann, F., Chan, S. & Mert, A. (Eds.) (2012). *Public-Private Partnerships for Sustainable Development. Emergence, Influence and Legitimacy.* Cheltenham: Edward Elgar.

Patton, M.Q., McKegg, K. & Wehipeihana, N. (Eds.) (2016). *Developmental Evaluation Exemplars. Principles in Practice.* New York: The Guilford Press.

Rahwan, I., Pasquier, P., Sonenberg, L. & Dignum, F. (2009). 'A formal analysis of interest-based negotiation', *Annals of Mathematics and Artificial Intelligence*, 55(3):253–276.

Ramalingam, B., Laric, M. & Primrose, J. (2014). *From best practice to best fit: Understanding and navigating wicked problems in international development.* ODI Working Paper. London: Overseas Development Institute.

Rawls, J. (1971). *A Theory of Justice.* Cambridge, MA: Harvard University Press.

Rittel, H.W.J. & Webber, M.M. (1973). 'Dilemmas in a general theory of planning', *Policy Sciences*, 4(2):155–169.

Rivera-Santos, M., Rufin, C. & Kolk, A. (2012). 'Bridging the institutional divide: Partnerships in subsistence markets', *Journal of Business Research*, 65(12):1721–1727.

Schenk, H. (2005). 'Organisational Economics in an Age of Restructuring, or: How Corporate Strategies Can Harm Your Economy'. In: De Gijsel, P. & Schenk, H. (Eds.) *Multidisciplinary Economics*, (pp. 333–365). Kluwer Academic Publishers.

Schneider, A., Wickert, C. & Marti, E. (2017). 'Reducing Complexity by Creating Complexity: A Systems Theory Perspective on How Organizations Respond to Their Environments', *Journal of Management Studies*, 54(2):182–208.

Spencer, F. (2013). 'Turning Wicked Problems into Wicked Opportunities', *Futurist Forum*, 15 May.

Stacey, R.D. & Mowles, C. (2015). *Strategic Management and Organisational Dynamic. The challenge of complexity to ways of thinking about Organisations* (7th edition). Essex: Pearson.

Stadtler, L. & Probst, G. (2011). 'How broker organizations can facilitate public–private partnerships for development', *European Management Journal*, 30(1):32–46.

Streeten, P.P. (2001). 'Comment'. In: Meier, G.M. & Stiglitz, J.E. (Eds.). *Frontiers of Development Economics. The Future in Perspective*, (pp. 87–93). New York: World Bank and Oxford University Press.

Utting, P. & Zammit, A. (2009). 'United Nations-Business Partnerships: Good Intentions and Contradictory Agendas', *Journal of Business Ethics*, 90(1):39–56.

Van Tulder, R. (2018a) *Getting all the Motives Right. Driving International Corporate Responsibility (ICR) to the Next Level*. Rotterdam: SMO.

Van Tulder, R. (2018b) *Skill Sheets. An Integrated Approach to Research, Study and Management*. Third Edition. Amsterdam: Pearson Education.

Van Tulder, R. & Keen, N. (2018). 'Capturing Collaborative Challenges: Designing Complexity-Sensitive Theories of Change for Cross-Sector Partnerships', *Journal of Business Ethics*, 150(2):315–332.

Van Tulder, R. with Van der Zwart, A. (2006). *International Business-Society Management. Linking Corporate Responsibility and Globalization*. London: Routledge.

Waddell, S. (2000). 'New institutions for the practice of corporate citizenship: historical, intersectoral, and developmental perspectives', *Business and Society Review*, 105(1)107–126.

Wartick, S. & Wood, D. (1999). *International Business and Society*. Oxford: Blackwell Publishers.

World Bank (1997). *World Development Report 1997. The state in a changing world*. Oxford: Oxford University Press.

Young, I.M. (2006). 'Responsibility and global justice: A social connection model', *Social Philosophy and Policy*, 23(1):102–130.

6 WHO?
THE GOVERNANCE CHALLENGE

DOI: 10.4324/9781003098355-8

P R I N C I P L E S

- **Responsible or good governance principles:** pertain to the system by which organizations are directed and controlled. It concerns structures and processes for decision-making, accountability, transparency, voice, equity, inclusiveness, control and behaviour at the top. Governance influences how an organization's objectives are set and achieved, how risk is monitored and addressed, and how performance is valued. Responsible leaders always act to optimize and sustain the societal value and potential of their organization and its people. Governance perspectives range from rules-based to principles-based and from compliance-driven to beyond compliance – mediating between liability and responsibility.

- **Fiduciary principles** can take various forms: narrow fiduciary duties directed towards 'shareholder value' creation; broad(er) fiduciary duties directed towards 'stakeholder value' creation; negative fiduciary duties aiming to 'avoid doing harm'; positive fiduciary duties aiming to 'enhance doing good'.

- **Hybridity principle:** stresses the relevance of organizational diversity for societal value creation. There is no one-size-fits-all governance type of sustainable enterprise, nor of corporate responsibility. No organizational form is perfect; all forms are part of the 'fabric' and overall resilience of societies.

- **Societal license principle:** societal acceptance or approval of organizations' activities is based on their abidance with approved standards and on responsively and responsibly taking stakeholder concerns into account. Four societal licenses can be obtained: the license to exist, to operate, to scale and to experiment.

- **'Level playing field' principle:** defines fairness not as an equal chance to succeed, but as the premise that all play by the same set of rules.

- **Rival governance principles** are context and culture dependent. Prevailing norms include 'precautionary' and 'subsidiarity' principles (the EU); 'substantial equivalence' principles (Anglo-Saxon countries), efficiency-driven pragmatism and, ethical-religious principles (e.g. stewardship, non-possessiveness, the prohibition to collect interest, sharing of profit and loss, reciprocity, zakat, harmony, compliance).

- **Hypernorms:** principles that function as minimum requirements for socially, ethically and ecologically responsible organizational conduct in the 'moral free space', by which all other norms are to be judged.

- **Universal principles:** include the UN General Principles on Business and Human Rights (Ruggie principles to Protect, Respect, Remedy), ILO Conventions, Environmental Conventions, UN Declarations (e.g. on the Rights of Indigenous Peoples).

■ **Treaty-based principles** are those included in bilateral treaties (e.g. on trade, investment and taxation), regional treaties (e.g. on trade, integration, environmental governance and protection; transboundary effects) and multilateral treaties (e.g. WTO principles: non-discrimination, reciprocity, transparency).

■ **Area-specific principles** have been introduced by multilateral organizations in areas such as health, food safety, human rights, labour conditions, anti-corruption, accountability, and a variety of other sustainability standards.

P R I N C I P L E S

6.1 INTRODUCTION: A MULTILEVEL HYBRID GOVERNANCE CHALLENGE

Transforming SDG frames from problems into opportunities presents a challenging organizational trial across societal sectors and levels. More specifically, it requires both a better understanding of the kind of governance principles that are needed to steer societal change in the right direction and an answer to the question of 'who' is going to take up what type of challenge. Having and taking responsibility for specific societal issues presents a subtle *agency* test that goes beyond the jagged distinction between state, market and civil society organizations (Chapter 5). Society has great diversity in organizational forms, each with their perspective on sustainability and progress. As wicked opportunities thrive on diversity in approaches, it is relevant to develop a greater insight into the various organizational forms that societies bring together. Many represent *hybrid governance* forms, combining or blending public (state) and private (market/communities), or profit and non-profit functions. Diversity in approaches and organizational forms can contribute to more *resilient* and more effective strategies, especially in the face of wicked problems. However, organizational diversity also creates significant intellectual and governance problems: What organizational forms work best for sustainable development and under what (governance) conditions?

The SDG endeavour itself has been organized as a hybrid governance model, with a relatively loose architecture of involved stakeholders. Part I explained why this hybrid multilevel approach can nevertheless be understood as a relevant governance response to the multiple challenges of the present VUCA world. With increased competition between societies and systems, it has become progressively difficult to find *rules-based* solutions to societal problems. National laws do not suffice to prevent the appearance of a 'race to the bottom' in most sustainability areas. This vicious race creates 'institutional voids' and 'trust gaps' at all levels of society by hollowing out what is in the common interest. Internationally, a 'global governance gap' exists that leaves the grand global challenges to a largely unregulated arena without rules, regulation or any type of effective supervisory organization to define laws and implement sanctions. How to deal with these gaps and guide all actors to move in 'the right' direction?

The 2030 Agenda and the 17 SDGs are grounded in a *principles-based* approach. They build on generally accepted international declarations and principles (for instance, on human rights) and guidelines drawn up by intergovernmental organizations (like the OECD), to fill governance gaps and institutional voids at all levels of society. These establish a floor of basic principles to 'do no harm' (negative duties). The ultimate ambition of the SDG-agenda, however, is to implement those principles that could trigger a 'race to the top' to 'do good' ('positive duties', *beyond* negative duties) to enhance the envisioned transformational change. The distinction between rules-based and principles-based approaches is not only relevant at the global level. It applies to all levels of society and to all situations in which organizations have to decide on interventions, and accordingly have to (re)consider what principles to adopt and what rules to abide by. In most instances, rules and principles combined create valid constraining and enabling motivators for sustainability. The more that systemic change and collective action is required, though, the more principles and values prevail over rules and laws as principal coordinating and governing mechanisms (Figure 6.1).

At all levels of society, various forms of 'hybrid governance' and 'hybrid organizations' have developed in response to societal challenges that

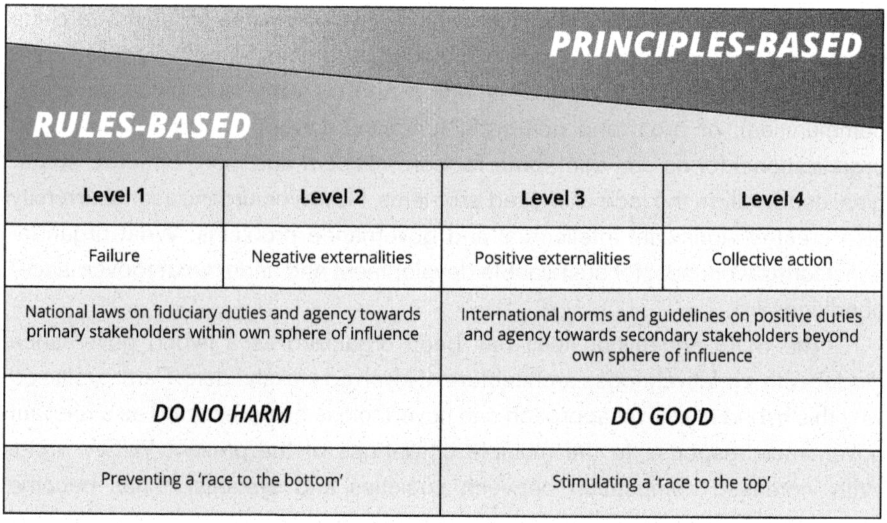

PRINCIPLES-BASED			
RULES-BASED			
Level 1	**Level 2**	**Level 3**	**Level 4**
Failure	Negative externalities	Positive externalities	Collective action
National laws on fiduciary duties and agency towards primary stakeholders within own sphere of influence		International norms and guidelines on positive duties and agency towards secondary stakeholders beyond own sphere of influence	
DO NO HARM		*DO GOOD*	
Preventing a 'race to the bottom'		Stimulating a 'race to the top'	

Figure 6.1 From rules-based to principles-based governance

necessitated a different take on organizing. The characteristics of these hybrid forms denote 'who' is probably well-positioned to act on what type of responsibility and related to what parts of the SDG-agenda. To some extent, one can claim that hybrids are better able to deal with certain types of sustainability problems. Hybridization is no panacea for absorbing increased societal complexity however. At the level of organizations, hybridization comes with comparable governance challenges as identified at the global level (Chapter 3): the risk of mixed identities, ambiguous actions, lack of focus, trailing progress and unclear distribution of responsibilities. These pitfalls are the equivalent of the strategic nightmare of organizations: being stuck in the middle, aiming for too many goals, or evolving into so-called 'garbage-can organizations' (Cohen et al., 1972).

This chapter considers three specific responsible governance challenges:

■ At the national level, what defines principles of sustainable governance for distinct organizational forms (section 6.3);

■ At the organizational level, what defines principles of sustainable governance for distinct types of intervention (section 6.4);

■ At the international level, how to select general principles defined by international organizations to enable the transition from a rules-based system to the principles-based system of the SDGs (section 6.5).

In all these discourses, we first need to establish a basic understanding of the relevant components of 'responsible governance' (section 6.2). Finally, the responsible governance principles are operationalized in a practical setting: the 'Wicked Problems Plaza'. This formula was developed as a 'safe space' to experiment with and apply responsible governance principles to the conditions for collaborative action in addressing wicked problems (section 6.6).

6.2 THREE APPROACHES TO RESPONSIBLE GOVERNANCE

The discourse on responsible governance has received input from three different streams of scientific and policy thinking: (1) the traditional focus on 'corporate governance', which emerged as an integrated field of knowledge for 'corporate control' from corporate law and corporate finance; (2) a broader discourse on 'responsible governance' that emerged from a growing, general interest in 'good governance', stakeholder thinking and corporate social responsibility (CSR); and (3) an even broader discourse on the institutional embeddedness of various organizational forms that focuses on the societal impact of different governance structures. These three streams of thinking largely complement each other. They present vital components in a holistic approach to the governance challenges of sustainable business models. This involves three basic levels of sustainable business and organizational practices: (a) at the *micro level*: ethics and compliance management; (b) at the *meso level*: responsible management; and (c) at the *macro level*: environmental- and sustainability-oriented management.

TRADITIONAL CORPORATE GOVERNANCE (LEVEL 1)

Traditional corporate governance discourse has mostly focused on the question of whether managers lead an organization in the best interest of its owners, and how to ensure that managers do so. Corporate governance thinking is strongly grounded in *agency theory* (Jensen and Meckling, 1976), which argues that when ownership and management become separated, interests start to diverge between the manager (the 'agent') and the owner (the 'principal'). The greater the disconnect between the interests of principals and agents, the more agents may behave opportunistically, abuse their discretionary powers for self-interested purposes, and engage in 'moral hazard'[1] when they can do so with impunity. Corporate governance then describes the institutional framework that regulates the division and exercise of power. It refers to the set of structures, mechanisms, relations and processes by which an organization is controlled and directed, with the objective of minimizing agency, goal divergence and conflicts of interests.

Conventional corporate governance literature deals with the *principal-agent* problem in terms of a narrowly defined scope of directly involved (primary) stakeholders. It centres on protecting capital-providing shareholders (owners) against value-destroying managers. 'Agency costs' then relate to monitoring costs (checks and balances), bonding costs (keeping managers aligned and accountable) and residual costs. The related principle of '*fiduciary duty*' or '*fiduciary responsibility*' is about the trust that the organization (the agent) will loyally, prudently (with due care, skill and diligence) and transparently act in the interest of its clients and beneficiaries (principals). The more trustworthy the fiduciary relationship is, the lower transaction costs are. In the corporate governance literature, fiduciary duties primarily relate to market relationships but in the CSR discourse, this element is particularly important for understanding how confidence, faith, reliance and, ultimately, societal legitimacy of corporations and organizations develop.

A narrow interpretation of both agency and fiduciary duty defines the challenge of corporate governance as dealing with *failure* (level 1) in the operation of

---

1   Moral hazard in economics refers to situations in which the agent has an incentive to increase their exposure to risk, because the agent does not bear the full costs of that risk. Applied to the financial crisis, for instance, moral hazard translated into 'too big to fail': the realization that systems banks were so crucial to the financial system that they would always be saved by the government. This provided an incentive for risky and even immoral behaviour.

organizations. Governance then focuses on preventing moral hazard, intentional misconduct by managers, and avoidance of unwanted consequences that arise from lacking diligence. The discussion in this discourse often boils down to whether organizational structures and disciplinary and incentivizing mechanisms of 'hierarchy and control' are effective in mitigating agency problems. Most of the traditional corporate governance literature has no reference to issues of sustainability, other than the realization that organizations need 'financial sustainability' to survive and be able to innovate and scale.

RESPONSIBLE GOVERNANCE (LEVEL 2)

The responsible governance discourse has gradually included a wider range of (primary) stakeholders who might be adversely affected by the actions of managers. The concept bears strong reference to public governance and questions of responsibility in implementing public policies. It entails rules, norms, processes and practices that incorporate *values* into decision-making, and combines accountability with discretionary action.

General concepts of 'good governance' have increasingly been applied to specific corporate governance challenges, mostly in reaction to public scrutiny of corporate practices. This constitutes a response to what is considered the 'crisis of shareholder governance' (Lamarche and Rubinstein, 2012). Standards and principles introduced around the world to deal with broader corporate governance issues have started to address *relational characteristics with society* and *longer-term value creation* as a starting position. These increasingly recognize the vital role of employees and other stakeholders in contributing to the performance and long-term success of companies. Examples include the OECD Principles of Corporate Governance and various national governance standards and codes, such as the Sarbanes-Oxley Act in the USA, the Tabaksblat Code in the Netherlands, or the European Green Paper on Corporate Governance. Many of these codes have formulated *principles* that provide a basis for extending principal-agent relations to include issues such as privacy, human rights, pollution, insider trading or lay-offs. These topics refer to negative externalities created by specific corporate behaviour and relate to responsibility challenges derived from global trends like digitalization (impact on privacy), global dynamic complexity (impact on international trade) or tensions that result from increased rivalry between 'varieties of capitalism' (Chapter 1). Mainstream literature on responsible governance tends to concentrate on level 2 type of issues.

MACRO-ORIENTED GOVERNANCE (LEVELS 3 AND 4)

The macro-oriented, societal discourse on governance takes an institutional approach. It looks into various organizational forms and how, and at what level, various organizations can effectively contribute to the functioning of societies.

Responsible governance then relates to the contribution that organizations can make to societal 'grand challenges' in general, and sustainable development in particular. The institutional perspective defines the logics that are prevalent in society, how these are enacted, undergo change and create certain institutional orders that lead towards a better (i.e. more resilient, sustainable, inclusive) society. The macro approach thus considers the more fundamental challenge of which institutional arrangements best serve the sustainability needs of society.

Broadening the concept of responsible governance to include wider societal spheres further builds on two types of institutional research: (1) (new) 'institutional economics' and (2) 'institutional logics' thinking. Institutional economics considers the concept of institutions as the formal and informal 'rules of the game' that shape, structure and constrain social, political and economic relations (North, 1990). Institutional logics thinking takes a more organizational perspective. It focuses on "socially constructed, historical patterns of cultural symbols and material practices, including assumptions, values and beliefs, by which individuals and organizations provide meaning to their daily activity, organize time and space, and reproduce their lives and experiences" (Thornton et al., 2013: 2). This definition reflects the dual view of culture in institutions as a system of both practices and meaning. Governance systems, in this discourse, provide a frame of reference in guiding the actor's choices in *sense-making*.

Institutions and logics delineate institutional *arrangements* (coalitions) and *organizations* (structures). They create collective terms of action that define which practices and governance procedures can be seen as effective and legitimate, whilst delineating who is authorized to intervene, take responsibility or show engagement with specific challenges (Reinecke and Ansari, 2016). Institutional arrangements thus relate to contextually embedded ways of doing things (Mair et al., 2012). Organizations, then, are the material expressions ('entities') of "groups of individuals bound by a common purpose to achieve objectives" (North, 1990: 5). The macro dimension of responsible governance depends on the context in which institutional arrangements can be linked to effective and legitimate types of action by specific organizational entities. The agency challenge can then be elaborated as the organization's *positive fiduciary duty* towards broader groups of primary and secondary stakeholders – now and in the future.

Different organizational forms consequently derive their legitimacy from two sources: (1) from the context in which they have been created and are operating in; and (2) in how they give shape and substance to different layers of duties and responsibilities that are, or can be, attributed to them. Formal organizations representing institutional arrangements can help actors to assign responsibility in ambiguous situations (e.g. 'institutional voids' and 'trust gaps'), and assist in constructing meaning and sense-making. This can be of particular importance when economic, social and emotional tensions create contradictory pressures, for instance in the absence of vital institutional structures or weak enforcement of formal institutions (such as laws). It can also be supportive in creating new (proto-) institutions (see Chapter 5), provided that actors can come to the formulation and implementation of a new 'social contract' – at the local, national and even global level (Sachs, 2015) – or create effective cross-sector partnerships.

Taking the institutional logics and institutional arrangements into account when considering responsible governance questions implies that we consider more complex organizational forms and relate them to ever broader topics of organizational responsibilities: limiting negative externalities (level 2), the creation of positive externalities and positive (fiduciary) duties (level 3), and how organizations can contribute to collective action challenges in general (level 4). *Complexity in organizational forms* involves 'hybridity' in two directions: horizontal (across societal spheres) and vertical (across levels of intervention).

6.3 HORIZONTAL HYBRIDITY: EIGHT ORGANIZATIONAL ARCHETYPES

Societies around the world have adopted a large variety of organizational and governance forms. These generally represent (a combination of) basic institutional characteristics: (1) public or private; (2) for-profit or non-profit; (3) governmental or non-governmental; (4) aimed at the provision of public or private goods/services. Each of these organizational and governance forms creates a different setting for responsible practices and sustainable 'business models'. Considerable confusion exists about the defining characteristics, roles and sources of success of organizations in contributing to society. For example, what to think of state-owned enterprises; do they serve the same goals as 'public' companies? What is the logic behind their existence and what societal value do they create? And what should we make of 'family-owned' firms, cooperatives, 'social enterprises' and the non-profit and informal sector? Who represents what kind of interests? Agency and agency costs relate to many organizational forms. Consequently, we need to broaden the discussion on agency to cover all manner of governance questions.[2]

Chapter 5 applied the principle of *societal triangulation* to define the basic institutional logics that create a balance between the three main sectors of society (state, market, civil society). It was explained that the functioning of these societal spheres – individually and in interaction with one another – determines how a

---

2   Part of this chapter was published in the *Handbook of Responsible Management* (Van Tulder and Van Mil, 2020, in Laasch et al., 2020). This handbook concentrates on the principles of responsible management praxis for individual managers. The excerpts from this contribution in the present chapter focus on organizational challenges at various levels of intervention.

society functions as a whole. This societal set-up of a country also defines the context, in terms of opportunities and constraints, in which policy and decision makers of organizations have to develop and implement sustainable policies and business models.

But institutional arrangements in the societal triangle are far more complex than that. None of the three institutional spheres operates in isolation of the others. Business, for instance, is grounded in society by legislation, competition and shared values and norms (Etzioni, 1988), and thus always finds legitimacy at the *interface of overlapping coordinating mechanisms* derived from public, private and non-profit orientations. As a result, many hybrid organizational forms have developed in response to societal challenges that required a different take on the organization of primary responsibilities and related governance (and institutional) arrangements. Hybrid forms, however, face responsible governance challenges as well. Accordingly, their role and functioning have given rise to questions related to the strengths and weaknesses in addressing agency problems effectively, the actual value (and side effects) created, the societal impact witnessed, and the most effective institutional arrangements and organizational forms for sustainability.

The hybridization trend in society has induced considerable conceptual ambiguity and confusion on how societal spheres (functions), inter-institutional logics (arrangements) and different organizational forms (entities) are related. This conceptual ambiguity can be tackled as a taxonomy challenge by distinguishing different organizational forms, based on a set of elemental societal and governance interface challenges that organizations have to address. The societal triangle can accordingly be recomposed along four basic interfaces (Figure 6.2) that define the organizational antecedents of responsible governance challenges:

1   **Organizational domain:** an organization can be identified as *governmental* or *non-governmental* (NGO). In the societal debate, this distinction is important yet also leads to confusion. Companies, for instance, are 'non-governmental organizations', but are rarely considered as such. From a responsible governance point of view, the discussion on the position and legitimacy of NGOs may be complicated because it is difficult to derive any meaningful purpose from the identity of an organization when it is defined by what it is *not* ('non-').

2   **Organizational means:** organizations are based on *for-profit* or *non-profit* (or *non-market*) principles. In most countries, communities are considered to be best represented by non-profit organizations (foundations). Yet 'non-profit' does not really define an identity, nor an aim – judging by the confusion in the hybridization debate on the status of, for instance, cooperatives and social enterprises.

3   **Legal form:** in most countries, a distinction is made between a *public organization* and a *private organization*. The confusion here is related to agency

questions in the market sphere that is split between market players with a public identity (such as joint-stock companies that have shares traded around the world in the public domain), and those with a private identity (such as family-owned enterprises, in which the agent can also be the principal).

4   **Functional/responsibility orientation:** at the primary level of responsibility (fiduciary duty), we can differentiate between organizations that focus on the provision of *public goods* and those that focus on *private goods*. This distinction splits up the sphere of civil society: some organizations take care of the provision of goods with an exclusive character (private or club goods), and other civil society organizations (like Greenpeace or Amnesty International) focus on the provision of public goods, for instance through advocacy.

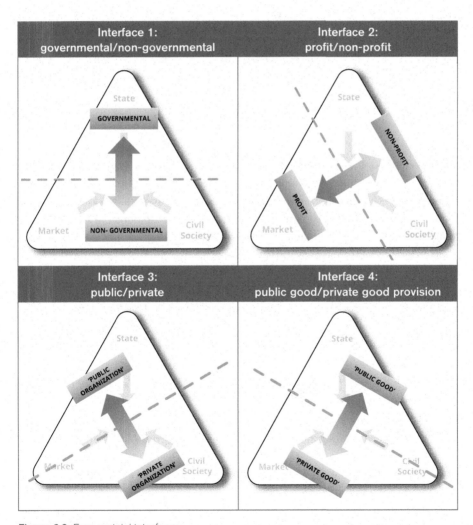

Figure 6.2 Four societal interfaces

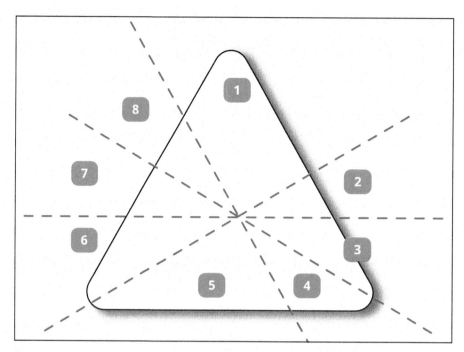

Figure 6.3 Eight organizational archetypes and responsible governance challenges

Combined, these four elementary interfaces present a regrouping of institutional functions and arrangements within the societal triangle. They define eight different *archetypical organizational forms* (Figure 6.3) that are (a) logically consistent, and (b) can be considered to face comparable responsible management challenges that – at the fundamental level of responsible governance – distinguish them from other archetypical organizational forms. Some of these challenges relate to what has been defined as ideal-typical roles of the state, market and communities sectors (organizational forms 1, 3 and 6); some of these challenges relate to the 'hybridization' realm (organizational forms 2, 4, 5, 7 and 8).

■ [1] This position represents the archetypical *state role*: a public organization, governmental, non-profit-oriented for the provision of public goods. This is the type of entity most people refer to when they talk about 'governments' or the 'public sector'.

■ [3] This position represents the archetypical *civil society or community role*: a private organization, non-governmental, non-profit-oriented, aimed at the provision of public or social/club goods. This is the type of entity most people would refer to when they talk about 'NGOs' or the 'third sector'. The more specialised literature nowadays prefers to use the term 'civil society organizations' (CSOs) to better delineate the archetypical community-based organization.

■ **[6]** This position represents the archetypical *market role* on which most of the corporate governance literature is centred: a public organization, non-governmental, profit-oriented for the provision of private goods. This is the type of entity most people refer to when they talk about 'firms' or 'corporations' or the 'private sector'.

Five additional archetypical organization forms can be identified along the four societal interfaces. They have developed in parallel to the others and sometimes in response to typical governance problems that the 'classic' archetypical organizational forms (market, state, civil society) faced, or created.

■ **[2] At the state-civil society interface**, we find private organizations that are non-profit-oriented, aimed at the provision of public goods, and (predominantly) funded by governments. We find most *public universities*, *public policy implementation bodies* and *public hospitals* in this category. Many of these organizations face governance challenges related to funding: how to develop business models that allow for 'cross-subsidization' between private activities (fees, wealthy patients) and non-profit or loss-making activities.

■ **[4] At the civil society-market interface**, we find private, non-governmental organizations that are *non*-profit-oriented and aimed at providing private goods. Most *cooperatives* and most *social enterprises* fit this category. Both types of organizations are impact driven and have been founded in response to a societal problem (poor working and income conditions of farmers, for instance). Cooperatives tend to have members rather than customers; many social enterprises are based on crowdfunding or other forms of blended finance.

■ **[5] At the market-civil society interface**, we find private, non-governmental organizations with a *for*-profit orientation that are aimed at the provision of private goods. Most *family-owned firms* appear in this category. Family-owned enterprises invest and expand on the basis of own capital. This makes them grow more slowly than joint-stock companies (archetype 3) that have better access to risk finance, but which also face greater basic governance challenges (e.g. due to opportunistic managers). Joint-stock companies that decide to 'go private' often do so to regain control vis-à-vis shareholders, and partly also to take more responsibility for the actions of their organization.

■ **[7] At the market-state interface**, we find public organizations that are (partly or wholly) government-owned or sponsored, with a for-profit orientation and aimed at producing private goods. Most *partly state-owned companies* that are also quoted on the stock exchange (and attract private capital) fall into this category.

■ **[8] At the state-market interface**, we find public organizations that are (partly) government-owned, for-profit-oriented and that produce a (semi-) public good such as infrastructure. We find most *public-private partnerships* in this category, as well as *majority-controlled state-owned enterprises (SOE)* with either a systems or public utility function, like banking, electricity, water, rail, internet or postal services.

6.3.1 Organizational strengths and weaknesses

Each of these eight organizational archetypes portrays typical organizational strengths and weaknesses. Strengths are derived from unique capabilities that each of these particular forms can more effectively align in comparison with other governance forms. However, aligning distinct spheres also comes with a broader span of specific responsibilities, and hence creates weaknesses as well. The specific combination of capabilities and responsibilities of each organizational form delineates its efficiency in producing specific types of value for society. Strengths and weaknesses play out differently over longer periods. No organizational form is perfect, yet all forms are part of the 'fabric' that have their function in the resilience of societies (Table 6.1).

Table 6.1 Strengths and weaknesses of eight organizational governance models

Governance/ organizational form	Typical strengths	Typical weaknesses
[1] STATE (government)	• Coordination in public goods provision; • Protecting public interest; • Coercion and enforcement measures to prevent free-riding, transgression, misbehaviour; • Redistributive, allocative and diffusing power (i.e. welfare, income, wellbeing, knowledge and information); • Creating stability/continuity; • Internalization of external effects.	• Lacking efficiency: public goods provision requires a high degree of transparency, accountability and organizational bureaucracy, which increases transaction and switching costs; • Increasing efficiency may compromise effectiveness, legality, (democratic) legitimacy and procedural and distributive justice; • The continuity of long-term programmes, due to short-term electoral cycles, political opportunism; populist promises during election.
[3] CSO (civil society organization)	• Creation and coordination of social capital; • Mutual support to cope with, mitigate, share or even out risk; • Advocacy, voice/articulation of interest, mobilization;	• Fragmentation (dealing with heterogeneity); • Access to sufficient funding; • Decision-making power (related to representation of diverse interests to prevent power abuse); • Degree of organizational professionalism;

Governance/ organizational form	Typical strengths	Typical weaknesses
	• Service-delivery: provision of social/club goods and services; • Organization of shared beliefs, values, norms, ideology (homogeneity in values, preference, focal point).	• Degree of efficiency in providing sufficient goods & services for members (transaction costs; difficulty of scaling opportunities); • Span of control (when too big, cohesion declines); • Continuity (dependency on volunteers; funds; support and goodwill) • Exclusiveness: tension between inclusion vs. exclusion/discrimination; • Ownership structures/ill-defined ownership.
[6] MARKET (joint-stock company)	• Relatively easy access to risk-bearing capital; • Mitigation of risk due to limited liability; • Transferability of shares/ownership; • No restriction of members; • Flexibility; • Efficient production and scaling; • Creation of (new) markets; • Competition; • Innovation (technologies; products; processes; organizational); • Risk-taking and risk management; • Generation of surpluses (profits); • Generation of spill-overs through applied mode of organizing: outsourcing, delegating, cooperating with suppliers.	• Short-term orientation (profit-driven); • Market concentration/monopoly surpluses/collusion/insider trading; • Fickle societal license to operate (trust; reputation); • Too big or too diversified to create value; • Too much risk-taking: high risk = high wins or high 'penalty'; • Deficient capacity to internalize external costs; • Global free trade excesses: 'race to the bottom', 'footloose capital', tax evasion and manipulation; natural resource exploitation; • Abuse of information asymmetries and market power (e.g. misuse of patents on medicine, seeds).
[2] STATE- CIVIL SOCIETY	• Quicker realization of social goals and the organization of social capital; • Lower marginal costs of public goods, while pursuing social welfare objectives; • Risk-sharing; investment in activities/ projects that the public authority or third sector would be unable or unwilling to complete alone; • Performance-based payment; • Contractual stipulation of risk bearing/ responsibilities/performance standard; • Access to networked solutions/ techniques/methods and specific target groups; • Leveraging private finance (voluntary contributions) with public funding.	• Complexity in, and duplication of steering mechanisms and monitoring; • Goal incongruence (different masters to serve); • Ambiguous or unclear performance criteria due to directive ambiguity; • Contracts/performance measures undermine autonomy, reducing short-term control over service delivery; • Confusion among management and employees, blame shifting and lack of real accountability; • Inefficiency due to monitoring duplicity, insufficient monitoring, increased coordination and transaction costs, • Risk transferred from taxpayer to semi-public organization (such as a university or hospital) to bear residual/unforeseen liabilities.

(Continued)

Table 6.1 (Continued)

Governance/ organizational form	Typical strengths	Typical weaknesses
[4] CIVIL SOCIETY- MARKET	• Active economic participation by members; • Solidarity /cooperation in meeting common economic, social, and cultural needs and aspirations; • Joining of forces (against market dominance; • Economic resilience by risk and profit-sharing, and by investing part of profits back into the community; • Voluntary, open membership; • Democratic member control and decision-making; • Autonomy and independence; • Education, training, information sharing; • Concern for community / values orientation (openness, social responsibility, caring, tradition); • The competitive advantage of mutuals	• Democratic decision-making (one man one vote, majority rule); • Accountability/ responsibility towards whole membership group hampers initiative and flexibility; • Less agile and thus less competitive; • Portfolio risk problem: different risk aversion levels and time horizons of members; • Shares not transferable, no or very restricted individual spread of risk possible; • Professionalism (hiring and retaining specialized staff, e.g. administrative capacity); • Tradition, conservatism; • Free-rider conflicts;
[5] MARKET- CIVIL SOCIETY	• Trust (alignment of ownership and management); • Stability: no shareholder influence that induces short-termism; • Strong leadership/direct influence in decision-making enables capability to take up issues quickly; • Flexibility (hands-on mentality) and commitment; • Long term outlook/focus on continuity reduces over-ambitious risk-taking; • Company interest prevails over personal gain; • Risk aversion supports steady growth strategy; • (Family) values-oriented; • Family owners often have a profound emotional investment and interest in their firms; their fortune, personal contentment, and reputation are tied to success of the firm.	• Limited access to capital; • Succession problem; • Relational aspects play an important role in decision-making (e.g. family conflict); • Inward looking/risk of groupthink/lack of checks & balances (family businesses are reluctant to allow outsiders into the top level, people are given jobs for which they may lack the skills, education, or experience); • Overly risk-averse (slow growth, stagnation); • Unstructured governance (related to formal decision-making; internal hierarchies; rules); • Deficient flexibility to internalize opportunities quickly (capacity and capabilities challenge); • Limited external accountability.
[7] MARKET- STATE	• Deep pockets of state (financial access and continuity); • Insider in local networks;	• Bureaucracy/loss in efficiency; • Suspicion of political agenda (industrial politics), especially in case of developing foreign activities;

Governance/ organizational form	Typical strengths	Typical weaknesses
	• Easier to make longer-term planning and thus increase strategic position within a sector; • Too big to fail; • Big influence on national policies, regulatory capture; • Stable /secure job environment for employees.	• Single shareholder influence (risk of bias in decision-making due to lack of sufficient checks and balances); • Lack of flexibility; • Risk aversion; • Target of political and ideological battles; • Pressure for corruption (if foreign influence is a focal point), rent-seeking behaviour by politicians, other non-pecuniary private benefits.
[8] STATE- MARKET	• Increased efficiency/operational performance/quicker realization; • Lower marginal costs of public goods, while pursuing social welfare objectives; • Risk-sharing; investment in activities/ projects that either the public authority or the private sector would be unable or unwilling to complete alone; • Performance-based payment; • Contractual stipulation of risk-bearing/ responsibilities/performance standard; • Access to innovative solutions/techniques/ methods (tendering selection process, market competition); • Leveraging private finance with public funding.	• Political interference may distort the public mission and commercial orientation; • Risk aversion/shirking in case of joint responsibilities or delegated (contracted) responsibilities; • Risk-bearing comes at a price: private party will ask for surplus, which may make a PPP costly; • Public party often still 'responsible' for realization (public goods provision), so considerable expense may be involved for a public authority where a project has gone wrong; or • Risk transferred from taxpayer to private company to bear residual/ unforeseen costs/contingent liabilities.

Sources: based on Voorn et al. (2019); Minguez-Vera et al. (2010); Foulke (2016); Smith et al. (2013); Milhaupt and Pargendler (2017).

6.3.2 Agency and responsibility challenges

The strengths and weaknesses of hybrid organizational forms can be associated with typical agency challenges that appear as diverging or conflicting interests between principal(s) and agent(s). Most hybrid organizational forms represent a multiplicity of interests that may be difficult to align, especially when under pressure. On the one hand, divergence in interests can be a source of substantial transaction costs. On the other hand, blended logics and hybrid ways of organizing may increase organizations' resourcefulness and success in addressing more complex responsibility issues, provided that related agency challenges can be effectively dealt with (Table 6.2). Agency challenges linked to the eight archetypical organizational forms include the adverse effects of such behavioural phenomena as moral hazard, adverse selection,[3] information-asymmetries, free-riding behaviour, risk aversion, shirking responsibilities, inadequate or perverse incentives, skewed loyalties, or signalling and reputation (how the agent can credibly convey some information about itself to the principal). Overlapping agency challenges across the hybrid organizational forms can partly be attributed to the fact that they share several basic institutional positions in society.

Responsible governance research on hybrid organizations has been limited. This prompted us to take the taxonomy development one step further to also include levels of responsibility (section 6.4) and deal with what we can call the 'vertical hybridity' challenge.

Table 6.2 Examples of responsible agency challenges per organizational form

Governance form	Examples of Agency Challenges (Conflicts of interest)
[1] STATE (government)	• Government officials act in their private interests (clientelism/power/influence/status/job aspirations); kleptocracy/enrichment; nepotism (appointing trustees to essential positions); • Regulatory capture, government officials are influenced by vested interests (lobby groups, corporate interests); • Government officials act in accordance with own convictions, ideology, priorities (not aligned with public cause/democratic majority)
[3] CSO (civil society organization)	• Information asymmetry between managers and members (fraud, expropriation of organizational resources; unacceptable risk-taking; mismanagement; moral hazard; acting in own interest/subversion); • Management acts in accordance with own convictions, ideology, priorities (not aligned with members' values and priorities); • Agency costs: monitoring & reporting, checks on staff trustworthiness; • Skewed representation of interests in decision-making by management • Dependency of members on volunteering staff and reliance on 'good intentions' can make control/sanctioning complicated (lack of effective control mechanisms); • Limited legal standing for members to file a lawsuit against managers (lack of juridical sanctioning instruments).
[6] MARKET (joint-stock company)	• Information asymmetries: How to protect shareholders (owners) against value-destroying managers (fraud, unacceptable risk-taking, mismanagement/moral hazard);

---

3 Adverse selection applies when sellers have information that buyers do not have, or vice versa, about some aspect of product quality. In the context of principles of sustainable business, adverse selection processes occur when organizations participate in initiatives (like the Global Compact) without the intention to really contribute; the adverse effects of the selection of 'unwilling' parties – parties that participate for defensive reasons – is that the initiative is frustrated from within, which will lower its potential impact considerably.

Governance form	Examples of Agency Challenges (Conflicts of interest)
	• 'Agency costs' relating to the costs of monitoring (checks and balances on information asymmetries), bonding costs (keeping managers aligned and accountable through contracts, profit-sharing and performance-related pay) and other residual costs; • Internal control mechanisms: Decision-making and representation structures/ corporate governance; • External control mechanisms: public financial statements and accountancy control.
[2] STATE- CIVIL SOCIETY	• Multiplicity in the responsibility to steer and monitor reduces steering and monitoring overall (increasing free-riding behaviour); • Inequity between principals may induce lobbying by the agent; • Conflict between principals increases the agent's autonomy: in the absence of clear directives, the agent has more freedom to choose its paths or to play out branches of government against each other; • Problems in building incentive schemes for agents when principals' objectives diverge and when there is a lack of coordination; • Individual principals have incentives to lobby agents to pursue their individual objectives; multi-principal nature of government can start to revolve more around individual principals' power and less around cooperation; • Leads to more significant inefficiencies: lobbying increases agency costs and brings a larger wealth transfer from principals to agent than would occur under a single principal; welfare loss that comes from monitoring duplicity when multiple principals do not coordinate.
[4] CIVIL SOCIETY- MARKET	• Members (e.g. in a cooperative) may play different roles simultaneously (owners, buyers and sellers, controllers, and beneficiaries) and thus may have very diverse objectives; • Multiplicity of objectives (e.g. social mission, financial stability, growth, flexibility, time horizon) means the objectives of the organization are not well defined, increasing managers' discretion; • Multiplicity of objectives makes it more difficult to establish incentives, performance metrics, and control mechanisms that minimize conflicts between members and managers; • Power of the (cooperative) managers, combined with the fact that property rights are not properly defined; • Boundaries between governance, management and operational matters can be very blurred.
[5] MARKET- CIVIL SOCIETY	• Conflict between owner and managers: driven by emotional ties to the business, shared family wealth, and nepotism; • Conflict of interest between controlling (family) shareholders and non-controlling shareholders, through 'private benefits of control' such as: excessive voting rights or board control, entrenched (family) managers, mismatch of control rights versus cash-flow rights, the transfer of profits or assets out of firms; • Conflict of interest between insider (e.g. family, founding) shareholders who may have an interest in non-financial aspects of the firm, including preserving reputation and legacy, giving back to the community, or protecting the environment, and (family) outsiders whose financial interests (e.g. maximizing share value or increasing the dividend) can conflict with these objectives.

(Continued)

Table 6.2 (Continued)

Governance form	Examples of Agency Challenges (Conflicts of interest)
[7] **MARKET-STATE**	• Exit options enjoyed by citizens (as the Ultimate Beneficiary Owners behind the state) are far weaker than those available to shareholders (in non-democratic societies, the voice option is virtually non-existent); • The lack of a clear consensus on which objectives the government should pursue (and on the means to accomplish these objectives) hinders the development of effective mechanisms of accountability; • The absence of a 'market check' on managerial agency costs; • Implicit state guarantees undermine the threat of bankruptcy as a source of managerial discipline; • The pursuit of social welfare objectives favours citizens, but not shareholders; • The appropriation of disproportionate financial benefits by the state (which favours citizens, but not shareholders); • The award of subsidies to SOEs, which favours shareholders, but not necessarily citizens; • Allocation of responsibilities and oversight/enforcement of duties may not be adequately separated, which may not be in the public interest (enforceability of the rule of law by the public);
[8] **STATE-MARKET**	• Level of transparency requested in tendering processes (information-asymmetries; information that is competition-sensitive); • Setting appropriate performance criteria related to risk-sharing/risk-bearing; • Exit option of government (taxpayer) is very limited, as it concerns public goods/services); • Handling contingent liabilities (fault finding/attribution); • Under-reporting by contractor of liabilities/unforeseen circumstances, risks; • Information-asymmetry in (technical, expert) knowledge between government officials and private party/contractor.

Sources: based on Voorn et al. (2019); Minguez-Vera et al. (2010); Foulke (2016); Smith et al. (2013); Milhaupt and Pargendler (2017).

6.4 VERTICAL HYBRIDITY: MULTILEVEL RESPONSIBILITY CHALLENGES IN ADDRESSING FAILURE

Agency is strongly related to the position of an organization in society, as are associated questions of fiduciary duty. In most countries, fiduciary relationships are legally defined. The exact breadth of duties defined by governance laws differs between countries and reflects more restrained or more extensive approaches to fiduciary responsibilities. A *narrow definition* of fiduciary duty is strongly related to a narrow view of the agency challenge, primarily confined to the relationship between capital provider(s) and the organization's management. A *broader approach* relates to the relationship between an organization and all relevant (societal) stakeholders.

The mainstream literature on responsible governance stays relatively close to the basic sources of failure of various organizational forms. As identified in section 6.3, it predominately focuses on *narrow* agency problems related to poor management, poor representation of the interests of principals, and poor realization of the primary fiduciary responsibility towards society – to sufficiently produce the type of (public, private, club/social) goods, services and value for which they were created. 'Market failure' then exists when firms do not supply goods and services that people want or can afford; 'government failure' exists when governments do not provide effective laws, regulation and sufficient enforcement to make society safe and prosperous; 'civic failure' exists when communities do not organize sufficient mutual support to make them secure and stable. As argued in Chapter 5, these '**level 1**' responsible governance challenges relate to primary responsibilities and narrowly defined fiduciary duties. Failure to abide by this basic level of fiduciary duty, in all societal spheres, contributes to low levels of societal trust.

Trust in organizations increases when they can demonstrate a better profile towards addressing broader stakeholder concerns and societal needs that goes beyond the direct sphere of solely internal operations. Responsible governance challenges then extend to addressing 'failure' at three additional levels of increasingly *broader fiduciary responsibilities* in response to direct and indirect stakeholder concerns, societal issues and sustainability:

- **Level 2:** failure to reduce the occurrence of negative externalities (e.g. pollution, corruption, unemployment) and to mitigate or internalize their consequences. This level of fiduciary responsibility relates in particular to affected secondary stakeholders and can be referred to as a *failure to protect*;

- **Level 3:** failure to create positive externalities (such as innovation, employment, poverty eradication, gender equality) that go beyond an organization's own direct interest to benefit others as well. This level of fiduciary responsibility extends to a broader range of direct and indirect secondary stakeholders, and can be labelled as a *failure to promote*;

- **Level 4:** failure to actively contribute to collective action problems (e.g. the climate crisis, pensions, ecological degradation and biodiversity loss, inclusiveness) and the sufficient provision of (global) common goods towards society at large; this can be dubbed a *failure to partner*.

The responsible governance challenge thus becomes *a multilayered challenge* that applies to all societal spheres and all eight archetypical organizational forms alike (Figure 6.4). These all face universal legitimacy and fiduciary duty problems at progressive levels of societal engagement. The higher the

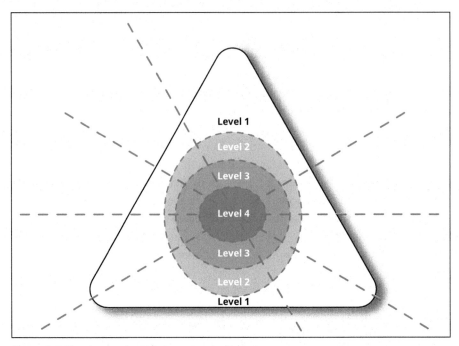

Figure 6.4 Four levels of societal governance challenges

degree of complexity of the societal problem an organization wants to address, the more the definition of what would constitute 'responsible governance' moves to higher levels of aggregation and institutional complexity. These levels are related to institutional voids, yet also constitute the most logical 'partnering space' (section 5.4). Institutional voids can be filled by hybrid organizations. However, at levels 3 and 4 in particular, the degree of institutional complexity that organizations would have to address creates an explosive mix of governance challenges that go beyond the direct sphere of influence of any individual organization.

A very logical extension of the responsible governance practice (and literature) thus implies that at levels 3 and 4 of society, goal-based institutions (Van Zanten and Van Tulder, 2018) and cross-sector partnering approaches (Van Tulder and Keen, 2018) need to be considered as the most viable and effective way to address collective action (common-pool) problems that transcend organizational boundaries and the scope of influence of individual societal sectors. By combining organizational identities, capacities and practices, cross-sector partnerships have the potential to provide innovative approaches – aimed at generating positive systemic effects (Googins and Rochlin, 2002) – that contribute to the forming of new proto-institutional arrangements (Lawrence et al., 2002) and structures of meta-governance. In institutional terms, the latter defines the responsible governance challenge for the transformational ambition of the SDG-agenda.

6.5 THE INTERNATIONAL HYBRIDITY CHALLENGE

As soon as organizations venture abroad and move their upstream or downstream activities beyond national borders, regulatory frameworks and domestic institutional contexts, they are faced with additional governance challenges. This is the realm of international or global governance that is largely covered by the international relations discipline (Dijkzeul, 1996). In general, global governance can be understood as 'governance without governments' (Reinalda, 2013), in which "the entire world hangs together through formal and informal governing techniques and processes" (Weiss and Wilkinson, 2014). Hybrid forms of governance have progressively appeared at the international level; the era of globalization has brought both rapid internationalization and increased multi-stakeholder scrutiny and engagement, leading to ways of governing international relations that supersede or replace the traditional way of governing 'global life' through diplomatic relationships between states (Wilkinson, 2005). Global governance scholars hence prefer to talk about *transitional governance*, thought of as "the processes of innovation that enable or obstruct societal actors to reconfigure and reconstitute governance roles and practices and establish new 'mechanisms' of cooperation and coordination and innovative hybrid organizational forms of governance" (Muldoon, 2018).

Chapter 3 took a 'top-down' approach to transitional governance by describing the endeavours of the United Nations in shaping a globally coordinated approach to sustainable development through the formulation and implementation of the SDGs. We described the goal-setting SDG-agenda as a form of multilevel hybrid or transitional governance, intended to navigate change in the 'right direction' through multi-sector engagement strategies. In this section, we take a *bottom-up perspective* by taking the national context (the 'home base') as the point of departure. What governance challenges do organizations face when they venture abroad? All organizations source internationally in ever more complex and hence fragile value chains. Many organizations have moved abroad to seek markets, exploit assets, or manage resources across borders (cf. Van Tulder with Van der Zwart, 2006). The institutional edges of the societal triangle should, therefore, be seen as 'dotted' and open to external influences. *Responsible governance* is not only bound by national regulatory frameworks, institutions and societal expectations but susceptible to 'international transitional governance' challenges as well (Figure 6.5).

The international environment confronts organizations with a variety of governance and circumstantial challenges that not only add considerable

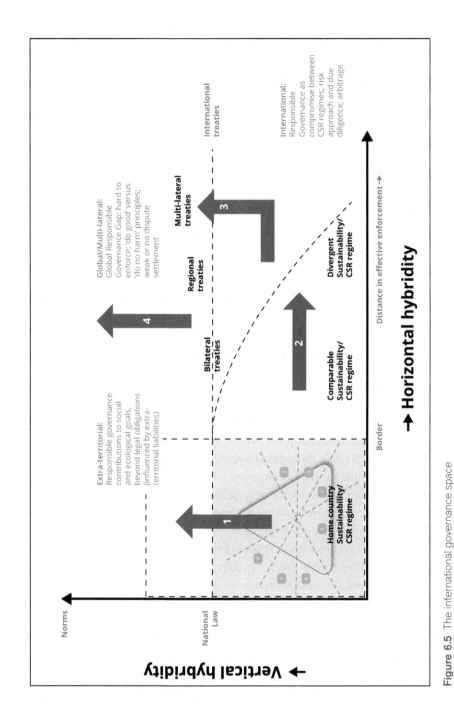

Figure 6.5 The international governance space

Source: inspired by an internal document of the Netherlands Ministry of Foreign Affairs

complexity to their activities, but also profoundly affect how responsible manage-ment principles can be operationalized across distinct countries:

■ **Governance gaps:** in many areas in the international arena, there are no laws; only norms, morals, principles, guidelines and voluntary initiatives. The international governance gap creates room for organizations to adopt higher, but also lower, standards of sustainability.

■ **Divergence:** laws, rules and informal practices (culture) differ between countries. This reality can present responsible managers with tough prob-lems. What principles should be used as the benchmark? How dominant should home country regulations and standards be? Should organizations adopt different practices per issue and country?

■ **Volatility:** the international environment is arguably more turbulent than the national environment. Laws change over time. Rules and regulations in countries can become stricter, but also more lenient. How flexible and adap-tive to changing circumstances should strategies be?

COPING WITH INTERNATIONAL HYBRIDITY – FOUR INTERNATIONALIZATION TRACKS

In the international arena, *hybrid governance challenges* of concurrently coping with distinct institutional contexts extend in both horizontal and vertical directions. Governance gaps materialize at various levels (national, international, global) and come with associated consequences for the ability of organizations to implement 'do no harm' (negative duties) and/or 'do good' (positive duties) principles. Starting from a home country – where the organization only has to reckon with national laws – organizations can adopt responsible strategies along four trajectories (see Figure 6.5), each susceptible to a different kind of governance challenge.

■ **Track 1 - International vertical hybridity:** organizations can move abroad based on extraterritorial principles; this implies the *extension of national norms and laws* into the international space, without adapting to local laws and practices. Extraterritoriality is usually applied to physical spaces, such as foreign embassies or military bases that are exempt from the jurisdiction of local law, following diplomatic negotiations. Extraterritoriality is also applied to maritime law; ships in international waters are governed by the laws of the jurisdiction in which that ship is registered (the flag under which it sails). Extraterritoriality principles are increasingly invoked by citizens in host countries who seek protection and justice by holding foreign corpora-tions accountable for (alleged) local environmental harms and human rights abuses. Taking the multinational enterprise to court in its home country, makes it possible to appeal to the domestic laws of that home country. Often, these are more stringent than the laws governing the host country. Companies headquartered in the US, the UK and the Netherlands, for instance, have regularly been held to account in domestic courts for their actions abroad. In the US, the application of extraterritoriality is based on the Alien Tort Statute (ATS). In this international space, 'do no harm' principles prevail. These principles can still raise the bar for responsible governance practice, as victims will prefer to hold the foreign company liable according to the jurisdiction with the strictest regulation.

- ■ **Track 2 - International horizontal hybridity:** here, organizations move beyond their national (home) regime into the institutional space of other countries, without any treaty or extraterritorial law to guide them or mitigate risks. In this space, the *degree of convergence and divergence* between the home country's and the host's sustainability/CSR regime becomes the most important factor to reckon with. This characteristic relates to formal and informal institutions around sustainability that guide the actions of organizations, primarily at levels 1 and 2 (avoid doing harm, according to national rules and principles). If organizations internationalize to countries with comparable regimes, they face a relatively short 'distance' between home and host regimes in what is considered 'responsible' governance and practice. In these instances, modest adaptations usually suffice. In case of diverging regimes, the adaptation challenge increases.

- ■ **Track 3 - Mitigated international space:** regime distance can be mitigated through treaties. Treaties between countries mediate between national and international law by creating *rules* that supersede national regulation and can be enforced in all participating constituencies. Treaties can lead to higher standards for CSR and sustainability but can also lead to lower (joint) standards ('lowest common denominator' outcomes), depending on the bargaining dynamics of the treaty parties and the adoption of principles.[4] They often include dispute settlement and arbitrage procedures that can affect the sustainability/CSR regimes of the treaty parties in different ways; in practice, private organizations have also used dispute settlement clauses to undermine the sustainability regime of one of the treaty parties. Bilateral and regional treaties present the most relevant types of governance regimes in the international space. They are always based on a combination of rules and principles.

---

4 See Box 5.2: treaties that are the result of 'interest-based negotiations' tend to aim for a compromise (and frequently lead to lowest common denominator outcomes), whereas treaties that are directed towards a collective vision tend to stimulate higher standards of sustainability.

■   **Track 4 - Largely unmitigated international space:** traditionally, the global space is weakly governed by essentially voluntary 'multilateral treaties' and their international (inter-governmental) organizations. In the global space, hardly any enforceable laws, mitigation measures or independent supranational dispute settlement panels are in force. This space is largely governed by 'soft law' principles and hence susceptible to what is called the 'global governance gap'. In particular, the production of 'global public and common goods' is at stake in this space. To fill this institutional void, two types of 'bottom-up' hybrid governance arrangements have been emerging: (a) international multi-stakeholder partnerships, and (b) semi-public organizations. Multi-stakeholder arrangements are important catalysts of change and innovation. They are rapidly "transforming the way decision-making is conducted and collective action is organized on the global level" (Muldoon, 2018). In addition, independent entities – some with quasi-governmental status – appear in the global governance void. A prime example is the Internet Corporation for Assigned Names and Numbers (ICANN) – a private, non-profit, public benefit corporation created in 1998 to take over the centralized coordination and management of the Internet's Domain Name System from the United States government. Nowadays, ICANN acts as the global internet governance agency for sustaining the open character of the global web. It functions as a regulator of a global public resource, with the ability to make national and international public policy decisions that are binding and independent of governments and treaty-based inter-governmental organizations (ibid).

In a world that is increasingly VUCA, bilateral treaties, in particular, have become popular as an instrument to govern international relations and preserve interests. A multitude of trade agreements between countries has emerged, concurrently with negotiations to create multilateral organizations with supranational arbitrage powers (World Trade Organization).[5] As a consequence, the tension between multilateral, bilateral and regional arrangements has increased. Trade economist Jagdish Bhagwati (1995) referred to the proliferation of agreements in the international space as a *spaghetti bowl* of arrangements that are often partial in their effect and at times counterproductive for reaching more comprehensive arrangements. The ensuing ambiguity influences the extent of guidance that private organizations operating across borders can derive from

---

5   The dispute panel of the WTO has stopped functioning since 2019 (due to US opposition). This creates a global governance gap in trade and reinforces the importance of bilateral dispute settlements.

international governance, especially with regard to sustainable behaviour, agency and responsible governance. Subsequent sections of this chapter elaborate related governance challenges to the four tracks.

6.5.1 International horizontal hybridity (tracks 1 and 2)

When organizations internationalize in a large number of countries and institutional systems, they foremost extend their horizontal hybridity challenge (Figure 6.5). In general, organizations that venture abroad have to *adapt* to several national governance principles and practices as defined in the formal laws and cultural practices of host countries. The horizontal hybridity challenge for these organizations then relates to managing the 'portfolio' of countries in which they operate. The prime governance challenge is mostly *rules-based* and specifies, in particular, level 1 and level 2 considerations.

Three portfolio characteristics define the international hybridity challenge: (1) the number of countries in which the organization operates; (2) the relative weight each of the countries represents in the consolidated activities of the organization; and (3) the basic characteristics of the sustainability/CSR regime each of these countries represents. The international business literature covers this discourse under the heading of the 'distance' between 'home' and 'host' countries.[6] The horizontal hybridity challenge then boils down to coping with the diversity of the administrative, economic and cultural regimes in which the organization operates (or sources from), and the implications for its agency and fiduciary duties. In the sustainability and CSR discourse, this type of governance challenge has been mapped primarily in terms of risks (Box 6.1).

<table>
<tr><td>

B
O
X

6.1

</td><td>

INTERNATIONAL HYBRIDITY: MANAGING RISKS AND RESPONSIBILITIES

The GTZ *CSR Navigator* in Germany maps countries in terms of their CSR policy 'maturity levels'. The *CSR Risk Barometer* in the Netherlands maps the CSR risks that companies face when venturing into less institutionally mature countries. These tools primarily serve as a *risk management tool*: doing business in more advanced CSR regimes requires companies to deal with more regulatory pressure; doing business in less advanced CSR regimes comes with less pressure, but might add substantial reputation-related CSR risks. For international civil society organizations, risks are particularly

</td></tr>
</table>

---

6 An extended discussion on salient dimensions of distance can be found in Van Tulder (2020).

linked to how they interpret and elaborate their 'advocacy' role (level 2) as a complement to national regulation and practices, or as a criticism to national policies.

Effectively managing distance dimensions across varying CSR regimes is what
delineates the responsible management strategy of managers (agents). Confronted
with the turbulence in the international regulatory environment and the associated risks
and opportunities, these managers must make realistic assessments of the (diverse)
context(s) in which they have to operate. The distance between the home base and the
various host countries defines whether the distance creates risks or opportunities.

Three types of risks can be distinguished: (1) operational, (2) strategic and
(3) sustainability risks (Van Tulder, 2018a; Van Tulder and Roman, 2019).

1 **Operational risks (level 1)** relate, for instance, to currency risks when
   conducting international business or in case of cultural differences between
   the countries of operation. Dealing with operational risks is the 'hygiene' factor
   of organizing across borders. It presents the difference between good and bad
   management, and can therefore be considered as the basics of responsible
   management. This aspect becomes more important if the 'distance' between
   home and host market increases, and when the relative weight of the host
   country portfolio becomes heavier than the home country activities.

2 **Strategic risks (level 2)** relate to political risks, which are prevalent in imma-
   ture or volatile political systems. Strategic risks can severely endanger the
   return on investments. Historically, the main concern for foreign companies in
   host countries was the risk that the state would capture their assets by expropriation or nationalization. Since the 1980s, direct expropriation has practically
   disappeared; governments now use more subtle measures, such as discriminatory regulations or contracts governing an investment. Internationally active
   NGOs (INGOs) have been facing increased opposition of host country governments since 2010. Their advocacy strategies triggered criticism for direct intervention in national policies. Domestic NGOs that receive foreign funding have
   become increasingly scrutinized as 'agents' of foreign interests.

3 **Sustainability risks (levels 3 and 4)** relate to the 'license to operate' that
   organizations can establish. In developing countries, the most salient sustainability risks are associated with poverty, human rights and income inequality. It is
   almost impossible to be structurally engaged in developing countries without
   adequately addressing many (related) sustainability risks. Generally speaking,
   the larger the 'development distance', the more sustainability risks must be
   taken into account.

For NGOs and companies alike, being confronted with diverging or even
conflicting values and norms (Hofstede and Hofstede, 2005) may create opportunities
as well. Tom Donaldson (1989), for instance, examined the manifold dilemmas created
by differences between home and host countries' norms and values. He concluded
that internationally operating organizations have considerable *leeway to develop their*

B
O
X

6.1

own standards and principles ('moral free space'), for example when dealing with repressive regimes. However, the perspective foremost holds that international firms should respect *principles that function as minimum requirements* for socially, ecologically and ethically responsible corporate conduct: so-called **hypernorms** (Donaldson and Dunfee, 1999). These principles are so fundamental that they constitute norms by which all others must be judged. Adopting hypernorms – which can be further developed as organizational cultures of ethically and socially accountable conduct – can help to overcome the dilemmas of fragmentation that multi-domestic organizations face in responsibly adapting to local norms and values. Hypernorms are an expression of the 'extraterritorial' ambitions of companies and, therefore, represent a 'vertical hybridity challenge' in particular (arrow 1 in Figure 6.5)

DISTINCT SUSTAINABILITY/CSR REGIMES

Different countries represent different institutional contexts for sustainability and (corporate) responsibility.[7] These 'sustainability/CSR regimes'[8] consist of both written and unwritten norms, rules and expectations that reflect the national societal 'selection environment' in which strategies of (foreign) organizations develop and are judged as legitimate and advantageous, or not. A sustainability/CSR regime comprises more than the roles adopted by national governments. It consists of all the actions, interactions and rules that influence the nature of the societal interfaces (Figures 6.2 and 6.3). It determines to what extent private sustainability strategies are voluntary or mandatory, and to what extent they can be considered successful or not. A sustainability/CSR regime can be thought of as consisting of three main elements:

■   **Legal requirements:** the legal tradition of the country; formal requirements for financial, social, environmental or sustainability reporting;

---

7   The comparative literature on sustainability governance is not well developed. Classifications often rely on written rules or perceptions measured in surveys, which renders a comparative overview of both written and unwritten rules problematic. Wayne Visser (2010; 2016) edited a series of volumes that consider the national contexts in which sustainable business has evolved. The main observation relevant in the realm of this book is: "sustainable business is becoming less about compliance and risk management and more about breakthrough opportunities and innovation management" (Visser, 2016: viii).

8   Both 'CSR' and 'sustainability' are terms that tend to be used interchangeably in national discourses. For practical purposes, we combine both terms and consider the national context as the 'sustainability/CSR' regime to consider how such a regime triggers specific approaches to sustainable 'business'. 'Business' here is to be understood as the 'activities' of a broader spectrum of hybrid organizational forms than merely the archetypical 'pure' market role [6] (see Figure 6.3), yet with the exception of the archetypical 'pure' state [1]).

extraterritoriality provisions (the degree to which organizations can be held liable in domestic courts for their practices abroad); other CSR relevant regulation, such as competition policy, intellectual property rights policy, security and safety regulations, transparency rules.

- **Government policy practices:** general strategies or roles of government ('partnering', 'mandating', 'endorsing', 'facilitating'); public procurement (CSR criteria incorporated into government procurement policies and subsidy schemes); public advocacy (promotion of sustainability awareness among the general public by local and central government); tolerance of corruption or 'clientelism'; adoption of sustainability regulation in national policy frameworks (defining a sustainability regime as more 'open' or 'closed').

- **Nature of interaction between business and civil society:** community involvement of companies (as embedded in tradition, legal provisions for philanthropy or sponsoring, religion); adoption and implementation of minimum standards for labour, supply chain responsibility and human rights in codes or business principles; corporate governance and accountability regimes (relevance of particular stakeholders; stimulation of social investment; voluntary transparency and accountability); receptiveness to labelling and trademarks.

Throughout the world, we can distinguish between five types of sustainability/CSR regimes, each with a distinct set of governance principles: (neo-)liberal (particularly Anglo-Saxon countries), (neo-)corporatist (mostly European countries), corporate-statist (mainly in East Asia), religious-autocratic (notably Islamic countries), and community-centric (local; Indigenous peoples; ethnic groups) regimes. Table 6.3 illustrates how these five regime types display typical institutional constellations in the societal triangle, as a result of the relative 'weight' that each institutional sphere has developed over time.

■ *The (neo)liberal archetype: CSR America*

The (neo)liberal approach to sustainability/CSR was pioneered in Anglo-Saxon countries – spearheaded by the United States. The American CSR regime originated foremost in antitrust regulation aiming to curb firms' abuse of power in consumer markets, more than in social regulation (as in Europe) opposing to firms' abuse of power in labour markets. The liberal sustainability/CSR regime is firmly rooted in the protection of property rights, including intellectual property and the rights of shareholders and creditors, within a political system that is mostly based on *winner-takes-all principles*. In liberal countries, the relatively antagonistic bargaining environment stimulated a legalistic sustainability/CSR regime based on common law that is shaped by jurisprudence, rather than strong (centralist) regulation.

Table 6.3 Relative weights in five sustainability/CSR regimes

(Neo)liberal regimes	
	• Common law • Strong voice and accountability • Winner takes all • Transparency • Accountability: comply with the rules • Substantial equivalence principle • Rules-based contracts • Fiduciary duty towards: shareholders • Strong property rights • Strong court independence
(Neo-)corporatist regimes	
	• Civil law • Proportional representation • Strong voice and accountability • Subsidiarity • Voluntarist • Precautionary principle • Principles-based contracts • Transparency: comply or explain • Fiduciary duty towards: stakeholders • Strong property rights • Strong court independence
Corporate-statist regimes	
	• (hybrid) Communist law • Hierarchical (mandatory CSR) • Weak voice and accountability • Pragmatic • Harmony • Relationship-based contracts • Fiduciary duty towards: owners • Limited transparency • Weak property rights • Weak court independence
Religious-autocratic regimes	
	• Islamic laws • Hierarchical • Zakat principle • Prohibition of interest • Weak voice and accountability • Relationship-based contract • Limited transparency • Fiduciary duty: based on moral considerations • Weak property rights • Weak court independence

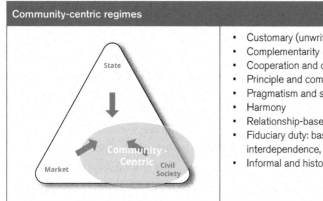

Community-centric regimes

- Customary (unwritten) law
- Complementarity
- Cooperation and co-optation
- Principle and communal rule-based
- Pragmatism and short-term survival mode
- Harmony
- Relationship-based partnering
- Fiduciary duty: based on mutual support, interdependence, reciprocity, loyalty
- Informal and historic property rights

The stance towards sustainability/CSR tends to be *compliance-oriented* rather than voluntarist. American companies are leaders in the formulation of *codes of conduct* as an expression of the Anglo-Saxon (business) culture of 'liability' and rules-based contracts. In general, governments have adopted a mandating and facilitating role to maintain their independence from societal groups. These roles entail a strong emphasis on sanctions (for instance, in combating corruption) and rules, and a less strong focus on enabling (financial and non-financial) policies or partnerships. A leading principle that guides many practical sustainability/CSR regulation discussions is that of *substantial equivalence.* The safety of food (or medical devices, or drugs) in the United States generally does not raise regulatory concern, as long as the new product does not differ materially from its predecessor. Labelling is therefore deemed unnecessary if it interferes with the free trade of the product.

The legalistic and compliance-oriented sustainability/CSR regime of liberal countries creates a mostly *reactive* and instrumentalist CSR orientation (levels 1 and 2). The liberal sustainability/CSR regime will only adopt higher labour or environmental standards if this is expected to boost short-term profitability – for instance, if consumers are willing to pay more for goods produced to higher standards. Corporate responsibility in liberal regimes is still primarily mediated through shareholders and the stock exchange. The increased attention to 'Corporate Social *Responsiveness* and Responsibility' has given rise to 'socially responsible investment' (SRI) initiatives, yet with strong reactive overtones (*don't do things wrong*).[9]

---

9   In August 2019, 181 CEOs of the American Business Roundtable endorsed a redefined statement on 'The Purpose of a Corporation'. The statement outlines a more modern US standard for corporate responsibility, acknowledging that companies should be run in the benefit of all stakeholders (customers, employees, suppliers, communities, shareholders), instead of principally serving shareholders. See also Box 9.8 Walking the Talk?

■ *The (neo-)corporatist archetype: CSR Europe*

The sustainability/CSR regime of continental European – 'Rhineland model' – countries is based on a different logic than the (neo)liberal American approach. Governments and well-organized NGOs have become deeply involved in the implementation of national and regional sustainability/CSR regimes. Consequently, governments adopted facilitating and partnering roles in an effort to work together with firms and other stakeholders on developing CSR practices. The political system in most European countries is founded on *proportional representation principles*, which tend to lead to coalition governments and a low 'power distance'.[10] Public advocacy of sustainability/CSR is hence relatively strong in most European countries. An inactive approach to sustainability is not really an option for any of the parties. As a rule, stakeholders from all three spheres of society are included in the formation of national and regional sustainability standards and principles. This *tripartite characteristic* of the formation process has an important impact on the implementation of the agreed standards and codes, in that it renders them 'more or less' obligatory.

This process is underpinned by the continental European practice of *civil law*, characterized by stricter rules that the authorities nevertheless often only marginally monitor. The latter is typical of (neo-)corporatist regimes: standards are formulated to conclude past negotiations and set a new floor, but also to facilitate future *bargaining* between societal stakeholders. Sanctions are relatively weakly formulated in the European sustainability/CSR regime, the objective being to encourage companies to adopt an active stance on sustainability, while discouraging 'evasive' behaviour (which often accompanies rules-based approaches). This logic is mirrored by the *comply or explain* corporate governance principle introduced in several European countries. It entails that if companies decide not to abide by a code as expected, they should publicly substantiate the grounds of that decision. This principle aims to increase transparency and accountability, while also creating some leeway for companies to *go beyond compliance* to formal regulation to develop and apply more active CSR practices. It is consistent with Europe's leading principle of 'subsidiarity'.[11]

As a result of institutionalized corporatist bargaining, the sustainability/CSR regime in European countries generally contains more and stricter stipulations on

---

10 'Power distance' is the degree to which less powerful members of institutions and organizations in a country accept that power is distributed unequally between elites and the rest of the population (Hofstede and Hofstede, 2005).

11 Subsidiarity is an organizing principle, contending that matters ought to be handled by the smallest, lowest or least centralized competent authority. Political decisions in the European Union are guided by the principle that they should be taken at a local level if possible, rather than by a central authority.

environmental reporting, labelling and codes of conduct than in liberal countries. This is reflected in specific reporting laws on environmental strategies in many European countries. The regulatory *precautionary principle* that guides the European sustainability/CSR regime requires that new products (ranging from genetically modified foods to refrigerators) are proven to be safe before being launched. The development of certification and labelling strategies as a means to ensure quality, safety and sustainability traits is encouraged. Free trade is not the most important factor in guiding international trade.

The European sustainability/CSR regime displays a relatively open stance and strong support for multilateral approaches and international standards (e.g. OECD guidelines; ILO conventions), especially with regard to social/labour rights and environmental protection. Principles of *stewardship*, culturally footed in the European Christian tradition, imply that private organizations should be managed in ways that best contribute to the fulfilment of all stakeholder interests. In general, corporatist European countries are inclined to be supportive to multilateral initiatives – like the SDGs and the Paris Climate Agreement – and to translate accepted international rules into national principles.

■ The corporate-statist archetype: CSR East Asia

According to the Heritage Foundation's Index of Economic Freedom,[12] the leading economies of (South) East Asia rate among the most liberal (Singapore, Hong Kong, Taiwan, South Korea,) and the least liberal (China, Vietnam) in the world. The most liberal regimes have a 'hub' function in the international political and economic position of the region, but also are very small. The more significant economies in the region are more 'closed' and present a more 'distant' regulatory environment for Western companies than, for instance, Singapore. East Asian countries, on average, share a *pragmatic* approach and a strongly *efficiency-oriented* sustainability/CSR regime that is inclined not to oppose how companies operate, unless this undermines the competitive position of the national economy. East Asian regimes share a high acceptance of hierarchies based on great power distances; most Asian countries lead the international charts in this respect. Governance values like 'harmony' and 'non-violence' are strongly articulated, but without agency for most stakeholders. Transactions in Asian countries are often *relationship-based* rather than on formal contracts, which is further reinforced by relatively weak institutions and poor property rights protection. Agency problems are linked to low corporate transparency (Claessens and Fan, 2002).

---

12 See www.heritage.org/index.

East Asian countries share a substantial heritage of European law due to previous colonial ties but have all developed distinct identities. In particular (former) communist countries (China, Vietnam) are starting to combine *socialist* or *communist* legal systems (which, for instance, give limited independence to courts), with efforts to open up to internationally accepted laws. This development has been influenced by calls by the United Nations to achieve the 'rule of law' at both the national and international level, as well as the ambition of countries like China to expand their economy internationally.

In most East Asian economies, close ties exist between the state and clusters of major companies (regulated, for instance, through state economic development programmes). In countries like Japan and China, public advocacy of sustainability/CSR and corporate citizenship is negligible or actively discouraged. The East Asian sustainability/CSR regime is primarily aimed at the efficiency and international competitiveness of their own industries. When sustainability creates a competitive advantage, East Asian countries provide a positive environment for investment in sustainable innovations, as demonstrated by the success of hybrid electric cars (Toyota) and the development of solar panel energy in China. In both areas, collaboration between government and companies – in terms of conducive regulation and effective barriers to foreign competition – has created a positive environment for innovation and scaling.

A number of the East Asian countries are still in a relatively early stage of economic development. Consequently, the East Asian sustainability/CSR regime is not only shaped by culture and institutions, but also by levels of development. Until recently, sustainability/CSR regimes in Asia hardly set any CSR relevant minimum standards of their own, except if these could be directly related to efficiency goals and control of their economies. East Asian sustainability regimes foremost implemented *pragmatic principles*. In the event that sustainability/CSR guidelines are adopted, this is often accompanied by close consultations with large firms and motivated by the need to secure the relevant industry's international competitiveness. Once adopted, however, implementation is actively pursued. The adoption of codes of conduct is not stimulated, neither is labelling – unless functional for the internationalization strategies of core companies. Regulation on sustainability/CSR has developed primarily in the area of environmental protection, the area that directly affects internationalization strategies. On labour, human rights and working conditions, the Asian sustainability/CSR regime generally exhibits an inactive orientation, largely because of weak civil society representation.

■ The religious-autocratic archetype: CSR Middle East

Middle Eastern countries exemplify the religious-autocratic approach towards sustainability/CSR. This approach is not very advanced if measured against the same benchmarks as the liberal and corporatist models. However, the religious-autocratic model represents a different philosophy of doing business, as embodied in the principles of zakat and Islamic banking. The act of zakat (almsgiving) purifies one's wealth and applies to both companies and individuals. It is obligatory for all Muslims to give away 2.5 % of wealth and assets above a certain threshold (*niṣāb*) to the poor annually. In Libya, Malaysia, Pakistan, Saudi Arabia, Sudan, and Yemen, zakat is mandated and collected by the state (Hasan, 2015). In many Muslim majority countries, zakat hence represents an institutionalised version of *philanthropy* and CSR and an alternative to taxes. The zakat regime for companies is rather detailed and well-specified. It encourages managers to adopt an active ethical stance towards business, with only limited reference to economic efficiency. The principles of Islamic banking include the *sharing of profit and loss* and the *prohibition of the collection and payment of interest* by lenders and investors.

Governments in these countries have mostly adopted a *mandating* role in order to support the appropriate implementation of religious codes and national security. Important industries are often *state-owned*, which makes it relatively easy to implement the principles adopted by government. In the Arab region, three types of legal frameworks related to commercial transactions can be found that accommodate particular sustainability/CSR regimes (cf. Kobeissi, 2005): (1) those following the Western system (Lebanon, Syria and Egypt); (2) those that have codified their laws, but mostly draw on sharia (Saudi Arabia, Oman and Yemen); (3) those that combine the previous two regimes by 'westernizing' modern law and continuing to draw on Islamic law in such areas as contracts (Iraq, Jordan, Libya). Multinational companies have targeted Arab countries primarily for their oil. This has resulted in a high degree of foreign direct investment (FDI) concentrated in a few resource-rich countries, and low inward investment in the remainder of these countries, reinforcing their relatively closed nature. FDI in these countries has occurred relatively independently of their sustainability/CSR regime. Only in Arab countries that have been host to market-seeking foreign investments have 'Western-style' sustainability/CSR initiatives been introduced. Egypt, for example, adopted an environmental policy with the objective to come to sustainable tourism by applying ISO14001 rules.

■ The community-centric archetype: Indigenous CSR

While Indigenous sustainability/CSR systems are globally dispersed, locally oriented, unique and, therefore, difficult to compare, they do share several characteristics. Strikingly, the interests of communities rather than shareholders prevail in these systems. Local governments tend to adopt partnering roles. The strongest advocates of this regime are Indigenous peoples whose demands are based on *unwritten customary law*.

In many countries, the conflict between national (written) and local (customary) law is at the heart of the conflict about the formulation and implementation of sustainability/CSR regimes. Indigenous peoples such as Native Americans, Aboriginals, Maori, Inuit, and African ethnic groups seek recognition for their *traditional legal institutions and practices*. The question of property rights, for instance, is a particularly controversial topic of debate. In Indigenous regimes, private property often does not exist and is considered inimical to the preservation of the local regime. The arrival of a third party, in particular multinationals originating from systems where common law (US, UK) or civil law (Europe) prevails, then creates severe tension (Whiteman and Mamen, 2002). In an attempt to maintain or create their own regime, Indigenous peoples have teamed up with NGOs with a grassroots orientation. Programmes developed through these partnerships seem to have a higher chance of success in the context of limited legal frameworks and/or weak enforcement traditions. As a result, companies in Latin America are investing in communities to achieve stable societies and to create an environment that is amenable to the production and trading of their products. CSR in Latin America and Africa represents a move towards *compassionate capitalism*, which implies setting up social initiatives to promote citizenship and develop civil society and local communities.

The UN Declaration on the Rights of Indigenous Peoples, adopted by the General Assembly in September 2007, emphasizes the rights of Indigenous peoples to maintain and strengthen their own institutions, cultures, traditions, and their economic and social development. It articulates that respect for Indigenous knowledge, cultures and traditional practices contributes to sustainable and equitable development as well as proper management of the environment. The non-legally binding Declaration is the result of over 20 years of UN-facilitated negotiations over rights, lands and resources. Many of the explicated rights in the Declaration imply participatory approaches to Indigenous issues, such as *partnerships* with local communities and *effective consultation*.

BOX 6.2

PROFILING COUNTRIES FOR THE SDGs

The sustainability/CSR regimes created by these distinct principles influence the national approaches of countries to the SDG-agenda, and arguably also their scores on specific SDGs. Extensive research on the relation between sustainability/CSR regimes and country progress on the SDGs has not yet been done, but information sources are becoming readily available to enable deeper insights. Three sources can help:

1   The first effects can probably be witnessed from the 'voluntary national reviews' (VNRs). In these reports submitted to the HLPF (see Chapter 3), countries are requested to provide information on how different stakeholders in society have

been participating, with chapters on the methodology and process, the creation of ownership of the SDGs, institutional mechanisms and means of implementation. We can expect weak CSR regimes to tend to report less on civic participation or on disputed issues. The UN databank on VNRs presently contains the (first and second time) reports of more than 100 countries.

2   The UN statistics hub created a more objective database on SDG progress, with trend lines on each of the SDGs, generic information (for instance on the degree of openness of countries, the trade balance), but without further analysis of the national governance regime.

3   A third source was developed by the UN Sustainable Development Solutions Network in collaboration with the Bertelsmann Stiftung. They present comparative scores for clusters of countries in their *SDG Index and Dashboard*, framing them in terms of six broad transformations. Salient conclusions from this exercise that can be linked to the above governance discourse, include:

●   The top-10 countries with the highest SDG index in 2019 (80–85) were all European neo-corporatist countries;

●   Anglo-Saxon countries rank lower than their European counterparts: New Zealand (11), UK (13), Canada (20), USA (35), Australia (38);

●   Asian countries reveal scores that are closely related to their level of development: Japan (15), Korea (18), China (39), Thailand (40), Vietnam (54), Singapore (66), Philippines (97), Myanmar (110), Cambodia (112), India (115);

●   Religious-autocratic countries score lower on average: Iran (58), UAE (65), Oman (83), Qatar 91), Egypt (92) Kuwait (106), Iran, Afghanistan (153);

●   The bottom-10 (score 51–39) are primarily African countries (and Afghanistan).

The SDG dashboard highlights the strengths and weaknesses of each country for each of the 17 SDGs. Their archetypical governance context partly explains the following patterns:

●   East and South Asia: present a mixed picture, but significant challenges exist in SDGs 2, 3, 5, 12–15 and 16. Negative trends can even be observed for SDGs 13 and 15;

●   Middle Eastern and North African countries show a declining performance on most of the SDGs, but in particular on SDGs 2, 3, and 16;

●   Within the OECD countries, significant challenges exist on SDG13, but overall the distinction between corporatist and liberal countries holds:

●   Corporatist countries score more positively on SDGs 1, 3, 7 and 17 than neoliberal countries, which can be explained by better social contracts, greater public goods provision and longer histories of institutionalized partnering;

●   Corporatist countries score (slightly) less poorly on average than neoliberal countries on SDG12 and SDG13, for the same reasons;

- On decent jobs and economic growth (SDG8), neoliberal countries (as well as some Asian OECD countries) score slightly better than the average of neo-corporatist countries, but challenges remain;

- The remaining SDGs show a mixed picture, with no clear, distinct patterns.

[1] Voluntary National Reviews	[2] Country Profiles	[3] SDG Index and Dashboards
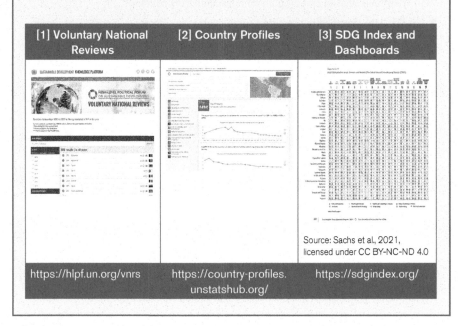		
		Source: Sachs et al., 2021, licensed under CC BY-NC-ND 4.0
https://hlpf.un.org/vnrs	https://country-profiles.unstatshub.org/	https://sdgindex.org/

6.5.2 Governance challenges under international treaties (track 3)

Beyond the national regime – across the border along the X-axis of track 3 (Figure 6.5) – lie two types of governance spaces, regulated through treaties that include arbitrage or dispute settlement procedures: (a) bilaterally governed spaces (through bilateral treaties in particular), and (b) regionally governed spaces (through regional agreements). The leading principle along the horizontal axis is the idea of a *level playing field*, which involves a conception of 'fairness'. It means that each player does not necessarily have an equal chance to succeed, but rather that all play by the same set of rules, that the playing field itself is not skewed in favour of any of the parties, and that an independent arbiter will see to it that all abide by the rules of the game.

BILATERAL TREATIES

Bilateral treaties have become increasingly popular under the influence of a VUCA world. Bilateral treaties are reciprocal, legally binding agreements concluded between two entities or countries that provide both with more control over the execution of the arrangement. For the organization of responsible governance of activities across borders, three types of treaties are particularly relevant: Free-Trade Agreements (FTAs), Bilateral Investment Treaties (BITs), and Double Taxation Treaties (DTTs).

■ **Free-Trade Agreements.** In 2019, the International Trade Centre (ITC) counted approximately 800 bilateral FTAs.[13] The contribution of free trade to sustainable development is not undisputed; worldwide, free trade has created economic growth for many countries but also contributed to a production system full of waste, inequality, pollution and poor labour conditions. If treaty parties negotiate and agree on a 'lowest common denominator', a trade treaty can stimulate a race to the bottom. The SDG-agenda hence contains important trade-related areas to prevent this from happening. According to the ITC, trade regimes can positively contribute to 10 of the 17 SDGs (1, 2, 4, 5, 8, 9, 10, 12, 16 and 17). (Note, however, that the ecological SDGs 13, 14 and 15 are not part of this narrative).

Trade agreements include dispute settlement procedures to ensure that agreements can be enforced and disputes can be settled. Notable disputes have been related to social and ecological issues such as wage levels, union rivalry, political interference, unfair labour practices, labour laws, safety and health rules, and environmental protection. So-called *Investor State Dispute Settlement (ISDS)* clauses, through which investors can sue governments for discriminatory practices through international tribunals, give multinational enterprises from any of the treaty parties the possibility of overriding (foreign) national laws. Critics have pointed to the ensuing diminished regulatory space for governments to implement policies that are in the public interest (e.g. health, safety, environment, human rights). During the 2018 CETA treaty negotiations (between Canada and the EU) for example, critical NGOs claimed that particularly the ISDS clause marks an attack on democracy, workers and the environment in Europe.

■ **Bilateral Investment Treaties.** In 2020, UNCTAD – the main UN body overlooking international investment treaties – assessed that around 2,334 BITs were in force.[14] An increasing number of trade agreements contain investment protection chapters. BITs offer protection to international companies by lowering some of the operational and strategic risks (e.g. takeover, seizure, nationalization; termination, non-renewal, interference with contracts;

13 http://www.intracen.org/
14 https://investmentpolicy.unctad.org/international-investment-agreements

revocation of licences or permits; free transfer of means; fair and equitable treatment) when investing in a different regulatory regime. In earlier stages, particularly developing countries were interested in BITs to prove themselves 'safe' and attractive destinations for investment. The discussion on the functioning of BITs in aligning governance regimes across treaty countries has mainly concentrated on how international arbitration has played out in the event of disputes. The number of settled treaty-based investment disputes climbed from 50 cases in 2000 to 674 by the end of 2019 (with 343 cases still pending).[15] Investors from developed countries are often the initiator of dispute procedures, with investors from the United States (174), the Netherlands (108) and the United Kingdom (78) the most frequent claimants in the period 1987–2018. 'Old-generation' BITs (dating from 1959–2011), in particular, have been claimed to impair the social and development interests of the host (developing) country and hence made them politically controversial. As a result, many developing countries and regional integration organizations have revised or are actively scrutinizing their model agreements (cf. Singh and Ilge, 2016). UNCTAD argues in favour of international investments as a significant source for filling the massive annual $2.5 trillion 'finance gap' related to achieving the SDGs; it concurrently underscores the need for a 'new generation' of investment policies, with reforms particularly in the areas of (1) safeguarding the right of states to regulate (while providing protection), (2) reforming investment dispute settlement, (3) promoting and facilitating investment, (4) ensuring responsible investment, and (5) enhancing systemic consistency (UNCTAD, 2019). UNCTAD's Investment Policy Framework for Sustainable Development builds on *ten core principles* and one overarching objective aimed at guiding investment policies and international investment agreements towards *inclusive growth and sustainable development* (UNCTAD, 2015).

■ **Double Taxation Treaties.** The basic principle of DTTs is one of *fairness*. It does not seem fair for companies or citizens with activities in two or more countries to be fully taxed in both. Double taxation may happen where two jurisdictions seek to tax the same transactions or activities. Tax treaties resolve issues that concern passive and active income of particularly non-resident companies or individuals. The UK, for instance, has double tax treaties with more than 130 countries; the USA with 58 countries.[16] Nevertheless, tax treaties are highly controversial as well. They provide openings for 'tax evasion' and 'tax avoidance' – through 'transfer pricing', 'debt shifting',

---

15 https://investmentpolicy.unctad.org/investment-dispute-settlement
16 https://www.ibfd.org/IBFD-Products/Tax-Treaties-Database

'phantom FDI' via empty corporate shells (Damgaard et al., 2019) and other tax engineering techniques used by multinational enterprises – to lower corporate taxes and shift profits from operating countries to tax havens. The IMF assessed that around $600 billion a year in tax revenues is lost due to profit-shifting, of which about $200 billion is borne by low-income countries – exceeding the approximate $150 billion these countries annually receive in development assistance (Shaxson, 2019).[17] OECD countries are estimated to lose 2–3% of their annual total tax revenue. Governments of developing countries rely on corporate income taxation much more than on private income taxation. Profit-shifting hence drains away the direly needed government resources for investments in sustainable development. To counter abuse, the OECD initiated the *OECD/G20 Inclusive Framework on Base Erosion and Profit Shifting (BEPS)*, in which 137 countries collaborate to "put an end to tax avoidance strategies that exploit gaps and mismatches in tax rules". The aim is to create consensus-based, long-term solutions to international tax challenges, for instance through mandatory disclosure, by equipping governments with domestic and international rules and instruments to address tax avoidance (15 Actions[18]), and by working towards policies to set minimum standards and get multinationals to pay a minimum level of tax. In October 2021, 136 countries and jurisdictions – representing more than 90% of the global GDP – signed a historic deal to ensure that multinationals pay a fairer share of tax. Countries agreed to enforce a corporate tax rate of at least 15% from 2023, and a fairer system of taxing profits where they are earned (regardless of whether firms have a physical presence there). According to OECD estimates, the deal could bring in an extra $150 billion of tax annually.

REGIONAL TREATIES

Regional treaties help in coordinating responsible governance across borders by providing policy credibility and more consistent criteria for investment, trade and operations. *Regional integration treaties* arrange varying degrees of regional cooperation in matters of international commerce, investment, private sector development, economic growth, infrastructure, strong (public) institutions, peace and security, and the region's interaction with other regions in the world. More specialized regional treaties exist that cover *specific areas* of concern with transboundary aspects.

---

17 The OECD calculated that profit-shifting practices of multinational enterprises costs developing countries between $100–240 billion in lost tax revenue annually.
18 See http://www.oecd.org/tax/beps/beps-actions/

- Some **Regional Integration Agreements** (RIAs) have formulated social, economic and ecological ambitions that support sustainable development in the region. Most RIAs, however, remain primarily aimed at economic goals, directed towards liberalizing trade and markets. The benefits of regionalism are then predominantly based on the premise of *open regionalism* and neoliberal principles, applied to *market integration* first. In developing regions such as ASEAN (Association of Southeast Asian Nations), the reference to sustainable development was found to remain largely rhetorical (Chandra, 2009). NAFTA (North American Free Trade Agreement) was renegotiated in 2019, partly because of protectionist sentiments in the United States. The resulting United States-Mexico-Canada Agreement (USMCA) is generally considered to widen the governance gap between the countries on sustainability issues. Already weak enforcement mechanisms (notably on workers' rights, living wages and ecological measures) were further weakened.

Arguably the furthest advanced regional integration initiative has been the **European Union** (EU), which since 1993 has developed a wide range of social, ecological and economic policies. Integration was gradually achieved – step by step – founded on shared values[19] and principles, represented by four 'freedoms': (1) free movement of goods; (2) free movement of capital; (3) freedom to establish and provide services; and (4) free movement of persons. Disagreement in particular on the exact bearing of the fourth freedom prompted the UK to opt out of the EU in 2019 ('Brexit'). The EU's explicit goal is "sustainable development based on balanced economic growth and price stability, a highly competitive market economy with full employment and social progress, and environmental protection". Areas for sustainability in which the European Commission (the governing body of the EU) has gained considerable relevance – or 'shared competences' as it is called in the European Treaty – include social policies, agricultural policies (Common Agricultural Policy), environment (for which it introduced the European Green Deal in 2020), energy, public health and development cooperation. In many of these areas, the European Commission can initiate policies that include legislation, funding and dedicated research programmes to stimulate coordinated progress. Regarding new challenges – notably the area of digital transformations – the formulation of common principles to navigate and guide progress is used as a governance approach to come to new standards. In 2020, the EU formulated three key principles in this

---

19 The EU values are common to the EU countries and form the basis of the EU, as laid out in the Lisbon Treaty and EU Charter of fundamental rights: human dignity, freedom, democracy, equality, rule of law, human rights.

domain: (1) technology that works *for people*, to improve every citizen's daily life; (2) a *fair and competitive* digital economy; and (3) an open, democratic and *sustainable* society, in which digital technologies help the EU reach climate neutrality and fight disinformation (European Commission, 2020).

■ Regional agreements increasingly include treaties around common-pool issues, such as fisheries and protecting the biosphere of seas. The *UN Division for Ocean Affairs and the law of the Sea* counts an indicative 37 regional treaties that cover most oceans and seas.[20] Most of them relate to the conservation of high fishery resources, with different regional practices in enforcement. A wide variety of regional environmental treaties, agreements, conventions and protocols apply, amongst others, on environmental governance, habitat protection, chemicals and waste, protection of species, migratory wildlife, air pollution, biological diversity and transboundary effects of industrial accidents.[21] Many represent a subset of international treaties.

6.5.3 Governance challenges under multilateral arrangements: the global governance gap (track 4)

Arguably the most challenging environment that organizations can enter into is the global space beyond national, bilateral or regional regulation. The global space is only partly regulated by multilateral treaties; a largely unregulated *global governance void* exists around 'global public goods', which leaves many 'collective action' issues inconclusively addressed. In this space – the *global governance gap* – principles prevail over rules. It is the space in which multilateral organizations operate, generally with a limited mandate and limited regulatory powers to formulate and enforce legally binding rules ('hard law'). Voluntary, non-legally binding initiatives ('soft law') based on negotiated agreements and commonly accepted principles, declarations and guidelines are then the prime mechanisms for filling global governance voids (see Box 6.3). Consequently, entering the global governance space slowly changes the governance discourse from one that is based on 'rules', to one based on 'resolutions', 'declarations, 'guidelines' and 'principles'. The ambiguity that characterizes this international arena provides ample reason to consider it a 'wicked problem' space. It also presents additional opportunities for organizations, however, to *move beyond*

---

20 https://www.un.org/Depts/los/biodiversity/prepcom_files/Indicative_list_of_regional_treaties.pdf
21 https://www.informea.org/en/treaties

CONFRONTING THE 'SOFT' AND THE 'HARD' SIDE OF GLOBAL GOVERNANCE

In filling the global governance gap, two types of coordination and intervention mechanisms interact: 'soft' versus 'hard' power, and 'soft' versus 'hard' law. These mechanisms define the dynamic between principles of international law and international diplomacy, in those areas where (a) no sovereign governing bodies exist, and (b) most relationships are based on negotiations between sovereign states with different power positions. In the global governance arena, weaker or stronger states set respectively more or less binding rules. How these rules are enforced, depends on how any of the participants exerts power before, during and after the negotiations.

Table 6.4 Likely combinations of power and law in the international arena

		INTERNATIONAL LAW	
		'SOFT'	**'HARD'**
INTERNATIONAL POWER	**'SOFT'**	• Resolutions of UN General Assembly (e.g. MDGs, SDGs) • Action plans (e.g. Agenda 21) • Non-treaty obligations (e.g. guidelines	• Customary international law • Weakly enforceable treaties
	'HARD'	• Framework treaties (including binding codes and principles) • Enforceable non-treaty obligations	• Enforceable treaties • Security council resolutions

Hard law in international relations refers to binding legal instruments between states and international actors. It includes treaties (conventions and other formal international agreements), UN Security Council resolutions and customary international law. Hard international law gives participants binding responsibilities as well as rights. Soft law refers to 'quasi-legal' instruments with no, or only a weak, binding effect. Soft law can also be associated with domestic law practice, but has been applied particularly to the international realm. Soft international law includes resolutions, declarations, statements of principles, codes of practice, action plans and all other non-treaty obligations.

The extent to which each of these practices is effective in stimulating coordinated international governance action, depends on the exercise of power in the formulation and implementation of either soft or hard law. Hard power may take the shape of the use (or threat of using) military and economic means to influence the behaviour or interests of others. Joseph Nye (2004) defines 'soft power' as the ability to co-opt and seduce, rather than coerce, the preferences of others through appeal and attraction. Means of soft power include culture, shared political values, but also joint development cooperation programmes that favour one country over another.

In order to overcome the tension between soft and hard power, the term *smart power* was introduced by the Center for Strategic and International Studies as "an

BOX 6.3

approach that underscores the necessity of a strong military, but also invests heavily in alliances, partnerships, and institutions of all levels to expand one's influence and establish legitimacy of one's action" (CSIS Commission on Smart Power, 2007: 7). The extent to which SDGs can be transformed from a relatively soft to a smarter power exertion practice will probably define its effectiveness.

compliance and develop strategies as 'wicked opportunities' (Chapter 5) – provided that 'hypernorms' (Donaldson and Dunfee, 1999) and principles can be embraced that effectively fill the void.

The extent to which the international space can be considered to be open, non-regulated or 'ambiguous', depends on the degree of *convergence* and *divergence* between national governments and international organizations operating in this space. Multilateralism as a system of treaties and practices is under increased pressure through unilateral (or bilateral) actions of countries that are seeking greater control over national affairs. Countries often compete on regulation, in order to incentivise companies to invest in or trade with them. Rivalry and divergence between countries for short-term gains or protection of national interests – signs of a VUCA logic – create a 'non-level playing field'. Rival and protectionist dynamics trigger a *race to the bottom* that leads countries and organizations to converge to the lowest denominator on sustainability issues. Such eroding dynamics tend to reinforce reactive strategies by companies and organizations operating across borders (at level 1 and 2). This fear has materialized for issues like ecology (creation of pollution havens), taxation (tax havens) and social affairs (labour rights violations, for instance, regarding 'cheap labour' and unsafe working conditions). If countries and organizations converge to higher standards of sustainability, however, they can encourage a *race to the top* in support of more active responsibility strategies (at levels 3 and 4). Principles-based efforts like the SDGs should, therefore, be understood not only as a constructive way to fill the global governance gap but also as an answer to the erosion of multilateralism that characterizes the present stage of the VUCA world.

MULTILATERAL INITIATIVES

International initiatives can be a stimulating force for institutional and regulatory convergence on sustainability issues between countries. In the global space, governance can rarely be based on enforceable supranational rules. Most international governance is susceptible to negotiation and voluntary agreements that can still create level playing fields and provide a positive stimulus for companies to embrace higher ambitions for sustainability. Exemplary multilateral initiatives that have developed *principles for action* are listed in Table 6.5. They can be classified

Table 6.5 Illustrative global initiatives since 2000

Aimed at preventing a 'race to the bottom' – Addressing levels 1 and 2	Aimed at stimulating a 'race to the top' – Addressing levels 3 and 4
• OECD Guidelines for Multinationals • UN Global Compact • UN General Principles on Human Rights ('Ruggie Principles') • PARIS Climate Agreement • OECD: Base Erosion and Profit Shifting (BEPS) project (the 2021 'Two Pillar Solution', minimum 15% corporate tax rate) • Extractive Industries Transparency Initiative (EITI) • Revised Equator Principles	• ISO 26000 • GRI: G3, G4 • Sustainable Development Goals (SDGs) • World Business Council for Sustainable Development (WBCSD) • Business & Sustainable Development Commission (BSDC)

as primarily directed towards *preventing* a 'race to the bottom' ('avoid doing harm') or *stimulating* a 'race to the top' (improve 'doing good').

Global initiatives aimed at preventing a 'race to the bottom' have been considered only moderately successful and supportive of relatively reactive approaches to sustainability. Inter-governmental organizations establish most of these initiatives; their implementation so far is seen as patchy and arduous. In case of multilateral treaties, ratification processes and actual integration into national law and regulatory frameworks generally encounter immense barriers. A prominent example is the Paris Agreement (adopted at the 2015 UN Climate Change Conference) that faces major enforcement problems. Industry-led initiatives have been formulated primarily as a result of advocacy campaigns and largely concentrate on 'do no harm' principles. The Equator Principles, for instance, serve as an environmental and social risk management tool for the projects financed by 105 financial institutions active in 38 countries. The Extractive Industries Transparency Initiative (EITI) – launched in 2002 by then British Prime Minister Tony Blair at the World Summit on Sustainable Development in Johannesburg, and since adopted in 53 'implementing countries' – requires full government disclosure of mineral revenues streams and related (foreign) company payments, as part of accountable management of the country's oil, gas and mineral resources. The 'Ruggie Principles' rest on three pillars: (1) the state's duty to *protect* against human rights abuses; (2) the corporate responsibility to *respect* human rights; (3) greater access by victims to effective *remedy*. The Ruggie Principles are not enforced but depend on their integration in national regulation, while providing 'due diligence' guidance for companies that want to avoid being part of human rights violations, by guiding them in becoming aware of, preventing and mitigating adverse human rights impacts in their strategies.

'Race to the top' initiatives more often constitute international multi-stakeholder efforts in which representatives of civil society, firms and governments participate. In recent years, the role of coalitions of frontrunner companies in these initiatives – notably organized in the World Business Council for Sustainable Development and (until 2018) in the Business & Sustainable Development Commission[22] – has grown in importance. 'Race to the top' efforts are generally directed towards spurring on and facilitating level 3 and 4 types of action (scaling positive externalities, initiating collective action and creating global public goods) and hence are primarily founded on voluntary commitments. The ISO 26000 guideline on the 'social responsibility' of organizations, for example, was developed with the consensus of more than 450 experts from 99 countries and 42 international liaison organizations. It presently serves as a 'repository of good practice' on how organizations can operate in an "ethical and transparent way that contributes to sustainable development while reckoning with the expectations of stakeholders, applicable laws and international norms of behaviour". The upgraded guidelines of the Global Reporting Initiative enable businesses, governments and other organizations to understand and communicate the impact of business on vital sustainability issues through universally applicable reporting guidance. Founded on multi-stakeholder engagement, GRI works with governments, international organizations and capital markets around the world to foster sustainability in policies and corporate reporting.

New kinds of global initiatives are enacted that not only build on multi-stakeholder approaches but also explicitly call on countries to translate specific, preferably quantifiable, ambitions into official policy. The SDGs are the most prominent example. The Paris Agreement also leaves room for states to move 'beyond' the formal agreement, by recognizing the possibility of inter-state cooperation to allow for higher ambitions. Even when regulation and implementation around the world diverge, a global agreement still creates a common minimum reference to monitor the extent to which the 'race the bottom' can be stopped.

6.6 CONCLUSION, TOOLS AND RESOURCES

The organizational set-up of societies proves rather complex and diverse. Part of the complexity is caused by the large number of hybrid forms that have emerged, notably: (1) as a means to deal with different economic principles, (2) as a means for escaping organizational stasis through the fusion of different institutional identities and practices (Jay, 2013; Battilana et al., 2009), or (3) as sources for

---

22 The Commission – a two-year initiative created to make the business case for sustainable development in general and the SDGs in particular – was launched at the World Economic Forum (WEF) in January 2016, co-chaired by former UN Deputy Secretary-General Mark Malloch-Brown and then Unilever CEO Paul Polman.

institutional and organizational change that can provide solutions for societal challenges. This chapter accordingly developed a 'multilayered' and 'multidirectional' approach to responsible governance. Following the wicked problems/opportunity frame of Part II, it makes sense to take multidimensionality and societal complexity into the realm of governance, agency and fiduciary duties. Responsible governance increasingly involves a solid understanding of the phenomenon of 'hybridization', both within society (across societal interfaces) and across societies (beyond national borders). We, therefore, distinguished between three types of hybridization that can be linked to different levels of responsible governance:

■   *Organizational or horizontal hybridization:* pertains to the merging of distinct organizational forms and/or formal organizations at or along the societal interfaces. 'Horizontal' hybridization often represents a response to developments that require a different take on a more effective organization of primary responsibilities and related governance arrangements (i.e. which organizational structure and governance constellation delivers the least negative externalities). Horizontal hybridization predominantly plays out at levels 1 and 2 of the societal triangle, both nationally and internationally.

■   *Societal or vertical hybridization:* relates to the multilayered concept of broadening up fiduciary responsibilities in addressing sources of failure that progressively transcend sectoral boundaries. Particularly at levels 3 and 4, 'vertical' hybridization considers organizational responsibilities linked to cross-sectoral challenges of meta-sectoral governance (i.e. which novel institutional arrangements create the biggest positive externalities), and the effectiveness of approaches in cross-sector coalitions to contribute to the creation of common goods.

■   *Global hybridization:* constitutes an intricate combination of both vertical and horizontal governance challenges, related to how to fill in the global governance gap by constructive arrangements that can create 'global public goods' or prevent 'global public bads' (race to the bottom) from appearing. In this global space, top-down approaches by UN organizations (Chapter 3) and bottom-up approaches (as specified in Chapters 5 and 6) come together in new (transitional) governance arrangements. The SDG-agenda is one of the most prominent areas where new forms of governance are developing around common principles (people, planet, prosperity, peace and partnering) to guide all organizations in *taking* responsibility as (corporate) leaders. Whether the SDGs will materialize, significantly depends on how private organizations develop effective initiatives in this space.

Broadening the realm of fiduciary duty and related (corporate) governance questions inherently implies a new 'conception of control' (Lamarche

Table 6.6 Four levels of responsible governance principles

Responsibility level:	Fiduciary duty	Failure to . . .	License to . . .	Prime beneficiaries
1. Primary responsibility	• Narrowly defined • Negative duty	Produce	Exist	Primary stakeholders
2. Negative externalities	• *Having* responsibility • Obligation to deliver (results-based)	Protect	Operate	Secondary stakeholders
3. Positive externalities	• Broadly defined • Positive duty	Promote	Scale	Societal (and international) stakeholders
4. Common goods creation through collective action	• *Taking* responsibility • Responsibility to commit (effort-based)	Partner	Experiment	Future generations

and Rubinstein, 2012) and legitimacy. It requires moving beyond ethics and morals, towards dealing with collective phenomena. It also calls for both formal and informal rules, principles and arrangements that go beyond the direct sphere of influence of the (corporate) organization. The organizational legitimacy literature refers to the social 'license to operate' (Kraemer and Van Tulder, 2012) to explain the societal acceptance or approval of organizations' operations based on their abidance by approved standards and on responsibly taking stakeholder concerns into account. This chapter, and the previous one, have introduced and consistently elaborated four distinct intervention and responsibility levels at which principles of responsible governance materialize. In line with these four levels, we can distinguish four types of 'societal licenses' that societies may grant to organizations. 'Higher-order' licenses should be understood as conditional to taking responsibility *beyond* the direct sphere of influence. They build on proven and ongoing responsible conduct at levels 1 and 2 (see Table 6.6).

■ **At level 1**, organizations have a *license to exist*, provided that they produce no controversial products (tobacco) or poor services (pyramid games). Failure to produce safe and healthy products in the longer run reduces their license to exist. If they abuse their (market) power, they create an even bigger fiduciary duty problem.

■ In particular **at level 2**, organizations can earn their *license to operate*, that is, gain legitimacy towards key external stakeholders that are faced with the negative externalities the organization creates. If primary and secondary stakeholders are satisfied with how the organization handles responsibility issues (and protects their interests), the license to operate is granted and sustained.

- **At level 3**, we can speak about a *license to scale* if the organization not only limits its negative externalities but actively promotes its positive externalities. In terms of an ethical theory of stakeholder relations, an organization that produces sufficient positive externalities (spill-over or agglomeration effects, as they are called in regional economic theory) may earn a license to internationalize and scale, even when this happens at the expense of employment in the home base.

- Finally, **at level 4**, a different type of license emerges. We call this the *license to experiment*. This license applies to developing new products and services for unserved needs and people. It requires 'out-of-the-box' and paradoxical thinking (Chapter 4, Box 4.3). The concept implies that a (corporate) organization may initially fail in its efforts to effectively create a new product or service to serve these needs, but nevertheless gains in credibility and goodwill in support of a business case for further expansion and experimentation. The license to experiment is particularly relevant for organizations that embrace the ambition to contribute to common and global goods creation, as envisioned in the SDGs. The required innovation and experimentation then become an integral part of the responsible governance challenges at level 4: creating effective, cross-sectoral alliances (partnerships) with strategically, tactically and operationally 'fit' parties.

In particular for level 3 and 4 ambitions, the *Wicked Problems Plaza* was developed as a technique that brings together stakeholders from all sides of society to engage on societal challenges in a structured way of deliberation and 'out-of-the-box' thinking (Box 6.4).

BOX 6.4

WICKED PROBLEMS PLAZA: METHOD AND PRINCIPLES

The governance challenge of altering wicked problems into wicked opportunities has a literal bearing on the 'space' in which stakeholders have to approach these issues. From the insights gained in all three chapters of Part II, we derived a number of **principles** for the design and operation of such a space: the Wicked Problems Plaza.

1 Create a safe space;

2 Adopt a systemic and collaborative approach: search for approaches, not (necessarily) for solutions;

3 Create an environment that does not judge on interests, problems or solutions;

4 Get the 'whole system' into the room: identify relevant stakeholders and their interests, and make sure that they are represented – either in person or in spirit;

5 Work on coalitions of the needed, rather than coalitions of the willing;

6 Don't stick to your position. Do not engage in position-based or interest-based negotiations, work on collective visions and collaborative approaches;

7 Don't shy away from complexity; create and develop a high 'tolerance for ambiguity', start thinking in paradoxes rather than trade-offs;

8 Understand your own responsibilities and core activities; don't be a sucker (i.e., don't take up responsibilities that you do not have in all reasonableness);

9 Distinguish between technical, organizational and societal approaches to a problem;

10 Get your own dilemmas out of your system by sharing them with others;

11 Open your mind: understand what biases you have; get the facts right or invite stakeholders that can help you in shedding light on the unknowns;

12 Respect and thrive on diversity as an art of 'thinking independently together'; each stakeholder has different interests, but also different ideas and possible solutions; work with that;

13 Be clear about the consequences of not acting; try to identify the indirect effects of your solutions;

14 Be creative: create a host of potential solutions; pay due attention to unintended consequences; failure is an option;

15 Be modest: nobody knows the solution;

16 Work towards the 'partnering space' and define the road you would like to take; define 'markers for change' to further fine-tune your approach in the future.

Synthesizing

The Wicked Problems Plaza stimulates paradoxical thinking through a method called synthesizing. In the plaza, participants first frame the wicked problem in terms of dilemmas and trade-offs. The facilitator then guides them in looking critically at these problem statements. Are they really either/or, or does the problem resemble a paradox more? How to consider the paradox in such a way that two positive outcomes can be reached? Synthesizing helps to facilitate this reframing by linking multiple, contradictory paradigms to generate new insights, through which opportunities can be found (Chapter 5).

Synthesizing is paradoxical by nature: the inconsistencies that define paradoxes oppose the compulsive effort to solve them with approaches that are based

BOX 6.4

on conventional logic only. Any framework focusing on logical analytics should simultaneously provide sufficient space for creative work and free-thinking in the process. Hence, using logic *and* creativity in approaching wicked problems must not be seen as a trade-off, but rather as two means; both have to work in synthesis. This reflective and reflexive practice stimulates participants to reconsider their own and others' baggage of value assumptions and predispositions. From this process for exploring paradoxes, engaged managers and stakeholders can construct shared meaning and clarify 'relational responsibilities' to each other.

Spaces

To structure positive interactions, the Wicked Problems Plaza created four 'spaces' that participants can go through in a particular sequence:[23]

- **Interest space:** 'head' – landscaping of stakeholders;
- **Equity space:** 'heart' – brainstorming on ideals;
- **Efficiency space:** 'hands' – thinking about practical ways and examples for dealing with (a part of) the problem;
- **Partnering space:** bringing 'hands-heart-head' together in a collaborative effort, aimed at effectively addressing the problem.

More on the 'Wicked Problems Plaza' method: https://repub.eur.nl/pub/93223

---

23 For each of these spaces, a variety of practical techniques are available. One excellent overview of techniques for multi-stakeholder partnering processes is Brouwer et al. (2015).

T
A
K
E
A
W
A
Y
S

- The increasing importance of hybrid organizations for sustainability makes it essential to (a) develop a deeper understanding of causes and consequences of hybridity and (b) to grasp the distinction between horizontal and vertical hybridity;

- Hybridity also points at the relevance of *organizational diversity* for sustainability; there is no 'one-size-fits-all' form of sustainable enterprise, nor of corporate responsibility;

- We can distinguish between an outside-in and an inside-out approach to responsible governance: insights from 'institutional logics' (i.e. contextually embedded arrangements of responsibility and action) and 'institutional economics' (i.e. societal functions and organizational forms) need to be combined for a full understanding of responsible governance questions;

- Along four basic societal interfaces (profit/non-profit; governmental/nongovernmental; public/private organization; public/private good provision), we can distinguish eight archetypical organizational forms; each form has strengths and weaknesses and faces a variety of agency and governance problems;

- 'Distance' adds the international dimension to governance challenges (governance gaps; divergence; volatility), along four internationalization tracks: international, bilateral, regional, and multilateral/global;

- Managing distance dimensions across varying sustainability/CSR regimes (international horizontal hybridity) comes with operational risks (level 1); strategic risks (level 2); and sustainability risks (levels 3 and 4); it calls for setting organizational 'hypernorms';

- Five archetypical sustainability/CSR regimes were discerned (as distinct environments for SDG approaches) to mark the responsible governance challenges of simultaneously coping with distinct institutional contexts;

- In the international space, a proliferation of bilateral, regional and multilateral treaties and arrangements can be witnessed (Bhagwati's 'spaghetti bowl'). These international governance instruments can be classified along a continuum of 'hard law' (legally binding and enforced rules) to 'soft law' (quasi-legal instruments with weak binding force);

- The multilateral governance system is losing strength; instead, many countries favour unilateral and bilateral approaches;

- If countries and organizations compete at the level of the lowest denominator on sustainability issues, they trigger a 'race to the bottom'; if countries and organizations converge on higher standards of sustainability, they can encourage a 'race to the top';

T A K E A W A Y S

■ The largely unregulated global space – the global governance gap/void – can only be filled by 'principles-based' multilateral commitments and multi-stakeholder alliances that create global hybrid or transitory responsible governance arrangements;

■ Their effectiveness depends for a large part on how private organizations deal with this gap: in a defensive (reactive) way, or in a positive (proactive) way. Part III will further explore the strategic and operational dimensions of this challenge.

■ *CSR Risk Check Tool:* quick scan to identify international CSR risks of business activities upstream and downstream in the value chain (exporting, importing, production facilities in foreign countries). Supports a quick assessment (eight-step 'due diligence' roadmap) of what can be done to prevent, reduce and manage them. https://www.mvorisicochecker.nl/en

■ *OECD Guidelines for Multinational Enterprises:* recommendations addressed by governments to multinational enterprises operating in or from adhering countries. They provide non-binding principles and standards for responsible business conduct in a global context, consistent with applicable laws and internationally recognized standards. The Guidelines are the only multilaterally agreed and comprehensive code of responsible business conduct that governments have committed to promoting. Additional publications are available to guide due diligence (by sector) and provide practical support on the implementation of the guidelines. http://mneguidelines.oecd.org/guidelines/

■ *UN Treaty Collection:* the depositary of more than 560 multilateral treaties covering a broad range of subject matters – categorized along 29 chapters – such as human rights, disarmament, health, international trade and development, commodities, and protection of the environment. https://treaties.un.org/

■ *UNCTAD International Investment Navigators:* global policy databases on international (bilateral) investment agreements (3,287); investment dispute settlement cases (1,023); investment policy measures (1,017); and national investment laws (177): https://investmentpolicy.unctad.org/

■ *WTO Dispute Settlement:* Resolving trade disputes is one of the core activities of the WTO. A dispute arises when a member government believes another member government is violating an agreement or a commitment that it has made in the WTO. The WTO has one of the most active international dispute settlement mechanisms in the world. Since 1995, 595 disputes have been brought to the WTO, and over 350 rulings have been issued. Provides a basic introduction to dispute settlement information (interactive course, the process, working procedures) and access to dispute documents. https://www.wto.org/english/tratop_e/dispu_e/dispu_e.htm

■ *UNCTAD Investment Policy Framework for Sustainable Development:* provides guidance for policymakers in the evolution towards a New Generation of investment policies. The updated Framework includes six sets of transformative measures aimed at promoting investments in pursuit of sustainable development goals. Six instruments shape policymaking in the area of investment and enterprise development at the global, regional and national levels. https://investmentpolicy.unctad.org/investment-policy-framework

■ *The Human Rights Guide to the SDGs:* developed by the Danish Institute for Human Rights. Illustrates the human rights anchorage of the 17 SDGs by making concrete links between the 169 targets and the relevant range of (1) international and regional human rights instruments; (2) international labour standards; and (3) key environmental instruments. https://sdg.humanrights.dk/en/instruments/overview/list

SELECTED WEB RESOURCES

■ *World Bank's Doing Business – measuring business regulation:* presents quantitative indicators on 12 areas of business regulation that can be compared across 190 economies and over time. World Bank's Doing Business website also provides regional, subnational and thematic business regulation reports and data (e.g. on taxes, access to finance, women's entrepreneurship). As of September 2021, the World Bank is formulating a new approach to assessing the business and investment climate in economies worldwide, under the working title 'Business Enabling Environment (BEE)'. https://www.doingbusiness.org/

■ *OECD Trust in Business Initiative:* gathers leaders from the private sector, state-owned enterprises, investors, governments and civil society organizations who are committed to championing responsible leadership, fostering environments of integrity and developing insights to improve trust. It promotes coordinated action through public-private cooperation, in the following areas: (1) promoting partnerships; (2) capacity-building solutions that draw upon international treaties and guidelines (reflecting sectoral and regional specificities); (3) ensuring implementation of guidelines and standards; (4) a forum for cooperation and collaboration. http://www.oecd.org/corporate/trust-business.htm

REFERENCES

Battilana, J., Leca, B. & Boxenbaum, E. (2009). 'How Actors Change Institutions: Towards a Theory of Institutional Entrepreneurship', *Academy of Management Annals*, 3(1):65–107.

Bhagwati, J.N. (1995). *US Trade Policy: The Infatuation with FTAs*, Department of Economics Discussion Papers, 726, April, Columbia University.

Brouwer, H. & Woodhill, J., with Hemmati, M., Verhoosel, K. & Van Vugt, S. (2015). *The MSP Guide. How to Design and Facilitate Multiple-Stakeholder Partnerships*. Centre for Development Innovation, Wageningen University.

Chandra, A.C. (2009). *The Pursuit of Sustainable Development through Regional Economic Integration: ASEAN and Its Potential as a Development-oriented Organization*, Trade Knowledge Network, International Institute for Sustainable Development.

Claessens, S. & Fan J. (2002). 'Corporate Governance in Asia: A Survey', *International Review of Finance* 3(2):71–103.

Cohen, M.D., March, J.G. & Olsen, J.P. (1972). 'A Garbage Can Model of Organizational Choice', *Administrative Science Quarterly,* 17(1):1–25.

CSIS Commission on Smart Power (2007). *A Smarter, More Secure America*. Washington D.C.: Center for Strategic and International Studies.

Damgaard, J., Elkjaer, T. & Johannesen, N. (2019). *What Is Real and What Is Not in the Global FDI Network?*, IMF Working Paper No. 19/274, 11 December.

Dijkzeul, D. (1996). *The Management of Multilateral Organizations*. The Hague, London and Boston: Kluwer Law International.

Donaldson, T. (1989). *The Ethics of International Business*. The Ruffin Series in Business Ethics. New York/Oxford: Oxford University Press.

Donaldson, T. & Dunfee, T.W. (1999). 'When Ethics Travel: The Promise and Peril of Global Business Ethics, *California Management Review*, 41(4):45–63.

Etzioni, A. (1988). *The Moral Dimension, Toward a New Economics*. New York: The Free Press.

European Commission (2020). *Shaping Europe's Digital Future*, February. Luxembourg: Publication Office of the European Union.

Foulke, D. (2016). 'Thinking About Corporate Governance In Family-Owned Firms', 6 January. Retrieved from: https://alphaarchitect.com/2016/01/06/thinking-about-corporate-gover nance-in-family-owned-firms/.

Googins, B.K. & Rochlin, S.A. (2002). 'Creating the Partnership Society: Understanding the Rhetoric and Reality of Cross-Sectoral Partnerships', *Business and Society Review*, 105(1):127–144.

Hasan, S. (Ed.) (2015). *Human Security and Philanthropy: Islamic Perspectives and Muslim Majority Country Practices*. New York: Springer.

Hofstede, G.H. & Hofstede, G.J. (2005). *Cultures and Organizations: Software of the Mind*. Third Edition. New York: McGraw-Hill.

Jay, J. (2013). 'Navigating Paradox as a Mechanism of Change and Innovation in Hybrid Organizations', *Academy of Management Journal*, 56(1):137–159.

Jensen, M.C. & Meckling, W.H. (1976). 'Theory of the firm: Managerial behavior, agency costs, and ownership structure', *Journal of Financial Economics*, 3(4):305–360.

Kobeissi, N. (2005). 'Foreign Investment in the MENA Region: Analyzing Non-Traditional Determinants', Perspectives On International Corporate Responsibility, *International Corporate Responsibility Series*, (2):217–233.

Kraemer, R. & Van Tulder, R. (2012). 'A license to operate for the extractive industries? Operationalizing stakeholder thinking in international business'. In: Lindgreen, A., Kotler, P., Vanhamme, J. & Maon, F. (Eds.) *A Stakeholder Approach to Corporate Social Responsibility. Pressures, Conflicts and Reconciliation* (pp. 97–120). Surrey: Gower Publishing.

Lamarche, T. & Rubinstein, M. (2012). 'Dynamics of corporate social responsibility: Towards a new conception of control?', *Journal of Institutional Economics*, 8(2):161–186.

Lawrence, T.B., Hardy, C. & Phillips, N.W. (2002). 'Institutional Effects of Interorganizational Collaboration: The Emergence of Proto-Institutions', *The Academy of Management Journal*, 45(1):281–290.

Mair, J., Battilana, J. & Cardenas, J. (2012). 'Organizing for Society: A Typology of Social Entrepreneuring Models', *Journal of Business Ethics*, (111):353–373.

Milhaupt, C.J. & Pargendler M. (2017). *Governance Challenges of Listed State-Owned Enterprises around the World: National Experiences and a Framework for Reform*, European Corporate Governance Institute (ECGI) Law Working Paper N° 352/2017.

Minguez-Vera, A., Martin-Ugedo, J.F. & Arcas-Lario, N. (2010). 'Agency and property rights theories in agricultural cooperatives: evidence from Spain', *Spanish Journal of Agricultural Research* 8(4):908–924.

Muldoon, J.P. (2018). 'International Organizations and Governance in a Time of Transition', *Journal of International Organizations Studies*, 9(2):13–26.

North, D.C. (1990). *Institutions, Institutional Change and Economic Performance*. Cambridge: Cambridge University Press.

Nye, J.S. Jr. (2004). *Soft Power: The Means to Success in World Politics*. Public Affairs.

Reinalda, B. (Ed.) (2013). *Routledge Handbook of International Organization*. London and New York: Routledge.

Reinecke, J. & Ansari, A. (2016). 'Taming wicked problems: The role of framing in the construction of corporate social responsibility', *Journal of Management Studies*, 53(3):299–329.

Sachs, J.D. (2015). *The Age of Sustainable Development*. Columbia University Press.

Sachs, J.D, Kroll, C., Lafortune, G., Fuller, G. & Woelm, F. (2021). *Sustainable Development Report 2021. The Decade of Action for the Sustainable Development Goals*. Cambridge: Cambridge University Press. DOI 10.1017/9781009106559.

Sachs, J.D., Schmidt-Traub, G., Kroll, C., Lafortune, G. & Fuller, G. (2019). *Sustainable Development Report 2019*. New York: Bertelsmann Stiftung and Sustainable Development Solutions Network (SDSN), June.

Shaxson, N. (2019). 'Tackling Tax Havens. The billions attracted by tax havens do harm to sending and receiving nations alike'', *Finance & Development*, 56(3):7–10.

Singh, K. & Ilge, B. (Eds.) (2016). *Rethinking Bilateral Investment Treaties: Critical Issues and Policy Choices*. Both Ends, Madyam, and Centre for Research on Multinational Corporations (SOMO). New Delhi: KS Designers.

Smith, W.K., Gonin, M. & Besharov, M.L. (2013). 'Managing Social-Business Tensions: A Review and Research Agenda for Social Enterprise', *Business Ethics Quarterly* 23(3):407–442.

Thornton, P.H., Ocasio, W. & Lounsbury, M. (2013). *The Institutional Logics Perspective: A New Approach to Culture, Structure, and Process*, Oxford University Press.

UNCTAD (2019). 'Taking Stock of IIA Reform: Recent Developments', *International Investment Agreements (IIA) Issues Note*, Issue 3, June 2019.

UNCTAD (2015). *Investment Policy Framework for Sustainable Development*. New York and Geneva: United Nations Conference on Trade and Development.

Van Tulder, R. (2020). 'In search of an integrative approach to managing distance', *EIBAzine*, Spring-Summer, 26:8–16.

Van Tulder, R. (2018a). *Getting all the Motives Right. Driving International Corporate Responsibility (ICR) to the Next Level*. Rotterdam: SMO.

Van Tulder, R. & Van Mil, E. (2020). 'Responsible governance: broadening the corporate governance discourse to include positive duties and collective action'. In: Laasch, O., Suddaby, R., Freeman, R.E. & Jamali, D. (Eds.), *Research Handbook of Responsible Management* (pp. 175–194). Cheltenham: Edward Elgar Publishing.

Van Tulder, R. & Roman, M. (2019). 'Re-assessing risk in international markets: a strategic, operational, and sustainability taxonomy'. In: Leonidou, L.C., Katsikeas, C.S., Samiee, S. & Leonidou, C.N. (Eds.), *Socially Responsible International Business: Critical Issues and the Way Forward* (pp. 158–183). Cheltenham UK: Edward Elgar.

Van Tulder, R. & Keen, N. (2018). 'Capturing Collaborative Challenges: Designing Complexity-Sensitive Theories of Change for Cross-Sector Partnerships', *Journal of Business Ethics*, 150(2):315–332.

Van Tulder, R. with Van der Zwart, A. (2006). *International Business-Society Management. Linking Corporate Responsibility and Globalization*. London: Routledge.

Van Zanten, J.A. & Van Tulder, R. (2018). 'Multinational enterprises and the Sustainable Development Goals: An institutional approach to corporate engagement', *Journal of International Business Policy*, (1):208–233.

Visser, W. (Ed.) (2016). *The World Guide to Sustainable Enterprise. Four Volume Set*. London: Routledge.

Visser, W. & Tolhurst, N. (Eds.) (2010). *The World Guide to CSR. A Country-by-Country Analysis of Corporate Sustainability and Responsibility*. London: Routledge.

Voorn, B., Van Genugten, M. & Van Thiel, S. (2019). 'Multiple principals, multiple problems: Implications for effective governance and a research agenda for joint service delivery', *Public Administration*, 97(3):671–685.

Weiss, T.G. & Wilkinson, R. (Eds.) (2014). *International Organizations and Global Governance*. Abingdon: Routledge.

Whiteman, G. & Mamen, K. (2002). 'Examining justice and conflict between mining companies and indigenous peoples: Cerro Colorado and the Ngäbe-Buglé', *Journal of Business and Management,* 8(3):293–310.

Wilkinson, R. (Ed.) (2005). *The Global Governance Reader*. London: Routledge.

PART III: HOW?
STRATEGIC AND OPERATIONAL PRINCIPLES

How to accelerate corporate action for the SDGs?

"If I had to select one sentence to describe the state of the world,
I would say we are in a world in which global challenges are
more and more integrated
and the responses are more and more fragmented,
and if this is not reversed, it's a recipe for disaster".
António Guterres, Secretary-General of the United Nations

Part I and II explored *Systemic, Societal and Dynamic Principles* of sustainable business. We discussed these principles in general, but also linked them to the Sustainable Development Goals (SDGs) – the leading global agenda to collectively and collaboratively deal with the world's grandest challenges in a transformative way. We covered foundational 'why', 'what' and 'who' questions and contended that sustainability issues are not only material from a 'negative duty' point of view (wicked problems, immediate and slow-burning crises, 'avoid doing harm'), but also hold significant (wicked) opportunities for navigating much-needed progress towards a more balanced and resilient global society. In that universal ambition, the goal-oriented SDG framework provides a unifying and actionable positive change agenda that has proved instrumental in mobilizing, coordinating and pooling the commitment, efforts and means of large groups of stakeholders from all societal sectors (state, market, civil society) around the world.

The first four-year cycle of the SDG trajectory (2015–2019) also showed that implementation of the SDGs comes with sizable conceptual, empirical and governance challenges. Progress towards achieving the SDGs has been too slow. The

DOI: 10.4324/9781003098355-9

2020–2030 period has consequently been declared a **Decade of Action**. Faced with a series of paralleled systemic crises – with the Covid-19 pandemic, heightened global economic uncertainty, hunger, a refugee and migration crisis, ecological degradation and climate-related crises as the most tangible symptoms of system fragilities – the urgency of transitioning towards a more resilient society is becoming rapidly clear. But how can such profound transitions be accelerated through actions of the private sector? How can the SDGs be meaningfully incorporated into the business models, corporate strategies and day-to-day operations of (multinational) companies and other private organizations in an actionable and forward-thinking way? How to use the power base and position of companies in (global) value chains for effecting positive, scalable and more impactful change – alone and together with others? With these key questions in mind, Part III concentrates on *Strategic and Operational Principles* for placing societal value creation, sustainability and the SDGs at the heart of corporate decision-making, functional-level processes and coherent strategy implementation.

AGENTS OF CHANGE?

From the outset, the active participation of private organizations has been considered pivotal for achieving the SDGs by 2030. *Transforming Our World: The 2030 Agenda for Sustainable Development* explicitly acknowledges "the role of the diverse private sector, ranging from micro-enterprises to cooperatives to multinationals" in the implementation of the new Agenda (UN, 2015: para. 41). Then UN Secretary-General Ban Ki-moon ascribed the most dynamic role in the SDG endeavour to the private sector: "Governments must take the lead in living up to their pledges. At the same time, I am counting on the private sector to drive success."[1] Likewise, then head of the United Nations Development Programme Helen Clark affirmed that "the new sustainable development agenda cannot be achieved without business" (ibid). These statements underline a significant shift from earlier thinking about sustainability that considered development issues predominantly 'government territory' (Part I). Corporate leaders themselves strongly supported the positioning of business as an active contributor to the achievement of the SDGs, and not surprisingly so. If taken on vigorously, the SDGs could unlock an estimated annual $12 trillion in business opportunities by 2030, while creating hundreds of millions of much-needed jobs. In the corporate community, the SDG-agenda was received as "a compelling

---

1   UN News Centre, 26 September 2015. https://www.un.org/sg/en/content/sg/statement/
2015-09-26/secretary-generals-remarks-united-nations-private-sector-forum

growth strategy for individual businesses, for business generally and for the world economy" (Business & Sustainable Development Commission, 2017: 11). In the words of Paul Polman, former CEO of Unilever: "the SDGs provide the world's long-term business plan by putting people and the planet first. It's the growth story of our time."

Private organizations, as was outlined in Chapter 6, come in different shapes, sizes and governance structures, and can epitomize combined (hybrid) functions across societal interfaces (Figures 6.2 and 6.3) and across national borders. Private organizations in general – and large multinational corporations specifically – are relevant 'agents' in addressing the SDGs, for a variety of reasons:

- They are able to innovate through their ability and willingness to take risk. Companies – in addition to governments – are the largest investors in (new) technologies;

- They create jobs, products and services and can help develop new organizational practices and standards – alone, within their sector or together with other societal actors;

- Stimulated by productive competition, they show great ability in scaling activities and in boosting efficiency, thereby (potentially) enhancing cheaper solutions for more affordable and accessible (needs-based) products and services;

- They can mobilize substantial and timely financial resources, either on the open stock market or as part of other financial arrangements;

- Reaching the SDGs requires a sizable increase in targeted public and private investments (estimated between $5 to $7 trillion per year); the annual 'financing gap' of $2.5 trillion that is to be bridged, pales in comparison with the more than $200 trillion of global assets under private management;

- Multinational organizations are able to correct 'market failures' across borders, by *internalizing* markets and organizing practices on an international scale;

- Due to their often powerful positions in networks, technologies and sectors, large companies can be a vital enabler, but also be a formidable *barrier to change* if they are not involved in the change process.

Large (internationally active) companies tend to be better positioned to innovate, standardize and scale; smaller and locally embedded businesses are often more capable of flexibly responding to immediate challenges; start-ups and social enterprises are usually better able to take up social challenges in an inventive and entrepreneurial manner, but often have difficulty in scaling and reaching sufficient impact on the more wicked sustainability problems.

WALKING THE TALK . . .

These core competences give companies promising potential to contribute to the SDGs and create added societal value. Their perceived commitment to actually deliver on that potential is nevertheless surrounded with considerable scepticism and low levels of trust (Chapter 5). Merely espousing general principles of 'good governance' and 'responsible management' is not enough. Society expects companies to define, commit to and deliver on far more concrete *strategic and operational principles* of sustainable business, translated into measurable (and verifiable) sustainable practices, outcomes and impacts. But even with sustainability-oriented and SDG-committed companies, a certain disconnect between 'intention' and 'realization' in the implementation of strategic aims is still probable (Mintzberg, 2015). *Walking the talk* and closing the *promise-performance gap* proves exacting in practice, especially when confronted with the more 'wicked' dimensions of sustainability challenges (Chapter 4).

Companies face barriers – of various kinds, at different responsibility and ambition levels, and in subsequent organizational transition phases – in incorporating the SDGs into their core activities. The UN Global Compact, for instance, found that 67% of their corporate signatories are committing to sustainability at the CEO level, yet only 48% are actually implementing sustainability into operations (UN Global Compact and Accenture, 2019). While 71% of the CEOs recognize the critical role that business could play in contributing to delivery of the SDGs, a mere 21% believe that business is indeed playing that role. The Sustainable Development Solutions Network (SDSN) and Bertelsmann Stiftung have repeatedly pointed to the problem of companies 'not walking the talk'. UN Secretary-General Guterres hence called upon businesses to significantly raise their efforts (September 2019): "Business leaders have a critical role to play in the Decade of Action. I urge all companies to drive ambitious SDG actions throughout their operations and supply chains, embedding human rights, labor, environment and anti-corruption into core business. Business and finance can lead through their actions and investment decisions an economic transformation that leaves no one behind."

OVERCOMING STRATEGIC AND OPERATIONAL SUSTAINABILITY CHALLENGES . . .

Even well-disposed 'agents of change' can in fact become 'agents of stagnation' – or fall prey to the *incumbent's curse* – if they are not able to seize the momentum provided by the SDGs. The early experience of companies in operationalizing and integrating the SDGs into their sustainability strategies and operations (summed up in section 3.4.3), indicates that companies are struggling with at least five interrelated challenges:

- **Materiality challenge:** what constitutes 'sustainability' and 'long-term value creation' is continuously evolving. Companies have trouble with exploring, selecting and prioritizing those (sets of) SDGs and SDG-targets most relevant for directing the organization towards a more resilient business model that aligns with (tomorrow's) societal expectations and needs. If there is insufficient fit between the organization's SDG-portfolio, its longer-term strategy and operational activities, sizable intention-realization gaps are bound to appear. This is reflected in the fact that many companies have experienced great difficulty in defining viable SDG-related 'business cases', at various sustainability ambition levels.

- **Legitimacy challenge:** especially large multinationals with substantial vested interests and powers encounter the challenge of having to overcome considerable trust gaps when they communicate and attempt to implement sustainability aspirations to 'do good'. Studies on the CSR intentions of companies are littered with *failure to walk the talk*, feeding into public distrust. Stakeholder pressure for more detailed measurement and sustainability reporting that should corroborate SDG performance and impact claims, is mounting accordingly. Gaining societal legitimacy requires convincing, dedicated and results-oriented SDG efforts, while averting the pitfall of the self-promotor paradox and related allegations of *SDG-washing*.

- **Transitioning challenge:** early practice shows that companies incline to 'avoiding harm' SDG-targets in particular, as part of a (reactive) reputation-driven and risk-mitigation approach to *limiting negative externalities*. 'Doing good' SDG-targets (aimed at creating and *scaling positive externalities*) can provide promising investment opportunities with great potential for transformational change, yet require a (pro)active and forward-looking approach to sustainability, a more sophisticated value orientation, new business concepts (inclusive, circular, sharing, regenerative, fair), as well as profound adjustments in present business models and modes of (value chain) organizing. Overcoming the many *internal barriers* and tipping points to organizational transitioning is challenging enough as it is. However, the *external business environment* (e.g. competitive forces, market push/pull, regulatory frameworks, industry standards, stakeholder expectations, consumer behaviour) is always part of the equation and hence must be positively influenced in parallel to enable accelerated change at scale.

- **Nexus challenge:** companies have been found to cherry-pick the SDGs, selecting those SDGs that appear more 'easy to achieve' while largely ignoring the SDG-framework's *integrative logic*. Due to such siloed practices, companies have only scratched the surface of using the SDGs to map and leverage nexus interactions for synergetic effects. An integrated yet well-targeted approach to the SDGs reveals options to minimize negative externalities while optimizing positive externalities. The link between micro-interventions and macro-effects has yet to be convincingly connected to actionable business strategies.

■ **Partnering challenge:** the inclusion of societal actors around SDG-related challenges has remained fragmented. Companies are struggling (or neglecting) to develop and integrate coherent cross-sector partnering strategies that match their SDG portfolio, and fall short in organizing sufficient institutionalization and organizational learning that would allow for greater outcomes and impact. Sharing responsibilities and engaging in issue-driven 'partnerships for the SDGs' comes with an array of internal and external coordination problems that have been constraining the full potential of collaborative arrangements.

These challenges translate into six strategic and operational 'how' questions, which constitute the chapters of Part III.

MAKING IT RESILIENT

Business cannot thrive in a society that fails; societies cannot be resilient where businesses blunder. Societies are probing for 'resilience' – the capacity to survive, adapt and grow in the face of societal stresses and shocks. A resilient society requires resilient organizations that are able to act upon different levels of 'failure', as identified in Chapters 5 and 6. A VUCA world with destabilizing tendencies triggers and exacerbates incidents, conflicts and (systemic) crises. Triggering events (incidents, structural, systemic) prompt organizational change, but to what extent can bouncing back from adversity result in positive change trajectories? Can corporate strategies effectively contribute to sustainable development and advance social, economic and ecological resilience in the process? **Chapter 7** develops general principles of **organizational resilience**. It synthesizes the history of managerial and scholarly thinking on sustainable business models (the CSR ambition of companies) and zooms in on the mutual dependence of business and society in preventing, coping with, and recovering from triggering events with ascending scopes of impact. The chapter distinguishes between more resilient/balanced and more vulnerable/fragile business models, by considering four levels of intervention at which organizations take on responsibilities in the face of grand challenges.

MAKING IT STRATEGIC

Chapter 8 looks into opportunities and viable ways for aligning organizational and societal ambitions in a sustainable manner: the quest for the sustainable 'business case'. It delineates a basic strategic framework for private organizations to implement the SDGs at all four levels of intervention as identified in Part II: (1) addressing failure; (2) limiting negative externalities; (3) creating and scaling positive externalities; and (4) fostering collective action. The chapter contends that a wealth of **business cases for sustainability** exist – each with their own rationale – that can be defined at four intervention levels and approached from two distinct angles: starting from a for-profit and a non-profit base. For-profit and non-profit-oriented private, semi-private or semi-public organizational forms represent distinct competences, governance logics and strategic 'repertoires', resources and business models for addressing sustainability challenges. The observed *hybridization* trend (Chapter 6) points to an expedient blending of logics: for-profit organizations are trying to achieve greater societal impact, while non-profit organizations are trying to become more efficient in achieving their impact. Chapter 8 shows that seven different governance models all present complementary approaches to the SDG challenge – each with their own strengths and potential pitfalls.

MAKING IT MATERIAL

Chapter 9 considers how the business case for sustainability can be linked to the 'materiality challenge' of business model innovation. How can companies break through a passive or reactive attitude towards sustainability issues and timely overcome the 'incumbent's curse'? Building on synthesized insights from extant literature on key drivers of business model innovation, stakeholder theory, societal legitimacy and stage models of organizational transitioning, this chapter introduces the notion of *reversing materiality*. This outside-in perspective takes societal needs as the starting point for future-oriented strategizing and serves as a useful lens in organizational goal-setting that aligns with the SDGs. Chapter 9 additionally presents an *extended value theory* of the firm: 'the CANVAS+ model'. By including 'value destruction' (level 2), 'value spreading' (level 3) and 'value co-creation/sharing' (level 4) dimensions – in addition to creating, designing, capturing and scaling value (level 1) – the upgraded business model canvas helps organizations to define a *richer/broad* **value proposition** as well as identify those aspects of their business model that are more vulnerable or more resilient. Defining **Key Value Indicators (KVIs)** guides the process of redefining the value orientation and purpose of the organization in order to become more resilient, generate greater societal value and contribute to a sustainability ecosystem that is circular, inclusive, sharing and social. The chapter concludes with what such ambition implies for dynamic and sustainable leadership.

MAKING IT POWERFUL

Ambitions to integrate the SDGs into core business remain elusive unless organizations are able to translate their aspirations into effectual corporate strategies. **Chapter 10** considers how sustainability ambitions can be made 'actionable' at scale, by exploring the 'power dimension'. In a VUCA world – packed with power imbalances and power exertion that add to the wickedness of problems – *not taking corporate power into account would present a naive position. Power abuse* is perhaps one of the most *overrated* aspects in the critical discourse on sustainable business, feeding into almost ideological cynicism on the 'greenwashing' nature of CSR efforts. Smart *power use*, on the other hand, is one of the most *underrated* aspects in the constructive discourse on sustainable business model innovation, feeding into overly optimistic and gullible expectations of companies' willingness to engage in sustainability at a sufficiently ambitious level. This chapter connects **corporate power exercise** – at the societal level, in value chains and across borders – to realistic strategies for impact-driven change. It operationalizes the power base of core/lead/focal organizations in terms of positioning, discursive and normalizing powers, spheres of influence, and 'hard', 'soft' and 'smart' power use. It also identifies **Key Decision-making Indicators (KDIs)** that define the nature of the strategic decisions that must be taken to overcome critical 'tipping points' in upgrading and upscaling sustainable business models. SDG alignment is accordingly elaborated as a strategic 'prioritization' and 'nexus' challenge: how to create leverage through smart combinations of SDG-targets that fit the corporate strategy. The design of an empowering **sustainable corporate story** conveying the 'logic' of societal value creation can provide a powerful means to mobilize and engage stakeholders.

MAKING IT FUNCTIONAL

'Walking the talk' and bridging the **intention-realization gap** also holds an operational challenge. Effective implementation of corporate sustainability ambitions into daily practice presents an *internal alignment challenge* in search of **operational fit**, while concomitantly maintaining a dynamic balance with the ever-changing business environment. Organizational transitioning affects different parts of the organization differently. Strategizing and organizing become intertwined, representing a formidable vertical and horizontal alignment challenge. How to govern change and manage internal processes of *integration, coordination and coherence*? And in parallel, how to *map, measure, report and communicate* on SDG-relevant progress, performance and impact amidst a 'metrics jungle'? **Chapter 11** operationalizes the corporate sustainability approach at the level of functional departments. It dives into the diverse ambition levels, practices, drivers, balancing acts, barriers to action and key tipping points of seven functional management areas: purchasing, operations management, marketing, finance, HRM, innovation management and communication. It elaborates how Key Decision-making Indicators (Chapter 10) can be translated into **Key Performance Questions (KPQs)** and contextualized **Key Practice and Performance Indicators (KPIs)** to help companies navigate operational coherence across functional departments and guide transition processes towards higher levels of sustainability. The chapter shows how vertical and horizontal alignment around *internally actionable SDG-targets* can be used to leverage organizational processes of sustainability integration, coordination and coherence. SDG fiches per functional department provide entries for further exploring leads towards an SDG portfolio that is both strategically and operationally 'fit'.

MAKING IT COLLABORATIVE

Chapter 12 then moves on to the meso level: how to develop effective and impact-driven SDG partnering strategies? Cross-sector partnerships (CSPs) are widely recognized as a key enabler and the principal way forward to serve the SDGs. For many companies, the question is not *whether* CSPs are relevant in operationalizing and implementing their SDG ambition, but rather *how* such partnerships can be successfully formed, organized, governed, intensified and eventually phased out. Cross-sector collaboration is complex – and *collaborative value* challenging to create and harness – which is among the primary reasons why on the ground progress on the SDGs has been slow. This chapter addresses the kind of motivational drivers, choices, tensions and dynamic complexities to anticipate in processes of **(re)configuring, managing and upgrading SDG-fit partnerships**. It looks into foundational organizational, relational and adaptive design challenges, varying ambition levels and governance logics among organizational partners, partnership 'fit' dimensions for impact, and CSP efficiency and effectiveness considerations. Effective partnering for the SDGs calls for 'complexity-sensitive' intervention strategies ('Theory of Change') and developmental evaluation methods that allow for 'learning and adjusting while doing', to develop ever more effective interventions along the way. Accordingly, this chapter delineates four **impact loops** for learning and partnership upgrading, and concludes with a corporate level strategic challenge: how to reconfigure and manage a **portfolio of partnerships** by using the SDGs as reference frame for partnership portfolio improvements.

REFERENCES

Business & Sustainable Development Commission (2017). *Better Business, Better World.*

Mintzberg, H. (2015). *Rebalancing Society. Radical Renewal Beyond Left, Right and Centre.* Oakland, CA: Berrett-Koehler Publishers.

UN (2015). *Transforming Our World: The 2050 Agenda for Sustainable Development.* New York: United Nations.

UN Global Compact & DNV GL (2020). *Uniting Business in the Decade of Action. Building on 20 Years of Progress.* UN Global Compact 20th Anniversary Progress Report.

UN Global Compact & Accenture Strategy (2019). *The Decade to Deliver. A Call to Business Action. The United Nations Global Compact – Accenture Strategy CEO Study on Sustainability 2019*, September.

7 MAKING IT RESILIENT

DEALING WITH TRIGGERING EVENTS

DOI: 10.4324/9781003098355-10

P
R
I
N
C
I
P
L
E
S

- **Foundational Principles of Sustainable Business:** micro-elaboration and application of the SDG-agenda's five basic (macro) principles: *People*, *Planet*, *Prosperity*, *Peace* and *Partnering* – from the 'Triple-P' bottom line, to the 'Quintuple-P' bottom line.

- **Resilience principle:** a sustainable business model is a resilient business model, able to anticipate and effectively respond to shocks and crises.

- **Subsidiarity principle:** applied to triggering events; distinguish between incidents, structural events and systemic crises for attributing responsibilities and identifying adequate intervention levels.

- **Proportionality principle:** ensure a reasonable balance between the event and adopted response. An intervention should not be more severe than is necessary for the objective pursued ('overshooting'), neither should it be less severe than the situation requires ('undershooting'). Actions must be in line with the direct aim/need and the longer-term purposes pursued.

- **Accumulation and legitimacy principles:** no responsibility taken at the societal level (levels 3 and 4) can substitute for *not* taking sufficient responsibility within the direct sphere of influence (levels 1 and 2). Trust-building is accumulative; it is founded on convincingly taking care of primary responsibilities ('fiduciary duties'), and continuing to build from there.

- **'Total recall' principle:** if you have direct responsibility, take it unconditionally.

- **Charity principle:** privileged people should protect the interests of the less privileged.

- **Stewardship principle:** refers to the confidence interested parties place in decision makers and managers to act responsibly and take into account the interests of those affected by business decisions.

- **Managerial discretion principle:** individual managers are moral actors who are capable of moral reasoning in reaching specific decisions.

7.1 INTRODUCTION: FAILURE AND RESILIENCE – AN EVOLVING AGENDA FOR THE PRIVATE SECTOR

"Never let a good crisis go to waste"
Winston Churchill

"By failing to prepare, you are preparing to fail"
Benjamin Franklin

Covid-19: "We're all in this together"
SDGs: "No one left behind"

Nowadays, the world is experiencing a rapidly increasing number of 'events' that are difficult to fathom or act upon. Chapter 1 characterized the present stage as Volatile, Uncertain, Complex and Ambiguous. A VUCA world confronts us with many diverging tendencies and fragmenting dynamics that trigger incidents, conflicts and even outright crises. Amidst this turbulent unpredictability, societies are seeking 'resilience' – the capacity to survive, adapt and grow in the face of societal stresses and shocks. Such 'stresses and shocks' come in different shapes and forms, and with varying scopes of impact. There are incidents, which are relatively 'easy' to repair; there are structural problems, which usually require more concerted action; and there is systemic failure, which necessitates a profound rethinking of the very design of conventional ways of organizing and accordingly calls for transformational change. Parts I and II delineated societal and systemic principles that – together – define vital conditions for more resilient pathways towards sustainable development. Part II (Chapter 4) identified multiple sources of ambiguity and wickedness, and concluded that where analytical, contextual, institutional and distributional aspects become entangled, resilient strategies are exceedingly difficult to draw out. Nonetheless, Part II (Chapter 5) also delineated ways out of real or perceived crises, notably through collaborative arrangements.

Societal and systemic resilience ultimately depend on the resilience of the *organizations* that constitute society. In addition to a broader (macro) perspective on societal dynamics, the search for societal resilience hence additionally requires an intimate understanding of the role that *private organizations* play in the strengthening or weakening of societal resilience. When are these organizations part of the problem? How can they become part of 'the solution'? The management literature looks at these questions as an *epistemic* challenge: how can private organizations become an agent for positive change in the wider *social-ecological system* (SES) in which they are embedded (Williams et al., 2017), and how to cover for the wider effects of specific micro-interventions of organizations on the whole system (Hahn et al., 2017)? More concretely: can corporate sustainability strategies effectively contribute to sustainable development and enhance social, economic and ecological resilience at the same time?

The resilience of organizations, societies and people hinges to a significant degree on how they cope with and bounce back from so-called 'triggering events' that prompt them to reconsider 'business as usual' and start addressing 'failure' at various levels of intervention (Box 7.1). As Milton Friedman stated: "Only a crisis – actual or perceived – produces real change. When that crisis occurs, the actions that are taken depend on the ideas that are lying around" (Friedman, 1962: xiv). This chapter synthesizes which ideas on sustainable and resilient organizing have been lying on the table and how effective these have been in the past. The main aim of this chapter is to link corporate approaches to triggering events and define what can be considered more or less 'resilient' strategies – not only in theory, but also in practice.

BOX 7.1

RESILIENCE QUALITIES

Achieving resilience presents a multilayered challenge:

- **Personal resilience:** "the process of adapting well in the face of adversity, trauma, tragedy, threats or significant sources of stress – such as family and relationship problems, serious health problems, or workplace and financial stressors" (American Psychological Association);

- **Social or group/community resilience:** "the ability of groups or communities to cope with external stresses and disturbances as a result of social, political and environmental change" (Adger, 2000), which calls for "the ability of community members to take meaningful, deliberate, collective action to remedy the effect of a problem, including the ability to interpret the environment, intervene, and move on" (Pfefferbaum et al., 2005);

- **Organizational resilience:** "the ability of an organization to absorb and adapt in a changing environment to enable it to deliver its objectives and to survive and prosper. More resilient organizations can anticipate and respond to threats and opportunities, arising from sudden or gradual changes in their internal and external context" (International Organization for Standardization);

- **Societal resilience** "is the capacity to survive, adapt and grow in the face of societal stresses and shocks". This requires the ability to analyse complex societal problems; collect, analyse and interpret big data; allowing people to collaborate with societal stakeholders to achieve sustainable solutions for societal issues (Institute for Societal Resilience, Free University Amsterdam);

- **Systems resilience** (related to social-ecological systems) is the capacity "to absorb or withstand perturbations and other stressors such that the system remains within the same regime, essentially maintaining its structure and functions. It describes the degree to which the system is capable of self-organization, learning and adaptation" (Resilience Alliance).

B
O
X

7.1

Principles of organizational resilience

The perspective taken in this chapter is on how organizational resilience can contribute to societal and systems resilience. We follow the argumentation of the International Organization for Standardization (ISO), which states that: "Climate change, economic crises and consumer trends are just some of the pitfalls that can dramatically affect the way an organization does business and survives."[2]

Although there are many definitions, most concepts of 'resilience' focus on capacities to 'absorb', 'adapt' and 'recover' from shocks. Resilience, to some extent, overlaps with attributes such as robustness, fault-tolerance, flexibility, survivability and agility (Hosseini et al., 2016). In the sustainability discourse, however, the ***regenerative capacity*** of resilience for renewal, reorganization, development and the potential to create opportunity for doing new things and to innovate is of particular importance. "Managing for resilience enhances the likelihood of sustaining desirable pathways for development in changing environments where the future is unpredictable and surprise is likely" (Folke, 2006: 254).

In 2017, the ISO introduced an 'organizational resilience' standard (ISO 22316), a framework developed with experts around the world to guide organizations in future-proofing their business to be better placed to respond to potential risks and harness opportunities as well. The standard is based on seven principles for developing organizational resilience attributes.

An organization's resilience . . .

■   . . . is enhanced when behaviour is aligned with a shared vision and purpose;

■   . . . relies upon an up-to-date understanding of an organization's context;

■   . . . relies upon an ability to absorb, adapt and effectively respond to change;

■   . . . relies upon good governance and management;

■   . . . is supported by a diversity of skills, leadership, knowledge and experience;

■   . . . is enhanced by coordination across management disciplines and contributions from technical and scientific areas of expertise;

■   . . . relies upon effectively managing risk.

THE VARIOUS FUNCTIONS OF WAKE-UP CALLS

Triggering events have regularly acted as a 'wake-up call' for organizations, pointing out that they had been heading down the 'wrong track' – sometimes even without knowing it. Managers came to understand that their 'business and management as usual' way of operating was no longer accepted or deemed legitimate. Many organizations consequently adopted reactive strategies and invested in communication

---

2   https://www.iso.org/news/Ref2189.htm

activities, issues management practices and CSR departments. In the aftermath of events, international organizations responded by issuing guidelines (OECD guidelines), voluntary standards (ISO 26000) and compacts (UN Global Compact). Governments pioneered more strict regulation, demanded more transparency in reporting and penalized companies for obvious misbehaviour. Companies adopted codes of conduct, engaged in 'roundtables' (e.g. Caux, Sustainable Palm Oil and Soy), embraced trademarks or labels (e.g. Fairtrade, Rainforest Alliance), and developed philanthropic strategies to deal with increased demands for scrutiny.

Arguably, many of these initiatives have had limited effects on sustainable development. Critical studies on the actual behaviour of companies suggest a considerable gap between 'talk' and 'walk', or between 'promise' and 'performance'. These phenomena have been explained by the *disconnect* between the nature of the triggering event and how companies acted on it. Authors like George Frynas even speak about the "false developmental promise of Corporate Social Responsibility" when covering multinational oil companies' response to a variety of direct triggering events (Frynas, 2005).

Triggers can be internally or externally induced, and can create positive or negative change; they can represent incidents, but can also be a sign of systemic failure. In a VUCA world, the number of issue-related 'risks' that companies are faced with has noticeably increased. But how to distinguish between incidents as incidents, and incidents as a sign of more persistent and systemic root causes? How to address various types of triggering events and ruminate resilient approaches? Chapters 4 and 5 defined ways to map the complexity of problems (Scoreboard #1) and possible ways to approach this complexity at four levels of intervention (Scoreboard #2). Chapter 5 also identified partnering approaches as, in practice, often 'overshooting' or 'undershooting' the actual complexity of the problem, leaving the problem insufficiently addressed, with regular re-emergence of issues and additional problems popping up in later phases. This chapter applies the conceptual and analytical models of Part II to explore first lessons on 'how to organize' a case-sensitive approach that connects issue to intervention.

First, this chapter will describe how the scientific thinking on the role of 'business in society' has been triggered by societal issues and events over time. The accumulated insights of decades of scholarly attention are synthesized as *foundational principles of sustainable business* (section 7.2). Management thinking on effective and resilient responses to societal challenges has largely developed along these lines as well. Section 7.3 then classifies various events that companies have been facing in the 21st century as incidents, structural problems or systemic crises. Sections 7.3.1–7.3.4 present illustrative cases and ways to analyse triggering episodes, by using the analytical models as elaborated in Part II. Section 7.4 considers the most recent systemic crisis: the Covid-19 pandemic that rapidly spread across the globe in the first half of 2020. The pervasive effects triggered by the pandemic have exposed the manifold vulnerabilities and system risks of a highly interconnected (global) society and economy. It unfolded a new landscape of (VUCA) challenges that lie ahead in the decade to come. With the future left highly uncertain, successful acceleration of the SDG-agenda for the 2020–2030 period will – more than before – depend on accumulated societal resilience for sustainable organizing (section 7.5).

7.2 MAINSTREAMING SUSTAINABLE BUSINESS: ACCUMULATING TIMELY INSIGHTS

Recent scholarly and societal thinking on the role of the private sector in dealing with societal issues has mostly run parallel with major societal developments: the end of the cold war, highlighted by the fall of the Berlin wall in 1989, the consecutive rise of globalization, the emergence of the fourth industrial revolution since the turn of the millennium, the advent of corporate scandals, and the increase in rivalry resulting from ascending economic and political powers (in particular, China) since 2015. Over the years, trust in corporations as 'societal actors' alternately increased and decreased, following incidents and scandals – as did trust in governments, NGOs, the media and even science. Since the 1960s, the societal role companies play has evolved from a marginal topic in social sciences (including management studies) into a core theme. In different stages, studies have focused on different aspects of corporate behaviour: from fraud and power abuse, via broader governance and value chain issues, to – nowadays – companies' more systemic contributions to the provision of global public goods.

What is currently referred to as 'corporate social responsibility' and customarily abbreviated as 'CSR', has been an umbrella term that encompasses a hodgepodge of concepts and meanings that date back to the second phase of the industrial revolution in the mid-19th century (Van Tulder with Van der Zwart, 2006). Over time, the meaning and content of CSR as a concept have become contested (Carroll, 1999) to the extent that in 2003, strategic management professor Michael Porter referred to the CSR field as "a religion with too many priests" (European Business Forum, 2003). Nonetheless, it is both instructive and necessary to select the most relevant insights in this field that have been accumulated in scientific thinking, relate them to the period in which they matured (and the managerial thinking they enticed), and then apply them to the most recent events in which companies have been involved.

SOCIETAL ORIGINS OF CAPITALISM
The notion of the social responsibility of corporations and of companies operating beyond their immediate (market) boundaries is as old as capitalism itself.

In the constituting phases of global capitalism and mass production during the second industrial revolution in the 19th century, business leaders were often also societal leaders, actively involved in the shaping of a new society and new societal structures – regularly at odds with societal interests as represented by churches, trade unions or the government. The founders of large industrial companies – many of them still key economic players today – became active in council housing and sometimes even built entire city quarters for their employees, including kindergartens, schools, libraries, sports facilities and shops. All over the world, 'enlightened' industrialists like Siemens, Krupp, Philips, Edison (General Electric), Carnegie, VanderBilt, Rockefeller and Lever Brothers (Unilever) developed initiatives that ranged from corporate philanthropy to setting up entire villages. Their motives were more or less identical: fear of labour unrest and radicalism; keeping rising trade unions at bay; a sense of duty, based in religious convictions; attracting labour forces from the countryside; using the initiatives for promotional purposes (McEwen, 2001). Interestingly, the modern 21st-century discourse on the role of companies in society still contains many of these fundamental historical elements: can companies be held responsible for societal issues? Can they become agents of change? What about the role of other societal actors, and how to interpret the heightened attention of many companies to public goods provision and systemic resilience? Can CEOs be trusted to walk their talk? How to create societies in which companies contribute to societal resilience? In the 19th and 20th centuries, society defined a multitude of approaches to these fundamental questions, often after considerable struggles (including world wars and class conflicts, succinctly discussed in Chapter 1). These struggles eventually resulted in a variety of societal arrangements and distinct sustainability/CSR regimes in regions around the world (see section 6.5).

BUSINESS 'AND' SOCIETY: 1960–1994 (CSR 1.0)

Fast forward to the 20th century, the post-World War II period. Since 1960, the paternalism of the 19th century has been making way for a more reactive stance of corporations towards society. This ran parallel with the development of the welfare state in many of the developed countries, and the rapid internationalization and separation of the 'market' sector from other sectors in society. Management scholars started to talk about 'business *and* society'. The establishment of critical consumer organizations in the 1950s and 1960s and the first protests against environmental degradation in the 1970s focused the spotlight on companies' responsibilities vis-à-vis other societal actors. Howard Bowen's book *Social Responsibilities of the Businessman* (1953) started off the 'modern era' of CSR thinking (cf. Carroll, 1999).

In the 1980s, specialized corporate departments were created to pursue 'bridging' activities. External/Public Affairs departments were set up to deal with so-called 'issues management' and various 'community relations' functions, including media, customer and investor relations, and governmental affairs. Ed Freeman was the first to point out that the corporate relationship with *stakeholders* contains important strategic elements. He defined stakeholders as "any group or individual who can affect or is affected by the achievement of the organization's objective" and argued that they have an important role to fulfil in defining the mission and aims of a company (Freeman, 1984: 64). An underlying thought of Freeman and others was that there is a direct correlation between the (financial) performance of a company and the relationship with its stakeholders.

BUSINESS 'IN' SOCIETY: 1995–2006 (CSR 2.0)

But the real thinking on CSR originated in the 1990s. This period runs more or less parallel with the coming of age of globalization. Most overviews consider the globalization era as the point of departure for modern thinking on corporate responsibilities (Blowfield and Murray, 2019). The fall of the Berlin wall in 1989 signalled the 'start of the end of the cold war'; the formalization of the World Trade Organization (WTO) in 1995 ushered in the *era of globalization* and triggered an unprecedented increase in international trade and investment. An increasingly interdependent world economy, with one dominant economic model (capitalism), became more vulnerable to the behaviour of the most important carriers of globalization: multinational enterprises.

The start-up phase of scholarly thinking on *corporate responsiveness* to societal concerns (CSR 2.0) can, therefore, be traced back to the second half of the 1990s, when significant triggering events occurred around oil spills and human rights violations. No country or region was spared. Major questions were raised about the responsibility of companies and corporate leaders for their own (mis) behaviour and fiduciary duty to society. In this period, companies were engaging in CSR primarily for fear of losing reputation (and thus societal legitimacy). The media started to cover a growing number of scandals in which companies were involved (Box 7.2). The question on the nature of these events popped up: stand-alone incidents or a sign of structural wrongs? The societal discussion consequently concentrated around codes of conduct, better corporate governance regulation, and higher penalties for company leaders who did not abide by their fiduciary duty. This duty foremost involved primary stakeholders (shareholders, financiers, employees, customers) who were directly affected by their actions, but increasingly also came to include the effects on stakeholders who were indirectly affected (such as suppliers, communities and other stakeholders susceptible to the negative externalities of corporate action – see Chapter 5).

TURBULENT TIMES (1995–2006): REVEALING INCIDENTS AT LEVELS 1 AND 2

Corporate scandals that reached the international media:

1995–2001

Rico; OSC; TEPCO; nuclear plant scandal; WorldCom; Funeral Industry; Enron; Crean; Bcom3; SEC; Ottawa; Manley; Cheney; Halliburton; Harvey Pitt; Chaebol; Samsung; Shell (Brent Spar, Nigeria); Hyundai; Xerox; Bloomberg; Big Biz; CPP; GE; GOP; GBP telecom scandal; O'Neill; Peregrine; Walmart; TSX; PwC; Manulife; Nasa; Probe; Stonewall; DaimlerChrysler; Mitsubishi; General Motors; Labatt's; Sokaiya; Nomura; Keidanren; Cadbury; ADM; Long-Term Capital Management (LTCM); ASIC; Osler, Ernst & Young; YBM; McDowell; CBN; internet security firms; Barings Bank; Bre-X, Livent; Equitable Life Assurance Society; HIH Insurance; WorldCom; Waste Management;

2002–2006

NYSE; pension accounting; Keidanren; Arthur Andersen; Tyco; WorldCom; Livent; KPMG; Adelphia Communications; TwoSons; Nigeria, Atiku, Ican; Bush, Cheney; XEROX; Enron; McCormicks; Ernst & Young; SACOB; TD; Telegraph; Keidanren; Tyco; NYSE; Grasso; Enron; Citigroup; JP Morgan; WorldCom; Deloitte; HKSA; PIMCO; Viacom; Phyllis Davis; HealthSouth; Boston Globe; Evergreen; Ahold; Dow Jones; Scrushy; Putnam; Tsang Yam Pui; HKSA; Zambia, BoZ; ABA; WorldCom; ASIC; Fedsure; Ebbers; Hannover settlement; Partnoy; HealthSouth; Whetstone; Kebble; Adelphia; Freddie Mac; Enron; Marsh; Morningstar; Tyco; Shell; MMC scandal; Nortel; Seibu; Parmalat; Omaha Charitable Group; SK; Enron; NCFE; Tyco; BDO; Leisurenet Saga; Ebbers; Samsung; Doosan; Royal Dutch Shell; Refco; Kanebo; PERAC; Chaebol; Westport ZO; Forex; Gomery; François Beaudoin; Donaldson; Fannie Mae; AIG scandal; Nortel, Susan Shephard; MCI; Enron; ASIC; WorldCom; CFTC; DPP; Oates; Hollinger fraud charges; Ebbers; HealthSouth, Richard Scrushy; Fraud-i Ltd; Adelphia; Tyco, Kozlowsky, Swartz; Black; Radler; Hollinger intl.; Bayou Hedge Fund; Refco; IBM; Siemens; Howard; Hurd, HP; McKesson Case; Lender; Shenzhen Expressway; CPPCC; Ocean Grand scandal; CJ; Murakami; Enron; Freddie Mac; Chaebol; Hyundai Automotive Group; TSE; Chen Jiulin; Bourse; Enron; WorldCom Scandal; Livedoor; McKesson Execs; Zambia, money laundering; Tyco; Westar; AIG; CipherTrust

Source: based on LexisNexis (corporate and scandal/fraud)

The origins of *business ethics* can also be traced back to this period. The dilemmas that companies noticeably faced have been extensively covered in a wide body of literature – ranging from corporate integrity considerations related to failed products, transparency in accounting, insider trading and the trade-off between employee safety and profits, to the extent to which a law-abiding company can still be held responsible and liable for the consequences of its behaviour. It became acknowledged that the ethical foundations of CSR ultimately rest on two principles: the *charity* principle and the *stewardship* principle (Frederick, Post and Davis, 1992). The *charity* principle refers to the notion that privileged people should protect the interests of the less privileged. The *stewardship* principle refers to the confidence interested parties place in managers to take into account the interests of those affected by business decisions. Firms should not only create wealth for themselves; they should also meet their social, ethical and ecological responsibilities, and publicly account for it. The fulfilment of these responsibilities requires companies to undertake initiatives that promote economic welfare, social well-being and a healthy environment beyond what is legally required. The principle of *managerial discretion* (Carroll, 1979) complements these principles, in that it views individual managers as *moral actors* who are capable of moral reasoning in reaching specific decisions.

The 'business *in* society' (BiS) school of thought further developed the academic foundations of these ideas. An apparent strong connection between financial and social performance encouraged managers to pay more attention to 'corporate communication' and 'business ethics', which in turn gave rise to the formulation of ethical guidelines for responsible management and company conduct (Kaptein and Wempe, 2002). The communication with stakeholders became based upon ethical/moral concepts like 'trust', 'reliability', 'social involvement', 'cooperation', 'accountability' and 'responsible entrepreneurship'. In this period, management also started to recognize the more visible role of business in society (McWilliams and Siegel, 2001). In many countries around the world, businesses entered into various societal dialogues to discuss how to add social and ecological value for both the company and society. Stakeholder management in BiS approaches was further enhanced by insights from *social contract theory*. A smoothly running economy and society are dependent on explicit as well as implicit contracts that are based on norms, trust, previous transactions, agreements and expectations (Donaldson and Dunfee, 1999). Anglo-Saxon countries started referring to the idea of corporate sustainability as the quest for 'corporate social responsibility' or CSR. Donna Wood (1991: 693) developed the first definition of *corporate social performance* (CSP) as "a business organization's configuration of principles of social responsibility, processes of social responsiveness, and policies, programs, and observable outcomes as they relate to the firm's societal relationships".

John Elkington's work on the exploration of CSR concepts became particularly influential and popular. In his book *Cannibals with Forks* (1999), Elkington distinguished between three dimensions of CSR, the so-called *Triple Bottom*

Line of *People*, *Planet* and *Profit* (see section 1.4.1). The Triple-P concept – introduced to reflect the 'triple helix' for corporate value creation to spur a 'new capitalism' of regenerating economies, societies and the biosphere – has since been used in a much more instrumental way than Elkington had intended (Elkington, 2018). This is not an isolated phenomenon in management thinking and practice: in reality, original and popular concepts are regularly misrepresented or 'flattened' to such an extent, that the original thinkers behind the concept distance themselves from their own legacy.

BUSINESS-SOCIETY MANAGEMENT: 2006–2014 (CSR 3.0)

Since the beginning of the 21st century, an increasing number of authors started avoiding a narrow interpretation of the term 'social responsibility', in particular "when translated into Continental European cultures and languages, as applying to social welfare issues only" (Andriof and McIntosh, 2001:15). With the introduction of the broader concept of *corporate social responsibility*, CSR shifted from a largely instrumental and managerial approach to one aimed at *managing strategic networks* where longer-term relationships with stakeholders are prominent in the strategic planning of the company. In the words of Björn Stigson, then president of the World Business Council for Sustainable Development: "Sustainable development is too big for companies to handle individually because it is critical to develop the right framework conditions, which can only be done by companies working together along the value chain. It also requires a broad interaction with stakeholders, to come to an understanding with society about how to address the challenge" (Stigson, 2000: 2).

This broader view was not a luxury, but rather an advisable necessity. The Edelman Trust Barometer revealed a crisis of leadership in companies, but also in governments (Edelman Trust, 2007). The need for a more strategic approach to corporate responsibilities was evident; for many companies, corporate *social* responsibility needed to further evolve into corporate *strategic* responsibility. Well-known business scholars had started to talk about the 'fortune at the bottom of the pyramid' (Prahalad, 2004) or emphasized the link between competitive advantage and corporate social responsibility (Porter and Kramer, 2006). Later on, this became better known as the need to think in terms of 'shared value creation' (Porter and Kramer, 2011).

A 'business-society' approach developed, along with techniques like (strategic) stakeholder dialogue, balanced scorecards, impact investment, sustainable supply chain, and the mainstreaming of trademarks, labels (MSC, FSC, Fairtrade). It became recognized that it is only through the systematic and structural exchange of facts, opinions and values with stakeholders that companies can stay in touch with evolving or new responsibilities imposed upon them. This development signalled the quest for the *balanced company*: a company that has not only a moral identity, but also combines medium-term profitability and longer-term sustainability (Kaptein and Wempe, 2002).

In this timespan, major incidents still occurred. Companies and corporate leaders showed that they continued to struggle with the execution of their primary fiduciary duties (Box 7.3). Closer scrutiny of many of these events reveals that the responses of society, regulators and of companies themselves had changed to become more critical generally. Trust in companies to 'do the right thing' decreased. The fall of the 'celebrity CEO' emerged as a novel phenomenon, with several high-profile cases of CEOs – previously heralded for sectoral 'leadership' – who became exposed for mal-behaviour (in particular, related to accountancy issues).

CONTINUED TURBULENT TIMES – REVEALING STRUCTURES?

Corporate scandals that reached the international media:

BOX 7.3

2007–2011:

Samsung; Siemens; Nortel scandal; Nigeria Stock Exchange; oil companies; Misuzu; Nortel; World Bank; SFO; Adelphia, Rigases; Harris Scarfe trials; Midland frauds; BDO; Bloomberg; Tiger brands; KL; Boyd Johnson, Spitzer Tap; Volkswagen; Samsung Electronics; News Corp; Bear Stearns; Northern Rock; Lehman Brothers; AIG; Washington Mutual; Royal Bank of Scotland; ABN AMRO; Mukasey, mortgage fraud; ABCP; Graft Bothers, James Ogoola; Johnson Sirleaf; Matthew Hammond; Bernard Madoff Investment Securities; Transmile; NRL; Niehaus; King (South Africa); Satyam affair, India IT scandal; Enron; Nortel; Drabinsky; AWB fraud; Conrad Black; Anglo; Bre-x, Hollinger, Livent; TCF corporate; FBI; Satyam; Bursa; SGX; Hong Kong Bourse; Rockfort Finance; SFO; GFC; Conrad Black; Bournville Trust; AFH; F&C Investments; Olympus; Asia inc.; James Murdoch; News Corp; ISS; AMP; AFRA scam; BSkyB; phone hacking scandal; News of the World; Telecoms scam; Sino Forest; ACFE

2012–2018:

Sky; James Murdoch; Florida SBA; BSkyB; BBC; Hermes; News Corp; Rupert Murdoch, phone hacking scandal; Olympus; RBA; ASIC; Walmart; Leveson inquiry; Rabobank's Libor scandal; Vince Cable; Tony Blair, Gordon Brown, News of the World; Orange scandal; Madoff; Pension fund scandal Japan; AIJ investment firm; Patricia Dunn; corporate credit card fraud; Dynergy; Rana Plaza; China Medical Technologies; ASIC; the Leighton files; Sias; BBC; Cipla Medpro; PetroSA, Kaizer Nyatsumba; News Corp; phone hacking and Shine deal; Rupert Murdoch; Edelman (trust barometer); NHS, (Sir) David Nicholson; SNC; Demo Africa; BBC; SAC; NDIC; Olympus; China North East Petroleum; ENRC; Rabobank (Libor); Petrobras; Cashbet; ASIC; STX; Addleshaw Goddard; KWM; Glaxo; Mr Tomana (Zimbabwe); SFO; Banco

BOX 7.3

Espirito Santo (BES); VW (Volkswagen) diesel emissions, Martin Winterkorn; Exxon; Brazil's mining disaster (Samarco-Vale); Toshiba, Hisao Tanaka; Deepwater Horizon (BP); Moody's; Pimco Sues; Daimler; Deutschland AG; Deutsche; Hermes; Petrobras (corruption); Japan Inc.; Rupert Murdoch News UK; Crown Prosecution services; Phone hacking scandal; BCCI; Enron; Olympus; Barclays; HSBC; Tesco; FIFA; Orix; Sony; LatAm; ColTel; Shkerli; White & Case; Dechert; EFCC; 1MDB; Satyam; BHS; SGX; Sky; James Murdoch; BHS; Beachcroft; Green Scandal; Volkswagen; AGM; Hermes; Mitsubishi Motors; car industry emissions scandal; bank scandal; big oil investigation; Fox; SFC; HK bourse; Steinhoff; JSE; Deloitte; Olympus Scandal; Kobe Steel; Mitsubishi Materials; Paradise Papers; Japan Inc.; Uber; Sky; Bradley letters; Fox (phone hacking scandal); Ofcom; Chris Jordan; Plutus payroll fraud scandal; Volkswagen; Sky; Christopher Williams; AFP; Hill and Knowlton; Apple; Equifax; NNPC; VimpelCom; Panama Papers; Gangs-LinkedIn; HBOS; Wells-Fargo; Scott Pruitt; Wan Azizah; Get Back; Korean Air; Steinhoff; Absa; AMP; Dieselgate Volkswagen; Kobe Steel; Hiroya Kawasaki; Marks & Spencer; Starbucks; Heathrow Airport; Vale (dam); Visa; Samsung; Edgewise; Microsoft; Facebook (privacy); Google, Apple, Amazon (tax evasion); ING (whitewashing); Uber; BCLP; Macfarlanes; AVID

Source: based on LexisNexis (corporate and scandal/fraud); *Forbes* and other media coverage (the worst accounting scandals of all time).

Structural factors gradually became more apparent. Scandals were increasingly related to entire sectors – e.g. finance, the oil industry, mining – and to global value chains, particularly in commodities due to generally poor labour conditions. Rapid globalization opened up opportunities for expansion, but also created heightened risk and turbulence. The financial crisis of 2007 made audiences around the world aware of the (potential of) major flaws in how entire sectors had organized their transboundary activities and associated responsibilities. In 2012, the collapse of a garment factory in Bangladesh – with more than 1,000 deaths (Rana Plaza) – reiterated the dark side and vulnerability of international value chains. The list of scandals that reflect structural flaws is extensive and includes oil spills in the Gulf of Mexico (BP Deep Water Horizon, 2010 and its aftermath); slavery and child labour in the cocoa chain in Ivory Coast (2012); corruption and human rights violations (Foxcom-Apple, 2012); selling bad mortgages and spreading risks through securitization to other countries (origins of the global financial crisis, 2008); tax evasion in developed and developing countries (since 2010 topic of congressional hearings around the world); the illicit harvesting of personal data, privacy issues and election tampering (Facebook, 2016); security and intellectual property concerns (Huawei, 2019).

In most of these cases, companies and their managers largely complied with the laws of the country in which, or from which, they were operating. In a strict sense, they did nothing 'illegal'. But the public discourse nevertheless started to seriously question the sustainability of these business models and their potentially debilitating impact on the resilience of societies. Laasch and Conaway (2015), for instance, note that "the second millennium has seen not only an increase in the number of global issues and crises, but also an increasing inter-relatedness and convergence of those crises towards a global mega-crisis trig-gered by multiple causes. Such systemic challenges are increasingly interrelated, which makes solving them more complex" (ibid: 10).

MAINSTREAMING: SUSTAINABLE BUSINESS (CSR 4.0)

This short historical overview shows that the thinking on the role of companies in society has been intimately related to, and influenced by, societal develop-ments. Accordingly, the CSR concept has been assigned different meanings over time for contextual, historical and disciplinary reasons. The focus gradually shifted: from CSR 1.0 (Corporate *Self* Responsibility), through CSR 2.0 (Corporate Social *Responsiveness*), to CSR 3.0 (Corporate *Social and Strategic* Responsibility), and nowadays towards CSR 4.0 (Corporate *Societal/ Sustainable* Responsibility).

With each period, the understanding of the 'fiduciary duties' of companies expanded (Figure 7.1), from a narrow focus on mere 'shareholder value', via 'stakeholder value', to also include 'future stakeholders' (next generations) and their needs. With a broader view on the scope of relevant stakeholders and related business cases, an expanding view on the *societal license* companies are expected to embrace developed: from a license to exist, via a license to operate, towards a license to scale and experiment (section 6.6). Despite progressing insights on the actual and potential role of companies in society, corporate scan-dals kept on reoccurring. Scandals related to breaches of primary (narrow) and secondary fiduciary duties (negative externalities), increasingly revealed structural and systemic patterns and flaws. Societal trust in companies to 'do the right thing' changed over time. Scandals were not confined to for-profit organizations only however. Many state-owned enterprises, public-private utility companies and non-profit organizations (hospitals, NGOs, universities) were faced with similar events (see Chapter 6 on governance/organizational hybridity and the influence of various regulatory regimes).

Periods and meanings overlap in the scientific and popular discourse. The CSR abbreviation is used in different – and often confusing – connotations in various places around the world. An increasing number of managers and manage-ment scholars hence prefer not to use the CSR abbreviation at all. The OECD embraced the term *responsible business conduct* (RBC); the International Organization for Standardization (ISO) uses the term *responsible organizing* (RO) to avoid confusion around the CSR acronym. This book adopts a

Topic	Start-up phase: globalization	Interim phase: turbulence	Present phase: increased turbulence
Focus of CSR discourse	1.0 →2.0 Corporate Social Responsiveness	2.0 →3.0 Corporate Strategic/Social Responsibility	3.0 →4.0 Corporate Societal/Sustainable Responsibility
Stakeholder orientation	Shareholder value: inform/prove it to me	Stakeholder value: engage me	Strategic stakeholder value: empower me
Fiduciary duty	Narrow fiduciary duty (to primary stakeholders)	Broad fiduciary duty (to secondary stakeholders)	Prospective fiduciary duty (to future stakeholders)
License	License to exist (reponsibly serving markets)	License to operate (better serving needs)	License to scale and experiment (with unmet needs); common goals (SDGs); grand challenges
Corporate scandals	'Incidents': fraud, spills and human rights violations Leading topics: ecological	'Structures': corruption and accounting standards; self-regulation Leading topics: social and ecological	'Systemic': value chains, taxation and global goods provisions Leading topics: economic, social, ecological
Trust in business to do the 'right thing'*	Under the influence of NGOs: lowered trust	Fall of celebrity CEOs; business more trusted than governments and media (2007); crisis of leadership	'Fake news'; business to lead the debate for change; trust is essential for innovation; 2017/18: trust crisis; battle for trust

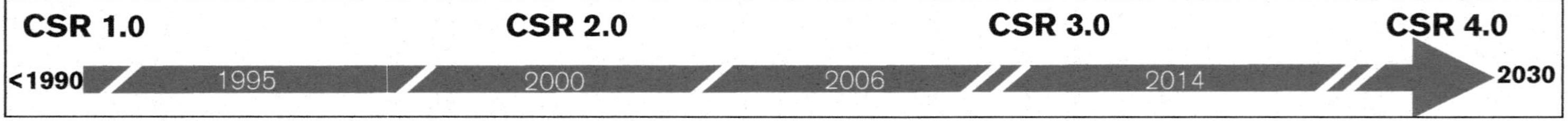

* Edelman Trust Barometer

CSR 1.0   CSR 2.0   CSR 3.0   CSR 4.0

<1990   1995   2000   2006   2014   2030

Figure 7.1 Phases of societal and disciplinary thinking on CSR

comparable logic but aims to synthesize all relevant insights of the past decades, rather than replace them with yet another new concept.

The present era – heading towards CSR 4.0 – has seen a stronger emphasis on the inclusion of societal goals and on contributing to a common purpose. The enhanced attention for sustainability and societal responsibility aligns with the SDG-agenda that materialized in 2014–2015, partly as the result of a more active role played by frontrunner companies (Chapter 2). The *purpose-driven company* emerged as a concept in the management discipline – with an increasing body of literature showing that organizing in a 'purposeful' way could foster more resilient organizations.[3] Both in the management sciences and in practice, *grand challenges* became topical and gained in relevance. The SDGs and the Paris Climate Agreement – both adopted in 2015 – signalled a breach in the silo-thinking of previous periods that considered business and society to be largely separate fields. Companies, with their innovative and scaling capacities, were acknowledged as playing an important role in achieving the SDGs – as partners in joint development goals. But the story so far remains mixed: in areas such as privacy, pollution (emissions, spills, plastics, chemicals), human rights violations and tax evasion, major companies are still a target for public indignation.

The thinking on the role of corporations in society – both in science and society – is presently reaching a new stage. Over the years, knowledge on the dilemmas that companies face and ways of dealing with them have (arguably) sufficiently accumulated. Basic textbooks on ethics, corporate responsibilities, responsible management and the like cover an abundance of cases. Strategic management thinkers have formulated new and innovative business ideas. In more specialized business research (e.g. on innovation, logistics, supply chain, human resource management, finance and marketing), sufficient knowledge has been gained to have a decent idea on partial strategies. The present challenge is to *combine* these insights with a new layer of ambitions, by which corporations and other private sector organizations can act as drivers of positive societal change, and as resourceful and vigorous contributors to sustainable development.

This is why we use the concept of 'sustainable business' as the synthesis of three generations and five decades of CSR thinking. *Principles of sustainable business* should then accumulate and integrate insights from three different corporate responsibility discourses: (a) societal developments and their impact on businesses (B&S); (b) the position of business in society (BiS); and (c) the interaction between business and society for common goals (B-SM).

3　Chapters 9, 10 and 11 will plug into this literature to show how the value proposition of an organization can have positive effects on a 'sustainable' or 'future-resilient' business model.

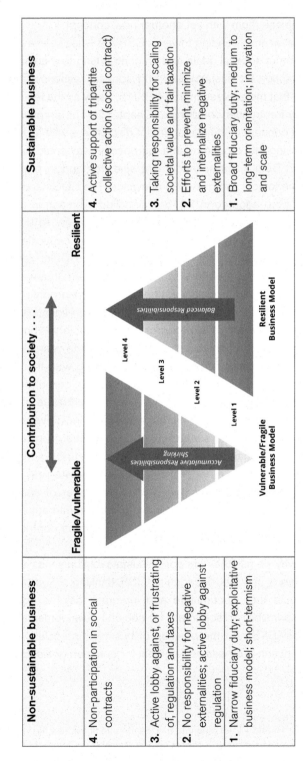

Figure 7.2 The pyramid of sustainable business: four intervention levels

FOUR DEFINING LEVELS OF SUSTAINABLE BUSINESS

Sustainable business contributes to the resilience of societies. Consistent with the frameworks elaborated in Part II that defined the basic characteristics of resilient and balanced societies, we distinguish four levels of intervention at which private organizations contribute to either a more, or a less, resilient society (Figure 7.2).

■ Levels 1 and 2

The resilient organization ultimately contributes to a resilient society by attaching importance to abiding by a broad set of fiduciary duties towards stakeholders, and by the development of an innovative business model that adds value to society. This creates a broad foundation – as an essential hygiene factor – for its 'license to exist' in that society. The fragile organization, on the other hand, adopts an 'exploitative' model; all responsibilities for the proper functioning of society that go beyond its narrowly defined fiduciary duty (e.g. making profits) are passed on to society ('shirking' fiduciary responsibilities). If this orientation is combined with limited own value added (e.g. exploiting market dominance, adopting extensive exploitative value chains, producing sin goods) and without bearing any responsibility for the costs of this business model for society (level 2), the organization is vulnerable to reputational damage and societal condemnation at some stage. Fragile companies operate on the brink of losing their societal license to produce – or to exist altogether.

■ Levels 3 and 4

Vulnerable companies further contribute to a more fragile society if they also actively lobby against regulation, frustrate change trajectories towards a more balanced society, or try to avoid taxes. In doing so, they put the responsibility of a well-functioning society entirely in the hands of others (in particular, governments and societal groups). The resilient organization, on the other hand, can be expected to actively contribute to the spurring of positive externalities and collective goods creation, even if it bears no direct responsibility. Resilient organizations take on shared responsibilities in partnerships, actively support the creation of social contracts, and understand the importance of fair taxation to enable governments to create a functioning, more balanced and resilient society. Resilient organizations understand that they are part of a societal ecosystem in which it is easier to innovate and engage in longer-term planning based on collective goals. Well-functioning companies need well-functioning governments to thrive in well-functioning societies. Chapter 5 elaborated the sources of societal failure at each level in more detail.

A sustainable business model takes the societal agenda as leading for its orientation and takes a balanced, layered approach that includes *all four levels* of intervention. As argued in Part I and II, the 17 Sustainable Development Goals and 169 targets of the 2030 Agenda can be considered a good proxy for cross-checking on the organization's degree of societal alignment. We hence propose to upgrade Elkington's Triple-P approach to encompass the **'Quintuple-P'** foundational principles of the SDGs as **leading principles of sustainable business: People, Planet, Prosperity, Peace and Partnering.** Applying these five leading principles on the level of the private sector organization then defines the basic architecture of 'sustainable business'. How to design and implement sustainable business models is the ultimate focus of Part III. How to make them resilient to triggering events at various levels of intervention, is the remaining topic of this chapter.

7.3 MAPPING THE NATURE OF TRIGGERING EVENTS AND (CORPORATE) RESPONSES

Oil spills, allegations of fraud, product liability, contested labour practices, stakeholder criticism, fear of stepped-up regulation. Responding to negative triggers and external events that could create reputational damage constitutes the basis of conventional *issue management techniques*. Throughout the years, companies have increasingly been confronted with sizable trust gaps, notably for taking insufficient action on failures of their own making, exploiting loopholes, denying responsibility, or for not 'walking their talk'. Organizations that repeatedly entice criticism or structurally underperform in external triggering events, lose societal legitimacy and ultimately the strategic and operational resilience needed to continue activities and engage in higher levels of sustainability.

In economics and finance research, so-called *event studies* have been used to (statistically) measure the effects of an economic event on the value of firms. Such an event can be *self-created*, for instance in the case of the announcement of a merger. An event analysis then tries to establish whether investors believe the merger will create or destroy value for shareholders, and how the timing of the announcement could manipulate stock prices (Ball and Brown, 1968). In sustainability research, event studies have often focused on cases of fraud and other breaches of (primary) fiduciary duties, and whether these harmed the company's reputation. Corporate communication studies have traditionally focused on how companies can repair damage inflicted by these self-created incidents (Van Riel and Blackburn, 1995). Increasingly, events studies are also used to assess the impact of *external events* – such as financial crises or the impact of market volatility – on the value of the company, and the adequacy of the company's response. Sustainability research is increasingly focusing on the 'resilience' of organizations in coping with external effects. The literature on *agile companies* and *agile leadership*, for instance, focuses on comparable issues, however without explicit reference to sustainable business. In most instances, event studies concentrate on the responsive side of joint-stock companies, for which effects are measured in terms of changes in stock returns, consumer preferences, and employee satisfaction ratios.

Within the framework of sustainable business, considering the adequacy of organizational responses to (external) triggering events by relating these to the resilience of business models is of key interest. The *proportionality principle* – mainly applied to weigh the impact of policy interventions, laws or the exercise of power in international relations – is relevant in that context. Proportionality, in general, implies that an action should not be *more* severe than is necessary for the objective pursued. Neither should an intervention be *less* severe than the situation requires; actions must be in keeping with the aim pursued. If the ultimate aim is to thrive in a well-functioning society – within a healthy ecosystem conducive to value creation, innovation and collaboration – what does this imply for dealing with various triggering events?

The management literature shows that it is much easier to adequately respond to an incident than to a structural or even systemic event. The worst responses were observed for issues that appeared to be an 'incident' but actually were a sign of a deeper (root) cause. To take proportionate and appropriate action, it is thus important to be able to distinguish between an incident and structural or systemic problems as well as to understand the problem's source. Is the triggering event: (1) a sign of a systemic (wicked) problem/opportunity; (2) a structural (complex) problem/opportunity; or (3) a (relatively simple) incident? The second dimension to a proportional action is the degree to which the company is, or can be held, (partially) responsible for the event. A layered and balanced approach to both having and taking responsibility (Chapter 5), put to use in good time, is a vital characteristic of a resilient business model.

Part II introduced a tool (Scoreboard #1) to assess whether an event can be considered a sign of relatively simple (level 1), complicated (level 2), complex (level 3) or wicked (level 4) problems. It also provided a tool (Scoreboard #2) to come up with preferred lines of responses (intervention logics). Table 7.1 links these dimensions together, provides some examples and describes preferred lines of response that management research has suggested over the years. The next sections will discuss exemplary events.

7.3.1 Corporate incidents

Incidents that represent particular flaws in the internal organization of the company's (core) activities can create an immediate and severe short-term reputation problem. Examples include unsafe products (e.g. glass found in a food product, as happened with Gerber and Heinz baby food products; problems with the engine control system in Toyota cars), or news media that report

Table 7.1 Distinct types of trigger events

Type of trigger event	Nature of trigger event	Examples/indications	Usual or preferred line of response
Corporate incident (7.3.1)	Related to own business model; own responsibility, and directly related to consumer	Technical problems; glass in baby food bottles; internal organization: accountancy fraud	Complete recall action; no fundamental change in business model needed, provided penalties are paid
Value chain incident (7.3.2)	Incidents in supply chain; own direct responsibility	Pollution; addictive products (cigarettes, alcohol); oil spills	End-of-pipeline mitigation; prevention; self-regulation; change in business model needed
	Incidents in supply chain; indirect responsibility	Supplier provides wrong (unsafe) equipment; poor working conditions in supply chain	Supplier code of conduct; recall actions; compensation payment; change in procurement practice
Structural and sectoral incident (7.3.3)	Incidents created by others in the same sector	Mad cow disease; speculation; corporate buy-backs; patent abuse; misinformation (fake news); data breaches/ personal data harvesting; flexible contracting of independent contractors	Entire sector and/or government need to take (radical action) to save the sector's reputation
	Actions of external societal stakeholders; created trigger events	Tax evasion schemes; deforestation; plastic soup; child labour	Code of conduct or accreditation schemes for the entire sector; structural adaptations in business models
Systemic trigger events: crisis (7.3.4)	Creeping crisis: smaller crises leading (beyond a tipping point) to collapse of entire system; wicked problem	Financial crises; debt/ currency crises; migration/ refugees; food system crises; climate crisis; ecological crisis; health crises (SARS, Ebola, Covid-19)	All societal parties need to act: common-pool problem; fundamental change in business model/value proposition needed

about a fraudulent employee. In principle, corporate incidents can be addressed by responsive strategies – that is, 'reactive' strategies aimed at avoiding (further) harm – that reflect the degree of responsibility the individual company *has* and hence can be expected to *take*. If the incident is within the realm of the company's *direct responsibility* (fiduciary duty), the effective way to respond to the incident is to convincingly take responsibility, for instance by means of a complete recall. Denial or awaiting the results of investigations on cause, fault and liability generally increases the reputational damage. Taking immediate and appropriate action can restore trust in the company – provided the company had a decent reputation before and communicates correctly throughout the event (Case #7.1).

CASE #7.1 THE VOLKSWAGEN DIESELGATE AFFAIR

The case

In 2015, the United States Environmental Protection Agency (EPA) found that Volkswagen (VW), the world's largest car producer from Germany, had been violating the Clean Air Act. The agency found that VW had intentionally manipulated its turbocharged direct injection diesel engines to cheat on emission controls during laboratory testing. During testing, the vehicles would score NOx output that met US standards, while in practical use emitting up to 40 times more NOx. VW had been deploying the related software in about 11 million cars worldwide since 2007.

The issue appears relatively simple: fraud. The response from different societal stakeholders around the world was varied: in the US, strict penalties and reputational damage; in Germany and Europe, the company was criticized, but not penalized. VW recalled millions of cars worldwide and set aside $6.4 billion to cover costs. In October 2016, the company posted its first quarterly loss in 15 years: $2.5 billion. In 2020, VW was reported to have paid 30 billion euros in claims and fines. The company twice replaced its CEO and stepped up its regulations and oversight on internal processes (level 1) and its supply chain (level 2).

A more strategic response was also triggered, with a radical shift towards battery-electric mobility in 2017. The company presently aims to roll-out almost 70 new electric models by 2028, in an effort to produce zero-emission cars and become CO_2-neutral by 2050 (level 3). In the meantime, focal stakeholders continue to hold the company responsible in courts around the world. In the UK, 90,000 car owners successfully issued a class action against the company, deemed to be the 'biggest consumer claim in UK history'. Important suppliers like Bosch have also been seen as part of the problem, with an off-court settlement in 2007 in the US for €303 million. Other European and American car companies like Fiat, Chrysler, Renault, Daimler, PSA and General Motors have been subject to investigation for comparable issues.

Analysis

In terms of the analytical frameworks presented in Chapters 4 and 5, the sequence of events that followed Dieselgate since 2015 can be portrayed as follows. The

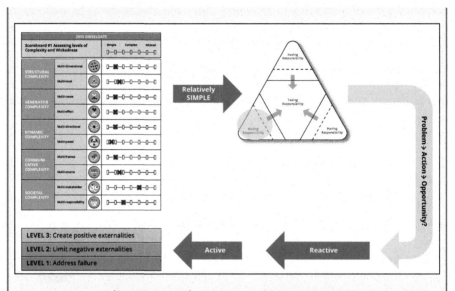

wickedness scale (Scoreboard #1) points to a relatively simple issue and a reasonably clear responsibility attribution (Scoreboard #2). Addressing the issue requires an appropriate response to avoid further harm: at level 1 (solving failure in core activities) *and* level 2 (negative externalities related to emissions). But because of strategic considerations – and its powerful position in the car industry, Germany and its supply chain (see Chapter 10) – the company decided to take additional action together with significant stakeholders (state, family, shareholders, trade unions). It adopted a change ambition (level 3, creating positive externalities) to speed up the transformation of the car industry in order to become more sustainable and serve societal needs for zero emissions, and a different approach to mobility. The company initiated a TOGETHER Strategy, directed towards '*sustainable growth*', by which the company aims to become an "excellent employer and a role model for the environment, safety and integrity, to excite customers". By 2025, VW endeavours to be the "world's number one in e-mobility". The company formulated a 'code of collaboration' for this strategy that encapsulates accompanying core values: 'open and honest', 'uncomplicated', 'without prejudice', 'on an equal footing', 'for one another'.

Reversing the odds?

Whether this intention, along with the formulated core values, will materialize, depends on the concrete internal and external alignment actions taken in practice. In 2017, the company explicitly embraced all SDGs, with the following argument: "as a global corporation, Volkswagen is committed to the SDGs and is actively contributing to the actualization of these global development goals through its innovative vehicles, intelligent mobility solutions and wide-ranging activities in support of sustainability." On its website, the company provides examples of its contributions to all SDGs, but frames this largely as part of its CSR projects (https://csrprojects.volkswagenag.com/dell/facts-and-figures/sustainable-development-goals.html).

7.3.2　Value chain incidents

Triggering events related to how companies source, produce and sell what kind of products – and under what conditions – potentially have a more profound effect on reputation and are less 'simple' to address than corporate incidents. Cases related to the long-term adverse effects of a particular production method (e.g. polluting or resource-inefficient industries; poor labour conditions; discards; deforestation; animal welfare; human rights abuses; use of pesticides, hormones, antibiotics in food chains); of a particular product or service (e.g. physical, emotional, psychological health impact; indebtedness; disinformation; privacy infringements); or endemic fraud in specific sectors, point to a weak motivation of companies to actively address the negative effects of their operations. It constitutes grounds for a fickle to rather poor reputation that – sooner or later – may seriously jeopardize the company's societal license to operate, or even to exist.

Value chain incidents cannot be solved by incidental (temporary) action. Companies can either ignore these effects – and be susceptible to low levels of trust – or take strategic action, in which case their business model needs to change. In the polluting industries, for instance, a common reactive approach has been to look for mitigating 'end-of-pipeline' solutions. Increasingly, however, regulation in many countries has stepped up under the influence of popular pressure. This has motivated many companies to look for more structural solutions in their business model to *prevent*, rather than just mitigate, pollution and waste.

Once confronted with a triggering event, an organization generally cannot persist with an inactive attitude. It must choose between reactive and proactive approaches. Companies that adopt a reactive approach – for instance, by denying (partial) responsibility while the case develops within their 'sphere of influence' (Case #7.2) – run the risk of greater and longer-lasting damage. Under proactive management, a company seriously considers the impact of events in a much earlier stage; it comes up with measures and takes steps in conjunction with relevant stakeholders. The more the company can rely on relevant stakeholder relationships built and maintained prior to a triggering event, the more it will be able to proactively manage and cushion further societal (and thus reputational) damage. The closer potential issues come to core activities, the greater the need for a proactive attitude.

A typical life cycle for an issue moves through the phases of birth, growth, development and maturity (Figure 7.3). The sooner the company is able to identify the issue for what it is (incident, structural or systemic), the easier it becomes to define a 'proactive' strategy that will dampen the amplitude of the societal discontent and related distrust. Simple triggering events are easier to proactively manage than systemic events; the proactive management of simple events can be implemented within the corporate sphere of influence. Proactive management of

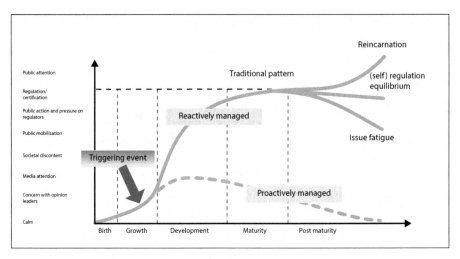

Figure 7.3 Issue life cycle

CASE #7.2 BP DEEPWATER HORIZON – A POORLY MANAGED TRIGGER EVENT

The case

In 2010, British company BP faced an immediate crisis. On 20 April, an explosion and subsequent fire on its drilling rig Deepwater Horizon, 64 km south-east of the Louisiana (US) coast, caused the death of 11 workers, injured 17 people and resulted in the sinking of the rig. Moreover, the explosion caused a massive offshore oil spill in the Gulf of Mexico. The oil spill was later assessed as the largest accidental marine oil spill in the world, and the largest environmental disaster in the history of the United States.

The corporate response

BP's CEO Tony Hayward immediately adopted a reactive approach. He initially denied that the disaster would cause severe ecological problems by stating that the oil spill was minor compared to "all the water in the sea". He caused a further kickback reaction when he later tried to put the blame with his US suppliers. After the event, it was found that BP had already been warned several times that the rig experienced problems and that rig workers had not raised their safety concerns from fear of getting fired or delaying drilling. Furthermore, the offshore industry had been lobbying successfully for deregulation of the entire sector – arguing that the companies themselves were sufficiently capable of self-regulation – which they clearly were not. Minor oil spills can potentially be reactively managed through a quick and thorough clean up but then it is also important to react promptly – not defensively. Major oil spills are a sign of more structural problems.

Source: courtesy of © Roberto De Vido

The business case for sustainability

The issue BP saw itself confronted with was not just the massive environmental disaster but also the fact that the company had made earlier decisions to put efficiency and price before safety (saving an approximate $1 million in safety precautions). This mistake is all the more interesting considering that BP had previously been perceived as one of the greenest oil companies. It had changed its value proposition accordingly, and even its logo (representing a green flower). The reputational damage was enormous, not in the least because the oil spill damaged American waters, making the company susceptible to the US liability regime (see Chapter 6). In 2015, BP reached an $18.7 billion settlement with various American government authorities. The costs for the clean-up came to around $54 billion. A detailed estimate of the ultimate costs of the oil spill (including fines, penalties, contingent liabilities, legal fees, SEC settlements and the like) was assessed at $145 billion in the US (Lee et al., 2018).

A proactive case would have involved the company aligning early on with critical partners, adopting higher levels of self-regulation and precautionary measures, and co-designing shared value creation models. Other companies that deployed these types of strategies were much less hit by popular outrage when they – unintentionally – created negative externalities.

systemic events, however, always requires collective action and stakeholder engagement. Making this functional implies that companies not only have to communicate strategic action ('talk') but also have to make this functional ('walk') and coherent, integrated across different areas of management.

7.3.3　Structural events

Structural events are related to how the entire industry is organized. Even if trigger events are created by others in the same sector, they tend to affect the credibility of the sector as a whole. This is the case, for instance, with diseases in fragile food chains in which many specialized producers compete on the basis of low prices and standardized products. In the event of an outbreak, the entire sector (often together with the government as the guardian of public health) needs to take rather radical actions. In the case of 'mad cow disease', for instance, even unaffected farms were ordered to cull large numbers of healthy animals – not only to reduce the risk for public health but also to restore trust in the sector. The more regularly such incidents occur, the more it points to structural elements at play, or even an underlying systemic problem of the entire food system. Structural events signal the fragility of the system and reinforce existing tacit expressions of discontent.

If an event involves and affects the entire sector, it becomes more difficult to attribute responsibility: there is no single 'issue owner'. Consequently, individual companies might be less inclined to bear and take responsibility, even when it is clear that they have partial responsibility.[4] Because of their structural nature, issues like child labour, deforestation or tax evasion remain somewhat hidden and 'silent' until critical stakeholders make it explicit and public by *creating a trigger event*. Many of the social problems that arise as the result of structural or systemic problems in the supply chains of companies – notably child labour, poor wages, poor working circumstances and human rights issues – are addressed by critical NGOs. They find ways of mobilizing and directing public discontent about structural problems that many people are probably already aware of, but so far have not explicitly acted upon.

Trigger events that draw and unleash sufficient public attention can be reinforced by a widely broadcast human disaster, such as took place in 2013 when a garment factory in Bangladesh – a supplier to a large number of clothing chains – collapsed. The Rana Plaza catastrophe killed more than 1,134 people (Case #7.3). If NGOs can make the case that the highlighted problem is not a stand-alone 'incident' but part of a structural or systemic problem, the urgency and motivation to act (among politicians, regulators, policymakers, opinion leaders, consumers, industry leaders) increases. Individual companies, however, are often insufficiently capable of effectively dealing with the issue – even if they are morally motivated – because it is part of a bigger system (in which companies compete based on price). This means that the entire sector needs to take action and change its business model in order to restore a level playing field at a higher level of societal value. Individual codes of conduct – the usual approach – prove relatively inadequate for systemic problems.

---

4   Chapter 5 discussed this as the challenge of 'conditional morality' (Box 5.2).

CASE #7.3 RANA PLAZA – THE COSTS OF CHEAP CLOTHES

The case

On 24 April 2013, the Rana Plaza building collapsed, killing 1,134 people and leaving thousands more injured. The origins of the collapse were relatively straightforward: safety regulations had been repeatedly violated and were not monitored; the building was poorly constructed, with too many floors and too much heavy equipment, with too many people working. The building housed a bank, shops and, in particular, garment factories supplying many global garment brands.

Until today, the exact names of all brands remain obscure, but the Clean Clothes Campaign identified at least 29 global brands that had orders with the factories in the Rana Plaza building. Amongst them were Benetton (Italy), Bonmarché (UK), Cato Fashions (US), The Children's Place (US), El Corte Inglés (Spain), Joe Fresh (Canada), Kik (Germany), Mango (Spain), Primark (UK/Ireland) and Texman (Denmark). The Clean Clothes Campaign called "each of these brands a complicit participant in the creation of an environment that ultimately led to the death and maiming of thousands of individuals".

The defence of many garment manufacturers was the 'cut-throat' competition in the clothing industry, due to customers' desire for cheap clothes, as well as the practice of competing with 'fast fashion'. At the same time, it was revealed that the Bengali government had not monitored safety regulations. One reason for this omission may have been that the owner of Rana Plaza, Sohel Rana, was a member of the local chapter of Jubo League, affiliated to the political party in power.

Wicked questions

The collapse triggered a global debate on 'who should be held responsible' and what actions should be taken to prevent reoccurrence. Was it the corrupt political system in Bangladesh? Was it the 'race to the bottom', in which Bangladesh had been competing with other countries to be the preferred source of low wage garments? The police, who had earlier advised – but not forced – the owners to close the factory after serious construction problems occurred? Western consumers who go for the lowest prices? Garment producers who engage in fast fashion aimed at the lowest consumer segments of society? Asked by CNN, the Bangladeshi prime minister dismissed the tragedy as 'accidents happen'. Bangladesh had already been criticized by the International Labour Organization (ILO) for failing to protect labour unions and, consequently, for not guaranteeing the workers' safety.

C A S E

7.3

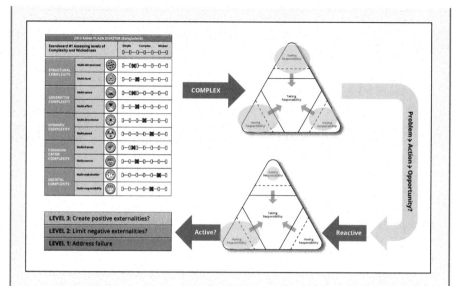

What happened after the disaster?

Sohel Rana received a three-year sentence for "failing to declare his personal wealth to Bangladesh's anti-graft commission"; not for his involvement in the disaster. No one took direct responsibility for the tragedy. The victims were offered a modest financial compensation. In the garment industry, initiatives were taken to 'never again' experience a similar tragedy. Three initiatives were set up in Bangladesh: (1) the Bangladesh Accord – a multi-stakeholder collaboration involving NGOs, brands and unions; (2) the Alliance for Bangladesh Worker Safety, which is corporation-led and primarily controlled by North American brands; (3) the National Tripartite Plan of Action on Fire Safety and Structural Integrity in the Garment Sector of Bangladesh – a government-led initiative supported by the ILO and foreign states. Around 250 companies signed the first two initiatives. According to the Asser Institute (2018), these initiatives have led to quantifiable improvements to workers' safety in Bangladeshi garment factories.

In two consumer countries, further-reaching initiatives were set up. In France, a 'due diligence' plan was released to deal with human rights risks (more or less in accordance with OECD guidelines). The Netherlands pioneered an Agreement on Sustainable Garments and Textile, bringing together a broad coalition of businesses and societal organizations, more or less following the OECD 'Responsible Business Conduct' principles (see Chapter 8). Both initiatives are primarily aimed at level 1 and level 2 (avoid doing harm) approaches (Chapter 5).

Some progress has been made following 2013, but is it sufficient and will it solidify? Safety initiatives may not be continued, unions are still being stifled and wages are still the lowest in the world, according to Clean Clothes research. Other studies report that progress is less obvious for workers in at least 2,000 factories that do not supply major Western brands. What will happen after the Accord and the Alliance ends, is unclear. Level 3 effects (enhancing and scaling positive externalities) have not yet emerged.

Sources: *The Guardian*; Clean Clothes Campaign; CNN; The Asser Institute – Doing Business Right Blog Antoine Duval (2018); https://www.imvoconvenanten.nl/en/garments-textile

C
A
S
E

7.3

7.3.4 Systemic events: the butterfly defect

A long series of consecutive smaller events hints at a systemic problem. In a VUCA world, apparent 'incidents' can be a sign of underlying systemic weaknesses. An increasing number of authors have convincingly argued that systemic risks are endemic at the present stage of global capitalism. Systemic issues appear, amongst others, in supply chains (trade), health issues (e.g. pandemics, antibiotic resistance), finance, (geo)politics, climate, natural ecosystems, digital technologies, energy, employment and critical infrastructures. Goldin and Mariathasan (2014) dubbed this the *butterfly defect* – pointing at the widening gap between the systemic risks generated by a 'turbo-charged' globalization and effective management approaches. They argue that – unless effectively addressed – these phenomena will "lead to greater protectionism, xenophobia, nationalism, and, inevitably, de-globalization, rising inequality, conflict, and slower growth" (see also Chapter 1).

Butterfly defect mechanisms have particularly manifested themselves in the financial sector (with repeated smaller banking and currency crises since the turn of the century) and the food and health industry (with recurring public health issues related to intensive livestock farming, dietary health – e.g. obesity, diabetes, cardiovascular diseases – and systemic food waste problems). The climate crisis is still in the phase of smaller yet accumulating 'events' (floods, rising temperatures, desertification, changes in biodiversity), which has not (yet) resulted in the collapse of the whole system. This slow-burning characteristic explains why it has generally been easier to create a 'sense of urgency' around finance and health, whereas the climate issue still seems susceptible to 'apocalypse fatigue' (Chapter 1).

Once a crisis hits the public realm and jeopardizes the entire system, the 'wake-up call' becomes real. It has proven difficult, however, to redress systemic events without profound and direct intervention by the only actor that is expected to serve the public interest: the state. Since the turn of the millennium, this has happened in at least two crises with global reach: (1) the *global financial crisis* that started in 2007 in the United States as a subprime mortgage lending crisis (trigger event: the bankruptcy of Lehman Brothers on 15 September 2008); and (2) the *global Covid-19 pandemic* that started in the Chinese city of Wuhan in December 2019 (section 7.4). What can we learn from these events in terms of organizational and societal resilience in dealing with the root causes of a systemic event?

CASE

7.4

CASE #7.4 CRISIS ... WHAT CRISIS?

"I'm proposing a Financial Crisis Responsibility Fee to be imposed on major financial firms until the American people are fully compensated for the extraordinary assistance they provided to Wall Street."

President Barack Obama, January 2010

The case

In 2008, the crisis of the financial system resulted in a global economic recession. The global (credit/mortgage) crisis commenced in 2007 with the bursting of the US 'housing bubble' and depreciation in the subprime mortgage market. The system event had been precipitated by a long sequence of smaller national crises, like the peso/ rubel/real crisis, the savings and loans crisis in the US, the Asian currency crisis ... Some observers counted as many as 150 financial crises since 1987. The liberalization of the financial markets had been one of the strongest forces in support of globalization. But the long sequence of smaller financial crises alluded to major governance and regulatory deficiencies within and across borders.

The sources of the 2008 financial crisis were attributed to irresponsible behaviour of banks (overleveraging) and consumers (overborrowing), but also pointed to failing regulation, both by governments and the financial sector itself. Regulatory voids appeared, in particular for new financial products and techniques – such as derivatives and securitization (mortgage-backed securities, often combined with credit default swaps). These instruments were primarily created to evade or frustrate effective regulation, not for the sake of financial innovation. The trade-off between 'risk appetite' (creating uncertainty) and 'responsibility' (managing uncertainty) was settled in favour of the risk-takers.

The financial crisis showed that deregulation had left policymakers and regulators ill-prepared to foresee the crisis; they lacked a thorough understanding of the financial system they oversaw. The same was true for players in the financial sector: even the most sophisticated risk management models at the level of financial corporations were not functioning properly. An insider at Lehman Brothers – the investment bank whose bankruptcy triggered many of the global butterfly effects – characterized the financial crisis as 'a colossal failure of common sense' (McDonald, 2009). Governments around the world responded with massive support and bailout programmes, nationalizations of banks that were considered 'too big to fail', and other monetary and fiscal public measures to prevent a collapse of the world financial system.

The corporate response

The financial crisis was addressed primarily by rescue actions from governments. But how did companies respond? The financial corporations had been the most directly involved in the proliferation of the financial crisis; one could expect them to experience the strongest urge to become active in the search for structural and preventative solutions. Also for non-financial multinationals, the predictive functioning of the global financial system is of existential importance. In general, however, the global top 100 largest companies showed a rather inactive to reactive response (Van Tulder, 2011).[5] Most American financials did not even adopt the word 'crisis', but instead referred to a 'challenging environment'. The American 'liability' context tends to create strong disincentives for firms to move beyond denial and take a more active approach. Two non-American banks took a more active stance:

■ *Crédit Agricole – a French cooperative bank:* "For us, the main conclusion is that we need a new international framework for banking and finance. In addition, the crisis has given us a stronger sense of our responsibility as a bank, of our obligation to look at the long-term consequences of our business and financial decisions" (Annual report, 2008: 7).

■ *HSBC – a Hong Kong/UK publicly listed global bank:* "The banking industry has done many things wrong. Inappropriate products were sold inappropriately by many. Compensation practices ran out of control and perverse incentives led to dangerous outcomes. There is genuine and widespread anger that the contributors to the crisis were in some cases amongst the biggest beneficiaries of the system. Underlying all these events is a question about the culture and ethics of the industry. The industry needs to recover a sense of what is right and suitable as a key impulse for doing business" (Annual report, 2008: 8).
"One of the consequences of the crisis – and rightly – is that we are going to see a fundamental reevaluation of the rules and regulations that govern our business. But we should remember that no amount of rules and regulations will be sufficient if the culture does not encourage people to do the right thing. It is the responsibility of Boards to supervise and management to embed a sustainable culture into the very fibre of the organization. For HSBC, there is nothing more important" (ibid: 10). "We are living through a genuinely global crisis; it cannot be solved by one nation alone" (ibid: 11).

What happened after the financial crisis?

Systems banks and vital sectors were (temporarily) nationalized, interest rates lowered, central banks issued enormous amounts of debt. A limited number of

---

5 The study explored how multinationals (global top 100 – including both financial and non-financial corporates) immediately responded to the global financial crisis in terms of inactive, reactive, active and proactive corporate responsibility narratives, and whether this response had been influenced by earlier positioning decisions taken in internationalization and corporate responsibility strategies.

CASE 7.4

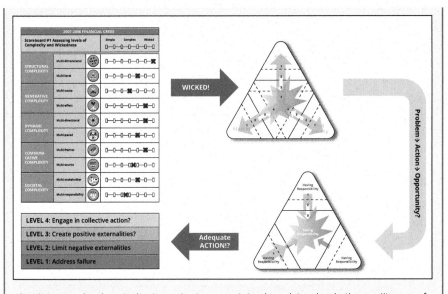

banks were bankrupted; stress tests were introduced to check the resilience of banks in order to cope with future crises. The systemic nature of the problem was not really addressed, however, not even at the level of regulating the bonus culture of major financial institutions. The result, according to many observers[6]: a 'ticking time bomb' with a global debt that increased from $180 trillion in 2008 to $255 trillion by year-end 2019 (over 322% of global GDP and 40% higher than at the onset of the crisis); with zero interest rates, making money almost free and private debts increasing in many countries. Joint-stock corporations used the low interest rates not for investments in innovative or more sustainable products, but for massively buying back shares. This brought share prices to all-time records, but – according to the Institute for International Finance – also increased corporate debts from $48 trillion to $75 trillion, of which $19 trillion was represented by so-called 'zombie companies' (companies that will collapse at the slightest setback). The government deficit receded in only a handful of countries.

Linking responses to societal resilience
The financial system as a whole did not become more resilient. On the contrary: in 2020, the debt trap had reached all corners of the societal triangle and made the

---

6   Peter de Waard, *Volkskrant*, 19 March 2020; *The Economist*, September 2018, header: "The world has not learned the lessons of the financial crisis."

financial system even less resilient and less prepared to deal with the pervasive financial and economic consequences of the Covid-19 pandemic, let alone the next imminent global crisis (climate). Linking the response to the financial crisis to the four
levels of intervention that resilient sectors have to take into account, we can observe
the following:

- **On level 1:** the interventions made (e.g. bailing out, nationalizing banks)
  solved *some* of the failures created by the combined activities of financial
  corporates, governments and private citizens; consequences for individual
  banks and citizens were relatively limited ('too big to fail, too big to jail'); it was
  foremost governments that acted. The actual sources of failure have not been
  resolved, according to many observers.

- **On level 2:** *some* of the adverse effects were 'channelled' through policy
  measures (stress tests, slightly higher reserve positions, rescue funds for future
  crises), but the risks of indebtedness remain largely uncovered. Pension funds
  suffer as a result of the near-zero interest rates policies by central banks. In
  general, financial institutions *relapsed* to a largely 'reactive' attitude towards
  sustainability.

- **On level 3:** it is difficult to define any positive externalities created, other than
  the realization of the relevance of a *positive investment agenda* to (1) safeguard
  future returns on investment, and (2) base growth on innovation and real
  economic growth, rather than debt. Attention for 'impact investment' and 'social
  enterprise' has grown, but is still relatively marginal. In particular, sustainable
  niche banks (e.g. Triodos) and cooperative banks – that had already been critical about the banking system – have embraced the SDGs.

- The latter is partly the result of lacking activities on **level 4**: on a global scale,
  no noticeable collective action was taken to make the financial system more
  resilient. The Basel regulation[7] has been stepped up, but global financial volatility remains. The G20 was effective in handling the immediate crisis following
  2007, but in the aftermath of the crisis has not been effective in triggering
  further systemic change.

---

7   The Basel Committee on Banking Supervision (BCBS) is the primary global standard setter
     for the prudential regulation of banks. It provides a forum for regular cooperation on banking
     supervisory matters. Its 45 members comprise central banks and bank supervisors from 28
     jurisdictions. The Basel III framework (completed in December 2017) is to address the
     shortcomings of the pre-crisis regulatory framework. It provides a regulatory foundation –
     minimum requirements that apply to internationally active banks – for the purpose of a more
     resilient banking system that supports the real economy.

7.4 LOOKING AHEAD – ON THE GLOBAL TIDES OF A PANDEMIC

"Had we been investing – in the MDGs and SDGs – we would have a better foundation for withstanding shocks" (UN, 2020: 11). This distressing conclusion was drawn by the United Nations, just three months after the outbreak and rapid global spread of the Covid-19 virus disease that began in December 2019. For years, the disruptive societal impact of spreading infectious diseases had been included in the Top 10 of Global Risks, annually listed by the World Economic Forum. Scenarios of a pandemic outbreak had been repeatedly sketched as part of economic and public health policy discussions.[8] Yet the world was caught ill-prepared for the exponential spread of Covid-19 and the pervasive, multiple impacts of consecutive policy measures to suppress transmitting of the virus. What appeared to be a global health crisis with a scary and uncertain outlook within three months also developed into a global social and economic crisis, projected to develop into the "worst recession since the Great Depression, surpassing that seen during the global financial crisis a decade ago" (IMF, 2020: v).

In April 2020, the IMF projected that the global economy – already fragile, indebted and slow-growing – would contract sharply in response to the pandemic. Possible recovery in 2021 would be dependent on *the world* succeeding in containing the virus and taking the necessary economic, financial and fiscal measures to forestall a wave of bankruptcies and layoffs. Aptly, IMF's intermediate World Economic Outlook was named *The Great Lockdown*, reflecting the sudden stop of the world economy. The ILO estimated in April 2020 that the second quarter of 2020 would see a loss equivalent to 195 million full-time jobs, following the 130 million full-time jobs already lost in the first three months since the Covid-19 outbreak. Small and medium enterprises, the self-employed, daily wage earners, migrant workers and those working in the informal economy – nearly half of the global workforce – were being hit the hardest (ILO, 2020a). The *Financing for Sustainable Development* report (Inter-Agency Task Force on Financing for Development, 2020) stated the expectation that the financial and economic shocks triggered by the pandemic – e.g. disrupted industrial production, falling commodity prices, financial market volatility, rising insecurity, pressure on foreign exchange

---

8   A few years earlier, in March 2015, Bill Gates – as a philanthropist with major health-related investments – presented his experience with the Ebola crisis in a TED talk entitled *The next outbreak? We're not ready*. Earlier, in 2006, epidemiologist and philanthropist Larry Brilliant who worked with the World Health Organization to eradicate smallpox (which killed 300 million people in the 20th century alone), described what the next pandemic could look like in terms of spread, death toll, socioeconomic impact and global recession in the TED talk *Help me stop pandemics*.

rates, falling tax revenues, pressure on reserves – would further reinforce financial risk, disruption of global value chains, and public and private debt distress, particularly for low- and middle-income countries. Investors had already removed $90 billion out of emerging markets in the first quarter of the Covid-19 outbreak, the largest capital outflow ever recorded. Middle-income countries – representing 75% of the world's population and one-third of the global GDP – are significant engines of global growth, yet are also home to 62% of the world's poor.[9] They are highly vulnerable to debt crises, lost market access and capital outflows. The report warned that the compounded and destabilizing global effects of the pandemic threatened to derail sustainable financing and investment, not in the least due to increased risk of geostrategic tensions, retreat from multilateralism, debt distress, soaring inequality, and heightened discontent and distrust of globalization.

CASE #7.5 COVID-19 – THE OUTBREAK OF A GLOBAL PANDEMIC

C
A
S
E

7.5

The case

December 2019, the wet markets of the Chinese city of Wuhan were, according to most accounts, the breeding ground for the outbreak of a novel coronavirus: Covid-19. The virus disease causes a severe and acute respiratory syndrome. It spreads among people in close contact, often via small droplets produced by coughing, sneezing or talking.
Initially, China did not release information on the disease, nor its risks. On 30 January 2020, however, the World Health Organization (WHO) declared the Covid-19 outbreak a 'public health emergency of international concern'. Following rapid worldwide spreading of the virus, the WHO declared Covid-19 a 'pandemic' on 11 March 2020. Nearly all countries became infected, some countries and regions more than others. As there was no vaccine yet, suppressing transmission and preventing deaths proved extremely difficult. Immediate parallels were drawn with the outbreak of the Spanish Flu in 1918, which infected about 500 million people – one-third of the world's population – in four waves (1918–1920) and resulted in an estimated death toll of at least 50 million people worldwide.

The initial response

As soon as Covid-19 was classified as a pandemic, stock markets plunged. A 'state of emergency' was declared in 84 countries; forceful social measures

9   https://www.worldbank.org/en/country/mic

CASE 7.5

were taken around the world (lockdowns; social distancing; quarantines; surveillance; international transport restrictions) at a level of intervention not seen since World War II. Governments were forced to come to the rescue – again (see Case #7.4) – with massive financial support programmes, cash injections and loan guarantees. The size of the financial interventions that were readily adopted had been dismissed as 'unfeasible' in previous periods when proposed by politicians and experts as ways to 'fix' the (global) public health system and prevent epidemics and pandemics from arising. Immediate support packages now amounted to trillions of dollars. In the United States, for instance, a $2 trillion support package was agreed on 26 March 2020, the single largest economic stimulus package in US history (most Western countries followed suit with massive financial packages). Only a few months earlier, proposals for 'universal health' provision schemes – of comparable cost and the topic of the US presidential election campaigns – were denounced as 'unrealistic'.

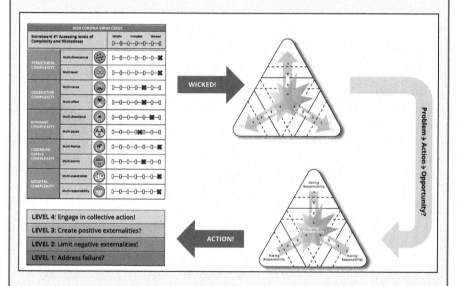

Meanwhile . . . ongoing crises

The early spread of the coronavirus in the first quarter of 2020 primarily took place in the 'developed' world (from China to Italy, Europe and the United States). This created significant media attention, but also suppressed attention for ongoing crises in 'slow motion' that had not made it to the front page of leading media. One example is the sheer scale of acute hunger in the world. At the same time as the Covid-19 crisis unfolded, around 135 million people in 55 countries faced acute hunger – mainly as a result of conflict, the effects of climate change, economic crises and massive voracious desert locust swarms in eastern Africa (World Food

Programme, 2020). Another slow-motion crisis: 6.1 million children under the age of 15 still die every year, mostly from preventable causes.

The effects of the Covid-19 pandemic further fed these 'silent' crises, with 88 to 115 million people on the brink of falling back into extreme poverty (World Bank, 2020) – the first increase in global poverty since 1998. Had the pandemic not convulsed the globe, the poverty rate was expected to drop to 7.9% in 2020. Acute hunger was projected to double to more than a quarter of a billion people by the end of 2020 due to interrupted trade flows and supply chains, price swings, sharp declines in purchasing power, hoarding of food supplies, lockdowns and loss of income. As an indirect result of the pandemic, cases of HIV, tuberculosis and malaria were expected to increase, due to interruptions in medical supply chains, obstructed access to (preventative) care and overwhelmed health services. For tuberculosis alone, an estimated 6.3 million additional cases and 1.4 million additional deaths were projected.[10]

Compounded systems fragility

Not only were people with pre-existing health conditions and marginalized socio-economic positions hit the hardest by the virus, the pandemic also exposed some significant 'pre-existing' systemic risks: dependencies, fragilities and inequalities within and across developed and developing societies, as the downside of globalization ('the butterfly defect'). Underlying systemic risks had made the world ill-prepared – most literally manifested in the scarcity of protection equipment, ventilators, hospitalization and testing capacity – to prevent the health crisis from rapidly 'infecting' the global economy. The compounded health, social, economic, financial and political effects are bound to last for a long time. Even when sufficiently effective vaccines are made readily available for every global citizen, managing the colossal debts will burden societies for decades to come. The effects of the pandemic have been impacting everyone and affected all societal dimensions, leaving the future landscape highly uncertain.

An early assessment by UN DESA (March 2020) of the pandemic's nexus effects on the SDGs, portrays the world community's fears for the devastating impacts triggered by Covid-19 in many interrelated areas of sustainable development, which may instigate divergence, growing inequalities, conflict and further VUCA dynamics (Chapter 1).

---

10 https://www.imperial.ac.uk/mrc-global-infectious-disease-analysis/covid-19/report-19-hiv-tb-malaria/

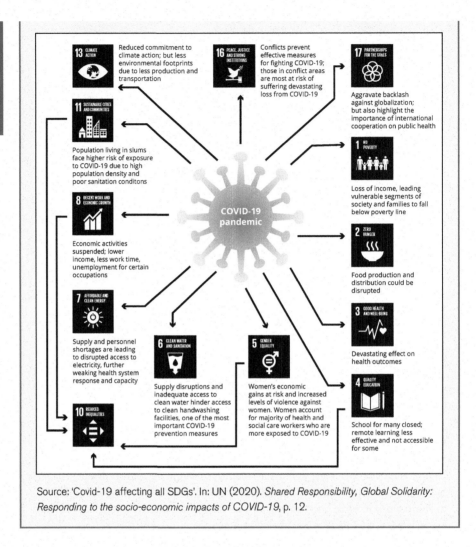

Source: 'Covid-19 affecting all SDGs'. In: UN (2020). *Shared Responsibility, Global Solidarity: Responding to the socio-economic impacts of COVID-19*, p. 12.

SOCIETAL TRIANGULATION CONSIDERATIONS; ADDRESSING TOUGH QUESTIONS

After rapid responses to suppress, remedy and stabilize the imminent effects of the pandemic, societies (governments, businesses, and citizens) need to plan for recovery. Covid-19 not only emphasized the urgency of better organizing global public health; it also raised fundamental, even existential challenges on how 'society at large' can re-emerge from the interlinked crises and its aftershocks. How will societies cope with the experienced chaos, loss and insecurity, and regain their perspective and control again? Will the aftermath drive disillusionment, distrust, anger, populism and nationalist-protectionist reflexes that trigger polarization and intensified VUCA dynamics? Will a collective sense of how 'we are in this together' prevail? Can it reverse the trend of underinvestment in common goods creation and spur collaborative and collective action? How to address systemic flaws, frailties and root causes, and build back better for healthier, safer, inclusive and more resilient societies? What kind of approaches and interventions are needed to bounce back and come out stronger?

Some preliminary responses to the immediate effects of the crisis could be noted that link to the analytical frameworks presented throughout Part I and II: societal triangulation, dimensions of wickedness, addressing sources of failure, having and taking responsibility, and levels of intervention. Early responses reflect, amongst others:

■ Renewed attention to the importance of **balanced and resilient societies** (Chapter 1) – at the global, regional, national and local level – combined with a rethinking of the characteristics of 'resilient' value chains. What defines the resilience of societies in times of extreme imbalances, shocks and destabilization? What are 'critical' or 'vital' sectors that are too important to fail? To what extent do patterns of public and private investment match the critical role and functioning of these sectors? How does society 'value' workers in those sectors (e.g. health, care, education, infrastructure and transport, utilities, cleaning, waste collection, agriculture, retail)?

■ A rethinking of the value of **open or closed societies** and reconsiderations on the present **mode of globalization**, its systemic vulnerabilities and nexus risks (e.g. extended supply chains, extreme efficiency and division of labour, fragile just-in-time production systems, 'lack of slack'); reaffirmation of the importance of knowledge and information sharing; open-source and collaborative research and development efforts that enable people to find answers to collective problems, be timely responsive and innovate;

■ A reassessment of the role of governments and the public sector, of the notion of **shared responsibilities**, and of the value of the **common good**; revaluation of the importance of the so-called **third sector** ('volunteers' and 'mutual support') in cushioning shocks that affect private lives (local resilience, community resilience) and as a vital part of a vibrant and balanced society;

■ A rethinking of the **trade-off between curation and prevention** – not only in health systems, but also with regard to social, economic, financial and ecological systems – as imminent crisis distracts from slow-burning crises with even more pervasive systemic consequences; how to prevent that 'the cure is worse than the disease' (the unintended spiralling effects of rapid responses, creating path dependencies, lock-ins and long-term, intergenerational consequences);

■ The importance of dealing with **global governance gaps** (Chapter 6): a reappraisal of the coordinating, facilitating and supporting role of global (multilateral) institutions as organized by, for instance, the WHO and the United Nations system; renewed awareness that in times of destabilization and confusion, strongmen can use governance voids as an excuse to grab more **power** (*The Economist*, 26 April 2020), which jeopardizes **checks and balances**, with severe institutional, societal and geopolitical repercussions;

- The importance of **organizational diversity**: the understanding that coping with systemic crises requires a healthy ecosystem of varied types of organizations that provide distinct yet **complementary inputs** and competences from different organizational backgrounds (see archetypes 1–8, Chapter 6) to cover all relevant dimensions of systemic risks: public/private; profit/non-profit; governmental/non-governmental; common values;

- A more acute understanding of what **failure** and **negative externalities** constitute (Chapter 4): the realization that markets do not always function well in distributing timely and fairly to those in need; intellectual property right protection schemes that prevent sharing of technologies (vaccines); lock-in effects in supply chains that create logistical problems and lower the system's resilience; competition between governments (internationally or federal-local) for scarce resources (e.g. vaccines; ventilators; protective equipment; medicines; food supplies); low reserves of highly profitable companies due to corporate buy-backs and the primacy of shareholder value, leading to layoffs and bankruptcies; multinationals evading corporate taxation while depending on state support or bailout in times of shock;

- Reiteration of the importance of **collaborative initiatives** that provide an important (global) infrastructure for mobilizing capabilities, pooling resources and coordinating collaborative approaches to face common challenges, addressing (global) governance gaps and common needs, and navigating change towards enhanced resilience and sustainability (Box 7.4);

- A reconsideration of 'best' ways of **organizing of a sustainable society**: what do distinct approaches to the Covid-19 crisis tell us about the resilience of various societal models (Chapter 6): the East Asian, North American, mainland European, Islamic, or community-centred models.

The discussion on what the pandemic's aftershocks imply for transition pathways towards more sustainable business models – in global health and interconnected sectors – will linger on for a long time. The public debate on 'what kind of society to rebuild' at least initially spurred policies for making financial support measures for companies conditional on their sustainability actions. The French government, for example, demanded that Air France cut carbon emissions by half by 2030 in return for a €7 billion bailout. The EU's Covid-19 recovery and support package had the Green Deal and the digital transformation at its core to kick-start the economy again, acknowledging that society would lose out twice if investments were to restore 'the old economy' instead of transforming it to a green and sustainable one.

NAVIGATING POSITIVE CHANGE TOWARDS RESILIENCE

The Covid-19 crisis reiterated the importance of several collaborative initiatives that had already been established before the pandemic outbreak. These initiatives all recognize the nexus challenge (trade-offs and synergies) related to the systemic risks of a globalized world and the SDGs as an agenda for positive change towards more resilient societies.

■ **The Global Fund** has aligned with the SDG-agenda to explore how systemic change can help the global health system to become both more resilient and innovative. It was launched in 2002 as a novel partnering mechanism to finance a massive and rapid international effort to drive back AIDS, tuberculosis and malaria as epidemics – "three diseases which stand as some of the greatest impediments to the sustainable development of much of the world". It raises and invests a yearly $4 billion in public and private funds to support sustainable health programmes in 100 countries. The fund has taken up an active role to identify how the capabilities and infrastructure it has been investing in can be adapted to strengthen responses to the Covid-19 pandemic (accelerating the development, production and equitable distribution of vaccines, diagnostics, and therapeutics for Covid-19). https://www.theglobalfund.org/

■ **The World Economic Forum**, a platform initiated by the private sector that brings together leaders of society to address the world's most pressing challenges. The WEF underlines that "Globalization 4.0 has only just begun, but we are already vastly underprepared for it. Clinging to an outdated mindset and tinkering with our existing processes and institutions will not do. Rather, we need to redesign them from the ground up, so that we can capitalize on the new opportunities that await us, while avoiding the kind of disruptions that we are witnessing today." The WEF's 'Shaping the Future' collaborative platforms aim to inform and advance "prosperous, inclusive and equitable economies and societies that provide opportunity for everyone to fulfil their potential." https://www.weforum.org/platforms

■ **The World Business Council for Sustainable Development,** a prominent global CEO-led community of over 200 leading businesses working together to accelerate the systems transformations needed for a net zero, nature positive, and more equitable future. WBCSD has pleaded for global responses to the multiple effects triggered by the Covid-19 pandemic that help accelerate the transition towards a more inclusive, resilient and sustainable society:

• "Shifting to a more stakeholder-oriented form of capitalism becomes more, not less important in the wake of Covid-19."

- "Only by ensuring the recovery is inclusive – benefitting all stakeholders – can we avoid a populist backlash against 'capitalism' that would ultimately make the recovery slower and more unequal."
- "Covid-19 has also provided a stark reminder of the scale of systemic risks that can build up – and the exponential impact these can have – when we allow negative externalities to accumulate over time. It is clear that deforestation, biodiversity loss, climate change and inequality all contributed either to increasing the risk of a crisis like the one we're in or making our societies and economies more vulnerable in the face of it. Given this, there is an opportunity post-crisis to accelerate work that was already underway to enable markets to integrate social and environmental impacts into financial valuations, helping to create stronger incentives for resilience-building, decarbonization and inclusive growth" (WBCSD, 2020: 14).

7.5 CONCLUSIONS, TOOLS AND RESOURCES

Business cannot thrive in a society that fails; societies cannot be resilient where businesses blunder. In essence, the Covid-19 pandemic painfully exposed the numerous vulnerabilities and system risks of a highly interconnected (global) society and economy. This chapter focused on the interaction and mutual dependence of business and society in preventing, coping with, recovering and bouncing back from different 'levels of triggering events', and the co-creating roles and shared responsibilities needed to future-proof society in the face of grand challenges. It defined principles of 'sustainable business' in more general terms: as principles of 'future-resilient organizing' by balancing responsibilities at multiple intervention levels.

The concept of organizational resilience applies broadly, essentially to all forms of private sector organizations: fully private, partly public, hybrid organizations (see Chapter 6). A healthy and more resilient societal ecosystem – conducive to developing novel approaches to fundamental human needs, desires and societal challenges – is versatile and consists of many organizational forms. Diversity provides stronger regenerative capacity for renewal, reorganization and the development of innovative solutions. The concept of sustainable 'business models' – as the materialization of 'sustainable business' and corporate societal/sustainable responsibility – can therefore be considered relevant to a variety of forms of private sector organizing.

The challenge of creating a resilient society lies in the complementary contributions that resilient private organizations are willing and able to make at various levels of intervention (Figure 7.4). This chapter focused on (a) the

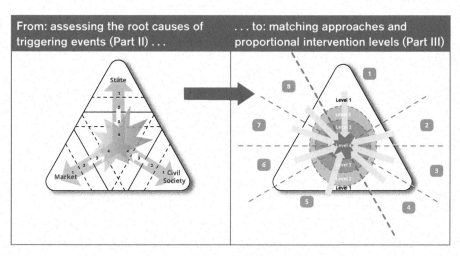

Figure 7.4 Dynamic fit: between event and intervention

proportionality, and (b) the levels of intervention at which organizations take on responsibilities for core fiduciary duties, negative externalities and broader societal issues. It enabled a distinction between more resilient business models (sustainable business) and more vulnerable/fragile business models (non-sustainable business). A sustainable business model makes the societal agenda leading for its orientation and, accordingly, reflects a balanced, layered approach that encompasses all four levels of intervention: (1) preventing failure; (2) minimizing negative externalities; (3) maximising positive externalities and enhancing spillovers; (4) engaging in collective action to collaboratively contribute to sufficient 'common goods' creation. The subsequent chapters will consider how to elaborate strategic and operational principles of 'sustainable business' in core activities and organizational interventions.

T A K E A W A Y S

■ In a VUCA world – characterized by triggering events and shocks – resilience is an important concept that applies to all levels of analysis: personal, group/community, organizational, societal, systemic;

■ Resilience is the capacity to absorb, adapt and recover from shocks. In the light of sustainability, the *regenerative* capacity to renew, reorganize, develop, create opportunity and innovate is vital to resilience;

■ Societal and systems resilience can only be achieved as the accumulated effect of (complementary forms of) organizational resilience; sustainable business is essential to the resilience of societies;

■ The scientific and management thinking on corporate responsibilities has developed along societal events; it gradually moved from ethical, via strategic, towards societal approaches; and from 'inside-out' ethical principles – e.g. charity, stewardship, subsidiarity – to 'outside-in' strategic principles of stakeholder management, stakeholder value and societal goal-setting;

■ To take proportionate and appropriate action in good time, an important strategic and analytical challenge is to define the nature of the event and to gauge dynamics (being able to 'read the signs'): incidents, structural or systemic;

■ Proportionality implies that an intervention should not be more severe than is necessary for the objective pursued ('overshooting'); neither should it be less severe than the situation requires ('undershooting'); actions must be in keeping with both the direct aim/need and the longer-term purposes pursued;

■ Proportionality of intervention is linked to a clear understanding and proper attribution of having and taking responsibilities, both direct and indirect, and within or beyond the direct sphere of influence;

■ Higher-level interventions (at systems levels 3 and 4) can never be a substitute for not addressing lower-level sources of failure (at levels 1 and 2);

■ A sustainable business model makes the societal agenda leading for its orientation and takes a balanced, layered approach that includes all four levels of intervention;

■ The Sustainable Development Goals present a leading societal agenda until 2030; they enhance societal resilience by addressing major systemic risks to sustainable development. In line with the SDG-agenda, the leading principles of sustainable business are: *People, Planet, Prosperity, Peace* and *Partnering*.

**S
E
L
E
C
T
E
D

W
E
B

R
E
S
O
U
R
C
E
S**

■ ***The Global Resilience Partnership:*** a partnership of public and private organizations joining forces towards a resilient, sustainable and prosperous future for vulnerable people and places. It aims to increase the attention for and investment in resilience and to further knowledge on what policies, practices and innovations are needed to build resilience (the capacity to persist, adapt and transform in the face of change). Resources provided include reports and case studies; learning webinars; a resilience guide for navigating sustainable futures ('Wayfinder'); and a mapping of global and regional resilience initiatives and funds. http://www.globalresiliencepartnership.org/

■ ***The Resilience Alliance:*** a networked international, multidisciplinary research organization that focuses on resilience in social-ecological systems as a basis for sustainability. Research and practical themes encompass the concepts of resilience, adaptation and transformation (between different levels or scales, from the household to the globe; comparisons and synthesizing information across different sectors and regions). Provides an open-access database of many (peer-reviewed) publications (articles, books, discussion papers), a practitioner's workbook for resilience assessment, and a glossary with key terms, concepts and definitions. https://www.resalliance.org/

■ ***ISO Organizational Resilience Standard:*** provides a framework to help organizations future-proof their business, detailing key principles, attributes and activities. The standard takes a broad view of the things that can drive resilience in an organization. Many of these are behavioural; the standard should help develop a culture that supports resilience, building upon existing forms of risk management, having shared values and an awareness of changing contexts, underpinned by strong and empowered leadership. https://www.iso.org/obp/ui/#iso:std:iso:22316:ed-1:v1:en

■ ***Case repository:*** Classic cases on international clashes between companies and societal stakeholders (including Shell-Brent Spar, Heineken in Myanmar) can be found on the website of the book *International Business-Society Management* (under 'cases'). http://www.ib-sm.org

■ ***World Business Council for Sustainable Development:*** a prominent global, CEO-led community of over 200 of the world's leading businesses – representing $8.5 trillion in combined revenues, 19 million employees and 70 global network partners – working together to accelerate the system transformations needed for a net zero, nature positive and more equitable future. The vision is "to build a world where more than nine billion people are living well and within the boundaries of the planet, by 2050". WBCSD has a three pillared strategy: (1) Imperatives (climate action, nature action, equity action); (2) Pathways (collaborative solutions in food, energy, products & materials, transportation & mobility, built environment, and 'health & wellbeing' value chains); and (3) Redefining value (aimed at the reinvention of capitalism). https://www.wbcsd.org/

In response to the covid-19 triggered crises, WBCSD started a global business response programme and three projects – vital supply chains; return-to-'normal' scenarios; long-term impacts. https://www.wbcsd.org/COVID-19/WBCSD-COVID-19-Response-Program

■ **TED talks:** many TED talks have been recorded on 'resilience' and 'how to deal with crises' at a personal, organizational, national and global level. A series of TED interviews on how to cope with the pandemic, how to restart the global economy and what to learn from responses has been released since the outbreak. Amongst others, philanthropist and Microsoft cofounder Bill Gates (*How we must respond to the coronavirus pandemic*); professor in the economics of innovation and public value Mariana Mazzucato (*The covid-19 crisis is a chance to do capitalism differently*); and global economist Dambisa Moyo (*What we get wrong about global growth*). https://www.ted.com/series/the_ted_interview

REFERENCES

Adger, W.N. (2000). 'Social and Ecological Resilience: Are They Related?', *Progress in Human Geography*, 24(3):347–364.

Andriof, J. & McIntosh, M. (2001). *Perspectives on Corporate Citizenship*. Sheffield: Greenleaf Publishing.

Ball, R. & Brown P. (1968). 'An Empirical Evaluation of Accounting Income Numbers', *Journal of Accounting Research*, 6(2):159–178.

Blowfield, M. & Murray, A. (2019). *Corporate Responsibility*, 4th edition. Oxford University Press.

Bowen, H.R. (1953). *Social Responsibilities of the Businessman*. University of Iowa Press (new edition).

Carroll, A.B. (1999). 'Corporate Social Responsibility: Evolution of a Definitional Construct', *Business & Society*, 38(3):268–295.

Carroll, A.B. (1979). 'A Three-Dimensional Conceptual Model of Corporate Performance', *Academy of Management Review*, 4(4):497–505.

Donaldson, T. & Dunfee, T.W. (1999). 'When Ethics Travel: The Promise and Peril of Global Business Ethics, *California Management Review*, 41(4):45–63.

Elkington, J. (2018). '25 Years Ago I Coined the Phrase "Triple Bottom Line." Here's Why It's Time to Rethink It', *Harvard Business Review*, 25 June.

Elkington, J. (1999). *Cannibals with Forks, the Triple Bottom Line of the 21st Century Business*. Oxford: Capstone Publishing.

European Business Forum (2003). 'CSR: a religion with too many priests', issue 15, Autumn.

Folke, C. (2006). 'Resilience: The emergence of a perspective for social-ecological systems analyses', *Global Environmental Change*, 16(3):253–267.

Frederick, W.C., Post, J.E. & Davis, K. (1992). *Business and Society: Corporate Strategy, Public Policy, Ethics*. New York: McGraw-Hill.

Freeman, R.E. (1984). *Strategic Management: A Stakeholder Approach*. Boston M.A.: Pitman Press.

Friedman, M. (1962). *Capitalism and Freedom* (40th Anniversary Edition). Chicago and London: The University of Chicago Press.

Frynas, J.G. (2005). 'The false developmental promise of Corporate Social Responsibility: evidence from multinational oil companies', *International Affairs*, 81(3):581–598.

Goldin, I. & Mariathasan, M. (2014). *The Butterfly Defect: How Globalization Creates Systemic Risk, and What to Do about it*, Princeton University Press.

Hahn, T., Figge, F., Aragón-Correa, J.A., & Sharma, S. (2017). 'Advancing Research on Corporate Sustainability: Off to Pastures New or Back to the Roots?', *Business & Society*, 56(2):155–185.

Hosseini, S., Barker, K. & Ramirez-Marquez, J.E. (2016). 'A review of definitions and measures of system resilience', *Reliability Engineering and System Safety*, (145):47–61.

ILO (2020a). *ILO Monitor: COVID-19 and the world of work. Third edition. Updated estimates and analysis*, International Labour Organization, 29 April 2020.

IMF (2020). *World Economic Outlook: The Great Lockdown*. Washington DC: International Monetary Fund, April.

Inter-Agency Task Force on Financing for Development (2020). *Financing for Sustainable Development Report 2020*. New York: United Nations, April.

Kaptein, M. & Wempe, J. (2002). *The Balanced Company. A Theory of Corporate Integrity*. New York: Oxford University Press.

Laasch, O. & Conaway, R.N. (2015). *Principles of Responsible Management: Glocal Sustainability, Responsibility, Ethics*. Mason: Cengage.

Lee, Y., Garza-Gomez, X. & Lee, R.M. (2018). 'Ultimate Costs of the Disaster: Seven Years After the Deepwater Horizon Oil Spill', *Journal of Corporate Accounting & Finance*, 29(1):69–79.

McDonald, L.G. with Robinson, P. (2009). *Colossal Failure of Common Sense. The Incredible Inside Story of the Collapse of Lehman Brothers*. Crown Business.

McEwen, T. (2001). *Managing Values and Beliefs in Organisations*. New York: Financial Times/ Prentice Hall.

McWilliams, A. & Siegel, D.S. (2001). 'Corporate Social Responsibility: A Theory of the Firm Perspective', *The Academy of Management Review*, 26(1):117–127.

Pfefferbaum, B.J., Reissman, D.B., Pfefferbaum, R.L., Klomp, R.W. & Gurwitch, R.H. (2005). 'Building Resilience to Mass Trauma Events'. In: Doll, L., Bonzo, S., Mercy, J. & Sleet, D. (Eds.) *Handbook on Injury and Violence Prevention Interventions*. New York: Kluwer Academic Publishers.

Porter, M.E. & Kramer, M.R. (2011). 'Creating Shared Value: How to Reinvent Capitalism and Unleash a Wave of Innovation and Growth', *Harvard Business Review*, January/ February. 30.

Porter, M.E. & Kramer, M.R. (2006). 'Strategy and Society: The Link Between Competitive Advantage and Corporate Social Responsibility', *Harvard Business Review*, December.

Prahalad, C.K. (2004). *The Fortune at the Bottom of the Pyramid. Eradicating Poverty through Profits*. Wharton, PA: Wharton School Publishing.

Stigson, B. (2002). *WBCSD Sector Projects*. Geneva: WBCSD.

UN (2020). *Shared Responsibility, Global Solidarity: Responding to the socio-economic impacts of COVID-19*, March. New York: United Nations.

Van Riel, C. & Blackburn, C. (1995). *Principles of Corporate Communication.* Prentice Hall.

Van Tulder, R. (2011). 'Crisis . . . what crisis? (revisited): Exploring multinational enterprises' responsiveness to the financial crisis'. In: Claes, D.H. & Knutsen, C.H. (Eds.). *Governing the Global Economy: Politics, Institutions and Economic Development*, (pp. 247–276). London: Routledge.

Van Tulder, R. with Van der Zwart, A. (2006). *International Business-Society Management. Linking Corporate Responsibility and Globalization.* London: Routledge.

WBCSD (2020). *The consequences of COVID-19 for the decade ahead. Vision 2050 issue brief.* World Business Council for Sustainable Development, May.

Williams, A., Kennedy, S., Philipp, F. & Whiteman, G. (2017). 'Systems thinking: A review of sustainability management research', *Journal of Cleaner Production*, (148):866–881.

Wood, D. (1991). 'Corporate Social Responsibility Revisited', *Academy of Management Review*, 16(4):691–718.

World Bank (2020). *Poverty and Shared Prosperity 2020. Reversals of Fortune.* Washington, DC: World Bank.

World Food Programme (2020). *Global Report on Food Crises 2020*, April. Food Security Information Network (FSIN) and Global Network Against Food Crises.

8 MAKING IT STRATEGIC

BUSINESS CASES FOR SUSTAINABILITY

DOI: 10.4324/9781003098355-11

■ **Ten Principles of the UN Global Compact:** universal principles of corporate behaviour derived from the Universal Declaration of Human Rights; the ILO Declaration on Fundamental Principles and Rights at Work; Rio Declaration on Environment and Development; and the UN Convention Against Corruption.

■ **ILO Principles:** based on tripartite agreements (employees, employers, governments) concerning such fundamental rights as 'rights at work', 'the right to collective bargaining' and 'elimination of forced or compulsory labour'.

■ **UN Guiding Principles on Business and Human Rights** (the 'Ruggie Principles'): the state's duty to *protect* (against human rights abuses), the corporate responsibility to *respect* human rights, and the need to help victims achieve *remedy*.

■ **Principles of Responsible Business Conduct** (RBC): formulated as part of the OECD Guidelines for Multinational Enterprises; includes principles, general policies and standards that comprise human rights, environment, bribery, labour practices, information disclosure, consumer interests, competition, taxation.

■ **Due diligence principles** (also known as CSR Risk Management): key element in RBC as an ongoing, responsive process through which companies identify, prevent and mitigate their actual and potential negative impacts on society.

■ **Universal service principle:** applies in particular to 'regulated' industries with a public utility function (and a business case dependent on network effects). Pertains to the fiduciary duty to deliver services, including to non-commercially viable segments of an economy.

■ **Principles of responsible organizing** (ISO 26000: Guidance on Social Responsibility): seven principles, for all types of organizations, referring to their positive duty to maximize contributions to sustainable development, with due respect to 'accountability', 'transparency', 'ethical behaviour', 'respect for stakeholder interests' and 'human rights', an organization's reasonable 'sphere of influence', pursued in an integrative approach.

■ **Investment principle:** short-term costs precede longer-term benefits.

■ **Principles of civil society organizations:** relate to the non-profit side of society to produce 'social capital'. They include elemental principles as 'mutual support', 'risk-sharing', 'equality', 'solidarity', 'inclusiveness' and 'democracy'.

■ **Accountability principles of international NGOs:** are grounded in the 'International NGO Charter of Accountability', specifying transparency, engaging stakeholders and continuous improvement, and using power responsibly as foundational principles. The notion of 'dynamic accountability' underpins the '12 Commitments of the Global Standard for CSO Accountability', through which CSOs aspire to further human rights, social justice, good governance and sustainability; address vulnerability and the exclusion of marginalized populations, and improve the lives of the poorest in society.

■ **Principles of purposeful management** (Peter Drucker): which include making sure that management serves a higher purpose that embeds the ideas of community and citizenship in management systems.

■ **Five principles of blended finance** (OECD): anchor to a development rationale; address market failure; tailor to the local context; focus on effective partnering; monitor for results; and ensure transparency and accountability.

8.1 INTRODUCTION: A MISGUIDED QUEST FOR 'THE' UNIVERSAL BUSINESS CASE FOR SUSTAINABILITY

"Sustainability begins with a principles-based approach
to doing business"
UN Global Compact website – the Power of Principles

"For those who think business exists to make a profit,
I suggest they think again.
Business makes a profit to exist.
Surely it must exist for some higher, nobler purpose than that."
Ray Anderson, founder of Interface

In the unsettling aftermath of systemic crises (Chapter 7), the rationale for future-proof organizing is perhaps more clear-cut than ever: more resilient societies are sustainable societies; sustainable societies call for sustainable businesses. The 'business case' for private sector organizations to align with the societal agenda seems compelling. The costs of inaction – in terms of market disruption, burdens to growth, resource shortages, low trust, stringent regulation, access to finance, decreased competitive edge – are mounting. For those able to grasp the opportunities that arise from addressing global needs and systemic risks, the prospect of future markets, an extended 'license to operate', innovative edge, access to finance, competitive advantage and longer-term profitability emerges.

Amidst heightened risk and uncertainty on the 'right' way to move ahead, the Sustainable Development Goals (SDGs) have been providing a guiding lens through which to translate imminent sustainability risks, societal needs and global ambitions into 'business solutions' for sustainability (Business & Sustainable Development Commission, 2017). In the words of former Unilever CEO Paul Polman: "the SDGs provide the world's long-term business plan by putting people and the planet first. It's the growth story of our time." Nevertheless, blending 'purpose and profits' in a meaningful and truly viable manner has proved a pressing challenge for most private sector organizations. Reconciling enhanced *societal value* with financially sustainable business is imperative, but complicated in a highly competitive and performance-driven setting. It not only demands recalibrating one's business strategy and core operations, but also involves market transformation, a shift in economic incentives and concerted action – of the whole sector, along the value chain, and in collaboration with key societal stakeholders.

THE QUEST FOR 'THE' UNIVERSAL BUSINESS CASE – WHY IS IT MISGUIDED?

Despite the evident necessity of embracing more sustainable and inclusive economic models – and the prospect of at least $12 trillion in market opportunities per year by 2030 in business savings and revenue (Business & Sustainable Development Commission, 2017) – progress on aligning 'business' with the SDGs has been lagging. It is widely recognized that if the private sector is to drive the success of the SDG-agenda, more vigorous private sector commitment *beyond incremental actions* is essential; corporate support for the SDGs needs to be matched by the stepped-up integration of the Global Goals into core business activities. This, however, is where the quest for *'the universal business case'* for sustainability proves a key area of contention, misconceptualization and impediments. A 2018 World Business Council for Sustainable Development survey among its members found that "lack of thorough understanding of the business case" was the main barrier to aligning core operations with the SDGs. Although the SDGs were broadly acknowledged as a strategic opportunity, they still represented a relatively marginal activity within organizations. Companies "are struggling to articulate the business case within their own operations" (WBCSD and DNV GL, 2018). A 2019 survey by UN Global Compact and Accenture among 1,000 CEOs of the world's largest companies corroborated that finding. It observed that one in three CEOs cite 'lack of market pull' as the top barrier to sustainable business; over half said they faced the 'key trade-off' of operating under extreme cost-consciousness versus investing in longer-term strategic objectives that are at the heart of sustainability (UN Global Compact & Accenture Strategy, 2019).

This recurrent ambivalence reflects a longstanding misconception in the popular discourse on the business case for sustainability. Aspiring sustainability managers have always had to legitimize their CSR ambitions and interests – or any other concept of sustainable business – along three conventional rationales: (1) sustainable activities should contribute to *profit maximization*; (2) should lead to distinct *competitive advantages* (compared to less sustainable competitors); and (3) should preferably have *proved and immediate* short-term positive effects on the operations of the organization. If a 'project' neatly abided by these three benchmarks, investing in sustainability was a 'no-brainer'. The search for *the* business case for sustainability defined as such became a search for the 'holy grail' in sustainable management thinking (Van Tulder with Van der Zwart, 2006: 141).

THE ROBUST BUSINESS CASE FOR SUSTAINABILITY – WHY IS IT AMBIGUOUS?

In the scientific discourse, this quest became operationalized as the *robust business case* for sustainability: the search for scientific evidence of a positive relationship between enhanced 'corporate social performance' (CSP) and increased 'corporate financial performance' (CFP). Over the years, many studies have tried to map the CSP-CFP relationship statistically. One of the most thorough studies – a meta-analysis of 52 empirical studies on the CSP-CFP relationship, carried out over 30 years – was executed by Orlitzky, Schmidt and Rynes (2003). The authors found a positive performance relationship, more so for social responsibility than for environmental responsibility. More robust statistical follow-up studies, however, persisted in more ambiguous findings; the empirical evidence was too mixed to allow for any firm to act upon (Orlitzky, 2009). Recent research again finds evidence of positive CSP-CFP relations. After a second-order meta-analysis, Busch and Friede (2018: 583) conclude that "based on the extant literature, the business case for being a good firm is undeniable".

Where managers and corporate leaders have to convincingly legitimize their ambition and prove their case as straightforwardly as possible, the desire for 'robust evidence' as a footing for prospective performance is understandable. But the search for the 'holy grail' remains quite disconnected from both the real meaning of a business case, as well as from actual practice – even when the accumulated evidence appears rather positive. This happens for a variety of reasons: first, because most of the research specifically concerns publicly listed companies, which – in absolute numbers or in terms of employment – only represent a small part of the entire private sector (Chapter 6). Second, because most studies were executed independently of context (in an attempt to arrive at general conclusions). In practice, however, regulatory context matters considerably as a selection or enabling environment for organizations to perform and thrive. Third, because of the ambition to generalize and define 'universal antecedents' of sustainable business models and best practice cases. In the past, the search for 'best practice' cases has often proved a futile and scientifically dangerous exercise; the ambition for statistical robustness has proved methodologically troublesome. Fourth, because 'sustainability' increasingly became equated with ecological sustainability, thereby creating a selection bias. Over the last decade, the financial business case for many ecological investments already turned out positive: investment in solar panels, for instance, reaps a positive return on investment (RoI). For other areas of sustainability, evidence has been less easy to gather or difficult to interpret, due to short-term switching costs and the discrepancy between positive macro (societal) effects and micro-level investments by individual organizations. Finally, but most importantly: in a VUCA context, it has become increasingly clear that the narrow CSP-CFP ambition represents only part of what a business case for a societal *resilient* business model (Chapter 7) would constitute. The conceptualization of 'the business case for sustainability' hence requires further elaboration.

This chapter covers the 'richness' of the business case for sustainability along three lines: (a) general principles of sustainable business cases and their contextualization under the influence of the 'hybridization' movement; *for*-profit and *non*-profit considerations are increasingly merged (section 8.2); (b) specific sustainable business cases along four levels of intervention/SDG engagement for organizations starting from a 'for-profit' orientation (sections 8.3 and 8.4); (c) specific sustainable business cases along four intervention/SDG engagement levels for organizations starting from a 'non-profit' orientation (sections 8.5 and 8.6). Many business cases for sustainability exist, each with a specific logic that reflects the societal positioning of an organization (see Chapter 6), and each with advantages and disadvantages at different intervention levels.

8.2 IN SEARCH OF A MORE COMPREHENSIVE SUSTAINABLE BUSINESS CASE

In essence, a business case captures the reasoning, logic and justification for initiating an undertaking, project, programme, portfolio or task. It defines – either formally or informally – the *business need* (in relation to its societal context) and the basic reasoning (a compelling motivation for change) behind a strategy. Furthermore, it delineates the *financial feasibility and sustainability* of a project or strategy. The business case for sustainability ultimately defines the financial foundation and continuity of a private organization in terms of benefits, costs and risks of investments. Profits – or positive earnings – remain vital for the longer-term financial resilience of an organization. Profit *maximization*, however, presents too narrow a frame for strategy development. Profits are a means, but a poor aim in themselves. The presumption that the pursuit of financial profit will inevitably improve social welfare lacks any theoretical or empirical support, and is arguably founded on an economic model that "bears no resemblance to the realities of twenty-first-century market capitalism" (Jones et al., 2016: 226). Last but not least, a proper business case explicitly considers the option of *doing nothing* and includes the costs and risks of *inactivity*.

The business model and business strategy, then, define *how* the business case should be organized in practice and at what level of intervention. It specifies the organizational structures and processes for creating, delivering and capturing the envisioned societal value or opportunity pursued. In Chapter 5, we defined four *intervention levels* on sustainability issues that require elaboration in terms of business cases and business models: (1) addressing failure; (2) preventing/limiting negative externalities; (3) creating/scaling positive externalities, and (4) stimulating collective action. These translate into *four levels of engagement* with the SDGs that can be attributed to organizations. Accordingly, the sustainable business case for private sector organizations generally materializes along the following lines:

■ **General principles:** the rationale and justification of the business case should be well-grounded in the five foundational principles of sustainable business as derived from the SDG-framework: people, planet, prosperity, peace, partnering (see Chapter 7);

■ **Societal positioning and contextualization:** the business case needs specification for the organizational form (governance structure) in which – or through which – the envisioned societal value should be organized or implemented. The private sector is diverse, consisting of many types of organizations with distinct organizational logics, means and competences (Chapter 6). The societal positioning of an organization matters for the viability of a particular business case;

■ **Levels of intervention/SDG engagement:** the sustainable business case should be specified for the level of intervention (1, 2, 3, 4) at which the private organization pursues contributing to a more resilient society. Distinct intervention levels may require different business cases; each engagement level has a distinct bearing on subsequent organizational principles.

GENERAL PRINCIPLES

To set in motion positive change, the SDG-agenda has been based on a 'goal-setting' and 'principles-based' approach (Chapter 2). It builds on various international initiatives that – since World War II – have laid the foundation for *universal principles* that are at the core of sustainable development: various iterations of the Universal Declaration of Human Rights (after 1948), several International Labour Organization (ILO) conventions (since 1948), and various international

Environmental conventions, enacted in particular after 1990. Arguably the most relevant initiative for private sector involvement in upholding these universal principles has been the *UN Global Compact* initiative, launched in 2000. The Global Compact developed a principles-based framework for responsible corporate behaviour to guide businesses, regardless of their size, complexity or location (Box 8.1). It encourages businesses to integrate these principles into corporate strategies, policies and ways of organizing, and to report annually on progress to societal stakeholders.

BOX 8.1

GLOBAL COMPACT: TEN UNIVERSAL PRINCIPLES OF CORPORATE BEHAVIOUR

The UN Global Compact – the world's largest corporate sustainability initiative based on voluntary CEO commitments – organizes more than 13,000 participants (over 10,000 companies and 3,000 non-business signatories) in nearly 160 countries. The public-private multi-stakeholder initiative has two main objectives: (1) mainstreaming ten universal principles on human rights, labour, environment and anti-corruption in business activities around the world; and (2) catalysing action in support of broader UN societal goals, notably the SDGs. The initiative aspires to "lead the largest-ever business model transformation towards a new normal" (UN Global Compact, 2020: 6). The main narrative of the UN Global Compact on sustainable business reads as follows:

"Corporate sustainability starts with a company's value system and a principles-based approach to doing business. This means operating in ways that, at a minimum, meet fundamental responsibilities in the areas of human rights, labour, environment and anti-corruption. Responsible businesses enact the same values and principles wherever they have a presence, and know that good practices in one area do not offset harm in another. By incorporating the Ten Principles of the UN Global Compact into strategies, policies and procedures, and establishing a culture of integrity, companies are not only upholding their basic responsibilities to people and planet, but also setting the stage for long-term success."

The Ten Principles of the Global Compact are derived from the Universal Declaration of Human Rights, the ILO Declaration on Fundamental Principles and Rights at work, the Rio Declaration on Environment and Development, and the UN Convention Against Corruption. Over 90% of business signatories have embedded the Ten Principles and have policies and practices in place (UN Global Compact, 2020: 14). Nevertheless, there is still ample room for deepening corporate efforts, and for extending and integrating policies across their supply chains: "companies need to understand and act on their impacts more" (ibid: 16).

Human Rights	Principle 1	Businesses should support and respect the protection of internationally proclaimed human rights; and . . .
	Principle 2:	. . . make sure that they are not complicit in human rights abuses.
Labour	Principle 3	Businesses should uphold the freedom of association and the effective recognition of the right to collective bargaining;
	Principle 4	The elimination of all forms of forced and compulsory labour;
	Principle 5	The effective abolition of child labour; and
	Principle 6	The elimination of discrimination in respect of employment and occupation.
Environment	Principle 7	Businesses should support a precautionary approach to environmental challenges;
	Principle 8	Undertake initiatives to promote greater environmental responsibility; and
	Principle 9	Encourage the development and diffusion of environmentally friendly technologies.
Anti-corruption	Principle 10	Businesses should work against corruption in all its forms, including extortion and bribery.

Mandatory public disclosure on corporate sustainability performance

As a voluntary initiative, UN Global Compact does not monitor or enforce the sustainability performance of its business signatories. It does, however, require business participants to annually produce and **publicly disclose** a Communication on Progress (COP) report.

In its yearly COP, a company details the *practical actions* undertaken and the **measurable outcomes** of embedding the Ten Principles into its strategies and operations. Furthermore, it includes a **CEO statement**, expressing ongoing commitment to Global Compact's societal priorities and its principles. As a publicly disclosed document, the purpose of a COP is to substantively inform societal stakeholders on a company's sustainability performance and progress, while also reflecting a company's commitment to transparency and accountability. According to DNV GL, 83% of corporate signatories participate in Global Compact as a way to **increase societal trust** through their public commitment to sustainability (UN Global Compact and DNV GL, 2020: 14).

The mandatory disclosure requirement for business participants also serves as Global Compact's 'integrity measure' to forestall potential misuse for bluewashing purposes. Failure to timely submit a COP on the Global Compact website will result in a downgrading of the participant's status – from 'active' to 'non-communicating'. Two consecutive years of non-disclosure will lead to the expulsion of a business from the initiative, with the names of expelled businesses published on the Global Compact's website.

Since implementation of a 'delisting policy' in January 2008, the **Delisted Participants database** contains the names of 13,002 expelled companies, many of which are classified as SME. The Global Compact **COP Database** presently contains over 50,700 submitted disclosures: 46,306 so-called 'Active' COPs that meet the minimum reporting requirements, and 4,428 'Advanced' COPs that provide additional information on the implementation of the Ten Principles into their core strategy and operations, active support of broader UN Goals and issues, and corporate sustainability governance and leadership.

Catalysing action on the SDGs

Over the 2001–2020 period, the Global Compact's principles-based framework has guided many UN initiatives that involve private sector engagement. Global Compact and its partnering network have played a leading role in framing a positive discourse around the SDGs, in creating broad corporate awareness, and in defining ways for companies to align with the SDGs. As of 2020, UN Global Compact's **SDG Ambition initiative** (launched at Davos in January 2020) pursues raising the bar and speeding up corporate action in the 'Decade to Deliver'. It challenges companies to align with a higher level of ambition to deliver on the SDGs by translating the SDGs into specific business targets, for which a series of **SDG Ambition Benchmark Reference Sheets** have been developed to accelerate action (https://unglobalcompact.org/library/5790).

Further information on the **Ten Principles**	• https://www.unglobalcompact.org/what-is-gc/mission/principles
Global Compact **COP Database**: 'Active' and 'Advanced'	• https://www.unglobalcompact.org/participation/report/cop/create-and-submit/active • https://www.unglobalcompact.org/participation/report/cop/create-and-submit/advanced
Delisted Participants database	• https://unglobalcompact.org/participation/report/cop/create-and-submit/expelled

SOCIETAL POSITIONING: DIVERSITY IN APPROACHES,
DIVERSITY IN BUSINESS CASES

General principles of sustainable business have universal application, but are to be embedded in different types of private sector organizations. Chapter 6 identified distinct (archetypical) organizational forms that are relevant in considering private sector contributions to the SDGs. Private, semi-private or semi-public organizational forms have a different, yet complementary, societal positioning. Accordingly, they represent distinct organizational 'logics', competences and governance challenges, and provide distinct strategic 'repertoires', resources and business models for addressing sustainability challenges.

In the sustainable business discourse, a pervasive *hybridization* trend can be observed. 'For-profit' organizations are trying to achieve societal impact and purpose (Porter and Kramer, 2011), whereas 'non-profit' organizations are trying to enhance their efficiency and financial resilience (Figure 8.1). Legislative innovations have started to provide special legal status for hybrids in many countries, while widespread recognition of auditing and certification organizations – such as B-Lab and the Global Reporting Initiative (GRI) – is improving their legitimacy (Battilana and Lee, 2014). 'Social enterprises', for instance, have experienced significant growth in numbers and popularity, indicating that 'non-profit/for-profit' hybrids are gradually becoming mainstream. This trend promises fresh impetus to the debate on how 'businesses' can address social and societal issues. But there are also concerns. Is this hybridization trend – as a new organizing and governance principle – not running the risk of getting *stuck in the middle* by combining a social goal with limited efficiency and low scaling possibilities? The danger of so-called *mission-drift* is looming for non-profit/ for-profit hybrids that do not effectively make the transition to a financially viable organizational (governance) form. Regardless of whether an organization serves the needs of private consumers, corporate clients, members, beneficiaries or patients (hospitals), it should always devise a viable business case for its longer-term survival.

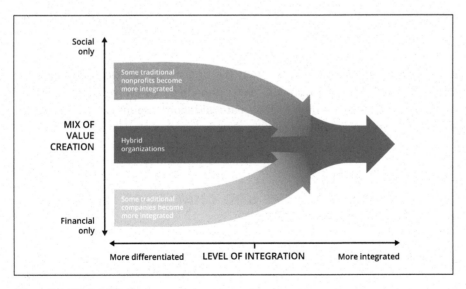

Figure 8.1 The hybridization movement

Source: adapted from Battilana et al., 2012: 54.

In order to better understand the rationale of the diversity of organizations that constitute the private sector, a fundamental distinction needs to be made between their origins: (1) the 'for-profit', and (2) the 'not-for-profit' orientation of organizations. For-profit organizations essentially generate revenue through 'sales' of produced goods and delivered services, and through financial rewards for risk-taking (return on investment). They are *profit-seeking* entities that have no legal obligation to work for the welfare of anyone but the organization and its owners. Non-profit organizations essentially generate value by 'sharing': risk-sharing, redistribution of surpluses of revenues, and the pooling and sharing of goods and services. They have a duty/obligation – either formal or informal – of working for the welfare of society, and can accordingly be considered *purpose-* or *cause-driven* entities.

Both origins have a bearing on how organizations can contribute to the sustainable development agenda. At both ends, the viability of the organization depends on how it is organized (the appropriateness of its business model), which in turn is strongly influenced by its position in society (in terms of distinct governance challenges and related governance principles; outlined in Chapter 6). Hybridization has been blurring the for-profit/non-profit interface, partly as a strategic response to sustainability challenges that require cross-sectoral partnering, collective action and novel modes of organizing in order to create societal value. Both sides of the for-profit/non-profit interface are thus relevant for exploring strategic and operational principles of sustainable business; each 'hybrid' defines different 'organizational logics', different types of business cases, and different approaches at the four levels of intervention/engagement.

The remainder of this chapter focuses on the 'principles of sustainable business' that private organizations need to consider in order to fully profit from, by contributing to, the SDG-agenda. It does so by taking the for-profit and non-profit origins as entry points: how to approach business cases for sustainability – the SDG challenge – from the *for-profit* side of society (sections 8.3 and 8.4); and how to approach them from the *non-profit* side of society (sections 8.5 and 8.6). Their further materialization in terms of value propositions, business models, operationalization and partnering will be elaborated in subsequent chapters.

8.3 APPROACHING THE SDG CHALLENGE FROM THE FOR-PROFIT SIDE

At the for-profit side of society, companies try to create societal impact through their commercial operations and the production of predominantly private goods (Porter and Kramer, 2011). For-profit companies have a starting position in the left corner of the societal triangle: the market sector. The diversity of companies

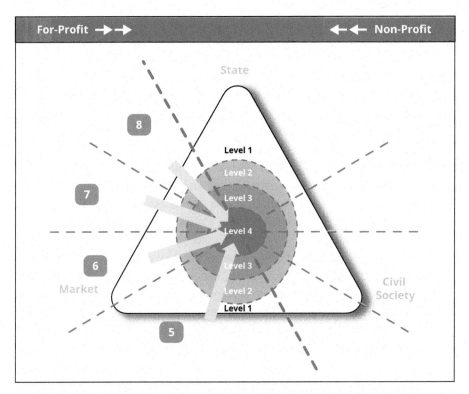

Figure 8.2 Four levels of for-profit involvement in the SDGs

in terms of size, governance and ownership structure, degree of internationalization, legal forms and responsibility orientation is considerable.

Along the societal interfaces specified in section 6.3, we distinguished four *archetypical organizations* with a for-profit (market) orientation: fully private organizations (type 5), publicly listed companies (type 6), semi-private organizations (type 7) and semi-public organizations (type 8). In line with the intervention levels elaborated in Chapter 5, Figure 8.2 also shows four levels of engagement for each of these organizational forms to contribute to sustainable development. Each level of engagement with the SDGs represents a different type of business case for sustainability.

■   **Type 5: family-owned or family-controlled enterprises** (at the market/civil society interface) classify as private, non-governmental organizations with a for-profit orientation, aimed at the provision of private goods. Family-owned firms range from sole proprietors to large international enterprises. As a group, they are estimated to contribute between 70–90% of the world's GDP[1] and

---

1   https://www.gvsu.edu/fobi/family-firm-facts-5.htm

to generate more employment than publicly listed companies. On average, family-owned enterprises tend to be more explicitly orientated towards longer-term continuity than profit maximization; they are also more strongly rooted in shared (family) values, vision and culture. The vast majority of the world's family-owned businesses are small and local. They constitute the bulk of the corporate population in most countries, often with limited financial capabilities to invest in sustainability on their own (unless for cost-reduction reasons). Although family ownership prevails in the group of small and medium-sized enterprises (SMEs), big 100% family-owned enterprises also thrive in many countries.[2] These large corporations generally generate slightly lower revenues than state-owned or publicly listed companies, but include high-profile company names, such as Koch, Mars, Cargill, Chanel and Aldi (Table 8.1). Some of the largest family-controlled companies are actually hybrid. High-profile hybrid family-controlled enterprises that are listed on the stock exchange (type 6) include Walmart, Arcelor Mittal, Heineken and Reliant Industries. Some companies are even more hybridized, such as Volkswagen Group. The German car producer represents a mixture of family ownership, publicly listed, and state ownership (the state of Lower-Saxony owns 20%).

■ **Type 6: publicly listed or 'joint-stock' companies** classify as public, non-governmental profit-oriented organizations that are aimed at the provision of private goods and services. At the end of 2017, the OECD counted around 41,000 publicly listed companies worldwide, with a combined market value of approximately $84 trillion (De La Cruz et al., 2019). Four main categories of investors dominate the ownership of publicly listed companies: institutional investors (e.g. insurance companies, mutual funds, mostly *profit-maximizing* intermediaries that invest on behalf of their beneficiaries), public sector owners (e.g. governments, public pension funds), private corporations (e.g. holdings), and individual strategic investors (ibid). Joint-stock companies – like Apple, Amazon, Alphabet, JPMorgan, British American Tobacco, Shell, Unilever, BP – are amongst the biggest, most focal and most international companies in the world. Nevertheless, they are not necessarily the most profitable. Table 8.1 illustrates that different governance forms and 'success' criteria (sales, market capitalization) lead to different lists of 'top performers'. An interesting *value paradox* exists: the companies with the highest 'market capitalization' – their value on the stock market – are not necessarily identical to the companies with the highest revenues or highest profits. Take, for instance, car producer Tesla, in comparison to its two most important American competitors: Ford Motor Corp. and General Motors. In 2019, Ford and GM respectively sold six times and twenty times

---

2   See the 'Global Family Business Index' of EY and University of St Gallen: http://familybusi nessindex.com/

as many cars as Tesla did. In 2020, however, Tesla's stock market value eclipsed the combined value of GM and Ford ($692 billion, compared to $59 billion for GM and $35 billion for Ford). Throughout most of its history, Tesla has not earned any profits from its car production.[3] But the stock market sentiment is more guided by future market expectations and the vision of the company's leader (Elon Musk), than by present profits and sales. According to stock market experts, the success of Tesla (and the return on investments of its shareholders) depends on its ability to seize a dominant position in the electric car market.

■ **Type 7: semi-private, state-controlled enterprises** (at the market/state interface) classify as for-profit organizations that are (partly or wholly) government-owned, with a public character, aimed at the production of *private goods and services*. They are typically found in strategic resources industries in emerging economies, notably oil (e.g. CNPC, China; Aramco, Saudi Arabia; Q8, Kuwait; Petrobras, Brazil; PDVSA, Venezuela). Many of these companies are hybrid: partly state-owned and partly publicly listed. State-controlled companies can also be found in the financial sector. Following the 2007–2008 financial crisis, large banks and mortgage companies were nationalized in many countries. Typical examples are Freddie Mac and Fannie Mae in the United States, or ABN AMRO and ASN Bank in the Netherlands. Considerable differences exist in state control across countries and industries, depending on a country's regulatory regime, privatization trends (e.g. in telecommunications, air transport sectors) and industrial policy. Mining companies like Alexkor in South Africa, BCL in Botswana, or Punjab Mineral Development Corporation in Pakistan, for instance, are structured like a private sector company, but are 100% state-owned.[4]

■ **Type 8: semi-public organizations** (at the state/market interface) are for-profit public organizations, (partly) government-owned, producing *(semi-)* *public goods and services*. Many public utility organizations are either state-owned, hybrid (public-private partnerships) or split up into a public network provider and a private products/services provider. Public utilities include

---

3 In the 2012–2020 period, Tesla derived its profits primarily from selling its 'regulatory credits' (given by the state California and US federal government for contributing zero pollution to the environment) to other carmakers who need to comply with emissions regulations. Tesla accumulated these credits from having an all-electric line-up, and earned $360 million (2017), $419 million (2018), $594 million (2019) and more than a billion dollars as of 3Q 2020 from their sales.

4 According to the International Finance Corporation, state-owned enterprises (SOEs) account for around 20% of investments, 5% of employment, and up to 40% of domestic output in countries around the world. SOEs can be found in high-income countries, in major emerging market economies, and in many low- and middle-income countries. Many SOEs rank among the world's largest companies, investors and capital market players.

water, electricity, energy, postal services, rail and roads. They represent regulated industries, often with a legal provision to deliver 'universal services'. Depending on the national regulatory regime, public utilities are also organized as 'non-profit' organizations, which then qualifies them as a 'type 2' organization (see section 8.5). In a growing number of countries, utility companies are also listed on the stock exchange (Table 8.1), representing market capitalization values between $30 billion (Exelon) and $50 billion (Duke Energy). The longer-term financial viability of these organizations then depends on their ability to provide a public service while operating in oligopolistic and often heavily regulated markets. The majority of the utility companies in the US and Europe are listed on the stock exchange – giving them access to private capital but also making them susceptible to short-term market sentiments. Semi-public organizations can also include development and investment banks that have a public role to invest in private sector projects, intended not to make a loss.

Table 8.1 Top 10 'for-profit' companies in the world – distinct scores (January 2020)

Market Capitalization	Revenues (*majority state)	Family ownership (100%)
1. Saudi Aramco (S.A.)	1. Walmart (US)	1. Schwarz Gruppe (Ger)
2. Apple Inc. (US)	2. Sinopec (China)*	2. Cargill Inc. (US)
3. Microsoft (US)	3. Royal Dutch Shell (Neth/UK)	3. Tate Sone Ltd (India)
4. Alphabet Inc. (US)	4. China National Petroleum	4. Koch Industries (US)
5. Amazon.com (US)	(China)*	5. Pacific Construction Group
6. Facebook Inc. (US)	5. State Grid (China)*	(US)
7. Alibaba Group (China)	6. Saudi Aramco (Saudi	6. Aldi Group (Ger)
8. Berkshire Hathaway (US)	Arabia)*	7. Amer International (Neth)
9. Tencent (China)	7. BP (UK)	8. Auchan Holding SA
10. JPMorgan Chase (US)	8. ExxonMobil (US)	(France)
	9. Volkswagen (Germany)	9. Gunvor Group ltd (Sw)
	10. Toyota (Japan)	10. Hinduja Group Ltd (India)

Utility companies (by market capitalization)	Hybrid family-controlled enterprises (owner)	Most profitable (2018)
1. Duke Energy (USA)	1. Walmart (Walton)	1. Apple
2. Engie (France)	2. Volkswagen AG (Porsche,	2. British American Tobacco
3. National Grid (UK)	Piech)	3. Berkshire Hathaway
4. NextEra (US, Canada)	3. Berkshire Hathaway (Buffett)	4. Industrial & Commercial
5. EDF (France)	4. Exor NV (Agnelli)	Band of China
6. Enel (Italy)	5. Ford Motor (Ford)	5. Samsung Electronics
7. Dominion Energy (USA)	6. BMW (Quandt, Klatten)	6. China Construction Bank
8. Iberdrola (Spain)	7. Comcast Corp. (Roberts)	7. Verizon
9. Southern Company (USA)	8. Dell Technologies (Dell)	8. AT&T
10. Exelon (USA)	9. Arcelor Mittal (Mittal)	9. Agricultural Bank of hina
	10. Reliance Industry (Ambani)	10. Bank of China

Sources: Investopedia, Fortune Global 500, Stock Exchanges

8.4 FOUR FOR-PROFIT BUSINESS CASES FOR SUSTAINABILITY

For each of these typical for-profit organizations, four distinct types of business cases for sustainable development can be distinguished at four levels of intervention/engagement. Each type of business case has its own logic, attitude, positive rationale and, essentially, a different meaning of the CSR acronym (Table 8.2).

8.4.1 Level 1: the classic business case

In mainstream management thinking, the 'classic' business case is generally considered as not oriented towards sustainability. Instead, it suggests 'business as usual', pursuing maximum profits, and essentially an 'inactive' or 'passive' attitude towards sustainability. But even at this basic level, businesses are faced with sources of 'market failure' (Chapter 5) for which specific aspects of sustainability might trigger relevant corporate strategies that suit a 'business as usual' approach. The 'inactive' business case is based on the logic that largely self-interested and profit-maximizing corporate behaviour can still contribute to addressing basic market failures that obstruct progress on sustainability. At least two rationales exist for an 'inactive' business case for sustainability: (a) 'know your customer' considerations to better serve consumers with sustainability preferences, and (b) boosting net returns through cost-saving investments related to enhanced resource-efficiency.

Table 8.2 Four for-profit business cases for sustainability

Level	CSR meaning	Basic attitude	Need for intervention	Main source of profit
1	Corporate Self-Responsibility	Inactive; passive	Addressing sources of market failure	Cost minimization, cost saving
2	Corporate Social Responsiveness	Reactive	Minimizing negative externalities	Enhanced reputation/ goodwill, or mitigation of reputational damage
3	Corporate Strategic/Social Responsibility	Active	Creating/scaling positive externalities	Extension of markets to serve latent *needs* for sustainable products (e.g. BoP)
4	Corporate Sustainable/ Societal Responsibility	Proactive	Creating common goods (through collective action)	Creation of new markets (new economy); serving collective *needs*

(A) CONSUMER SEGMENTATION – ADDRESSING CONSUMER PREFERENCE FOR SUSTAINABILITY

The classic argument underneath the inactive/passive attitude relates to the finding that the overwhelming majority of consumers are largely 'price-driven' and lack the willingness to pay for more sustainable products. This rationale applies in particular to markets where companies decided to compete on price only. Research indeed shows that it is difficult to change the behaviour of mainstream consumers towards choosing more sustainable over unsustainable products, especially when more sustainable products are (perceived as) more expensive.[5] It has also been found, however, that sustainability can add a 'selling point' to segments of mainstream consumers, but only if the products are competitively priced and of sufficient quality. Poorly designed but 'sustainable' sneakers do not sell. The literature speaks of *ethical* or *alternative hedonism* (Soper, 2008) in reference to specific consumer groups for products that are both sustainable and appeal to certain self-worth and self-realization motives of people. The business case for more sustainable products can thus be particularly relevant for high-end markets – like fashion or smartphones – where identity, status, aspiration, quality, uniqueness/exclusivity and experience of products are more distinctive features than price.

(B) COST-MINIMIZATION AND COST-SAVINGS

Arguably the most interesting category of the 'inactive' business case for sustainability relates to the *cost-minimizing potential* of more resource-efficient ways of operating. In nearly all management fields, efficiency and inherent cost-saving present a compelling business case: lower costs boost the net return of a business. Market failure occurs in case of an inadequate appreciation of the substantial *cost-saving* potential of such investments. Pollution, for instance, is often linked to the waste of valuable (natural) resources (materials, energy, water, fertilizer). An increasing number of 'ecological' investments have the potential to substantially reduce the operational costs of companies (e.g. reduction in energy use through insulation; cheaper energy provision through solar power; smart water and recycling systems that lower costs), with a decent return on investment. For that matter, investing in resource efficiency for cost-saving purposes is actually 'business as usual'. *Not* investing in cost-saving sustainable technologies could even be seen as proof of poor management judgement. A surprisingly large

---

5   Consumer research has shown a negative perception bias (primed) among many consumers towards products that are branded as 'sustainable'. When asked to double-blind compare products on price and quality, people considered products with, for instance, a fair trade label – like chocolate of coffee – more expensive and less tasty, even when the labels were switched between the fair trade and the non-fair trade product.

number of incumbent companies nevertheless still suffer from a mistaken form of conservatism. Anecdotal evidence shows that some managers are not reaping the fruits of already existing eco-friendly technologies because they consider ecology (or social sustainability aspects) 'soft', non-financial, or not directly related to 'profit maximization'.[6] By not understanding and harnessing the cost-saving potential of sustainable investments, companies and their managers add to market failure.

Accordingly, the CSR acronym at the basic level of intervention stands for (well-understood) **Corporate *Self*-Responsibility**.

---

18 CASES OF CLASSIC WAKE-UP CALLS

B O X 8.2

Classic cases of companies facing a 'wake-up' call on the limitations of their 'business as usual' approach materialized in the early 1990s – at the start of the globalization era. Many of these wake-up calls were initiated by demands from activist civil society organizations that confronted in particular large (multinational) enterprises with issues of (lacking) corporate responsibility. Confrontations emerged around four main issue clusters:

1   Health (food safety, genetic modification, access to medicine);

2   Labour and human rights conditions (forced labour, child labour);

3   Environment (waste dumping, global warming);

4   Dictatorship and wars (Burma/Myanmar, Nigeria, 'blood diamonds').

Eighteen exemplary cases illustrate landmark events of growing awareness of corporate responsiveness – CSR 2.0 (Chapter 7). Some cases show how issues can evolve (the treatment of dictatorship in Burma, for instance); other cases illustrate evolving strategies of NGOs (e.g. Greenpeace, the Clean Clothes Campaign). The case descriptions comprise:

a)   An analysis of the societal interfaces that are at stake: public/private; for-profit/non-profit; efficiency/ethics;

---

6   Managers of Walmart, the world's largest company by revenues, found out that annual costs could be lowered by US$1 billion if their lorry drivers would switch off the motor during loading. Walmart's managers could have initiated this cost-saving measure decades earlier, but – as the story goes – did not want to be associated with a 'tree-hugging' mentality that would not fit their image and identity as efficiency-driven, profit-maximizing managers. The biggest barrier to this cost-saving – and emissions-reducing – measure thus turned out to be their own mindset.

b) The company's governance characteristics (or the subsidiary in question) and the key stakeholders in the conflict at hand;

c) A description of the conflict;

d) The effects of the conflict on the company's reputation in three relevant 'markets': (1) consumer market; (2) capital market; and (3) labour market;

e) The company's response to the conflict, in terms of disciplining measures taken in the area of labelling, reporting, codes of conduct or otherwise;

f) An assessment of the outcome of the conflict, and of its contribution to resolving the issue.

INTERNATIONAL
BUSINESS-SOCIETY
MANAGEMENT
Linking corporate responsibility and globalization

Rob van Tulder with Alex van der Zwart

The selected cases include the following **companies** (in historical sequence): C&A, Schiphol, PepsiCo, Heineken, Nike, Shell (Brent Spar, Nigeria), Adidas, Cargill, GlaxoSmithKline, IHC Caland, ExxonMobil, IKEA, ABN AMRO, Triumph, Nutreco, Unilever, McDonald's. **Advocacy groups** include: Clean Clothes Campaign, Friends of the Earth, XminY, Greenpeace, Amnesty International, India working group, Oxfam, Burma Centre, Stop Exxon Coalition, Fatal Transactions, Bharti and VLAN.

The cases show that reputational damage has distinct effects on different types of organizations: the effects on family-owned enterprises or cooperatives differ from those on publicly listed companies; business-to-business companies face different effects than business-to-consumer companies; internationalized companies encounter a different effect than local companies. A responsive approach (level 2) in many instances only temporarily redressed the issue. For full case descriptions: www.ib-sm.org.

8.4.2 Level 2: the defensive business case

At this level, the company tries to make sure that *negative externalities* it inflicts upon society are limited, or will not negatively influence its operations. The degree to which society is willing to bear the costs created by the company's negative externalities defines, to a large extent, whether a company decides to include this intervention/engagement level in its sustainability strategy. There are five interrelated logics to the 'defensive' business case: (a) avoiding or dealing with reputational losses; (b) reputational gains from preserved goodwill; (c) longer-term corporate resilience; (d) access to more 'patient' finance; and (e) coping with increased screening activities of private and institutional investors.

(A) AVOIDING REPUTATIONAL LOSSES

A very strong incentive for companies to address negative externalities comes from (the risk of) reputational losses (Van Tulder with van der Zwart, 2006; Laasch and Conaway, 2015) and classic 'wake-up call' trigger events (Box 8.2). By building and protecting their reputation, companies can avoid stricter and more costly legislation or regulatory scrutiny. Businesses with a predominantly reactive stance towards sustainability tend to prioritize end-of-pipe technologies and pollution control measures, in contrast to clean technology and prevention (Lin, 2012). Reactive approaches focus on *risk management, risk mitigation* and *minimizing the added costs of measures* that would limit negative externalities, instead of searching for value maximization (Hengelaar, 2017). A reactive attitude towards sustainability has been found to lead to a decoupled, un-aligned or piecemeal approach (Grosvold et al., 2014).

(B) GAINING FROM REPUTATION: MANAGING GOODWILL

Preserving the corporate reputation also provides a positive argument: the 'value' of many companies depends on the level of trust that society puts in them. Societal trust substantially lowers transaction costs and diminishes regulatory scrutiny. Moreover, many companies base their prices (and thus their profit margins) on brand image and 'goodwill'. Without beneficial reputational effects, their market value and profit margins would be substantially lower. This applies to banks and institutional investors, but also high-end market companies like Nike (publicly listed), or low-end market companies like Coca-Cola (publicly listed) or C&A (family-owned). The value of goodwill presents a relevant category on the balance sheet of famous brands. The flipside, however, is that reputation, brand value and goodwill are prone to stakeholder influence and public sentiment, and therefore fragile. Companies that take limited responsibility for the negative externalities they inflict upon society, put their reputation at stake. The larger the negative externalities, the higher the odds of conflicting with society at some point. Loss of the societal 'license to operate' will then not only adversely affect short-term profit margins, but most likely also have longer-term disadvantageous impacts on access to finance, shareholder value, market expansion and ultimately competitive edge.

(C) LONGER-TERM RESILIENCE

Companies with a better sustainability outlook prove more resilient during reputational crises. Research on effective stakeholder dialogues, for instance, finds that companies that had been able to make their stakeholders 'partners' in the dilemmas they were struggling with in earlier stages of their strategies, tend to achieve a more emphatic response from stakeholders if problems arise. Heath (2001) uses the term 'co-created meaning' for this situation, to point to a certain level of mutual understanding built up prior to an event. The business case for greater stakeholder involvement appears fairly straightforward, as it helps firms to: (1) increase their sensitivity towards stakeholder concerns; (2) develop a heightened sense of responsibility for social issues; and (3) avoid, or better manage,[7] incidents that may receive wide public and media attention (Kaptein and Van Tulder, 2003). Companies that have delegated their corporate responsibility to their corporate foundation – separate from their core business activities – were found unable to seize the opportunities of this level of commitment (Box 8.3).

<table>
<tr><td>B
O
X

8.3</td><td></td></tr>
</table>

ON THE PRINCIPLE OF CHARITABLE GIVING – THE PHILANTHROPY TRAP

Many companies around the world have categorized the execution of their corporate responsiveness strategy under their corporate foundation, a separate (private) non-profit entity in support of charitable activities or community engagement. Philanthropists who respond to the ethical principle of *giving back to society* – a practice particularly established in the Anglo-Saxon (liberal) countries – mostly do so after leaving their company. In both instances, philanthropic activities are separated from core business operations, which tends to create a 'philanthropy trap'. Research on the degree of integration between corporate responsibility activities and the financial and societal outcomes thereof, indicates that philanthropic activities that are outside the core business of the company reap the least impact on society (Halme and Laurila, 2009).

World's Top 10 Foundations*	Country	Assets	Fiscal Year End Date
Stichting INGKA Foundation	Netherlands	$58.6 bn	31/08/2016
Bill & Melinda Gates Foundation	USA	$47.9 bn	31/12/2018
Wellcome Trust	UK	$39.7 bn	30/09/2019
Howard Hughes Medical Institute	USA	$22.5 bn	31/08/2019
Novo Nordisk S/A	Denmark	$18.3 bn	31/12/2019
The MasterCard Foundation	Canada	$17.4 bn	31/12/2018
Lilly Endowment	USA	$15.1 bn	31/12/2018
Ford Foundation	USA	$13.1 bn	31/12/2018
The Garfield Weston Foundation	UK	$12.5 bn	05/04/2018
Robert Wood Johnson Foundation	USA	$11.1 bn	31/12/2018

Source: * https://www.arcolab.org/en/worlds-100-largest-philanthropic-foundations-list/ (April 2020)

---

7   Companies can ward off or minimize the damage of campaigns by critical stakeholders if they adopt a less confrontational (buffering) stance and exhibit a willingness to enter into dialogue and seek solutions in consultation with stakeholders (bridging) instead (Heugens, 2001). This approach – also known as 'strategic issues management' – can have direct modifying effects on reputational crises.

Major American philanthropists – among the most prominent philanthropists in the world – donated to health, education and climate-related causes while still in charge of their companies, but without linking their societal engagement to core business activities. In 2020, for example, Jeff Bezos – CEO of Amazon and the richest man in the world ($189bn net worth in July 2020) – initiated the Bezos Earth Fund to address climate change. Bezos received considerable criticism due to his much less ambitious strategy to make Amazon's own operations (a significant contributor to CO_2 emissions) climate-neutral and to tackle poor working conditions and low payment in the Amazon distribution centres (social sustainability issues). The critics argued that Bezos' goal of the fund was primarily PR-related. Comparable arguments have been presented to CEOs who donated to non-profit causes during times of great reputational turmoil that concerned their companies or leadership. Examples include the societal discontent on privacy breaches (Zuckerberg, Bezos), antitrust violations (Gates, Walton), tax evasion schemes (Bezos), or currency manipulation (Soros).

Examples of major philanthropists	Net worth (2020)*	Giving (2018)**	Sustainable development issues focus
Warren Buffett	$80.3 bn	$3.4 bn	Health and poverty alleviation
Bill & Melinda Gates	$113.6 bn	$2.6 bn	Economic development, healthcare and education
George Soros	$8.6 bn	$ 585 mln	Open Society Foundation: human rights; economic development
Michael Bloomberg	$54.9 bn	$767 mln	Public health and gun control, climate change
Walton Family	$225.6 bn	$596 mln	Building charter schools
Jim & Marilyn Simons	$23.5 bn	$397 mln	Education
Li Ka-Shing	$25.7 bn	n.a.	Education and healthcare
Jeff Bezos	$188.7 bn	$131 mln	Climate Change: Bezos Earth Fund

Sources: * https://www.forbes.com/real-time-billionaires/; ** https://www.forbes.com/top-givers/

(D)   ACCESS TO MORE 'PATIENT' FINANCE

Investors are becoming more activist. Rather than relying purely on financial considerations and short-term financial returns, an increasing number of asset owners and institutional investors weigh long-term investment value drivers and risk factors – which include environmental, social and governance (ESG) aspects – in their investment decision-making and ownership. Investing in more sustainable companies is progressively perceived to be 'less risky' than investing in companies with an 'inactive' (level 1) or 'defensive' (level 2) corporate responsibility orientation. The rationale: ESG-friendly portfolios are considered 'more resilient in downturns' (BlackRock Investment Institute, 2019). "*To ignore ESG factors is to ignore risks and opportunities that have a material effect on the returns delivered to clients and beneficiaries*" (PRI, 2019: 4). The longer-term financial returns on investment portfolios ultimately depend on a sustainable and stable economy.

According to the Global Sustainable Investment Alliance (2019), 'sustainable investing' already represented $30.7 trillion at the start of 2018, a 34% increase since 2016.[8] More than 2,250 asset investors – collectively overseeing around $80 trillion in assets – had signed on to the Principles for Responsible Investment by 2019 (PRI, 2019: 6). By 2019 the Sustainable Stock Exchange initiative represented 90 exchanges around the world, together listing 50,000 companies valued at $86 trillion.[9] Integration of ESG considerations in private and institutional investment decisions is by now considered 'mainstream', while sustainable investing is poised to further accelerate (see section 11.7 on 'sustainable corporate finance'). Policymakers and consumers (especially millennials) demand more attention to company values and sustainability. Those active on capital markets foresee a significant reallocation of capital, driven by a profound reassessment of risks and asset values. *Sustainability risks* are increasingly considered *investment risks*, and this awareness is reshaping the world of finance and investment. Gradually, unsustainable corporate practices are being penalized. Larry Fink, chairman and CEO of BlackRock – the world's largest asset manager with $7.43 trillion in assets (2019) – announced BlackRock's policy of *divesting in risky, non-sustainable industries*: "We will take action against investee companies that do not consider sustainability. . . . Given the . . . growing investment risks surrounding sustainability, we will be increasingly disposed to vote against management when companies have not made sufficient progress" (14 January 2020).[10] BlackRock stated it would veto investments in any mining company that continues to extract coal for burning in thermal power plants.

(E) INCREASED RELEVANCE OF SCREENING

More generally, asset managers and institutional investors operationalize their selection strategies for 'sustainable investing' through a variety of approaches: (1)

---

8   For comparison: the market capitalization of the entire S&P500 was worth $25.75 trillion (28 February 2020).

9   https://sseinitiative.org/sse-event/un-sse-initiative-10-year-anniversary-celebration/

10 https://www.blackrock.com/corporate/investor-relations/larry-fink-ceo-letter

negative screening[11] or 'avoid strategies', which exclude certain sectors, practices or companies from their potential investment portfolio; (2) *positive screening* or 'advance strategies', which select and include companies with superior sustainability performance; (3) *norms-based screening*, which excludes companies with practices that are not in line with international norms (Boxes 8.1 and 8.4); (4) *ESG integration*, which systemically includes ESG risks and opportunities in financial analysis and investment decisions; (5) *sustainability-themed investing,* with a focus on specific sustainable development issues (e.g. low carbon, renewable energy, social diversity); (6) *impact investing*, which intends to achieve positive measurable ESG impact; and (7) *corporate engagement*, which uses active shareholder engagement with companies to influence their corporate behaviour on ESG issues (cf. Uzsoki, 2020). Concurrently, the call for a shift from voluntary to mandatory sustainability reporting is gaining momentum, aiming to push an accelerated scaling of private sector investments in sustainable development.

CSR at intervention/engagement level 2 (minimizing negative externalities, 'avoid doing harm', preventing or mitigating reputational damage) stands for **Corporate Social *Responsiveness*.** Guidelines for corresponding 'risk-mitigation' strategies to address both actual and potential negative impacts are best represented by the Principles of Responsible Business Conduct (RBC), as defined by the OECD (Box 8.4).

PRINCIPLES FOR RESPONSIBLE BUSINESS CONDUCT (RBC) – OECD GUIDELINES FOR MULTINATIONAL ENTERPRISES

BOX 8.4

The Organization for Economic Cooperation and Development (OECD) initiated general principles and standards for 'Responsible Business Conduct' – consistent with applicable laws and internationally recognized standards – as part of its OECD

---

11   The rating methodology of *Corporate Knights' Global 100 Index* of most sustainable corporations, for instance, contains '*Exclusionary Screens*' based on 21 metrics. Metrics include: 'access to medicine laggards' (pharmaceutical companies in the bottom quartile of the Access to Medicine ranking); 'access to nutrition laggards' (food companies in the bottom quartile of the Access to Nutrition index); 'blocking climate policy' (companies flagged for opposing Paris-aligned climate policy); 'cement carbon laggards'; 'civilian firearms' (companies that manufacture civilian automatic and semi-automatic firearms, magazines or parts); 'deforestation and palm oil laggards' (companies engaging in deforestation); 'energy' (fossil fuel companies with less than 20% of new investments in themes consistent with decarbonisation); 'farm animal welfare laggards', 'gambling'; 'oil sand laggards', 'severe human rights violations', 'thermal coal', and 'tobacco'. See: https://www.corporateknights.com/wp-content/uploads/2021/03/2021-Global-100_Methodology_Updated.pptx.pdf

**B
O
X

8.4**

Guidelines for Multinational Enterprises (Chapter 6). Although primarily aimed at multinational companies (state-owned enterprises included), the RBC principles can also be of relevance for small and medium-sized businesses.

RBC is based on the notion that businesses have a responsibility to adopt responsible business practices that take into account both the bottom line (i.e. contributing to economic, environmental, and social progress with a view to achieving sustainable development), as well as the impact of their activities on society. The guidelines are intended to provide a clearer understanding of the baseline standards for how businesses should understand and address the **risks of their operations**, and to equip them with the necessary processes to meet their responsibilities. They also enable societal stakeholders to hold companies accountable for reasonable expectations. The guidelines cover RBC principles and standards related to information disclosure, human rights, employment and labour, environment, anti-corruption, consumer interests, science and technology, competition and taxation.

Risk reduction

Although businesses are seen as the engine of the economy – creators of economic and social development through job creation, development of skills, technology, and the provision of goods and services – the prevailing take of the RBC principles and standards is *risk reduction*. The guidelines acknowledge the positive contribution of business, but seek to ensure that corporate activities do not have adverse impacts on people, the environment and society at large. This may include, for example, when operating in 'host countries' where laws on human rights, environmental protection, labour relations and financial accountability may be poorly enforced.

The guidelines for RBC hence aim to **avoid and address adverse impact** of corporate behaviour related to their operations, supply chains and other business relationships. Accordingly, a key element of RBC is **risk-based due diligence** as an integral part of core business policies and activities. In this area, due diligence is to be understood as an ongoing, responsive process – informed by meaningful engagement with relevant stakeholders – through which companies "**identify, prevent and mitigate** their actual and potential negative impacts, and account for how those impacts are addressed". It applies to a company's own operations and throughout their supply chains; it relates to all types of companies, operating in all countries and all sectors of the economy. The nature and extent of due diligence can be influenced by factors such as the size of the enterprise, the context of operations, its business model, its position in supply chains, the nature of its products or services.

As regards the *scope* of corporate responsibilities, the OECD guidelines specify that enterprises should:

- ■ "*Avoid causing or contributing to* adverse impacts on matters covered by the Guidelines, through their own activities, and address such impacts when they occur."

- ■ "Seek to *prevent or mitigate* an adverse impact where they have not contributed to that impact, when the impact is nevertheless directly linked to their operations, products or services by a business relationship. This is not intended to shift responsibility from the entity causing an adverse impact to the enterprise with which it has a business relationship."

- ■ "*Encourage*, where practicable, business partners including suppliers and sub-contractors, to apply principles of responsible business conduct compatible with the Guidelines", in addition to addressing adverse impacts on matters covered by the guidelines.

Sources: OECD (2014) *OECD Guidelines for Multinational Enterprise – Responsible Business Conduct Matters*; OECD (2018) *OECD Due Diligence Guidance for Responsible Business Conduct*; OECD (2011) *OECD Guidelines for Multinational Enterprises*.

8.4.3   Level 3: the strategic business case

The societal legitimacy of a company to a large extent depends on the net outcome of positive and negative externalities. Companies that produce products or services that (also) provide a solution for a societal problem or latent need, create positive spill-over effects or positive externalities as part of their regular activities. The strategy literature speaks of 'shared value creation' (Porter and Kramer, 2011): to have a positive return on investment for the company *and* society. Here, the business case is oriented towards *seizing the various opportunities* that active engagement with, and investment in, specific dimensions of sustainability imply. At least three rationales exist for an 'active' business case: (a) strategic resource-seeking: safeguarding sufficient resources for continued production and future operations; (b) market entry: developing a 'sustainable' niche in an existing market; (c) market extension, based on meeting an unserved or underserved need.

(A)   STRATEGIC RESOURCE-SEEKING

Resource-seeking considerations provide an important rationale for an active sustainability strategy in many sectors. The prospect of depleted vital natural resources (e.g. fish, minerals, wood, energy, food crops) forces companies operating in these sectors to act more decisively. The business case is both simple and compelling: if resource-dependent companies fail to act now, there will be no product to sell or source in the near future. This is why, for instance, Unilever in

1997 initiated the Marine Stewardship Council (MSC) – in partnership with many non-market agents – to foster 'sustainable fisheries'. Confronted with rapid depletion of fish stocks around the world, the MSC programme was rolled out for strategic rather than ideological or philanthropic purposes. Increasingly, *product stewardship* is mentioned as the primary motivation for an active CSR strategy, along with *life cycle analysis* approaches (from farm to fork), *supplier and stakeholder involvement* and a *competitive differentiation focus* (Hengelaar, 2017). The more immediate and systemic the shortage becomes (Chapter 7), the more incumbents have an interest in searching for strategic, rather than piecemeal approaches to sustainability issues.

(B) MARKET ENTRY

Reliance on market entry considerations particularly applies to start-ups that use sustainability as their unique selling point. When entering an existing and mature market, companies are often faced with oligopolies: markets that are dominated by a few established big players. As these companies can reap sizable economies of scale, they are able to sell their product at very low prices. Large, dominant companies have generally based their success on other logics than 'sustainability', and this presents 'entry opportunities' for newcomers with alternative value propositions. Ben & Jerry's and The Body Shop are both classic cases of newcomers that made a successful entry in the mature ice cream and personal care markets respectively, primarily based on their sustainability concept and image. More recently, California-based Beyond Meat successfully entered the American burger market with its meatless, plant-based alternative and mission to make protein from animals 'obsolete'. It rapidly extended its meatless 'meat' product assortment, its alliances with American 'fast food' and restaurant chains (e.g. McDonald's, Subway, DelTaco, Dunkin) and expanded to new market outlets (supermarkets in the United States, Canada, United Kingdom, the Netherlands) and became a foreign co-producer (in the Netherlands) to serve the European market. Typically, new entrants use the sustainability claim of their product (fair trade, animal-friendly, social, eco-friendly) to legitimize higher prices, at least initially. Marketing research shows that only a limited number of people are willing to pay 'premium prices' for sustainable products, however, confronting many newcomers with serious scaling problems. Most new entrants consequently remain 'niche' players. Some have been taken over by incumbents, as was the case with Ben & Jerry's (by Unilever) and The Body Shop (by L'Oréal, and later by Natura). Beyond Meat, after ten years, went public in 2019. It offered at $241 million and went public with a $1.5 billion valuation. Three months later, Beyond Meat was worth over $13 billion – a rise of 859% from its initial IPO price of $25. Beyond Meat's IPO turned out to be the best-performing IPO of US companies since 2000.

(C) EXTENSION OF MARKETS

Meeting as yet unserved or underserved *needs* provides the third rationale for an active business case. In 'rich' and saturated markets, 'created demand' and over-consumption of mostly non-sustainable products and services is a regular practice. Only more recently have major multinational companies been dedicating innovative capacity to expanding their business to unserved communities. In many cases, the strategic rationale for such a move has plainly been stagnating growth in their core markets. Enter the notion that the 'bottom of the pyramid' (BoP) consists of billions of people across many countries, whose daily needs for certain goods and services have largely been overlooked. The BoP offers potential for growth in 'new markets', provided that companies are able to develop reliable, good quality, yet sufficiently cheap products that actually serve the needs of impoverished people. Profitability is then to come from utilizing *economies of scale* – because of necessarily low margins, required investments in product/service development and the costs of doing business associated with entering new markets.

The BoP strategy has been linked to the idea of 'frugal innovation', which involves the (design) process of optimally reducing the complexity and costs of a certain good and its production. BoP and frugal innovation strategies have brought forth adjusted products and services developed to fit the needs – and improve the conditions – of unserved or underserved poor and low-income consumer segments. Common examples include microfinance, micro-insurance, 'mobile money' (MPesa), sanitation and hygiene products, water purification and lighting solutions for those without access to the electricity grid. These products and services not only reach new customers, but also contribute to more inclusive (sustainable) development, because of their positive effects on empowerment, education, health, entrepreneurship, gender equality and job creation. When serving *societal needs* also means 'good business', level 3 sustainable develop-ment considerations can become an integral part of a company's long-term competitive positioning and survival strategy.

At the third level of intervention/SDG-engagement, the CSR acronym gets its best-known connotation: **Corporate Social *Responsibility***. This type of CSR strategy presents a strategic business case aimed at the *scaling and optimization of positive externalities*. It requires companies to go beyond 'liability-oriented' reasoning, and more into responsibility and 'positive duty'-oriented reasoning. If that mindset has truly taken hold, the CSR acronym can be elaborated as **Corporate *Strategic* Responsibility**. The business case then resembles an 'ordi-nary' investment curve (Box 8.5), with CSR as an integral part of strategic decision-making. Necessary measures to reap the full strategic benefits from an active sustainability orientation in any case involve an effective 'internal alignment' of employees and functional areas of management (Chapters 9 and 11). This requires the alignment of policies and rewards schemes (Chiappetta et al., 2010) and training of employees (Asgary and Li, 2016), in order to embed awareness of CSR in *all* aspects of the business. Not as a response, but *in anticipation* of potential legislation, societal needs or customer demand.

SUSTAINABLE BUSINESS MODELS AS AN INVESTMENT CURVE: BREAKING THROUGH THE RESPONSIVE PHASE

Research into the relationship between societal (CSP) and financial performance (CFP) does not produce universal patterns, nor straightforward business cases (section 8.1). When linked to the transition phases of companies and the levels of operationalization of corporate responsibility, however, a U-shaped pattern can be revealed.

At level 1, cost savings resulting from environmental measures such as resource efficiency can be related to relatively strong financial performance (Ambec and Lanoie, 2008). At level 2, costs generally precede benefits. Investments in minimizing negative effects to enhance (or not damage) reputation may improve the company's 'goodwill', but initially lower direct profit margins. Companies that focus *solely* on levels 1 and 2 thus face a downward slope in their return on sustainable investments (Figure 8.3). Their investment curve points in the wrong direction, which can make it difficult to legitimize – to shareholders or top management – why the next phase of enhanced sustainability should be entered.

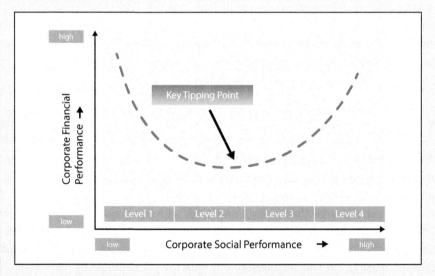

Figure 8.3 The U-shaped correlation between financial and societal performance

Source: based on Van Tulder et al., 2014

Key tipping point

The interface between level 2 (avoiding 'doing harm', minimizing negative externalities) and level 3 (enhancing 'doing good', optimizing positive externalities) represents a key tipping point in the adopted business model of a company. Overcoming it requires a fundamentally different logic of the business case (Van Tulder, 2018a). Interestingly, research related to higher levels of corporate societal engagement shows an upward Rate-of-Return slope, after companies have successfully overcome the internal and external barriers related to this threshold. Taken as a whole, the correlation between financial and societal performance shows a 'U-shape', like any 'regular' investment curve in the long run. Taking the basic principle of investment – costs precede benefits – on board can help in defining more sophisticated sustainable business models.

A universal pattern

The U-shape between financial and social/societal responsible performance is not only found in developed economies; similar correlations have been noted in developing markets like China (Ye and Zhang, 2011). Apparently, a higher score on sustainability performance in time reduces the associated costs. Companies must generally pass through a transition phase to be able to fully profit from their efforts to integrate all three dimensions of sustainability: social, economic and ecological. Lower financial results from investments in sustainability should thus be assessed critically: they may be an indication of investments not paying off, but can also point to being in the middle of a vital transition, for which it is difficult to determine exactly how long that phase will last. Chapter 11 further specifies the type of functional tipping points a company has to master to facilitate the transition to higher degrees of sustainability. For the financial strategy of a company – the basis of the business case – several tipping points can be defined that must be resolved and passed, in order to make a 'sustainable enterprise' a reality. Entrepreneurs who want to head towards sustainability, must work out whether they can take steps with and within their organization to shift:

- From shareholder value to stakeholder value
- From adversarial to constructive, longer-term stakeholder relationships
- From low to high involvement and share of sustainable investment funds
- From quarterly profits (and reporting) to longer-term profits (and reporting)

8.4.4   Level 4: the systemic ('new economy') business case

Wicked societal challenges particularly play out at the level of whole systems. Part II showed that most SDGs are systemic in nature – although often caused by basic failures in primary responsibilities – and accordingly require a distinct type of corporate approach. The more companies recognize that the whole system 'fails', the more they will be interested in developing strategies that not only create a competitive advantage for themselves (level 3), but also contribute to 'fixing' the system (level 4). As former DSM CEO Feike Sijbesma stated: "I cannot successfully operate a business in a society that fails"; to which former Unilever CEO Paul Polman added: ". . . nor can business be a bystander in the system that gives them life in the first place" (Foreword in: Elkington, 2020). Many corporate leaders formulated a comparable motive for their involvement in the SDGs: the present system fails, is not resilient enough, and involves risks of disruption that are simply too big and too pervasive to ignore (Chapter 7).

The business case at level 4 is also known as the *proactive business case* for sustainability. The management literature uses a large variety of synonyms to indicate its content, ranging from 'integrated' (Slawinski and Bansal, 2012) and 'sustaincentric' (Valente, 2012), to 'transformational' and 'radical'. Most refer to the *new economy* business case, which relates to a vision on the outlook of the fourth industrial revolution (Chapter 1). The proactive business case requires systems thinking, holistic approaches, and anticipative and long-term focus (Walls et al., 2011). It always includes a keen eye on innovation – especially breakthrough innovations (Valente, 2012; Chen et al., 2012). – and the acknowledgment that cooperation – specifically in the form of cross-sector partnerships – is needed to make the transition stick at the systems level. The business case of proactive companies is in the *creation of new markets*, inspired by a long-term vision on sustainable development and a more resilient society, to serve the (latent) *needs of both present and future generations*.

Why would companies be interested in radical or transformative change? Proactiveness, after all, is not a guarantee for positive performance in each setting (Aragón-Correa and Rubio-López, 2007). Transition research shows that radical systems innovation is a precondition for societal transition.[12] For individual companies, however, the business case for driving disruptive innovation processes is often only positive from a long-term perspective. Substantial and risky investments are needed first; frontrunners might not survive. Management research (Bansal and Roth, 2000) finds that the values and motivations of the corporate leadership strongly influence the business case for proactive behaviour. Drivers for proactive behaviour are external, in terms of societal awareness

---

12 In the successful spread of new technological paradigms, frontrunner companies – and their home economies – were able to seize a long-term strategic advantage. This happened around the introduction of cotton and machinery (first industrial revolution), oil, cars and infrastructure (shaping the American economy), and telecommunication and the internet (Chapter 1).

of systems risks and a shared sense of urgency. But successful proactive behaviour always needs to be complemented by internal drivers: critical capabilities to make change material; dedicated commitment of employees; agility in strategically aligning functional areas of management. It is in the *mix of internal and external drivers* for sustainability that positive 'antecedents of change' are developed. External drivers – such as critical stakeholder pressure – might actually help the organization to speed up the formulation and implementation of proactive business cases. Whilst the active business case for sustainability is mostly intrinsically motivated, the proactive business case always requires a combination of intrinsic and extrinsic value drivers (Van Tulder, 2018a) to become successful.

Two distinct, yet often complementary and mutually reinforcing, types of business cases for level 4 interventions/engagement can be distinguished: (a) an *ecosystem approach* and (b) a *network approach*.

(A) ECOSYSTEMS APPROACHES: FROM JOINT AMBITIONS TO INDIVIDUAL ACTION

The creation of ecosystems is usually attributed to the action of governments – as the logical guardians of the 'public good'. But their primary intervention powers (laws and subsidies) are rarely sufficient to create vibrant, resilient and sustainable ecosystems. Ecosystems can be described as constantly co-evolving communities of diverse (public and private) organizations that create new value through sophisticated models of both collaboration and competition. The creation of 'sustainable ecosystems' that are conducive to collaboration and co-creation has become an integral part of building the proactive business case. It helps companies to implement a variety of business models – circular, inclusive, sharing (see Chapter 9) – that they cannot develop on their own. A precondition for the success of an ecosystem approach is the complementarity of its networked actors, and the extent to which they share a common purpose orientation. The ecosystem benefits from integrating complementary logics (market, state, civil society) and various capacities to create, mobilize, organize and scale. The sustainable ecosystem is bound together by the shared interest of various actors to: (1) create 'common pool' goods, (2) change the rules of economic interaction, (3) actively facilitate collaboration, and (4) work towards interconnected approaches and solutions for sustainable development. The better functioning and the more purpose-oriented an ecosystem is, the more resilient it becomes. Governments are vital in the creation of an *enabling environment* for collaborative and innovative action by private organizations, for instance by explicitly endorsing the transformative ambition of the SDG-agenda (and actively reporting on progress, as explained in Box 6.2). But governments cannot create or plan an ecosystem 'top-down'.

Individual organizations that are part of a vibrant ecosystem can profit from *collaborative advantage* and a selection environment that 'rewards' proactive business models and bold innovation for transformative change. It also provides an enabling environment for companies to further explore, co-create and develop a more sophisticated *nexus approach* to sustainable development. A nexus approach (see section 2.3.4) is aimed at smartly linking and leveraging relevant social, ecological, economic, institutional and collaborative aspects in order to *synergize* sustainability effects. By adopting a *portfolio* of SDG-related activities that optimizes the positive effects of their business model while reducing the negative effects (Van Zanten and Van Tulder, 2020), companies can have a positive societal impact and contribute to societal resilience. Furthermore, an ecosystem enables proactive companies to reap *insider advantages*'. Streamlined flows of ideas, capabilities, 'capital' and activities between the ecosystem's networked partners tend to create strong barriers to entry by new competitors.

Ecosystems thinking is increasingly used to mainstream sustainable business models and to help organizations – both public and private – understand and measure how they increase, decrease or transform 'stocks of value' through their activities. In the accountancy and reporting practice, ecosystems thinking has become related to business case development by looking at the *return* on various types of capital investments. The IIRC[13] (2013b) distinguishes six sources of 'capital' in this area, ranging from 'tangible' to 'intangible': natural capital, industrial (working) capital, human capital, cultural capital, social capital, and creative capital. These capitals are stocks of value that are increased, decreased or transformed through the activities and outputs of an organization. An *integrated perspective* on the business case that considers *all* relevant stocks of value is fundamental to a better understanding of the resources and relationships used, affected and created by an organization (elaborated in section 11.7).

Examples of ecosystem developments include 'inclusive port development' projects, 'sustainable/smart/resilient cities', 'circular economies' or 'inclusive value chains'. For individual companies, the viability and contours of a level 4 business case depend on their *embeddedness* in relevant networks and local collaborative arrangements, as well as on their *credibility and prior performance* on level 1 (addressing market failure) and level 2 (minimizing negative externalities) types of corporate responsibilities.

---

13 The International Integrated Reporting Council (IIRC) is a global coalition of regulators, investors, companies, standard setters, the accounting profession, academia and NGOs promoting communication about value creation as the next step in the evolution of corporate reporting and 'mainstreaming' sustainable business practice.

(B)   NETWORK EFFECTS: FROM INDIVIDUAL ACTION TO COMMON POOL PROVISIONS

Common-pool provisions can also be initiated by the actions of individual private organizations. Proactively contributing to collective goods creation can actually pay off for individual companies, if the effort leads to system-wide advantageous effects *and* generates further opportunities for commercially viable spinoffs or first-mover advantages. Building a business case that contributes to the creation of mostly non-rivalrous, non-excludable goods or services may appear counterintuitive. For so-called *disruptive innovations*, however, it has been proved feasible. Disruptive innovations make products and services more accessible, affordable and available to a larger population, with positive transformative effects across industries and areas of society. Disruptive innovations create potential first-mover advantages along three strategic venues: *network effects, positive lock-ins* and *(open) standard-setting*. When organized well, individual organizations can set 'new rules' and 'redefine norms' that help them to compete based on higher levels of sustainability (Chapter 10), without relying on governments to create a level playing field through (stricter) regulation or financial support.

Network effects arise if the value of a specific product or service depends on the number of others using it. The effect refers to the incremental benefit gained by an existing user for each new user that joins the network. Classic examples of network effects are the telephone system and social networks. Whether an organization can reap a positive return from the provision of 'network goods', hinges on the adoption rate beyond a critical mass of users needed for the network effect to take hold. As a user network scales up, the costs per unit decrease logarithmically, to the extent that the initial offering can be provided nearly 'for free'. 'Freemium' business models are based on this network effect. A company then provides the basic-level service for free – thereby creating a 'collective' good – while offering optional (future) additional services at an extra cost.

Network effects are substantially reinforced if the product or service evolves towards a new common standard. The more users accept or apply the same standard, the more network effects can contribute to a financially feasible business case. Successful initiators of a *de facto standard* brought about by massive (consumer) acceptance can profit from 'first-mover advantages', while creating a **positive lock-in effect** towards a higher level of sustainability.[14] Positive lock-in

---

14 Note that network effects and 'de facto standards' can also trigger *negative* 'lock-in' effects that initially speed up specific applications but, in later stages, limit further innovation and spinoffs due to limited further participation of stakeholders, proprietary issues or reinforcement of monopoly positions.

effects have notably been triggered by the initiation of **open standards,** for instance related to technologies (e.g. software), systems (the World Wide Web), processes, and ways of organizing (open formats). An open standard is initially developed by an individual organization (or group of cooperation partners), and, at a later stage, made publicly available for others to adopt, implement and extend. The open standard then becomes a public good that defines a new level playing field and selection environment within which organizations can compete and innovate.

Viable sustainable business models have been built around leveraging 'opensource' and 'open-access' standards that advanced innovations in the field of, for instance, medicine and vaccine development (tropical diseases, neglected diseases), software development (free applications), research (open-access journals) and education (massive open online courses). Through decreased R&D costs, faster-paced innovation and accelerated product development, many innovative *access to* provisions have been developed that serve the needs of many and contribute to enhanced inclusiveness and the provision of 'common-pool' goods.

The business case for more systemic sustainability efforts thus depends on the potential of a newly developed technology, product or service to: (a) sufficiently trigger network effects, and (b) to set a new (open) systems standard for its sustainability offering as a new threshold for next-stage competition. The business case for individual companies depends on their ability to reap first-mover advantages based on their ability to set standards – alone, or together with others – that are adopted by a large number of stakeholders. Level 4 business cases for sustainability include disruptive innovation with substantial *scale effects* due to successful network creation of sustainable products, services and technologies. At this level of intervention/engagement, CSR is to be understood as **Corporate *Societal (or Sustainable)* Responsibility**.

8.5 APPROACHING THE SDG CHALLENGE FROM THE NON-PROFIT SIDE

The business case for sustainability ultimately defines the financial foundation and continuity of a private organization in terms of benefits, costs and risks of investments. A non-profit organization is thereby characterized by the act of investing its surplus revenues back into the further support of its primary (civic) purpose or mission, rather than distributing it to the organization's shareholders or owners for the sole purpose of financial gain. The non-profit side of society produces 'social capital' (Putnam, 2000) by adding different organizational approaches to sustainable development challenges. In the management literature, these non-profit approaches are only occasionally taken into account in terms of business models and business cases. The non-profit side is an under-researched area for business models and business cases, partly due to the prevalence of *for*-profit cases in management studies and training. Nevertheless, a wide and versatile range of fascinating organizations operate at the state/civil society and civil society/market interface, including universities, hospitals, charities, trade unions, public pension funds, mutual insurance companies, NGOs, cooperatives, activist groups, voluntary associations, clubs, community foundations, religious organizations, political parties and social enterprises. On the non-profit side of society, too, many hybrid organizational forms have developed that combine for-profit and non-profit dimensions in their strategies and operations. All non-profit organizations face financial viability issues in securing a solid base for their continuity and contribution to inclusive and sustainable development. In this respect, they are not that different from for-profit organizations. But their strategic 'repertoire', as well as their 'logic' in addressing sustainability issues, is decisively distinctive from for-profit organizations.

On the non-profit side of the societal triangle (Figure 8.4), we can distinguish three basic organizational forms: civil society organizations (CSOs), which are primarily aimed at mobilizing and organizing volunteers and members around

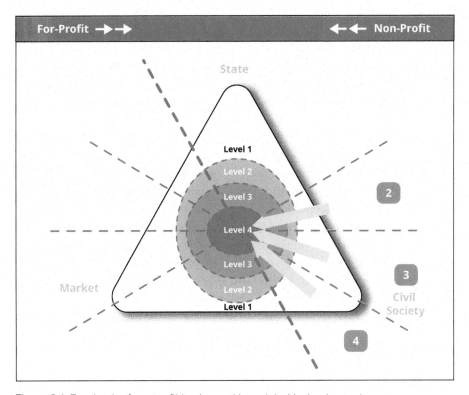

Figure 8.4 Four levels of non-profit involvement in sustainable development

a shared cause (type 3); cooperatives and social enterprises that produce products and services (type 4); and semi-public organizations – such as hospitals, universities, mutual insurance companies and public pension funds – that serve wider communities (type 2). The paramount characteristic these organizations all have in common is *mutual support* and the *sharing of risk.* Notwithstanding their non-profit orientation, many of these organizations are capable of generating (sizable) revenues and positive returns ('profits'). Profits are, in principle, reinvested to sustain the growth or enhancement of mutual activities, or given back to members, for instance through reduced membership contributions. Generally, non-profit organizations are more strongly embedded in national and local ecosystems and less internationally orientated than for-profit organizations. They also tend to be more risk-averse, since they represent and act in the longer-term interests of their members.

■ **Type 2**: at the public/private interface, we find non-profit-oriented private organizations that are directed towards the provision of public goods and services, and operate within the realm of government (often regulated under public law). This category contains surprisingly large organizations, such as public pension funds, mutual funds, and some public utilities.

■ **Public pension funds** present a particular category of semi-public organizations: they invest money based on collectivized investment risk, representing the longer-term benefits of their 'members'. Pension funds are amongst the world's biggest institutional investors, with passive and active investment portfolios that include both national and international companies (stocks) and countries (government bonds). The 'profit' that public pension funds accumulate is aimed at providing longer-term dividends for their members (principals) in the form of pensions (retirement income). Public pension funds generally seek stable investment returns with minimal risks; they operate on a long-term investment horizon while securing sufficient liquidity to pay out pension benefits. Government pensions funds are among the largest asset funds in the world. The Social Security Trust Funds (US) – the world's largest public pension fund – holds around $2.89 trillion in total assets, the Government Pension Investment Fund in Japan manages $1.55 trillion and Stichting Pensioenfonds ABP (the Netherlands) around $455 billion (Table 8.3).[15]

More hybrid forms exist as well: some public pension funds combine their public status with a 'cooperative' governance form, like PGGM in the Netherlands. They may, therefore, also be classified as

---

15 https://www.swfinstitute.org/fund-rankings/public-pension, 28 May 2020.

'semi-private'. The Norway Government Pension Fund Global (Norway's oil fund) is not a pension fund in the conventional sense, but rather a 'sovereign wealth fund' (SWF) – pools of assets owned and managed directly or indirectly by the government to achieve national objectives for the benefit of the country's economy and citizens. With $1.18 trillion in total assets, Norway's Global is the world's largest SWF.[16] The purpose of its existence is "to help finance the Norwegian welfare state for future generations". Global derives part of its revenues from Norwegian oil and gas production that is transferred to the fund. Nevertheless, over half of revenues come from its investments in equities, fixed income (government bonds in over 70 countries) and real estate (rental income). The fund holds around 1.5% of all shares in the world's listed companies, with investments in around 9,200 companies worldwide. It is managed independently from government by Norges Bank Investment Management, part of Norway's central bank.[17]

■ **Mutuals:** a mutual is a private organization that is collectively owned and governed by its members (customers, policyholders). Mutuals exist and operate with the sole purpose of benefitting their members, based on the principle of solidarity (mutual support) to overcome the effects of risks. Financial surpluses accrue to members/policyholders (for instance, through reduced premiums), rather than external shareholders (as is the case with 'stock insurers', which are owned by shareholding investors). The mutualist movement gained momentum in the second half of the 19th century – more or less parallel to the introduction of many cooperatives – as a response to social deprivation and insecurity, caused by the low wages of the upcoming capitalist companies (types 5 and 6). Workers decided to organize solidarity funds by putting aside a portion of their pay to support those in destitute situations (sickness, disability, old age, death). As an alternative to public assistance or charity, the mutual movement became the cornerstone of social insurance schemes and the funding of social security.[18] The concept of *mutual insurance* originated in late 17th-century England, following the Great Fire of London in 1666, to cover losses as a result of the fire. Presently, mutual property/casualty insurance companies exist in nearly every country. Their policyholders

---

16 https://www.swfinstitute.org/fund-rankings/sovereign-wealth-fund
17 https://www.nbim.no/en/
18 See the International Association of Mutual Benefit Societies (AIM), an international umbrella organization of federations of health mutuals and health insurance bodies, counting 59 members from 30 countries in Europe, Latin America and Africa and the Middle East: https://www.aim-mutual.org/

collectively fill the roles of both owners and customers. Some mutual insurers are among the world's largest insurance companies.

Globally, more than 5,100 active mutual insurers collectively wrote $1.3 trillion in insurance premiums in 2017.[19] They present 27% of the global insurance markets, serve 922 million members/policy-holders, and employ 1.16 million people. The ten largest mutual insurance markets in terms of market share are in Europe, ranging from Austria (59.9%) to Hungary (43.6%).[20] Mutual business also has a significant presence in the world's two largest insurance markets: the US (39.9%) and Japan (42.2%). The US is the largest mutual market in the world in terms of total premiums, assets and number of companies. The total investments of the global mutual insurance sector in 2017 – notably in bonds (60%), stocks and shares (18%), mortgages and loans (12%) – were valued at $7.42 trillion. In 2017, mutual insurers held $8.9 trillion in total assets (ICMIF, 2019).

- **Public utilities:** in most countries, public utilities – such as postal services, telecom, water – are to be classified as 'type 2' organizations (depending on country-specific regulation, utility companies may also classify as type 7). These organizations deliver public services to private customers under a legal obligation. It is part of their duty to deliver a 'universal service', even to remote areas that are not commercially viable for for-profit organizations. Take, for instance, the postal services, a public utility that in many countries belongs to the largest organizations measured by revenue. In 2014, postal revenues of the world's top 15 postal operators amounted to $245 billion.[21] From this top 15, twelve organizations are 'government-owned' (with the state owning more than 50% of the company's shares). In 2014, US Postal Services and China Post (the largest government-controlled postal operators) each had revenues over $60 billion. Three of the 15 largest postal companies have been privatized (Deutsche Post, Royal Mail, PostNL) and are presently publicly listed, albeit strictly regulated with regard to their national postal services. In some countries (such as Brazil), the postal service is a government agency.

- **Type 2/3:** along the government/non-government interface, we find non-profit-oriented **hybrid organizations** directed towards the provision of

---

19 https://www.icmif.org/publications/global-mutual-market-share/global-mutual-market-share-10
20 Europe's regional mutual market share was estimated at 32.7% in 2017 (25.4% in the life insurance business and 42.1% in the non-life insurance business).
21 https://www.ttnews.com/articles/us-postal-service-tops-list-largest-postal-operators

public and/or social/club goods and services, in particular hospitals and universities. These organizations often use *cross-subsidization* schemes to fund loss-making activities (their provision of public goods, based on mutual support) with profit-making activities (fees of students, executive courses, private health treatments, commercial activities). Other hybrids that fall into this category include international sports organizations such as FIFA (football), IOC (Olympic Games) and IAAF (athletics) that organize big semi-commercial sports events, which they use to sponsor sports and community development projects around the world.

■ **Type 3: civil society organizations (CSOs)** can be classified as private, non-governmental organizations that are non-profit oriented and aimed at the provision of public or social/club goods and services. This category includes formal and informal entities, voluntarily formed by people in the social sphere ('the 3rd sector'). CSOs represent a wide range of interests and ties. They include both 'community-based organizations' (sports clubs, church groups, neighbourhood associations, food banks), as well as internationally operating NGOs. According to NGO Advisor,[22] the 'social profit' sector amounts to nearly 12 million organizations worldwide. Examples of leading civil society organizations include Amnesty International, the International Trade Union Confederation (ITUC), the World Wide Fund for Nature (WWF), Greenpeace and the Danish Refugee Council (DRC). The World Economic Forum even refers to some of the largest as 'civil society brands', because of their broad international presence, reputation and name recognition.

In many countries, legitimate non-profit organizations are often exempt from taxes on income, sales or property if their operations exclusively serve their charitable, scientific, religious or public safety mission. In particular the larger organizations are highly efficient in revenue generation. The 'richest' non-profit organizations include Catholic Charities, the Salvation Army, United Way Worldwide, Goodwill Industries International and the YMCA, with revenues of between $3.7 billion and $7.4 billion in 2019.[23] The world's largest NGO – with over 97,000 employees – is BRAC from Bangladesh. Its operations are focused on economic development, education, public health and disaster relief programmes in conflict-prone and post-disaster settings. Organizations such as CARE, Oxfam and WorldVision are amongst the largest International NGOs in development cooperation, and active supporters of the SDG-agenda.

■ **Type 4** organizations operate at the civil society/market interface. They represent non-profit-oriented, non-governmental organizations aimed at the

---

22 NGO Advisor researches, evaluates and ranks NGOs worldwide to showcase best practices and innovative thinking. See https://www.ngoadvisor.net/about

23 https://www.tharawat-magazine.com/facts/top-5-richest-nonprofit-organizations/

provision of *private* goods and services. Type 4 organizations notably include **cooperatives**, which come in all sorts and shapes and are present in every type of economy – developed or developing. Cooperatives are people-centred, value-driven enterprises that are owned, governed and operated by and for their members, to realize their common economic, social and cultural needs and aspirations. Principles and values around fairness, equality, democratic member control ('one member, one vote'), autonomy, self-responsibility, social justice and cooperation/solidarity are at the heart of these enterprises. Surpluses accrue to the group; profits are generally reinvested in the continuity or the enhancement of the enterprise, or returned to the member-owners.

According to the International Co-operative Alliance (ICA), there are around 3 million cooperatives across the world that together employ approximately 280 million people (10% of the world's employed population). The 300 largest cooperative businesses together generated nearly $2.1 trillion in total turnover in 2017 (World Cooperative Monitor, 2019). Cooperatives can be classified as: (1) *producer cooperatives*, in which members cooperate in a joint production activity as an enterprise (prevalent in agriculture, crafts, fishing, energy, industrial sector); (2) *worker cooperatives*, in which members have a common interest in the work provided by or ensured through the cooperative (notably in construction, utilities, green energy); (3) *consumer/user cooperatives*, where members are the consumers/users of the goods and services made available by the cooperative, by purchasing and supplying at competitive conditions in the interest of their members (for instance, banking and credit services, agricultural products, education, housing); and (4) *multi-stakeholder cooperatives*, which have more than one type of member – none dominant, none with veto power – represented in the governance structure (for instance, in health and social work).

Large cooperatives particularly appear in the financial services, insurance sector, agriculture, food industries, and wholesale and trade sectors (Table 8.3). The world's top 10 of the largest cooperatives, measured in turnover, ranges from nearly $39 billion (Nonghyup, Republic of Korea) to over $96 billion (Groupe Crédit Agricole, France). Because cooperatives operate at the interface between for-profit and non-profit, they often compete directly with commercial organizations. It has been found that during an economic downturn, cooperatives in the finance sector tend to remain more stable than commercial banks (World Cooperative Monitor, 2019: 27). Because of their value-based and mutual orientation, large cooperative banks like Rabobank or Groupe Crédit Agricole are also more likely to embrace sustainability ambitions. Groupe Crédit Agricole, for instance, calls this ambition its "mutualist commitment to inclusive development", and considers its green finance activities as one of the Group's 'growth drivers'.

■ **Type 4/5: social enterprises** are generally described as a hybrid between a non-profit and a 'traditional' for-profit business (Galaskiewicz and Barringer, 2012). Social enterprises aim to create both societal and financial value, but do not explicitly put profit before all other goals (Yunus, 2007). Typically, social enterprises seek business solutions and commercial strategies that not only generate profits, but concurrently 'solve' social problems and maximize benefits to society and the environment. They explicitly aspire to achieve 'positive societal impact'. The majority of their profits are principally reinvested in pursuit of their mission on a voluntary basis. Financial viability and safeguarding a sustainable revenue stream are some of the greatest challenges for social enterprises. The initial funding of smaller organizations is often based on 'crowdfunding', in-kind contributions or grants. Social enterprises typically derive their revenues from a combination of 'market sources' (producing and selling goods and services to the public sector, the private sector, and consumers) and 'non-market sources' (for instance, government subsidies or grants for project-based activities, private donations, volunteers as staff). But many face longer-term funding problems if operations cannot be sufficiently commercialized and scaled. The literature on social enterprises calls this the *valley of death* – the looming trap of not having sufficient income to create the level of efficiency and scale required to make it to the next phase of activities.

Around the world, a great variety exists in the legal entity and organizational structures (for-profit, non-profit) of social enterprises. A recent development has been the introduction of **B-Corps** and *benefit corporations* – the latter referring to a new type of for-profit corporate entity that is legally empowered to pursue positive stakeholder impact alongside profit. Both aim to 'use business as a force for good', guided by the principle of 'do well by doing good'. B-Corps represents a third-party certification scheme (administered by B-Lab) for for-profit companies – regardless of size, industry, corporate structure, location – that voluntary commit to higher standards of transparency, accountability, performance and positive impact in the area of sustainability. Over 2,500 certified B-Corps in over 50 countries existed in 2020. Many are relatively small, representing community platforms, consultancy firms or retailers. The number of large and international B-corps – such as Danone or Patagonia – is growing however. Danone's CEO expressed his choice for 'B-Lab accreditation' as follows: "in an increasingly complex world, big brands and companies are fundamentally challenged as to whose interests they really serve. . . . Accreditation is a great way to express our long-time commitment to dual economic and social progress."[24]

---

24 https://bcorporation.net/certification/large-multinational

Table 8.3 Top non-profit organizations in private and public goods provision (2019)

10 Largest cooperatives * (turnover – employees)			10 Largest public pension funds ** (by total assets)	
• Groupe Crédit Agricole (France)	Financial service	$96.25 bn / 139,000	• Social Security Trust Fund (USA)	$2,889 bn
• Groupe BPCE (France)	Financial service	$59.03 bn / 106,463	• Government Pension Investment Fund (Japan)	$1,549 bn
• REWE Group (Germany)	Wholesale & retail	$55.85 bn / 345,434	• Military Retirement Fund (USA)	$896 bn
• BVR (Germany)	Financial service	$55.29 bn / 177,248	• Federal Employees Retirement System (USA)	$687 bn
• Zenkyoren (Japan)	Insurance	$51.69 bn / 6,282	• National Pension Service of Korea (South Korea)	$609 bn
• Nippon Life (Japan)	Insurance	$48.36 bn / 86,394	• Federal Retirement Thrift Investment Board (USA)	$601 bn
• State Farm (USA)	Insurance	$42.42 bn / 65,664	• Zankyoren (Japan)	$523 bn
• ACDLEC – E. Leclerc (France)	Wholesale & retail	$42.01 bn/	• Stichting Pensioenfonds ABP (Netherlands)	$455 bn
• Zen-Noh (Japan)	Agriculture & Food Industry	$41.37 bn / 7,446	• California Public Employees Retirement System (USA)	$394 bn
• Nonghyup (NACF) (South Korea)	Agriculture & Food Industry	$38.82 bn / 100,594	• Canada Pension Plan Investment Board (Canada)	$387 bn

Sources: * World Cooperative Monitor (2019); **https://www.swfinstitute.org/fund-rankings/public-pension

8.6 FOUR NON-PROFIT BUSINESS CASES FOR SUSTAINABILITY

For each of these (hybrid) types of non-profit-oriented organizations, four distinct rationales or types of business cases for sustainable development can be discerned, each at a different level of intervention and with a different interpretation of 'responsible organizing' (Table 8.4). At level 1, sustainable business cases for non-profits are defined by their ability to (self-)organize mutual support for a specific aim, which is jeopardized if the organization is unable to attract sufficient (financial) resources. At level 2, sustainable business cases deal with the ability of 'responsive' organizing, related in particular to the 'advocacy' role of non-profits. Depending on their exact societal positioning (type 2–4/5 organizations), the level 2 business case for sustainable development involves either the ability to fund campaigns against the non-sustainable action of other actors in society, or the capacity to effectively deal with negative externalities within one's own sphere of responsibilities. Business cases for non-profits at level 3 depend on their ability and willingness to successfully expand their mutual support activities towards

Table 8.4 Four non-profit business cases for sustainability

Level	Responsible organizing – meaning	Basic attitude	Need for intervention	Sources of 'income'
1	Self-organizing	Inactive; inward-looking	***Civic failure:*** addressing poor support/lacking mutual support	Membership fees; church tax; collections/donations; in-kind contributions; subsidies; crowdfunding
2	Responsive organizing	Reactive	***Advocacy:*** solidarity; minimizing negative externalities (own or induced by others)	Reputation/goodwill based on public advocacy campaigns; subsidies; campaign contributions
3	Service-driven organizing	Active	***Service delivery:*** diversification; filling voids left by others	Sales of goods and services; expansion of activities (into the private or public sphere); cross-subsidization
4	Collective organizing	Proactive	***Collective action*** and cross-sector partnering	New social contracts and social economy; partnerships with private and public sector; blended finance

for-profit areas and private-service provision. The business case for level 4 activities is delineated by the ability and willingness of non-profits to engage in collective action that creates an enabling environment for the longer-term collective interests of their constituencies. We will discuss each of these intervention/engagement levels by using examples from exemplary segments of the non-profit side of society (type 2–4/5 organizations).

8.6.1   Level 1: mutual support as a sustainable business case

The basic function of non-profit organizations, first and foremost, is to organize *mutual support* for groups of people. Non-profit organizations are essentially 'mutual support organizations' (MSOs). Mutual support has proved an important factor in organizational resilience, particularly during crises (Box 8.6). The level 1 business case for sustainability of MSOs is, therefore, defined by how these organizations create the foundations and sources of continuity – in terms of shared benefits, costs and risks – for the provision of sufficient levels of mutual support. Just as governments are vulnerable to 'government failure' and companies to 'market failure', MSOs are susceptible to (interrelated) forms of *civic failure* (Chapter 5) that adversely affect their (financial) foundations, efficacy and continuity. Failure to organize sufficient numbers of people to create a sustainable 'club good' reinforces failure in gathering sufficient sources of funding for the continuation and possible upscaling of mutual support aims, and vice versa. The business case for sustainability accordingly involves two vital dimensions, each with its advantages and disadvantages: (a) (re-)alignment and reconfiguration: with the needs, values and interests of social (member) groups, in a financially sustainable manner; and (b) broadening: attracting additional financial resources to sustain a sufficient creation of 'social value' at level 1.

(A) (RE-)ALIGNMENT AND RECONFIGURATION

In many countries, traditional social movements – like trade unions, churches and political parties – have faced a serious reduction in their members' ability or willingness to contribute, either through the payment of fees, voluntary action (in-kind), sponsoring or donating. A comparable trend has been witnessed for MSOs predominantly managed by volunteers, such as community-based sports clubs or community centres. Their business case has been eroding from within. This reality not only jeopardizes the continuity of their activities but also their contribution to socially cohesive and resilient societies. In the past, various MSOs were able to attract government support to sustain or even expand their activities in specific areas. Retreating governments (as a result of neoliberal policies) have prompted non-profits to search for other forms of organizing to secure sufficient levels of revenues to sustain an adequate scale of club good provisions. This works in two directions: creating new organizing and funding models, or downsizing.

The first involves the development of novel types of community-based activities and related funding arrangements: crowdfunding for a wide range of risk-bearing social activities, new forms of citizen cooperatives in areas such as energy (cooperatives around the production and use of wind and solar energy), food (guerrilla gardening, urban farming, food collectives) or other services based on largely non-financial transactions (repair shops, clothing and food banks). They form an increasingly interesting group of bottom-up initiatives that can fill some of the voids left by the old social movement. Many of these initiatives can be counted as expressions of a *new social movement* that taps into the support of younger generations, who are increasingly interested in sustainability on a non-profit basis. What distinguishes the new social movement from the old is that they are more loosely coupled, event-driven and often less well-organized on a national scale, which lowers their external lobbying power as a group at level 2.

The second option is downsizing. This manoeuvre does not have to be a bad strategy. Downsizing in business strategies can be a way to recover from *mission drift* as a result of two interrelated mechanisms: overly big ambitions (imperial overstretch) or the influence of external funding by organizations with a different purpose or interest (watered-down identity). Many large CSOs (type 3) have fallen prey to mission drift because of *over-reliance* on external funding. It alienated them from their original constituencies who became less committed to the goals, values, and strategies of the organization. It made the organization even more dependent on external finance and the associated mission drift. Government or company sponsorship comes with strings attached. Less funding from external parties can, therefore, be a purifying 'blessing in disguise', provided that the MSO is able to (1) *downsize* in a controlled manner, and (2) *re-align* with the intentions, needs, values and interests of their original support groups. It involves thorough reflection on and reconsideration of the organization's identity. In the words of Peter Drucker (1990), one of the most influential management thinkers: "The non-profit organization exists to bring about a change in individuals and in society. . . . the ultimate test is not the beauty of the mission statement. The ultimate test is the right action." A more compact MSO that is better aligned with its core mission and has closer connections with its members, can be highly effective – independent of size.

(B) BROADENING THE FINANCIAL BASE WITHOUT LOSING PURPOSE

In essence, there are two approaches MSOs can take to serve and strengthen their business case at level 1: (a) cross-subsidization, and (b) attracting risk-bearing capital. Both come with benefits and risks.

Many hybrid 'type 2/3' organizations (hospitals, educational institutes) have started to search for *commercial income* to better serve their primary constituency, through *cross-subsidization*. Cross-subsidization is the practice of charging higher prices for certain types of activities or customers, to pay for another activity that is losing money – or making less money – for instance, as a result of applying artificially lower prices for specific customer segments. If this practice remains a relatively marginal activity that does not erode the service provision to original beneficiaries, the business case for an MSO can indeed be strengthened. A riskier approach to broadening the financial base has been implemented by (wealthy) non-profits that started to invest their accumulated capital in stocks or other risk-bearing activities, as a means to compensate for withered funding by their members. Several types of MSOs have experienced a similar inclination: (a) the investment portfolios of public or cooperative pension funds have gradually moved from less risky government bonds to more risky equity investments; (b) trade unions and churches have invested in equity to cover for finance gaps resulting from dwindling membership contributions; (c) cooperatives have considered moving to the stock market to gain access to easier capital; (d) mutual insurance companies have become more commercial to sustain their activities.

Well-managed portfolios of risk-bearing investments can strengthen the business case for the MSO, provided that the core aims, values and interests of its member group are not compromised. Public pension funds and large cooperatives, for instance, have the management capabilities to professionally handle more complex investment portfolios. Nevertheless, this approach also increases the risk of 'unsustainable' investments (e.g. in highly profitable companies involved in dodgy practices), mission drift, and legitimacy or reputation problems with own constituencies (at level 2). Pension funds, for instance, have been under pressure from their members to better scrutinize their investment portfolios and divest from unsustainable companies. At the same time, present and future beneficiaries are increasingly concerned about their (prospective) retirement income: low-risk investments – like government bonds – in times of overall low interest rates, will probably not suffice to accumulate the return on investment that is required to safeguard future retirement liabilities.

Social enterprises (type 4/5) present an interesting separate logic. Social enterprises often face financial sustainability problems because of (initial) difficulties in reaping economies of scale. Predictable continuity problems in serving their primary constituencies ensue if they are not capable of broadening their base of investors, contributors and (corporate or public) clients. In specific cases, it can be considered a smart strategy to *get incorporated* by larger cash-rich companies, as a means to broaden leverage and pursue the intended societal impact. For some social enterprises, the 'takeover scenario' is actually part of their purpose-driven strategy. Their raison d'être is to present a viable alternative business model to conventional business. Incorporation of that alternative business model by a financially more vigorous and resilient (commercial) organization can provide the opportunity of targeting *market failure* at scale. For some social enterprises, the ultimate business case – for instance, in case of fair trade or waste management – is actually to make themselves redundant.

| BOX 8.6 | **SUSTAINABLE BUSINESS CASES IN TIMES OF CRISES: THE EMPLOYEE COMMITMENT FACTOR** |

Management challenges of the 21st century, according to Peter Drucker (2001):

- Ensure that the work of the management serves a higher purpose.
- Fully embed the ideas of community and citizenship in management systems.
- Reconstruct the management's philosophical foundations.
- Eliminate the pathologies of formal hierarchy.
- Reduce fear and increase trust.
- Reinvent the means of control.

Non-profit organizations have one clear 'competitive advantage' compared to the for-profit sector: more committed employees, members and other primary stakeholders. This factor for instance explains for the remarkable commitment shown by health workers and others in vital societal functions during the ongoing Covid-19 crisis. It also reveals a different logic to the sustainable business case, from the non-profit angle of society:

B O X 8.6

■ **Easier recruitment and retention:** it has repeatedly been found that 'purpose-driven' organizations form a more attractive prospect for existing and potential employees. It lowers recruitment and retention costs (Figure 8.5). Workers of *non-purpose*-driven organizations are prepared to leave when the occasion arises if the opportunities they are offered – such as skills development, higher pay and other investments – do not speak to their passion and purpose. Research by Deloitte (2018) among millennials showed that about 60% of millennials value 'purpose' more than 'profits' in a working environment of their choosing.

■ **Leadership:** leadership recruitment studies found that prospective leaders of non-profit organizations accept lower salaries; not just for idealistic reasons, but also to gain and retain credibility about their sustainability motives amongst employees and stakeholders. They are also aware that loyalty and 'mutual support' – key assets of purpose-driven organizations – tend to decline, as soon as the income differential between 'the top' and 'the bottom' of the organization becomes too large.

■ **Increased loyalty:** working for a purpose-driven organization increases loyalty in a variety of ways: (1) employees tend to be less demanding regarding payment and raises (no financial compensation needed for controversial reputation), (2) during crises, employees stay loyal to the extent of voluntarily accepting longer working hours, lower income, postponed leave, extended or more demanding task portfolios.

■ **Lowering perverse incentives:** higher salaries tend to attract less loyal employees and leaders (the agency problem) and induce upward pressure on organization-wide remunerations, while stimulating 'share buy-back' actions in the case of publicly listed companies. Both trends have been found to compromise the financial resilience of organizations.

Not only do these effects make it easier for non-profit organizations to include higher levels of societal engagement in their strategies and operations, it also contributes to their longer-term resilience. The strategic value of employee commitment, especially in transition processes, is increasingly emulated by *for*-profit companies that seek to develop business cases at levels 3 or 4. Committed employees have been found to be more willing and dedicated to giving their best efforts – beyond task description and comfort zone – for instance, by developing their skills, acquiring new fields of experience and *creating* new opportunities. These are vital elements for enhanced value creation approaches, such as accomplishing effective 'co-creation' strategies with industry and value chain partners, customers, NGOs and other external stakeholders.

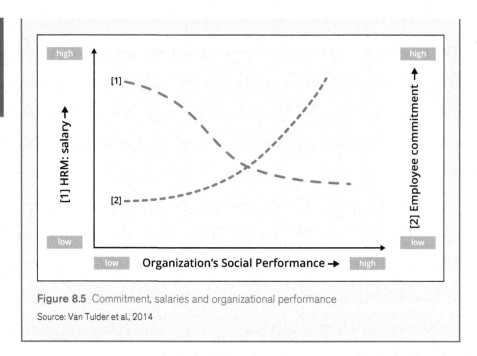

Figure 8.5 Commitment, salaries and organizational performance

Source: Van Tulder et al., 2014

8.6.2 Level 2: advocacy as a sustainable business case

Level 2 sustainable business cases for non-profits are primarily related to their 'advocacy' role and their 'responsive organizing' ability. Depending on the type of organization (type 2–4/5), it involves either their capacity to mobilize adequate support and attract sufficient funding for campaigns against the non-sustainable actions of other actors in society, or the ability to effectively resolve negative externalities within their own sphere of responsibilities. The *advocacy* role of non-profits is conditioned by the actual influence the organization can exert over other societal actors. The business case for this advocacy role is ultimately defined by the (financial) resources the organization can attract, and the ways in which their actions can contribute to the accumulation of sufficient (financial) means to sustain this role. The *responsive role* of non-profits is determined by how they deal with (potential) negative effects of their actions on their own stakeholders, which is mediated by their reputation. Not all non-profit organizations (type 2–4/5) are equally well-positioned to effectively apply each of these roles.

(A) ADVOCACY TO ADDRESS THE NEGATIVE EFFECTS OF OTHER SECTORS
The advocacy role of traditional CSOs (or NGOs) is usually aimed at influencing the problems created by other societal sectors: in particular companies and governments. Advocacy towards governments is commonly exerted by human

rights organizations – such as Amnesty International, Defence for Children, Human Rights Watch – that publicly denounce such aberrations as discrimination, impunity, armed conflict and violence, democracy deficits, inequality, poverty and weak institutions. Development NGOs – such as CARE or Oxfam – consider advocacy a key aspect of their efforts, in the knowledge that it does not suffice to address the immediate needs of the poor without pointing out the root causes of poverty and the obstacles to its elimination. Advocacy towards firms is most commonly exerted by labour unions and other social movement CSOs, such as ATTAC. CSOs such as Greenpeace or Friends of the Earth try to influence both business and governments.

Many advocacy-oriented CSOs use 'confrontation and debate' as techniques to draw attention to single – often simplified – issues. This strategy is aimed at maximum impact, yet also holds a funding strategy. In the highly competitive 'market' for attention, CSOs have to ensure that their message is effectively picked up by the media and reaches a critical mass of supporters. It often prompts them to start 'blaming-and-shaming' campaigns. In a way, some advocacy-driven CSOs might be trapped in this role due to financial considerations. CSOs that are not run as a membership-based organization (no level 1 MSO function) depend on contributions by supporters for a considerable part of their income. The number of active supporters then becomes intimately related to the media action they can generate for particular actions. As a result, financial resources can become relatively fickle, ad hoc and susceptible to fashionable types of action that gravitate to relatively minor causes that attract more contributions than more complex causes. When action-oriented CSOs are not able to attract sufficient media attention, their financial foundations become weaker and their impact smaller.

Other advocacy roles adopted by CSOs towards companies, in particular, include *supervisory* roles (for instance, related to overseeing and granting sustainability labels, such as fair trade); *active ownership* (CSOs that use their role as a shareholder to exert influence over a publicly listed company during shareholder meetings); or an *incentivising* role, by developing benchmarks and publishing rankings on the sustainability performance of companies (e.g. Rank a Brand; Access to Medicine Index; Access to Seed Index; Corporate Human Rights Index; the World Benchmark Alliance). The funding needs of these supervisory, certifying or benchmarking organizations can confront them with a considerable dilemma: how to remain independent, while (partly) being financed by service fees paid by (corporate) 'customers'. Supervisory and certification bodies are expected to take on a semi-public role; their independence and discretionary power to address unsustainable behaviour of actors, however, has also been found to be influenced by funding conditions.

Public pension funds and mutuals (type 2) have taken on advocacy roles as *activist investors*. They adopted so-called *exit or voice strategies* – active engagement with their investees to address their negative externalities and ESG performance ('voice'), or altogether divest from them ('exit'). They also integrated 'avoid doing harm' criteria in their investment portfolios. Their objective is dual: discouraging unsustainable practices of their publicly listed investees, while enhancing the sustainability of their own business model (reduced investment risk; enhanced reputation; improved alignment with their constituencies). Influential examples of this practice include the Norwegian Government Pension Fund Global, that started to divest from unsustainable businesses (163 companies between 2011–2014) as early as 2011, for reasons of "environmental, social and governance issues" and "high levels of uncertainty about the sustainability of their business model". Ever since, Global's divesting and investing decisions have been closely watched by other public pension funds and institutional investors. The Californian civil servants pension fund CalPERS has been known for its shareholder activism, in particular towards corporate governance topics, such as workers' rights and corporate executive 'compensation' practices. CalPERS' shareholder activism has had positive effects on its return on investment and has even been referred to as the 'CalPERS effect'.

(B) RESPONSIVENESS TO SELF-CREATED REPUTATION EFFECTS

Comparable to for-profit organizations, non-profits have to earn and sustain a societal 'license to operate'. As explained for the for-profit side of society, this license to operate is directly related to the organization's reputation and the legitimacy of its actions to a wider audience than their own group. Reputation effects can be positive (improving the sustainable business case) and negative (undermining it). Managing these effects is directly related to the various roles played by MSOs: (a) internally: in how they manage their basic function as mutual support organization; and (b) externally: in how they exercise their advocacy roles.

First, how MSOs organize 'club goods' for group members not only involves the inclusion, but inherently also the exclusion of non-group members. If the principles of inclusion/exclusion are considered 'fair' and 'just', the MSO is likely to face limited controversy. Exclusion based on biased, wrongful or illicit criteria – such as race, gender, age, sexual orientation – gives room to discrimination and will negatively affect the organization's reputation, especially if it is geared towards addressing (social) sustainability issues by denouncing irresponsive conduct of other actors (advocacy). Exclusion based on financial contributions (membership fees) lowers the number of beneficiaries of the MSO and, accordingly, limits its societal role. The reputation of an MSO is positively influenced by the *efficiency* of its organization, its transparency and the accountability of its operations. Negative reputational effects – with serious consequences for membership, income and legitimacy – have appeared because of: (a) excessive (perceived) bureaucracy at the organization (leading to inefficiency and high overhead costs); (b) excessive (perceived) remuneration of the organization's leadership (inducing allegations of irregularities and bonus culture with, for instance, Foster Parents Plan, the International Red Cross, Save the Children, a large number of cooperatives); (c) moral indignation because of misbehaviour within the organization (e.g. covered-up allegations of sexual misconduct and bullying at Oxfam). The negative reputational effects are usually more significant for non-profits than for for-profits, due to higher societal expectations of their social and moral profile.

Secondly, reputation effects can be related to the general *portfolio of activities* the MSO organizes, their advocacy role included. When the media found out that several public pension funds invested in so-called 'vice funds' (with stocks in tobacco, alcohol, gambling, defence equipment industries) or other unsustainable activities (e.g. food speculation, causing huge price swings in staple foods), members protested. It forced them to embrace their advocacy role more coherently and, ultimately, to divest from unsustainable or 'sin' sectors. When the media uncovered that the Rabobank cooperative had engaged in corrupt practices in the more speculative parts of its business (the Libor scandal), the bank lost the legitimacy of its sustainable image, which it could only repair by boosting its sustainability profile. When it was revealed that Greenpeace had won in the 'Brent Spar' affair – its successful campaign against Shell in 1995 – by grossly overestimating the amount of remaining oil in Brent Spar's storage tanks, Greenpeace's reputation with the media as a reliable source of information was severely affected.

Similar to the accountability approach taken by for-profit organizations, leading international advocacy CSOs have been adopting several accountability principles (Box 8.7).

ACCOUNTABILITY PRINCIPLES OF INTERNATIONAL ADVOCACY ORGANIZATIONS

BOX 8.7

Confronted with the general challenge of reduced legitimacy of the entire sector, several leading international advocacy CSOs started to consider how to embrace principles of accountability. They did so primarily to safeguard and uphold their joint reputation: in order to build shared influence, they had to acknowledge their interdependence as international NGOs on something that could be called *sector legitimacy* (Batliwala and Brown, 2006). Trust and accountability – to donors, governments, (local) partners and society at large – are central to CSOs' ability to work and thrive. It was recognized

B
O
X

8.7

that the bad reputation of one organization could negatively affect the credibility and influence of the entire sector.

Several CSO self-regulatory measures have developed since the 1990s, both internationally and on national levels. Nonetheless, the growing power and responsibility positions of CSOs and some high-profile scandals have given rise to increased demands from societal stakeholders for CSOs to be more accountable for their actions and impact. In response, ten leading international CSOs (including development, humanitarian, environmental, rights-based and advocacy organizations) in 2008 adopted an *International NGO Charter of Accountability*. The charter was to ensure that the high standards NGOs demand from others were also respected within their own organizations. It specified the following accountability principles:

- Being transparent on what the organization is, what it commits to doing, and progress achieved;
- Engaging key stakeholders in meaningful dialogue to enable continuous improvement for those we serve;
- Using power responsibly and enabling stakeholders to hold us to account effectively.

Members signed up to ten commitments related to respecting human rights, taking responsibility for the environment, and engaging in these principles in an ethical and professional way. The initial platform was rebranded as *Accountability Now*. Over the years, it organized about 25 internationally operating CSO active in over 150 countries – many of them well-known organizations with a global 'brand', including Greenpeace, CARE, Oxfam, Amnesty International, Transparency International, Civicus, World Vision, Terre des Hommes, Plan International, Action Aid and SOS Children's Villages International.

More recently, nine CSO accountability initiatives from around the world have been joining forces to develop the *Global Standard for CSO Accountability*. It is to serve as a reference standard of good CSO accountability practices that CSOs can adopt and implement to strengthen their accountability commitments to the public, build trust, and leverage impact. The Global Standard uses a 'dynamic accountability' approach that is "grounded in processes of meaningful engagement with all stakeholders that are inclusive, participatory and continuously practiced" (Baranda and Büchner, 2019).

The Global Standard's *12 Commitments* describe what CSOs aspire to achieve and how they work to implement positive change (Table 8.5). Because of its focus on human rights obligations, social justice, good governance, sustainability, reducing vulnerability, addressing the exclusion of marginalized populations and improving the lives of the poorest in society, it also takes into account the various dimensions of *the SDGs*.

BOX 8.7

Table 8.5 12 Commitments of the Global Standard for CSO Accountability

What CSOs want to achieve	CSOs' approach to change	What is done internally
1. Justice and equality "We will address injustice, exclusion, inequality, poverty and violence to create healthy societies for all"	**5. People-driven work** "We will ensure that people we work with have a key role in driving our work"	**9. Empowered and effective staff and volunteers** "We will invest in staff and volunteers to develop their full potential and achieve our goals"
2. Women's rights and gender equality "We will promote women's and girls' rights and enhance gender equality"	**6. Strong partnerships** "We will work in fair and respectful partnerships to achieve shared goals"	**10. Well-handled resources** "We will handle our resources responsibly to reach our goals and serve the public good"
3. Healthy planet "We will protect the natural environment and enhance its ability to support life for future generations"	**7. Advocating fundamental change** "We will address root causes by advocating for fundamental change"	**11. Responsive decision-making** "We will ensure our decisions are responsive to feedback from people affected by our work, partners, volunteers and staff"
4. Lasting positive change "We will deliver long-term positive results"	**8. Open organizations** "We will be transparent about who we are, what we do and our successes and failures"	**12. Responsible leadership** "We will ensure our management and governing body are accountable"

Sources: https://accountablenow.org/; https://www.csostandard.org/; Global Standard for CSO Accountability (2017) *12 Commitments for dynamic accountability. Guidance material.*

Combining advocacy and 'normal' MSO activities thus proves a challenging proposition. When handled well, positive reputation effects can be gained that reinforce the financial foundations of the business case. When this is handled poorly, however, the organization risks losing part of its legitimacy and financial sustainability, at least in the short run.

8.6.3 Level 3: service provision and product development

To actively enhance their impact on larger sustainability areas – as well as to cover for some of the financial gaps experienced at the very core of their activities (level 1) – various MSOs have been expanding their operations towards 'level 3'. Non-profits generally apply two types of (overlapping) strategies to scale their positive externalities: (a) diversification into *new areas* of service provision; and (b) expanding existing services into *for-profit* areas.

(A) DIVERSIFICATION OF SERVICES INTO PUBLIC AND PRIVATE AREAS

At level 3, a non-profit organization has to consider how to enhance the positive externalities of its activities, while strengthening its own business case. One way of diversifying is to start offering *cause-related products* or services at a profitable rate in order to strengthen core operations at level 1. Several CSOs (type 3) sell merchandise or products – for instance, made by local producers in partner countries – to supplement their income streams. If they stay close to their core mission (as WWF, Oxfam or Amnesty are doing), peripheral sales can actually contribute to public awareness, attract new (younger) target audiences, and strengthen their cause-driven profile. Diversifying into commercial ventures, however, can also cause CSOs to lose their societal legitimacy as a non-profit, fall prey to mission drift or induce role ambiguity. Commercial megachurches, for instance, that have been exploiting peoples' faith as a lucrative commercial business – particularly in deprived areas in the United States, Nigeria and many other countries – have been widely criticized and condemned for self-enrichment and malpractice.

By diversifying into service delivery beyond the original mutual support function, CSOs move into the realm of either (non-profit) governments or (for-profit) businesses. The provision of private goods and services – e.g. through *social entrepreneurship* or *third-party labelling services* – brings a CSO inside the sphere of the 'market sector' and can make it susceptible to 'market logics' and 'market failure'. Societal boundary-spanning activities do not necessarily pose a problem as long as a CSO can account for its independence, identity, mission and core values. CSOs that receive corporate funding – for instance, to carry out a community or ecological project – with the overarching purpose of representing the company's interests, may face a credibility problem however. CSOs that diversify into the provision of *public services* operate inside the sphere of 'the state'. They partly take over what is traditionally regarded as government responsibilities, and can become prone to 'government logics' and 'government failure' (e.g. excessive bureaucracy, procedural requirements, politics). Many development NGOs (or *co-financing organizations)* have received government financing to carry out socioeconomic and sustainable development projects in foreign countries. This 'contracting' relationship can bring NGOs in direct conflict with host country governments, who may consider these NGOs as 'foreign agents' and accuse them of interference in domestic affairs.

(B) EXPANDING INTO THE FOR-PROFIT SECTOR

The approach chosen, notably by type 2/3 organizations to make their mutual support ambition financially sustainable, has developed in two directions: (1) scaling their business case by integrating cross-subsidization opportunities, and (2) enhancing their effectiveness and impact by creating spill-over effects in the for-profit sector.

'Cross-subsidization' models have been part and parcel of the business model of educational and health organizations. Educational institutes can ask specific student segments for higher fees. Universities have engaged in executive training as 'profit centres' to cross-subsidize regular educational activities. Hospitals have been dedicating part of their facilities to 'private' patients who pay more. In such cases, the additional income is used to serve more students and patients who are unable to pay the full amount, thereby creating positive externalities (equal opportunity). But there are risks involved as well. If poorly managed, unintended adverse effects may occur, such as long-term debt burdens with 'premium-fee' students, discriminatory practices on campus (privileged treatment), or 'rich-man' and 'poor-man' wings in hospitals.

Another way for non-profits to generate positive spill-over effects is to set up *separate for-profit activities* to reach underserved communities. This practice has been observed in developing countries with poorly organized public health and schooling systems, where many people (and children) remain untreated, uneducated and, therefore, deprived and impoverished. Under these circumstances, *private schools and private hospitals* have increasingly proved a viable alternative. Social enterprises and foundations (type 3/4) have set up relevant concepts that start with non-profit-oriented investments and should eventually develop into self-reliant business models. Successful examples in healthcare include Sankara, a US-based non-profit active in India as a social enterprise in free eye care for poor people. The organization works towards eliminating curable blindness. It manages 11 highly specialized hospitals that together have performed over 1.5 million free eye surgeries. The finance model is based on an 80:20 model, whereby 20% of the paid surgeries fund 80% of the free surgeries.[25] In the area of schooling, Spark schools in South Africa complement the public school system with their blended learning concept. Spark is based on a hybrid funding model that combines funding from non-profit foundations with a high-impact philanthropy focus, with investments from for-profit impact investors. The organization opens a new Spark school every year.[26] Several CSOs – such as Amref-Flying Doctors, WWF, PharmAccess,

---

25 https://www.giveindia.org/nonprofit/sankara-eye-foundation-india
26 https://www.sparkschools.com

WorldVision, CARE and Plan International – are increasingly aligning with companies to set up joint partnering initiatives (at level 4). In order to make that work, they are gradually becoming more hybrid, with ventures and 'social enterprise' spin-offs (at level 3) based on blended finance and cross-subsidization models.

8.6.4 Level 4: collective goods provision through partnering

The business case for level 4 intervention/engagement relies on non-profits' ability and willingness to engage in collective action. Social movements and CSOs (type 3) have traditionally been very active in enacting (and implementing) *social contracts* that provide *collective goods* in such areas as universal health provision, access to proper schooling, equality, inclusiveness, decent work, social security, justice and, internationally, the SDGs. Social contracts have generally been the result of *combined strategies* applied by these organizations across all intervention levels: mutual support and mobilization/organization of interests groups (at level 1); advocacy, including peaceful action and confrontation (e.g. strikes, protests) (at level 2); and venturous efforts to scale positive externalities beyond one's own group (at level 3). Successful social contracts often guarantee an enabling environment and some form of financial support (for instance, through redistributed tax income) to serve the broader constituencies represented by the mission of a (coalition of) CSO(s). In many countries, social contracts are part of institutional (tripartite) bargaining arrangements – many of them safeguarded by formal and informal regulation (see Chapter 6). Social contracts are based on acts of *collective commitment* and *collective funding*.

   In order to address various institutional voids and enhance progress in sustainable development, many non-profits have sought to improve their direct influence by engaging in targeted partnerships 'for the common good' with governments and for-profit organizations (see Chapters 5 and 12). At this level, so-called *blended finance* constructions – which mobilize a multitude of financial sources to fund risk-bearing development projects – have been implemented. The OECD refers to the 'blended finance' concept as "the strategic use of development finance for the mobilization of additional finance towards sustainable development in developing countries".[27] The basic idea behind blended finance is to leverage (public) aid spending by *crowding in private investment* from a variety of for-profit and non-profit organizations, to overcome investment gaps

---

27 http://www.oecd.org/development/financing-sustainable-development/blended-finance-principles/

and catalyse sustainable development. To that end, the OECD formulated *principles of blended finance* in support of strengthening the sustainable business case of a level 4 partnership:

1   Anchor blended finance use to a development rationale – as a driver to maximize development outcomes and impact; with defined objectives and expected outcomes; based on high ESG standards and responsible conduct;

2   Design blended finance to increase the mobilization of commercial finance – seek context and conditions-based leverage; address market failure and potential market distortion; pursue commercial sustainability;

3   Tailor blended finance to local context – support local development priorities that meet people's needs; create an enabling environment for blended finance to work;

4   Focus on effective partnering for blended finance – within each partner's mandate; with balanced and targeted risk allocation; aim for scalability;

5   Monitor blended finance for transparency and results – agree on performance/result metrics; track progress; dedicate resources for monitoring and evaluation; ensure transparency and accountability.

Governments have been experimenting with forms of blended finance when engaging in sustainable development projects, often together with development CSOs and companies. It has prompted development CSOs to experiment with their *partnering or brokering role* at the interface with business and governments. In doing so, partnering-oriented CSOs face the challenge of how their partnering strategy is perceived by their members/constituents. Scaling societal impact through 'collaboration' can be (perceived to be) at odds with 'independence from corporate or state interests' and thus should be carefully considered and effectively dealt with.

Non-profits not only engage in cross-sector partnering initiatives to contribute to collective action but also as a means to improve risk management (PrC, 2011; 2015). Mutual insurance companies and public pension funds (type 2), for instance, increasingly apply *dual strategies* to address investment risks related to 'super-wicked' problems such as climate change mitigation. As an institutional investor, they use the threat of (or actual) withdrawal from specific sectors ('voice or exit' advocacy at level 2), while concurrently engaging in coalitions (level 4) to work on the development and implementation of alternative approaches and incentive frameworks to effectuate broader transformation at systems level. Chapter 12 further explains how effective cross-sector partnerships for the 'common good' can be organized.

The principles of 'social responsibility' as developed by the International Organization for Standardization (ISO) provide guidance for organizations that seek to take up responsibilities at intervention levels 3 and 4, by engaging stakeholders in joint processes of co-creation (Box 8.8).

BOX 8.8

PRINCIPLES OF RESPONSIBLE ORGANIZING (RO) – ISO 26000: GUIDANCE ON SOCIAL RESPONSIBILITY

Key principles of civil society organizations are the promotion of individual and collective human rights, including right to life, freedom, education, development, dignity, decent work, social justice and equality among human beings. These principles focus on **positive duties** and involve mutual support, solidarity, inclusiveness and democracy. In ethical terms: they represent 'doing good' principles. This orientation requires 'responsible organizing' principles that add to the predominant risk minimization or 'negative duty' approach ('avoid doing harm' principles) as covered by the OECD Guidelines (Box 8.4).

The International Organization for Standardization (ISO) in 2010 launched ISO 26000 to provide guidance on how **organizations in general** can operate in a responsible way. ISO 26000 is intended to provide a multi-stakeholder-backed, common understanding of 'social responsibility' (rather than '*corporate* social responsibility') and to be applicable to all types of organizations – profit *and* non-profit, public *and* private, regardless of their size and location.

ISO 26000 is built on **seven principles of social responsibility** to serve this need, with the overarching goal to **maximize** the contribution of organizations to sustainable development. The seven principles reflect two fundamental practices of 'responsible organizing': (a) the recognition – by any organization – of its social responsibility pertaining to the impacts of its decisions and activities on society and the environment; and (b) the identification of – and active engagement with – its stakeholders. Organizing for social responsibility explicitly includes respecting the **interests of stakeholders** and taking their expectations into account.

ISO 26000 pursues a holistic approach. It offers practical guidance on the relationship between an organization, its stakeholders and society; on recognizing the core subjects and issues of social responsibility; and on an organization's reasonable **sphere of influence** – including due responsibility to influence the behaviour of other actors. It addresses seven core subjects of social responsibility that are relevant to every organization: organizational governance; human rights; labour practices; the environment; fair operating practices; consumer issues; and community involvement and development (see graphic). Detailed guidance (further principles, considerations, related actions, expectations) is provided on 37 issues related to social responsibility.

7 Principles of Social Responsibility	Holistic Approach to Core Subjects of Organizational Social Responsibility

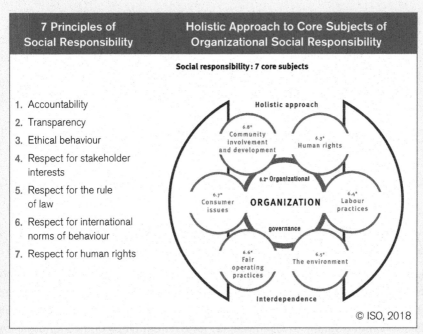

1. Accountability
2. Transparency
3. Ethical behaviour
4. Respect for stakeholder interests
5. Respect for the rule of law
6. Respect for international norms of behaviour
7. Respect for human rights

© ISO, 2018

Source: ISO (2018). *ISO 26000. Guidance on Social Responsibility. Discovering ISO 26000*, p. 9

ISO and the SDGs

ISO actively supports organizations in linking with the SDG-agenda. It recommends to identify societal stakeholders not solely from a 'due diligence' (risk) point of view, but also from the prospect of 'opportunity' (who is needed to effectuate change) and as a vital part of a continuous learning and feedback process. ISO identifies several steps in linking with the SDGs, by integrating the ISO 26000 approach:

- **Step 1:** use the seven main principles to make a quick analysis of *your performance* in relation to each of the seven core subjects. What is *your role in society* and what impacts, especially negative impacts, do your activities have? *What value do you create* for sustainable development?

- **Step 2:** create a stakeholder map, i.e. a list of expectations from those stakeholders that affect, or are affected by, your organization. *What is expected from you* through the rule of law, international norms of behaviour and your own organization?

- **Step 3:** refine your self-analysis through due diligence or developing a *gap analysis* between your current operations and the detailed guidance (found in clause 6 of the standard). Are there recommendations that you need to act on immediately?

- ▪ **Step 4:** define your *objectives and targets after stakeholder input*. How will you show continual improvement of your socially responsible behaviour over the short and long term?

- ▪ **Step 5:** *integrate social responsibility in all relevant parts of the organization.* How, for example, will you reach relevant parts of top management and the board, line managers and procurement functions?

Sources: ISO (2017). *Practical overview of the linkages between ISO 26000:2010, Guidance on social responsibility and OECD Guidelines for Multinational Enterprises (2011)*; ISO (2018a) *ISO 26000 and the SDGs.*

8.7 CONCLUSION, TOOLS AND RESOURCES

The bad news of this chapter is that *the* business case for sustainability does not exist. The good news, on the other hand, is that rather than one single business case, this chapter showed that a 'wealth' of business cases for sustainability exists: (1) with a variety of rationales, (2) for different types of (hybrid) organizations (archetypes 2–8), and (3) at distinct intervention/engagement levels. This broader scope creates leeway for organizations to resourcefully examine viable ways and opportunities for aligning organizational and societal ambitions in a sustainable manner. It also creates a significant strategic challenge: how to link a proper business case for sustainability to a suitable organizational form. 'Hybridization' of different 'governance logics' potentially enables more apt approaches towards the SDG-agenda at a higher level of ambition (see Chapter 6). But blending distinct governance logics may also elicit the risk of getting 'stuck in the middle' if it results in a blurred business model that eventually turns out to be financially unsustainable.

This chapter argued that business cases for sustainable development materialize along two pathways: a *for-profit* and a *non-profit* approach. Both pathways reveal four intervention levels with corresponding logics to delineate a sustainable business case. Profit-oriented and non-profit-oriented organizations alike can define (complementary) business cases at various levels of intervention/engagement. All can potentially contribute to the SDG-agenda; and all are needed, in order to address the full spectrum of the SDGs. For-profit or non-profit-oriented private, semi-private or semi-public governance forms represent distinct organizational competences and strategic 'repertoires', resources and business models for addressing sustainability challenges. Organizations with different societal positioning also tend to have a distinct 'hierarchy' in prime interests with specific SDG goals and targets. For-profit organizations initially tend to prioritize the more economic targets among the SDGs, predominantly defined by

SDGs 7–12, with the preconditions of their effective implementation generally lying in the ecological and social area. Mutual support organizations usually prioritize the more socially oriented goals, defined by SDGs 1–6, for which the preconditions of their effective implementation lie in the economic and ecological realm. Both orientations come together at levels 3 and 4, with increasingly overlapping business rationales. How the SDGs can be managed by organizations, prioritized and linked with core operations and activities is further covered in the next chapters.

- The business case for sustainability captures the reasoning, logic and justification for initiating an undertaking, project, programme, portfolio or task that should effectuate a relevant contribution to sustainable development. It defines the motivation for change behind a strategy, considers the *consequences of inaction*, and delineates the *financial feasibility and sustainability* in terms of benefits, costs and risks of investments in sustainable activities.

- Prospective costs of inaction include market disruption, burdens to growth, resource shortages, low trust, stringent regulation, difficult access to finance, withered competitive edge. Among the opportunities of (pro)active sustainability strategies are future markets, extended 'license to operate', innovative edge, access to patient finance, competitive advantage and longer-term profitability.

- A business case for sustainability should be well-grounded in the five foundational principles of sustainable business as derived from the SDG-framework: *People, Planet, Prosperity, Peace, Partnering*.

- A large variety of sustainable business cases exist, each with their own rationale, at four levels of intervention/SDG engagement. What distinguishes them is whether the basic approach is founded on *for*-profit principles and orientation (types 5–8) or *non*-profit principles and orientation (types 2–4/5).

- The non-profit side of society – characterized by *mutual support* and the *sharing of risk* – is an underexposed area for relevant business models and business cases. It comprises a wide range of fascinating and germane organizations operating at the interface between state and market, including universities, hospitals, NGOs, trade unions, public pension funds, mutual insurance companies, cooperatives, social enterprises.

- The hybridization trend points to a blending of logics between for-profits and non-profits. The more the business case of for-profit and non-profit organizations pertains to the creation of positive externalities and common goods, the more they overlap and become susceptible to hybridization processes.

- For non-profit/for-profit hybrids, the risk of getting *stuck in the middle* and *mission-drift* looms large, if they are unable to effectively transition to a financially viable organization.

- The business case for the cost-saving potential of resource efficiency and many eco-friendly investments (level 1) is compelling, to the point of being a no-brainer. Not reaping this cost-saving potential can be considered as contributing to market failure, and proof of poor management judgement.

- The business case for sustainability is often shaped as an 'ordinary' investment curve: a U-shape.

- The business case for non-profit organizations reveals the importance of employee engagement and commitment; this factor is increasingly relevant for profit-oriented companies, especially during times of crises.

- The OECD Principles of Responsible Business Conduct are particularly relevant for for-profit organizations, but largely aimed at risk mitigation and 'avoiding harm' (level 1 and 2); the ISO 26000 principles of 'social responsibility' are particularly relevant for 'responsible organizing' at non-profit organizations, and more helpful for level 3 and 4 approaches towards sustainability.

T A K E A W A Y S

- **SDG Business Hub:** an online portal of the World Business Council for Sustainable Development (WBCSD) that offers the latest insights, key (country and sector-specific) developments, useful tools ('SDG Essentials for Business'), guides, and emerging best practice (business perspectives and approaches), with a view to helping business to effectively navigate the dynamic SDG landscape: https://sdghub.com/

- **SDG Compass:** developed by the Global Reporting Initiative (GRI), UN Global Compact and the WBCSD. A navigating tool that provides guidance for companies in aligning their strategies with the SDGs, and in measuring and managing their contribution to the realization of the SDGs. The 'SDG Compass Guide' presents five steps to align the company course with the SDGs, to ensure that sustainability is an outcome of core business strategy. The website also provides an inventory of 58 key 'Business Tools' that are relevant for assessing company impact on the SDGs, and an inventory of over 1,550 'Business Indicators': https://sdgcompass.org/

- **Business Call to Action:** a multilateral alliance aimed at accelerating progress towards the SDGs, by challenging companies – from multinationals to social enterprises – to develop 'Inclusive Business Models' that engage people at the base of the economic pyramid (BoP) as consumers, producers, suppliers, distributors and employees. A total of 249 companies in over 70 countries have committed to improving the livelihoods of millions through commercially viable business ventures. By 2030, these aggregated commitments should result in increased 'access to financial services' for 59 million people, improved 'access to energy' for 80 million people, improved 'access to healthcare' services for over 617 million people and a 635-million-tonne reduction in greenhouse gas emissions. The website provides a variety of 'Inclusive Business' Toolkits (human rights included), 'Impact Lab' resources, case studies, and tools for impact measurement and management to support companies in understanding, proving, and improving their societal and sustainability impact: https://www.businesscalltoaction.org/business-call-action

- **UN Global Compact:** is a call to companies everywhere to align their operations and strategies with Ten Universal Principles in the areas of human rights, labour, environment and anti-corruption. Launched in 2000, the mandate of the UN Global Compact is to guide and support the global business community in advancing UN goals and values through responsible corporate practices. The website provides extended resources via its library on human rights, labour and social sustainability; global governance; action for the SDGs; environment and climate; sustainable management practice; sustainable finance. https://www.unglobalcompact.org/library. In addition, the *UN Global Compact Academy* offers learning experiences, virtual sessions, e-learning courses and an online community designed to enhance knowledge and skills for meeting sustainability objectives: https://www.unglobalcompact.org/academy

- **Global Opportunities and Global Solutions Explorer:** Rooted in research involving over 17,000 business leaders and 17 expert panels, the Explorer guides through hundreds of sustainable solutions and market opportunities which address the SDGs. The Global Opportunity Explorer is a joint project initiated by Sustainia, DNV GL and the UN Global Compact, created based on the conviction that the SDGs offer a myriad of business opportunities with great value for companies, society, and the environment: https://goexplorer.org/about/

- **_UNLEASH:_** a global non-profit talent programme and platform for innovative, implementable and scalable solutions to the SDGs aimed at developing new business models to ignite change for a better and more sustainable world. Next generation solutions for the SDGs will need to be commercially viable as well as deliver value to society. UNLEASH (a) mobilizes young innovative talents with fresh perspectives, open minds, different values and an appetite for disruption; (b) provides them access to an ecosystem of corporations, think tanks, research institutions, foundations, non-profits and angel investors; (c) curates resources and provides the support needed to bring the best ideas to life. UNLEASH annually organizes a Global Innovation Lab for the SDGs that gathers 1,000 young people, a Storyteller Lab for emerging impact journalists and localized hackathons to collaborate on solutions that meet the SDGs. It also provides an online platform and network for collaboration comprised of over 3000 talents, facilitators, experts, mentors, masters and participants in the UNLEASH programme: https://unleash.org/

- **_Sustainable Stock Exchanges Initiative:_** a global platform for exploring how exchanges – in collaboration with investors, regulators and companies – can enhance corporate transparency and performance on ESG (environmental, social and corporate governance) issues, and encourage sustainable investment. The SSE is organized by the UN Conference on Trade and Development (UNCTAD), the UN Global Compact, the UN Environment Program Finance Initiative (UNEP FI) and the Principles for Responsible Investment (PRI). Its goal is for all stock exchanges to provide listed companies with guidance on sustainability reporting. The SSE compiles the world's most comprehensive, publicly available database of stock exchanges worldwide on: (1) sustainability information on stock exchanges; (2) regulatory initiatives, and (3) sustainability reporting guidance documents: https://sseinitiative.org/

SELECTED WEB RESOURCES

REFERENCES

Aragón-Correa, J.A. & Rubio-López, E.A. (2007). 'Proactive Corporate Environmental Strategies: Myths and Misunderstanding', *Long Range Planning*, 40(3):357–381.

Asgary, N. & Li, G. (2016). 'Corporate Social Responsibility: Its Economic Impact and Link to the Bullwhip Effect', *Journal of Business Ethics*, 135(4):665–681.

Bansal, P. & Roth, K. (2000). 'Why Companies Go Green: A model of Ecological Responsiveness', *Academy of Management Journal*, 43(4):717–736.

Baranda, E. & Büchner, I. (2019). *Dynamic Accountability: Changing approaches to CSO accountability*. UK, Germany: Accountable Now.

Batliwala, S. & Brown, L.D. (2006). *Transnational Civil Society: An Introduction*. Bloomfield, CT: Kumarian Press.

Battilana, J. & Lee, M. (2014). 'Advancing Research on Hybrid Organizing – Insights from the Study of Social Enterprises', *Academy of Management Annals*, 8(1):397–441.

Battilana, J., Lee, M., Walker, J. & Dorsey, C. (2012). 'In Search for the Hybrid Ideal', *Stanford Social Innovation Review*, (10):51–55.

BlackRock Investment Institute (2019). 'Sustainability: The future of investing', *Global Insights*, report BIIM0219U-733437, February.

Busch, T. & Friede, G. (2018). 'The Robustness of the Corporate Social and Financial Performance Relation: A Second-Order Meta-Analysis', *Corporate Social Responsibility and Environmental Management*, 25(4):583–609.

Business & Sustainable Development Commission (2017). *Better Business, Better World*.

Chen, Y.S., Chang, C.H. & Wu, F.S. (2012). 'Origins of green innovations: The differences between proactive and reactive green innovations', *Management Decisions*, 50(3): 368–398.

De La Cruz, A., Medina, A. & Tang, Y. (2019). *Owners of the World's Listed Companies*, OECD Capital Market Series. Paris: OECD.

Deloitte (2018). *Deloitte Millennial Survey. Millennials disappointed in business, unprepared for Industry 4.0*.

Drucker, P.F. (2001). *Management Challenges for the 21st Century*. Paperback edition, Harber Business.

Drucker, P.F. (1990). *Managing the Non-profit Organization: Principles and Practices*. Harper Business.

Elkington, J. (2020). *Green Swans. The coming boom in regenerative capitalism*, Fast Company Press.

Galaskiewicz J. & Barringer S.N. (2012). 'Social Enterprises and Social Categories'. In: Gidron, B. & Hasenfeld, Y. (Eds.) *Social Enterprises. An Organizational Perspective*, (pp. 47–70). London: Palgrave Macmillan.

Grosvold, J., Hoejmose, S.U. & Roehrich, K.K. (2014). 'Squaring the circle: Management, measurement and performance of sustainability in supply chains', *Supply Chain Management*, 19(3):292–305.

Halme, M. & Laurila, J.S. (2009). 'Philanthropy, Integration or Innovation? Exploring the Financial and Societal Outcomes of Different Types of Corporate Responsibility', *Journal of Business Ethics*, (84):325–339.

Heath, R.L. (Ed.) (2001). *The Handbook of Public Relations*. Thousand Oaks, CA: Sage Publications.

Hengelaar, G.A. (2017). *The Proactive Incumbent. Holy Grail or Hidden Gem? Investigating whether the Dutch electricity sector can overcome the incumbent's curse and lead the sustainability transition*. Rotterdam: Erasmus Research Institute for Management.

Heugens, P. (2001). *Strategic Issues Management. Implications for Corporate Performance*. (No. EPS-2001–007-STR). ERIM Ph.D. Series Research in Management. Erasmus University Rotterdam.

ICMIF (2019). *Global Mutual Market Share. The Global Insurance Market Share Held by Mutual and Cooperative Insurers*, International Cooperative and Mutual Insurance Federation.

IIRC (2013b). *Capitals – Background Paper for <IR>*. The International Integrated Reporting Council, March.

ISO (2018). *ISO 26000. Guidance on Social Responsibility. Discovering ISO 26000*. Geneva: International Organization for Standardization.

ISO (2018a). *ISO 26000 and the SDGs*. Geneva: International Organization for Standardization.

ISO (2017). *Practical overview of the linkages between ISO 26000:2010, Guidance on social responsibility and OECD Guidelines for Multinational Enterprises (2011)*, version 7 February 2017. Geneva: International Organization for Standardization.

Jones, T.M., Donaldson, T., Freeman, R.E., Harrison, J.S., Leana, C.R., Mahoney, J.T. & Pearce, J.L. (2016). 'Management Theory and Social Welfare: Contributions and Challenges', *Academy of Management Review*, 41(2):216–228.

Laasch, O. & Conaway, R.N. (2015). *Principles of Responsible Management: Glocal Sustainability, Responsibility, Ethics*. Mason: Cengage.

Lin, H. (2012). 'Cross-sector Alliances for Corporate Social Responsibility Partner Heterogeneity Moderates Environmental Strategy Outcomes', *Journal of Business Ethics*, 110(2): 219–229.

OECD (2018). *OECD Due Diligence Guidance for Responsible Business Conduct*, 31 May.

OECD (2014). *OECD Guidelines for Multinational Enterprise. Responsible Business Conduct Matters*.

OECD (2011). *OECD Guidelines for Multinational Enterprises*. OECD Publishing.

Orlitzky, M. (2009). 'Corporate Social Performance and Financial Performance: A Research Synthesis'. In: Crane, A., Matten, D., McWilliams, A., Moon, J. & Siegel, D.S. (Eds.). *The Oxford Handbook of Corporate Social Responsibility*, Oxford University Press.

Orlitzky, M., Schmidt, F.L. & Rynes, S.L. (2003). 'Corporate Social and Financial Performance: A Meta-Analysis', *Organization Studies*, 24(3):403–441.

Porter, M.E. & Kramer, M.R. (2011). 'Creating Shared Value: How to Reinvent Capitalism and Unleash a Wave of Innovation and Growth', *Harvard Business Review*, January/ February.

PrC (2015). *The State of Partnerships Report – 2015. Civil Society Organisations (CSOs) Under Siege – can partnerships provide new venues?* Rotterdam: Partnerships Resource Centre at RSM-Erasmus University.

PrC (2011). *The State of Partnerships Report – 2011. Dutch Development NGOs facing the Partnering Challenge*. Rotterdam: Partnerships Resource Centre at RSM-Erasmus University.

PRI (2019). *Principles for Responsible Investment. An investor initiative in partnership with UNEP Finance Initiative and the UN Global Compact*.

Putnam, R.D. (2000). *Bowling Alone: The Collapse and Revival of American Community*. New York: Simon & Schuster.

Slawinski, N. & Bansal, P. (2012). 'A Matter of Time: The Temporal Perspectives of Organizational Responses to Climate Change', *Organization Studies*, 33(11):1537–1563.

Soper, K. (2008). 'Alternative Hedonism, cultural theory and the role of aesthetic revisioning', *Cultural Studies*, 22(5):567–587.

UN Global Compact (2020). 'UN Global Compact defines new level of ambition for corporate sustainability', 9 June 2020.

UN Global Compact & DNV GL (2020). *Uniting Business in the Decade of Action. Building on 20 Years of Progress*. UN Global Compact 20th Anniversary Progress Report.

UN Global Compact & Accenture Strategy (2019). *The Decade to Deliver. A Call to Business Action. The United Nations Global Compact – Accenture Strategy CEO Study on Sustainability 2019*, September.

Uzsoki, D. (2020). *Sustainable Investing: Shaping the future of finance.* Winnipeg, Manitoba CA: International Institute for Sustainable Development (IISD), February.

Valente, M. (2012). 'Theorizing Firm Adoption of Sustaincentrism', *Organization Studies*, 33(4):563–591.

Van Tulder, R. (2018a). *Getting all the Motives Right. Driving International Corporate Responsibility (ICR) to the Next Level.* Rotterdam: SMO.

Van Tulder, R., Van Tilburg, R., Francken, M. & Da Rosa, A. (2014). *Managing the Transition to a Sustainable Enterprise. Lessons from Frontrunner Companies.* London: Routledge.

Van Tulder, R. with Van der Zwart, A. (2006). *International Business-Society Management. Linking Corporate Responsibility and Globalization.* London: Routledge.

Van Zanten, J.A. & Van Tulder, R. (2020). 'Towards nexus-based governance: defining interactions between economic activities and Sustainable Development Goals (SDGs)', *International Journal of Sustainable Development & World Ecology*, 28(3):210–226.

Walls, J.L., Phan, P.H. & Berrone, P. (2011). 'Measuring Environmental Strategy: Construct Development, Reliability, and Validity', *Business & Society*, 50(1):71–115.

WBCSD & DNV GL (2018). *Business and the SDGs: A survey of WBCSD members and Global Network partners.* World Business Council for Sustainable Development, July.

World Cooperative Monitor (2019). *Exploring The Cooperative Economy Report 2019.* International Cooperative Alliance (ICA) and the European Research Institute on Cooperative and Social Enterprises (Euricse), December.

Ye, K. & Zhang, R. (2011). 'Do Lenders Value Corporate Social Responsibility? Evidence from China', *Journal of Business Ethics*, 104(2):1–10.

Yunus, M. (2007). *Creating a World Without Poverty: Social Business and the Future of Capitalism.* New York: Public Affairs.

9 MAKING IT MATERIAL

DESIGNING SUSTAINABLE BUSINESS MODELS

DOI: 10.4324/9781003098355-12

- **Principles of management:** are summarized in the vision, mission and value statements that guide the behaviour of people in the organization.

- **Principle of materiality:** materiality covers all relevant aspects that reflect an organization's significant economic, environmental and social impacts that substantively influence the assessments and decisions of stakeholders (GRI). Determining materiality is the basis for establishing the legitimacy of the corporation's role in society (Eccles and Youmans, 2015).

- **Principle of 'reversing materiality':** taking societal issues as the point of departure for strategic decision-making on value generation in six value dimensions. The perspective shifts from company-centric to societal, and from an 'inside-out' performance orientation to an 'outside-in' impact orientation in determining materiality.

- **Principles of sustainable business model innovation:** capture economic value while creating and providing natural and social value. Outcomes should add to societal value.

- **Principles of circularity:** "design out waste and pollution; keep products and materials in use; regenerate natural systems" (Ellen MacArthur Foundation).

- **Principles of inclusiveness:** accessibility, availability, affordability, awareness, appropriateness (5As).

- **Principles of regenerative capitalism:** looking beyond net-zero to a net-positive impact on the planet: (1) in the right relationship (humanity as integral and interconnected part of the biosphere); (2) views wealth holistically; (3) innovative, adaptive, responsive; (4) empowered participation; (5) honours place and community (resilient communities and regions); (6) learning and development sourced from diversity; (7) robust circularity flow; (8) seeks to balance efficiency and resilience, collaboration and competition, diversity and coherence (Fullerton, 2015).

- **Principles of purpose and value generation:** the value proposition of companies needs broadening, from short-term 'shareholder value' to one that includes all (present and future) stakeholder interests. Companies' understanding of their societal value generating potential can spark and guide processes of organizational repurposing.

- **Principles for protecting the common good:** such as the 'Contract for the Web', which includes nine principles establishing a 'new social contract' between government, companies and civil society for preserving the internet as a 'force for good for all'.

■   **Ten strategic principles of business model innovation for sustainability:**

1   Reverse materiality – the SDGs are a vital source for informing materiality analysis;

2   Make sustainability core – deal with the philanthropy trap;

3   Walk the Talk – define the promise-performance gap (zero measurement);

4   Deal with the incumbent's curse – reckon with overcoming critical tipping points;

5   Aim to add *societal* value – define a broadened value portfolio: design, create, capture, avoid destruction, spread and share value;

6   Develop a 'rich' value proposition – repurpose to guide the direction of change;

7   Identify vulnerable parts of the business model to strengthen resilience;

8   Distinguish 'narrow' from 'broader' business model elaborations – aim for the latter;

9   Identify relevant 'Key Value Indicators' (KVIs) and 'Key Decision-making Indicators' (KDIs) to guard coherence and progression in transitioning towards higher levels of value creation and sustainability;

10   Recognize the distinct types of leadership required in each transition phase.

9.1   INTRODUCTION: THE MATERIALITY CHALLENGE OF SUSTAINABLE BUSINESS MODEL INNOVATION

"Your talk talks and your walk talks,
but your walk talks louder than your talk talks."
John C. Maxwell

Although most private organizations consider sustainability issues to be of strategic importance, it has proven challenging for many to embrace the Sustainable Development Goals (SDGs) in a meaningful, integrated and transformative way. Organizations struggle with the strategic choices that must be made to design a *sustainable, resilient business model* that reckons with (tomorrow's) societal needs, path dependencies, vital tipping points and related switching costs. This class of strategic considerations is generally known as the *materiality challenge*. It concerns the deliberation and strategic decision-making on what (societal) issues to focus on and how to integrate these in the organization's strategic ambitions and core operations. An issue becomes 'material' if it "could substantially affect the organization's ability to create value in the short, medium or long term" (IIRC, 2013: 33). In determining whether or not a matter is material, "senior management and those charged with governance should consider whether the matter substantively affects, or has the potential to substantively affect, the organization's strategy, its business model, or one or more of the capitals it uses or affects" (IIRC, 2013a: 2).[1] Material issues are, therefore, described as "items that are relevant to decision-making" (Eccles et al., 2012: 66). They are 'entity-specific', 'stakeholder and time frame dependent', ultimately based on the judgement of the board directors, and "the basis for establishing the legitimacy of the corporation's role in society" (Eccles and Youmans, 2015: 3).

Throughout the previous chapters, we referred to consecutive (global) survey and research findings, all pointing to the hurdles that companies experience in making the SDGs 'material'. Since 2015, many organizations have embraced the SDGs, but in a fragmented manner and foremost as a risk-mitigation strategy to deal with reputational issues, rather than as a future-oriented investment agenda linked to the 'business opportunity' of addressing societal needs. Most multinational companies have been found to focus primarily on SDG-targets that 'avoid harm' (minimize adverse effects and negative externalities). Their engagement in 'doing good' SDG-targets – through the scaling of positive contributions and public goods provision *beyond* avoiding harm, for which multi-stakeholder partnerships are critical – has remained remarkably low however (Van Zanten and Van Tulder, 2018). Companies also find it challenging to link the SDGs to their core activities and define a proper business case for their SDG approach (WBCSD and DNV GL, 2018). It proves particularly difficult to prioritize specific SDG-targets and to manage the interactions between them (a 'nexus' approach), in order to advance multiple SDGs simultaneously and reduce the risk of trade-offs. Notably, companies tend to engage in 'cherry-picking' SDGs without a clear strategy or vision on the kind of systemic priorities they aim for (UN Global Compact and DNV GL, 2020). In other words: most are willing, but not (yet) 'walking their talk'.

These findings hint at a set of common, interrelated challenges that organizations in the private sector all encounter when striving to make the SDGs material and integral to their business model:

(a) **Strategic gap:** how to understand the process of formulating and implementing strategies for sustainability; or, more specifically: what type of strategic thinking is needed to overcome the 'intention-realization' gap?

---

1   The IIRC (2013b) identifies six categories of capital, all referring to "stores of value that, in one form or another, become inputs to the organization's business model": financial, manufactured, natural, intellectual, human, social & relationship capital.

(b) **Trust and legitimacy gap:** how to assess the context in which to express intentions; what stakeholder dynamics influence the various combinations of 'walking' and 'talking'?

(c) **Basic attitudes and stages:** how to map motivations to engage at a particular ambition and intervention level (levels 1, 2, 3, 4) regarding sustainability challenges?

(d) **Pace and direction of change:** how to identify ambitions and drivers of change (incremental or radical) behind business model innovation strategies, and how to align these?

(e) **Antecedents of change:** how to understand change as materializing along several distinct 'tipping points' and phases that imply change mechanisms that are fundamentally different from evolutionary (gradual) trajectories?

This chapter operationalizes 'strategic principles of sustainable business' that link the four levels of 'business cases' for sustainability (Chapter 8) to the materiality challenge. It identifies key dimensions and strategic considerations for translating a 'sustainable business case' into a 'sustainable business model', by addressing the following 'how' questions:

■ Materiality and the practice of issues management: how to move beyond a reactive mode (related to triggering events, defensive and tactical motivations) towards a (pro)active (transformational, strategic) mode of approaching societal issues (section 9.3);

■ Purpose-related questions: how to design broader value-adding, more resilient business models and 'richer' value propositions that (a) cover the four intervention levels of sustainability engagement, and (b) allow for linking the SDGs to the organization's value(s) portfolio (section 9.4);

■ The societal level: how do business model strategies and elaborations fit into different 'systemic' sustainability ambitions that aim to 'redesign' capitalism (e.g. circularity, inclusiveness, the we/sharing/social economy) (section 9.5);

■ What set of key value and decision-making indicators do organizational leaders need to take into account to set the direction of change, guard coherence and drive transition phases towards higher levels of sustainability (section 9.6).

The chapter starts with a synthesis of main insights from the extant CSR and business model innovation literature to create a basic understanding of what drives organizations to adopt sustainable business models – at various levels of ambition and implementation (section 9.2). It will serve as a basis for addressing the strategic questions addressed in this and subsequent chapters on how to make sustainability ambitions 'material' and 'actionable', in view of accelerating corporate contributions to realizing the SDGs.

9.2 BUSINESS MODEL INNOVATION: BASIC CONCEPTS OF KEY DRIVERS

The myriad of strategy challenges that private organizations face in aligning their corporate practice with societal issues has been the topic of decades of theoretical and applied management research focusing on CSR/sustainable business models. Section 7.2 covered the evolving discourse in general terms, along the generations CSR 1.0, CSR 2.0, CSR 3.0 and CSR 4.0. Different strands of management research have produced relevant, complementary insights that shed light on such matters as strategic intent, drivers and barriers of corporate responsibility, contextual and internal dynamics of change, interdependencies within the broader business ecosystem. Consequently, we can make (eclectic) use of complementary and accumulative insights from, inter alia, strategic management, stakeholder and issue management theory, motivational theory, transition theory, ethical theories and business model innovation literature. This section synthesizes relevant basic concepts on key drivers for organizations to adopt sustainable business models. Chapters 9 and 10 will continue to build on this basic understanding of the dynamics at play and their implications for strategic decision-making.

9.2.1 Strategic and motivation insights: overcoming the 'intention-realization' gap

Strategic thinking starts with a desired end in mind and is followed by efforts to overcome the gap between ambition and achievement. In the dedicated CSR discourse, the 'intention-realization' gap is also known as the gap between 'promise' and 'performance' (Rasche and Waddock, 2014). Combining the business case for sustainability (Chapter 8) with the actual business model adopted requires a solid understanding of the key decisions, organizational processes and contextual dynamics that come into play to close the gap in all its iterations.[2] Henri Mintzberg portrayed overcoming the gap as a dynamic navigation process – a 'strategy safari' (Mintzberg et al., 2009) – through several phases (Figure 9.1). During the implementation phase of *intended strategies*, some activities prove

---

2 The management literature has been covering this gap with many comparable synonyms that reveal comparable materiality challenges from different analytical angles: the hypocrisy-sincerity continuum; formulation-implementation gap, attitude-behaviour(al) intention gap, attitudes-action gap, intention-behaviour gap, intention-achievement gap, value-action gap, sustainability gap, engagement gap, habit discontinuity, corporate dissonance, strategic dissonance, disclosure-performance gap, strategy-performance gap (cf. Peeters, 2019).

unfeasible (*non-realized strategies*). New realities may emerge out of experiential knowledge (*emergent strategies*) that boil down to more *deliberate strategies* and, ultimately, to the actually realized strategy – which, during the process, has usually taken on a different shape than the initially intended strategy.

Confusing realized strategy with intended strategy often leads to reproaches of ill intent with companies when they are not exactly 'walking their talk', but are trying to. It also underestimates the very reality of (successful) strategic management, which generally resembles more of a *learning by doing* and *tinkering* exercise than one of strategic planning towards an envisaged outcome, exhaustively mapped out upfront. Strategy scholars have found that *muddling through* can actually be a highly effective strategy, particularly in such complex areas like sustainability (Crilly et al., 2012). Most strategy scholars, therefore, denounce the so-called 'planning school': the idea that a strategy can be fully and meticulously planned, after which implementation is only a matter of tracking checklists, schedules, and Key Performance Indicators (KPIs). They recognize that most organizations are in a perpetual state of transition, which requires a 'realistic' understanding of where in the strategy implementation process organizations actually are.

As for the SDG-agenda, most private sector organizations are still in the phase of translating their SDG-engagement ambition into an 'intended strategy'. This partly explains the trailing performance of companies, but also makes it difficult to empirically assess *how* – and with what vision and vigour – organizations are actually implementing the SDGs; let alone to deduce which approaches are

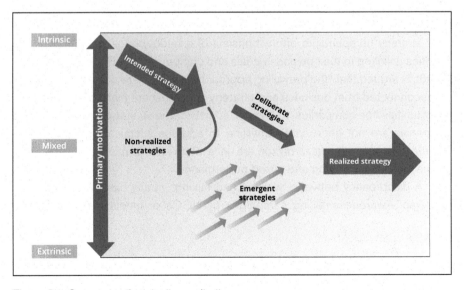

Figure 9.1 Overcoming the intention-realization gap

Source: based on Mintzberg and Waters, 1985

successful and which are not. Most overview studies (e.g. PwC, 2016; UN Global Compact and Accenture, 2016; WBCSD and DNV GL, 2018; UN Global Compact and Accenture, 2019; UN Global Compact and DNV GL, 2020) have mainly covered the *intent* of corporate leaders and how their organizations communicate on the SDGs in their public statements and annual reports. Studies on the intermediate progress on working towards the SDGs show less convincing results however. Simply mentioning support for the SDGs is not enough; leadership and a longer-term view on integrating the SDGs into corporate strategies are crucial, which touches on the origins of *corporate motivations*. Motivation theory adds the question of whether companies (and their leaders) are triggered by *intrinsic, mixed* or *extrinsic* motivations, and by short-term or longer-term considerations (Van Tulder, 2018a). Intrinsic motives are driven by the interest and ambitions of the companies themselves. Extrinsic motivations are primarily caused by external influences. As most strategies represent an interplay between intrinsic and extrinsic motivations, it should not come as a surprise that most realized strategies are based on 'mixed motives'.[3]

9.2.2 Stakeholder theory insights: trust and legitimacy gaps – 'walking the talk'

The trust gap that the private sector faces in many countries (Chapter 5) is intimately linked to companies' (perceived) inability and unwillingness to actually contribute to those issues relevant to society, and to substantively communicate on their efforts to achieve these. Research on the societal record of companies shows mixed results as to whether this actually portrays a lack of intent. McElhaney (2009: 34), for instance, indicates that a company's responsibility/CSR strategy compendium often "consists of a hodgepodge of disconnected activities unlinked to their business goals and competencies". Porter and Kramer (2006: 2) argued that "the prevailing approaches to CSR are so fragmented and so disconnected from business and strategy as to obscure many of the greatest opportunities for companies to benefit society". These statements imply that companies are not necessarily unwilling to address sustainability issues, but *organize activities haphazardly* or are in a state of transition that inherently comes with fragmentation and mixed performance.

A discrepancy between 'walking and talking', in any case, feeds into the trust gap. Awareness-raising campaigns by NGOs or media may further fuel

---

3   For a short animation that further explains the interplay between primary, secondary, intrinsic, extrinsic and mixed motivation, see: http://www.robvantulder.nl/projects/skills/skills-moocs/

scepticism. Low trust tends to create or reinforce barriers to change and may frustrate the implementation of sustainability-motivated business models for which the involvement of other stakeholders is vital. *Stakeholder theory* helps in addressing the right audiences at the right moment of transition. Ed Freeman's classic Stakeholder Theory (1984) put stakeholder thinking on the map. Central to his theory is the idea that doing business can be seen as 'a set of relationships' between groups with an interest in business activities, the stakeholders. The active and timely involvement of stakeholders in company activities lies at the heart of sustainable business. Taking (legitimate) stakeholder needs, interests and expectations on board in corporate decision-making ensures that ethical, social and environmental issues can be better anticipated and more effectively acted upon. Accordingly, business scholars increasingly talk about 'co-created value' (Prahalad, 2004) or 'shared value creation' (Porter and Kramer, 2011). Interest in stakeholder engagement has grown significantly since the mid-1990s, in parallel with the growing involvement of companies in sustainability issues.

Stakeholders can be *primary* or *secondary*. Primary stakeholders are of crucial importance to the organization and – as they usually invest substantial time, effort and means into the organization – directly affected by its actions. Examples of primary stakeholders include shareholders, employees, customers, suppliers, vendors and business partners. Secondary stakeholders are groups or individuals who do not hold direct interests in an organization, but may still have a reasonable influence over its dealings. The organization does not directly depend on these stakeholders for its continuity. Business competitors, trade unions, media groups, pressure groups, and state or local government organizations are generally considered examples of secondary stakeholders. The exact delineation of primary and secondary stakeholders in stakeholder thinking is increasingly debated, particularly when and where sustainability issues are at stake. Why should communities, governments, 'future generations', 'animals' or 'the environment' not be considered primary stakeholders as well? Triggering events and systemic crises can, after all, influence entire sectors and regions to the extent that a wide range of societal actors are affected, who are also needed to find adequate answers, help remedy and mitigate (longer-term) effects and (structurally) forestall reoccurrence. Especially at intervention/engagement levels 2, 3 and 4, the classic distinction between primary and secondary stakeholders becomes increasingly fluid.

Various (societal) stakeholders may have overlapping, divergent or outright conflicting interests, demands and expectations. The more divergent interests are (see Chapters 4 and 5 on 'societal complexity'), the more challenging it becomes for an organization to reconcile all demands and dynamically evolving expectations and decide on 'the right' strategy and actions. In their classic article, Mitchell,

Agle and Wood (1997) identified three factors to define the relevance of various stakeholder groups to the organization – power, legitimacy and urgency:

■ *Power:* the greater the power of the stakeholder group, the greater its influence. Stakeholders with economic relationships (primary stakeholders) can be very powerful if they are dominant investors, big customers, or suppliers of products and services that are difficult to procure elsewhere;

■ *Legitimacy* is the extent to which a group of stakeholders can justify its claim on a company. When it comes to moral issues, for instance, secondary stakeholders may be in a position to frame an issue in such a way that the company is forced to respond;

■ *Urgency* is the extent to which a claim provokes immediate action; for example, when an NGO comes knocking on the door to demand immediate action to stop polluting the soil and drinking water. Delay in attending the issue will be unacceptable to the stakeholder.

The most influential stakeholder groups are those that unite all three features and represent both primary and secondary interests. The nature of the relationship with these 'salient' stakeholders largely determines what strategic priorities the company is willing, able or forced to set in order to 'walk the talk'. In a complex and dynamically changing environment, even frontrunner companies find it difficult to prioritize between all issues relevant to their stakeholders. Particularly for the more ambitious targets in a multi-domestic or international setting, organizations need to figure out how to operate in regulatory voids with limited coordination, conflicting values, interests and competition between stakeholders (e.g. taxation, environmental regulation, human rights, quality standards). When to walk

Table 9.1 Walking the talk: four options

| | | TALK ABOUT SUSTAINABILITY | |
		NO	*YES*
WALK SUSTAINABLY	*NO*	• Narrow fiduciary duty approach; • Low expectations/low trust; • Focused on shareholder relations.	• Greenwashing; bluewashing; SDG-washing; • Lack of action confirms scepticism and increases trust gap; • Focused on 'salient' primary stakeholders.
	YES	• Broad fiduciary duty approach; • Fear of reputational damage; • (Re)gaining trust with powerful secondary stakeholders.	• Alignment of trust; • Building trust in collaboration (co-creation) with important primary and secondary stakeholders.

and when to talk? Or, put differently: what to do, what to communicate, in which phase, and with whom? In this discourse, organizations can take four positions (Table 9.1).

1   *Don't talk and don't walk* reflects a traditional (neoclassical) view in which companies adopt a narrow fiduciary duty, with responsibility only towards shareholders and owners, and relatively simple goals like profit maximization. This position goes hand in hand with and feeds into low stakeholder expectations and low levels of societal trust in the organization's ability to contribute to sustainability. Still, it does not necessarily create a trust 'gap', as long the organization does not create or pass on major costs (negative externalities) to society.

2   *Talk, but don't walk* represents the archetypical reason why sceptics refer to 'greenwashing', 'bluewashing', 'whitewashing' and 'SDG-washing' activities. It arises when organizations do not take their contribution to sustainability seriously, but still suggest the opposite. 'Talk, but don't walk' can also apply to organizations that are more serious about sustainability issues but have limited their sustainability strategy to marginal activities (for instance, organized as philanthropy or through their foundation), or find it difficult to implement their ambitions (overcoming the intention-realization gap). Both trends, to varying extents, feed into a widening trust gap. Secondary stakeholders (media, activist NGOs) may voice harsh critique; primary stakeholders (e.g. investors, employees, banks, consumers, vendors) may implicitly or indirectly be held jointly responsible.

3   *Talk and walk* establishes an alignment of trust in well-communicated processes. However, as most sustainability issues are complex and hence take considerable time, there is no guarantee that willing organizations are actually able to integrate all facets of their sustainability ambition into their core strategies. If their ambition fails to succeed, for whatever reason, the sceptics may consider their arguments confirmed ('I told you so'), and the trust gap may increase. Talking and walking is a delicate process. The managerial challenge is not only to prioritize sustainability issues in a well-thought-out manner, but also to carefully consider what, when and how to communicate, and with whom. Engaging with primary and secondary stakeholders can help to implement a more active and innovative strategy that requires co-creation.

4   *Walk, but don't talk* may seem a surprising combination, but is actually increasingly applied by frontrunner companies. Faced with the societal trust gap, several frontrunners choose *not* to talk (too much) about their societal ambition, for fear of not being able to satisfy all critics. For instance, when operating in countries with corrupt or religious regimes, it is not always wise to be explicit on certain human rights ambitions, like gender equality or democracy.

9.2.3 Stage models insights: basic classifications of levels of engagement

Since Archie Carroll's classic paper on the philosophy of social responsiveness (1979), the sustainable business literature has been focusing on two interrelated classification questions: (1) how to classify 'archetypical' sustainable business models and link them to a 'behavioural theory' of the firm; and (2) how to understand major 'triggers for change' and identify 'stages' that companies go through in reaching higher levels of sustainability. Several stage models have been developed since the 1990s, notably related to corporate environmental strategies, underlying value systems, organizational learning (Zadek, 2004), communication and corporate citizenship (Mirvis and Googins, 2006), supply chain management, innovation (Nidumolu et al., 2009; Klewitz and Hansen, 2014), and HRM practices.[4]

Considerable congruence exists on the underlying definitions and logic of stages (Maon et al., 2010). Most models start with an *inactive stage,* in which the firm does not respond to societal issues at all, or only in a dismissive way. Most then include one or two *reactive stages*, alternately named legalistic, compliance-seeking or liability-oriented. Next, one or two *active* or accommodative stages are defined. Most studies qualify these as differentiation-seeking and profit-oriented, stressing that in the active stages, companies start to recognize that active sustainable behaviour could create 'win-win' outcomes and a strategic competitive advantage within their sector. Some studies identify that active behaviour can also be driven by ethical concerns and designate a separate 'caring' stage, 'stewardship' attitude, or 'concerned citizen' stage (Hunt and Auster, 1990). Both moral and strategic motives can thus trigger an active corporate attitude towards sustainability. Additionally, all models consider one or two stages *beyond* active behaviour. In delineating this *proactive* or transformational stage, the literature provides two qualifications. The first refers to (performance-based) strategic behaviour, which extends profit-oriented (resource-based) corporate behaviour with a long-term mindset (Zadek, 2004). The second presents the impact-driven ideal type – described in terms of 'holistic', 'integrated' or 'transforming' (Mirvis and Googins 2006) – aimed at sustainable development (Hart, 1995). So, despite the existence of many classifications of sustainable business models, stage models tend to converge around four archetypical stages: inactive, reactive, active and proactive. By and

---

4 Hengelaar (2017) considered the most influential publications on archetypes and stages in the CSR discourse since 1979. He identified around 15 studies, cited more than 100 times over years. All studies by and large converge around four archetypes and find that reactive and (pro)active CSR strategies are based on very distinctive drivers.

large, these relate to the four intervention levels that define principles of sustainable business as developed throughout this book.

These four archetypical CSR strategies (inactive, reactive, active, proactive) can be linked to companies' underlying motives to engage in sustainability at various levels of intervention. Primary motivations (intrinsic – mixed – extrinsic) can be complemented with 'secondary motivations', which relate to the aim of action (level 1, 2, 3, 4 views on fiduciary duty/ responsibility) and its orientation: short-term (tactical) or longer-term (strategic). The interaction between primary and secondary motivations defines companies' basic *attitude* and *drive* with respect to their ambition and determination to pursue sustainability. The resulting classification, depicted in Figure 9.2, typifies whether an organization considers sustainability primarily a *short-term liability* (leaning towards an inactive attitude); a longer-term *competitive advantage* (triggering an active attitude); a short-term *tactical challenge* (triggering a reactive attitude), or a longer-term *societal challenge* (feeding into a proactive attitude and involving the combined motives of a pool of stakeholders).

This classification does not define how long it takes to move from one corporate attitude (and business model) to another and whether change is evolutionary or radical; nor does it reveal the nature of the drivers that explain the direction of the change. Section 9.2.5 addresses the dynamics, phases and critical tipping points in evolving from one stage to the next.

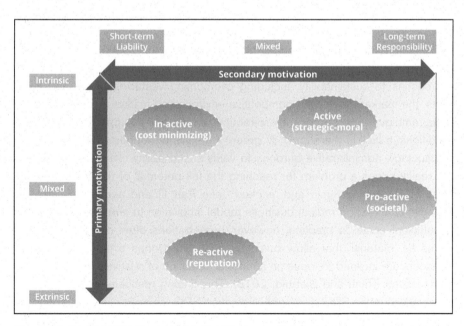

Figure 9.2 Sustainable business model strategies and underlying motives

Source: Van Tulder (2018a)

9.2.4 Insights on business model innovation processes

Sustainable business models aim to capture the logic of how an organization creates economic value while providing natural and social value as well (Schaltegger et al., 2016). Sustainable business model innovation aims to define and design business models that create positive and/or reduce negative impacts on the environment and society (Bocken et al., 2014). Essentially, companies can adopt two approaches to sustainable business model innovation: a performance-driven or impact-driven approach (Van Tulder and Lucht, 2019). *Performance-driven* innovation approaches start from the existing business model and seek ways to improve (components of) it, with a focus on present markets and needs. *Impact-driven* innovation strategies anticipate new business models for future markets and needs; they take a societal issue as the point of departure and consider novel ways to effectively resolve it. Furthermore, business model innovation studies distinguish between business model 'adjustment', 'adoption', 'improvement' and 'redesign'. The first three categories fall within the realm of largely reactive strategies and incremental approaches. The 'redesign' category is based on questioning the organization's dominant logic of 'doing business' in view of future needs and anticipated markets, and accordingly requires (pro-)active strategies and transformative approaches directed towards *shaping or creating new markets*.

In practice, companies often adopt incremental approaches that add environmental protection and social support elements to their existing business model, while gradually phasing out unsustainable components. More radical approaches to sustainable business model innovation are highly uncertain, risky and, therefore, far more challenging (high risk, high pay-off). Scholars have identified a range of barriers to adopting more radical and systemically integrated approaches to sustainability, including overcoming vested interests and sunk costs, the market model (the competitive environment; market incentives), time, costs, ambiguity on the desirable direction of change, unsupportive regulatory conditions, a lack in the supply of 'green' materials or supportive infrastructure, bureaucracy, administrative burdens to verify sustainability claims. Dealing with this reality poses a problem for reaching the full potential of the SDG-agenda. Most SDGs are systemic and 'wicked' (see Part II) and accordingly require systemic change and radical business model innovation to *timely* address them at sufficient scale. In practice, however, organizations often only select those issues as 'material' that allow business continuity (Jones et al., 2016), while managers are inclined to focus on a modest selection of relatively 'easy' sustainability issues (Raith and Siebold, 2018). This finding resonates with reiterated observations in the SDG discourse, indicating SDG 'cherry-picking' and reactive modes of hesitant, fragmented and even ill-conceived implementation. To spark and accelerate the transformation needed, nexus-oriented and proactive strategies for business model innovation should prevail instead.

9.2.5 Dynamic insights on the antecedents of change: phases, drivers and tipping points

Implementing sustainability ambitions into core business strategies and operations represents a dynamic and multilevel process. Aligning intention/promise and realization/performance in a competitive, complex and dynamically changing environment will never be a smooth and gradual change process. Instead, it portrays a bumpy road of overcoming internal and external barriers, 'business as usual' mindsets and habituated practices, relapse mechanisms, and learning by trial and error. The final challenge, therefore, is to identify vital drivers of change and define critical 'tipping points' along transition pathways that must be overcome, to move from one stage to another (while preventing relapse).

When making societal challenges material to core operations, organizations generally go through three basic phases along dominant pathways and related tipping points (Figure 9.3):

■ **Phase 1:** usually, a **triggering event** motivates the organization to move from a relatively passive attitude to sustainability towards a *reactive* outlook. The trigger can be (a) external and negative (e.g. public outrage in response to an oil spill, fraud, harmful products, polluting production processes, poor labour conditions in the supply chain – involving reputational risk); (b) external and positive (e.g. the SDG-agenda, green 'New Deals'); or (c) internally induced (e.g. new management or leadership). Chapter 7 discussed various triggering events – incidents, structural events, systemic crises – in more detail. In all cases, the business model needs to take level 2 challenges (negative externalities) into account and integrate policies and processes to effectively address them. Motivational research has found that, at this stage, negative triggers tend to provide a stronger incentive than positive triggers and hence represent a more potent driver of 'willingness to change'. The dominant pathway, therefore, moves from an inactive to a reactive attitude.

■ **Phase 2:** in order to evolve from a business model shaped by extrinsically driven considerations and reactive strategies into one that is based on values, core competencies and longer-term strategic goals (the 'active' business case), **internal alignment** is required. Mainstream management literature (cf. Trevor and Varcoe, 2017) describes the internal alignment challenge as one that connects the 'business purpose' with business strategy, organizational capabilities, resource architecture and performance assessments. Well-executed internal alignment ensures that all parts of the business model are *coherent*. When strategy matches structure, internal stakeholders are aligned, vital dynamic capabilities developed, and communication and monitoring processes in order, companies are better able to 'unlock capabilities' for change (ibid), and act on sustainability challenges in an integrated manner. The dominant motivation at this stage is 'intrinsic' and related to positive change (values and purpose-based). The dominant pathway tends to develop from 'reactive' into 'active' (more so than from 'inactive' directly into 'active').

▪ **Phase 3:** moving towards an impact-driven attitude to sustainability issues at a systemic level requires companies to **align with external stakeholders** (the *proactive* business case). Such external alignment is generally more effective if companies and their leaders have developed sufficient capabilities, intrinsic motivation and internally aligned efficacy to address the structural causes of societal challenges. For external stakeholders, an active corporate attitude is more credible and worthwhile to engage with than a reactive one. The dominant pathway, therefore, is from 'active' to 'proactive'. The least common transition direction is that of 'leap-frogging' from a reactive to a proactive attitude, which would imply a massive change in attitude, without the vital internally built-up capacities to match it.

Figure 9.3 shows the dominant pathways that most organizations go through. In each phase of moving towards a new stage, they encounter critical 'tipping points' that must be overcome to embed 'points of no return' and successfully evolve towards higher levels of engagement in sustainability (Van Tulder, 2018a).[5] In particular large (incumbent) organizations face challenging tipping points on their journey; they may find themselves confronted with having to overcome significant sunk costs and switching costs, while also risking their assets becoming stranded if they stagnate. The reactive stage can be considered the most critical juncture. Here, organizations will have to decide whether to restrict their materiality challenge to level 1 and 2 sustainability issues (addressing 'market failure' and 'negative externalities'), or to take on board level 3 and 4 societal challenges as well ('scaling positive externalities', 'collective action' for systemic challenges). This juncture presents a 'mixed' (secondary) motives game, in which companies can easily get stuck between tactical (short-term) and strategic (long-term) considerations, or actually manage to break through this critical threshold.

---

5   A tipping point represents a breakthrough at which a new balance is achieved. Reaching a tipping point is not necessarily based on big or sudden changes; minor changes are often accumulative and reach a critical point at which they become an irreversible reality (Gladwell, 2001). Tipping points in corporate transition processes arise when business case and business model match up.

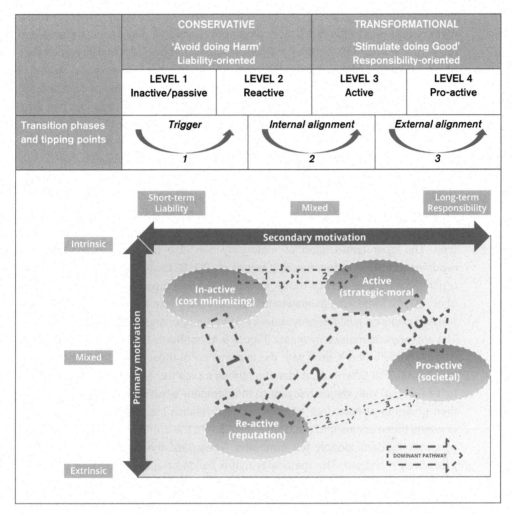

Figure 9.3 Transition phases of sustainable business model innovation

9.3 ISSUES MANAGEMENT: FROM A REACTIVE PRACTICE TO A PROACTIVE APPROACH

Private organizations are always confronted with a large number of sustainability issues at the same time. This reality creates sizeable dilemmas in determining what to prioritize – and what not. In particular for-profit organizations have started using so-called *materiality assessments* to determine the threshold for issues deemed so important to relevant stakeholders that they should be addressed in their strategy. The practical goal of materiality analysis has been to identify those matters that reflect the firm's economic, environmental and social impacts and have a substantive influence on the assessments and decision-making processes of stakeholders.[6] Materiality analysis should help to select the information that is critical for the business (Eccles et al., 2012). This information is not only relevant for reporting purposes and to manage expectations but, importantly, has strategic meaning as well. Since a materiality assessment helps prioritize those *issues with the most impact* (Schönherr et al., 2017), it is essential for contributing to sustainable development in a sensible and meaningful way.

The process for determining 'material issues' is not regulated by law. Neither is there a universally accepted definition of materiality in the sustainability context. Whether an issue is deemed material in practice depends on the context (e.g. the industry, regulatory environment, multi-stakeholder perspectives) and varies over time. The operationalization of materiality has also been found to differ per reporting standard or framework (Guix et al., 2018; Lai et al., 2017). In practice, organizations often select those issues that allow business continuity (Jones et al., 2016). Materiality assessments typically start from the *company's perspective* and prioritize sustainability issues in direct response to stakeholder pressure. The *archetypical materiality matrix* (Figure 9.4) confronts the importance of issues to stakeholders (the Y-axis) with the importance of these issues to the company (the X-axis). Put differently, it identifies those topics the organization is supposed to 'talk' about, with issues relevant to the company's 'walk'. The materiality matrix then presents at least four combinations of relative importance. The 'top right' contains those issues that are both significant to the company and to the company's stakeholders' deeply felt concerns. These are the issues that should be proactively managed. The materiality matrix builds on a long-standing corporate practice of 'issues management', which used issue-priority matrices to position issues in terms of 'importance' and 'likelihood of occurrence'.

---

6   GRI (2018: 10) defines *materiality* in the context of sustainability reporting. GRI's Materiality Principle holds that "a report should cover aspects that reflect the organization's significant economic, environmental and social impacts; or substantively influence the assessments and decisions of stakeholders". Materiality, then, is defined as "the threshold at which aspects and other topics become sufficiently important that they should be reported". In reference to the materiality of non-financial information, the European Commission uses the term *double materiality* to distinguish between two 'risk perspectives': (a) non-financial elements that affect the company's "development, performance and position" and, therefore, the company's value (indicating financial materiality); and (b) non-financial elements that relate to the "external impacts" of a company's activities (indicating social and environmental materiality) that are of the most interest to the company's stakeholders (European Commission, 2019: 6–7).

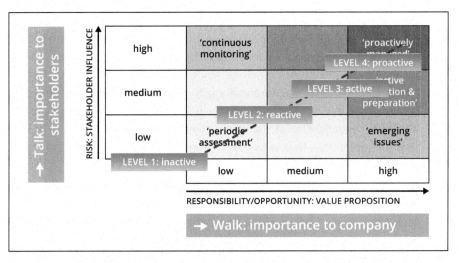

Figure 9.4 Materiality matrix and issue prioritization
Source: Based on Steiner and Steiner (2000); Van Tulder et al. (2014)

9.3.1 The reactive practice of materiality

The practice of prioritizing issues based on materiality matrices has revealed several pitfalls:

■ **Risk-related motives prevail.** By using the materiality matrix to map 'salient' stakeholders and 'salient' issues, priorities became selected only (1) when represented by powerful stakeholders, and (2) if related to those issues that could adversely affect corporate operations. The technique has been primarily used as a risk-management strategy to anticipate where impactful operational risks (or potential scandals) could be exposed by powerful stakeholders. A study by AccountAbility (2015) showed that most companies use stakeholder engagement and materiality as a risk-based tool to manage reputation, rather than as an *opportunity-seeking* technique. In many organizations, issue management has primarily been aimed at identifying 'threats' to the continuity of the organization: issue management as an 'inward-oriented' technique.

■ **Biased 'framing' of sustainability issues.** Over the years, companies also started to include issue-priority matrices in their external sustainability reporting to communicate on their CSR efforts: issue management as an 'outward-oriented' search for legitimation. The inherent risk of sustainability reporting, however, lies in selectivity and framing. Companies may only publish what management deems relevant while reflecting a subjective – even opportunistic – interpretation and selection of stakeholders' concerns.

On many accounts, sustainability communications have become more of an exercise in PR, telling feel-good stories about irrelevant issues, rather than a meaningful story about value creation. Likewise, organizations may focus on good performance on 'immaterial' issues instead of poor performance on material issues, diverting stakeholder focus from vital and far more strategic sustainability issues (Maniora, 2018). A low propensity for transparency about the determination of 'material' issues, as well as low quality or lack of data on contentious issues, pose challenges that require continuous attention and scrutiny.

■ **A challenging relation with transparency.** Firms have to manage conflicting interests and objectives inside and outside of the organization. Sharing dilemmas and conflicts can potentially drive learning and innovation, but is challenging to manage. To communicate effectively, companies have to determine the scope and range of information provided, stakeholder groups, and the timeframe (KPMG, 2014). Whether the information provided serves the information need of various stakeholder groups is a delicate balance between intent, timing and transparency. Furthermore, the impacts of sustainability efforts are usually not immediately visible; effects may be cumulative, slow to materialize or occurring at a distance from stakeholders, which obscures causal relations (Jones et al., 2016).

Critical studies on the use of materiality or issue-priority matrices found that these are more about intent than about performance. Implementation – even of stated objectives – is rarely guaranteed. Matrices tend to be relatively static rather than based on (latent or future) needs, whereas priorities shift year on year due to changing stakeholder engagement. Neither do they take stakeholder diversity between and within stakeholder groups sufficiently into account. This has a practical reason: materiality matrices are mainly accumulated through consultation with a selected group of (friendly) stakeholders, who are not necessarily the most critical or relevant ones. In such encounters, the most important topics are predetermined by the company. Moreover, it has been found that there is often a difference between the 'public' matrix and the version used for internal decision-making. Most matrices are individualized assessments of the organization's performance with no reference to other practices used by peers and investors. Materiality assessments rarely make use of key sustainability performance indicators used within an industry (Bouten and Hoozée, 2015). Both practices make it difficult to assess where an organization stands in comparison to others. KPMG (2014), in addition, found that (a) senior management is frequently not involved in the materiality assessment process, (b) businesses are generally too complex for a meaningful materiality assessment, (c) material topics generally tend to be too broad or overlap, and (d) there are more material issues than the company can (or wants to) manage. This range of findings corroborates the relatively reactive practice of issue and stakeholder management.

9.3.2   Reversing materiality: overcoming the incumbent's curse

The result of the fairly reactive practice of materiality exercises is that the materiality analysis itself can become a barrier for business model innovation. The materiality matrix is primarily used to identify *threats rather than opportunities*; it examines *risks rather than responsibilities*. Consequently, the strategic potential of materiality analysis for sustainability is underutilized, whereas stakeholder needs are insufficiently addressed and their complementary competencies insufficiently tapped into. This indicates that the practice can be improved *if* organizations are able and willing to *break through the reactive threshold* by *shifting focus*: from the prevailing attention to short-term threats and risk, towards an outlook that defines future-oriented issues, needs and opportunities as 'material'. The latter would imply that economically sustainable business models should be built around an environmental or social mission (Raith and Siebold, 2018).

   To overcome the reactive approach, the prevailing materiality logic needs to be reversed: from the company's perspective to a societal perspective (Van Tulder and Lucht, 2019). 'Reversing' the materiality implies that companies move from an 'inside-out' to an 'outside-in' orientation that takes societal issues as the starting point for future-oriented strategizing (see Chapter 5). It can be argued that the SDGs are more useful in informing a company's materiality analysis than the existing practice of materiality approaches. The SDG-framework provides the relevant social, economic and environmental goals and specifies specific indicators to measure progress (see Part I). It serves as a lens in goal-setting – also embraced by other societal actors – that supports a unified sense of priorities and purpose that facilitates communication with stakeholders for at least a decade. Reversing the materiality, however, is not the same as 'repackaging' the present 'material' issues into SDG language. Instead, it involves deliberate engagement in identifying and prioritizing those societal challenges with which the organization can create value for the common good – not as a philanthropic activity, but as an integral part and outcome of its business model. By making the 'reversed materiality' approach part of a back-casting technique, companies can involve stakeholders in co-creation and co-strategizing exercises for a shared future (also referred to as 'world views') (Box 9.1).

FROM 'FORECASTING' TO 'BACK-CASTING'

The reactive practice of stakeholder and issue management is based on the view that present relations define the drivers of change. Forecasting future materiality concerns then tends to develop as an extrapolation of present 'trends' in this relationship. Most forecasting methods use **scenario planning** methods as part of a strategic risk mitigation approach. However, in a complex (VUCA) world, forecasting methods can only help define a *limited set* of possibilities. Particularly when fore-casting emphasizes 'doom scenarios', it provides limited guidance or motivation for concrete interventions.

To get out of this predicament, **foresight** (or 'scoping') studies have been introduced. Foresight studies started to include the social dimension of change by operationalizing the inputs and concerns of social actors (Georghiou, 2001) as the major drivers of change. Foresight techniques are aimed at a better understanding of 'the future' by extrapolating (forecasting) the consequences of present strate-gies or trends, but also by 'back-casting' from a desirable or feared future to the present. To overcome a reactive or defensive approach to societal issues, **back-casting** has been suggested as a way to improve future-oriented decision-making together with stakeholders.

Back-casting starts with a predetermined end point: a plausible and desirable future or future (world) vision, like the SDGs. Next, possible pathways to that point are devised and investigated. Storylines work back from the 'desirable future' or 'future vision' towards the present. The back-casting method is commonly used in **aspira-tional scenario** workshops, where it involves (co-)creating a 'desired future' and, from there, imagining all the events and actions that need to happen for that future to be achieved. Some people consider back-casting a less extensive version of 'road-mapping'; both methods require setting up a timeline of key events and measurable goals to be reached. Other objectives are to identify strategies and policies needed to work towards the desired future, and the identification of relevant stakeholders with whom the intended ambitions can best be achieved (Chapter 12).

The potential of the SDGs will only materialize if companies can align their strategies with the SDGs in a *forward-looking* manner. The most challenging yet critical threshold to overcome in this respect is twofold: (a) to move from theory and intention ('talk') to practice and implementation ('walk'), and (b) to shift from a reactive/responsive attitude towards an active/proactive one. Notably for large established companies ('incumbents'), embedding the SDGs in strategic activities and core operations may pose significant challenges. It not only requires them to rethink and transform the existing business model – while in full operation and under the magnifying glass of public scrutiny – but also to rethink and reconfigure the business ecosystem in which they operate. In the face of such dynamic challenges, established companies may find themselves confronted with the so-called *incumbent's curse* (Box 9.2). The curse applies to those companies that are too big to fail, yet also too conservative to go beyond 'business as usual' and lead the change. Because of their size, market position and de facto (economic and political) hindrance power, incumbents are capable of creating sizeable barriers to change within their sector and along supply chains. 'Business model innovation' is, therefore, more often associated with start-ups. Starting basically from scratch, start-ups find it easier to embrace a riskier novel business model, but typically face scaling problems at a later stage (section 8.4.3).

Incumbents' inability or unwillingness to 'reverse materiality' partly explains why progress towards sustainability is generally slow. There is some reason for (modest) optimism, however. The Business & Sustainable Development Commission (2017) points to the emergence of so-called *radical incumbents* – big and leading companies that 'talk and walk'. The Commission observed that 30 *Global Goal unicorns* – as they call them – exist already, with market valuations topping $1 billion. These leading companies actually *co-shape* the SDGs by more actively deploying new types of business models: 'sharing', 'circular', 'lean service', 'big data' and 'social enterprise'. These companies have made the SDGs 'material' by integrating them into corporate strategy, while – as part of their deliberate strategy – engaging with others to create an enabling environment that accelerates uptake and realization.

THE INCUMBENT'S CURSE

BOX 9.2

Incumbent companies are established companies that often occupy a dominant position in their sector. Their market position implies that they have a vested interest in the 'old way' of doing things and may experience – or anticipate – great difficulties in changing. Incumbents are inclined to bar change towards higher levels of sustainability, even if their leadership were convinced of the need for change. Consequently, the role of incumbents in sustainability transitions is highly contested in the public (and academic) debate. To what extent are they *agents of stagnation*, and to what extent *agents of impact-oriented leverage* and scaling?

Research on the 'incumbent's curse' shows that lack of adaptation to new realities is an important reason why seemingly 'big and powerful' companies may eventually disappear altogether. The incumbent's curse is also known as the **Kodak effect**. Kodak was by far the leading company in the photographic industry. It had all the technology in-house to go digital, but failed to organize this properly. Managers clung to old success formulas and the associated business model, and were not prepared to reorganize quickly enough. When the leading paradigm of the industry changed – from analogue to digital – the company was too slow in adapting. Kodak went bankrupt.

Incumbents' failure to adapt has been related to their inability and lack of motivation to master new competencies and routines – so-called 'cognitive locks' (Benner and Tripsas, 2012) – and their embeddedness within an established industry network that initially does not value new technologies and societal ambitions. As central actors in the current 'regime', incumbents favour stability, select incremental paths and often resist more radical change emerging from niches. Motivated by their 'status quo' bias, incumbents will try to block any change that may threaten their vested interests or, alternatively, get stuck in 'pilot paralysis' (UN Global Compact & Accenture Strategy, 2013; Hengelaar, 2017). Such reactive strategies can lead to massive value destruction, stranded assets, and may risk the firm's longer-term survival.

Both internal company and sector conservatism pose significant challenges for proactively motivated leaders of incumbent firms. There is some evidence, however, that incumbents can indeed succeed in actively creating and co-shaping transformative change. More future-oriented and anticipating incumbents have been found to: (1) actively invest in internal capabilities and innovation portfolios; (2) develop a proactive vision and value proposition that provides focus on what to aim for; (3) co-create conducive innovation and change environments; and (4) leverage their innovative capabilities in new technological and market domains with the potential to drive radical transformations, for instance in the energy sector (Hengelaar, 2017).

In conclusion, using the SDGs to broaden the materiality approach as an input for strategic planning and innovation almost always requires a more specific 'societal goal' and mission statement, with clear markers and ambitions. The challenge is not to pick the easiest, most positive, most marketable or obvious goals, but to select those SDG-targets that are 'material' to the core business. By prioritizing the right global goals in their strategy agenda, companies are not only better equipped to anticipate disruptions emerging in the future, but also to *shape contextual trends and the direction of change* to their competitive advantage (Business & Sustainable Development Commission, 2017). The strategic challenge is how to link the 'right' portfolio of SDGs to the company's value proposition and related business model.

9.4 A VALUE THEORY OF THE ORGANIZATION: BREAKING THROUGH THE REACTIVE THRESHOLD

Overcoming the critical threshold between lower levels (1 and 2) and higher levels (3 and 4) of engagement with the SDGs can be related to the real characteristics of the issue at at hand, but is also influenced by internal (mindset) barriers. Entrepreneurs may be more reactive than actually needed – or than may be expected from them in view of their risk-taking and value-adding profession. An overly conservative and defensive response creates barriers to societal change. What is needed to break through this barrier of passiveness and lacking entrepreneurial spirit?

First and foremost, as detailed in Chapter 5, the corporate definition of 'fiduciary duty' and 'fiduciary responsibilities' needs to broaden. The business opportunity to address societal needs will not be (as clearly) visible if an organization's dominant view remains restricted to adhering to primary responsibilities (level 1) and limiting negative externalities (level 2). To create and capture the business opportunities that the SDG-agenda offers, companies will additionally have to come up with entrepreneurial answers on how to increase positive externalities beyond their organizational boundaries (level 3) through redesign of their business model and their relationship with society as a whole (level 4) – their legitimacy-providing ecosystem. This requires a much *broader definition* of what aspects to include in the organization's 'business model' and 'value proposition' (section 9.4.1). Designing a business model based on a broader value proposition also has repercussions for whether an organization's purpose is aimed at short-term or longer-term value creation (section 9.4.2), which ultimately defines the extent to which a business model can be considered fragile or resilient (section 9.4.3).

9.4.1 Broadening the business model: an extended value theory of the firm

The principles of management define the activities that plan, organize and control the operations of participants in the organization, "providing direction and coordination, and giving leadership to human efforts, so as to achieve the sought objectives of the enterprise" (Graham, 1995). The principles of strategic management are summarized in the *vision, mission, and values statements* that guide people's behaviour in the organization. More recently, this line of thinking has found a very popular template in the 'business model CANVAS', as introduced by Alexander Osterwalder (Osterwalder and Pigneur, 2010). The core concept in this model is an organization's *value proposition* – defined as "the collection of products and services a business offers to meet the needs of its customers" – that distinguishes an organization from its competitors (see Figure 9.5, [4]). The value proposition can be quantitative or qualitative. The original CANVAS model specifies seven additional building blocks of activities that an organization can develop, adjust and improve around its value proposition.

The CANVAS model can be rephrased in terms of specified *value dimensions* – as defined by Philip Kotler, the founding father of the marketing profession. In *Principles of Marketing*, Kotler considered how to build profitable relationships with targeted audiences by offering a value proposition: "the set of benefits or *values* a company promises to deliver" (Kotler and Armstrong, 2018). Key elements in this approach are: (1) designing value, (2) creating value, and

(3) capturing and scaling value. Combining Kotler's value approach and Osterwalder's CANVAS model, leads to the following clustering:

■ **Value design** is customer-oriented and – in Osterwalder's model – involves 'customer relationships' [5] that materialize through different (marketing) 'channels' [6] aimed at specific 'customer segments' (mass markets, niche markets, etc.) [7].

■ **Value creation** is organized in the actual production process, which operationalizes how 'key activities' are internally organized [2], based on what kind of 'key resources' – assets – are needed to sustain and support the organization [3], and the 'partner network' [1] of vital suppliers that enables the organization to focus on its core (value-creating) activities.

■ **Value capturing and scaling** represents the basic financial side of the business model, which is defined by the cost structure [8.1] necessary to create the value (fixed costs, variable costs, economies of scale and scope) and the revenue streams [9.1], the income generated from each customer segment. The net effect of 'cost structure' and 'revenue streams' defines whether the organization is profitable or not.

The business model CANVAS has developed into a powerful tool for assisting firms in aligning their activities, by illustrating potential trade-offs in capturing value. Nonetheless, it is rather static, based on traditional business thinking and too narrow a representation of what private organizations – affecting and being affected by complex societies – are all about (Chapter 8). Capturing the full picture of *sustainable business models* requires an *upgraded* CANVAS model, in particular with regard to the 'value-capturing' dimension. In traditional business models, value-capturing is often defined in terms of financial value only. Sustainable business models focus on social and environmental value as well, which implies a shift from short-term to long-term value creation. The simultaneous focus on creating multiple forms of 'value' or capitals can be derived from the definition of a 'sustainable business model' as formulated by Schaltegger, Hansen and Lüdeke-Freund (2016: 6):

> "A business model for sustainability helps describing, analysing, managing, and communicating (i) a company's sustainable value proposition to its customers, and all other stakeholders, (ii) how it creates and delivers this value, (iii) and how it captures economic value while maintaining or regenerating natural, social, and economic capital beyond its organizational boundaries."

Thinking in terms of sustainable business models requires that the conventional CANVAS model is extended beyond the 'profit' purpose to also include a

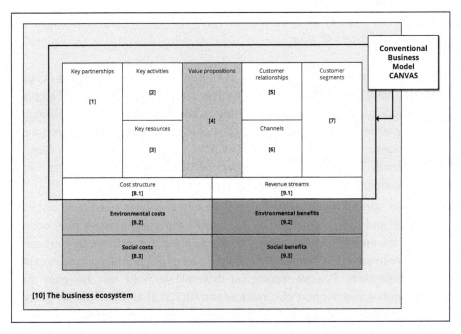

Figure 9.5 Upgraded CANVAS model: CANVAS+

social and environmental purpose. This implies that the 'value proposition' is broadened accordingly. Furthermore, the financial account ('cost structure' and 'revenue streams') needs to include both the positive and negative externalities of the business model. A successful (sustainable) business model achieves a positive net value in terms of profits as well as social and environmental value added, which to a considerable extent depends on an organization's relationship with its broader business ecosystem [10].

BROADENING THE 'VALUE PROPOSITION':
CREATING, DESTROYING AND SPREADING VALUE[7]

By extending the conventional CANVAS model to encompass negative and positive externalities, it can accommodate a broader set of vital (societally relevant) value dimensions that link to higher levels of intervention, beyond level 1 (Figure 9.6). Level 1 interventions, in this area, relate to the basic functions of any organization (largely following Osterwalder's model): creating, designing and capturing value.

---

7 A specification of the six value dimensions of the CANVAS+ model for Sustainable Business is provided in Tool #9.2 at the end of this chapter.

A broader value proposition and business case should additionally include level 2, 3 and 4 types of value:

- **Value destruction** occurs when an organization creates negative ecological, social and economic externalities (section 5.2 and 5.3). Negative *ecological* externalities [8.2] include pollution and waste; negative *social* externalities [8.3] include lay-offs and (local) crowding-out effects. Negative *economic* (cost-related) externalities [8.1] involve, for instance, tax evasion schemes. The accumulated impact of all these activities defines the 'value destruction' effects of a particular business model (level 2).

- **Value spreading** arises when an organization creates positive ecological, social and economic externalities. Positive *social* externalities [9.3] constitute the impact created beyond customer value, for instance by increasing employment in the value chain, enhancing employees' education or investing in innovation. Positive *ecological* externalities [9.2] can be generated through active support of climate action (SDG13) and biodiversity protection and improvement (SDGs 14 and 15). Positive *economic* externalities [9.1] can be created through enhanced competitiveness of the entire community. The accumulated effect defines the value-spreading potential of a business model (level 3).

- **Co-created/shared value** is generated when social, ecological and economic value is co-created together with the communities that constitute the business ecosystem (level 4). Designing business models that aim for shared value creation is the ultimate ambition of sustainable business models. In this area, a growing body of literature is developing on so-called *purpose ecosystems* (Hervieux and Voltan, 2018). Rather than considering the ecosystem merely as a contextual factor, individual organizations can actively weave and co-shape conducive systems that support their purpose-driven activities. This strategy requires developing cross-sector partnerships (section 5.4). The purpose ecosystem often has a social entrepreneurial approach and provides an infrastructure to enable social and economic change. It connects and brings together actors from multiple areas and educates new and potential actors to be social innovators (ibid: 285).

The more intervention levels (levels 1, 2, 3, 4) are included in the business model, the more *societal value* can be generated. Applying the CANVAS+ model to a practice of reversing materiality implies that companies link the SDGs to their entire '*value portfolio*' of value creation, value design, value capturing, value destruction, value spreading and value sharing.

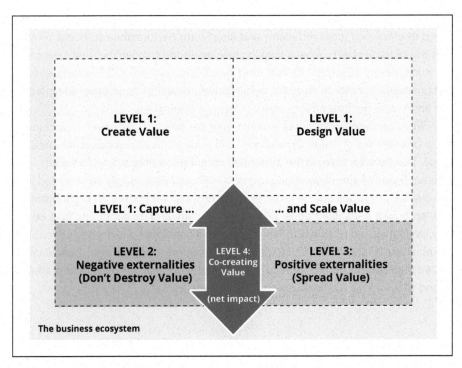

Figure 9.6 Upgraded CANVAS model: CANVAS+ and value dimensions

9.4.2   Poor versus rich value propositions: guiding the purpose

Depending on their motivation and ultimate sustainability ambition, companies are confronted with fundamental questions of what goals to aspire to, what trade-offs to consider and what synergies to pursue. Many face a strategic crossroads – the critical threshold between reactive and (pro)active – and recognize that choosing a direction is not without consequences: there are 'sunk costs' and 'switching costs' involved, while raised expectations and path dependencies will make it difficult to change track intermediately. These insights reiterate the importance of defining a guiding value proposition – as a key value driver and monitoring mechanism – at the start of a transition trajectory. What values does the organization promise to deliver? In whose interest? To what end?

Business models based on inspiring value propositions can spur the development of organizations and reshape entire industries. The steering potential of meaningful 'value drivers' goes to the very heart of management principles and the purpose of an organization. The classic idea of the 'purpose of a firm' – that "the business of business is business", the famous dictum of Nobel Laureate Milton Friedman – has broadly been understood as: firms should aim for profit maximization. This classical view represents a *narrow value proposition*, primarily aimed at efficiency, cost reduction and short-term performance to boost profits. This line of traditional business thinking was extended to how 'the' business case for sustainability (Chapter 8) has long been approached: CSR efforts should demonstrably contribute to profit maximization, distinct competitive advantages and short-term positive effects on a company's operations.

Management thinking has evolved (see section 7.2), however, to include a much broader set of 'value dimensions' and relevant business cases for sustainability. This broader take on the (potential) contribution of business to society – at different levels of intervention/engagement – should accordingly be reflected in a *broader value proposition*. A broader value proposition mirrors an organization's view on how it sees itself positioned within society and its sector, its take on its fiduciary duties and responsibilities, and whom it considers primary and secondary stakeholders (Table 9.2). Customers then become communities, benefits are related to people's 'needs' (instead of marketable propositions only), and 'markets' extend to future generations, needs and markets as well.

Table 9.2 'Poor' versus 'rich' value propositions

	Poor/narrow value proposition	Rich/broad value proposition
General characteristics	Instrumental, simplistic, managerial, risk averse, quantitative, easy to measure, company-oriented only, 'don't do harm', short-term value creation	Resilient, inspirational, entrepreneurial, risk-taking, qualitative, societal orientation, long-term value creation
Cost of 'doing nothing'	Costs and risks of inactivity are not considered	Costs and risks of inactivity are part of the business case
Marketing	Sell as much as possible; explicit (marketable) demand orientation; appeal to impressionable groups	Sell consumer value; support latent demand; needs orientation; appeal to all ages
Finance	Profit maximization; cost minimization; increase (short-term) shareholder value ('biggest return on investment')	Enable the financial means for a company to thrive; creating increased societal value ('social return on investment')
Purchasing/ supply chain	Purchase as cheaply and as flexibly as possible (no commitment to suppliers)	Empower suppliers (for instance, through innovation) to contribute to your value creation process
HRM	Produce the highest possible output with the lowest possible number of people	Organize inspired and committed staff; empowerment and creativity
Strategic management	Being the biggest, the first	Being innovative, creating the most value for society, solving specific societal problems

A basic characteristic of a poor value proposition is that it does not consider the company's effects on societal stakeholders, which renders it overly simplistic. Value propositions like 'being the first', 'being big', 'being the biggest' or 'maximum profits' – in various forms – belong to this category. For instance, Enron – an American energy, commodities and services company that went bankrupt in 2001 – positioned itself as "the world's leading company"; Barclays – a London-based multinational investment bank and financial services company – advertised itself as "a Big world needs a Big Bank".[8] Ironically, some companies, particularly in the financial sector, have become 'too big to fail'. In 2007–2008, banks created a notoriously vicious problem for society (the financial crisis) when it turned out that

---

WHAT MARK WILL YOUR VALUE PROPOSITION SET?

B O X 9.3

Vintage advertisements illustrate how the vision and mission of companies – as portrayed in advertisement campaigns – indicate a value proposition that, in a different era, would not be considered acceptable. Consider, for example, the following advertisements from the 1950s, showing a particular vision on 'health' and 'safety'. Ask yourself: what current ads might signal the wrong value propositions two decades from now?

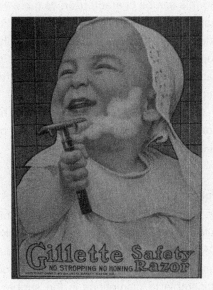

Source: courtesy of University of Alabama Center for the Study of Tobacco and Society (https://csts.ua.edu/)

---

8   Barclay's 'Big', directed by Tony Scott (2000) https://www.youtube.com/watch?v=_39b8e5PXWw

they had been taking too much risk, anticipating that the costs would probably be borne by society ('socializing losses' through bailouts; also known as the 'moral hazard problem', see section 7.3.4). Size and profitability are indeed valid *means* for the financial and competitive longevity of a company, but in themselves do not represent a valid 'value' in terms of societal legitimacy ('license to exist/operate'). A similar problem applies to negatively formulated value propositions, like "Don't be evil" (Google) or "Don't violate privacy" (WhatsApp). In practice, negatively formulated intentions prove difficult to sustain. Google faced problems with implementing its value proposition after entering the Chinese market; WhatsApp after its takeover by Facebook.

9.4.3 Fragile or resilient?

Triggering events (Chapter 7) and the dynamics of the present VUCA era (Chapter 1) have revealed the relevance of developing *resilient business models*. In a highly interconnected yet uncertain world, triggering events can sprawl unanticipated effects at great speed, scope and scale. How triggering events (incidental, structural, systemic) spread and develop indicates the fragilities within organizations, value chains, sectors or entire systems. Business models can be characterized as more vulnerable to or more resilient against, for instance, changing consumer expectations, shifting stakeholder/societal expectations, changes in international regulatory environments, disruptions (e.g. in supply chains, technology, markets), unanticipated shocks (e.g. pandemics, natural disasters) or systemic crises (e.g. financial, economic, climate, social, ecological, geopolitical).

The CANVAS+ business model helps to identify those parts of the *value portfolio* that can be considered more or less vulnerable/resilient aspects of the business model (Table 9.3).

CREATING VALUE

At the level of the business model, one of the most evident characteristics of vulnerability can be found in the supply chain – the 'value-creating' part of the CANVAS+ model. The more companies outsource large parts of the production (and added value) to suppliers, the more their entire business model becomes vulnerable to disruptions in the supply chain. Global value chains that start in fragile or unstable countries further reinforce that vulnerability. Just-in-time (JIT) production models – which align raw material orders directly with demand-driven production schedules to cut back on inventory costs and increase efficiency – are relatively fragile. These models depend on precise coordination and prompt delivery throughout the entire value chain and do not reckon with eventualities or shocks ('just in case'). In other words, 'lack of slack' is resource- and cost-

Table 9.3 Vulnerable versus resilient organizations

LEVEL	Value dimension	Vulnerable organization	Resilient organization
LEVEL 1	**Creating value**	Just-in-time (JIT), global value chains; specialized and dependent suppliers	Circular and local (or glocal) value chains; diversification
	Designing value	Fast (food, fashion, tourism); fast-moving consumer goods; 'manufactured' demand	Slow (food, fashion, tourism); circular designed goods; solutions to 'needs' (as opposed to created demand)
	Capturing value	Shareholder value; stock buy-backs	Stakeholder value; long-term return on investment
	Scaling value	Rapid internationalization and growth; mergers and acquisitions (M&A) based on external capital, debt-financed	'Organic' or 'evolutionary' internationalization and growth processes; based on own capital and reserves
LEVEL 2	**(not) Destroying value**	Exploitative business models, in search of and actively creating pollution/taxation/wage havens	Explorative business models; internalization of costs and 'true pricing' strategies
LEVEL 3	**Spreading value**	Competitiveness based on scale and specialization only; aimed at 'license to exist'	Competitiveness based on resilience and scope; 'license to operate and experiment'
LEVEL 4	**Sharing/ co-creating value**	Short-term; philanthropic; Ad hoc partnering; marginal activity	Medium-term; SDG priorities; aligned with the national or local agenda; core business; partnering and co-creation

efficient in stable environments (where all goes well and to plan), but is fragile and can be extremely 'expensive' under unpredictable circumstances (the present VUCA world). Globalized 'lean production' and just-in-time delivery systems have arguably increased the vulnerability of the entire system (Box 9.4), as became painfully apparent during the Covid-19 pandemic (section 7.4).

THE INFLUENCE OF (RE)FRAMING: FROM 'VULNERABLE' TO 'LEAN'

The JIT model was first introduced in Japan in the 1980s, in the Toyota production system. 'Toyotism' presented a competitive alternative to the prevailing 'Fordism' model, in which companies organized large parts of their supply chain in-house (vertical integration). Ever since, the JIT concept has spread around the world to become the leading frame of globally organized value chains.

B O X

9.4

BOX 9.4

The global success of the Toyota production model has partly been the result of its framing. Originally, the leading authors on the Toyota production model (Womack, Jones and Roos, 1990) called the Japanese model the *vulnerable production system* to characterize the just-in-time, hierarchical supply chains that heavily relied on the flexible capabilities of loyal and dependent suppliers. Company-loyal trade unions and an ecosystem of intricate stakeholder relations were required to manage this vulnerability (Ruigrok and Van Tulder, 1995). The authors on the Toyota production model decided that 'vulnerable' production would not resonate well with American and European car producers. They reframed 'vulnerable production' as 'lean production'. The concept of 'lean production' (and related JIT inventory systems) has become one of the most dominant frames in business model approaches since the 1990s. In network theory, the model has been referred to as the 'strength of weak ties'.

DESIGNING VALUE

The distinction between more vulnerable and more resilient organizing can also be made for other value dimensions of the CANVAS+ model. In designing value (the marketing side of the business model), the key distinction applies to the difference between 'fast' and 'slow'. *Fast food* and *fast fashion*, for instance, are two business models that require an ecosystem of short-term or instant need satisfaction. Sociological research on the broader impact of the instant gratification model speak of the 'McDonaldization of society' (Ritzer, 1993) or the existence of a 'fast food nation' (Schlosser, 2005). These societal models often go hand in hand with low wages, low added value, poor nutrition (and obesity, diabetes, cardiac and vascular diseases), and competition based on 'created' or 'manufactured' demand – as is the case with considerable segments of so-called 'fast-moving consumer goods'. Fast consumption patterns contribute to an unhealthy, wasteful, and relatively fragile society. The alternative has become known as 'slow food' and 'slow fashion'. These movements not only seek to develop more resilient business models but also more aware, responsible and resilient societies. They tap into people's more fundamental needs for 'self-realization' (the top of Maslow's pyramid), related to lifestyle decisions around health, well-being, quality of life, and being a 'responsible/good' person.

CAPTURING AND SCALING VALUE

Value capturing based on 'shareholder value' feeds into short-termism and the global trend of 'speculative capital' prevailing over 'productive capital'. It is related to the erosion of own capital by massive stock buy-backs to increase shareholder value. A focus on *stakeholder value*, on the other hand, enables companies to consider longer-term resilience, for instance by investing in innovation that goes beyond efficiency enhancement only. Research on the operation of hedge funds hints at the bias of these funds against more sustainable companies (DesJardine et al., 2020).

Scaling value also involves financial decisions related to the nature and direction of growth: through autonomous growth and/or takeovers. Growth based on mergers/acquisitions and rapid takeover strategies has often resulted in greater vulnerabilities, as integrating different organizational cultures often proves complicated. Two out of three mergers and acquisitions eventually fail (Chapter 6), thereby *destroying value*, even for many shareholders. Organic or autonomous growth, on average, proves more resilient and sustainable, because it is founded on a company's internal capabilities that trigger growth (instead of the other way around). Comparable logics apply to internationalization strategies. Rapid internationalization through acquisitions can lead to 'imperial overstretch' and is riskier than gradual or evolutionary internationalization strategies (Van Tulder, 2018a). Cooperatives and family-owned companies fund their scaling and internationalization strategies with their own capital, rather than by issuing shares (external capital). It has made their scaling strategies less extensive, but also more deliberate, resilient and stable. The phenomenon of *de-internationalization* – retreating from a rapid expansion strategy that has proved vulnerable – has also been observed, in particular related to externally funded rapid takeover strategies (Van Tulder with Van der Zwart, 2006).

DESTROYING AND SPREADING VALUE: EXPLOITATIVE VERSUS EXPLORATIVE MODELS

When it comes to how private organizations include externalities in their business models, one can distinguish between 'exploitative' and 'explorative' business models. *Exploitative* business models capitalize on scale and cost-reducing opportunities, by actively searching for regulatory environments where companies only minimally contribute to the social and ecological costs of their chosen business model. Exploitative strategies induce competition between locations to minimize costs, contribute to the creation of tax, wage and pollution 'havens', and instigate 'race to the bottom' mechanisms (Chapter 6). By not paying for value destruction – and not contributing to 'value spreading' either – these companies not only contribute to *less resilient societies* around the world (Chapter 7), but also make themselves vulnerable to waning societal acceptance of their limited contribution, exploitative operations and shirking on key responsibilities. Low trust creates low societal legitimacy, which will eventually restrict the possibilities of companies to scale, grow and experiment, to the extent of eroding the company's innovative and dynamic capabilities.

Explorative business models, on the other hand, are aimed at 'rethinking value', how it is created and how value is distributed. Explorative firms seek ways to internalize negative externalities and optimize positive externalities and, therefore, usually gain higher levels of trust and societal legitimacy. Societal legitimacy increases a company's 'scope' to experiment – with innovative concepts, novel approaches, differentiated operations – and to dynamically adapt its business model to challenges. Legitimacy also fosters vital stakeholder support (from government, suppliers, customers, NGOs) in case of, for instance, hostile takeover bids or in times of crises. The relevance of the *scale* versus *scope* dimensions for the resilience of business models goes back to the original thinking on the 'dynamics of industrial capitalism' by Alfred Chandler (1990).

SHARING/CO-CREATING VALUE

The 'sharing value' dimension links the business model to an organization's wider ecosystem, societal expectations and societal challenges. When primarily operationalized through philanthropic efforts, corporate engagement becomes vulnerable to short-term considerations and (fashionable) preferences of the management of the day. Resilient value sharing, as a level 4 type of engagement, requires co-creation, strategic involvement and integration in the core business of the organization. If organizations are able to 'align' with the societal (SDG) priorities of the country or ecosystem in which they operate, they will gain in legitimacy, be better able to tap into collaborative competencies and opportunities, and grow more resilient.

B O X

9.5

'ZOMBIE COMPANIES' – RETURN OF THE 'LIVING DEATHS'?

The link between 'business models' and 'value dimensions' of companies and the resilience or fragility of the entire system is perhaps best illustrated with the growing phenomenon of so-called 'zombie companies'. Zombie companies are indebted "low-productivity firms that would typically exit in a competitive market" (Andrews et al., 2017). These weak firms earn just enough to continue operations and service the interest on their loans, but are unable to pay off their debts in any meaningful way – making them, in a sense, 'living deaths'.[9] Other than the 'valley of death' – which defines the *upscaling* problems that many social enterprises encounter – the 'zombie' problem covers the challenge of *downscaling* activities, *restructuring* the business model, or

---

9   The OECD defines 'zombie firms' as those aged ten years or older, with an interest-coverage ratio (the ratio of operating income to interest expenses) of less than one, in each of the preceding three years (Andrews et al., 2017).

B
O
X

9.5

ultimately facing *creative destruction* by competitive business models with more vigorous and resilient *value portfolios*.

The 'zombie' phenomenon started in Japan, where large Japanese banks – instigated by the government – continued to support lingering firms after the 'asset price bubble' burst around 1990. Many of the supported companies were considered 'too big to fail'. In the aftermath of the 2008 financial crisis, the 'zombie' status also applied to many American and European companies. Following the Chinese stock market crash in 2016, it even pertained to publicly listed state-owned enterprises in industrial sectors with massive overcapacity. State support packages in response to the Covid-19 pandemic in 2020 – which unleashed trillions of dollars in government spending and newly created money for bailout programs – have further increased concerns that financially fragile companies are supported to forestall (short-term) friction problems (e.g. safeguarding jobs and consumption levels). More promising investment opportunities – notably in sustainable business – that would accelerate systemic change may be left underfunded.

Continued support for 'zombie' companies may crowd out investment by non-zombie firms and stall technological diffusion. Furthermore, it distorts efficient resource allocation by preventing more efficient, more future-proof and more sustainable companies from gaining market share. According to research by the Bank of America, around one-fifth of US and EU companies can be considered 'zombie' firms. The Bank for International Settlement (BIS) calculated that the number of zombie companies around the world increased from 2% at the end of the 1980s, to 12% of all companies in 2016 (Banerjee and Hofman, 2018). In the aftermath of the Covid-19 crisis, society's urgent call to effectively address systems fragilities and increase resilience to future shocks will have its repercussion on prospective resource allocation. Pairing the massive recovery actions with 'building back stronger' policies raises the fundamental question of what business models one should bet on. Choosing between reanimating fragile business models or stimulating future-oriented resilient ones, then reflects the choice for more 'sustainable' or 'non-sustainable' societal change trajectories.

9.5 SUSTAINABILITY ECOSYSTEMS AND RELATED BUSINESS MODELS

There is considerable confusion as to what the ultimate ambition of sustainable business models actually entails at the societal level. Exactly what kind of 'ecosystem' do they seek to co-shape and/or contribute to? The sustainable business model literature discusses a wide variety of socioeconomic and societal aspirations, including circular economies, inclusive growth, prosperity without growth, sustainable development, moral or humanistic capitalism, creative capitalism, the 'sharing economy', the 'we economy'. All emphasize the relevance of 'business' in engendering societal change; all recognize that sustainability issues cannot be effectively addressed by government alone, nor taken up by individual societal actors. *Purpose-driven* business models are considered to drive the 'New Economy' (Hollensbe et al., 2014). Under different sustainability headings and claims, most sustainable business models represent complementary elaborations of the same ambition: to advance financially sustainable business models that contribute to societal and ecological sustainability by addressing many of the shortcomings of the present societal model – including external costs and benefits. All emphasize the combination of two leading motives: profit motives (positive returns) and societal motives have to be reconciled in an entrepreneurial manner, in order to create the positive and innovative change needed to drive sustainability to the next level.

9.5.1   Sustainable paradigm ecosystems

Generally, sustainable business models are framed as contributing to an alternative to existing but failing economic and organizational paradigms. Leading, partly overlapping paradigms that are expected to contribute to sustainable development include: 'circular', 'inclusive', 'sharing' or 'social', and 'creative capitalism'.

CIRCULAR

A circular economy is often presented as an answer to the linear economy, with its extractive 'take-make-dispose' models that lead to wasteful production systems in a world with finite resources. A circular economy is restorative and regenerative by intention and design. Ecosystems in which the waste of one system is the food or input for another form the basic philosophy of the circular economy. The Circle Economy (2016) introduced a 'value hill' concept – a categorization based on the lifecycle phases of a product (pre-, in- and post-use).[10] In this approach of *circular design*, *optimal use* and *value recovery*, a product is kept on its highest value (top of the hill) for as long as possible through proper maintenance and repair, while the product's downhill journey seeks to 'retain value' through *reuse/redistribution, refurbishment, remanufacturing* and *recycling*. The Ellen MacArthur Foundation – one of the leading think tanks and charities aimed at inspiring a generation to "re-think, re-design and build a positive future through the framework of a circular economy" – bases their circular model on three principles: (1) design out waste and pollution; (2) keep products and materials in use; (3) regenerate natural systems.[11]

---

10   https://www.circle-economy.com/resources/master-circular-business-with-the-value-hill
11   Source: https://www.ellenmacarthurfoundation.org/circular-economy/concept

INCLUSIVE

An 'inclusive economy' is an answer to the 'exclusive' production model of, in particular, large private firms (types 5, 6, 7 in Chapter 8) that produce only for those customers that can afford the products, thereby ignoring the poor segments of society. Perhaps the most famous elaboration of the paradigm was presented by Prahalad and Hart (2002), with their vision of the business fortune to be gained at the 'Bottom of the Pyramid' (BoP). Inclusive business models aim to develop *scalable innovations* that address market failures and fulfil the needs of resource-constrained communities. These models include low-income communities as clients or consumers on the 'demand side', and as producers, entrepreneurs or employees on the 'supply side'. In order to reach marginalized groups, inclusive businesses need to remove constraints that inhibit BoP communities from entering the market and getting access to public goods. In a 2011 article, Prahalad proposed to replace the commonly used four Ps of marketing (*product, price, place* and *promotion*) with four As that are relevant when doing business at the BoP: *awareness, access, affordability* and *availability*. Follow-up studies on the BoP concept suggested that a fifth 'A' be added to the framework – *appropriateness* – since context-specific and sociocultural factors play a crucial role in the potential uptake of products and services. Accordingly, five As characterize 'inclusive innovations' and differentiate 'inclusive business' from 'business as usual' (Lijfering and Van Tulder, 2020):

1   Accessibility: enabling access to products and services to reach marginalized consumers.

2   Availability: establishing an uninterrupted supply of high-quality products and services.

3   Affordability: providing solutions that are affordable for low-income groups.

4   Awareness: ensuring that consumers know what is on offer and how to use the solution.

5   Appropriateness: adapting products and services to local needs and requirements.

SHARING/WE/SOCIAL ECONOMY

A 'sharing/we/peer economy' aims for collaborative consumption, shared ownership and replacing buying by renting. This paradigm is presented as an answer to markets organized around individualistic preferences and short-term consumption-oriented interests. In very general terms, the 'sharing economy' is often defined as 'collaborative consumption'; sharing products and services lowers the price of using these products and services. A community can share tools (a lawn mower), goods (cars) or services (collective energy contracts) as a way of mutual support.

In a similar vein, the 'we economy' or 'collaborative economy' is based on the notion of interdependence. Individuals can only thrive if the network around them is thriving as well. According to observers, the 'we economy' can create a 'next level of value creation' by combining and coordinating networks of contributors, co-creating contextual solutions, and drawing on connected sources and skills. Trust, confidence, fair sharing and societal cohesion are vital preconditions in the 'we economy' (Hesseldahl et al., 2015). In both the 'sharing economy' and the 'we economy', activities are typically organized through community-based platforms and by coordinating solutions enabled through digital technology. The 'social economy' overlaps with the sharing/we/collaborative paradigm, with its primacy to social values and objectives of the rich diversity of organizations that constitute it. The European Commission classifies 'social economy' organizations as cooperatives, mutual societies, voluntary organizations, foundations and social enterprises (types 2, 3, 4 in Chapter 8).

RETHINKING CAPITALISM

Over the years, a variety of upgraded versions of 'capitalism' have been proposed: creative, moral or normative, humanistic, responsible and even regenerative capitalism. All contributions argue that the value proposition of companies needs to be broadened. Moral or humanistic capitalism[12] has been presented as an answer to 'purposeless capitalism' that puts the burden of negative externalities with society as a result of its one-sided orientation to shareholder capitalism and profit maximization. 'Creative capitalism' is a term introduced by Bill Gates, the former Microsoft CEO and one of the world's biggest philanthropists. Gates presents creative capitalism as "an approach where governments, businesses, and non-profits work together to stretch the reach of market forces so that more people can make a profit, or gain recognition, doing work that eases the world's inequities".[13] In 2019, the US Business Roundtable – an association of Chief Executive Officers of America's leading companies – issued a 'Statement on the Purpose of the Corporation' with a distinct stakeholder flavour. The statement was signed by 181 CEOs, representing almost all members of the Business Roundtable. For the first time, the statement departed from the original principles of shareholder primacy in the US system (see section 6.5.1) – that corporations principally exist to serve shareholders – towards one comprising "a fundamental commitment to

---

12 The term 'moral capitalism' was coined by Adam Smith (founder of economics as a science); 'humanistic capitalism' by Mohammed Yunus (microfinance and Nobel peace prize laureate).
13 https://www.gatesfoundation.org/Media-Center/Speeches/2008/01/Bill-Gates-2008-World-Economic-Forum

all of our stakeholders".[14] The latter includes the interests of shareholders, employees, retirees and pensioners, creditors, consumers and governments, the environment, and the long-term interests of the corporation. The statement's signatories committed to the following principles: (1) delivering value to customers, including meeting or exceeding customer expectations; (2) investing in employees, including through fair compensation and fostering diversity and inclusion, dignity and respect; (3) dealing fairly and ethically with suppliers, including serving as good partners with those companies that help them meet their missions; (4) supporting the communities in which they work, including by embracing sustainable practices; (5) generating long-term value for shareholders, including through transparent and effective engagement.

The World Business Council for Sustainable Development (WBCSD) – which convenes more than 200 global companies committed to advance the sustainability agenda – argues in favour of a far more ambitious and transformative role for business in society. In its *Vision 2050: Time to Transform* report, WBCSD calls upon businesses and their leaders to change their mindsets towards building *long-term resilience*, towards a *regenerative approach* to business and towards *reinventing capitalism*. Such a foundational mindset shift is to "ensure that the economic system, our incentives, the global accounting standards and the capital market valuations will no longer be based on the financial performance of business but integrates the impact on the planet and people as part of how we define success and determine enterprise value. The move to a capitalism of true value for all will accelerate the transformation towards 9+ billion people all living well, within planetary boundaries" (WBCSD, 2021: 1). Since "change is not happening at the speed and scale required", the WBCSD urges businesses to take on their role to lead, forge the collaborations required to drive change, move beyond a 'doing no harm' mindset, and invest in realistic transition trajectories.

9.5.2 From paradigm to business model elaboration: distinguishing narrow from broad

The crux of understanding to what extent different paradigms contribute to changing trajectories at the societal level lies in understanding (a) how the business model labelled by any of these paradigms is operationalized, and (b) the type of motivation underlying the business model: reactive with modest change ambitions, or more proactive with transformational ambitions (Lüdeke-Freund and Dembek, 2017). Following on from sections 9.3 and 9.4, the elaboration of the sustainability ambition of any business model – operating under any of these paradigms – can reflect a level 1+2 or a level 3+4 type of engagement (Table 9.4).

---

14 https://s3.amazonaws.com/brt.org/BRT-StatementonthePurposeofaCorporationwith SignaturesApril2022.pdf

Table 9.4 From narrow to broadly defined sustainable business models

Sustainability paradigms	Sustainability ambition of the business model	
	Key Tipping Points →	
	Narrow/Reactive elaboration LEVEL 1 + 2	Broad/Proactive elaboration LEVEL 3 + 4
General ambition	Avoid doing harm Narrow fiduciary duty/responsibility Value propositions based on markets Shareholder value Risk-aversion Reactive and tactical	Doing good Broad fiduciary duty/responsibility Value propositions based on needs Stakeholder value Risk-taking Proactive and strategic
Circular economy	Maximize waste reduction; minimize waste; recycle; limit capital destruction; climate/CO_2-neutral	Closing production and consumption loops; regenerative; build economic, natural, social capital; climate/CO_2-positive
Inclusive business	Including poor/excluded people as consumers (BoP 1.0)	Including poor/excluded people as communities, empowering people (BoP 3.0)
We/sharing economy	Centralized, lower pricing strategies (Airbnb, Facebook, Uber)	Decentralized and open source: co-creation of social goods (energy cooperatives; Wikipedia; Linux; 'Fairbnb')
Social Enterprise	Filling gaps left unaddressed by society, hybrid companies (compromise)	Developing scalable purpose-driven companies
Rethinking/ reinventing capitalism	Repairing deficiencies of capitalism; Giving back to society, philanthropy; Normative capitalism or creative capitalism	Create innovative, entrepreneurial solutions for societal challenges as part of core business; Progressive, responsible, regenerative capitalism
Sustainable development [Brundtland Commission]	"Development that meets the needs of the present *without compromising* the ability of future generations to meet their own needs."	Meeting the needs of present generations *while enhancing* the ability of future generations to meet their own needs.

CIRCULAR BUSINESS MODELS

Circular business models are often defined as 'minimizing' waste emissions, resource inputs and energy leakages, through recycling and slowing down energy loops; they primarily cover the technological aspects of circularity (the supply-side of the business model), whereas consumer-oriented and behavioural aspects (e.g. consumer education, reducing unsustainable consumption; moderating consumer demand) are far less emphasized (Bocken and Short, 2016). More integral circularity approaches seek to fully close material and energy loops to contribute to a completely circular economy – one that gradually decouples economic activity from the use of finite resources. Making a distinction between the 'narrow/reactive' and 'broader/integral' version of circularity proves vital for understanding the antecedents of progress. Some circularity practices have become questioned. Recycling waste, for instance, might provide an excuse for not investing in structural waste prevention. Zink and Geyer (2017) have called this the *circular economy rebound* effect, which implies that recycling actually increases the production of wasteful materials, with potentially a worse (net) effect. A comparable logic was already observed several decades ago when – due to emission standards – companies invested in 'end-of-pipe' technologies (filters on chimneys) rather than profoundly rethinking production systems. Combined with poorly implemented sanction mechanisms, end-of-pipe measures actually aggravated the problem. The 'plastic soup' problem shows a comparable logic: initiatives to 'clean up the oceans' – sometimes sponsored by big plastics producers – run the risk of de-incentivizing more structural/systemic solutions. Effective and ambitious circular practices that advance the decoupling of prosperity from environmental degradation have been pointed out as a vital precondition for achieving the SDGs (Sachs et al., 2019a). Vice versa, linking circular business models to specific SDG-targets can positively affect circularity practices and create traction for more proactive sustainability ambitions. (Box 9.6).

CIRCULAR ECONOMY AND THE SDGs

BOX 9.6

The circular economy (CE) and the SDGs are linked. Schroeder, Anggraeni and Weber (2018) considered the relationship between CE practices, the 17 SDGs and the 169 SDG-targets, in particular for developing countries. Based on literature review, an exploratory matching exercise and qualitative relationship assessment, they concluded that CE practices could potentially *directly* contribute to achieving 21 SDG-targets, and *indirectly* an additional 28 SDG-targets.

The strongest **direct relationships** exist between CE practices and the targets of SDG6 ('clean water and sanitation'), SDG7 ('affordable and clean energy'), SDG8 ('decent work and economic growth'), SDG12 ('responsible consumption and production'), and SDG15 ('life on land'). Furthermore, CE practices were assessed to provide **potential synergies** between SDGs that promote economic growth and (green) jobs (SDG8), eliminating poverty (SDG1), ending hunger and sustainable food production (SDG2) and SDGs 14 and 15 (biodiversity protection below water and on land). The authors also considered several **potential trade-offs** between present CE practices (e.g. relating to recycling of municipal waste, e-waste and wastewater) and SDG-targets related to decent work, safe working environments and human health, with suggestions for overcoming them.

A reversed relationship (progress on an SDG-target supports the broader uptake of CE practices) was identified for SDG4 ('quality education'), SDG9 ('industry, innovation and infrastructure'), SDG10 ('reduced inequalitie's'), SDG13 ('climate action'), SDG16 ('peace, justice and strong institution's'), and SDG17 ('partnerships

B
O
X

9.6

for the goals'). This category of reversed causality covered 52 SDG-targets. According to the authors, progress on SDG16 and SDG4 represents the vital 'software' elements of governance and (technical and vocational) skills that will benefit the uptake of CE practices globally; progress on SDG9 provides the necessary 'hardware' elements (facilities, infrastructures) for a circular economic system.

INCLUSIVE BUSINESS MODELS

In practice, inclusive business models are often narrowly defined as creating products for the bottom of the pyramid, providing cheap products to poor people or creating a minimum wage – often slightly above subsistence level. A broader view takes the entire production system into account and regards the social side of the economy as a trigger for advancing human well-being at a higher level of prosperity. The largely market-driven elaboration of the original 'inclusive business' concept by Prahalad and Hart (2002) claimed to solve poverty through 'profit maximization' (Prahalad, 2004). They referred to the 'fortune' to be found at the bottom of the pyramid. The idea that the poor would present a huge untapped market was heavily criticized; it was considered to represent an exploitative and imperialistic model that identified the poor as underserved consumers only. It was acknowledged that entire communities of both customers and producers should be included to support the claim that BoP business models can actually contribute to inclusive development.

The criticism on the supply-driven 'selling to the poor' approach led to a BoP 2.0 version, which put more emphasis on addressing local needs through 'business co-venturing'. By involving local communities, entirely 'new markets' of more innovative, embedded, sustainable and high-quality products and solutions were to be created to enhance 'mutual value'. Later on – in response to early findings on the negative effects on local communities of integration in global value chains (cf. Dembek et al., 2019) – an even more fundamental BoP 3.0 frame was proposed (Cañeque and Hart, 2015; London, 2016). The BoP 3.0 version acknowledges the need to: embed BoP-ventures into wider innovation ecosystems; come up with more relevant value propositions that address a broader portfolio of value dimensions (section 9.4.1); evolve from a poverty alleviation orientation to a holistic take on sustainable development; adopt a bottom-up and multisector partnerships approach, rather than 'outsourcing' the customer-facing functions of the business model to NGOs.

WE/SHARING ECONOMY BUSINESS MODELS

One of the most contentious parts of the 'shared' or 'platform' economy has been whether it is premised on centralized or decentralized provision models, and on commercial or non-commercial logics (Figure 9.7). If 'shared' services and products are centrally provided for profit purposes (e.g. Airbnb, Uber or Facebook), they in practice create negative externalities for society as well (e.g. bypassing the middlemen, infringing on privacy, triggering a 'race to the bottom' that erodes social protection and fair wages, antitrust issues). The 'sharing economy' can also be organized as a decentralized system of networks and marketplaces to "unlock the value of underused assets by matching needs and haves" (Botsman and Rogers, 2010). In a decentralized, non-extractive sharing economy, the metaphorical argument is that 'Airbnb' should be a 'Fairbnb' that enhances 'community-powered tourism'.[15] More fundamentally, the present state of use of the World Wide Web has compelled the formulation of new principles to save it from non-sustainable, exploitative use by centralized platform incumbents (Box 9.7).

A 'CONTRACT FOR THE WEB': NINE PRINCIPLES TO PROTECT AND EXPAND A COMMON GOOD

B O X 9.7

In 1989, the World Wide Web was designed by Tim Berners-Lee "to bring people together and make knowledge freely available. It has changed the world for good and improved the lives of billions." At that time, Berners-Lee worked for a public institute (CERN) and decided to make his brainchild a *common good* by designing it as an open-access platform, non-profit, without imposing any patent protection on its use.

The further build-up, spread and completion of the web in a largely unregulated global environment revealed several significant weaknesses however. Over the years, the web has become dominated by a few profit-driven 'platform' firms with non-sustainable business models that exploit, divide and undermine, which – according to Berners-Lee – has severe repercussions for the web's future and integrity. "Half of the world's population still can't get online. For the other half, the Web's benefits seem to come with far too many unacceptable risks: to our privacy, our democracy, our health and our security." Instead of enriching people's life, a digital dystopia looms large.

Berners-Lee's intention in creating the web was to stimulate open-access and cooperative business models. Wikipedia and Linux – non-profit centralized (top-down) – and, for instance, energy and solar panel cooperatives (decentral users of the web) reflect its original philosophy. However, the web has also been open to commercial initiatives – of which Bitcoin represents a decentral (bottom-up) initiative.

---

15 https://www.meetup.com/nl-NL/FairBnB/.

Berners-Lee did not anticipate that a few centralized internet platform companies like Uber, Alibaba or Facebook (and a few others) would be able to dominate the web for commercial purposes only.

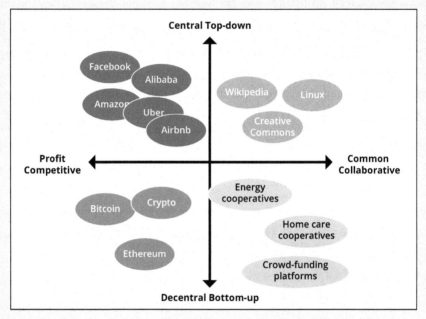

Figure 9.7 Shared economy business model logics

In 2019, 30 years after the birthday of the web, Berners-Lee initiated a global plan of action – the 'Contract for the Web' – as the result of a multi-stakeholder engagement process. The contract is guided by past work on digital and human rights. It contains nine principles that hold each of the three societal sectors (government, companies, citizens) accountable for doing their part "to ensure that the online world is safe, empowering and genuinely for everyone", and to protect the web as a 'force for good'. The principles combine both 'avoid harm' (negative duties) and 'doing good' (positive duties) values and propositions.

Contract for the Web

Governments

- **Principle 1:** Ensure everyone can connect to the internet – *so that anyone, no matter who they are or where they live, can participate actively online;*

- **Principle 2:** Keep all of the internet available, all of the time – *so that no one is denied their right to full internet access;*

B
O
X

9.7

- **Principle 3:** Respect and protect people's fundamental online privacy and data rights – *so everyone can use the internet freely, safely, and without fear*;

Companies
- **Principle 4:** Make the internet affordable and accessible to everyone – *so that no one is excluded from using and shaping the Web*;
- **Principle 5:** Respect and protect people's privacy and personal data to build online trust – *so people are in control of their lives online, empowered with clear and meaningful choices around their data and privacy*;
- **Principle 6:** Develop technologies that support the best in humanity and challenge the worst – *so the Web really is a public good that puts people first*;

Citizens
- **Principle 7:** Be creators and collaborators on the Web – *so the Web has rich and relevant content for everyone*;
- **Principle 8:** Build strong communities that respect civil discourse and human dignity – *so that everyone feels safe and welcome online*;
- **Principle 9:** Fight for the Web – *so the Web remains open and a global public resource for people everywhere, now and in the future*

At its launch in November 2019, the 'Contract for the Web' – with its 76 implementation clauses – already had the backing of over 160 organizations, including Microsoft, Google, Electronic Frontier Foundation, DuckDuckGo, CIPESA, AccessNow, Reddit, Facebook, Reporters Without Borders and Ranking Digital Rights, and several governments (Germany, Ghana, France). Just one month later, over 1,100 organizations from over 50 countries had signed it and promised to take action to uphold the commitment. More information: https://contractfortheweb.org/#main

SOCIAL ENTERPRISES
The social enterprise represents a specific part of the 'social economy' that can be susceptible to a relatively narrow or broader operationalization of its sustainability ambitions. In Anglo-Saxon countries, social enterprise can be interpreted as an organizational form that fills gaps that result from modest government

involvement in the social economy and a smart tax deduction scheme. The social enterprise business model can also be interpreted as a purpose-driven hybrid form of organizing aimed at an enhanced positive impact on society. A significant challenge for social enterprise business models is their scalability and, consequently, their modest impact on major sustainability issues. Social enterprises run the risk of remaining niche players (see section 8.5, archetype 4/5).

REINVENTING/RETHINKING CAPITALISM

The operationalization of different views on capitalism can also portray a narrow, broader or transformative orientation. A narrow elaboration of the idea of creative capitalism boils down to a profit orientation, complemented by philanthropic efforts that provide 'recognition' (as a reputation-based market incentive). The concept of 'normative capitalism' is applied to make conventional business models less exploitative or less harmful. 'Responsible capitalism' seeks the integration of the 'needs of the wider community'. More transformative thinkers on capitalism – with relevance for business models based on broader value propositions – speak of 'rethinking capitalism', stressing the importance of new social contracts and common goods (Mazzucato, 2018; see also Chapter 1). Comparable concepts – like 'progressive capitalism' in the elaboration of Joseph Stiglitz (2019) or 'regenerative capitalism' in that of John Fullerton (2015) – represent the search for a better balance of government, markets and civil society and imply more transformational, societal ambitions beyond the corporate 'bottom line'.

SUSTAINABLE DEVELOPMENT

Following the logic of relatively narrow and broader elaborations of sustainability ambitions in the business model, even the most quoted definition of sustainable development by the Brundtland Committee (UN World Commission on Environment and Development, 1987) may be classified as relatively defensive. It defines sustainable development as "meeting the needs of the present without compromising the ability of future generations to meet their own needs". A more proactive elaboration would read "meeting the needs of present generations while *enhancing* or *improving* the ability of future generations to meet their own needs". The latter elaboration is less about limitations and more about opportunities.

So, seemingly similar terms for sustainable business models can demarcate completely different practices. As a consequence, the discussion on sustainable business models regularly becomes clouded by – arguably sympathetic – frames that turn out to have less positive effects than suggested, because broader societal, longer-term and indirect effects were not taken into account. In the scientific discourse on sustainable business models, taking these societal effects on board has led to the upgrading of many of the original concepts. This happened with the discussion on the bottom of the pyramid, which moved from a BoP 1.0, via a BoP 2.0 to a BoP 3.0 approach. Comparable discourses evolved around the concept of 'shared value creation' and its claim on 'how to fix capitalism' (Crane et al., 2014), and the concept of 'creative capitalism' and its claim on the positive role of philanthropic efforts. Nonetheless, any of the sustainability ambitions might still turn out to be difficult to implement due to the intention-realization gap. Any claim on the changed purpose of a company and its effect on society – whether it is circular, inclusive, social or stakeholder-orientated – therefore has to be closely scrutinized and critically pursued. How likely are companies to be able to 'walk the talk'? How to move beyond superficial ambitions and value propositions (Box 9.8)? Chapter 10 relates these questions to the strategic scope for manoeuvre of companies to make the SDGs 'material' by considering their strategic positioning, power base, responsibilities and sphere of influence. Chapter 11 then considers the *operational* challenges of implementing the sustainability ambitions into functional areas of management.

WALKING THE TALK? A CHANGED 'PURPOSE OF THE CORPORATION'?

BOX 9.8

The 'Statement on the Purpose of the Corporation' of 2019, signed by 181 American CEOs, immediately drew comments. They ranged from 'transformational' to 'nothing new', 'we have to wait and see', and 'they are forced to do that to regain trust'. In view of the prevailing neoclassical narrative, the Business Roundtable's statement can be considered a considerable breach with dominant thinking in the US, and the start of a continued debate on the purpose of corporations.

One of the most vocal critics of the statement was Robert Reich, former US Secretary of Labor. He followed the actions of several leading signatories and critically questioned the extent to which their CEOs are actually "prepared to sacrifice share values (as well as all the executive pay tied to those shares) in order to raise worker pay, achieve greater diversity, remain in communities even when somewhere else on the globe becomes a cheaper place to do business, and better protect the environment" (Reich, 2020: 35). The response to the Covid-19 crisis of many of the signatories, for instance, and their constant lobbying for large corporate tax cuts made him rather sceptical about the prospect of these companies 'walking their talk'.

BOX 9.8

Whether the statement's signatories will operationalize their pledged ambition ('talk') by making it 'material' at both the strategic and operational level ('walk') remains to be seen. Concrete translation of their stated ambition should be reflected in adjusted value statements addressing broader 'value portfolios', and 'internalization' into all functional areas of management that operationalize the business model (discussed in Chapter 11). Strategic checkpoints for critical scrutiny include:

■ **What specific 'value dimensions'** does the company address in its value statement (see section 9.5.1; Chapter 10 elaborates this further as 'the sustainable corporate story').

■ **'Having' responsibility:** to what extent does the company acknowledge its role (broader fiduciary duty and related responsibility) in systemic problems?

■ **'Taking' responsibility:** to what extent does the company aim to 'reverse materiality' – taking societal concerns on board, beyond addressing market failure and negative externalities (levels 1 and 2), to also embrace societal themes (like the SDGs) at engagement levels 3 and 4?

■ **How (openly, transparently, materially) does the company communicate** about where it is now, the dilemmas it faces, the progress it is making, its de facto impact?

9.6 CONCLUSIONS, TOOLS AND RESOURCES – KEY MATERIALITY CHALLENGES

This chapter started by recapping one of the biggest challenges of the SDG-agenda: getting private organizations to align their business models with the *transformational* ambitions of the SDGs. But how can that ambition be made 'material'? How can one specify *strategic intent* and select those values that enable progress towards higher levels of sustainable business? The chapter delineated a value theory that should help organizations to consider six value dimensions – at four levels for value creation – for making their business model more 'sustainable' and aligned with the principles of the SDG-agenda.

Materiality challenges generally evolve around two strategic considerations: (1) how can the chosen strategy "substantially affect the organization's ability to create value in the short, medium or long term" (IIRC, 2013: 33); and (2) what items are consequently relevant to decision-making (Eccles et al., 2012). This chapter argued that perhaps the most vital challenge in determining 'materiality' lies in reversing the prevailing materiality logic: from a primarily company-centric perspective (inside-out) to a societal perspective (outside-in) as the point of departure. *Reversing materiality* implies that organizations take an explicit societal view in determining what issues would establish the legitimacy of their value-generating role in society – both in the present and in the longer run. It also implies that organizations move beyond their focus on 'Key Performance Indicators' (KPIs) – which tend to provide largely quantitative, technical, one-dimensional and often oversimplified benchmarks on sustainability performance – towards *Key Value Indicators (KVIs)* and *Key Decision-making Indicators (KDIs)*.

The materiality challenge of driving change towards sustainable and more resilient business models lies foremost in identifying those vital 'value' and 'decision-making' dimensions that would empower corporate leadership in setting the 'right' direction, in ensuring the pursuance of goals, and in overcoming critical tipping points. KVIs and KDIs facilitate deliberation and decision-making on intricate trade-offs, hurdles and alignment challenges that organizations and their leaders encounter in their change trajectories towards higher levels of sustainability and 'value creation' (Table 9.5). KVIs and KDIs will, therefore, serve as a general frame for consecutive elaborations in Chapter 10 ('making it powerful') and Chapter 11 ('making it functional').

Table 9.5 From triggering event to business model – the alignment challenge

KVIs ➡	LEVEL 1 Tipping point ➤	LEVEL 2 Key tipping point ➤	LEVEL 3 Tipping point ➤	LEVEL 4
	VALUE ORIENTATION			
Purpose of the organization	Short-term (primary) shareholder value		Longer-term (societal) stakeholder value	
Business model innovation aim	Gradual/incremental innovation		Radical/transformative innovation	
Ultimate ambition	Profit maximization	Limiting negative externalities	Enhance positive externalities	Take up collective action challenges
Value dimension emphasis	Designing, creating and capturing value	Minimize destroying value	Maximize spreading value	Co-creating value
CSR-orientation	Corporate *Self* Responsibility	Corporate Social *Responsiveness*	Corporate *Social/ Strategic* Responsibility	Corporate *Societal/ Sustainable* Responsibility
Fiduciary duty: stakeholder orientation	Limited: towards owners (shareholders)	Narrow: primary stakeholders (depending on salience)	Broader: primary and secondary stakeholders	Broad: society at large; future generations
License to...	Exist	Operate	Scale and internationalize	Experiment

(Continued)

Table 9.5 (Continued)

Main narrative and motto	Doing things right	Don't do things wrong	Doing the right thing	Doing the right things right
	Doing well	Doing well, don't do harm	Doing good	Doing well by doing good
Generic SDG orientation	Limited materiality Forecasting and use as issue management tool		Reversing materiality Back-casting and reformulation of value proposition	
	LEADERSHIP			
Phases and KDIs	1. Trigger	2. Internal alignment		3 External alignment
Primary motivation	Intrinsic	Extrinsic	Intrinsic	Mixed
Secondary motivation	Liability; short-term; cost-minimizing	Liability; reputation	Strategic; moral	Long-term societal
Attitude	Inactive/passive	Reactive	Active	Pro-active
Performance: walking the talk	'No talk, no walk'	'Talk, no walk'	'Walk, don't talk'	'Walk and talk'
Main leadership challenge	Becoming effectively responsive	Creating internal (dynamic) capabilities		Engaging and empowering external stakeholders
Prevalent leadership style	Transactional, situational, charismatic leadership	Servant, shared, agile, moral, visionary leadership		Strategic, thought, connected, paradoxical, transformational leadership
SDG principles for sustainable business				

KEY VALUE INDICATORS:
RE(DE)FINING THE PURPOSE OF THE ORGANIZATION

The popular discourse on the purpose of organizations is often narrowed down to a simple dichotomy: is the ultimate 'purpose of the firm' to create 'shareholder value' or 'stakeholder value'? This chapter provided a framework for a broader and more nuanced understanding of the value-generating *potential* of companies, by taking six value dimensions into account – creation, design, capturing, destroying, spreading and co-creating/sharing. Aligning the corporate ambition with this broadened set of value dimensions should help in sparking insights for the refinement – or redefinition – of a longer-term, societally aligned and more inspiring 'purpose' of the organization. *Repurposing* stands or falls, however, with the interplay of motivations (intrinsic-mixed-extrinsic; tactical-strategic) of organizations and their leaders to engage at higher or lower ambition levels of societal 'value creation'.

KVIs reflect the organization's value orientation, its value(s) portfolio and value proposition, which relate to the four engagement levels at which the 'business case' for sustainability needs to materialize (levels 1, 2, 3, 4, as defined in Chapter 8). KVIs also operationalize the purpose of the organization in terms of the 'societal license' to which it aspires: a license to exist, to operate, to scale/internationalize or to experiment. As such, KVIs define the value frame within which sustainable business models can be further elaborated and finetuned. KVIs, therefore, also mark the level of ambition at which an organization and its leaders embrace, select and prioritize specific (combinations of) SDGs and SDG-targets.

The concrete operationalization of KVIs is organization-specific. Table 9.5 summarizes key dimensions – synthesized from this chapter and the previous ones – from which customized elaborations of KVIs can be derived. Different types of organizations are likely to display different types of purpose, value orientations, value portfolios and value-generating potential, depending on their societal positioning and prevailing governance form (for-profit/non-profit/hybrid, see Chapters 6 and 8).

An organization's public statement on its value orientation (e.g. espoused intentions, ambitions, the corporate narrative) may divert from its prevailing purpose in practice. The public narrative might be about broader societal challenges, whereas the actual value orientation and basic purpose may still be formulated in terms of quarterly earnings and shareholder value. An organization might use the term 'corporate social responsibility' (CSR) – signalling a level 3 value orientation – but, in practice, may only operationalize its corporate responsibility in terms of 'limiting negative externalities' – at level 2. A first 'materiality challenge' that can be derived from applying KVIs is the *extent of coherence* between purpose, ambitions, value portfolio (reflected in the business model and value proposition), and the level (1, 2, 3, 4) at which the impact thereof primarily materializes. More coherently aligned KVIs smoothen decision-making on the strategic course of action to be set.

KEY DECISION-MAKING INDICATORS:
THE DYNAMIC LEADERSHIP CHALLENGE

This chapter argued that many organizations are still inclined to a reactive (level 2) stance towards sustainability issues. Moving beyond reactivity was identified as probably the most difficult yet crucial threshold – the key tipping point – to overcome in evolving towards a future-oriented, sustainable and more resilient business model. Adopting a transformational approach (as needed to achieve many of the SDGs) would imply a significant transition process for most organizations. 'Repurposing' the organization – in alignment with 'material' societal issues and longer-term business-critical developments – first and foremost represents a leadership challenge. Leaders define the road to be travelled, the longer-term goals to be pursued, the values and principles to guide core strategies, and the relevant value portfolio to be developed and strengthened. Leadership in times of transition is an inherently dynamic process. It involves complex change processes amidst uncertainty, ambiguity and emergence. It also entails the timely involvement and empowerment of relevant followers, and effective collaboration with sector and cross-sector peers. In order to persistently progress in a fickle environment, leaders have to consider Key Decision-making Indicators (KDIs) that document how to move from one level to the next.

The dynamic leadership challenge materializes along the five dimensions identified in section 9.2: (1) overcoming the intention-realization gap; (2) 'walking the talk' to (re-)establish legitimacy and trust; (3) understanding the motivations for short-term or long-term ambition levels for value creation; (4) understanding the distinction between incremental and transformative/radical approaches to change. Taken together, these dimensions ultimately define (5) the key tipping points that effective leaders should be able to help overcome. The more leaders are able to define a coherent set of values, the easier it becomes to design the proverbial road sign that indicates the direction of the transition trajectory. The materiality challenge then becomes one of defining the strategic tipping points and related Key Decision-making Indicators that an organization has to surpass in order to reach the next stage of value creation (Table 9.5):

■ ***Phase 1:*** represents a universal tipping point that all organizations are confronted with – the extent to which an organization is willing and able to respond effectively to societal pressures, general trends and triggering events to become more sustainable by minimizing negative externalities (transition towards level 2);

■ **Phase two:** represents the decisive (key) tipping point in the orientation of organizations: to aim for transformative (and often more radical) change, or modest change through incremental adjustments. How leaders deal with this tipping point indicates their receptiveness to reversing materiality. This phase requires the development of internal capabilities and an organization-wide integrated broader value orientation, which fosters value spreading and the scaling of positive externalities – in addition to upholding level 1 and 2 responsibilities (transition towards level 3);

■ **Phase three:** represents a complex and often confusing tipping point, in which organizational leaders have to move beyond their direct sphere of influence. To effectively address societal challenges that affect the business ecosystem, leaders will have to align with cross-sector stakeholders to co-create societal value. The most transformational SDG ambitions require the organization to transition towards level 4. External alignment with stakeholders also occurs at level 2, but then for defensive reasons (as discussed in section 9.3). Leaders find it difficult to discern between the two approaches, particularly when the strategic gap between intention and realization in the business model is large (see section 9.2.1).

PREFERRED LEADERSHIP STYLES

Leadership studies indicate that in each of these transition phases, different types of leaders prevail. Leaders can suppress change by stressing conservative values or encourage change by establishing values that are founded on, for instance, societal consciousness, a sense of collectiveness or moral considerations. Effective leadership is influenced by situational factors, timing and individual traits and motivations. This influence makes leaders more or less '(pro)active' and more or less inclined to actively take responsibility for sustainability issues. Furthermore, contextual and organizational developments tend to alter the appreciation of particular leadership styles over time: what is considered visionary or radical in an early stage of sustainability, may become 'normal' and 'business as usual' in later stages.

Table 9.5 summarizes the key orientations developed in this chapter that are required in each transition phase. Each phase represents different kinds of challenges, requires the development and integration of different value dimensions, and comes with different types of key decisions (KDIs) to be taken. Each phase, therefore, implies a different type of leadership:

■ **Phase 1: gradual transition to a reactive attitude**

The leadership within inactive (level 1) companies is often classified as *transactional*. This leadership type is characterized by a contract-based kind of relationship between leader and followers that arranges the exchange of rewards for efforts, a dominant efficiency orientation, and a 'business as usual' mindset. Transactional leaders only take decisive action if there is a straightforward business case for sustainability – one that will increase profits or decrease costs in the short run. In the face of an – unexpected – triggering event (Chapter 7), transactional leaders will generally find it difficult to respond timely, proportionately and effectively. So-called *situational leaders* or *charismatic leaders* have been found to be more effective in responding to triggered challenges and to drive the organization to a 'level 2' mode of operating. Situational leaders adjust their leadership style to the needs of their followers – based on the changed situation. Charismatic leaders thrive on a sense of urgency, which can be effective in realigning the organization in times of external threat and pressure, through charm and persuasion.

■ Phase 2: decisive transition to an active attitude

When a defensive line of reasoning does not suffice, a process of internal alignment and capabilities development commences that initially requires 'servant', 'shared', 'participative' or 'agile' leadership. Fully transitioning to 'level 3' engagement implies 'moral' and 'visionary' leadership as well. *Servant* and *shared leaders* share power, put the need of employees first, and facilitate their optimal development and performance. *Agile* and *participative leadership* styles are particularly related to the creation of the right context for self-organization. Self-organization requires quick feedback, mutual and continuous learning, both between and within teams. In consecutive stages of internal alignment, visionary and/or moral leadership gains in prominence. *Visionary leaders* are capable of sketching an inspiring, perhaps even daring picture of the future that provides direction (but not a drawn-out plan of action). If the sustainability vision creates a common base for all primary stakeholders, it can significantly speed up change due to increased motivation, enthusiasm and internal traction to come up with ideas that help shape action. *Moral leadership* entices similar effects but is primarily guided by respect for ethical values and convictions. Both leadership styles need to be complemented or followed up by *strategic leadership* in order to translate vision into a longer-term (level 3) course of action. Strategic leadership brings in the ability of strategic goal-setting, prioritization, and dealing with ambiguity and uncertainty. It provides the vital configurational and ownership conditions for alignment within and across the various functional departments of the organization.

■ Phase 3: deliberate transition to a proactive attitude

Whereas the necessary change processes in phase 2 stress inward-oriented leadership styles, phase 3 ('external alignment') additionally requires outward-oriented leadership. External stakeholders have to be involved; not (only) for defensive reasons, but for real engagement, collective action and co-creation. The leadership literature refers to several leadership styles that are potentially relevant for guiding and managing this transition phase: transformational, thought, connected and paradoxical leadership. *Transformational leadership* – the most generic style – aims to broaden and elevate the interest of its followers. It sees the societal challenge of sustainability and the organization's longer-term resilience as important reasons to develop radically new business models, in alignment with relevant stakeholders. Transformational leaders create awareness and acceptance of the group's purpose and mission and stimulate stakeholders within the business ecosystem to look beyond self-interest to include the collective good. They are keenly aware that the success of their organization depends on structural and systemic changes that reach beyond their direct sphere of influence – and, therefore, develop integrative or connected leadership. *Connected leadership* concerns the ability to bridge divides between different groups of primary and secondary stakeholders, and create a partnering strategy to collaboratively address a societal challenge. The literature refers to the ability to overcome conflicting interests by formulating creative goals that supersede the contradiction and serve the collective interest as *paradoxical leadership*. Paradoxical leaders have a keenly developed capacity for embracing uncertainty, ambiguity, complexity and tension, to make sense out of it, and to creatively come up with a new take on the matter that resolves the tension. *Thought leadership* is attributed to those who put a societal (sustainability) issue on the agenda, link it to their own business model, and resourcefully work towards a resolution. If their frame becomes established within the business ecosystem and wider society, the organization can derive a strategic advantage from serving this need.

T
A
K
E
A
W
A
Y
S

- *'Material' issues* are those issues that could substantially affect the organization's ability to create value in the short, medium or long term. Material issues have a substantive bearing on the organization's strategy, its business model, and the capitals the organization uses or affects. The selection of issues an organization deems 'material', ultimately establishes the legitimacy of its (value-generating) role in society;

- *'Reversing materiality'* implies a shift in perspective when considering materiality: from a company-centric perspective (inside-out orientation) to a societal perspective (outside-in orientation). Reversed materiality takes societal issues (e.g. the SDG-agenda) as the point of departure for strategic decision-making; conventional materiality approaches are limited in substantive and relevant stakeholder engagement;

- Interrelated challenges in making the SDGs 'material' and integral to the business model: (a) overcoming the 'intention-realization' gap; (b) 'walking the talk', to (re)establish legitimacy and trust; (c) understanding the motivations for short-term or long-term ambition levels (1, 2, 3, 4) for value creation; (d) understanding the pace and direction of change (incremental vs transformative approaches); (e) surpassing key tipping points towards higher levels of value creation, sustainability and resilience;

- Depending on their primary motivation (intrinsic-extrinsic-mixed) and secondary motivation (liability-responsibility-mixed) for sustainability, archetypical CSR attitudes of organizations can be classified as inactive (efficiency-driven), reactive (reputation-driven), active (strategic or morally driven) and proactive (societally aligned). These attitudes align with the four levels of intervention/engagement;

- Breaking through the reactive threshold involves transitioning from a *narrow definition* of fiduciary duty, responsibilities, view on relevant stakeholders, purpose and value creation, towards a *broader definition* of what aspects to include in the business model. Especially for incumbent companies, this critical threshold is the most difficult, yet most vital one to overcome;

- An extended view on the value-generating potential of companies considers six value dimensions in designing, finetuning or innovating the business model (CANVAS+ model): value design, value creation, value capturing and scaling, minimizing value destruction, optimizing value spreading, value co-creation/sharing;

- Applying the CANVAS+ model to a practice of 'reversing materiality' implies that companies seek to link the SDG-agenda to their entire *value portfolio* (value creation, design, capturing, destruction, spreading and sharing);

- A *'rich' value proposition* reflects the organization's *broader* take on its value-generating potential. It mirrors how the organization sees itself positioned within society and its sector, its take on its fiduciary duties and responsibilities, whom it considers primary and secondary stakeholders, and how it contributes to the outlook of a positive ecosystem (e.g. inclusive economy, we/sharing economy, circular economy; regenerative capitalism);
- The CANVAS+ model helps to identify those parts of the *value portfolio* that can be considered more vulnerable or more resilient aspects of the business model;
- Different sustainable paradigm ecosystems exist in which sustainable business models are operationalized. The label in itself is no guarantee for sustainability impact however. The actual contribution of a 'circular', 'sharing', inclusive' or 'social' business model at a societal level depends on how it is elaborated: narrowly or broadly;
- The materiality challenge of driving change trajectories towards higher levels of sustainability and resilience is an intricate alignment challenge; it requires identification of 'Key Value Indicators' (KVIs) and 'Key Decision-making Indicators' (KDIs) that enable corporate leadership to guard coherence, set the 'right' direction and drive change effectively;
- Each transition phase favours distinct leadership styles to align organizational ambitions with key tipping points and related strategic decision-making.

■ ***WBCSD SDG Learning Platform: SDG Essentials for Business:*** provides a 'crash course' in the SDGs and their relevance to business: the challenges they aim to solve, the vital role business has to play in realizing the SDGs, the opportunities it can harness along the way. Designed to help companies raise awareness and understanding of the SDGs to empower meaningful contributions, and to explore ways of becoming more involved – from ambition to action – in contributing to the transformational SDG-agenda. https://sdgessentials.org/

■ ***WBCSD CEO Guide to the SDGs:*** strong and visionary CEO leadership is essential for realizing the SDGs. This *CEO Guide to the SDGs* "succinctly lays out the implications of the SDG agenda for the private sector while positioning clear actions that business leaders can take to begin to integrate this agenda into their organizations". https://sdghub.com/ceo-guide/

■ ***WBCSD SDG Sector Roadmaps:*** the ambitions of the SDGs call for coordination and collective efforts from entire industry sectors. The SDG Sector Roadmap Guidelines aim to inspire and support leading companies within sectors to come together, plot a shared SDG vision for their industries, and develop detailed 'roadmaps' to guide their industry's shift towards sustainable development in line with the SDGs. The sector roadmaps (1) identify tangible ways in which a sector impacts the SDGs; (2) set sector-specific targets and KPIs; (3) flag barriers and explore solutions; (4) lay foundations to advocate for policy enablers. https://www.wbcsd.org/Programs/People/Sustainable-Development-Goals/SDG-Sector-Roadmaps

■ ***UN Global Compact 'Take Action':*** provides a platform for, inter alia, 'building the business of tomorrow', by helping to navigate 'opportunities to take action across a breadth of sustainability issues'; 'new technologies with potential to enable sustainable business models of the future'; 'engaging with responsible investors'; 'activities to advance sustainability in the boardroom'. https://www.unglobalcompact.org/take-action

■ ***The Capital Institute:*** builds on the concept of 'regenerative capitalism': the acknowledgement that today's greatest challenge is to address the root cause of the world's systemic crises – the prevailing economic paradigm and the financial system that 'fuels and rules' it. The institute encourages a fundamental transformation of the current economic system by redefining wealth and reimagining finance in service to the emergence of an ecologically and socially regenerative economy. The institute focuses on "thought leadership, deep analysis of successful and transformative Regenerative Economy models, and the collaborative sharing of knowledge with partners and an expanding community around the world": https://capitalinstitute.org/about-us/. Also provides an interesting library of recommended reading: https://capitalinstitute.org/book-library/

TOOL #9.1 THE BETTER BUSINESS SCAN – OVERCOMING THE INTENTION-REALIZATION GAP

The **Better Business Scan (BBS)** provides a free quick-scan technique (15 minutes) – for managers of any type of private organization – to assess the kind of sustainable transition trajectory the organization is in. The BBS scores 'the gap' between intention (business case) and realization (business model), and the organizational 'tipping points' that the present stage represents  for seven functional areas of management. This assessment ultimately enables advice on the leadership style needed to progress. Every manager receives a personalized and confidential feedback document.

The BBS serves as a 'zero measurement' in often complex transition processes: 'where does the company stand'. Companies have used the scan internally to get the – often complementary – perspectives of a larger group of managers, which can feed into a strategic conversation on how to overcome internal barriers to change (elaborated in Chapters 10 and 11). Visit: https://www.betterbusinessscan.org/

TOOL #9.2 THE CANVAS+ MODEL FOR SUSTAINABLE BUSINESS – SPECIFICATION[16]

Key partnerships [1]	Key activities [2]	Value propositions	Customer relationships [5]	Customer segments
	Key resources [3]	[4]	Channels [6]	[7]

Cost structure [8.1]	Revenue streams [9.1]
Environmental costs [8.2]	Environmental benefits [9.2]
Social costs [8.3]	Social benefits [9.3]

[10] The business ecosystem

✎ *DESIGNING VALUE*

[7] Customers: this segment represents the direct users of the product or service. The customers – which could be individuals, communities, companies, or organizations – have a direct relation to the value delivered. For sustainable businesses, the customers represent the segment of the community the company aims to reach.

[4] Extended value proposition: a 'narrow' value proposition is the core element of the business model and describes the value that is delivered to 'customers'. An 'extended' value proposition also examines the business model's broader repercussions in the community. A value proposition helps identify and assess the benefits of the solution for customers and communities. It also includes the trade-offs between (social, environmental and economic) costs and benefits.

[6] Channels: this component describes the consumer interface, i.e. how the business reaches its customers to deliver the value proposition. This

16 This summary of the CANVAS+ model was taken from: Lijfering and Van Tulder (2020).

includes communication and marketing, as well as distribution channels. Channels are the customer contact points that raise awareness about the offered solution and play an important role in the customer experience. Especially for sustainable business ventures, organizing 'last mile distribution' is key in order to deliver the solution to marginalized consumers.

[5] Customer relationships: managing customer relationships is a crucial aspect of embedding the business model in the local context. Customer relations can range from personal, face-to-face engagement to self-service or automated contact. Investing in social embeddedness helps companies create local buy-in and credibility for the solution, thereby providing a competitive advantage in the market.

⬩ CREATING VALUE

[2] Key activities: are the pivotal actions the business must take to deliver the value proposition – i.e. reaching its customer segments, sustaining customer relationships, and ultimately creating long-term revenue streams and social impact. Identifying all activities that are needed to implement the business model, helps the company decide which activities to take up itself and which to outsource to third parties.

[3] Key resources: are the most important inputs required to make a business model work; it constitutes both tangible and intangible resources. Tangible resources include assets such as infrastructure and other materials and equipment. Intangible resources consist of human resources, such as local knowledge and skills. In addition, financial resources are needed to carry out the key activities listed before.

[1] Key partners: are the stakeholders the business needs to engage in order to implement and sustain the business model in the community context. These partners can range from public actors to civil society organizations, but, in particular, pertain to subcontractors and supplying companies in the value chain. Through partnerships, the organization can leverage key resources, capabilities and local networks. Choosing partners that complement the skills and expertise of the company is crucial in creating value for specific beneficiaries.

⬩ CAPTURING VALUE

[9.1] (Financial) revenue streams: represent the money the organization generates from each customer segment and the additional financial resources it can mobilise, such as grants and other external funding. As many low-end communities experience affordability constraints, it is important to understand which value the customer segments are willing and able to pay for, and for which aspects alternative sources of finance have to be found.

[8.1] (Financial) cost structure: describes the monetary consequences of implementing and sustaining the business model. The costs are linked to the key activities and key resources needed to create and deliver the value to the customers. Costs are likely to vary over time, so it is important to determine at which phase (e.g. the investment or start-up phase or implementation phase) in the process the business model is currently operating and adjust the cost structure accordingly.

✎ DESTROYING VALUE

[8.2] Negative externalities – environmental costs: in addition to potential negative social outcomes, possible negative environmental impacts need to be addressed. Issues such as climate change, deforestation and pollution need to be addressed and mitigated in the sustainable business strategy.

[8.3] Negative externalities – social costs: in addition to identifying social needs the business model can alleviate, it is also crucial to identify factors that could potentially have negative social impacts and formulate strategies that can mitigate or prevent those outcomes. Developing a good risk-management strategy and allocating potential risks to various partners is, therefore, an important aspect of the sustainable business model.

✎ SPREADING VALUE

[9.2] Positive externalities – environmental benefits: in addition to social impact, sustainable businesses strive to create environmental sustainability with their business model. Therefore, identifying potential aspects where the company can minimize its ecological footprint and integrate climate change measures into its sustainable business strategy to contribute to climate action (SDG13), life below water (SDG14) and life on land (SDG15) is a crucial aspect of sustainable business.

[9.3] Positive externalities – social benefits: the impact that is created beyond customer value. Identifying critical social issues and formulating approaches to cater for those needs is a crucial aspect of sustainable business. To make the business model inclusive, the company needs to address the five As of inclusiveness. Companies can use the SDGs as a benchmark to formulate sustainable business objectives for the medium-run and determine their sustainable business strategy to reach those targets.

⚲ *SHARING VALUE*

[10] Business ecosystem; co-creating shared value: sustainable businesses do not operate in a vacuum; many factors outside the scope of the business can affect the successful implementation of the business model. The final building block, therefore, consists of those factors that (can potentially) influence the embedding of the business model in the local context, including such aspects as a given policy, a lack of available professionals, or competition. Especially in developing country contexts characterized by institutional voids, low trust levels and resource constraints, mapping the variables in the business ecosystem can make the business model more robust.

Finally, note that the Canvas+ model provides a *snapshot* of the business model at one point in time. To account for changes in the developing country context, companies need to adjust their business model accordingly. Monitoring and evaluation are also beneficial for measuring progress in order to change business strategies and address issues of inclusiveness more effectively.

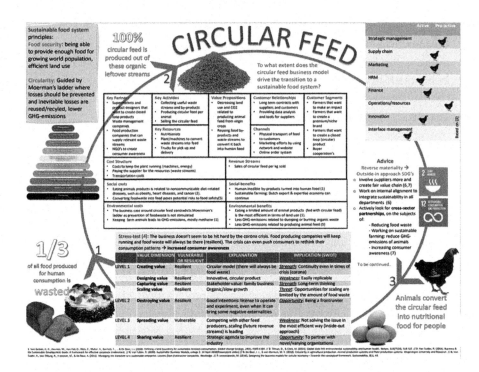

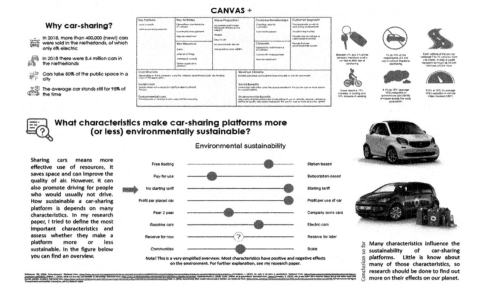

Illustrative CANVAS+ posters

REFERENCES

AccountAbility (2015). *Beyond Risk Management – Leveraging Stakeholder Engagement and Materiality to uncover Value and Opportunity*. Research paper, March.

Andrews, D., McGowan, M. & Millot, V. (2017). 'Confronting the Zombies: Policies for Productivity Revival', OECD Economic Policy Papers No. 21, December.

Banerjee, R. & Hofmann, B. (2018). 'The Rise of Zombie Firms: Causes and Consequences', *BIS Quarterly Review*, September, 67–78.

Benner, M.J. & Tripsas, M. (2012). 'The influence of prior industry affiliation on framing in nascent industries: the evolution of digital cameras', *Strategic Management Journal*, 33(3): 277–302.

Bocken, N. & Short, S. (2016). 'Towards a sufficiency-driven business model: Experiences and opportunities', *Environmental Innovation and Societal Transitions*, (18):41–61.

Bocken, N., Short, S., Rana, P. & Evans, S. (2014). 'A literature review to develop sustainable business model archetypes', *Journal of Cleaner Production*, (65):42–56.

Botsman, R. & Rogers, R. (2010). *What's Mine Is Yours: The Rise of Collaborative Consumption*. New York: HarperCollins.

Bouten, L. & Hoozée, S. (2015). 'Challenges in sustainability and integrated reporting', *Issues in Accounting Education Teaching Notes*, 30(4):83–93.

Business & Sustainable Development Commission (2017). *Better Business, Better World*.

Cañeque, F.C. & Hart, S.L. (Eds.) (2015). *Base of the pyramid 3.0. Sustainable Development through Innovation and Entrepreneurship*. Sheffield: Greenleaf Publishing.

Carroll, A.B. (1979). 'A Three-Dimensional Conceptual Model of Corporate Performance', *Academy of Management Review*, 4(4):497–505.

Chandler, A.D. (1990). *Scale and Scope: The Dynamics of Industrial Capitalism*, Harvard University Press.

Crane, A., Palazzo, G., Spence, L.J. & Matten, D. (2014). 'Contesting the Value of 'Creating Shared Value', *California Management Review*, 56(2):130–153.

Crilly, D., Zollo, M. & Hansen, M.T. (2012). 'Faking It or Muddling Through? Understanding Decoupling in Response to Stakeholder Pressures', *Academy of Management Journal*, 55(6):1429–1448.

Dembek, K., Sivasubramaniam, N., & Chmielewski, D.A. (2019). 'A Systematic Review of the Bottom/Base of the Pyramid Literature: Cumulative Evidence and Future Directions', *Journal of Business Ethics*, (165):365–382.

DesJardine, M.R., Marti, E. & Durand, R. (2020). 'Why Activist Hedge Funds Target Socially Responsible Firms: The Reaction Costs of Signaling Corporate Social Responsibility', *Academy of Management Journal*, in press.

Eccles, R.G. & Youmans, T. (2015). 'Materiality in Corporate Governance: The Statement of Significant Audiences and Materiality', Working Paper 16–023, Harvard Business School.

Eccles, R.G., Krzus, M.P., Rogers, J. & Serafeim, G. (2012). 'The Need for Sector-Specific Materiality and Sustainability Reporting Standards', *Journal of Applied Corporate Finance*, 24(2):65–71.

European Commission (2019). *Guidelines on reporting climate-related information*. Directorate-General for Financial Stability, Financial Services and Capital Markets Union.

Freeman, R.E. (1984). *Strategic Management: A Stakeholder Approach*. Boston M.A.: Pitman Press.

Fullerton, J. (2015). *Regenerative Capitalism. How Universal Principles and Patterns Will Shape Our New Economy*. Whitepaper, The Capital Institute.

Georghiou, L. (2001). 'Third generation foresight – integrating the socio-economic dimension', Proceedings of the International Conference on Technology Foresight. The Approach to and Potential for New Technology Foresight, NISTEP Research Material No. 77, March.

Gladwell, M. (2001). *The Tipping Point. How Little Things Can Make a Big Difference*. New York: Back Bay Books.

Graham, P. (Ed.) (1995). *Mary Parker Follett: Prophet of Management. A Celebration of Writings from the 1920s*. Boston: Harvard Business School Press.

GRI (2018). *GRI 101: Foundation 2016*. GRI Sustainability Reporting Standards. Amsterdam: Global Reporting Initiative.

Guix, M., Bonilla-Priego, M.J. & Font, X. (2018). 'The process of sustainability reporting in international hotel groups: an analysis of stakeholder inclusiveness, materiality and responsiveness', *Journal of Sustainable Tourism*, 26(7):1063–1084.

Hart, S.L. (1995). 'A Natural-Resource-Based View of the Firm', *The Academy of Management Review*, 20(4):986–1014.

Hengelaar, G.A. (2017). *The Proactive Incumbent. Holy Grail or Hidden Gem? Investigating whether the Dutch electricity sector can overcome the incumbent's curse and lead the sustainability transition*. Rotterdam: Erasmus Research Institute for Management.

Hervieux, C. & Voltan, A. (2018). 'Framing Social Problems in Social Entrepreneurship', *Journal of Business Ethics*, (151):279–293.

Hesseldahl, P., Nielsen, I., Abrahamsen, M., Jensen, M. & Hansen, I. (2015). *Your Business in the WE-Economy. Navigating the waters of the new collaborative economy*, June.

Hollensbe, E., Wookey, C., Hickey, L., George, G. & Nichols, V. (2014). 'Organizations with Purpose', *Academy of Management Journal*, 57(5):1227–1234.

Hunt, C.B. & Auster, E.R. (1990). 'Proactive Environmental Management: Avoiding the Toxic Trap', *Sloan Management Review*, (31):7–18.

IIRC (2013). *The International <IR> Framework*. The International Integrated Reporting Council, December.

IIRC (2013a). *Materiality – Background Paper for <IR>*. The International Integrated Reporting Council, March. 18.

IIRC (2013b). *Capitals – Background Paper for <IR>*. The International Integrated Reporting Council, March.

Jones, P., Comfort, D. & Hillier, D. (2016). 'Materiality in corporate sustainability reporting within UK retailing', *Journal of Public Affairs*, 16(1):81–90.

Klewitz, J. & Hansen, E.G. (2014). 'Sustainability-Oriented Innovation of SMEs: A Systematic Review', *Journal of Cleaner Production*, (65):57–75.

Kotler, P. & Armstrong, G. (2018). *Principles of Marketing. 17th Global Edition*. Pearson Education.

KPMG (2014). *Sustainable Insight: The essentials of materiality assessment*. KPMG International, October.

Lai, A., Melloni, G. & Stacchezzini, R. (2017). 'What does materiality mean to integrated reporting preparers? An empirical exploration', *Meditari Accountancy Research*, 25(4):533–552.

Lijfering, S.M. & Van Tulder, R. (2020). *Inclusive Business in Africa. A business model perspective*, The Partnerships Resource Centre. Rotterdam: Rotterdam School of Management, Erasmus University.

London, T. (2016). *The Base of the Pyramid Promise: Building Businesses with Impact and Scale*. Stanford: Stanford University Press.

Lüdeke-Freund, F. & Dembek, K. (2017). 'Sustainable Business Model Research and Practice: Emerging Field or Passing Fancy?', *Journal of Cleaner Production*, (168):1668–1678.

Maniora, J. (2018). 'Mismanagement of Sustainability: What Business Strategy Makes the Difference? Empirical Evidence from the USA, *Journal of Business Ethics*, (152):931–947.

Maon, F., Lindgreen, A. & Swaen, V. (2010). 'Organizational Stages and Cultural Phases: A Critical Review and a Consolidative Model of Corporate Social Responsibility Development', *International Journal of Management Reviews*, 12(1):20–38.

Mazzucato, M. (2018). *The Value of Everything. Making and Taking in the Global Economy*. Allen Lane.

McElhaney, K.A. (2009). 'A Strategic Approach to Corporate Social Responsibility', *Leader to Leader*, (52):30–36.

Mintzberg, H., Ahlstrand, B. & Lampel, J. (2009). *Strategy Safari: A Guided Tour Through The Wilds of Strategic Management*. Second Edition, FT Press.

Mintzberg, H. & Waters, J.A. (1985). 'Of Strategy: Deliberate and Emergent', *Strategic Management Journal*, 6(3):257–272.

Mirvis, P.H. & Googins, B.K. (2006). 'Stages of Corporate Citizenship', *California Management Review*, 48(2):104–126.

Mitchell, R.K., Agle, B.R. & Wood, D. (1997). 'Toward a Theory of Stakeholder Identification and Salience', *Academy of Management Review*, 22(4):853–886.

Nidumolu, R., Prahalad, C.K. & Rangaswami, M.R. (2009). 'Why Sustainability Is Now the Key Driver of Innovation', *Harvard Business Review*, September.

Osterwalder, A. & Pigneur, Y. (2010). *Business Model Generation: A Handbook for Visionaries, Game Changers, and Challengers*. John Wiley & Sons.

Peeters, D. (2019). *Moving from 'Wanting' to 'Doing': The Intention-Realization Gap of Sustainable Business Model Innovation – a systemic literature review*. Excerpt from Master Thesis, October. Rotterdam School of Management (RSM), Erasmus University.

Porter, M.E. & Kramer, M.R. (2011). 'Creating Shared Value: How to Reinvent Capitalism and Unleash a Wave of Innovation and Growth', *Harvard Business Review*, January/February.

Porter, M.E. & Kramer, M.R. (2006). 'Strategy and Society: The Link Between Competitive Advantage and Corporate Social Responsibility', *Harvard Business Review*, December.

Prahalad, C.K. (2011). 'Bottom of the Pyramid as a Source of Breakthrough Innovations', *Journal of Product Innovation Management*, 29(1):6–12.

Prahalad, C.K. (2004). *The Fortune at the Bottom of the Pyramid. Eradicating Poverty through Profits*. Wharton, PA: Wharton School Publishing.

Prahalad, C.K., & Hart, S.L. (2002). 'The fortune at the bottom of the pyramid', *Strategy + Business*, (26):2–14.

PwC (2016). *Navigating the SDGs: a business guide to engaging with the UN Global Goals.*

Raith, M.G. & Siebold, N. (2018). 'Building Business Models around Sustainable Development Goals', *Journal of Business Models*, 6(2):71–77.

Rasche, A. & Waddock, S. (2014). 'Global Sustainability Governance and the UN Global Compact: A Rejoinder to Critics', *Journal of Business Ethics*, 122(2):209–216.

Reich, R.B. (2020). *The System. Who Rigged It, How We Fix It*. London: Picador.

Ritzer, G.D. (1993). *The McDonaldization of Society. An Investigation into the Changing Character of Contemporary Social Life*. Pine Forge Press.

Ruigrok, W. & Van Tulder, R. (1995). *The Logic of International Restructuring*. London: Routledge.

Sachs, J.D., Schmidt-Traub, G., Mazzucato, M., Messner, D., Nakicenovic, N. & Rockström, J. (2019a). 'Six Transformations to Achieve the Sustainable Development Goals', *Nature Sustainability*, 2(9):805–814.

Schaltegger, S., Hansen, E.G. & Lüdeke-Freund, F. (2016). 'Business Models for Sustainability: Origins, Present Research, and Future Avenues', *Organization & Environment* 29(1):3–10.

Schlosser, E. (2005). *Fast Food Nation. The Dark Side of the All-American Meal*. Harper Perennial.

Schönherr, N., Findler, F. & Marinuzzi, A. (2017). 'Exploring the Interface of CSR and the Sustainable Development Goals', *Transnational Corporations*, 24(3):33–47.

Schroeder, P., Anggraeni, K. & Weber, U. (2018). 'The Relevance of Circular Economy Practices to the Sustainable Development Goals', *Journal of Industrial Ecology*, 23(1):77–95.

Steiner, G.A. & Steiner, J.F. (2000). *Business, Government and Society*, 9th edition. New York: McGrawHill.

Stiglitz, J.E. (2019). *People, Power, and Profits: Progressive Capitalism for an Age of Discontent*. New York: Allen Lane.

Trevor, J. & Varcoe, B. (2017). 'How Aligned Is Your Organization?', *Harvard Business Review Digital Articles*, February.

UN World Commission on Environment and Development (1987). *Our Common Future: Report of the World Commission on Environment and Development*. Oxford: Oxford University Press.

UN Global Compact & DNV GL (2020). *Uniting Business in the Decade of Action. Building on 20 Years of Progress*. UN Global Compact 20th Anniversary Progress Report.

UN Global Compact & Accenture Strategy (2019). *The Decade to Deliver. A Call to Business Action. The United Nations Global Compact – Accenture Strategy CEO Study on Sustainability 2019*, September.

UN Global Compact & Accenture Strategy (2016). *The United Nations Global Compact – Accenture Strategy CEO Study 2016. Agenda 2030: A Window of Opportunity*, June. UN

UN Global Compact & Accenture Strategy (2013). *The UN Global Compact – Accenture CEO Study on Sustainability 2013. Architects of a Better World*. September.

Van Tulder, R. (2018a). *Getting all the Motives Right. Driving International Corporate Responsibility (ICR) to the Next Level*. Rotterdam: SMO.

Van Tulder, R. & Lucht, L. (2019). 'Reversing materiality: From a Reactive Matrix to a Proactive SDG Agenda'. In: Bocken, N., Ritala, P., Albareda, L. & Verburg, R. (Eds.), *Innovation for Sustainability: Business Transformations Towards a Better World* (pp. 271–289). Cham: Palgrave Macmillan.

Van Tulder, R., Van Tilburg, R., Francken, M. & Da Rosa, A. (2014). *Managing the Transition to a Sustainable Enterprise. Lessons from Frontrunner Companies*. London: Routledge.

Van Tulder, R. with Van der Zwart, A. (2006). *International Business-Society Management. Linking Corporate Responsibility and Globalization*. London: Routledge.

Van Zanten, J.A. & Van Tulder, R. (2018). 'Multinational enterprises and the Sustainable Development Goals: An institutional approach to corporate engagement', *Journal of International Business Policy*, (1):208–233.

WBCSD (2021). *Vision 2050. Time to Transform. How business can lead the transformations the world needs*. Geneva: World Business Council for Sustainable Development.

WBCSD & DNV GL (2018). *Business and the SDGs: A survey of WBCSD members and Global Network partners*. World Business Council for Sustainable Development, July.

Womack, J.P., Jones, D.T. & Roos, D. (1990). *The Machine that Changed the World*. New York: Rawson Associates.

Zadek, S. (2004). 'The Path to Corporate Responsibility', *Harvard Business Review*, 82(12): 125–132+150.

Zink, T. & Geyer, R. (2017). 'Circular Economy Rebound', *Journal of Industrial Ecology*, 21(3): 593–602.

10 MAKING IT POWERFUL

USING POWER AS A FORCE FOR POSITIVE CHANGE

DOI: 10.4324/9781003098355-13

- **The Peter Parker principle:** 'With great power comes great responsibility'. Power is accumulated potential; it is never absolute, always contested, and strongly dependent on the legitimacy of one's past and intended future actions. The greater the power base, the greater one's responsibilities. With greater shared powers, greater shared responsibilities can be achieved.

- **Principle of 'smart power' exertion:** creating a timely balance between the use of 'hard' and 'soft' powers for maximum impact on sustainability issues; reflects the recognition of different forms and mechanisms of power and the appropriateness of their use in different settings.

- **Principle of 'sphere of influence':** acting in accordance with one's scope of political, contractual, economic or other relationships through which one has the ability to affect the decisions or activities of other individuals or organizations; embraces both 'avoid doing harm' and 'doing good' dimensions of responsibility, and includes both direct and indirect influence and impact.

- **Ruggie Principles:** due diligence principles adopted by the UN and OECD that reflect the state duty to *protect*, the business responsibility to *respect*, and the role of both state and business to ensure peoples' right to *remedy*. To foster progression, the 'protect, respect, remedy' trinity requires an additional principle: the duty to *empower*.

- **Principles of sustainable multinational business:** internalize market failure across borders; internalize normative failure across borders; move beyond compliance; aim at maximizing corporate (value) contribution to societies; engage in 'race to the top', counter 'race to the bottom'.

- **Principles of responsible governance:** are aimed at fostering an environment of trust, stability, integrity and inclusiveness, by adhering to key principles of accountability, fairness, transparency, assurance, leadership and stakeholder management.

- **Principle of free, prior and informed consent:** a vital aspect of 'procedural justice' that pertains to mutually agreed and culturally appropriate community engagement for granting – or withholding – consent on an action that affects community interests. Stipulates that consent-seeking processes should: (1) be self-directed and free of manipulation or coercion; (2) guarantee sufficient time for meaningful consultation; (3) be based on relevant, complete and understandable information.

- **Principle of indivisibility** in the context of the SDGs, denotes that their implementation should (1) be based on integrated approaches rather than siloed knowledge, policymaking and strategies, and (2) be anchored in the '5Ps' – *People, Planet, Prosperity, Peace, Partnering*. A nexus approach to sustainability takes the interdependencies between the SDG-targets – and in relation to the business ecosystem – into consideration.

■ **Principle of ambidexterity:** the (paradoxical or integrative leadership) ability to overcome contradictions, conflicts or trade-offs by simultaneously engaging in two seemingly opposed directions: strengthening while loosening, running while reinventing, being efficient and innovative, exploiting while exploring, cooperative while competing.

■ **Principle of coopetition:** (precompetitive) collaboration between competitors to achieve higher levels of sustainability in the near future; involves raising the bar for a new level playing field to create innovative and competitive markets for sustainable products, services and integrated systems solutions; grounded in the 'broad welfare' concept and 'citizens welfare'.

■ **Principle of choice architecture:** the responsibility to thoughtfully design decision-making processes in ways that minimize biases and errors arising from bounded rationality. By responsibly organizing the decision-making context (default-setting, framing, sequencing) to 'make the better choice the easier choice', people can be empowered to make better choices and engage in more sustainable behaviour, without restricting them.

■ **Seven principles of a 'sustainable corporate story':** (1) acknowledge systems failure and your own role and responsibilities; (2) understand the 'sunk cost' of your starting position, power base and sphere of influence; (3) understand the switching costs/benefits and path dependencies of strategic decisions; (4) be explicit about your values and powers; (5) use them to overcome organizational and institutional barriers in attaining higher levels of sustainability; (6) design a portfolio of SDGs and SDG-targets linked to your core ambitions and core activities, and (7) design a compelling narrative to frame beneficial change and set agendas.

10.1 INTRODUCTION: MAKING THE SDGs ACTIONABLE

"Power is the ability to produce intended effects"
Bertrand Russell, 1938

"Power without ethics is worthless;
Ethics without power is powerless"
The claim of this chapter

Ambitions to integrate the SDGs into core business remain elusive unless organizations are able to translate their ambition into effectual corporate strategies. On paper, an organization can design an aspirational sustainable business model that covers all six value-generating dimensions, at all four levels of intervention, as specified in Chapter 9. That is no guarantee, however, for driving change at a sufficiently strategic level, nor for fostering sustainability impact at the scale and pace needed to achieve the SDGs by 2030. In their pursuit of effective strategies towards higher levels of societal value creation, organizations face a dual strategic challenge: (a) how to align the *complexity of issues* (section 5.5.1) with adequate interventions that translate into in a future-oriented, more resilient and sustainable business model; and (b) how to deal with *switching costs* related to more profound change processes of strategic renewal and redirecting that condition the organization's strategic *scope for manoeuvre*. In short: how to make the SDGs not only 'material' to the core business, but also 'actionable' in order to overcome the intention-realization gap (section 9.2.1)?

Most companies – start-ups aside – do not start from a *tabula rasa*. They are confronted with sunk costs resulting from prior decisions, which can create significant (mental) barriers in adjusting course. In practice, an organization's *realistic* scope for manoeuvre is conditioned by strategic positioning decisions – notably based on market, resources, efficiency and asset-seeking considerations – that were carried through and further strengthened in the past. Today's consequences of these prior decisions may confront organizations and their leaders with confined options to adjust their business model in a more radical manner. On the other hand, however, a strong positioning sculptured throughout the years may also unlock promising opportunities for initiative and leverage. Three relevant positioning dimensions for strategic decision-making can be discerned in this context:

a   **Societal positioning:** an organization's governance model provides it with a distinct societal and legal legitimacy while presenting certain regulatory boundaries and specific agency issues (Chapter 6);

b   **Value chain positioning:** an organization's product portfolio and value chain position may provide it with market and innovation power that potentially reach beyond its direct 'sphere of influence', both horizontally and vertically;

c   **International positioning:** the implemented internationalization strategy defines an organization's 'country portfolio', with possibilities to overcome individual countries' regulatory boundaries through 'internalization' processes.

Each of these positioning dimensions defines a particular *power base* within societies and the business ecosystem. An organization's power base comes with societal expectations on its reasonable scope of responsibilities vis-à-vis other actors: upstream and downstream in the value chain, within the broader ecosystem, and within foreign regulatory regimes. 'Power base' explains why certain organizations are insistently expected to use their weight and leeway more effectively and take up greater responsibility for SDG-related action accordingly. 'With great power comes great responsibility' – as the popular aphorism appropriately states.

MAKING IT 'POWERFUL': A DUAL CONNOTATION

If we want to consider how transformational societal ambitions such as the SDGs can be made 'actionable' – vigorously and at scale – we have to explore the 'power dimension' further. In a VUCA world – filled with power imbalances and power exertion reinforcing the wickedness of problems (see Parts I and II) – *not* taking power into account would, in any case, present a naive position. *Power abuse* is perhaps one of the most *overrated* aspects in the critical discourse on sustainable business, feeding into almost ideological cynicism on the 'greenwashing' nature of CSR efforts of big and multinational enterprises in particular. *Power use*, on the other hand, is one of the most *underrated* aspects in the constructive discourse on sustainable business model innovation, feeding into overly optimistic or naive expectations of companies' willingness to engage in CSR at a sufficiently ambitious level.

Sustainable business model research rarely considers the power dimension. For instance, a systematic overview covering all academic studies on sustainable business models over the 2008–2018 period (Nosratabadi et al., 2019) found four main approaches that have emerged in the literature on designing sustainable business models (emphasizing value propositions, value creation, value-delivering and generating partnership networks); no reference was made to the exertion of 'power'. Neither have concepts of power been applied in the mainstream literature on corporate responsibility and responsible management (cf. Laasch et al., 2020). Both discourses primarily relate to governance and ethical questions on the moral foundations of decision-making and achieving results, with hardly any reference to the exact use of power in making sought-after goals actionable. The 'strength-based approach' (Sekerka, 2020) developed in responsible management, for example, refers to 'moral courage' and 'moral competency', rather than the power base of managers and organizational leaders.

Notwithstanding the vast importance of ethical decision-making and a strong moral compass in leaders, managers and employees alike, accelerated progress on the SDGs at the societal level critically hinges on how organizations use their various power bases in practice. Impact-driven change requires organizational approaches that are firmly grounded on an internalized awareness of broader societal responsibilities *beyond* good intentions and espoused SDG commitments. In addition to a clearly (re)defined purpose, delineated key values and a 'rich' value proposition (Chapter 9), it calls for decisive leadership and realistic strategies to enact potent, *viable* change trajectories. Not by keeping 'power' undefined under a veil of moral statements, but rather by making power bases explicit as '*assets of potential change*'; not by downplaying the organization's 'means of power', but by making responsible and optimal use of positioning, direct and indirect spheres of influence, and smartly combined means of 'hard' and 'soft' powers. With good reason: *power without ethics is worthless; ethics without power is powerless.*

PUTTING POWERS TO (GOOD) USE

In particular large, established organizations (incumbents) have built up vested power bases, interests and spheres of influence. Over the years, they have fine-tuned their business models for optimal efficiency to consolidate their market position. They now have to rebuild their ship while sailing. Redirecting operations in alignment with changing societal expectations, needs, values and ambitions may confront them with considerable anticipated switching costs. In the face of shifting economic models and changing success criteria, organizations can deploy their power base in three directions, basically:

- To withstand, defy and hinder transition processes in order to preserve their 'business as usual' – as *agents of frustration*;

- To reactively adapt to external pressures by piecemeal adjustments in the business model to become less *un*sustainable – as *agents of stagnation*;

- To speed up, transform and co-create future-orientated sustainable business models and ecosystems that contribute to more resilient societies (the transformational parts of the SDG-agenda) – as *agents of change*.

Powerful companies act as 'agents of frustration' if they actively use their strengths for strategies of resistance and obstruction. For example, by persistently lobbying against regulation that raises the bar of ecological, social and fair taxation standards. Alternatively, through 'regulatory capture' that seeks to influence government intervention so as to preserve the company's or industry's short-term interests. In the second scenario, powerful organizations can become 'agents of stagnation' if they primarily invest in strategies and technologies that superficially mitigate only certain negative aspects of their operations while leaving the root causes of their adverse impact largely unattended. A response-driven approach of merely modest adjustments stalls real progress at the required pace, scope and scale. Especially when effectuated by *lead companies*, a reticent strategy of piecemeal adjustment tends to slow down progress in the entire sector or value chain since it takes away actors' incentives to also invest in more ambitious change initiatives. Only in the third scenario – where organizations use their power base to (1) lead by example, (2) work with and within their sector to formulate transition trajectories, and (3) engage the broader business ecosystem to enact enabling change environments – can companies be considered 'agents of change'. In contrast to start-ups, many incumbents have the means of power, the position and access to vital resources to bolster transitions at scale.

MAKING THE SDGs ACTIONABLE; USING THE POWER BASE FOR POSITIVE CHANGE

The SDG-agenda confronts all organizations (archetypes 2–8) with strategic decisions on their future-oriented ambition, their relationship with relevant stakeholders, and their responsibilities towards society at large. Each organization has to decide to what extent it is willing and able to harness its specific power base as a *force for positive change* in driving the business ecosystem into a sustainable direction. In doing so, organizations can relate to the SDGs in four distinct ways:

- Not adopting the SDGs at all, for instance because of lack of awareness or commitment, unclear actionability as to how the SDGs could be operationalized to fit into the business, or lacking power base (which applies to small and medium-sized organizations, in particular);

- Supporting the SDGs in a general manner (without prioritization), disconnected from core operations and value proposition (the initial phase of consideration and adaptation);

- Prioritizing specific SDGs or SDG-targets that relate to core operations. This phase of SDG portfolio delineation is intimately linked to an organization's reorientation on its longer-term value-generating potential (see section 9.4), its ambition to align with societal needs at the strategic level, and processes of strategic renewal and redirecting;

- Developing a 'nexus approach' to prioritized SDGs or SDG-targets in order to identify and elaborate opportunities for leverage, synergy and reduction of potential trade-offs. This phase of more sophisticated analysis and strategic decision-making fosters a more clearly delineated direction of change and, therefore, enables more actionable strategies for renewal, redirecting and reconfiguration of the business model towards enhanced sustainability.

The empirical evidence – as presented by consecutive global surveys referred to throughout this book – shows that most companies experience significant barriers in moving beyond the level of 'general support' for the SDGs. The need for clearer guidance on direction, prioritization and operationalization of SDG-targets has recurrently been voiced as grounds for hesitant corporate action (UN Global Compact and DNV GL, 2020). Additionally, the absence of sufficient 'enablers' – supportive public policies, apt regulatory frameworks, an incentivizing business environment – has consistently been asserted to keep companies from more forceful action. This state of affairs raises at least two questions: (1) to what extent have organizations been making effective use of their own powers to overcome the critical 'reactive-active' threshold, and (2) how can companies responsibly deploy their power base and use their scope for manoeuvre to strategize for more transformational approaches?

This chapter starts with a condensed outline of key dimensions of power, power exertion and 'sphere of influence' as elemental ingredients of using the organizational 'power base' as a force for positive change (section 10.2). Next, we take a deeper dive into three types of 'bargaining arenas' in which organizations exercise their powers simultaneously: agency in societal positioning, value chain positioning, and international positioning (section 10.3). By building on structural, relational and discursive/normalizing aspects of 'positioning' and organizational power exertion, this section seeks to lay the foundation for an understanding of vital strategic decisions on responsible 'smart power' use as a force for driving transformative change. Section 10.4, then, links the 'context and conduct-shaping' implications of conducive power exercise to three organizational 'transition phases'. How to loosen one's grip on the old paradigm of organizing, while strengthening one's grip on changing societal expectations and environments? How to redirect organizational powers and realign core operations with societal needs, goals and values amidst fierce competition? 'Key Decision-making Indicators' (KDIs) define the nature of the strategic decisions that must be taken (at the societal level, related to value chains and the international country portfolio) to overcome critical 'tipping points' in processes of sustainable business model innovation. Section 10.5 subsequently considers what effective management of organizations' power bases could imply for making their SDG ambitions 'actionable'. The concluding section (10.6) integrates all components into (1) a (powerful) *sustainable corporate story*, (2) the 'logic framework' to attune multiple alignment 'fits', and (3) a final KDI checklist.

KPIs, KVIs OR KDIs?

"Most of the things you can measure aren't interesting . . .
Most of what's interesting you cannot measure"
Marcia Angell

"Not everything that can be counted, counts,
and not everything that counts can be counted."
Attributed to Albert Einstein

In his book *Out of the Crisis* (1982), leading management scholar William Edwards Deming – the inventor of 'Total Quality Management' – debunked the popular premise that 'you can't manage what you can't measure'. In fact, he identified it as one of the 'seven deadly diseases' of management. His argument: *"Nothing becomes more important just because you can measure it. It becomes more measurable, that's all."* But what to rely on, then, when tasked with decision-making on 'the right' direction to follow and the correct strategies to pursue in effectuating higher levels of sustainability? How to deal with qualitative indicators that may not seem as 'solid' as quantitative indicators suggest to be, but nevertheless are vital in taking sensible decisions?

A *principled approach* to sustainable business requires a variety of relevant metrics, matched by a keen understanding of when to use what type. To complement the common use of Key Performance Indicators (KPIs), this book introduces two additional types of 'calibration points' that should support decision makers and managers in dealing with strategic 'how' questions: *Key Value Indicators (KVIs)* and *Key Decision-making Indicators (KDIs)*.

The 'Performance Paradox': the problematic practice of KPIs

Most studies on sustainability-oriented change processes are packed with *quantitative* performance indicators, such as CO_2-emission levels, waste reduction rates, water footprints, minimum wages, diversity measures and CEO-remuneration benchmarks. The search is for *Key Performance Indicators (KPIs)* to keep track of progress. However, the many dimensions of sustainability are intricately linked (see Chapter 4). Clear and unambiguous indicators are, therefore, difficult to develop. In practice, KPIs not seldom turn into Key Performance *Illusions* (Box 4.2). By emphasizing only those aspects that can be measured, they tend to induce perverse incentives and skew the allocation of investments, time and energy. Eventually, this may stall rather than foster progress. Sustainable business rankings that score companies on their sustainability performance, for instance, tend to be strongly biased towards those environmental dimensions of sustainability that are relatively 'easy' to measure: CO_2 reduction, the number of solar panels and wind turbines realized, the volume of CO_2 storage and the like. The *performance-driven* focus on KPIs creates several problems:

■ Not all sustainability issues can be adequately quantified or 'monetized' – either for practical or moral reasons. This predicament ranges from applied questions like 'what monetary value does a tree represent' and 'how to value ecosystem services', to existential questions such as 'how to price the loss of one human life' or 'what monetary value to put on quality of life'. In an increasing number of industries (e.g. insurance, health) and in legal trials, these questions are far from theoretical but no less controversial.

■ Quantitative measures oversimplify the problem by reducing it to a technical or measurement problem. An artificial reduction of complexity does not provide the proper guidance for making informed decisions on the integration of *all* sustainability dimensions however. Intricate *trade-offs* between sustainability aspects remain undefined, giving rise to power battles as the choice for one measure happens at the expense of another.

■ By oversimplifying complexity, KPIs tend to foster *bounded awareness*, *bounded ethicality* and, therefore, morally ambiguous decision-making within organizations that may even be inconsistent with consciously held ethical values. Zhang et al. (2015), for instance, note that "individuals who are assigned specific goals are less likely to notice relevant information in uncertain and ambiguous environments" (ibid: 311). The resulting biases unconsciously influence proper moral judgment, moral decision-making and moral behaviour. To counter such 'inattentional blindness', Zhang and colleagues suggest instilling an inquisitive mindset that triangulates on focal issues with multiple questions and multiple sources. Furthermore, individuals' inclinations towards *intentional* unethical behaviour could be decreased by defining corporate goals more broadly "at levels that are perceived as fair and relatively attainable by employees" (ibid).

From performance illusions to societal value creation

An ***impact-seeking focus*** goes beyond output performance. Where transformational change processes are at stake, scholars are increasingly looking at *both qualitative and quantitative* change data (Rasche and Waddock, 2014). An organization's performance is then related to its ability and willingness to *internalize* societal values and longer-term goals – such as the SDGs. This is reflected in a broader take on corporate responsibilities, a reconsideration of 'value-generating potential', adjustment of the organization's purpose and enrichment of the value proposition to align societal needs with the organization's sustainability ambition. The identification and operationalization of a relevant set of *Key Value Indicators (KVIs)* help the organization to set the 'right' direction, as well as calibrate and guard the internal coherence between purpose, sustainability ambitions, values portfolio and societal expectations. Chapter 9 identified vital dimensions for designing KVIs to guide this alignment process.

From Key Value Indicators to Key Decision-making Indicators

Values and ambitions have to be operationalized and implemented – within the organization, the value chain and the broader business ecosystem. Effective change in the right (principle-based) direction requires 'calibration points' to decide and check on the strategic course of action. *Key Decision-making Indicators* (KDIs) should facilitate an enhanced understanding of the phase the organization is in, the transition steps to be taken, the strategy options and the scope for manoeuvre to effectuate a chosen strategy. Here, the leadership challenge becomes more 'wicked' and ambiguous: how to identify and steer on apt indicators that enable the organization to move forward, overcome critical tipping points, deal with intricate trade-offs and business-critical developments, leverage synergies and responsibly manage power relations. KDIs specify the nature of the decisions to be taken in order to move from one phase of sustainable business to the next.

Sustainable business requires complementary metrics

Each of the three types of metrics has merit, but in a specific sequence: KPIs are inspired by KVIs and the operationalization of KDIs, not the other way around.

Key Performance and Practice Indicators (KPIs)	Key Value Indicators (KVIs)	Key Decision-making Indicators (KDIs)
• 'Simple'	• 'Complex'	• 'Wicked'
• Output-oriented	• Purpose-oriented	• Outcome-oriented
• Performance-driven	• Intention-driven	• Impact-driven
• Technical solutions	• Corporate mission, vision and direction	• Strategy, goal-setting, scope for manoeuvre
• Implementation progress	• Value-generating ambition	• Trade-offs, synergies, leverage, negotiation
• Instructing /informing stakeholders	• Inspiring stakeholders	• Involving stakeholders
• Management principles	• Societal leadership	• Strategic leadership
Chapter 11	Chapters 9 and 12	Chapters 10, 11 and 12

10.2 ORGANIZATIONAL POWER AND POWER EXERTION

The exertion of power by individual organizations is habitually framed in a rather negative sense: how to contain (potential) power abuse through either regulation or mechanisms of countervailing powers. In classical economic thinking, for instance, market concentration and the related corporate monopolistic powers have been assumed to solidify into higher prices due to lacking competition – at odds with consumer interests. Alternatively, innovation economists argue that size and market dominance can also create the necessary scale to reap sufficient profits that enable companies to innovate – which would be in the longer-term interest of both consumers and society. A similar dual signification applies to organizations' lobbying powers. These can be exercised to preserve vested interests and (fore)stall progress towards sustainability, but also to activate new initiatives that catalyse advancement in a societally desirable direction.

Questions on how to direct the active use of various powers to ensure that corporate strategies and actions bring about the envisioned beneficial impact at both the sector and systems level should, therefore, address both sides of the same coin: *restricting power abuse* while *unleashing and guiding its conducive potential*. How organizational power can be put to use for positive change critically depends on its sources (section 10.2.1) and an organization's direct and indirect spheres of influence (section 10.2.2).

10.2.1 Dimensions of power

Power in social sciences generally refers to the ability of individuals to exert their will over others to bring about the outcomes they desire (Salancik and Pfeffer, 1977). It comprises a range of distinct sources that includes *coercive power* and *reward power*; *legitimate power* (derived from an elected, selected or appointed position in a structure of formal relationships); *expert power* (based on level of skill, competence and experience); *referent power* (derived from being valued and respected in affiliations) and *informational power*, based on the ability to control sources and flows of relevant information (French and Raven, 1959; Raven, 1965). Power is relative; people tend to compare their powers with those of others. Power differences trigger pressure towards an increased degree of conformity or, alternatively, independence. The area of organizational power adds two specific dimensions to these general observations: (1) a resource base perspective and (2) a stakeholder perspective, involving discursive powers.

In economics and business studies, definitions of organizational power generally refer to some form of *resource base*, which includes, among others, size, money, access to scarce yet vital resources, ownership, technology, patents, positioning, trust and knowledge. The more these various capacities are spread across many actors, the less individual actors can exert dominant influence. There is *purchasing power* (for customers to influence the production and features of certain goods), *bargaining power* (skills and abilities to influence the outcome of negotiation processes), *monopoly power* (the ability of an organization to set prices) and *managerial power* (influence over employees). In these contexts, power is often framed with a negative connotation – to influence other actors in directions they would normally (without the exertion of power) *not* choose. Questions of 'market power' are an area of industrial economics and industrial organization research. Research in these fields focuses on the appropriate mix of competition and collaboration in markets for creating wealth. Other forms of resource-based power exertion are topical in the disciplines of political economics, business and international relations.

The second dimension of power exertion by organizations concerns the *process* of influencing other (groups of) actors. Such processes can take place under relatively calm circumstances in which power is used to prevent or pre-empt conflict, or in the presence of overt conflict (power/interest battles) where power is used to deal with opposition. Power in this context is related to an organization's *relationship* with its primary and secondary stakeholders (see section 9.2). Both the structure and nature of ties between organizational actors determine their ability to influence each other's actions. Primary stakeholders – such as suppliers, buyers, employees, capital providers – are directly influenced by the organization's actions, but can also exert influence on the corporation themselves. Secondary stakeholders – e.g. NGOs, the media, local communities, society at large – are not necessarily directly affected by the organization's actions but can nevertheless exert substantial influence on its legitimate scope for action. Technologies such as social media have given even seemingly powerless stakeholders new means of influence over the sustainability strategies of big multinational enterprises.

Power, both in a stakeholder and societal context, can be used to affect the interests of other (groups of) actors by actively shaping and influencing perceptions, interpretations, ideas, values and norms. Such *discursive powers*[1] may be subtle, diffuse and rather unobservable but can nevertheless have profound repercussions on processes of *sense-making*, social interaction, trust-building, and enacting legitimacy and confidence. In political and sustainability discourses, for instance, discursive powers have proved strong instruments for introducing, magnifying or maintaining specific topics on the agenda, with the objective to

---

1   Reed (2013: 203), for instance, defines 'discursive power' as "the degree to which the categories of thought, symbolizations and linguistic conventions, and meaningful models of and for the world determine the ability of some actors to control the actions of others, or to obtain new capacities".

(a) shift conventional frames in the desired direction, (b) craft new meaning to existing norms, or (c) ward off pressure from societal expectations. Lack of (definitional) clarity – on the precise meaning of 'sustainability', 'corporate responsibility' or 'fair wages', for instance – elicits a bargaining environment in which (groups of organized) actors exercise their discursive powers to establish frames, norms and principles that provide legitimacy to their actions. In practice, the use of discursive powers can take many different shapes. Organizations with direct or indirect *agenda-setting powers*, for example, can influence the inclusion, exclusion or suppression of certain issues or (groups of) actors in signification and decision-making processes. Discursive power has also been exercised to prevent people from having voiced interests or grievances at all – known as *unobtrusive power* (Hardy, 1985) – "by shaping their perceptions, cognitions and preferences in such a way that they accept their role in the existing order of things" (Lukes, 1974: 24). This *manufacturing of consent* is used in attempts to establish legitimacy and justification for certain preferred arrangements, actions or outcomes to avoid them being questioned. Discursive power has also been labelled as *narrative power* or in terms of *symbolic power* to denote that political language, framing, symbols and rituals can be important tools in the use of power.

10.2.2   Can powers be(come) a force for positive change?

With its connotations of coercion, expediency and domination, power remains a highly contested concept. In an overview study on the conceptualization of 'power' in management and organization sciences, Fleming and Spicer (2014) argued that power could nevertheless be used as a positive force to serve progressive ends, as long as it is linked to responsibilities. Expressions of organizational power, the authors assert, can play out in four distinct settings: 'within', 'through', 'over' or 'against' organizations. Their taxonomy categorizes power as either (1) *episodic*: through explicit and overt acts of power exertion (with power abuse linked to coercion and manipulation, and positive use of power linked to effective resource mobilization); or (2) *systemic*: through more implicit and covert acts of power exercise related to the mobilization of institutional, ideological and discursive resources (ibid: 240). A more commonly used distinction – derived from the realist school in international relations theory – is that between 'hard power' and 'soft power' (see also Box 6.3).

(a)   **Hard organizational powers** are primarily founded on the *resource base* of organizations. Hard power relates to ownership of, or dominant control over, tangible (e.g. infrastructure, land, machines) and intangible assets (e.g. patents, intellectual property, data), financial means, (raw) materials and information, as well as competitive strength, size and key positions in (international) value chains.

(b) **Soft organizational powers** are primarily founded on the *relational base* of organizations. Soft power relates to social mechanisms, network positioning, discursive powers and other non-economic means of influence, such as co-optation, the power of initiative, framing and agenda-setting powers, the power of example, and legitimacy through constructive relationships with stakeholders.

Balancing hard and soft power for the common good constitutes a 'smart power' challenge (Nye, 2004). A smart power exercise reflects the recognition of *different forms and mechanisms of power* and the *appropriateness of their use* in different settings, in an organization's quest for maximum impact on sustainability issues.

(c) **Smart power exertion** focuses on creating a timely and contextualized balance between the use of hard and soft powers and often involves investing in strategic alliances and partnerships. It requires (1) a well-developed sense of purpose, direction and strategic priorities; (2) skilful alignment of internal and external needs and interests; and (3) smart ways of both synthesizing and synergizing intervention levels and practices (see Chapters 5 and 6). Furthermore, it demands organizations to (4) effectively deal with *key strategic decisions* along transition trajectories, and to (5) create room for manoeuvre and momentum towards positive change. In practice, this implies (6) a solid understanding of *key tipping points* and *Key Decision-making Indicators* for realizing the organization's strategic intent (section 10.4).

EXTENDING THE 'SPHERE OF INFLUENCE' AS A FORCE
FOR POSITIVE CHANGE

A bold effort to bring 'power' into the CSR discourse was the introduction of the concept of *sphere of activity and influence* by the UN in their 2003 *Draft Norms on the Responsibilities of Transnational Corporations and other Business Enterprises with regard to Human Rights* (UN, 2003). The 'sphere of influence' concept was subsequently incorporated in UN Global Compact's pragmatic frameworks for CSR guidance on corporate codes of conduct and international responsibility standards (Chen, 2018). Essentially, the concept seeks to establish the reasonable scope and boundaries of an organization's responsibilities towards an array of actors with whom it has a certain (contractual, economic, political) relationship, or that are affected by its activities. It suggests that an organization's degree of direct influence – and, therefore, responsibility – diminishes as the scope of its sphere stretches outwards: from core operations to business partners (value chain), local communities and society at large.

Following requests for a more precise operationalization of the concept, the UN appointed John Ruggie as Special Representative to clarify the implications of 'sphere of influence' and 'complicity' for (international) business. Ruggie concluded that sphere of influence is "too broad and ambiguous a concept to define the scope of due diligence with any rigor" (UN, 2008: 3),[2] and hence susceptible to strategic manipulation. The concept was abandoned. The Ruggie Principles that followed – the state duty to *protect*, the business responsibility to *respect*, and the role of states and business to ensure peoples' right to *remedy* – primarily focused on 'negative duties', 'avoid doing harm' and due diligence processes as essential ingredients for firms to ensure *compliance* with UN Human Rights Principles (see Chapter 6).

Initiatives that also emphasize the 'doing good' dimension of responsible business – particularly the ISO 26000 guidance standard on social responsibility (see Box 8.8) – chose to further elaborate the 'sphere of influence' concept.[3] ISO 26000 defines it as the "range/extent of political, contractual, economic or other relationships through which an organization has the ability to affect the decisions or activities of individuals or organizations" (clause 2.19). Sphere of influence is thereby articulated as a *relational* concept, to be operationalized in *contextual* factors, that embraces both the negative ('avoid doing harm') *and* positive ('doing good') dimensions of organizations' social responsibility (ISO, 2017; Wood, 2011). For practical relevance, Wood (2011) suggested four varieties of *'influence-based social responsibility'* to clear up the conceptual ambiguity on influence understood as 'impact' and influence understood as 'leverage'. The typology is based on two dimensions: (a) the character of influence ('impact' or 'leverage'), and (b) the character of responsibility (negative/'do no harm', or positive/'do good'):

- **Impact-based negative responsibility:** an approach in which the organization has a responsibility to avoid or minimize the negative impacts *of its own* activities and decisions, directly or through its relationships with other actors;

- **Leverage-based negative responsibility:** an approach in which the organization has a responsibility to use its leverage to avoid or minimize the negative impacts of the activities or decisions *of other actors* with whom it has a relationship;

---

2 The conceptual discussion on an organization's 'sphere of influence' has been related to such concepts as *'impact'* (the link between activities and negative/ positive outcomes); *'leverage'* (the influence over other actors through relationships), and the spatial metaphor of *'proximity'* (political, contractual, economic or geographic distance).

3 Sphere of influence still features in the Ten Principles of the UN Global Compact.

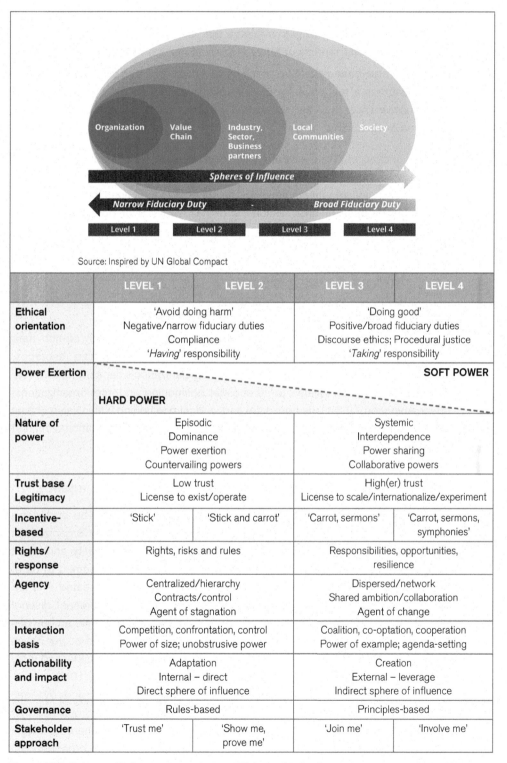

Source: Inspired by UN Global Compact

	LEVEL 1	LEVEL 2	LEVEL 3	LEVEL 4
Ethical orientation	'Avoid doing harm' Negative/narrow fiduciary duties Compliance 'Having' responsibility		'Doing good' Positive/broad fiduciary duties Discourse ethics; Procedural justice 'Taking' responsibility	
Power Exertion	HARD POWER			SOFT POWER
Nature of power	Episodic Dominance Power exertion Countervailing powers		Systemic Interdependence Power sharing Collaborative powers	
Trust base / Legitimacy	Low trust License to exist/operate		High(er) trust License to scale/internationalize/experiment	
Incentive-based	'Stick'	'Stick and carrot'	'Carrot, sermons'	'Carrot, sermons, symphonies'
Rights/ response	Rights, risks and rules		Responsibilities, opportunities, resilience	
Agency	Centralized/hierarchy Contracts/control Agent of stagnation		Dispersed/network Shared ambition/collaboration Agent of change	
Interaction basis	Competition, confrontation, control Power of size; unobstrusive power		Coalition, co-optation, cooperation Power of example; agenda-setting	
Actionability and impact	Adaptation Internal – direct Direct sphere of influence		Creation External – leverage Indirect sphere of influence	
Governance	Rules-based		Principles-based	
Stakeholder approach	'Trust me'	'Show me, prove me'	'Join me'	'Involve me'

Figure 10.1 Spheres of influence, power base and intervention levels

■ **Impact-based positive responsibility:** an approach in which the organization has a responsibility to maximize the positive impacts *of its own* actions and decisions, directly or through its relationships with other actors;

■ **Leverage-based positive responsibility:** an approach in which the organization has a responsibility to use its leverage to increase or maximize the positive impacts of the activities or decisions *of other actors* with whom it has a relationship.

By and large, Wood's typology corresponds well with the four intervention/engagement levels developed throughout this book. Figure 10.1 incorporates the 'power' dimension into the framework. The subsequent sections further elaborate on the power base of organizations and the dynamics of power exercise as leverage for positive impact.

10.3 THREE POWER BASES AS A FORCE FOR POSITIVE CHANGE

By 'smartly' combining hard and soft powers, organizations can stretch their scope for action – alone or together with partners – by leveraging resources, integrating activities and aligning positions. An organization's capacity for leverage and impact intimately relates to its societal positioning and inter-organizational agency (section 10.3.1), its horizontal and vertical positioning within value chains (section 10.3.2), and its international positioning through internalization of market failure and operating norms (section 10.3.3).

10.3.1 Societal positioning and inter-organizational agency

Society grants substantial freedom and power to companies. The underlying basic idea is that it provides the leaders (agents) of private sector organizations with the requisite room and autonomy to take risks, create opportunity, and invest in solutions and innovations that add value to society. What is deemed to be of societal value – and the conditions under which value can be created – is the result of the interaction between different organizations that represent distinct governance logics (see Chapter 6). Each of the eight organizational archetypes portrays complementary organizational strengths, weaknesses and power bases that delineate the scope and leverage for positive impact. This societal and institutional setting is best characterized as a *bargaining arena* (Figure 10.2).

Power, in this societal bargaining domain, is a complex and dynamic concept. It comprises both *context shaping* and *conduct shaping* qualities that affect structure as well as practice. In the bargaining arena – where no single organizational actor is in charge – power can be understood as organizational

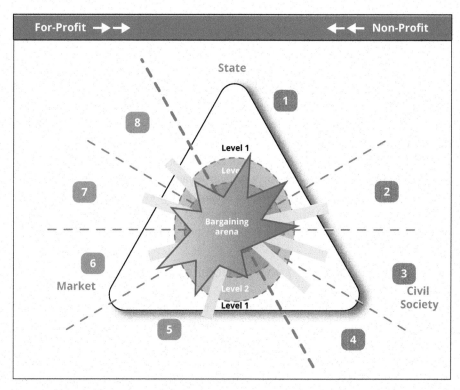

Figure 10.2 Governance entries for sustainability strategies

controls of ideas, resources, rules, modes, media and methods in inter-organizational dynamics (Ran and Qi, 2018; Crosby and Bryson, 2005). Within this multi-organizational arena, the conditions for legitimacy (the 'license to operate') are established within a framework of societal arrangements and regulation that guides agency, ownership and the acceptable use of (accumulated) power. The arena represents the setting in which *countervailing powers* and *societal checks and balances* are exercised and organized. American economist John Kenneth Galbraith introduced the concept of 'countervailing power' in 1952, suggesting that the market power of companies can be balanced by that of other (groups of) actors.[4]

The arena also constitutes the setting in which patterns of *dependencies and interdependencies* unfold. Depending on how formal authority, control over key resources and discursive legitimacy are distributed among the organizational

---

4   This premise is also known as the 'political modification of markets', and states that the (vertical) market power of, for instance, manufacturers can be balanced by the (horizontal) market power of retailers, and vice versa.

actors, strategies of 'collaboration', 'compliance', 'contention' and 'contestation' develop (Hardy and Phillips, 1998). An asymmetrical diffusion of critical sources of power creates dependencies between those in stronger and in weaker power positions. The sharing or pooling of complementary power sources in collaborative arrangements fosters more balanced ties of organizational *inter*dependencies. In practice, asymmetric power relations and power-sharing arrangements usually coexist. What constitutes 'relevant power' in a given setting is context-specific and dependent on the specific societal *need* – at levels 1, 2, 3 and 4 – to be addressed. Ultimately, the dynamics of inter-organizational power exertion shape the conditions for a more or a less balanced and resilient ecosystem (Chapter 1), as well as the parameters (organizing principles, operating principles, values and norms) for more or less synergistic ways of societal value creation.

POWER SOURCES AND SOCIETAL POSITIONING: A SOCIETAL SWOT ANALYSIS

The potential of an organization to achieve beneficial outcomes within a multi-organizational bargaining domain depends to a large extent on how it directs and makes 'smart' use of its multifaceted power base. Each societal position (archetypes 1–8, in Figure 10.2) combines unique capabilities and, accordingly, sources of power to contribute to a more sustainable society. In practice, various organizational power sources are concurrently at play, reflecting different mixtures of formal authority, control over critical resources and discursive legitimacy. These include:

- **Value-generating powers**, which relate to the control over – and effective use of – scarce material and non-material resources, vital assets and key channels to develop, consolidate and scale beneficial business models. It pertains to economic, structural and dispositional powers, power over critical capitals (financial, manufactured, human, intellectual, natural, social), the power of size and of ownership.

- **(Re)distributive powers,** derived from authoritative and decision-making powers on how (societal) value, resources and revenues are to be allocated, distributed or redistributed, and based on what mechanisms, principles and criteria.

- **Representative powers,** relating to the ability to mobilize and organize 'critical mass' (members, citizens, customers, employees), as well as the power to 'hold out' or veto the acts of others. Representative powers strongly rest on relational and structuring mechanisms and include associational and formational powers (e.g. workers' right to assemble), coalitional powers, lobbying powers, and demonstrating or protesting powers.

- **Moral powers,** which pertain to normative and discursive powers that define the dominant (societal) narrative, perceptions of 'truth', values and norms that establish what is deemed as 'acceptable'. Moral powers imply the capacity to steer towards a particular course of action, which de facto sets boundaries to (inter-)organizational agency. Moral powers rest on a mixture of ideological, political, sense-making, symbolic, framing, agenda-setting, exemplary and preference-shaping powers, with 'trust' and 'legitimacy' as the most important social capitals.

- **Innovation powers,** linked to the capacity to come up with – or mobilize – new ideas, innovative approaches and realistic ways of (re)solving societal problems. They involve visionary, imaginative, conceptual and creative capacities, rest on unique access to relevant knowledge, expertise and information, and include standard-setting powers with the potential to gradually change or disrupt the structural order.

- **Execution powers,** which refer to the instrumental power to achieve intended outcomes. This power source rests on the capacity to timely, forcefully and efficiently decide, organize and realize. It involves (formal) decision-making powers based on clear and effective governance of roles and responsibilities, as well as coordinating powers that drive and align internal and inter-organizational structures, processes, procedures and resources, to reduce complexity and uncertainty.

Organizations can contribute most to positive change if they can harness a timely and societal needs-oriented mix of their unique organizational power sources. The more organizations are able and willing to pool their complementary power bases for the common good in a 'smart' fashion, the higher the level of societal resilience that can be achieved (see Chapter 7).

SOCIETAL SWOT ANALYSIS

B O X 10.2

The extent to which an organization can position itself within the societal bargaining arena as a force of positive change rests on whether it can make smart use of its unique set of power sources. A societal 'SWOT' framework – building on the insights developed in Chapters 5 and 6 – helps to identify, analyse and strategize on an organization's societal positioning, power base, inter-organizational dynamics, and potential impact and leverage within a multi-organizational setting.

- **[SW] Strengths-Weaknesses:** whether an organization can develop and effectively wield its hard and soft powers in essence depends on the degree to which it masters primary governance processes (fiduciary duties and responsibilities) related to its societal position. Potential strengths are mitigated by how the organization handles its internal weaknesses (see Table 6.1) and sources of failure (Chapter 5), in particular at level 1 ('fiduciary duty to create value') and level 2 ('fiduciary duty not to destroy value') (see Tables 5.2, 5.3 and 5.4). How organizations manage these strengths and weaknesses – individually and in comparison with other organizations – defines the degree of legitimacy, credibility and trust with which they can enter the bargaining arena and claim to add value to society.

- ■ **[OT] Opportunities-Threats** subsequently relate to how an organization wields its powers in a societal context to seize opportunities for societal value creation, while mitigating risks and threats. In Chapter 6, we dubbed this the *'responsible agency challenge'* (Table 6.2). It pertains to an organization's capability to direct its societal positioning and related power sources 'smartly', in order to effectively deal with societal failures at intervention levels 2, 3 and 4 (which require dynamic interaction with other organizations). Whether these inter-organizational dynamics develop as collaborative, competitive, compliant, conflictual or countervailing interactions depends on the specific nature of the societal challenge, the transition phase, and the regulatory and institutional context ('sustainability regime', see section 6.5). Section 10.4 will elaborate this further in terms of Key Decision-making Indicators (KDIs).

10.3.2 Value chain positioning powers

Value chains can be defined as a set of activities that organizations that operate in a specific industry or segment of society perform in order to deliver a valuable good or service for 'users' or 'markets'. Value-adding activities within such input-output structures commonly include research and development, design, manufacturing, distribution and logistics, sales and marketing, services, and materials recovery for reuse or recycling purposes. Power and power dynamics, in the context of value chains, are intimately related to an organization's positioning within a particular chain and to the mechanisms through which the chain is structured, controlled and coordinated. Organizations with dominant positioning powers can actively shape the distribution of profits and risks through their activities along the value chain. They are also essential in providing leadership to steer the entire supply chain in a more sustainable direction (Seuring and Müller, 2008).

Value chain power can come from any position, can take many shapes, and can be exerted both *vertically* (upwards and downwards in the value chain), *horizontally* (dominance within industries and markets) and *diagonally* (as cross-industry conglomerates). How value chain power can be exercised is (1) sector-specific, (2) affected by national regulatory regimes (for instance, the extent to which organizations are allowed to exert monopolistic powers or to collaborate) and (3) conditioned by a complex interplay of structural, relational, and discursive or 'normalizing' aspects (Ponte et al., 2019). Ownership, asset specificity, switching costs, knowledge intensity, as well as access to information, technologies, capital and markets, amongst others, all affect power positions in the – often uneven – relationship between buying, supplying and intermediating value chain actors. Accordingly, value chain dynamics are prone to bargaining processes and organizational agency.

Dominance in vertical (chain), horizontal (industry and market) or diagonal (cross-industry) positions represents a so-called 'small numbers game', in which just a few organizations determine the formal and informal 'rules of the game'. The strong positioning of *core/lead/focal/flagship/keystone* organizations[5] in setting these rules has given them considerable sway over the course and pace of technological development, production requirements, information flows, and the distribution of costs, risks and revenues. It also gives them significant influence over *entry and exit conditions* in chains and markets, thereby affecting supply chain configurations. As central 'directors' and 'coordinators' of value chains, these organizations are deemed well-positioned to drive the transmission of sustainability standards, to incorporate responsible operating principles, and to establish organizing principles that reflect a broader take on responsibilities and *societal* value added (Box 10.3). How and to what purpose core organizations use their powers within chains and markets ultimately defines them as agents of change, frustration or stagnation (section 10.1).

GREAT POWER, GREAT RESPONSIBILITY?

High degrees of market concentration indicate significant positioning power and, therefore, point to key nodes for leveraging *societal value creation*. Accumulated vertical, horizontal or diagonal positioning powers imply higher degrees of responsibility to be attributed to (groups of) core companies for promoting, initiating and transmitting action throughout their chains and across industries and markets. Consider, for example, the following areas for leverage:

■   *Addressing pollution.* Just 100 companies have been the source of more than 70% of the world's greenhouse gas emissions since 1988, according to a 2017 Carbon Majors Report of the Climate Accountability Institute (CDP, 2017).

BOX 10.3

---

5   Studies on value chain organization use comparable concepts to characterize those organizations with dominant positioning power and significant control over value chain decisions and activities that function as 'directors', 'managers' or 'coordinators' of risk and performance of, and within, value chains.

- *Challenging privacy.* The five largest information technology companies in the US – Google-Alphabet, Amazon, Facebook, Apple and Microsoft – constitute an oligopoly that, according to most observers, appears to take control of the internet. They accumulate market and financial power, for which they (ab)use patent rights, copyrights provisions and behavioural data of their 'customers', while actively discouraging – or buying up – new market entrants. Their dominance is being countered by regulatory agencies (within the United States, the European Union) and by Chinese state-owned or state-influenced enterprises.

- *Sustainable energy provision.* In 2019, Chinese firms produced 72% of the world's solar modules, 69% of lithium-based batteries and 45% of wind turbines. They also control much of the refining minerals that are critical to clean energy, such as cobalt and lithium (*The Economist*, 17 September 2020).

- *Industrial innovation.* According to OECD figures, global business R&D expenditure is concentrated with just 250 firms (out of the global top 2000 of R&D investor companies). Together, they account for around 72% of total R&D investments, 71% of publications and 65% of patents (Dernis et al., 2019). In many countries, industrial innovation is concentrated with less than four companies that de facto define the *selection environment* in which countries develop their technology strategies. In some high-tech value chains, key nodes are even represented by a single company. B2B company ASML, for instance, holds a near monopoly in chip-producing machinery. The number of chip manufacturers at the industry's cutting edge has fallen from over 25 in the year 2000 to just three in 2021 (*The Economist*, 23 January 2021). In 2019, the world's top 10 ranked companies in terms of R&D expenditure (no.1 Alphabet; no. 10 Johnson & Johnson) together invested more than $145bn (2020 EU Industrial R&D Investment Scoreboard – R&D ranking of the world top 2500 companies).

- *Concentration of ownership.* Index funds Blackrock, Vanguard and State Street – the Big Three in asset management – together hold the majority of shares of 88% of all S&P500-listed companies.

STRUCTURAL POWERS: VALUE CHAIN POSITIONS

An organization's degree of structural power relates to its position within or towards value chains. Five archetypical value chain structures can be distinguished, each depicting a distinct position of the 'core organization' that delineates its power base (Figure 10.3).

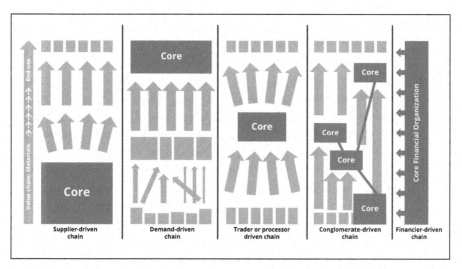

Figure 10.3 Structural power – five core positions

■ **Supplier-driven value chains** are dominated by the powerful position of 'upstream' companies. They derive their (hard) powers predominantly from their control over strategic resources and materials, which may include land, oil and minerals, raw materials, exploitation rights, mining concessions, food crops and other vital commodities. The dominance in supplier-driven chains remains relatively 'silent' where the core supplier has no need for 'forward integration' towards end-product markets – which could make them more susceptible to reputational damage with the general public – to uphold their dominant position. A core company's positioning power may extend over multiple 'downstream' suppliers in various separate value chains.

■ **End-market and demand-driven value chains** are dominated by organizations at the B2C end of the value chain. They derive an important part of their power base from their relationship with end users and their ability to shape (mass) consumption patterns. This applies, for instance, to merchandisers in food, clothing and consumer electronics, which base their dominant position on a mixture of economies of scale, locational advantage, brand awareness and loyalty, and high costs for new entrants. Core firms' power may extend across suppliers in various separate value chains, depending on their end-market dominance (as a measure of the strength of their brand, product, service or organization relative to competitive offerings). Size, price-setting powers and the revenues that accrue as a result enable core firms in demand-driven value chains to be active in acquisitions and international expansion processes. Market dominance can be further reinforced by *preference-shaping* and *market-creation powers*.

- **Trader and processor-driven value chains.** The intermediary function of traders and contractors that procure from many dispersed or smaller suppliers *(multiple-sourcing)* and sell to many dispersed or smaller buyers can provide a powerful position, particularly in global commodity trade. The position is often reinforced by the presence in spot markets around the world. Core intermediary firms channel most of the traded goods efficiently through their facilities or may act as *systems or components integrators*. This applies, for instance, to multinational food processing companies that organize a network of various global commodity chains. In the digital economy, platform companies have established a comparable strategic coordinating position. Core platform companies have accumulated significant market power, derived from their *channelling powers* and reinforced by massive network and lock-in effects.

- **Conglomerate-driven value chains.** Conglomerates are multiple-industry organizations that operate in *cross-industry* structures. They organize companies in several sectors and industries and concurrently hold strategic positions in different segments of various value chains. Their portfolio of activities is often highly diversified – in scope and spread over focus – and their presence in complementary industries is not necessarily founded on synergistic relatedness. Conglomerates' diagonal positioning power can be based on family ties, cross-ownership, minority or majority holdings and political support, through which barriers of entry can be overcome more easily. Especially in developing and Asian countries, conglomerates still thrive. In South Korea, so-called *chaebol* (family-controlled conglomerates like Daewoo, Samsung, LG, Hyundai) exercise considerable economic power. In Japan, vertical *keiretsu* (e.g. Toyota, Nissan, Toshiba) dominate specific industries, such as cars and electronics. Horizontal keiretsu – which include vertical and diagonal chain relationships – are often organized around a bank or general trading company – so-called *sogo shosha*, which engage in trade, logistics, plant development and resource exploitation. They include conglomerates like Mitsubishi and Sumitomo. Family-controlled conglomerates in India (e.g. Mittal, Tata) and in the Philippines (e.g. Ayala, Jollibee, San Miguel) also structure and dominate considerable parts of the economy.

- **Financier-driven chains** are under the strong influence of financial organizations (e.g. commercial and investment banks, pension funds, asset management companies, impact investors, insurance companies) that enable firms along the value chain to capture, design, add, destroy, scale and spread value (see section 9.4.1). Although positioned outside the value chain, financial organizations can derive significant structuring powers from their intermediary *access to finance* position by *selecting* those organizations and activities that they deem financially sustainable (see section 8.4.2). Financial intermediaries reduce the transaction costs and information asymmetries in markets for finance by *reallocating* and *leveraging* otherwise uninvested financial capital to selected enterprises, by granting loans, providing credit, managing equity and through financial arbitrage across countries. Banks have been able to significantly stretch and reinforce their structural power base by leveraging their actual capital reserves, often more than tenfold.[6] How financial intermediaries manage their portfolio of activities – in terms of screening and selecting, enabling, mitigating, withdrawing – has a great impact on the financial viability of individual companies and on the structure, stability and resilience of entire value chains, industries and markets.

RELATIONAL POWERS: MANAGING CONTRACTUAL AND DEPENDENCY RELATIONSHIPS

How core organizations use their positioning powers within and across value chains defines their relational power exertion. Resilient supply chains are based on inter-organizational governance arrangements that advance efficient as well as sustainable and fair relationships (Seuring and Müller, 2008). In essence, five types of governance (Gereffi et al., 2005) and related dependency arrangements (Ruigrok and Van Tulder, 1995) can be discerned in managing value chain relationships (Figure 10.4).

At the two extremes of the relational continuum, we find 'markets' and 'hierarchies'. Transaction costs economics distinguishes between 'markets' – based on competition – and 'hierarchies' – based on vertical integration and control – as efficient distribution and allocation mechanisms between organizations in value chains (Williamson, 2008). Networked ways of organizing fill the analytical void between these two extremes (Powell, 1990). Networks involve varying degrees of interdependence between organizations based on reciprocal patterns of communication and exchange. Value chain governance can accordingly be expanded with 'modular', 'relational' and 'captive' types of inter-organizational arrangements, each reflecting varying degrees of *mutual influence* and strategies for organizational agency (competition, compliance, coalition, direct control, structural control).

---

6   Under Basel III, the minimum capital adequacy ratio (CAR) that banks must maintain was raised to 8%. CAR measures a bank's capital in relation to its risk-weighted assets.

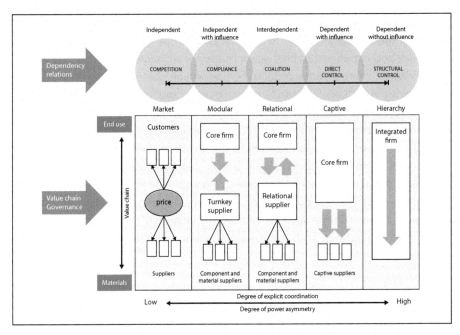

Figure 10.4 Relational power: Governance and dependencies in value chains
Sources: Gereffi et al. (2005), p. 89; Ruigrok and Van Tulder (1995), p. 116

Both value chain orientation and organizations' strategic positioning within it define the relational antecedents of power exertion. Modes and patterns of chain governance can alter over time, for instance, as the result of changing end-market needs, (disruptive) technological advancements, new market entrants, and economic, social and environmental *upgrading* processes within or across value chains.[7] Dynamics in value chain governance are contingent on three key variables in particular: (a) the degree of information complexity and knowledge intricacy shared between chain actors for the production of a good or service; (b) the extent to which this information and knowledge can be codified for

---

7 Various types of upgrading have been distinguished in the global value chains literature (e.g. Humphrey and Schmitz, 2002; Barrientos et al., 2011), including: *process upgrading* (increasing efficiency through the reorganization of production activities or introducing superior technology); *product upgrading* (moving into more sophisticated product lines with increased unit value); *functional upgrading* (acquiring new functions that increase the skill content of activities); *inter-chain or inter-sectoral upgrading* (moving into new yet related activities of different chains or sectors; *social upgrading* (enhancing the rights and entitlements of workers as social actors, and the quality of their employment); and *environmental upgrading* (altering of production systems and practices that result in positive or less negative environmental outcomes).

transmission (e.g. product specifications, operating procedures, industry-wide standards); and (c) chain actors' level of competence to source, design, produce and distribute efficiently and reliably, in accordance with standards and specifications (Gereffi et al., 2005: 85–87):

- **Market governance** involves relatively simple, *arm's length* transactions with *price* as the central governance mechanism between many (interchangeable) suppliers and buyers. Market governance represents the textbook example of *perfect competition*. However, in the real world, the conditions for perfect competition – no information asymmetries, identical products, rational economic behaviour, no economies of scale, open competition without entry, exit or switching costs – hardly ever exist. Value chains in which market mechanisms prevail notably pertain to food crops and commodity chains in which many suppliers and buyers operate. But even in these chains, traders, food-processing firms and retailers have been able to take on and exert significant powers. Trader-driven chains – with the core company positioned in the centre – instigate competition on both sides of the chain, which enables them to set prices that do not necessarily reflect real value, nor 'true' costs (of externalities to society that remain hidden, or are missing, in the market price).

- **Hierarchical governance** mechanisms are found in *vertically integrated* value chains where the lead organization develops and manufactures products and services *in-house*. Vertical integration is typical in chains where product specifications cannot be codified, where products are complex or highly strategic, or where specialized suppliers cannot be found. Vertical integration can be established downstream (e.g. branded oil companies that have integrated forwards, from well to service station), or upstream (e.g. food companies that have integrated backwards to control the value chain from 'farm to fork'). Globalization has prompted vertical *dis*integration in many value chains, which has made them more fragile and susceptible to disruptions (see Chapter 7).

- **Captive governance** arrangements appear in value chains where smaller suppliers are dependent on one or a few powerful buyers (*monopsony, oligopsony*). In these settings, core buying companies can wield significant power in setting specific conditions (e.g. product requirements, processing standards, operating principles and protocols, delivery time provisions). Power asymmetries in captive supply networks create *lock-in effects* (which can be positive or negative) and high *switching costs*, mostly for suppliers who have to specialize and structure their activities to meet specific conditions. Captive suppliers can also exert a certain degree of influence, as the core company is reliant on its suppliers' competence, efficiency and customized quality to uphold its brand value, reputation and competitive position. In view of enhancing overall supply chain efficiency, performance and resilience, core companies are inclined to support their suppliers in *upgrading* their production capabilities. Core companies have also used their purchasing strategies to discipline their suppliers and increase dependencies however. Under the pretext of sustainability, the (hidden) costs and risks of implementing CSR practices have regularly been transmitted to suppliers (e.g. Ponte, 2020).[8]

- **Modular governance** pertains to transactions that are complex yet relatively easy to codify. Arrangements typically entail contractual relationships between a core company and *independent, highly capable* modular ('turnkey') producers that make complete and ready-to-use products in compliance with customers' specifications. It usually involves process technology on generic machinery that can flexibly serve a wide customer base. Hence, switching costs and transaction-specific investments are relatively limited. An example is the production of off-patent medicines by non-branded drug manufacturers that offer a portfolio of generic drugs and active pharmaceutical ingredients. When a turnkey supplier manages to upgrade its competences, develop superior technology, enhance efficiency or produce more sophisticated (e.g. certified fair or organic) products or services, relational arrangements may alter. Semiconductor chip manufacturer Intel, for example, positioned itself to the greater public with its 'Intel Inside' trademark, which flipped its dependency and power relation with leading computer system manufacturers. Similarly, the spark plugs of equipment manufacturer Bosch are used by most car and motorcycle producers around the world and in various industrial applications because of their technological sophistication (safeguarded by patents).

- **Relational governance** occurs when complex and context-specific information exchange is needed, for instance, when *knowledge sharing and learning* are essential to produce a certain product or boost overall chain performance. Such exchanges require a considerable degree of *trust and reliance*, leading to strong ties of *mutual dependencies* between core organization and independent supplier, commonly regulated through social, networking, kinship (e.g. family, ethnic group) and reputational mechanisms. Producers in relational arrangements more often have a differentiation focus; their related asset-specificity and tacit knowledge is complementary

---

8   Walmart, for instance, was criticized for how it rolled out its 2006/2007 green 'packaging scorecard' at the expense of its 2,000 private-label brands and 60,000 global value chain suppliers.

to that of the core organization and hence vital in achieving mutually beneficial goals and gains. As relational linkages take time to build, the *switching
costs* of moving to a new partner – in terms of search, setup, execution,
learning and sunk costs – are also relatively high.

Supply chain management studies increasingly examine how to create
governance structures that make the entire value chain more sustainable and
resilient. Accordingly, attention has shifted from a focus on the core organization's (responsible) procurement function in particular to one that focuses on the
sustainability performance of the entire chain within the broader context of societal actors affecting and shaping value chain governance dynamics. The *sustainable supply chain management* (SSCM) discipline especially considers the
position of upstream suppliers (e.g. farmers, smallholders, small-scale miners,
labour-intensive manufacturing) by investigating venues for improved and more
equitable value creation, value capturing and (re)distribution of costs, risks and
revenues – through processes of social, economic and environmental upgrading,
integrated/inclusive participation, co-creation strategies and collaborative
approaches. Ultimately, a sustainable supply chain can be characterized by
(1) the degree to which environmental considerations, social performance
measures and economic contributions are integrated, (2) whether it achieves a
circular, inclusive and/or fair value chain, and (3) whether it provides each chain
participant with sufficient scope for manoeuvre to articulate a sustainable value
proposition and implement a sustainable business model (Chapter 9). What can
be considered 'sustainable' depends on context: the segment or node the organization holds within the chain, the nature of the trade-offs considered, and the
national context in which (relative) performance is measured. Core organizations
can drive the achievement of higher levels of sustainability by continuously reconsidering the right balance between 'formalization' and 'collaboration' (cf. Panigrahi
et al., 2019). In non-collaborative contexts, core organizations may wield their
contractual powers to set higher sustainability standards; collaborative arrangements, however, usually provide more robust and sustainable ways for upgrading
chain participants. The degree of interdependence in sustainability-oriented value
chains increases either way.

DISCURSIVE POWERS: MOBILIZING AND ALIGNING CHAIN ACTORS
FOR POSITIVE CHANGE

Finally, power exertion within and across value chains is influenced by core organizations' discursive and normalizing powers through which they 'frame' and
reframe buyer-supplier relations and the legitimacy of associated transmission,
capturing, and (re)distribution mechanisms. Framing, agenda-setting and demonstrative powers (the 'power of example') have proved strong instruments for

shifting conventional frames in desired directions, crafting new meaning to existing norms, and warding off pressure from societal expectations. They are among the strongest of discursive powers that lead organizations can exercise in bolstering sustainability – within society, along the value chain, and across the industries and sectors in which they operate. Hence, discursive powers have also been labelled as the 'language of leadership' (Fairhurst, 2010). *Thought leadership*, *sense-making* and the *manufacturing of consent* (section 10.2.1) then relate to a lead organization's ability to credibly convince actors along the chain of (1) the necessity of, (2) opportunities for, and (3) feasible trajectories towards higher levels of societal value creation.

If exercised smartly (section 10.2.2), discursive powers can function as effective coordination mechanisms in *mobilizing* value chain actors around goals and gains and in the *convergence* of their operational practices to prevailing expectations, norms and standards. Ponte et al. (2019: 126), in that context, point to the 'normalizing' nature of chain governance through the establishment of *conventions* – such as standards, certification schemes, supplier codes of conduct, labels and quality marks, best practices, expectations and norms – that 'travel' along the value chain to steer organizational agency (Box 10.4). The value chain thereby represents yet another *bargaining arena*, in which actors interact based on their discursive and normalizing powers. The extent to which specific sustainability conventions (a) prevail as more 'legitimate' than conventional practice, (b) effectively align value chain actors around core values, principles and goals, and (c) provide feasible venues for leverage, depends on the set of discursive and normalizing instruments used by the core organization. Transmission mechanisms may include broadly accepted norms developed in loosely affiliated (societal, sector or industry) groups, quality conventions accepted by all value chain members, or '*issue advertisement*' to broadly 'signal' how a lead organization's or industry's ambition, thought leadership or sustainability performance should be understood.

BOX 10.4

KEY CONVENTIONS IN VALUE CHAIN COORDINATION – ALIGNMENT, SIGNALLING AND ASSURANCE INSTRUMENTS

■ **(Supplier) code of conduct:** a system of agreements and basic principles through which an organization communicates the kind of conduct it expects from its members – and in a more extended version, its upstream and downstream business partners – in specific situations. Codes have a signalling, clarifying, guiding and alignment function of outlined norms, rules, responsibilities and practices. *Performance-oriented codes* define minimum standards of desired outcomes of sustainable behaviour. *Process-oriented codes* outline the procedures an organization should follow (e.g. in non-financial reporting, stakeholder consultation, communities' free and prior informed consent). Codes can range from general (mission statement, values statement, business principles) to specific (code of conduct), and from narrow (addressing a few issues) to extensive (addressing over a hundred issues). Most large (multinational) organizations have codes; all cover internal processes, about half of them also encompass responsibilities towards customers (Babri et al., 2021).

- **Standards and guidelines:** whereas codes are specific to a firm, industry or issue, standards are applicable across a wide range of sectors and geographical regions and accountable to a much broader constituency. CSR-related standards usually comprise a series of norms based on some degree of consensus among stakeholders on values, principles, criteria and indicators. Sustainability standards can be 'de facto', 'de jure', open or closed. *Guidelines* – such as Global Compact and OECD guidelines (Chapters 6 and 8) – comprise more generic principles that provide direction to action or organizational behaviour.

- **Voluntary sustainability standards (VSS):** VSS are "requirements that producers, traders, manufacturers, retailers or service providers may be asked to meet, relating to a wide range of sustainability metrics, including respect for basic human rights, worker health and safety, the environmental impacts of production, community relations, land use planning and others" (definition by the UN Forum on Sustainability Standards). VSS are also referred to as sustainability standards, ecolabels, certification schemes, eco-certification, or voluntary market-based certification programmes.

- **Quality marks and labels:** organizations' efforts to address specific (sustainability) issues can be made recognizable – particularly to end-market users – through quality marks and labels that communicate their commitment. A wide range exists, for instance, related to a specific sector, labour conditions (Oké bananas, Fair Wear, Rugmark, Fairtrade), production conditions (FSC, MSC, RSPO and RSSO certificates, Rainforest Alliance, UTZ), recycling or organic (Eco, EKO, Grüne Punkt), human resource policy (Investors in People).

- **Certification and monitoring:** pertain to the (voluntary) verification and approval by an (accredited) party on performance conformity (of products, practices, systems) to a specific standard (e.g. SA8000, ISO14001), code or norm. The assurance-providing certification body that performs the audit is usually an expert (independent) *third party*. *Second-party* monitoring relates to an organization auditing its suppliers to ensure conformity or to (voluntary) peer audits performed within business alliances. *First-party* monitoring refers to internal organization audits, usually with the primary aim to identify areas for improvement.

BOX 10.4

- **Accreditation:** the entire set of activities that should lead to confirmation by an independent accreditation body of the *independence, impartiality and expertise* of a conformity-assessing certification organization, based on internationally harmonized standards and norms (e.g. ISO, ISO/IEC). Certifying organizations found compliant with these standards use an accreditation logo on their certificates to signal additional assurance. Accreditation systems are designed to provide confidence in the credibility of certification schemes and conformity attestations, by *supervising the supervisors*.

More information and overviews: Leipziger (2016); Van Tulder with Van der Zwart (2006); Kaptein (2020); Babri et al. (2021); UN Forum on Sustainability Standards (https://unfss.org/).

Within value chains, discursive powers and normalizing mechanisms can be directed downstream (towards end-market customers) and upstream (towards suppliers). Towards end markets, discursive powers are generally used for the purpose of *justification*, *mobilization* and *alignment* with (societal) expectations, values, principles and governance arrangements. Towards upstream suppliers, normalizing mechanisms primarily operate as coordinating instruments that go beyond formal contractual arrangements and which can vary in their degree of formalization and de facto coercive effect. Discursive and normalizing mechanisms at the chain level materialize in the dynamic context of bargaining processes in four (nested) 'bargaining arenas': [1] within organizations, [2] the value chain (upstream-downstream), [3] the sector/industry, and [4] society at large. In each of these arenas, power exertion develops in two directions: *inside-out* and *outside-in* (Figure 10.5).

- **Inside-out discursive and normalizing influence.** To instigate positive change, lead organizations' discursive challenge boils down to questions on how to mobilize, align, incentivize and empower all relevant stakeholders – in various layered bargaining arenas – around a shared vision and common values. Sustainability strategies are hence increasingly framed in terms of *corporate stories*: rich narratives in which key strategic challenges are portrayed and contextualized, agenda-setting and framing powers exerted, and choices, arrangements and actions towards enhanced sustainability legitimized by values statements and reference to guiding principles, standards and codes. At the sectoral level, organizations have been using the 'power of example' to inspire their industry peers in developing a future-oriented sustainability vision for the entire sector, or to 'lead the way' in navigating transition strategies by disinvesting from the 'old' organizational paradigm. At the value chain level, the discursive challenge amounts to (co-) shaping a common frame and convincing value proposition for the

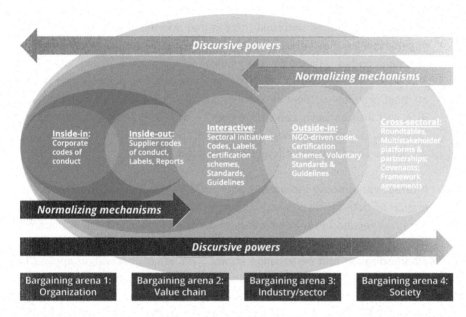

Figure 10.5 Bargaining arenas, discursive powers and normalizing mechanisms

organization of the entire chain (e.g. inclusive, circular, fair, sharing, see Chapter 9), to drive sustainable value creation in the right direction. But without normalizing mechanisms, discursive powers would lack implementation, legitimacy and credibility. The normalizing powers of lead organizations particularly unfold in negotiations and dialogues at the value chain and industry/sector level. Here, scope, stretch and effectiveness of their discursive and normalizing powers depend on (a) the strength of their *convening powers* to elicit convergence of norms and establish industry-wide standards, and (b) their implementation powers – related to their direct and indirect 'sphere of influence' (section 10.2.2), the smart use of hard and soft power sources, and (horizontal, vertical, diagonal) positioning powers to create sufficient traction and leverage.

■ **Outside-in discursive and normalizing influences.** The outside-in perspective involves exertion of societal *countervailing powers* – by NGOs, organized communities, governments – that materialize around and within (international) platforms, multi-stakeholder initiatives and the formulation of (generic and sectoral) codes, guidelines and standards. *Transparency*, *accountability* and *reputation effects* are key instruments of outside-in power exercise (see Chapter 7 on *triggering events* and the emergence of CSR, and Chapter 9 on *reversing materiality*). The discursive and normalizing powers of multi-stakeholder initiatives notably lie in their convening, framing and agenda-setting powers. By establishing international campaigns, platforms and round tables that address targeted (clusters of) societal issues, they have been able to drive the development of numerous voluntary codes, standards and guidelines for a wide variety of critical sustainability issues. Initiatives that identify, assess, benchmark and report on 'best practice' or 'best in class' organizations – for which metrics, rankings and indices have been developed – further drive these normalizing dynamics, eventually making societal 'soft' power exertion fairly coercive, disciplinary and 'hard' in effect, once adopted at scale.

■ **Interactive: aligning inside-out and outside-in norm-setting.** The proliferation of both inside-out and outside-in 'signalling' and normalizing initiatives has resulted in a fragmented landscape of thousands of (company-, industry-, issue-) specific norms, codes and quality marks, and hundreds of standardization and certification efforts. The same observation applies to reporting practices. The convergence of norm-setting initiatives has been identified as pivotal to creating greater transparency, effectiveness and sustainability impact. This vital harmonization challenge – playing out at the sectoral level, in particular – represents a struggle between (1) the need for convergence to simplify the large number of codes and standards and (2) the need to leave sufficient room for innovation and novel approaches that foster societal value creation (Leipziger, 2016). Associated with this is the challenge to enhance the level of trust with societal stakeholders in sustainable business initiatives (at levels 2, 3, 4) by establishing effective and credible certification processes.

Convergence in *performance standards* (e.g. on child labour, biodiversity, decent wages, discrimination, inequality) has proved more difficult to establish than convergence in *procedural issues* (e.g. non-financial reporting, guidelines, systems standards). Mixed effectiveness, fragmentation, overlap and rival applications of normalizing instruments have been eroding their credibility, dissemination and acceptance (see Box 10.5). This state of affairs has prompted NGOs, business alliances and international organizations alike to push for greater convergence in the certification, accreditation and reporting landscapes. The Global Reporting Initiative (GRI), for instance, joined with CDP, Climate Disclosure Standards Board (CDSB), International Integrated Reporting Council (IIRC) and Sustainability Accounting Standards Board (SASB) in 2020 to achieve progress towards a single set of comprehensive and global reporting standards.[9] The

---

9   https://www.globalreporting.org/public-policy-partnerships/the-reporting-landscape/

ISEAL alliance – which brings together accreditation bodies covering fair trade, social accountability, living wage, organic agriculture, and sustainable fishing and forestry – works on common frameworks for sustainability standards. Its *Credibility Principles* represent the fundamental qualities, values and concepts embraced by affiliated sustainability standards systems and certification schemes, to achieve positive social, environmental and economic impacts while decreasing negative effects.[10] Taking the *SDGs as the overall reference framework* can be considered the latest, most widely disseminated trend in attaining greater convergence between the myriad sustainability initiatives.

THE NORMALIZATION JUNGLE

BOX 10.5

The origins of SSCM normalizing measures

The history of normalizing efforts has developed in phases, primarily in response to challenges in effective codification, reporting and labelling of companies' responsible behaviour in supply chains. In the 1970s, organizations such as the OECD, ILO and UN pioneered the idea of (voluntary) 'codes of conduct' for multinationals, followed in the 1980s and 1990s by initiatives of critical NGOs (trade unions, religious organizations, human rights and ecological movements) that called for *mandatory codes*. The challenge of 'good practices' codification was first met by business associations – like the joint Chambers of Commerce and the Japanese employers' organization Keidanren – in the 1990s. Parallel initiatives for sustainability labels (e.g. Fairtrade, Eko-labels) and reporting (Global Reporting Initiative) also originated in this period. Mandatory requirements for companies proved difficult to implement however; governments were unable or unwilling to regulate, whilst certification and standardization efforts rarely surpassed the 'voluntary' status – which, in practice, curtailed their effectiveness.

The hazards of divergence

From the 1990s onward, core companies introduced their own codes, labels and reports on a massive scale. A 'cascade' of corporate codes materialized on such topics as child labour, human rights and environmental issues – partly in defensive response to external initiatives, partly to wield discursive powers vis-à-vis stakeholders in the face of mounting media attention. This *proliferation phase* intensified in the early decade of the millennium; it resulted in a 'jungle' of divergent normalizing initiatives. Some beneficial effects emerged from (best in class) examples and experiments. But

---

10 https://www.isealalliance.org/defining-credible-practice/iseal-credibility-principles/

lacking transparency, confused signalling and poor comparability also eroded the credibility and effectiveness of many norm-setting initiatives. Leipziger (2016), in that context, pointed to the simultaneous existence of two 'paradoxes': (1) many of the best codes and standards are not well known, whereas some well-disseminated ones are not very effective; (2) it is possible to have comprehensive codes of conduct that nonetheless achieve nothing, and rather vague codes that are well-embedded into the organization and that foster innovation and change. This confusing and muddled state of affairs led others to observe that "*a code is nothing, coding is everything*". Both *hard and soft controls* prove pivotal in designing effective business codes; the right mix is context-dependent and changes over time (Kaptein, 2020).

Challenges to clarity, uniformity and credibility

- *Labelling and quality-marks.* Organizations' unilateral issuing of (proprietary) labels and quality marks for sustainability-related causes has become a widespread practice. As a result, the sheer diversity of (competing) labels and the 'vagueness' of their content have hampered their effectiveness considerably. Consumer research on the clarity of their visualized sustainability message repeatedly pointed to consumers' lack of recognition and knowledge of the exact meaning of distinct labels. Moreover, it led some consumers to perceive sustainability-labelled products as being (far) more expensive or of lower quality than non-certified products. An additional challenge with labelling is the difficulty in communicating composite sustainability characteristics and complex trade-offs in product qualities, for instance, between fair and ecologically responsible, or animal-friendly and a decent income.

- *Sustainability standards, predominantly voluntary.* Most sustainability standards and guidelines rely on a 'voluntary' uptake. According to UNFSS estimates, over 400 'voluntary sustainability standards' (VSS) currently exist, with the largest numbers found in the (tropical) agricultural commodities, consumer products and processed foods sectors. Most are *private VSS*, developed by NGOs, industry and multi-stakeholder groups to provide indications on the safety, social and environmental conditions behind products and on efforts made to enhance sustainability. *Public VSS'* have emerged from public sector initiatives (e.g. Blue Angel of the German Government, the EU's Ecolabel). Annually, several VSS disappear "due to low uptake levels or unsustainable economic models" and several new ones emerge (UNFSS, 2020: 8). The *adoption intensity of various VSS* around the world (in number and by type) varies considerably per country – depending, for instance, on a country's trade diversification, reliance on imports and exports, its governance, level of development and globalization characteristics (ibid: 17–18).

- *Reporting: ambiguous transparency and benchmarking.* Non-financial reporting grew rapidly under various designations (environmental, social, 'responsible care', 'citizenship', sustainability reports), signalling organizations' growing willingness – and experienced pressure – to show greater transparency on selected sustainability issues in the value chain. More sophisticated 'due diligence' and 'track and trace' methods have created avenues to better assess, address and report on both risks and opportunities for enhanced sustainability performance. In parallel, institutional investors and rating agencies gradually included sustainability indicators as part of their *risk management* strategies. This reinforced their tendency to particularly focus on 'avoiding harm' dimensions, more than rewarding greater transparency on change trajectories towards improved *sustainability impact* and related dilemmas (Chapter 9). Rankings, in general, have been biased in favour of larger companies that have the capacity to respond repeatedly to extensive questionnaires used in various benchmarking initiatives. 'Playing the ranking game', however, has also been found to feed into *complacency and lowest denominator dynamics* that crowd out organizations' motivation to further improve overall sustainability performance and impact. Ranking initiatives such as the Dow Jones Sustainability Index have tried to limit such unintended side effects by *not revealing* their benchmarking criteria, in turn diminishing their legitimacy and dependability, however.

■ *Certification: the risk of false solutions.* Private standards, codes and proprietary labels not only led to a divergence in norm-setting initiatives but also resulted in the emergence of 'private certification' schemes with limited assurance. Especially where such standards encompass superficial, less crucial or controversial issues – while seeming to provide a solution – the risk of 'greenwashing' exists. The credibility of (competing) semi-private certification in industrial timber, pulp and palm oil production has been questioned and criticized.[11] Also, where the gains of *cheating* are high – in organic agriculture, for instance, where higher prices are paid for certified products – free-riding on consumers' sustainability intentions will eventually erode fragile consumer trust (Nuttavuthisit and Thogersen, 2017).

The need for convergence: the SDG-agenda leading the next normalizing phase

Authoritative norm-setting organizations have considered the SDG-agenda a promising framework and platform for creating greater convergence in sustainability benchmarks. Value chains figure prominently in the SDG-framework. SDG-target

---

11 The World Rainforest Movement, for instance, characterized the many competing certification schemes in sustainable forestry as the 'greenwashing' of logging activities: https://wrm.org.uy/about-wrm/.

12.6 (on responsible consumption and production) in particular calls upon companies to adopt sustainable practices and integrate sustainability information into their reporting cycle. Accordingly, they have started to align their normalizing efforts, frameworks and indicators with the SDG-framework. Leading examples on vital *transparency and accountability* areas include:

- GRI-SDG alignment on integrated reporting;
- OECD-SDG alignment regarding responsible business guidelines;
- ISO26000-SDG alignment on social responsibility;
- World Benchmarking Alliance-SDG alignment to entice a 'race to the top' among 2000 'keystone companies' in transition-critical industries;
- ISEAL-SDG alignment regarding value chain-orientated labelling and certification;
- ESG-metrics-SDG alignment by large accountancy firms and impact investors.

10.3.3 International positioning: the powers of multinationals

Companies can create considerable positioning power through cross-border organizing (see Chapter 6). This is the area of multinational enterprises (MNEs) and the topic of international business research. A company's international positioning strongly hinges on strategic choices related to (a) its *market, resource, efficiency, and asset-seeking strategies* (Dunning and Lundan, 2008), and (b) *country portfolio optimization* processes, through which it seeks to overcome individual countries' regulatory constraints by internalizing risks and norms (see Box 6.1). Positioning power, in this context, can be understood as derived from a context-specific interplay of *structural* (e.g. locational, contractual, investment, transfer-pricing and profit-shifting choice sets), *instrumental* (actor-centred relational use of lobbying and bargaining powers), and *discursive* and normalizing aspects (Fuchs, 2013). An organization's international position is thereby conditioned by:

- The number of countries it operates in or from. The larger the number of countries, the greater the need for coordination. A company's country portfolio, then, represents the set of countries selected for: (1) sourcing inputs and materials, (2) customer markets, and (3) the degree of standardization or adaptation to each of these markets;
- The overall degree of volatility the country portfolio presents. The higher the volatility in distinct regulatory regimes, the more important operational, strategic and sustainability risk management becomes (see Box 6.1);

- The country portfolio's diversity in CSR/sustainability regimes and the extent to which that presents risks to, and opportunities for, positive impact (section 6.5.1).

In the popular discourse, MNEs are often treated with considerable distrust, in particular because of their size and related power base (Box 10.6). Media and business-society management literature (section 7.2) is filled with cases of MNEs that abuse their powers for strategies considered to be manipulative (tax evasion), corrupt (colluding with governments to achieve investment goals), or irresponsible (e.g. polluting, human rights abuse, forced labour in global value chains). MNEs often have considerable bargaining power over local authorities, which they can wield to pressure local governments, for instance to create or sustain 'tax havens', 'pollution havens' or policy arrangements that provide a competitive advantage vis-à-vis rivals. MNEs can actively (ab)use the governance gaps and regulatory voids that exist between countries, but they can also constructively draw on their power base in support of beneficial societal impact (Chapter 6).

A CONTROVERSIAL ISSUE: THE POWER OF MULTINATIONAL CORPORATIONS – HOW 'BIG' ARE THEY REALLY?

BOX 10.6

A particularly threatening aspect for citizens and governments of corporate power is the sheer size of certain MNEs and their assumed inherent ability to manipulate governments. Over the years, the world's largest companies have become larger as the result of the consolidation trend that followed from 'shake-outs' and a wave of mergers and acquisitions in many sectors. The number of large companies consequently increased, with concentrated power in the hands of a limited number of firms in most sectors and economies. Due to their size, reach, resources and relative powers derived thereof, MNEs have received particular attention in relation to sustainability issues. Being beyond national regulatory authorities' direct sphere of influence, MNEs have proved susceptible to allegations of power abuse and of undermining democratic institutions.

The intellectual protagonists of the anti-globalist movement have habitually gauged MNEs' powers in terms of relative economic size. The compelling frame: many of the world's largest 'economies' are corporations rather than nation states. David Korten (*When Corporations Rule the World*), Joshua Karliner (*The Corporate Planet*), Noreena Hertz (*The Silent Takeover*), in varying words, compare companies to countries as an indication of their power and far-reaching impact. The death of democracy, then, is illustrated by the claim that "of the world's 100 largest economies, 51 are now corporations, only 49 are nation states" (Hertz, 2002).

Comparing the size of countries' GDP with corporate sales and revenues – or, sometimes, with market capitalization – has since been a recurring theme in the popular discourse. It has led to the redrawing of world maps, in which country names are replaced by corporate names to display comparable economic size, with the suggestion of similar economic and political power. Comparing companies' turnover with countries' GDP proves seriously flawed, however. 'Gross domestic product' measures the accumulated *value-added* produced by domestic companies. Sales and revenues do not present their value added; market capitalization even less so (see section 8.3). For example, big retailers commonly add around 15% value to the products they sell; the greatest proportion of value-added comes from their (foreign) suppliers. Estimates of MNEs' actual value-added (De Grauwe and Camerman, 2002; UNCTAD, 2002) hence give cause to a downward adjustment of popular representations by at least a factor two (in Europe) to three (in the United States and Japan). Of the world's 100 largest 'economies' – when adjusted for value added – around twenty to thirty would be companies, with many of them ranked in the second half of the list.

ENTRY/EXIT POWERS

In his book *Power in the Global Age*, Ulrich Beck (2005) sketched the 'meta-power' of MNEs vis-à-vis nation states. Meta-powering is commonly described in terms of its structural impact on institutional arrangements and (international) exchange relationships. The 'meta-power' of MNEs notably rests on the threat of their *exit option*: the (partial) withdrawal of vital activities and their relocation to states that would offer more conducive investment and operating conditions. The implication of withdrawal is the exclusion of a host economy from the world market – as represented by that MNE, with affiliates located in diverse countries. The more *footloose* the industry is (such as textile), the more persuasive the exit option as a bargaining chip.

In practice, bargaining positions in MNE-state relations are sector-dependent and contingent on the degree of (dis)similarity in strategic goals, stakes, resources and constraints of both parties involved (Eden et al., 2005).[12]

---

12 In their 'political bargaining model', Eden, Lenway and Schuler (2005) explain that the potential bargaining power in MNE-state relations is determined by the valuation each party places on the other's resources (e.g. firm-specific assets, a country's location-bound assets). The existence of economic, political, and institutional constraints, then, may strengthen or weaken each party's actual bargaining power, depending on: (a) the (specificity of) resources controlled by one party and demanded by the other, (b) the similarity of interests and stakes related to the negotiation, (c) the specific constraints on each party, and (d) the ability of either party to limit the behaviour of the other directly, through economic or political coercion.

Mineral-rich but less diversified host economies, for instance, may find themselves overly dependent on MNEs' foreign direct investments (FDI) to spur vital private sector development in non-mineral sectors. Furthermore, relative bargaining powers may shift over time. Raymond Vernon's (1971) *obsolescing bargain* concept argues that an MNE's strong 'before-entry' bargaining position may weaken once firm-specific capital-intensive investments are made. Sunk costs would then inhibit the MNE from using its exit option. Conversely, knowledge-seeking MNEs – notably from emerging economies – that go abroad to learn may find their weaker 'at entry' bargaining position strengthened over time, once they have gained from technology spillovers and location-bound resources in foreign business ecosystems. Where the interests of an MNE and host country partly converge as mutual dependencies, the exit threat is often used as *voice strategy* to influence government action towards preferred outcomes. Both *exit and voice* are part of the power exertion repertoire (Hirschman, 1970) in iterative MNE-state bargaining processes.

Notorious areas of exit/entry and related MNE lobbying and bargaining strategies include tax regulation, health and safety regulations, and local relationships to trade unions. MNEs have also used the exit option to sway improvements in national regulation – in favour of minimum wage and labour standard provisions, for instance – or to pressurize governments to respect basic human rights. MNEs' broader scope for manoeuvre and, often, competitive advantage over local companies enables them to adopt international initiatives (such as the OECD Guidelines on MNEs) and integrate stricter sustainability standards into their host country operations. This positively affects their legitimacy, potential leverage and bargaining position, both locally and internationally.

POSITIVE POWER EXERTION – THE VALUE-ADDING POTENTIAL OF MNEs

MNEs engage in social, economic and environmental *arbitrage*, through which they manage imperfect global regulatory architectures (section 6.5). MNEs can use arbitrage to manipulate – divide and rule – countries, thereby instigating a spiralling 'race to the bottom'. They may also harness their arbitrage powers to overcome regulatory voids, however, to drive sustainability to higher levels (inciting a 'race to the top').

The so-called *internalization theory*, developed in the international business (IB) discipline, explains why – in an imperfect world – MNEs, under certain conditions, can be considered a lesser evil compared with non-multinational corporations. The most important argument in this line of reasoning is that MNEs correct for 'market imperfections' or 'market failure' in international product markets. MNEs *internalize markets* and hence mitigate risks between countries. The internalization theory builds on the *general theory of the firm*, as introduced by Nobel

Laureate Ronald Coase, which argues that markets, in general, are not good at efficiently directing resources. Firms, then, are a response to the high costs of using markets. Many of the imperfections in international markets – trade barriers, quota arrangements and other protectionist measures – appear because of 'government failure'. The potential to profit from international trade and open exchange relations is consequently limited. Multinationals set up facilities around the world to internalize part of the market inside their organization and, by bridging regulatory boundaries, potentially provide solutions to market and government imperfections. If multinationals organize the interaction between headquarters and subsidiaries well, they can contribute to greater wealth through enhanced efficiency and greater exchange of knowledge.

Ethical theory has added another dimension to this argument: in an imperfect world in which norms and values compete, the multinational corporation can also *internalize norms* and create an environment that resolves some of the rivalries between cultures, norms and values. MNEs can provide a *normative free space* and develop *hypernorms* (Donaldson and Dunfee, 1999) that potentially enhance ways of doing business beyond competing for national systems and cultures. Companies manage their international corporate responsibilities by aligning their internal organizing and operating principles with the norms and values of their external stakeholders. If they do this right, they can also be considered a force for good. Effectively bridging host countries' regulatory voids with international initiatives that foster both 'avoid doing harm' and 'doing good' approaches potentially provides MNEs with the leverage to credibly engage in level 3 and 4 activities (Box 10.7).

BOX 10.7

THREE PRINCIPLES OF SUSTAINABLE MULTINATIONAL MANAGEMENT

An extended theory of the multinational enterprise (1) looks at both risks and responsibilities, (2) defines the trade-offs between risk and responsibility, and (3) tries to assess whether the synthesis, as created by an MNE, adds value. It reveals three constituting principles for a 'sustainable MNE':

- **Principle #1:** internalize market failures across borders
- **Principle #2:** internalize normative failures across borders
- **Principle #3:** move *beyond* compliance and aim at maximizing *societal* value contribution (the overarching goal of the SDG-agenda).

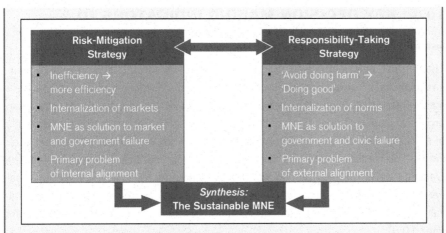

Supranational initiatives

Multinational enterprises have operationalized these three principles in a variety of ways. On a strategic level, MNEs have developed normative institutional initiatives to make their operations more environmentally sustainable and socially responsible. Norms, rules and standardized procedures for sustainable business conduct were established that surpass national regulatory regimes. Four types of normative institutional initiatives that encourage companies to contribute to sustainable development have become particularly widespread (Rasche et al., 2013):

1) *Principle-based initiatives*, such as UN Global Compact and the OECD Guidelines for Multinational Enterprises, which urge companies to commit to specific norms in their day-to-day operations;

2) *Certification and labelling initiatives* that address developmental issues associated with the production of specific products, including the Marine Stewardship Council (MSC), Social Accountability 8000, Fairtrade, Fair Wear; Forest Stewardship Council (FSC);

3) *Reporting initiatives* (e.g. the Global Reporting Initiative, SASB Standards) that seek to advance the disclosure of companies' (industry-specific) social and environmental information;

4) *Process-based initiatives*, such as AccountAbility's AA1000 series of standards, that set up procedures for managing corporate responsibility.

Because institutional initiatives seek to govern corporate outcomes on the environment and society at large, they have been understood as an institution for *transnational governance* (Barkemeyer et al., 2015).

10.4 KEY DECISION-MAKING INDICATORS TO ACTIVATE POSITIVE CHANGE

The context- and conduct-shaping implications of structural, relational and discursive powers – exercised directly or throughout the wider sphere of influence – make their 'smart' and balanced use contingent on the transition phase an organization is in. Trajectories of business model innovation towards higher levels of societal value creation confront organizations with very specific transition challenges, centred around critical *tipping points* (section 9.2.5). These delineate *Key Decision-making Indicators (KDIs)* for rethinking how the organization could best harness its various (hard and soft) power sources and recalibrate its (societal, value chain, and international) positioning to attain its sustainability ambitions (Box 10.8).

BOX 10.8

DECISION-MAKING FOR POSITIVE CHANGE

Decision-making theory – or the theory of choice – has a normative and a descriptive bearing. *Normative thinking* focuses on the outcome of decisions and seeks to determine whether decisions are optimal; *descriptive thinking* analyses how people come to (better) decisions. Normative and ethical approaches to decision-making stress how to 'balance conflicting expectations of stakeholders in an adequate way', and gear organizational activities to ethical principles (Constantinescu and Kaptein, 2021). Descriptive approaches link these insights to game theoretical and organizational behavioural notions of actors' (intrinsic and extrinsic) motivations and power play to decide on apt interventions in overcoming key tipping points (section 9.2). Behavioural research underlines the importance of a *realistic* understanding of decision-making processes under the influence of inherent 'bounded rationality'. Smart power use takes both normative and descriptive dimensions into account. It applies the principles of 'choice architecture' (Thaler and Sunstein, 2008) in a 'nudging' approach, as the thoughtful design of interventions for positive change that reckon with the flaws and flavours of boundedly rational decision-making.

Key dimensions for KDIs

KDIs for sustainable business specify *the nature* of decisions to be taken in order to surpass critical thresholds and tipping points, adjust the business model and move from one level of sustainability to the next. KDIs highlight four dimensions critical to strategic decision-making:

■ **Decision-making under uncertainty and complexity** involves an understanding of the gap between intention and realization (section 9.2) and requires a solid assessment of the nature of the issues at stake (Chapter 7). It reiterates the relevance of *contextualization*: key decisions must take societal, value chain and international factors into account and reckon with stakeholder diversity, their needs and interests (Chapters 4 and 5).

- **Decision-making under behavioural constraint** acknowledges the ambiguity inherent to a VUCA world (Chapter 1), the bounded rationality in the actions of internal and external stakeholders, the psychological processes that induce indecisiveness, and the associated paradoxical effects. For instance, the more one cares, the more indecisive one generally becomes (Ariely and Wertenbroch, 2002), whilst the tendency to procrastinate or postpone decisions intensifies when faced with complex situations (De Cremer, 2013).

- **Prioritizing decisions:** faced with over 10,000 decisions a day (Hertz, 2014), people – and organizations – rely on *routines* ('business as usual') to prevent stress and deal with choice paralysis. But 'non-decisions' also induce path dependencies. Deliberate choices – on what to sustain, what to change and to what intended end – steer goal-setting and organizational focus, as well as time, energy and resource allocation. What are relevant thresholds, trade-offs and tipping points to consider in strategizing on the 'right' course of action and for making informed decisions?

- **Sequencing decisions** require a solid understanding of how various decisions are interrelated and may lead to different outcomes at different stages over time; it involves a deliberate consideration of trade-offs (or synergies) between short-term and long-term implications and profound insights into the various stages of – and dependency relations between – strategy implementation processes.

Strategic fit, alignment and tipping points

How organizations and their leaders arrive at certain strategies defines the 'antecedents' of change. The alignment theory of strategic management refers to the challenge of *creating a strategic fit* (Chorn, 1991). 'Strategic fits' – along various organizational dimensions – express the degree of matching between the external environment and an organization's resources, capabilities and sphere of influence to create and harness opportunities. Strategic alignment goes beyond 'responsive adaptation'; an active approach implies that an organization is able to smartly wield its power base to dynamically co-shape its competitive environment and steer the business ecosystem in a sustainable direction.

BOX 10.8

Strategizing in organizational transition processes entails a 'paradoxical leadership' challenge of finding ways to concurrently reckon with ethical choices, the need for timely and decisive action, and meaningful involvement of relevant stakeholders while taking diverse institutional and operating contexts into account. Foremost, it involves timely resolving of the tension between *loosening* grip on the 'old' paradigm and *strengthening* traction on an evolving sustainable 'new' one by navigating change trajectories of *'loosening while strengthening'*. How to loosen one's grip on the present mode of organizing – the bedrock of hitherto accumulated powers and competitive positioning – while using this same power base to strengthen one's grip on changing expectations and environments? How to redirect organizational powers and realign core operations with societal needs, goals and values amidst fierce competition? Reconciling such tensions calls for *ambidextrous leadership* capacities: loosening while strengthening, adapting while creating, running while reinventing, staying efficient yet innovative. In short, the strategic challenge of transitioning towards enhanced sustainability boils down to how to shift:

- From a negative duty approach ('having' responsibility), to a positive duty approach ('taking' responsibility);
- From restricting power abuse ('compliance'), to using principles, powers and positioning for good (beyond compliance);
- From primarily applying hard powers, to a 'smart' use of powers to attain intended (societal, sustainability, resilience) effects;
- From a liability and risk orientation, to a responsible opportunity-seeking orientation;
- From governance mechanisms that elicit countervailing powers, to governance that entices collaborative powers.

This section builds on the three transition phases delineated in section 9.2.5 in moving away from an inactive (level 1) or reactive approach (level 2), towards an active (level 3) or proactive (level 4) orientation. Each phase presents a combination of strategic tipping points that require a fundamental rethinking of the business case (see Chapter 8) and business model (Chapter 9):

1   **The trigger-induced phase** (tipping point 1); change trajectories start with the ambition to *escape* from a prevailing negative duty approach ('avoid doing harm'), 'hard power' exertion, and a risk, rules, control and compliance-driven orientation (focussed on addressing failure, restricting power abuse and limiting negative externalities to avoid liability). In this phase, the pace and amplitude of change usually follow the dynamics of the external triggering events (see Chapter 7) the organization is confronted with.

2   **The internal alignment phase** (tipping point 2); advancing to an active, positive duty ('do good') approach to societal value creation requires a

rearrangement of internal structures, processes and capabilities. This phase presents a *decisive shift* from a reactive to an active orientation to addressing sustainability challenges. It requires an organization to reorient externally (industry, market, competitive, regulatory environment dynamics) as well as realign all internal stakeholders.

3 **The external alignment phase** (tipping point 3); a proactive and transformational orientation towards societal challenges additionally requires a *deliberate strategy* of seizing a competitive advantage in alliance with external stakeholders (partners). It calls for the development of strategic partnerships with various societal stakeholders (elaborated in Chapter 12), through which complementary sources of power can be mobilized, aligned, leveraged and directed, in collaborative approaches that address societal needs and challenges – within and beyond the organization's direct sphere of influence.

Each phase highlights different areas of KDIs (Table 10.1) to guide strategic positioning questions: how to approach the regulatory environment (section 10.4.1); how to approach present and prospective value chain participants (section 10.4.2); and how to approach internationalization processes (section 10.4.3)?

Table 10.1 Phases in activating positive change

	LEVEL 1 Inactive	LEVEL 2 Reactive	LEVEL 3 Active	LEVEL 4 Proactive
				STRENGTHENING
	LOOSENING			
				TRANSFORMATION
	ADAPTATION			
	Tipping point	Key Tipping point	Tipping point	
Transition phases	Phase 1: *Gradual*	Phase 2: *Decisive*	Phase 3: *Deliberate*	
	Trigger	*Internal alignment*	*External alignment*	
KDIs centred around:	**Adaptation ambition:** Loosening grip on fragile, unsustainable paradigms of doing business ('business as usual')	**Strategic ambition:** Strengthening while loosening; value propositions that deal with negative while aiming at positive effects	**Transformational ambition:** Strengthening traction on new paradigm of sustainable/resilient business	

10.4.1 Societal KDIs – dealing with the regulatory context

KDIs in the area of societal positioning (see section 10.3.1) are foremost centred around issues of regulation and self-regulation under competitive or more collaborative conditions. In most countries, regulation is primarily aimed at preventing market failure (see Table 5.3), negative externalities (Table 5.4) and 'power abuse' by organizations – for which society usually bears the costs. Organizations with higher sustainability ambitions will need to gain additional levels of societal trust ('license to operate, scale, experiment', Table 6.6) in order to create sufficient leeway – and support – for novel approaches to enhanced sustainability. Such

Table 10.2 Society-related KDIs

	LEVEL 1 *Tipping point*	LEVEL 2 *Key tipping point*	LEVEL 3 *Tipping point*	LEVEL 4
KDIs related to:	1. Gradual: *triggering*	2. Decisive: *internal alignment*	3. Deliberate: *external alignment*	
	REGULATION/COMPLIANCE		SELF-REGULATION	
Governance approach	Self-regulation and within-sector compliance: 'comply or explain'	Strict(er) and clear regulation; creation of level playing field to prevent free-rider behaviour	Smart regulation; hybrid/partnering governance principles for learning, sharing and accountability	
	COMPETITION		COLLABORATION	
Competition regime	Support countervailing powers of competitors and new entrants; support policies to prevent power abuse	Support collaborative competition policies that stimulate precompetitive collaboration	Support coordinated (international) coopetition policies that facilitate precompetitive and pro-competitive collaboration for future markets	
	CLOSED		OPEN	
Intellectual property regime	Closed innovation: Use of patent regimes for the development and scaling of sustainability-enhancing innovations	Shared innovation: Use of joint patents in support of sustainable technologies for unmet demands and needs (e.g. frugal innovation)	Open innovation: engage in collaborative research and open innovation; support co-ownership and pooled ownership of patents; Open standards	

'new rules of engagement' require an orientation *beyond* compliance to rules and regulation; they call for transparent, responsible and principled approaches to effective self-regulation as well as taking initiative to constructively co-shape a business environment conducive to advancing sustainability. Three prominent areas of societal contention can be distinguished, in which organizations may opt for different repertoires of regulation and self-regulation (Table 10.2): corporate governance, orientation to competition and intellectual property regime (IPR) approaches.

GOVERNANCE KDIs

Matters of responsible governance relate to the regulation of 'principal-agent' relations (see section 6.2) for the effective management of sustainability-related issues. Responsible governance can be interpreted narrowly – primarily directed at the prevention, containment and correction of irresponsible practices (e.g. insider trading, perverse executive incentives, transfer price manipulation, pollution, tax evasion, disregard of workers' and human rights, whistle-blower procedures, violation of privacy). Operationalized more broadly, responsible governance provides an organization with a coherent set of principles to guide, empower and incentivize responsible practices that are aligned with societal needs, norms and values and contribute to addressing societal challenges.

- **Phase 1 KDIs**: organizations in the process of overcoming tipping point 1 face the challenge of deciding on the scope of their voluntary (good) governance codes. 'Comply or explain' principles (section 6.2), as developed in some Western countries, are intended to foster greater compliance with voluntary commitments through transparency. They give organizations some leeway to explain the specific circumstances behind deviant behaviour, provided that derogation is not structural and does not violate the code's spirit. In practice, however, 'comply or explain' decision-making can also result in adverse effects. Transparency on CEO remunerations, for instance, was supposed to discourage excessive executive pay; in practice, the code triggered an upward effect: it instigated CEOs to compare their income with the 'highest' salaries in the sector on a global scale.

- **Phase 2 KDIs**: organizations in the process of attaining level 3 ambitions are usually in favour of more strict and clear regulation that raises the bar for the entire sector. The aim is to press for *a level playing field* that fades out free-rider behaviour so that those organizations that are serious about their sustainability strategies are enabled to distinguish themselves with their positive agenda – instead of being dragged into a competitive 'race to the bottom'. Accordingly, phase 2 type of KDIs seek effective combinations of rule-based and principles-based governance that strike a balance between an organization's responsibility ambition and the dynamic (competitive) reality of the business ecosystem; for instance, by actively supporting legal provisions on minimum diversity 'quota' in management and corporate boards, absolute caps on emissions to air, soil and water, or strict regulation of transfer price management.

▪ **Phase 3** governance challenges present additional steps in facilitating change towards level 4 strategies. KDIs then relate to effective arrangements for the management of hybrid governance principles, applicable to cross-sector partnerships (section 5.4.2 and Chapter 6). Relevant questions pertain, for instance, to the degree of goal congruence between prospective partners; the degree of formalization of collaborative efforts; choices regarding structural or occasional arrangements; the division of responsibilities, allocation of means and accountability on actions. A major barrier to effective partnerships is the design of governance principles that enable accountability/control and learning/flexibility at the same time (see Chapter 12). Phase 3 governance includes decisions on arrangements that support greater transparency and the sharing of good 'responsible governance' practices to bolster transformational change on a larger scale (using the power of example).

ORIENTATION TO COMPETITION

One of the 'hottest' areas of contention in curbing or boosting sustainability efforts concerns the regulation of competition and collusion. Competition and 'antitrust' policies around the world differ in their definition of monopoly power, collusion, cartels and what can be considered 'abuse of power'. Competition policies can be founded on a *narrow* or a *broad welfare* perspective. A narrow welfare perspective focuses on *consumer welfare* only. It is based on the premise that consumer interest is best served by 'low prices' in existing markets that are efficient and competitive. In this view, cartel agreements are assumed to always lead to higher prices and should thus be restricted. A broader welfare perspective is oriented towards *citizens' welfare* and, in addition to consumer interest, also considers *citizens' needs* – including those of future generations. In this view, *precompetitive collaboration* can be beneficial and may be allowed if it enables the development of technologies and innovative products that raise overall welfare without stifling competition in the longer run.

Policymakers struggle with including broader welfare dimensions into their antitrust policies. To what extent can 'agreements between competitors' to concertedly address sustainability-relevant externalities be tolerated if this could initially lead to higher consumer prices? If applied too restrictively, competition regulation may considerably constrain the emergence of *novel markets* for more sustainable products in the face of fierce price competition. To overcome this conundrum, organizations will have to substantively convince regulatory authorities of how their *coopetition strategy* will result in a higher level of value creation that increases societal welfare and well-being in the longer run.[13] Relevant KDIs on balancing competition and collaboration for positive change vary according to transition phase, orientation and envisaged outcome:

- *Phase 1 KDIs* acknowledge the relevance of fair competition as a force that enables distinctiveness and efficiency in existing markets, and reflect the willingness not to abuse market power (even in weakly enforced regulatory environments, or in relation to as yet insufficiently regulated areas, such as the digital economy). Countervailing powers are recognized as a functional force in steering markets, sectors and innovations towards more resource-efficient solutions with less harmful impacts. Studies on the role of competition in this transitioning phase suggest a positive correlation between competition and, for instance, reduction of industrial pollution releases at the facility level (Simon and Prince, 2016). Limiting competition in this phase might lead to 'greenwashing'.

- *Phase 2 KDIs* support competition policies and sector initiatives that stimulate precompetitive collaboration to establish a 'level playing field' for the production of goods and services at a higher level of sustainability while preventing a 'race to the bottom'. Precompetitive collaboration and 'coopetition strategies' can enhance competition in later stages in ways that increase the competitiveness of the entire industry, at a higher level of societal value creation.

- *Phase 3 KDIs* are oriented towards a constructive lobby for changes in competition rules that curtail meaningful progress towards sustainability. They address precompetitive collaboration for future markets – joint efforts in the development of knowledge, capacity, standards, technologies and systems – that address societal needs based on the principles of *citizens' welfare* (sustainability impact here/there, now/later). In phase 3, companies also have an interest in greater international coordination in competition policies (to raise the bar internationally and address systems challenges more coherently).

---

13 The concept of 'coopetition', developed by Brandenburger and Nalebuff (1996), is based on game theoretical insights of 'cooperative games'. Coopetition materializes between organizations with a partial congruence of interest. They cooperate so that all parties can attain a higher level of value creation that cannot be reached by focussing on individual competitive advantage alone.

ORIENTATION TO INTELLECTUAL PROPERTY RIGHTS

The protection of intellectual property rights is a vital element in encouraging organizations to invest substantial time, effort and resources in finding innovative solutions to societal needs and sustainability challenges. Patent systems are intended to create societal value and spark innovation by granting inventors a time-limited exclusive right over their invention (*appropriability function*) in exchange for public disclosure of detailed enabling information on the invention (*disclosure function*). This transitory legal monopoly position provides the patent holder with a certain leverage over competitors to recover costs and earn a reasonable return on (uncertain) investment.[14]

But patent protection can also stall further progress. Especially in patent-intensive sectors, patents may be (ab)used as a strategy to stifle innovation and reap monopoly profits through excessive pricing strategies. Patents can "reinforce monopolies and intensify abuse of market power, block the diffusion of knowledge and follow-on innovations, and make it easier to privatize research that is publicly funded and collectively created" (Mazzucato, 2018: 206). By ignoring the deeply collective and cumulative processes behind innovation – often funded by governments through subsidies and grants – unbalanced patent regimes may, in fact, facilitate *societal value exploitation* by rewarding 'unproductive entrepreneurship' (Baumol, 1990). This can have a profound effect on the innovativeness of the economy and the degree and pace of dissemination of sustainability-relevant technological discoveries.

The idea of *open innovation* – first coined by Henry Chesbrough (2003) – emphasizes the relevance of distributed innovation processes, based on principles of *collective intelligence* and *co-production* across organizational boundaries, in order to be able to respond flexibly and concretely to societal challenges. Open innovation – supported by shared patents, open standards or no patents at all – is increasingly considered a precondition for the proliferation of innovative systems integration in, for instance, recycling and waste prevention systems (circular or Cradle-to-Cradle® principles), or in developing products, services or systems for unmet needs (e.g. 'bottom of the pyramid' approaches, see section 8.4.3). Balancing the positive forces of both (closed) competition and (open) collaboration in intellectual property rights arrangements results in the following KDI orientations:

- **Phase 1 KDIs** involve closed, self-reliant innovation strategies that use the patent system to develop sustainable and competitively priced innovations to meet existing demand. Patents are aimed at enabling and protecting

---

14 Firms use patents mostly for strategic reasons (Cohen et al., 2000). Informal appropriation methods of '*closed innovation*' – such as secrecy, confidentiality agreements, lead-time – were found to be more commonly used to protect intellectual property (Levin et al., 1987).

efforts to scale and diffuse sustainability-enhancing concepts and technologies, in particular those that lower negative externalities of present devices, services and systems.

■ *Phase 2 KDIs* involve purposive arrangements for shared innovation strategies, aimed at generating (complementary) new ideas for the development, application and diffusion of sustainability-enhancing solutions that address as yet unmet needs and demands. To resolve unmet, often basic needs in developing countries in a context-specific way, the development of 'frugal innovation' (sections 8.4.3 and 11.8) and joint patenting strategies is of particular relevance for successful uptake and diffusion.

■ *Phase 3 KDIs* include strategic decisions on arrangements that enable collaborative research for the provision of collective goods (see section 8.4.4). The more open and co-created 'innovation ecosystems' become, the more joint patents and 'open standards' will be applied. The competitive advantage then lies not so much in protecting the patent but rather in setting up a unique and scalable network of collaborating parties. Success in developing innovations for transformational change strongly hinges on the degree to which each of the collaborating parties can have 'ownership' of the project's outcomes for follow-on innovation.

10.4.2 Value chain KDIs – changing horizontal and vertical relations

Transitioning towards a sustainable business model requires organizations to consider at least *five key dimensions* in deciding on the strategic orientation – and ultimate configuration – of their value chain: (1) linear – circular; (2) exploitative – inclusive; (3) closed – open; (4) efficient – fair; and (5) global – local (Chapters 8 and 9). Some of these orientations are mutually exclusive; most represent tensions and trade-offs that delineate KDIs according to transition phases.

The scope to structurally reorganize for enhanced sustainability is conditioned by the business environment however. The power base of an organization (societal, structural, relational, normalizing, international), as well as the specific characteristics of horizontal (industry, market), vertical (value chain) and lateral (cross-industry) dynamics (section 10.3.2), significantly determine the leeway for redirecting the course of action. For instance, governance mechanisms and dependency relations across the value chain may have to change drastically in order to facilitate positive change. *Switching costs* – the economic, financial, procedural and relational cost associated with changing suppliers, locations, products or services – may initially appear to compromise competitive or financial performance and discourage value chain actors from adjusting their operations. Conversely, *switching benefits* (Guandalini et al., 2019) – the rewards of timely transitioning towards greater societal value creation – may prove a vital lever for creating competitive advantage by driving capabilities development, the innovativeness and sustainability performance of the entire value chain.

As central 'directors' or 'coordinators' of value chains, core organizations will have to reflect on whether their sustainability intent and strategic positioning give cause to either (a) a gradual transitioning process of *chain adaptation*, by adjusting to the 'pace of change' and 'rules of the game' as dictated by industry efforts and the business environment; or rather (b) *transforming* the industry (and value chain) to attain systems change, by shaping novel industry rules and (co-)creating a 'fitting' business environment that is supportive to the level of sustainability sought. Chain adaptation foremost requires flexibility and the capacity to continuously change the product/service offering, the configuration and governance of (value chain) activities, the resource base and capabilities development. Transformation for systems change presumes a compelling conception of what a more sustainable, resilient and future-proof industry could look like. It demands leadership, clear vision and a profound assessment of the ('first-mover') opportunities that can be derived from the innovative strength and competitive power of the value chain.

FIVE COMPETITIVE FORCES, THREE DYNAMICS

KDIs that inform strategic choices on value chain transitioning concentrate on industry dynamics, innovative capacity, competitive performance and longer-term resilience. The strategic implications of an industry's structure and the nature of horizontal and vertical interactions can be classified according to Michael Porter's (1985) classic 'five forces' framework. The framework provides an insightful decision-making support tool to analyse the underpinnings of industry dynamics as the overall outcome of:

1   **Horizontal dynamics:** related to the structure, nature and degree of 'rivalry' within the industry or market segment an organization is operating in; horizontal dynamics have a particular bearing on the *scaling* potential of (sustainable) value chains;

2   **Vertical dynamics:** related to the bargaining powers of 'buyers' [2a] and 'suppliers' [2b], which have a bearing on the *upgrading* potential of (sustainable) value chains;

3   **Lateral dynamics:** related to the 'threat' of 'new entrants' [3a] and 'substitute offerings' (3b), which have a bearing on the *innovative potential* of (sustainable) value chains in combining scaling and upgrading effects.

Power exertion along these five forces is furthermore influenced by normalizing and discursive strategies to influence, enact and pursue what constitutes legitimate and sustainable practice. Normalizing and discursive conditions affect the extent to which 'switching costs' can be reframed as 'switching benefits' and transaction costs lowered by investing in well-aligned and collaborative supply chain relationships. KDIs that can help organizations navigate beyond key tipping points then relate to finding the right balance between processes of adaptation and transformation, and between switching costs and benefits along the three transition phases (Table 10.3).

Table 10.3 Value chain KDIs and five competitive forces

	LEVEL 1 *Tipping point*	LEVEL 2 *Key tipping point*	LEVEL 3 *Tipping point*	LEVEL 4
KDIs related to:	1. Gradual: triggering	2. Decisive: internal alignment	3. Deliberate: external alignment	
Change orientation	CHAIN ADAPTATION		SYSTEMS TRANSFORMATION	
Cost-benefit approach to change	SWITCHING COSTS		SWITCHING BENEFITS	
HORIZONTAL KDIs	COMPETITION/RIVALRY		COOPETITION/PARTNERING	
Scaling Potential	DOWNSCALING		SCALING ACROSS	
[1] Approach to rivalry among competitors	**Competition as a means to lower prices** for sustainable products and services in existing markets; adapt product portfolio to increase demand for sustainability. Scaling focus: down, up and deep	**Build strategic alliances and support** within industry co-opetition: to create level playing field, seize scaling and network effects, and lower information asymmetries. Scaling focus: deep and wide	**Engage in cross-sector partnering** between complementary organizations: aimed at innovative products, services and systems integration. Scaling focus: wide and across	
VERTICAL KDIs	LINEAR/EXCLUSIVE/EFFICIENT		CIRCULAR/INCLUSIVE/FAIR	
Upgrading potential	PROCESS		INTER-CHAIN	

(continued)

Table 10.3 (continued)

	LEVEL 1	LEVEL 2	LEVEL 3	LEVEL 4
	Tipping point ⟫	*Key tipping point* ⟫	*Tipping point* ⟫	
Downstream: [2a] **Bargaining power of buyers**	**Efficiency/price-driven:** labelling strategy to inform clients about activities undertaken for inclusive/ fair/eco-efficient chains; preference shaping and nudging	**Value-driven:** support buyer cooperatives; coordinate labelling to contain the normalization 'jungle' (Box 10.5); industry level preference shaping		**Integration-driven:** aimed at servitization, co-creation in support of needs and a 'sharing' (we) economy (Chapter 9)
Upstream: [2b] **Bargaining power of suppliers**	**Involve individual suppliers** in a more fair/ inclusive/eco-efficient approach; Differentiation of products Prime upgrading focus: process, environmental and social	**Create industry effects:** improve transparency and industry standards; Additional upgrading focus: functional and product		**Inter-chain platform:** diversification, coproduction and co-development for optimizing sustainable chain ambitions: circular (closed loops), fair, inclusive, resilient (Chapter 9); Additional upgrading focus: inter-chain
LATERAL KDIs	*- -* SUBSTITUTION			**COMPLEMENTARITY**
Innovative potential	*- -* PRODUCT DEVELOPMENT			**SYSTEMS INTEGRATION**
[3a] **Relation to 'new entrants'**	**Exploration and intra-chain organization** in dealing with large rivals and small innovative start-ups	**Inter- and intra-chain alliances:** Co-opetition and collaboration to create vital linkages with innovative entrants		**Cross-industry and cross-sector alliances:** Innovative partnerships for systems change
[3b] **Function of 'substitutes' and complements**	**Trigger change:** Adaptive transformation based on and market dynamics; Substitution effect: organize for better sustainable product/ service offerings at greater scale; Complementarity effect: sustainable niche innovations and market niches	**Accelerate change:** Progressive transformation based on industry dynamics; Substitution effect: Business model innovation and 'creative destruction'; Complementarity effect: internalization of 'best-in-class' innovations to raise industry-wide sustainability standards		**Institutionalize change:** Deliberate transformation based on societal dynamics; Search for complementary capabilities and organizational logics to facilitate systems change at scale

HORIZONTAL KDIs – MAKING RIVALRY SUPPORTIVE FOR CHANGE [1]

The characteristics of an industry – in terms of the nature, dynamics and intensity of rivalry among competitors – delineate the conditions under which organizations are able to develop (financially) sustainable business models. Strategic management scholars have long discussed whether 'the firm' or 'the industry' matters most in defining the room for manoeuvre to (autonomously) create change. Does it matter whether organizations operate in a 'growing', a 'mature' or a 'declining' industry? To what extent are the fortunes of a business closely tied to its industry? In this discussion, Charles Baden-Fuller and John Stopford (1992: 13) presented the general consensus: "There is no such thing as a mature industry, only mature firms. Industries inhabited by mature firms often present great opportunities for the innovative." In other words, the dynamics and performance of an industry – and the extent to which it provides conducive conditions to spur systems change for sustainability – ultimately depends on imaginative organizations that: (1) know how to use their creative capabilities, (2) thoroughly understand the drivers of change within their industry, and (3) dare to articulate, defend and adopt novel approaches to reshape the rules of the 'old competitive game'.

To impact industry dynamics, sustainable business propositions hinge on the successful scalability of their approach to demonstrate both commercial viability and sustainability performance in practice. Horizontal *scaling approaches* consist of increasing the market share through strategies of replication, rolling out and growth. 'Rival' organizations can thereby be treated as direct competitors or as potential collaborators and strategic alliance partners in present and prospective markets. How organizations adopt various sustainability scaling strategies (Box 10.9) and balance *competition and cooperation* influences the pace with which they can trigger *chain adaptation or systems transformation*. Combined, these factors delineate the most strategic (horizontal) KDIs.

SCALING STRATEGIES FOR INCLUSIVE AND SUSTAINABLE BUSINESS

B
O
X

10.9

A core underlying assumption of the 'sustainable business' proposition is the potential to develop *scalable innovations* that create both commercial viability for the business and systemic impact to meet the (unmet) needs of the (unserved) global population. 'Sustainability scaling' requires the *downscaling* of non-sustainable practices while scaling sustainable practices by increasing the share of existing markets for sustainable offerings, entering new markets, developing new sustainability solutions, products or services, or a combination. Four scaling strategies and associated risks can be discerned (London and Hart, 2011; Lijfering and Van Tulder, 2020):

[1] **Scaling up (market penetration):** selling existing products or services to more consumers in the current market. This is a relatively low-risk strategy because companies can leverage current resources and capabilities to increase the market share in familiar contexts.

[2] **Scaling wide (market development):** targeting additional (geographical) markets, distribution channels or customer segments with existing (or slightly adapted) products or services. This 'differentiation' approach is riskier as it involves entering relatively uncharted territory and forces an organization to rethink their business and distribution models.

[3] **Scaling deep (product development):** offering new products or services to existing consumer segments. This typically requires the development of new competencies, access to additional resources and research and development while concurrently downscaling certain existing activities. Downscaling and upscaling at the same time is a higher-risk strategy; it presents a leadership and transition challenge also known as the 'incumbent's curse' (see Box 9.2).

[4] **Scaling across (diversification):** developing new products or services for new markets and value chains. Diversification requires divergence of current products and markets simultaneously, often across countries and value chains. The success of this strategy depends on the degree to which organizations are able to create an enabling business ecosystem and conducive institutional conditions, alone or in collaboration with strategic partners.

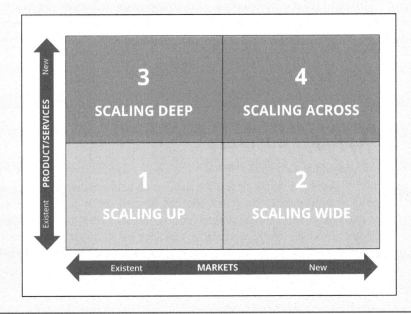

■ *Phase 1 horizontal KDIs* focus on optimally using rivalry as a positive force to drive sustainable product/service offerings and related upscaling, down-scaling and deep-scaling strategies. Competition then primarily revolves around level 2 value propositions (see section 9.4): designing, creating, capturing and scaling value while limiting 'value destruction' (negative exter-nalities) as much as possible. In a competitive environment for sustainable products and services, rivals can distinguish themselves by the innovative-ness of their sustainability solutions and products, the user attractiveness and convenience, competitive pricing as the result of scaling effects, higher productivity levels and better use of (over)capacity. The positive effects of this type of rivalry predominantly materialize in existing markets. Relevant KDIs, then, pertain to strategies that induce an upward spiral for enhancing core competencies and creative capabilities by using competition as a prolific means to (a) lower prices for sustainable products and services in existing markets (upscaling), (b) differentiate and adapt the product port-folio to demand improved sustainable offerings (scaling deep), (c) lower the production costs of sustainable offerings (upscaling), or (d) all the above.

■ *Phase 2 horizontal KDIs* revolve around forging *strategic alliances* with competitors to elevate the level playing field to a higher level of sustainability and deep- and wide-scaling strategies. Coopetition reflects the recognition that rivals must cooperate to some degree in order to *all* overcome vital sustainability thresholds that cannot be surpassed by focusing on one's own competitive advantage alone. Balancing competition and cooperation may take the shape of a frontrunner organization deciding to 'lead by example', in order to instigate industry-wide adoption of sustainability practices. By wielding its discursive and framing powers – to mobilize, normalize and pressurize – the rules of the competitive game can be altered and new benchmarks for success established. KDIs in this phase are hence aimed at pursuing network (wide-scaling) effects: supporting a de facto or de jure (enforced by regulation) level playing field that (a) raises the price for organi-zations of 'destroying value' (negative externalities) or (b) raises the *switching benefits* for organizations to 'scale and spread value' (positive externalities). An example of the first is the collective support for CO_2 taxation by rival companies; emission pricing provides the less polluting companies with a competitive advantage and hence induces an entirely different industry dynamic. An example of the latter is coopetition among health insurance companies to lower the costs of healthcare; by incentivizing prevention rather than curation, new benchmarks for success create first-mover advan-tages for service providers who are active in the prevention segment.

■ *Phase 3 horizontal KDIs* concern cross-sector collaborative and wide- or across-scaling strategies to effectuate systems change. At this stage, coopetition and cross-sector cooperation are aimed at 'co-creating (net) societal value' (section 9.4) by finding novel ways to resolve societal problems. Heading for systems change calls for more radical transformations, which may involve reconfiguring or redesigning entire value chains (e.g. circular, open, inclusive). It may even question the relevance of the 'core organization' concept for industry dynamics, with the recognition that the *interdependencies in the entire network* ultimately define sustainability performance, resilience and 'success'. KDIs, in this context, hence revolve around (a) how to balance one's 'core' and competitive position amidst profoundly changing industry and value chain structures and new 'rules of engagement' and (b) which dynamic capabilities to develop to enhance the effectiveness of cross-sector partnering strategies. Building open, inclusive and effective cross-sector partnership arrangements between key organizations from different societal positions (for-profit/non-profit, Figure 10.2) presents the most important set of KDIs to take into account for progress at this stage. Chapter 12 will further elaborate relevant antecedents of partnering for systems change.

VERTICAL KDIs – REASSESSING BARGAINING POWERS AND VALUE CHAIN ORIENTATIONS [2]

At present, linear – often global – value chains prevail in the economy. Linear value chains are generally organized for optimal efficiency: cost minimization, flexibility and speed through extreme labour division and squeezed lead times, in exclusive and often exploitative relationships. This may make them quite profitable for well-positioned core organizations (section 10.3.2), but also rather fragile, unfair and unsustainable (section 9.4.3). *Intra-chain rivalry* is part and parcel of the market economy, where competition is considered to be a healthy distribution mechanism. *Inter-chain* competitiveness, however, strongly hinges on the degree of alignment, cooperation and capabilities development of and between intra-chain actors. Hence, greater involvement of upstream and downstream organizations in ascending the value ladder for enhanced sustainability implies: (a) modifying intra-chain relationships to foster *upgrading* and *scaling* along the value chain (Box 10.10) and (b) the consequential willingness to redistribute power, benefits and burdens between value chain actors in order to (c) move from linear and exclusive chains focused on maximum efficiency towards circular and inclusive value chains, aimed at ecological sustainability and social fairness.

Vertical KDIs (Table 10.3), therefore, involve the conditions under which the powers of intra-chain suppliers and buyers can be enhanced: to upgrade their business models in order to strengthen the sustainability performance and resilience of the entire value chain – from upstream sourcing to downstream end markets.

INTRA-CHAIN 'UPGRADING' AND VALUE CHAIN 'DEVELOPMENT PATHS'

BOX 10.10

Meeting advanced sustainability requirements can have an ambiguous effect on chain actors. Contingent on chain-specific characteristics of governance, bargaining dynamics and power relations (see section 10.3.2), modifications in operating standards, management systems and product requirements may create significant *barriers* for B2B and B2C chain participants by increasing costs and risks (dependency, lock-in) that restrict business opportunities. Enhanced requirements can also *catalyse* capacity development, however, and improve access to new market segments. For core organizations, applying the principles of *sustainable supply chain management* (SSCM) entails that each chain participant is provided with sufficient scope to develop, fine-tune and articulate a sustainable value proposition and implement a sustainable business model (see section 9.4).

The effects of intra-chain bargaining dynamics can be measured as the firm-level 'upgrading' possibilities provided along the value chain. Upgrading can be defined as augmenting the relative competitive position of a firm to provide it with higher returns (*'value capturing'*) and a more steady and secure income through the development of knowledge, competencies and ability to respond to changing market conditions. Core organizations can create enabling conditions and support systems for intra-chain upgrading as part of a *purposive strategy* to boost the sustainability-driven performance and competitiveness of the entire value chain. For instance, by:

■ Removing barriers or facilitating (easier) access to particular markets, infrastructure, finance, technologies, knowledge and training;

■ Managing risks, volatility and uncertainties in the business environment to establish a certain level of predictability and stability in investment horizons;

■ Fostering intra-chain trust, cooperation and information sharing;

■ Incentivizing sustainable, responsible and inclusive practices by striking a fair balance between 'value creation' and 'value capturing'.

Six types of upgrading have been distinguished in the global value chains literature (Humphrey and Schmitz, 2002; Barrientos et al., 2011):

■ **Process upgrading:** increasing efficiency through the reorganization of production activities or by introducing superior technology;

■ **Product upgrading:** moving into more sophisticated product lines that increase per-unit value;

■ **Functional upgrading:** acquiring new functions (or abandoning existing functions) that increase the skill content of activities;

■ **Inter-chain or inter-sectoral upgrading:** horizontally moving into new yet related activities in different value chains or sectors;

B
O
X
10.10

- **Social upgrading:** enhancing the rights and entitlements of workers as social actors, and the quality of their employment;
- **Environmental upgrading:** altering of production systems and practices that result in positive or less negative environmental outcomes.

Sustainable value chains can develop in different directions as they mature, depending on the characteristics of the chain, the opportunities present, its production base, market demand and the capabilities of chain actors. In general, three paths can be pursued, each with distinct repercussions for intra-chain bargaining relations:

- **The upscaling path** that is based on greater volumes, leading to the possibility of reductions in per-unit cost for a particular product or service (e.g. solar panels);
- **The value-added path** (scaling deep and/or wide), based on greater degrees of integration and cooperation between chain actors for the development of value-adding functions and additional services;
- **The diversification path** (scaling across), whereby inter-chain or inter-sectoral synergies are explored and created, for instance, in the direction of systems integration for fully circular (local) value chains.

Value chain transitioning for sustainability implies that the focus of core organizations on the desired type of supplier (upstream) and buyer (downstream) upgrading, changes per phase:

- **Phase 1 KDIs** focus on upscaling the market potential of existing (more) sustainable products and services; KDIs consequently stress process, environmental and social upgrading efforts along the value chain;
- **Phase 2 KDIs** aim to increase the societal value added of the whole chain; KDIs *additionally* attend to functional and product upgrading efforts along the chain, building on already established minimum levels of social and environmental upgrading;
- **Phase 3 KDIs** centre on inter-chain and inter-sectoral upgrading efforts to enable systems integration and transformational change.

- *Phase 1 downstream KDIs* ultimately pertain to boosting (end-market) buyers' ability and willingness to: (a) pay a higher price ('premium') for products with certified sustainability features, and/or (b) influence consumer behaviour in favour of sustainable products and services. The first factor outlines KDIs on how to reorganize the value chain and 'upgrade' and 'scale' in order to optimally serve and grow this (niche) market. The second dimension involves KDIs on *preference shaping*, *choice architecture* and *nudging strategies* that make the better (more sustainable, responsible) choice 'the easier choice' (Thaler and Sunstein, 2008). Individual consumers have limited ability to discriminate between the manifold sustainability labels and to oversee all sustainability trade-offs involved. Moreover, their fickle motivation to prefer sustainable products over non-sustainable alternatives implies that companies must still take prime responsibility for a sustainable offering at sufficiently competitive prices through strategies of upscaling and environmental, social and process upgrading along the value chain. Under the 'right' conditions, a strategy of forward and/or backward integration could strengthen the efficient provision and continuous improvement of sustainable products.

■ *Phase 1 upstream KDIs* centre on intra-chain approaches that (a) involve individual suppliers in improving the chain's sustainability performance and related differentiation and upscaling strategies; (b) through trajectories of process upgrading (e.g. efficiency, cost-cutting), environmental upgrading (eco-efficiency, recycling) and social upgrading (basic workers' rights, establishing minimum wages); (c) in ways that *preclude* risk externalization, lock-in effects, or reductions in suppliers' upscaling and upgrading potential. Pressing issues include: how to develop, roll out and leverage SSCM codes – and associated sustainability metrics, track and trace systems, monitoring, audit and certification procedures, sustainability reporting – throughout the chain? How to responsibly deal with supplier non-compliance (trade-off between longer-term relationship and reputational damage)? How to support current suppliers in their upgrading process while bonding sustainable suppliers with hard-to-substitute sustainability solutions to the shifting business model? How to prevent that compliance costs result in cost-squeezing trade-offs that undermine improvements in, for instance, labour conditions? Redirecting the orientation of the value chain (e.g. circular, inclusive, fair) requires suppliers to take up part of the responsibility. Accordingly, KDIs in phase 1 must address the enabling function of greater supplier bargaining power to facilitate their own sustainability upscaling, differentiation and upgrading strategies as part of longer-term relationships with lead organizations.

■ *Phase 2 downstream KDIs* involve avenues for engaging buyers in strategies that curtail the general acceptance of non-sustainable products and entice bandwagon effects in end markets. Horizontal alliances for raising overall minimum sustainability requirements can be significantly reinforced by effective vertical alliances along the chain. To that end, downstream KDIs include approaches for: (a) empowering end market buyers to amass a collective demand for sustainable products, and (b) increasing the general level of transparency in competitive offerings of (certified) sustainable products.

The first type of KDIs involves the facilitation of buyer cooperation. Cooperation between independent end-market buyers particularly materialized in food chains, with retailer cooperatives (like Spar or Coop) establishing central buying organizations to enlarge their combined purchasing power vis-à-vis manufacturers, engage in joint promotion efforts and achieve economies of scale. Buyer cooperatives are gaining importance in various domains of the 'sharing economy' (e.g. energy cooperatives) and collective purchasing activities (e.g. housing and consumer cooperatives). The more successful buyer cooperatives are in organizing themselves in professionally managed (sustainable) business models, the more effective they become in creating *positive pull effects* that trigger beneficial intra-industry rivalry and coopetition for sustainable offerings. For those organizations able to serve these pooled markets at scale, first-mover advantages beckon.

The second type of KDIs relates to coordinated approaches to *containing the normalization jungle* (Box 10.5). Harmonized, accredited labelling initiatives lower information asymmetries, facilitate better-informed choice and reduce options for 'cherry-picking' noncommittal labels by (end-market) buyers. In this phase, branding and labelling initiatives are oriented towards meaningfully informing buyers and end users on, for instance, *true pricing* efforts that internalize the costs of negative externalities while upscaling and pushing for positive externalities (e.g. 'fair trade' and 'living wage' initiatives) along the chain.

■ *Phase 2 upstream KDIs* centre on reorganizing the chain's supply side to create positive *push effects* through increased intra-chain alignment and cooperation for sustainability. Two approaches are particularly relevant in this context: (a) empowering suppliers at the base of the value chain to increase their value-adding capacity, and (b) implementation and continuous upgrading of (accredited) standards in SSCM codes.

The first type of KDIs aims to empower suppliers at the sourcing end of the value chain by facilitating the formation of supplier cooperatives. Notably for smallholders, joining forces in cooperatives strengthens their position and ability to scale 'up', 'deep' and 'wide', to purchase and sell at better prices, to increase productivity through process upgrading and also deliver to other buyers and markets (local and global). 'Fair trade' purchasing practices along the chain enable supplier cooperatives to capture their legitimate share of created value and to reinvest their gains in environmentally and socially upgraded and higher value-adding business models. However, fluctuating world market prices easily undermine the empowering effects of smallholder cooperatives. Positive effects can only last if core organizations choose to engage in relationship-based longer-term contracts rather than have the value chain governed by short-term market dynamics (section 10.3.2). Organizations that facilitate supplier cooperatives to materialize and thrive, in fact, invest in sourcing stability, high input quality, and the value chain's overall resilience.

The second type of KDIs concerns intra-chain alignment around implementation and continuous upgrading of sustainability-enhancing standards in ways that beneficially reinforce B2B relationships and expand already established basic levels of environmental, social and value-adding upgrading. Once adopted and *responsibly* implemented (without externalizing burdens to suppliers), standards can considerably lower transaction costs and increase the scaling opportunities ('up' and 'wide') for all chain actors. SSCM codes and sustainability-oriented standards resulting from industry-wide engagement commonly have the highest adoption rate, as these enable suppliers to gain easier access to additional markets (and expand and/or differentiate), rather than create lock-in effects. When regularly fine-tuned and upgraded based on shared experience with the advantages and disadvantages in practice, these standards develop to become progressively effective over time. ISO standards, for instance, are reviewed every five years to establish whether a revision is required, which has triggered 'series' of more detailed elaborations.[15]

■ *Phase 3 downstream KDIs* steer on viable approaches to the provision of *integrated solutions* that serve end users' 'needs'. This ambition requires a redefinition of existing 'markets' as well as aligned *inter-chain upgrading* efforts. Collaborative consumption, 'access over ownership' and peer-to-peer rentals (phenomena of the 'we' and 'sharing' economy) confront suppliers with the challenge of phasing out or downscaling production volumes for present products while redesigning and reorganizing for new types of offerings. In this phase, the relationship with buyers develops into one of co-creation, shared responsibility and *servitization* – the provision of 'outcome as a service' rather than a one-off sale. Leasing constructions are an example of the latter. As ownership resides with the service provider, there is a strong incentive to supply durable, repairable, reusable and recyclable products and systems that are *built to last* rather than *designed to*

---

15 The ISO 14001 series on designing and implementing effective environmental management systems, for instance, is one of the most widely used tools to guide the development of integrated systems in supply chains. It has been expanded into a range of ISO 14000 standards (with ISO 14064 specifically aimed at reducing greenhouse gas emissions).

fail.[16] Servitization business models generally require an integrative systems approach in which core organizations function as 'systems integrators' that orchestrate inter-chain, needs-oriented solutions development. For example, the integrated systems and services strategy of Signify (Philips Lighting) focuses on renting out connected LED-lighting systems for buildings and public spaces – such as cities, airports and shopping malls – rather than selling large volumes of light bulbs. By combining 'internet of things' (IoT) solutions and sensor-driven data, 'smart' integrated systems meet the need for light and public safety in an energy-efficient and sustainability-enhancing way. Similarly, the gradual shift from combustion engine cars to (shared) electric vehicles is stimulating car companies to alter their value proposition from 'selling as many cars as possible', to becoming a *mobility provider*. This switch also comes with a growing interest to co-invest in a sufficiently dense (cross-border) infrastructure of battery-charging stations. Vehicle-to-grid systems that enable battery-electric cars to store and discharge electricity imply further integrative steps between mobility and (renewable) energy generation, storage and provision systems.

▪ ***Phase 3 upstream KDIs*** are directed to organizing (adjacent) value chains to enable the above 'integrated systems' effects in a sustainable manner. This requires greater inter-chain alignment, collaboration between chain actors, and processes of continuous 'inter-chain upgrading' for diversification (across-scaling). The ambition to realize ever higher degrees of circularity, fairness and supplier inclusivity implies that a core organization's relationship with (groups of) suppliers develops into one of *co-production* and *co-development*. A typical organizational approach thereto is the engagement of suppliers in strategic 'platforms'. *Joint platform development* provides a shared set of common design, technological, engineering or production efforts to generate distinct products and services based on similar underpinnings. In some industries, platforms are used to create efficiency (such as the car industry) or to accumulate power and network effects

---

16 *Right-to-repair* legislation that requires companies to make their parts, tools and information available to consumers and repair shops is gaining ground in Europe and the United States. In 2020, the European Commission announced plans for a comprehensive set of right-to-repair rules that includes mobile phones, tablets and laptops. These rules should remove obstacles that prevent repair, resale and reuse by making repairs more appealing, systematic (through producer's guarantees) and cost-efficient. The plans aim to foster sustainable consumer choices, a culture of reuse, support for second-hand goods and raw material markets, improved reparability, extended lifespan of products (by harmonized mandatory labelling of product durability and estimated lifespan) and reduction of electronic waste to push for sustainable production.

(as with internet companies). However, platform approaches can also be used to bolster the sustainability performance and differentiation potential of an entire industry. KDIs then relate to defining viable strategies that merge suppliers from different value chains into one platform, with the purpose of boosting synergistic effects and the development of high value-added – but competitively priced – solutions to societal needs. Platform alliances can be found in a variety of sectors. For example, the LiveKindly Collective – an alliance of mission-aligned plant-based brands aspiring to a sustainable global food system – leverages expertise on strategy, expansion, marketing and open innovation to scale plant-based food production by affiliated firms – at speed while creating relationship-based partnerships across the supply chain (from seed to fork) to enable growth.[17] In pharmaceuticals, innovative platforms have become a pivotal condition for accelerated vaccine development, diagnostic capacity and large-scale vaccine deployment to contain rapidly spreading and adapting viruses – such as Covid-19.[18] Collaborative vaccine and diagnostic platforms create flexibility, speed and scale, which enables boosted development, manufacturing and distribution in parallel. Purpose-driven platform creators may become the next 'core' organization in value chains (as has been the case in the internet economy).

LATERAL KDIs – USING THE INNOVATIVE POWERS OF NEW ENTRANTS [3]

When the value chain is seen as a closed system of relationships, the destabilizing arrival of new entrants and substitute products, services and technologies might be defined as a 'threat' – as Porter does. In transition processes, however, new entrants and substitutes should also be appraised for their potential to unlock opportunities and 'complementary' inputs for societal value creation and conducive change. Two types of relevant 'new entrants' can thereby be distinguished. First, incoming core organizations that introduce a 'new way' of doing business and possess all the crucial resources, means and capabilities to develop their 'alternative' at scale. Such new entrances usually have an instant effect on incumbents and alter the chain's horizontal dynamics – with further repercussions for vertical value chain dynamics. Second, social enterprises and start-ups that carve out 'market niches' on the merits of their (technological or organizational) sustainable 'niche innovation', purpose-driven value proposition and/or novel sustainable business model. These 'pioneering entrepreneurs' can be(come) an innovative force with the potential to impact mainstream practice, industry dynamics and, ultimately, the pace and direction of sustainability transitions. A growing body of

---

17 https://thelivekindlyco.com/the-collective/#about.
18 "This is how we prevent the next pandemic", https://youtu.be/OJtblo12Uxl.

sustainability literature documents how relatively small actors from outside the value chain can play a vital role in sparking and furthering systems change, both direct and indirectly: (a) by showcasing the commercial viability of their (alternative or complementary) value proposition in the market, and by providing 'proofs of concept'[19] for their business model; (b) by raising awareness about societal issues and entrepreneurial ways to address them – with consumers, clients, prospective employees and impact investors; and (c) by instigating improvements in industry standards, certification and labelling initiatives, and fuelling discussions on the need to change government policy (Van Dijk et al., 2020).

Lateral KDIs focus on the potential role that new entrants – big and small – can play in affecting an incumbent's business model, either as 'substitutes' or as 'complements' to existing practice. How incumbents respond to (more sustainable) newcomers is contingent on their sustainability ambition, industry dynamics in different transition phases and actors' resource base, capabilities and strategic repertoire, whilst conditioned by intellectual property and competition policy regimes for acquiring knowledge and companies (section 10.4.1). Lateral KDIs ultimately cover two dimensions, each related to intricate trade-offs (Table 10.3):

- *The relation with new entrants:* from closed and competitive interaction primarily motivated by protecting one's market position and preventing substitution effects, to more open and mutually reinforcing relationships that build on – and make optimal use of – complementarities;

- *The function of the relationship* (combining upgrading and scaling potential): ranging from directed at product development to pursuing systems change.

BOX 10.11

LATERAL SCALING AND UPGRADING STRATEGIES – SUSTAINABLE INNOVATION JOURNEYS FOR SYSTEMS CHANGE

In transition processes to sustainability, the arrival of 'new entrants' can be considered both a consequence and an enabler of transformative change. The lateral influence of newcomers adds new ideas, innovations, organizational models and systems dynamics to the value chain and, accordingly, functions as a trigger for either stepwise (evolutionary) or more profound (radical) change of markets and industries. The literature on socio-technical transitions speaks of *sustainable innovation journeys* to refer to the

---

19 'Proof of concept' refers to the process of testing innovations in real-life settings to validate assumptions and making improvements so that investment decisions on scaling can be made more confidently.

(long-term) trajectories that 'sustainable niche innovations' travel – and the various barriers, lock-in and scaling challenges they must overcome – before they finally become integrated, institutionalized and anchored in mainstream markets and provisioning systems (Geels, 2019). Innovations are thereby broadly defined: they comprise not only technical but also social, organizational and business model innovations.

In the context of horizontal and vertical value chain dynamics, the 'sustainable innovation journey' can be understood as the outcome of combined *'upgrading' and 'upscaling' effects* in consecutive phases along an S-shaped path (Figure 10.6). These effects result from the interplay between 'incumbents' and 'new entrants' (incoming core organizations, start-ups, social enterprises). Their dynamic interaction and strategies in different phases define the *potential*, *pace and direction* of sustainability-oriented upgrading and upscaling processes as either incremental adjustments or as more radical and disruptive change. Basically, new entrants can induce two types of positive effects on sustainability transitioning:

- **Substitution:** replacing existing technologies, practices and business models with more effective, better (societally) valued/accepted, and/or more efficient (price/performance) sustainable alternatives.

- **Complementarity:** adding technological and/or organizational capabilities to already existing practices to augment the overall sustainability performance of the value chain. Complementary solutions and practices can be symbiotic – by filling 'voids' in the value chain or by enabling novel resource combinations – and in consecutive phases can become incorporated without major switching costs.

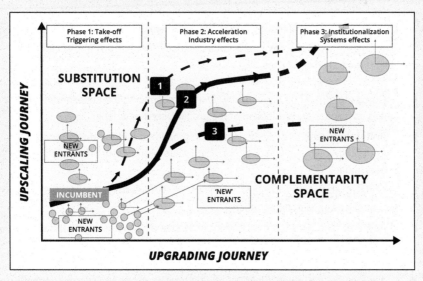

Figure 10.6 Interaction effects in the upgrading-upscaling journey

Inspired by: Geels (2019); Geels and Schot (2007); Grin et al. (2010); Simons and Nijhof (2021).

B
O
X

10.11

Substitution effects are typically created by (large) incoming core organizations that have all vital resource combinations available to introduce their 'alternative' offering at scale. Complementarity effects are typically created by (smaller) start-ups and social enterprises that have innovative solutions for (specific) value chain activities but lack resources – especially in early phases – to organize and introduce their sustainable niche innovation at sufficient scale (and competitive prices).

Strategic games and repertoire

While navigating their 'sustainable innovation journey', incumbent organizations must decide how to make beneficial use of new entrants' innovative potential, to achieve their own sustainability objectives more effectively, at greater scale, smarter, faster or better. *Driving the S-curve* upwards implies that incumbents enter into 'strategic games' with newcomers – of varying size, power base and positioning – with the aim of reinforcing positive outcomes for sustainability (positive-sum games). To that end, incumbents have to manage substitution and complementarity effects, along with influencing industry dynamics, by (a) timely balancing *pull* (scaling) and *push* (upgrading) effects in markets and the value chain, while (b) managing the relationships with newcomers in their changing roles as competitor, supplier or partner, in different phases of the journey. If successful, the core organization can establish a steeper S-curve (accelerated 'upgrading' and 'upscaling', path 1); when less successful, a more flattened and elongated innovation journey lies ahead (for instance, as a result of 'mainstreaming' difficulties, path 3). The ultimate consequence of trailing behind is decline.

Core organizations have five strategies at their disposal in their approach to new entrants. They have to figure out what strategy to use, at what moment in transaction phases, towards or with whom, to engender what type of effect. Table 10.4 reflects some of the most likely strategies deployed under circumstances of substitution or complementarity, vis-à-vis core new entrants and smaller start-ups and social enterprises, in three transition phases.

- **Compete:** enter into direct rivalry, aimed at enhancing the price/performance and sustainability contribution of the product, service or technology;
- **Imitate:** emulate or copy the innovation presented by the newcomer in order to upgrade own sustainability practices, value proposition, offering, and business model;
- **Collaborate:** forge a strategic alliance to scale the effects of complementary capabilities in each organization;
- **Acquire:** take over the new entrant or technology, to accelerate the downscaling and phasing-out of less sustainable practices while upscaling more sustainable practices;
- **Accept and co-exist:** allow the new entrant to thrive as a relevant complement to the own business model and value chain – also referred to as the 'symbiosis' option.

Table 10.4 Using lateral dynamics as a force for positive change: strategic repertoires

INNOVATION THROUGH		NEW ENTRANTS							
		CORE				SOCIAL / START-UP			
	SUBSTITUTION	Preferred strategy	Phase 1	Phase 2	Phase 3	Preferred strategy	Phase 1	Phase 2	Phase 3
		Compete	■			Compete	■		
		Imitate				Imitate			
		Collaborate		■		Collaborate			■
		Acquire			■	Acquire			
		Accept				Accept	■		
	COMPLEMEN-TARITY	Preferred strategy	Phase 1	Phase 2	Phase 3	Preferred strategy	Phase 1	Phase 2	Phase 3
		Compete		■		Compete			
		Imitate			■	Imitate		■	
		Collaborate		■		Collaborate		■	■
		Acquire				Acquire			
		Accept	■			Accept	■		

B O X 10.11

■ *Phase 1 lateral KDIs* focus on optimally using the (potential) rivalry of new entrants as a driving force to organize for better sustainable product/service offerings at a greater scale. It denotes a 'take-off' of the sustainable innovation journey in search of scaling and upgrading opportunities in a dynamic and ambiguous environment. Triggering events (Chapter 7) stir up (societal) needs for more resilient, attainable and affordable solutions (pull effects), and so create 'space' for innovations as competitive sustainable offerings (push effects) to emerge, enter the market, establish a foothold and gain market share. An increasing number of newcomers can thus be anticipated, but their impact on relevant push (upgrading) and pull (scaling) factors – and the implications thereof for the pace and direction of sustainability paths – is often far more difficult to read, particularly in early phases. Since the potential of various new technologies and concepts – either as substitute or complement to current practices – is yet to crystallize, deciding on the intensity with which to pursue the sustainable innovation trajectory is challenging. Hence, the preliminary approach towards newcomers is likely to be exploratory and focused on gaining experiential knowledge. To navigate and balance between substitution and complementarity effects in phase 1, two types of KDIs should be considered: (1) relevant approaches for making full use of the 'pull effects' (upscaling potential) that entrants' substitute offerings can incite; (2) apt approaches for using the 'push effects' (upgrading potential) of complementary sustainable solutions.

The first type of KDIs pertains to *substitute offerings* presented by large entrants from adjacent industries. Rivalry and increased competition may prove a beneficial force *if* they induce downward pressure on prices for sustainable products. Affordability makes sustainable products attainable and more appealing to a larger number of customers. Successful expansion of the market segment may gradually erode demand for non-sustainable alternatives and, over time, replace it altogether. What can be considered as an effective (positive-sum game) strategy towards entrants with substitute offerings is contingent on the extent to which: (a) rival sustainable offerings and innovative practices can be emulated; (b) new entrance (notably by recognized brands) adds legitimacy, positive reputation and value to the market segment for more sustainable products, leading to greater customer acceptance and further market development; (c) increased competition can trigger beneficial scaling effects with upstream suppliers; (d) increased competition raises the barrier for aspiring new entrants.

The second type of KDIs concerns the beneficial use of *complementary sustainability solutions*, primarily developed by entrepreneurial start-ups and social enterprises. These smaller entrants pioneer, develop and nurture 'sustainable niche markets' that are largely overlooked by incumbents or disregarded as insufficiently attractive. The technological and organizational innovations developed in these niches may point to interesting 'upgrading' opportunities to enhance the sustainability performance of the existing value chain. Specific niche innovations may qualify as a pivotal 'missing link' in enabling novel combinations of capabilities, resources and methods for improved societal value creation. Relevant KDIs in this phase accordingly focus on learning and on gaining experiential knowledge from niche developments by start-ups. This could include providing financial means to selected start-ups ('seed funding') and access to relevant knowledge and infrastructure in return for hands-on experiential knowledge. Another – low-profile – approach is to closely monitor developments and observe whether start-ups and social enterprises prove capable of scaling their sustainable niche innovation in the market and make it through the 'valley of death'.

▪ *Phase 2 lateral KDIs* are geared to acceleration. Decisions include the conditions under which vital linkages with innovative entrants can be established to boost upgrading (sustainable innovation push) and upscaling (market pull) effects while concurrently allowing for controlled processes of 'creative destruction' of unsustainable practices in the value chain and business model. Coupling their own sustainable innovation path with the innovation pathways of innovative entrants inherently involves a delicate balancing act: between timely substitution (the replacement, downscaling or phase-out of unsustainable practices) and complementarity effects (the uptake, integration and synergetic use of novel capacities and concepts). The acceleration effect thereof depends on the availability of relevant *best in class practices* and the organization's internal 'absorptive capacity' for their internalization in core operations. If advanced sustainability practice can be successfully demonstrated, new industry-wide benchmarks and upgraded sustainability standards can be established for broader diffusion and uptake. In phase 2, strategic alliances and forms of coopetition with innovative actors are both a conditional and enabling factor for speeding up change, expanding the market, and advancing broad customer/consumer acceptance (critical mass). Accordingly, KDIs should reveal the trade-offs of and logic for choosing specific strategies, arrangements and allies.

The *complementarities-oriented* relationship with newcomers can thereby develop along three routes: by emulation, strategic alliances or acquisition. *Emulating* the 'best practice' of start-ups becomes vital if their sustainable niche innovations represent scalable business models and successful 'proofs of concept' that are of relevance to the whole industry. Tesla, for example, induced significant push effects on conventional car producers to emulate its lead after it had accumulated sufficient capital to develop a competitive electric car market. *Allying* with best in class social enterprises can be relevant if an alliance could broaden the product portfolio to include a more sustainable offering or provide experiential knowledge on serving and growing a specific niche market. Alliances risk losing momentum, however, if partnering crowds out impetus to internalize gained insights for their own deep and wide-scaling purposes.[20] The relevance of *acquiring* 'best practice' initiatives as an auspicious strategy to accelerate change depends on the extent to which successful integration of acquired capabilities can boost economies of scale, learning, expansion of new market segments and the potential to diversify towards more advanced sustainable solutions.[21]

---

20 Dutch incumbent telecom provider KPN allied with FairPhone in the distribution of conflict-mineral free, fairly produced and repairable and recyclable smartphones, supported by a guaranteed delivery contract. The alliance enabled KPN to immediately tap into a niche market of conscious consumers and gain additional (experiential) knowledge on the complexities of responsible smartphone production, which fitted its CSR ambition. KPN failed to successfully internalize and mainstream the FairPhone principles in its business model. Progress on further scaling stalled with both companies.

21 Positive examples of successful internalization strategies include the acquisitions of Ben & Jerry's and the Vegetarian Butcher by Unilever and Natura's acquisition of The Body Shop. In contrast to L'Oréal −former owner of The Body Shop − Natura had already progressed further on the sustainability upscaling/upgrading curve, which presumably makes internal alignment easier to achieve.

Substitution-oriented innovations offered by (more) sustainable entrants from adjacent industries may constitute a direct alternative for mainstream business models. Incumbents have to determine how to speed up change for *more sustainable business models* and how to facilitate the formation of new 'innovative combinations' – of capabilities, resources, methods and partners – to effectuate upgraded provisioning at a competitive scale. Consequential decisions involve (1) the controlled but decisive 'creative destruction' of unsustainable practices, models and technologies, (2) managing 'cannibalizing effects' on the existing business model 'in flux', and (3) reorganization of (value chain) activities to internalize the changes, standardize new practices and maximize 'increasing returns to adoption' along the value chain. Intensified intra-chain cooperation (vertical dynamics) and inter-chain coopetition/collaboration (horizontal dynamics) can accelerate the search for scalable 'innovative combinations'. Acquiring or partnering with successful start-ups can feed into that process. Alliances, covenants and industry platforms are another way to press for stepped-up efforts through industry-wide initiatives and commitments in such contested areas as, for instance, the transition to healthier diets (lowering the sugar, fat, and salt content in food products); the shift to sustainable apparel (from 'fast' fashion to 'slow' fashion); the transition to inclusive access to pharmaceuticals (a responsible mix of patented medicine production and generic medicines). Key decisions thus focus on how to forge inter-chain alliances that (a) stress the innovative potential of new combinations and new entrants,[22] and (b) are capable of internalizing game-changing trade-offs related to transformational change within industries.

▪ *Phase 3 lateral KDIs* focus on *institutionalization* as an enabling condition for continued progression on *systems integration*. Relevant decisions at this stage relate to collaborative *cross-industry* scaling and upgrading strategies to effectuate broader systems change, and approaches for 'societal embedding' anchored in mainstream markets, regulatory frameworks, user habits, views of 'normality', professional standards and technical capabilities (Geels, 2019). Opportunities for systems integration rely on the synergistic potential of cross-industry initiatives to leverage 'complementarity effects' (Figure 10.6) that address (wicked) societal needs (Chapter 5).

---

22 Safaricom – a large telecom company minority-controlled by Vodafone from the UK – entered the banking industry in Kenya by making 'mobile money' available to all, including the poor, through an extensive value chain of small kiosks. In doing do, they revolutionized the financial sector by addressing the needs of the majority of the population for 'access to finance', at the expense of the regular banking sector.

Cross-sector collaboration with key players from different societal origins (archetypes 1–8, section 6.3) can significantly reinforce that ambition and significantly broaden the scope for auspicious opportunities. Phase 3 KDIs hence revolve around (pro)active approaches for mapping, selecting and bonding key organizations from relevant societal sectors that bring in vital complementary capabilities to facilitate systems change at scale. Relevant KDIs should inform: (1) the degree of complementarity to be achieved in terms of capabilities, positioning, power base and sectoral origins; (2) the 'fit' of the partnership configuration in view of the societal need it seeks to address; (3) the conditions under which collaborative arrangements will be conducive to all; (4) the degree of internalization within each participating organization, at sufficiently strategic levels of decision-making; and (5) how to remain receptive to substitute innovations with the potential to provide even more sustainable solutions. Collaborative arrangements that create entry barriers to prospective new partners run the risk of becoming static and stifling constructive competition (Chapter 12).

10.4.3 International KDIs – managing distance and country portfolios

Within an international arena, 'institutional voids' confront organizations with the challenge of delicately balancing *rights and responsibilities* and *rules-based and principles-based* approaches across national borders (Chapter 6). Internationally active companies have to work with these conditions and, correspondingly, manage relevant 'distance' dimensions (e.g. institutional, administrative, developmental, cultural, normative, geographic, see section 6.5) – concurrently and in a responsible way. Amidst ever-changing geopolitical developments, international businesses are challenged to find operative strategies that uphold the corporate sustainability ambition as well as appropriately reckon with local realities and divergent CSR regimes in various host countries. Applying the principles of 'sustainable multinational business' (Box 10.7) hence entails an inherently complex harmonizing and synthesizing act between: (a) *internalization of markets* and related *liabilities and risks* – as a solution to market and regulatory failure; and (b) *internalization of norms* and associated *responsibilities and duties* – as an answer to institutional failure.

International business literature discerns four 'logics' of corporate internationalization that condition the scope for implementing sustainability approaches across borders: *trading, multi-domestic, global* and *glocal* (Van Tulder, 2015). Companies that primarily engage in international sourcing and export activities – the 'trading' model – operate from their home base with a minimal local presence abroad. The 'market-seeking' (sales) and 'efficiency-seeking' (low prices) logic of trade-driven companies imply that they have limited vested interest in local sustainability and relationships. Once organizations set up substantial assets abroad that they actively manage (e.g. factories, plantations, mines, wholly owned sales and distribution channels), they become a 'multinational enterprise' (MNE). Investing in long-term local presence suggests that organizations must consider in far more detail whether to adapt to host country practices – or not, but with good reason – and what principles to sustain, customize or emphasize. This type of consideration reflects, in particular, the *'at-entry' dynamics* that many MNEs face when starting preliminary negotiations with local representatives (section 10.3.3).

After entry, strategic challenges change. The focus then shifts to how to upgrade and upscale (or downscale) the *portfolio of countries* in taking next steps to higher levels of sustainability. The established country portfolio thereby defines the starting position from which to consider paths of strategic changes and the associated *switching costs and benefits* these would entail. Change trajectories include a range of possible options and outcomes. In practice, adjustments could involve disinvesting from certain activities in specific countries (sales, sourcing, assembly, customer support services, finance) while increasing investments in others. They could comprise a reshoring strategy, the relocation of activities, expansion of the international presence, or withdrawal from certain regions to correct for 'international overstretch' and inherent fragilities in order to restore focus, performance and resilience.

Distinct 'internationalization logics' suggest different conditions and options for using international (re)positioning powers as a positive force. Essentially, all MNEs face two types of coordination challenges that determine their strength in effectuating change: (1) *vertical integration* – how to manage the relationship between corporate headquarters and local subsidiaries (centralized/decentralized decision-making; hierarchical/dispersed prioritization, programming, learning; standardized/fragmented policies, norms, procedures, codes); and (2) *horizontal coordination* – how to coherently align activities across all countries of operations. Both dimensions affect the extent to which an MNE can internalize market, regulatory and institutional failures (Box 10.7) and leverage norms for better outcomes across borders. The *integration-responsiveness grid* – introduced by Christopher Bartlett and Sumantra Ghoshal (1989) – provides a relevant conceptual frame on combining global integration and local responsiveness.

Accordingly, KDIs for managing the country portfolio concentrate on establishing the appropriate combination of vertical integration and local responsiveness to facilitate the implementation, upgrading and upscaling of the international sustainability ambition. KDIs on what cross-border sustainability approach to adopt inform decisions on: (a) the type of 'societal license' to pursue and applicable principles to adopt; (b) responsibly dealing with differences in regulatory regimes (e.g. taxation, human rights, labour standards); and (c) how to prevent a race to the bottom and foster a race to the top (Table 10.5).

Table 10.5 Internationalization-related KDIs

	LEVEL 1	LEVEL 2	LEVEL 3	LEVEL 4
	Tipping point ⟹	Key tipping point ⟹	Tipping point ⟹	
KDIs related to:	*1. Trigger*	*2. Internal alignment*	*3. External alignment*	
	LIABILITY/RIGHTS/RISK		RESPONSIBILITY/DUTIES/ OPPORTUNITY	
Internationalization logic	Multi-domestic: adaptation of business model and norms to locations	Regional or Global: standardization of markets and norms across locations	Glocal: balancing standardization and local adaptation across locations	
Integration - responsiveness	Low vertical integration, high local responsiveness	High vertical integration, limited local responsiveness	High vertical integration, high local responsiveness	
ICR approach	**ICR 2.0: International Corporate** *Responsiveness*	**ICR 3.0: International Corporate** *Responsibility*	**ICR 4.0: International** *Community* **Responsibility**	
Positive use of international power	Internalization of markets to mitigate market and regulatory failure	Internalization of norms to mitigate governance and ethical failure	Synthesis: internalizing markets and norms for societal value creation across borders	
License to	. . . Operate	. . . Scale	. . . Experiment	
Orientation to principles	Do no harm, 'Respect' and 'Remedy' (ex post) negative externalities	Help to 'Protect' as act of 'corporate citizenship'	'Empower' local communities and business ecosystems	
Envisaged outcome (Chapter 6)	Preventing race to the bottom by adopting international '*rules*' on taxation, responsibility, transparency, etc.	Supporting race to the top by (also) adopting international *principles* on taxation, technology protection, labour rights	Supporting race to the top by contributing to *effective global governance* for sustainability	

IMPROVING LOCAL RESPONSIVENESS – PHASE 1 KDIs

A *multi-domestic approach* to sustainability rests on an adaptation strategy; the organization takes the local CSR/sustainability regime of each host country as a given, adjusts its norms and principles accordingly, and tries to be accepted as a loyal corporate citizen. In practice, this orientation to country portfolio management creates sizable coordination and integration problems, as sustainability regimes vary widely around the world. Dispersed realities make it challenging to establish a sufficient level of coherence and coordination in corporate sustainability ambition, implementation strategies, pace and practice. Furthermore, an approach of cultural or moral 'relativism' ('when in Rome, do as the Romans do') makes an organization susceptible to pressures to abide by lower standards in countries where human and workers' rights, gender equality, environmental protection, bribery and transparency are considered of subsidiary importance. By practising different standards in different countries, the risk of reputational damage looms large.

Phase 1 KDIs hence emphasize strategies for responsively limiting, mitigating and remedying the negative effects that are prone to emerge from coordination, integration and harmonization difficulties. A multi-domestic approach to sustainability heavily relies on well-organized risk and reputation management across borders. An important strategic alignment challenge, therefore, lies in upgrading headquarters' coordination powers to establish a sufficient level of societal trust *(license to operate)* – in all countries of operations – while enhancing local subsidiaries' responsiveness to national sustainability issues and societal needs. This ambition involves three types of KDIs:

- **Vertical KDIs** pertain to the establishment of effective coordination mechanisms between the headquarters and subsidiaries to mitigate the operational, strategic, sustainability-related risks inherent to a dispersed portfolio of decentralized operations. KDIs should include policies for responsible and accountable use of internal 'arbitrage' mechanisms, which are commonly applied by MNEs to manage operational risks (e.g. currency exchange rates, internal transfer prices, taxation rates); they also cover harmonization of internal policies and procedures through an organization-wide adoption of applicable international rules and due diligence principles – such as the OECD Guidelines for MNEs.

- **Horizontal KDIs** focus on supporting local subsidiaries in effectively managing their national stakeholder relations, by making local experiences with stakeholder engagement strategies relevant to other subsidiaries ('leveraging lessons learned'). Both corporate and subsidiaries' 'license to operate' critically depend on the capability to translate and apply elemental international principles – such as 'free, prior and informed consent' – into national contexts and internalize (experiential) good practice for continuous improvement.

- **Strategic KDIs** cover avenues for improving the congruence (strategic 'fit') between the country portfolio and overall ICR ambitions from an efficiency and optimization point of view. Such strategies should increase the level of cohesion and simplify management processes. Consequential adjustments could imply a reduced spread of countries to better manage risks or, for instance, an intensified presence in certain regions to leverage (nexus) opportunities (see section 10.5.4).

UPGRADING GLOBAL COORDINATION – PHASE 2 KDIs

A *global approach* to sustainability pursues a centrally coordinated yet globally applicable corporate sustainability approach – based on universal principles – to which an organization commits in all host bases. Instead of taking the various national CSR/sustainability regimes as a given, the global approach selects those *supranational* (global or regional) standards, norms and values that can be implemented in *all* countries of operations. 'Moral universalism' and 'hypernorms' (Donaldson and Dunfee, 1999, see Box 6.1) make it easier to coordinate and coherently manage across countries. The global approach enables high levels of vertical integration between corporate headquarters and subsidiaries and capitalizes on efficiency effects derived from 'top-down' coordination processes, global brand image, and standardized policies, procedures and codes. Nevertheless, central coordination also restrains corporate responsiveness to local customs, needs and realities and, therefore, is prone to eliciting tense relationships with local stakeholders.

Global MNEs that implement higher levels of sustainability than a local CSR regime requires, may activate 'upgrading' dynamics that encourage local industries and regulatory bodies to follow suit. In practice, however, standardized norms may also reflect a form of 'ethical imperialism', with the foreign company superimposing its norms, principles and practices on host country stakeholders, irrespective of local customs and country-specific (business ecosystem) contexts. Global MNEs like McDonald's or Coca-Cola – with standardized products for 'standardized' tastes – have hence been treated with considerable distrust and opposition from local stakeholder groups.[23] To overcome the consequential trust gap, global MNEs with sustainable leadership ambitions must earn their 'legitimacy', principally by creating *tangible* 'positive externalities' (level 3 effects) – such as job creation, improved working conditions, decent wages, equal opportunity, skills development, and knowledge and technology transfer.

Phase 2 KDIs for positive change, therefore, emphasize strategies for the continuous 'upgrading' of the *overall* level of sustainability in *all global operations*. A global approach to societal value creation critically hinges on the general acceptance of standardized practices and norms at a sufficiently high and

---

23 Failure to adapt to local CSR-regimes explains, for instance, the retreat of Walmart in a number of European markets. After entering Germany, Walmart was unwilling or unable to adapt to the German co-determination regime that provides trade unions with a place on the board, and raise minimum wage levels to German standards. Walmart retreated. The global expansion of (platform) companies like Uber and Amazon encounters comparable bottlenecks where the business model infringes on nationally established 'social contracts'.

exemplary ('brand image') level of sustainability. This societal *license to scale* ambition involves three types of KDIs:

- **Vertical KDIs** focus on the strengthening of headquarters' *dynamic capabilities* to drive continuous improvements in adopted ICR principles and sustainability standards, and to coordinate their effective implementation in *all* operational contexts. KDIs should include criteria for the selection of applicable supranational standards, norms and principles that enable the sustainability 'upgrading' ambition at a global scale. The universal principles of the Global Goals (SDGs) – which match the supranational scope – are of particular relevance for global MNEs. The choice for specific standards, norms and principle should reckon with strategic and reputational risks that are integral to centralized decision-making and local embedding in dispersed realities.

- **Horizontal KDIs** include the selection of promising pilot projects around the world that provide relevant insights for internationally scalable, sustainability-enhancing change trajectories. Relevant 'proofs of concept' established in one subsidiary should be replicable for other subsidiaries in different local contexts and preferably have a positive impact on local business ecosystems and host regulatory regimes.

- **Strategic KDIs** particularly concentrate on managing the global intention-realization gap. Penalties for not 'walking the talk' – or being slow in internalizing international principles on just taxation, labour and human rights, decent wages or ecological protection – are especially high for global MNEs, as global brands are highly vulnerable to reputational effects. Global MNEs with reputable, strong brands are well-positioned to develop and leverage their exemplary role as 'agents for positive change'. To credibly substantiate that ambition, KDIs should cover strategies for the establishment of cross-sector partnership arrangements on substantive sustainability issues and active management of strategic partnership portfolios, preferably with stakeholders that match the supranational presence.

SYNTHESIZING GLOBAL COORDINATION AND LOCAL RESPONSIVENESS – PHASE 3 KDIs

A *glocalization* approach to sustainability seeks to harmonize global integration and local responsiveness. It applies universal principles (such as the UN Global Compact, see Box 8.1) in such a way that local contexts, needs and realities are accommodated as much as possible. This 'best of both worlds' synthesis makes the *glocal* approach a better fit as a flexible response to the many complexities and conflicting expectations, demands and pressures that are an integral part of global operations. It also provides an expedient position for identifying and creating opportunities for societal value creation.

Glocal MNEs are committed to achieving a long-term (sustainable) competitive advantage in all countries in which they are active. Local embedding and active engagement with local stakeholders allow them to differentiate the global sustainability approach to specific local needs to meet that end. Glocal MNEs that *think global, and act local* are best positioned to synthesize the dual internalization challenge (markets/risks and norms/responsibilities) and maximize social value creation across borders (see Box 10.7). But they are also prone to sizable coordination challenges. An ever-broadening involvement in a large number of local alliances necessitates sophisticated internal coordination, advanced levels of external stakeholder management, and ample absorptive capacity to probe, internalize and harness opportunities for shared value creation. Accordingly, phase 3 KDIs for glocal MNEs are threefold:

■ *Vertical KDIs* focus on coordinated approaches that facilitate the integration of relevant local experiences into one global ICR approach. KDIs include the continuous upgrading of subsidiaries' *responsive capabilities*, societal legitimacy and their local embeddedness through meaningful stakeholder engagement. KDIs also cover the establishment of structures for internal learning to enable (1) internal absorption of 'best practices' and experiential insights from dispersed activities, and (2) their subsequent translation into scalable sustainability approaches to be leveraged across borders – where and when applicable.

■ *Horizontal KDIs* encompass strategic approaches to effectively organize stakeholders for localized shared value creation. When managed well (see section 5.5 and Chapter 12), glocal MNEs can wield their convening powers to activate collective action on societal issues that reach across borders (Chapter 6). KDIs concern avenues for meaningful engagement in 'hybrid' forms of governance that involve (local) representative groups of stakeholders, which ideally provide the MNE with a (local) societal '*license to experiment*' with more transformational sustainability ambitions. Such approaches call for strategic stakeholder dialogue and active community involvement, directed at collaborative advantage and the creation of common-pool goods (section 5.2.2).

■ *Strategic KDIs* synthesize horizontal and vertical KDIs into a sophisticated, international cross-sector partnership portfolio that is aligned with the organization's country portfolio. Two approaches can thereby be considered: (1) to ally with international NGOs – which can lower internal coordination costs, but at the expense of local embeddedness; or (2) to create a diverse and representative network of local strategic partnerships, which increases the local 'license to experiment', yet significantly increases internal coordination costs.

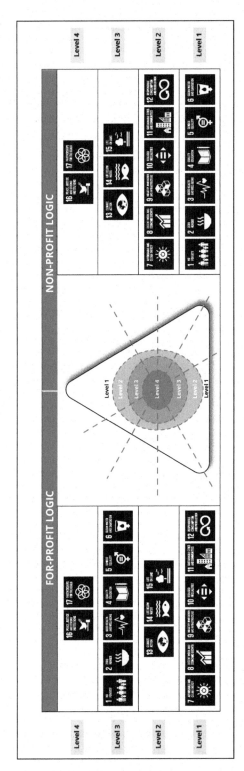

Figure 10.7 Prioritizing SDGs along responsibilities lines

10.5 USING POWERS TO MAKE THE SDGs ACTIONABLE

The SDGs have developed into a leading frame for sustainable development that gradually changes the business ecosystem – and selection environment – in which private sector organizations operate. The SDG framework has given impetus to convergence in norm-setting mechanisms within the standardization, certification, accreditation and (non-financial) reporting landscapes (section 10.3.2). It also increasingly functions as a 'benchmarking frame' to discern to what extent organizations have aligned their ambitions, business model, value chain and core activities with their sustainable development context. Those organizations that are able to co-shape and co-evolve with their changing environment – in terms of societal expectations, needs, values, norms, dynamics and performance – can be expected to be more successful in the longer run than those that fail to anticipate and adapt to change (see Chapters 7 and 8). Hence, the challenge that particularly large organizations manifestly face is how to make the SDGs 'actionable' within the contours of their direct and indirect spheres of influence, in a meaningful and 'powerful' way.

In this section, we identify four 'entry points' for the process of navigating prioritization and strategic decision-making that follows from the ambition to align core operations with the SDGs. These stepping stones for analysis can be used in conjunction; all require an informed consideration of contexts, organizational 'logics', business models and operational realities. Used sequentially, they encourage the process of identifying vital nodes for leverage that (1) enable a more insightful strategizing and coherent management of sustainability trade-offs and synergies, and (2) reveal opportunities for a more impactful use of the organization's power base for the achievement of sustainability ambitions.

10.5.1 SDG prioritization along 'primary responsibilities' lines

The SDG-agenda does not prioritize specific SDGs over others. Rather, the framework of 17 SDGs and 169 SDG-targets are intentionally presented as a unified and indivisible whole to stress that they are fundamentally interdependent and interlinked (Chapter 2). Still, for organizations to meaningfully align their sustainability ambitions with the SDG-agenda, certain (sets of) SDGs and SDG-targets will appear more proximate and imminent to their core operations and hence closer to the direct sphere of influence to address than others. Not all SDGs are equally 'actionable' for all types of organizations (see archetypes 2–8, section 6.3); not all SDG-targets are equally proximate to all sectors. Accordingly, for-profit and non-profit organizations are predisposed to prioritize different (sets of) SDGs at distinct levels of engagement (levels 1, 2, 3, 4). Depending on an organization's societal position and governance logic, a certain 'hierarchy' in interests for specific SDGs can be discerned (Figure 10.7).

On a general level, organizations grounded in a *for-profit logic* initially focus foremost on the SDG framework's economic targets. Their level 1 priorities are predominantly defined by SDGs 7–12, which tend to be closest to their day-to-day activities, primary responsibilities and direct sphere of influence. Most ecology-oriented SDGs (13–15) – associated with the negative impacts of their operations – are a second-level priority (limiting, mitigating, preventing negative effects). Addressing these SDGs commonly requires a proper business case (presenting the business opportunity with a decent return on investment, see section 8.4), or is pressed for by societal stakeholders that demand corporate policies – matched by concrete actions – that structurally forestall further harm. Less prominent priority tends to be given to the social or people-oriented SDGs (1–6) – unless, of course, these SDGs are directly linked to core operations (e.g. the food industry and SDG2; the health sector and SDG3; freshwater companies and SDG6). Because SDGs 1–6 are also part of the core activities of many non-profit or semi-public organizations, for-profit interest to energetically address this category is easily crowded out. Level 3 prioritization ('enhancing positive effects') may then induce a 'wait-and-see' mindset that leaves the initiative for action to others (see Box 5.1 on 'conditional morality'), even if this may happen at the expense of the business model's longer-term resilience. The lowest priority for direct action (level 4) tends to be given to SDGs aimed at good governance and partnerships at the level of institutions (SDGs 16–17). Although important to for-profit organizations and conditional to conducive operating environments, these SDGs are least likely to be prioritized in terms of dedicated resources and 'action-able' spheres of influence.

Organizations founded on a *non-profit logic* are initially bound to prioritize the social and people-centred SDGs (1–6), as their core activities ('mutual support', see section 8.5) are intimately linked to the social agenda embedded in these goals. However, most will acknowledge that the preconditions for their effective implementation often lie in the economic realm, which makes SDGs 7–12 a relevant second-level priority. The ecological realm (at level 3) and institutional realm (at level 4) may pose less of an imminent priority for direct action unless these SDGs are directly related to the core activities of organizations (e.g. ecology-directed NGOs and SDGs 13–15; human rights groups, trade unions, pension funds and SDG16).

10.5.2 SDG prioritization at target level – internal and external actionability

The 17 SDGs and 169 SDG-targets define highly diverse sustainability challenges. An assessment of their actionability at a strategic level requires a profound understanding of the organization's power base (power sources, positioning, spheres of influence) as well as the various responsibilities ('having' and 'taking', at levels 1, 2, 3, 4) that come with the strength and scope of their powers. Actionability and responsibility orientation are two sides of the same coin. *Actionability*, in this context, describes an organization's ability to decisively act on an SDG-target; *responsibility orientation* denotes the intended behaviour towards an SDG-target: a 'negative duty' approach of 'avoiding harm', or a 'positive duty approach' of using organizational powers to create and act on opportunities to 'do good'.

The actionability of specific SDGs can best be assessed at the target level. SDG-targets can be characterized as being 'internally actionable' or 'externally actionable' (Van Zanten and Van Tulder, 2018). *Internally actionable* SDG-targets are those that can be meaningfully engaged with within an organization and throughout the value chain; they are relevant to core activities and day-to-day operations and fall within the organization's direct sphere of influence. *Externally actionable* SDG-targets are those that cannot be meaningfully advanced within the organization's internal and value chain operations; significant contributions towards their achievement can only be made when working in (cross-sectoral) partnership with other societal actors (see section 5.4.2). Externally actionable SDG-targets hence go beyond an organization's direct sphere of influence but can nevertheless be affected *indirectly*. Organizations often find it easier to focus on those sustainability challenges and SDG-targets that are 'internally actionable'. These help them to *self-regulate* and apply principles of responsibility and sustainability to their own operations and value chains, for instance, to reduce their negative environmental and social footprints.

Even for ambitious organizations, the sheer breadth of 169 SDG-targets can be too unclear and impractical to guide deliberate decision-making on sustainability strategies. This volume can be condensed, however, to a representative listing of 59 SDG-targets of relevance to the private sector in particular. By (1) excluding SDG-targets primarily aimed at governmental action, (2) merging multiple SDG-targets into one target that captures their essence, or summarizing similar SDG-targets under one header, and (3) coupling each (aggregated) target to its related SDGs, a listing of 59 targets could be obtained that covers 100 linkages with specific SDGs. Subsequently, each of these listed 59 SDG-targets was characterized according to (a) being internally or externally actionable, and (b) its responsibility orientation.[24] Targets in the category 'doing good' were defined as helping organizations exceed expectations by generating positive externalities; targets in the category 'avoiding harm' as

---

24 See Van Zanten and Van Tulder (2018) for explanation and validation of the methodology used to arrive at this representative listing and categorization of SDG-targets.

seeking to reduce negative externalities – indicating outcomes that are expected of any responsible organization. Table 10.6 provides two examples from each of the resulting four categories. The entire listing can be found at the end of this chapter (Tool #10.1).

To illustrate, the ambition to 'reduce air, water and soil pollution' (related to SDGs 3, 6 and 12) and 'manage waste sustainably' (linked to SDGs 3, 6, 8, 11 and 12) can, in principle, be implemented throughout the organization with relatively little support being required from government or other societal actors. These targets are internally actionable. In contrast, contributing meaningfully to the provision of 'affordable and safe housing for all' (related to SDG11) requires collective efforts and partnerships between the private sector, states and civil society. Even for large companies in the construction industry, this target is largely *beyond* their direct sphere of influence and, therefore, indicated as externally actionable. Meaningful contributions to this SDG-target would necessitate a smart use of organizational powers in order to influence, co-shape and accelerate courses of action (for instance, by wielding convening, mobilizing, demonstrative, agenda-setting and collaborative powers). Early empirical insights (Van Zanten and Van Tulder, 2018) reveal that although companies supportively embrace the SDGs, there are still many gaps in their engagement

Table 10.6 Business-relevant SDG-targets and actionability – examples

Examples of SDG-targets	Relevant SDGs	Actionability	Responsibility orientation
• Reducing air, water, and soil pollution	3, 6, 12	Internal	Avoiding harm
• Sustainable waste management	3, 6, 8, 11, 12	Internal	Avoiding harm
• Transfer of (sustainable) technologies to developing countries	12, 17	Internal	Doing good
• Fair payment to small-scale suppliers	1	Internal	Doing good
• Actual and potential impact on local communities	1, 2	External	Avoiding harm
• Marine, coastal, and other water-related ecosystems	6, 14	External	Avoiding harm
• Access to financial services for all, including the most vulnerable	1, 8, 9, 10	External	Doing good
• Access to affordable and safe housing for all	11	External	Doing good

with SDGs that aim to 'avoid harm' but are 'externally actionable' – such as environmental degradation.

A further refinement for assessing the actionability of SDG-targets along the lines of direct and indirect spheres of influence can be obtained by considering distinct types of 'economic activities' (Van Zanten and Van Tulder, 2020; 2021). Sinkovics and colleagues (2021), for instance, propose a 'responsibility matrix' that classifies four types of corporate activities (representing the 'width' of responsibilities) and their potential contribution to the SDGs (positive, neutral or negative in effect). In their classification, *associative activities* refer to an organization's engagement in partnerships or in networks formed to further a specific cause; *peripheral activities* denote voluntary actions undertaken to support a sustainability objective beyond the organization's core activities; *operational activities* represent an organization's core activities linked to day-to-day operations, and *embedded activities* encompass its products and services. Each of these activity types can be linked to one or several SDGs. Whether the performed action makes a positive, negative or neutral contribution ultimately depends on the 'depth' of the activity: the *degree of responsibility* reflected in a particular action.

10.5.3 SDG prioritization as a 'nexus challenge'

The nexus concept is a direct implication of the '*principle of indivisibility*' that underlies the SDG-agenda. The principle denotes that implementation of the SDGs should be based on integrated approaches rather than siloed knowledge and policymaking (Bennich et al., 2020), and be entrenched in the 5Ps (*People, Planet, Prosperity, Peace, Partnerships*). Accordingly, the 'nexus challenge' (see sections 2.2.3 and 2.3.4) at the level of organizations pertains to an integrated approach to sustainability that does not focus on individual SDGs and SDG-targets, but instead explicitly takes their *interactions and interdependencies* – in the context of the entire business ecosystem – into consideration. A nexus approach helps organizations develop insights on SDG-relevant actions that may create *opportunities* for reducing trade-offs or for leveraging synergies, to support more coherent and deliberate decision-making. The rationale is that by identifying such vital 'nodes for leverage', an organization can advance multiple SDG-targets simultaneously – at reduced costs or with greater impact across a larger scale ('co-benefits') – while reducing the risk that contributions to one SDG-target undermine progress on another ('trade-offs'). Applying the '*nexus principle*' can thus enhance the impact of an organization's sustainability strategy; it informs optimal directing of organizational efforts, resources and incentives for greater attainment of its sustainability ambition and contribution to the SDGs.

Understanding the range of possible positive and negative interactions between the SDGs is critical for unlocking their full potential. The field of SDG interactions studies is still fairly young but rapidly emerging. Various conceptualization, assessment and modelling approaches have already been developed that seek to explore, map, qualify or quantify SDG interactions. They range from relatively simple, intuitive (cross-impact) mapping and scoring exercises to extensive network analyses of interactions at various levels, and the quantitative or conceptual modelling of their potential systems effects.[25] So far, however, few – if any – approaches take an action-focused perspective at the level of economic activities performed by individual organizations (Van Zanten and Van Tulder, 2020). To explore opportunities for leveraging SDG-relevant action, organizations can perhaps best start with mapping and assessing SDG interactions at a more general (macro) level.

EXPLORING AND MAPPING SDG INTERACTIONS

Approaches to SDG interaction mapping can be performed at various levels of sophistication, from various perspectives and with varying scopes (all SDGs or demarcated subsets). There are goal-goal interactions, goal-target interactions, target-target interactions and approaches that include SDG-indicators (see section 2.2.2), specific policies (e.g. forest conservation, resource efficiency) or external variables (Bennich et al., 2020). A useful starting point for initial nexus exploration at the goal-target level is provided by ECOSOC (2016), which distinguishes between *explicit* and *substantive* SDG interactions (Figure 10.8). Explicit links are those connections that follow directly from how targets have been formulated within the SDG framework ('linkage by design'); substantive links are those connections that can be expected to generate interaction effects. For example, ECOSOC's nexus identification shows that SDG8 and SDG12 – both vital for realizing circular economies – are explicitly linked via SDG-target 8.4: 'decouple economic growth from environmental degradation in accordance with sustainable consumption and production frameworks'. In addition, SDG8 and SDG12 are both substantively linked to SDG-targets 7.1 and 7.2 ('increase share renewable energy', 'increase energy efficiency'), which in turn are substantively linked to SDGs 1, 10, 9 and 13. SDG8 is substantively connected to SDG2 ('zero hunger') via SDG-targets 2.3 and 2.4 ('sustainable food

---

25 A helpful overview and classification of the (scientific) literature on approaches to conceptualize and assess SDG interactions is provided by Bennich et al. (2020). Scharlemann et al. (2020) and Breuer et al. (2019) provide additional reviews and a discussion of various SDG interaction frameworks developed to date.

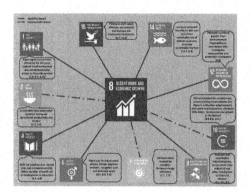

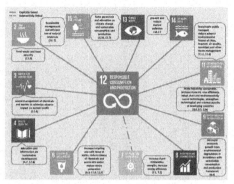

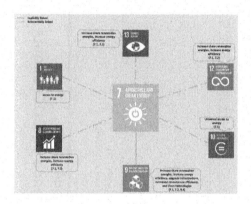

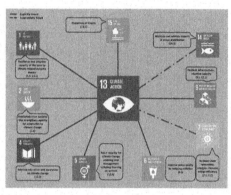

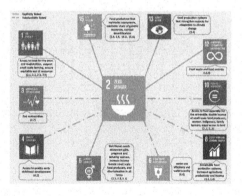

Figure 10.8 Examples of interlinked goals and targets – ECOSOC[26]

Source: ECOSOC (2016). *A Nexus Approach for the SDGs. Interlinkages between the goals and targets.*

26 ESOSOC (2016) identified prominent SDG interlinkages for all SDGs, with the exception of SDG17 and its underlying targets (which relate to the 'means of implementation' that concern all SDGs). For the full overview, see https://www.un.org/ecosoc/sites/www.un.org.ecosoc/files/files/en/2016doc/interlinkages-sdgs.pdf.

Table 10.7 Alignment of economic activities with the SDGs

Core: Scaling Need	Mixed: Decoupling Need

□ Renewable electric power generation, transmission and distribution
□ Financial services
□ Insurance
□ Legal activities
□ Scientific research and development
□ Security and investigation sercivces
□ Education
□ Human health and social work
□ Arts, entertainment and recreation
	□ Manufacture of:
	  □ Computer, electric, optical products
	  □ Agri, agriforestry machinery
	  □ Machinery for mining and construction
	  □ Motor vehicles
	  □ Railway locomotives
	  □ Medical and dental instruments
	□ Retail sale of pharma and medical goods
	□ Water collection, treatment & supply
	□ Sewerage
	□ Waste collection, treatment and disposal
		□ Growing non-perennial crops
		□ Growing of perennial crops
		□ Fishing
		□ Manufacture of fertilizers, pesticides, other agrochemical products
		□ Manufactur of basic phrmaceutical products
		□ Manufacture of cement, lime and plaster
		□ Manufacture of basic metals
		□ Contruction of utility projects

Source: Van Zanten and Van Tulder (2021).

production systems', 'increased agricultural productivity and income'), whereas SDG12 is explicitly connected to SDG2 through SDG-target 12.3 ('food waste and food security'), and via various targets explicitly linked to eight additional SDGs (3, 4, 6, 9, 11, 13, 14, 15). Although this identification of relatedness does not inform on *the nature* of SDG interactions (in terms of their directionality, polarity, dependencies, strengths and effects), the obvious implication is that a holistic approach to analysing SDG interactions is a prerequisite for taking a strategic view on an organization's sustainability potential and relevant venues for meaningful impact.

EXPLORING INTERACTIONS BETWEEN SDG-TARGETS AND ECONOMIC ACTIVITIES

Another way of looking at relevant interactions is to consider how various positive and negative impacts of different 'economic activities' relate to the SDGs. Economic activities represent industries and sectors (the meso level) and can be used as a proxy for assessing the private sector's diversified influence on sustainable development. Confronting 67 economic activities – as an indication of the 'core activities' companies undertake – and 59 business-relevant SDG-targets rendered a total of 3,953 interactions (67 x 59). By using a qualitative scoring technique (based on Nilsson et al., see section 2.3.4) and network analysis to assess all interactions, indications could be obtained on: (1) those economic activities most central in impacting most SDG-targets; (2) economic activities with similar impacts on the same SDG-targets; (3) SDG-targets most frequently impacted by economic activities; and (4) SDG-targets being impacted by the same economic activities (Van Zanten and Van Tulder, 2021). The analysis found, for instance, that economic activities with the most positive influence on SDG-targets are 'human health and social work activities' and 'education'. In contrast, 'mining of coal, lignite and extraction of natural gas' and 'quarrying of sand, stone, and clay' were found to exert the most negative net influence on the SDGs. SDG-target 9.2 ('promotion of industrialization') appeared to benefit the most from economic activities, whereas SDG-target 13.2 ('mitigation of climate change') was found to face the strongest net negative influence from economic activities.

Based on this analysis, four groups of economic activities could be classified according to their alignment (degree of positive influence; degree of negative influence) with the SDGs: *core, mixed, opposed* and *peripheral* economic activities (Table 10.7). For organizations undertaking these economic activities, the classification implies four distinct types of *strategic challenges* in future-proofing their core operations and business models in alignment with the SDG-agenda (ibid):

■ Activities that are 'core' to the SDG-agenda have many positive (synergistic) and few negative interactions (trade-offs) with the SDG-targets. For organizations, the strategic challenge here is to exploit their present business model to *expand and scale* positive impacts;

■ Activities that play a 'mixed' role have a moderate to high degree of both negative and positive interactions with SDG-targets. As the positive interactions of these activities cannot be missed in a sustainable future, the strategic challenge for organizations undertaking them is to improve alignment by *decoupling* positive impacts from negative impacts;

■ Activities 'opposed' to the SDG-agenda have few positive but significant negative interactions with SDG-targets and a potentially strong influence on holding back or reversing progress on the SDGs. For organizations, the strategic challenge is to *transform* in order to abandon economic activities that are negatively aligned with the SDGs, and shift towards activities with positive alignment;

■ Activities 'peripheral' to the SDG-agenda have few positive and few negative interactions with SDG-targets and are hence less relevant for achieving the SDGs. Here, the strategic challenge is to further *explore* options for generating positive impact.

10.5.4 SDG prioritization through country portfolio management

What constitutes an optimal portfolio of 'actionable' SDGs is highly contextual. The set of SDGs, SDG-targets and 'nodes for leverage' that come into view as 'opportunities' or 'challenges' strongly depends on the perspective taken. To inform strategic decision-making, an appraisal of relevant options for SDG impact should – in any case – include a sectoral focus ('economic activities'), but is additionally bound to such factors as geographical presence, the spatial scale of operations (local, national, regional, global), and the scope, scale and diversity of people and stakeholders affected. As multinational organizations integrate various economic activities within their value chain, they 'spread and connect' SDG impacts across continents and national borders. Each economic activity impacts different SDGs in different locations around the world.

Internationally operating 'core' organizations determine what is produced, how it is produced, by whom, when and where (see section 10.4.3). Through the management of their country portfolio, multinationals have the ability to decide in which countries they can best organize what type of economic activities. Their strategic choices regarding geographical presence, value chain governance and responsibility orientation ('avoid doing harm', 'doing good') influence how countries perform on the SDGs – in absolute and relative terms. Conversely, local conditions and countries' prevalent CSR regimes (section 6.5) affect whether a multinational considers a particular country foremost as a risk or as conducive to its operations and sustainability ambition.

Managing across borders can be approached as a risk-mitigation or as an opportunity-enhancing strategy; a complex world probably requires both. For multinationals, the strategic challenge is how to align their country portfolio with the SDGs in a way that (a) is sensitive to local 'SDG gaps', (b) enhances their strategic positioning, and (c) fosters the transformational ambitions of the SDG-agenda. Depending on their responsibility orientation and the sustainability ambition pursued (level 1, 2, 3, 4), multinational organizations can approach this strategic alignment challenge in three ways:

■ *A risk-mitigation approach*, which is foremost oriented to the multi-domestic management of operations' (potential) negative externalities and hence focused on those SDGs that pursue the 'avoidance of harm'. The alignment challenge then implies (1) the mapping of countries' SDG-relevant risks, and (2) an assessment of the (potential) negative impacts of local operations ('due diligence'), in order to prevent, reduce or mitigate the incidence of harmful events;

■ *An opportunity-seeking approach* that seeks to strategically link the SDGs to the country portfolio by considering which SDGs can be meaningfully engaged with in global operations (prioritization based on the 'potential' for internal and external actionability). The alignment challenge then involves the mapping of relevant SDG gaps across countries in order to minimize overall negative impacts and scale positive contributions to the SDG-agenda.

■ *An optimizing approach*, which seeks the best possible synthesis of the country portfolio and prioritized SDGs by contextualizing the corporate sustainability strategy to country-specific SDG realities. The alignment challenge involves the search for those country-specific SDG nodes and interactions (trade-offs, synergies) for which its (localized) operations can attain the greatest 'net impact', in view of optimizing overall contributions to the SDGs.

Several tools exist to support the mapping of 'CSR risks', potential SDG opportunities and SDG gaps at the country level (Box 10.12), and for mapping positive and negative SDG interactions that facilitate a target-level nexus approach (Box 10.13).

BOX
10.12

MAPPING CSR RISKS AND OPPORTUNITIES – COMPARING SOUTH AFRICA AND THE USA

■ **The CSR Risk Check** (developed by CSR Risk Check and MVO Nederland)

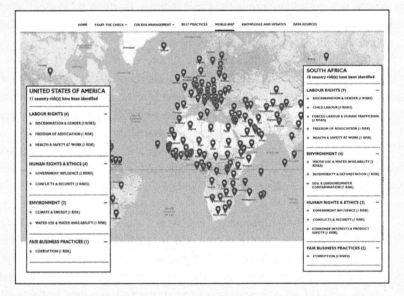

Source: https://www.mvorisicochecker.nl/en/worldmap

■ **Interactive Map and Country Profiles** (by SDSN's Sustainable Development Report)

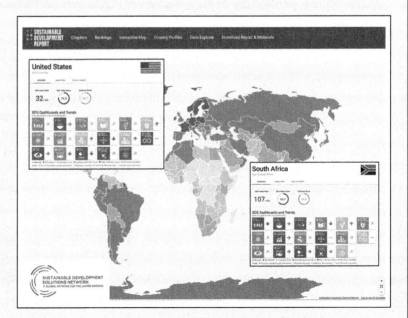

Source: Sustainable Development Solutions Network, https://dashboards.sgindex.org/map

MAPPING SYNERGIES AND TRADE-OFFS AT TARGET LEVEL

South Africa: SDG8 ('decent work and economic growth') and SDGs 1–16

■ Positive linkages (synergies)

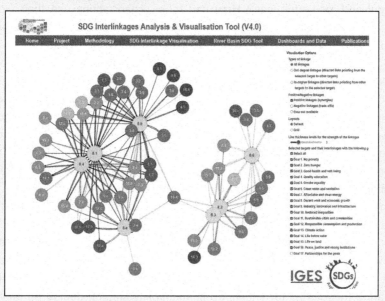

■ Negative linkages (trade-offs)

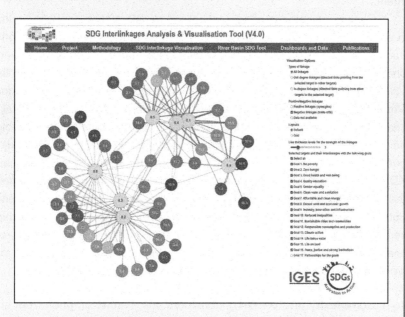

Source: Institute for Global Environmental Strategies (IGES). Data and visualisation charts are provided by the courtesy of the IGES SDG Interlinkages Analysis & Visualisation Tool (V4.0) – https://sdginterlinkages.iges.jp/visualisationtool.html

10.6 CONCLUSION, TOOLS AND RESOURCES – DESIGNING A POWERFUL 'SUSTAINABLE CORPORATE STORY' FOR THE SDGs

How can organizations make the SDGs 'actionable' to core activities in a meaningful and 'powerful' way? How can focal organizations use their weight as catalysts for transformative change – rather than as agents of 'stagnation' or 'frustration' – to drive accelerated progress on the pressing systems challenges of our time (Chapter 1)? This chapter explored how organizations can purposively use their power base and spheres of influence to drive, guide, support and co-shape trajectories of positive change towards higher levels of sustainability. It argued why and how a 'smart' and responsible use of organizational powers – strategically exercised as a driving force for advanced value creation – is a prerequisite for overcoming critical tipping points in the process of aligning core operations with societal needs, values and expectations. As analytical building blocks, we discerned (a) structural, relational and discursive/ normalizing dimensions of power; (b) direct and indirect spheres of influence (for 'having' and 'taking' responsibility); and (c) societal, value chain and international 'bargaining arenas' in which organizations exercise their positioning powers. Together, these arenas comprise the 'selection environment' as well as the 'collaborative space' in which organizations navigate opportunities and change trajectories for enhanced sustainability impact, decide on their strategies and positioning, and seek to establish leeway to realize their strategic intent.

Change trajectories of adaptation and transformation confront incumbents in particular with complex balancing challenges of loosening and strengthening traction on multiple fronts. Concomitant alignment challenges vary per transition phase and according to various positioning decisions. Following up from the *Key Value Indicators (KVIs)* distinguished in Chapter 9, this chapter identified elemental areas of *Key Decision-making Indicators (KDIs)* at the societal, value chain and international level. KDIs specify the nature of the strategic choices to be made in each transition phase in order to surpass critical thresholds, adjust the business model and move from one level of sustainability to the next. In essence, KDIs inform the probing of strategic 'fits' between the business ecosystem and the use of organizational resources, capabilities and spheres of influence for optimal outcomes and beneficial impact. The 'logic framework' – introduced in section 5.5 in relation to societal intervention strategies – provides a relevant analytical framework to examine the degree of consonance between distinct types of 'fits' so as to enhance their attunement (Figure 10.9):

1   **Complexity fit (0⬅→A)**; considers the nature of prioritized societal issues/portfolio of SDGs and their congruence with the organization's

purpose and mission. The complexity of the challenge is defined by the degree of wickedness of prioritized issues (Chapters 4 and 5); their relevance to core activities ('materiality', Chapter 9) can be expressed in terms of (anticipated) triggering events and longer-term resilience (Chapter 7).

2   **Value-orientation fit (F→A+0)**; calibrates responsibility orientation (having, taking) and envisioned impact on prioritized societal issue(s)/SDG portfolio, in relation to issue complexity. Responsibility orientation can be narrow and reactive (engagement level 1 or 2), or broad and transformational (level 3 or 4). The 'business case' for sustainability (Chapter 8) should mirror the organization's value orientation (section 9.6) and match the value-generating potential of the business model, value proposition and motto (Chapter 9).

3   **Strategic fit (E←→B1)**; considers the degree to which the power base (power sources, positioning, sphere of influence) is in line with envisaged effects. The feasibility of the 'business case' and value proposition hinges on (a) the context-specific *conditions* under which espoused sustainability ambitions can be made actionable, and (b) the switching costs related to business model innovation and adjustment. KDIs cover elemental strategic parameters to direct strategy implementation and the implications thereof (in terms of societal, value chain, international positioning) in the dynamic interaction with other organizational agents (sections 10.2–10.4).

4   **Operational fit (B→C→D)**; relates to the formation, alignment and leveraging of inputs and core activities in order to effectively and efficiently deliver on the sustainability strategy and meet intended outcomes at the desired level of impact. Output performance is expressed in terms of KPIs. The alignment of internal operations pertains to functional areas of management (elaborated in Chapter 11).

5   **SDG alignment (F←→0 + A; → B → C → D → E)**; involves the dynamic fit between the manifold sustainability challenges integral to the business ecosystem and the extent to which prioritized SDG interactions match the organization's purpose, mission and power base – in order to purposively address them at appropriate levels of responsibility, intervention and engagement (1, 2, 3, 4). Ultimately, the better the fit between core activities (represented by fits 1–4) and the SDG-agenda, the more an organization will be able to positively contribute to beneficial SDG impact. Table 10.8 synthesizes how different choices on issue prioritization, KVIs and KDIs relate to organizations' SDG alignment challenge. Table 10.8 also identifies prevalent opportunities, challenges and risks associated with SDG alignment in different phases of organizational change.

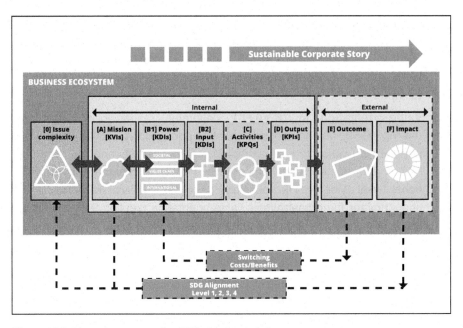

Figure 10.9 Managing power – the SDG alignment challenge

BUILDING ALIGNMENT – DESIGNING AN EMPOWERING SUSTAINABLE CORPORATE STORY

Sustainability strategies are increasingly framed in terms of 'corporate stories': narratives that communicate the strategic challenges an organization faces, portray the dilemmas for day-to-day operations, convey key binding organizational values and legitimize choices in support of change. A corporate story has the function of aligning internal and external stakeholders in a way that is consistent with the core principles of effective corporate communication (Van Riel and Blackburn, 1995).

A *sustainable corporate story* is a narrative that conveys the organization's sustainability ambitions in support of addressing critical systems challenges (Chapter 1), the envisaged way forward to achieve these ambitions, and the motivation (in terms of key values, responsibility orientation and strategic considerations) for doing so. It communicates *why* prioritized SDGs are deemed 'material' to core activities – now and in the longer run – and *what* approaches and efforts the organization commits itself to in order to make its SDG ambition (powerfully) actionable. Essentially, a sustainable corporate story concisely communicates the organization's *intervention logic* and *Theory of Change* for attaining its sustainability ambitions with impact – in a convincing, coherent and stakeholder-mobilizing manner. Mission statements and corporate stories are increasingly developed in collaboration with groups in society; proactive organizations will seek to include critical stakeholders in strategic dialogue.

Designing a connective and powerful sustainable corporate story implies integrating all relevant steps and fits of the 'logic framework' (Figure 10.9) into a compelling narrative. Relevant elements include (Table 10.8):

1   The nature of today's challenges, the systems transformations needed, and a vision on 'the kind of world' the organization wants to operate in (a 'VUCA world' or an 'SDG world', Chapter 1);

2   The organization's view on its 'corporate responsibilities' and the kind of dilemmas the organization faces (purpose and values orientation);

3   The value proposition the organization aims for (explanation of its motto);

4   How it will use its organizational power sources, positioning and spheres of influence to organize for positive change, alone and with others (restricting negative effects, scaling beneficial effects, contribution to systems transformation);

5   The prioritized portfolio of SDGs and how this selection is linked to core operations and medium-turn ambitions;

6   The commitments, efforts and results to which the organization is responsive and accountable.

Table 10.8 Mapping the SDG alignment challenge – building a sustainable corporate story

	LEVEL 1	LEVEL 2	LEVEL 3	LEVEL 4
	Tipping point	Key tipping point	Tipping point	
	1. ISSUE AND PROBLEM DEFINITION			
Root causes of challenge (Chapters 4, 7)	Market failure – needs to be addressed by individual companies	Sectoral failure – needs to be addressed within the sector	Systemic – can be addressed on individual basis	Systemic – address on sectoral and societal level
Sources of failure; having/taking responsibility (Chapter 5)	Power abuse creating failure; poor management practices; poor value proposition	Defensive adjustment strategies, including denial and lobbying to feed doubt	Active lobbying against regulation; denial of sectoral role in structural events	Free-rider and bystander effect: denial of collective responsibility
Nature of triggering event (Chapter 7)	Incident	Sectoral incident/event	Structural/systems crisis	(Imminent) Systems crisis
Nature of risk/opportunity	Managing in a VUCA world (Chapters 1 and 4)		Managing in an SDG world (Chapter 2, 3, 5 and 6)	

(continued)

Table 10.8 (continued)

	LEVEL 1 — Tipping point	LEVEL 2 — Key tipping point	LEVEL 3 — Tipping point	LEVEL 4
2. PURPOSE AND VALUE ORIENTATION — Key Value Indicators (KVIs)				
Sustainability orientation (Chapter 8)	Corporate *Self* Responsibility	Corporate Social *Responsiveness*	Corporate *Social/ Strategic* Responsibility	Corporate *Societal* Responsibility
Value dimension emphasis (Chapter 9)	Designing, creating, capturing value	Minimize destroying value	Maximize spreading value	Co-creating value
Stakeholder approach	'Trust me'	'Show me'	'Inform me'	'Involve/Engage me'
License to …	… Exist	… Operate	… Scale	… Experiment
Vision and motto	'Doing things right' 'Doing well' 'Just do it'	'Don't do it wrong and doing well' 'Just do it right'	'Doing good and doing well' 'Do the right thing'	'Doing good by doing well' 'Do the right thing right'

	3. STRATEGY — Key Decision-making Indicators (KDIs)		
KDIs	*1. Trigger*	*2. Internal alignment*	*3 External alignment*
Societal orientation	Regulation/rivalry/competition/closed		Self-regulation/coopetition/cooperation/open
Use of position	Adaptation/downscaling/substitution/product orientation		Transformation/scaling across/complementary/systems integration
International strategy	Liability/risk		Responsibility/opportunity

	4. SDG PORTFOLIO ALIGNMENT		
Portfolio of SDGs	• General support for SDGs without prioritization; *or*	• Prioritization of specific SDGs/SDG-targets related to core activities	• Prioritization of SDGs/SDG-targets based on optimization of impact (nexus approach)

	LEVEL 1 Tipping point	LEVEL 2 Key tipping point	LEVEL 3	LEVEL 4 Tipping point
	• Prioritization based on risk mitigation	• Prioritization based on market opportunities		• Prioritization addresses here/elsewhere, present/ future needs
Strategic opportunity	• Exploration of how core activities relate to SDGs (inside-out adjustment) • Signalling sustainability ambition to internal and external stakeholders (reputation effect)	• Re-orientation on organization's longer-term value-generating potential and resilience; • Identification of unmet needs and new (future) markets • Feeds/informs strategic renewal and redirection; • Creating first-mover advantages		• Sharper delineation of required business model change (and value proposition); • Identification of actionable strategies; • Informs strategic reconfiguration of business model/ activities/value chain • Better targeted allocation of invested time, efforts, resources
Challenge	• Prioritizing those SDGs/ SDG-targets most material to core activities • Translation of SDGs into value proposition and product/market portfolio	• Implementing strategic approaches that link internally and externally actionable SDG-targets to activities (core, value chain, sector, cross-sector) • Instigating bandwagon effects (mobilizing value chain and sector actors) • Establishing an SDG-conducive level playing field		• Understanding the complexity between SDG-interactions and business activities; • Optimizing net impact by reducing trade-offs and leveraging synergies • Learning while doing • Building a conducive innovation ecosystem (open innovation)
Risk	• SDG washing • SDG cherry-picking • SDG discontinuation	• Too much focus on 'avoiding harm' SDGs (risk mitigation) and neglect of opportunities to meet unmet needs (doing good SDGs); • Insufficient transparency and accountability		• Overstressing the negative effects (trade-offs) while not using the full potential of positive effects (synergies). • Tension between learning, performance and accountability

- Power can be a force of stagnation but also a force for positive change to catalyse sustainable development and create societal value. Organizations can wield their powers (resource base, positioning, sphere of influence) in three directions: as 'agents of frustration', 'agents of stagnation' or as 'agents of change'.

- Effective power exertion for positive change includes the responsible use of (1) 'hard powers', based on resources; (2) 'soft powers', based on relationships and discursive/ normalizing influence; and (3) 'smart powers', based on a timely and contextualized balancing of both hard and soft powers.

- 'Sphere of influence' defines the reasonable scope of an organization's responsibilities towards various actors with whom it has a (political, contractual, economic, other) relationship, or that are affected by its actions. The concept embraces both 'avoid doing harm' and 'doing good' dimensions of 'responsible business', and connects power exercise to four levels of intervention/engagement (levels 1, 2, 3, 4).

- The 'agency power' of organizations materializes in 'bargaining arenas' (at the societal level, within value chains, in markets, across borders) of 'countervailing powers', in which they seek to create 'scope for manoeuvre', stakeholder support, and strategic alliances for more or less actionable strategies.

- The dominant positioning powers of core/lead/focal/flagship/keystone organizations in vertical (value chain), horizontal (industry/market) or diagonal (cross-industry) relations point to greater responsibilities to drive transformative change and (co)shape conducive conditions for higher levels of sustainability – 'with great powers, come great responsibilities'.

- Discursive powers and normalization mechanisms are powerful instruments for mobilizing and aligning a variety of actors for positive change. However, an expanding 'normalization jungle' and related cherry-picking practices risk eroding transparency, accountability and credibility. To drive greater convergence, authoritative norm-setting organizations have started to align their normalization frameworks and indicators to the SDG-framework.

- Multinational enterprises (MNEs) have two kinds of 'powers' that (potentially) can correct for market, regulatory and institutional failures around the world: internalization of markets and internalization of norms. The *sustainable MNE* seeks to find a synthesis of both by combining global coordination with local responsiveness ('glocalization approach').

- Effective power exertion requires a solid understanding of change trajectories and related Key Decision-making Indicators (KDIs) that delineate critical tipping points to move from one transition phase to the next. KDIs define the nature of the strategic decisions to be taken in each phase: how to direct organizational power sources and recalibrate (societal, value chain, and international) positioning for positive change.

■ Transitioning to higher levels of societal value creation involves purposive processes of 'scaling' (of sustainable products, services, solutions) and 'upgrading' (technological and organizational capabilities) through strategies of competition, coopetition, strategic alliances, collaboration and cross-sector partnering.

■ Many frontrunner companies are embracing a portfolio of SDGs, but face the challenge of how to make the selected SDGs 'actionable' within the contours of their direct and indirect spheres of influence – in a meaningful and 'powerful' way. SDGs and SDG-targets can be prioritized in several ways: (1) along 'primary responsibility' lines; (2) according to assessed potential for their internal and external actionability; (3) via a 'nexus approach', to maximize synergies and minimize trade-offs; and (4) in alignment with country portfolio risk-mitigation, opportunity-seeking or optimizing approaches.

■ A 'sustainable corporate story' communicates the organization's *'intervention logic'* and *'theory of change'* for attaining its sustainability ambitions with impact – in a convincing, coherent and stakeholder-mobilizing manner.

- **GRI Sustainability Disclosure Database:** online application that provides free access to all types of sustainability reports (GRI-based or otherwise) and information on reporting organizations until December 2020 https://database.globalreporting.org/search/. GRI's *SDG Target 12.6 Global-Tracker* displays an interactive world map to explore which countries have market regulations, policies or legislation in place with requirements for companies to disclose or report on non-financial factors: https://database.globalreporting.org/SDG-12-6/Global-Tracker

- **International Trade Centre Sustainability Standards Map:** provides verified information on over 260 standards on environmental protection, worker and labour rights, economic development, quality and food safety, and business ethics. The database can be searched by sector/product, producing region/country, destination region/country, and standard name. It includes private, public and international standards and can be specified to type of mandate, position in the value chain and sustainability theme. Each voluntary sustainability standard (VSS) displayed provides specific information on 'what' the standard is about, 'the requirements' per sustainability area covered and 'how' the standard operates (audits, claims and labelling, support and membership; recognition or compliance with international standards). Information is reviewed and quality-controlled by each participating standard organization. https://standardsmap.org/en/identify

- **ITC The State of Sustainable Markets:** displays visualized market trends (e.g. certified area of land; number of certified producers) for certified commodities, specific to 12 major VSS for bananas, cocoa, coffee, cotton, palm oil, soybeans, cane sugar, tea and forest products. Data can be explored per country, by commodity and by VSS. https://www.sustainabilitymap.org/trends

- **State of Sustainability Initiatives (SSI):** SSI is an international transparency and capacity-building project that aims to improve strategic planning and sustainable development outcomes related to voluntary sustainability standards. Exponential growth in the demand and supply of standard-compliant products has led to a proliferation of VSS. SSI publishes independent, evidence-based reports on VSS characteristics, market performance and potential opportunities for VSS to move commodity sectors more effectively towards sustainability. https://www.iisd.org/ssi/reviews/

- **SEI-SDG Synergies:** free online tool developed by the Stockholm Environment Institute for understanding how groups of policy areas and SDG-targets interact using systems thinking. SDG Synergies helps to record, visualize and analyse how multiple targets are likely to interact in a given context. Based on a discussion-based scoring process, SDG Synergies develops a cross-impact matrix of target interactions to gain insight into how progress on one might affect progress on the other. The tool can be used to inform strategic decisions about how to prioritize or sequence implementation of different targets or how best to manage potential trade-offs between them. It can also help to identify what cross-sectoral collaborations would be most productive. https://www.sdgsynergies.org/

- **SDG-Interlinkages Analysis & Visualisation Tool:** free web tool, developed by the Institute for Global Environmental Strategies (IGES), to visualize the interlinkages between SDG-targets and explore the data for monitoring SDG progress. Relations between relevant targets are quantified for 27 selected countries from East Asia (China, Japan, Mongolia and Republic of Korea), South Asia (Afghanistan, Bangladesh, Bhutan, India, Maldives, Nepal, Pakistan and Sri Lanka), and South East Asia (Brunei, Cambodia, Indonesia, Lao PDR, Malaysia, Myanmar, Philippines, Singapore, Thailand and Vietnam), as well as from Africa (Ethiopia, Ghana, Malawi, South Africa and Tanzania) based on the target-level indicators and corresponding time series data. https://sdginterlinkages.iges.jp/visualisationtool.html. For cross-impact matrices per country on synergies and trade-offs: https://sdginterlinkages.iges.jp/Dashboards%20and%20Data.html

■ ***CSR Risk Check Tool:*** quick-scan to identify international CSR risks of business activities upstream and downstream in the value chain (exporting, importing, production facilities in foreign countries). Supports a quick assessment (eight-step 'due diligence' roadmap) of what can be done to prevent, reduce and manage them: https://www.mvorisicochecker.nl/en. CSR risks per country can also be explored via an interactive world map: https://www.mvorisicochecker.nl/en/worldmap

■ ***SDSN's Interactive Map and Country Profiles:*** Based on its annual Sustainability Development Report, the Sustainable Development and Solutions Network visualizes global developments of countries' progress towards achieving the Sustainable Development Goals. Countries' performance (overall score, ranking and progress per SDG) can be explored via an interactive world map https://dashboards.sdgindex.org/map. For each of the 193 UN Member States, country profiles provide a more detailed, dashboard overview of trends in their progress on each SDG: https://dashboards.sdgindex.org/profiles

■ ***UN SDG Country Profiles:*** Developed by the Statistics Division of the UN Department of Economic and Social Affairs, this online database provides a country profile (basic characteristics such as population and migration, national account and labour market, trade and balance of payments, environment) as well as visualized longer-term trends on each country's progress for each of the SDGs: https://country-profiles.unstatshub.org

■ ***WBA's SDG2000:*** Based on seven systems transformations (social; decarbonization and energy; food and agriculture; circular; digital; urban; financial) vital to meeting the SDGs by 2030, the World Benchmarking Alliance has identified and listed 2,000 'keystone companies' that are assumed to have a disproportionate influence – and impact – on meeting the SDGs. Five principles guide their identification as potential 'catalysts for change'. A keystone company (1) dominates global production revenues and/or volumes within a particular sector; (2) controls globally relevant segments of production and/or service provision; (3) connects (eco)systems globally through subsidiaries and their supply chains; (4) influences global governance processes and institutions; (5) has a global footprint, particularly in developing countries. The SDG2000 list can be filtered by transformation, industry, headquarter and region: https://www.worldbenchmarkingalliance.org/sdg2000/#company-overview

T O O L

10.1

MAKING SDGs ACTIONABLE AT TARGET LEVEL: THE CORPORATE ALIGNMENT CHALLENGE – SDG TARGETS AS NEXUS

Indicator	Nexus of relevant SDGs						Actionability	Responsibility orientation
Socially responsible and environmentally sustainable sourcing	1	2	8	12	14	15	Internal	Doing good
Fair payment to small-scale suppliers	1						Internal	Doing good
Goods and services for those on low incomes	1						Internal	Doing good
Access to financial services for all, including the most vulnerable	1	8	9	10			External	Doing good
Sustainable food production	2	13	15				Internal	Doing good
Healthy and sufficient food for those on low incomes	2	3					External	Doing good
Agricultural productivity of small-scale suppliers	1	2					External	Doing good
Small-scale producers' ownership over land and other property	1	2					External	Doing good
Actual and potential impacts on local communities	1	2					External	Avoiding harm
Occupational health and safety	3	8					Internal	Avoiding harm
Mental health and well-being	3						External	Avoiding harm
Health-care services and medicines for all	3	5					External	Doing good
Employee training and education	4	8					Internal	Doing good
Education to promote sustainable development	4	12	13				External	Doing good
Children's access to education	4						External	Doing good
Water, sanitation and hygiene	6						External	Doing good
Water use efficiency	6						Internal	Avoiding harm
Energy efficiency	7	8					Internal	Avoiding harm
Energy infrastructure	7						External	Doing good
Renewable energy	7						External	Doing good
Access to energy for all	7						External	Doing good
Labour rights and practices in the supply chain	8						Internal	Avoiding harm
Elimination of forced labour and child labour	8						Internal	Avoiding harm
Economic growth and productivity, particularly in developing countries	8						External	Doing good
Employment for all, particularly young people and people with disabilities	8						Internal	Doing good
Resilient and sustainable infrastructure	9						External	Doing good
Sustainable technologies and sustainable industrial processes	9						External	Doing good
Responsible finance	10						External	Doing good
Investment (e.g. FDI) in developing countries	10	17					Internal	Doing good

Topic						Internal/External	Approach
Access to information and communication technology for all	9					External	Doing good
Access to affordable and sustainable transport for all	11					External	Doing good
Access to affordable and safe housing for all	11					External	Doing good
Cultural and natural heritage and diversity	11					External	Doing good
Greenhouse gas emission reductions	13					Internal	Avoiding harm
Funding for developing countries' climate change actions	13					Internal	Doing good
Transfer of (sustainable) technologies to developing countries	12	17				Internal	Doing good
Resilience to climate-related hazards	13					External	Avoiding harm
Disaster and emergency planning	1	11	13			Internal	Avoiding harm
Reducing air, water and soil pollution	3	6	12			Internal	Avoiding harm
Sustainable waste management	3	6	8	11	12	Internal	Avoiding harm
Marine, coastal and other water-related ecosystems	6	14				External	Avoiding harm
No overfishing and illegal, unregulated and destructive fishing	2	14				External	Avoiding harm
Ecosystems and biodiversity on land	15					External	Avoiding harm
Halt poaching and trafficking of protected species	15					External	Avoiding harm
Halt or reverse deforestation and/or desertification	15					External	Avoiding harm
No corruption and bribery	16					Internal	Avoiding harm
Accountable and transparent governance	16					Internal	Avoiding harm
Responsive and inclusive decision-making at all levels	16					Internal	Avoiding harm
Equal pay and opportunities for men and women, at all levels	5	10				Internal	Avoiding harm
No discrimination, and anti-discrimination laws and policies	5	8	16			Internal	Avoiding harm
No workplace violence and harassment	5	16				Internal	Avoiding harm
Childcare services and benefits	4	5				Internal	Doing good
Collective bargaining for wages and benefits along the supply chain	1	8				Internal	Avoiding harm
Social protection systems for all	1	10				External	Doing good
Protection of privacy	16					Internal	Avoiding harm
External reporting on sustainability	12					Internal	Avoiding harm
Data availability and public access to information	16	17				Internal	Doing good
Tools to monitor impacts on sustainable development	12	17				Internal	Avoiding harm
Partnerships with the public and civil society sectors	17					Internal	Doing good

REFERENCES

Ariely, D. & Wertenbroch, K. (2002). 'Procrastination, Deadlines, and Performance: Self-control by Pre-commitment', *Psychological Science*, 13(3):219–224.

Babri, M., Davidson, B. & Helin, S. (2021). 'An Updated Inquiry into the Study of Corporate Codes of Ethics: 2005–2016', *Journal of Business Ethics*, (168):71–108.

Baden-Fuller, C. & Stopford, J. (1992). *Rejuvenating the Mature Business: The Competitive Challenge*. London: Routledge.

Barkemeyer, R., Preuss, L. & Lee, L. (2015). 'On the effectiveness of private transnational governance regimes – Evaluating corporate sustainability reporting according to the Global Reporting Initiative', *Journal of World Business*, 50(2):312–325.

Barrientos, S., Gereffi, G. & Rossi, A. (2011). 'Economic and social upgrading in global production networks: A new paradigm for a changing world', *International Labour Review*, 150(3–4):319–340.

Bartlett, C. & Ghoshal, S. (1989). *Managing Across Borders: the Transnational Solution*. Boston: Harvard Business School Press.

Baumol, W.J. (1990). 'Entrepreneurship: Productive, Unproductive and Destructive', *Journal of Political Economy*, 98(5):893–921.

Beck, U. (2005). *Power in the Global Age: A New Global Political Economy*, Polity Press.

Bennich, T., Weitz, N. & Carlsen, H. (2020). 'Deciphering the scientific literature on SDG interactions: A review and reading guide', *Science of the Total Environment*, 728:138405.

Brandenburger, A. & Nalebuff, B. (1996). *Co-Opetition: A Revolution Mindset that Combines Competition and Cooperation*, Crown Business.

Breuer, A., Janetschek, H. & Malerba, D. (2019). 'Translating Sustainable Development Goal (SDG) Interdependencies into Policy Advice', *Sustainability* 11(7):2092.

CDP (2017). *The Carbon Majors Database CDP Carbon Majors Report 2017*, CDP Report June.

Chen, S. (2018). 'Multinational Corporate Power, Influence and Responsibility in Global Supply Chains', *Journal of Business Ethics*, (148):365–374.

Chesbrough, H.W. (2003). *Open Innovation: The New Imperative for Creating and Profiting from Technology*. Boston, Massachusetts: Harvard Business School Press.

Chorn, N.H. (1991). 'The "Alignment" Theory: Creating Strategic Fit', *Management Decision*, 29(1).

Cohen, W.M., Nelson, R.R. & Walsh, J. (2000). *Protecting Their Intellectual Assets: Appropriability Conditions and Why U.S. Manufacturing Firms Patent (or Not)*. NBER Working Paper No. 7552.

Constantinescu, M. & Kaptein, M. (2020). 'Ethics management and ethical management: mapping criteria and interventions to support responsible management practice'. In: Laasch et al. (2020), *Research Handbook of Responsible Management*, (pp. 155–174). Cheltenham: Edward Elgar.

Crosby, B.C. & Bryson, J.M. (2005). *Leadership for the Common Good: Tackling Public Problems in a Shared-Power World*, second edition. San Francisco, CA: Jossey-Bass.

De Cremer, D. (2013). *The Proactive Leader: How to Overcome Procrastination and be a Bold Decision-Maker*, Palgrave Macmillan.

De Grauwe, P. & Camerman, F. (2002). 'How Big are the Big Multinational Companies?', *Review of Business and Economic Literature*, 0(3):311–326.

Deming, W.E. (1982). *Out of the Crisis*. MIT Press.

Dernis, H., Gkotsis, P., Grassano, N., Nakazato, S., Squicciarini, M., Van Beuzekom, B. & Vezzani, A. (2019). *World Corporate Top R&D investors: Shaping the Future of Technologies and of AI*. Luxembourg: Publications Office of the European Union.

Donaldson, T. & Dunfee, T.W. (1999). 'When Ethics Travel: The Promise and Peril of Global Business Ethics, *California Management Review*, 41(4):45–63.

Dunning, J. & Lundan, S. (2008). *Multinational Enterprises and the Global Economy*, Second Edition. Cheltenham: Edward Elgar.

ESOSOC (2016). 'A Nexus Approach for the SDGs. Interlinkages between the goals and targets', Retrieved from: https://www.un.org/ecosoc/sites/www.un.org.ecosoc/files/files/en/2016doc/interlinkages-sdgs.pdf.

Eden, L., Lenway, S. & Schuler, D.A. (2005). 'From the obsolescing bargain to the political bargaining model'. In: Grosse, R. (Ed.), *International Business and Government Relations in the 21st Century* (pp. 251–272). Cambridge: Cambridge University Press.

Fairhurst, G.T. (2010). *The Power of Framing: Creating the Language of Leadership*. San Franciso, CA: Jossey-Bass.

Fleming, P. & Spicer, A. (2014). 'Power in Management and Organization Science', *Academy of Management Annals*, 8(1):237–298.

French Jr., J.R.P. & Raven, B. (1959). 'The Bases of Social Power'. In: Cartwright, D. (Ed.), *Studies in social power* (pp. 150–167). University of Michigan.

Fuchs, D. (2013). 'Theorizing the Power of Global Companies'. In: Mikler, J. (Ed.) *The Handbook of Global Companies* (pp. 77–95), John Wiley & Sons.

Galbraith, J.K. (1952). *American Capitalism. The concept of countervailing power*. Houghton Mifflin.

Geels, F.W. (2019). 'Socio-technical transitions to sustainability: a review of criticisms and elaborations of the Multi-Level Perspective', *Current Opinion in Environmental Sustainability*, (39):187–201.

Geels, F.W. & Schot, J.W. (2007). 'Typology of sociotechnical transition pathways', *Research Policy* 36(3):399–417.

Gereffi, G., Humprey, J. & Sturgeon, T. (2005). 'The Governance of Global Value Chains', *Review of International Political Economy*, 12(1):78–104.

Grin, J., Rotmans, J. & Schot, J. (2010). *Transitions to Sustainable Development. New Directions in the Study of Long Term Transformative Change*. London: Routledge.

Guandalini, L., Sun, W. & Zhou, L. (2019). 'Assessing the implementation of Sustainable Development Goals through switching cost', *Journal of Cleaner Production*, (232):1430–1441.

Hardy, C. (1985). 'The Nature of Unobtrusive Power', *Journal of Management Studies*, 22(4):384–399.

Hardy, C. & Phillips, N. (1998). 'Strategies of Engagement: Lessons from the Critical Examination of Collaboration and Conflict in an Interorganizational Domain', *Organization Science*, 9(2):217–230.

Hertz, N. (2014). *Eyes Wide Open. How to Make Smart Decisions in a Confusing World*, Harper Business.

Hertz, N. (2002). *The Silent Takeover. Global Capitalism and the Death of Democracy*, Cornerstone.

Hirschman, A.O. (1970). *Exit, Voice, and Loyalty: Responses to Decline in Firms, Organizations, and States*, Harvard University Press.

Humphrey, J. & Schmitz, H. (2002). 'How does insertion in global value chains affect upgrading in industrial clusters?' *Regional Studies*, 36(9):1017–27.

ISO (2017). *Practical overview of the linkages between ISO 26000:2010, Guidance on social responsibility and OECD Guidelines for Multinational Enterprises (2011)*, version 7 February 2017. Geneva: International Organization for Standardization.

Kaptein, M. (2020). 'Business Codes: A review of the literature'. In: Van Rooij, B. & Sokol, D.D. (Eds.), *Cambridge Handbook of Compliance*. Cambridge University Press.

Karliner, J. (1997). *The Corporate Planet. Ecology and Politics in the Age of Globalization*, Sierra Club Books.

Korten, D.C. (2001). *When Corporations Rule the World*, 2nd Revised Edition, Kumarian Press.

Laasch, O., Suddaby, R., Freeman, R.E. & Jamali, D. (Eds.) (2020). *Research Handbook of Responsible Management*. Cheltenham: Edward Elgar.

Leipziger, D. (2016). *The Corporate Responsibility Code Book*, Third Edition, Greenleaf Publishing.

Levin, R.C., Klevorick, A.K., Nelson, R.R. & Winter, S.G. (1987). 'Appropriating the Returns from Industrial Research and Development', *Brookings Papers on Economic Activity* 3(1987):783–831.

Lijfering, S.M. & Van Tulder, R. (2020). *Inclusive Business in Africa. A business model perspective*, The Partnerships Resource Centre. Rotterdam: Rotterdam School of Management, Erasmus University.

London, T. & Hart, S.L. (Eds.) (2011). *Next Generation Business Strategies for the Base of the Pyramid: New Approaches for Building Mutual Value*. Upper Saddle River, NJ: Pearson Education.

Lukes, S. (1974). *Power: A Radical View*. London: MacMillan.

Mazzucato, M. (2018). *The Value of Everything. Making and Taking in the Global Economy*. Allen Lane.

Nosratabadi, S., Mosavi, A., Shamshirband, S., Zavadskas, E.K., Rakotonirainy, A. & Chau, K.W. (2019). 'Sustainable Business Models: A Review', *Sustainability*, 11(6):1663.

Nuttavuthisit, K. & Thogersen, J. (2017). 'The Importance of Consumer Trust for the Emergence of a Market for Green Products: The Case of Organic Food', *Journal of Business Ethics*, (140):323–337.

Nye, J.S. Jr. (2004). *Soft Power: The Means to Success in World Politics*. Public Affairs.

Panigrahi, S.S., Bahinipati, B. & Jain, V. (2019). 'Sustainable supply chain management: A review of literature and implications for future research', *Management of Environmental Quality: An International Journal*, 30(5):1001–1049.

Ponte, S. (2020). 'The hidden costs of environmental upgrading in global value chains', *Review of International Political Economy*, DOI: 10.1080/09692290.2020.1816199.

Ponte, S., Sturgeon, T.J. & Dallas, M.P. (2019). 'Governance and power in global value chains'. In: Ponte, S., Gereffi, G. & Raj-Reichert, G. (Eds.) *Handbook on Global Value Chains*, (pp. 120–137). Edward Elgar Publishing.

Porter, M.E. (1985). *Competitive Advantage: creating and sustaining superior performance*. New York: The Free Press.

Powell, W. (1990). 'Neither Markets Nor Hierarchy: Network Forms of Organization', *Research in Organizational Behavior*, (12):295–336.

Ran, B. & Qi, H. (2018). 'Contingencies of Power Sharing in Collaborative Governance', *American Review of Public Administration*, 48(8):836–851.

Rasche, A. & Waddock, S. (2014). 'Global Sustainability Governance and the UN Global Compact: A Rejoinder to Critics', *Journal of Business Ethics*, 122(2):209–216.

Rasche, A., Waddock, S. & McIntosh, M. (2013). 'The United Nations Global Compact: Retrospect and Prospect', *Business and Society*, 52(1):6–30.

Raven, B.H. (1965). 'Social influence and power'. In: Steiner, I.D. & Fishbein, M. (Eds.), *Current studies in social psychology*, (pp. 371–382). New York: Holt, Rinehart, Winston.

Reed, I.A. (2013). 'Power: Relational, Discursive, and Performative Dimensions', *Sociological Theory*, 31(3):193–218.

Ruigrok, W. & Van Tulder, R. (1995). *The Logic of International Restructuring*. London: Routledge.

Salancik, G.R. & Pfeffer, J. (1977). 'Who Gets Power – And How They Hold on to It: A Strategic-Contingency Model of Power', *Organizational Dynamics*, Winter 77, 5(3):3–21.

Scharlemann, J., Brock, R., Balfour, N., Brown, C., Burgess, N., Guth, M., Ingram, D., Lane, R., Martin, J., Wicander, S. & Kapos, V. (2020). 'Towards understanding interactions between Sustainable Development Goals: the role of environment-human linkages', *Sustainability Science* (15):1573–1584.

Sekerka, L. (2020). 'A strength-based approach to responsible management: professional moral courage and moral competency'. In: Laasch, O, Suddaby, R. Freeman, R.E. & Jamali, D. (Eds.), *Research Handbook of Responsible Management*, (pp. 549–565). Cheltenham UK: Edward Elgar.

Seuring, S. & Müller, M. (2008). 'From a literature review to a conceptual framework for sustainable supply chain management', *Journal of Cleaner Production,* 16(15):1699–1710.

Simon, D.H. & Prince, J.T. (2016). 'The effect of competition on toxic pollution releases', *Journal of Environmental Economics and Management*, (79):40–54.

Simons, L. & Nijhof, A. (2021). *Changing the game. Sustainable Market Transformation Strategies to Understand and Tackle the Big and Complex Sustainability Challenges of our Generation.* London and New York: Routledge.

Sinkovics, N., Sinkovics, R.R. & Archie-Acheampong, J. (2021). 'The business responsibility matrix: a diagnostic tool to aid the design of better interventions for achieving the SDGs', *Multinational Business Review*, 29(1):1–20.

Thaler, R.H. & Sunstein, C.R. (2008). *Nudge: Improving decisions about health, wealth and happiness.* New Haven, CT: Yale University Press.

UN (2008). *Clarifying the concepts of "sphere of influence" and "complicity",* Report of the Special Representative of the Secretary-General on the Issue of Human Rights and Transnational Corporations and Other Business Enterprises, A/HRC/8/16.

UN (2003). *Draft Norms on Responsibilities of Transnational Corporations and Other Business Enterprises with Regard to Human Rights.* Geneva: United Nations, 30 May

UNCTAD (2002). 'Are some TNCs bigger than countries?', *World Investment Report 2002. Transnational Corporations and Export Competitiveness* (pp. 90–91). Geneva: United Nations Conference on Trade and Development.

UNFSS (2020). *Scaling up Voluntary Sustainability Standards through Sustainable Public Procurement and Trade Policy.* 4th Flagship Report of the United Nations Forum on Sustainability Standards (UNFSS/4/2020).

UN Global Compact & DNV GL (2020). *Uniting Business in the Decade of Action. Building on 20 Years of Progress.* UN Global Compact 20th Anniversary Progress Report.

Van Dijk, S., Hillen, M., Panhuijsen, S. & Sprong, N. (2020) *Social Enterprises as Influencers of the Broader Business Community. A scoping study.* Amsterdam: Social Enterprise NL.

Van Riel, C. & Blackburn, C. (1995). *Principles of Corporate Communication.* Prentice Hall.

Van Tulder, R. (2015). 'Getting all motives right: a holistic approach to internalization motives of companies', *Multinational Business Review*, 23(1):36–56.

Van Tulder, R. with Van der Zwart, A. (2006). *International Business-Society Management. Linking Corporate Responsibility and Globalization.* London: Routledge.

Van Zanten, J.A. & Van Tulder, R. (2021). 'Analyzing Companies' Interactions with the SDGs through Network Analysis: Four Corporate Sustainability Imperatives', *Business Strategy and the Environment*, 30(5):2396–2420.

Van Zanten, J.A. & Van Tulder, R. (2020). 'Towards nexus-based governance: defining interactions between economic activities and Sustainable Development Goals (SDGs)', *International Journal of Sustainable Development & World Ecology*, 28(3):210–226.

Van Zanten, J.A. & Van Tulder, R. (2018). 'Multinational enterprises and the Sustainable Development Goals: An institutional approach to corporate engagement', *Journal of International Business Policy*, (1):208–233.

Vernon, R. (1971). *Sovereignty at Bay: The Multinational Spread of US Enterprises.* New York: Basic Books.

Williamson, O.E. (2008). 'Outsourcing: Transaction Cost Economics and Supply Chain Management', *Journal of Supply Chain Management,* 44(2):5–16.

Wood, S. (2011). 'The Meaning of "Sphere of Influence". In: Henriques, A. (Ed.), *Understanding ISO 26000: A Practical Approach to Social Responsibility* (pp. 115–130). London, UK: British Standards Institution.

Zhang, T., Fletcher, P.O, Gino, F. & Bazerman, M.H. (2015). 'Reducing Bounded Ethicality: How to Help Individuals Notice and Avoid Unethical Behavior'. *Organizational Dynamics* 44(4):310–317.

11 MAKING IT FUNCTIONAL

THE INTERNAL ALIGNMENT CHALLENGE

(continued)

DOI: 10.4324/9781003098355-14

(continued)

■ **Strategic tinkering principle:** navigating organizational progress towards enhanced sustainability performance and impact requires iterative processes of top-down and bottom-up interactions, in which gaps between strategic intent and realization will regularly appear. Steering towards strategy coherence calls for sophisticated progress and performance measures as reference points, and an understanding of organizational change as a 'balancing act' between intrinsic and extrinsic motivations.

■ **Operational fit principle:** internal alignment materializes from successfully managing: (a) dynamic processes of integration, coordination and coherence; (b) within, between and across all functional departments, business units and local offices; (c) each with their own drivers, levers, timescales and barriers to change.

■ **Operational principles for sustainable business:** in order to manage organizational transition processes coherently, 'Key Practice and Performance Indicators' (KPIs) have to be linked to 'Key Value Indicators' (KVIs) and 'Key Decision-making Indicators' (KDIs). The formulation of 'Key Performance Questions' (KPQs) helps managers identify vital tipping points for next-level progress. KPIs always require appropriate 'contextualization' – related to transition phases and implemented as part of a synergy ambition – to coordinate 'vertical' and 'horizontal' alignment processes.

■ **Sustainability context principle:** organizations need to consider their performance at the micro (organizational) level within the context of demands, limits and thresholds at the macro level (the 'carrying capacity' of the ecosystem). Metrics should be used in a context-relevant manner to reflect this understanding.

■ **Net Positive principles:** twelve principles – accompanied by seven measurement principles – that define a way of doing business that puts back more into society, the environment and the global economy than it takes over the life cycle.

■ **Principle of impact integrity:** impact claims must be objectivized and substantiated with context-specific and relevant data to provide a whole, complete, sound and uncorrupted picture of all material impacts that business, investment activities and decisions have – or may have in future – on people or the planet (UNDP, 2021).

■ **Dynamic materiality principle:** what constitutes 'sustainability' and 'long-term value creation' is continuously evolving. Once considered societally relevant, non-financial or pre-financial topics can rapidly become material in financial terms. Metrics should evolve likewise.

- **Integrated management systems (IMS) principles:** (1) systemic management (integrated responsibilities; identification of synergies and trade-offs between systems; inclusion of stakeholder needs); (2) standardization (of concepts, processes, documentation); (3) integration of systems at the strategic, tactical and operational levels; (4) organizational learning; (5) de-bureaucratization; (6) continuous improvement.

- **Principles for sustainable supply chains:** operational, strategic, integrative and interactive principles related to sustainable supply chain management and 'sustainable procurement', which ISO 20400 defines as "procurement that has the most positive environmental, social and economic impacts possible over the entire life cycle".

- **Principle of extended producer responsibility:** a widely adopted policy instrument that holds producers financially and/or physically responsible for the proper end-of-life treatment of their products; encourages the production of goods that are 'built to last' rather than 'designed to fail' (planned obsolescence).

- **Principles of sustainable finance:** an expanding range of principles-based channeling efforts, including: Principles for Responsible Investment (PRI); Principles for Positive Impact Finance; Principles for Responsible Banking (PRB); Principles for Sustainable Insurance (PSI); The Equator Principles; principles for green bonds, social bonds, sustainability bonds and sustainability-linked bonds; CFO Principles on Integrated SDG Investment and Finance.

- **Principled prioritization:** strategizing and reporting approach introduced in the *SDG Compass* that sets out the process of principled prioritization: linking up to a selection of international principles through which an organization can identify priority SDG-targets to focus on, while applying the GRI standards on sustainability reporting.

- **Principles for sustainability reporting and disclosure:** rest on (1) principled prioritization; (2) standardized frameworks for 'true cost' and 'value accounting' (Greenhouse Gas, Natural Capital and Social & Human Capital Protocol); (3) IIRC's guiding Principles for Integrated Reporting; and (4) global standards for sustainability reporting (GRI, SASB, CDSB, TCFD) that define report structure, content elements, metrics, and quality dimensions.

- **ILO Tripartite Declaration of Principles concerning Multinational Enterprises and Social Policy:** delineates the nature of company-union relationships and how companies can provide inclusive, responsible and sustainable workplace practices around the world.

- **Principles of Decent Work for All:** relate to ILO's Fundamental Principles and Rights: (1) freedom of association and the right to collective bargaining; (2) elimination of forced and compulsory labour; (3) effective abolition of child labour; (4) elimination of discrimination in respect of employment and occupation. For establishing decent wage levels, a variety of benchmarks exist: minimum wage, living wage, living income, fair wage.

- **Innovation management principles:** eight principles defined in ISO 56000:2020, with an emphasis on future-focused realization of value that meets the overall objectives of securing prosperity, sustainability and the organization's long-term relevance and survival.

- **Design thinking principles** for sustainability-oriented innovation include: (1) defining a problem statement in an appropriate context, (2) a human-centric, needs-based user focus; (3) diversity and multidisciplinary approaches; (4) visualization to make abstract ideas tangible; and (5) experimentation and iteration.

- **SHIFT principles:** framework for shifting consumer attitudes, choices and behaviours towards (ecologically) sustainable outcomes, built around five key dimensions: 'social influence', 'habit formation', 'individual self', 'feelings and cognition' and 'tangibility'.

- **Principles of stakeholder participation:** a framework of 15 principles to facilitate effective multi-stakeholder processes. Principles include: accountability, effectiveness, equity, flexibility, inclusiveness, learning, legitimacy, ownership, participation and cooperative management, transparency, and 'voices' rather than 'votes'.

- **Principles of corporate citizenship** apply social, civil and political principles of 'civic membership' to corporate entities. To be accepted as a 'fellow citizen', companies should: (a) demonstrate a profound understanding of community needs; (b) develop 'interactive' capacity, accountability and credibility in supporting community activities; and (c) incorporate 'good citizenship' in the culture of their organization and the ethos of firm representatives.

P R I N C I P L E S

11.1   INTRODUCTION: CREATING OPERATIONAL FIT THROUGH STRATEGIC TINKERING

"The road to hell is paved with good intentions"
Attributed to Samuel Johnson (1775)

"The discipline of ensuring that business practices incorporate and support sustainability is the essence of internal alignment."
Business for Social Responsibility (BSR) (2007)

Translating a sustainability strategy into meaningful action necessitates that it is implemented as an integral part of the business model – embedded in all core operations and functional areas of management and supported by appropriate organizational structures, systems, policies, processes and progress measurement. Strategy, after all, is not something an organization *has*, but something an organization *does* (Jarzabkowski, 2004; Engert and Baumgartner, 2016). The effective implementation into corporate practice presents an *internal alignment challenge* in pursuit of coherence and 'operational fit', while concurrently maintaining a dynamic balance with the ever-changing business environment. Sustainable strategy implementation includes a range of factors tied to organizational governance, structure, culture, leadership, management control, capabilities development, communication and reward systems. Moreover, it vitally entails the effective management of 'internal stakeholder' dynamics throughout different phases of change. Organizational transitioning processes affect different parts of the organization differently and (temporarily) increase ambiguity and uncertainty. The ensuing divergence in expectations and motivation among separate departments and business units, the appearance of new trade-offs and dilemmas to be resolved, internal power battles, vested interests, fragmented action, and disparate progress and performance levels can constitute considerable barriers to greater sustainability performance.

Sustainability integration and related strategic renewal processes come with a certain degree of 'disorder' that must be *navigated*, directed and monitored. Strategizing and organizing become intertwined. The concept of strategic *tinkering* (Mintzberg, 1980), introduced in section 9.2.1, is helpful here. It refers to dynamic processes of alignment and realignment that allow for the pursuit of strategic intent in an agile, flexible and iterative way. Tinkering acknowledges that strategic 'intent' and 'realization' – or 'talk' and 'walk' (Chapter 9) – are not sequentially separate activities, but rather parallel processes that can converge over time into a *coherent* sustainability strategy – of proper operational fit and integral to the business model. Transition processes rarely develop in a linear or evolutionary trend; they usually evolve in an iterative way, with leaps and bounces, as *learning by doing* processes. Correspondingly, the involvement of internal stakeholders cannot be planned, but requires being 'aligned' and 'navigated'. Coherence and organizational alignment materialize from dynamic initiation and adaptation processes between functional areas of management and from smart and timely interventions. Resilient organizations are 'elastic' organizations (Carayannis et al., 2017). Internal alignment hence focuses on the (dynamic) conditions under which organizations can leverage sustainable performance and positive impact.

Organizations' slow implementation of the SDGs reflects two internal alignment problems in particular: (a) a weak link of selected SDGs with core activities, reinforced by (b) the decision to put the management of the organization's SDG approach in the hands of specialized CSR departments (WBCSD and DNV GL, 2018; UN, 2019; UN Global Compact, 2020). Nonetheless, companies are increasingly judged on their ability to 'make positive impact' – material, measurable, attributional and substantiated – whilst society's call for ramped up corporate action on the SDGs becomes louder and louder. Especially for incipient 'SDG adopters', external pressure for swift and tangible results may not leave sufficient room for strategic tinkering. Prioritizing relevant SDGs, therefore, not only poses a strategic (Chapter 8), visionary (Chapter 9) and positioning (Chapter 10) challenge, but also comprises an intricate operational challenge. Moving from strategy intent ('SDG promise') to strategy realization ('SDG performance and impact') at sufficient speed and scale requires sophisticated processes of integration and coordination between all functional areas of management, departments and business units. Organizations face two elementary challenges with a bearing on realistic ways to apply *operational principles of sustainable business*: (1) how to govern dynamic change and manage internal alignment (relating to processes of *integration, coordination* and *coherence*); (2) how to measure, report and communicate on relevant progress, performance and impact.

DYNAMIC GOVERNANCE – MANAGING INTERNAL STAKEHOLDERS

Strategic tinkering represents a 'top-down' as well as a 'bottom-up' alignment challenge. Sustainability strategies involve all business units – not only the executive board (Schaltegger et al., 2014). All functional areas of management contribute to dynamic learning and improvement processes. Failing to appreciate and utilize the drive, insights, practical expertise and competences of the organization's 'human capital', will eventually undermine effective integration, coherence, motivation and performance. Core to an effective sustainable business model is the advancement of 'dynamic capabilities', 'adaptive capacity' (Aggarwal et al., 2017) and 'self-correction' mechanisms conducive to organizational learning (Lozano, 2015). Successful sustainability trajectories hence distinguish a variety of internal *decision-making or bargaining arenas* in which managers and (informal) leaders negotiate implementation strategies. Jeffrey Pfeffer's (1993) classic study *Managing with Power* showed the importance of appropriately accounting for the varying interests represented within an organization – the 'political landscape' as he called it – in order to adopt realistic ways to operationalize feasible change pathways.

Most internal bargaining arenas are organized around *functional areas of management*. Transitions for positive change affect these areas in dissimilar ways and, accordingly, can engender internal friction, conflicts of interest, divergent ambitions and differences in paces of change – conditions that must all be skillfully navigated. Organizations have to resolve internal coordination and integration questions like: how to integrate (old and new) activities; how to deal with *competing values* (Quin and Rohrbaugh, 1983); how to create *cohesion* and *synergies* across functional areas and departments; how to identify and deal with internal *frontrunners* and *laggards*; how to also internalize the more challenging (SDG) ambitions for societal value creation; how to address switching costs and tipping points while sustaining longer-term financial viability? In either case, navigating organizational progress based on (iterative) tinkering principles instead of (top-down) planning, involves a solid understanding of: (a) internal levers of control, integration and coordination, (b) as organized in functional areas of management, (c) that influence drivers, timing and pathways of change, (d) as well as barriers to action (e) in overcoming organizational tipping points.

ORGANIZING AMIDST AN INTERNAL AND EXTERNAL MEASUREMENT JUNGLE
Managing dynamic transition processes, furthermore, requires effective internal and external communication and reporting strategies based on relevant progress measures – commonly referred to as Key Performance Indicators (KPIs) or sustainability 'metrics'. Metrics are standards of measurement by which efficiency, performance, progress or quality of a plan, process or product can be assessed. The 'metrics challenge' in sustainable business models lies in discriminating between ambiguous, nonsensical metrics that distract from material and meaningful progress on strategic goals (see Box 10.1), and those that are relevant enablers in purposive decision-making processes. Most sustainability KPIs used within private sector organizations have been developed as part of accounting and controlling efforts. They represent a subset of accounting and reporting metrics that deal with activities, methods and systems to record, analyse and report on environmental, social and economic performance – often in an isolated way. These (mostly quantitative) measures capture sustainability 'performance' primarily in terms of short-term *output* and *outcome*. Reliance on one-dimensional performance measures may induce fixated 'targetism' and myopia, however. The use of metrics that reflect the positive and negative *impacts* of corporate activities on medium-term societal goals (such as the SDGs), is nevertheless still incipient. The UN Global Compact (2020), for instance, found that only 13% of its signatory companies measure the impact of operations throughout the supply chain, 10% extend their impact assessments to raw materials, and 10% into product use.

A reported 31% of signatory companies were monitoring negative impacts, while 18% were conducting impact assessments for human rights, 25% for anti-corruption, and 29% for labour rights (ibid: 14). Considerable gaps in effective performance and impact measurement – especially with regard to more complex and multidimensional measures of sustainability – still make it challenging to systematically track progress on the integration of sustainability in business strategy.

An additional challenge for organizations is to keenly see through the complex and ever-expanding ecosystem of sustainability-related management systems, impact assessment methods, tools, performance indicator sets and impact metrics developed for management and reporting purposes. The area presents a 'jungle' comparable to the one observed for international normalization efforts (Box 10.5). Over the years, a "plethora of management system standards and guidelines" has emerged that address different corporate sustainability perspectives differently (Gianni et al., 2017: 1279). The observed result, so far, is that "integrated management systems are managed yet not measured", whereas "corporate sustainability is measured yet not managed". In other words, it remains largely unclear how the corporate 'black box' is managed, where results come from, and how they are used to improve sustainability performance (ibid). In response to the call for clarity, compatibility, comparability and harmonization – and under the influence of impact investors, accountants and rating agencies – initiatives for greater coordination in indicator development are under way. On most accounts, however, the landscape of management systems and sustainability performance management, measurement and evaluation is still overly diverse, confusing and fragmented (Box 11.1).

THE SUSTAINABILITY MANAGEMENT AND METRICS JUNGLE

B O X

11.1

The lack of practical frameworks and models to holistically operationalize sustainability in organizations has been observed as a major hurdle in attaining higher levels of sustainability performance and impact. In that light, Nawaz and Koç (2019) mapped the sustainability themes, functional areas and management tools used by 20 'best practice' companies – a selected sample from the *Corporate Knights' Global 100* most sustainable organizations. Which available management/metrics 'tools' do 'best practice' companies use for internal alignment and operational fit?

The picture of frontrunner best practice that Nawaz and Koç draw (Figure 11.1), illustrates the complexity of managing sustainability integration amidst a jungle of certifiable and non-certifiable (thematic) management systems, standards, programmes, (disclosure) guidelines and tools. The authors observe a relatively uncoordinated landscape, in which organizations additionally introduce customized tools and systems – developed in-house or outsourced – to address their organization-specific

BOX 11.1

Certified and Assured Tools

- Quality MS (ISO 9001)
- Environmental MS (ISO 14001)
- Safety MS (OHSAS 18001)
- Social Responsibility (ISO 26000, SA 8000)
- Energy MS (ISO 50001)
- Information Security MS (ISO 270001)
- Risk MS (ISO 31000)
- Food Safety (HACCP, GFSI)
- Green Building (LEED, BREEAM)
- Life Cycle Assessment (ISO 14040/44)
- Responsible Management of World's Forests (FSC, PEFC)
- Laboratory MS (ISO 17025)
- Bonsucro Production Standard
- EU Eco-Management and Audit Scheme (EMAS)
- Energy Star Certification
- AccountAbility Principles Standard (AA1000)
- Carbon Footprint of Products (ISO 14067)
- Water Footprint of Products (ISO 14046)
- Integrated MS (PAS 99)
- European Energy Certificate System (EECS)
- Standard for Assurance (ISAE 3000)
- Carbon Trust
- International Water Stewardship Standard
- The Industry Green (for Creative Industries)
- Certified B Corporations
- Sector Specific Standardized Guidelines (e.g., ISO/TS 16949:2009, ISO/TC 17, ISO/ TR 14062:2002, EN50581, ISO3834, ISO 12100, IEC 62061, IEC 61882, IEC 82079-1, IEC 62430 etc.)

Non-Certified Tools

- Policy MS
- Idea MS
- Enterprise Content MS
- Performance MS
- Data MS
- Emergency and Security MS
- Risk MS
- Project MS
- Transport MS
- Freight MS
- Carbon MS
- Water MS
- GHG Target MS
- Product Life Cycle MS
- Lost-Time Incident MS
- Enterprise Feedback MS
- Learning MS
- Compliance MS (ISO 19600)
- Six Sigma
- Lean Manufacturing
- Eco-design (ISO 14006)
- PAS 2060 (Carbon Neutral)
- Substance MS (EN50581)
- Global Salary MS

Disclosure

- Global Reporting Initiative (GRI)
- Carbon Disclosure Project (CDP)
- International Integrated Reporting Council (IIRC) Framework
- Corporate Accounting and Reporting Standard

Other Management Programs

- Stakeholder Management
- Enterprise Risk Management
- Operational Risk Management
- Project Management
- Crisis Management
- Supply Chain Management
- Supplier Relationship Management
- Customer Relationship Management
- Industrial Hygiene Management
- Stress Management
- Campaign Management (for brands)
- Integrated Performance Management

International Guidelines

- ILO Fundamental Conventions
- Universal Declaration of Human Rights
- European Convention on Human Rights
- UN International Convention on the Rights of the Child
- EU Charter of Fundamental Rights
- UNESCO Convention on the Protection and Promotion of the Diversity of Cultural Expressions
- OECD Guidelines for Multinational Enterprises
- UN Guiding Principles on Business and Human Rights
- The Ten Principles of the UN Global Compact
- Children's Rights and Business Principles by UNICEF, UN Global Compact, and Save the Children
- UN Sustainable Development Goals

Other Tools and Systems

- SAM-DJSI Evaluation Criteria
- WBCSD – Global Water Tool
- Carbon Accounting and Emissions Verification System
- Life Cycle Inventory Analysis
- Fieldprint® Platform
- SMETA – Sedex
- Efficient Logistics – Load Optimization
- Prince's Accounting for Sustainability
- Building Information Modeling
- ICTI CARE
- Oiva-Evira
- Energy Saving Opportunity Scheme (ESOS)
- Life Cycle (GaBi, HSC Thermochemical)
- Net Promoter Score (Customer Satisfaction)
- Employee Pulse Survey
- Yammer
- SIL Allocation Assessment
- SafExpert Risk Assessment
- Stage-Gate Process
- Eco Vadis Ratings & Scorecards
- Big Data Analytics
- Eco TransIT World
- Environmental Product Declaration
- ManagerReady® (management assessment)
- Trucost – SDG Evaluation Tool
- London Benchmarking Group Framework
- Web Content Accessibility Guidelines
- Environmental Profit and Loss
- Gallup Q12 (Employee Engagement Survey)
- Schneider Performance System
- Centrica's Green Deal Program
- Enbridge's Leak Survey MS
- Siemens Global Engagement Survey

Figure 11.1 A representative list of tools used by the most sustainable organizations to manage sustainability

Source: Nawaz and Koç (2019), p. 25; licensed under CC BY 4.0

needs. The sheer number and diversity of extant (and still evolving) sustainability-related management systems indicate the challenge related to: (1) the *integration* of relevant systems into an organization-wide holistic approach; (2) the *coordination* thereof among all functional areas of management, business units and local offices; (3) in ways that establish *coherence*, to enhance the organization's ability to leverage sustainability performance and impact, through synergetic effects and improved management of trade-offs.

B O X 11.1

Although harmonization and a certain degree of standardization could provide a welcome way out of '*the management and metrics jungle*', organization-specific ambitions, characteristics, structures and circumstances still call for appropriate '*contextualization*'. Contextualization recognizes that not every performance indicator is 'key' to all organizations or strategies. Not every *relevant* indicator can be quantifiably measured or monetized, nor does every indicator apply equally to all functional areas or to every organizational transition phase. Studies on the pros and cons of sustainability KPIs show how important it is to contextualize KPIs along four lines, related to: (1) the 'key decisions' an organization is faced with; (2) the transition phase it is in; (3) the functional area of management the KPIs apply to; and (4) the performance areas and SDG impact aimed at.[1]

CREATING OPERATIONAL FIT AS A MAPPING EXERCISE

In conclusion, achieving 'operational fit' and 'internal alignment' to enhance overall sustainability performance and impact entails processes of strategic tinkering and advanced navigating. Organizational 'mapping' enables corporate leaders to: (a) appreciate where their organization stands, (b) plot where the

---

1   Contextualization is one of the key elements that many benchmarking and measurement initiatives have been struggling with. The Global Reporting Initiative (GRI) established the so-called *Sustainability Context Principle,* which calls on organizations to consider their performance at the micro (organizational) level within the context of demands, limits and thresholds at the macro level (the 'carrying capacity' of the ecosystem as introduced by the Club of Rome). Applying this principle to business models in value chains implies that the sustainability performance of all chain actors is assessed as a function of relevant ecological, social and economic sustainability measures and thresholds within that particular value chain and related ecosystem. UNRISD, the United Nations Research Institute for Social Development, uses this principle to develop context-relevant performance indicators (in particular adding new types of indicators to Tier II and III), that can be linked to the SDGs (see Chapters 2 and 3).

organization needs or wants to be, (c) assess the possible routes to take to reach envisaged goals, and (4) anticipate internal barriers and possible short-cuts along the way. Applying the *principle of contextualization* requires that the 'maps' are specified for functional areas of management. This chapter puts an approach of mapping and contextualization centre stage.

Section 11.2 centres on the conditions under which organizations can leverage performance at the intended level of societal value creation. It sets out the 'intervention logic' through which coherence and operational fit across functional areas of management can be navigated. The section addresses the appearance of 'intention-realization' gaps in the change process, identifies five 'transition routes' and conditions for their feasibility, and introduces mapping techniques to assess the degree of operational coherence at four ambition levels. Throughout, the section highlights the relevance of meaningful reference points for establishing operational fit at higher ambition levels: the 'sustainability metrics challenge'.

Sections 11.3 through 11.9 take a (bottom-up) functional-level perspective. They focus on operationalizing sustainability ambition levels for seven functional areas of management. For each area, key trade-offs, dilemmas and tipping points are distinguished that play out in 'Key Performance Questions' (KPQs) and the identification of relevant principles to integrate into functional-level strategies. Each section concludes with a selection of 'Key Practice and Performance Indicators' (KPIs) and a synthesizing 'practice mapping' framework (Tables 11.1–11.7).

Section 11.10 maps the SDG alignment potential of organizations as a function of bottom-up processes that can be initiated by separate functional departments. The main argument: vertical and horizontal alignment around *internally actionable*, cross-linked SDG(-target)s can leverage organizational processes of sustainability integration, coordination and coherence. We introduce 'SDG alignment fiches' as a technique to explore leads towards an SDG-portfolio that is strategically and operationally 'fit'.

Section 11.11 synthesizes top-down and bottom-up 'alignment mapping' techniques, by illuminating ways to integrate functional-level and corporate level SDG prioritization into a coherent corporate SDG strategy: the SDG Compass 'Plus'.

NAVIGATING A 'BOOK WITHIN A BOOK'

To emphasize the interrelated nature of functional level strategies and operational choices, this chapter considers seven functional areas of management within one chapter (sections 11.3 through 11.9). Each section follows the same structure, to enable the reader to get a concise and systematic overview of the most salient discussions related to implementing sustainable management practices in each of these areas. By doing this in one integrated chapter, we created a 'book in a book' that might require some navigation guidance. There are three tracks:

- **A fast track:** which first identifies key dimensions for establishing vertical and horizontal alignment, to integrate sustainability across the organization in a coherent manner (section 11.2). Operational fit can be leveraged by exploring functional-level SDG entries to identify actionable SDG-fits (section 11.10), synthesized at the level of the whole organization (SDG Compass Plus; section 11.11).

- **A deep dive:** which, additionally, considers the trade-offs, dilemmas, tipping points, Key Performance Questions (KPQs) and Key Practice and Performance Indicators (KPIs) per functional area (sections 11.3–11.9); each overview of functional-level sustainability ambitions, considerations and choices can be studied separately.

- **A clustered track:** to broaden the perspective, gain further insights on related areas of management, and draw attention to the various interdependencies and internal linkages between operational and organizational decisions:

  - Functions with a direct bearing on organization of the value chain: sustainable purchasing (section 11.3), sustainable operations management (section 11.4), sustainable marketing (section 11.5);

  - Functions that are central to internal coordination and integration processes: sustainable HRM (section 11.6), sustainable finance (section 11.7), sustainable innovation (section 11.8);

  - Functions that manage the organization's societal license to operate: strategy (Chapter 10) and communications (section 11.9).

11.2 NAVIGATING INTERNAL CHANGE: MAPPING INTEGRATION, COORDINATION AND COHERENCE

Sustainable business model innovation studies emphasize a variety of performance 'drivers' and 'success factors' for effective organizational change: (1) coherence across strategies, organizational structure and management systems; (2) formulation of measurable goals; (3) capabilities development and allocation of sufficient resources to the process; (4) organizational learning (including safe 'failure' spaces); (5) top management commitment; and (6) effective employee motivation through co-creation and co-ownership. Appropriately dealing with these factors implies that organizational reform should not solely be instigated 'top-down' but be accompanied by 'bottom-up' approaches and

initiatives to ensure effectiveness and acceptance in the long run. The internal alignment question focuses on the conditions under which organizations can leverage
sustainable performance at the intended level of sustainability. A key management
challenge thereby is how to create *organizational synergies,* best manage (limited)
resources and adaptively 'fit' with the needs of society. This challenge poses three
types of navigating questions: (a) how to define the organizational 'logic' through
which coherence and operational fit can be achieved between functional areas of
management; (b) how to identify relevant organizational tipping points and barriers
that either facilitate or frustrate positive change; and (3) how to classify indicators
and measures relevant for monitoring progress and navigating change?

11.2.1 Mapping operational fit: creating an intervention logic

Creating 'operational fit' presents the next step in translating KVIs and KDIs into
organizational dimensions (see section 10.6). The operational fit challenge involves
the formation, alignment and leveraging of inputs and core activities to effectively
and efficiently deliver on the strategy and meet envisaged sustainability outputs,
outcomes and impact (as defined in the mission). Figure 11.2 recaps the logic
framework – introduced in previous chapters – to specify the components portraying
the drivers of organizational sustainability performance and impact, in a sequence
of interventions. Figure 11.2 zooms in on the relevant elements for *internal
alignment* – inputs, activities, output (B2 → C → D) – that relate to an organization's

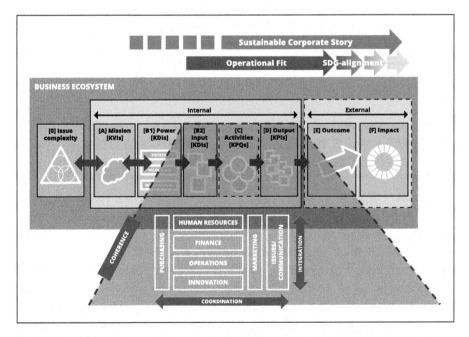

Figure 11.2 A logic model of operational fit and SDG alignment

core operations and functional areas of management and the extent to which these components are *integrated* and *coordinated,* to establish *coherence.*

INTEGRATION: VERTICAL ALIGNMENT

Integration is generally considered a 'design' and 'implementation' process that should result in a *decisional logic* – pertaining to substantive, temporal and organizational aspects – being consistently applied at every level of management (strategic, tactical and operational) and every stage of the change process (Cejudo and Michel, 2015). In the field of strategic management, integration is also known as *vertical alignment*, referring to the "configuration of strategies, objectives, action plans and decisions throughout the various levels of the organization" (Kathuria et al., 2007: 505). Asif et al. (2013) describe vertical integration of corporate sustainability in terms of the organizational strategy 'cascading down' to all levels, so that a 'fit' is created among organizational objectives, targets and processes.

Vertical integration hence concerns organizational 'hierarchies' of top-down and bottom-up approaches for strategy implementation. Integration processes are *dynamic* processes through which corporate sustainability ambitions become embedded into functional level strategies, systems, activities, programmes, priorities and performance indicators. Well-developed and well-articulated sustainability ambitions can be powerful integrating factors to steer the ideas, capabilities and motivations of employees, and for creating the vital organizational support and commitment needed to drive enhanced sustainability integration. Co-creation, monitoring and evaluation of sustainability approaches and targets have been found important components for incorporating *sustainability principles* into organizational culture (Riccaboni and Leone, 2010). Furthermore, high levels of integration reduce redundancies and lead to better results. Lock and Seele (2016), for instance, found that more successful sustainable companies were those that had vertically 'institutionalized' their CSR strategies – anchored in the governance as well as the operational level, within the close reach of top management.

Increasingly, organizations seek to integrate their various management systems to strengthen their sustainability performance and achieve higher levels of societal value creation (Box 11.2).

THE SUSTAINABILITY MANAGEMENT AND METRICS CHALLENGE [1] – INTEGRATING MANAGEMENT SYSTEMS

BOX 11.2

Effective sustainability management requires that strategy, structure and management systems are aligned. An integrative approach to sustainability implementation and management supersedes the scope of most (thematic) management system standards in areas of, for instance, quality management (ISO 9001), environmental management (ISO 14001), health and safety (OHSAS 18001), sustainable procurement (ISO 20400), accountability assurance and stakeholder relations (AA 1000), social accountability (SA 8000), energy (ISO 50001), anti-bribery (ISO 37001) and social responsibility (ISO 26000).

Managing multiple management systems (see Box 11.1) makes sustainability management as a whole more complex. Not only does the number of activities to be managed multiply, it also comes with an expanding number of performance measures across organizational functions, unsystematic lists of indicators, inconsistencies and redundancies, and high costs related to control, administration, audits, maintenance and excessive bureaucracy (Nunhes et al., 2019). Accordingly, it has become arduous and complex for organizations "to prove that internal operations deal with sustainability issues yielding results that come out as improvement in sustainability indicators" (Gianni et al., 2017: 1298). Organizations increasingly seek to unify their internal systems in support of integrative sustainability implementation and reporting to more effectively meet the needs of internal and external stakeholders.

Management systems integration fuses two or more management systems into a single, multifunctional system based on a holistic approach – operationalized at the strategic, tactical and operational levels. Companies have been found to use different models and approaches to IMS implementation, and to achieve different levels of integration and sustainability results. Empirical studies indicate several **benefits from IMS**, including optimization of resource use, improved efficiency, higher levels of employee satisfaction and teamwork, improvement in knowledge sharing, systematization of procedures, clearer definition of tasks and responsibilities, and better stakeholder relationships. But IMS development does not happen overnight. **Barriers to effective IMS implementation** – as identified in overview studies (Ikram et al., 2020; Nunhes et al., 2019) – include: (1) insufficient resources and management support (e.g. lack of financial and human resources, time, information, technology, expertise, training); (2) 'people factors' (lack of proper attitude, perception, awareness, motivation; resistance to change); (3) implementation issues (reduced flexibility after integration, diversity of constituent management system standards, misunderstanding integration concepts); (4) economics (insufficient drivers and benefits); (5) social and legal (e.g. varying stakeholder demands, lack of support schemes); and (6) cultural (lack of communication and team work, cultural conflicts).

To date, there is no standardized one-size-fits-all approach to IMS. Based on systematic content analysis, Nunhes et al. (2019) identified 28 elements for IMS development and implementation, from which they deduced six pillars or **guiding IMS principles** to develop and manage an IMS in a balanced way: (1) *systemic management* (e.g. integrated responsibilities, identification of synergies and trade-offs between systems, inclusion of stakeholder needs); (2) *standardization* (of concepts, processes, documentation); (3) *integration of systems at the strategic, tactical and operational level* (and integrated audits); (4) *organizational learning* (capacity development for innovation, knowledge sharing, investment in education);

(5) *de-bureaucratization* (elimination of redundancies and inconsistencies between processes and procedures); and (6) *continuous improvement*.

SDG alignment through ISO standards

ISO management system standards and guidelines are widely adopted by organizations around the world to manage the environmental, economic and societal dimensions of sustainability in their operations. In 2019, certification bodies reported 1,357,240 valid ISO certificates – covering a total of 1,973,475 sites – for twelve of the most used ISO management system standards (ISO Survey, 2019). To date, ISO has published more than 22,000 international standards and related documents. ISO indicates a considerable number of standards that are substantively linked to the SDGs (Figure 11.3), and which could support organizations in implementing their SDG strategy across functional areas of management. SDG9 has the largest number of linkages with applicable ISO standards and guidelines (12,197), whereas the least-aligned SDG (SDG16) still has 133 linkages with applicable ISO standards.

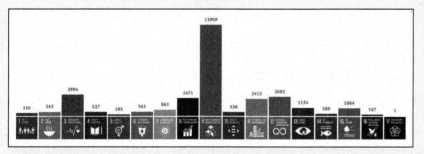

Figure 11.3 Number of ISO standards directly applicable to each SDG
Source: https://www.iso.org/sdgs.html

COORDINATION: HORIZONTAL ALIGNMENT AND SPAN OF CONTROL

The coordination dimension (Figure 11.1) refers to the degree of *horizontal alignment* and characterizes the scope and nature of an organization's operational 'span of control'.[2] Coordination pertains to the interrelation between functional areas of management in delivering on the sustainability strategy (the *input-output*

---

2   'Flat' and 'broad' organizations can be more flexible in dealing with societal triggering events (Chapter 7), but require greater levels of coordination. 'Narrow' and 'tall' organizations may display greater levels of integration and may be easier to coordinate, but usually face less flexibility in quickly responding to sudden external challenges. All combinations of organizational responsiveness and adaptation are possible and feasible. 'Big' and 'hierarchical' is not necessarily 'slow', while 'small' and 'flat' is not necessarily 'swift'.

fit). This includes the spread of activities across different countries and industries (sections 10.3.2 and 10.3.3). Effective coordination ensures smooth processes and a coherent pursuit of corporate objectives to efficiently use resources and competencies (Asif et al., 2013). Horizontal alignment requires appropriate mechanisms for exchange and cooperation – both *across and within* functional areas, departments and local business units (Kathuria et al., 2007) – as well as arrangements and structures of well-defined *responsibilities, ownership, tasks and efforts*. Communication and systems for information and knowledge sharing are key enablers for horizontal or 'lateral' alignment.

The degree of horizontal alignment established has a direct bearing on the relation between sustainability performance management, measurement and reporting (Morioka et al., 2017). The orientation and coordination of sustainability-related metrics has become a typical function of the functional department in charge of its operationalization. Moving from isolated or partial performance indicators to more holistic progress measurement, presents one of the horizontal alignment challenges that organizations face (Box 11.3).

BOX 11.3

THE SUSTAINABILITY MANAGEMENT AND METRICS CHALLENGE [2] – MOVING BEYOND ISOLATED INDICATORS AND PARTIAL MEASURES

Key Performance Indicators (KPIs) are sets of measures that organizations use to gauge their performance and assess progress towards strategic goals and desired sustainability results. KPIs can include a wide variety of indicators for varying purposes. They may be aimed at tracking efficiency, effectiveness, quality, timeliness, governance, compliance, behaviour, performance, resource utilization and various impact dimensions. KPIs can be leading (predicting outcomes) or lagging (measuring results), input or output orientated, process or outcome related, directional (evaluating trends) or actionable (involving timeframe dimensions). Furthermore, KPIs may serve internal or external concerns for sustainability management. The orientation and coordination of sustainability-relevant metrics has become a typical function of the department in charge of their operationalization. The finance department focuses on monetized KPIs to cover the costs/benefits of all activities; the operations department concentrates on emission levels, energy use and water footprint metrics; the HRM department seeks to cover health and safety-related, (gender) equality, wage and capacity development metrics; the communications/CSR department coordinates the measurement of issues relevant in the relationship with external stakeholders. Enhancing the degree of alignment across all functional activities serves three parallel purposes (Figure 11.1):

■ An *inside-in purpose*: increasing the operational efficiency of input, throughput and output activities;

- An *inside-out purpose*: serving the information needs of shareholders and investors on specific output, outcome and – increasingly – impact categories;

- An *outside-in purpose*: better serving the information needs and wider (outcome- and impact-related) concerns of societal stakeholders, pertaining to the organization's input (e.g. purchasing), throughput (e.g. operations, finance, HRM) and output (e.g. marketing, communications) activities.

In the course of over 20 years, an abundance of 'Corporate Sustainability Performance Measures' (CSPM) has been introduced to cover the operational performance of organizations. Most sustainability KPIs have come with considerable flaws, however. They tend to be partial, biased, largely focused on output rather than impact, and mostly unrelated to organizational transition phases (see Box 10.1 on the problematic practice of KPIs and the *performance paradox*). Knowledge on which sustainability management aspects should be considered to account for 'meaningful' CSPM is still limited and the development of *integrated sustainability performance measures* at the 'firm level' relatively unchartered territory – surrounded by both conceptual and methodological ambiguity. Inconsistencies, deficiencies and measurement disparities abound. Measurement tends to be primarily related to environmental performance management, "promoting initiatives to prevent, mitigate or control negative environmental impacts and compliance with regulation" (Morioka et al., 2017: 138). Based on a comparison of 108 CSPMs, Antolín-López et al. (2016) observed that most metrics do not integrate economic, social and environmental dimensions in a holistic manner. The social, economic and organizational dimensions – and the trade-offs involved – are often left open.

Composite measures – such as *ecology, social and governance (ESG) metrics* – create similar problems. As especially social factors (e.g. corporate culture, equality, support of human rights throughout the value chain) are hard to quantify, ESG metrics foremost focus on inputs and intentions (e.g. documented corporate policies and codes of conduct) rather than realized outputs and outcomes (*The Economist*, June 6 2020). Due to their industry-agnostic character, ESG metrics are commonly "too coarse-grained to be closely aligned with any particular firm's capabilities and strategy" (Young and Reeves, 2020). Hence, most ESG metrics largely miss out on the 'organizational context' in which these metrics should gain analytical and managerial meaning. The emphasis is on reporting and compliance, rather than on strategy, action and attaining sustainable competitive advantage. This state of affairs leaves managers without an "acceptable, practical and comprehensive framework that combines and informs on distinct management processes, holistic perspectives, materiality of sustainability initiatives and processes, and extent of integration" within, between and among functional areas and organizational activities (Whitelock, 2019: 925).

SDG alignment: towards 'dynamic materiality'?

The World Economic Forum (WEF) and the International Business Council (IBC) also flagged the lack of consistency among various ESG metrics as a risk for companies' long-term value creation. Together with accountancy firms Deloitte, EY, KPMG and PwC, they developed a set of *Stakeholder Capitalism Metrics (SCM)* as 'common metrics' to enable companies to consistently report on their performance against ESG indicators and track their contributions to the SDGs. The set draws from existing frameworks and standards, and is composed of metrics selected for (1) their universality across industries and business models, (2) their materiality to long-term value creation, and (3) their extent of actionability. However, "the intention is not to replace relevant sector- and company-specific indicators" for sustainable value creation (WEF, 2020: 6).

The selected set of 21 'core metrics' and 34 'expanded metrics' is organized under four pillars that are aligned with the SDGs[3] and principal ESG domains: *Principles of Governance, Planet, People and Prosperity*. With reference to the concept of *dynamic materiality*, the SCM metrics were developed in the acknowledgment that what constitutes 'sustainability' and 'long-term value creation' is continuously evolving. Once considered societally relevant, non-financial or 'pre-financial' topics may quite rapidly become material in financial terms.

The WEF/IBC initiative complements the evolving harmonization efforts within the standard-setting ecosystem, in particular that of five voluntary framework- and standard-setters – the CDP, the Climate Disclosure Standards Board (CDSB), GRI, IIRC and SASB.

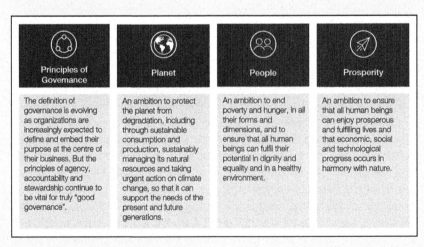

Principles of Governance	Planet	People	Prosperity
The definition of governance is evolving as organizations are increasingly expected to define and embed their purpose at the centre of their business. But the principles of agency, accountability and stewardship continue to be vital for truly "good governance".	An ambition to protect the planet from degradation, including through sustainable consumption and production, sustainably managing its natural resources and taking urgent action on climate change, so that it can support the needs of the present and future generations.	An ambition to end poverty and hunger, in all their forms and dimensions, and to ensure that all human beings can fulfil their potential in dignity and equality and in a healthy environment.	An ambition to ensure that all human beings can enjoy prosperous and fulfilling lives and that economic, social and technological progress occurs in harmony with nature.

Figure 11.4 WEF's four pillars for common metrics of sustainable value creation

Source: World Economic Forum (2020), p. 12. Licensed under CCPL

---

3   Note, that the White Paper does not make explicit reference to SDG2 (zero hunger) and SDG11 (sustainable cities and communities).

COHERENCE: ORGANIZING AN INTERNAL NEXUS

Coherence appears when various components of the strategy and organizational structures, systems, processes, instruments and incentives correspond. It is obtained when high levels of both vertical and horizontal alignment are achieved across all functional areas of management and business units, such that they conjointly serve a *larger goal* than each individual department could attain separately. Organizational coherence involves: (1) consistency of decisions across organizational levels, (2) effective coordination of all activities, (3) appropriate resource allocation, and (4) attentive management of trade-offs and potential conflicts of interest. It is accompanied by systems for monitoring and evaluation, in order to keep track on progress and to enable adaptive and timely decision-making.

A coherent business model adds efficiency and effectiveness to an organization's activities. Organizational coherence, in a sense, presents the micro-equivalence of macro-level 'policy coherence' for sustainable development and SDG implementation (see Chapters 2 and 3). Coherence creates an *internal nexus* between functional areas that provides opportunities to leverage organizational resources and capabilities by eliminating redundancies, minimizing trade-offs and harnessing synergistic effects (see section 10.5.3). Coherence thus increases an organization's potential to attain higher levels of societal value creation. In contrast, *lack of organizational coherence* induces goal ambiguity, diminishes effectivity and tends to discourage commitment, support and employee motivation – all vital to the realization of the intended sustainability strategy.

Coherence is not a static 'state of being', however. Change processes commonly lead to (temporarily) lower levels of coherence as a necessary condition for transitioning towards the next sustainability level. *Coupling and decoupling* processes are an inextricable part of dynamic change, equivalent to the *loosening while strengthening* balancing act (and related power, positioning and leadership dimensions) elaborated in Chapter 10. *Coupling* denotes the extent to which decisions made in one functional area, department or business unit are congruent with – and supported or reinforced by – decisions made in other parts of the organization. This requires high degrees of vertical and horizontal alignment. *Decoupling*, on the other hand, appears when formal strategy and action plans differ substantially from everyday practice, conflict with departments' own goals (Weaver et al., 1999) or are subject to divergent interpretations, applications and practices in different parts of the organization. Although often associated with intra-organizational power battles, *decoupling while coupling* processes also enable strategic 'tinkering' for reaching next level sustainability and, therefore, should be navigated and smartly managed. A too tight coupling of strategy, structure and practice – especially when applied in a top-down manner and with low levels of commitment – will cut out the flexibility an organization needs to timely adapt to changing circumstances. Decoupling, to a certain extent, may provide more flexibility and adaptive capacity. But if functional departments are 'out of sync' – all organizing sustainability differently, yet with the same (perceived) purpose in mind – an organization may become its own major obstacle in realizing positive change. Considerable gaps between sustainability intention and realization are then bound to appear.

Linking steering principles to organizational transition phases and sustainability 'performance and impact' measures, presents a next mapping and management challenge (Box 11.4).

BOX 11.4

THE SUSTAINABILITY MANAGEMENT AND METRICS CHALLENGE [3] – MAKING IT IMPACTFUL THROUGH SDG ALIGNMENT

Greater coherence – through higher degrees of vertical and horizontal alignment – increases organizational capacity for enhanced sustainability outcomes and positive societal impact (see Figure 11.1). But how to integrate 'impact management' into decision-making in a way that optimizes corporate contributions to sustainable development and the SDGs? What 'steering principles' to use, how to see through 'the jungle' of impact management tools, metrics, taxonomies and valuation models, and how to translate these into actionable activities?

To facilitate organizations in achieving higher levels of strategic sustainability integration and SDG outcomes – and counter 'SDG-washing' as well – the United Nations Development Programme developed **SDG Impact Standards for Enterprises** (UNDP, 2021). The impact standards set out a decision-making framework that should help organizations to coherently integrate 'impact management' into their strategy, management approach, disclosure, governance and decision-making

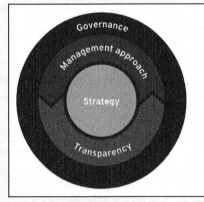

Standard 1 (Strategy): Embedding foundational elements into purpose and strategy

Standard 2 (Management Approach): Integrating foundational elements into operations and management approach

Standard 3 (Transparency): Disclosing how foundational elements are integrated into purpose, strategy, management approach and governance, and reporting on performance

Standard 4 (Governance): Reinforcing commitment to foundational elements through governance practices

Figure 11.5 UNDP's SDG impact standards categories for enterprises

Source: UNDP (2021) SDG Impact Standards, https://sdgimpact.undp.org/practice-standards.html

practices. They are intended as **practice and decision-making standards** – not performance or reporting standards – to help organizations operationalize and link existing principles frameworks, standards and sustainability management tools in a consistent way. The standards are aimed at providing organizations with a 'best prac-tice' guide and self-assessment tool for internal gap analysis and improvement over time, and to connect organizational sustainability and SDG practice to consistent reporting. Each of the four SDG Impact Standard categories – (1) Strategy, (2) Management approach, (3) Transparency, (4) Governance – is accompanied by **Practice Indicators** that "demonstrate what achieving each standard looks like" (UNDP, 2021).

Aligning around 'impact measurement' of SDG contributions

Not only is the development of SDG Impact Standards a timely effort to give impetus to accelerated corporate action on the SDGs in the 'Decade of Action', it is also a reflection of the progressive trend for organizations' willingness to act sustainably. The **Impact Management Project (IMP)** – an international public interest forum convening over 2,000 organizations and 16 international standard-setting organiza-tions around **impact management norms** – reached global consensus on how to define, measure, manage and report on sustainability impact. IMP defines four levels of impact related to corporate sustainability intentions – the so-called **ABC Impact Classification** – and five dimensions for impact measurement, encompassing 15 categories of data for assessing and substantiating sustainability and SDG impact (Figure 11.6).

The increasing attention for measuring and reporting on SDG impact also raises the issue of the legitimacy of impact claims, the relevance (materiality) of reported direct and indirect effects, and the completeness and accuracy of infor-mation provided. The emergence of **SDG-washing** and **SDG cherry-picking** – with organizations overestimating their positive contributions while understating or disregarding their negative impact – has repeatedly been pointed out with serious concern. In 2020, the UN Global Compact's progress report emphasized that "a key gap in analysing impacts across the Ten Principles" remained, with merely 31% of signatory companies reporting on their negative impact. Measuring and reporting on SDG contributions requires that impact claims are objectivized, substantiated with context-specific and relevant data, and made with due regard to **impact integrity** – by "acting to provide a whole, complete, sound and uncorrupted picture of all material impacts that business and investment activities and decisions have (or may have in future) on people or the planet" (UNDP, 2021). In this chapter, these insights will be further 'contextualized', by linking each of the four impact levels to functional areas of management, SDG alignment and internal nexus challenges.

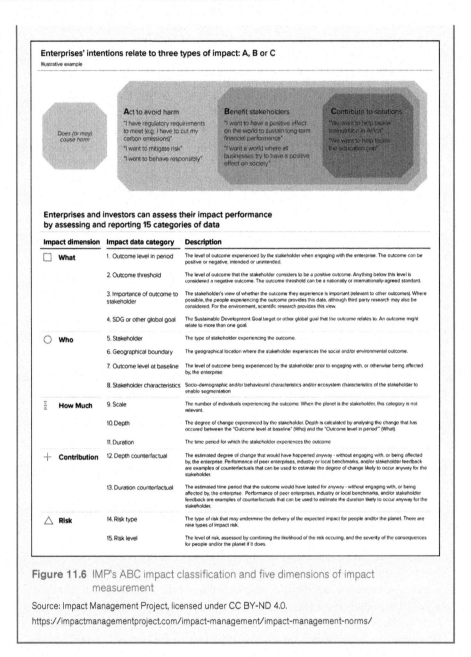

Enterprises' intentions relate to three types of impact: A, B or C
Illustrative example

Act to avoid harm
"I have regulatory requirements to meet (e.g. I have to cut my carbon emissions)"
"I want to mitigate risk"
"I want to behave responsibly"

Benefit stakeholders
"I want to have a positive effect on the world to sustain long-term financial performance"
"I want a world where all businesses try to have a positive effect on society"

Contribute to solutions
"We want to help tackle malnutrition in Africa"
"We want to help tackle the education gap"

Does (or may) cause harm

Enterprises and investors can assess their impact performance by assessing and reporting 15 categories of data

Impact dimension	Impact data category	Description
What	1. Outcome level in period	The level of outcome experienced by the stakeholder when engaging with the enterprise. The outcome can be positive or negative, intended or unintended.
	2. Outcome threshold	The level of outcome that the stakeholder considers to be a positive outcome. Anything below this level is considered a negative outcome. The outcome threshold can be a nationally or internationally-agreed standard.
	3. Importance of outcome to stakeholder	The stakeholder's view of whether the outcome they experience is important (relevant to other outcomes). Where possible, the people experiencing the outcome provides this data, although third party research may also be considered. For the environment, scientific research provides this view.
	4. SDG or other global goal	The Sustainable Development Goal target or other global goal that the outcome relates to. An outcome might relate to more than one goal.
Who	5. Stakeholder	The type of stakeholder experiencing the outcome.
	6. Geographical boundary	The geographical location where the stakeholder experiences the social and/or environmental outcome.
	7. Outcome level at baseline	The level of outcome being experienced by the stakeholder prior to engaging with, or otherwise being affected by, the enterprise
	8. Stakeholder characteristics	Socio-demographic and/or behavioural characteristics and/or ecosystem characteristics of the stakeholder to enable segmentation
How Much	9. Scale	The number of individuals experiencing the outcome. When the planet is the stakeholder, this category is not relevant.
	10. Depth	The degree of change experienced by the stakeholder. Depth is calculated by analysing the change that has occured between the "Outcome level at baseline" (Who) and the "Outcome level in period" (What).
	11. Duration	The time period for which the stakeholder experiences the outcome
Contribution	12. Depth counterfactual	The estimated degree of change that would have happened anyway - without engaging with, or being affected by, the enterprise. Performance of peer enterprises, industry or local benchmarks, and/or stakeholder feedback are examples of counterfactuals that can be used to estimate the degree of change likely to occur anyway for the stakeholder.
	13. Duration counterfactual	The estimated time period that the outcome would have lasted for anyway - without engaging with, or being affected by, the enterprise. Performance of peer enterprises, industry or local benchmarks, and/or stakeholder feedback are examples of counterfactuals that can be used to estimate the duration likely to occur anyway for the stakeholder.
Risk	14. Risk type	The type of risk that may undermine the delivery of the expected impact for people and/or the planet. There are nine types of impact risk.
	15. Risk level	The level of risk, assessed by combining the likelihood of the risk occuring, and the severity of the consequences for people and/or the planet if it does.

Figure 11.6 IMP's ABC impact classification and five dimensions of impact measurement

Source: Impact Management Project, licensed under CC BY-ND 4.0.
https://impactmanagementproject.com/impact-management/impact-management-norms/

11.2.2 Mapping intention and realization: mind the gap!

The process of developing, implementing and managing a coherent 'sustainable business' strategy, ultimately boils down to a confrontation between *intention and realization* or sustainability *promise and performance*. As discussed in Chapter 9 (Figure 9.3), sustainability intentions are the upshot of both primary (intrinsic/extrinsic) and secondary (short-term/long-term) motivations, resulting in level 1 (inactive), level 2 (reactive), level 3 (active) or level 4 (proactive) value propositions and related KVIs (Chapter 9) and KDIs (Chapter 10). The degree of strategy integration and operational coordination established across the entire organization explains for the actual realization of sustainability intentions. In practice, integration and coordination are not necessarily aligned, nor do strategic intent and realization go hand in hand. The proverbial road to hell is paved with good intentions. Dynamic transition processes – almost by definition – portray considerable intention-realization gaps (section 9.1) as a reflection of the size and complexity of the internal alignment challenge. This gap can be graphically mapped, by juxtaposing intention and realization scales (Figure 11.7):

■ *Intentions* are represented by the upper and upper-left scales. The interplay of primary (intrinsic-extrinsic) and secondary (short-term/long-term) motivations generates level 1, 2, 3 and 4 sustainability ambitions. Ambition levels define the intended sustainable business strategy and business case (and associated KVIs that guide KDIs).

■ *Realization* of ambitions in the concrete organization of a business model can be assessed as the (intermediate) outcome of two 'realization scales', representing vertical (integration) and horizontal (coordination) alignment dimensions.

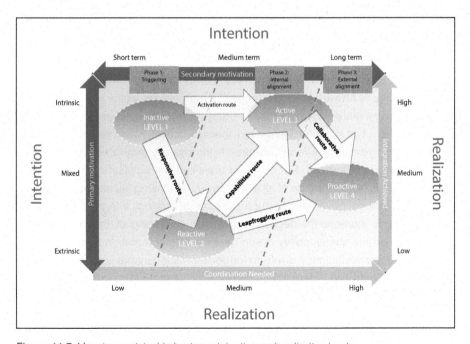

Figure 11.7 Mapping sustainable business intention and realization levels

EXPLORING TRANSITION ROUTES

The confrontation of intention and realization reveals five distinct transition routes – related to four motivational 'logics' (inactive, reactive, active, proactive, see section 9.3.2) – that organizations go through when moving from one level of (societal) value creation to the next. Each transition route delineates distinct organizational tipping points that are rooted in different combinations of integration-coordination:

- **The responsive route** represents the prevalent route taken by organizations that see themselves confronted with *external triggering* events (Chapter 7). Mounting stakeholder pressure and the threat of stricter regulation can be decisive reasons to move away from a passive stance to sustainability (level 1), towards a level 2 (reactive) sustainability approach and organization of the business model. Cost considerations, reputation and brand value are generally the main motivational drivers (Chapter 8). Along the responsive route, the critical operational challenge lies in altering the dominant *tactical and short-termism* practice that is grounded in how the business model is orientated, organized and incentivized. The internal momentum for change risks to cease, however, as soon as the external pressure from stakeholders disappears. Loss of traction jeopardizes the internal *decoupling and recoupling* processes needed to coherently organize around 'level 2' corporate responsibility (*minimize negative effects, avoid doing harm*). The reactive logic – with its inherent need to swiftly respond to external concerns – commonly arrives at a lower degree of integration (as a *consistent* sustainability strategy is yet to be determined and internalized) and a higher need for operational coordination (Figure 11.7).

- **The activation route** entails a more exceptional path: from level 1 (inactive), directly onward to level 3 (active). It materializes as the result of *internal triggering* events – for instance, visionary strong new leadership drafting the contours of a sustainability-driven mission. Level 3 ambitions (*do good, enhancing positive effects*) are mostly intrinsically motivated and aimed at longer-term outcomes. Successfully travelling the activation route involves a strategic (re)orientation of all activities by: (a) making full use of the already strong internal governance structures to drive strategy integration, while (b) seeking to increase the degree of coordination among all units to conjointly deliver on the sustainability-driven mission. Implementation of more radical change (from efficiency-driven to longer-term sustainable outcomes) entails that core activities, operational practice and managerial mindsets are altered accordingly – a sizable leadership challenge. Major barriers to change are mostly internal, as drastic shifts in value orientation imply profound alterations in activities and organizational structures, day-to-day routines, required capabilities and the responsibilities assigned to managers.

■ **The capabilities route** is the common route organizations take in moving from level 2 (reactive) to level 3 (active) sustainable business approaches. Adaptive and managerial capabilities are developed along the way (*learning by doing*), whilst viable and more strategic sustainability approaches gradually take shape. Integration into core operations progresses in a step-by-step manner as the organization works towards overcoming key organizational tipping points. Major internal barriers include the *recoupling* of varying practices, motivational drivers, values and interests. Because resource, responsibility and budget allocations will change in accordance with new priorities, power battles over vested interests are bound to appear. The focus along this route is on developing greater levels of internal alignment: more effective coordination and cooperation between functional areas of management, and a consistent uptake of the sustainability approach into systems, policies, processes and incentive mechanisms. External stakeholder pressure may actually help to speed up internal alignment. As experience grows, more confident decisions on fundamental organizational changes move the organization from relatively low, to higher levels of integration, coordination and coherence. Accordingly, the strategic intent shifts *from do no harm to do good* – in all areas of management. The successful completion of this route should result in a long-term *strategic advantage* for the organization in order to solidify (Chapter 8).

■ **The leapfrog route** leads directly from a reactive (level 2) to a proactive (level 4) sustainability approach. The leapfrog route is a *high-risk* trajectory that rarely succeeds, due to external influences. Regardless of the sincerity of intentions, external stakeholders will be suspicious of any company claiming to contribute to *transformative change* when that claim is not convincingly substantiated by a track record of consistent sustainable practice. Critical stakeholders will suspect 'window dressing' and 'SDG-washing' if strategy, operational practice and corporate conduct appear insufficiently aligned for meaningful outcomes. Organizations that opt for the leapfrog track should critically ask themselves whether the requisite levels of (a) strategy integration, (b) operational coordination (functional alignment), (c) intrinsic drive and stamina, and (d) dynamic capabilities are in place to, in all reason, be able to deliver on 'level 4' ambitions. The more secure and common route is to establish sufficient internal alignment and adaptive capabilities first, in order to build trust, credibility, societal legitimacy and vital stakeholder support in addressing sustainability challenges.

■ **The collaborative route** is the transition process that leads organizations from level 3 (active) to level 4 (proactive) sustainability approaches. Following the collaborative track stems from the understanding that no single organization can effectively resolve the more complex sustainability challenges alone – no matter how operationally coherent and internally aligned the business model. Organizations with *transformational* (level 4) ambitions recognize that their business cannot thrive in a society that fails and that joint efforts are imperative for systems change. Taking *societal needs* as the starting point for future-oriented strategizing – a *reversed materiality approach* (section 9.3.2) – requires effective external alignment and collaborative strategies in partnership with relevant stakeholders. Managing a portfolio of strategic partnerships may come with a significantly lower degree of strategy integration however. A certain degree of flexibility is vital for being able to respond, adapt and commit to (dynamically evolving) joint approaches. More loosely (or less tightly) coupled vertical alignment increases the need for coordination – both internally (between functional areas of management) and externally (the interaction with strategic partners) – in order to sustain sufficient operational coherence and deliver on envisaged sustainability outcomes and impact.

BOX 11.5

MIND THE GAP!

The graphical confrontation of (strategy) intent and (business model) realization (Figure 11.8) enables an assessment of the gap between *intention* and *realization*. 'Mapping the gap' helps to: (a) figure out what the sources of motivational and organizational misalignment are, (b) reflect on the relevant transition route to take, and (c) anticipate the kind of integration-coordination challenges to be addressed along the way.

Research among more than 1,200 managers of a representative sample of 718 companies in the Netherlands[4] – applying the *Better Business Scan* (Tool 9.1) – reveals several patterns:

- About 70% of companies report level 3 or 4 ambitions;

- 87% of companies face a gap between strategy intention and realization, of which 46% self-assessed a sizable gap;

- Interestingly, 13% of companies have realized sustainability strategies beyond their initial intention (which can be explained by contextual factors, such as stakeholder pressure);

- The majority of companies (60%) are operating along the 'capabilities route', progressing as they go while working on overcoming primarily internal alignment challenges.

---

4   Intermediate results of ongoing research, based on the number of assessments until March 2021.

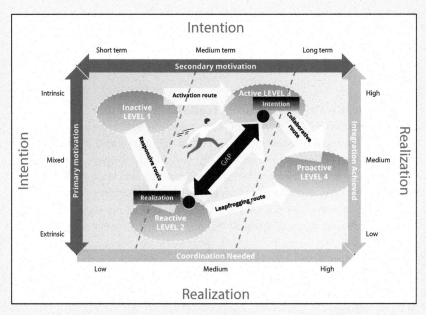

Figure 11.8 Mapping the intention–realization gap

Understand the route to take

For executives, one of the most unfortunate blind spots is *not* knowing where in the transition the organization finds itself in. Figure 11.8 shows the 'internal alignment' gap that is typical for phase 2 transitioning. The organization and its leaders aspire a 'level 3' (active, intrinsically driven) sustainability ambition, but so far have only been able to achieve a 'level 2' (reactive, extrinsically driven) organization of their business model. This 'internal alignment' gap is notoriously known to evoke allegations of 'greenwashing' as the company is not 'walking the talk' (see section 9.1). However, the internal alignment gap does not necessarily reflect a lack of commitment. It may well represent an intermediate 'snapshot' of a dynamic process still unfolding – a moment in time universal to any transition process, as intentions almost always precede realization. The gap analysis merely indicates the transition route that leaders and managers should commit to in order to (operationally) align sustainability intent and realization at level 3 ambitions.

As depicted in Figure 11.8, 'walking' the capabilities route entails working towards higher degrees of both strategy integration and operational coordination. Successful navigation thereby relies on the selection of appropriate metrics and measures to track progress and shed light on both dimensions. Performance indicators might, misleadingly, *suggest* a relatively linear or evolutionary path – for example, increasing CO_2-reduction targets from 30% to 60%. But to achieve such reduction targets, most organizations face a bumpy road of having to surpass *fundamental organizational tipping points.*[5] The path from level 2 to level 3 essentially entails the coherent operationalization of a *reconceptualized business model* (see section 9.4). Accordingly, breaking through the reactive threshold requires inherently different organizational capabilities.

'Bears on the road' – pitfalls, traps and barriers

Along each transition route, a variety of barriers and enablers materialize that organizations should reckon with.[6] Although every transition route is marked by its own typical challenges, the *capabilities route* has a particularly high number of 'bears on the road'. Most pertain to changing relationships between 'leading' and 'lagging' departments, alterations in the roles and responsibilities of managers, and adjustments in value propositions (Chapter 9) that develop amidst internal power struggles (related to conflicting values, the course and pace of action, reallocation of resources and budgets). Barriers are 'manageable' and can be overcome, provided that all functional areas of management can be aligned to a sufficient degree and indicators of organizational friction are attentively addressed. Practical pointers for dealing with intention-realization gaps along the capabilities route include:

▪ **Confront trade-offs.** Transition processes rarely present unequivocal win-win situations. Most organizations encounter difficult trade-offs – for instance, whether to prioritize: ad hoc responsiveness to market demand over future-oriented planning and investment, avoiding liability over taking responsibility, or ecological sustainability over social and economic sustainability. The starting point is to create a strategic vision that provides guidance (a 'decisional logic') on how these trade-offs should be weighed and addressed. It is important not to postpone unavoidable choices; delaying them can cause the organization to *get stuck in the middle* of the route. Internal stakeholders are the most

---

5   In his book *How to avoid a climate disaster: the solutions we have and the breakthroughs we need*, Bill Gates (2021) sets out why, in the short run, policies and strategies need to be in place that will put all on the path to deep decarbonization. "It might seem like 'reduce by 2030' and 'get to zero by 2050' are complementary. Isn't 2030 a stop on the way to 2050? Not necessarily. Making reductions by 2030 the wrong way might actually prevent us from ever getting net zero. Why? Because the things we'd do to get small reductions by 2030 are radically different from the things we'd do to get to zero by 2050" (p. 196).

6   Nearly 150 motivational triggers and barriers along the five transition trajectories were identified in *Getting all the motives right. Driving International Corporate Responsibility (ICR) to the next level* (Van Tulder, 2018).

important target group in this transition process: they can frustrate, facilitate or greatly accelerate change.

■ ***Deal with the 'Kodak effect'.*** The implementation of sustainability strategies creates a new internal reality. Some activities need to be stepped up, others restructured, downscaled or discontinued altogether (see section 10.4). Companies that fail to timely do so, miss out on opportunities. In the management discourse, this mechanism is known as the 'incumbent's curse' or the 'Kodak effect' (see Box 9.2). It refers to organizations that cling to their long-standing business model, fail to keep pace with changing societal needs and expectations, and eventually face loss of competitiveness, marginalization and even bankruptcy. Large companies, in particular, often find it difficult to change how they 'do business'. Developing a strategic vision of where the company wants to go *and why*, is essential in reducing fears of radical change, uncertainty and related internal interest battles. It is also vital for mobilizing internal support and empowering bottom-up initiatives as important enablers of organizational change (see section 10.6 on developing a *sustainable corporate story*).

■ ***Beware of techno-optimism.*** Techno-optimism relates to overly optimistic expectations on the potential of technologies to solve societal problems. *The Economist* (10 February, 2018) referred to this as *techno solutionism*, pointing to 'techies' with the naive belief system that problems in, for instance, health, education, nature conservation, consumer behaviour or waste reduction can be solved with whatever technology is in vogue. The danger of techno-optimism lies in the path dependencies, unintended side effects and blind spots it creates when technology (e.g. artificial intelligence, 'big data', blockchain) is introduced as the primary or ultimate solution for complex organizational and behavioural challenges. Faced with a large number of integration and coordination challenges at the same time, management may try to 'fit' the organization of activities into the design of a particular IT system or, conversely, design an IT system that is supposed to solve integration and coordination complexities. Organizational change becomes geared towards 'making the system' work, rather than 'making the organization' work. More successful organizations first establish the fundamental fit with the sustainability ambition, so that technology 'follows' the organization rather than the other way round. Take the example of 'blockchain' – a peer-to-peer distributive ledger system that promises to improve security, reliability and manageability of ICT networks. Blockchain can be used in the organization of, for instance, sustainable supply chains. Nine out of ten blockchain projects presently fail, however, mainly because they are too complex, too expensive or unaligned with the core activities and needs of the organization that introduced it. The history of innovation shows that organizational change usually precedes successful technological innovation.

11.2.3 Mapping coherence: identifying leaders and laggards

Addressing the organizational implications of the gap between sustainability intent and realization requires one more mapping exercise: an assessment of the realized strategy of each functional area of management to indicate the degree of operational coherence across the organization. Plotting the position of all functional departments (Figure 11.9) reveals the 'span of control' in achieving the intended sustainable business model. It provides a snapshot of (intermediate) organizational characteristics, pointing to: (1) 'leaders' and 'laggards' within the organization; (2) the level of organizational coherence this reflects; and (3) the routing challenges ahead in overcoming critical organizational tipping points.

IDENTIFYING INTERNAL CHANGE AGENTS: LAGGARDS AND LEADERS

The process of establishing a sustainable business model is a trajectory ridden with internal alignment and operationalization challenges. Both the course and pace of change are strongly influenced by how functional departments – with varying levels of sustainability engagement – interact. All organizations, especially larger ones, face *internal bargaining arenas* in which the desirability, conditions for and implications of organizational change are negotiated (section 11.1). Divergence in motivation and commitment levels can be the result of board-level 'top-down' strategy choices that prioritize some departments over others. It may also be a reflection of constrained 'bottom-up' interactions, with some departments facing difficulties in the operationalization of sustainability ambitions, or resisting the initiated change trajectory altogether. Whatever the exact background of considerations, divergence in departments' commitment levels materializes in divergent operational clock speeds and progression on sustainability realization. Over time, progress and performance disparities eventually reveal a pattern of leading and lagging departments.

The influence that leading and lagging departments de facto have on the course, pace and viability of change depends on their internal positioning and (informal) power base.[7] The relevant question, therefore, is which department(s) – or which corporate function(s) – is decisive in determining the tempo and way forward: the leaders or the laggards? Which parts of the organization can be identified as 'agent of change' or 'agent of stagnation'? In relative terms, the finance and purchasing departments often occupy a (prudent) lagging position,

---

7　So-called 'Stackelberg games' – repeated dynamic 'leader-follower' games indicative for internal alignment processes – suggest that cooperation can be improved in a value-adding direction, provided that leaders consider followers' strategies and constraints, and followers respond to the leader's strategy (Nie et al., 2019).

whilst the interface departments (communications and CSR) – tasked with the management of external stakeholder relations – are often at the forefront of sustainability ambitions. To sustain both positions would imply that the sustainability strategy and core activities become detached. 'Talk and walk', then, are no longer in line and the organization risks to lose its credibility.

ASSESSING ORGANIZATIONAL COHERENCE

Keeping track of organizational coherence is a vital element for navigating effective change strategies. Internal alignment ensures that all parts of a business model are coherently organized: the strategy matches the structure, culture and activities of the organization. Greater coherence generally leads to better performance on intended outcomes as strategic priorities are consistent, linked and mutually supporting. A *coherent business model* has achieved high levels of both strategy integration and operational coordination between and across all functional areas of management. High coherence is not necessarily similar to an advanced sustainable business model however. Coherence can be achieved at a low ambition level (inactive, level 1), at a high ambition level (proactive, level 4), and any level in between. In contrast, an *incoherent business model* is characterized by a low degree of vertical and horizontal alignment between functional areas of management. The less coherent the business model is operationalized – represented by a wide spread of functional activities, as plotted in Figure 11.9 – the higher the 'span of control'. Organizational incoherence makes it extremely arduous and complicated to get anything done inside the business model. Major differences in realized sustainability levels between functional departments have been found to negatively impact an organization's overall sustainability performance.

Figure 11.9 shows: (1) a relatively coherent business model, challenged by a relatively low span of control, and (2) a relatively incoherent business model, challenged by an extremely high span of control.

DECIDING ON VIABLE TRANSITION ROUTES

By (1) mapping the realization positions of all functional areas of management, (2) identifying leaders and laggards, and (3) assessing the degree of operational coherence, a clearer picture of the viability of each transition route unfolds. The mapping exercise should also provide a better insight into those functional departments best positioned to play a leading role in determining the pace of change and orchestrating adaptive organizational learning. Depending on the level of coherence, an organization may focus its strategy on one transition route that it considers the most feasible. Alternatively, it may opt for a combination of routes – geared to the dynamics in distinct parts of the organization – which eventually should all converge around achievement of the overall sustainability ambition.

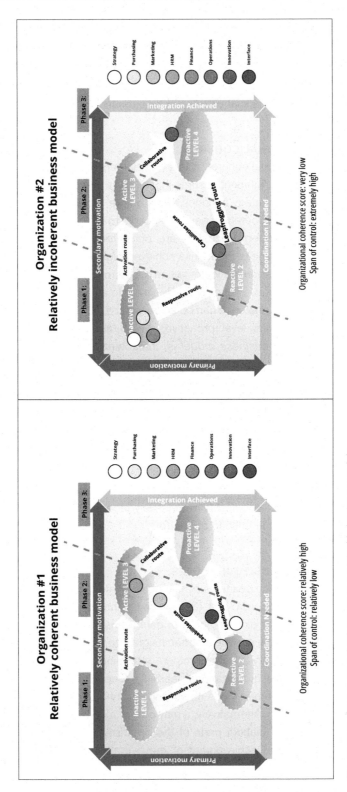

Figure 11.9 Organizational coherence in sustainable business models

Source: Better Business Scan, https://www.betterbusinessscan.org/

Research on successful business model innovation strategies (see Chapter 9) has not yet developed robust results on the antecedents of change and the potential role of specific functional areas in shaping and driving organizational transitions. However, observations on a case-by-case basis (Van Tulder et al., 2014) provide applicable insights on the conditions under which organizations can drive internal alignment for positive change (Box 11.6).

TWO CASES OF COHERENCE AND TRANSITIONS

B
O
X

11.6

Figure 11.9 maps two types of organizations with distinct levels of coherence across their functional areas of management. Organization #1 realized a relatively coherent business model at ambition level 2, with only one functional area (HRM) portraying a more active position (level 3). Organization #2 has a very active marketing department (focusing on the bottom of the pyramid) and an R&D department that aims at level 4 innovations, organized in open-innovation processes. However, organization #2 is also faced with quite powerful conservative departments (finance, purchasing and strategy) that have a dispiriting effect on the overall sustainability ambition and a dampening influence on the pace of progress. Which organization to put your sustainability hopes on?

■   **Organization #1** has the greatest chance to organize a reasonably coordinated transition process, provided it chooses to actually pursue it. Organization #1 represents a far more coherent environment for change processes than organization #2. The *intention-realization gap* is relatively narrow and, under the right conditions, probably attainable to overcome. Although the organization is not yet convincingly 'active' (level 3), there is a general sense of responsiveness to societal challenges and a reasonable awareness of the need to future-proof the business model. The main challenge is to develop a company-wide internal alignment approach and a strategic business case for sustainability. In case the C-suite decides to move beyond level 2 – with a clear vision and operationalization plan –major internal opposition probably does not need to be anticipated. The HRM department and most employees are already motivated to take a more active (level 3) stance on societal issues. It might even be advisable to assign the HRM department an internal accelerator's role. The preferred transition route for this organization is the *capabilities route*, for which the active involvement of the HRM department is always a necessary condition.

■   **Organization #2** faces major integration and coordination problems. The span of control between functional areas is wide, as is the gap between sustainability intent and realization. Due to its incoherence, the organization has great difficulties in prioritizing and aligning corporate efforts. In this particular case, the organization is highly dedicated to sustainable innovations, but experiences considerable internal opposition from its financial and purchasing departments – both largely efficiency-driven and aimed at short-term results (level 1). The marketing department wants to move ahead. It has already started campaigns on specific sustainable products, but the communications department fears to be confronted with serious criticism from external stakeholders who may reproach the company for using its BoP approach as PR. The interface with society is driven by reputation considerations. This has made it susceptible to defensive motives, reflected in a limited willingness to embrace an integrated reporting approach. Organization #2 has a hard time deciding on any transition route. Because strategy, finance and purchasing do not seem sufficiently triggered to take a next step, any transition trajectory risks getting stuck on these three powerful agents of stagnation. Pressure from external stakeholders, strong leadership or a convincingly 'hard' business case for sustainability, could help to overcome the organizational stalemate.

11.2.4 The functional management challenge: operationalizing progress

Progressive strategy-making for enhanced sustainability requires that strategic and functional priorities are linked in ways that leave sufficient leeway for bottom-up initiative and functional spearheading. 'Leading' functional departments can inspire, push, and accelerate organizational transitioning. But if internal dynamics lead to operational friction and barriers to change, realization of a next-level sustainable business model may prove an overstretch. Decisions on the course and pace of transitioning can, therefore, only be effective when based on a thorough understanding of the internal levers, barriers, phases and critical tipping points – for each functional area of management. The organizational challenge is to establish what would constitute 'progress' in each functional area, and then to consider effective levels of operationalization that can take the whole organization to higher levels of sustainability.

Scholarly thinking in various disciplines (e.g. supply chain, operations, marketing, finance, HRM) points at the potential – and necessity – of functional areas of management to move beyond the 'compliance' phase of sustainability:

- Supply chain and operations management approaches increasingly look at *closed loops of resources and materials* to raise efficiency, sustainability and inclusiveness at the same time;

- The marketing discipline is shifting towards a *theory of needs* that reaches beyond market demand, 'want' and peoples' identity as consumers to also include choice-editing, latent demand, needs-based approaches to serve underserved populations, and the creation of future markets;

■ HRM approaches are reassessing *the value of purpose, vision and commitment* in personnel management, as impact-driven sustainability strategies contribute to motivated, creative and agile employees;

■ In financial management, the search is for how finance can enable a shift away from short-termism, shareholder focus and retention of 'stranded assets', towards a resilience-oriented investment agenda focused on longer-term opportunities and societal value creation – also known as *Sustainable Finance 3.0* (Schoenmaker and Schramade, 2019).

■ The innovation management discipline has been exploring *disruptive, breakthrough* and *open innovation* concepts for function and systems innovation, through joint platform development, networked approaches and sustainable innovation design cycles.

■ In the fields of corporate communications and investor relations, the search is for ways to *co-create* with societal stakeholders in addressing societal themes. Communication moves from a functionalist approach to a 'formative' approach; 'issue management' increasingly revolves around *reversed materiality* and (pro)active forms of *corporate citizenship*, whilst non-financial reporting is increasingly emphasizing *integrated reporting* approaches.

Sections 11.3–11.9 zoom in on the functional level to consider the operationalization challenges faced by functional departments in aligning their motivational logic (inactive, reactive, active, proactive) and functional sustainability approach with the organization's overall transitioning ambition.

THE OPERATIONAL ASSESSMENT CHALLENGE: FIRST ASK
KEY PERFORMANCE QUESTIONS

Navigating along transition routes requires an organization to adopt relevant indicators as reference points that help to keep track of progress. The selection and implementation of indicators, metrics and measures enables leaders and managers: (a) to monitor and assess how well each functional area is performing in relation to strategic goals and objectives; (b) to track the organization's overall progress on (coherently) achieving the sustainability ambition; (c) to identify vital internal tipping points for organizational change; and (d) to learn, adjust and improve.

It is important that strategic, functional and operational indicators are aligned, so that there is a clear connection between organizational sustainability ambitions and functional strategies, performance and progress. Furthermore, proper *contextualization matters* since no sustainable business model is identical in its options, levers and barriers to change, nor in its potential to contribute to particular sustainability outcomes. Contextualized indicators enable better decision-making, because they are customized to: (1) the 'key decisions' and realities specific to the organization, (2) the transition phase it is in, (3) the functional areas they apply to, and (4) the level of impact aimed at (see section 11.1). Nevertheless, under stakeholder pressure and amidst a jungle of already existing sustainability metrics (Box 11.1–11.4), organizations still far too often jump straight to designing indicators before they are clear about what it is they need to know.[8] Obviously, it is vital to first ask the right questions, establish supportable goals and delineate information needs, before defining performance indicators and related metrics. The formulation of *Key Performance Questions (KPQs)* – suggested and defined by Bernard Marr as management questions that capture what managers need to know when it comes to each of their strategic objectives[9] – can be a helpful intermediate step to connect boardroom level KVIs (Chapter 9) and KDIs (Chapter 10) to functional level *Performance and Practice Indicators (KPIs)*. In the following sections, we adopt the concept of KPQs to identify strategically relevant measures for each functional area of management. The logic framework in Figure 11.2 reflects how KVIs, KDIs, KPQs and KPIs are related.

In sections 11.3–11.9, we apply this reasoning for seven functional areas of management: purchasing, operations, marketing, HRM, finance, innovation and communications management. For each functional area, a selected set of KDIs, KPQs and KPIs is identified, linked to four levels of sustainability orientation and value creation (levels 1, 2, 3, 4). The classifications should inspire and facilitate managers to: (a) understand the logical steps needed to translate organizational ambition levels into functional strategies, (b) delineate the trade-offs and dilemmas related to moving from one sustainability level to another, and (c) identify relevant 'output' measures (e.g. sustainability-related management systems, tools, impact assessment practices) that help to monitor progress and enable dynamic vertical and horizontal alignment processes.

---

8   https://www.youtube.com/watch?v=IX4nkkcYmW8.
9   https://www.bernardmarr.com/default.asp?contentID=1008.

11.3 THE SUSTAINABLE PURCHASING CHALLENGE: TOWARDS SUSTAINABLE SUPPLY CHAINS

Key Performance Questions for sustainable purchasing

■ On what leading principles is your relationship with suppliers based?

■ Who bears prime responsibility for sustainable practices: you, your suppliers or jointly held?

■ What degree of fragility or resilience do you allow in your supply chains?

■ How far into the supply chain do you want your 'sphere of control/influence' to reach? Do you know your suppliers (and operating conditions) at the base of the chain?

■ What SSCM configuration helps your sustainability ambitions best?

■ What role do supplier codes of conduct play in achieving your sustainability ambitions?

■ To what extent does certification help you in ensuring the effective implementation of your sustainability priorities and standards?

■ How does your SSCM strategy affect wage levels and value-capturing capabilities along the supply chain?

■ How do you deal with supplier non-compliance: do you terminate the contract, or invest in progress-oriented development programmes?

■ Should key practice and performance indicators be developed and implemented jointly between buyers and suppliers?

KEY DECISIONS: AN EFFICIENCY-DRIVEN OR RELATIONAL PERSPECTIVE?

The purchasing or sourcing function is tasked with managing the company's upstream supply-demand system. Since a considerable part of all production activities take place within supply networks, the purchasing function represents one of the most important dimensions of an organization's sustainability strategy. The function is conditioned by (past) positioning and outsourcing decisions in (international) value chains and markets, and contingent on the various (multi-tier) supply chain configurations the company operates (Chapter 10, sections 10.3.2 and 10.4.3 in particular). Major controversies – relating to child labour, conflict minerals, labour and human rights violations, health and safety issues, deforestation and other ecological concerns – exist around supply chains organized in ways that optimally serve core companies' 'lowest material cost', 'security of supply' and 'strategic resource-seeking' strategies. The purchasing function hence has a pivotal role to play in developing and operationalizing sourcing strategies that prevent social and ecological harm from occurring, and which contribute to enhanced sustainability outcomes along the chain. This multifaceted management challenge has been covered by a variety of concepts, including 'sustainable purchasing and sourcing', 'socially responsible or ethical purchasing', 'sustainable procurement' and 'ethical procurement and sourcing'. Key to all is the nature of the relationship with suppliers, which may be predominantly guided by market-driven measures (e.g. price, risk, quality, delivery speed), or be geared towards longer-term objectives (e.g. resilience, reliability, ongoing improvement, innovativeness, mutual gains, sustainable competitive advantage).

Sustainable supply chain management (SSCM) has been defined in terms of "the management of material, information and capital flows as well as cooperation among companies along the supply chain while taking goals from all three dimensions of sustainable development, i.e., economic, environmental and social, into account which are derived from customer and stakeholder requirements" (Seuring and Müller, 2008: 1700). SSCM involves a broad range of activities and (bundles of) practices. Purchasing and supplier management strategies can thereby be grounded in a narrow or a broader interpretation of what SSCM would require in different institutional and industry settings. A narrow interpretation is mostly motivated by risk-management and compliance-driven considerations in the relationship with suppliers. A broader interpretation suggests collaborative, developmental and risk- and opportunity-sharing approaches beyond the 'avoid doing harm' logic, in pursuit of positive spill-over effects ('do good' logic) that contribute to societal value creation. The broader take on SSCM is based on the tenet that if each supplier is encouraged and enabled to operate a sustainable business model, the whole value chain eventually benefits from becoming more capable, sustainable and resilient. Sustainability performance, then, is not so much a reflection of the core company's purchasing function alone, but rather the outcome of the performance of all suppliers along the chain (sections 10.3.2 and 10.4.2). The broader interpretation accordingly emphasizes longer-term buyer-supplier relationships, supplier upgrading (Box 10.10), shared value creation and fair modes of value capturing over efficiency, transactional and market-driven measures only.

In view of deciding on distinct supplier management approaches, Akhavan and Beckman (2017) distinguish between *supplier screening* and *supplier development* SSCM strategies. Supplier screening-oriented approaches stress practices of supplier assessment, selection, monitoring and performance evaluation – weighed against predetermined minimum requirements and sustainability-related standards – as well as mechanisms for dealing with non-compliance. A focus on supplier screening is typical for risk-oriented, liability-driven sourcing companies "where selecting and evaluating alternative suppliers against a set of given sustainability criteria is the main focus to avoid supplier related risks" (ibid: 139). In contrast, a supplier development approach gives prominence to training and education, collaboration and joint development, follow-up activities, supplier diversity and reinforcing supplier incentives. These practices are indicative of an 'opportunity-oriented' sourcing strategy that proactively seeks to advance suppliers' capabilities and sustainability performance. Supplier upgrading and joint development activities potentially lead to product and process innovations that are beneficial for the longer-term performance on both sides (see Box 10.10 on value chain development paths). The choices a company makes in combining and implementing various supplier screening and development practices in its (international) sourcing activities delineate the potential impact of its SSCM strategy on supply chain sustainability.[10]

KPQs: WHAT TO FOCUS ON?

Key Performance Questions, then, focus on what kind of practices, measures and instruments to consider in operationalizing narrow or broader SSCM ambitions. Not all SSCM practices are applicable to all types of supply chain configurations; not all SSCM configurations are fit for advancing multiple sustainability dimensions jointly. In their review on how (multi-tier) supply chain structures, relational mechanisms and sustainability outcomes relate, Koberg and Longoni (2019) differentiate between *open*, *third-party* and *closed* types of SSCM configurations (Figure 11.10).

■   *Open SSCM configurations* represent those supply chains where the buying company engages only first-tier suppliers in its sustainability efforts, but has no direct contact with sub-suppliers. The buying firm may task first-tier suppliers with extending SSCM further upstream, yet lacks direct control over effective implementation and sustainability outcomes. Open configurations are characterized by relatively high supplier turnover and relatively low degrees of structural stability (section 10.3.2). This makes them ill-suited for effectively addressing social issues in particular – which often require repeated on-site verification of labour conditions and compliance to minimum requirements and standards – and for actively supporting sub-suppliers in improving their sustainability performance.

---

10 In their study – based on a cross-regional, cross-sectoral sample of 100 companies drawn from the Financial Times Global 500 list – Akhavan and Beckman (2017) found that the transition from a reactive to a more (pro)active sourcing practice is characterized by: (1) a greater internal integration of the sourcing practice (e.g. through top management support), (2) greater inter-organizational collaboration, and (3) very high levels of combined screening and development of suppliers on environmental as well as social issues.

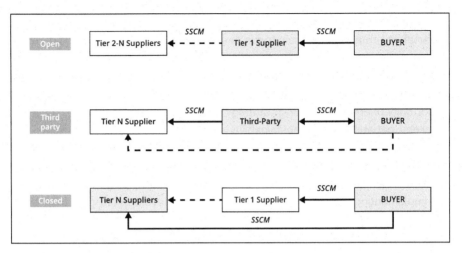

Figure 11.10 SSCM configurations – direct and indirect relationships

Source: based on Koberg and Longoni (2019), p. 1089

- *Third-party SSCM configurations* relate to supply chains where the buying firm either: (a) collaborates with a third party (e.g. an NGO, multi-stakeholder initiative or producer association) to provide suppliers with training and assistance, or (b) delegates the assessment of suppliers to (industry-specific or multi-industry) standardization and certification bodies. Empirical findings suggest that buying firms with a high number of suppliers are more likely to opt for a third-party configuration for facilitating SSCM implementation and managing upstream sustainability outcomes (ibid: 1091).

- In *closed SSCM configurations*, the buying firm engages directly with both first-tier and sub-suppliers (e.g. smallholder cooperatives, local SMEs) to help improve their social and environmental capabilities and to manage sustainability outcomes throughout the supply chain. Closed configurations are characterized by relatively high structural stability and a limited number of key suppliers, which makes them better suited for managing multiple sustainability outcomes in complex (local) settings.

Key questions hence revolve around how to effectuate the aspired level of SSCM through direct and indirect supplier relationships and combinations of 'supplier screening' and 'supplier development' practices – in distinct types of SSCM configurations. This challenge includes the creation of enabling conditions, support systems and reinforcing incentives along the chain for supplier upgrading, so that all suppliers – smallholders and SMEs included – can capture sufficient (net) value, effectively limit any negative social and ecological externalities and optimize the positive effects. We touch upon three types of SSCM mechanisms, each with a different bearing on suppliers' sustainability performance and supply chain sustainability outcomes: (a) the use of 'supplier codes of conduct' and other normalizing arrangements, (b) the practice of certification schemes; and (c) collaborative, developmental practices supportive to supplier upgrading.

■ Supplier codes and compliance likelihood

Supplier codes of conduct – as a complement to contracts – provide the most direct instrument for influencing suppliers' sustainability practices. A supplier code represents a set of rules and principles defining the 'tolerated processes' and minimum standards of desired outcomes in areas like occupational health and safety, wages and working hours, respect of human and labour rights, ethical conduct, environmental standards and documentation management. Supplier codes vary in their *specificity* and *compliance* mechanisms included. Accordingly, codes differ in the implementation and 'compliance likelihood' they induce among suppliers localized in different institutional and operational settings (Van Tulder, Van Wijk and Kolk, 2009). The 'specificity' of a code indicates how elaborated and *strict* the code is, reflected by the breadth of issues covered, the extent to which the code refers to international standards and guidelines (e.g. ILO conventions, ISO standards, OECD guidelines, UN Global Compact principles) and industry-specific standards, and the extent to which the code is subject to monitoring and evaluation. The compliance likelihood of a code is generally enhanced by clear monitoring systems in place, an independent position of the monitoring agency, and inclusion of procedures for enforcing credible improvements and/or proportional sanctions (fines, reduced business, termination of contract) in case of non-compliance.

Strict codes that address many issues can be difficult to enforce and relatively easy to evade – especially in the context of globally organized sourcing and production networks. Furthermore, the implementation of strict codes may trigger adverse side effects, especially when insufficient attention is given to contextual conditions and the complex root causes of a societal problem, as has been the case with banning child labour.[11] Codes that put the implementation burden (and auditing costs) on their suppliers, lower suppliers' margins which can be particularly harmful for smallholders and SMEs at the base of the supply chain. Strict codes with an extensive scope of sustainability-related stipulations also reduce the flexibility of the buying firm and increase the costs of auditing for the issuing party. Moreover, highly specific codes tend to create (mutual) 'lock-in' effects that

---

11 In the 1990s, Nike faced negative publicity around child labour, poor wages and poor working conditions with its suppliers in South East Asia. Nike responded by raising the minimum age of workers beyond the 16-year threshold agreed upon by the ILO. The immediate effect of this approach, however, was that children were fired and eventually ended up in prostitution or criminality for lack of local opportunities. The company had underestimated the 'wickedness' of the child labour problem.

increase suppliers' dependency on the lead company's commercial success and market approach, for instance with regard to certification-based consumer labelling (discussed in section 11.5).

In response to the various flaws in codification practice, a variety of complementary *principles-based* and *progression-oriented* codification approaches have been developed in multi-stakeholder networks. This has resulted in new generations of supplier codes and standards that are part of collective normalization practices (Box 11.7).

BOX 11.7

DEVELOPING PRINCIPLES OF SUSTAINABLE SUPPLY CHAINS

■ **Phase 1: from bilateral supplier codes to operational principles**
Since the 1990s, various international principles and frameworks for global procurement and supply chain management have developed, organized through multi-stakeholder processes. Well-known frameworks include *SA8000* (social standards for humane workplaces, introduced in 1989), *Sedex* (working conditions in global supply chains, 2004) and *BS8903* (sustainable procurement, 2010). The mechanisms used in these schemes for fostering SSCM practice vary: from (accredited) certification based on performance and process standards, to web-based data exchange, peer-based audits and 'best practice' guidance – each with advantages and disadvantages. SA8000 and BS8903 included performance elements (e.g. related to labour criteria) as well as specified process elements for embedding the standard into day-to-day management practice. The BS8903 framework was designed to cover each stage of the procurement process and be applicable to organizations of all size and from all sectors, under the motto 'good procurement is sustainable procurement'.

■ **Phase 2: from operational to strategic principles**
Since 2010, the UN Global Compact (UNGC) has given special attention to international supply chains as central levers for businesses to advance human rights, fair labour practices, environmental protection, inclusive economic growth and ethical conduct. Together with Business for Social Responsibility (BSR), UNGC developed strategic guidance materials to help companies implement the *Ten Principles* (see Box 8.1) in supply chain programmes and operations. Extending the principles into companies' supply chains proved "a daunting challenge", however, because of the scale and complexity of many supply networks. Hence, the UNGC seeks the active involvement and commitment of company leaders, so that 'supply chain sustainability' and 'responsible procurement' are given sufficient strategic priority. The UNGC encourages businesses to look at their supply chain 'as a whole' and to create a broader understanding within their organizations of how decisions beyond

the procurement function affect supply chains. Practices of *traceability* and *continuous improvement* are considered integral to SSCM.

■ **Phase 3: from strategic to integrative and interactive principles**
In 2017, ISO launched the first international guidance standard on delivering sustainability objectives through the supply chain, to facilitate 'buying for a better world'. **ISO20400** defines sustainable procurement as "*procurement that has the most positive environmental, social and economic impacts possible over the entire life cycle*". ISO20400 is aligned with **ISO26000** (see Box 8.8), and hence places great emphasis on social responsibility, ethical processes and stakeholder involvement. It also highlights the need for organizations of all size and sectors to *exercise their capacity to influence* the behaviour of suppliers and other stakeholders, and to go beyond basic legal compliance in their procurement strategy, policies and due diligence processes. ISO20400 uses *relevance* (i.e. which sustainability issues apply to the organization and its stakeholders) and *significance* (analysis of which relevant issues are most impacted by an organization's activities and decisions) as key aspects for procurement strategy priority-setting. It also recommends cost analysis *beyond whole life costing*, to also include positive or negative impacts on society as far as these can be monetized (e.g. carbon emissions, job creation and losses, ecosystem services). ISO20400 supersedes the BS8903 frameworks and is linked to the SDGs.

■ **Phase 4: from interactive principles to sector covenants**
The latest development in enhancing the effectiveness of corporate purchasing strategies is the conclusion of 'covenants' that cover entire sectors and supply chains, to establish a new and more sustainable level playing field (Chapter 10). A supply chain covenant is a non-legally binding normalization instrument that engages all sector players in formulating shared goals for supply chain sustainability and for holding each other accountable for progress in achieving these goals. Pivotal is the extent to which the covenant is aimed at 'avoid doing harm' (level 2) ambitions or actually sets the conditions for 'doing good' (level 3 and 4) ambitions. The International Responsible Business Conduct (IBRC) agreements, pioneered in the Netherlands since 2014, are a case in point. They include multi-stakeholder agreements for responsible procurement and business conduct in international value chains like garment and textiles, gold, natural stone, metals, food products, horticulture and forestry. Key performance measures for the success of a supply chain covenant relate to the level of transparency created by participants, how lessons learned are shared and implemented, and outcomes in terms of (living) wages earned and (net) value captured by the most vulnerable participants at the supply chain's base. More information: https://www.imvoconvenanten.nl/en/agreements.

▪ Certification and labelling dilemmas

Certification schemes, certification-labels and voluntary sustainability standards (VSS) have become a significant additional mechanism for ensuring and communicating compliance with responsible sourcing practices (Box 10.4 and 10.5). Certification labels are mostly directed at end customers and hence partially overlap with the marketing function (see section 11.5). Still, the traceability of materials and intermediate product streams, certification requirements and audits, progress monitoring and follow-up activities remain a prime responsibility of the purchasing department with most organizations.

The effectiveness of certification systems as a credible instrument to help companies meet their sustainability commitments has, for years, been topic of debate. Large differences exist between various certification schemes in terms of their scope, governance, the rigour of their standards (principles, criteria, verifiable indicators), implementation modes and enforcement. A recent study by Greenpeace International (2021) on the experience of nine major commodity certification schemes,[12] concludes that: "while some certification schemes have strong standards, weak implementation combined with a lack of transparency and product traceability means even these schemes have major failings. Too many certified companies continue to be linked to forest and ecosystem destruction, land disputes and human rights abuses" (ibid: 11). The report points at several limitations inherent to certification systems: (a) they rest on market-based mechanisms directed at market access, positioning and sales, and pass the ultimate responsibility for driving sustainability onto consumers; (b) schemes are not designed to address the expanding demand for certified commodities, which puts additional pressure on land use and ecosystems and so risks to offset the positive effects of implemented measures; (c) certification for 'niche markets' does not take away the problem of 'leakage' – unsustainable producers still find alternative markets for non-certified goods.[13] On the whole, major certification systems still have limited ability *to prevent* companies from breaching the agreed upon standard. Weak implementation and enforcement are reiterated by lack of transparency and source-to-end product traceability, which proves difficult to address even by third-party auditors.

---

12 Certification schemes included in the study are: International Sustainability and Carbon Certification (ISCC), Fairtrade, Rainforest Alliance/UTZ, Roundtable on Sustainable Palm Oil (RSPO), Indonesian Sustainable Palm Oil / Malaysian Sustainable Palm Oil (ISPO/MSPO), Round Table on Responsible Soy (RTRS), ProTerra, Forest Stewardship Council (FSC), and Programme for the Endorsement of Forest Certification (PEFC).

13 For instance, only 21% of global palm oil production was RSPO-certified by 2017, according to RSPO data.

■ *Collaborative practices and supplier upgrading – specialization or diversification*

Supplier audits shed light on non-compliance and areas for improvement, but usually do not provide suppliers with practical training and process-oriented guidance on how to accomplish greater sustainability performance. There are companies that have done away with traditional supplier audits and, instead, have started working with 'development teams' on the ground. Supplier development efforts involve systematic approaches to encourage, assist and reinforce suppliers – particularly those at the base of the chain – in improving their capabilities and sustainability performance.

Supplier upgrading initiatives can differ in the objectives pursued (Box 10.10). *Performance-driven* SSCM approaches emphasize process, functional, environmental and social upgrading, with the aim of boosting productivity, quality or yields within the conditions of better environmental and social outcomes. Productivity gains may benefit both supplier and buyer. However, an instrumental mode of capabilities upgrading may also induce greater supplier dependence on the buying firm and one specific value chain. Higher productivity requires suppliers to *specialize*, which increases the risk of 'lock in'. *Impact-driven* upgrading practices, in contrast, also explicitly consider the longer-term economic conditions for smallholder cooperatives and SMEs in global (commodity) chains. Capabilities development then includes objectives of empowerment and improved earning capacity, for instance by teaching and training suppliers how to meet more general sustainability and quality standards and how to successfully diversify their product offering (e.g. crop diversification[14]) and market outlet (e.g. local, next to global). *Diversification* makes the business model of suppliers more resilient and less susceptible to market volatility, the supply chain as a whole more stable and innovative, and the lead firm more trusted and attractive as preferred buyer.[15]

---

14 Crop diversification refers to the addition of new crops or cropping systems to agricultural production on a particular farm, taking into account the different returns from value-added crops with complementary marketing opportunities. Crop diversification helps to: increase the income on small farm holdings, withstand price fluctuations, mitigate the effects of increasing climate variability, balance food demand, improve fodder for livestock animals, conserve natural resources, minimize environmental pollution, reduce dependence on off-farm inputs, decrease insect pests, crop diseases and weed problems, and increase community food security.

15 The longer-term effects of these relationship-based developmental strategies depend on (a) whether suppliers can withstand short-term opportunistic behaviour of switching to a competitor buyer that temporarily offers higher prices, and (b) the degree to which the lead buying firm can guarantee sufficient growth possibilities in end markets. Fairtrade-certified smallholders in selected commodities, for instance, face insufficient demand for their produce as long as fair trade products are subject to 'niche' marketing strategies and fickle consumer demand.

Supplier upgrading can be part of a direct buyer-supplier relationship or be organized through the involvement of an NGO or multi-stakeholder initiative. The Fair Wear Foundation (FWF) provides a case in point. Founded in 1999 as an independent (third-party) multi-stakeholder labelling initiative for the garment industry, it currently organizes 128 garment brands in improving working conditions in sewing factories located in Asia, Africa and Eastern Europe. FWF engages directly with factories, trade unions, NGOs and governments, in the recognition that "no single factory, brand or government can improve things alone". Fair Wear member brands acknowledge that (women) worker welfare is a responsibility shared between brand and sewing factory and that they must work together to accomplish sustainable improvements. Brands are required to keenly monitor conditions in their supply chain, adapt management practices to support safe, dignified and properly paid employment, and resolve reported problems – instead of terminating the factory's contract, which does not help factory workers. FWF conducts regular brand performance checks and factory audits, runs a complaints helpline system ('access to remedy') and organizes on-site training programmes to educate workers, supervisors and factory management on (a) labour rights and relevant resources available to them, (b) Fair Wear labour standards, and (c) effective methods for communicating and resolving workplace-related problems. Furthermore, FWF develops tools and resources that enable garment brands, suppliers and workers' representatives to compare wages to estimated 'living wage' levels as a start for negotiations on how to move wages 'up the ladder' in regular steps.[16]

SELECTED KPIs

Key Practice and Performance Indicators for SSCM can be based on two distinct rationalities: (1) a *linear maturity logic*, which measures progress in terms of gradual improvements ('from less to more'), and (2) a *configuration logic*, which emphasizes the structural and relational arrangements needed to establish the conditions for durable improvements along the supply chain. The configuration logic implies that the value chain is viewed as a whole, and that the impacts of SSCM strategies on suppliers' business models, their room for manoeuvre and their earning and value-capturing capacity are explicitly taken into account. Disregard of these micro-economic dimensions is likely to eventually undermine any environmental (e.g. forest and ecosystem conservation) or social (e.g. safe, dignified, properly paid employment, human rights, child labour) progress made. Hence, the effects – and side effects – that supplier codes, certification systems, and compliance and performance monitoring can have on supply chain participants should not be limited to one-off or occasional 'due

---

16   https://www.fairwear.org/about-us/get-to-know-fair-wear.

diligence' procedures, but rather be part of continuous (on-site) monitoring and be followed up by targeted, progress-oriented action for lasting improvements.

Assessment of SSCM performance and outcomes can be geared to the direct relationship with first-tier suppliers, involve the direct relation(s) with third-party actors, and be extended to the (smaller) suppliers at the supply chain base (Figure 11.10). Indicators that measure the quality and outcomes of relationships require the involvement of both partners. Qualitative performance measures like trust, open communication, information and knowledge sharing, empathy, developmental competencies and shared value creation have become more relevant in the purchasing function than non-relational measures such as contract management, contract administration, purchase-to-pay and vendor rating (PwC, 2013). An important precondition for *strategic* SSCM is the involvement of cross-functional teams (organizational internal alignment) and sufficient strategic alignment between the buying firm, key suppliers and/or third party involved.

The effectiveness of SSCM strategies for the base of the supply chain is moderated by committed participation in the development, implementation and continuous reinforcement of industry-specific standards (joint codification), progressive sector covenants and multi-stakeholder initiatives. A necessary yet insufficient condition for driving further progress is the extent to which SSCM strategies create structural breakthroughs in the wages and incomes earned by workers along the chain: from at least a minimum wage, to a 'decent', 'fair' and/or 'living' wage. A living wage is the income level that allows individuals or families to afford adequate shelter, food and other necessities. Providing people with decent working conditions and paying them a living wage underpins many of the wider (nexus) ambitions represented by the SDGs, including good health and well-being, quality education and gender equality.

Table 11.1 Mapping sustainable purchasing practice

KVIs ➡	LEVEL 1	LEVEL 2	LEVEL 3	LEVEL 4
			Key tipping point ⟩	
Functional KDIs	1. Trigger	2. Internal alignment	3. External alignment	
Main trade-off	Price/cost-driven			Value/relationship driving
Leading frame	Narrow interpretation of Sustainable Supply Chain Management		Broad interpretation of Sustainable Supply Chain Management	
	Chain liability, risk orientation, compliance-driven		Chain responsibility, opportunity orientation, shared value creation	
	Emphasis on supplier screening		Emphasis on supplier development	

(Continued)

Table 11.1 (Continued)

Responsibility for sustainability	... lies with suppliers	Compliance with buying firm's supplier code	Lead company uses sphere of influence for positive outcomes	Joint responsibility along the supply chain
KPQs	**Inactive**	**Reactive**	**Active**	**Proactive**
Supplier management	Supplier competition, selection on price and efficiency		Longer-term relationship, selection on value	
SSCM configuration	Open	Open and strict supplier code	Third-party, indirect relation with supply base	Closed, direct relation with supply base
Supplier code of conduct based on...	Contract	Open and strict supplier code	Third-party, indirect relation with supply base	Closed, direct relation with supply base
Supplier assessment, verification and follow-up	Organization-internal audit	External audit (second party); non-compliance is sanctioned /prompt improvement imposed	Independent (third-party) auditing. Progress-oriented follow-up through training and capacity-building	Progress-oriented joint capacity building and investment; multi-stakeholder verification
Supplier upgrading–capability development	Efficiency-oriented process upgrading	Additional: environmental and social upgrading	Additional: product and functional upgrading	Additional: inter-chain or inter-sectoral upgrading, empowerment
Impact on business model supplier	Specialization	Specialization, differentiation	Differentiation/ diversification	Diversification
Income along supply chain	No policy	Minimum wage	Decent/fair wage	Living wage
KPIs	**Inactive**	**Reactive**	**Active**	**Proactive**
Supplier management system	• Contract and cost management • No or basic indicators for supplier relations developed • Basic measures for tracking and reporting on supplier sustainability performance (one-way) • Limited information exchange with suppliers • Risk-mapping; mitigation approach ambiguous		• Continuous improvement management • Strategic indicators for supplier relations • Critical measures for tracking and periodically reporting on sustainability performance measures (two way) • Value-mapping and joint development of performance measures to cover all relevant aspects; • Exchange of operational, tactical, strategic information • Insight into relevant risks (joint-risk mapping), mitigation approach developed with supplier and/or third party	
Certification/ standards	**'Do no harm'-oriented** e.g., SA8000, Sedex, FSC, RSPO		**'Do good'-oriented** e.g., ISO20400, Fairtrade, MSC, ISEAL	
Typical KPIs	• Spend reduction, optimization of total lifecycle costs, ROI • Security of supply, reduced supply and operational risk exposure • Order fulfilment lead time, time-to-market		• Constructive membership in industry-initiative, active engagement/partnership with NGO/multi-stakeholder initiative • Trust, transparency, quality of relationship; 'customer of choice'/ preferred buyer	

• Supplier segmentation, vendor rating, 'performance to contract' • Inventory reduction (just-in-time), flexibility, efficient purchase-to-pay	• Long-term security of better quality/ sustainable supply • Early involvement in product and process development (joint innovation, complexity reduction) • Joint learning/knowledge development, continuous improvement • Increased resilience, responsiveness, innovativeness of supply chain, enhanced competitive advantage • KPIs related to supplier development programmes, outcomes achieved in supporting suppliers, improvements in sustainability of their business model

11.4 THE SUSTAINABLE OPERATIONS CHALLENGE: REGENERATIVE NATURAL RESOURCES MANAGEMENT

Key Performance Questions for sustainable operations management

■ What leading principles guide your natural resource management strategy?

■ What is your take on 'natural capital' and other natural resource-based dimensions, such as biodiversity and 'planetary boundaries'?

■ What logic drives your activities: a linear rationality of 'take, make, dispose', or a restorative and regenerative logic based on circularity and nature-inclusive approaches?

■ What business case for sustainable operations: cost-cutting, natural resource efficiency and preventing future costs from stricter regulation, or securing long-term availability of strategic natural resources while preventing negative impacts?

■ What type of business model, innovations and investments are needed to move away from 'limiting waste' and 'risk mitigation', towards 'net positive impact', renewables and dematerialization?

■ What sourcing, logistic and value chain approaches are necessary to operationalize your sustainable operations ambitions?

■ What international agreements and regulatory instruments do you endorse for your natural resource management strategy?

■ How to move beyond reactive environmental management and pollution control systems, and related KPIs?

KEY DECISIONS: A DEGENERATIVE OR REGENERATIVE LOGIC?

Closely related to sustainable purchasing is the sustainable operations management challenge. Whereas purchasing particularly relates to the economic and social dimensions of the supply chain, operations management is primarily concerned with the use and handling of 'natural resources', which adds the ecological dimension to value chain management. Operations management deals with the efficient input-output conversion of materials into goods and services by making optimal use of an organization's capabilities and capitals. *Sustainable operations management (SOM)* has been defined in terms of: "the set of skills and concepts that allow a company to structure and manage its business processes to obtain competitive returns on its capital assets without sacrificing the legitimate needs of internal and external stake-holders and with due regard for the impact of its operations on people and the environment" (Kleindorfer et al., 2005: 489). SOM encompasses a broad field of topics: from environmental management and performance, *low-carbon economy* and *closed-loop supply chains (CLSC)*, to innovation (in technologies, processes, products and materials), *eco-design* (for durability, remanufacturing, disassembling, materials recovery) and *reverse logistics* (Atasu et al., 2020). SOM essentially spans the 'core activities' of a company and is hence closely related to purchasing, marketing, innovation and HRM management.

A narrow take on SOM is foremost efficiency-driven, based on a 'linear' logic ('take, make, dispose') and founded on 'doing less harm' to achieve better value returns. In this logic, efforts are geared to risk mitigation and the reduction of negative externalities (e.g. pollution, waste, harm to biodiversity). Narrow approaches typically involve technical 'end-of-pipe' solutions at the last stages of production, such as filtering toxic substances out of residual water or 'carbon capture and storage' (CCS). A (pro)active approach to SOM directs attention to achieving varying degrees of recovery and circularity – at the production facility, supply network, and integrated systems level (section 10.5.2) – to create *restorative* and *regenerative effects* in natural resources and ecosystems (Figure 11.11).

KPQs: WHAT TO FOCUS ON?

Key performance questions for sustainable operations management relate to the nature of 'the business case'. In other words, how can a shift away from conventional 'linear' activities towards more circular and regeneration-driven approaches be substantiated as: (a) a strategic operational priority to safeguard future natural resource availability, and (b) an opportunity for leveraging capabilities and competitiveness through *sustainable value creation*. Both dimensions directly relate to the longer-term resilience of an organization.

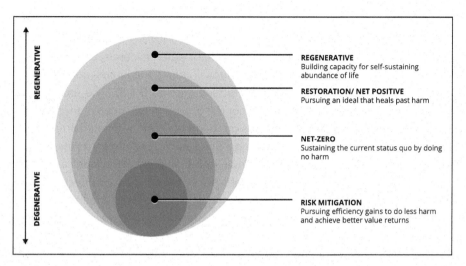

Figure 11.11 Evolving toward a regenerative mindset

Source: WBCSD (2021). *Vision 2050: Time to Transform*, p. 86

■ *The business case for internalizing negative externalities*

The business case for pollution and waste reduction lies in the potential for cost-cutting, efficiency-maximization and the restriction of *prospective cost increases* (see sections 8.4.1 and 8.4.2). Foreseeable cost increases for instance relate to CO_2 emissions pricing, upward price pressures from rising resource scarcity, more stringent environmental regulation and Extended Producer Responsibility (EPR).[17] Advanced environmental planning, sourcing, manufacturing and distribution reduces the need for raw materials, energy and water – thereby curbing avoidable costs and waste. An increasing number of studies furthermore show that environmental achievements are coupled with improvements in costs, efficiency and quality. Environmental management (supported by ISO 14000 certification, pollution prevention, recycling and waste reduction) has been found to have a positive effect on four key operational performance areas: quality, delivery speed, flexibility and costs (Schoenherr, 2012). In a supply chain setting, 'lean and green' management proved to enhance environmental performance and waste management, to reduce costs by eliminating non-value activities, and to boost competitiveness as well (Galeazzo et al., 2014; McDougall et al., 2021).

---

17 Extended Producer Responsibility (EPR) is a policy instrument that holds producers financially and/or physically responsible for the proper end-of-life treatment of their products. It is widely adopted due to its potential to incentivize eco-designs. Examples of EPR (or 'take-back') legislation include: the Waste Electrical and Electronic Equipment (WEEE) Directive (2012/19/EU) established by the European Commission; the Specified Household Appliance Recycling (SHAR) Law in Japan, and the e-waste legislation adopted in 25states across the United States (Gui et al., 2016).

▪ *A business case for creating positive externalities?*

Resource efficiency and pollution prevention for *net zero impact* reduces the risk of depleted natural resource availability (e.g. water, minerals, energy, timber, food crops, fish). Conservation of strategic natural resources constitutes a pressing business case in most sectors (see section 8.4.3). The prospect of ecosystem degradation and natural resource depletion has been a driving force for innovations in clean-tech, eco-design, dematerialization, material recovery, upcycling and closed-loop organizing. Sustainable resources management focuses on *eco-effectiveness* rather than eco-efficiency. Prominent examples include the replacement of non-renewables (oil, natural gas, coal) with renewables (e.g. solar, wind and geothermal energy, hydropower, green hydrogen, plant-based packaging) to limit negative externalities and secure long-term availability of natural resources as well. The premise of *net positive* goes beyond net zero, and relates to approaches that "put back more to society, the ecosystem and the global economy than they take out" over the life cycle of produced goods and services (Box 11.8). 'Net positive impact' practices notably pertain to: (1) climate and the low-carbon economy: removing more CO_2 emissions and other greenhouse gasses from the atmosphere than generated; (2) water scarcity: replenishing dwindling levels of available water in a specific location; and (3) biodiversity: nature-inclusive approaches that, over a quantified timescale, outweigh biodiversity disturbances and damage associated with activities (cf. Van Oorschot et al., 2020).

BOX 11.8

'NET POSITIVE' PRINCIPLES

In 2013, Forum for the Future, WWF-UK and The Climate Group convened the 'Net Positive Group' (NPG) – a collaboration of companies with an aim to have a positive societal impact. In the absence of established net positive (NP) standards, the group recommended 12 NP principles along with 7 measurement principles for more accurate impact measuring. The initiative culminated in the 'Net Positive Project' that gathered a breadth of businesses, NGOs and academics. It developed resources, guidance and tools to foster mindset, behaviour and outcome shifts – aligning NP with parallel movements such as the 'circular economy'.[18]

---

18 See https://www.netpositiveproject.org. A relevant follow-up initiative is the 'Science-based Targets Network' (SBTN), which is part of the Global Commons Alliance – a partnership of more than 50 of the world's most forward-looking organizations in science, business, philanthropy and advocacy. SBTN "enables companies and cities to play a vital role in creating an equitable, nature positive, net-zero future using science-based targets", https://sciencebasedtargetsnetwork.org/.

Twelve net positive principles

■ *Material impact:* the organization aims to make a positive impact in its key material areas.

■ *Evidence:* the positive impact is clearly demonstrable if not measurable.

■ *Best Practice:* the organization also shows best practice in corporate responsibility and sustainability across the spectrum of social, environmental, and economic impact areas, in line with globally accepted standards.

■ *Innovation:* the organization invests in innovation in products and services, enters new markets, works across the value chain, and in some cases, challenges the very business model it relies on.

■ *Big shift:* a net positive impact often requires a big shift in approach and outcomes, and cannot be achieved by business-as-usual.

■ *Transparency:* reporting on progress is transparent, consistent, authentic, and independently verified where possible. Boundaries and scope are clearly defined and take account of both positive and negative impacts. Any trade-offs are explained.

■ *No trade-off:* net positive is delivered in a robust way and no aspect of a net positive approach compensates for unacceptable or irreplaceable natural losses, or ill treatment of individuals and communities.

■ *Partnerships:* organizations enter into wider partnerships and networks to create bigger positive impacts.

■ *Throughput:* every opportunity is used to deliver positive impacts across value chains, sectors, systems, and throughput to the natural world and society.

■ *Influence:* organizations publicly engage in influencing policy for positive change.

■ *Restorative:* where key material areas are ecological, robust environmentally restorative and socially inclusive methods are applied.

■ *Inclusive:* an inclusive approach is adopted at every opportunity, ensuring affected communities are involved in the process of creating positive social and/or environmental impacts.

Net positive measurement principles

1   *Transparency:* rules and standards cannot be developed for every eventuality – but being transparent will enable others to compare and contrast and hence, allow appropriate rules to emerge;

2   *Consistency:* capturing positive and negative impacts in a consistent way and across the value chain, allows organizations to compare like with like;

3   *Completeness:* where information isn't available for a material area it is better to use a conservative estimate than to leave a gap. Be transparent about assumptions and lay out intentions for acquiring this data;

BOX 11.8

4   ***Keep different types of impact separate:*** we don't yet have a clear understanding of how to balance or trade off different impacts against each other (e.g. water and social), so compare them at an individual project level but keep them separate;

5   ***Keep positive and negative impact separate:*** positive impacts don't always compensate for negative impacts (e.g. social: high levels of staff training don't compensate for poor working conditions);

6   ***Use existing methods where possible:*** there are a number of tried and tested methods such as the Greenhouse Gas Protocol that can be useful when analysing net positive carbon impacts;

7   ***Sharing data is vital:*** sharing data and building up libraries of data will accelerate this process and avoid wasted time and effort.

Source: https://www.forumforthefuture.org/net-positive

SELECTED KPIs

Sustainable operational practice has been supported by a wide range of environmental management (e.g. ISO14000), energy management (e.g. ISO 50001), quality management and safety management systems, life cycle assessments (LCA) and environmental impact assessments (EIAs). Leading measures predominantly document improvements in 'reactive' approaches: limiting waste, lowering energy and water usage, and bringing down toxicity, pollution, emission and material content levels. The prevalence of level 1 and 2 metrics – and the risk of complacency when certain targets for negative impact reduction have been met – easily take away companies' incentives to more decisively engage in extended life cycle, circular and net positive (level 3 and 4) approaches. A 'risk mitigation' logic implies a completely different business model than a restorative or regenerative logic involving cross-functional integration and co-creation with suppliers and customers for circularity and net positive *solutions*. Costly investments in end-of-pipeline technologies can make it extremely difficult in later stages to transition into eco-effective practices. The sunk costs of investments in 'intermediate' risk-reducing technologies are known for creating 'path dependencies' that get organizations 'stuck' in the wrong transition route (section 11.2.2).[19] The potential for organizational resilience and competitive leveraging far more likely lies in future-oriented *dynamic*

19 The steel industry, for instance, is presently the largest industrial consumer of coal, which provides around 75% of its energy demand (IEA, 2020). To achieve 'net zero' carbon emissions by 2050, investments in carbon capture and storage (CCS) are considered necessary, but will also crowd out much needed investments in more advanced technologies, such as hydrogen-based direct reduced iron (DRI).

capabilities advancement – e.g. investing in innovative capacity, effective stakeholder engagement, collaborative intelligence, ecological leapfrogging and a global lifecycle perspective of operations (Machado et al., 2017; McDougall et al., 2021). This should be reflected in optimized material recovery practices, closed-loop approaches and net positive impact measurement.

Table 11.2 Mapping sustainable operations practice

KVIs ➡	LEVEL 1	LEVEL 2	LEVEL 3	LEVEL 4
		Key tipping point ➤		
Functional KDIs	*1. Trigger*	*2. Internal alignment*	*3. External alignment*	
Main Trade-off	**Efficiency-driven**			**Regenerative effects-driven**
Orientation	Linear, Exploitative: 'Take, make, waste'	Pollution reduction; End-of-pipeline; Carbon capture and storage as 'solution'	Product stewardship and life cycle perspective; Clean technologies preventing pollution and depletion; Decoupling; Net zero impact; Restoration	Closed-loop supply chains; Full circularity; Regeneration
Performance goals[20]	Value protection; (compliance and conformity)	Process control	Value creation	Long-term value
KPQs	**Inactive**	**Reactive**	**Active**	**Proactive**
Business case for ecology	Resource efficiency and limiting waste; Reduced costs, 'Lean'	Reputational; Eco-efficiency; By-product and waste exploitation	Development of new/advanced technologies and substitutes for non-renewable inputs; creative redesign of processes and products; waste-to-energy plants; upcycling	Resilience, Collaborative advantage through reconfigured or recombined assets and value chain; Partnerships for systems integration
Strategic frame	Lower use of non-renewables		Create net positive impact	
Support for agreements	Kyoto and Paris Agreement; Carbon emission trading schemes; CO_2 taxation		Inclusive green growth, Natural capital coalitions; Circular economy platforms	

(Continued)

---

20 Derived from the sustainable operations management 'maturity framework' as conceptualized by Machado et al. (2017).

Table 11.2 (Continued)

KPIs	Inactive	Reactive	Active	Proactive
Measures, management systems, practices	LCA, EIA, OH&SM/QMS/EMS; Waste management and pollution control; Chemicals-alternatives analysis; ISO 14000; EMAS; Continuous improvement and optimization of processes, machinery and technologies. Direct energy consumption; Energy saved and efficiency improvements; CO_2-emission and pollution levels (direct/indirect greenhouse gasses; ozone-depleting substances; NO + SO); Water (re)usage; Use of virgin plastics, Plastics/packaging reduction; percentage of recycled input materials: GRI Environmental performance Indicators		Global LCA, circular LCA, resource-impact assessment; Cross-functional integration (closed-loop systems, eco-design, reverse logistics; materials and energy recovery); Green/responsible sourcing, green distribution and design for the environment (e.g. durability, disassembly and remanufacturing). Net positive impact measures on: water, biodiversity, soil, climate, carbon; Renewables created (e.g. energy); Material circularity indicator (MCI) and extended lifecycle metrics.	

11.5 THE SUSTAINABLE MARKETING CHALLENGE: FOSTERING SUSTAINABLE CONSUMPTION

Key Performance Questions for sustainable marketing

- On what leading principles is your relationship with customers based?
- What markets do you aim for: demand-driven, needs-based, present, future?
- Who is to take prime responsibility for sustainability in your value chain: you or your customer/consumer?
- What role do you want trademarks and labels to play and how do you organize this effectively: as voluntary initiative, alone, in the sector or regulated by governments?
- How do you inform your customers of your sustainability intentions and achievements?
- To what extent do you use marketing (or de-marketing) to influence your customers to make more sustainable choices?
- How can advertisements be responsibly used in support of your sustainability strategy?
- What about cause-related marketing: can it create sustainable impact?
- What pricing strategy to adopt and how to communicate about it?

The marketing function constitutes the interface between an organization's offerings and customer needs. Much of marketing theory and practice has developed around distinctive and competitive market positioning (segmentation, targeting, channelling, branding), customer experience, customer relationships and marketing mix strategies (product, pricing, promotion, place) to affect buying behaviour. Because of its function in both providing and encouraging consumption opportunities – as well as its sophisticated understanding of how to influence consumer behaviour[21] – marketing has a pivotal role to play in affecting production-consumption activities for the better.

Sustainable marketing has been defined as the process of creating, communicating and delivering value to customers in such a way that both natural and human capital are preserved or enhanced throughout (Martin and Schouten, 2012). This definition reinforces the view that the role and responsibility of marketing management does not end with the transaction exchange, but extends to life cycle usage and the societal effects of consumption behaviours triggered (see section 9.4). Already in 1969, it was posited that: "marketing must serve not only business but also the goals of society. It must act in concert with broad public interest . . . Marketing shares in the problems and goals of society and its contributions extend well beyond the formal boundaries of the firm" (Lazer, 1969: 3). An important task of marketing hence is "to redirect [customer] needs and wants towards consumption that is socially and ecologically least harmful" while altering "prevailing unsustainable consumption cultures" (Sheth and Parvatiyar, 2021: 156). Such efforts inherently include: (1) the *de-marketing* of harmful products and planned obsolescence,[22] (2) actively enabling customers to make *better choices* (responsible consumption of sustainable products and services), (3) encouraging customers to consume *less instead of more* (contentment and needs-based, rather than impulse- and want-driven), (4) fostering sustainable *habit formation*, and (5) communicating *societal value*.

---

21 See, for instance, the SHIFT framework for conceptualizing and encouraging sustainable consumer behaviour change, developed by Katharine White and Rishad Habib (2018; 2019). The framework outlines a *set of principles* drawn from behavioural science (marketing, psychology, economics) for shifting consumer attitudes, choices and behaviours towards (ecologically) sustainable outcomes.

22 Planned obsolescence refers to the strategy of producing and marketing goods with uneconomically short useful lives so that customers will have to make repeat purchases. Notorious examples include irreplaceable batteries in tech products, limited lifespans of light bulbs, insignificant updates in new products (smartphones, cars) and software upgrades incompatible with older hardware. Products, then, are *designed to fail* rather than *built to last* (see section 10.4.2), contribute to a *throwaway society,* and instigate consumerism.

Perhaps the biggest challenge in sustainable marketing practice is to antici-pate and channel fickle consumer behaviour (White et al., 2019). On the whole, customers' positive attitude to environmental and social sustainability, animal welfare, well-being and quality of life is only sparsely reflected in their actual buying behaviour. This *attitude-behaviour gap* confronts companies with a classic chicken-and-egg question: to wait until demand for sustainable products and services rises, or to generate demand by making sustainability an integral part of the offering (mainstreaming). This conundrum comes with two related marketing challenges: (1) how to identify, inform and engage customers that are willing and able to buy sustainably produced products, and (2) how to help articulate, channel and serve the *needs* (rather than wants) of present, potential and future customers in a sustainable way – the unmet needs of underserved and underprivileged people included (sections 8.4.3 and 9.5.1 on BoP approaches and inclusive business models).

The first challenge relates to the *responsive* marketing practice (and litera-ture) that mainly follows consumer trends and fads, sells 'lifestyles' ('green', 'ethical', 'responsible') and seeks to satisfy customer demand for choice, self-expression, novelty and preferences (see section 8.4.1). The responsive approach centres on how to identify 'green' and 'fair' consumer segments that are willing to pay extra for products with specific sustainability features (e.g. organic, fair, free of micro-plastics, GMO free, animal-welfare friendly, responsibly sourced). Marketing, then, for an important part becomes a matter of labelling and commu-nication. Marketing research shows that mainstream customers value firms' sustainability efforts, but are limitedly willing to pay a premium. The purchasing decisions of a large proportion of consumers with limited purchasing power are of necessity driven by price rather than environmental and social justice consid-erations. More sustainable but higher-priced products, therefore, seldom reach sufficient scale and often remain a 'niche' product (Box 10.9 and 10.11).

The second challenge pertains to a *transformational* approach to marketing that is purpose- and impact-driven, humanistic (Varey and Pirson, 2014) and firmly grounded in *societal value creation* (sections 9.4 and 9.5). This approach seeks to actively shape and enable needs-based demand for (co-created) sustainable solu-tions that are in the *long-term mutual benefit* of society and the firm. The respon-sible use of 'choice architecture' – positive nudges, preference-shaping, choice-editing and other instruments for *making the better choice the easier choice* – are essential techniques for guiding consumers to more sustainable consumption behaviour (Thaler and Sunstein, 2008). The transformational approach entails that companies themselves take prime responsibility for driving change in production-consumption activities, by *internalizing sustainability* in their value proposition, business model, core activities and (global) value chain (section 10.4.2). This is in sharp contrast to the premise that individual consumers are sufficiently willing, knowledgeable and positioned to drive sustainable demand.

WHAT THE PEOPLE WANT

DO NOT GIVE ME ANY CHOICE!

CHEAP!

SUSTAINABLE

© 2018 Rotterdam School of Management / Auke Herrema

KPQs: WHAT TO FOCUS ON?

The key tipping point in marketing strategies is marked by a shift away from a responsive approach toward a transformational approach of (co-)creating, communicating and delivering *societal value*. A repurposing of the corporate mission and value proposition (sections 9.4 and 9.5) inherently calls for a reorientation of the marketing mix to account for the societal impact of products and services offered. Prominent areas of attention include advertisement, labelling and pricing strategies, branding, and positioning strategies as part of broader stakeholder management approaches (see section 11.9).

■ *Advertisement*

Advertisement campaigns have traditionally been used to inform consumers about product characteristics and purchase opportunities, in ways appealing to targeted consumer segments to improve – and influence – their purchase decision-making process. Increasingly, for-profit and non-profit organizations use multimedia advertising to signal their core values, explain their role in society, convey their stance on a controversial issue or to communicate their engagement with a societal cause. Well-known examples include the campaigns of Patagonia ('Don't Buy this Jacket'; 'Buy Less, Demand More'; 'The Earth Tax'), United Colors of Bennetton ('UnHate'; 'HIV Positive') and Dove ('Real Beauty'). *Issue advertising* seeks to raise awareness and sway people to change their opinions or behaviour by putting social and environmental issues on the 'societal agenda' (advocacy). If such efforts are supported by a genuine *sustainable corporate story* (section 10.6) and geared towards cooperation with other societal groups, issue advertising can be a powerful instrument for mobilizing *thought leadership* and *collective action*. The responsible use of *discursive powers* can catalyse much-needed positive change beyond the 'direct sphere of influence' (section 10.3.2). However, if merely deployed as *virtue signalling* to improve corporate image and public relations, the effects of issue advertising are usually short-lived and may even backfire.[23] This also applies to *cause-related marketing* campaigns, which are often used as a positioning strategy to enhance brand image.

▦ *Positive-duty or negative-duty labels*

A particular challenge in the marketing strategy is how to use *(private) labels* and *trademarks* to communicate sustainability policies and facilitate customers in making responsible choices. Product labelling is an instrument for ensuring and communicating specific characteristics and responsible practices that are unobservable or difficult to assess for consumers. Companies and governments have introduced a myriad of sustainability-related labels (Figure 11.13).[24] Many involve initiatives that seek to *limit the negative externalities* of products or services on the environment (e.g. recycling claims, use of packaging materials, CO_2 and water footprints), marking performance claims on a specific set of operational metrics. The main responsibility for sustainable consumption is thereby passed on to consumers, who are supposed to make the right decision once properly informed. However, the lack of national and international coordination and regulation has given rise to a confusing labelling jungle (see Box 10.4) and an environment of mixed and even competing messages. As a result, most consumers have a limited understanding of what each label factually

---

23 There are many examples of companies that received criticism for inconsistency in their issue advertising. Lacoste, for example, launched its 'Save Our Species' campaign in 2019 as part of its three-year partnership with the International Union for Conservation of Nature (IUCN). Lacoste swapped its crocodile-logo for ten limited-edition polo shirts featuring various endangered species instead, with the number of polo shirts produced matching the number of animals known to remain in the wild. The campaign received criticism for being inconsistent with the company's product line of gloves and handbags made from deer and cow leather. In 2017, Audi's Super Bowl advertisement supporting gender equality and equal pay backfired, when it was revealed that Audi itself had a poor track record on promoting women in leadership roles (below the average of 20% for female representation on corporate boards of Fortune 500 firms). Several companies have been criticized for *woke-washing* as they associated themselves with LGBTQ rights, gender-neutrality and anti-racism (following the Black Lives Matter marches).

24 See, for instance, the Ecolabel Index – a global directory of ecolabels that tracks 455 eco-labels in 199 countries and 25 industry sectors: http://www.ecolabelindex.com/ecolabels/.

Figure 11.12 Example of issue advertising, Patagonia

Source: courtesy of Patagonia

stands for. Does an eco-label for recycling, for example, signify that a product is made of recycled materials, that it can be recycled, that it should be returned to the shop to dispose of, or that the producer is trying to recycle 'as much as possible' (85%)? Is the label due to regulation or self-declared as part of a voluntary approach? Who oversees and ensures the correct use of the label to preclude greenwashing? Who is responsible for the recycling: the consumer, the producer, someone else?

Labels based on a positive-duty approach – such as fairtrade, organic, sustainable fisheries (MSC) and timber (FSC) – are a means to mobilize consumer demand for responsibly sourced commodities and manufactured products. They are geared to *enhancing positive externalities* while preventing the negative effects in production-consumption systems as much as possible. Positive-duty labels indicate the certification requirements of voluntary sustainability standards (VSS) that producers, traders, manufacturers and retailers commit themselves to – for instance, with regard to ecosystem conservation, land use, worker health and safety, fair wages and decent working conditions (section 11.3 on sustainable purchasing). Certification schemes vary considerably in terms of their governance, principles and criteria, transparency,

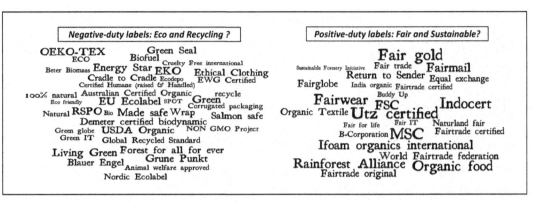

Figure 11.13 Negative-duty and positive-duty labelling initiatives

implementation and effectiveness. Even well-informed consumers may find themselves ill-equipped to distinguish between stronger and weaker certification schemes in the face of an overwhelming labelling jungle. Under these circumstances, certification-based labelling is easily equated with 'sustainability' despite marked differences in the quality and effectiveness of varying approaches, whilst public perception and trust are easily affected by 'incidents' – which always appear in complex change trajectories. Furthermore, positive-duty labels are received differently by distinct consumer segments. Consumers have been found to associate positive labels with (1) mediocre product quality compared to non-labelled products; (2) higher prices; (3) elite products; (4) an excuse for less sustainable lifestyles ('moral self-licensing'); and (5) confusion, in case a label addresses more than one issue and hence embodies intricate dilemmas and trade-offs. So far, the effectiveness of positive-duty labelling has remained relatively low. Companies that are serious about mainstreaming sustainability hence seek to create a new 'level playing field' by developing and internalizing *sectoral or industry standards* that apply to all organizations (see section 10.4).

Still another sustainable marketing approach can be to monetize the negative effects of the production-consumption system that are not accounted for in the market price – the unpaid external costs borne by underpaid workers, taxpayers and future generations. Once transparent and quantified, customers can be better informed about the *true price gap* to raise awareness. The True Price initiative, for instance, strives to calculate the per-product 'true costs' by including the external ecological costs from (air, soil, water) pollution, depletion of scarce resources, contribution to climate change and degradation of land, biodiversity and ecosystems. On the social side, external costs considered include health and safety risks (occupational, public, consumer), underpayment, forced and child labour, discrimination, breaches of basic rights (union rights, land,

Indigenous, human, privacy), tax evasion, corruption and lack of transparency.[25] Being transparent about true costs while showing stakeholders how negative externalities are actively being addressed over time, can positively affect brand loyalty of conscious and responsible consumers in particular. Some companies and impact investors have taken over the metrics.[26]

■ *Pricing strategies: segmentation and differentiation*

Along with quality and availability, price is a decisive factor in influencing purchasing decisions and consumption behaviour. Companies have come up with various pricing strategies that rely on consumers' willingness to pay a premium, for instance, to offset their consumption footprint (e.g. carbon compensation fees for planting CO_2-absorbing trees) or to pay a fair price that internalizes the costs of responsible sourcing and smallholder 'upgrading' (section 11.3). Sustainable products have been found to be 75% to 85% more expensive than conventional products.[27] The 'production part' of the value chain that has the largest direct impact on sustainability typically accounts for just 10% to 30% of final product costs. The largest markups tend to come from brand owners, wholesalers and retailers that have far less impact on sustainability. The suggestion is that the retail prices of sustainable products could be more consumer-friendly – with the premium set at a *reasonable and responsible level* – in order to encourage a wider range of consumers to opt for sustainably produced products over unsustainable products. Adjustments in pricing strategies, combined with a fairer distribution of profit margins along the value chain, can have an amplifying effect on the potential to mainstream sustainability in production-consumption systems.

For a considerable part of the world population, however, purchasing power and choice with regard to consumption are an unobtainable luxury. The often basic needs of vast groups of underprivileged people are largely underserved. The Covid-19-related economic downturn has exacerbated this situation; in 2020, the pandemic pushed an additional 119 to 124 million people into extreme poverty whilst the equivalent of 255 million full-time jobs were lost (see section 7.4). To what extent can *differential pricing strategies* enhance the

---

25 Monetizing has the potential to raise awareness and to help consumers compare the social and environmental performance of brands based on standardized information, if adopted more widely (True Price et al., 2017). See https://trueprice.org/true-price-resources for the monetization methodology and underlying principles.

26 International distributor of fresh organic and fair fruits and vegetables Eosta, for example, applies the principles of True Cost accounting to educate consumers about the real cost of fruit and vegetable production. https://eosta.com/en/search/content/True%20cost%20accounting.

27 Analysis by consultancy firm Kearney, *Why today's pricing is sabotaging sustainability* (2020).

social welfare of less privileged consumers in such areas as food, healthcare, educational books, computer software, cell phones, high-yield seeds, fertilizer and other agricultural inputs? Famous cases of mispricing have been documented in the area of high-priced pharmaceuticals (Vachani and Smith, 2004; Smith and Jarisch, 2019) with developing countries facing serious problems in getting access to affordable life-saving medicines. Pharmaceutical companies have regularly argued that lowering drug prices for developing countries would be an untenable strategy in the face of competitive pressures of generic drugs, regulated prices set by national governments, substitute products and parallel imports eroding their business model and jeopardizing the investment needed for new medicine development. The pressure from societal (ranking) initiatives such as Access to Medicine Foundation[28] and Access to Seeds[29] that are increasingly backed by institutional investors, stimulates companies to implement more inclusive business models that allow for *socially responsible pricing* to also serve the world's poorest.

SELECTED KPIs

Sustainable marketing performance can be assessed along a wide range of (direct and indirect) outcomes and (positive and negative) impacts on present, potential and future customers, markets and communities. Prevailing marketing metrics emphasize a rather narrow focus on performance, with sales revenue, market share, brand equity and customer equity as dominant KPIs – broken down along product categories, customer segments and distribution channels. In most areas, these measures show that sustainable products and services still occupy a niche market (< 5%) and constitute a (very) modest share of the overall product portfolio of most companies. Cause-related marketing campaigns do not substitute for *integrating* sustainability into the marketing strategy; rather, they reinforce the *niche market trap*. A broader view on sustainable marketing practice and performance takes a *production-consumption systems perspective* and focuses on *mainstreaming sustainability*. It smartly uses the wider influence that the sustainable marketing function can have in communicating values and social norms, raising awareness, guiding responsible and sustainable consumer behaviour and

---

28 The Access to Medicine Index analyses how the world's largest pharmaceutical companies are addressing access to medicine in 106 low- and middle-income countries for 82 diseases, conditions and pathogens https://accesstomedicinefoundation.org/access-to-medicine-index.

29 The Access to Seeds Index – currently part of the World Benchmarking Alliance – measures and compares the efforts of the world's leading seed companies to enhance the productivity of smallholder farmers.

initiating collective action. Measuring and evaluating the success of marketing strategies can be part of corporate reporting strategies (GRI). Increasingly, practice and performance are also assessed by external benchmarking initiatives – such as the Access to Medicine Index and Access to Seeds Index – that assess (and rank) whether companies have been capable to use inclusive pricing strategies to also provide in the needs of underprivileged people.

Table 11.3 Mapping sustainable marketing practice

KVIs ➡	LEVEL 1	LEVEL 2	LEVEL 3	LEVEL 4
		Key tipping point ▷		
Functional KDIs	*1. Trigger*	*2. Internal alignment*	*3. External alignment*	
Main Trade-off	Market-driven			Market-driving
Market orientation	Exchange-driven and responsive: existing markets and *demand*; satisfying momentary desires; expanding production-consumption		Impact-driven and humanistic: addressing present and future *needs*; creating collective prosperity; transforming product-consumption	
Customer viewed as	Cost minimizer	Preference optimizer	Responsible consumer	Co-creator/partner in creating prosperity
KPQs	Inactive	Reactive	Active	Proactive
Issue advertising and awareness raising campaigns	No issue campaigns	Cause-related campaigns	Explanation of core values and vision	Broad awareness raising; societal issue advertising; thought leadership; collective action-oriented
Customer approach	Mass production	Mass customization of niche markets based on green, ethical, responsible customer segments	Active nudging, choice-editing and preference-shaping; enabling customer to make responsible choices and change consumption habits	Co-producer/ co-designer for enhanced well-being
Main pricing strategy	Low prices	Price premiums	Fair prices based on true costs and value	Needs-based pricing
Consumer labelling strategy	Negative-duty labels		Positive-duty labels	
	No sustainable labelling policies other than legally required labels	Own (private) labels; limited relation with core mission	Sector labels, coordinated with competitors and NGOs	Societal labels developed together with stakeholders

(Continued)

Table 11.3 (Continued)

KPIs	Inactive	Reactive	Active	Proactive
Measures, management systems, practices	GRI 417 (product and service information, labelling and marketing communications); ISO14020 (guiding principles for development and use of environmental labels, self-declarations and third-party certification); Sustainable packaging indicators (Global Protocol on Packaging Sustainability). Negative-duty labelling.		ISO 26000 Guidance on social responsibility; ISO/TS 26030 Guidance on using ISO26000 in the food chain; Positive-duty labelling (e.g. Fairtrade, UTZ/ Rainforest Alliance, MSC, FSC, B-Corps certification, On the way to PlanetProof).	
	Exchange and market growth-oriented practice & performance:		**Prosperity and impact-oriented practice & performance:**	
	Sustainable life-style segmentation linked to new product development (NPD); Market share of sustainable products & services; Percentage of products with sustainability labelling; Sales revenues per product category; Brand awareness; Brand equity; Customer satisfaction; Customer loyalty; Growth in segmented (sustainable) customer groups; Share of promotional/ advertisement budget allocated to sustainable products.		Creation of needs-based markets; Growth in needs-based markets; De-marketing of unsustainable production-consumption activities; Sustainable habit formation programmes; Demonstrating and communicating long-term societal value, societal engagement, human dignity, inclusion; Transparency and supply chain accountability on progress made, trade-offs, dilemmas; Issue awareness related to brand; Relational equity; Long-term customer engagement, trust and commitment; Score on Access to Medicine Index, Access to Seeds Index, Seafood Stewardship Index and other impact-oriented sustainability benchmarks.	

11.6 THE SUSTAINABLE HRM CHALLENGE: VIBRANT HUMAN AND SOCIAL CAPITAL

Key Performance Questions for sustainable HRM

- What leading principles and values guide your relationship with employees?

- What orientation characterizes your HRM approach: performance, compliance and reputation-driven, or developmental, values and impact-driven?

- What societal issues, labour standards and stakeholders do you consider in designing HRM policies and in evaluating performance, outcomes and impact?

- How to deal with conflicting roles, needs and interests? Can the HRM department be a 'linchpin' in facilitating organization-wide integration of sustainability efforts?

- How to foster change and a sustainability-oriented organizational culture – in view of 'competing values' and diverse subcultures – locally and across borders?

- What breadth of instruments do you have to embed sustainability-related goals in recruitment, training and capabilities development, appraisal and reward?

- To what extent do you give voice to internal 'agents of change' that can accelerate positive change?

- What do you consider a fair compensation floor for employees across the globe – and those indirectly employed in supply chains?

- What is your approach towards worker representation and organized labour?

KEY DECISIONS: EMPLOYEES AS 'COST FACTOR' OR
AS 'HUMAN AND SOCIAL CAPITAL'?

The HRM function is concerned with the efficient and effective management of work and employment relations to achieve the organization's goals and commitments, while keeping in mind the needs of employees (Malik, 2018). HRM develops and implements policies that link an organization's strategy and changing business needs – in various institutional settings and operating contexts (see section 6.5) – with suitable recruitment and retention, capabilities development, performance management and compensation practices. The role of the HRM department depends heavily on the company's vision for employees and people in general. Are employees considered as a 'cost factor' or as a valuable asset in creating both business and societal value? Should HRM be primarily focused on coordinating personnel management systems – contracts, hiring and firing, occupational training – or be strategically concerned with the organization's culture and wider business context, the needs of – and impacts on – wider communities and related leadership challenges too?

Transactional ('hard') approaches to HRM focus on establishing performance-driven cultures and work practices, tight strategic and managerial control and instrumental 'market value of employee', 'excellence' and 'best practice' type of metrics. The transactional approach emphasizes economic rationality, operational efficiency, financial performance (productivity, profitability, growth, shareholder value) and a view on employees as a 'production factor' needed for generating added value and ensuring business continuity. The focus on efficiency is reflected in such practices as labour rationalization and work intensification, the relocation of jobs to cheaper labour markets, minimization of labour costs (skimping on pensions, employee benefits, health and safety, skills development) and excessive workforce flexibilization. On-call zero-hour contracts and gig economy platform jobs, for instance, shift most transactional risk to 'self-employed' labour, mediated by technology (Dundon and Rafferty, 2018). Such arm's length employer-employee relations easily solidify into *human costs*, embodied in 'mini-jobs' and in-work poverty. The transactional mode is furthermore manifested in performance-based incentives and compensation schemes (e.g. bonuses, variable wages, sizable wage gaps), fierce talent competition ('the war for talent') and in the criteria applied for selection, appraisal, reward and career development that drive a self-reinforcing and often exploitative performance culture geared to maximizing profits and shareholder returns.

Strategic HRM takes a context-based ('best fit' or contingency) approach to the design and implementation of HRM policies. It seeks to align HRM with the company's strategic (multi-domestic) business environment, so that specific institutional (cultural, social and legal) settings are duly taken into account. Strategic HRM links economic rationality with relational rationality and social responsibility. It strives to balance financial/economic outcomes for the firm with well-being outcomes for employees while trying to harmonize strategic competitive advantage with stakeholder interests and legitimacy (Paauwe and Farndale, 2017). Employees are viewed as valuable stakeholders ('human capital') and 'resourcing partners' in attaining 'mutual gains', in the acknowledgement that organizations can only create value with and through skilled and motivated employees. High-involvement relationship management, proper investments in capabilities development, ensured compensation schemes, employee participation and well-being are hence considered vital factors to foster enhanced commitment, competence, goal congruence and cost-effectiveness. Still, the ultimate focus is on the long-term organizational needs of the business itself. The premise is that socially responsible HRM serves human capital conservation and, in turn, the firm's competitive positioning and longer-term performance.[30]

Sustainable HRM approaches seek to contribute to the long-term success of an organization by taking a *multidimensional performance outcomes* perspective that reckons with the interests and needs of a broader range of stakeholders, both within and beyond the boundaries of the firm. This view recognizes that HRM strategies can play a vital supportive role in wider community development and welfare creation. It also sees that HRM extends to the needs of workers *indirectly employed* in the company's supply chains. For instance, by incorporating HRM policies related to wage levels, working conditions, decent work and labour rights into supplier codes of conduct, or advising on and assisting in capabilities development in intra-chain upgrading trajectories (section 11.3). Sustainable HRM has been defined as: "the adoption of HRM strategies and practices that enable the achievement of financial, social and ecological goals, with an impact inside and outside the organization and over a long-term horizon while controlling for unintended side effects and negative feedback" (Ehnert et al., 2016: 90). Correspondingly, HRM practices can be considered "responsible or sustainable in so far as they contribute to social welfare, environmental protection and long-term economic prosperity, and irresponsible or unsustainable if they harm social, environmental, and economic wellbeing" (Stahl et al., 2020: 5). Sustainable HRM, then, reflects the aim of 'value creation' (at levels 3 and 4) while avoiding 'value destruction' (level 1 and 2). Organizations' internal and external impacts can pertain to a wide range of issues involving job security, job creation, employee health and well-being, decent work, fair wages, human rights, diversity and equality, quality education and capabilities development inclusive to low-skilled and low-paid workers.

KPQs: WHAT TO FOCUS ON?

Studies on the sustainability/CSR-HRM interaction suggest several avenues through which the HRM function can contribute to the delivery of a company's sustainability strategy and commitments. These include: (1) the integration of sustainable business values and principles into all areas of HRM policy, structure and procedures; (2) developing an organizational culture conducive to corporate responsibility and sustainability; (3) identifying and recruiting agents of change

---

30 The AMO model, for instance, suggests that if HRM practices are designed to advance employees' ability, motivation and opportunities to contribute, (goal congruent) performance outcomes will ensue.

(leadership development); (4) building human capital (competencies, skills, knowledge and attitudes) and employee motivation that fosters good practice, stakeholder engagement and the ability to manage sustainability impacts capably and responsibly; and (5) aligning appraisal, reward and incentive systems with sustainability-related performance outcomes.

Going by these entry points, it would seem that the HRM function is well-positioned to facilitate and reinforce the corporate sustainability strategy. In practice, however, the HRM department is mostly peripherally involved in the design and implementation of sustainability strategies and rarely regarded as a vital *linchpin* and major contributor to sustainability ambitions (Stahl et al., 2020). HRM professionals appear uncomfortable in taking ownership of HRM issues related to corporate responsibility. They see themselves confronted with role conflicts, trade-offs and balancing challenges in serving the divergent objectives and needs of various internal and external stakeholders. What leading perspective to take, how to delineate the scope of HRM-related responsibilities in view of an ever-changing (international) operating context, and what sustainability issues to prioritize? Should the angle be on *inside-in* HRM domains (such as talent management, training, performance and reward policies), on *outside-in* matters (e.g. recruitment, trade union involvement, local labour laws, rights and customs), or take an *inside-out/outside-in* societal viewpoint (e.g. forging social contracts, promoting diversity and equality, capacity building, job creation, community development and well-being)? Can the HRM function support sustainability at higher levels of commitment (levels 3 and 4)? What tenets to adopt for developing and implementing a coherent 'sustainable HRM strategy' across borders?

▪ *Juggling with HRM roles*

The degree of sustainability involvement of the HRM department can be perceived to mirror the development stage and level of sophistication of the company's commitment to corporate sustainability (Stahl et al., 2020). Against that backdrop, HRM scholars notice an emphasis in HRM approaches on short-term business performance and shareholder value (levels 1 and 2), with still too little attention to its human costs and the positive contributions HRM policies can have on social and economic progress (levels 3 and 4). HRM professionals are faced with the challenge of translating contradictory yet interrelated objectives into coherent HRM practices that harmonize the tensions between shareholder, employee and stakeholder orientations. Various roles in performing a sustainability-oriented HRM function can thereby be distinguished (Podgorodnichenko et al., 2020), each with a distinct take on and prioritization of HRM-related activities:

▪ The *strategic support role*, in which the HRM department acts as a 'business partner' in facilitating the achievement of environmental and social goals, in addition to the company's traditional economic objectives. In this role, the focus is on adapting existing HRM practices to incorporate CSR-related goals in recruitment and selection, training and development, rewards and performance management;

■ The *employee advocate role*, which emphasizes employees' needs and interests and the responsibilities of the organization in creating a humane work environment and developing a sustainable workforce. Here, the priorities for sustainable HRM are directed at responsible and inclusive workplace practices, labour rights and benefits, trustful employment relationships, job security, work-life balance, wellbeing and employability;

■ The *social support role*, which takes the needs of employees and those of the wider community as a prime concern. Priorities for sustainable HRM are accordingly geared to the development of policies and practices that address the broader impacts and (negative and positive) spill-over effects of the corporate strategy on both internal and external (societal) stakeholders.

A *hybrid model* that reconciles these roles such that the multiple goals and needs of various stakeholders are accommodated, is the most sophisticated yet most challenging approach. The synthesizing of roles calls for HRM approaches that are flexible, participative, tolerant to complexity and suited to coping with paradox (see Box 4.3).

■ *Fostering a sustainability-oriented organizational culture:*
dealing with competing values

Sustainability-oriented 'culture change' is generally seen as one of the most central conditions for an organization to transition towards higher levels of societal value creation. If the HRM department is regarded as the 'guardian of the organizational culture', then empowering sustainability-related culture change is within the HRM remit too. The concept of 'corporate culture' broadly refers to the set of shared values, beliefs and patterns of meaning and understanding among organizational members that is reflected in the behavioural rules, norms and rituals accepted. The concept suggests the existence of one unified organizational culture. In practice, however, various 'competing values' and subcultures co-exist within one organization (Quinn, 1988), clustered around hierarchical levels, organizational departments, occupational disciplines or across business units located in different countries and regions. Each subculture can be thought of as representing an own set of valued outcomes and managerial ideology about how to understand, enact, organize and achieve corporate sustainability (Linnenluecke and Griffith, 2010).

The co-existence of various subcultures implies that different (groups of) organizational members may hold contrasting views on the nature and scope of responsibilities vis-à-vis various internal and external stakeholders, and society at large. Divergent subcultures may emphasize different transition paths and modes of directing, coordinating and controlling change. Managers and employees representing 'competing values' (Box 11.9) may – openly or covertly – question the need, relevance or adequacy of the instruments chosen to establish sustainability-related transformation, as well as their role in it. While some perceive of change as a welcome opportunity to make progress, others may disagree with the course, pace, priorities and projected outcomes, or resist (top-down) imposed organizational change altogether.

Accordingly, the HRM department faces the delicate challenge of finding the sweet spot between: (a) the *strength of diversity*, by accommodating various competing values and employee motivations; and (b) the *strength of an overarching organizational culture* that is to guide 'unity of purpose and action' for enhanced sustainability performance and outcomes. The appropriate balance can be expected to differ in subsequent transitioning phases (dynamic alignment) and – in case of international presence – should reckon with the national cultures, norms and customs of the business units located across the world (cross-cultural alignment).

BOX 11.9

COMPETING VALUES AND ORGANIZATIONAL SUBCULTURES

In their 'Competing Values Framework', Cameron and Quinn (2011) outline four archetypical organizational cultures denoting how people in organizations think, organize their values and process information. The classification is based on two dimensions: (a) dominant orientation to either internal organizational or external organizational dynamics, and (b) preference for either 'flexibility and discretion' or 'stability and control' in organizational structures. The resulting cultural orientations highlight different organizational aspects that affect day-to-day operations, influence social interactions and mark corporate practice:

■ *Adhocracy ('create') cultures* nurture innovation, agility and willingness to improve, pioneer, take risks, think out of the box and break through existing norms;

■ *Bureaucracy ('control') cultures* foster a formal, rules-based and compliance-driven administrative approach with detailed procedures, processes and task descriptions that ensure predictability, stability and efficiency;

■ *Clan ('collaborate') cultures* emphasize interpersonal relations, cohesion, loyalty and morale and coordinate through social interaction, participative decision-making, consensus and group thinking;

■ *Market ('compete') cultures* are results- and reward-driven and pursue productivity, competitive actions and goal and task achievement, coordinated through central decision-making, instructional communication, targets and planning.

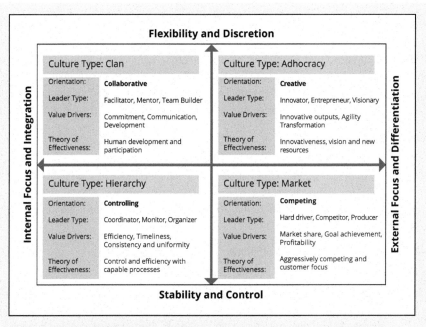

Figure 11.14 Competing values: leadership, effectiveness and organizational theory
Source: Cameron and Quinn (2011)

Sustainability-oriented culture change represents an 'internal alignment' challenge between co-existing subcultures, within the context of a changing business environment and shifting business needs. The prevalence of one dominant organizational culture may turn out to be too rigid and dysfunctional in view of the agility, mindset and competencies required to aptly adjust, while the orientation of strongly rooted subcultures may prove tenacious and hard to alter. The search, then, is for a new functional balance. Which organizational subcultures – or specific elements from them – should be given more prominence and active encouragement in driving, shaping and meeting sustainability ambitions?

A *bureaucracy/control* culture, for instance, can pose significant adjustment problems in a dynamic environment due to its deficient flexibility to swiftly respond to sudden challenges. Still, its procedural focus is well-suited for integrating sustainability standards and protocols into organizational guidelines and operational processes. Nurturing a *collaborative* culture can be very effective in trajectories of joint capabilities development aimed at internalization of an 'active' sustainability mindset (phase 2), particularly when combined with those elements from the *market/competition* culture that emphasize resource efficiency, goal accomplishment and the firm's competitive position. An *adhocracy/create* culture provides the traits to adapt, innovate and transform – instrumental for phase 3 transitioning – but is less suited for fostering cultural coherence, internalization and the establishment of organizational procedures that provide stability and efficiency gains.

For the HRM function, the internal alignment challenge implies the composition of a coherent set of programmes, tools, procedures and incentives that can facilitate different organizational needs in different phases of change. Such change management approaches should allow the organization to find an appropriate balance between: (1) 'adaptation vs. stability' of organizational structures; (2) 'formalized vs. informal' procedures; (3) 'centralized vs. decentralized/participative' decision-making; (4) 'vertical vs. horizontal' modes of coordination and communication; (5) 'human relations vs. task accomplishment'; and (6) 'control and enforcement vs. motivation and encouragement'.

Building a coherent sustainability-oriented culture across borders adds a delicate integration-coordination challenge that spans diverse (competing) national cultures, rooted in distinct CSR/sustainability regimes (section 6.5.1). Similar to approaches for 'managing distance' – and depending on the internationalization strategy of a company (section 10.4.3) – a 'cross-cultural sustainability management' (CCsM) approach can opt for:

- **Adaptation** to cultural differences;
- **Mitigation** of cultural differences (managing clashing cultures between dispersed organizational units/members);
- **Integration,** by developing a coherent overarching corporate culture that supersedes national cultures – communicated, internalized and upheld through internal codes of conduct and employee rotation;
- **Differentiation**, by nurturing a dynamic and diverse corporate culture that thrives on constructive interaction between global and local practices.

▨ *Agents of change: leaders, pioneers, advocates and activists*

Through its central role in recruitment and selection, talent management, skills and leadership development and employee commitment, the HRM department is well-positioned to identify and support relevant 'agents of change' needed to help the organization overcome critical tipping points in evolving to next level sustainability. Agents of change can be frontrunning functional departments (section 11.2.3), but also individuals that can make a difference in the organization's internal 'decision-making bargaining arena'. Giving voice to fresh perspectives and ambition, novel ideas and practices, bridging capacity and 'productive dissent' can provide the organization with the kind of acumen vital to aligning organizational effectiveness with employee wellbeing and societal welfare – and for catalysing action accordingly (Box 11.10).

In the area of *recruitment for change*, there is still a remarkable disconnect between companies' espoused sustainability ambition and actual recruitment and selection practice. Noteworthy are the findings of Russell Reynolds – a global leadership advisory and senior executive search firm – that in 2019 looked at how frequently sustainability was a factor in board appointments and senior-level executive hiring. From the 4,000 role specifications across industries analysed,[31] just 15% were found to make reference to sustainability, whereas in only 4% of specifications sustainability experience or sustainability mindset were an actual requirement (UN Global Compact & Russell Reynolds, 2020). An additional HRM challenge lies in attracting and retaining impact-driven *young professionals* with sustainability-oriented values and aspirations. Deloitte research among millennials and Generation Z (2019; 2021) indicates that 60% of younger generations around the world seek *purpose beyond profit* in their employer of choice, with 44% of millennials and 49% of GenZ having made work-related choices accordingly. These younger generations are the people most likely to call out *racism, sexism, pay and wealth inequality, climate change and social injustice*, and to shun companies whose actions conflict with their personal values. Unimpressed with companies' impact on society, fewer than half see business as a force for good.[32] Younger generations want to work for companies that share their values so that they "feel more empowered to make a difference as part of organizations" (2021: 33). In order to attract and retain younger talent, a strong corporate sustainability profile helps but does not suffice. Recruitment should preferably be followed by active support that channels and further develops their drive for positive impact – notably with purposeful starter positions, training, mentoring and on-the-job coaching that helps them grow into their 'agent of change' or 'sustainability leader' potential.

IDENTIFYING AGENTS OF CHANGE – WHAT AND WHOM TO FOCUS ON?

B
O
X

11.10

■ **Sustainable leadership?** Leadership is a personal attribute, but also a qualification conditional on organizational context and transitioning phase. Sustainable leadership denotes a social process: within a given context, an individual (the 'leader') proves effective in influencing a group of individuals ('followers') to surpass an organizational tipping point (intermediary goal), and overcome relevant intention-realization gaps on the pathway to greater sustainability (the ultimate goal). KPQs for HRM include: Does the envisaged change process call for formal or informal leadership roles? What leadership style aligns best with the organization's needs, challenges, transition phase and sustainability ambition? Can 'sustainable leaders' be handpicked and trained to achieve the intended outcomes? In view of competing values and organizational subcultures, what type of leadership is accepted for what type of purpose?

---

31 Specifications for non-profit organizations and Chief Sustainability Officer roles were excluded from research.

32 Based on the solicited views of 14,655 millennials and 8,273 'GenZs' from 45 countries across the globe, between January–February 2021.

BOX
11.10

■ **Middle managers?** Although middle managers are often seen as the conservative 'clay layer' of organizations, *effective* middle managers are found to have great 'tolerance for ambiguity' (Whetten and Cameron, 2004). Aligning social, ecological and economic values is laden with ambiguities and trade-offs, which makes tolerance for ambiguity an indispensable competence. 'Sustainable middle managers' are versatile, goal and role flexible, and able to change their team's orientation with each transition phase in a motivational manner. KPQs involve: How to empower those middle managers capable of effectuating timely change in the required direction? Can tolerance for ambiguity, versatility and agility be trained? Should rotation schemes be used to develop managers' adaptive capabilities and to prevent them from accruing vested interests that lowers their willingness to change course?

■ *Intrapreneurs?* To address specific sustainability challenges, organizations can opt to assign *intra*preneurs: proactive, resourceful and impact-oriented individuals working inside the company on innovative ideas, projects and pilots that should enhance the organization's sustainability performance. Intrapreneurs are given relative autonomy and access to the company's resources, infrastructures and capabilities to eventually deliver organizational, business and societal value. Many inventive young professionals choose to work for an established organization rather than set up their own (niche) business. KPQs concern: How to create a conducive and appreciative internal space for (young) intrapreneurs to make a positive contribution to sustainability and the good of the entire organization? How to ensure they can optimally collaborate with likeminded people, inside and outside the organization? How to focus their time and energy on ideas that directly link with the organization's contextual realities and actual business needs?

■ **Women?** To what extent does 'gender' shape the motives, means and opportunities for more aspirational sustainability outcomes? Women, compared to men, are generally considered to be more supportive of sustainability ambitions. Whether this insight should lead to, for instance, quota for the representation of women on corporate boards, is heavily debated. Multi-year research of McKinsey finds that creating a better balance between women and men on all hierarchical levels leads to more growth, innovation and stability within organizations. KPQs include: How does diversity affect the value creating potential and sustainability ambition of your organization? Should the focus be specifically on women, or on inclusion and diversity (e.g. ethnic, cultural, age) in general? How to enable inclusion, strengthen representation of diverse talent and ensure equality of opportunity at all levels?

■ **Whistle-blowers?** Whistle-blowing refers to an organizational member raising concern about misconduct within the organization (e.g. illegal practice; improper, immoral or unprofessional behaviour; violation of ethical code of conduct) to persons or organizations in the position to effect (corrective) action. Their fair treatment is an important part of corporate governance arrange-

**B
O
X**

11.10

ments. Dutiful whistle-blowers have an important signalling function on the organization's blind spots and can act as important agents of change, provided they are correctly supported, protected from repercussions (retaliation, intimidation, social isolation, dismissal) and their signals followed up by appropriate action. The position of whistle-blowers is vulnerable and not to be envied: in many countries, there are only weak legal provisions to protect them. Related KPQs include: How to create a sufficiently open culture and trusted procedures to safeguard the position of whistle-blowers? How to ensure that signals of potential misconduct are appreciated as an opportunity to improve responsible practice, rather than as acts of disloyalty? How to facilitate a culture of 'dilemma sharing' and constructive counterbalancing, revive codes of conduct, and support ongoing internal discussion on adjusting values, perspectives and practices in subsequent transitioning phases?

■ **Trade union members?** Freedom of association and the right of collective bargaining are universal rights that apply to all people in all countries. By organizing themselves in trade unions, workers can protect and improve collective goals related to working conditions, occupational health and safety standards, wages, labour contracts, working hours and benefits (e.g. provisions for retirement, health insurance, training), equality and non-discrimination, social protection, employability and just procedures for dispute resolution and remedy. At the company level, relations with trade union representatives and the works council hinge on whether they are viewed as a *conservative and antagonistic force* to articulate workers' discontent, rights and demands, or as a *social partner and cooperative force* in pursuing employee wellbeing, organizational effectiveness and societal welfare. The extent to which the company subscribes to ILO's International Conventions and the *Tripartite Declaration of Principles concerning Multinational Enterprises and Social Policy* (ILO, 2017) delineates the nature of the company-union relationship and the role that organized labour can play in advancing value creation. Related KPQs cover: How can the relationship with union representatives help to overcome key tipping points (1) in distinct operating countries, (2) company-wide, across countries, (3) extended to supply chains? Is the relationship based on meaningful dialogue, good faith and shared commitment, or on disputed adherence to labour standards, principles of decent work and workers' rights?

■ *Decent work and fair compensation*

Central to fostering productive employment and decent work – and thus a key concern of the HRM function – is the development of human-centred HRM policies that ensure: "a fair income, security in the workplace and social protection for families, better prospects for personal development and social integration, freedom for people to express their concerns, organize and participate in the decisions that affect their lives and equality of opportunity and treatment for all women and men."[33] Wages are among the most important conditions of work. Nonetheless, in-work poverty is a reality for a substantial part of workers, despite having a paid job in the formal economy. In 2020, ILO reported that 266 million wage earners – representing 15% of global wage earners – are paid less than the (statutory or collectively negotiated) hourly minimum wage level set in their country, either because they are not legally covered or because of non-compliance.[34] Women, young workers, workers with lower education, rural workers and workers with dependent children are overrepresented in this group (ILO, 2020). Sub-minimum wages are found across all continents, with Europe and Central Asia counting 45 million (13%) underpaid employees; Asia and the Pacific 134 million (16%), the Americas 58 million (17%) and Africa 28 million (21%).

Matters of 'quality of employment' encompass many contextual labour market factors, institutional settings and national labour laws. However, providing employees with adequate earnings is a fundamental precondition in enabling them to secure decent living conditions for themselves and their families. This applies to workers *directly employed* – at the headquarters and across all countries of operations – and extends to workers *indirectly employed* throughout the supply chain (section 11.3). For the HRM department, KPQs on compensation policies include whether to set the absolute floor at:

■ *The minimum wage level*, as established by national standards (statutory or negotiated). In many countries, however, gross minimum wage levels are too low to protect workers and their families to unduly low pay or poverty; these thresholds do not include the cost of living, nor the relative living standards of other social groups (ILO, 2020); [35]

■ *The living wage level* reflects the minimum income, at the local living standard, needed for an individual and her/his family to meet basic needs. A living wage reckons with the costs of food, water, housing, transport, education, healthcare, phone costs, clothing and other essential needs. As such, it indicates that workers earning above this income level are out of absolute poverty and can afford a modest yet decent life in dignity.

---

33 https://www.ilo.org/global/topics/decent-work/lang--en/index.htm.

34 The ILO (2020) notes that an estimated 18% of countries with statutory minimum wages exclude agricultural workers and/or domestic workers from minimum wage regulations.

35 Only in a small number of high-income countries is the minimum wage above the living wage level: Australia, Austria, France, Germany, Ireland, Oman, Netherlands, New Zealand, Saudi-Arabia, United Kingdom. For information on definitions, visit: https://wageindicator. org/salary/living-wage/faq-living-wage/.

■   *A decent compensation* additionally offers a set of social benefits, typically involving provisions for medical and social insurance, pension, parental leave and vocational training. Decent compensation for workers fosters positive effects on the families, the wider community and economy through greater social security, employability, purchasing power and (indirect) social and economic spill-over effects that contribute to empowerment, socio-economic progress and societal prosperity.

ILO'S 'FUNDAMENTAL PRINCIPLES' AND 'DECENT WORK FOR ALL'

ILO's Fundamental Principles and Rights at Work are universal, inalienable and indivisible human rights. The ILO principles also represent key enabling conditions for 'decent work' and sustainable economic growth: they are the foundation for effective social dialogue, better conditions for workers, rising enterprise productivity, increased consumer demand, more and better jobs and social protection, and for formalizing the informal economy.

1   ***Freedom of association and the right to collective bargaining*** is a crucial vehicle in enabling employers and workers to negotiate key aspects of their relationship and to promote the 'fair sharing of wealth' they have helped to generate. Still, more than 40% of the world's population lives in countries that have not (yet) ratified the freedom of association and collective bargaining conventions (ILO, 2019). Especially in these countries, employers can play an active role in explicitly recognizing and promoting workers' right to organize.

2   ***Elimination of forced or compulsory labour***, in all its forms, entails that workers "will neither be robbed of their dignity nor their right to freely-chosen employment". Currently, 40.3 million people are in modern slavery, including 24.9 million in forced labour – 25% of whom are children (ILO, 2019).

3   ***Effective abolition of child labour***, to ensure that all children have access to education and can fulfil their creative and full potential – and the intergenerational transmission of poverty and social exclusion can eventually be broken. Global estimates indicate that 160 million children were in child labour at the beginning of 2020, of whom 79 million were in hazardous work directly endangering their health, safety and moral development. Almost half are aged 5–11 years, which represents a rise of 16.8 million more children aged 5–11 in child labour compared to 2016 (ILO and UNICEF, 2021).

4   ***Elimination of discrimination in respect of employment and occupation*** would unlock the potential of women, men and youth presently excluded or undervalued because of their sex, age, ethnic or social origins, religion, political opinion, sexual orientation or identity, disability or health status. Presently, women are paid an averaged 23% less than their male counterparts while millions of people suffer from work-related discrimination (ILO, 2019).

B O X

11.11

As a guidance to companies in providing inclusive, responsible and sustainable workplace practices around the world, the ILO elaborated the *Tripartite Declaration of Principles concerning Multinational Enterprises and Social Policy* (the **MNE Declaration**). Adopted in 1977 – and lastly updated in 2017 – the MNE Declaration is the only principles-based global instrument on international labour standards adopted by governments, employers and workers from around the globe. The guidance framework is grounded in key ILO Conventions and Recommendations. It encompasses both negative-duty (avoid doing harm) and positive-duty (doing good) principles in the fields of employment, training, conditions of work and life, and industrial relations.

Since 1999, the ILO has actively promulgated a **Decent Work Agenda** founded on four positive-duty pillars: rights at work; employment creation; social protection; and social dialogue and tripartism. 'Decent work for all' is the ultimate goal guiding all of ILO's present work. It is intimately linked with implementation of **SDG8** ('decent work and economic growth'). The basic argument is: "quality jobs along with social protection and respect for rights at work contribute to sustainable and inclusive economic growth, and eliminate poverty". The principles of the MNE Declaration provide the elemental entry points for enhancing positive social and labour effects of the operations and governance of multinational enterprises to achieve decent work for all, in line with the SDG-agenda.

- Operational tools and the ILO 'helpdesk for business': https://www.ilo.org/empent/areas/business-helpdesk/lang--en/index.htm.

- The complete list of ILO standards (by subject and status), the NORMLEX database: https://www.ilo.org/dyn/normlex/en/f?p=NORMLEXPUB:12030:0::NO:::

- Country profiles and national legislation database on labour standards: https://www.ilo.org/dyn/normlex/en/f?p=NORMLEXPUB:11003:0::NO:::

▪ *Employee motivation and rewards*

Sustainability-oriented organizational change entails that employees are (a) *knowledgeable* about the societal challenges and corporate responsibilities the organization seeks to address, and (b) *motivated* to contribute to enhanced sustainability performance and outcomes. Motivated engagement, then, is typically assumed to be derived from 'intrinsic benefits' that employees receive by contributing to society – an enhanced sense of fulfilment and meaning, being true to one's values and ethics, inspiring experiences and greater self-esteem for instance. This intrinsic drive certainly holds true for most impact-driven *initiators* of sustainability projects, but not necessarily applies to all participating employees tasked with carrying them out. Especially when implementation comes with increased workload, tougher working conditions, self-sacrifice and challenging performance targets, a better understanding of the diverse motivations that drive employee commitment is in order. For the HRM department, related KPQs include: How to appropriately motivate and *crowd-in* all organizational members? To what point can the organization appeal to employees' intrinsic motivation? When should *motivation-enhancing* practices be included that meet employees' instrumental needs for recognition and reward? Reliance on financial rewards is known for its adverse effect of *crowding-out* intrinsic motivation, work morale, reciprocity, social relations and creativity (Frey and Jegen, 2001). However, unexpected rewards not contingent on task behaviour may actually stimulate morale. How to avoid the *hidden costs of reward* and tailor appraisal and reward policies that: (1) recognize the fine line between crowding-in and crowding-out motivation, and (2) reckon with diverse organizational cultures and locational realities (see Box 11.9)?

Research in the field of strategic human capital management indicates that employees engaging in corporate sustainability initiatives have *mixed motives* (intrinsic and extrinsic motivations) for their commitment, which explicitly include self-focused benefits. Additional to fulfilment, personal meaning and a 'fit' between their own values and those of the organization ('the warm glow'), employees also seek skills development and improved career prospects (Bode and Singh, 2018). Their commitment to corporate sustainability projects is motivated significantly by professional development opportunities that increase their future earnings potential. For instance, through acquiring problem-solving skills, gaining confidence in stretch roles, and working with diverse internal and external stakeholders. As such, self-focused motivation can be an important lever for human capital development and talent management programmes that meet employees' needs for positive contributions, recognition and reward.

The balance between intrinsic and self-focused motivation may be breached, however, under the influence of 'relative rewards' and the *perceived legitimacy* of reward policies. A 'bonus culture' that leads to unsubstantiated compensation differentials may seriously crowd-out intrinsic motivation and undermine employee commitment. Exorbitant CEO pay, for instance – tied to stock value rather than to corporate sustainability performance – signals normalization of inequality, priorities unrelated to dedicated societal value creation, and the wrong kind of 'performance' message to organizational members.[36] In the same vein, Dundon and Rafferty (2018: 383) point to the *vicious cycle of demotivation* that may ensue from talent competition. Employees who do not receive the label 'top talent' or

---

36 Research by the Economic Policy Institute found that inflation-adjusted CEO compensation of the largest US public firms grew 940% since 1978, while typical worker compensation rose only 12%. The ratio of CEO-to-worker compensation was 320-to-1 in 2019, compared to 21-to-1 in 1965. https://www.epi.org/publication/ceo-compensation-2018.

'high potential' and accordingly receive fewer resources and less training, may become alienated and disengaged.

SELECTED KPIs

Key Practice and Performance Indicators for HRM are contingent on the organization's view of employees as 'factors of production' or as 'pockets of human and social capital' that drive its ability to create sustainable value and contribute to socially cohesive, vibrant and resilient societies. At the heart of *value creation* lies the degree of proficiency to effectively tap into the knowledge, skills, competencies, resourcefulness and dedication embodied in individuals. The extent to which diverse talent can be recruited, developed and motivated in line with the company's strategic goals, ultimately determines organizational performance in terms of productivity, innovation and sustainability outcomes. At the heart of *value destruction* – particularly in terms of human costs and eroding social fabric – lie practices of poor people management, disregard of diverse talents, exploitative work relations, 'union-bashing', toxic organizational cultures and inadequate investment in training and employee development.

According to observers, the *performance imperative* and compliance with labour laws prevail in most of today's HRM approaches. A narrow view on human capital management reduces HRM practice to a more efficient allocation of human resources, which all the same is supposed to contribute to higher skills levels, increased productivity, greater innovation and strategic performance. The purpose of HRM, then, is mostly economically driven. Against the 'performance imperative' backdrop, new conceptualizations of HRM are emerging and steadily gaining in influence. *Green HRM*, *triple bottom line HRM* and *common goods HRM* approaches (Aust-Ehnert at al., 2020) – to varying degrees of sophistication – use human capital management to integrate environmental, social and societal values into HRM practices. For instance, through capabilities and leadership development, building a learning culture, training awareness, encouraging active employee engagement and rewarding initiative and dedication in ways that advance sustainable workplace practices, stakeholder engagement and positive contributions to society. 'Common goods' HRM, in particular, emphasizes the importance of principles and objectives such as workplace democracy, equal opportunity and fairness, distributive justice, youth employment creation, job security, decent work and earnings for workers and societal resilience. It considers a broad range of stakeholders and acknowledges a wider scope of impact that can be affected via the HRM function. The common goods approach (section 5.4.2) considers both international and local contexts, stresses *the imperative of constructive business-society interactions* and seeks to establish 'social contracts' that serve the common interest of involved societal stakeholders.

Table 11.4 Mapping sustainable HRM practice

KVIs ➡	LEVEL 1	LEVEL 2	LEVEL 3	LEVEL 4
		Key tipping point		
Functional KDIs	*1. Trigger*	*2. Internal alignment*	*3. External alignment*	
Main Trade-off	Employees as cost			Employees as human and social capital
Approach	Transactional HRM	Strategic HRM		Sustainable HRM
Orientation	Performance, compliance and reputation-driven		Developmental, value(s) and impact-driven	
Classification	Traditional HRM	Socially responsible HRM; Green HRM	Triple bottom line HRM	Common goods HRM
KPQs	Inactive	Reactive	Active	Proactive
Perspective	Inside-in	Outside-in	Inside-out	Outside-in/inside-out
Role emphasis	Cost/performance optimizer	Strategic support/business partner	Employee advocate & social support	Hybrid: strategic, employee advocate & social support
Building organizational culture	Consolidation of efficiency/performance culture	Adaptation to and mitigation of cultural differences	Integration of cultural diversity; 'unity of purpose and goals'	Contextualized differentiation; combining 'strength of diversity' and 'unity of purpose'
Agents of change?	Whistleblowers; trade union representatives	Middle managers, intrapreneurs; young professionals; diverse talents (women, ethnic, cultural, age)		Individuals' sustainable leadership; intrapreneurs with external partnership mandate; trade union social partners
Worker representation	Limited voice; hostile relations; dissuasion of representation; union-bashing	Confined involvement of works council; company unions	Employee participation; works council timely informed and consulted; sectoral union representatives	Active involvement of works council; company-union industrial relations at national level, social contracts
Compensation	Minimum wage	Living wage (individual level)	Living wage (household level)	Decent wage
Motivation and rewards philosophy	Market-based incentives; employees as status-seeking, self-focused and income-driven individuals	Mutual gains incentives; employees as professional development-driven and wellbeing-oriented individuals		Impact-based incentives: employees as purpose-driven and societal welfare-oriented individuals

(Continued)

Table 11.4 (Continued)

KPIs	Inactive	Reactive	Active	Proactive
Implementation of ILO Labour Standards (conventions & recommendations)	**Avoiding harm**		**Advancing good**	
	• Elimination of forced labour • Abolition of child labour (e.g. minimum age) • Non-discrimination (equal remuneration, employment and occupation) • Industrial relations: grievances, arbitration • Protection against unemployment • Security of employment • Conditions of work: e.g. working hours; housing • Protection of workers' claims (employer's insolvency) • Occupational safety and health (working environment; chemicals; industrial accidents; mines; radiation protection; guarding of machinery; cancer and occupational diseases) • Social protection (minimum standard of social security; employment injury; social protection floors) • Governance: labour inspection		• Freedom of association and collective bargaining • Industrial relations: workers' representatives; co-operation; social dialogue) • Employment promotion and job creation • Equality of treatment • Training: human resources development • Governance: tripartite consultation • Indigenous and tribal peoples	
Typical practices and metrics	• Composition of the workforce (e.g. analysis by gender, age, full/part-time; contingent labour) • Recruitment costs; internal hire rate • Employee compensation, benefits entitlements, retirement benefit plans • Training on health & safety • Accident rates; work-related fatalities; days lost to injury • Training and employee development spend (average hours training per employee category; numbers of courses taken) • Reward schemes aligning employee performance with strategic goals • Employee health, motivation and engagement (absence rates, work satisfaction surveys) • Stability of the workforce; rate of employee turnover (voluntary and regrettable turnover rates) • Retention rates after parental leave; health-related absenteeism • Industrial relations issues; employee representation and voice • Revenue per headcount; productivity gains made		• Work-life balance; flexible work arrangements; job rotation • Workforce health, well-being and vitality metrics • Organizational culture metrics (respectful relationships; fairness; diversity; equality; cooperation) • Performance evaluation in alignment with sustainability-related criteria • Voice giving; effective employee participation, engagement and initiative (e.g. impact-teams) • Employee representation in decision-making beyond statutory requirements • Employee leadership development, capabilities training, experience and knowledge sharing; employability • On-boarding, on-the-job coaching; off-boarding; responsible and supportive outplacement trajectories • Community involvement, volunteering and external partnerships • Employee commitment, job satisfaction, trustful employee-employer relationship • Decent working conditions in supply chains; (youth) employment creation	

11.7 THE SUSTAINABLE FINANCE CHALLENGE: INTEGRATED VALUE BEYOND THE BALANCE SHEET

Key Performance Questions for sustainable finance

■ What leading principles guide the finance function in your organization?

■ What sources of external funding best fit your fiduciary duty, ESG profile and preferred capital structure?

■ What principal cost/benefit and return-on-investment assessments do you make?

■ What time horizon do you take in your capital allocation decisions?

■ What role can 'monetizing' (attaching a monetary value to externalities) play in mitigating ESG risk or identifying new sources of income and ways of organizing?

■ How to deal with the vast number of ESG criteria, reporting standards, disclosure requirements and protocols, on top of emerging regulation on non-financial disclosure?

■ How do you approach internal transfer pricing and taxation across borders?

■ What capitals and reporting scope do you take into account when disclosing on performance, impacts and prospects?

■ How is integrated reporting helpful in surpassing key tipping points?

■ What focus to encourage as Chief Financial Officer and what 'value' to pursue?

KEY DECISIONS: PROFITS AS A GOAL OR MEANS?

The corporate finance function is concerned with the management of financial resources to ensure the long-term viability of the organization's value generating activities. It operates at the interface with the financial sector (e.g. banks, institutional investors, stock markets, venture capital and impact investors, insurance companies), which constitutes the external valuation context for assessing corporate performance, potential, resilience and risk. Corporate finance deals with the effective and efficient planning, organizing, directing and controlling of financial activities and processes to attain the company's strategic goals and objectives over time. Finance interferes with practically all decisions in a firm. The function encompasses a cluster of related activities that include: (a) *financial planning and budgeting*, based on a proper understanding of the needs and priorities of the organization within its wider business context; (b) *capital management*, which links the organization's investment-related capital needs with appropriate capital structures and sources of additional funding (e.g. equity, bonds, loans); (c) *investment* of funds in profitable ventures in ways that provide a reliable and adequate rate of return; (d) *cash flow management*, for sufficiently meeting operational expenses; (e) *financial risk management* and control; (f) *disposal of net profits*, distributed as shareholder dividends or retained within the company for investment purposes; and (g) *financial reporting* and disclosure of (financial and non-financial) information.

The traditional approach to corporate finance is grounded in the private property theory of finance, in which the company pursues profit maximization and shareholder value without much consideration to social, environmental or broader welfare dimensions. The primary goal is to optimize expected financial returns at the lowest risk possible. The 'refined shareholder view' recognizes that it is instrumental to maintain good relations with other stakeholders ('license to operate') in order to preserve shareholder value in the longer run (Schoenmaker and Schramade, 2019). This 'enlightened' version of shareholder value maximization reconciles maximum profits with the reduction of obvious negative effects – for instance, by investing in cost-reducing, energy-saving and efficiency-enhancing technologies that require less (natural) resources and material inputs and thus generate cost-savings (see section 8.4.2 on the 'defensive business case').[37] Classical financial models and valuation methods reiterate the one-dimensional economic objective. They only include financial variables in considering the present value of future cash flows that activities are expected to bring in, but ignore the wider (social, environmental, economic) repercussions of investment decisions outside the firm. The costs of externalities and future liabilities, asset stranding (see Box 9.2 on 'the incumbent's curse') and operational disruptions, for instance, are not incorporated in financial forecasts, discount rates and capital budgeting decision criteria. Outdated financial decision-making models that fail to reflect the risk and timing of future payoffs, the potential cost savings from avoided future losses and the value of intangible

---

37 The financial business case for sustainability was portrayed in Box 8.5 as a 'normal' U-shaped investment curve in which financial performance measures – such as 'return on investment' (ROI) – should be considered in relation to the transition stage of the organization. The business case for sustainability proves easiest to make for ecological performance (Ambec and Lanoie, 2008).

resources,[38] have been pointed out as a key culprit in hampering corporate investments in sustainability (Siegrist et al., 2020).

Sustainable corporate finance (SCF), as a concept, emerged as part of the broader notion of business sustainability. It has been defined as "a multi-attribute approach to finance the company in such a way that all the company's financial, social and environmental elements are interrelated and integrated" in ways that explicitly connect the firm's present and future stakeholders (Soppe, 2004: 213). SCF implies a fundamental rethinking of 'agency' and related fiduciary duties and responsibilities (see section 6.2 on 'responsible governance'), and realignment of the company's purpose, mission and value proposition with societal needs and expectations (Chapter 9). Does the company steer on maximizing profits and shareholder value, or rather strive for optimizing stakeholder value, societal value creation and long-term viability through the private provision of common goods at a 'fair' rate of return? Interconnecting business strategy and purpose with finance and sustainability objectives implies that 'extra-financial' aspects are fully integrated into corporate finance instruments and decision-making processes. The 'sustainable corporate finance' challenge hence lies in incorporating both negative and positive externalities in the company's financial forecasts, valuation methods and capital budgeting decision frameworks in ways that demonstrate and optimize *integrated value* – that is, financial, social and environmental value combined – so that the interests of current and future stakeholders are ranked equally (Schoenmaker and Schramade, 2019).

The role of finance has traditionally been aimed at allocating funding to its most productive use. However, what should be considered 'the most productive' is open to change and subject to the context-specific challenges an organization faces in distinct transitioning phases. The role of the corporate finance department has been shifting accordingly: from primarily focused on funding activities, towards a partnering role in strategic decision-making, informing on investment opportunities that allow the company to innovate and overcome key tipping points in reaching the next sustainability level. In line with the sustainable finance (SF) typology of Schoenmaker and Schramade (2019: 20), corporate finance strategies, policies and practices can be classified along three ambition levels: (1) an *SF1.0 orientation*, geared to (short-term) 'financial value' maximization that meets optimal 'refined shareholder value' by avoiding risks from environmentally and socially harmful activities; (2) an *SF2.0 orientation* that incorporates social and

---

38 It is estimated that at least 80% of enterprise value remains hidden from the balance sheet. As a result, the value of a firm's (strategic) intangible assets – such as innovation, culture, trust, a talented workforce, effective corporate governance and other vital sources of competitive advantage that provide the bases for expected value but are difficult to measure – is poorly understood by both internal and external stakeholders (IFAC, 2020; EPIC, 2018).

environmental externalities into finance decisions to optimize 'integrated value' and 'stakeholder value' and so avoid (medium-term) risk; and (3) an *SF3.0* approach, which seeks to create long-term 'societal value' through investments that optimize the provision of common goods at a sufficient rate of return. The interaction with the financial sector – itself subject to a 'sustainable finance landscape' in flux (Migliorelli, 2021) – determines the pace with which organizations can move through these transition phases.

KPQs: WHAT TO FOCUS ON?

Sustainability is progressively permeating the domain of corporate investments and finance. An array of financial instruments and products has emerged to support private investments in sustainability-related activities and projects – including green, social, sustainability, SDG- and sustainability-linked corporate bonds and loans. Concurrently, principles frameworks and good practice standards for corporate governance and board oversight, internal controls, verification and disclosure of sustainability performance have been proliferating. Institutional investors, asset managers and loan providers are increasingly weighing long-term value drivers and risk factors in their screening, credit rating and index-ranking practices. ESG investing is fast becoming mainstream (OECD, 2020). According to PwC (2020), "there is a wide body of evidence indicating that CFOs recognize the impact of ESG performance on their cost of capital, clearly placing ESG in the remit of the corporate finance function".[39] This raises the question to what extent the company's investment and finance strategies are effectively aligned with 'sustainable finance' landscape developments, changing investor preferences, and opportunities to leverage corporate finance for societal value creation (Box 11.12).

B O X 11.12	**NAVIGATING THE SUSTAINABLE FINANCE JUNGLE** Sustainable finance (SF) has steadily been gaining worldwide attention from financial markets, political actors and the broader public alike. Asset managers, institutional investors and banks are increasingly aligning their investment and financing strategy with environmental, social and responsible governance (ESG) aspects, in the recognition that: (1) non-financial risks can have a material impact on risk-adjusted returns and long-term value, and (2) financial instruments, such as thematic bonds and sustainable lending products, can channel capital to investments and activities with positive sustainability impacts.

39 https://www.pwc.com/jp/en/knowledge/column/integration-into-corporate-finance.html.

At year-end 2019, over $30 trillion of institutional investments in corporate bonds and equity was actively managed under ESG-based considerations – an increase of more than 30% compared to 2016 (OECD, 2020). The market size of green, social and sustainability corporate bonds passed $500 billion,[40] whereas the estimated size of the global impact-investing market amounted to $715 billion as of year-end 2019 (Global Impact Investing Network, 2020).[41] Furthermore, 67% of global banks reported to screen their loan portfolios for ESG risk.[42] The growth rates in SF markets notwithstanding, there is still considerable ambiguity on how corporate non-financial performance can be effectively recognized and what type of corporate activities and (transition) investments should be eligible for what type of sustainable financing. So far, there is no universal definition of what constitutes 'sustainable finance', nor on the composition of vital ESG aspects and implementation standards (Migliorelli, 2021). Terminology and practices vary considerably (OECD, 2020).

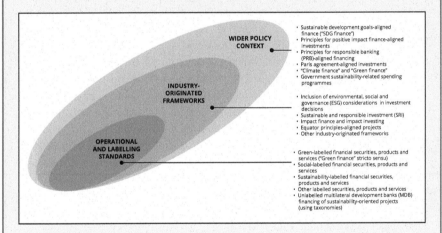

Figure 11.15 The sustainable finance landscape
Source: Migliorelli (2021), licensed under CC BY 4.0

The evolving SF landscape

Initiatives to redirect capital flows to socially responsible and sustainability-related investments have given rise to a complex landscape of novel financial securities, products and services alongside a range of policy and industry frameworks, guidelines, taxonomies and labelling standards (Figure 11.15). The SDG-agenda and the

---

40 https://www.climatebonds.net/resources/reports/sustainable-debt-global-state-market-2020.
41 https://thegiin.org/impact-investing/need-to-know/#what-is-the-current-state-of-the-impact-investing-market.
42 https://investesg.eu/2020/12/15/scaling-sustainable-finance-through-integrated-corporate-finance-jerome-lavigne-delville-ifc-un-global-compact/.

Paris Climate Agreement have spurred developments in regional SF strategies (e.g. the European Green Deal), financial innovations and (voluntary) commitments by financial institutions and investor networks to contribute to a fundamental shift. Various guidelines and taxonomies for financiers and investors have emerged to establish a 'common language' and increase transparency across categories of financial instruments and business activities.

Challenges in the SF chain

The financial intermediation chain that converts SF concepts into sustainable investment practice is growing increasingly complex too, as more financial service providers – notably of ESG ratings, indices and benchmarks – are becoming engaged (Figure 11.16). At the end of 2019, about 70 different ESG-rating providers were identified on top of the vast array of investment banks, government bodies and research organizations (Li and Polychronopoulos, 2020). ESG ratings are used by asset managers, institutional investors and financial institutions to inform their portfolio composition decisions. However, ESG ratings have been found to vary markedly among distinct rating providers. In its *Business and Finance Outlook 2020*, the OECD observed a proliferation of methodologies, ratings, frameworks and metrics on ESG performance – with consequential challenges for consistency, comparability and assessing related financial materiality, and for aligning private investments with sustainable, long-term value. According to the OECD, "current market practices, from ratings to disclosures and individual metrics, present a fragmented and inconsistent view of ESG risks and performance" (ibid: 15). Such divergences are confusing for end investors and may distort investment decisions. For companies, this state of affairs makes it challenging to efficiently attract (transition) financing at a competitive cost that considers all relevant ESG factors and potential for sustainability impact.

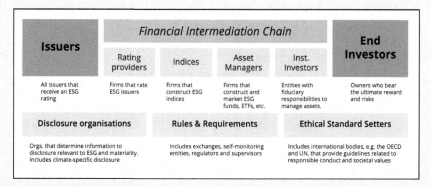

Figure 11.16 The structure of the ESG financial ecosystem

Source: adapted from OECD (2020) *OECD Business and Finance Outlook 2020. Sustainable and Resilient Finance*, p. 23. © OECD.

Principles-based channelling efforts

Over the years, a variety of internationally recognized principles, guidance frameworks and standards have been developed with the intention to: (a) accelerate the channelling of private investments into sustainability-enhancing projects and activities, and (b) spur commitment, coordination, transparency and accountability among actors within the SF landscape. Leading industry-based standard-setting initiatives with global reach include:

- *The UN Principles for Responsible Investment (PRI):* a set of investment principles that demonstrate signatories' commitment to including ESG factors in investment decision-making and ownership. The principles reflect the understanding that "an economically efficient, sustainable global financial system is a necessity for long-term value creation. Such a system will reward long-term, responsible investment and benefit the environment and society as a whole". At year-end 2020, PRI counted more than 3,000 signatory organizations, together representing over $100 trillion in assets under management. https://www.unpri.org/pri/what-are-the-principles-for-responsible-investment

- *The UNEP-FI Principles for Responsible Banking (PRB):* a six-point framework launched in 2019 "for ensuring that signatory banks' strategy and practice align with the vision society has set out for its future in the SDGs and Paris Climate Agreement". The principles are designed to embed sustainability at the strategic, portfolio and transactional levels across all business areas. Over 230 banks – representing more than a third of the global banking industry – have committed to taking a leadership role in transforming the banking industry by using their products, services and relationships to accelerate the fundamental changes needed to achieve shared prosperity. Signatory banks are required to self-assess and report on their transitioning efforts and to have implemented their targets within a maximum of four years. https://www.unepfi.org/banking/bankingprinciples/

- *The UNEP-FI Principles for Positive Impact Finance:* provide a 'meta' set of guidelines for financiers, investors and auditors that defines 'Positive Impact Business & Finance' as "that which serves to deliver a positive contribution to one or more of the three pillars of sustainable development (economic, environmental and social), once any potential negative impacts to any of the pillars have been duly identified and mitigated". The principles articulate inclusive, holistic and transparent impact analysis and management of both processes and outcomes, at the portfolio, corporate, asset or project level. They are applicable to all forms of financial institutions and financial instruments, and come with impact mapping and analysis tools developed for banks, investors and investee companies. https://www.unepfi.org/positive-impact/principles-for-positive-impact-finance/.

- *The UNEP-FI Principles for Sustainable Insurance (PSI):* a framework for ensuring that all activities in the insurance value chain are done in a responsible

BOX 11.12

and forward-looking way by identifying, assessing, managing and monitoring risks and opportunities associated with environmental, social and governance issues. 'Sustainable insurance' aims to reduce risk, develop innovative solutions, improve business performance and contribute to environmental, social and economic sustainability. Since its launch in 2012, PSI has been adopted by 140 organizations worldwide, including insurers representing over 25% of world premiums and $14 trillion in assets under management. The principles are part of the insurance industry criteria of the Dow Jones Sustainability Indices and FTSE4Good. https://www.unepfi.org/psi/the-principles/

- **The Equator Principles:** a risk management framework adopted by financial institutions for determining, assessing and managing environmental and social risk in projects. The principles provide a minimum standard for due diligence and monitoring to support responsible risk decision-making. They particularly focus on social/community standards and responsibility, including standards for indigenous peoples, labour and consultation with locally affected communities. The EPs have been officially adopted by 118 financial institutions in 37 countries, covering the majority of international project finance debt within developed and emerging markets. https://equator-principles.com./about/

- **International Capital Market Association Bond Principles:** The Green Bond Principles (GBP), the Social Bond Principles (SBP), the Sustainability Bond Guidelines (SBG) and the Sustainability-Linked Bond Principles are a collection of voluntary, internationally recognized frameworks and process guidelines with the stated mission of promoting the role that global debt capital markets can play in financing progress towards environmental and social sustainability. The principles outline best practices when issuing bonds serving social and environmental purposes, through guidelines that promote transparency and disclosure, thereby underpinning the integrity of the market. In 2020, 97% of global sustainable bonds (representing $580 billion) were aligned with the principles. https://www.icmagroup.org/sustainable-finance/the-principles-guidelines-and-handbooks/

- **The CFO Principles on Integrated SDG Investments and Finance:** launched in September 2020 to supplement the UN Global Compact's Ten Principles. By committing to the principles, CFOs and Corporate Treasurers recognize: (1) their responsibility to support their companies in the transition to sustainable development and to leverage corporate finance and investments towards realization of the SDGs; and (2) the opportunity to 'create a market' for corporate SDG investments and finance that is sufficiently diverse and transparent to "channel trillions in financial investments towards private-sector solutions for the SDGs". The four CFO Principles comprise:

1   SDG impact thesis and measurement;

2   Integrated SDG strategy and investments;

3   Integrated corporate SDG finance;

4   Integrated SDG communication and reporting.

CFOs commit to work with their companies and board members to adopt best practices suggested for each principle, to set ambitious targets, and to annually disclose their progress in implementing the principles, targets and (verified) results on key performance indicators. In due course, the KPIs for progress measurement and target-setting should become an integral part of the accountability mechanism in the implementation of the UN Global Compact's Ten Principles.[43] By 2021, 58 companies with a market capitalization of over $1.6 trillion had committed to measure their progress on implementing the principles. https://www.unglobalcompact.org/take-action/action/action-platforms/cfo-taskforce.

The SF orientation is reflected in at least three key aspects of the corporate finance role: (a) attracting sustainability-oriented external funding; (b) accounting for future-oriented decision-making, transition risk management and capital(s) budgeting (e.g. internal carbon pricing); and (c) reporting and disclosing financial and non-financial information on performance, progress, prospects and impacts.

■ *Managing a portfolio of financiers and investors*
Demand for sustainable investment opportunities is on the rise, instigated by the growing number and size of sustainable, responsible and impact-oriented investment initiatives and the emergence of sustainability-related regulation in the financial sector.[44] Also public sources of finance – e.g. soft loans, revolving

---

43 See the UN Global Compact's CFO Taskforce for the SDGs report *CFO Principles KPIs and Definitions for Progress Measurement and Target Setting*, June 2021, https://unglobalcompact.org/library/5929.

44 By 2020, 24 stock exchanges around the world – including the Hong Kong Exchange, Euronext London and the Johannesburg Stock Exchange – already had mandatory ESG listing requirements. Another example is the EU regulation on *sustainability-related disclosure in the financial services sector* (EU 2019/2088), which established harmonized rules for financial market participants and financial advisers on transparency regarding integration of sustainability risks and impacts in their information on financial products. The regulation is binding in all EU member states. Furthermore, the European 'Sustainable Finance Taxonomy' – Regulation (EU) 2020/852 – defines the conditions that an economic activity has to meet in order to qualify as 'environmentally sustainable'. Through technical screening criteria and the listing of environmental sustainable activities, the EU taxonomy pursues to "create security for investors, protect private investors from greenwashing, help companies to become more climate-friendly, mitigate market fragmentation and help shift investments where they are most needed". The taxonomy sets a Europe-wide standard for sustainable investments, https://ec.europa.eu/info/business-economy-euro/banking-and-finance/sustainable-finance_en.

	Traditional investing	Sustainable and Responsible Investing (SRI)/ ESG Investing strategies				Impact Investing			Philanthropy
		Negative screening	ESG Integration & engagement	Positive or best-in-class screening	Sustainability themed	Market rate	Concessional	Concessionary capital	
Key features	Invest to maximize financial returns, regardless of ESG factors	Exclude activities or industries with clearly defined negative impacts from an investment portfolio (e.g. arms)	Integrate ESG factors into investment decisions to better manage risk and possibly enhance financial returns	Selecting best performing companies accros industries in terms of sustainability performance	Invest in themes or assets constructed around the SDGs (e.g. water, gender)	Invest with the intention to generate positive measurable social and environmental impact alongside a financial return		Grants and donor-driven development projects (e.g. PPP's, blended finance, seed funds, revolving funds)	Address societal challenges by donating private money to good causes
Return expectation	Financial market rate only	Financial market rate focused				Social return & market financial return	Social return & sub-market financial return	Societal return & uncertain financial return	Social return only
Impact		**Do no harm** ▶ ▶ ▶ ▶ ▶ **Investment likely to create positive sustainable development outcomes**							

Figure 11.17 Sources of external finance for sustainability investments

Source: based on UN Inter-agency Task Force on Financing for Development (2020), p. 73.

funds, grant schemes, seed funding, blended finance and other (concessionary) financial arrangements – extend companies' financing options for expanding their portfolio of sustainability activities beyond the reactive threshold. Assessing the various conditions and avenues for attracting sufficient external funding to break through the 'responsive phase' of the investment curve (see Box 8.5) is a vital function of the finance department. Related KPQs are twofold: (a) how best to finance sustainability-related activities for which the business case and 'return on sustainability investment' (ROSI) is relatively clear (often involving level 1 and 2 sustainability ambitions); and (b) how to finance more innovative and risky activities that will have a positive sustainability impact (at levels 3 and 4), but for which the business case and ROSI is less clear-cut – at least in the short run – and/or contingent upon the continued involvement of (co-) financing partners?

By linking different forms of sustainability investing to various impact ambitions – ranging from 'do no harm' to 'doing good' – UN DESA and Global Investors for Sustainable Development mapped the landscape of potential investors and financiers relevant to corporate external funding needs. The landscape includes traditional investing, various ESG investing strategies, (market rate and concessional) impact investing and philanthropy, yet can be complemented with government co-financing and concessionary capital arrangements to support otherwise non-viable corporate investments in projects and activities with desirable sustainability outcomes (Figure 11.17). Each of these external financial sources comes with conditions, risks and requirements that have a bearing on the organization's degree of autonomy in strategy implementation. For instance, participating in grant schemes can create a perverse incentive for the company to abide to specific requirements of the sponsor that may impinge upon the firm's longer-term ambitions. Financial arrangements may also come with extensive impact measurement, assurance and disclosure requirements, which can significantly increase transaction costs.

For companies, the external funding challenge lies in strategically linking the organization's sustainability ambitions and related capital needs with suitable financial arrangements and different sources of (patient) funding. As financiers and investors increasingly integrate ESG and ESG+ factors into their investment, lending and project grant decisions, *unsustainable* companies, in due course, are likely to encounter more trouble raising financing – eventuating in higher transaction and financing costs and affecting their preferred capital structure. A growing body of empirical studies suggests that better ESG performance is rewarded by investors, with high ESG-scoring companies facing lower average costs of capital (both of equity and debt) than firms with poor ESG scores. In developed markets, lower scoring companies were found to experience reduced costs of capital upon credibly improving their sustainability profile, indicating that firms may financially benefit from upgrading their sustainability performance.[45] For CFOs and investor/creditor relation officers, it is hence important to ensure effective engagement with relevant capital providers so that they do not operate on exclusion ('negative screening'), but rather on constructive and longer-term engagement for stronger sustainability performance and outcomes – based on concrete goals and meaningful indicators for impact and progress measurement. It also requires that firms take a longer-term horizon in their investment decisions and find ways to resist short-term pressures from shareholders looking for immediate returns. Rather than fixate on quarterly or year-end financial reporting, CFOs need to think in time-frames extending a decade or several decades in the future.

▪ Strategic planning, capital(s) budgeting and forecasting: internalizing externalities

The *internal* corporate finance challenge revolves around how to organize for well-informed forward-looking decision-making (e.g., on acquisition, investment and divestment), effective risk management and optimized revenue streams such that (a) realization of the organization's sustainability ambitions is fittingly enabled, and (b) its potential for long-term value creation reinforced. Future-proofing the organization's strategy requires a thorough understanding of how the use of and investment in natural, social and human capitals affect the company's business model, its financial performance and its long-term value (SASB, 2020). It also calls for valuation, measurement and modelling methods that can help identify and project the longer-term costs and risks of existing practices, weighed against the forecasts of more sustainable and resilient alternatives.

Various valuation and measuring methods have emerged that seek to internalize the hidden costs and benefits of business impacts normally not reflected in companies' profit and loss statements and balance sheets (Box 11.13). *Monetization* – i.e. attaching a monetary value to externalities and non-financial capitals – is increasingly used by firms as a quantitative valuation or 'internal pricing' tool to measure, model and manage ESG *risks* associated with regulatory and market regimes in order to better inform financial and investment decisions. Monetization enables companies to see 'value creation' and 'value destruction' in

---

45 Results from MSCI analysis, based on a four-year study period of the MSCI World Index (1,552 companies) and MSCI Emerging Markets Index (960 companies) between 2016 and 2020. The relationship between ESG-scores and the cost of capital was the strongest in the US. https://www.msci.com/www/blog-posts/esg-and-the-cost-of-capital/017265 13589. Research on the link between corporate social/environmental performance and costs of capital is generally supportive of an inverse relationship, although context-specific factors at the country, industry and firm levels affecting the strength and direction of the relationship should always be considered (Gianfrate et al., 2019; Garzón-Jiménez and Zorio-Grima, 2020; Gerwanski, 2020).

the terms they are conversant with. Used in a forward-looking and (pro)active way, monetized valuation and internal pricing methods can also be supportive to *anticipate and prevent* operational and strategic risks. By calculating the 'true costs' and 'true values' of activities to see how, where and when these are affected, *opportunities* for new sources of income and ways of organizing can be identified early on, so that technologies, strategies, business models and supply chain configurations can be timely adjusted accordingly. Relevant KPQs, then, relate to whether *to await* externally imposed mitigation measures (e.g. taxation, compliance costs, risk premiums, fees, fines, reputational damage), or rather *be ahead* of developments in the recognition that non-financial issues are in fact *pre-financial*, and may shortly become financially material.

CONVERGENCE IN THE 'VALUE ACCOUNTING' LANDSCAPE

BOX 11.13

Starting in the 1970s with the social audit movement, various approaches to *full cost, true cost* and *true value* accounting emerged – at the level of a product, project, process or whole organization – that seek to record the impact of mostly thematic externalities (e.g. carbon emissions, water and land use, biodiversity, forests) arising from the activities of organizations (cf. Unerman et al., 2018). Awareness of both the impact and dependence of firms on natural capital accelerated after the release of the 'TEEB for Business' report (2010),[46] which emphasized the vast (economic) value of nature's 'biodiversity and ecosystem services' (BES) to business and humanity. Because these benefits are not reflected in market prices of goods and services, the value of BES is generally neglected or undervalued in private decision-making, leading to actions that result in biodiversity loss and ecosystem degradation. The TEEB report argued that the *integration of BES into business* could create significant cost reductions and added value for companies. For instance, by ensuring the sustainability of supply chains, inspiring new value propositions and creating new markets.

Decision-making support tools for measuring, valuating and managing externalities rapidly developed since then. The range includes Environmental Profit and Loss (EP&L) methodologies – developed by PUMA (in 2010) and further elaborated by Kering (in 2016);[47] PwC's 'Total Impact Measurement and Management'

---

46 The Economics of Ecosystems and Biodiversity (TEEB) synthesizes knowledge from ecology, economics, policy, and social sciences to provide recommendations to governments and businesses on integrating biodiversity and ecosystem services into their decision-making processes through 'natural capital accounting', http://www.teebweb.org/.
47 The first-ever EP&L was published by IT company BSO/Origin (Eckart Wintzen) in 1990, which included the hidden environmental costs of the company's atmospheric emissions and waste.

BOX 11.13

(TIMM) model; KPMG's 'True Value' method; the Impact Institute's 'Integrated Profit and Loss Assessment Methodology' (IAM); and the 'Impact Statement' methodology of the Value Balancing Alliance.[48]

In response to companies' call for a harmonized and internationally recognized approach, the Capitals Coalition released its *Natural Capital Protocol* and *Social & Human Capital Protocol* after four years of global consultation and collaborative development. The protocols provide a standardized framework to understand, measure and valuate natural, social and human capital – expressed in qualitative or quantitative terms – to inform actionable and holistic (corporate) decisions "that create value for nature, people and society alongside businesses and the economy". 'Accounting for a Living Wage' is the Coalition's next step in fuelling the practice of 'value accounting'. Furthermore, the Value Accounting Network, launched by the Capitals Coalition mid-2021, will endeavour to build further consistency in the burgeoning 'value accounting' landscape. In a collaborative effort, the initiative intends to harmonize how various concepts, methodologies, valuation techniques and classification are applied within organizations. More information: https://capitalscoalition.org/

One example of how a growing number of multinational companies are anticipating business-critical transition risks is the practice of 'internal carbon pricing' (ICP).[49] As the climate crisis worsens, companies can expect more stringent regulatory and pricing measures.[50] Putting an *internal* cost on carbon – i.e. monetizing the carbon impact to reflect anticipated *external* carbon emission prices and compliance costs within and across jurisdictions – can provide a useful decision-making support tool for risk mitigation and externality internalization. An ICP can be used in several ways: (1) as an *actual fee* levied on business units within the company to incentivize emission reductions and fund further investments in more sustainable technologies; (2) to create an *internal cap-and-trade market* that

48 The Value Balancing Alliance (VBA) was founded mid-2019 as a non-profit organization representing several international companies. The alliance is supported by Deloitte, EY, KPMG and PwC, the OECD, the University of Oxford and the 'Impact Weighted Accounts Initiative' at Harvard Business School.

49 Disclosures on ICP policies are documented by the Carbon Disclosure Project (CDP), a global organization focused on promoting corporate disclosures of environmental risks and impacts. Of the 2,600 companies reporting to CDP in 2019, 23% indicated to use an internal carbon charge whereas an additional 22% planned to do so in the next two years. ICP is most prevalent in energy, materials and financial services industries, followed by the technology and industrial sectors. The internal prices companies set per metric ton of carbon vary widely by region and industry (McKinsey & Company, 2021).

50 As of April 2020, 44 countries and 31 provinces or cities are operating a carbon pricing scheme through a carbon tax and/or an Emissions Trading System (ETS). Together, these jurisdictions account for around 60% of global GDP, https://www.i4ce.org/download/global-carbon-account-in-2020/.

drives emission cutbacks towards internally set targets; (3) as a *scenario-based theoretical price* reflecting expected future carbon prices in different countries of operations to inform business decisions with long-term impacts; or (4) as a *shadow price* to be incorporated into project or investment budgets to create the business case for investing in net zero or net positive carbon options. ICP is also helpful for gauging the impact of regulatory changes and assessing carbon risk exposure throughout the supply chain, beyond the operations directly controlled by the company (Aldy and Gianfrate, 2019). This would involve that both the quantity and geographical location of direct (scope 1) and indirect (scope 2 and 3) carbon emissions are determined – for which the *Greenhouse Gas Protocol* created standardized approaches.[51] Subsequently, ICP-based calculations and benchmarks can be the start for developing carbon-reducing collaborations with supply chain partners and end market users.

The mechanisms underlying ICP can be applied to externalities such as water, waste and pollutants in a similar fashion. In fact, internal pricing ('transfer pricing') and arbitrage mechanisms are common instruments used by multinational companies in day-to-day routines for mitigating financial risk (related, for instance, to currency and interest rate fluctuations), managing financial transactions and for optimizing tax payments across borders (tax scheme engineering). Internal transfer pricing – an accounting practice that relates to the cross-border exchange of goods, services, technology and capital within and between enterprises under common ownership or control – is part of multinationals' competitive advantage as it helps them to internalize cross-border market failure (Box 10.7), thereby adding value to societies (section 10.3.3). However, the practice of internal transfer pricing is also notoriously being misused by companies to maximally reduce their effective tax burden by charging a higher price to divisions in high-tax countries (reducing profit), while charging lower prices (increasing profits) for divisions in low-tax countries (section 6.5.2). Even when compliant with the letter of tax laws, manipulative profit-shifting practices erode the tax base and national income of countries. Multinationals that avoid 'fair taxation' principles while conveying a message of local citizenship and sustainability, create sizable trust gaps.

■ *From financial reporting to integrated reporting on performance and value*

The ability of companies to create value relies on more than financial capitals alone. Understanding value 'beyond the balance sheet' (IFAC, 2020) implies a more holistic comprehension of the financial, manufactured, human, intellectual, relational and natural capitals the company manages, affects and depends upon

51 Building on a partnership between the WBCSD and World Resources Institute (WRI), the GHG Protocol establishes comprehensive global standardized frameworks to measure and manage GHG emissions from private and public sector operations, value chains and mitigation actions. See: https://ghgprotocol.org/.

as well as how these interconnections relate to the company's key 'value drivers' (Figure 11.18). With the lion's share of business value being comprised of intangible assets, non-financial reporting has become progressively important. But at the same time, reporting on financial and non-financial performance, business value and societal impact in a robust and consistent way has presented finance departments with a significant measurement and alignment challenge. They face a complex and dynamically evolving landscape of reporting standards, assurance and disclosure requirements and burgeoning regulation on non-financial impact disclosure. The Reporting Exchange, for instance, counted more than 2,000 voluntary reporting frameworks, mandatory reporting requirements, methodologies and protocols across 71 countries for the measurement and disclosure of ESG-related information as of 2020 – a tenfold increase since the early 1990s.[52] In the EU, existing rules for sustainability and diversity reporting as laid down in the Non-Financial Reporting Directive (Directive 2014/95/EU) are being revised and strengthened, while the European Commission is also planning to extend mandatory sustainability reporting to include all large and all listed companies. Under the proposed Corporate Sustainability Reporting Directive (CSRD), 50,000 companies in the EU will be required to follow detailed EU sustainability reporting standards, an increase from the 11,000 'public interest entities' subject to the existing non-financial disclosure requirements.[53]

Over the years, the finance function has become increasingly vital in calibrating *external* disclosure requirements with *internal* company sustainability efforts and related metrics. Typical KPQs pertain to the form, substance, scope, specificity and degree of (integrated) reporting, required to: (a) meet the information needs of all relevant stakeholders; (b) safeguard access to sufficient external funding at favourable conditions and competitive costs; and (c) steer internal company actions to deliver on the sustainability outcomes and level of value creation that investors, financiers, governments and societal stakeholders expect or demand. Accordingly, a key challenge involves identifying those metrics that are both internally and externally decision useful and that provide a reliable insight into present, forecasted and future material performance dimensions (Box 11.14).

---

52 The Reporting Exchange is an Arabesque initiative, originally developed and founded by the WBCSD. It provides freely available resources on ESG reporting requirements across more than 70 countries, https://www.reportingexchange.com/.

53 The European Commission adopted the CSRD proposal in April 2021. It is expected that companies apply the sustainability reporting standards for the first time to reports covering fiscal year 2023. https://ec.europa.eu/info business-economy-euro/company-reporting-and-auditing/company-reporting/corporate-sustainability-reporting_en#review /.

PRINCIPLES OF INTEGRATED REPORTING

Since the 1990s, financial reporting started to be complemented by a spate of voluntary non-financial reports covering environmental, social and ethical aspects of doing business. By 2020, the concept of 'integrated reporting' had been embedded by over 2,500 companies in more than 70 countries, with more than 40 stock exchanges referring to it in their guidance.[54] Integrated reporting is more than the combining of financial and non-financial information into one single corporate annual report. Rather, in the definition of the International Integrated Reporting Council (IIRC), integrated reporting is "a process founded on integrated thinking that results in a periodic integrated report by an organization about value creation over time and related communications regarding aspects of value creation". It is a reflection of how an organization optimizes (net) value over the short, medium and long-term, by basing its business decisions and day-to-day management practices on a cohesive multi-capitals approach that recognizes the vital interdependencies (synergies and trade-offs) between them. The approach (1) builds on notions of value creation, preservation and erosion, (2) takes multiple time horizons and value perspectives into account in assessing business performance and impacts, and (3) reckons with a wider set of stakeholders than just the company's shareholders, financiers and customers. Ultimately, "the cycle of integrated reporting and thinking" should result in efficient and productive capital allocation that serves business resilience, financial stability and sustainable development (IIRC, 2021).

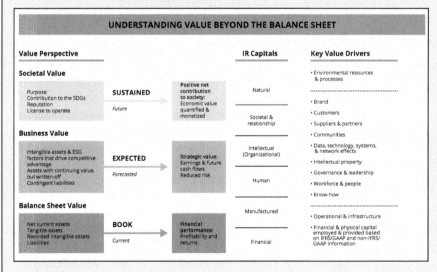

Figure 11.18 IFAC – Integrated View of Performance and Value

Source: IFAC (2020). *The CFO and Finance Function Role in Value Creation*, p. 8. © 2020 by the International Federation of Accountants (IFAC).

---

54 https://integratedreporting.org/10-years/10-years-summary.

B
O
X

11.14

Guiding Principles for integrated reporting

The IIRC (2013; 2021) delineated seven principles – the <IR> framework – that guide the preparation, content elements and presentation of an integrated report:

1. *Strategic focus and future orientation:* what is the organization's strategy on creating value in the short, medium and long term (using and affecting multiple capitals);
2. *Connectivity of information:* provide a holistic picture of the interdependencies between the factors affecting the organization's ability to create value over time;
3. *Nature and quality of stakeholder relationships:* how and to what extent does the organization understand, take into account and respond to legitimate needs and interests of its key stakeholders;
4. *Materiality:* disclose information (for determined reporting boundaries) about matters that substantively affect the organization's strategic focus and ability to create value;
5. *Conciseness:* accommodate to the user's need for sufficient context, logical structure and clearness of concepts, but refrain from less relevant or too detailed information;
6. *Reliability and completeness:* include all material matters, both positive and negative, without material error;
7. *Consistency and comparability:* presented in a way that is consistent over time and enables relevant comparison with other organizations.

Aligning principles and standards, paving the way towards harmonization

The principles-based <IR> framework provides industry-agnostic guidance that strikes a balance between high-level content prescription on the one hand and, on the other hand, flexibility for appropriate contextualization that reflects the various realities of different sectors, types of organizations, operating circumstances and environmental contexts. The <IR> framework does not prescribe the metrics and methodologies to be used nor the KPIs to report on, but rather clarifies *how* to structure relevant information on a set of broad and interconnected topics relevant to processes of value creation. More detailed guidance on what topics and metrics to select, is typically provided by standard frameworks. Standards for sustainability reporting – such as the *Global Reporting Initiative (GRI) Standards*, the *Sustainability Accounting Standards Board (SASB) Standards*, the *Climate Disclosure Standards Board (CDSB) Framework*, and the *Task Force on Climate-related Financial Disclosures (TCFD) Recommendations* – present either universal, industry-specific or thematic requirements on *what* to report on for each relevant subject matter. Standards, to a certain degree, facilitate comparability of quantified sustainability-related performance, which enables benchmarking over time and across peer companies.

In March 2021, IIRC and the SASB decided to strengthen their complementary approaches to sustainability reporting and disclosure, by merging into the *Value Reporting Foundation*. The collaboration is intended to offer a comprehensive suite of tools to assess, manage and communicate 'value', in ways that provide comparable and reliable data relevant to investors (Figure 11.19). In September 2020, CDP, CDSB, GRI, IIRC and SASB announced their intent to work together on comprehensive corporate reporting, by identifying how their present frameworks, standards and platforms can be aligned to advance corporate disclosures on how sustainability matters relate to enterprise value.

International <IR> Framework	SASB Standards
• Industry-agnostic • Principles-based • Preparation and presentation • High-level content elements and guiding principles • Drives connectivity of information	• Industry-specific • Metrics-based • Standards application guidance • Disclosure topics and metrics • Enables comparability of information

Figure 11.19 Value reporting and disclosure standards

Source: https://integratedreporting.org/news/strengthening-an-integrated-report-using-sasb-standards

SELECTED KPIs

Key Practice and Performance Indicators for corporate finance can be directed at financial performance, or be geared towards ascending degrees of business and societal value creation, grounded in a broader notion of productive, impacted and impacting 'capitals'. Much hinges on the time horizon of the company's leadership – the CFO included – and that of its shareholders, investors and financiers. Breaking through the reactive threshold, in any case, requires a consistent tone from the top for integrating sustainability into the business model and mandating the finance function to embed societal value creation into its role. Conversely, by pointing out the 'hidden value' behind the balance sheet, finance officers can play a vital role in convincing the board of the economic viability of long-term sustainability investments hitherto overlooked. Surpassing the key tipping point also calls for organizational structures, processes and methods that enable the corporate finance department to consistently integrate relevant non-financial aspects into budgeting, forecasting, reporting and disclosure practices. Increasingly, new accounting measures and capitals protocols are being developed to support companies in credibly valuating negative and positive externalities, and to inform forward-looking decision-making for (net) value creation in a more holistic way.

Table 11.5 Mapping sustainable corporate finance practice

KVIs ➡	LEVEL 1	LEVEL 2 *(Key tipping point)*	LEVEL 3	LEVEL 4
KDIs	**1. Trigger**	**2. Internal alignment**	**3. External alignment**	
Main trade-off	**Profit as goal**			**Profit as a means**
Value proposition	Shareholder value		Stakeholder value	
	Profit maximization	Shareholder value maximization	Stakeholder/shared value creation	Societal value creation (common good)
Generation	Sustainable Finance 1.0		Sustainable Finance 2.0	Sustainable Finance 3.0
Fiduciary duty	Narrow: shareholders and owners	Limited: primary stakeholders	Broader: primary and secondary stakeholders	Society: relevant (present and future) stakeholders
KPQs	**Inactive**	**Reactive**	**Active**	**Proactive**
Search for external funds dependent on	Negative screening policies (exclusion of negative ESG-impact activities)	General ESG screening by (institutional) investors (ESG risk sufficiently managed)	Best-in-class ESG screening; impact investors; active engagement with institutional investors	Impact investors, governments, concessional and concessionary funding
Cost of capital/ funding conditions	Financial market rate. Higher cost of capital/risk premium in case of poor ESG profile	Financial market rate focused. Potentially lower cost of capital/ risk premium in case of agreeable ESG profile	Patient finance at competitive cost; issuance of sustainability-themed bonds	Patient finance at (submarket) rates, seed funds, (project) grants, blended finance, revolving funds, soft loans, etc.
Externalities accounting	No externalities considered	Negative externalities considered ('true cost') to mitigate or avoid ESG risk/harm	Negative and positive externalities ('true value') to identify new ways of organizing and value creation	Net positive impact for long-term societal value creation
Appraisal scope	Own operations; limited scope of issues considered	Extended to direct suppliers and /or customers; obvious issues included	Extended to relevant parts of value chain; obvious capitals (natural, social) included	All relevant parts of the value chain; integrated approach to wide range of capitals
Transfer pricing and tax management	Tax avoidance, optimized tax scheme engineering	Tax management, limit base erosion (OECD BEPS, G7 and G20)	Fair and transparent tax management (publish what you pay)	Pressurize for fair taxation and international regulation; (e.g. participate in global alliances on fair /minimum taxation levels)

Reporting and disclosure	Financial only	Financial and non-financial (selected ESG topics)	Sustainability reporting using standards frameworks (GRI, SASB, CDSB and TCFD)	Integrated reporting using IIRC Principles and relevant standard frameworks
KPIs	**Inactive**	**Reactive**	**Active**	**Proactive**
Role finance director	Chief Financial Officer (CFO)		Chief Value Officer (CVO)	
The balance sheet and beyond [55]	*Book value;* Financial performance; Quarterly profits; Short-term returns	*Business value;* Profitability and returns; Intangible assets and ESG factors; Contingent liabilities; Reduced ESG risk	*Strategic value;* Forecasted earnings and cash flows derived on intangible assets driving future competitive advantage; Return on sustainability investment (ROSI)	*Societal value;* Optimized value from managing the use of and impacts from/on multiple capitals. Performance, impact and prospect quantified and monetized (proxy for economic value), or expressed in qualitative terms

---

55 Based on IFAC (2020), see Figure 11.18.

11.8 THE SUSTAINABLE INNOVATION CHALLENGE: DEALING WITH PARADOXES

Key Performance Questions for sustainable innovation management

- What leading principles guide your (sustainable) innovation strategy?

- What approach do you take in addressing the 'innovation paradox', 'design paradox' and 'openness paradox'?

- What choices and tensions drive your sustainable innovation approach: technology-push or market-pull factors; existing or future markets; 'simple' or 'wicked' challenges; performance-enhancing (incremental) or impact-driven (radical) innovation; collaborative/open or appropriation-driven/closed; centrally planned or emergent processes; linear ideation-validate-solution, or an iterative innovation journey?

- How do you internalize stakeholder needs in sustainable innovation practices?

- What dynamic capabilities present within your organization need further development?

- Where in the innovation cycle do you involve internal and external stakeholders, in what innovation spaces, with what objective, and based on what selection criteria?

- What position does the R&D department take in open, collaborative innovation?

- What role for innovation managers and sustainable *intra*preneurs?

- What trade-offs do you consider in appropriating, managing and protecting intellectual property?

KEY DECISIONS: DOING THINGS DIFFERENTLY
OR DOING DIFFERENT THINGS?

Nowadays, the only constant of business is change. New regulatory require-ments, demanding societal stakeholders and customers, innovation-oriented industrial and value chain relations, fierce (global) competition and the emergence of new technologies necessitate companies to continuously adapt and develop in order to remain relevant, meet expectations and secure continuity. Companies' potential to contribute to sustainable development critically depends on how successful they manage their innovation activities and techno-organizational capabilities to *design, operationalize and scale value for society*. The innovation function of enterprises provides the fundamental basis of their societal legitimacy (Table 5.2) and should position them to "be future-focused and effectively deliver on [their] overall objectives of securing prosperity, sustainability and longer-term relevance and survival" (ISO, 2020: 13). *Sustainability-oriented innovation (SOI)* has thereby been defined as "the intentional creation and realization of new (or improved) products, services, processes or practices which aim at environmental and/or social benefits in addition to economic returns throughout the physical life-cycle" (Buhl et al., 2019: 1249; Adams et al., 2016).[56] SOI can target 'green', 'eco' and 'clean-tech' solutions that mostly contribute to the ecological environment, but also 'social', 'inclusive', 'frugal' innovations that add to social cohesion and economic viability. The effective management of the organization's innovation processes – covering all activities involved in the process of idea generation, technology development, manufacturing and commercialization – is a precondition for sustainable business model innovation (section 9.2).

Innovation processes typically consist of a set of interrelated activities that are executed iteratively and in a non-linear order (ISO, 2020). The dynamic interplay between *technology-push, market-pull and regulatory-push/pull* factors (see Box 10.11) can be quite erratic in its effect on innovation processes, giving rise to "false starts, recycling between stages, dead ends and jumps out of sequence" (Tidd, 2021). Accordingly, effective innovation management is increasingly portrayed as an unfolding *innovation journey* – purposive and determined, yet sensitive to the nature, complexities and uncertain context of the challenge – rather than a conventional (top-down) linear planning exercise of sequenced functional activities, in which organizations seize opportunities by way of leveraging their established (core) competencies. Modern innovation management insights highlight the importance of scanning and scouting, absorptive capacity and flexibility, the continuous upgrading of dynamic capabilities for innovation, learning from mistakes and tolerance of failure, and adjustment of the business model if needed (Tidd and Bessant, 2021). The cost of *not* effectively managing knowledge accumulation, organizational learning and dynamic capabilities development can be considerable – as the 'incumbent's curse' literature compellingly shows.

Sustainable innovation management (SIM) takes these insights one step further by explicitly taking sustainability performance and the integration of ecological, social and economic dimensions as guiding principles for pursued innovation outcomes. Accordingly, SIM can be understood as the management

---

56 Sustainability-oriented innovation is also referred to as 'sustainability innovation', 'sustainable innovation', sustainability-driven innovation', 'responsible innovation', 'responsible research and innovation' or 'sustainable technology development'.

of "the dynamics through which organizations progressively structure them-selves in order to address the systemic nature, complexity and ambiguity of sustainable innovation and implement solutions that holistically address internal and external sustainability challenges" (Pellegrini et al., 2019: 1046). The incor-poration of sustainability concerns tends to add further *complexity, uncertainty and ambiguity* to companies' innovation strategy. Due to its multipurpose nature, steering on successful SOI outcomes requires that a broader set of target criteria is identified, integrated and made mutually compatible. Under society's dynamically changing expectations and evolving insights on what constitutes 'sustainability', however, 'success criteria' are prone to shift over time. Moreover, sustainable innovation often implies a departure from the company's present knowledge base and market relations ('decoupling') in order to move beyond technological borders, realize novel (re)combinations of resources, functions and structures, and develop 'future markets'. SIM hence entails an *uncertainty and ambiguity reduction process.* It stands or falls with the effective alignment of intra-organizational and inter-organizational processes that should inform and catalyse the innovation process. Concomitant manage-ment challenges to that end include: (1) the organization of inter-functional involvement and collaboration across internal departments; (2) the timely involvement of relevant external stakeholders (e.g. prospective customers, value chain partners, universities, tech companies, regulators, civil society groups) to reduce uncertainty, ensure commercial viability, share risk, and gain access to critical information, knowledge, technology and capital; (3) the development of a new or modified business model that integrates ecological, economic and social dimensions (section 9.4.1); and (4) "orchestrating a business ecosystem that serves the sustainable innovations the conducting firm develops" (Mousavi et al., 2018: 383) – notably through collaborative (open) innovation strategies carried out in, and facilitated by value networks.

SOI initiatives range in their envisaged degree of novelty and scope of sustainability impact. Strategies targeted at *doing things differently* (incre-mental innovation) are mostly motivated by efficiency-driven, cost-cutting, risk-reducing or compliance-oriented considerations that prolong the lifespan of current activities, market positions and product lines. Product and process improvements are based on the deployment of applicable 'off-the-shelf' tech-nologies and/or product redesigns that yield direct sustainability effects (e.g. enhanced resource efficiency, substitution of hazardous substances, emission reduction, prolonged product and material life cycles) while also meeting short-term business priorities (e.g. efficiency gains, supply chain optimization, lower costs while assuring quality, market appeal, competitiveness, conformity to regulations and sustainability standards). Incremental innovation generally pertains to level 1 and 2 ambitions, reflecting a 'reducing harm while continuing business as usual' logic.

A longer-term, future-oriented perspective to SOI recognizes that the delivery of societal value at sufficient scale and pace necessitates paradigm-shifting solutions. A *doing (entirely) different things* ambition hence aims at breakthrough innovations with the potential to disrupt markets and transform the business ecosystem for *systemic effects*. Radical innovation involves the development of new technologies (e.g. biotechnology, green hydrogen, quantum computing), new competences and new organizational models (e.g. closed-loop value chains, systems integration) that reach *beyond sustainability performance improvement* on a product/technology level. Radical SOI typically extends to 'function innovation' (level 3) and 'systems innovation' (level 4), which profoundly affect user practice and lifestyles, markets and business models, policies, regulations and infrastructures as well.

A MULTILEVEL CHALLENGE: INNOVATION FOR THE COMMON GOOD?

BOX 11.15

Throughout the chapters of this book, different facets – and internal and external drivers – of sustainable innovation challenges have been highlighted, all with a bearing on the dynamic capabilities that organizations have to develop and organize in order to meaningfully contribute to positive change, sustainable development and the common good:

At the systems and societal level:

■ Reckoning with 'the degree of wickedness' of the sustainability challenge throughout the innovation process (Chapters 4 and 5) – a 'simple' techno-fix that disregards the level of societal complexity at hand will not suffice: simplification eventually complicates.

■ Seizing the value (collaborative advantage) of complementary roles and competences in 'fit-for-purpose' cross-sector partnerships (coalitions of the willing/needed) for collective action on the common good (Chapter 5).

■ Developing 'breakthrough', 'disruptive' and 'systems' innovations that make products and services accessible, affordable and available to a larger population – through network effects, positive lock-ins and (open) standard-setting – with positive transformative effects across industries and areas of society (section 8.4.4; Table 9.5; section 10.3.2).

■ Building a conducive innovation ecosystem. Being conscious of the effects of 'societal positioning' decisions and related responsibilities. Anticipating how corporate power and positioning affects societal trust and the licence to operate, scale and experiment (section 10.4.1; Table 6.6).

BOX 11.15

At the sectoral, industry, value chain level:

- Managing intra-sectoral and inter-sectoral collaborations that stimulate positive spill-over and network effects (Chapter 8; section 10.4.2).

- Managing substitution ('creative destruction') and complementarity effects in upgrading/upscaling sustainable innovation journeys (section 10.4.2; Box 10.9).

- Managing the tension between open/collaborative innovation and appropriation and protection of intellectual property rights (section 10.4.1).

At the organizational level:

- Moving from performance-driven to impact-driven innovation strategies (section 9.2.4) that seek 'regenerative' and 'net positive' outcomes (section 11.4).

- Building the business case for innovation around opportunities to: (a) minimize harm while maximizing good; (b) scale up positive spill-over effects; and (c) serve people's unmet or latent needs (Chapter 8; Table 9.3).

- Developing competencies and business models for frugal and inclusive innovation to also reach underserved poor and low-income segments (sections 9.4.1, 9.5.1 and 9.5.2).

- Anticipating, assessing and addressing potentially harmful consequences, unintended side effects and negative externalities that may flow from radical or disruptive innovation (Tables 5.3 and 5.4).

- Dealing with the 'incumbent's curse' and the 'Kodak effect' (Box 9.2).

- Developing paradoxical, (co-)creative, out-of-the-box thinking skills as well as ambidexterity in strategic decision-making (Box 4.3 and 5.2).

- Organizing 'checks and balances' to prevent undue 'techno-optimism' (Box 11.5).

KPQs: WHAT PARADOXES TO FOCUS ON?
How to organize for innovation strategies that, over time, materialize in *societal value-adding* business models (see section 9.4.1), capable of contributing to sustainable development at a relevant scale while ensuring business continuity? On the whole, an organization's innovation capacity for sustainability can be thought of as contingent on the strategic direction and operational logic opted for in dealing with six 'classic' tensions: (1) taking either technology-push (supply-driven) or market-pull (demand-driven) drivers as starting point; (2) targeting existing or future markets and needs; (3) aiming at performance-enhancing (incremental) or radical and impact-driven innovation; (4) preferring open (collaborative) or closed (ownership) innovation; (5) choosing for centralized organization or

decentralized and emergent processes; (6) applying a linear 'ideation-validate-solution' logic (Tidd, 2021), or an iterative approach of exploring and exploiting new knowledge simultaneously. The fundamental trade-offs and key tipping points that organizations face in deciding on the most appropriate course of action, can be summarized along three types of (interrelated) paradoxes:

a) An **innovation paradox**, which holds that the very processes, structures, mindsets and practices that underpin an organization's enduring operational excellence, also prevent it from developing breakthrough innovations (Davila and Epstein, 2014). Managing this paradox implies a balancing act between the 'need for stability' and the 'need for creativity', between 'sustaining' and 'sustainable' innovation activities, and between short-term and long-term time horizons;

b) A **design paradox**, which entails that essential knowledge – notably on unforeseen negative impacts or under-utilized opportunities for scaling positive spill-overs – may only then become available when the design is already too constrained to be modified according to these vital insights. Managing this tension has a bearing on how innovation processes can be organized and improved;

c) An **openness paradox** – also known as the 'double externality' problem – which denotes that much-needed investments in 'common good' innovations are discouraged – even in the presence of conducive push and pull conditions – when the 'societal return' resulting from each party's investment in collaborative/open innovation cannot be sufficiently translated into private returns and benefits. Whereas the *creation* of innovations often necessitates openness because of its resource intensity, the *commercialization* of innovations requires appropriability of the returns from innovation activities. Openness, then, may demand more attention to protection (Laursen and Salter, 2014).

■ *Dealing with the innovation paradox*

In his classic work *The Innovator's Dilemma*, Clayton Christensen (1997) explained why successful companies eventually fail precisely because they do everything right: "an excessive customer focus prevents firms from creating new markets and finding new customers for the products of the future". In a similar vein, Davila and Epstein (2014) argued in *The Innovation Paradox* why a strategy of pursuing operational excellence and incremental innovation – "adding a feature here, cutting a cost there" – unintendedly reduces the likelihood of realizing much-desired breakthrough innovations. Both works stress the internal barriers that firms must overcome to avert that their focus on operational excellence and (short-term) market-driven preoccupation blinds them to longer-term strategic priorities, future relevance and business continuity. Both lines of reasoning highlight the importance of moving away from a single-track incremental innovation strategy, to build organizational structures, cultures, mindsets and practices more apt to stimulating breakthrough innovation, 'strategic discoveries' and future-oriented solutions instead. Breakthrough innovations are highly uncertain and take time to mature, however, whilst their business case is hard to visualize up-front ('high risk/high payoff'). Dealing with the innovation paradox consequently calls for running a *shadow-track* strategy that allows an organization to remain competitive within present markets while innovating for future markets that meet society's multifaceted sustainability needs.

Efforts to overcome the innovation paradox require thorough insight in (a) how to mediate the timeframes required for innovations with short-term and long-term time horizons, and (b) relevant internal sources, drivers and structures needed to organize for innovations with varying degrees of sustainability impacts. Effectively managing for SOI implies that the organization regularly reconsiders its core activities and competencies and sufficiently invests in the continuous development of its *dynamic capabilities for innovation* – that is, the strategic activities by which firms scan and monitor for new business opportunities, explore ideas, prioritize and choose between them, mobilize resources and recombine technologies, functions and structures, and then create and capture value. Based upon insights from high-tech innovation in companies and along the lines of David Teece's (2007) three-fold 'sensing, seizing, reconfiguring' classification, Mousavi et al. (2019) indicated essential organizational practices ('micro-foundations') underlying the dynamic capabilities that constitute innovative capacity for sustainability:

- *Sensing:* developing intrapreneurial resources and organizational structures for recognizing innovation opportunities for sustainability; taking sustainability as guiding principle and value proposition of the innovation strategy; monitoring developments inside and outside the organization to anticipate – and make informed decisions on – sustainability opportunities;

- *Seizing:* developing internal capabilities for cross-functional collaboration; a profound understanding of the value chain and its positioning dynamics to identify opportunities and potential leverage points; engaging customers (and other important external stakeholders) during the innovation process to elicit preferences and overcome uncertainties and ambiguities related to market acceptance of innovative technologies; prototyping and demonstration to inform future markets; sufficient resource allocation and investment in internal R&D activities, market research and acquisitions; gathering specialized resources and competencies scattered in diverse value chain actors around the sustainability opportunity; delineating new business models and market structures around integrated ecological, economic and social dimensions to facilitate commercialization.

■ *Reconfiguring:* pursuing co-innovation strategies with relevant external stakeholders; establishing a supporting business ecosystem and value chain to build demand; investing in marketing and service teams in conjunction with technology development; integrating market expectations by moving technology development forward in a step-by-step manner, to absorb the latest information, options and possibilities.

Building innovative capacity for SOI is a dynamic and unfolding process that hinges on the organization's ambition level, time horizon, risk management posture and effective commitment to finding viable solutions to societal needs (Box 11.16). It is subject to organizational change processes that develop over time. Pellegrini et al. (2019), in this context, point to the catalysing role of *networks* and *sustainable intrapreneurs* in "sparkling dynamic cycles that gradually shift organizations to adapt their structures and processes in ways that support the adoption of sustainable innovation" (ibid: 1046). They found that collaborative networks and sustainable intrapreneurship can act as spurring mediating factors in linking 'external drivers' (regulatory pressure, stakeholder demands, market transformations) with the organization's 'internal drivers' of innovation. In particular, sustainable intrapreneurship was identified to play a vital role in: (1) sensing external opportunities for addressing sustainability challenges and envisioning potential benefits; (2) identifying alternative or new solutions to targeted societal challenges that fit organizational infrastructures; (3) overcoming organizational barriers, inspiring colleagues and gathering top-level management consensus on taking the risk of experimenting and piloting; and (4) scaling solutions within and beyond the organizational level.

INNOVATION MANAGEMENT PRINCIPLES – ISO 56000:2020

B O X 11.16

1 **Realization of value:** the purpose of innovation management is to realize value. Value is realized by the process of identifying, understanding and satisfying needs of interested parties. Realizing value, both financial and non-financial, is vital to the sustainability of organizations.

2 **Future-focused leaders:** conscious efforts to challenge the status quo enable the organization to balance the current focus and short-term performance with attention to innovation opportunities in order to anticipate and create the future. Leaders, at all levels, across the organization inspire and engage employees and other interested parties to innovate.

3 **Strategic direction:** commonly shared and understood innovation objectives and strategy, that are aligned with the overall objectives and strategic direction of the organization, provide the basis for allocating people and resources. The

<table>
<tr><td>

**B
O
X

11.16**

</td><td>

strategic direction is used for prioritizing innovation activities, as well as for setting the scope for monitoring and evaluating innovation performance and impact.

4   **Culture:** traditional management practices focus on efficient execution. For innovation management, it is also necessary to develop values, beliefs and behaviours supportive of the creation and execution of new ideas. To achieve innovation, the culture should enable the coexistence of the behaviours of creativity and execution.

5   **Exploiting insights:** the development of innovative solutions depends on the identification of stated and unstated needs. Identifying insights that can be exploited to realize value requires a systematic approach, drawing on diverse sources of knowledge. Effective insights go beyond the obvious and incorporate strategic foresight about future needs and conditions.

6   **Managing uncertainty:** balancing the exploitation of opportunities and management of risks increases the potential for value realization. The application of a portfolio approach, combining experimentation and exploitation, generates confidence and builds resilience to manage uncertainties.

7   **Adaptability:** changes in the context of the organization are addressed by timely adaptation of structures, processes, competences and value realization models to maximize innovation capabilities. The ability to systematically anticipate and understand the need for change and respond to changes is an essential innovation capability.

8   **Systems approach:** the innovation performance of an organization is dependent on processes that operate towards a common purpose. Measuring the interaction between elements develops the understanding of their interrelation. Managing these elements as a system improves organizational learning, effectiveness and efficiency.

Source: https://committee.iso.org/sites/tc279/home/projects/published/ongoing-3.html ISO (2020).

</td></tr>
</table>

▪ Dealing with the design paradox

The design paradox adds a timing challenge to the innovation paradox: full information on the effects of (product) design variants is often hard to screen *ex ante*. The concurrent pursuit of environmental, social and economic objectives entails 'directional risks'. Additionally, future market conditions, user behaviour, unfolding social contexts and sustainability impacts throughout the life cycle are – to various degrees – uncertain or ambiguous, and hence difficult to anticipate. Consequently, a too narrow focus on ill-considered 'success criteria' in the early stages of the design process may very well eventuate in a 'solution' with built-in 'failure': the innovation does not accurately meet (prospective) user needs, comes with unforeseen yet significant side effects and harmful socio-ecological impacts, or leaves the potential for sustainability-enhancing 'function' (level 3) or 'systems integration' (level 4) untapped. In later stages of the innovation process, modifications in accordance to newly acquired insights can be highly costly and have major repercussions on the allocation of organizational resources, especially when commercialization processes are already implemented at scale.

Dealing with the design paradox has direct implications for the organization of the innovation process. To *design out risk* under dynamic conditions and to produce real outcomes and assure positive sustainability effects, the process must allow for open-minded exploration, 'zooming in and out' for context, sufficient knowledge accumulation, experimentation and learning – enabled by iterative feedback cycles and flexible processes – to incorporate relevant insights early on and timely adjust to new realities. Design thinkers have looked at this creative and iterative problem-solving process as orchestrating a system of *overlapping spaces* (Brown, 2008) – rather than a sequence of siloed activities along predefined and orderly steps – which, when properly managed, can induce self-reinforcing processes through feedback loops, team interactions and scaling activities, within and beyond the organization. To this end, the innovation cycle is organized according to different phases of 'uncertainty and ambiguity reduction' activities, in a way that offers space for imagining, creativity, exchange and experiential learning (Box 11.17) while providing appropriate structure to work towards desired goals and 'complexity fit' design outcomes. Each phase culminates in a go/no-go decision for progressing to the next, to mark sufficient confidence that (a) intended effects and discovered potential have been maximized, and (b) foreseeable, identified or experienced negative side effects minimized.

Figure 11.20 portrays four phases of common design activities in the innovation process as well as possible iteration loops for incorporating relevant insights at each stage: (1) problem definition; (2) working towards 'proof of concept'; (3) working towards 'proof of business'; and (4) evaluating 'proof of success'.

■ **Phase 1: problem (re)definition: simple or complex?** Built-in 'failure' may already materialize in the problem definition phase if the targeted sustainability challenge is unduly defined as either too complex or too simple (Chapters 4 and 5). Delineation of the problem frame has direct implications for both 'design outcome' and 'innovation process' dimensions. It determines: (a) the innovation scope within which to search for complexity fit solutions (a narrow or broad space); (b) the approach chosen for organizing the innovation process (the higher the degree of complexity,

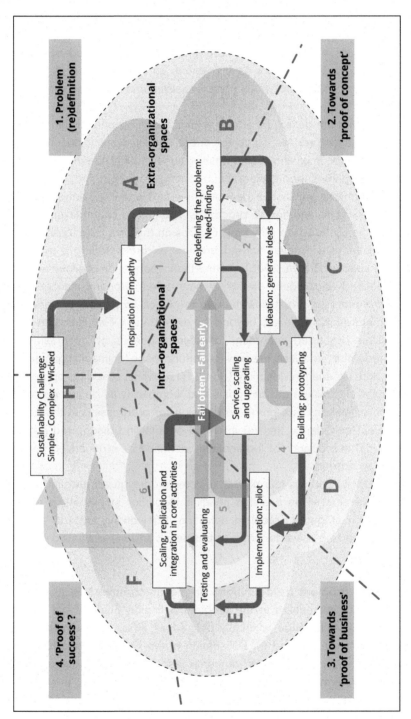

Figure 11.20 Linking phases, spaces and stakeholders in the innovation proces

the more vital it is to build in feedback mechanisms, checkpoints and itera-tions, involve external stakeholders in addition to intra-organizational stake-holders, and incorporate multiple perspectives, insights and experiences); (c) the type of 'solutions' that come to mind (fixing the current, or creating entirely new alternatives). The problem/opportunity context explored and the problem frame adopted profoundly affect how 'needs' of people are understood, defined and approached in the further course of the innova-tion process (Box 11.17).

If the innovating organization addresses a 'complex/wicked' sustain-ability problem as a mere technical challenge (section 4.2), it runs the risk of being confronted with unforeseen (side) effects that may only become apparent in the 'scaling and replication' stage (phase 3) – when consider-able costs and investments have already been made. Conversely, if a rela-tively 'simple' sustainability challenge is addressed with an overly complex approach involving a large number of external stakeholders (spaces A–F in Figure 11.20), the risk of undue delay, inertia or inaction looms large – accompanied by a disproportionate amount of time, means and efforts spent to align internal and external stakeholders around a shared course of action. In practice, sustainable innovation often constitutes simple (tech-nical) and more complex (behavioural) dimensions at the same time. This makes it all the more relevant to allocate sufficient time and means for exploration in order to build a thorough understanding of the problem, problem context and the 'intensity of wickedness' involved (section 4.4).

■ **Phase 2: towards 'proof of concept': quick wins or deep appreciation?**
The next critical moment for identifying blind spots and reducing the odds of built-in failure revolves around the time and resources freed up for 'ideation' and 'prototyping'. A narrow ideation-validation approach focuses in particular on eliciting users' opinion about proposed ideas and product concepts before committing further investments. When the experiment is well-executed, possible negative externalities or surprising potential can already be identified at this stage – leading to modifications, redesign or problem redefinition. For more complex sustainability challenges, however, the involvement of external stakeholders from diverse backgrounds in co-creative ideation and prototyping is vital. Effective selection of stake-holders with cutting-edge ideas, contrasting logics and out-of-the-box perspectives should help the organization to broaden the design perspec-tive, think up and explore novel concepts, and develop complexity fit proto-types that optimally incorporate stakeholder needs and interests. Possible ways to engage external stakeholders include inviting social start-ups to participate, or organizing collaborative 'living labs' in advance of the pilot stage. The specific tension that organizations face in phase 2 is whether to adopt a 'quick win' ideation-validation logic and rapidly proceed to the next

stage, or a more resource-intensive diverging-converging search approach of iterative 'concept testing', geared towards deeper appreciation of what would constitute long-term societal value.

■ **Phase 3: towards 'proof of business': scaling or redefining?** The third phase revolves around 'market testing' activities that should materialize in a 'proof of business'. Piloting, testing and evaluation are aimed at exploring whether and how to scale, replicate and integrate design outcomes into core business activities, reinforced by supporting service and sales activities. A narrow approach to market testing probes existing customers to assess whether the design outcome delivers the intended value. Testing and evaluation then should shed light on additional – or previously misinterpreted or overlooked – user needs and may give cause to problem redefinition and design modifications. For complex sustainability challenges, a more extensive and collaborative market testing approach is usually required. Selected external stakeholders are engaged in piloting and assessing activities to help identify what aspects should be modified to 'design out' encountered or anticipated negative externalities (in the production, distribution, retail, usage, maintenance, repair and end-of-life stages) while optimizing for positive effects. Living labs in collaboration with start-ups, local communities, knowledge institutes and other types of cross-sector partnerships can create a dynamic and innovative 'ecosystem' around the organization, conducive to developing, implementing and scaling solutions for greater sustainability impact.

■ **Phase 4: assessing 'proof of success': user-centric or societal value?** The (temporary) final stage of a design cycle involves evaluation for 'proof of success', which takes place after the final product/service has been launched at scale in targeted markets. This is the stage where the initial aims of the design effort (*ex ante*) are assessed against the design outcome's real-life impact (*ex post*). The proof of success indicates the degree of 'complexity fit' between intention and realization and whether user-centric or societal value has been created. A successfully navigated first-loop design cycle can still fail to deliver on its full potential in the after-sales phase. For instance, because the design outcome does not sufficiently reckon with product-service-systems constructions required to accommodate the design's envisaged 'sharing', 'circular' or 'inclusive' objectives (section 9.5). Innovations that are eventually not adopted or incorrectly used imply waste: of energy, natural resources, materials and financial means used for their production, storage, marketing, distribution and disposal.[57]

---

57 The literature on 'sustainable product development and services' (SPDS) presents relevant insights on this challenge (cf. Wang et al., 2021).

DESIGN THINKING FOR SUSTAINABILITY – PRINCIPLES AND CAPABILITIES

Design thinking (DT) for sustainability has increasingly attracted the interest of practitioners as an approach for finding relevant solutions to societal problems that meet users' actual needs. Rather than focusing on optimizing products or services, making them more efficient and elaborating their features, *system-conscious design thinking* takes a human-centric, creative and iterative problem-solving approach to open-ended, complex innovation challenges. DT-based approaches typically involve multidisciplinary teams that – throughout the innovation cycle (Figure 11.20) – actively engage and convene stakeholders from various backgrounds to include multiple perspectives, expertise and experiences. Depending on (1) the organization's ambition level to sustainability-oriented innovation, and (2) the degree of complexity of the challenge involved, system-conscious design efforts can be aimed at *product/service design* (incremental innovation), *product-service-systems* design (function innovation) or even *systems-shifting design* (systems innovation).

Design thinking principles

The praxis of DT to date, indicates several common approaches to system-conscious design. Buhl et al. (2019), for instance, elaborate five highly intertwined 'DT key principles' for sustainability-oriented innovation:

■ **Problem-framing:** defining a problem statement and appropriate problem context that delimits the scope for the ideation phase (taking a system perspective). The problem frame must sufficiently 'fit' the degree of wickedness involved (Chapters 4 and 5) and be continuously questioned and reframed, until it is adequately set. Problem framing facilitates the definition of an appropriate innovation scope (the space within which innovation teams can search for possible solutions).

■ **User-focus:** adopt a human-centred, needs-based and user-centric approach, based on a thorough understanding of users, their (articulated and unarticulated) needs, behaviours, routines, experiences and contexts. User feedback and information on usage in real-life contexts should be continuously gathered for further design iterations.

■ **Diversity:** collaborate in multidisciplinary, cross-functional innovation teams to assure complementarity of skills, worldviews, personalities and hierarchical positions. Ensuring early and (inter)active involvement of diverse internal and external stakeholders, engaging them as co-designers in the design process.

■ **Visualization:** make abstract ideas visible and tangible to test preconceived ideas, validate assumptions and facilitate collaboration, by developing (low-cost, rough) prototypes and allowing for 'thinking by doing'.

■ **Experimentation and iteration:** diverge and converge iteratively. Explore and rapidly test multiple options. 'Fail often, fail early' and learn from mistakes. Allow for emergence. Integrate sustainability 'checkpoints' in the process to assess positive and negative sustainability effects.

Capabilities for system-conscious design thinking

Based on literature study and the insights of 38 pioneering designers on topics such as 'collective intelligence design', 'regenerative practice', 'deep emotional learning' and 'non-physical design', the Design Council published its *System-Shifting Design. An Emerging Practice Explored* (Design Council and The Point People, 2021). The report identifies how 'next practice' design for deeper sustainability impact and 'possibility-giving' systems change could look like. In addition to an array of design tensions, dilemmas, values, characteristics and emerging developments in design thinking and practice, the report points out six capacities that design practitioners and innovation managers need to develop, if they seek to create sustainable innovations. These capacities include (ibid: 26):

■ **Integrative thinking:** the ability to hold the tension between opposing constraints or points of view, and generate a new model that transcends both.

■ **Abductive reasoning:** discovering 'what could be', rather than departing from the status quo ('what is'). Designers progress by forming an idea of the 'what' (the value that could be produced) concurrently with the 'how' (the means of producing it). The interaction between 'what and how' helps to unfold a systemic opportunity.

■ **Perspective-taking:** the ability to move between the subjective and objective, which helps to take on different vantage points, see how patterns at a micro level are reflected at a macro level, and keep both in play when designing.

■ **Propositionality:** making 'propositions' for how the future could be, which depends on 'the capacity for daringness and non-conformity' that allows designers to focus energy on 'the possible and the promising', rather than 'the right or the certain'.

■ **Reflexivity:** the ability to reflect-in-action and improvise in real time, in dialogue with a dynamic context (e.g. through sketching, prototyping).

■ **Synthesis through making:** the ability to take in diverse information, be changed by it, synthesize it, and give form and expression to this new understanding.

More information: www.designcouncil.org.uk/

■ *Dealing with the openness paradox*

A classic tension in technology and innovation management is the complex relation between a company's degree of openness to external parties and the strategy it chooses to protect and appropriate the fruits of its R&D investments. To innovate for impact, companies rely on 'harnessing the collective genius' (Davila and Epstein, 2014) present within their organization while making effective use of relevant ideas, insights and knowledge embedded in diverse external actors (*spill-in effects*). Drawing from external knowledge sources requires some degree of openness and (informal or formal) collaboration (sections 10.4.1 and 10.4.2). But with the need for spill-ins, also comes the risk of 'leakage' and unwanted *outgoing spill-over* of competitive knowledge – which could put the company's reward for its resource-intensive R&D efforts at stake. Innovative companies face a so-called *double externality problem* (Rennings, 2000): dedicated investments in sustainability-driven R&D activities are inhibited when (a) innovations from these investments tend to spill over to competing firms (at a much lower cost for the emulator); and (b) there is substantial 'societal value' flowing from the R&D activities, but not enough private return on the investment made.

The openness paradox suggests that external collaboration is associated with greater attention to protection and appropriability mechanisms. Conversely, legal appropriability methods may enable more openness (Laursen and Salter, 2014). Depending on the nature and level of cooperation, a firm will have (technological) knowledge it wishes to share or co-develop, and competitive knowledge it does not want to disclose (*selective revealing*). Firms use different combinations of appropriability mechanisms to protect and profit from their innovations, ranging from *legal property rights* (patents, copyrights, registered designs and trademarks) and the out-licensing of technologies against royalties, to *informal methods* such as lead time advantage, secrecy, hard-to-copy complementary assets, and product complexity. Registered intellectual property rights (IPR) are part of a company's intangible assets, which for science-driven companies may constitute up to 70–80% of their market capitalization. However, the costs involved for filing and upholding IPRs are considerable, whereas in many industries product-related patents are not perceived as effective to prevent imitation, nor the royalties sufficient to recoup the filing costs (*Forbes*, November 13, 2017). Enforcing patent rights in court can be problematic in terms of the timespan and financial resources involved, especially for smaller businesses and start-ups. Moreover, threatening to strictly protect and enforce patents that – if shared – could greatly benefit the 'common good', may create serious reputational damage and lower the firm's license to operate – as for instance has been the case with pharmaceutical companies in times of crisis (Covid-19, HIV/Aids).

Organizations hence search for new ways to appropriate the results of their R&D efforts, deal with the double externality problem, and capture sufficient value needed for further investments in systems change. Examples include the *releasing of patents* and *royalty-free licensing* to engender network externalities (section 8.4.4). Companies that started out with 'closed innovation' for radical SOI, may eventually decide to release their patents and share their technological knowledge in view of accelerating research and development towards a new technology standard. Tesla, for instance, in 2014 "irrevocably pledge[d] that it will not initiate a lawsuit against any party for infringing a Tesla Patent through activity relating to electric vehicles or related equipment for so long as such party is acting in good faith". Toyota quickly followed in 2015, by sharing 5,680 patents related to its fuel cell electric vehicles to promote 'Global Vehicle Electrification', followed in 2019 by royalty-free licenses on 24,000 of its patents. Toyota provides fee-based technical support to manufactures developing and selling electric vehicles based upon Toyota's technology. Ford followed suit and was the third automaker to release patents on its electric vehicle technology, including its 'battery balancing' and 'regenerative braking' related patents.

BOX 11.18

THE CHANGING ROLE OF THE CORPORATE LAB

The corporate lab has been the traditional locus of innovation for 'high-tech' industries. An in-house R&D department makes it possible to maximally control the innovation process (and related investments) as well as appropriate the outputs of R&D activities through patents and other forms of intellectual property right (IPRs). Corporate innovation labs have been critical in staying ahead of the product innovation curve in the face of market disruption from start-ups or new technologies (Box 10.11). Notable historical examples include Bayer's scientific laboratory established in 1878 (the development of aspirin), Philips's Natlab established in 1914 (pioneering cassette tapes, VCRs, compact disks) and IBM's Watson Lab established in 1945 (pioneering mainframe computing, software standards and artificial intelligence). Although these labs were costly to operate, they served as a powerful incubator for radical ideas and provided their companies with unique products, based on in-house breakthrough inventions. They also enabled companies to amass large patent portfolios – which can serve as an independent source of income – and even garnered Nobel Prize winners in areas like chemistry, medicines and physics. Over the years, however, basic research has increasingly been financed by governments, either directly – through public labs (housed by universities) – or indirectly, through subsidized private R&D (Mazzucato, 2018a).

Reassessing the function of corporate labs

The role of in-house labs has nevertheless remained relevant. The focus on 'core activities' to increase competitiveness – accompanied by 'unbundling' processes of selling-off and spinning-off activities – prompted established innovative companies

B
O
X

11.18

to reassess the position of their labs, often in support of more open innovation approaches. Presently, the majority of innovation labs concentrate on applied research and application of existing technologies for new product development. This focus aligns in particular with marketing ambitions (reaching more customers, expanding product lines, enhancing 'user' experience, developing the next generation of mobile devices) and operations-enhancing strategies (packaging, processing innovations, implementing digital innovations, blockchain, artificial intelligence, robotics and the like). Several corporate labs prioritize sustainability-oriented innovations, systems change and 'open innovation' as explicit part of their value proposition/mission.

Open spaces in support of open innovation

In the recognition that successful (sustainable) innovations require collaboration, knowledge sharing and an ecosystem of complementary products, technologies, services and infrastructures built around them, a number of companies have taken a next step towards 'openness'. They are stimulating inter-organizational collaboration by creating interfaces and 'open spaces' for (sustainability-oriented) innovation and product development, inside and outside their organization. Examples include:

■ **Nike's 'innovation kitchen':** "an open, laid-back space conducive to free thinking, experimentation, and self-expression". Nike speaks of 'getting the whole system in the room' in order to diagnose problems, understand system complexity, build trust, identify possible levers for change, and develop common thought processes.

■ **3M innovation centre:** organizes "collaborative spaces and exhibit halls, featuring solutions for industries ranging from energy to healthcare to defence".

■ **Accor's Disruption & Growth centre:** "drives collaboration between start-ups and major groups in its business" by bringing them together in a space with "an open innovation laboratory on one side and a vast industrial testing ground on the other."

■ **Bayer CoLaborator:** is an "incubator space for life science [start-ups]". The incubator offers start-ups laboratory and office space, to work on and develop new research in both pharmaceuticals and agriculture. Members can network with other professionals in research and academia, access shared communal space, and gain access to Bayer's experts.

■ **Philips High-Tech campus Eindhoven:** Philips Natlab was transformed in 2000 into an open innovation facility for technology companies, of which Philips Research (former Natlab) is only a relatively small one, aimed at the new direction of Philips: Health and Lifestyle. The Philips innovation strategy is closely related to its core mission and its alignment with SDG3: "We are striving to make the world healthier and more sustainable through innovation, with the goal of improving the lives of 2.5 billion people a year by 2030."

SELECTED KPIs

Sustainability-oriented innovation is a strategic priority for many organizations, yet it is not very clear how to measure it in an effective way. Measurement scales to evaluate sustainable innovation performance are lacking (Calik and Bardudeen, 2016), as is hard evidence about cause-effect relations between input and impact measures (Cillo et al., 2019). Conventional innovation metrics have been rather narrowly defined, mostly in terms of *inputs* (absolute or relative R&D budgets; number of projects in pipeline), *outputs* (patents filed, citations, protectable property rights; market introduction of new products/services) and organizational-level *outcomes* (percentage of revenues from new products/services; cost reduction realized from process improvements; royalties and licensing income from intellectual property). Innovation economics added positive *spill-over and diffusion effects* to the equation, whilst sustainability considerations brought a variety of life cycle-related, socio-economic and ecological *impact* measures. On the 'do no harm' side, typical measures relate to the extent to which technology improvement and product/service (re)design contribute to eco-efficiency, emission reduction, substitution of harmful substances, dematerialization, waste minimization, extended product life cycles and recycling. On the 'doing good' side, (proxy) measures include the extent to which innovations deliver on eco-effectiveness, health and well-being, frugal/inclusive solutions, shared/collective knowledge accumulation and new technology/industry standards for sustainable practice – developed and diffused through open innovation efforts.

SOI management is about linking technology, market and organizational capabilities in inventive and system-conscious ways to create, scale and deliver societal value – with due regard for *socio-ethical aspects* and the world's *regenerative capacity* – in a dynamic and competitive environment. Orientation, strategic positioning, regulatory-push/pull factors, innovative capacity and time horizon (short-term, long-term outlook) all affect how the trade-off is made between 'incremental' and 'breakthrough' SOI initiative. Companies typically allocate at least 70% of their overall R&D budget to incremental innovations, and 5–10% to activities investigating long-term technologies and future breakthrough innovation (Davila and Epstein, 2014). However, 'invention of new options' does not straightforwardly translate into return on sustainable investment (ROSI) or higher ESG ratings. KPIs for breakthrough ambitions are invariably more 'soft' than the quantifiable metrics for new product/service development or technology improvements in the short run. In addition to having an innovation strategy and enabling innovation management system in place, one way to assess an organization's innovative capacity for radical SOI, is the extent to which it has succeeded in effectively organizing (co-creative) innovation spaces that align internal and external stakeholders around key SOI objectives. This presents an indication of the organization's 'innovative culture', 'intrapreneurship', 'change awareness', 'capacity to sense and seize' external and internal drivers of SOI, and 'relational capital' in relevant innovation/value networks.

Table 11.6 Mapping sustainable innovation practice

KVIs ➡	LEVEL 1	LEVEL 2	LEVEL 3	LEVEL 4
			Key tipping point ➤	
KDIs	*1. Trigger*	*2. Internal alignment*		*3. External alignment*
Main trade-off				'Doing different things'
	'Doing things differently'			
Innovation focus	Product improvement (based on off-the-shelf technology)	Product redesign (based on new technological competences)	Function innovation (new technology and organizational models)	System innovation (based on societal, organizational and technological change)
KPQs	Inactive	Reactive	Active	Proactive
Dominant logic	Existing markets /regulatory push Performance-driven, incremental Closed innovation approach Sustaining technology Need for stability Short-term horizon		Needs-based, future markets Impact-driven, radical Open innovation approach Sustainable technology Need for creativity Long-term horizon	
1. Innovation paradox	'Continuous progress' for operational excellence	'Emergent improvements' from capabilities enhancements	'Strategic bets' for breakthrough innovation with disruptive effects in markets	'Strategic discovery' for systems integration with transformational effect in society
• **SOI change approach** *Pellegrini et al. (2019)*	**Phase 1: 'Reactive'** • Routine management; • Compliance-driven; • Passive involvement in networks; • Absence of sustainable intrapreneurship; • Loosely coupled internal drivers of innovation (strategy, structure, financial resources, procedures, knowledge, competences, relations).	**Phase 2: 'Embedding'** • High sensitivity to external drivers (market, regulation, stakeholder demand/ pressure); • Active involvement in networks; • Presence of sustainable intrapreneurship • High interaction among internal innovation drivers (clear innovation strategy, knowledge/capabilities building, formalized procedures for identifying needs and (technology) scouting, selecting, experimenting, adopting internal and external solutions; • Radical hard and soft innovation.	**Phase 3: 'System change'** • High sensitivity and interaction with external drivers; • Strategic involvement in networks (search for new ideas, solutions, co-creators of solutions); • Strong presence of consolidated sustainable intrapreneurship; • High interaction among internal drivers (innovation strategy fully integrated; dedicated organizational structures, cross-departmental collaboration, informal knowledge/competences); • Implementation of radical changes that impact internal operations, business practice and external context.	

(Continued)

Table 11.6 (Continued)

2. Design paradox	Routine product-service improvements	Product-service redesign	Product-service-system design	System-shifting design
• **Problem framing**	'Simple' (technical) innovation challenge: avoid doing harm Design-out negative effects		'Complex/wicked' (technical, behavioural) innovation challenge: doing good Problem-solving and possibility-giving design	
• **Innovation spaces**	Internal: cross-functional collaboration and alignment		Internal and external: intra-organizational and extra-organizational collaboration in co-creation processes	
• **Proof of concept**	Prototype: no negative externalities		Prototype: no negative externalities, optimized positive externalities	
• **Proof of business**	Successful in existing (niche) market, integration in present business model		Successful for integration in upgraded or new business model	
• **Proof of success**	User-centric value created		Societal value created	

3. Openness paradox	Closed: Appropriation and strict protection of IPR	Shared: Joint appropriation of IPR and pre-competitive collaboration	Open: No patent protection or other forms of open, networked collaboration

KPIs	Inactive	Reactive	Active	Proactive
Performance measurement focus:	• Economic aspects: innovation expenditure (R&D; training and commercialization); number of new sustainable products introduced; cost reduction realized from implemented process improvements; number of patents and citations; income from royalties and sales of licenses • Environmental aspects: material/energy/resource usage; end-of-life management; certification and eco-labelling; waste, emission and pollution reduction • Social/societal aspects: health and safety; durability and quality; end-of-life management; ergonomics		• Economic: frugal products, lease constructions; percentage of R&D budget allocated to breakthrough SOI • Ecological: eco-design, eco-effectiveness • Societal: successful scaling of needs-based products/services; networking effects and positive (technology, knowledge) spill-overs, full circularity, net positive, successful introduction of open standards and effective partnerships	

11.9 THE SUSTAINABLE COMMUNICATION CHALLENGE: 'TALKING WHILE WALKING'

Key Performance Questions for sustainable communication management

■ What leading principles guide your communication strategy?

■ How do you deal with the limited trust society bestows on companies and their brands to 'do the right thing'?

■ What is the prime orientation of your communication strategy: functionalist, informative and instrumental, or formative and geared to meaningful negotiation, sense-making and stakeholder alignment for greater sustainability outcomes?

■ How do you deal with the gap between 'talk' and 'walk' and the effects thereof on perceived credibility, reputation and corporate legitimacy?

■ How do you approach external stakeholders and communities: as sources of liability and risk, or as potential co-creators of the sustainability strategy and corporate narrative?

■ What function does the communications department have in the identification of (material) sustainability topics, the formulation of the corporate narrative and the development of a sustainable corporate story?

■ What 'societal license' does your organization aim at in the relationship with stakeholders?

■ How can this approach be translated into an effective sustainability reporting strategy and frame?

KEY DECISIONS: BUFFERING OR BRIDGING?

The corporate communications function acts as a liaison between the organization, diverse publics and the media – with a particular bearing on the organization's reputation, its brand, activities and products. Communication plays a central role in how internal and external stakeholders (e.g. employees, investors, consumers, NGOs, regulators, the general public) perceive and evaluate the organization and are aware of its mission, values and sustainability efforts. Vice versa, effective business-stakeholder communication is an important means for firms to 'make sense' of – and appropriately respond to – the societal contexts in which they are operating. The communications department hence often assumes the function of 'CSR management', 'investor relations', 'interface management', 'public affairs/relations' or 'issues management' (see sections 7.3 and 9.3). It monitors and scrutinizes what various stakeholder groups are saying about the organization, manages and meets information needs, builds and maintains relationships with constituent and societal stakeholders, and disseminates deliberate messages on the organization's positioning and (sustainability-related) outputs, outcomes and impacts among various audiences in a controlled and coordinated manner.

Communicating on responsible corporate action serves a variety of often parallel purposes. To varying degrees, CSR communication strategies are commonly aimed at influencing perceptions, attitudes and image/identity enhancement; at controlling the business environment (reputation and issues management); at persuading, activating and engaging stakeholders through rhetoric, narratives and other meaning-creating discursive practices (sections 10.2 and 10.6); and at gaining knowledge about stakeholders, their values and ways of looking at the world. Ultimately, CSR communication is about establishing good stakeholder relationships through practices of accountable 'dissemination and deliberation' in ways that build, repair, sustain and enhance *societal legitimacy* (section 6.6). The thinking on CSR communication practice thereby distinguishes between two perspectives: (a) the *functionalist view* and (b) the *formative view* (Crane and Glozer, 2016; Schoeneborn et al., 2020).

In the *functionalist view*, CSR communication is instrumental to the purposes of the organization. It primarily serves as a means to transmit information on existing sustainability-related strategies, activities and realized performance and for 'signalling' appropriate business conduct. A key concern is whether the communication department accurately reflects the firm's sustainability practice to inform and persuade targeted audiences. Functionalist communicative practices emphasize content and one-directional communication methods and channels – such as CSR reports, press releases, corporate websites, issue advertisement, position papers, CEO statements – that can be maximally controlled to substantiate corporate sustainability actions and to reinforce brand image and corporate identity. A one-way mode of CSR communication de facto functions as a communicative and relational *buffer* between the organization and critical stakeholders. A 'buffering approach' that wards off external criticism runs the risk, however, of feeding into the already dominant frame that many companies are more interested in 'window dressing' and 'SDG-washing' than in actually addressing the root causes of sustainability issues.

By contrast, the *formative view* portrays a more interactive and dynamic perspective. It takes CSR communication as an iterative, ongoing process of sense-making and sense-giving between an organization and its stakeholders, in the recognition that pursued sustainability practice can be 'co-constructed' and 'talked into being' (Schoeneborn et al., 2020) through effective dialogue. In this view, two-way communicative processes of 'meaning negotiation', strategic stakeholder dialogue (Kaptein and Van Tulder, 2003) and democratic, multi-vocal participation (Hemmati, 2002) shape how CSR is understood and sustainability activities prioritized and practiced. A formative approach takes stakeholder needs and concerns as vantage point and considers how to make societal challenges material for the company (see section 9.3 on *reversing materiality*). It combines an outside-in approach with a thoughtful inside-out response and, vice versa, continuously probes how inside-out approaches resonate with engaged stakeholder groups. The corporate communications department then serves as an (interactive) *bridge* between the sustainability ambitions of the company and the articulated needs and concerns of society. This potentially makes it well-positioned to play an active role in the development and formulation of a *sustainable corporate story* (section 10.6) and the continuous upgrading and fine-tuning thereof in interaction with multiple stakeholders. A key question about the position and function of the communication department is what role it should take in the integration and coordination of the sustainability strategy *within* the organization. Can the communications department escape from being a 'passive' or 'reactive' buffer, to serve as a '(pro)active' bridging force for sustainable transformations instead? Can it carve out a conducive strategic position, or will it remain a marginal activity?

In the practical discourse, the formative approach is denoted under the heading of *sustainable communication* (as opposed to 'sustainability communication'). It has been described as: "a communicative practice, which corporations undertake to integrate social, environmental, ethical, human rights and consumer concerns into their business operations and core strategy in close collaboration with their stakeholders" (Nielsen and Thomsen, 2018: 493). Internally, 'sustainable communication' addresses corporate sustainability as a *strategy topic* that fuels sustainable marketing, sustainable supply chain management, sustainable HRM, sustainable innovation and sustainable finance strategies in a way that fosters *integration and coherence*. In the relationship with external stakeholders – beyond the organization's direct 'sphere of influence' (see Figure 10.1) – sustainable communication is geared towards framing, agenda-setting and the 'smart' use of the organization's discursive powers (section 10.3.2) to support its societal positioning, mobilize and align stakeholders, and enhance normalization efforts for positive change (section 10.3.1).

KPQs: WHAT TO FOCUS ON?

Effective sustainable communication in times of low societal trust in corporations to 'do the right thing' is challenging in multiple ways. Section 4.4 on 'wickedness dimensions' already pointed to *communicative complexity* as a complicating dynamic in addressing societal challenges. The omnipresence of social media has profoundly reshaped the communications landscape. A broad range of (vocal) societal stakeholders increasingly require that companies substantiate their sustainability ambitions and justify their actions in a concrete, transparent and accountable way – especially at the outcome and impact level (Box 11.4). The intricate, multilayered character of most societal challenges – as well as the company's role, influence and responsibilities therein – is generally not suited to be captured in episodic or simple content. And the practice of 'managing issues' may actually reinforce negative reputation effects in case the company is caught ill-informed or ill-prepared and feels forced to react in a defensive mode. When confronted with triggering events (section 7.3) and negative media coverage, the communication department usually becomes the focal point of an organization.

To effectuate transition processes beyond reactive strategies, companies need to thoroughly understand the concerns, interests, expectations and information needs of their multiple stakeholders – domestically, abroad, in various fora, and up and down the value chain. How can diverse stakeholder groups be effectively informed? How will they probably respond? How can they be constructively engaged and timely involved in the development and execution of the organization's sustainability strategy (see section 9.2.2)? How will the firm's communication practice affect its 'license to exist/operate/expand/experiment' (Table 6.6) in the short and longer run? How to gain a basic level of trust, build constructive relationships with critical stakeholders on truly material matters, and establish a responsible 'corporate identity' that consistently attunes sustainable communication, perception, brand positioning and corporate reputation in a credible and authentic way? What leading narrative (sustainable corporate story) to develop and how to meaningfully report on it?

▪ Talking and walking

The formative view implies that the communication department fulfils a more strategic role in the communicative, relational and organizational processes of internal and external alignment. In addition to the four *positions* that organizations can take in 'walking the talk' (see Table 9.1), Schoeneborn, Morsing and Crane (2020) discern three formative approaches to the walking-talking *dynamic interaction*. Each approach represents a distinct communicative 'intervention' sequencing and accentuates different cause-effect dynamics in adjusting, accelerating and advancing sustainability practice (Figure 11.21).

- **Talking-to-walk:** reflects an 'outside-in' approach to communication as 'aspirational talk' in which sustainability ambitions and intent ('talk') precede practice and performance ('walk'). The function of this communication strategy is that talk must pave the way for the materialization of aspirations. By communicating envisaged sustainability practice, an organization raises

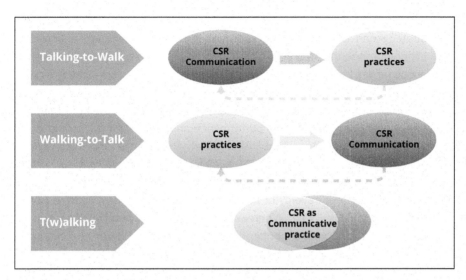

Figure 11.21 Three formative views on 'talk and walk'
Source: adapted from Schoeneborn et al., 2020

stakeholder expectations and consequently commits itself to being held to account for delivering on its promises. At the risk of reputational damage in case of intention-realization discrepancies, this formative dynamic can provide a powerful driver for organizational change. CSR practice is 'talked into being'. 'Talking-to-walk' can be used as a deliberate approach for both internal and external CSR communication. The formative mechanisms for progression then are twofold: (a) *creating a productive stretch* between 'talk' and 'walk' that challenges the status quo and incentivizes the organization to adjust its ways in order to meet raised expectations; and (b) *pursuing societal legitimacy* for espoused ambitions through stakeholder dialogue and deliberation ('talk'), in order to establish mutual understanding, rational agreement and *free, prior and informed* consent on the proposed walk. By and large, the 'talking-to-walk' approach corresponds with the drivers needed to overcome *phase 1 tipping points*. Key question is whether the communication department is in a position to timely identify and internally address default, discrepancies and greenwashing practices, so that the tension between 'lived reality' and 'future aspiration' can be effectively managed and the organization safeguarded from foreseeable reputational backlash.

■ **Walking-to-talk:** represents an 'inside-out' approach to CSR communication in which practiced and reported 'walk' precedes future-oriented 'talk'. Here, the organization's established track record provides a confident stepping stone for stakeholder dialogue on ways to improve and further extend sustainability ambitions. Externally, the 'walking-to-talk' communication strategy can be an effective approach for stakeholder mobilization and alignment (agenda-setting, pushing for a new level playing field at a higher sustainability level, upgrading sector standards), or for convincingly signalling 'leading by example' aspirations (see section 10.1). A pitfall to avoid, however, is the risk of *moral self-licensing*, which may flow from complacency over past sustainability performance and, unintentionally, could jeopardize further advancement. Alternatively, *walking-but-not-(yet)-talking* about progress on experimental sustainability activities with uncertain outcomes may be a sensible communication strategy to avoid disappointment, untimely controversy or to keep cynical media at bay, yet may come with drawbacks as well. Whereas it creates the necessary discretion to steadily work on 'proof of concept', it may also evoke distrust – for instance, in case of operating 'silently' in countries with a weaker CSR regime (Box 10.7). Internally, a 'walking-to-talk' approach may be used to boost further integration of the sustainability strategy into business activities, by providing confidence, purpose and a reinforced sense of 'corporate identity'. How sustainable practice is propagated influences how CSR is understood within and around the organization. Framing, rhetoric and 'issue-selling' – as 'sense-giving' instruments – can create a new understanding among employees, customers and value chain partners as to what CSR *could or should* constitute. A key question is whether the communication department can help shape an organizational atmosphere of purpose, pride and activation that: (1) provides clarity of values, identity and direction; (2) enhances employee motivation and commitment; and (3) accelerates internal alignment processes (*phase 2 transitioning*) through sense-making.

■   **T(w)alking:** involves an 'inside-out/outside-in' approach, based on the notion that "CSR talk and walk coexist in a mutually constitutive relation of co-occurrence" (Schoeneborn et al., 2020: 22). Rather than following a linear past–present–future progression, the t(w)alking approach recognizes that CSR is only valued as such if 'talk and walk' move in sync with changing stakeholder expectations, shifting societal norms and ongoing developments in the business environment. Accordingly, t(w)alking emphasizes *meeting while shaping expectations*. It (pro)actively uses input-inviting formative practices – such as informed stakeholder interaction aimed at *dilemma sharing,* deliberation on intricate *trade-offs* encountered in strategy implementation, and organizational learning ('learning by doing', 'doing while learning') – as a way to deal with competing frames, co-existing realities and to address the feasibility of farther-reaching sustainability ambitions (*phase 3 transitioning*). External 'ideation' and interactive 'out-of-the-box' thinking processes are a vital part of innovation and organizational 'learning loops' needed for addressing 'wicked problems' (see Part II). A key question, then, is whether the communication department is placed in a sufficiently strategic position – and provided with adequate means, mandate, time, flexibility and skills – to align a variety of (contrasting) external expectations with internal change processes, and vice versa.

■ *Issue communication and stakeholder dialogue*

At every level of engagement, organizations have to figure out how best to manage the communication relationship with multiple stakeholders. Sustainable communication plays an important role in (a) informing and engaging stakeholders on issues that are immediately material, and (b) identifying and selecting issues that, in due course, could *become* material (processes of 'reversing' and 'dynamic' materiality). Mainstream stakeholder theory has thereby mainly focused on 'salient stakeholders' that are of particular relevance to the organization from a reactive point of view (section 9.2.2). The precept then is to target those societal stakeholders that have the power, legitimacy and willingness to influence the existing corporate strategy or to significantly affect planned implementation. Strategic stakeholder management goes beyond the organization's reactive purposes. It deliberately seeks to timely engage diverse stakeholders in identifying societal issues and crafting a balanced, well-aligned sustainable corporate story (section 10.6) that helps the organization break through its reactive barriers. It contrasts from conventional stakeholder management in that it is forward-looking, based on continuous relationships and geared to societal challenges, rather than company-centric, preoccupied with handling controversies, and resting on occasional interactions.

For quite some time already, effective stakeholder dialogue has been acknowledged as a powerful catalyst for change. It promotes greater transparency, information sharing, mutual understanding and inspires to work together (WBCSD, 2002). Stakeholder trust generally tends to increase when stakeholders are made partner in the dilemmas an organization faces. *Strategic stakeholder dialogue* can be defined as a structured, interactive and proactive process aimed at creating sustainable strategies for societal challenges, in which the company and engaged stakeholders seek to reconcile societal values and needs with pragmatic and solution-oriented approaches (Van Tulder et al., 2004). It involves a substantive and respectful exchange of viewpoints and frames on present concerns, an informed discussion on (future) interests and expectations, and the exploration and development of shared principles, norms and frames for the functioning of organizations. Entering into a stakeholder dialogue is not a non-committal exercise however. By opting for stakeholder dialogue over a 'buffering' or confrontational approach, an organization expresses its willingness to learn, adjust, include and cooperate.

The practice of stakeholder dialogue can prove quite troublesome however – good will notwithstanding. Because of bad timing, unmatched or unaligned expectations, low trust, unclear mandates or significant power differences, dialogue can easily turn into a 'collective monologue'. If the process is ill-conceived or starts out badly, continuous rounds of dialogue, deliberation and negotiation will cease prematurely – without sufficient common ground for a sustainable way forward. A precondition for effective stakeholder dialogue, therefore, is that process contours, content, ambition and expectations and guiding *principles of stakeholder participation* are well-considered in the setup and agreed upon upfront.[58]

As the character of the business-stakeholder relationship changes along the consecutive organizational transitioning phases, the communication and negotiation frames used require adjustments as well.

- **'Show/prove it to me'.** In transitioning from an 'inactive' to a 'reactive' level of engagement (phase 1), the emphasis in stakeholder communication shifts from unilaterally *informing* a targeted set of stakeholders (e.g. investors, employees, customers, NGOs), to a setting of *debate, discussion* and *framing contests* (Kaplan, 2008) in which each party states and stresses its own case and pursues to win the other party over. In negotiation theory, this communication practice is denoted as 'position-based negotiations' (Box 5.2). KPQs relate to whether the 'hot' issues successfully pushed by the most salient, powerful or noisiest stakeholders are truly the most relevant (material) issues to focus on – or best 'solutions' to implement – from a longer-term perspective. How can the process of 'issue prioritization' (Figure 9.4) be organized such that it builds corporate legitimacy and stakeholder trust, rather than serve as a risk management tool for interacting and negotiating with powerful stakeholders?

- **'Inspire/engage me'.** In transitioning from a 'reactive' to an 'active' level of engagement (phase 2), the focus shifts from 'debate and discussion' with the most vocal stakeholders, to initiating *consultation and deliberative dialogue* with the most important stakeholders. Stakeholder communication becomes aimed at exploring the expert opinion, worldviews, knowledge and insights of selected stakeholders as a way to develop the company's vision on – and approach to – sustainability issues. It serves to fill in the blank and blind spots and to enhance legitimacy and commitment. It also provides the basis for 'interest-based negotiations' (Box 5.2), directed at creating a

---

58 In her book *Multi-Stakeholder Processes for Governance and Sustainability – Beyond Deadlock and Conflict*, Mina Hemmati (2002) outlined 15 principles of stakeholder participation that provide a helpful framework in considering the contours and organization of multi-stakeholder processes. Key principles include: accountability, effectiveness, equity, flexibility, inclusiveness, learning, legitimacy, ownership, participation and cooperative management, transparency and 'voices' rather than 'votes'.

satisfactory situation that accommodates the interests of all parties involved. KPQs relate to the identification and selection of 'win-win' opportunities with the potential to bridge internal and external interests. Notorious pitfalls to avoid, however, include relapsing into compromise at a lower ambition level, or involving primarily lenient and amenable stakeholders. Soliciting lip service eventually backfires, as a lack of constructive criticism takes away the felt urgency and opportunity to learn, adjust and accelerate change.

■ **'Involve/co-create with me'.** In phase 3 (from 'active' to 'proactive'), the weight shifts towards *strategic stakeholder dialogue*. Strategic stakeholder dialogue creates an opportunity to develop shared ambitions, principles and criteria through processes of 'collective vision-based negotiations' (Box 5.2) – aimed at goal alignment, mutual gains, societal benefit and 'positive-sum' outcomes. Phase 3 communication on complex issues acknowledges the interdependencies, complementarities and joint responsibilities between the company and involved stakeholders. Continued conversation in a series of meetings should build a shared understanding and deepen trusted relationships as a basis for vision and strategy development, implementation criteria and the definition of agreed upon performance and outcome benchmarks. KPQs include: how to build up trust, even when short-term interests are opposed; which strategic stakeholders to engage at what stage of the dialogue process; to what extent can stakeholder relationships remain informal (or even confidential) and when should they be formalized in partnership agreements and reported on (Chapter 12)?

■ *Sustainability reporting, framing and narrative development*
CSR reports are among the most prominent communication instruments used by companies to respond to the information needs and expectations of stakeholders and, by doing so, manage corporate image, perceived credibility and organizational legitimacy. CSR reports provide an important means to: (a) *look back* and reflect on realized performance and impacts, set against the corporate sustainability ambitions; and (b) to *look forward* and communicate how the organization plans to organize for further sustainability progress, in view of 'lessons learned', developments in the business environment and changing stakeholder expectations, norms and needs. The practice of CSR reporting hence has a functionalist ('reflecting reality') as well as a formative ('constructing reality') side to it (Crane and Glozer, 2016). On the one hand, the degree of transparency and accuracy of disclosed information has a direct bearing on the credibility that external publics ascribe to the organization (Box 11.19). On the other hand, the framing used to communicate aspirations and sustainability commitments contains 'performative power': it shapes the context and conditions for future action.

SUSTAINABILITY REPORTING – GRI REPORTING PRINCIPLES

Non-financial reporting has a long history, ranging back to US and Australian compa- nies reporting on social issues already before WWI (Blowfield and Murray, 2019). Partly stimulated by laws that required companies to report on social and environ- mental matters in response to corporate scandals (section 7.2), and partly as a means to communicate responsible intentions, large companies started to issue separate CSR reports in the early 1990s, additional to their financial reports. KPMG has been covering the state of affairs on sustainability reporting since 1993. In 2020, its 'KPMG Survey of Sustainability Reporting' found that 96% of the world's 250 largest companies by revenue (the G250) report on their sustainability performance, whereas 80% of the top 100 largest firms in 52 countries across the continents (the N100) do so – up from 18% in 2002.

The practice of sustainability reporting involves a number of challenges that require careful consideration (Blowfield and Murray, 2019). First, a CSR report has to address a much wider and more diverse stakeholder base than the financial commu- nity alone, which raises the matter of appropriate 'positioning': what is the company's take on 'corporate responsibility', 'sustainability', 'societal value creation' and 'perfor- mance'? Second, CSR is a highly contested frame and continuously evolving concept. Mandatory non-financial disclosure requirements aside, companies are largely free to determine how they report on CSR.[59] Considerations of 'positioning' and 'image enhancement' can have a bearing on the selection of material issues to report on (section 9.3), the scope and boundaries applied, and the level of transparency adopted. Third, in order to be perceived as accountable, transparent and credible among various audiences, the relevance and reliability of disclosed information requires external verification. Independent assurance on the veracity of claimed sustainability performance, outcomes and impacts can be arduous to organize, however, whilst the development of relevant performance indicators is still in flux. Lastly, corporate commitments and ambition levels communicated in CSR reports are mostly voluntary and, therefore, prone to low levels of implementation likelihood if comparability over time (progress) and between and across companies (competitive benchmarking) is not facilitated.

The Global Reporting Initiative (GRI) Standards have been developed to help organizations understand and disclose their sustainability impacts in a consistent, credible and comparable way that "meets the needs of multiple stakeholders". The

---

59 To promote transparency and reduce information asymmetries, government-mandated non-financial disclosure (NFD) requirements specify the information that corporations must disclose. NFD legislation nonetheless grants businesses complete discretion regarding the nature of socially 'responsible' business practices. To date, it does not usually prescribe specific reporting formats, nor verification by an external auditor (Jackson et al., 2020).

GRI Standards have become the leading global standard for organizations to report on topics related to their economic, environmental and social impacts. By 2020, around three-quarters (73%) of the G250 and two-thirds (67%) of the N100 used GRI as reporting standard (KPMG, 2020). Companies that claim to report in accordance with GRI Standards, must specify how they have implemented the ten *Reporting Principles* for defining 'report content' and 'report quality' – as indicated in GRI 101.

B O X 11.19

Reporting Principles for defining report content:

1   *Stakeholder inclusiveness:* the reporting organization identifies its stakeholders and explains how it has responded to their reasonable expectations and interests. An organization typically initiates different types of stakeholder engagement as part of its regular activities. To whom does the organization consider itself accountable? How does the report content relate to, and draw upon, the outcomes of stakeholder engagement processes?

2   *Sustainability context:* the report presents the organization's performance in the wider context of sustainability. What is the organization's understanding of sustainable development? How does its performance and impacts relate to broader sustainable development conditions and goals (as reflected in recognized sectoral, local, regional, or global instruments)? How do long-term strategy, risks, opportunities and goals, including in the organization's value chain, relate to these topics?

3   *Materiality:* the report covers topics that reflect the organization's significant economic, environmental and social impacts and topics that substantively influence the assessments and decisions of stakeholders. Materiality can be determined by considering internal and external factors: broader societal expectations, the organization's influence on upstream (suppliers) or downstream (customers) entities, and the expectations expressed in international standards and agreements with which the organization is expected to comply.

4   *Completeness:* coverage of material topics and their boundaries must be sufficient to reflect economic, environmental and social impacts, and to enable stakeholders to assess the organization's performance in the reporting period. Does the report include all relevant impacts it causes, contributes to, or is linked to through business relationships? Does it include reasonable estimates of foreseeable future impacts that can become unavoidable or irreversible?

Reporting Principles for defining report quality:

5.   *Accuracy:* reported information is sufficiently accurate and detailed for stakeholders to assess the organization's performance. Data, data measurement methods, and bases for calculations are adequately described, as are the underlying assumptions, techniques and sources used for estimated data.

6   **Balance:** reported information reflects both positive and negative aspects of the organization's performance to enable a reasoned assessment of overall performance. Does the report cover favourable as well as unfavourable results, trends and topics, instead of aggregate 'net' outcomes? Does the emphasis on various topics reflect their relative priority?

7   **Clarity:** information is made available in a way that is understandable and accessible to stakeholders using that information. Excessive and unnecessary detail is avoided (as are technical terms and jargon).

8   **Comparability:** information is reported consistently and presented in a manner that enables stakeholders to analyse changes in the organization's performance over time (on a year-to-year basis), and that supports analysis relative to other organizations.

9   **Reliability:** information is gathered, recorded, compiled, analysed and reported in a way that establishes its quality and materiality. Decision-making processes are documented such that they allow for the examination of key decisions. The scope and extent of external assurance is identified. The report provides unambiguous explanations of any uncertainties associated with the information, as well as reliable evidence and original sources and data to support assumptions or calculations.

10 **Timeliness:** reporting is consistent in its frequency so that information is available in time for stakeholders to make informed decisions. The organization balances the need to provide information in a timely manner with the need to ensure that the information is reliable. The information in the report clearly indicates the time period to which it relates, when it will be updated, and when the latest updates were made.

Over the years, CSR has become a highly institutionalized field of corporate activity (see Box 11.12; 11.14). With regulation by governments and stock exchanges rapidly developing, sustainability reporting is becoming a standard corporate practice, while external verification of reported sustainability information is on the rise as well. The number of G250 companies with a formal assurance statement increased from 30% in 2005, to 71% in 2020. Of the group N100 companies, 33% sought independent third-party assurance in 2005, ascending to 51% in 2020 (KPMG, 2020). Assurance statements vary in their scope and depth of application, however. Some assurance engagements only look at selected sustainability indicators or topics, whereas other verification approaches asses the entire sustainability report and underlying processes.

More information: GRI 101: Foundation (2016). https://www.globalreporting.org/standards/media/1036/gri-101-foundation-2016.pdf.

Companies have adopted a variety of reporting frames for communicating sustainability aspirations, actions and results. Next to the neutral frame of 'sustainability report', one can find analogue titles like 'corporate citizen report' (Box 11.20), 'responsible care report', 'CSR report', 'social report', 'impact report' and 'partnering report'. The frame is not to be taken lightly. It signals the company's ambition level, expresses the depth of societal commitment and reflects anticipated stakeholder perceptions. The development and formulation of a compelling organizational narrative – a coherent *sustainable corporate story* that clarifies the contextual why's, what's, how's, and with whom's behind the organization's sustainability strategy (section 10.6) – should provide a solid basis for credibly communicating sustainability intentions and outcomes, and for channelling goal priorities and organizational learning. A sufficiently sophisticated frame of how the organization understands societal challenges and the multilevelled contexts in which it operates, can also help to overcome simplification tendencies among internal and external stakeholders. In a sense, a sustainable corporate story provides a 'platform' for negotiating competing frames and sharing progressive insights on the urgency, responsibilities, threats and opportunities involved in responsibly addressing societal needs. A misguided frame, however, can make the communication department complicit in alleged window dressing and greenwashing practices and undermine the formative potential of sustainability reporting.

THE 'CORPORATE CITIZENSHIP' FRAME – COMPANIES AS 'GOOD CITIZENS'?

Along with diverse reporting frames emphasizing 'stakeholder focus', 'meeting conflicting expectations', 'legitimacy', 'partnering' and 'the business case' for sustainability, the popular concept of *'corporate citizenship'* has been of particular relevance to the communications department for framing business-society relations. Citizenship refers to the rights and duties of individuals in the communities of which they are part. The notion of 'corporate citizenship' extends social, civil and political principles of 'civic membership' to corporate entities. To be accepted as 'fellow citizen', then, (multinational) companies should prove themselves responsible members of the local communities in which they operate and, by virtue of their participation, earn their basic 'license to operate' (section 6.6). First coined in 1969, the corporate citizenship concept particularly gained in popularity since 2003 to denote the societal engagement and social behaviour of companies. Equivalent concepts include 'ethical citizenship', 'discretionary citizenship' and 'citizenship behaviour'. All

BOX 11.20

B
O
X

11.20

make special reference to social and human rights, philanthropic activities, community support and volunteering programmes as part of the 'citizenship' commitment.

The aptness of the 'citizen' metaphor in the context of 'market logics' has been intensely debated among academics, however (Moon et al., 2005). As a frame, corporate citizenship particularly underlines "that the corporation sees – or recaptures – its rightful place in society, next to other 'citizens', with whom the corporation forms a community" (Matten et al., 2003: 111), whereas corporations do not share a similar status of citizenship as individuals, nor do citizens share comparable economic and (locational) positioning powers as multinational companies hold (see Chapter 10). The limited liability of a company as a 'juristic person', for instance, provides it with judicial leeway that individual citizens – as 'natural persons'– generally do not have.

Nonetheless, the corporate citizenship frame is regularly embraced in communication and reporting strategies to signal societal involvement and commitment. The widespread uptake of the concept among companies reflects the growing importance of local 'embeddedness' in legitimacy-seeking considerations. To be viewed as a valued and contributing community member, corporates are more outspokenly expected to: (a) have a profound understanding of community needs; (b) develop 'interactive' capacity, accountability and credibility when supporting community activities; and (c) incorporate 'good citizenship' in the culture of their organization and the ethos of firm representatives. For the communications department, the challenge lies in convincingly portraying how the company manages to bridge 'market logic' and 'civic logic' (section 5.2) by taking a broader view on the company's fiduciary duties (sections 6.2 and 6.6), in each of the CSR regimes in which it operates (section 6.5).

SELECTED KPIs

Key Practice and Performance Indicators for the communication function are contingent on whether the organization views CSR communication mainly as: (a) an *instrumental driver* for protecting and enhancing corporate reputation, brand equity and market capitalization; or (b) also, as an important *constitutive driver* for building trusted stakeholder relationships, gaining legitimacy and nurturing engagement, participation and empowerment ('social capital') for sustainability-oriented action. The level of legitimacy an organization might obtain, hinges on "a generalized perception or assumption that the actions of an entity are desirable, proper, or appropriate within some socially constructed system of norms, values, beliefs and definitions" (Suchman, 1995: 574). In other words, 'reputation', 'public trust' and 'corporate legitimacy' – as pursued outcomes of communication strategies – all rely on the *perceived credibility* of communicated sustainability aspirations, actions and justifications. Perceived credibility, in turn, strongly rests on the company's 'walking-talking' track record, the sophistication of its sustainable corporate story (section 10.6), and its willingness and ability to enter into meaningful dialogue with stakeholders on effective ways for addressing societal issues.

KPIs accordingly reflect the extent to which the corporate communication strategy contributes to the company's envisaged CSR outcomes, including: the extent to which diverse stakeholder groups are effectively informed and involved in the corporate strategy; how corporate reputation and 'license to operate' are enhanced (or repaired, regained and restored after reputational damage, see Chapter 7); and among which stakeholder groups additional trust is created – notably through effective sustainability reporting and corporate narrative development (Table 11.7).

Another way to measure the effects of the CSR communication strategy is by considering external benchmarks related to reputation and trust. Several corporate reputation benchmarks are available – most of them with scant reference to sustainability however. Fortune's 'World's Most Admired Companies' ranking, for instance, uses nine attributes to assess relative reputation[60], of which one directly relates to companies' CSR strategy: 'social responsibility to the community and the environment'. The Reputation Institute's Global RepTrak™ 100 identifies four factors – admiration, trust, good feelings and overall esteem – to assess how stakeholders perceive a company, which feed into seven reputation pillars (Van Riel and Fombrun, 2007). Three pillars – 'governance', 'citizenship' and 'workplace' – contain CSR-related metrics of the company being perceived as 'behaving ethically', 'environmentally responsible', 'supporting good causes' and having a 'positive influence on society', while 'rewarding employees fairly' and considering 'employee well-being'. More dedicated indices rank companies according to the perceived sustainability of their corporate brand. The Sustainable Brand Index™, for instance, measures and analyses the effect of branding, communication and business development of over 1,400 brands across 34 industries in eight European countries, as perceived by their most important stakeholders: consumers.

---

60 Fortune's nine attributes of reputation are: ability to attract and retain talented people; quality of management; social responsibility to the community and the environment; innovativeness; quality of products and services; wise use of corporate assets; financial soundness; long-term investment value; effectiveness in doing business globally. Interpretation of the meaning of the attributes within a specific industry is left to respondents, that is top executives and directors from eligible companies, along with financial analysts.

Table 11.7 Mapping sustainable communication practice

KVIs ➡	LEVEL 1	LEVEL 2	LEVEL 3	LEVEL 4
		Key tipping point ➡		
KDIs ⬇	*1. Trigger*	*2. Internal alignment*	*3. External alignment*	
Main trade-off	**Buffering**			**Bridging**
Orientation	Liability – Risk Monitoring & Controlling		Responsibility – Opportunity Exchanging & Collaborating	
	Functionalist view on comunication function		Formative view on communication function	
	'Sustainability Communication'		'Sustainable Communication'	
Communication focus	Inside-in; Informative	Outside-in; Persuasive	Inside-out; Aspirational	Interactive; Participatory
KPQs	Inactive	Reactive	Active	Proactive
Walking-Talking dynamics	Talking *to* walk	Walking *to* talk		T(w)alking
Stakeholder approach	'Inform me'	'Show/prove it to me'	'Inspire/engage/consult me'	'Involve /co-create with me'
Communication mode	Debate: Deliberation; discussion; competing frames; pressure		Dialogue: Deliberative dialogue; strategic dialogue; shared understanding	
Narrative rationale	Doing well by doing things right: 'Just do it'	Doing well by *not* doing things wrong: 'Just don't do it'	Doing good *and* doing well: 'Do the right thing	Doing good *by* doing well: 'Do the right things right'
Narrative characterized by	Corporate *Self* Responsibility	Corporate Social *Responsiveness*	Corporate *Social/ Strategic* Responsibility	Corporate *Sustainable/ Systems/Societal* responsibility
Societal license sought (see section 6.6)	License to exist	License to operate	License to scale	License to experiment
Corporate citizenship (see section 6.2)	Embeddedness based on narrow view on fiduciary duties: e.g. paying due taxes, philanthropy, community sponsoring, volunteering, 'avoid doing harm'		Embeddedness based on broad view on fiduciary duties: e.g. building social capital, mobilizing for the common good, fostering voice, participation and empowerment; joint agenda-setting initiatives, 'doing good'	
KPIs	Inactive	Reactive	Active	Proactive
Management system in place for…	Coordination and timely collection of KPIs from all departments and business units for issue management, sustainability communication and CSR reporting		Coordination, integration and internal/external alignment of sustainability KPIs for continuous conversation and integrated sustainability reporting	

Established Walk-Talk track record	Timely identification of greenwashing (prevented reputation risk)		Clarity on purpose, values, identity and direction; enhanced employee motivation and commitment		Degree to which dilemmas are shared and external ideation is achieved
Stakeholder interaction outcome	Successful issue prioritization		Successful initiation of deliberative dialogues		Strategic dialogues, partnership formation with strategic stakeholders
Reporting approach	Financial reporting only	Financial and separate non-financial reporting (selected topics)	Sustainability reporting using standards frameworks (e.g. GRI, SASB, CDSB, TCFD)		Integrated reporting using IIRC Principles and relevant standard frameworks
Branding and trust level	Brand recognition	Brand sentiment	Positive brand reputation		Local citizenship recognition
	Low trust, or not relevant	Low-moderate trust	Moderate-high trust		High trust

11.10 INTERNAL SDG ALIGNMENT: ENTRIES FOR BOTTOM-UP APPROACHES

An effective integration of the corporate sustainability strategy is a dynamic process of 'strategic tinkering' and 'navigating', in search of vertical and horizontal alignment (sections 11.1 and 11.2). So too is the process of aligning core business activities with a strategically and operationally 'fit' SDG portfolio (sections 10.5 and 10.6). The identification of relevant SDG(-target)s is not necessarily reserved to 'top-down' strategy-making, however. In fact, functional departments – from their obvious area of responsibilities and competences – may provide valuable *bottom-up windows* for recognizing the potential of specific SDGs that may have been overlooked, or not (yet) prioritized, in 'top-down' decision-making. Functional departments can inspire, push and accelerate internal change processes by pointing out those SDGs and SDG-targets that are particularly close to their functional-level strategy and comprise interlinkages with other organizational functions as well. Vertical and horizontal alignment around such cross-linked SDGs can greatly enhance organizational processes of sustainability integration, coordination and coherence. In a way, these SDGs can be considered to represent an *internal nexus* for organizing corporate sustainability, as they help shed light on potential synergies, trade-offs and ways to operationalize feasible change trajectories. Anticipating internal nexus effects can help develop more fine-grained sustainable business models in which negative and positive interlinkages can be actively leveraged within the organization.

The research on SDG alignment and nexus effects – especially at the level of functional areas of management – is still in its infancy however. Moreover, the SDG-framework itself is not without gaps (see Part I). Many areas need to be further developed, particularly at the micro-level of analysis, as the SDG-framework does not provide detailed indicators tailored to be applicable to organizations. So, where to start then from the *bottom-up perspective* of the functional department?

This section introduces *SDG alignment fiches* as an aid for identifying obvious SDG entries for each functional area, and as a stepping stone for subsequent conversations on internal nexus mapping. The fiches present suggestions for making selected SDGs material in organizational functions.[61] They build on Tool #10.1, which sublimated the 169 SDG-targets in 59 business-relevant targets, of which 31 were marked as *internally actionable.* Section 10.5.2 described internally actionable SDG-targets as those that can be meaningfully engaged with *within* an organization and throughout the value chain. They are (1) relevant to core business activities and day-to-day operations; (2) fall within the organization's *direct sphere of influence*; and (3) help organizations to 'self-regulate' and apply principles of responsibility and sustainability ('avoid doing harm', 'do good') to their own operations and those in the value chain (Van Zanten and Van Tulder, 2018). Internally actionable targets not only present leads for SDG alignment at the corporate level, but also for decentralized sustainability efforts organized within functional departments.

11.10.1   SDG entries for sustainable purchasing

The SSCM approach of the purchasing department can be directly linked to at least six SDGs representing vital *social-economic dimensions* of supply-demand relationships. As elaborated in sections 10.4.2 and 11.3, SSCM strategies aim at more equitable value capturing and (re)distribution of costs, risks and revenues, as well as supportive approaches to enhance suppliers' sustainable value creation and earning capacity. Supplier upgrading strategies

---

61 Note, that the functional SDG alignment fiches and specified suggestions require contextualization, including for (1) country/countries of operations, (2) sector/industry, (3) position in the value chain (see sections 10.3.2 and 10.4.2), and (4) organizational governance type (section 6.3). The fiches suggest selected lenses for looking at the SDG-framework – not prescribed sets of generally applicable SDG-targets.

SDG ALIGNMENT FICHE #1 Sustainable Supply Chain Management (SSCM)						
Selected SDG lenses	**1** NO POVERTY	**2** ZERO HUNGER	**8** DECENT WORK AND ECONOMIC GROWTH	**9** INDUSTRY, INNOVATION AND INFRASTRUCTURE	**10** REDUCED INEQUALITIES	**12** RESPONSIBLE CONSUMPTION AND PRODUCTION
SDG-targets	1.1; 1.2	2.3	8.2; 8.5; 8.7; 8.8	9.3	10.1	12.a
Internally actionable targets (Tool #10.1)	**Avoid doing harm**	• Labour rights and practices in the supply chain • Elimination of forced labour and child labour • Collective bargaining for wages and benefits along the supply chain • Equal pay and opportunities for men and women, at all levels				
	Doing good	• Fair payment to small-scale suppliers • Sustainable food production • Socially responsible sourcing • Transfer of sustainable technologies to developing countries				

(Box 10.10), effective supplier codes and sustainability certification schemes, co-development approaches, small-scale supplier income and wage levels earned by workers along the chain, were highlighted as key topics for enhancing sustainability outcomes and strengthening the resilience of supply networks. In the light of these SSCM ambitions, purchasing managers can opt for multiple internally actionable 'avoiding harm' and 'doing good' targets (Fiche #1) to explore viable ways for aligning their functional-level strategy with the SDG-agenda.

SDG9 is the only SDG that makes explicit reference to value chains. **SDG-target 9.3** underlines the need to increase the access of small-scale industrial and other enterprises, in particular from developing countries, into value chains and markets. **SDG12** (on responsible production and consumption) would seem an obvious entry for SSCM, yet hardly contains elements that relate to the socio-economic conditions in supply networks, with the exception of **SDG-target 12.a.** Subscribing to 12.a would imply commitment to transferring sustainable technologies and know-how to suppliers in developing countries, which may well match existing or planned supplier upgrading programmes. Potential side effects to consider include whether technological upgrading efforts could unintendedly result in increased dependency, 'lock-in' and 'crowding out' effects.

With regard to income dimensions along the supply chain – a litmus test for effective SSCM strategies – **SDG-target 8.5** defines a relative target ('equal pay for work of equal value'), whereas **SDG-targets 1.1+1.2** ('no poverty') and **SDG-target 10.1** ('reduced income inequality') add absolute income dimensions to SSCM practice. **SDG-target 2.3** additionally underscores the 'incomes of small-scale food producers', emphasizing the position of women and indigenous peoples in particular. Combined, these dimensions provide general indicators for checking on desirable and effective SSCM approaches. Linking SDG-targets 2.3+1.1+1.2, for instance, would translate into an actionable 'positive duty' target: 'fair pay to small-scale suppliers'. Taking this ambition one step further requires contextualized metrics on 'minimum income', 'living wage' and 'decent wage' levels. Furthermore, **SDG8** is a particularly relevant entry for SSCM strategies due to its emphasis on 'decent work' (**8.5**), the protection of labour rights and promotion of safe working conditions (**8.8**), elimination of forced and child labour (**8.7**), and the observed relevance of diversification and upgrading strategies (**8.2**) along the supply chain.

11.10.2   SDG entries for sustainable operations management

Operations management can be linked to a considerable number of obvious SDG entries, as evidenced by the central role that protecting the 'regenerative capacity of nature' and the eco-efficient and eco-effective management of vital natural resources play in the SDG logic. Sustainable operations management adds the *ecological dimension* to value chain management, with great weight given to clean technologies; regenerative and nature-inclusive approaches; circularity, dematerialization and upcycling; renewable sources of energy and emission-neutral or 'net positive' solutions and product life cycles. Internally actionable targets for sustainable operations management most prominently concentrate on 'avoid doing harm' goals and preventing, mitigating or minimizing 'negative externalities'.

SDG ALIGNMENT FICHE #2 Sustainable Operations Management								
Selected SDG lenses	2 ZERO HUNGER	3 GOOD HEALTH AND WELL-BEING	6 CLEAN WATER AND SANITATION	7 AFFORDABLE AND CLEAN ENERGY	12 RESPONSIBLE CONSUMPTION AND PRODUCTION	13 CLIMATE ACTION	14 LIFE BELOW WATER	15 LIFE ON LAND
SDG-targets	2.4	3.9	6.3; 6.4; 6.6	7.2; 7.3; 7.b	12.2; 12.3; 12.4; 12.5	13.2	14.1	15.1; 15.2; 15.3; 15.4; 15.5; 15.9
Internally actionable targets (Tool #10.1)	**Avoid doing harm**	• Water use efficiency • Energy efficiency • Reducing air, soil and water pollution • Sustainable waste management • Greenhouse gas emission reductions • Disaster and emergency planning						
	Doing good	• Environmentally sustainable sourcing • Sustainable food production • Transfer of sustainable technologies						

SDG12 ('responsible consumption and production') provides the most obvious SDG entry, as it makes explicit reference to 'sustainable management and use of natural resources' (**12.2**), 'reducing food losses along production and supply chains' (**12.3**), 'environmentally sound management of chemicals and all wastes throughout their lifecycle' (**12.4**), and 'substantial reduction of waste generation through prevention, reduction, recycling and reuse' (**12.5**). Circularity and responsible production can have positive impacts on **SDG-target 2.4** ('sustainable food production and resilient agricultural practice'), **SDG-target 3.9** ('reduced illness and death from hazardous chemicals and air, water, soil pollution'), **SDG7** ('renewable energy'), **SDG-target 8.4** (decoupling growth from environmental degradation); **SDG13** ('climate action'), **SDG14** ('life below water'), and **SDG15** ('life on land').

SDG15 provides another evident entry. The protection, restoration and sustainable use of freshwater and terrestrial ecosystems (**15.1**), the halting of deforestation and the sustainable management of forests (**15.2**), as well as counteracting and reversing desertification (**15.3**), land degradation, biodiversity loss and harm to natural habitats (**15.4; 15.5; 15.6**) are all directly related to the company's sourcing strategies and the eco-efficient and eco-effective management of input-output processes – both within the company and along the value chain. SDG15, in turn, has clear linkages with, for instance, **SDG6** ('clean water'). Fresh water should be sufficiently available and safe to drink, which can be attained by eliminating pollution from wastewater (**6.3**), 'increasing water-use efficiency' (**6.4**), and 'protecting and restoring water-related ecosystems' (**6.6**).

A third logical entry point for sustainable resource management systems can be found in the 'water-energy-food' and 'food-water-energy-climate' nexus (see Box 4.4). Linking **SDGs 2, 6, 7** and **13** enables an assessment of important trade-offs and possible synergies that appear between the different uses of water, energy and land for the purpose of food production, and the effects thereof in terms of greenhouse gas emissions (**13.2**).

11.10.3   SDG entries for sustainable marketing

Sustainable marketing can be linked to those SDGs that particularly emphasize 'access to' dimensions in relation to an affordable and sufficient fulfilment of people's (unmet or latent) need for health and wellbeing, and (responsibly and sustainably produced) food, products and services. Furthermore, marketing has a vital role in: (a) 'raising awareness' on the responsible (life cycle) usage of products and the societal effects of consumption behaviour; (b) enabling better choices through effective labelling and sustainable certification schemes, choice editing and differential pricing strategies (that reckon with the limited purchasing power of people on low income in developing and developed economies); and (c) communicating 'societal value'.

SDG ALIGNMENT FICHE #3
Sustainable Marketing Management

Selected SDG lenses	1 NO POVERTY	3 GOOD HEALTH AND WELL-BEING	4 QUALITY EDUCATION	6 CLEAN WATER AND SANITATION	7 AFFORDABLE AND CLEAN ENERGY	8 DECENT WORK AND ECONOMIC GROWTH	9 INDUSTRY, INNOVATION AND INFRASTRUCTURE	11 SUSTAINABLE CITIES AND COMMUNITIES	12 RESPONSIBLE CONSUMPTION AND PRODUCTION	13 CLIMATE ACTION	14 LIFE BELOW WATER	15 LIFE ON LAND
SDG-targets	1.4	3.4; 3.5; 3.7; 3.b	4.2; 4.3; 4.7	6.1; 6.2	7.1; 7.a	8.3; 8.9; 8.10	9.3	11.1; 11.2	12.8	13.3	14.4	15.2

Internally actionable targets (Tool #10.1)

Avoid doing harm
- Reducing pollution
- Energy efficiency
- Labour rights and practices in the supply chain (labelling)
- Greenhouse gas emission reduction
- Protection of privacy

Doing good
- Goods and services for those on low incomes
- Access to financial services for all, including the most vulnerable
- Sustainable and healthy food production
- Socially and ecologically responsible sourcing
- Partnerships with public and civil society sectors

SDG12 ('sustainable consumption and production systems') provides the most obvious entry to the SDG-framework. **SDG-target** 12.8, perhaps closest to the marketing function, stresses the provision of 'relevant information' and 'awareness for sustainable development and lifestyles in harmony with nature'. Related SDG-targets with an equivalent objective are, for instance, the promotion of 'sustainable tourism' (**8.9**), disease prevention and promotion of health and well-being (**3.4**), prevention of the harmful use of alcohol (**3.5**), awareness-raising on climate change (**13.3**) and on human rights, gender equality, non-violence and diversity (**4.7**), ending overfishing (**14.4**), and the promotion of the sustainable management of all types of forests (**15.2**).

Another powerful entry is provided by the overarching principle of the SDG-agenda: **no one left behind**. This leading *inclusiveness principle* has a direct bearing on the 'market creation' dimension of sustainable marketing: to serve the explicit needs of people (but latent effective demand in terms of buying power), in a way that effectively includes them as (potential) customers. In different places around the world, underserved groups may concern city dwellers and rural poor, women and young girls, youth, the elderly, the undernourished, the under-treated, the undereducated or the physically challenged. The SDGs provide ample alignment possibilities to create affordable 'access' to specific product and service markets for yet underserved customer groups, including: basic services for those on low incomes (**1.4**); health services (**3.7**); affordable essential medicines and vaccines (**3.b**), childcare and (vocational) education (**4.2; 4.3**), affordable sanitation, hygiene and drinking water (**6.1; 6.2**); affordable energy/electricity (**7.1**); access to clean energy (**7.a**); financial services for micro-, small- and medium-sized enterprises, including banking, insurance and affordable credit (**8.3; 8.10; 9.3**); safe and affordable housing (**11.1**) and transport (**11.2**).

11.10.4   SDG entries for sustainable HRM

Sustainable HRM pertains to a broad range of employment-related issues, including job security, job creation, decent work and working conditions, fair wages, employee health and well-being, human and labour rights, diversity and equality, quality education, and capabilities development inclusive to low-skilled and low-paid workers. The SDG-framework provides a considerable number of powerful and internally actionable targets to align with, in order to "support livelihoods that enable people to live well and work with dignity, security, freedom and opportunity" (Shift and WBCSD, 2018: 4). Obvious entries are spread over SDGs that stress 'productive employment and decent work for all' (**SDG8**), poverty and income levels (**SDG1**), health and well-being (**SDG3**), 'quality education' (**SDG4**), gender equality (**SDG5**), inclusion and reduced income inequalities (**SDG10**).

SDG ALIGNMENT FICHE #4							
Sustainable Human Resources Management							
Selected SDG lenses	1 NO POVERTY	3 GOOD HEALTH AND WELL-BEING	4 QUALITY EDUCATION	5 GENDER EQUALITY	8 DECENT WORK AND ECONOMIC GROWTH	10 REDUCED INEQUALITIES	16 PEACE, JUSTICE AND STRONG INSTITUTIONS
SDG-targets	1.4	3.8; 3.c	4.2; 4.3; 4.4; 4.7	5.1; 5.2; 5.5; 5.c	8.3; 8.5; 8.6; 8.7; 8.8	10.3; 10.4	16.2; 16.7

Internally actionable targets (Tool #10.1)	**Avoid doing harm**	<ul><li>Elimination of forced labour and child labour</li><li>Labour rights and practices in the supply chain</li><li>Occupational health and safety</li><li>Equal pay and opportunities for men and women, at all levels</li><li>No discrimination</li><li>No workplace violence and harassment</li><li>Responsive and inclusive decision-making at all levels</li><li>Protection of privacy</li></ul>
	Doing good	<ul><li>Employee training and education</li><li>Childcare services and benefits</li><li>Promote empowerment of women through technology</li><li>Employment for all; particularly young people and people with disabilities</li></ul>

HRM departments can align with these SDGs from a positive duty ('doing good') ambition, particularly by creating decent jobs that help counter youth unemployment (**8.5; 8.6**), informal employment (**8.3**) and precarious employment (**8.8**), and in doing so, induce related spill-over effects conducive for *inclusive* economic growth (**10.1; 10.2**). In addition, providing technical and vocational training and education (**4.3**) – in a safe, inclusive and secure working environment (**8.8**) – can considerably add to workers' relevant skills level and employability in decent and fairly paid jobs (**4.4; 2.3**), their literacy and numeracy (**4.5**), their knowledge of sustainable development, gender equality and human and labour rights (**4.7**), as well as to employee retention in for instance the health sector (**3.c**). Offering health insurance (**3.8**) and childcare services (**4.2**) is furthermore supportive to job security, gender equality, and economic and social inclusion.

SDG alignment possibilities in the 'avoid doing harm' (negative duty) realm generally relate to issues involving 'inequality' and 'human rights'. Corporate action to prevent or counter discrimination (**1.4; 5.1; 10.3**), workplace violence, in particular against women (**5.2; 8.8**), gender disparities in income, opportunity and leadership positions, (**8.5; 5.5; 5.c**), and forced labour, modern slavery and child labour (**8.7; 16.2**) are typical matters that the HRM function can influence for the better – as are upholding labour rights, representation and voice (**8.8; 10.6; 16.7**) and equal opportunity and reward (**10.3; 10.4; 8.5**).

PUTTING PEOPLE FIRST

B
O
X

11.21

A nexus approach to the SDG-agenda can become particularly effective if 'human rights' and 'employee empowerment' are used as point of departure. In 2018, Shift – the leading centre of expertise on the UN Guiding Principles on Business and Human Rights (UNGPs) – and the World Business Council for Sustainable Development published a compendium on the potential of companies to contribute to the SDG-agenda by taking a people-centred, human rights-based approach as part of a 'holistic SDG strategy'. The principal argument: "Business respect for human rights is more than a requirement to 'do no harm'. By proactively implementing the key tenets of the UNGPs, companies have the potential to break down significant barriers to development and positively impact the lives of millions of the most vulnerable individuals in society" (Shift and WBCSD, 2018: 4).

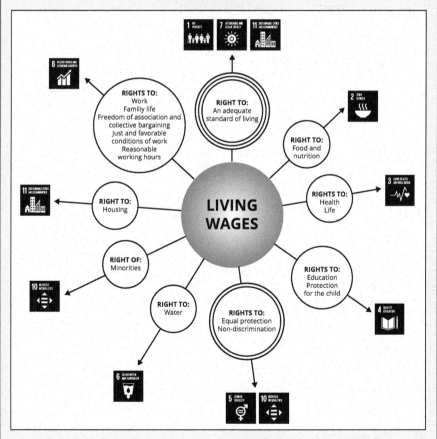

Figure 11.22 The Human Rights connection: living wages and gender equality

Source: Shift and WBCSD (2018), p. 13 and p. 49, (http://www.shiftproject.org). © 2018 Shift Project Ltd.

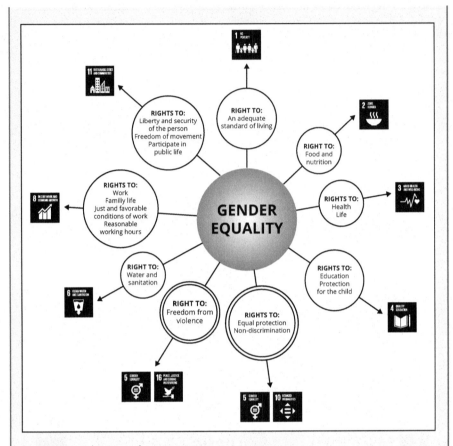

Figure 11.22 (Continued)

Illustrated by 15 real-life cases of evolving corporate sustainability strategies, the Shift/WBCSD compendium identifies four key human rights tenets, each with a considerable number of potentially powerful SDG nexus connections: (a) living wages; (b) forced labour; (c) gender equality; and (d) land-related human rights. Living wages and gender equality are most close to 'positive duty' ambitions in the direct sphere of influence of the HRM function. Effective practice on both will not only positively impact people's lives and contribute to the 'People' part of the SDGs (Figure 11.22), but also benefit HRM purposes through "improved recruitment and retention of staff; increased productivity and business continuity; a more secure and enhanced reputation; and the opportunity to become an investment, a business partner and a brand of choice" (ibid: 7).

▪ **The potential of living wage:** the Shift/WBCSD study finds that providing employees with a living wage – defined as "the provision of wages that are enough to meet basic needs and to provide some discretionary income" – could help advance as many as 11 SDGs through 24 connected SDG-targets. The study concludes that freedom of association, collective bargaining and non-discrimination play a central role in corporate action on living wages, as does participation in collaborative initiatives (for instance, in producer-buyer partnerships).

■ **The potential of gender equality:** gender equality and women's empowerment are generally considered critical conditions for sustainable economic progress (see Box 4.4). The Shift/WBCSD study points out that advancements in gender equality have a ripple effect on nearly all areas of sustainable development: from reducing poverty, hunger and even carbon emissions to enhancing the health. It finds that by addressing gender-related issues in its daily activities and value chain, a company could help advance up to eleven SDGs and 29 related SGD-targets.

More information: https://www.shiftproject.org/SDGs

11.10.5 SDG entries for sustainable finance

The sustainable finance function is geared to raising, facilitating and allocating funding to its most productive use in order to optimize 'integrated' or 'societal value'. The various SDG-targets denoted as **Means of Implementation** (MoI) have a similar function. MoI refer to all SDG17-targets and the 43 alphabetic SDG-targets spread among the other SDGs. They comprise an interdependent mix of enabling and means-mobilizing 'instruments' for realizing the SDGs: public and private finance, technology, capacity-building, trade as an engine for inclusive economic growth, policy coherence, public-private partnerships, and monitoring and accountability-related targets. Although most MoI-targets relate to public policymaking, a subset provides alignment opportunities for corporate initiative as well (**SDG-targets 17.1; 17.3; 17.5**). Long-term investments (e.g. FDI), the correct payment of corporate taxes, international trade and mobilization of financial resources through 'blended finance and investment', concessionary capital and creation of reliable SDG investment opportunities for institutional investors, are all actionable topics within the ambit of the corporate finance function.

To align the corporate strategy and investments with the SDG-agenda, three types of entries to the SDG-framework can be explored, representing (a) opportunity-drivers, (b) activity-drivers and (c) value-drivers.

■ **Opportunity-drivers:** concern those SDGs for which considerable public finance gaps exist that cannot be covered through domestic taxation and other means for governmental revenue collection. The financial link with the SDG-agenda particularly runs through the private (or blended) provision of *merit and public goods*, where public sources are lacking or trailing behind.

SDG ALIGNMENT FICHE #5
Sustainable Corporate Finance

Selected SDG lenses		Soft infra-structure			Hard infrastructure						
1 NO POVERTY; 2 ZERO HUNGER		3 GOOD HEALTH AND WELL-BEING; 4 QUALITY EDUCATION		10 REDUCED INEQUALITIES	6 CLEAN WATER AND SANITATION; 7 AFFORDABLE AND CLEAN ENERGY; 9 INDUSTRY, INNOVATION AND INFRASTRUCTURE; 11 SUSTAINABLE CITIES AND COMMUNITIES				12 RESPONSIBLE CONSUMPTION AND PRODUCTION	13 CLIMATE ACTION; 15 LIFE ON LAND	17 PARTNERSHIPS FOR THE GOALS
SDG-targets	1.4; 1.b; 2.a	3.c	4.a	10.4; 10.a; 10.b	6.a; 7.1; 7.2; 7.3; 7.a; 7.b 9.1; 9.3; 9.4; 9.5; 9.a; 9.b; 9c 11.1; 11.2; 11.4; 11.5; 11.b 11.c				12.6; 12.a;	13.1; 15.a; 15.b	17.1; 17.3; 17.5; 17.7;

Internally actionable targets (Tool #10.1)	**Avoid doing harm**	<ul><li>Accountable and transparent governance</li><li>No corruption and bribery</li><li>Monitoring tools on impact</li><li>External reporting on sustainability</li><li>Investment in developing countries</li></ul>
	Doing good	<ul><li>Adopt fiscal and social policies that promote equality</li><li>Funding for developing countries' climate change actions</li></ul>

The IMF estimated that meeting the SDGs in five priority areas – education (**SDG4**), health (**SDG3**), roads (**SDG9**), electricity (**SDG7**), and water and sanitation (**SDG6**) – will require an additional private and public annual spending of US$528 billion for low and lower middle-income countries, and US$2.1 trillion for emerging economies (Gaspar et al., 2019). Investments in vital 'soft' (social) infrastructure typically pertain to healthcare (**SDG3**) and education (**SDG4**). Investments in 'hard' (economic) infrastructure relate to 'power and renewable energy (**7.1; 7.2; 7.3; 7b**); affordable housing and resilient infrastructure for transport, IT and communication (**9.1; 9.a; 9c; 11.1; 11.2; 11.c**); and climate change mitigation (**13.1; 11.5; 11.b**).[62]

■ **Activity-drivers:** providing access to financial services and microfinance (**1.4; 9.3**) in countries with less developed financial markets – or for SDG-related projects that are too small to attract portfolio investors – can be part of the financial arrangements companies can adopt to enable the integration of smaller-scale enterprises in supply chains and markets (**SDG12**). Furthermore, corporate investment strategies can be aligned with, or scale SDG finance for specific SDG-targets, including: 'accelerated investments in poverty eradiation actions' (**1.b**); agricultural, rural infrastructure and technology development to enhances agricultural productivity (**2.a**); water harvesting, efficiency, recycling and reuse technologies (**6.a**); energy efficiency and clean energy technology (**7.a; 7.b**); innovation, the retrofitting of industrial sectors and upgrading technological capabilities (**9.5; 9.4; 9.b; 12.a; 17.7**); foreign direct investment (**10.b**); and investment in cultural and natural heritage in support of sustainable tourism (**11.4; 8.9**), reforestation (**15.b**) and conservation of biodiversity and ecosystems (**15.a**).

■ **Value-drivers:** adoption of the CFO Principles on Integrated SDG Investment and Finance contributes to expanding the market for corporate SDG investments (section 11.7). Two recent SDG alignment initiatives support this ambition: (a) the creation of SDG-linked bonds; and (b) IIRC's effort to link integrated reporting principles to SDG impact (Figure 11.23), which reiterates the importance of transparent corporate reporting on their sustainability practices (**SDG-target 12.6**) and how this contributes to achieving the SDGs.

---

62 The UNDP 'SDG Investor Platform' provides market intelligence on SDG-related private and blended investment opportunities around the world. Its searchable 'Investment Opportunity Area' database compiles over 300 investment projects in various sectors – ranging from consumer goods manufacturing, food & beverage, pharmaceuticals and communication & technology, to healthcare, education, affordable housing, transport and renewable energy. Each investment project comes with a description of the project's business model, expected impact, indicative rate of return, investment timeframe, market size, ticket size, and relation to direct and indirect SDG impacts. The SDG Investor Platform also features some ventures as case studies and regularly adds projects that are ready for investment in emerging economies. See https://sdginvestorplatform.undp.org/market-intelligence.

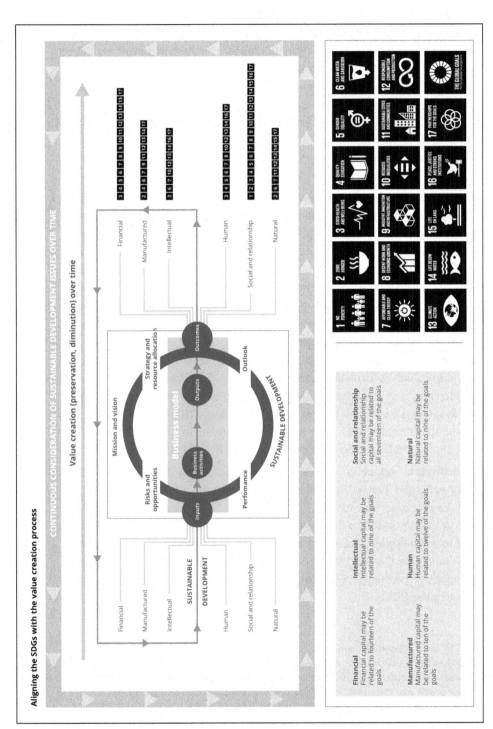

Figure 11.23 Aligning the SDGs with the value creation process

Source: Adams (2017), p. 14, www.integratedreporting.org/resource/sdgs-integrated-thinking-and-the-integrated-report/.

Copyright © September 2017 by the International Integrated Reporting Council (IIRC).

11.10.6   SDG entries for sustainable innovation

Sustainable innovation management is concerned with the development, operationalization and dissemination of new products, practices, services and technologies that bring sustainable and scalable value for society. Innovations in the field of clean-tech, eco-effective and closed-loop production particularly contribute to resource efficiency, the decoupling of economic growth from environmental degradation (**SDG-target 8.4**) and greenhouse gas emission reduction (**SDG13**), while social, health-related and frugal innovations can significantly contribute to fulfilling people's need for social and economic inclusion (**1.4**), health and well-being (**SDG3**).

SDG9 ('industry, innovation and infrastructure') provides an obvious point of reference for many innovation activities. SDG9 reiterates the importance of a functioning and conducive domestic R&D infrastructure (with a sufficient number of skilled R&D workers) as a critical condition for sustainable industrialization and diversification, technological capabilities upgrading (**9.5, 9.b**) and higher productivity levels (**8.2**) for inclusive and sustainable economic growth (**SDG8**). In addition, **SDG17** comprises several SDG-targets that further emphasize the centrality of access to 'enabling technologies', knowledge sharing, technology transfer and innovation capacity-building mechanisms (**17.6; 17.7; 17.8; 17.16**) for achieving the SDGs.

Environmentally sound, new or upgraded technologies are mentioned in the SDG-framework as part of: people's access to, in particular, information and communication technology (**1.4; 5b**); agricultural production in supply chains (**2a**); sustainable (fresh) water management (**6.a**); renewables, clean energy and energy efficiency (**7a; 7b**); industrial process retrofitting (**9.4**); more sustainable patterns of consumption and production (**12a**); climate change action (**13.3**) and marine technology (**14.a**). Furthermore, advancement of technical and vocational skills of employees and young people – an explicit target of **SDG4** – to strengthen the domestic development, implementation and diffusion of sustainability-enhancing solutions, is within direct reach of companies' approach to innovation management.

11.10.7   SDG entries for sustainable communications

Among the core elements of the communication function are 'sustainability reporting and disclosure', 'transparency' and 'accountability' in the relationship with internal and external stakeholders. To that end, **SDG-target 12.6** provides a directly applicable entry to the SDG-framework: it explicitly calls on (multinational) companies to integrate information on their sustainable practices into their reporting cycle, in a way that "builds on existing initiatives to develop measurements of progress on sustainable development" (**17.19**). The degree of sophistication of SDG reporting is a vital element in catalysing progress on the

SDG ALIGNMENT FICHE #6
Sustainable Innovation Management

Selected SDG lenses	1 NO POVERTY	3 GOOD HEALTH AND WELL-BEING	4 QUALITY EDUCATION	7 AFFORDABLE AND CLEAN ENERGY	8 DECENT WORK AND ECONOMIC GROWTH	9 INDUSTRY, INNOVATION AND INFRASTRUCTURE	12 RESPONSIBLE CONSUMPTION AND PRODUCTION	13 CLIMATE ACTION	17 PARTNERSHIPS FOR THE GOALS
SDG-targets	1.4	3.b	4.4; 4.b	7.a; 7.b	8.2; 8.3; 8.4	9.4; 9.5; 9.b	12.a	13.3	17.6; 17.7; 17.8 17.16
Internally actionable targets (Tool #10.1)	**Avoid doing harm**	▪ Water use efficiency ▪ Energy efficiency ▪ Greenhouse gas emission reduction ▪ Reducing air, water and soil pollution ▪ Sustainable waste management							
	Doing good	▪ Goods and services for those on low incomes ▪ Transfer of (sustainable) technologies to developing countries ▪ Employee training and education ▪ Sustainable technologies and sustainable industrial processes ▪ Data availability and public access to information ▪ Partnerships with the public and civil society sector							

SDG-agenda. It demonstrates corporate commitment, provides a source for stake-holder engagement, may strengthen the company's societal legitimacy, and fosters both organizational and collective learning for enhancing SDG-related impacts. Accordingly, an honest picture of the company's level of SDG alignment and SDG performance demands that both realized contributions and setbacks or unexpected side effects are accounted for. Preventing (alleged) **SDG-washing** from appearing implies that 'positive' as well as 'negative' material impacts are transparently reported – separate, not as compounded 'net effect'– with due regard to the principle of **impact integrity** (Box 11.4). It also calls for a well-conceived balance between: (a) using the activating power of *positive framing* for internal and external formative purposes (sections 10.6 and 11.9), and (b) reporting on *controversies* as a stepping stone for reflection, dialogue and structural improvement.

■ **Positive frames:** the most pervasive frames in the formulation of SDG-framework are fivefold: (1) 'sustainable'; (2) 'inclusive'; (3) 'resilient'; (4) 'equal'; and (5) 'access to'. The *sustainable frame* obviously underlies all SDGs, but is explicit in nine of them, ranging from sustainable agriculture (**SDG2**), sustainable management of water and sanitation (**SDG6**), sustainable energy (**SDG7**), economic growth (**SDG8**) and industrialization (**SDG9**), to cities and communities (**SDG11**), consumption and production (**SDG12**), oceans, marine resources (**SDG14**), and the management of forests and ecosystems (**SDG15**). At the target level, 'sustainable' further-more refers to management practices in relation to buildings, tourism, food production, fisheries, forests, biodiversity, energy, livelihoods, infrastructure, industrialization and urbanization. The *inclusiveness frame* is prevailing in five SDGs: inclusive education (**SDG4**), economic growth (**SDG8**), indus-trialization (**SGD9**), cities and communities (**SDG11**), and societies and institutions (**SDG16**). *Resilience* is used in reference to infrastructure (**SDG9**) and cities and communities (**SDG11**) and – at the target level – to agricultural practices and buildings. *Equality* has a positive framing in **SDG5** (gender equality) and a negative frame in **SDG10** (reduce inequalities). At the target level, equality is mostly used in the context of 'equal rights' (to economic resources), 'equal pay' (for work of equal value), 'equal access' (to education and justice) and 'equal opportunities'. Closely related to inclu-siveness and the 'no one left behind' philosophy that underlies the entire SDG-agenda, is the *access to* frame. 'Access' is stressed in **SDG7** (afford-able, reliable and sustainable energy) and **SDG16** ('access to justice for all'). At the target level, however, no less than 37 references to 'access' can be found – ranging from access to 'safe and nutritious food', 'safe and affordable drinking water', 'land', 'marine resources', 'genetic resources and seed', to 'health-care services', 'essential medicines and vaccines', 'quality education', 'financial services', 'the Internet', 'safe and affordable housing', 'transport systems', 'public spaces' and 'markets'.

SDG ALIGNMENT FICHE #7
Sustainable Communications Management

Selected SDG lenses	12 RESPONSIBLE CONSUMPTION AND PRODUCTION	16 PEACE, JUSTICE AND STRONG INSTITUTIONS	17 PARTNERSHIPS FOR THE GOALS	5Ps
SDG-targets	12.6	16.5; 16.7; 16.10; 16.b	17.14; 17.16; 17.19	
Internally actionable targets (Tool #10.1)	Avoid doing harm	• External reporting on sustainability • No corruption and bribary • Accountable and transparent governance • Responsive and inclusive decision-making at all levels • Tools to monitor impacts on sustianable development		
	Doing good	• External reporting on sustainability • Data availability and public access to information • Partnerships with the public and civil society sector		

■ **Controversy reporting:** all 'sustainable corporate stories' contain decisive moments of reflection and redirection that were triggered by incidents and controversy (Chapter 7) – the so-called 'wake-up call'. Accountable and credible SDG reporting implies that harmful incidents are analysed and reported on, preferably in conjunction with a plan for structural improvements. Typical controversies with damaging SDG impact include tax evasion (**17.1**), corruption and bribery (**16.5**), human rights violations in the value chain (**8.7**), sexual harassment (**5.2**), food safety issues (**2.1**), privacy infringements (**16.10**); child labour (**16.2; 8.7**), oil spills and pollution (**SDG13; 14; 15**); substance abuse, alcohol and drug-induced addiction (**3.5**), power abuse in markets and value chains – such as insider trading (**SDG16**), outright collusion (**SDG17**), and all controversies related to reliably and truthfully reporting on the organization's SDG approach.

11.10.8 The internal SDG nexus challenge: exploring the potential for leverage

Adopting the SDG-agenda presents an organization with a great number of internal alignment options. By (vertically) integrating and (horizontally) coordinating 'top-down' and 'bottom-up' sustainability approaches around cross-linked SDG(-target)s, organizations are better able to create leverage, manage trade-offs, and achieve greater coherence to overcome intention-realization gaps. Ultimately, the real-world impact of any corporate SDG strategy hinges on the ability to identify those SDG-targets that can be meaningfully and action-ably implemented across functional-level strategies. By making full use of the 'internal SDG nexus' potential, organizations may carve out change trajectories that are both more efficient and effective, as well as lead to greater SDG performance.

This section listed suggested SDG entries for each functional area of management. The 'SDG alignment fiches' indicate that all functional areas can be substantively linked to the SDG-framework, although some functional areas show greater potential to align with SDG-targets than others. The opportuni-ties for internal 'bottom-up' synergies – as embodied by cross-linked SDGs and SDG-targets – can be mapped by combining all functional 'SDG align-ment fiches'. Such an exercise should result in an overview comparable to Figure 11.24.

There is no one-size-fits-all outcome to this mapping exercise. The rele-vance of specific SDG-targets for each functional area – as well as their 'nexus potential' for actionable internal alignment and synergistic value – is organization-specific and context-dependent. Five basic steps can help navigate this process further:

1   **Organize an internal stakeholder meeting.** Comparable to the method of the Stockholm Environmental Institute (SEI) for exploring macro-level link-ages between the SDGs (Box 3.8), a first step can be to organize an internal *SDG synergies* meeting. Representatives of all core functional departments thereto get together to discuss their first selection of relevant SDG-targets, identified and explored on the basis of their functional-level SDG fiche.

2   **Draw a nexus matrix.** Based on the assessments of relevant SDG-targets per functional area, an internal nexus matrix can be composed that shows which SDG-targets are anticipated to reflect a relatively large number of cross-departmental linkages, for which Figure 11.24 provides a basis.

3   **Assess the nature and strength of identified cross-departmental link-ages.** The seven-point scale for weighing SDG interactions – developed by Nilsson and colleagues (Nilsson et al., 2016; 2018). and elaborated in section 2.3.4 – may be used as a tool to assess the positive, negative or neutral character of cross-impacts of SDG-targets on the *functional activi-ties* concerned. The SEI method advises the use of a guiding question to support a cross-impact assessment (Box 3.8). A basic guiding question at the functional level could be: if progress is made by functional department X on SDG-target A, how does that influence progress on the core activities of functional department Y?

SDGs	Purchasing	Operations	Marketing	HRM	Finance	Innovation	Communication
1 NO POVERTY	1.1; 1.2		1.4	1.4	1.4; 1.b;	1.4	
2 ZERO HUNGER	2.3	2.4			2.a		
3 GOOD HEALTH AND WELL-BEING		3.9	3.4; 3.5; 3.7; 3.b	3.8; 3.c	3.c	3.b	
4 QUALITY EDUCATION			4.2; 4.3; 4.7	4.2; 4.3; 4.4; 4.7	4.a	4.4; 4.b	
5 GENDER EQUALITY				5.1; 5.2; 5.5; 5.c			
6 CLEAN WATER AND SANITATION		6.3; 6.4; 6.6	6.1; 6.2		6.a		
7 AFFORDABLE AND CLEAN ENERGY		7.2; 7.3; 7.b	7.1; 7.a		7.1; 7.2; 7.3; 7.a; 7.b	7.a; 7.b	
8 DECENT WORK AND ECONOMIC GROWTH	8.2; 8.5; 8.7; 8.8		8.3; 8.9; 8.10	8.3; 8.5; 8.6; 8.7; 8.8		8.2; 8.3; 8.4	
9 INDUSTRY, INNOVATION AND INFRASTRUCTURE	9.3		9.3		9.1; 9.3; 9.4; 9.5; 9.a; 9.b; 9.c	9.4; 9.5; 9.b	
10 REDUCED INEQUALITIES	10.1			10.3; 10.4	10.4; 10.a; 10.b		
11 SUSTAINABLE CITIES AND COMMUNITIES			11.1; 11.2;		11.1; 11.2; 11.4; 11.5; 11.b; 11.c		
12 RESPONSIBLE CONSUMPTION AND PRODUCTION	12.a	12.2; 12.3; 12.4; 12.5	12.8		12.6; 12.a	12.a	12.6
13 CLIMATE ACTION		13.2	13.3		13.1	13.3	
14 LIFE BELOW WATER		14.1	14.4				
15 LIFE ON LAND		15.1; 15.2; 15.3; 15.4; 15.5; 15.9	15.2		15.a; 15.b		
16 PEACE, JUSTICE AND STRONG INSTITUTIONS				16.2; 16.7;			16.2; 16.5; 16.7; 16.10; 16.b
17 PARTNERSHIPS FOR THE GOALS					17.1; 17.3; 17.5; 17.7;	17.6; 17.7; 17.8; 17.16	17.1; 17.14; 17.16; 17.19

Figure 11.24 Exploring alignment potential – the internal SDG nexus

4   **Combine top-down and bottom-up approaches to the SDGs.** In case 'bottom-up' selections of the most relevant SDGs and SDG-targets substantively diverge from the 'top-down' corporate SDG strategy, extra rounds of internal alignment conversations are needed, in which the degree of (a) complementarity, (b) subsidiarity, and /or (c) conflict between prioritized SDG-targets is identified, analysed and resolved, in order to establish an appropriate level of coherence.

5   **Identify those nodes of activities with the greatest potential to drive the company's SDG performance and societal value creation capacity.** A horizontal (cross-functional) and vertical (top-down/bottom-up) assessment of the potential for strategic alignment with the SDGs, should help reveal which organizational functions are best positioned to take the lead in specific SDG-related activities, as part of the company's *overall* SDG portfolio (elaborated in sections 10.5 and 10.6).

11.11   CONCLUSION, TOOLS AND RESOURCES: FROM TINKERING TO COHERENT FIT

One of the most vicious blind spots for executives is not knowing where in the transition process their organization finds itself – and how big the gap between sustainability intention and realization actually is (Box 11.5). It increases the likelihood of adopting *Key Performance Illusions* – quantifiable targets that do not represent truly relevant intervention points and, therefore, are not very helpful in driving organizational change to higher levels of societal value creation. This chapter introduced a mapping technique to navigate 'operational fit' across organizational activities by linking 'internal alignment' challenges to Key Value Indicators (KVIs) and Key Decision-making Indicators (KDIs) in seven distinct functional areas of management (Figure 11.2). We introduced Key Performance Questions (KPQs) and Key Practice/Performance Indicators (KPIs) for each organizational function, to specify the indicative challenges, questions and choices – at four levels of engagement and three transitioning phases – that companies face when trying to operationalize their strategic intent. Combined, these functional-level 'maps' help create insight into the degree of (vertical) integration achieved and the (horizontal) coordination needed to establish operational coherence in the company's sustainability approach. 'Practice mapping' informs the dynamic process of strategy-making ('strategic tinkering') by revealing patterns of – and frictions between – 'leading' and 'lagging' functional departments that affect the course and pace of organizational transitioning and, consequently, the feasibility of the transition route envisaged (Figure 11.7).

The operational fit between – on the one hand – the company's strategic intent and – on the other hand – realization of the sustainability strategy across functional departments, can be plotted as relative scores on a continuous scale from 1 to 4. By mapping and scoring the 'position' of each corporate function – along the logic, trade-offs and pointers synthesized in Tables 11.1 to 11.7 – an overview comparable to that of Figure 11.25 can be compiled. The organizational snapshot derived from this practice mapping exercise reflects the degree of 'internal alignment' and operational coherence (or incoherence) of the business model. The degree of coherence can be considered as an indicator of the company's vigour, efficiency and effectiveness in organizing for enhanced sustainability performance and meaningful SDG impact.

Figure 11.25 shows an assessment outcome of two hypothetical situations. Organization #1 portrays a reasonably high degree of coherence across all functional departments around a modest strategic intent (at level 2), with the marketing department running ahead of the corporate sustainability ambition. In contrast, organization #2 presents a relatively *in*coherent organization and low degree of strategy integration (at level 3) among the organizational functions. Whereas the innovation and marketing departments are ahead of the curve and HRM appears to be nearly on course, the purchasing, operations, finance and communication functions are all significantly trailing behind on the corporate ambition level. Accordingly, the odds of having to deal with sizable intention-realization discrepancies seem highest for organization #2. To steer towards greater coherence, then, implies going back to the functional-level maps (Tables 11.1 to 11.7) so as to identify relevant intervention points conducive to overcoming key tipping points, organizational 'barriers' and 'bears on the road' in the corporate functions concerned (Box 11.5). Due care is in order, however, not to attenuate the driving force of frontrunning departments too much. The traction and internal dynamics that 'leading' departments create, may be exactly what is needed for taking the next steps to progression.

In this chapter, we furthermore argued that a well-considered adoption of the SDG-agenda can actually function as a lever for internal alignment. We

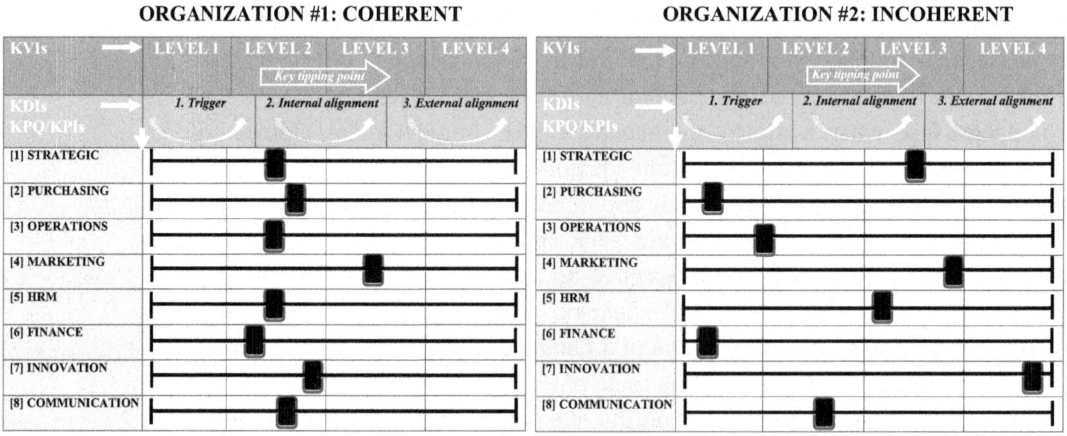

Figure 11.25 Mapping internal alignment challenges

introduced 'SDG alignment fiches' as a practical tool to support the navigation process of aligning core business activities with a *strategically and operationally fit* SDG portfolio. Combined, the 'bottom-up' SDG fiches should help to identify, explore and select internally actionable SDG(-target)s with the potential to: (a) reinforce the ('top-down') corporate SDG portfolio, and (b) streamline and optimize business activities for greater SDG impact. The basic rationale behind this SDG-mapping approach is that by (horizontally) coordinating and (vertically) integrating 'bottom-up' and 'top-down' approaches around 'cross-linked' SDG-targets – denoted in this chapter as *internal nexus* – organizations are better able to exploit synergies, manage trade-offs and achieve enhanced operational coherence in contributing to the SDGs. The real-world impact of any corporate SDG strategy ultimately hinges on the organization's ability to identify those SDG-targets that can be meaningfully and actionably implemented across functional-level strategies such that it adds efficiency and effectiveness to societal value creation (Figure 11.26).

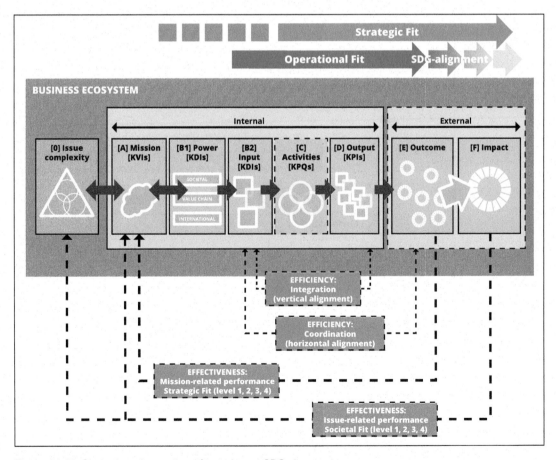

Figure 11.26 Strategic and operational fit – coherent SDG alignment

SDG COMPASS 'PLUS' – SYNTHESIZING TOP-DOWN AND BOTTOM-UP TECHNIQUES

Since the launch of the SDG-agenda in September 2015, a considerable number of tools and guidance frameworks have been devised to stimulate and facilitate SDG implementation by private sector organizations. Throughout the chapters of this book, we mentioned quite a few of them. Of particular relevance for SDG prioritization, alignment and measurement purposes, is the *SDG Compass*. It was prepared by a coalition of three key global stakeholders in the SDG discourse – the UN Global Compact, the Global Reporting Initiative (GRI) and the World Business Council for Sustainable Development (WBCSD) – following a trajectory of multi-stakeholder engagement and "feedback received through three consultation periods from companies, government agencies, academic institutions and civil society organizations worldwide".

The SDG Compass aims to provide guidance for (multinational) companies on how they can align their strategies and measure and manage their contributions to achieving the SDGs. The guide uses a 'five steps' process approach for identifying and prioritizing SDGs, taking action (operationalizing, integrating), and transparently communicating and reporting on realized SDG performance. The SDG Compass Guide thereby emphasizes an approach of *principled prioritization*, in alignment with key international frameworks, principles and guidelines as defined by the ILO, UN Global Compact, UN, ISO, OECD and GRI. Application of the five-step approach is further supported by a comprehensive inventory of existing business tools and business indicators from widely recognized sources – all mapped against the SDGs and SDG-targets.

The SDG Compass presents a 'top-down' guidance instrument for corporate action. It was designed for use 'at entity level' and, accordingly, begins (step 1) with understanding SDG-related opportunities and responsibilities from the angle of the company as a whole. Its logic model (step 2) takes the value chain as analytical starting

STEP 1	Understanding the SDGs	• What are the SDGs? • Understanding the business case • The baseline responsibilities for business
STEP 1A	Take a step back: contextualize for actionability	• Determine the value orientation and KVIs (Chapter 9) • Determine the power base and KDIs (Chapter 10) • Consider the interventions needed to establish 'complexity fit', 'value orientation fit', and 'strategic fit' (section 10.6)
STEP 2	Defining priorities	• Map the value chain to identify impact areas • Select indicators and collect data (using a logic model) • Define (strategic) priorities

B
O
X

11.22

STEP 2A	Take a deep dive: assess bottom-up dynamics and SDG entries (Chapter 11)	• Determine the intention-realization gap (section 11.2) • Map the sustainability practices of each functional area of management (Key Performance Questions and Key Practice Indicators, at levels 1, 2, 3, 4 (sections 11.3–11.9) • Explore internal SDG synergies (using SDG alignment fiches) by defining internally actionable (cross-linked) targets, through internal stakeholder involvement (section 11.10.8)
STEP 3	**Setting goals**	• Define scope of goals and select KPIs • Define baseline and select goal type (inside-out; outside-in) • Set level of ambition • Announce commitment to SDGs
STEP 4	**Integrating**	• Anchoring sustainability goals within the business • Embed sustainability across all functions • Engage in partnerships
STEP 5	**Reporting and communicating**	• Effective reporting and communication • Communicating on SDG performance

point for mapping high-impact areas of present business activities, to identify strategic priorities across the SDG-framework. This exercise then boils down to goal-setting, establishing ambition levels and the definition of KPIs to drive performance (step 3), after which 'lead from the top' should ensure that sustainability goals are effectively integrated into the core business and embedded into all functional areas concerned (step 4). Step 5, finally, is to effectively report and communicate about material sustainability performance and SDG contributions.

The SDG Compass 'five-steps' method can be further fine-tuned and complemented with the frameworks and (mapping) techniques introduced in Part III of this book:

■ First, by realizing that the search for coherent SDG alignment requires processes of strategic tinkering to navigate both *strategic and operational fit* (section 10.6). Value orientation, sphere of influence and strategic power base – captured in KVIs and KDIs (Chapters 9 and 10) – define strategic intent, the degree of actionability and the level of SDG engagement envisaged.

■ Second, overcoming the *intention-realization gap* necessitates a more fine-grained understanding of how ('top-down', strategic) KDIs translate into functional-level practices, such that *key tipping points* and organizational barriers to greater sustainability performance and SDG impact can be successfully surpassed. Concrete, actionable and meaningful goals – in terms of Key

Practice and Performance Indicators (KPIs) – can only be established when input from *bottom-up approaches* has been taken into due account.

Integrating the insights of this chapter into the SDG Compass method, requires companies to: (a) 'take a step back' and *contextualize* for meaningful *actionability*, and (b) 'take a deep dive' into the sustainability ambitions, practices and realities of their functional departments, to consider *functional-level (cross)linkages with the SDGs* as well. To this end, we added two additional steps to the five-step approach of the SDG Compass (step 1a and 2a). Figure 11.27 portrays top-down and bottom-up approaches to SDG alignment as mutually complementary and mutually reinforcing processes.

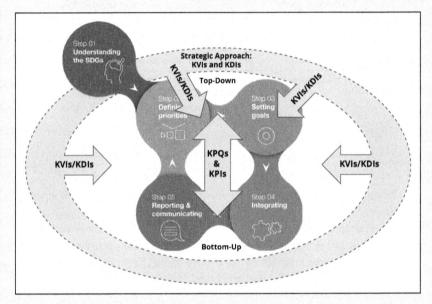

Figure 11.27 Complementary approaches to prioritizing SDGs: SDG Compass 'Plus'

More information on SDG Compass: see https://sdgcompass.org/

■ **GRI and UN Global Compact:** provide essential tools and guidance for integrating the SDGs into sustainability reporting. Recent tools include: (1) *Analysis of the goals and targets* – a handbook of indicators to make reporting on the SDGs straightforward and simple to execute; (2) *Integrating the SDGs into corporate reporting: A practical guide* – a three-step guide to embed the SDGs in existing business and reporting processes; (3) *Linking the SDGs and the GRI Standards* – shows the disclosures within the GRI Standards that can be used to report on specific SDGs and their targets; (4) *In focus: Addressing investor needs in business reporting on the SDGs* – a guide to addressing investor needs within reporting. GRI's resource centre provides access to the latest GRI Standards, as well as articles, research and videos supportive to sustainability reporting. https://www.globalreporting.org/how-to-use-the-gri-standards/resource-center/

■ **International Integrated Reporting Council (IIRC):** a global coalition of regulators, investors, companies, standard-setters, the accounting profession, academia and NGOs that promotes sustainability-aligned 'integrated reporting and thinking' within mainstream business practice as the norm in public and private sectors. It encourages businesses to align their value creation models with the SDGs and to use relevant metrics. IIRC's *International Integrated Reporting Framework* (January 2021) guides organizations in bringing together material information about strategy, governance, performance and prospects for value creation, in a way that: (a) reflects the commercial, social and environmental context; (b) enhances accountability and stewardship for the broad base of capitals; and (c) promotes an understanding of their interdependencies. https://integratedreporting.org/resources/

■ **UNDP's SDG Impact Standards Enterprises:** are provided as a best practice guide and self-assessment tool for integrating impact management into organizations' internal management and decision-making processes to optimize their contributions to the SDGs. The standards are *for all organizations* – regardless of size, geography, sector, for-profit and non-profit orientation. They are not reporting standards, but 'management standards' that focus on the alignment of internal processes, practices and decision-making in line with achieving sustainable development outcomes. Voluntary, independent assurance against the standards and an SDG Impact Seal and associated governance are being developed. https://sdgimpact.undp.org/enterprise. html. UNDP has also developed SDG Impact Standards for Bond Issuers and Private Equity Funds https://sdgimpact.undp.org/sdg-bonds.html; https://sdgimpact.undp. org/private-equity.html

■ **The Impact Management Project (IMP):** a public interest forum for building global consensus on measuring, managing and reporting impacts on sustainability, of relevance for organizations that want to manage environmental, social and governance (ESG) risks as well as contribute positively to Global Goals. IMP convenes over 2,000 practitioners (enterprises and investors) and facilitates the IMP Structured Network – a collaboration of 16 global standard-setting organizations (including GRI, GIIN,

UNGC, SASB, CDP, WBA, IIRC, OECD, PRI, UNDP) to build consensus on standards in three areas: (1) processes for managing impacts (practice); (2) frameworks and indicators for measuring and reporting impacts (performance); and (3) valuation for comparing impacts (benchmarking). Provides resources, examples, worksheets and an extensive 'impact management' glossary. https://impactmanagementproject.com/about/

■ **SDG Compass:** an essential guide for business action on the SDGs, developed by GRI, UN Global Compact and WBCSD. Provides a useful five-step framework for companies, offering guidance on aligning their strategies and measuring and managing contributions to achieve the SDGs. Further, the *Inventory of Business Indicators* searchable database maps around 1,600 existing, commonly used, robust and applicable business indicators against the SDGs, https://sdgcompass.org/business-indicators/. Furthermore, the *'Inventory of Business Tools'* provides an overview of 58 business tools that are useful when assessing your organization's impact on the SDGs, https://sdgcompass.org/business-tools/

■ **WBCSD SDG Sector Roadmaps:** a set of guidelines which provide a structured approach that companies can follow as they embark upon SDG road-mapping for their sector. The framework seeks to lead companies through a process of establishing their sector's current level of SDG engagement throughout the value chain, identifying the sector's most significant opportunities for impact, and establishing key action items and monitoring systems to chart a course for action. https://www.wbcsd.org/Programs/People/Sustainable-Development-Goals/SDG-Sector-Roadmaps/Resources/SDG-Sector-Roadmaps. The WBCSD Business Hub further informs on developments, latest insights and trends on the SDG to support business in navigating their course of SDG action. https://sdghub.com/

■ **The Future-Fit Business Benchmark:** a free business tool designed to understand, set, measure and disclose "real progress toward a flourishing future – and make the SDGs a reality". The Benchmark is a self-assessment approach which equips companies to manage and improve their social and environmental performance, in alignment with the SDGs. A *Methodology Guide*, *Positive Pursuit Guide*, *Implementation Guide* and *Action Guide* help organizations to analyse opportunities and risks, by quantifying the social and environmental impacts of all day-to-day decisions in a holistic way. The Benchmark consists of 23 'Break-Even Goals' (which all companies must strive to reach) and 24 'Positive Pursuits' (to create and contribute to positive impacts), to assess and communicate the extent of a company's negative and positive societal contributions. https://futurefitbusiness.org/benchmark-documents/

■ **SDG Action Manager:** a (multi-user) web-based 'impact management' tool – developed by B Lab and the UN Global Compact – that enables businesses to identify risks areas, track improvement, access resources, and manage impact on the SDGs throughout their operations, supply chain, business model, and collective action. The 'SDG Action Manager' brings together *B Impact Assessment* and the *Ten Principles* *of the UN Global Compact*, to enable meaningful business action through self-assessment, benchmarking, and improvement. https://bcorporation.net/help-build-better-world-sdg-action-manager

■ *UNDP's Business Call to Action Impact Lab:* helps companies develop an SDG-focused impact framework for data collection, analysis and reporting. Four self-paced modules support companies to drive business value while also delivering impact by understanding, proving, and improving their contributions to the SDGs. Through a step-by-step process, the tool facilitates the process of defining a theory of change linking business operations to the SDGs, designing an SDG impact framework with a plan for collecting data that will allow you to measure, manage and communicate business impact. Case studies illustrate how inclusive businesses are measuring and managing their impact. https://impactlab.businesscalltoaction.org/

■ *Science Based Targets Network:* (part of the 'Global Commons Alliance') aims to transform economic systems and protect the global commons – air, water, land, biodiversity and ocean – by developing methods (for cities and companies) to set science-based, integrated targets for an *equitable, nature positive, net zero future*. By developing measurable, actionable, and time-bound objectives based in the best available science, SBTN equips businesses with guidance to move from doing "a little less bad" to "doing its fair share" to maintain the global commons and societal sustainability goals. https://sciencebasedtargetsnetwork.org/resources/

■ *IRIS+ Catalog of Metrics:* provides generally accepted core metrics (numerical and qualitative values) aligned to common 'impact themes' and the SDGs (at the target level). It can be searched by impact category, specific SDGs, dimensions of impact (what, who, scale, depth, duration contribution), operational impact, environmental or social focus, etc. IRIS+ is the generally accepted system for impact investors to measure, manage, and optimize their impact in a detailed, contextualized, consistent and powerful way. The full catalog is offered as a free, publicly available resource (searchable and downloadable) – managed by the Global Impact Investing Network (GIIN) and aligned with over 50 standards bodies to cover diverse industry types and disclosure requirements. IRIS+ can be used by investors, companies, researchers and others to implement and produce data according to any framework, assessment or reporting tool. https://iris.thegiin.org/metrics/

■ *The Value Balancing Alliance:* a non-profit alliance of multinational companies, founded in 2019, coming together with a common goal: to create a reliable global impact measurement standard for disclosing positive and negative impacts of corporate activity on people and the environment, and to provide guidance on how these impacts can be integrated into business steering. Companies play a crucial role to enable sustainable and inclusive value creation; it is hence paramount to identify, understand and ultimately manage businesses multiple impacts on society. The alliance is supported by major accounting firms, researchers and academia, in close cooperation with standard-setters. https://www.value-balancing.com/en/downloads.html; https://www.value-balancing.com/en/our-work.html

SELECTED WEB RESOURCES

- **Climate Disclosure Project (CDP):** a not-for-profit organization that runs the global disclosure system for investors, companies, cities, states and regions to manage their environmental impacts. CDP works with intergovernmental agencies, governments, business and regional associations, NGOs and financial organizations around the world to drive action for a sustainable economy. In 2020, 9,600+ companies – representing over 50% of global market capitalization – disclosed through CDP on their environmental performance. CDP annually discloses its *A List* of companies and cities that managed to score an 'A' on climate change, forests and/or water security actions. https://www.cdp.net/en/companies/companies-scores. CDP's *Open Data Portal* provides access to climate-related datasets (e.g. emissions, climate actions, climate risks) for 812 cities and 131 states and regions: https://data.cdp.net/

- **The Human Rights Guide to the SDGs:** open-access searchable database – developed by the Danish Institute for Human Rights – that demonstrates how the SDGs relate to 35 human rights and labour conventions and more than 50 global and regional human rights instruments. An essential tool to help: (1) understand the linkages between the SDGs and human rights, labour standards and environmental treaties and instruments; (2) develop a human rights-based approach to sustainable development programming, implementation, monitoring, evaluation and reporting; (3) understand the linkages between regional and international human rights instruments and environmental treaties https://sdg.humanrights.dk

- **Human rights tools:** the Danish Institute for Human Rights provides an extensive set of business-relevant, instructive tools and guidance instruments aimed at fulfilling responsibilities to protect and promote human rights. Tools include: (1) human rights-related environmental, social and health impact assessments; (2) country-specific guidance on human rights; (3) assessments for state-investor negotiations; (4) Indigenous Navigator Tools Database; (5) due diligence processes; (6) learning hub on human rights, https://www.humanrights.dk/tools, and (7) *Human Rights Indicators for Business*, https://www.humanrights.dk/projects/human-rights-indicators-business. The Institute's *Human Rights Guide to the SDGs* provides a searchable database – with entries via 17 SDGs and 169 SDG-targets – that shows the concrete linkages between the SDGs and the relevant range of: (a) international and regional human rights instruments; (b) international labour standards, and (c) key environmental instruments with human rights dimensions, https://sdg.humanrights.dk/

- **WageIndicator Foundation:** promotes labour market transparency for the benefit of employers, employees and workers worldwide, by sharing and comparing information on wages, labour law and career. It is active in more than 140 countries, includes both the formal and informal sector, and maps the labour market also in countries where information is not on paper or digital. WageIndicator organizes several databases on international comparable 'minimum wages', 'living wages', actual wages, wages in Collective Agreements, 'decent work', and international comparable labour laws. https://wageindicator.org/salary/wages-in-context

■   ***Better Business Scan:*** helps to gain insight into the sustainability ambitions of yourself and your company and how you can take these ambitions further. It maps out where in the change process you and your company currently are, and what challenges this position entails. The answers given to a concise survey are placed in several analytical frameworks based on insights from recent scientific research into sustainable business models. The scan covers: (a) your ambition and motivation for sustainability, (b) which sustainable business case you are currently embracing, (c) what the associated barriers and success factors are, (d) which functional management areas may need additional attention, and (e) which leadership challenges you are facing. https://www.betterbusinessscan.org/resources-towards-a-better-understanding/

S E L E C T E D   W E B   R E S O U R C E S

REFERENCES

Adams, C.A. (2017). *The Sustainable Development Goals, integrated thinking and the integrated report*, published by IIRC and ICAS.

Adams, R., Jeanrenaud, S., Bessant, J., Denyer, D. & Overy, P. (2016). 'Sustainability-oriented Innovation: A Systematic Review', *International Journal of Management Reviews*, 18:180–205.

Aggarwal, V.A., Posen, H.E. & Workiewicz, M. (2017). 'Adaptive Capacity to Technological Change: A micro-foundational approach', *Strategic Management Journal*, 38(6):1212–1231.

Akhavan, R.M. & Beckmann, M. (2017). 'A configuration of sustainable sourcing and supply management strategies', *Journal of Purchasing & Supply Management* (23):137–151.

Aldy, J.E. & Gianfrate, G. (2019). 'Future-Proof Your Climate Strategy', *Harvard Business Review*, May-June issue, pp. 86–97.

Ambec, S. & Lanoie, P. (2008). 'Does It Pay to be Green? A Systemic Overview', *Academy of Management Perspectives*, 22(4):45–62.

Antolín-López, R., Delgado-Ceballos, J. & Montiel, I. (2016). 'Deconstructing corporate sustainability: a comparison of different stakeholder metrics', *Journal of Cleaner Production*, 136(A):5–7.

Asif, M., Searcy, C., Zutshi, A. & Fisscher, O.A. (2013). 'An integrated management systems approach to corporate social responsibility, *Journal of Cleaner Production*, 56(1):7–17.

Atasu, A., Corbett, C.J., Huang, X.N. & Toktay, L.B. (2020). 'Sustainable Operations Management Through the Perspective of Manufacturing & Service Operations Management', *Manufacturing & Service Operations Management*, 22(1):147–157.

Aust-Ehnert, I., Matthews, B. & Muller-Camen, M. (2020). 'Common Good HRM: A paradigm shift in Sustainable HRM?', *Human Resource Management Review*, (30):100705.

Blowfield, M. & Murray, A. (2019). *Corporate Responsibility*, 4th edition. Oxford University Press.

Bode, C. & Singh, J. (2018). 'Taking a hit to save the world? Employee participation in a corporate social initiative', *Strategic Management Journal*, 39:1003–1030.

Brown, T. (2008). 'Design Thinking', *Harvard Business Review*, June.

Buhl, A., Schmidt-Keilich, M., Munster, V., Blazejewski, S., Schrader, U., Harrach, C., Schäfer, M. & Süßbauer, E. (2019). 'Design thinking for sustainability: Why and how design thinking can foster sustainability-oriented innovation development', *Journal of Cleaner Production*, 231:1248–1257.

Calik, E. & Bardudeen, F. (2016). 'A measurement scale to evaluate sustainable innovation performance in manufacturing organizations', *Procedia CIRP*, (40):449–454.

Cameron, K.S. & Quinn, R.E. (2011). *Diagnozing and Changing Organizational Culture: Based on the Competing Values Framework*, 3rd edition. San Francisco, CA: Jossey-Bass.

Carayannis, E.G., Grigoroudis, E. & Stamati, D. (2017). 'Re-visiting BMI as an Enabler of Strategic Intent and Organizational Resilience, Robustness, and Remunerativeness', *Journal of the Knowledge Economy*, 8(2):407–436.

Cejudo, G.M. & Michel, C. (2015). 'Addressing fragmented government action: Coordination, coherence, and integration'. *Paper presented at the 2nd International Conference in Public Policy*, Milan, July.

Christensen, C.M. (1997). *The Innovator's Dilemma. When New Technologies Cause Great Firms to Fail*. Boston: Harvard Business School Press.

Cillo, V., Petruzelli, A.M., Ardito, L. & Del Giudice, M. (2019). 'Understanding sustainable innovation: A systematic literature review', *Corporate Social Responsibility and Environmental Management*, 26(1):1012–1025.

Crane, A. & Glozer, S. (2016). 'Researching Corporate Social Responsibility Communication: Themes, Opportunities and Challenges', *Journal of Management Studies*, 53(7):1223–1252.

Davila, T. & Epstein, M.J. (2014). *The Innovation Paradox*. San Francisco: Berrett-Koehler Publishers.

Deloitte (2021). *The Deloitte Global 2021 Millennial and Gen Z Survey: A call for accountability and action.*

Deloitte (2019). *Deloitte's Global Millennial Survey: Exploring A 'Generation Disrupted'.*

Design Council & The Point People (2021). *System-shifting design. An emerging practice explored*, October.

Dundon, T. & Rafferty, A. (2018). 'The (potential) demise of HRM?', *Human Resource Management Journal*, 28:377–391.

Ehnert, I., Parsa, S., Roper, I., Wagner, M. & Muller-Camen, M. (2016). 'Reporting on sustainability and HRM: A comparative study of sustainability reporting practices by the world's largest companies', *The International Journal of Human Resource Management*, 27(1):88–108.

Engert, S. & Baumgartner, R. (2016). 'Corporate sustainability strategy–bridging the gap between formulation and implementation', *Journal of Cleaner Production*, 113:822–834.

EPIC (2018). *The Embankment Project for Inclusive Capitalism Report*. Coalition for Inclusive Capitalism.

Frey, B.S. & Jegen, R. (2001). 'Motivation Crowding Theory', *Journal of Economic Surveys*, 15(5):589–611.

Galeazzo, A., Furlan, A. & Vinelli, A. (2013). 'Lean and green in practice: interdependencies and performance of pollution prevention strategies', *Journal of Cleaner Production*, 85.

Garzón-Jiménez, R. & Zorio-Grima, A. (2020). 'Corporate Social Responsibility and Cost of Equity: Literature Review and Suggestions for Future Research, *Journal of Business Accounting and Finance Perspectives*, 2(3):1–19.

Gaspar, V., Amaglobeli, D., Garcia-Escribano, M., Prady, D. and Soto, M. (2019). *Fiscal Policy and Development: Human, Social, and Physical Investments for the SDGs*. IMF Staff Discussion Note, SDN/19/03.

Gates, B. (2021). *How to Avoid a Climate Disaster: The Solutions We Have and the Breakthroughs We Need*. Allen Lane.

Gerwanski, J. (2020). 'Does it pay off? Integrated reporting and cost of debt: European evidence', *Corporate Social Responsibility Environmental Management*, (27):2299–2319.

Gianfrate, G., Schoenmaker, D. & Wasama, S (2019). 'Cost of capital and sustainability: a literature overview', *Working paper series 03*. Erasmus Platform for Sustainable Value Creation, Rotterdam School of Management/Erasmus University.

Gianni, M., Gotzamani, K. & Tsiotras, G. (2017). 'Multiple perspectives on integrated management systems and corporate sustainability performance', *Journal of Cleaner Production*, 168:1297–1311.

Greenpeace International (2021). *Destruction: Certified. Certification; not a solution to deforestation, forest degradation and other ecosystem conversion*, March.

Gui, L., Huang, N., Atasu, A. & Toktay, L.B. (2016). 'Design Implications of Extended Producer Responsibility Legislation' In: Atasu, A. (Ed.), *Environmentally Responsible Supply Chains* (pp. 339–358). Springer Series in Supply Chain Management.

Hemmati, M. (2002). *Multi-Stakeholder Processes for Governance and Sustainability – Beyond Deadlock and Conflict*. London: Earthscan.

IEA (2020). *World Energy Outlook 2020*. Paris: International Energy Agency.

IFAC (2020). 'The CFO and Finance Function Role in Value Creation'. New York, International Federation of Accountants.

IIRC (2021). *International <IR> Framework, January 2021*. International Integrated Reporting Council.

Ikram, M., Sroufe, R. & Zhang, Q. (2020). 'Prioritizing and overcoming barriers to integrated management system (IMS) implementation using AHP and G-Topsis', *Journal of Cleaner Production*, 245(1): 120121.

ILO (2020). *Global Wage Report 2020–21: Wages and minimum wages in the time of COVID-19*. Geneva: International Labour Organization.

ILO (2019). *Integrated Strategy on Fundamental Principles and Rights at Work 2017–2023*. Geneva: International Labour Office.

ILO (2017). *Tripartite Declaration of Principles concerning Multinational Enterprises and Social Policy*, Fifth Edition, March. Geneva: International Labour Office.

ILO & UNICEF (2021). *Child Labour: Global estimates 2020, trends and the road forward*. New York: International Labour Office and United Nations Children's Fund.

ISO (2020). *ISO 56000, Innovation management – Fundamentals and vocabulary*, First edition, 2020–02.

Jackson, G., Bartosch, J. Avetisyan, E., Kinderman, D. & Steen Knudsen, J. (2020). 'Mandatory Non-financial Disclosure and Its Influence on CSR: An International Comparison', *Journal of Business Ethics*, 162(2):323–342.

Jarzabkowski, P. (2004). 'Strategy as Practice: Recursiveness, Adaptation, and Practices-in-Use', *Organization Studies*, 25(4):529–560.

Kaplan, S. (2008). 'Framing Contests: Strategy Making under Uncertainty', *Organization Science*, 19(5):729–752.

Kaptein, M. & Van Tulder, R. (2003). 'Toward Effective Stakeholder Dialogue', *Business and Society Review*, 108(2):203–224.

Kathuria, R., Joshi, M. & Porth, S. (2007). 'Organizational Alignment and Performance: Past, Present and Future', *Management Decision*, 45(3):503–517.

Kleindorfer, P.R., Singhal, K. & Van Wassenhove, L.N. (2005). 'Sustainable Operations Management', *Production and Operations Management* 14(4):482–492.

Koberg, E. & Longoni, S. (2019). 'A systematic review of sustainable supply chain management in global supply chains', *Journal of Cleaner Production*, (207):1084–1098.

KPMG (2020). *The Time has Come: The KPMG Survey of Sustainability Reporting 2020*, December.

Laursen, K. & Salter, A.J. (2014). 'The paradox of openness: Appropriability, external search and collaboration', *Research Policy*, 43(5):867–878.

Lazer, W. (1969). 'Marketing's changing social relationships', *Journal of Marketing*, 33:3–9.

Li, F. and Polychronopoulos, A. (2020). 'What a Difference an ESG Ratings Provider Makes!', *Research Affiliates*, January.

Linnenluecke, M.K. & Griffiths, A. (2010). 'Corporate sustainability and organizational culture', *Journal of World Business*, 45(4):357–366.

Lock, I. & Seele, P. (2016). 'CSR governance and departmental organization: a typology of best practices', *Corporate Governance*, 16(1):211–230.

Lozano, R. (2015). 'A Holistic Perspective on Corporate Sustainability Drivers', *Corporate Social Responsibility and Environmental Management*, 22(1):32–44.

Machado, C.G., De Lima, E.P., Da Costa, S.E.G., Angelis, J.J. & Mattioda, R.A. (2017). 'Framing maturity based on sustainable operations management principles', *International Journal of Production Economics*, (190):3–21.

Malik, A. (2018). *Strategic Human Resource Management and Employment Relations. An International Perspective*. Springer Nature Singapore.

Martin, D. & Schouten, J. (2012). *Sustainable marketing*. Harlow: Pearson Education.

Matten, D., Crane, A. & Chapple, W. (2003). 'Behind the Mask: Revealing the True Face of Corporate Citizenship', *Journal of Business Ethics*, 45(1/2):109–120.

Mazzucato, M. (2018a). 'The entrepreneurial state: socializing both risks and rewards', *Real-World Economics Review*, (84):201–217.

McDougall, N., Wagner, B. & MacBryde, J. (2021). 'Leveraging competitiveness from sustainable operations: frameworks to understand the dynamic capabilities needed to realise NRBV supply chain strategies', *Supply Chain Management: An International Journal*, February.

McKinsey & Company (2021). 'The state of internal carbon pricing', Strategy & Corporate Finance, February 10.

Migliorelli, M. (2021). 'What Do We Mean by Sustainable Finance? Assessing Existing Frameworks and Policy Risks', *Sustainability*, 13(2):975.

Mintzberg, H. (1980). 'Structure in 5's: A Synthesis of the Research on Organization Design', *Management Science*, 26(3):322–341.

Moon, J., Crane., A & Matten, D. (2005). 'Can Corporations be Citizens? Corporate Citizenship as a Metaphor for Business Participation in Society', *Business Ethics Quarterly*, 15(3):429–453.

Morioka, S.N., Bolis, I., Evans, S. & Carvalho, M.M. (2017). 'Transforming sustainability challenges into competitive advantage: Multiple case studies kaleidoscope converging into sustainable business models', *Journal of Cleaner Production* (167):723–738.

Mousavi, S., Bossink, B. & Van Vliet, M. (2018). 'Microfoundations of companies' dynamic capabilities for environmentally sustainable innovation: Case study insights from high-tech innovation in science-based companies', *Business Strategy and the Environment*, (28):366–387.

Nawaz, W. & Koç, M. (2019). 'Exploring Organizational Sustainability: Themes, Functional Areas, and Best Practices', *Sustainability*, 11(16):4307.

Nie, P., Wang, C. & Cui, T. (2019). 'Players acting as leaders in turn improve cooperation', *Royal Society Open Science* 6(7):190251.

Nielsen, A.E. & Thomsen, C. (2018). 'Reviewing corporate social responsibility communication: a legitimacy perspective', *Corporate Communications: An International Journal*, 23(4):492–511.

Nilsson, M., Chisholm, E., Griggs, D., Howden-Chapman, P., McCollum, D., Messerli, P., Neumann, B., Stevance, A., Visbeck, M. & Stafford-Smith, M. (2018). 'Mapping interactions between the sustainable development goals: lessons learned and ways forward', *Sustainability Science*, 13(6):1489–1503.

Nilsson, M., Griggs, D. & Visbeck, M. (2016). 'Map the interactions between Sustainable Development Goals', *Nature*, 534(7607):320–322.

Nunhes, T., Bernardo, M. & Oliveira, O. (2019). 'Guiding principles of integrated management systems: Toward unifying a starting point for researchers and practitioners', *Journal of Cleaner Production*, (210):977–993.

OECD (2020). *OECD Business and Finance Outlook 2020: Sustainable and Resilient Finance*, OECD Publishing, Paris.

Paauwe, J. & Farndale, E. (2017). *Strategy, HRM, and Performance: A Contextual Approach*, second edition. Oxford: Oxford University Press.

Pellegrini, C., Annunziata, E., Rizzi, F. & Frey, M. (2019). 'The role of networks and sustainable intrapreneurship as interactive drives catalyzing the adoption of sustainable innovation', *Corporate Social Responsibility and Environmental Management*, 26(5):1026–1048.

Pfeffer, J. (1993). *Managing with Power. Politics and Influence in Organizations*. Harvard Business Review Press.

Podgorodnichenko, N., Edgar, F. & McAndrew, I. (2020). 'The role of HRM in developing sustainable organizations: Contemporary challenges and contradictions', *Human Resource Management Review*, (30):100685.

PwC (2013). *Supplier Relationship Management. How key suppliers drive your company's competitive advantage*.

Quinn, R.E. (1988). *Beyond rational management: Mastering the paradoxes and competing demands of high performance*. San Francisco, CA: Jossey-Bass.

Quinn, R.E. & Rohrbaugh, J. (1983). 'A spatial model of effectiveness criteria: towards a competing values approach to organizational analysis', *Management Science*, (29):363–377.

Rennings, K. (2000). 'Redefining innovation – eco-innovation research and the contribution from ecological economics', *Ecological Economics*, 32(2):319–332.

Riccaboni, A. & Leone, E.L. (2010). 'Implementing strategies through management control systems: the case of sustainability', *International Journal of Productivity and Performance Management*, 59(2):130–144.

SASB (2020). 'Exposure draft of the SASB Conceptual Framework', August 28, Sustainability Accounting Standards Board.

Schaltegger, S., Harms, D., Windolph, S.E. & Hörisch, J. (2014). 'Involving Corporate Functions: Who contributes to Sustainable Development? *Sustainability*, 6(5):3064–3085.

Schoeneborn, D., Morsing, M. & Crane, A. (2020). 'Formative Perspectives on the Relation Between CSR Communication and CSR Practices: Pathways for Walking, Talking, and T(w)alking', *Business & Society*, 59(1):5–33.

Schoenherr, T. (2012). 'The role of environmental management in sustainable business development: A multi-country investigation', *International Journal of Production Economics*, 140(1):114–128.

Schoenmaker, D. & Schramade, W. (2019). *Principles of Sustainable Finance*. Oxford University Press.

Seuring, S. & Müller, M. (2008). 'From a literature review to a conceptual framework for sustainable supply chain management', *Journal of Cleaner Production*, 16(15):1699–1710.

Siegrist, M., Bowman, G., Mervine, E & Southam, C. (2020). 'Embedding environmental and sustainability into corporate financial decision-making', *Accounting & Finance*, (60):129–147.

Sheth, J. & Parvatiyar, A. (2021). 'Sustainable Marketing: Market-Driving, Not Market-Driven', *Journal of Macromarketing*, 41(1):150–165.

Shift & WBCSD (2018). *The Human Rights Opportunity. 15 real-life cases of how business is contributing to the Sustainable Development Goals by putting people first.* New York: Shift.

Smith N.C. & Jarisch, D. (2019). 'GSK: Profits, Patents and Patients: Access to Medicines'. In: Lenssen G., Smith N. (eds) *Managing Sustainable Business.* Springer, Dordrecht.

Soppe, A. (2004). 'Sustainable Corporate Finance', *Journal of Business Ethics,* 53(1):213–224.

Stahl, G.K., Brewster, C.J., Collings, D.G. & Hajro, A. (2020). 'Enhancing the role of human resource management in corporate sustainability and social responsibility: A multi-stakeholder, multidimensional approach to HRM', *Human Resource Management Review,* (30):100708.

Suchman, M.C. (1995). 'Managing legitimacy: strategic and institutional approaches', *Academy of Management Review,* 20(3):571–610.

Teece, D. (2007). 'Explicating dynamic capabilities. The nature and microfoundations of (sustainable) enterprise performance', *Strategic Management Journal,* 28(13):1319–1350.

Thaler, R.H. & Sunstein, C.R. (2008). *Nudge: Improving decisions about health, wealth and happiness.* New Haven, CT: Yale University Press.

Tidd, J. (2021). 'A review and critical assessment of the ISO56002 innovation management systems standard: evidence and limitations', *International Journal of Innovation Management,* 25(1).

Tidd, J. & Bessant, J. (2021*). Managing innovation. Integrating technological, market and organizational change,* 7th edition, Wiley.

True Price, Deloitte, EY & PwC (2017). The Business Case for True Pricing; Why you will benefit from measuring, monetizing and improving your impact, second edition.

Unerman, J., Bebbington, J. & O'Dwyer, B. (2018). 'Corporate reporting and accounting for externalities', *Accounting and Business Research,* 48(5):497–522.

UNDP (2021). *SDG Impact Standards Enterprises. Integrating impact management into Enterprises' decision-making to optimize their contributions to sustainable development and the SDGs.* Second public consultation draft, March.

UN Global Compact (2020). 'UN Global Compact defines new level of ambition for corporate sustainability', 9 June 2020. https://www.unglobalcompact.org/news/4575-06-09-2020.

UN Global Compact & Russell Reynolds Associates (2020). *Leadership for the Decade of Action,* New York.

UN Inter-agency Task Force on Financing for Development (2020). *Financing for Sustainable Development Report 2020.* New York: United Nations.

Vachani, S. & Smith, N.C. (2004). 'Socially Responsible Pricing: Lessons from the Pricing of AIDS Drugs in Developing Countries', *California Management Review,* 47(1):117–144.

Van Oorschot, M.M.P., Kok, M.T.J. & Van Tulder, R. (2020). *Business for biodiversity. Mobilising business towards net positive impact.* PBL Netherlands Environmental Assessment Agency, The Hague.

Van Riel, C. & Fombrun, C. (2007). *Essentials of Corporate Communication: Implementing Practices for Effective Reputation Management,* Routledge.

Van Tulder, R. (2018a). *Getting all the Motives Right. Driving International Corporate Responsibility (ICR) to the Next Level.* Rotterdam: SMO.

Van Tulder, R., Van Tilburg, R., Francken, M. & Da Rosa, A. (2014). *Managing the Transition to a Sustainable Enterprise. Lessons from Frontrunner Companies.* London: Routledge.

Van Tulder, R., Van Wijk, J. & Kolk, A. (2009). 'From chain liability to chain responsibility, *Journal of Business Ethics,* (85):299–412.

Van Tulder, R., Kaptein, M., Van Mil, E.M. & Schilpzand, R. (2004). *De Strategischeet Stakeholderdialoog. Opkomst, succesfactoren, toekomst.* Erasmus University Rotterdam, Schuttelaar & Partners.

Van Zanten, J.A. & Van Tulder, R. (2018). 'Multinational enterprises and the Sustainable Development Goals: An institutional approach to corporate engagement', *Journal of International Business Policy*, (1):208–233.

Varey, R.J. & Pirson, M. (2014). *Humanistic Marketing*. London: Palgrave Macmillan.

Wang, S., Su, D., Ma, M. & Kuang, W. (2021). 'Sustainable product development and service approach for application in industrial lightning products', *Sustainable Production and Consumption,* (27):1808–1821.

WBCSD (2021). *Vision 2050. Time to Transform. How business can lead the transformations the world needs*. Geneva: World Business Council for Sustainable Development.

WBCSD (2002) *Stakeholder dialogue: the WBCSD approach to engagement,* Switzerland.

WBCSD & DNV GL (2018). *Business and the SDGs: A survey of WBCSD members and Global Network partners*. World Business Council for Sustainable Development, July.

Weaver, G.R., Trevino, L.K. & Cochran, P.L. (1999). 'Integrated and decoupled corporate social performance: Management commitments, external pressures, and corporate ethics practices', *Academy of Management Journal*, 42(5):539–552.

Whetten, D.A. & Cameron, K.S. (2008). *Developing Management Skills*, 7th Edition. Upper Saddle River: Prentice Hall.

White, K., Habib, R. & Hardisty, D.J. (2019). 'How to SHIFT Consumer Behaviors to be More Sustainable: A Literature Review and Guiding Framework', *Journal of Marketing*, 83(3):22–49.

White, K. & Habib, R. (2018). *SHIFT. A review and framework for encouraging environmentally sustainable consumer behaviour*, Sitra Studies 132. Erweko, Helsinki.

Whitelock, V.G. (2019). 'Multidimensional environmental social governance sustainability framework: Integration, using a purchasing, operations, and supply chain management context', *Sustainable Development*, (27):923–931.

WEF (2020). *Measuring Stakeholder Capitalism: Towards Common Metrics and Consistent Reporting of Sustainable Value Creation*, White Paper, September.

Young, D. & Reeves, M. (2020). 'The Quest for Sustainable Business Model Innovation', *BCG Henderson Institute Newsletter*, March 10.

12 MAKING IT COLLABORATIVE

THE PARTNERSHIP CHALLENGE

DOI: 10.4324/9781003098355-15

■ **'Partnering' as a principle:** cross-sector collaboration has become a defining concept for sustainable and inclusive development. *Partnering* is one of the five foundational principles underpinning the SDGs – next to *People*, *Planet*, *Peace* and *Prosperity*.

■ **Partnership 'fit' principles:** cross-sector partnerships that are impact-driven, adaptively optimize for (1) issue-partnering fit; (2) dynamic fit; (3) partner fit; (4) cultural fit; (5) strategic fit, (6) complexity fit, (7) SDG-fit. Effective partnerships are 'fit for purpose'.

■ **Collaborative value principle:** value-adding cross-sector partnerships build on the core activities, capabilities, power bases and distinct strengths of partners. The *additionality* and collaborative value that can ultimately be created comes from appreciating, harnessing and leveraging partners' *complementarities*, whilst also supporting the needs, interests and 'value proposition' of each participating partner. Partners share the risks and benefits of the partnership's investments, accomplishments and societal legitimacy.

■ **What a cross-sector partnership is *not*:** ≠ a project; ≠ a sponsoring relationship; ≠ a supply-chain relationship based on transactional market principles only; ≠ an unequal relationship; ≠ an alliance without complementary capabilities and/or shared goals.

■ **The 'missing partner' principle:** 'coalitions of the willing' are the easiest partnerships to strike but seldom meet the necessary 'fit' conditions to be effective, efficient and impactful (because of crowding out, overshooting or undershooting effects). Timely identification of missing yet crucial stakeholders allows for purposive reconfiguration to evolve into a 'coalition of the needed'.

■ **Principles of Partnership:** a principles-based approach to cross-sector partnering includes defining, adopting and committing to partnership-specific principles. Fundamental CSP principles at least cover: (1) equality and mutual respect, irrespective of size and power; (2) transparency, information-sharing, dialogue and timely consultation; (3) a result-oriented and reality-based approach grounded in effective capabilities and operational capacities; (4) responsibility, integrity, commitment; (5) complementarity that builds on partners' comparative advantage, (6) development of a 'common language', mutual understanding and trust-building.

■ **Principles of developmental evaluation (DE):** recognize that *ex ante* formulated intervention strategies ('Theory of Change') must be designed in a 'complexity-sensitive' way and allow for timely adaptation as needs, findings and insights emerge. DE takes a 'learning and adjusting while doing' approach to partnership interventions: fast learning cycles in order to co-create, implement and integrate ever more effective intervention approaches along the way. Instituting an *Impact Team* – as a practical approach to applying DE principles – can help partnering organizations navigate and keep track of *impact loops*.

■ **Ten partnership brokering principles:** internal and external partnership brokers have a pivotal role in *raising the bar* for effective partnering and optimizing collaborative action for the SDGs. Relevant principles to guide the intermediary role of partnership brokers in shaping and driving transformational change include: (1) break through assumptions, be prepared to challenge; (2) relish diversity; (3) properly value different contributions; (4) develop skills in collaboration brokering and collective leadership; (5) understand systems and contexts; (6) apply the highest standards, rigour and accountability; (7) invest in optimal partnering processes, but refrain from promoting partnering in case of alternatives; (8) learn, and be prepared to change course; (9) understand own limitations and abilities; (10) understand that partnering is a means, not an end in itself.

12.1 INTRODUCTION: MAKING THE COLLABORATIVE PARADIGM WORK FOR THE SDGs

"If, working apart, we are a force powerful enough to destabilize our planet, surely working together we are powerful enough to save it"
Richard Attenborough, COP26 (1 November 2021)

If you want to go fast, go alone;
If you want to come far, go together
African proverb

You don't partner because you trust each other;
You trust each other because you (try to) partner
The claim of this chapter

For effective sustainability strategies and their operationalization, effective external alignment with a wide diversity of stakeholders has become imperative. Harvard professor James Austin (2000) was the first to label the emergent phenomenon of strategic collaboration between business and non-profit stakeholders as "the collaborative paradigm of the 21st century". Stakeholder engagement around a common goal has taken many forms: from platforms, coalitions, councils and networks, to roundtables covenants and compacts. They range from relatively loose alliances to highly formalized arrangements. The frame most commonly used for these alliances is 'partnerships'. Those collaborations that bridge different societal sectors (public, private, for-profit, non-profit) are denoted as 'cross-sector partnerships' (CSPs). CSPs represent an increasingly important strategic and operational area for those organizations that want to push for transformational change and address societal (wicked) problems in an impactful way (Part II). The potential is clear: by sharing information, linking resources and combining complementary capabilities, organizational logics and activities, CSPs can attain issue-specific outcomes that no organization (or sector) could achieve on its own. CSPs can provide access to different competencies, means and alternative ways of 'getting things done', and offer a space in which organizations from various societal backgrounds can build new sources of trust (section 5.4). Partnerships, therefore, present a dedicated next phase in external alignment *beyond* generic and oftentimes reactive 'multi-stakeholder engagement' and 'stakeholder management' processes that many organizations have adopted as part of their CSR and issues-management strategy (Chapter 9).

CSPs are by now widely recognized as a key enabler and the principal way forward to serve sustainable development goals. Already in 2002 – as an outcome of the Johannesburg World Summit on Sustainable Development – the global development community introduced 'partnering' with the private sector as one of the Millennium Development Goals (MDG8). The SDG-agenda gave further impetus to this effort by designating 'partnerships for the goals' as a separate goal (SDG17) and *Partnering* as one of the five foundational principles underlying all 17 SDGs – next to *People*, *Planet*, *Peace* and *Prosperity* (Part I). In practice, however, effective CSPs prove difficult to operationalize and to sustain. A global survey on 'external engagement' (McKinsey, 2020), for instance, found that nearly 60% of CEOs rank stakeholder engagement among their top three priorities. However, the survey also indicates vast 'intention-realization' gaps, with merely 7% of respondents stating that their organization regularly aligns the interests of stakeholders and their business. Moving on from external stakeholder engagement to a committed, formal and embedded CSP strategy proves even more challenging – which probably explains why many companies still underutilize the potential of partnerships. UN Global Compact and Russell Reynolds (2020) assessed that only 52% of their signatories are engaging in partnership projects with public or private organizations, whilst endorsing that multi-stakeholder collaboration is key to achieving the transformations and systemic effects needed. Cross-sector collaboration is complex and *collaborative advantage* challenging to create and harness, which is among the primary reasons why progress on the SDGs has been slow. In 2019, UN DESA concluded that despite the strong rhetoric and overwhelming efforts put into partnering around the world, "the reality is that we are still only scratching the surface in terms of the number, and quality, of partnerships required to deliver the SDGs" (UN DESA, 2019).

For many companies, the question is not so much *whether* CSPs are relevant, but rather *how* they can be effectively formed, organized, governed, intensified and phased-out after successful completion – or in case of 'failure'. Partnering is no panacea, and CSP practice has been criticized accordingly. First, for not adequately – or not measurably – addressing those problems that gave rise to the partnership's initiation in the first place. Second, partnerships have underperformed due to sub-optimal partnering configurations and limited ambitions that did not do justice to the actual complexity of the problem (insufficient *issue-complexity fit, issue-partnering fit, partner fit, culture fit* and/or *dynamic fit*, see section 5.5). More than producing 'collaborative solutions' (Hart and Sharma, 2004), ill-aligned partnerships are prone to creating 'collaborative complexities' (Schneider et al., 2017) that get them sidetracked. Third, ill-conceived partnerships have been criticized for undermining the very legitimacy of the CSP phenomenon, owing to overly optimistic or superficial claims, subdued responsibilities or poor governance structures. Concerns over unsubstantiated over-optimism even led to discussions whether the collaborative paradigm should not be rescued from its staunchest supporters and early adopters (Van Tulder, 2017). Lastly, numerous external stakeholder relationships popularly labelled as 'partnerships', are not really partnerships. Prominent examples include sponsoring relations framed as partnership, or buy-sell relations in value chains which, in fact, are market-based transactional relations based on competitive contracts and tenders (sections 10.3.2 and 11.3). Skewed financial relations often create power imbalances and dependencies that may run counter to building a longer-term relationship, creating shared value, and working towards the realization of transformational goals.

WHAT DEFINES A CROSS-SECTOR PARTNERSHIP?

B O X

12.1

Since the start of the millennium, thousands of 'partnerships' were initiated by organizations from all spheres of society (section 5.4.2). Governments introduced developmental-oriented ('soft') public-private partnerships. Companies allied with civil society organizations (CSOs) – and vice versa – to form 'profit-nonprofit' partnerships in order to increase the scale, efficiency and effectiveness of their activities (Seitanidi and Crane, 2014). Partnerships have become part and parcel of corporate strategies seeking 'shared value creation', 'reaching the bottom of the pyramid' and creating 'circular' or 'inclusive' business models (section 9.5). Global multi-stakeholder platforms were established to work towards more sustainable and fair value chains, while numerous non-competitive partnerships and strategic alliances in and across industries have been forged to develop and agree on sustainability-enhancing standards. Over time, a veritable 'jungle' of local, sectoral, national and global collaborative initiatives has emerged – all with varying partner configurations, governance mechanisms, ambitions, scope, leverage, results and impacts.

Reputation Matters...   Size Matters...

One of the conclusions that can be drawn from extant CSP research, however, is that not all stakeholder relationships denoted as 'partnership' can be considered a 'true' partnership, nor are all well-disposed partnerships 'fit for purpose' (section 5.5). It is generally agreed that the notion of 'partnership' should be reserved for collaborations characterized by a high degree of commitment and active involvement from all parties, in contrast to non-committal membership or occasional action. The following features are commonly considered to make a 'true' CSP distinguishable from other forms and notions of multi-stakeholder engagement (e.g. alliances, platforms, cooperations) and non-descript gatherings. These elements constitute defining *starting dimensions* of a CSP. The more (prospective) partners are able (and willing) to create clarity and transparency on these dimensions, the easier it becomes to classify a collaborative relationship as an actual 'partnership'.

■　The partners originate from different societal spheres, which provides them with distinct organizational logics, strengths and core competencies needed for addressing the issue;

- The partners share (sustainable development) objectives, goals and a common vision;
- They benefit from complementarity in resources and competences;
- Partners acknowledge that they cannot address the issue on their own;
- The partners have no problem in becoming (partly) interdependent for the issue at stake;
- Rewards and profits are shared;
- Risks, responsibilities and accountability are shared;
- There is voluntary collaboration and contractual agreement;
- There is a mutually agreed division of labour;
- Decision-making is shared and non-hierarchical;
- Initial trust is not a necessary condition, but all parties should work on building trust-based relationships − based on mutual respect − alongside formalized relationships;
- Each partner works on institutionalizing the partnership in their own organization;
- There is the will to learn from successes and mistakes, and for open discussion if mistakes appear;
- There is an appropriate monitoring and evaluation system in place.

ENHANCING THE TRANSFORMATIONAL POTENTIAL OF CSPs

Effective cross-sector partnering comes with a range of strategic, formational and operational challenges that call for careful consideration. First, partnerships are highly context-dependent, susceptible to change and − like all *strategic* alliances − require considerable formation time. Second, as most societal issues can be qualified as complex 'moving targets', a 'dynamic fit' between the targeted issue and partnership configuration needs to be established (section 5.5), which is not easy to orchestrate or 'design' upfront. Third, partnerships tend to be organized around (practical) 'coalitions of the willing' rather than (strategic) 'coalitions of the needed' that would enable far more optimal results. Lastly, building partnering experience requires a *learning approach*, which calls for an open and reflexive attitude on the part of practitioners, as well as a wider corporate portfolio of sometimes experiential partnerships to enhance learning opportunities. Facilitating learning and adaptation while running partnership implementation processes comes with methodological difficulties in monitoring and evaluation, especially for partnerships that target complex/wicked societal challenges − such as the SDGs. Fortunately, over two decades of research and accumulated practical knowledge on CSPs has yielded helpful insights on partnering processes, goal alignment in collaborative relationships, hybrid governance mechanisms, and developmental evaluation.

Making partnerships work for the SDGs – from the perspective of companies – will be the main concern of this chapter. We further build on the 'partnership configuration' concept and various 'fit' dimensions that were elaborated in Chapter 5, by applying relevant insights and operationalizing key principles of cross-sector partnering. We focus on three aspects that provide fundamental insights on how organizations can initiate, manage and enhance the effectiveness of CSPs for the SDGs, by considering: (1) the kind of choices to be made and the tensions to be addressed along the *partnering cycle* (section 12.2); (b) the 'learning challenge': measuring and improving the impact of the CSP by accounting for four *impact loops* (section 12.3); (c) the strategic challenge: how to reconfigure and manage a *portfolio of diverse partnerships* by using the SDGs as reference frame for partnership portfolio improvements (section 12.4)? Being the last chapter of this book, section 12.5 concludes with an ultimate **personal challenge**: what does it take to become an *SDG professional*?

BOX 12.2

CROSS-SECTOR PARTNERING CASES

Real-life case descriptions on illustrative cross-sector partnerships have been developed for this chapter, each with a specific bearing on key partnering topics and the use of partnerships for the SDGs. The cases are available on this book's accompanying website, which is regularly updated. Each case description contains questions for in-class discussion as well as further reading tips. The footnotes in this chapter indicate when best to use the cases.

- **Case #12.1** – *Jollibee:* getting the system in the room. Creating an inclusive value chain in the Philippines (SDGs 1, 2, 8, 10, 12, 15, 16, 17).

- **Case #12.2** – *Football for Water (F4W):* managing a broad multi-stakeholder alliance (SDGs 3, 4, 6, 17).

- **Case #12.3** – *Upgrading sponsoring relations:* Why is it so difficult?

- **Case #12.4** – *World Ports Sustainability Programme (WPSP):* creating ecosystems for inclusive development (selecting the right portfolio of SDGs).

- **Case #12.5** – *Chevron's partnering portfolio approach:* the challenge of an early and extensive partnership approach (ultimate selection of SDGs 3, 4, 7, 8, 13).

- **Case #12.6** – *TNT-WFP partnership:* moving the world. The problem of trailing institutionalization of one of the earliest global partnerships (SDG2).

- **Case #12.7** – *Safaricom-MPesa:* financial inclusion through partnership; filling the institutional void through partnering (ultimate aim: SDGs 8, 12, 16; intermediary SDGs: 3, 4, 7, 9, 10, 17).

- ■ **Case #12.8** – *Philips-Amref Health Africa:* enhancing and scaling access to primary health care through local pilots (SDGs 3, 12, 13).

- ■ **Case #12.9** – *AkzoNobel-Plan:* strategic realignment. How to learn from misalignment and improve the partnership (SDGs 5, 11)

- ■ **Case #12.10** – *Unilever's Sustainable Living Plan:* the function of an extensive portfolio of partnerships (all SDGs)

Download: www.principlesofsustainablebusiness.nl/cases/

12.2   MANAGING DRIVERS, ADDRESSING TENSIONS ALONG THE PARTNERING CYCLE

Cross-sector partnerships are not easy to build, nor straightforward to manage. There is no 'one-size-fits-all' formula. Most CSPs do not develop as a neat evolutionary 'cycle' of clear-cut stages with a clear beginning (a trigger) and a measurable end; partnerships may already exist and new ones created around a common problem. Partnering cycles – from scoping, scouting and formation, to execution and scaling (or collapse) – are dynamic, and at times even outright chaotic. For obvious reasons: CSPs are formed to deal with complex issues and institutional voids (section 5.4), oftentimes in challenging contexts. All sorts of eventualities can thus be expected. Over time, the initial partners may prove insufficiently geared to address an evolving issue. For some participants, established CSP goals may turn out too ambitious or not ambitious enough. Partnering agreements may be formulated too strictly, be based on mutual distrust, or imbued with control and accountability measures that hamper collaboration and learning. Signing a partnering agreement may turn out to be the start of negotiations, rather than the end of it. In practice, CSP dynamics much resemble strategic tinkering processes (sections 9.2.1 and 11.1) – they are susceptible to all complications that 'hybrid governance' entails (Chapter 6).

Consequently, there are many operational roadblocks along the journey that have to be taken into account. The partnering process confronts organizations with an array of relational and organizational challenges: power differences between parties, trust gaps, funding inequalities, varying ambitions and expectations, transparency and accountability challenges, issues on ownership of the partnering results, (in)equity in the relationship, issue management, profiling desires towards constituencies and financial backers, the need for flexibility and adaptation under VUCA conditions, the proper selection of partners, the direction and optimal pace of progressing, adequate goal-setting and goal alignment, efficiency versus effectiveness considerations, and measurement problems related to ambition and impact levels. The list is long, and increasingly topic of research on the dynamics of CSPs (Gray and Purdy, 2018; Austin and Seitanidi, 2014; Seitanidi and Crane, 2014; Stott, 2019; Murphy and Stott, 2021).

Some of the operational barriers require attention at the start of a new partnership cycle, others can only be managed during implementation and revision phases, while still other developments necessitate a complete redrafting – or termination – of the CSP. Managing these processes from the perspective of an individual organization is part of 'partnership portfolio management' (section 12.4). Cross-sector partnering, in all cases, implies a keen understanding of a whole range of interrelated challenges that affect why, how, and to what end organizations with distinct 'organizational logics' and societal positions interact along various phases of the 'partnering cycle' – as defined by Tennyson (2019).[1]

---

1 Various open-source toolbooks are available: (1) the Partnership Brokers Association (PBA) has produced the classic toolbook in which typical characteristics per node of the partnering cycle are elaborated, as well as the roles that partnership brokers can play in each phase; (2) The Partnering Initiative (TPI) published an SDG Partnership Guidebook in 2020 that uses similar life cycle phases; (3) Herman Brouwer, Jim Woodhill and colleagues developed The MSP Guide (2016) for designing and facilitating effective multi-stakeholder partnerships.

■ *When to start?*

In the so-called **scoping and building phase**, drivers, needs, options and potential partners are identified, which should eventuate in building proper relationships with aligned partners and the signing of a partnering agreement. In this formation phase, foundational decisions are made with significant implications – both intended and unintended – for the CSP's further course of action as well as its effectiveness. It matters, for instance, whether participants are 'opportunity-driven' or 'issue-driven' with regard to the targeted issue. Who has taken the initiative, for what reasons, and how does that influence the choice of partners that were approached – and relevant parties that were not? During the 'building phase', prospective partners are to define their individual and common ambition levels, figure out how they can achieve goal alignment, build up trust, and then strike a proper agreement based on a shared understanding of the partnership's 'intervention logic' – a so-called Theory of Change (see section 5.5). Power imbalances, differences in cultures, organizational logics, ambition levels and expectations may already split up 'needed' partners in this early phase. Partnership building activities are conditioned by already existing partnership configurations and by each party's estimation of whether, how and under what conditions next steps can be satisfactory organized in order to attain the CSP's overall objectives, as well as each organization's own goals.

■ *How to proceed and adapt?*

The second phase of the partnering cycle centres on **managing and maintaining**, which entails processes of governance and structuring, execution and deepening engagement for delivering the intended outcome. The third phase then revolves around **reviewing and revising** processes. The two phases are often presented as separate and sequential. However, this underestimates the relevance of 'reviewing' and 'revising' feedback loops for continuously improving the actual management of the partnership. Increasingly, phase two and three are therefore presented as integrated and reflective. Governance and structuring decisions agreed upon in an earlier stage may need adjustment in view of changing circumstances, goals and 'success criteria'. Partners may decide to withdraw, activities may need restructuring, more dedicated engagement and additional capacities may be required, and learning may prove more important in bringing about the envisaged change than a focus on accountability and control. Are the established governance mechanisms sufficiently flexible to anticipate unforeseen changes, shifting goals, arising tensions, and partners' evolving interests and needs?

■ *When to phase out?*

The fourth phase of the partnering cycle (**sustaining outcomes**) represents the stage in which organizations consider whether to continue, terminate or scale their collaborative activities. Although implying an *ex post* question, in practice it is difficult to define at what point a partnership has actually achieved its goals. Assessments of 'success' and landmarks achieved may differ per participant, depending on whether they consider the partnership as a finite project (with finite funding) or as an continuous relationship. To what extent have ambitions been realized through the partnership, what societal and organizational value has been created, and what effectuated impact is attributable to the CSP? Dimensions for each partner to consider are the extent to which attained outcomes (a) have been the result of their individual contributions and efforts, and (b) could not have been achieved without the collaborative efforts and complementary inputs of others. What 'collaborative value' has been created, seized upon and leveraged, or has the partnership been demanding repeated investments in time, effort and resources without really matching the scale of change intended? If the partnership were to continue, under what conditions could it achieve greater impact in a next cycle?

CAPITA SELECTA

Cross-sector partnering initiatives rarely develop along a neatly defined sequential partnering (life) cycle. Bearing in mind the multifaceted partnering complexities, we can identify *four key themes* that cover basic insights on (1) how partnerships materialize, (2) what factors and dynamics to reckon with to create focus, (3) the type of tensions CSPs generally face, and (4) how fickle processes can be navigated to (iteratively) fine-tune, deepen and upgrade partnering processes, seize 'collaborative advantage' and create impact for the issues at stake:

- **Drivers of CSPs** indicate how initial drivers of inter-organizational collaboration affect strengths and weaknesses of the partnership configuration, and what actions can be considered to create a better 'issue-complexity fit' (section 12.2.1);

- **Goal alignment** requires an understanding of own motivational drivers for a partnership and how to align these with the goals of (potential) partners, to create 'collaborative value' at four ambition levels (section 12.2.2);

- **Tensions** between partnering organizations – arising out of varying objectives and interests, power imbalances, organizational interdependencies and distinct organizational logics and cultures – affect the results-orientation, management and governance of the partnership. Bridging tensions is a balancing act that requires a 'paradox view' on governance approaches and mutual trust-building (section 12.2.3);

■ **The design challenge** for CSPs entails the design of an adaptive intervention strategy – i.e. a 'complexity-sensitive' Theory of Change – the formulation of partnering principles and a comprehensive partnering agreement that articulates the partners' common understanding of the collaborative relationship (section 12.2.4).

12.2.1 Drivers of CSPs: exploration, exploitation and reconfiguration

Partnerships are formed when several stakeholders encounter an urgent problem – or detect a promising opportunity – which they feel they cannot or should not approach on their own. We can distinguish between two types of triggers that, initially, create separate points of departure for successive steps in partnership formation: (1) an 'issue-driven' route, and (2) an 'opportunity-driven' route. The issue-driven route starts from the notion that the targeted societal challenge should be approached as part of a 'wicked problem' (Chapter 4). The opportunity-driven route, on the other hand, departs from the notion that the targeted challenge (also) poses 'wicked opportunities' (Chapter 5). Both routes have a bearing on the mobilization and selection of prospective partners in the 'scoping and building' phase of the CSP, as both routes initially focus the attention on different drivers, motivations, interests, capabilities and risks.

■ **The wicked problem / issue-driven route** is activated by a *sense of urgency* on a specific societal problem felt by several parties, who consider the issue too complex to address on their own, but nevertheless have not yet established any meaningful coalition around this theme. The need, experienced pressure or desire to act upon the issue – felt by at least one (lead) organization – then prompts action to further explore and analyse the issue's nature, scope and degree of complexity (sections 4.3 and 4.4). The impossibility of this issue being solved by one (type of) organization forms a trigger to start searching for partnering solutions. The kind of relationship scouted for is typically based on *co-exploration* motives (Parmigiani and Rivera-Santos, 2011): a cooperative voluntary agreement to *create new* knowledge, tasks, functions or activities, through exchange of ideas, learning and the co-development of solution-oriented novel approaches to the problem as perceived by the parties involved. A co-exploration logic can be motivated by the anticipated benefit of sharing tacit knowledge and combining vital competences and resources possessed by potential partners. Additionally, it may be driven by the need to "develop a reputation with new or different stakeholders on new or different issues", in order to gain legitimacy in environments often characterized by new or underdeveloped institutions (ibid: 1126).

■ **The (wicked) opportunity-driven route** is activated by a more positive prospect: *a sense of opportunity* and the potential to develop a sustainable business case (Chapters 5, 8, 9). This route usually rests on ongoing dialogues between organizations already working together, who wish to leverage the experience and collaborative advantage that their existing partnership could bring to a new challenge. The deepening of the collaborative relationship then rests on *co-exploitation* motives (Parmigiani and Rivera-Santos, 2011): to *execute existing* knowledge, tasks, functions and expand existing activities, in order to seize greater efficiency and derive value from the better use of resources, capacities and investments. Co-exploitation strategies typically seek to leverage resources, connections and reputations with known stakeholders on known issues, in order to harness and transfer their existing legitimacy within or across familiar institutional environments.

RISK FACTORS

Both routes face a number of vulnerabilities stemming from a too strong focus on either 'exploration' or 'exploitation' that could jeopardize the partnership's effectiveness over time. A prominent risk factor of the 'issue-driven route' (and related 'co-exploration' approaches) is that the initiating parties may not succeed in mobilizing the 'right' kind of partners around the issue. Deciding whether or not to participate in cross-sector partnering implies that each party must weigh the (strategic, operational, reputational) risks of *not taking joint action*, versus the *collaborative risk* inherent to reliance on other parties' dedicated commitment to collaboratively work towards resolving the issue. Defensive motivations might prevail, which could restrict partners' willingness to dedicate sufficient time and resources to the collaborative effort, thereby curtailing the possibilities to exploit and leverage each partners' complementary capabilities to their full potential. In later phases, this reticence and a too open set-up can result in an *insufficient dynamic fit* of the partnership configuration (section 5.5.3).

Risk factors of the opportunity-driven route (and related co-exploitation approaches) include the possibility of underestimating – undershooting – the actual complexity of the issue. An opportunity-driven focus may be blind for *contextual risk* and unexplored or ill-considered root causes. Offensive motivations might prevail – reflected in a 'closed' partnership set-up – which can constrain the willingness to explore whether additional partners could add to the effectiveness of the collaboration. In later phases, overoptimism and a closed set-up may eventuate in an *insufficient complexity fit* (section 5.5.3) between the established partnership and the targeted sustainability challenge. There are indications that a considerable number of registered SDG partnerships have taken the 'opportunity-driven route' (Box 12.3).

PARTNERSHIPS FOR THE SDGs: WHAT CHALLENGES EXIST?

The United Nations hosts an online platform that serves as a global registry of voluntary commitments and multi-stakeholder partnerships as a means to facilitate "global engagement of all stakeholders in support of the implementation of the Sustainable Development Goals". The UN defines partnerships as: "voluntary and collaborative relationships between various parties, both public and non-public, in which all participants agree to work together to achieve a common purpose or undertake a specific task and, as mutually agreed, to share risks and responsibilities, resources and benefits". In January 2022, the global registry noted 6,220 partnership commitments, spread as follows over the 17 SDGs:

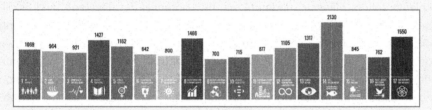

The registry adds considerable legitimacy to the SDG effort, but also reveals a number of weaknesses in listed SDG partnerships – which attests an earlier conclusion of UN DESA in 2019, that the number and quality of partnerships required to timely deliver on the SDGs leaves a lot to be desired.

A considerable number of registered 'Partnerships for the SDGs' show a relatively vague linkage to specific SDGs, lack clear strategic prioritization of SDG-targets, and provide limited transparency on status, progress, impact and lessons learned. Around 1,900 listed partnership commitments already existed before the SDGs. Many were launched or were initiated in relation to other UN conferences (notably the 2017 Ocean Conference, the 2016 Global Sustainable Transport Conference, the 2014 SIDS Conference, and the 2012 Rio+20 Conference). These partnerships appear to have taken the *opportunity-driven route* offered by the SDG-agenda, to 'reframe' their commitment under the SDG label. Furthermore, partnership commitments are voluntarily registered; almost all constitute 'coalitions of the willing'. Whereas nearly half of the partnership initiatives target one specific SDG and approximately 25% aim at 2–4 SDGs, several initiatives state to have embraced an extensive portfolio of practically all SDGs – which suggests potential nexus effects (sections 10.5 and 11.10). Yet most initiatives remain vague on the rationale behind their SDG selection, and on whether and how nexus effects can be achieved. Regular submission of progress reports is an (informal) requirement for keeping the partnership published on the 'UN Partnerships for SDGs' platform. In May 2020, however, just 195 progress reports were submitted 'on time', while 3,419 (66%) were already 'two years overdue'.

Many of the pending progress reports related to partnerships that existed already before the launch of the SDGs, or that are tagged as 'inactive'. By September 2021, one in five partnerships had provided progress updates.

More information: https://sdgs.un.org/partnerships

STAKEHOLDER (RE)CONFIGURATION PROCESSES

Although collaborative relationships may have sprung from distinct triggers and motivations, in the end an effective CSP always involves a combination of exploration and exploitation functions. A one-sided focus on co-exploration lacks implementation efficacy, underutilizes the potential for leverage and is ill-equipped to scale. A one-sided focus on co-exploitation risks underestimating contextual complexities and the pitfall of short-sighted overconfidence in own competencies and 'proven approaches'. An effective CSP seeks to mitigate both deficiencies by striking an appropriate balance between co-exploration and co-exploitation, in line with the partnership's overall purpose and the motivational drivers of all partners involved. Complex challenges require a partnership configuration that sufficiently matches the degree of complexity it seeks to address: with complementary competencies, motivational drivers, cultures, roles, interests and explorative as well as exploitative capacities that make the partnership 'fit for purpose'.

The higher the level of complementarity and interdependence between the partners, the higher the likelihood that organizations are willing to collaborate (Vangen and Huxham, 2012) and mobilize the capacities needed to work towards the intended level of change (Vellema et al., 2019). That does not imply, however, that the CSP has to include each relevant stakeholder as participant. On the contrary: to keep the partnership's span of control manageable and ensure that the intent of the initiating partners is not watered down, the size of the configuration and the number of involved participants should not be overstretched. The balancing of co-exploration and co-exploitation motivational drivers poses an internal governance challenge (discussed in section 12.2.4), as well as a (re) configuration challenge: how to move from a 'coalition of the willing' to a 'coalition of the needed' (section 5.5.3)? Depending on the partnership's initial trigger and drivers, two key reconfiguration questions appear: *who* is needed and *what* is needed (Figure 12.1)?

■ **[1] Who is needed?** Issue-driven partnerships have to consider whether the CSP they are constructing will create sufficient 'partner fit' and commonality in attitudes and approaches ('cultural fit') to be able to *exploit* mutual competencies (section 5.5.3). Stakeholder mapping (or 'landscaping') can

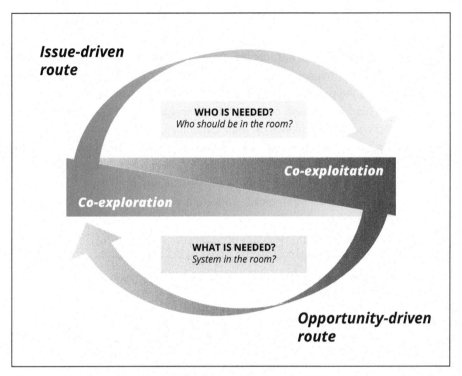

Figure 12.1 Reconfiguration: what and who is needed?

help overcome early configurational deficiencies. One technique for exploring the fit of the initial partnership – and for identifying strategically relevant potential partners needed to enhance the CSP's ultimate impact – is to organize a 'wicked problems plaza' (Box 6.4), to discuss 'who should be in the room'. Landscaping informs initiating partners whether the interests of all relevant stakeholders and essential complementarities are represented in the present CSP set-up, or whether adjustments still need to be made before proceeding to the next phase of the partnering cycle. Stakeholder mapping is ideally done *before* partners get to the building phase (Box 12.4).

■ **[2] What is needed?** Opportunity-driven partnerships have to further *explore* whether their current configuration organizes the 'right' kind of connections, capacities and insights needed to fully grasp and successfully address the societal issue(s) they are interested in. The formation of opportunity-driven partnerships is often a relatively closed process, based on existing ties and shared prior experiences. Deficiencies in the roll-out of familiar approaches to a 'new' context may only become apparent during execution. Here, the 'wicked problems plaza' technique can be used to 'get the system in the room' in order to figure out *what is needed* to enhance the partnership's ultimate (local) impact. By inviting all stakeholders directly influenced by the partnership's actions, negative and positive externalities can be identified and approaches explored to address voids, flaws and blind spots – or missed opportunities for scaling. 'Getting the system in the room' helps the partnership to properly contextualize and come to grips with different *worldviews* and *opinions.*[2] Such insights can inform further analysis and review processes of what capacities, critical competences and interests are still underrepresented or entirely missing in the present partnership. It may result in a *re*configuration by inviting key stakeholder to join the CSP – for instance, to ensure more effective embedding of (local) activities, or to internalize strategically important complementary competencies, values and capacities.

BOX 12.4

STAKEHOLDER MAPPING – WHO SHOULD BE 'IN THE ROOM'?

A Wicked Problems Plaza simulation

How to define which stakeholders are needed to address a particular societal problem? Master students simulated a 'Wicked Problems Plaza' session (Box 6.4) on the issue of water pollution around the Rhine river in Europe (streaming through Switzerland, Germany and the Netherlands). In the first round of deliberations, participants made a stakeholder map based on two questions: (1) which stakeholders are *present* and in what corner of the *societal triangle* are they positioned; (2) which stakeholders are *not present,* and how could this affect the deliberations.

Participants drew a societal triangle and stickered the identity and societal position of each of the stakeholders 'present'. From this overview, it became clear to all participants that several 'key stakeholders' were not represented in the session. The group defined the following missing groups that might have different interests than the stakeholders 'in the room':

o   Some of the upstream civil stakeholders
o   Companies that are intense users of water (and thus might have conflicting interests)
o   The fish (!)

---

2   The Jollibee case in the Philippines (**Case #12.1**) illustrates what 'getting the system in the room' could entail in practice. The case describes the experience of a large, multinational retailer that tried to develop an inclusive value chain through partnering. Applying the 'getting the system in the room' principle resulted in the identification of surprising 'agents of change', such as local mayors, young entrepreneurs or not-yet-involved financial institutions that helped the partnership succeed.

○   'Future generations' (!) of people living near the river
○   The European Commission

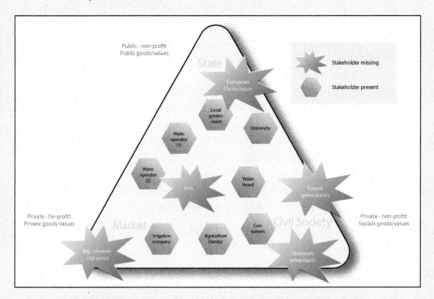

Additionally, it turned out that a number of stakeholders were not adequate in defining their societal position (section 6.3) and related power base (section 10.3.1). For instance, water operator companies defined themselves as 'private companies' whereas most of them were in fact owned by regional or local authorities – making them semi-public non-profit organizations with a different business model than fully private for-profit organizations. Citizens defined themselves as 'consumers', but in a narrow sense (water drinkers, but not as beneficiaries of the natural environment). Government organizations defined themselves as legislator, regulator, tax collector and subsidy provider, but not as potential partner of the other stakeholders.

Following-up

In consecutive rounds, participants shared their sources of failure (dilemmas and trade-offs), judged their willingness to take up responsibilities (investment in projects, for instance) and challenged each other to share risks in common projects. During these rounds, each of the participants was challenged to take the interests of missing stakeholders into account. In particular, the 'European Commission' and 'the fish' turned out to be vital stakeholders to come up with creative solutions for several wicked problems related to waste and water treatment. Consumers faced major conflicts with 'future generations' of river shore inhabitants, but these could be mitigated by the (semi-private) water boards that were able to forge a compromise between local governments along the river, and potential recreative users of the river. The 'willingness to pay' for particular approaches proved a vital consideration that – on the one hand – limited the bandwidth of solutions (narrow interests related to water management) and – on the other hand – broadened the opportunities, because the river could be defined as a 'public good' that provided substantial positive externalities to the surrounding inhabitants (higher ground prices, more recreational facilities).

The SDG-framework – the nexus approach, in particular – was then used to identify positive and negative interlinkages at the meso level (section 10.6). From this assessment, a different business case could be developed with participants: a cluster of stakeholders pooled complementary resources and delineated a 'blended finance' approach to cover common ambitions for the medium-term (2030). The 'local university' was asked to do a follow-up study to explore: (1) the financial and ecological sustainability of a number of the ideas that popped up in the meeting; (2) develop a monitoring and evaluation system that would link KPQs and KPIs to a selection of SDGs; and (3) define a hybrid governance system that could serve the interest of all stakeholders, while being flexible enough to learn from implementation experiences.

12.2.2   Reaching goal alignment

"Even when parties agree to pool their efforts, they frequently do not see eye to eye on the aims of collaborations" (Gray, 2007: 33). In other words, partnerships face the challenge of reaching a sufficient degree of 'goal alignment' to make them fly. For a functioning CSP, the outcome of a formation process always involves (formal or informal) agreement on a common purpose, shared goal(s) and level of commitment by all participants involved. Effective goal alignment is a dynamic process, however, that usually materializes over extended periods of time – iteratively, and throughout the partnering cycle. In practice, the existence of a minimum level of commitment commonly marks the beginning of partnership negotiations, from which further alignment, deepened commitment and higher ambition levels can be established as the partner relationship evolves.

To indicate the level of engagement of each party in a collaborative relationship, James Austin and May Seitanidi (2014) developed a 'collaboration continuum'. On this continuum, they identified four nodes defining the 'nature' of the partnering relationship along increasing intensities of *collaborative value creation*: 'philanthropic', 'transactional', 'integrative' and 'transformational'. The continuum helps delineate to what degree the motivational drivers of each partnering organization can be considered more or less strategic, and more or less geared to effecting systems change. Philanthropic relations are relatively ad hoc, peripheral and skewed (unilateral dependence), whereas a transformational ambition generally involves a far greater degree of interdependence, collective action and synergistic modes of organizing. Three 'value drivers' underpinning the collaboration continuum explain how the partnering organizations can be propelled to more deeply engage in higher levels of collaborative value creation: (1) 'alignment drivers', which explain the (strategic) relevance of the collaboration to each of the partners; (2) 'engagement drivers', which characterize the structure, intensity and interaction between the partners; and (3) 'leverage drivers', which assess the magnitude, linkages and nature of involved capabilities and resources required to make the partnership (more) effective.

The four nodes of the collaborative continuum can almost one-on-one be linked to the four levels of intervention, engagement and value creation (levels 1, 2, 3, 4) consistently developed throughout this book. Combined, the two approaches constitute a 'cross-sector partnering continuum' (Table 12.1).

Table 12.1 Cross-sector partnering continuum: linking intervention levels with collaboration value drivers

Level of engagement:	LEVEL 1	LEVEL 2	LEVEL 3	LEVEL 4
Motivation for collaboration	Passive	Reactive	Active	Proactive
Nature of relationship	Philanthropic	Transactional	Integrative	Transformational
■ Alignment driver				
– Mission relevance – Strategic importance – Values connection – Problem knowledge – Value creation frames – Benefit focus	Peripheral Insignificant Shallow Unbalanced Disparate Partners	⟸⟹		Central Vital Deep Synchronous Fused Society
■ Engagement driver				
– Emotional connection – Interaction focus – Involvement – Frequency – Active scope – Structure – Managerial complexity	Light Procedural Few Occasional Narrow Dyad Simple	⟸⟹		Profound Substantive Top to bottom Intensive Broad Multiparty Complex
■ Leverage driver				
– Magnitude of resources – Resource type – Resource link – Synergism – Learning – Innovation – Internal change – External system change	Small Money Separate Weak Low Seldom Minimal Rare	⟸⟹		Big Core competencies Conjoined Predominant Continual Always Great Common
Summary	Ad hoc ⟸			⟹ Strategic

Source: based on Austin and Seitanidi (2014)

Goal alignment appears when all collaborative parties have the same understanding of their partnership, share the same ambition level, and have comparable degrees of engagement and motivation. Goal alignment can be established at each of the four ambition levels. In that regard, engaging in a transformational relationship is not necessarily 'better' or preferable to being involved in a philanthropic relationship. It all depends on the converged expectations of involved partners, the overall purpose the partnership is to serve, and the 'complexity fit' that the CSP is supposed to establish. Philanthropic partnerships (alignment at ambition level 1), for instance, are characterized by 'charitable' and sponsoring relations that are often short-term orientated, forged for opportunistic and instrumental reasons, and generally involve modest commitment from both sides. Sponsoring relationships can be terminated any year.[3] Termination does not necessarily have to be a bad thing, however, as long as each party has understood and agreed – right from the outset – that the established relationship was intended to be temporary. The same applies for transactional relationships (alignment at ambition level 2) characterized by reciprocal exchanges, which can be phased out as soon as the relationship has served the purpose of the initiating partner. Transformational partnerships (alignment at ambition level 4), on the other hand, are inevitably strategic; achieving societal impact at a meaningful scale requires a long-term horizon and enduring and dedicated engagement of all partners. Integrative partnerships (alignment at ambition level 3) are strategic to the mission and activities of the partnering organizations too, but directed at harnessing 'collaborative advantage' to scale positive effects, and the co-creation of mutually beneficial outcomes (shared value creation).

Problems of *goal misalignment* appear when intentions of partners differ and are either not understood or not communicated.[4] Goal alignment challenges tend to grow with the number of participants and the degree of 'issue complexity' involved. The more the ambitions of individual partners vary, the more difficult it becomes to manage the partnership. Low-fit partnerships can be extremely cumbersome, intense and time-consuming to manage. For partnerships with a limited number of participants, it is often easier to reorganize and become strategically aligned. For more extensive partnerships, however, reaching strategic alignment usually requires considerable investments in time, money and effort, for

---

3 **Case #12.3** addresses the phenomenon of 'sponsoring relations' and to extent to which these relationships need to be upgraded to become more effective. It presents two cases of partnerships between an International NGO and a multinational company: International Red Cross and FrieslandCampina; Unicef and H&M.

4 **Case #12.9** addresses the challenge of misalignment between a multinational company (AkzoNobel) and an international NGO (Plan International). It describes how both organizations realigned their partnership to enhance the impact for themselves and for the issue at stake.

instance because it takes years to attain a high level of reciprocal trust, mutual understanding and operational efficiency between the partnering organizations. Strategic (re)alignment in more complex partnerships might also involve a change in leadership from one CSP participant to another.[5]

12.2.3 Dealing with partnering tensions: governance and trust-building

Despite having agreed on the overall purpose, ambition and objectives of the partnership, the CSP's actual management can still run into inter-organizational tensions that tend to play out particularly against the backdrop of power differences and organizational interdependencies between participants. We zoom in on two types of partnering tensions: (1) those resulting from differences in the emphasis individual partners put on either 'co-exploration' or 'co-exploitation', and (2) those resulting from emphasizing either 'accountability and control' or 'learning and trust' in the collaborative relationship. Both fields of tension can be constrained and managed through sensible governance and trust-building practices.

INTER-ORGANIZATIONAL TENSIONS

Tensions linked to the 'balancing act' between co-exploration and co-exploitation originate in the initial trigger for the partnership (issue/opportunity) and in the motivational drivers of each partner to engage in a collaborative relationship (section 12.2.1). Did participants join the partnership mostly for co-exploration or for co-exploitation purposes? When the partnership's overall approach is: (a) not unequivocally understood by engaged parties, (b) not entirely suitable or valid anymore in the light of new developments, or (c) not sufficiently aligned with the evolving needs, motivations and interests of (some of the) participants, this will inevitably lead to underperformance. Certainly in later stages of the partnership, views of individual partners on what approach and activities would best serve the ambition of the partnership – and the goals of their own organization – may start diverging. Based on a meta-review of studies on inter-organizational collaborative relationships, Parmigiani and Rivera-Santos (2011) distilled a set of partnership traits based on two 'pure' forms of co-exploration and co-exploitation. Their helpful typology portrays the areas of tension that, over time, may arise between the various partners of a collaborative effort (Table 12.2).

---

5   **Case #12.2** reveals the experience of a complex multi-actor partnership – 'Football for Water' – in which representatives of all societal sectors participated. The leadership had to change over time to increase the partnership's efficiency and effectiveness.

Table 12.2 Inter-organizational partnering tensions

CO-EXPLORATION	◀ AREAS OF TENSION ▶	CO-EXPLOITATION
Voluntary cooperative agreement to create new knowledge, tasks, functions or activities	AMBITION	Voluntary cooperative agreement to execute existing knowledge, tasks, functions or activities
Learning	KEY ACTIVITY	Expansion
Innovation	TYPE OF VALUE CREATION	Efficiency
Tacit	KEY KNOWLEDGE TYPE	Explicit
Set	DURATION	Ongoing
Appropriation	KEY HAZARD	Slacking
Uncertainty	ENVIRONMENTAL STATE	Risk
Reciprocal	TYPE OF INTERDEPENDENCE	Pooled or sequential
Joint	DECISION-MAKING	Divided
Rich, ongoing, few people	COMMUNICATION	Thin, routine, more people
Interpersonal	COORDINATION	Routines, standard operating procedures

Source: based on Parmigiani and Rivera-Santos (2011)

Most partnerships reflect a combination of co-exploration and co-exploitation traits, by either adopting a 'balanced' or a 'focused' approach (Parmigiani and Rivera-Santos, 2011). Focused partnerships emphasize co-exploration over co-exploitation, or vice versa, whereas balanced partnerships seek to establish an optimal combination of features from both approaches – or cycle between co-exploration and co-exploitation activities to provide balance over time (Figure 12.1). The particular combination established for the CSP not necessarily reflects the intention that each individual partner holds for the partnership, however. Certainly in more complex partnership configurations with many participants, this can cause tension and ultimately conflict.

A restructuring of activities may restore a certain balance. For instance, exploration and exploitation activities may be separated and performed by different organizations that either aim at exploration or exploitation functions. Balance can then be found by conceiving the CSP as a portfolio of different activities. This option should be carefully assessed, however, as its feasibility most likely depends on the partnership's ambition level of value creation. Notably partnerships with level 3 and 4 ambitions are bound to *integrative and synergetic* approaches to be able to achieve the kind of outcomes and societal impact for which they were created. Another venue to address inter-organizational tensions is to create a 'bridge' organization to help partners interpret each other's motivations and actions and deal with power imbalances – in particular when partners do not share a history of collaboration, are not yet familiar with the distinct organizational logics of their (cross-sector) partners, or face low levels of initial trust. This is the role often played by 'partnership brokers' (Box 12.11).

TENSIONS FROM DIFFERENT GOVERNANCE LOGICS

Another source of tension between partners concerns the steering logic and the result-oriented mechanisms applied to ensure that the partnership's objectives are realized and 'collaborative value' is generated. Partnering organizations bring in contrasting organizational logics and cultures, varying expectations and different power positions – factors that all have a bearing on *how* results are achieved, *what kind* of results are valued, and *under what conditions* engagement can be intensified as the partnership evolves. Governance logics – and related monitoring practices – can emphasize *formal* 'control and accountability' or emphasize more *informal* principles of 'cooperation and mutual learning' (Pfisterer and Van Tulder, 2020). The extent to which either logic prevails finds its origin in the initial level of mutual trust between partners. Trust, in itself, is not a necessary nor a sufficient condition to establish a successful partnership. On the contrary, section 5.4.1 argued that cross-sector collaboration is often elemental to bridge sizable societal trust gaps (Figure 5.4). The practice of partnering hence gives cause to a somewhat philosophical question underpinning the type of governance applied to manage a CSP: "Do you partner because you trust each other, or do you trust each other because you partner?"

CSPs that emphasize a 'control logic' assume a certain degree of *mutual distrust*. Distrust can be based on unequal organizational size and power positions, the different sectors partners come from, differences in funding commitments, or perhaps a different anticipation of who is going to profit from the partnership (anticipated opportunistic behaviour). As a result, more formalized governance structures are implemented that particularly stress accountability aspects. The focus of this governance logic is on collecting timely performance information according to predefined 'result indicators', as set in the planning and design phase of the partnership. Generally, the prime focus is on project activities and outputs, comparing results with targets, and using performance information for (partnership) reorientation decisions – often steered by the organization with the greatest financial stake in the partnership (the funding agency). Control approaches emphasize contracts and other forms of rules and procedures (e.g., monitoring, reporting, penalties on default), creating a partnering framework through which organizations can protect themselves from opportunism and conflict.

A collaborative governance logic, on the other hand, emphasizes collective behaviour and places a high value on *initial goal symmetries*. It departs from the assumption that long-term relationships are developed on the basis of trust, reputation, collective goals and involvement, in which alignment between actors is an outcome of relational reciprocity. CSPs that follow a collaborative governance logic emphasize mutual learning, seek to actively involve the target group (i.e., beneficiaries) and apply holistic monitoring systems that are multilevel and adaptable if and where required. This take on CSP governance is more sensitive to contextual factors, power dynamics, inclusion and exclusion issues, and empowerment and disempowerment (Lennie and Tacchi, 2014).

Tensions between control/accountability and cooperation/learning are inherent to the hybrid nature of cross-sector collaboration. All CSPs – certainly those geared to level 3 and 4 ambitions – need structures for sound control/accountability as well as cooperation/learning. Combining both is a dynamic balancing act; finding the right fit a necessary condition for effective CSPs. Strict and too rigid accountability requirements easily run counter to 'mutual learning' and partnership upgrading and so may hamper greater impact. Conversely, a prevailing focus on mutual learning may not bring the envisaged outcomes at the pace, scale and scope required. Sophisticated reporting and monitoring mechanisms (section 12.3) are therefore often highlighted as critical formal implementation structures for ensuring the continuation of ongoing efforts (Clarke and Macdonald, 2019). The more partners can deal with these governance tensions not as a trade-off but as a constructive paradox (see Box 4.3), the more practitioners will be able to recognize the strength and weaknesses of both, and design novel governance structures, steering principles and monitoring and evaluation (M&E) systems that facilitate a synthesis of control and collaboration (Vangen, 2017). A hybrid governance logic combines formal and informal rules as well as procedural and learning approaches in order to assess, fine-tune and continuously upgrade impact over longer periods of time (see section 12.2.4).

A benchmark of whether partners are able to deal with fundamental governance tensions is their approach towards trust – as either *trust-building* in case of low-trust partnerships or *trust repair and restoring* in the case of higher-trust partnerships turning sour. Trust levels will need to be built over time – in consecutive phases of the partnering cycle – to raise the partnership's effectiveness while lowering transaction costs. Building up trust is greatly facilitated by smart governance structures, but also involves developing a common language. In complex CSPs, notions like 'value', 'impact', 'performance', 'efficiency', 'synergy', 'profits' or 'benefits' receive remarkably different connotations in distinct sectors. Even when such concepts seem to denote similar dimensions of organizing, they can still lead to misapprehensions and confusion (Box 12.5). Building trust, therefore, requires investing in conversations: to foster mutual understanding, to develop a *common language*, to encourage the willingness to *share dilemmas*, and to carve out an approach for dealing with common misunderstandings. An answer to the earlier posed 'trust conundrum' could therefore be: "You trust each other, because you all agree on implementing governance modes in the partnership to raise the level of trust – and by doing so, attain higher levels of goal alignment."

COMMON MISAPPREHENSIONS

Trust-building during formation'

Goal symmetry: 'Speaking the same language'

Sharing Dilemmas...

Source: PrC/Department of B-SM

12.2.4 Design challenges: a 'complexity-sensitive' and principled approach to partnering

An essential part of the formation phase is alignment between the partnering organizations on *how* they think their partnership can affect the aspired short-term, intermediate and longer-term outcomes. What defines success? What does it take to get there? How to know whether actions lead to envisioned results? A Theory of Change (ToC) outlines the partnership's *intervention strategy* through which participants seek to address the targeted issue and bring about the desired change. A ToC explains the rationale as to why certain outcomes can be expected, along what outcome pathways and intervention processes, under what conditions, and the kind of (risk) factors that might undermine assumed causal relations (section 5.5.1).

The process of drawing up a sophisticated ToC poses comparable challenges as were noted with regard to the 'design paradox' (section 11.8): a ToC is developed *ex ante* – before the actual start of the CSP. It rests on chains and stages of *assumed* cause-effect relations, *expected* plausibility and *projected* feasibility – all based on present insights, experience and anticipated conditions. Funding organizations often demand 'evidence-based' ToCs before deciding to fund or not. Most ToCs are accordingly portrayed as a programmatic linear process, tailored to project control and co-exploitation activities, with measurable output indicators along charted timelines. This practice challenges in particular the formation of CSPs that aim at *transformative change* – which inherently calls for novel approaches, partly off the beaten track, as systems change trajectories are not paved on clear solutions (Chapter 4). In addition to proven methods, CSPs targeting more complex societal challenges also rely on co-exploration activities, experiential learning, adapting while doing, and qualitative outcome indicators next to measurable results.

Drawing up the partnership's 'intervention strategy' is a process of negotiation between the partnering organizations on the longer-term course of action: purpose, ambition level, goal orientation, means and governance mechanisms all come together in the design of a ToC – as explicit objectives and milestones, and as explicit and implicit assumptions on the time, resources, efforts and ultimate benefits that goal achievement could entail for each participant. Different views and fundamental tensions are likely to become apparent during negotiations and may be sufficiently addressed before the actual start of the partnership. Other tensions may only arise during execution and need to be resolved in the partnering process, for which adequate structures and modes of interaction need to be in place. The end of a proper CSP formation phase takes these contextual, relational and organizational eventualities into account, resulting in: (1) the design of a 'complexity-sensitive' Theory of Change; (2) the formulation of shared principles on which the partnership is founded; and (3) the formulation of a sound partnering agreement.

DESIGNING A COMPLEXITY-SENSITIVE ToC

The Theory of Change underpinning a partnership cannot be used as a 'planning tool', but rather serves as a 'navigation' instrument (Ramalingam et al., 2014) that should leave room for an evolving understanding of how change comes about. A *complexity-sensitive* approach to working with ToCs basically acknowledges that the partnership is subject to constant change, which makes effective impact assessment all but a static exercise (Van Tulder and Keen, 2018). A complexity-sensitive ToC (Box 12.6) helps participants: (a) to diagnose and better appreciate the dynamic complexity of the various contexts in which they operate; (b) to fine-tune and upgrade the partnership configuration, if needed, to sufficiently match the level of complexity involved; and (c) to shift the partnering strategy from a planning approach to a continuous 'learning and adapting' approach (see section 5.5.3 on 'dynamic fit').

A complexity-sensitive ToC departs from the notion that the partnership itself is part of a continuous learning exercise: the pooled intelligence and experience of the CSP participants is used in a process of 'co-creation' to come up with ever more effective approaches along the way. In that view, a ToC is both a set of assumptions on how change could be realized as well as an approach to making these assumptions better informed – by applying, testing and upgrading them in practice. In the monitoring and evaluation (M&E) literature, this 'learning and adapting' approach is known as *developmental evaluation* (Patton et al., 2016). Developmental evaluation techniques stress the importance of collecting and analysing real-time data, bringing in multiple stakeholders and 'triangulating' learning. Quick and ongoing learning thereby guides timely adaptation of the intervention strategy to emergent realities in ways that lead to informed and embedded actions towards the aspired change. A related technique is *outcome harvesting* (Wilson-Grau et al., 2016), an evaluation approach that collects evidence of what has been achieved and then works backward to determine whether and how the intervention strategy contributed to that change, in order to improve the partnership's transformative capacity.

KEY COMPONENTS OF A COMPLEXITY-SENSITIVE THEORY OF CHANGE

B O X 12.6

A complexity-sensitive ToC approach can support partnerships to (1) achieve an alignment of ambitions, (2) create a 'complexity fit' partnership configuration, and (3) develop a proper intervention and learning strategy. Eight components of a complexity-sensitive ToC for CSPs could be identified (Van Tulder and Keen, 2018). Half of these relate to issue analysis and design questions – i.e. whether the partnership adequately captures the degree of complexity of the targeted issue and has been able to align the partnership configuration accordingly. The other half concerns process and learning components – i.e. how the ToC allows for effective learning (monitoring and evaluation) during the partnering process.

Issue/design components:

■ A *problem and context analysis,* investigating underlying (root) causes of the problem, its context, and the degree to which the problem can be perceived as systemic.

B
O
X

12.6

■ A **stakeholder analysis,** identifying key stakeholders, both in terms of being part of the solution (coalition of the willing) or being part of the problem (coalition of the needed).

■ An **analysis of the intended change,** ensuring goal alignment and a collective appreciation of the level of complexity of the intended change.

■ Critical reflection on **assumptions** underlying the ToC, determining whether these assumptions are grounded in evidence, practices or whether they need to be validated during implementation.

Process/learning components:

■ **Intervention strategy and markers for change,** using a backwards mapping approach to identify the best strategy and set-up of relevant monitoring structures.

■ Reflection on the **critical conditions,** determining the risks and potential changes in the enabling environment that cannot be influenced, but could affect the ToC.

■ A **reflective approach,** aligning expectations that the ToC is likely to evolve. Will the partnership ask evaluators to prove the validity of the ToC based on *the results* of the partnership, or will it adjust and (drastically) change its ToC as the partnership *unfolds?*

■ A **graphical presentation,** depicting an easy-to-understand representation of the ToC. Visual strategy mapping (Bryson et al., 2016) aids in action research and mutual learning projects. Narratives, combined with mapping techniques, create frames.

The effectiveness of a cross-sector partnership can be greatly enhanced if the participants see their collaborative effort as a *series of consecutive interventions and learning steps* from which they can learn (as evaluation of 'impact loops', discussed in section 12.3), but which also prompts them to: (1) improve mutual understanding of the wickedness of the problem; (2) realign the partnership's governance during the process, if and when needed; (3) engage other stakeholders, when and where needed; (4) share dilemmas; (5) build up trust; and (6) embed and institutionalize the partnership in each organization. Impact Teams can facilitate vital learning steps along the partnering cycle (Box 12.9).

DEFINING PARTNERSHIP PRINCIPLES

To mark the end of the scoping and building phase, partners have to agree on the conditions, ambitions, main goals and governance of the partnership, and define leading principles on which their collaboration is based. The specification of partnership principles helps to manage relationships and guide collaboration processes. Developing partnership principles also proves a powerful tool for partners to define the value of their collaboration and to keep their 'eyes on the ball' during the further implementation of the partnership project. Partnering principles capture the uniqueness of the collaboration – why can this particular partnership configuration be considered well-positioned to deal with the complexity of the issue – and link it with the partnership's purpose and the aspired impact. The discussion and formulation of 'principles' also serves as the starting point for a continued dialogue about how to assess 'progress' and enhance the quality of the relationship. Partnering principles are usually not part of formal (legally binding) agreements, but their publication has an important *formative* communication function in support of level 3 and 4 ambitions that require active participation of both internal and external stakeholders (see section 11.9).

DEFINING PRINCIPLES FOR A CROSS-SECTOR PARTNERSHIP

Partnering principles usually make reference to one or more existing guiding frameworks, to which contextualized and partnership-specific principles are then added – if and as agreed by all partners involved. Humanitarian organizations, for instance, may choose to endorse the 'Principles of Partnership' (PoP) as defined by the UN Global Humanitarian Platform (GHP) – a framework for all actors active in the humanitarian realm, committed to building and nurturing effective partnerships. The GHP principles highlight partnership fundamentals:

- **Equality:** mutual respect between partnership members, irrespective of size and power; participants respect each other's mandates, obligations and independence and recognize each other's constraints and commitments; mutual respect must not preclude organizations from engaging in constructive dissent.

- **Transparency:** achieved through dialogue on equal footing, with an emphasis on early consultations and early sharing of information; communications and (financial) transparency increase the level of trust among organizations.

- **Result-oriented approach:** action must be reality-based and action-oriented; this requires result-oriented coordination based on effective capabilities and concrete operational capacities.

- **Responsibility:** partnership members have an ethical obligation to each other to accomplish their tasks responsibly, with integrity and in a relevant and appropriate way; they must make sure they commit to activities only when they have the means, competencies, skills and capacity to deliver on their commitments; decisive and robust prevention of abuse must also be a constant effort.

- **Complementarity:** building on comparative advantages and complementing each other's contribution; language and cultural barriers must be overcome.

The defining characteristics of a specific CSP then zoom in on the following aspects, to further specify:

BOX
12.7

- Problem and impact statement: why is collaboration necessary
- Working for mutual benefit
- Commitment, including to joint learning
- Complementarity in resources and capabilities, and how this can add to impact
- The right to disagree and the conditions of an exit strategy

- Clarity, integrity, transparency and accountability
- Creating a culture of openness
- Building equity/equal footing
- Celebrating diversity
- A motto or statement that summarizes the ambition

Below, two examples are shown of concisely formulated 'CSP principles' for an education (GPE) and a Food (WFP) partnership.

Example 1: Global Partnership for Education *"Improving learning and equity through stronger education systems"*	Example 2: WFP Corporate Partnership Strategy (2014–2017) *"We deliver better together"*
1. **Education as a public good,** a human right and an enabler of other rights. It is essential for peace, tolerance, human fulfilment, and sustainable development.	1. **Equality:** "Respect differences in focus and methods but strive for a common vision around a shared objective"
2. Focusing our resources on securing **learning, equity and inclusion** for the most marginalized children and youth, including those affected by fragility and conflict.	2. **Transparency:** Freely share information on resources, objectives and expectations at the outset
3. Achieving **gender equality.**	3. **Results-oriented approach**: Agree on a clear exit strategy based on a mutual understanding of what will constitute completion (or abandonment) of the partnership.
4. Enabling inclusive, evidence-based **policy dialogue** that engages national governments, donors, civil society, teachers, philanthropy and the private sector.	
5. Providing support that promotes **country ownership** and nationally identified priorities, and is linked to country performance in achieving improved equity and learning.	4. **Responsibility**: Review human resources to ensure that WFP and its partners can supply and support individuals with appropriate skills.
6. Improving **development effectiveness** through harmonization and aligning aid to country systems.	5. **Complementarity**: Gather data on potential partners to provide insight into knowledge, skills and scope complementary to those of WFP.
7. Promoting **mutual accountability** and transparency across the partnership.	
8. Acting on our belief that **inclusive partnership** is the most effective means of achieving development results.	
Source: www.globalpartnership.org	Source: www.icvanetwork.org

More information: PrC Insight Series, No.1 (2020), *Partnership Principles.*

DESIGNING AGREEMENTS

Written agreements signal the end of the formation negotiation phase and may take various forms: memorandum of understanding (MoU), letter of intent (LoI), partnership agreement (PA), collaboration agreement (CA), grant decision (GD), covenant or purchasing agreement (PA). Written agreements are intended to provide the proper mechanisms to cope with relational, situational and performance risk, and to coordinate interaction dynamics in ways that are supportive to the collaborative relationship. They establish the aim of the collaboration, the values and principles underpinning the partnership, the contributions of each partner, how decisions are made, how the partnership will be managed, what will happen when the partners disagree, matters of confidentiality and how the partnership may be dissolved. Written agreements provide a means to encourage institutional buy-in while offering an explicit way of recognizing the various (financial and in-kind) contributions of partners and recording the commitment of resources.

An agreement should be comprehensive enough to clarify how partners' roles and responsibilities are coordinated, how appropriation concerns are safeguarded, and what to do in case of uncertainty, conflict, withdrawal or a drastic change of plans. At the same time, agreements need to be flexible enough to allow for alterations in the partnership and partnership configuration; change can be considered a given in the face of dynamic and complex operating environments. If agreements do not adequately reckon with (1) the complexity of the partnership, (2) the areas of tension between co-exploration/co-exploitation drivers and between control/collaboration governance logics, or (3) disregard the reasonable leeway needed for evaluating, learning and adjusting, then partnership agreements can also hinder effective partnering processes. Comprehensive partnering agreements embrace a number of 'good partnering' principles that help organizations to timely address some of the basic tensions in the partnership (Box 12.8).

DEFINING ELEMENTS OF A COMPREHENSIVE PARTNERING AGREEMENT

BOX 12.8

A good partnering agreement will:

- ✓ Define the problem addressed
- ✓ Specify the mutual understanding of roles and responsibilities
- ✓ Articulate the commitments which partners must live up to

Designing Comprehensive Partnering Agreements
An Introduction to the Partnering Agreement Scorecard

THE PARTNERSHIPS
RESOURCE CENTRE
ROTTERDAM SCHOOL OF MANAGEMENT
ERASMUS UNIVERSITY

the partnering initiative

B
O
X

12.8

✓   Formalize the relationships between partners

✓   Provide a reference point for the collaboration that is to follow

✓   Support the partnering process by ensuring partners have correctly developed answers about all aspects of the partnership

✓   Reduce the likelihood of misunderstandings and disputes

✓   Serve as an overall framework to manage the partnership and guide decision-making

✓   Help maintain focus on the original activities and objectives

✓   Allow partners to keep track of project performance and review progress

✓   Allow for flexibility

More information: PrC Insight Series, No.2 (2021), *Partnership Agreements*. https://www.rsm.nl/research/centres/prc/prc-insight-series/

12.3   LEARNING AND UPGRADING: IDENTIFYING OPERATIONAL FIT AND IMPACT

Measuring the impact of a CSP in order to learn and enhance its transformative capacity has proven a challenging task. Many academics as well as practitioners have observed the risk of relying too much on 'scientific evidence' produced in highly controlled settings. The kind of evidence-based results accumulated in *randomized controlled trial* testing methods (Banerjee and Duflo, 2019), for instance, are much more difficult to establish in the far more complex, dynamic and uncertain real-life environments in which most CSPs materialize, adapt and evolve. Accordingly, the trend in contemporary 'monitoring and evaluation' (M&E) practice is to no longer speak of evidence-based impact, but rather to search for *plausible effects*. This approach is increasingly supported by impact investors and influential foundations, such as the Bill and Melinda Gates Foundation. In complex real-life environments, overly detailed ToCs are even considered counterproductive because they "stifle creativity and innovation" (Rogers, 2009).

A complexity-sensitive Theory of Change (ToC) seeks to capture the complexities of the CSP before the start of the project as a sequence of dynamic *fit questions* – organized along an (adaptive) intervention logic that can be portrayed as an *impact value chain*. Figure 5.7 presented the basic 'logic framework' to assess partnership configurations in terms of 'societal-complexity fit' and 'internal-partnering fit'. Figure 12.2 presents the next iteration. It considers

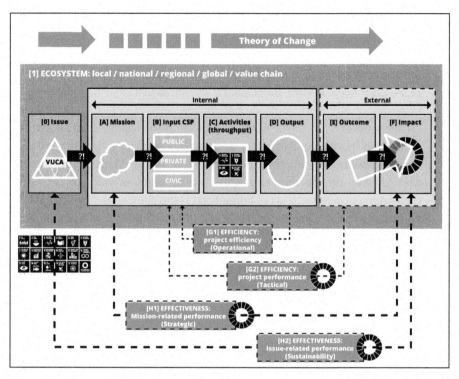

Figure 12.2 An impact value chain for CSPs – mapping plausible effects

Source: based on Van Tulder, Seitanidi, Crane and Brammer (2016); Van Tulder and Maas (2012)

the various 'fits' that need to be established – and upgraded along the way – to make a CSP (more) impactful.

■ **Issue-mission fit [0-A]:** The partnership's mission functions as the linchpin between the targeted societal issue and the inputs of all partners in terms of mobilized competences, resources, skills, finance, assets, time, staff and the like. Partners will only be able to seize the synergies of working together if they share a common vision, mission and understanding of the issue, and agree on shared partnership principles and objectives.

■ **Issue-partnering fit [0-B]:** considers the fit between the societal issue and cross-sector partners in terms of 'coalition of the needed'. Does the partnership configuration represent all requisite roles, mandates and responsibilities to be well-aligned with the societal issue it seeks to address? Do all partners uphold their commitment of bringing in the relevant functions, resources and capabilities? The composition of the partnership – including the societal positioning, power, representation of interests, involvement in other networks, and reputation of participants – influences both input and output *legitimacy* of the partnering project (Dellas, 2012). Section 5.6 outlined analytical steps that can be used to assess the issue-partnering fit.

▪ *Input-activities fit [B-C]:* is defined by the degree to which the activities of the CSP relate to each participant's 'organizational logic' and strategies – in terms of ambition, motivational drivers and intended level of value creation (level 1, 2, 3, 4). Factors such as governance, agency, power, accountability, transaction costs and decision-making structures particularly play out during project execution. The activities ('throughput') dimension focuses on the structure within which partners work towards the partnership objectives. It is contingent on (1) the number and nature of CSP participants, (2) the roles adopted by the participants, (3) the arrangements and degree of internal dependencies chosen, which in turn is influenced by (4) the position of participants as primary or secondary stakeholder in the project (Fransen and Kolk, 2007), and the degree to which the partnership is 'institutionalized' in the participating organizations (Van Huijstee and Glasbergen, 2010).

▪ *Input-output fit [B-D]:* basically concerns the operational cost/benefit dimension of the partnership. Outputs are tangible results that the participating organizations or project manager can measure or assess directly. Output represents the deliverables: what will be accomplished as a result of the combination of inputs, activities and established degree of goal alignment between the partners.

▪ *Output-outcome fit [D-E]:* outcomes are the benefits or changes for individuals, communities or society at large that the activities of the partnership can bring about. Unlike inputs and outputs, outcomes are more difficult to assess and even more difficult to *attribute* to specific partnership interventions. Outcome evaluations consider the wider and longer-term effects of the partnership. In both opportunity-driven and issue-oriented CSP approaches, the 'output-outcome fit' can be defined as the creation of as much as possible 'positive effects' while limiting 'negative effects' for directly and indirectly affected stakeholders and beneficiaries. The benchmark for measuring these externalities will be different for each approach.

▪ *Output-impact fit [D-F]:* impacts are the ultimate changes that indicate whether the partnership can be considered 'fit for purpose'. It addresses all positive and negative, short-term and longer-term effects produced by the partnership – directly or indirectly, intended or unintended. The impact of the partnership can be assessed at the level of the partners, the stakeholders, the value chain, the community and the system.

12.3.1 Monitoring performance and impact of CSPs

To inform continuous learning and ongoing decision-making on the best possible course of action, plausible effects of the cross-sector partnership project can be assessed in terms of performance or impact.[6]

[a] **The performance angle** focuses on the type of *efficiencies* that can be attributed to the actual management of the partnership (Figure 12.2):

■ G1 – project efficiency: operational efficiency [B→D]

■ G2 – project performance: tactical efficiency [B→E]

The **efficiency** dimension of a CSP can be understood as the *internal value added* of the partnership. This can be assessed using a straightforward cost-benefit analysis. What were the total costs of the partnership and what specific costs (transaction costs, operating costs) can be attributed to the partnership? For example, complex negotiations involving a large number of stakeholders initially impose more costs on the participants, but – in case of successfully embedded and institutionalized relationships – can lead to significantly lower operating costs later on. Weakly elaborated partnering agreements or contracts between the cooperating parties can result in considerable additional costs when the partnership runs up against 'collaborative complexities' and becomes 'problematic'. Also the extent to which the partnership could profit from operational synergies can be assessed. What costs could be saved by joining forces and combining competences, resources and activities in achieving the intended partnership outcome? An CSP efficiency assessment can pertain to two dimensions: (a) an *operational level* of 'project efficiency' that links 'input' with 'output' [G1]; and (b) a *tactical level* of 'project performance' that links 'input' with 'outcome' [G2].

[b] **The impact angle** centres on how *effective* the partnership is in addressing the complexity of the societal issue:

■ H1: mission-related performance (strategic) [A→F]

■ H2: issue/SDG-related performance (sustainability) [O→F]

The **effectiveness** of a CSP can be understood as the *additionality* and *the impact of the partnership* compared to individual activities of the different

---

6 Figure 5.7 in Chapter 5 depicted two 'schools of thought' in measuring the effects of CSPs: the 'performance school' and the 'impact school' The performance school prevails in M&E practice, but both approaches have to be combined if the effects and ultimate impact of the CSP are to be assessed.

partners. In other words, does the partnership provide additional ways of achieving societal ambitions (like the SDGs) that would not have been possible otherwise? Were other objectives attainable through the partnership? Were more resources allocated than otherwise possible? Did the partnership project trigger other activities of participants that proved relevant for obtaining (some of) the societal goals? Is an alternative partnering (or non-partnering) approach possible that would have brought about comparable results? To what extent is the experience reproducible and scalable? What would have happened in case the partnership project had not been implemented? The latter question defines the so-called *counterfactual* dimension. The counterfactual seeks to establish whether the effects of the partnership could have appeared anyway, or with much less effort, or whether other partnership configurations might have been more effective. The counterfactual is difficult to prove, however, for lack of representative 'control groups' or relevant benchmarks.

An CSP effectiveness assessment can be split into two dimensions: (a) a mission-related performance measure, which evaluates how the CSP made a difference in context and time, as articulated in the partnership's mission [H1, strategic]; and (b) an issue-related performance measure, which assesses the contribution of the CSP to providing solutions to the targeted issue in terms of impact [H2, sustainability]. Both efficiency and effectiveness are always highly dependent on the context [I] in which the partnership is initiated and operational (see Box 11.4 on impact measurement).

12.3.2 Four partnership impact loops for learning and upgrading

Partnerships define purpose-driven and impact-oriented collaborative relationships between parties that – on the basis of accumulated experience and insights gained during projects – can increase in efficiency and effectiveness over time. Effective learning from monitoring and regular (impact) evaluation is instrumental for enhancing the transformative capacity of the partnership. It helps practitioners, managers and partnering organizations to learn more about their intervention activities and gain a deeper understanding of why and how outcomes and impacts are realized – or not. Learning – at the individual, intra-organizational and inter-organizational levels – is a basic precondition and prime driver of fortifying increasingly complex (order) impact effects created by the partnership (Figure 12.3). Impact loops thereby indicate how 'feedback' (learning) may 'feed forward' (partnership upgrading) in order to bring about the aspired change.

Four partnership impact loops for learning and upgrading can be discerned: (1) at the level of individuals, (2) at the level of each participating organization (intra-organizational), (3) at the inter-organizational level of the

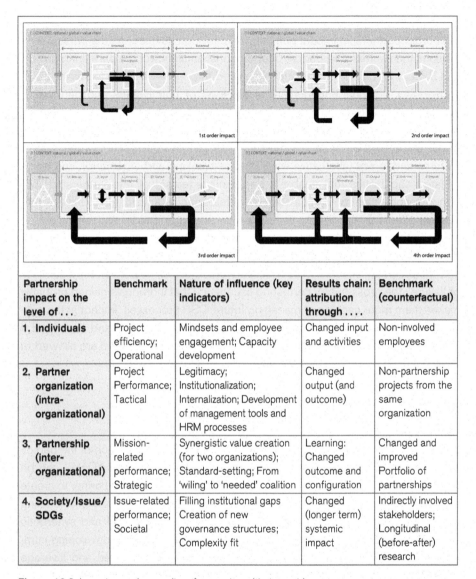

Partnership impact on the level of ...	Benchmark	Nature of influence (key indicators)	Results chain: attribution through	Benchmark (counterfactual)
1. Individuals	Project efficiency; Operational	Mindsets and employee engagement; Capacity development	Changed input and activities	Non-involved employees
2. Partner organization (intra-organizational)	Project Performance; Tactical	Legitimacy; Institutionalization; Internalization; Development of management tools and HRM processes	Changed output (and outcome)	Non-partnership projects from the same organization
3. Partnership (inter-organizational)	Mission-related performance; Strategic	Synergistic value creation (for two organizations); Standard-setting; From 'wiling' to 'needed' coalition	Learning: Changed outcome and configuration	Changed and improved Portfolio of partnerships
4. Society/Issue/SDGs	Issue-related performance; Societal	Filling institutional gaps Creation of new governance structures; Complexity fit	Changed (longer term) systemic impact	Indirectly involved stakeholders; Longitudinal (before-after) research

Figure 12.3 Learning and upgrading: four partnership impact loops

partnership, and (4) at the societal or 'issue' level. Each of these loops has a bearing on specific 'fits' along the 'impact value chain' (Figure 12.2). Learning effects on each of the four impact levels can be expected to create better 'fits' and provide upgrading possibilities for the partnership, which ultimately should lead to greater societal impact [F]. *Learning in, from and on the partnership* can be greatly enhanced through the formation of an 'Impact Team' that can guide vital learning and upgrading processes along the partnering cycle (Box 12.9).

1ST ORDER IMPACT LOOP: CHANGING MINDSETS

First order partnership impact primarily runs through its effect on the participating persons themselves. The degree of operational efficiency of the partnering project [fits B→C→D] can be significantly advanced through harnessing learning effects and greater personal engagement at the level of practitioners and partnership managers. Beneficial learning effects derived from the partnering experience may range from a strengthened 'collaborative mindset' and 'pro-social behaviour' to (leadership) skills development, new insights gained from distinct organizational cultures and logics (alternative ways of sense-making and organizing), and accumulated capabilities that enable a better management of the partnership. The (empowering) effect on participating individuals can be anticipated to have further positive effects on the performance of partnering organizations and, ultimately, on the societal issue addressed. The 'counterfactual' is relatively easy to establish by taking other employees that are not involved in the partnership as a benchmark. Individual learning effects can be assessed regardless of the partnership's success or 'failure': the cross-sector partnering experience that individuals gained probably makes them more capable of managing future CSP processes. Impact at the individual level comes with experience, yet can only be acquired and leveraged if partnership managers are provided with an adequate mandate and are allowed to invest sufficient time in the partnership to really learn from it.

2ND ORDER IMPACT LOOP: IMPROVED INTERNALIZATION AND INSTITUTIONALIZATION

Second order impact runs through the effects the CSP has on each of the participating organizations. The partnership's tactical efficiency [B→C→D→E] can be advanced through organizational learning effects that enable each partner to create a better fit between inputs, outputs and CSP outcome. Intra-organizational learning includes finding ways to internalize the operational, reputational and synergetic value (collaborative advantage) created by the partnership while developing intra-organizational infrastructures, processes and routines that embed and leverage these effects into own activities. Effects from 'institutionalizing' the partnership in intra-organizational processes may, for instance, result in a more effective management of the organization's 'partnership portfolio' (section 12.4) and the development of M&E methods, management tools and HRM practices that provide partnering managers with sufficient support (reinforcing 1nd order impact loops).[7]

<hr/>

7 **Case #12.6** discusses an application of using impact loops 1+2 to understand why one of the first global partnerships for a common goal – the TNT-WFP 'moving the world' partnership – failed, from the perspective of the private company. From the experience gained by WFP, the partnership can nevertheless be considered a success.

Efficiencies and organizational benefits derived from the partnering experience can be anticipated to reinforce organizational commitment ('buy-in) to the partnership from ever more experienced organizational partners. The counterfactual can be provided by comparing successful and less successful partnership efforts initiated by the same organization – and the extent to which these CSPs have been institutionalized within the organization.

3RD ORDER IMPACT LOOP: LEARNING AT THE PARTNERSHIP LEVEL

Third order impact loops appear at the level of the partnership itself and relate to the CSP's effectiveness in attaining its mission-related objectives [A→F]. The strategic performance of the partnership can be upgraded by identifying organizational, relational and contextual factors that, if modified, could create a more optimal fit between the partnership's internal workings [A→B→C→D] and the external effects induced [E→F]. Learning at the partnership level involves reckoning with intended and unintended, negative and positive, and long-term, intermediate and short-term effects. Section 12.2 defined several key CSP dimensions that can be used to assess learning and upgrading effects, including: the degree of goal alignment established between the partners, the capacity to build up sufficient levels of mutual trust and the effectiveness of established governance mechanisms to guide actions, results, decision-making and organizational tensions between the partners. Effects from inter-organizational learning processes may result in decisions to intensify or extensify the collaborative relationship, to develop additional partnering activities, scale current activities or terminate the partnering initiative altogether. Additional avenues for upgrading the CSP's strategic performance could involve modifications in the partnership configuration (upgrading the partnership's 'additionality' by optimizing partner complementarities), a restructuring of activities (adjusting the balance between co-exploration/co-exploitation), or adjustments in the partnership's Theory of Change to incorporate important lessons learned.[8] A benchmark for the relative performance of the partnership might be found in cross-checking the experience of comparable partnerships (for instance, within the same funding programme), by tracking the partnership's progress over time, or by considering organizations with a similar mission definition (e.g. SDG-related ambition).

8   **Case #12.8** applies these insights to the Philips-Amref Health Africa case. Both parties learned from their experience of the – unsuccessful – first partnering cycle to subsequently improve their partnership and enhance their impact on a wicked problem: 'access to primary health care' (SDG3).

4TH ORDER IMPACT LOOP: ULTIMATE IMPACT ON THE ISSUE

Fourth order impact refers to the overall impact effected by the partnership on the issue for which it was initiated. Learning and upgrading effects at this level include all stages – from input to impact – and cover the full extent of the CSP's contribution to the (societal) issue [O→F]. Fourth order effects are the most complex to assess, because of the multiple impact levels involved and the sizable number of interaction effects that play out over extended periods of time. In practice, 4th order impact loops – as the accumulated effects of 1st, 2nd and 3rd order impact loops – develop on the basis of continuous upgrading and scaling efforts.[9] Intermediate adjustments in the partnership configuration and intervention strategy, for instance, may allow for a more dynamic issue partnering fit [O→B] to bring about greater impact. One benchmark for establishing the CSP's societal performance is its effectiveness in formulating and operationalizing novel (transformational, paradoxical) approaches that successfully serve as a 'proto-institution', filling in an existing 'institutional void' and bridging related societal trust gaps (section 5.2). The counterfactual has to meet conditions of a comparable 'context' – either in the same country or supply chain – where stakeholders and/ or communities are differently affected by the partnership. A complementary approach is to take a longitudinal perspective and compare 'before-after' settings. For instance, the extent to which the existence of the partnership actually *prevented* a societal issue from proliferating could be explored.

BOX 12.9

KEEPING TRACK OF IMPACT LOOPS – CREATING AN IMPACT TEAM

The idea for an 'Impact Team' to help guide and reflect on partnering project processes, originates from the concept of a 'Red Team'. Red Teams are increasingly used by organizations that face transition problems and, therefore, decide to initiate "an independent group that challenges an organization to improve its effectiveness". An Impact Team consists of the representatives of each of the partnering organizations and is aimed at facilitating the operationalization and implementation of a 'complexity-sensitive' Theory of Change for the CSP, by applying principles of 'developmental evaluation' in a practical setting. The members of the Impact

---

9   One of the most relevant illustrations of a successful transformational strategy (level 4), using partnerships to enter an institutional void, is arguably provided by Safaricom and the successful introduction of a mobile money system (MPesa) in Kenya. **Case #12.7** uses impact loops 1–2–3–4 to illustrate how and why the partnership that created the MPesa system could become a success in addressing the issue of 'financial inclusion' of tens of millions poor people (SDG1).

Team serve as 'internal brokers' (see Box 12.11) within their respective organizations and engage in mutual learning processes to enhance the efficiency and effectiveness of the CSP. The Impact Team comes together at least twice (at the start and completion) during each of the four phases of the partnership cycle.

The Impact Team navigates the partnership through each phase, by using sets *of guiding questions* that keep the partnership focused on achieving maximum impact on society, both during and sustained after the partnership. The Impact Team should be able to identify and deal with two particular types of tensions in the partnership that – if not properly addressed – will have a negative influence on the relational, operational and outcome dimensions of the collaboration: (1) a performance-driven versus an impact-driven orientation (section 12.3.1), and (2) a focus on 'accountability and control' versus 'mutual learning and upgrading' (section 12.2.3). All partnerships suffer from the problem of an extended time horizon, as meaningful and lasting impact only materializes over longer periods of time. Nevertheless, sponsors and participants usually want to show for short-term 'results', preferably measurable and with a claim of impact. Accountability and control become more important than learning, even when this creates quasi-exactness (see Box 11.4 on 'impact integrity'). The Impact Team should be aware of this tension and make sure to ask *the right questions at the right time*, and search for *the right type of metrics at the right time*. Chapter 11 (section 11.2) introduced this method as a way to bridge the gap between Key Decision-making Indicators (KDIs) and Key Practice and Performance Indicators (KPIs) by formulating Key Performance Questions (KPQs).

The Impact Team systematically keeps track of progress on the four impact loops and related learning processes, in each consecutive phase of the partnership cycle. The focus of guiding questions consequently changes over time. Guiding questions should be agreed upon at *the start of each phase*, whilst reflections on achieved results (and pointers for further attention) serve as a *stoplight*. In case of agreement on having satisfactory tackled key considerations, the partnership can move on to the next phase (green light). In case of disagreement and remaining points of attention that need addressing (red or yellow light), sociocratic principles (section 5.6) can be applied to search for creative/common solutions, either at the level of individual partnering organizations or at the level of the partnership as a whole (see section 12.2.3–4). Typical guiding questions per phase include:

❏ Do you consider yourself a coalition of 'willing' or 'needed' partners? Who else should be involved and why?

❏ Have you made a shared analysis of the root-causes of the problem; if not, how can this become a problem later on in the project?

❏ Can you define aspired impact and formulate Key Performance Questions?

❏ How open are you towards change, and are you willing to share dilemmas and build up mutual trust?

❏ What M&E practices are presently in place and how effective are they?

❏ What expertise, experience and lessons have you accumulated from previous partnerships?

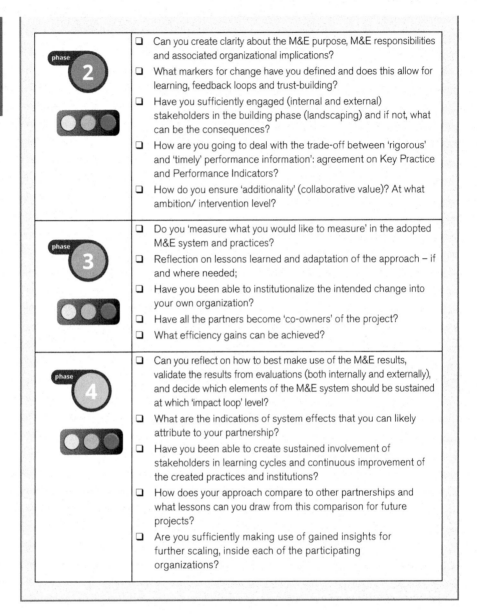

phase 2

❑ Can you create clarity about the M&E purpose, M&E responsibilities and associated organizational implications?

❑ What markers for change have you defined and does this allow for learning, feedback loops and trust-building?

❑ Have you sufficiently engaged (internal and external) stakeholders in the building phase (landscaping) and if not, what can be the consequences?

❑ How are you going to deal with the trade-off between 'rigorous' and 'timely' performance information': agreement on Key Practice and Performance Indicators?

❑ How do you ensure 'additionality' (collaborative value)? At what ambition/ intervention level?

phase 3

❑ Do you 'measure what you would like to measure' in the adopted M&E system and practices?

❑ Reflection on lessons learned and adaptation of the approach – if and where needed;

❑ Have you been able to institutionalize the intended change into your own organization?

❑ Have all the partners become 'co-owners' of the project?

❑ What efficiency gains can be achieved?

phase 4

❑ Can you reflect on how to best make use of the M&E results, validate the results from evaluations (both internally and externally), and decide which elements of the M&E system should be sustained at which 'impact loop' level?

❑ What are the indications of system effects that you can likely attribute to your partnership?

❑ Have you been able to create sustained involvement of stakeholders in learning cycles and continuous improvement of the created practices and institutions?

❑ How does your approach compare to other partnerships and what lessons can you draw from this comparison for future projects?

❑ Are you sufficiently making use of gained insights for further scaling, inside each of the participating organizations?

12.4 PARTNERSHIP PORTFOLIO MANAGEMENT: CREATING AN SDG-PARTNERING FIT

Over the years, companies have been engaging in an expanding and often highly diverse portfolio of cross-sector partnerships. In 2010, the world's 100 largest multi-national corporations reported involvement in 18 CSPs on average, representing a wide variety of sustainability goals (PrC, 2011). In the 'alliance portfolio' literature, the

engagement of firms in multiple simultaneous strategic alliances with different partners has been established as a "ubiquitous phenomenon" in the business landscape
(Wassmer, 2010). Classic insights on the reasons why firms are better off by
managing a 'portfolio' of alliances – rather than 'one-at-a-time' relationships – include
the management of risk and uncertainty; enhancement of firm resilience to changes
in the business ecosystem; opportunities for accelerated learning; access to complementary resources; extended relational capital and structural embeddedness in vital
networks; and leverage of power, influence and positioning. Nevertheless – and
perhaps more importantly – opposite effects have also been found: "a poorly
designed, mismanaged network can entangle the firm and waste scarce managerial
bandwidth" (Gomes-Casseres, 1998). Conflicts among partners will overshadow
any potential value to be gained from multiple partnerships. In order to bring about
the desired beneficial effects, Partnership Portfolio Management (PPM) needs to be
grounded in an *aggregate logic* underpinning all strategic and tactical partnering
activities, along with a dynamic view on portfolio (re)configuration and *effective portfolio coordination* to manage the interdependencies between partnering activities in
a coherent way (Duysters et al., 1999).

The insights from PPM bear relevance for the simultaneous engagement in
various CSPs too, and increasingly so. Managing a portfolio of CSPs – at all
relevant levels of intervention and sustainability ambitions (levels 1, 2, 3, 4) –
requires a constant reflection on the question whether the portfolio serves the
organization's strategic and society's sustainability needs. Empirical research on
companies' involvement in CSPs nevertheless indicates that few of the CSP portfolios have evolved on the basis of solid strategic choices. Most are grounded in
ad hoc reasoning and short-term considerations, resulting in a rather fragmented
assortment of partnering commitments that tend to be poorly linked to core
corporate activities. A clear 'logic' has often been difficult to ascertain.[10] Peripheral
and decentralized partnerships struck by individual departments or persons
brought considerable internal coordination and integration problems. Partnerships
were created, but subsequently also terminated on the basis of ad hoc decisions.[11] The size and complexity of early CSP portfolios even prompted

---

10 **Case #12.5** documents the portfolio strategy of an early adopter of the partnership
approach: American oil producer Chevron. In 2009, Chevron reported engagement in 48
different cross-sector partnerships. Although its CSR report was entitled 'The value of partnership', a clear 'logic' behind the established portfolio was difficult to distinguish. The case
explores what lacking coherence in the partnering strategy implied for the company's
'license to operate and scale' in the decade that followed.

11 **Case #12.6** (TNT-WFP) presents a case in which the leader of one organization developed
the partnership as a dedicated yet isolated commitment, resting on the core competences
of both organizations. The partnership was ended as soon as the company's leadership
changed.

'partnership fatigue' with managers, which made them less willing to start another partnership (Huxham and Vangen, 2004).

Difficulties in establishing and managing a sophisticated CSP portfolio do not take away its relevance, however. The key challenge companies face is how to create a *strategic partnering fit* between the organization's sustainability strategy and its overall partnership portfolio in a way that maximizes collaborative value for positive change. Formulated in more operational terms: whether and when to intensify or extensify specific partnering activities and on the basis of what considerations? Effective CSP portfolio management represents a balancing act between two parallel ambitions: meaningfully engaging in a portfolio of partnerships that adequately covers the company's *present* sustainability ambitions, while at the same time forging (new) partnerships that enable the company to move into *future* sustainability areas. The first PPM challenge requires partnership 'mapping' in order to optimize present CSP involvement (section 12.4.1). The second PPM challenge calls for 'strategizing' and the search for a forward-looking SDG-partnering fit (section 12.4.2).

12.4.1 Mapping gaps in the partnership portfolio

Aligning the established CSP portfolio with the organization's present sustainability strategy implies a periodic re-examination of the portfolio as a whole, viewed through a 'gap analysis' and optimization lens. Partnership portfolio mapping enables an organization to assess to what extent the standing portfolio corresponds with the organization's key sustainability issues, in terms of engaged partners; the scope and depth of the societal issues addressed; the ambition level, objectives, results and effects of each partnership; and the partnering complementarities and collaborative advantage involved. How 'material' are the issues as reflected by the CSP portfolio to the company (section 9.1)? Empirical research by the Partnerships Resource Centre indicates that CSP portfolio mapping – despite its strategic and operational merit – is still rarely practiced by organizations, nor used as a mechanism to support internal coordination or external communication (PrC, 2015). This finding applies to for-profit and non-profit organizations alike.

Partnership portfolio mapping takes the following dimensions into account: (1) the 'size' of the portfolio; (2) the effect of different partners on the 'diversity' of the portfolio; (3) 'density': interdependencies and features of weak and strong ties, flowing from the nature of the various collaborative relationships; (4) inter- and intra-partnership 'dynamics' between (different types of) partners over time; in order to (5) draw the CSP portfolio map as a stepping stone for portfolio optimization and future-oriented strategizing (Figure 12.4).

■ **Portfolio size:** the choice for a particular size of the partnering portfolio typically varies with the number and scope of issues the organization is

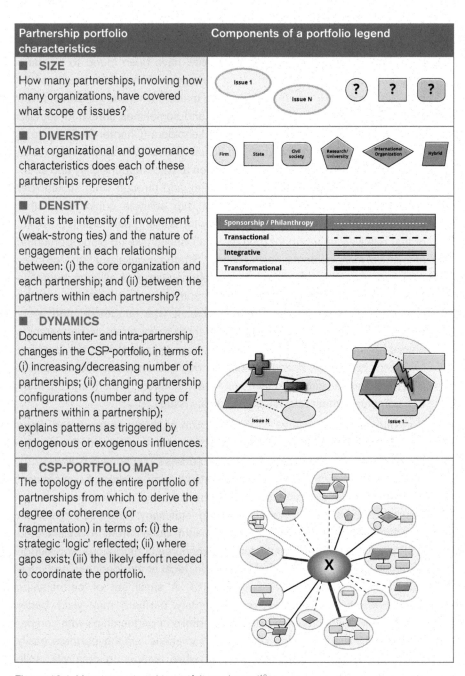

Partnership portfolio characteristics	Components of a portfolio legend
■ **SIZE** How many partnerships, involving how many organizations, have covered what scope of issues?	
■ **DIVERSITY** What organizational and governance characteristics does each of these partnerships represent?	
■ **DENSITY** What is the intensity of involvement (weak-strong ties) and the nature of engagement in each relationship between: (i) the core organization and each partnership; and (ii) between the partners within each partnership?	
■ **DYNAMICS** Documents inter- and intra-partnership changes in the CSP-portfolio, in terms of: (i) increasing/decreasing number of partnerships; (ii) changing partnership configurations (number and type of partners within a partnership); explains patterns as triggered by endogenous or exogenous influences.	
■ **CSP-PORTFOLIO MAP** The topology of the entire portfolio of partnerships from which to derive the degree of coherence (or fragmentation) in terms of: (i) the strategic 'logic' reflected; (ii) where gaps exist; (iii) the likely effort needed to coordinate the portfolio.	

Figure 12.4 Mapping partnership portfolios: a legend[12]

---

12 The original partnership portfolio mapping technique was developed together with Lisa Barendsen (2012), linked to the strategic alliance literature by Andrea da Rosa (2013), and applied and further validated with 20 Dutch frontrunner companies (Van Tulder et al., 2014).

faced with. A large number of partnerships does not necessarily provide an advantage. With size in numbers come considerable span of control problems. Factors such as 'partnership quality' have been found to be more important predictors of the partnering strategy's efficacy than the size of the portfolio alone. Numbers particularly matter when organizations are confronted with a vast array of diverse and sometimes unrelated sustainability issues represented by 'salient' stakeholders (Chapter 9). The size of the CSP portfolio then becomes a function of issue prioritization and materiality choices: which issues need attention at what responsibility and ambition level, how to effectively address them, and through what stakeholder engagement strategies? Conducting a gap analysis could reveal that several salient issues are not covered by the existing partnership portfolio, or that relatively unimportant (non-material) issues take up disproportionate amounts of management time and energy. Strategy consultant firm McKinsey even put a number on the observed phenomenon of alliance portfolios growing into 'a random mix' of partnering commitments assembled over the years. To keep the portfolio manageable, it was suggested that every company should typically identify two or three major strategic partnerships crucial for future success, five to seven that are important at an operating level and, potentially, dozens of tactical deals (Bamford and Ernst, 2002: 38). Prioritizing as such should ensure that managers give enough attention to a company's most relevant sustainability issues.

▪ **Portfolio diversity:** relates to the selection of those partners and those partnerships that enable sufficient 'dynamic/complexity fit' with the sustainability issues the organization seeks to address (sections 5.5 and 12.2). The 'portfolio diversity' dimension reiterates the importance of complementarities: of core competences, organizational logics, resources, power bases, networks, societal positioning and legitimacy. It reveals the breadth of potential benefits an organization might obtain from a multifaceted CSP portfolio – for instance in terms of resource contributions, knowledge accumulation, relational capital, reputation, local embeddedness and internationality of partners (Wassmer, 2010). A small set of partnerships comprised of well-selected complementary partners may yield better 'collaborative value' than an extended portfolio of partnerships with comparable organizations. A high degree of 'sameness' among partners easily leads to one-sided interest articulation while hampering creativity, spillovers and innovation. Portfolio optimization considerations then concentrate on defining a stakeholder portfolio that is: (1) *effective* in representing the 'needed' configurations of organizational partners for tackling specific issues, and (2) *efficient* in prioritizing those partners that cover a wider set of sustainability issues and could create synergy effects between various partnerships represented in the CSP portfolio.

- **Portfolio density:** involves the intensity of ties that the CSP portfolio consolidates. Dense portfolios consist of strong and mutually reciprocal connections between most partners, whereas dispersed portfolios reflect more loosely coupled, occasional connections. The nature of collaborative relationships generally varies per partnership, and can be based on provisional (philanthropic), transactional, integrative or more transformational goals and interactions (Table 12.1). Commitment levels vary accordingly, ranging from 'weak ties' reflecting lower levels of dependency and reciprocity to 'strong' or 'strategic' ties that rest on higher levels of interdependence and consequential interlocking effects. In network theory, weak ties have been found particularly instrumental in the diffusion of information and ideas by performing a 'bridging function' between partnerships within and networks outside the CSP portfolio. Strong and strategic collaborative ties, on the other hand, are pivotal in operationalizing and purposively implementing the (transformational) change envisaged. Extensive partnership portfolios are likely to contain both loosely and strongly coupled relational ties, as both can fulfil different organizational needs and 'functions'. A coherent CSP portfolio not only considers the degree of interdependencies, but also takes heed of the 'ecosystem' of adjacent networks.

- **Dynamics:** partnership portfolios evolve over time due to the formation of new and the termination of existing partnerships. Such changes can be the result of learning processes and optimization decisions based on size, diversity and density, but may also flow from rapidly changing situational, operational and organizational circumstances. Drivers of 'change' and 'stability' within the CSP portfolio notably relate to such factors as trust levels, conflict and goal alignment between partnering organizations, each partner's decisions on the intensification or extensification of specific partnering activities with time, and the 'entry and exit' conditions set for each partnership (formulated in partnering agreements). Interaction dynamics that play out at the level of individual partnerships may affect dynamics at the CSP portfolio level as well. For instance, trust levels across the portfolio of partners can be seriously compromised if one of the partners is concurrently involved in another network supporting competing goals. By contrast, organizations that – over the years – have managed to build up a well-functioning CSP portfolio, will find it easier to attract additional partners or to get support in times of crisis. This finding relates to the *trust dividend* organizations may obtain from societal stakeholders (including the critical ones) in reaction to genuine efforts to invest in meaningful collaborative relationships and credibly communicate about their CSR and related partnering strategy. Unilever, for instance, was able to withstand a hostile takeover bid in 2017 by a less sustainable food company (focused on short-term profits), "thanks in part to the goodwill it had painstakingly earned by investing in partners and working with stakeholders on their net positive journey" (Polman and Winston, 2021: 4).

- ■ **CSP portfolio map:** shows the accumulated characteristics of the entire CSP portfolio – as represented by the observed topology of all partnership relationships – at a certain moment in time. Drawing the topology in an unbiased and systematic manner reveals patterns, gaps, redundancies, possible overlaps and coordination challenges. The CSP portfolio map enables an assessment of the extent to which the company's sustainability strategy has resulted in a reasonably coherent partnership portfolio. It provides a means for benchmarking the *realized* partnering approach – the established CSP portfolio – against the organization's *intended* sustainability strategy (at levels 1–4). Ideally, the established CSP portfolio conveys a clear aggregate logic that is consistent and in line with the overall sustainability strategy. In practice, however, partnerships often materialize as decentralized, 'bottom-up' or locally enacted initiatives – not seldom in a relatively uncoordinated manner or as part of an emergent or strategic tinkering process (Chapter 11). Optimizing the assembled CSP portfolio then requires the organization to appraise the relevance and consequences of revealed gaps and mismatches, for instance in terms of coordination efforts needed, the risk management involved, underutilized potential for learning and internalization of collaborative value, and reputational or operational vulnerabilities due to disappointing results.

Voids in the CSP portfolio can appear on numerous fronts, but are arguably most prominent and immediate where: (a) issues, as targeted by individual partnerships, do not convincingly overlap with the organization's material sustainability issues; (b) partnership ambition levels, goals or intervention approaches do not match with the organization's key values, key positioning decisions and societal legitimacy pursued (Chapters 9 and 10); (c) stakeholders represented in the portfolio do not provide the complementarities needed to establish sufficiently 'complexity-fit' partnerships, thereby undermining the credibility of intervention approaches and projected outcomes. The more and the wider the identified gaps, the more likely it is that the 'logic' underpinning the CSP portfolio stems from tactical and ad hoc considerations, rather than a strategic course of action. Further evidence of this observation can be found in case the composition of the portfolio changes regularly without an obvious logic. Gaps may furthermore point to restrained senior management involvement and support, limited absorptive capacity or a view on CSPs as a relatively marginal corporate activity – indicating low levels of 'institutionalization' and internal coordination of PPM. The efforts needed to improve coordination of the CSP portfolio then not only require optimizing, but also strategizing decisions.

12.4.2 Strategizing for greater SDG-partnering fit

Strategizing for a more astute fit between CSP portfolio and sustainability ambitions implies a deliberate process of *rethinking* the original CSP approach, related choices and identified limitations posed by implementation processes, in order to narrow the gap between intended and realized partnering strategies. Strategizing "links aspirations and capabilities, issues and answers, problems and solutions" (Bryson, 2021), so that imminent sustainability challenges and unfolding opportunities can be more effectively addressed. Working towards a future-oriented CSP portfolio requires organizations to move beyond their presently 'material' issues and 'reverse' the materiality perspective in the strategizing process (section 9.3.2). By taking *societal needs* as the main point of departure, the strategizing question shifts: from portfolio optimization considerations alone, to how to use the SDGs to leverage change in a more sustainable direction and establish a greater 'SDG-partnering fit'.[13] Strategizing as such adds an *impact perspective* to Partnership Portfolio Management (PPM) considerations, operationalized in earlier sections as 'issue-related performance' and the ability to meaningfully contribute to the SDGs (section 5.5.3 and 12.3.1).

Strategizing the CSP portfolio is a dynamic process – 'strategizing in action' – that develops under the conditions of complexity: in interaction with internal stakeholders (functional-level sustainability initiatives and strategies, Chapter 11), in interaction with external stakeholders and (prospective) partners, and as part of the organization's value orientation, positioning and organizational transitioning processes (Chapter 10). Moreover, consequential PPM decisions to intensify, de-intensify or altogether terminate specific partnering commitments may have a bearing on the entire CSP portfolio in terms of its overall coherence, strength and efficacy in serving the organization's sustainability ambitions. PPM decisions can build or burn relational capital; they can drive or jeopardize future strategizing efforts; they may reinforce or cancel conducive 'part-whole' dynamics. What constitutes a resilient 'fit' is therefore difficult to determine upfront. The SDG-framework can nevertheless provide a useful 'reference frame' that adds 'strategic logic' to PPM decision-making directed at improving the organization's capacity for societal impact.

Portfolio strategizing can be approached as a sequence of analytical steps to gradually 'redraw' the CSP portfolio map (section 12.4.1) and facilitate (re-) configuration decisions. Guiding questions along three consecutive 'steps' can

---

13 **Case #12.10** describes the case of Unilever, which in the course of years developed a relatively coherent CSP portfolio strategy in support of its 'Sustainable Living Plan'. Unilever's PPM approach eventually not only allowed the organization to align with the SDGs, but also helped it to withstand a hostile takeover bid.

help navigate PPM decisions in working towards greater SDG-partnering fit: [1] rethinking the portfolio's issue orientation, [2] strengthening resilience by deepening capabilities, and [3] extending impact ambitions.

[1] RETHINKING THE PORTFOLIO'S ISSUE ORIENTATION

Taking 'issue-related performance' (Figure 12.2) as a benchmark for rethinking the CSP portfolio strategy, puts the identification, prioritization and management of *societal issues* at the core of the strategizing exercise. A critical reassessment of the organization's present issues management approach – as mirrored in the established partnership portfolio – includes questions like: what societal issues have as yet been considered 'material' to the organization and how does this issue prioritization relate to the identified patterns, gaps, redundancies and overlaps in the built-up partnership portfolio? Upon reflection, are these the issues, partner relations and partnership projects that the organization wants, should or needs to focus on – why exactly, or why not? Does the portfolio add up to the kind of societal value and scale of impact the organization strives to attain through its various partnerships? To what extent can the issues that were deemed material in the past, still be considered to drive the sustainability strategy in the years ahead? Do these particular issues support the organization's longer-term outcome and impact ambitions? What do these patterns imply for the effectiveness of the organization's sustainability strategy in the longer run? What changes in issue prioritization and partnering activities are probably needed to better align with societal expectations and needs?

Rethinking the CSP portfolio set against the corporate sustainability strategy can already give cause to drastic reconfiguration decisions to attain better congruence, optimize portfolio performance and bridge apparent intention-realization gaps. From a more forward-looking perspective, however, using the SDGs as a 'reference frame' could add *societal relevance* and a longer time horizon to the strategizing process and, therefore, increase the 'strategic logic'.

- To the extent that the SDGs are already integral to the organization's sustainability strategy (see section 10.5), rethinking the CSP portfolio implies (re)aligning (parts of) the portfolio around prioritized SDGs and SDG-targets – as defined in the corporate strategy and corporate sustainable story (section 10.6) – as well as an effective translation of SDG-related objectives into partnering strategies. Which of the present partnerships in the portfolio can be substantively aligned with the prioritized set of SDGs (Box 12.10)?

- To the extent that the SDGs are not yet explicitly part of the corporate strategy, clustering existing partnerships around applicable SDGs could entail a helpful (re)structuring logic for revealing issue-related commonalities between the organization's distinct partnership activities. Such

SDG-oriented clustering may, for instance, unveil that several partnership commitments – entered into by different functional departments or business units – all in some way relate to biodiversity, deforestation and land remediation ('life on land', SDG15), while others show substantive overlaps on living wage, gender equality and economic inclusion ('decent work and economic growth', SDG8 and 'reduced inequalities, SDG10). By classifying separate partnering initiatives under a common heading, patterns of functional-level ambitions and initiative, partnership objectives and emergent sustainability strategies become more apparent. As a result, they can be more strongly articulated, coordinated and (re)directed, and give further impetus to top-down/bottom-up strategy alignment (Chapter 11).

■ On closer consideration, there will be certain partnerships in the current CSP portfolio that neither quite match the organization's impact ambition, nor relate in a meaningful way to already prioritized or applicable SDGs. These partnerships may have been formed in the past as the result of ad hoc or tactical considerations, but lose their (strategic) relevance in the light of the organization's forward-looking sustainability strategy. If the strategizing objective is to increase the portfolio's issue-related performance ('SDG effectiveness'), the logical consequence would be to de-intensify, phase out or terminate those partnerships in the portfolio that do not, or cannot, add to SDG-relevant outcomes and impact.

[2] STRENGTHENING RESILIENCE, DEEPENING CAPABILITIES

Can rethinking lead to strengthening? A strengthening of the CSP portfolio is geared towards upgrading portfolio attributes and improving PPM capabilities, while addressing identified limitations and weaknesses. Strengthening objectives typically include: (1) an enhanced *ability to anticipate* and address risks, vulnerabilities and opportunities; (2) *greater coherence* (coordination and institutionalization of partnerships) to advance the portfolio's capacity for SDG-relevant impact ('issue-related performance'); and (3) a comprehensive understanding of the many *dependencies and interdependencies* that support the portfolio's strategic goals and the feasibility of impact objectives. Strengthening the partnership portfolio in a forward-looking manner implies that portfolio qualities such as 'balance', 'proportionality' and 'resilience' are taken into account (Chapter 7). A restructuring of partnerships around relevant SDGs (issue-related 'rethinking') is an essential and insightful first step in strategizing, but in itself does not necessarily result in a balanced or a resilient CSP portfolio.

■ **Balance:** a 'balanced' partnership portfolio implies that the selection of societal issues – as represented in the CSP portfolio – corresponds to an appropriate distribution of 'having' and 'taking' responsibilities (Box 5.1) and of 'avoiding harm' and 'doing good' objectives (Figure 5.2) in furtherance of a more balanced, resilient and regenerative society (Chapter 1). A partnership portfolio that predominantly consists of 'doing good' ambitions while largely ignoring – or insufficiently addressing – 'avoiding harm' objectives, holds a significant *credibility risk*. If an organization's 'doing good' partnering activities are detached from a proven capacity to conscientiously contribute to 'avoiding harm', it easily falls prey to the pitfalls of 'moral self-licensing', the 'self-promotor's paradox' and allegations of SDG-washing or cherry-picking (Table 10.8). A skewed portfolio of relatively 'easy' partnerships may lead the organization to lose – rather than gain – credibility and societal legitimacy. Alternatively, by taking up too many responsibilities in its CSP portfolio, an organization might fall prey to the 'sucker syndrome' (Box 5.1), which will fragment focus, time and effort and eventually jeopardize the portfolio's capacity for SDG impact. A balanced CSP portfolio consequently presents a *proportionate* compilation of 'avoiding harm'- and 'doing good'-oriented partnership commitments that mirror prioritized sustainability issues the organization cannot address alone – and for which it needs to *share responsibilities*.

- ▪ **Resilience:** a balanced CSP portfolio is a necessary but not sufficient condition for 'resilience' in the longer run. To reinforce its resilience, the CSP portfolio additionally needs to be aligned with *society's hierarchy* of priorities and needs – allowing the organization to collaborate with societal stakeholders on the conditions to achieve sustainable solutions for societal issues. In terms of Raworth's (2017) Doughnut Economics framework (section 1.3.6), strengthening resilience implies that an organization's partnership portfolio should be a proper reflection of endeavours that convincingly contribute to "an ecologically safe and socially just space for humanity" (ibid: 39) – ensuring the social foundation of human well-being (precluding shortfall on life's basics) within the confines of the earth's regenerative capacity ('planetary boundaries'). In terms of the 'Systemic Hierarchy of SDGs' as defined by the Stockholm Resilience Centre (Figure 12.5a), building a strategic and more resilient CSP portfolio entails that it is first and foremost firmly grounded in biosphere-related SDGs (6, 13, 14, 15), then prioritizes society-oriented SDGs (1, 2, 3, 4, 7, 11, 16), followed by economy-related SDGs (8, 9, 10, 12) – in that order, weight and proportion. In other words, a partnership portfolio that is one-sidedly focused on economy-related SDGs while disregarding (the nexus with) ecological and social SDGs, topples society's hierarchy of needs and, therefore, constitutes a vulnerable CSP portfolio that may be difficult to sustain and legitimize over the longer run. A less resilient CSP portfolio is less likely to be able to timely anticipate, absorb, respond and adapt to the threats and opportunities of a complex and changing societal context (Chapter 7).

■ **Legitimacy:** an SDG-aligned CSP portfolio that is both balanced and resilient, adds societal legitimacy to an organization's partnering efforts. The relation between portfolio balance, resilience and societal legitimacy can be depicted as a hierarchy of 'licenses' (Figure 12.5b) that society grants to organizations on the basis of their willingness, proven ability and solid commitment to societal value creation. *Strengthening the base* (deliberate efforts to uphold and solidify the foundational 'license to exist and operate') entails that addressing market failures, negative externalities and shared 'avoiding harm' responsibilities figure prominently in the CSP portfolio. At the top of the partnership pyramid, pursuing a 'license to scale or experiment' revolves around unlocking opportunities and mobilizing societal support for the creation and dissemination of positive externalities, common goods and 'doing good' (shared positive duty) goals. Such higher-order licenses are unsustainable, however, if the 'base of the pyramid' gets neglected. Societal legitimacy is accumulative, not an options menu. An unbalanced, 'top-heavy' and hence vulnerable CSP portfolio may not only cost the organization its higher-order license, but eventually could also erode its societal license to operate or exist. A sustained 'license to experiment' is only granted to organizations that have gained a sufficiently robust license to operate and scale, based on a proven capacity to serve basic societal needs. Strengthening the legitimacy and resilience of the CSP portfolio consequently starts at the base of the pyramid.

Consolidating the partnership portfolio in alignment with the SDGs is all but a static process and, therefore, relies heavily upon top management's

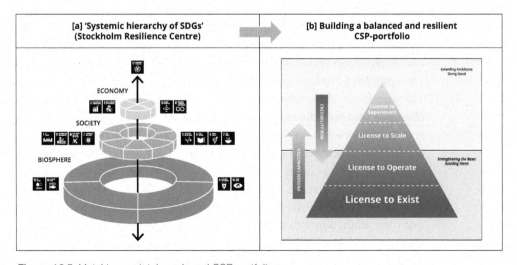

Figure 12.5 Matching societal needs and CSP portfolios

comprehensive and up-to-date understanding of the organization's diverse operating contexts (local, national, across borders, global). A regular reassessment of the portfolio's established balance and resilience is conditional to maintain a 'dynamic fit' with the needs, priorities and evolving expectations of both internal and external stakeholders.

▪ *Strengthening the portfolio's collaborative value*

A second strengthening aspect to consider in the strategizing process is how to enhance the portfolio's overall collaborative value and with it, its capacity for SDG-related impact. Answering this question starts with a critical reflection on the organization's own core responsibilities, power base and *direct sphere of control* (Chapter 10). As a general rule, partnerships are an excessive 'means of intervention' if used to address societal concerns that fully fall within the organization's fiduciary duty, primary responsibilities and capacity to resolve. Chapter 5 discussed the risks and costs involved in entering into collaborative arrangements that are not strictly needed or that 'overshoot' the complexity of the issue. Partnerships are no free lunch; they come with significant coordination, governance and communication complexities that translate into transaction costs. Where added collaborative complexities outweigh (potential) collaborative value, collaborative arrangements are not the reasonable way forward. In fact, continuation thereof may actually erode the organization's societal legitimacy, since it could be interpreted as unduly hiding behind a veil of 'societal engagement' while shirking on responsibilities for which the organization itself bears prime responsibility.

- **Intensifying:** for those SDG-related issues that are within the organization's *direct sphere of influence*, a further examination of the CSP portfolio along the lines of 'internal actionability' could indicate promising opportunities for collaborative value from working in partnership. In sections 10.5.2 and 11.10, *internally actionable SDG-targets* were denoted as those business-relevant targets that can be meaningfully engaged with and acted upon within the organization and throughout the value chain. The ambition to reduce air, water and soil pollution (related to SDGs 3, 6, 12) across the value chain, for instance, represents an 'avoiding harm' objective of which the main responsibility to act rests with the organization, but for which it may need cross-sectoral support to realize this ambition at speed, scale and with durable effect. The same goes for internally actionable 'doing good' SDG-targets – such as implementing fair payment to small-scale suppliers (related to SDG1). When properly internalized, learning effects derived from action-oriented partnering activities can both strengthen and broaden the organization's capacity to deliver on prioritized SDGs and, in turn, spur additional action. Partnerships in the CSP portfolio that add scale, speed and impact and which allow the organization to more effectively deliver on internally actionable SDG-targets, should therefore be prioritized and intensified.

■ **Amplifying:** searching for a strategic fit of the CSP portfolio with *externally actionable SDG-targets* can help organizations define ways and identify 'needed partnerships' to more purposively contribute to the collective safe-guarding and provision of common goods – a key function of CSPs (sections 5.4.2 and 5.5). Externally actionable SDG-targets are those that are *beyond the organization's direct sphere of influence* but nevertheless can still be affected indirectly by assuming one's 'leverage-based respon-sibilities' (section 10.2.2). Meaningful contributions to 'externally action-able' SDG-targets can only be made when working in partnership with diverse societal actors, while making optimal and responsible use of the organization's power base (e.g. societal position, resources and mobilizing, agenda-setting, convening, relational, discursive, normalizing powers) in support of advancing collaborative solutions for transformative change (section 10.5.2). Strengthening the CSP portfolio along the lines of exter-nally actionable SDG-targets hence involves an assessment of how the smart use of organizational powers could influence, co-shape and accel-erate courses of action that ensure a proper functioning of sustainable systems. Tool #10.1 identified 28 business-relevant 'externally actionable' SDG-targets (eight classified under 'avoiding harm' and twenty under 'doing good') that can be used to assess the CSP portfolio's potential for amplifying collaborative value.

■ *Deepening PPM capabilities*

The conditions for strengthening the portfolio's SDG performance rest on the organization's ability to integrate, build and adaptively reconfigure internal and external competences, such that (a) societal, (b) CSP portfolio and (c) individual partnership dynamics can be addressed in a timely and coherent manner. PPM capabilities are inextricably linked to the notion of 'dynamic capabilities' and to processes of intra- and inter-organizational learning, adjusting and upgrading that drive cumulative partnership 'impact loops' (section 12.3.2). They relate to the organization's absorptive capacity to institutionalize partnering-related activities, internalize operational, reputational and collaborative value and harness learning effects. They also relate to the organization's ability to anticipate, (co-)shape and respond to change, and the effective management of dependencies and interde-pendencies between the organization's internal and external contexts and stake-holders. Capabilities are especially valuable when they can be leveraged across the portfolio of partnerships.

If well-developed, PPM capabilities add 'decision-making intelligence' and 'operational performance' to the strategizing process, by linking organizational and inter-organizational competences to the portfolio's 'SDG-impact capacity' – along the four CSP portfolio dimensions outlined in section 12.4.1:

■ **Portfolio dynamics:** strategic decision-making capabilities are required to navigate and effectively manage the dynamics, resilience and societal legitimacy of the CSP portfolio as a whole – as it gets constructed in a continuous strengthening and balancing process; insufficiently developed strategic and communicative capabilities limit the organization's ability to strategize, leverage and mobilize for the SDGs;

■ **Portfolio density:** strategic, integrative and relational capabilities related to intensifying strategic partnerships (tight coupling) and managing interdependencies (goal alignment, governance, reciprocity, risk), in ways that advance the portfolio's potential for collaborative value for the SDGs;

■ **Portfolio diversity:** exploratory, exploitative and adaptive capabilities that are conditional to a deliberate search for 'needed' partners, the formation of fit-for-purpose partnerships and to ensure the portfolio's dynamic/complexity fit with prioritized SDGs over time;

■ **Portfolio size:** efficiency-related capabilities to deal with the portfolio's span of control in the context of to the organization's sustainability ambitions, whilst considering available internal capabilities, the need to develop or acquire new capabilities, and budgetary constraints.

Table 12.3 Partnership Portfolio Management: capabilities and competences

PPM Dimension	Selected Capabilities and Managerial Competences
DYNAMICS	• Strategic decision-making: extensifying, intensifying, amplifying (section 12.4.2);
	• Finding a balance between opportunity-driven and issue-driven partnerships (section 12.2.1);
	• Dealing with partnerships in various phases of the partnering cycle (section 12.2);
	• Weighing and prioritizing the relevance of specific partnerships for the organization (SDG alignment) (section 10.6; Table 10.8);
	• Connected and principles-based leadership capabilities (section 9.6);
	• Communication capabilities: formulating a coherent SDG-aligned corporate story that conveys the strategic and collaborative logic of the CSP portfolio (Table 10.8);
	• Using the organization's formative, discursive and normative powers to mobilize and engage relevant (prospective) partners (section 11.9);
	• Adaptive capabilities to anticipate, adjust and respond to changing societal priorities and needs;
	• Alignment capabilities to ensure the portfolio's 'dynamic complexity fit' over time (section 5.5);
	• Monitoring and evaluation capabilities for learning and upgrading (section 12.3).

PPM Dimension	Selected Capabilities and Managerial Competences
DENSITY	• Relational capabilities: managing tightly and loosely coupled networks and related high or low levels of dependencies and interdependencies;
	• Governance, trust & commitment and negotiation capabilities: managing tensions; co-exploitation vs. co-exploration; control vs. collaboration; trust building, repairing and restoring (sections 5.4.1, 12.2.3; Box 5.2);
	• Collective vision-based negotiation, reaching goal alignment (Box 5.2; section 12.2.2);
	• Design of comprehensive partnering agreements (section 12.3.4);
	• Learning, information-sharing, knowledge exchange (section 12.2.3).
DIVERSITY	• Leveraging collaborative advantage between complementary partners; search for additionality and collaborative synergies (sections 5.4.2; 5.5);
	• Managing diverse motivational drivers and overshoot/undershooting tendencies (section 5.5.3);
	• Managing stakeholder reconfiguration processes; organization of Wicked Problems Plazas; stakeholder mapping and scoping (Box 6.4; Box 12.4);
	• Organizational culture that enables collaboration, diversity and paradoxical thinking (section 11.6; Box 4.3).
SIZE	• Creation of internal management support systems that allow for institutionalization of partnerships; efficient organization of internal knowledge sharing (Chapter 11);
	• Sufficient budget for developmental evaluation capacity (section 12.3);
	• Sufficient budget to initiate, organize and coordinate (inter-organizational) impact teams (Box 12.9);
	• Dealing with span of control trade-offs, establishing CSP portfolio coherence (section 11.2);
	• Enforcement capabilities: managing 'exit' and 'entry' conditions as part of comprehensive partnering contracts (section 12.2.4);
	• Monitoring and evaluation capabilities to ensure operational efficiency and performance of the CSP portfolio (Figure 12.2).

[3] EXTENDING IMPACT AMBITIONS

Insofar as organizations have succeeded in strengthening the coherence, balance, resilience and performance capacity of their SDG-aligned partnership portfolio, further pathways for extending the portfolio's societal impact may be explored. A more solid 'base' of societal legitimacy and acquired PPM capabilities implies that an organization is better equipped to act upon unfolding opportunities that could broaden the scale and/or scope of its SDG contributions. With time and gained experience, an organization may have grown confident enough to take on systems-oriented partnering ambitions – aimed at effecting transformative change – that before it had deemed too complex, too ambitious or too risky. With increased knowledge and a deeper understanding of the interdependencies and positive and negative interactions among the SDGs incorporated in the CSP portfolio, a strategic view on actionable 'nodes for leverage' and 'key intervention points' could significantly advance the portfolio's potential for SDG impact (section 10.5.3).

Logical strategizing questions for extending the SDG ambition would accordingly include: what additional SDG-targets could be embraced to broaden the issue scope of the CSP portfolio? What concepts and proven effective partnering approaches lend themselves to be scaled – across borders, (prospective) partners or sectoral boundaries – and under what conditions? Who are missing stakeholders and 'needed' partners that could help blaze the trail to the aspired impact ambition and future-oriented CSP portfolio? What might be considered relevant 'nodes for leverage' that could add efficiency and effectiveness in a widening portfolio of partnerships directed at more extensive SDG implementation? What change trajectories can be carved out for the longer run if the organization were to make full use of identified SDG interactions within its portfolio? The options and directions for strategizing are manifold and inherently contextual. At least three leads to explore possible ways forward can be discerned.

■ **Broadening the issue scope.** Smartly selecting additional SDG-targets with a substantive or functional relation to already prioritized SDGs, not only broadens the issue scope of the CSP portfolio, but could also add to a reinforcement of positive interaction effects or the minimization of adverse interactions with perverse sustainability impact (see section 2.3.4 on the nexus challenge). For instance, health and well-being (SDG3) cannot be achieved without access to a sufficient quantity of nutritious food at affordable prices (SDG2). The impact potential of a partnership geared to SDG3 might be greatly enhanced by extending the partnering scope with SDG2-related objectives. In a similar vein, partnerships aimed at fresh water ecosystem services (SDG-target 15.1), sustainable forestry (SDG-target 15.2) or restoration of degraded land and soil (SDG-target 15.3) could be substantially reinforced by broadening the partnering scope towards fostering 'sustainable and resilient agriculture practices' (SDG-target 2.4). CSPs directed at scaling renewable energy (SDG-target 7.2) or diffusing energy-efficient technologies (SDG-targets 7.3) can spur – and be spurred – by extending partnering efforts towards the (vocational) training of (young) workers to become skilled employees in decent and higher-paying jobs (SDG8). In this line of reasoning, the following CSP portfolio considerations could be further explored:

▶ Could a related SDG-target be successfully incorporated in an already existing partnership, such that it would advance expected outcomes, collaborative value and SDG-relevant impact? This option would entail a broadening of the partnership's ambition and mission, a focus on strengthening beneficial interaction effects, and possibly a broadening of the current configuration with additional 'needed' partners that bring in complementary competences and expertise.

▶ Should an added SDG-target be addressed by initiating a completely new partnership endeavour, fully dedicated to attaining tangible results on this particular SDG-target? This option could be especially relevant in case of an 'internally actionable SDG-target' that lies within the organization's direct sphere of influence, and for which the stakes to show for attributable and undisputed results are high (for instance, elimination of forced labour and child labour in the organization's production chain, SDG-target 8.7).

▶ In case of adding an 'externally actionable SDG-target': would it be more effective to join an already existing partnering initiative – if any – and assume one's leverage-based responsibilities to advance the cause? Or is it more productive to actively use the organization's mobilizing and convening powers by initiating a platform to build momentum around a common initiative (local, national, international), from which to proceed further?

■ **Following through on the 'internal nexus'.** As outlined in Chapter 11, functional departments can inspire, push and accelerate organizational change processes by rallying around those SDG-targets that are close to their functional-level sustainability efforts and cross-linked with other functional departments (section 11.10). Such cross-cutting SDG-targets indicate 'internal actionability' density (Figure 11.24) – reflecting an emergent 'bottom-up' sustainability strategy that can be expected to become an integral part of the corporate sustainability strategy 'in the making'. By (vertically) integrating and (horizontally) coordinating 'top-down' and 'bottom-up' sustainability approaches around cross-cutting SDG-targets, organizations are better able to create leverage, manage trade-offs and achieve greater coherence to overcome their intention-realization gaps. Evidently, a future-oriented CSP portfolio should support such 'internal actionability' nodes. For example, if the sustainability efforts of the purchasing, operations, marketing, finance, innovation and communication departments all convergence on SDG12 ('responsible consumption and production'), then a strategic partnership aimed at achieving substantial 'reduction of food waste' (SDG-target 12.3) or at 'life-cycle approaches for the efficient use of natural resources' (SDG-target 12.4) could reinforce and help accelerate internal change processes, with greater sustainability results. In this line of reasoning, CSP portfolio strategizing starts with identifying those internally cross-linked SDG-targets that contain the greatest potential to drive the organization's SDG performance over a sustained period of time. The functional-level 'SDG-fiches' outlined in section 11.10 can support this strategizing exercise. Options for subsequent exploration include:

▶ Whether to energetically start a new partnering initiative around a strategic, internally cross-linked SDG-target – which would clearly signal the organization's dedicated commitment to advance, accelerate and scale its SDG performance;

▶ Whether it is feasible and effective to incorporate extended ambitions into an existing partnership, possibly complemented with additional 'needed' partners that share the required level of ambition;

▶ Whether to best proceed by joining an already successful partnering initiative or, instead, self-organize joint action by mobilizing and convening societal stakeholders and (prospective) partners on a common, sector-wide and ambitious way forward (for instance, aimed at jointly developing an SDG-aligned industry standard that could alter the 'level playing field' and facilitate a business ecosystem more responsive and conducive to societal value creation).

■ **Exploring opportunities from 'portfolio nexus'.** Is there strategic merit in exploring all interactions among the SDG-targets addressed in the CSP portfolio? Such an analytical exercise, at the 'portfolio level', would be aimed at identifying key intervention points and priority issues that – if timely and deliberately addressed – should increase the overall effectiveness of the PPM strategy in delivering on the SDGs. Understanding the nature, strength and dynamics of positive and negative SDG interactions under context-specific conditions, is an essential first step in identifying such cross-cutting intervention points (ICSU, 2017). At the 'partnership level', contextualized insights into the workings of SDG interactions can help anticipate unintended side effects, restrain vicious feedback loops and develop more sophisticated Theories of Change. At the 'portfolio level', it helps preclude goal, strategy and policy inconsistencies and avert investments in SDG-oriented partnerships from evaporating.

The ability to identify 'nodes for leverage' within the CSP portfolio adds *'intervention intelligence'* to strategic decision-making – which is key to unlocking opportunities for synergy effects. An integrative approach to portfolio interdependencies helps to determine what governance mechanisms could be put in place to manage trade-offs and constraining forces, and which cross-sector and cross-border partnering organizations should be brought together to maximize synergies. With well-targeted interventions, more than one SDG-target can be advanced at the same time – at reduced costs or with more substantial impact across a larger scale (sections 2.3.4; 3.3.3; 10.5.3). The consequential strategizing challenge is whether (and under what conditions) a 'nexus approach' to the CSP portfolio would allow for: (a) enhanced goal consistency; (b) more coherent and astute decision-making that ensures portfolio balance and resilience; (c) greater potential for synergy effects from actionable intervention nodes with powerful sustainability impact; (d) deliberate allocation of organizational means, time and efforts among prioritized partnership activities; and (e) fuelling the corporate sustainability strategy, by pointing out those SDG-targets most promising to boost the organization's SDG performance, progress and impact.

STRATEGIZING FOR AN 'SDG-FIT' PARTNERSHIP PORTFOLIO – A JOURNEY IN FOUR STAGES

A hypothetical case

Until 2016, *Food Company X* had adopted a largely reactive approach to issues management, reflected in a fragmented composition of tactical and mostly reputation-driven partnership commitments. In 2017, however, the board felt that this approach was no longer adequate to corroborate the organization's sustainability ambition. It anticipated new issues voiced by critical stakeholders, but found it difficult to define in what direction concerns and expectations would materialize. What was clear to all board members, though, was that the company should invest in a more robust societal license. In particular younger employees had expressed a growing desire for the company to become more sustainable and forward-thinking. The board also anticipated more demanding sustainability criteria from investors, impacting changes in the fields of value accounting and sustainability reporting, and new regulation on sustainability issues. These developments would require a completely different stakeholder approach. They decided that the organization not only had to make its portfolio of partnerships more coherent and strategic, but would also need to make it more resilient and impactful to join the bandwagon of more sustainable companies in their sector. An obvious start was to support the recently introduced SDGs. The board had already made the 'Global Goals' part of the corporate narrative, although in a general and rather superficial fashion. With the ambition to develop a more powerful and convincing SDG-aligned strategy, they decided to use the SDG-framework as a 'logic' to make sense of their diverse partnership relations, prioritize among them and to restructure the portfolio to make it more 'SDG-fit'. A journey along four strategizing steps followed (Figure 12.6).

Step 1 – CSP portfolio map (2017)

During a brainstorming weekend, the board members drew a first map of the existing CSP portfolio (Figure 12.6). They defined the scope of topics and nature of interactions with all perceived 'partners' by examining the CSP portfolio's size, diversity, density and dynamics. Looking at the created map, they deliberated on pertinent

B O X

12.10

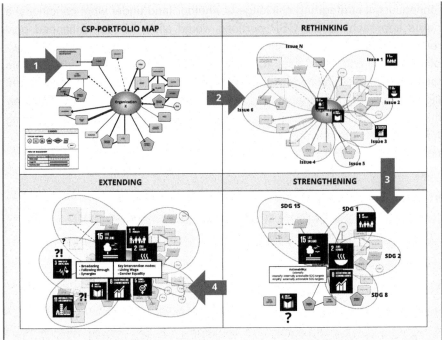

Figure 12.6 Increasing the SDG-fit of CSP portfolios

strategic questions: can we discern a clear 'logic' to the partnership practice so far? What societal issues had been selected over the last five years? Was this selection the result of stakeholder pressure (issue and stakeholder salience) or something else? They concluded that the portfolio reflected a haphazard pattern, more than a 'strategic logic': there were lots of gaps in the established portfolio; many partnerships were actually quite ad hoc and dependent on the action of single managers. In short: the portfolio did not seem particularly supportive for their sustainability ambition. The board decided that the organization's partnership approach required profound rethinking and strengthening. They agreed that one of them would take the lead in this dossier, with the explicit mandate to explore, design and implement an SDG-aligned CSP portfolio strategy for the next five to ten years.

Step 2 – rethinking (2018)

With that mandate, the assigned board member first engaged in more elaborate mapping. By clustering the existing partnerships around material issues, six key societal challenges could be identified (and several residual issues) on which the organization had apparently been acting. A first *strengths/weaknesses* analysis of the portfolio was conducted to identify gaps, (inter-)dependencies and (latent) vulnerabilities that could affect the portfolio's performance and with it, the organization's credibility. From this assessment, it appeared that some partnerships were not particularly 'dense' (issue 6), showed disproportionately strong ties for relatively marginal issues (issue 4), or represented a rather isolated effort (issue 5). Moreover, the analysis revealed some disturbing coordination problems inside the organization: partnership account managers did not share their knowledge, experiences or operational challenges in regular meetings, nor participated in joint training programmes. Some did not even know of each other's existence! Interesting, though, was that all partnership managers were familiar with the company's SDG ambition. But unfortunately, they had not been invited to make this ambition operational for their own activities. To set that straight, two dedicated meetings with all partnership managers were organized to first explore and then determine which issue-centred partnership clusters could be substantively, strategically or functionally linked to the organization's prioritized set of SDGs. A proper fit could be established with SDGs 1, 2 and 8. More than three clusters had no convincing link, whilst two SDGs (4 and 15) set out in the corporate sustainability strategy had not yet been operationalized in any CSP.

Step 3 – strengthening (2019)

Subsequent strategizing sessions revolved around the conditions for establishing a solid and credible CSP portfolio, resilient enough to address developments in the upcoming five to ten years. The sessions considered the measures that could be taken to strengthen the portfolio's 'SDG logic', its impact potential and operational feasibility. Participants assessed whether current partnering organizations were motivated to link up to the SDG-agenda at a sufficient ambition level. Both requisite and supportive measures to enhance the organization's PPM capabilities were identified, based on a thorough evaluation of constraining and enabling factors in the daily practice of partnership managers. The extent to which selected SDG-targets could be qualified as 'internally actionable' or 'externally actionable' was assessed – and discussed – in an intense and lengthy session. Participants appeared to have quite different interpretations of what they considered 'within' or 'beyond' the company's 'reasonable' sphere of influence.

Findings from the strategizing sessions were reported to the board. In the ensuing board meeting, it was decided that those partnering relationships that did not fit the organization's SDG ambition, would be gradually extensified. As one board member said: "strategizing is prioritizing". Furthermore, the board agreed on the intensification of partnerships clustered around SDG-target 2.4 (sustainable food production), SDG-target 8.2 (capacity-building and smallholder upgrading) and SDG-target 8.3 (smallholders' access to financial services). These SDG-targets had been marked as 'internally actionable' and were evidently strategic to the food company's core business. The partnerships clustered around SDG1 ('no poverty') proved more difficult to position in terms of 'actionability'. How to exactly direct the organization's sway and give shape to the ambition to help raise local communities' living standard and ease their harsh living conditions – in a truly meaningful way and with lasting effect – would have to be further explored. The board commissioned the design of a 'Theory of Change' and a feasibility study for a partnered local pilot project in one of their operating countries. In a similar vein, it decided that for the next two years, efforts on

SDG4 ('quality education') would be continued in its present form – in a philanthropic partnering relationship – yet with an assignment for the partnership account manager to investigate whether, how and under what conditions the commitment could be deepened over the longer run.

Reviewing the list of decisions just taken, it struck the board that SDG15 – one of the five prioritized SDGs incorporated the organization's sustainability strategy – had not been included in the proposed partnering strategy, despite the undeniable impact of agricultural production on deforestation, soil degradation and biodiversity loss. 'Internally actionable' or not, all board members almost intuitively felt that this inconsistency with their sustainability strategy and 'sustainable corporate story' (section 10.6) would be untenable and undermine the CSP portfolio's overall credibility. A convincing partnering approach to SDG15 simply was a *conditio sine qua non* – not only to safeguard the company's future relevance to society, but also to acquire explorative, exploitative and transformative knowledge on how to operationalize a restorative, or even regenerative, business model. To ensure the portfolio's resilience, capacity and societal support, the board decided to install an internal task force to (a) explore options and pathways for *strategic* partnering on SDG15, and (b) to implement the final recommendations from the strategizing team on internal capabilities development. Absolute priorities regarding the latter: a supportive internal infrastructure and upgraded management systems to enable proper institutionalization of strategic partnerships; adaptive and innovative capabilities; knowledge exchange and learning; and more sophisticated monitoring, evaluation and reporting capabilities. For this purpose, the board reserved sufficient funds.

Step 4 – extending (2022)

As of 2020, the company's 'SDG-fit' partnering approach figured prominently in its annual report and helped convey a more sophisticated 'sustainable corporate story' to both internal (employees) and external stakeholders (investors in particular). And by the looks of it, with success: the organization climbed the international sustainability rankings as 'best-in-class' and 'super-sector leader'. Almost weekly, the CEO – as acknowledged sustainability leader – was invited to present his vision in fora dedicated to systems change and the 'Decade of Action'. But high rankings notwithstanding, societal reception of the company's sustainability performance remained mixed at best. There were allegations of SDG-washing, fed by stories in the media on controversial tax rulings and regular 'incidents' in its value chains concerning human rights (child labour, sexual harassment, labour union suppression) and tense relations with workers and local communities. Furthermore, it proved challenging to extend the experience of piloted partnerships from one location to others. Creating scale and impact turned out to be more complex, arduous and time-consuming than anticipated.

Again, the adequacy of the CSP portfolio as a strategy to deliver on the organization's SDG commitment was topic of – somewhat disenchanted – debate in the board. It was undeniable that, so far, the portfolio strategy had not lived up to expectations. Had the board's pick of SDG-targets perhaps been too narrow, too broad, not ambitious or not aligned enough? Did the organization, despite its laudable efforts, still lack the required capabilities to absorb and leverage the experience gained from its partnerships into its operations? Had the company made responsible use of its societal, value chain and international position (Chapter 10), assumed 'leadership role' and power base? Upon reflection – and after having consulted two senior partnership managers, known among colleagues for their progressive mindset and strategizing acumen – the board concluded that its portfolio approach had lacked sufficient balance and coherence. It had not approached the SDG-aligned partnership portfolio in an integrative way and, accordingly, had overlooked 'key intervention nodes' within the CSP portfolio with the potential to dampen negative and leverage positive spill-over effects across SDG-targets. Making full use of the 'nexus potential' would enable more intelligent decision-making on what to prioritize and how best to allocate means, time and efforts across partnership activities for greater SDG performance. Identification of actionable 'nodes for leverage' would probably provide interesting clues for a more sophisticated and more effective CSP portfolio strategy, the senior managers advised.

Following up on that advice, several *SDG synergy meetings* (Box 3.8; section 11.10.8) were organized. Impact Team members, partnership (account) managers, functional managers engaged in SDG initiatives and board members all participated. The meetings focused on exploring the range of positive and negative relations, inter-actions and interdependencies between SDG-targets and the identification of action-able cross-cutting intervention points – by pooling the organization's strategic, tactical and operational knowledge. An additional motivation was the hope that these sessions would foster co-ownership of the emerging strategy and encourage the creation of an internal 'nexus community'.

The organization chose a combination of the *SEI method* (the seven-point scale for defining and weighing SDG interactions, see section 2.3.4) and *SHIFT's human rights-based approach to a 'holistic SDG strategy'* (Figure 11.22) to guide delibera-tions and explore, assess and identify SDG-targets expected to have the most prom-ising 'co-benefit' effects. After several rounds of engaged and diligent deliberation, two 'key intervention nodes' emerged that were deemed to have the greatest potential for leveraging nexus effects: *living wage* (related to SDG8) and *gender equality* (SDG5). Not only were these principle-based, cross-cutting topics positively related to all prior-itized SDGs (including SDG4 and SDG1); they also seemed to provide additional (part-nering) opportunities for extending the company's contribution towards: SDG-target 15.2 (sustainable forest management), SDG-target 15.3 (restoration of degraded land and soil), SDG-target 15.5 (protection of natural habitats), SDG10 ('reduced inequali-ties'), SDG11 ('sustainable communities') and SDG3 ('good health and well-being'). All participants agreed that the choice for these two nodes, as key leverage points, would add intervention intelligence and coherence to the CSP portfolio. It would certainly help in creating strategic focus, enable more effective coordination among partnership

B O X 12.10

activities across SDG-targets and to more deliberately explore and exploit (new) partnership options. But all participants also realized that success was not 'set in stone'. Effectiveness would be conditional on local circumstances, rest on complexity-sensitive implementation and depend on the ability to internalize and scale learning effects for ever greater impact. The CEO hence concluded: "the proof of the pudding is in the eating . . . . and in transparently publishing about our efforts and encountered dilemmas". An internal task force was formed with the assignment to develop an integrated management system to keep track of progress, report to the board about progress and bottlenecks and – if needed – to further strategize.

What happened next?

The organization is still in the middle of this transition. But its publications on the choice for 'living wage' as a key benchmark have been favourably received by a group of influential impact investors – organized in a Living Wage Platform. The company is presently investigating the converging initiatives on (SDG) impact measurement, value accounting (natural, social, human capital, living wage) and integrated reporting to figure out how these methodologies can be linked to reporting and disclosure on the portfolio's SDG performance. Looking at the reconfigured CSP portfolio map, the CEO confided to a journalist that he felt confident that this vital step had provided the company and its partners with better decision-making and coordinating powers which – he believed – added to the company' societal relevance and legitimacy. The 'nexus' approach had not only improved the CSP portfolio's coherence, but also made it more impactful and flexible. The future will tell . . .

12.5   CONCLUSIONS, TOOLS AND RESOURCES: MAKING IT PERSONAL

"We are living on this planet, as if we had another one to go to"
"I've seen smarter cabinets at IKEA"
"Why should we go to school, if you won't listen to the educated?"
"Bla bla bla . . ."
Protest signs at youth climate marches (2019–2021)

Cross-sector partnerships (CSPs) come in many shapes, at various ambition levels, driven by diverse motivations and with varying intensities of engagement and commitment. CSPs range from philanthropic projects and transactional relationships to more strategic partnerships with transformational potential (Austin and Seitanidi, 2014). The more complex the societal issues a company aims to address, the greater the need for a solid (cross-sector) partnership strategy – and supportive internal organizational infrastructures – to build, manage and optimize the portfolio of collaborative relationships. CSPs represent the more formal dimension of 'external alignment' and the most focused approach possible to 'multi-stakeholder engagement' strategies. Setting up, managing and further developing effective and impactful partnerships proves a necessary but challenging endeavour in effecting positive change.

In that light – and to further operationalize the 'partnership configuration' and 'fit' dimensions touched upon in Chapter 5 – we discussed the importance of understanding the difference between 'coalitions of the willing' and 'coalitions of the needed' for attaining the outcomes and sustainability impact envisaged. We did so by addressing a selection of fundamental insights related to: (a) the various phases of the partnering cycle; (b) drivers of partnering processes (issue-driven and opportunity-driven) and their ripple effects on the dynamics and effectiveness of collaborative relationships; (c) the significance of goal alignment, appropriate governance and trust-building processes; (d) creating a dynamic partnering fit through stakeholder mapping and reconfiguration processes; (e) tensions to reckon with during partnership execution; and (f) the imperative of partnering principles, comprehensive yet adaptive partnership agreements, and 'complexity-sensitive' Theories of Change (ToC) to guide learning and adapting for progressively greater impact. To facilitate 'developmental' monitoring and evaluation, we introduced four impact loops presented along an 'impact value chain', to assess learning and upgrading opportunities at four levels of partnering processes.

Bringing these insights together, from an organizational point of view, requires a new area of management: Partnership Portfolio Management (PPM). Instead of treating each partnership as a separate activity, there is considerable collaborative value to be gained from creating a 'strategic partnering fit' between the organization's SDG strategy and its partnership portfolio. A PPM approach enables more sophisticated strategizing for a more future-oriented SDG-partnering fit.

MAKING IT . . .

PART III of this book presented a sequence of strategic and operational challenges that organizations need to take heed of if they are serious about their sustainability ambitions, their long-term relevance, their contributions to the SDG-agenda and their societal license as 'a force for positive change': making it 'resilient' (Chapter 7), making it 'material' (Chapter 8), making it 'strategic' (Chapter 9), making it 'powerful' (Chapter 10), making it 'functional' (Chapter 11) and making it 'collaborative' (Chapter 12). None of these layered strategies will ever satisfactorily materialize, however, if one ultimate condition is not met as well: *making it personal*. In scholarly terms, this challenge pertains to behavioural matters of individual and organizational 'agency' related to 'having', 'taking' and 'sharing' responsibility (Chapter 5). In practical terms, it refers to how individuals can become **change agents**, capable of instigating, driving and shaping much-needed shifts in mindsets, 'value' perspectives, organizational logics and ways of doing business – within their organization, within the networks and communities of which they are part, and across their direct and indirect 'sphere of influence'.

Throughout Part III – with due reference to the multiple perspectives and analysing techniques gathered in Parts I and II – the vital role of change agents for effective transition processes was mentioned many times. Change agents should surely include those in central positions, such as CEOs of all sorts of organizations (section 6.3), strategists, and political and intellectual leaders. However, we also argued that people in leading positions may prove powerful 'agents of frustration' or even 'agents of stagnation' (Chapter 10), because of their vested interests in the 'old' ways of thinking, organizing and doing business – which has prompted many of the sustainability challenges the world is presently facing (Chapter 1). We asserted that agents of change can appear everywhere and involve all kinds of actors from all positions in society: proactive middle managers in functional areas of management (Chapter 11), critical stake-holders, (local) government officials, system-conscious consumers, young people, and young professionals (millennials, GenZ) acting as social *entrepreneurs* or social *intrapreneurs*.

What change agents have in common is their ability to (1) take a *systems perspective,* (2) act as a *responsible* community member, (3) take a proactive, creative and *collaborative* attitude to problem-solving, and (4) be engaging, inspiring and strong communicators. By mobilizing people and managing joint purpose-setting, they are capable of activating internal and external processes that trigger accelerated change. Throughout the book, we made the case that agents of change are those individuals who are able to effectively navigate a *principles-based approach* at multiple intervention levels: systemic, societal, strategic and operational (see Preface). Change agents were identified as dynamic (formal and informal) 'leaders' (section 9.6), capable of identifying and 'looking beyond' key tipping points – faced by themselves, their organization, the business ecosystem, and society at large. Change agents are not only able to motivate themselves but also inspire and empower others to overcome challenging intention-realization gaps. Rather than settling for compromise (interest-based negotiations), they engage in forward-looking *collective-vision-based negotiation* processes to create *future-resilient* pathways for turning 'wicked problems' (Chapter 4) into 'wicked opportunities' (Chapter 5).

BECOMING AN SDG PROFESSIONAL . . .

To be effective in the present (Volatile, Uncertain, Complex and Ambiguous) VUCA era (Chapter 1), aspiring change agents have to master so-called

21st-century skills (Van Tulder, 2018b; WEF, 2020c). These particularly prioritize skill sets in the realm of critical thinking, complex problem-solving, creativity, people management, coordination and negotiation, emotional intelligence, cognitive flexibility, service orientation, and judgment and decision-making. In rankings of relevant skills, these 21st-century skills score consistently higher than more instrumental skill sets – such as quality control, presenting, listening or ICT-related abilities. Many of the personal skills, competencies and insights needed to effectuate the SDG-agenda are building on 21st-century skills, in different combinations and in various guises. For instance: dealing with and engaging in multi-stakeholder processes (Part I); grasping, defining and addressing wicked problems and opportunities; organizing wicked problems plazas (Part II); understanding and operationalizing SDG-nexus (Part I, II, III); applying and developing dashboards, rather than relying on single measures (Chapter 2); assessing the nature of triggering events in real time, not afterwards (Chapter 7); coping with key performance *illusions* (Chapter 9); asking heuristic 'guiding questions' (Chapter 1, Chapter 11, Chapter 12); dealing with *hybrid* governance logics and processes (Chapter 6); properly defining values, purpose and ambition levels (Chapter 9); using power, positioning and narratives as a force for positive change (Chapter 10); and seeing through 'mixed motives' to navigate 'coherence' (Chapter 11).

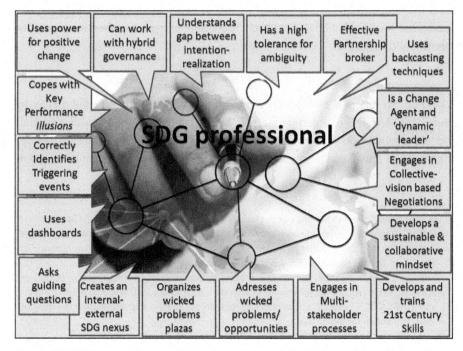

Figure 12.7 SDG professional profile

Practicing and further developing these skills requires a particular combination of *mindsets*, which we sought to capture across the chapters: an inquisitive mindset geared to triangulation (Chapter 5; Box 10.1); a collaborative mindset (Chapter 12); a regenerative mindset (Box 7.1); a long-term strategic yet adaptive mindset (section 9.2.3; section 11.1); a sustainable mindset (UN Global Compact & Russell Reynolds, 2020);[14] an entrepreneurial mindset (Chapters 8, 9); a paradox mindset (Box 4.3) with high tolerance for ambiguity; a multilevel mindset (Preface) capable of 'zooming in and out' on context and of reckoning with multiple 'clock speeds' and timespans (Chapter 4). The SDG-agenda provides societal 'purpose' to skill formation processes, which encourages continuous learning – alone and in groups.[15] Developmental evaluation was identified in this chapter as a 'learning and adjusting while doing' mindset for reinforcing impact loops in collaborative efforts (section 12.3; Box 12.9). Effective skills development always constitutes an act of combining individual and collaborative processes of reflection, learning and action. Developing and training this skill profile in real-life situations will support the aspiring change agent in becoming an 'SDG professional'. In this 'Decade of Action', the ultimate objective of any impact-driven SDG professional is to help accelerate the implementation of the SDG-agenda and help overcome the organizational tipping points, barriers and 'bears on the road' (Chapter 11) that could easily turn the 'Decade of Action' into a 'Decade of Stagnation'. A typical risk to be aware of is the occurrence of 'SDG-washing' and disregard for SDG 'impact integrity' (Box 11.4). Each SDG professional should be able to recognize the drivers and pitfalls of SDG-washing and unjustified impact claims, in order to support organizations in closing the analytical, motivational and organizational gaps between sustainability intention and realization.

. . . AND AN ENGAGED BROKER

Taking up the role of a *partnership broker* is one of the most impactful means to these ends. An SDG-oriented partnership broker is able to bring a 'developmental' and 'learning' attitude to partnering processes in order to enhance their efficiency, effectiveness and ultimate impact. Many tools introduced throughout this book

---

14 In the context of characteristics of sustainable business leaders, UN Global Compact and Russell Reynolds (2020) discern four dimensions of a 'sustainable mindset': multilevel systems thinking, stakeholder inclusion, disruptive innovation, and long-term activation.

15 The Good Life Goals lay out 85 ways anyone can contribute towards the objectives at the heart of the SDG-agenda. A multi-stakeholder collaboration – involving Futerra (a change agency), WBCSD, the governments of Sweden and Japan, SEI, IGES, UN Environment and UNESCO – created a repository of resources, guides and techniques to support 'personal action for the SDGs'.

actually entail partnership broker skills: organizing Wicked Problems Plazas; helping coalitions of the willing to progress into coalitions of needed partners; developing intervention logics, impact pathways and learning loops; supporting Impact Teams; mapping and help strategizing partnership portfolios; using strategic alignment techniques based on ambition levels, partnering continuums, dependency scales and partnership formation checks; applying navigating questions (used by Impact Teams) to check for relevant progress throughout the partnering cycle; drawing maps and designing info-graphics to make complex issues clear. Partnership brokers can act as internal or external brokers (Box 12.11).

THE ROLES OF A PARTNERSHIP BROKER

B O X 12.11

The term 'partnership brokering' refers to the process of supporting and strengthening partnerships through innovative and skilled management of collaborative processes. CSP brokering has become an increasingly relevant topic of research and practice (Stott, 2019; Tennyson and Mundy, 2019), especially with regard to the SDGs (Murphy and Stott, 2021).

A partnership broker can help organizations navigate their 'partnering journey' (Tennyson, 2019) by explicating what is needed, identifying (contextual, relational, organizational) dynamics, intervening in the right way, and steering on principles and common ground. Brokers have a key role to play in the creation of the right 'fit'

BOX 12.11

between prospective partners – the phase in which the majority of challenges to effective partnership formation appear (Van Tulder and Kahlen, 2019). But as issues and contexts change, the partnership's approach, its arrangements or configuration may need to evolve accordingly. Brokers thus have an important connective, guiding and enabling function in all phases of the partnering cycle – from managing expectations, risks, challenges and negotiating the terms of collaborative arrangements, to dealing with conflict, building capacity, co-creating implementation plans, and helping to alter the direction, pace and make-up of the partnership when necessary. The way partnership brokers can perform these roles depends on their position as either 'internal' or 'external' broker (Tennyson, 2019).

External partnership brokers operate as independent neutral 'third' parties, often involved on an 'episodic' basis and contracted to undertake specific tasks – which requires less personal involvement and appropriate distance from the partners. External partnership brokers are particularly helpful in the formation phase of the partnership, in reviewing the partnership's progress and effectiveness, to 'zoom out' (the broader perspective) and ask the sensitive/difficult questions, and to force breakthroughs in case of partnering tensions or power blockage.

Internal partnership brokers are those that carry the responsibility for shaping and supporting the partnership itself "whilst preparing their own organization to be effective partners". The internal broker is part of the 'institutionalization process' of the partnership becoming embedded in their own organization. The internal brokering role hinges on the kind of support (e.g. mandate, resources, access, time, personal backing) the broker receives from senior management levels, which in turn depends on the extent to which the partnership is considered strategic and related to core activities. In contrast to external brokers, internal brokers play a much more continuous role in organizational transition processes, for instance by enabling internal (impact) teams to collaborate,

EXTERNAL BROKER	
ANIMATOR Reactive	**PIONEER** Proactive
Mandate **COORDINATOR**	Mandate **INNOVATOR**
INTERNAL BROKER	

Figure 12.8 The roles of internal and external brokers
Source: Tennyson (2019), p. 23

building greater organizational coherence and creating internal management systems to support partnerships appropriately (Tennyson, 2019: 24).

Depending on their mandate and position inside or outside the organization, brokers can fulfil different functions: 'animator' or 'coordinator' in case of a *reactive* mandate, and 'pioneer' and 'innovator' in case of a more *proactive* mandate.

Partnership brokering principles

Partnering has become the default mechanism of sustainability efforts, but that does not necessarily make partnerships strategic, nor transformational in their effect. The partnership broker – whether internal or external – performs a pivotal role in *raising the bar* for effective partnering processes and in *optimizing collaborative action* for the SDGs (Stott, 2019). Additional to the 'Good Practice' principles – developed by the Partnership Brokers Association – that provide a standard for *professional* partnership brokering, the following principles have been proposed to guide the intermediary 'go-between' role of partnership brokers in shaping and driving ascending levels of sustainable change:[16]

1. **Break through** assumptions and preconceptions about each other;
2. **Recognize and relish diversity** as an asset rather than a problem;
3. **Properly value the many different contributions** each partner brings;
4. **Develop new skills** in partnership-building, collaboration brokering and collective leadership;
5. **Understand the system and contexts** in which partnerships operate;
6. **Apply the highest standards**, rigour and accountability to all partnering endeavours;
7. **Invest in the partnering process** in order to optimize engagement and create the conditions for efficiency, innovation and sustainability;
8. **Learn** and be prepared to change course on the basis of growing insights;
9. **Be modest** in understanding your own limitations and abilities to develop sustainable approaches;
10. **Keep your eyes on the ball:** partnering is a means to an end, not an end in itself.

More information: https://partnershipbrokers.org/w/resources/

---

16 These brokering principles were developed as part of the Principles of Effective Partnering (PEP) initiative (Box 5.3), in joint conversations between the initiators and largely based on the input of PBA (Ros Tennyson). More information: http://www.effectivepartnering.org/

T A K E A W A Y S

- Thousands of cross-sector partnerships (CSPs) have been created since the start of the millennium. Yet "the reality is that we are still only scratching the surface in terms of the number, and quality, of partnerships required to deliver the SDGs" (UN DESA, 2019).

- CSPs can provide a vital stepping stone for implementing the SDGs, provided that they (1) are appropriately aligned with the societal issue addressed (dynamic issue-partnering fit); (2) genuinely aspire and work towards realization of (sustained) *transformational* change; and (3) sufficiently invest in effective partnering practice.

- To become impactful, 'issue-driven' and 'opportunity-driven' partnerships must find a balance between 'co-exploration' and 'co-exploitation' motivational drivers.

- Reconfiguration entails that the partnership evolves from 'a coalition of the willing' into 'a coalition of the needed' in a purposive way, to: (1) create a fit-for-purpose CSP; (2) keep the partnership's span of control manageable; and (3) forestall that purpose, ambition level and focus are watered down.

- Establishing a good fit between 'what is needed' and 'who is needed' requires an understanding of partnering dynamics along the four phases of the (iterative) partnering cycle: (1) scoping and building; (2) managing and maintaining; (3) reviewing and revising; (4) sustaining outcomes.

- Inter-organizational tensions often result from a different emphasis of partners on (1) co-exploration or co-exploitation activities, (2) control/accountability or collaboration/learning-oriented governance. Managing these tensions implies a paradoxical lens to reconciling differences, the development of a common language and processes for trust-building.

- Effective partnering always involves a principles-based approach to collaboration, establishing sufficient goal alignment, and continuous 'learning and adapting while doing'.

- The Theory of Change (ToC) underpinning a CSP cannot be used as a planning tool, but serves as a navigation instrument for bringing about the aspired 'plausible effects'. A *complexity-sensitive ToC* anticipates that the partnership will be subject to constant change; it allows for the development of ever more effective interventions as an integral part of 'learning and adjusting' along the way.

- The *impact value chain* – portrayed as a logic framework – consists of a series of 'fits' and 'impact loops' that can be upgraded for greater efficiency and effectiveness. Opportunities for learning and upgrading can be assessed along four *impact loops*: (a) at the level of individuals (skills development, collaborative mindsets); (b) organizations (institutionalization, internalization of collaborative advantage); (c) the partnership (goal alignment, reconfiguration, additionality); (d) society (issue-partnering fit, partnership's societal performance).

■ The more complex/wicked the targeted issue is, the more 'developmental evaluation' is appropriate as technique to meaningfully assess the impact of the CSP. An Impact Team can facilitate these learning processes.

■ To seize the full potential of multiple partnerships, organizations need a strategic approach to the management of their portfolio of partnerships. Effective Partnership Portfolio Management (PPM) involves CSP portfolio 'mapping' and 'strategizing' to maximize the collaborative value, align with the SDGs and take informed decisions about extensifying or intensifying specific partnership activities.

- **The Partnerships Resource Centre (PrC):** research and knowledge centre on public-private collaboration for sustainable and inclusive development, embedded within Rotterdam School of Management (RSM) of the Erasmus University. PrC bridges science and practice by developing, connecting and sharing knowledge on: (1) how cross-sector partnerships work; (2) how they can contribute to sustainable transformations; and (3) how to enhance the transformative capacity of partnerships. PrC shares tools and publications to guide strategizing processes of partnering and mutual learning, https://www.rsm.nl/faculty-research/centres/partnerships-resource-centre/. The *PrC Insight Series* (on partnership principles, agreements, skills) is aimed to contribute to the professionalization of cross-sector partnerships and improve standards in effective partnering. https://www.rsm.nl/research/centres/prc/prc-insight-series/

- **The Partnership Brokers Association (PBA):** a non-profit, international professional body for practitioners who are managing and developing collaboration processes, that aims to: (1) challenge and change poor partnering practices so that multi-stakeholder collaboration can become truly transformational; (2) ensure those operating in partnership brokering roles are skilled, principled and work to the highest standards; (3) promote the critical importance of partnering process management to decision makers in all sectors. PBA supports partnership practitioners with vocational training (accreditation scheme, based on good practice principles) and open access handbooks, guides, publications, learning papers. https://partnershipbrokers.org/w/resources/

- **UN SDG Learn:** aims to bring relevant and curated learning solutions on sustainable development topics. Through collaborative efforts of the United Nations, multilateral organizations and sustainable development partners from universities, civil society, academia and the private sector, the platform provides a unique gateway that empowers individuals and organizations through an informed decision when selecting among a wealth of SDG-related learning products and services, for instance on partnering for the SDGs. https://www.unsdglearn.org/courses/?_sf_s=partnerships

- **The Multi-stakeholder Partnerships Guide:** links the underlying rationale for multi-stakeholder partnerships with a four-phase process model, a set of seven core principles, key ideas for facilitation, and 60 participatory tools for analysis, planning and decision making. The guide has been written for those directly involved in MSPs – as a stakeholder, leader, facilitator or funder – to provide both the conceptual foundations and practical tools that underpin successful partnerships. http://www.mspguide.org/

- **Action Networks for the SDGs:** action-oriented networks and communities maintained by UN system entities or actors that focus on accelerating progress in sustainable development thematic areas, typically contributing to multiple interlinked SDGs. Action networks are useful in mobilizing resources, generating momentum and creating awareness, spurring tangible results in support of the objectives of the network, scaling up existing initiatives or catalysing new SMART commitments and actions. https://sustainabledevelopment.un.org/partnerships/actionnetworks; https://sdgs.un.org/partnerships/browse

■ *2030 Agenda Partnership Accelerator:* a collaborative initiative by the UN Department of Economic and Social Affairs (UN DESA) and The Partnering Initiative, in collaboration with the UN Office for Partnerships (UNOP), UN Global Compact, and the UN Development Coordination Office. Aimed at supporting effective country-driven partnership platforms for the SDGs and building partnering skills and competencies. Provides a 'Learning Library' with various publications, tools and webinars that helps organizations to advance SDG implementation and organize partnerships for the SDGs. http://partnershipaccelerator.org/

■ *The Good Life Goals:* stresses the importance of individual action in achieving the ambitions of the SDGs. Lays out "85 ways anyone can contribute towards the huge planet-changing objectives", and provides materials and resources to help stakeholders explore and communicate around the Good Life Goals. Result of a multi-stakeholder collaboration between Futerra, the 10 YFP Sustainable Lifestyles and Education program, co-led by the governments of Sweden and Japan represented by the Stockholm Environment Institute (SEI) and the Institute for Global Environmental Strategies (IGES), as well as UN Environment, UNESCO and WBCSD, https://sdghub.com/goodlifegoals/

■ *The Inner Development Goals Initiative:* a co-creative initiative of 23 supporting organizations – involving academics, experts and collaborating business partners – that develops inner abilities, skills and qualities to contribute to a more sustainable global society and achieving the SDGs. The initiative aims at educating, inspiring and empowering people to be a positive force for change in society. The (work-in-progress, open-source) IDG framework represents five categories ('being', 'thinking', 'relating', 'collaborating', 'acting') of 23 skills and qualities to reach the SDGs and create a prosperous future for all humanity, https://www.innerdevelopmentgoals.org/

REFERENCES

Austin, J.E. (2000). 'Strategic Collaboration between Nonprofits and Businesses', *Nonprofit and Voluntary Sector Quarterly*, 29(1):69–97.

Austin, J.E. & Seitanidi, M.M. (2014). *Creating Value in Nonprofit-Business Collaborations. New Thinking and Practice*. San Fransisco, CA: Jossey-Bass.

Bamford, J. & Ernst, D. (2002). 'Managing an alliance portfolio', *The McKinsey Quarterly*, (3):28–39.

Banerjee, V. & Duflo, E. (2019). *Good Economics for Hard Times – better answers to our Biggest Problems*, Penguin Books.

Barendsen, L. (2012). *Unraveling the CSR Journey. Partnership Portfolio Configurations along the Corporate Social Responsibility Transition*, RSM/Erasmus University: Master Thesis.

Bryson, J.M. (2021). 'Strategizing as an organizing and integrating concept'. In: Ferlie, E. & Ongaro, E., *Strategic Management in the Public Sector: Concepts, Schools, and Contemporary Issues*, 2nd edition. New York: Routledge (forthcoming).

Bryson, J.M., Ackermann, F. & Eden, C. (2016). 'Discovering collaborative advantage: the contributions of goal categories and visual strategy mapping', *Public Administration Review*, 76(6):912–925.

Clarke, A. & Macdonald, A. (2019). 'Outcomes to Partners in Multi-Stakeholder Cross-Sector Partnerships: A Resource-Based View', *Business & Society*, 58(2):298–332.

Da Rosa, A. (2013). 'Cross-Sector Portfolio Management. Lessons Learned from the Strategic Alliance Portfolio Literature', RSM/Erasmus University: PrC memorandum.

Dellas, E. (2012). 'Partnerships for sustainable development in the water sector: Privatization, participation and legitimacy'. In: Pattberg, P., Biermann, F., Mert, A. & Chan, M. (eds.) *Public-private Partnerships for Sustainable Development: Emergence, Influence and Legitimacy* (pp. 183–208). Edward Elgar Publishing.

Duysters, G., De Man, A.P. & Wildeman, L. (1999). 'A network approach to alliance management', *European Management Journal*, 17(2):182–187.

Fransen, L.W. & Kolk, A. (2007). 'Global rule-setting for business: A critical analysis of multistakeholder standards', *Organization*, 14(5):667–684.

Gomes-Casseres, B. (1998). 'Do You Really Have an Alliance Strategy?', *Strategy & Leadership*, Sep/Oct pp. 6–11.

Gray, B. (2007). 'The process of partnership construction: anticipating obstacles and enhancing the likelihood of successful partnerships for sustainable development'. In Glasbergen, P., Biermann, F. & Mol, A.P. (2007). *Partnerships, governance and sustainable development. Reflections on Theory and Practice* (pp. 29–48). Cheltenham: Edward Elgar Publishing.

Gray, B. & Purdy, J. (2018). *Collaborating for Our Future: Multistakeholder Partnerships for Solving Complex Problems*, Oxford Press.

Hart, S.L. & Sharma, S. (2004). 'Engaging fringe stakeholders for competitive imagination', *Academy of Management*, 18(1):7–18.

Huxham, C. & Vangen, S. (2004). 'Doing Things Collaboratively: Realizing the Advantage or Succumbing to Inertia?', *Organizational Dynamics*, 33(2):190–201.

ICSU (2017). *A Guide to SDG Interactions: From Science to Implementation*. Paris: International Council for Science.

Lennie, J. & Tacchi, J. (2014). 'Bridging the Divide between Upward Accountability and Learning-Based Approaches to Development Evaluation: Strategies for an Enabling Environment', *Evaluation Journal of Australasia*, 14(1):12–23.

McKinsey (2020). 'The pivotal factors for effective external engagement', May 26, Survey.

Murphy, D.F. & Stott, L. (eds.) (2021). *Partnerships for the Sustainable Development Goals (SDGs)*. Basel, Switzerland: MDPI.

Parmigiani, A. & Rivera-Santos, M. (2011). 'Clearing a Path Through the Forest: A Meta-Review of Interorganizational Relationships', *Journal of Management*, 37(4):1108–1136.

Patton, M., McKegg, K. & Wehipeihana, N. (eds.) (2016). *Developmental Evaluations Exemplars. Principles in Practice*. New York: The Guilford Press.

Pfisterer, S. & Van Tulder, R. (2020). 'Navigating the governance tension to enhance the impact of Public-Private Partnerships for the SDGs', *Sustainability,* 13(1):111.

Polman, P. & Winston, A. (2021). *Net Positive. How courageous companies thrive by giving more then they take*, Harvard Business Review Press.

PrC (2015). *The State of the Partnerships Report – 2015*. The Partnerships Resource Centre.

PrC (2011). *The State of Partnerships Report 2010*. The Partnerships Resource Centre.

Ramalingam, B., Laric, M. & Primrose, J. (2014). 'From Best Practice to Best Fit: Understanding and Navigating Wicked Problems in International Development', Working Paper. London: Overseas Development Institute.

Raworth, K. (2017). *Doughnut Economics. Seven Ways to Think Like a 21st-Century Economist*. Cornerstone.

Rogers, P. (2009). 'Matching impact evaluation design to the nature of the intervention and the purpose of the evaluation', *Journal of Development Effectiveness*, (1):217–226.

Schneider, A., Wickert, C. & Marti, E. (2017). 'Reducing Complexity by Creating Complexity: A Systems Theory Perspective on How Organizations Respond to Their Environments', *Journal of Management Studies*, 54(2):182–208.

Seitanidi, M., & Crane, A. (eds.) (2014). S*ocial Partnerships and Responsible Business. A research handbook,* London: Routledge.

Stott, L. (ed.) (2019). *Shaping Sustainable Change. The Role of Partnership Brokering in Optimising Collaborative Action*. Abingdon: Routledge.

Tennyson, R. (2019). 'What do partnership brokers do'. In: Stott, L. (ed.). *Shaping Sustainable Change. The Role of Partnership Brokering in Optimising Collaborative Action*, pp. 20–34. London: Routledge/Greenleaf Publishing.

Tennyson, R. (2003). *The Partnering Toolkit*. Bangladesh: The Partnering Initiative.

Tennyson, R. & Mundy, J. (2019). *Brokering Better Partnerships Handbook*. London, United Kingdom: Partnership Brokers Association.

UN DESA (2019). *2030 Agenda Partnership Accelerator*, United Nations Department of Economic and Social Affairs. New York.

UN Global Compact & Russell Reynolds Associates (2020). *Leadership for the Decade of Action*.

Vangen, S. (2017). 'Developing Practice-Oriented Theory on Collaboration: A Paradox Lens', *Public Administration Review*, 77(2):263–272.

Vangen, S. & Huxham, C. (2012). 'The tangled web: unravelling the principle of common goals in collaborations', *Journal of Public Administration Research and Theory*, (22):731–760.

Van Huijstee, M. & Glasbergen, P. (2010). 'Business–NGO interactions in a multi-stakeholder context', *Business and Society Review*, 115(3):249–284.

Van Tulder, R. (2018b). *Skill Sheets. An Integrated Approach to Research, Study and Management*, 3rd edition. Amsterdam: Pearson.

Van Tulder, R. (2017). 'Rescuing the Collaborative Paradigm from its supporters?, *Annual Review of Social Partnerships*, (12):27–31.

Van Tulder, R, & Kahlen, T. (2019). 'Creating a better fit: a scoping role for partnership brokers'. In: Stott, L. (ed.). *Shaping Sustainable Change. The Role of Partnership Brokering in Optimising Collaborative Action* (pp. 35–50). Abingdon: Routledge.

Van Tulder, R. & Keen, N. (2018). 'Capturing Collaborative Complexities – designing complexity sensitive theories of change for transformational partnerships', *Journal of Business Ethics,* 150(2):315–332.

Van Tulder, R., Seitanidi, M., Crane, A. & Brammer, S. (2016). 'Enhancing the Impact of Cross-Sector Partnerships', *Journal of Business Ethics*, (135):1–17.

Van Tulder, R., Van Tilburg, R., Francken, M. & Da Rosa, A. (2014). *Managing the Transition to a Sustainable Enterprise. Lessons from Frontrunner Companies.* London: Routledge.

Van Tulder, R. & Maas, K. (2012). *The partnerships effectiveness model.* Rotterdam: Partnerships Resource Centre.

Vellema, S., Schouten, G. & Van Tulder, R. (2019). 'Four capacities configuring the transformative power of partnering for inclusive development', *Development Policy Review,* 38(6):710–727.

Wassmer, U. (2010). 'Alliance Portfolios: A Review and Research Agenda', *Journal of Management*, 36(1):141–171.

WEF (2020c). *The Future of Jobs Report 2020.* Geneva: World Economic Forum.

Wilson-Grau, R., Kosterink, P. & Scheers, G. (2016). 'Outcome Harvesting: a developmental evaluation inquiry framework supporting the development of an international social change network'. In: Patton, M.Q., McKegg, K. & Wehipeihana, N. (Eds.), *Developmental Evaluation Exemplars. Principles in Practice* (pp. 192–216). New York: The Guilford Press.

ACKNOWLEDGEMENTS

Sustainable business requires collaboration. The same principle applies to the development of societally relevant and rigorous academic research. Over the years, collaborations with a large number of colleagues in academia, with practitioners at companies, civil society organizations and governments, and with PhD, master's and postgraduate students have allowed us to develop an integrated vision on how corporations could effectively contribute to resolving complex societal problems. For more than 20 years, the Rotterdam School of Management (RSM) and the department of Business-Society Management provided an inspiring (collaborative) research environment in which we were able to develop many of the ideas that figure prominently in this book. The teaching environment of one of the leading business schools in the world and the cross-disciplinary contacts with colleagues around the globe, also created a need to devise teaching and action research formulas – suited to both graduate students and executives – and to validate and fine-tune developed frameworks and techniques under more practical circumstances.

At RSM, we would like to thank Eva Rood and her team – supported by the Dean's office and other faculty stakeholders – who have been leading the effort to make RSM a 'force for positive change' embracing the SDGs. At the Department of Business-Society Management, a growing group of scholars has been engaged in research on 'grand challenges' (Joep Cornelissen, Gail Whiteman, Corina Frey, Emilio Marti), business ethics and leadership (Muel Kaptein, Marius van Dijke), inclusive prosperity (Martin de Jong), regulation (Martin de Bree), social enterprises and collective action (Lucas Meijs, Tine de Moor, Lonneke Roza), sustainable development in teaching practice (Steve Kennedy, Maarten Wubben), responsible international business (Suzana Rodrigues, Frank Wijen) and corporate communication and stakeholder/issues management (Guido Berens, Cees van Riel, Flore Bridoux). For practical and teaching assistance, we thank Ronny Reshef. For design of icons and figures, we thank Thomas Bijen. Natalie Bowler-Geerinck helped us to improve the text from a native speaker's point of view. Martin de Reuver has been a tremendous support in co-creating the book's accompanying website and in helping to unlock all supportive materials relevant for teachers, students and practitioners. At Routledge, our publishers Rebecca Marsh and Lauren Whelan provided diligent support, while Matthew Twigg's hands-on approach guided us in getting through the last (production) mile.

In further developing the academic building blocks and insights used for this book, the joint projects with ambitious PhD students proved particularly helpful and stimulating: Jan Anton van Zanten (on SDG nexus), Gerbert Hengelaar (on the incumbent's curse), Maurice Jansen (inclusive ports), Romy Kraemer (on license to operate). A vibrant research community of post-docs and PhD students is forming around the SDGs and key themes of the book, which we feel is both inspiring and hopeful. Vital support was provided by the colleagues of the Partnerships Resource Centre (PrC) at RSM and directly involved colleagues abroad, who helped develop insights on topics like inclusive business strategies (Addisu Lashitew, Siri Lijfering, Andrea da Rosa), value chains and partnering (Jeroen van Wijk, Greetje Schouten, Marijn Faling, Sietze Vellema, Annette Balaoing-Pelkmans, Jane Capacio, Noel de Dios, Anne van Lakerveld, Kristine van Tubergen, Denise Carvalho), partnering in general (Stella Pfisterer, Marieke de Wal, Nienke Keen, Salla Laasonen, Ismaella Stöteler), partnership brokering (Ros Tennyson, Leda Stott, Timo Kahlen, Ken Caplan), international human rights (Cees van Dam, Heleen Tiemersma, Liesbeth Enneking, Martijn Scheltema), materiality thinking (Laura Lucht), impact measurement (Karen Maas, Kellie Liket, Marije Balt), shared value creation (Muriel Arts, Sander Tideman, Nienke Kloppenburg), the Wicked Problems Plaza concept (Rianne van Asperen, Jack van Ham), leadership (Annemieke Roobeek, Hans Reus, Herman Mulder) and the Better Business Scan (Thorben Kwakkenbos).

Our particular appreciation goes to the academic colleagues in the Cross-Sector Social Interactions (CSSI) network: May Seitanidi, Jim Austin, Sandra Waddock, Andrew Crane, Pieter Glasbergen, Barbara Gray, Ans Kolk. Colleagues in the International Business, Public Management and Business Ethics community have provided us with valuable insights and support (Lorraine Eden, Sarianna Lundan, Hafiz Mirza, John Bryson, Alain Verbeke). We also acknowledge the many unnamed but highly deserving colleagues in the scientific communities that show increasing interest in the SDGs, organized around international business, organization studies, political economy, public management and governance. As a co-editor of several special issues dedicated to the SDGs (*Journal of International Business Policy, Journal of Business Ethics, Critical Perspectives on International Business*), we have noticed the growing interest and ambition of (young) scholars to add to academic thinking on corporate contributions to the SDGs. We can look forward to a rich variety of upcoming scholarly contributions.

The policymaking community around the SDGs in the Netherlands – at the ministry of Foreign Affairs and several Dutch embassies, the African Study Centre (Ton Dietz), the Netherlands Environmental Assessment Agency (PBL, Mark van Oorschot), the UN Global Compact Netherlands (Jan Willem Scheijgrond), SDG House, the Dutch Sustainable Growth Coalition (Jan Peter Balkenende), GRI, Wage Indicator Foundation and the World Connectors – helped us test the relevance of concepts and frameworks. Organizations that shared their insights, experience and dilemmas include: Unilever, DSM, AkzoNobel, Philips (Saskia Verbunt, Ties Kroezen), KPN, Partos, ICCO, Cordaid, Max Havelaar Foundation, Amnesty International, DHV, World Wildlife Fund for Nature, Oxfam, Amref Flying Doctors (Marianne Hangelbroek), the United Nations Development Programme, Friesland Campina, Social Enterprise.NL, ABN Amro, the Netherlands Africa Business Council, Safaricom, Jollibee, Unifrutti, ESAMI (East African Business Schools, Michael Munkumba) and University of the Philippines (Manila). The collaboration with Change Inc. (Yoeri van Alteren) resulted in the launch of the Better Business Scan.

This book is part of a movement among business schools around the world that take up responsibility to educate, train and equip the next generation of change agents and business leaders to drive systems change. In that ambition, we feel supported by the global PRME (Principles for Responsible Management Education) network that is dedicated to "transform[ing] management education and develop the responsible decision-makers of tomorrow to advance sustainable development" (Mette Morsing, Wilfred Mijnhardt, Guénola Nonet). Last but not least, we are particularly indebted to Jeffrey Sachs, Paul Polman and Peter Bakker, and more than 50 thought leaders from business, government, NGOs and academia, who contributed to the May 2021 *Driving Systems Change, Corporate Leadership for the SDGs* conference, organized as a prelude to this book. Their contributions provided inspiring and powerful testimony that transformative change driven by companies is not only badly needed, but also feasible.

FURTHER READING

Making it logical

Covers the ongoing 'international restructuring race' between industrial complexes and the dynamism of dependency relations between 'core firms' and their bargaining partners (suppliers, workers, distributors, dealers, financiers, governments). The book addresses debates on post-Fordism, globalization, lean production and international trade policies. It presents historic data showing that none of the largest 100 core firms is truly 'global' or 'borderless'. All core firms have benefited decisively from government trade or industrial policies.

Winner of the 1996 Gunnar Myrdal Award (European Association for Evolutionary Political Economy)

Making it global

International Business-Society Management documents the institutional void between governments, international enterprises and civil society, and the appearance of a 'global bargaining society'. It shows how globalization and corporate responsibility strategies can be integrated across borders as part of 'societal interface' management. The book applies and further illustrates the framework with in-depth cases on Nike (labour conditions in value chains), Shell (waste dumping, resource curse), Triumph International (dictatorship and foreign direct investments), GlaxoSmithKline (HIV/Aids and patents) and ExxonMobil (global warming). More classic cases are included on the website.

Short-listed 'Management book of the year' in 2004 (for Dutch precursor)
Website: www.ib-sm.org (historical cases and issue dossiers)

Making it transformational
Combining practice and theory, this textbook provides a management perspective on the 'business case' for sustainability. Drawing on examples from 20 frontrunner companies – representing different business models and organizational governance forms – the book builds upon a unique research project in which 1,500+ CEOs and middle managers gave access not only to their decision-making process, but also revealed how their perceptions shaped the organizational transition process.

Short-listed 'Management book of the year' in 2014 (for Dutch precursor).

Making it purposeful
Grand challenges confront managers and corporate leaders with ambiguous environments that affect their own sustainability motivations – and those of their stakeholders. *Getting all the motives right* applies insights from organizational psychology, organization science and business model literature (amongst others) to help managers better understand their motivations to become more sustainable, and shows ways to effectively realize these ambitions. The book identifies 100+ 'bears on the road' and 'tipping points' that require the attention of companies. The book provided the foundation for the *Better Business Scan* – a validated tool used to map the gap between 'intention and realization', and for identification of tipping points and leadership choices along the way.

Website: https://www.robvantulder.nl/projects/global-business/global-business-books/

Making it personal
The third edition of *Skill Sheets* presents an integrated approach for acquiring 21st-century skills. It explains how these skills can be used to develop 'Societal Intelligence' and leadership skills required to address wicked problems like the Sustainable Development Goals. The Skill Sheets delineate basic principles of a holistic approach to skill development. The sheets are organized around seven comprehensive skills: research, study and self-management, reading, listening, writing, presenting, and team and project management. The specific challenge addressed in the formula is: how to combine 'head' (logic), 'heart' (passion and motivation) and 'hands' (practice) into the skill development equation.

Website: https://www.skillsheets.com

More information on the website:
https://www.principlesofsustainablebusiness.nl/

BIBLIOGRAPHY

Abell, P. (2009). 'History, Case Studies, Statistics, and Causal Inference', *European Sociological Review* 25(5):561–567.

AccountAbility (2015). *Beyond Risk Management – Leveraging Stakeholder Engagement and Materiality to uncover Value and Opportunity*. Research paper, March.

Acemoglu, D. & Robinson, J.A. (2017). *The Emergence of Weak, Despotic and Inclusive States* (No. w23657), National Bureau of Economic Research.

Acemoglu, D., Gallego, F.A. & Robinson, J.A. (2014). 'Institutions, Human Capital, and Development', *Annual Review of Economics* 6(1):875–912.

Acemoglu, D. & Robinson, J.A. (2012). *Why Nations Fail: The Origins of Power, Prosperity, and Poverty*. Profile Books.

Adams, C.A. (2017). '*The Sustainable Development Goals, integrated thinking and the integrated report*', published by IIRC and ICAS.

Adams, R., Jeanrenaud, S., Bessant, J., Denyer, D. & Overy, P. (2016). 'Sustainability-oriented Innovation: A Systematic Review', *International Journal of Management Reviews*, 18:180–205.

Adger, W.N. (2000). 'Social and Ecological Resilience: Are They Related?', *Progress in Human Geography*, 24(3):347–364.

Aggarwal, V.A., Posen, H.E. & Workiewicz, M. (2017). 'Adaptive Capacity to Technological Change: A micro-foundational approach', *Strategic Management Journal*, 38(6): 1212–1231.

Akhavan, R.M. & Beckmann, M. (2017). 'A configuration of sustainable sourcing and supply management strategies', *Journal of Purchasing & Supply Management* (23):137–151.

Aldy, J.E. & Gianfrate, G. (2019). 'Future-Proof Your Climate Strategy', *Harvard Business Review*, May-June issue, pp. 86–97.

Alford, J. & Head, B.W. (2017). 'Wicked and less wicked problems: a typology and a contingency framework', *Policy and Society*, 36(3):397–413.

Allen, C., Metternicht, G., & Wiedmann, T. (2018). 'Initial progress in implementing the Sustainable Development Goals (SDGs): A review of evidence from countries', *Sustainability Science*, 13(5):1453–1467.

Ambec, S. & Lanoie, P. (2008). 'Does It Pay to be Green? A Systemic Overview', *Academy of Management Perspectives*, 22(4):45–62.

Andrews, D., McGowan, M. & Millot, V. (2017). 'Confronting the Zombies: Policies for Productivity Revival', OECD Economic Policy Papers No. 21, December.

Andriof, J. & McIntosh, M. (2001). *Perspectives on Corporate Citizenship*. Sheffield: Greenleaf Publishing.

Antolín-López, R., Delgado-Ceballos, J. & Montiel, I. (2016). 'Deconstructing corporate sustainability: a comparison of different stakeholder metrics', *Journal of Cleaner Production*, 136(A):5–7.

Aragón-Correa, J.A. & Rubio-López, E.A. (2007). 'Proactive Corporate Environmental Strategies: Myths and Misunderstanding', *Long Range Planning*, 40(3):357–381.

Ariely, D. & Wertenbroch, K. (2002). 'Procrastination, Deadlines, and Performance: Self-control by Pre-commitment', *Psychological Science*, 13(3):219–224.

Asgary, N. & Li, G. (2016). 'Corporate Social Responsibility: Its Economic Impact and Link to the Bullwhip Effect', *Journal of Business Ethics*, 135(4):665–681.

Asif, M., Searcy, C., Zutshi, A. & Fisscher, O.A. (2013). 'An integrated management systems approach to corporate social responsibility, *Journal of Cleaner Production*, 56(1):7–17.

Atasu, A., Corbett, C.J., Huang, X.N. & Toktay, L.B. (2020). 'Sustainable Operations Management Through the Perspective of Manufacturing & Service Operations Management', *Manufacturing & Service Operations Management*, 22(1):147–157.

Aust-Ehnert, I., Matthews, B. & Muller-Camen, M. (2020). 'Common Good HRM: A paradigm shift in Sustainable HRM?', *Human Resource Management Review*, (30):100705.

Austin, J.E. (2000). 'Strategic Collaboration between Nonprofits and Businesses', *Nonprofit and Voluntary Sector Quarterly*, 29(1):69–97.

Austin, J.E. & Seitanidi, M.M. (2014). *Creating Value in Nonprofit-Business Collaborations. New Thinking and Practice.* San Fransisco, CA: Jossey-Bass.

Australian Public Service Commission (2012). *Tackling wicked problems: A public policy perspective*, March.

Babri, M., Davidson, B. & Helin, S. (2021). 'An Updated Inquiry into the Study of Corporate Codes of Ethics: 2005–2016', *Journal of Business Ethics*, (168):71–108.

Bäckstrand, K. (2012). 'Are partnerships for sustainable development democratic and legitimate?'. In Pattberg, P., Biermann, F., Chan, S. & Mert, A. (Eds.) (2012) *Public-Private Partnerships for Sustainable Development. Emergence, Influence and Legitimacy*, (pp. 165–183). Cheltenham: Edward Elgar Publishing.

Baden-Fuller, C. & Stopford, J. (1992). *Rejuvenating the Mature Business: The Competitive Challenge.* London: Routledge.

Ball, R. & Brown P. (1968). 'An Empirical Evaluation of Accounting Income Numbers', *Journal of Accounting Research*, 6(2):159–178.

Bamford, J. & Ernst, D. (2002). 'Managing an alliance portfolio', *The McKinsey Quarterly*, (3):28–39.

Banerjee, A.V. & Duflo, E. (2019). *Good Economics for Hard Times. Better Answers to Our Biggest Problems.* Penguin Books Ltd.

Banerjee, R. & Hofmann, B. (2018). 'The Rise of Zombie Firms: Causes and Consequences', *BIS Quarterly Review*, September, 67–78.

Bansal, P. & Roth, K. (2000). 'Why Companies Go Green: A model of Ecological Responsiveness', *Academy of Management Journal*, 43(4):717–736.

Baranda, E. & Büchner, I. (2019). *Dynamic Accountability: Changing approaches to CSO accountability.* UK, Germany: Accountable Now.

Bardi, U. (2015). 'Wicked problems and wicked solutions: the case of the world's food supply', blogpost on resilience.org, 15 July.

Barendsen, L. (2012). *Unraveling the CSR Journey. Partnership Portfolio Configurations along the Corporate Social Responsibility Transition*, RSM/Erasmus University: Master Thesis.

Barkemeyer, R., Preuss, L. & Lee, L. (2015). 'On the effectiveness of private transnational governance regimes – Evaluating corporate sustainability reporting according to the Global Reporting Initiative', *Journal of World Business*, 50(2):312–325.

Barrientos, S., Gereffi, G. & Rossi, A. (2011). 'Economic and social upgrading in global production networks: A new paradigm for a changing world', *International Labour Review*, 150(3–4):319–340.

Bartlett, C. & Ghoshal, S. (1989). *Managing Across Borders: the Transnational Solution.* Boston: Harvard Business School Press.

Basu, K. (2001). 'On the goals of development'. In: Meier, G.M. & Stiglitz, J.E. (Eds.) *Frontiers of development economics: The future in perspective.* Washington/New York: World Bank/OUP, pp. 61–86.

Batliwala, S. & Brown, L.D. (2006). *Transnational Civil Society: An Introduction.* Bloomfield, CT: Kumarian Press.

Battilana, J. & Lee, M. (2014). 'Advancing Research on Hybrid Organizing – Insights from the Study of Social Enterprises', *Academy of Management Annals*, 8(1):397–441.

Battilana, J., Lee, M., Walker, J. & Dorsey, C. (2012). 'In Search for the Hybrid Ideal', *Stanford Social Innovation Review*, (10):51–55.

Battilana, J., Leca, B. & Boxenbaum, E. (2009). 'How Actors Change Institutions: Towards a Theory of Institutional Entrepreneurship', *Academy of Management Annals*, 3(1):65–107.

Baumol, W.J. (1990). 'Entrepreneurship: Productive, Unproductive and Destructive', *Journal of Political Economy*, 98(5):893–921.

Beck, U. (2005). *Power in the Global Age: A New Global Political Economy*, Polity Press.

Beisheim, M. & Bernstein, S. (2020). 'Matching the HLPF's Ambition to Performance: Prospects for the Review', Guest article IISD SDG Knowledge Hub, 13 February.

Benner, M.J. & Tripsas, M. (2012). 'The influence of prior industry affiliation on framing in nascent industries: the evolution of digital cameras', *Strategic Management Journal*, 33(3):277–302.

Bennich, T., Weitz, N. & Carlsen, H. (2020). 'Deciphering the scientific literature on SDG interactions: A review and reading guide', *Science of the Total Environment*, (728):138405.

Bhagwati, J.N. (1995). *US Trade Policy: The Infatuation with FTAs*, Department of Economics Discussion Papers, 726, April, Columbia University.

Bhattacharya, A. & Kharas, H. (2015). 'Worthy of support', *The Economist*, 8 April.

Biermann, F., Mol, A.P.J. & Glasbergen, P. (2007). 'Conclusion: partnerships for sustainability – reflections on a future research agenda'. In Glasbergen, P., Biermann, F. & Mol, A.P.J. (Eds.), *Partnerships, Governance and Sustainable Development. Reflections on Theory and Practice*, (pp. 288–300). Cheltenham: Edward Elgar.

BlackRock Investment Institute (2019). 'Sustainability: The future of investing', *Global Insights*, report BIIM0219U-733437, February.

Blind, P.K. (2019). *How relevant is governance to financing for development and partnerships? Interlinking SDG16 and SDG17 at the target level.* United Nations, DESA Working Paper No. 162, ST/ESA/2019/DWP/162, October.

Blowfield, M. & Murray, A. (2019). *Corporate Responsibility*, 4th edition. Oxford University Press.

Bocken, N. & Short, S. (2016). 'Towards a sufficiency-driven business model: Experiences and opportunities', *Environmental Innovation and Societal Transitions*, (18):41–61.

Bocken, N., Short, S., Rana, P. & Evans, S. (2014). 'A literature review to develop sustainable business model archetypes', *Journal of Cleaner Production*, (65):42–56.

Bode, C. & Singh, J. (2018). 'Taking a hit to save the world? Employee participation in a corporate social initiative', *Strategic Management Journal*, (39):1003–1030.

Botsman, R. & Rogers, R. (2010). *What's Mine Is Yours: The Rise of Collaborative Consumption.* New York: HarperCollins.

Bouten, L. & Hoozée, S. (2015). 'Challenges in sustainability and integrated reporting', *Issues in Accounting Education Teaching Notes*, 30(4):83–93.

Bowen, H.R. (1953). *Social Responsibilities of the Businessman.* University of Iowa Press (new edition).

Brandenburger, A. & Nalebuff, B. (1996). *Co-Opetition: A Revolution Mindset that Combines Competition and Cooperation*, Crown Business.

Breuer, A., Janetschek, H. & Malerba, D. (2019). 'Translating Sustainable Development Goal (SDG) Interdependencies into Policy Advice', *Sustainability* 11(7):2092.

Brinkerhoff, D.W. & Brinkerhoff, J.M. (2011). 'Public-private partnerships: Perspectives on purposes, publicness, and good governance', *Public Administration and Development*, 31(1):2–14.

Brinkerhoff, J.M. (2002). 'Government-nonprofit partnership: a defining framework', *Public Administration and Development*, 22(1):19–30.

Brouwer, H. & Woodhill, J., with Hemmati, M., Verhoosel, K. & Van Vugt, S. (2015). *The MSP Guide. How to Design and Facilitate Multiple-Stakeholder Partnerships*. Centre for Development Innovation, Wageningen University.

Brown, T. (2008). 'Design Thinking', *Harvard Business Review*, June.

Brown, V.A., Harris, J.A. & Russel, J.V. (Eds.) (2010). *Tackling Wicked Problems: Through the Transdisciplinary Imagination*. London: Earthscan.

Bryson, J.M. (2021). 'Strategizing as an organizing and integrating concept'. In: Ferlie, E. & Ongaro, E., *Strategic Management in the Public Sector: Concepts, Schools, and Contemporary Issues*, 2nd edition. New York: Routledge (forthcoming).

Bryson, J.M., Ackermann, F. & Eden, C. (2016). 'Discovering collaborative advantage: the contributions of goal categories and visual strategy mapping', *Public Administration Review*, 76(6):912–925.

Bryson, J.M., Crosby, B.C. & Bloomberg, L. (Eds.) (2015). *Creating Public Value in Practice. Advancing the Common Good in a Multi-sector, Shared-Power, No-One-Wholly-in-Charge World*. CRC Press: Taylor and Francis Group.

Bryson, J.M., Crosby, B.C. & Stone, M.M. (2006). 'The Design and Implementation of Cross-Sector Collaborations: Propositions from the Literature', *Public Administration Review*, 66(s1):44–55.

B-SM (2018). *Mainstreaming sustainable business. 20 years Business-Society Management, 20 years impact?* SMO and Department of Business-Society Management, SMO-2018/3. Rotterdam: SMO.

Buhl, A., Schmidt-Keilich, M., Munster, V., Blazejewski, S., Schrader, U., Harrach, C., Schäfer, M. & Süßbauer, E. (2019). 'Design thinking for sustainability: Why and how design thinking can foster sustainability-oriented innovation development', *Journal of Cleaner Production*, (231):1248–1257.

Busch, T. & Friede, G. (2018). 'The Robustness of the Corporate Social and Financial Performance Relation: A Second-Order Meta-Analysis', *Corporate Social Responsibility and Environmental Management*, 25(4):583–609.

Buse, K. & Harmer, A. (2004). 'Power to the partners? The politics of public-private health partnerships', *Development*, 47(2):49–56.

Business & Sustainable Development Commission (2017). *Better Business, Better World*.

Calik, E. & Bardudeen, F. (2016). 'A measurement scale to evaluate sustainable innovation performance in manufacturing organizations', *Procedia CIRP*, (40):449–454.

Calton, J.M. & Payne, S.L. (2003). 'Coping With Paradox: Multistakeholder Learning Dialogue as a Pluralist Sensemaking Process for Addressing Messy Problems', *Business & Society*, 42(1):7–42.

Cameron, K.S. & Quinn, R.E. (2011). *Diagnosing and Changing Organizational Culture: Based on the Competing Values Framework*, 3rd edition. San Francisco, CA: Jossey-Bass.

Cañeque, F.C. & Hart, S.L. (Eds.) (2015). *Base of the pyramid 3.0. Sustainable Development through Innovation and Entrepreneurship*. Sheffield: Greenleaf Publishing.

Carayannis, E.G., Grigoroudis, E. & Stamati, D. (2017). 'Re-visiting BMI as an Enabler of Strategic Intent and Organizational Resilience, Robustness, and Remunerativeness', *Journal of the Knowledge Economy*, 8(2):407–436.

Carbon Disclosure Project (2019). *Major Risk or Rosy Opportunity. Are companies ready for climate change*, CDP Climate Change Report 2018, Global edition.

Carcasson, M. (2013). 'Tackling wicked problems through deliberative engagement', *Colorado Municipalities*, October, pp. 9–13.

Carroll, A.B. (1999). 'Corporate Social Responsibility: Evolution of a Definitional Construct', *Business & Society*, 38(3):268–295.

Carroll, A.B. (1979). 'A Three-Dimensional Conceptual Model of Corporate Performance', *Academy of Management Review*, 4(4):497–505.

CDP (2017). *The Carbon Majors Database CDP Carbon Majors Report 2017*, CDP Report June.

Cejudo, G.M. & Michel, C. (2015). 'Addressing fragmented government action: Coordination, coherence, and integration'. Paper presented at the 2nd International Conference in Public Policy, Milan, July.

Chandler, A.D. (1990). *Scale and Scope: The Dynamics of Industrial Capitalism*, Harvard University Press.

Chandra, A.C. (2009). *The Pursuit of Sustainable Development through Regional Economic Integration: ASEAN and Its Potential as a Development-oriented Organization*, Trade Knowledge Network, International Institute for Sustainable Development.

Chang, H.J. (2002). *Kicking Away the Ladder. Development Strategy in Historical Perspective.* Anthem Press.

Chattopadhyay, S. & Manea, S. (2019). *'Leave no one behind' index 2019*. Briefing note, September. London: Overseas Development Institute.

Chen, S. (2018). 'Multinational Corporate Power, Influence and Responsibility in Global Supply Chains', *Journal of Business Ethics,* (148):365–374.

Chen, Y.S., Chang, C.H. & Wu, F.S. (2012). 'Origins of green innovations: The differences between proactive and reactive green innovations', *Management Decisions*, 50(3):368–398.

Chesbrough, H.W. (2003). *Open Innovation: The New Imperative for Creating and Profiting from Technology.* Boston, Massachusetts: Harvard Business School Press.

Chorn, N.H. (1991). 'The "Alignment" Theory: Creating Strategic Fit', *Management Decision*, 29(1).

Chiappetta, C., Santos, F. & Nagano, M. (2010). 'Contributions of HRM throughout the stages of environmental management: Methodological triangulation applied to companies in Brazil', *The International Journal of Human Resource Management*, 21(7):1049–1089.

Christensen, C.M. (1997). *The Innovator's Dilemma. When New Technologies Cause Great Firms to Fail.* Boston: Harvard Business School Press.

Cillo, V., Petruzelli, A.M., Ardito, L. & Del Giudice, M. (2019). 'Understanding sustainable innovation: A systematic literature review', *Corporate Social Responsibility and Environmental Management*, 26(1):1012–1025.

Claessens, S. & Fan J. (2002). 'Corporate Governance in Asia: A Survey', *International Review of Finance* 3(2):71–103.

Clarke, A. & Macdonald, A. (2019). 'Outcomes to Partners in Multi-Stakeholder Cross-Sector Partnerships: A Resource-Based View', *Business & Society*, 58(2):298–332.

Clarke, A. & Fuller, M. (2010). 'Collaborative Strategic Management: Strategy Formulation and Implementation by Multi-Organizational Cross-Sector Social Partnerships', *Journal of Business Ethics*, 94(1):85–101.

Cohen, M.D., March. J.G. & Olsen, J.P. (1972). 'A Garbage Can Model of Organizational Choice', *Administrative Science Quarterly,* 17(1):1–25.

Cohen, W.M., Nelson, R.R. & Walsh, J. (2000). *Protecting Their Intellectual Assets: Appropriability Conditions and Why U.S. Manufacturing Firms Patent (or Not).* NBER Working Paper No. 7552.

Conklin, J. (2006). *Dialogue Mapping: Building Shared Understanding of Wicked Problems.* Chichester, UK: Wiley and Sons.

Constantinescu, M. & Kaptein, M. (2020). 'Ethics management and ethical management: mapping criteria and interventions to support responsible management practice'. In: Laasch et al. (2020), *Research Handbook of Responsible Management*, (pp. 155–174). Cheltenham: Edward Elgar.

Cornes, R. & Sandler, T. (1986). *The Theory of Externalities, Public Goods and Club Goods*, Cambridge University Press.

Crane, A. & Glozer, S. (2016). 'Researching Corporate Social Responsibility Communication: Themes, Opportunities and Challenges', *Journal of Management Studies*, 53(7): 1223–1252.

Crane, A., Palazzo, G., Spence, L.J. & Matten, D. (2014). 'Contesting the Value of 'Creating Shared Value', *California Management Review*, 56(2):130–153.

Crilly, D., Zollo, M. & Hansen, M.T. (2012). 'Faking It or Muddling Through? Understanding Decoupling in Response to Stakeholder Pressures', *Academy of Management Journal*, 55(6):1429–1448.

Crosby, B.C. & Bryson, J.M. (2005). *Leadership for the Common Good: Tackling Public Problems in a Shared-Power World*, second edition. San Francisco, CA: Jossey-Bass.

Crowley, K. & Head, B.W. (2017). 'The enduring challenge of 'wicked problems': revisiting Rittel and Webber', *Policy Sciences*, (50):539–547.

CSIS Commission on Smart Power (2007). *A Smarter, More Secure America*. Washington D.C.: Center for Strategic and International Studies.

Dabla-Norris, E., Kochhar, K., Suphaphiphat, N., Ricka, F. & Tsounta, E. (2015). *Causes and Consequences of Income Inequality: A Global Perspective*, IMF Staff Discussion Note, Strategy, Policy, and Review Department, SDN/15/13, 15 June.

Damgaard, J., Elkjaer, T. & Johannesen, N. (2019). *What Is Real and What Is Not in the Global FDI Network?*, IMF Working Paper No. 19/274, 11 December.

Da Rosa, A. (2013). 'Cross-Sector Portfolio Management. Lessons Learned from the Strategic Alliance Portfolio Literature', RSM/Erasmus University: PrC memorandum.

Davies, P. (2012). 'The State of Evidence-Based Policy Evaluation and its Role in Policy Formation', *National Institute Economic Review*, 219(1):R41–R52.

Davila, T. & Epstein, M.J. (2014). *The Innovation Paradox*. San Francisco: Berrett-Koehler Publishers.

Davis, K. (1973). 'The Case for and against Business Assumption of Social Responsibilities', *Academy of Management Journal*, (16):312–323.

Davis, K., Fisher, A., Kingsbury, B. & Engle Merry, S. (Eds.) (2012). *Governance by Indicators. Global Power through Quantification and Rankings*. Oxford: Oxford University Press.

Daviter, F. (2017). 'Coping, taming or solving: alternative approaches to the governance of wicked problems', *Policy Studies*, 38(6):571–588.

Daviter, F. (2017a). 'Policy analysis in the face of complexity: What kind of knowledge to tackle wicked problems?', *Public Policy and Administration*, 34(1):62–83.

De Bruijn, C. (2018). *Key Performance Illusions: pitfalls and loopholes in performance measurement*, Van Duuren Management.

De Cremer, D. (2013). *The Proactive Leader: How to Overcome Procrastination and be a Bold Decision-Maker*, Palgrave Macmillan.

De Grauwe, P. & Camerman, F. (2002). 'How Big are the Big Multinational Companies?', *Review of Business and Economic Literature*, 0(3):311–326.

De La Cruz, A., Medina, A. & Tang, Y. (2019). *Owners of the World's Listed Companies*, OECD Capital Market Series. Paris: OECD.

Dellas, E. (2012). 'Partnerships for sustainable development in the water sector: Privatization, participation and legitimacy'. In: Pattberg, P., Biermann, F., Mert, A. & Chan, M. (Eds.) *Public-private Partnerships for Sustainable Development: Emergence, Influence and Legitimacy* (pp. 183–208). Edward Elgar Publishing.

Deloitte (2021). *The Deloitte Global 2021 Millennial and GenZ Survey: A call for accountability and action*.

Deloitte (2019). *Deloitte's Global Millennial Survey: Exploring A 'Generation Disrupted'*.

Deloitte (2018). *Deloitte Millennial Survey. Millennials disappointed in business, unprepared for Industry 4.0.*

Dembek, K., Sivasubramaniam, N., & Chmielewski, D.A. (2019). 'A Systematic Review of the Bottom/Base of the Pyramid Literature: Cumulative Evidence and Future Directions', *Journal of Business Ethics*, (165):365–382.

Deming, W.E. (1982). *Out of the Crisis.* MIT Press.

Deneulin, S. & Shahani, L. (Eds.) (2009). *An Introduction to the Human Development and Capability Approach: Freedom and Agency.* London, Sterling, VA: Earthscan, International Development Research Centre.

Dernis, H., Gkotsis, P., Grassano, N., Nakazato, S., Squicciarini, M., Van Beuzekom, B. & Vezzani, A. (2019). *World Corporate Top R&D investors: Shaping the Future of Technologies and of AI.* Luxembourg: Publications Office of the European Union.

Design Council & The Point People (2021). *System-shifting design. An emerging practice explored*, October.

DesJardine, M.R., Marti, E. & Durand, R. (2020). 'Why Activist Hedge Funds Target Socially Responsible Firms: The Reaction Costs of Signaling Corporate Social Responsibility', *Academy of Management Journal,* in press.

Dijkzeul, D. (1996). *The Management of Multilateral Organizations.* The Hague, London and Boston: Kluwer Law International.

Dodds, F., Donoghue, D. & Leiva Roesch, J. (2016). *Negotiating the Sustainable Development Goals: A transformational agenda for an insecure world.* London: Routledge.

Donaldson, T. (1989). *The Ethics of International Business.* The Ruffin Series in Business Ethics. New York/Oxford: Oxford University Press.

Donaldson, T. & Dunfee, T.W. (1999). 'When Ethics Travel: The Promise and Peril of Global Business Ethics, *California Management Review*, 41(4):45–63.

Drucker, P.F. (2001). *Management Challenges for the 21st Century.* Paperback edition, Harber Business.

Drucker, P.F. (1990). *Managing the Non-profit Organization: Principles and Practices.* Harper Business.

Dundon, T. & Rafferty, A. (2018). 'The (potential) demise of HRM?', *Human Resource Management Journal*, (28):377–391.

Dunning, J. & Lundan, S. (2008). *Multinational Enterprises and the Global Economy,* Second Edition. Cheltenham: Edward Elgar.

Duysters, G., De Man, A.P. & Wildeman, L. (1999). 'A network approach to alliance management', *European Management Journal*, 17(2):182–187.

Dzebo, A., Brandi, C., Janetschek, H., Savvidou, G., Adams, K. & Chan, S. (2017). 'Exploring connections between the Paris Agreement and the 2030 Agenda for Sustainable Development, *SEI Policy Brief*, Stockholm Environment Institute.

Eccles, R.G. & Youmans, T. (2015). 'Materiality in Corporate Governance: The Statement of Significant Audiences and Materiality', Working Paper 16–023, Harvard Business School.

Eccles, R.G., Krzus, M.P., Rogers, J. & Serafeim, G. (2012). 'The Need for Sector-Specific Materiality and Sustainability Reporting Standards', *Journal of Applied Corporate Finance*, 24(2):65–71.

ECLAC (2019). *Quadrennial report on regional progress and challenges in relation to the 2030 Agenda for Sustainable Development in Latin America and the Caribbean.* Santiago: United Nations Economic Commission for Latin America and the Caribbean.

ESOSOC (2016). 'A Nexus Approach for the SDGs. Interlinkages between the goals and targets', Retrieved from: https://www.un.org/ecosoc/sites/www.un.org.ecosoc/files/files/en/2016doc/interlinkages-sdgs.pdf.

Eden, L. & Wagstaff, F.M. (2021). 'Evidence-based policymaking and the wicked problem of SDG5 Gender Equality', *Journal of International Business Policy*, 4(1):28–57.

Eden, L., Lenway, S. & Schuler, D.A. (2005). 'From the obsolescing bargain to the political bargaining model'. In: Grosse, R. (Ed.), *International Business and Government Relations in the 21st Century* (pp. 251–272). Cambridge: Cambridge University Press.

Ehnert, I., Parsa, S., Roper, I., Wagner, M. & Muller-Camen, M. (2016). 'Reporting on sustainability and HRM: A comparative study of sustainability reporting practices by the world's largest companies', *The International Journal of Human Resource Management*, 27(1):88–108.

Eisenhardt, K.M. (2000). 'Paradox, Spirals, Ambivalence: The New Language of Change and Pluralism', *Academy of Management Review*, 25(4):703–705.

Ellersiek, A. (2011). *Same Same but Different. Power in Partnerships: An Analysis of Origins, Effects and Governance*, published doctoral dissertation. Tilburg: Tilburg University.

Elkington, J. (2020). *Green Swans. The coming boom in regenerative capitalism*, Fast Company Press.

Elkington, J. (2018). '25 Years Ago I Coined the Phrase "Triple Bottom Line." Here's Why It's Time to Rethink It', *Harvard Business Review*, 25 June.

Elkington, J. (1999). *Cannibals with Forks, the Triple Bottom Line of the 21st Century Business*. Oxford: Capstone Publishing.

Elkington, J. (1994). 'Towards the Sustainable Corporation: Win–Win–Win Business Strategies for Sustainable Development', *California Management Review*, 36(2):90–100.

Engert, S. & Baumgartner, R. (2016). 'Corporate sustainability strategy–bridging the gap between formulation and implementation', *Journal of Cleaner Production*, (113): 822–834.

EPIC (2018). *The Embankment Project for Inclusive Capitalism Report*. Coalition for Inclusive Capitalism.

Espen Stoknes, P. (2015). *What We Think About When We Try Not To Think About Global Warming: Toward a New Psychology of Climate Action*. Chelsea Green Publishing.

Etzioni, A. (1988). *The Moral Dimension, Toward a New Economics*. New York: The Free Press.

European Business Forum (2003). 'CSR: a religion with too many priests', issue 15, Autumn.

European Commission (2020). *Shaping Europe's Digital Future*, February. Luxembourg: Publication Office of the European Union.

European Commission (2019). *Guidelines on reporting climate-related information*. Directorate-General for Financial Stability, Financial Services and Capital Markets Union.

European Parliament (2019). *Europe's approach to implementing the Sustainable Development Goals: good practices and the way forward*, Directorate-General for External Policies, EP/EXPO/B/DEVE/2018/01.

Expert Group Meeting (2019). 'The Way Forward – Strengthening ECOSOC and the High-level Political Forum on Sustainable Development', 3–4 December 2019.

Fadel, M. (2017). 'Fiduciary Principles in Classical Islamic Law Systems'. In: Criddle, E.J., Miller, P.B. & Sitkoff, R.H. (2019). *The Oxford Handbook of Fiduciary Law*, (pp. 525–544). New York: Oxford University Press.

Fahey, L. (2016). 'John C. Camillus: discovering opportunities by exploring wicked problems, *Strategy & Leadership*, 44(5):29–35.

Fairhurst, G.T. (2010). *The Power of Framing: Creating the Language of Leadership*. San Franciso, CA: Jossey-Bass.

Ferlie, E., Fitzgerald, L., McGivern, G. & Bennet, C. (2011). 'Public policy networks and 'wicked problems': A nascent solution?', *Public Administration*, 89(2):307–324.

Ferrant, G. & Kolev, A. (2016). *The economic cost of gender-based discrimination in social institutions*, OECD Development Centre, June.

Fischer, F. (1993). 'Citizen participation and the democratization of policy expertise: From theoretical inquiry to practical cases', *Policy sciences*, 26(3):165–187.

Fisher, R. & Ury, W. (1981). *Getting to Yes: Negotiating Agreement Without Giving In*. New York: Penguin Books.

Fleming, P. & Spicer, A. (2014). 'Power in Management and Organization Science', *Academy of Management Annals*, 8(1):237–298.

Folke, C. (2006). 'Resilience: The emergence of a perspective for social-ecological systems analyses', *Global Environmental Change*, 16(3):253–267.

Foulke, D. (2016). 'Thinking About Corporate Governance In Family-Owned Firms', 6 January. Retrieved from: https://alphaarchitect.com/2016/01/06/thinking-about-corporate-governance-in-family-owned-firms/.

Frame, B. (2008). 'Wicked, Messy and Clumsy: Long-Term Frameworks for Sustainability', *Environment and Planning C: Politics and Space*, 26(6):1113–1128.

Frank, A.G. (1966). 'The Development of Underdevelopment', *Monthly Review Press*, 18(4):17–31.

Fransen, L.W. & Kolk, A. (2007). ´Global rule-setting for business: A critical analysis of multistakeholder standards´, *Organization*, 14(5):667–684.

Frederick, W.C., Post, J.E. & Davis, K. (1992). *Business and Society: Corporate Strategy, Public Policy, Ethics*. New York: McGraw-Hill.

Freeman, C. & Perez, C. (1988). 'Structural crises of adjustment, business cycles and investment behaviour.' In: Dosi G., Freeman, C., Nelson, R.R., Silverberg, G. & Soete, L. *Technical Change and Economic Theory*, (pp. 38–66). London, New York: Pinter Publishers.

Freeman, R.E. (1984). *Strategic Management: A Stakeholder Approach*. Boston M.A.: Pitman Press.

French Jr., J.R.P. & Raven, B. (1959). 'The Bases of Social Power'. In: Cartwright, D. (Ed.), *Studies in social power* (pp. 150–167). University of Michigan.

Frenkel-Brunswik, E. (1949). 'Intolerance of ambiguity as an emotional and perceptual personality variable', *Journal of Personality*, 18(1):108–143.

Frey, B.S. & Jegen, R. (2001). 'Motivation Crowding Theory', *Journal of Economic Surveys*, 15(5):589–611.

Friedman, M. (1962). *Capitalism and Freedom* (40th Anniversary Edition). Chicago and London: The University of Chicago Press.

Frynas, J.G. (2005). 'The false developmental promise of Corporate Social Responsibility: evidence from multinational oil companies', *International Affairs*, 81(3):581–598.

Fuchs, D. (2013). 'Theorizing the Power of Global Companies'. In: Mikler, J. (Ed.) *The Handbook of Global Companies* (pp. 77–95), John Wiley & Sons.

Fukuda-Parr, S. (2016). 'From the Millennium Development Goals to the Sustainable Development Goals: shift in purpose, concept, and politics of global goal setting for development', *Gender & Development*, 24(1):43–52.

Fukuda-Parr, S. & McNeill, D. (2019). 'Knowledge and Politics in Setting and Measuring the SDGs: Introduction to Special Issue', *Global Policy*, 10(s1):5–15.

Fukuyama, F. (1992). *The End of History and the Last Man*. New York: Free Press.

Fullerton, J. (2015). *Regenerative Capitalism. How Universal Principles and Patterns Will Shape Our New Economy*. Whitepaper, The Capital Institute.

Galaskiewicz J. & Barringer S.N. (2012). 'Social Enterprises and Social Categories'. In: Gidron, B. & Hasenfeld, Y. (Eds.) *Social Enterprises. An Organizational Perspective*, (pp. 47–70). London: Palgrave Macmillan.

Galbraith, J.K. (1952). *American Capitalism. The concept of countervailing power*. Houghton Mifflin.

Galeazzo, A., Furlan, A. & Vinelli, A. (2014). 'Lean and green in practice: interdependencies and performance of pollution prevention strategies', *Journal of Cleaner Production*, (85):191–200.

Garzón-Jiménez, R. & Zorio-Grima, A. (2020). 'Corporate Social Responsibility and Cost of Equity: Literature Review and Suggestions for Future Research, *Journal of Business Accounting and Finance Perspectives*, 2(3):1–19.

Gaspar, V., Amaglobeli, D., Garcia-Escribano, M., Prady, D. and Soto, M. (2019). *Fiscal Policy and Development: Human, Social, and Physical Investments for the SDGs*. IMF Staff Discussion Note, SDN/19/03.

Gates, B. (2021). *How to Avoid a Climate Disaster: The Solutions We Have and the Breakthroughs We Need*. Allen Lane.

Geels, F.W. (2019). 'Socio-technical transitions to sustainability: a review of criticisms and elaborations of the Multi-Level Perspective', *Current Opinion in Environmental Sustainability*, (39):187–201.

Geels, F.W. & Schot, J.W. (2007). 'Typology of sociotechnical transition pathways', *Research Policy* 36(3):399–417.

Gennari, P. & Navarro, D.K. (2020). 'Are We Serious About Achieving the SDGs? A Statistician's Perspective', IISD SDG Knowledge Hub, 14 January. Retrieved from: https://sdg.iisd.org/commentary/guest-articles/are-we-serious-about-achieving-the-sdgs-a-statisticians-perspective/.

Georghiou, L. (2001). 'Third generation foresight – integrating the socio-economic dimension', Proceedings of the International Conference on Technology Foresight. The Approach to and Potential for New Technology Foresight, NISTEP Research Material No. 77, March.

Gereffi, G., Humprey, J. & Sturgeon, T. (2005). 'The Governance of Global Value Chains', *Review of International Political Economy*, 12(1):78–104.

Gerwanski, J. (2020). 'Does it pay off? Integrated reporting and cost of debt: European evidence', *Corporate Social Responsibility Environmental Management*, (27):2299–2319.

Gianfrate, G., Schoenmaker, D. & Wasama, S. (2019). 'Cost of capital and sustainability: a literature overview', *Working paper series 03.* Erasmus Platform for Sustainable Value Creation, Rotterdam School of Management/Erasmus University.

Gianni, M., Gotzamani, K. & Tsiotras, G. (2017). 'Multiple perspectives on integrated management systems and corporate sustainability performance', *Journal of Cleaner Production*, (168):1297–1311.

Gladwell, M. (2001). *The Tipping Point. How Little Things Can Make a Big Difference*. New York: Back Bay Books.

Glasbergen, P. (2011). 'Understanding partnerships for sustainable development analytically: The ladder of partnership activity as a methodological tool', *Environmental Policy and Governance*, 21(1):1–13.

Global Commission on the Economy and Climate (2018). *Unlocking the Inclusive Growth Story of the 21st Century: Accelerating Climate Action in Urgent Times*, The New Climate Economy.

Global Sustainability Investment Alliance (2019). *2018 Global Sustainable Investment Review*, fourth bi-annual edition.

Goldin, I. & Mariathasan, M. (2014). *The Butterfly Defect: How Globalization Creates Systemic Risk, and What to Do about it*, Princeton University Press.

Gomes-Casseres, B. (1998). 'Do You Really Have an Alliance Strategy?', *Strategy & Leadership*, Sep/Oct pp. 6–11.

Gomme, J. (2019). 'Lead, transform, succeed: Translating global needs and ambitions into business solutions on the path to 2030'. In: Sachs, J., Schmidt-Traub, G., Kroll, C., Lafortune, G., Fuller, G. *Sustainable Development Report 2019*. New York: Bertelsmann Stiftung and Sustainable Development and Solutions Network (SDSN).

Googins, B.K. & Rochlin, S.A. (2002). 'Creating the Partnership Society: Understanding the Rhetoric and Reality of Cross-Sectoral Partnerships', *Business and Society Review*, 105(1):127–144.

Graham, P. (Ed.) (1995). *Mary Parker Follett: Prophet of Management. A Celebration of Writings from the 1920s.* Boston: Harvard Business School Press.

Gray, B. (2007). 'The process of partnership construction: anticipating obstacles and enhancing the likelihood of successful partnerships for sustainable development'. In Glasbergen, P., Biermann, F. & Mol, A.P. (2007). *Partnerships, governance and sustainable development. Reflections on Theory and Practice* (pp. 29–48). Glos: Edward Elgar Publishing.

Gray, B. & Purdy, J. (2018). *Collaborating for Our Future: Multistakeholder Partnerships for Solving Complex Problems,* Oxford Press.

Greenpeace International (2021). *Destruction: Certified. Certification; not a solution to deforestation, forest degradation and other ecosystem conversion,* March.

GRI (2018). *GRI 101: Foundation 2016.* GRI Sustainability Reporting Standards. Amsterdam: Global Reporting Initiative.

Griggs, D.J., Nilsson, M., Stevance, A. & McCollum, D. (Eds.) (2017). *A Guide to SDG Interactions: From Science to Implementation.* Paris: International Council for Science (ICSU).

Grin, J., Rotmans, J. & Schot, J. (2010). *Transitions to Sustainable Development. New Directions in the Study of Long Term Transformative Change.* London: Routledge.

Grint, K. (2008). 'Wicked Problems and Clumsy Solutions: The Role of Leadership', *Clinical Leader,* 1(2):54–68.

Grosvold, J., Hoejmose, S.U. & Roehrich, K.K. (2014). 'Squaring the circle: Management, measurement and performance of sustainability in supply chains', *Supply Chain Management,* 19(3):292–305.

Guandalini, L., Sun, W. & Zhou, L. (2019). 'Assessing the implementation of Sustainable Development Goals through switching cost', *Journal of Cleaner Production,* (232):1430–1441.

Gui, L., Huang, N., Atasu, A. & Toktay, L.B. (2016). 'Design Implications of Extended Producer Responsibility Legislation'. In: Atasu, A. (Ed.), *Environmentally Responsible Supply Chains* (pp. 339–358). Springer Series in Supply Chain Management.

Guix, M., Bonilla-Priego, M.J. & Font, X. (2018). 'The process of sustainability reporting in international hotel groups: an analysis of stakeholder inclusiveness, materiality and responsiveness', *Journal of Sustainable Tourism,* 26(7):1063–1084.

Gupta, J. & Vegelin, C. (2016). 'Sustainable development goals and inclusive development', *International Environmental Agreements: Politics, Law and Economics,* 16(3):433–448.

Hahn, T., Figge, F., Aragón-Correa, J.A., & Sharma, S. (2017). 'Advancing Research on Corporate Sustainability: Off to Pastures New or Back to the Roots?', *Business & Society,* 56(2):155–185.

Hallegatte, S., Rentschler, J. & Rozenberg, J. (2019). *Lifelines: The Resilient Infrastructure Opportunity,* Sustainable Infrastructure Series. Washington DC: World Bank.

Halme, M. & Laurila, J.S. (2009). 'Philanthropy, Integration or Innovation? Exploring the Financial and Societal Outcomes of Different Types of Corporate Responsibility', *Journal of Business Ethics,* (84):325–339.

Hanson, L.L. (2019). 'Wicked Problems and Sustainable Development'. In: Leal Filho, W. (Ed.) *Encyclopedia of Sustainability in Higher Education,* (pp. 2091–2098). Switzerland: Springer Nature.

Hardin, G. (1968). 'The Tragedy of the Commons', *Science,* New Series, 162(3859): 1243–1248.

Hardy, C. (1985). 'The Nature of Unobtrusive Power', *Journal of Management Studies,* 22(4):384–399.

Hardy, C. & Phillips, N. (1998). 'Strategies of Engagement: Lessons from the Critical Examination of Collaboration and Conflict in an Interorganizational Domain', *Organization Science,* 9(2):217–230.

Hart, S.L. (1995). 'A Natural-Resource-Based View of the Firm', *The Academy of Management Review*, 20(4):986–1014.

Hart, S.L. & Sharma, S. (2004). 'Engaging fringe stakeholders for competitive imagination', *Academy of Management*, 18(1):7–18.

Hartmann, T. (2012). 'Wicked problems and clumsy solutions: Planning as expectation management, *Planning Theory*, 11(3):242–256.

Hasan, S. (Ed.) (2015). *Human Security and Philanthropy: Islamic Perspectives and Muslim Majority Country Practices*. New York: Springer.

Hawken, P. (2017). *Drawdown. The Most Comprehensive Plan Ever Proposed to Reverse Global Warming*, Penguin Books.

Head, B.W. (2019). 'Forty years of wicked problems literature: forging closer links to policy studies', *Policy and Society*, 38(2):180–197.

Head, B.W. & Alford, J. (2015). 'Wicked problems: the implications for public policy and management', *Administration & Society*, 47(6):711–739.

Heath, R.L. (Ed.) (2001). *The Handbook of Public Relations*. Thousand Oaks, CA: Sage Publications.

Hege, E., Barchiche, D., Rochette, J., Chabason, L. & Barthélemy, P. (2019). *Initial assessment and conditions for success of the 2030 Agenda for Sustainable Development*, IDDRI study, No. 7, October.

Hemmati, M. (2002). *Multi-Stakeholder Processes for Governance and Sustainability – Beyond Deadlock and Conflict*. London: Earthscan.

Hengelaar, G.A. (2017). *The Proactive Incumbent. Holy Grail or Hidden Gem? Investigating whether the Dutch electricity sector can overcome the incumbent's curse and lead the sustainability transition*. Rotterdam: Erasmus Research Institute for Management.

Henriques, A. & Richardson, E. (Eds.) (2004). *The Triple Bottom Line: Does it All Add Up. Assessing the Sustainability of Business and CSR*. Abingdon: Earthscan.

Hertz, N. (2014). *Eyes Wide Open. How to Make Smart Decisions in a Confusing World*, Harper Business.

Hertz, N. (2002). *The Silent Takeover. Global Capitalism and the Death of Democracy*, Cornerstone.

Hervieux, C. & Voltan, A. (2018). 'Framing Social Problems in Social Entrepreneurship', *Journal of Business Ethics*, (151):279–293.

Hesseldahl, P., Nielsen, I., Abrahamsen, M., Jensen, M. & Hansen, I. (2015). *Your Business in the WE-Economy. Navigating the waters of the new collaborative economy*, June.

Heugens, P. (2001). *Strategic Issues Management. Implications for Corporate Performance*. (No. EPS-2001-007-STR). ERIM Ph.D. Series Research in Management. Erasmus University Rotterdam.

Hirschman, A.O. (1970). *Exit, Voice, and Loyalty: Responses to Decline in Firms, Organizations, and States*, Harvard University Press.

Hofstede, G.H. & Hofstede, G.J. (2005). *Cultures and Organizations: Software of the Mind*. Third Edition. New York: McGraw-Hill.

Hollensbe, E., Wookey, C., Hickey, L., George, G. & Nichols, V. (2014). 'Organizations with Purpose', *Academy of Management Journal*, 57(5):1227–1234.

Hosseini, S., Barker, K. & Ramirez-Marquez, J.E. (2016). 'A review of definitions and measures of system resilience', *Reliability Engineering and System Safety*, (145):47–61.

Hudson, J.M. & Bruckman, A.S. (2004). 'The Bystander Effect: A Lens for Understanding Patterns of Participation', *Journal of the Learning Sciences*, 13(2):165–195.

Humphrey, J. & Schmitz, H. (2002). 'How does insertion in global value chains affect upgrading in industrial clusters?' *Regional Studies*, 36(9):1017–27.

Hunt, C.B. & Auster, E.R. (1990). 'Proactive Environmental Management: Avoiding the Toxic Trap', *Sloan Management Review*, (31):7–18.

Huxham, C. (Ed.) (1996). *Creating Collaborative Advantage*. London: Sage Publications.

Huxham, C. & Vangen, S. (2004). 'Doing Things Collaboratively: Realizing the Advantage or Succumbing to Inertia?', *Organizational Dynamics*, 33(2):190–201.

ICMIF (2019). *Global Mutual Market Share. The Global Insurance Market Share Held by Mutual and Cooperative Insurers*, International Cooperative and Mutual Insurance Federation.

ICSU (2017). *A Guide to SDG Interactions: From Science to Implementation*. Paris: International Council for Science.

ICSU & ISSC (2015). *Review of Targets for the Sustainable Development Goals: The Science Perspective*. Paris: International Council for Science.

IEA (2020). *World Energy Outlook 2020*. Paris: International Energy Agency.

IEAG (2014). *A World That Counts: Mobilising The Data Revolution for Sustainable Development*, The United Nations Secretary-General's Independent Expert Advisory Group on a Data Revolution for Sustainable Development.

IFAC (2020). *The CFO and Finance Function Role in Value Creation*. New York, International Federation of Accountants.

IIRC (2021). *International <IR> Framework, January 2021*. International Integrated Reporting Council.

IIRC (2013). *The International <IR> Framework*. The International Integrated Reporting Council, December.

IIRC (2013a). *Materiality – Background Paper for <IR>*. The International Integrated Reporting Council, March.

IIRC (2013b). *Capitals – Background Paper for <IR>*. The International Integrated Reporting Council, March.

Ikram, M., Sroufe, R. & Zhang, Q. (2020). 'Prioritizing and overcoming barriers to integrated management system (IMS) implementation using AHP and G-Topsis', *Journal of Cleaner Production*, (254):120121.

ILO (2020). *Global Wage Report 2020–21: Wages and minimum wages in the time of COVID-19*. Geneva: International Labour Organization.

ILO (2020a). *ILO Monitor: COVID-19 and the world of work. Third edition. Updated estimates and analysis*, International Labour Organization, 29 April 2020.

ILO (2020b). *World Employment and Social Outlook. Trends 2020*. Geneva: International Labour Organization.

ILO (2019). *Integrated Strategy on Fundamental Principles and Rights at Work 2017–2023*. Geneva: International Labour Office.

ILO (2017). *Tripartite Declaration of Principles concerning Multinational Enterprises and Social Policy*, Fifth Edition, March. Geneva: International Labour Office.

ILO & UNICEF (2021). *Child Labour: Global estimates 2020, trends and the road forward*. New York: International Labour Office and United Nations Children's Fund.

IMF (2021). *World Economic Outlook. Managing Divergent Recoveries*. Washington DC: International Monetary Fund, April.

IMF (2020). *World Economic Outlook: The Great Lockdown*. Washington DC: International Monetary Fund, April.

IMF (2019). *World Economic Outlook. Global Manufacturing Downturn, Rising Trade Barriers*. Washington DC: International Monetary Fund, October.

IMF (2019a). 'Follow the Money', *Finance and Development, A Quarterly Publication of the International Monetary Fund*, 56(3), September.

Inter-Agency Task Force on Financing for Development (2020). *Financing for Sustainable Development Report 2020*. New York: United Nations, April.

International Planning Committee on Food Sovereignty (2013). 'Informal Thematic Consultation Hunger, Food and Nutrition Post 2015'. Retrieved: 7 October 2013.

IPBES (2019). *Summary for policymakers of the global assessment report on biodiversity and ecosystem services of the Intergovernmental Science-Policy Platform on Biodiversity and Ecosystem Services*, approved by the IPBES Plenary, May 2019 (IPBES-7). Bonn, Germany: IPBES.

ISO (2020). *ISO 56000, Innovation management – Fundamentals and vocabulary*, First edition, 2020–02.

ISO (2018). *ISO 26000. Guidance on Social Responsibility. Discovering ISO 26000*. Geneva: International Organization for Standardization.

ISO (2018a). *ISO 26000 and the SDGs*. Geneva: International Organization for Standardization.

ISO (2017). *Practical overview of the linkages between ISO 26000:2010, Guidance on social responsibility and OECD Guidelines for Multinational Enterprises (2011)*, version 7 February 2017. Geneva: International Organization for Standardization.

Jackson, G., Bartosch, J. Avetisyan, E., Kinderman, D. & Steen Knudsen, J. (2020). 'Mandatory Non-financial Disclosure and Its Influence on CSR: An International Comparison', *Journal of Business Ethics*, 162(2):323–342.

Jackson, T. (2009). *Prosperity without growth? The transition to a sustainable economy*. Sustainable Development Commission, March.

James, C. (2011). *Theory of Change Review: A report commissioned by Comic Relief*. Retrieved from: https://www.dmeforpeace.org/wp-content/uploads/2017/06/James_ ToC.pdf.

Jarzabkowski, P. (2004). 'Strategy as Practice: Recursiveness, Adaptation, and Practices-in-Use', *Organization Studies*, 25(4):529–560.

Jay, J. (2013). 'Navigating Paradox as a Mechanism of Change and Innovation in Hybrid Organizations', *Academy of Management Journal*, 56(1):137–159.

Jensen, M.C. & Meckling, W.H. (1976). 'Theory of the firm: Managerial behavior, agency costs, and ownership structure', *Journal of Financial Economics*, 3(4):305–360.

Jones, P., Comfort, D. & Hillier, D. (2016). 'Materiality in corporate sustainability reporting within UK retailing', *Journal of Public Affairs*, 16(1):81–90.

Jones, T.M., Donaldson, T., Freeman, R.E., Harrison, J.S., Leana, C.R., Mahoney, J.T. & Pearce, J.L. (2016). 'Management Theory and Social Welfare: Contributions and Challenges', *Academy of Management Review*, 41(2):216–228.

Jordan, M.E., Kleinsasser, R.C. & Roe, M.F. (2014). 'Wicked problems: inescapable wickedity', *Journal of Education for Teaching*, 40(4):415–430.

Kabeer, N. (2010). *Can the MDGs provide a pathway to social justice?: The challenge of inter-secting inequalities*. Institute of Development Studies. New York: United Nations Development Programme.

Kahneman, D. (2012). *Thinking, Fast and Slow*. New York: Farrer, Strauss and Giroux Inc.

Kamau, M., Chasek, P.S. & O'Connor, D. (2018). *Transforming Multilateral Diplomacy. The Inside Story of the Sustainable Development Goals*. Routledge.

Kania, J. & Kramer, M. (2011). 'Collective Impact', *Stanford Social Innovation Review*, 9(1):36–41.

Kaplan, S. (2008). 'Framing Contests: Strategy Making under Uncertainty', *Organization Science*, 19(5):729–752.

Kaptein, M. (2020). 'Business Codes: A review of the literature'. In: Van Rooij, B. & Sokol, D.D. (Eds.), *Cambridge Handbook of Compliance*. Cambridge University Press.

Kaptein, M. & Van Tulder, R. (2003). 'Toward Effective Stakeholder Dialogue', *Business and Society Review*, 108(2):203–224.

Kaptein, M. & Wempe, J. (2002). *The Balanced Company. A Theory of Corporate Integrity*. New York: Oxford University Press.

Karliner, J. (1997). *The Corporate Planet. Ecology and Politics in the Age of Globalization*, Sierra Club Books.

Kathuria, R., Joshi, M. & Porth, S. (2007). 'Organizational Alignment and Performance: Past, Present and Future', *Management Decision*, 45(3):503–517.

Katz, N. & Pattarini, N.M. (2008). 'Interest-based negotiation: An essential business and communications tool for the public relations counselor', *Journal of Communication Management*, 12(1):88–97.

Kelly, E. (2015). 'Business ecosystems come of age'. In: Deloitte (2015). *Business ecosystems come of age*, Business Trend Report (pp. 3–15), Deloitte University Press.

Kennedy, P. (1989). *Rise and Fall of the Great Powers. Economic Change and Military Conflict from 1500 to 2000*. Random House.

Kharas, H. & McArthur, J. (2019). *Building the SDG economy. Needs, spending, and financing for universal achievement of the Sustainable Development Goals*, Global Economy & Development, Brookings Working paper 131, 21 October.

Klein, N. (2007). *The Shock Doctrine. The Rise of Disaster Capitalism*. Allen Lane/Penguin Books.

Kleindorfer, P.R., Singhal, K. & Van Wassenhove, L.N. (2005). 'Sustainable Operations Management', *Production and Operations Management* 14(4):482–492.

Klewitz, J. & Hansen, E.G. (2014). 'Sustainability-Oriented Innovation of SMEs: A Systematic Review', *Journal of Cleaner Production*, (65):57–75.

Kobeissi, N. (2005). 'Foreign Investment in the MENA Region: Analyzing Non-Traditional Determinants', Perspectives On International Corporate Responsibility, *International Corporate Responsibility Series*, (2):217–233.

Koberg, E. & Longoni, S. (2019). 'A systematic review of sustainable supply chain management in global supply chains', *Journal of Cleaner Production*, (207):1084–1098.

Koehler, G. (2016). 'Assessing the SDGs from the standpoint of eco-social policy. Using the SDGs subversively', *Journal of International and Comparative Social Policy*, 32(2):149–164.

Koehler, G. (2015). 'Seven Decades of 'Development', and Now What?', *Journal of International Development*, 27(6):733–751.

Kolk, A. & Van Tulder, R. (2010). 'International Business, Corporate Social Responsibility and Sustainable Development', *International Business Review*, 19(1):119–125.

Kolk, A., Van Tulder, R. & Kostwinder, E. (2008). 'Business and partnerships for development', *European Management Journal*, 26(4):262–273.

Korten, D.C. (2001). *When Corporations Rule the World*, 2nd Revised Edition, Kumarian Press.

Kotler, P. & Armstrong, G. (2018). *Principles of Marketing. 17th Global Edition*. Pearson Education.

KPMG (2020). *The Time has Come: The KPMG Survey of Sustainability Reporting 2020*, December.

KPMG (2014). *Sustainable Insight: The essentials of materiality assessment*. KPMG International, October.

Kraemer, R. & Van Tulder, R. (2012). 'A license to operate for the extractive industries? Operationalizing stakeholder thinking in international business'. In: Lindgreen, A., Kotler, P., Vanhamme, J. & Maon, F. (Eds.) *A Stakeholder Approach to Corporate Social Responsibility. Pressures, Conflicts and Reconciliation* (pp. 97–120). Surrey: Gower Publishing.

Kramer, M.R. & Porter, M.E. (2006). 'Strategy and society: The link between competitive advantage and corporate social responsibility', *Harvard Business Review*, 84(12):78–92.

Kroll, C. (2019). 'Long in words but short on action: UN sustainability goals are threatened to fail', press release 19 June 2019, Bertelsmann Stiftung.

Krugman, P. (2013). 'The New Growth Fizzle', *The New York Times,* 18 August. Retrieved from: https://krugman.blogs.nytimes.com/2013/08/18/the-new-growth-fizzle/.

Laasch, O. & Conaway, R.N. (2015). *Principles of Responsible Management: Glocal Sustainability, Responsibility, Ethics.* Mason: Cengage.

Laasch, O., Suddaby, R., Freeman, R.E. & Jamali, D. (Eds.) (2020). *Research Handbook of Responsible Management.* Cheltenham: Edward Elgar.

Lai, A., Melloni, G. & Stacchezzini, R. (2017). 'What does materiality mean to integrated reporting preparers? An empirical exploration', *Meditari Accountancy Research*, 25(4):533–552.

Lamarche, T. & Rubinstein, M. (2012). 'Dynamics of corporate social responsibility: Towards a new conception of control?', *Journal of Institutional Economics*, 8(2):161–186.

Lashitew, A.A., Bals, L. & Van Tulder, R. (2020). 'Inclusive Business at the Base of the Pyramid: The Role of Embeddedness for Enabling Social Innovations', *Journal of Business Ethics*, 162(1):421–448.

Laursen, K. & Salter, A.J. (2014). 'The paradox of openness: Appropriability, external search and collaboration', *Research Policy*, 43(5):867–878.

Lawrence, T.B., Hardy, C. & Phillips, N.W. (2002). 'Institutional Effects of Interorganizational Collaboration: The Emergence of Proto-Institutions', *The Academy of Management Journal*, 45(1):281–290.

Lazer, W. (1969). 'Marketing's changing social relationships', *Journal of Marketing*, (33):3–9.

Le Blanc, D. (2015). *Towards integration at last? The Sustainable Development Goals as a network of targets.* DESA Working Paper No. 141, United Nations Department of Economic and Social Affairs, ST/ESA/2015/DWP/141, March.

Lee, Y., Garza-Gomez, X. & Lee, R.M. (2018). 'Ultimate Costs of the Disaster: Seven Years After the Deepwater Horizon Oil Spill', *Journal of Corporate Accounting & Finance*, 29(1):69–79.

Leipziger, D. (2016). *The Corporate Responsibility Code Book*, Third Edition, Greenleaf Publishing.

Leleux, B. & Van der Kaaij, J. (2018). *Winning Sustainability Strategies. Finding Purpose, Driving Innovation and Executing Change.* Basingstoke: Palgrave Macmillan.

Lennie, J. & Tacchi, J. (2014). 'Bridging the Divide between Upward Accountability and Learning-Based Approaches to Development Evaluation: Strategies for an Enabling Environment', *Evaluation Journal of Australasia*, 14(1):12–23.

Levin, K., Cashore, B., Bernstein, S. & Auld, G. (2012). 'Overcoming the tragedy of super wicked problems: constraining our future selves to ameliorate climate change', *Policy Sciences*, 45(2):123–152.

Levin, R.C., Klevorick, A.K., Nelson, R.R. & Winter, S.G. (1987). 'Appropriating the Returns from Industrial Research and Development', *Brookings Papers on Economic Activity* 3(1987):783–831.

Lewis, M. (2000). 'Exploring Paradox: Toward a More Comprehensive Guide, *The Academy of Management Review*, 25(4):760–776.

Li, F. & Polychronopoulos, A. (2020). 'What a Difference an ESG Ratings Provider Makes!', *Research Affiliates*, January.

Lijfering, S.M. & Van Tulder, R. (2020). *Inclusive Business in Africa. A business model perspective*, The Partnerships Resource Centre. Rotterdam: Rotterdam School of Management, Erasmus University.

Lin, H. (2012). 'Cross-sector Alliances for Corporate Social Responsibility Partner Heterogeneity Moderates Environmental Strategy Outcomes', *Journal of Business Ethics,* 110(2): 219–229.

Lin-Hi, N. & Müller, K. (2013). 'The CSR bottom line. Preventing corporate social irresponsibility', *Journal of Business Research*, 66(10):1928–1936.

Linnenluecke, M.K. & Griffiths, A. (2010). 'Corporate sustainability and organizational culture', *Journal of World Business*, 45(4):357–366.

Lock, I. & Seele, P. (2016). 'CSR governance and departmental organization: a typology of best practices', *Corporate Governance*, 16(1):211–230.

Lomborg, B. (Ed.) (2018). *Prioritizing Development: A Cost Benefit Analysis of the United Nations' Sustainable Development Goals*. Cambridge University Press.

London, T. (2016). *The Base of the Pyramid Promise: Building Businesses with Impact and Scale*. Stanford: Stanford University Press.

London, T. (2011). 'Building Better Ventures with the Base of the Pyramid: A Roadmap'. In: London, T. & Hart, S.L. (Eds.), *Next Generation Business Strategies for the Base of the Pyramid: New Approaches for Building Mutual Value*. Upper Saddle River, NJ: Pearson Education.

London, T. & Hart, S.L. (Eds.) (2011). *Next Generation Business Strategies for the Base of the Pyramid: New Approaches for Building Mutual Value*. Upper Saddle River, NJ: Pearson Education.

Lozano, R. (2015). 'A Holistic Perspective on Corporate Sustainability Drivers', *Corporate Social Responsibility and Environmental Management*, 22(1):32–44.

Lüdeke-Freund, F. & Dembek, K. (2017). 'Sustainable Business Model Research and Practice: Emerging Field or Passing Fancy?', *Journal of Cleaner Production*, (168):1668–1678.

Lukes, S. (1974). *Power: A Radical View*. London: MacMillan.

Maani, K.E. & Cavana, R.Y. (2007). *Systems Thinking, System Dynamics: Managing Change and Complexity*. Prentice Hall.

MacFeely, S. (2019). *The Political Economy of Measuring the Sustainable Development Goals*, UNCTAD Research Paper No. 32, UNCTAD/SER.RP/2019/4, June.

MacFeely, S. (2019a). 'The Big (data) Bang: Opportunities and Challenges for Compiling SDG Indicators', *Global Policy*, 10(s1):121–133.

Machado, C.G., De Lima, E.P., Da Costa, S.E.G., Angelis, J.J. & Mattioda, R.A. (2017). 'Framing maturity based on sustainable operations management principles', *International Journal of Production Economics*, (190):3–21.

Madsbjerg, C. (2017). *Sensemaking: The Power of the Humanities in the Age of the Algorithm*. Hachette Books.

Mair, J., Battilana, J. & Cardenas, J. (2012). 'Organizing for Society: A Typology of Social Entrepreneuring Models', *Journal of Business Ethics*, (111):353–373.

Mair, J. & Marti, I. (2009). 'Entrepreneurship in and around institutional voids: A case study from Bangladesh', *Journal of Business Venturing*, 24(5):419–435.

Malik, A. (2018). *Strategic Human Resource Management and Employment Relations. An International Perspective*. Springer Nature Singapore.

Maniora, J. (2018). 'Mismanagement of Sustainability: What Business Strategy Makes the Difference? Empirical Evidence from the USA, *Journal of Business Ethics*, (152):931–947.

Mann, C. (2018). *The Wizard and the Prophet. Science and the Future of Our Planet*. New York: Alfred Knopf.

Maon, F., Lindgreen, A. & Swaen, V. (2010). 'Organizational Stages and Cultural Phases: A Critical Review and a Consolidative Model of Corporate Social Responsibility Development', *International Journal of Management Reviews*, 12(1):20–38.

Martin, D. & Schouten, J. (2012). *Sustainable marketing*. Harlow: Pearson Education.

Matten, D., Crane, A. & Chapple, W. (2003). 'Behind the Mask: Revealing the True Face of Corporate Citizenship', *Journal of Business Ethics*, 45(1/2):109–120.

Mazzucato, M. (2018). *The Value of Everything. Making and Taking in the Global Economy*. Allen Lane.

Mazzucato, M. (2018a). 'The entrepreneurial state: socializing both risks and rewards', *Real-World Economics Review*, (84):201–217.

McConnell, A. (2018). 'Rethinking wicked problems as political problems and policy problems', *Policy & Politics*, 46(1):165–180.

McDermott, W.B. (1996). 'Foresight is an illusion', *Long Range Planning*, 29(2):190–194.

McDonald, L.G. with Robinson, P. (2009). *Colossal Failure of Common Sense. The Incredible Inside Story of the Collapse of Lehman Brothers*. Crown Business.

McDougall, N., Wagner, B. & MacBryde, J. (2021). 'Leveraging competitiveness from sustainable operations: frameworks to understand the dynamic capabilities needed to realise NRBV supply chain strategies', *Supply Chain Management: An International Journal*, February.

McElhaney, K.A. (2009). 'A Strategic Approach to Corporate Social Responsibility', *Leader to Leader*, (52):30–36.

McEwen, T. (2001). *Managing Values and Beliefs in Organisations*. New York: Financial Times/Prentice Hall.

McKinsey & Company (2021). 'The state of internal carbon pricing', Strategy & Corporate Finance, February 10.

McKinsey (2020). 'The pivotal factors for effective external engagement', May 26, Survey.

McKinsey Global Institute (2015). *The Power of Parity: How Advancing Women's Equality Can Add $12 Trillion to Global Growth*, September.

McWilliams, A. & Siegel, D.S. (2001). 'Corporate Social Responsibility: A Theory of the Firm Perspective', *The Academy of Management Review*, 26(1):117–127.

Meadows, D.H., Meadows, D.L., Randers, J. & Behrens, W.W. (1972). *The Limits to Growth. A Report for The Club of Rome's Project on the Predicament of Mankind*. New York: Universe Books.

Merton, R.K. (1936). 'The Unanticipated Consequences of Purposive Social Action', *American Sociological Review*, 1(6):894–904.

Metlay, D. & Sarewitz, D. (2012). 'Decision Strategies for Addressing Complex, "Messy" Problems', *The Bridge*, 42(3):6–16.

Meyer, R. & Meijers, R. (2017). *Leadership Agility. Developing Your Repertoire of Leadership Styles*. London: Routledge.

Migliorelli, M. (2021). 'What Do We Mean by Sustainable Finance? Assessing Existing Frameworks and Policy Risks', *Sustainability*, 13(2):975.

Milhaupt, C.J. & Pargendler M. (2017). *Governance Challenges of Listed State-Owned Enterprises around the World: National Experiences and a Framework for Reform*, European Corporate Governance Institute (ECGI) Law Working Paper N° 352/2017.

Minguez-Vera, A., Martin-Ugedo, J.F. & Arcas-Lario, N. (2010). 'Agency and property rights theories in agricultural cooperatives: evidence from Spain', *Spanish Journal of Agricultural Research* 8(4):908–924.

Mintzberg, H. (2015). *Rebalancing Society. Radical Renewal Beyond Left, Right and Centre*. Oakland, CA: Berrett-Koehler Publishers.

Mintzberg, H. (1980). 'Structure in 5's: A Synthesis of the Research on Organization Design', *Management Science*, 26(3):322–341.

Mintzberg, H., Ahlstrand, B. & Lampel, J. (2009). *Strategy Safari: A Guided Tour Through The Wilds of Strategic Management*. Second Edition, FT Press.

Mintzberg, H. & Waters, J.A. (1985). 'Of Strategy: Deliberate and Emergent', *Strategic Management Journal*, 6(3):257–272.

Mio, C., Panfilo, S. & Blundo, B. (2020). 'Sustainable development goals and the strategic role of business: A systemic literature review', *Business Strategy and the Environment* 29(8):3220–3245.

Mirvis, P.H. & Googins, B.K. (2006). 'Stages of Corporate Citizenship', *California Management Review*, 48(2):104–126.

Mitchell, R.K., Agle, B.R. & Wood, D. (1997). 'Toward a Theory of Stakeholder Identification and Salience', *Academy of Management Review*, 22(4):853–886.

Moon, J., Crane., A. & Matten, D. (2005). 'Can Corporations be Citizens? Corporate Citizenship as a Metaphor for Business Participation in Society', *Business Ethics Quarterly*, 15(3):429–453.

Moore, H.L. (2015). 'Global Prosperity and Sustainable Development Goals', *Journal of International Development*, 27(6):801–815.

Morioka, S.N., Bolis, I., Evans, S. & Carvalho, M.M. (2017). 'Transforming sustainability challenges into competitive advantage: Multiple case studies kaleidoscope converging into sustainable business models', *Journal of Cleaner Production* (167):723–738.

Mousavi, S., Bossink, B. & Van Vliet, M. (2018). 'Microfoundations of companies' dynamic capabilities for environmentally sustainable innovation: Case study insights from high-tech innovation in science-based companies', *Business Strategy and the Environment*, (28):366–387.

Mroue A.M., Mohtar, R.H., Pistikopoulos, E.N. & Holtzapple, M.T. (2019). 'Energy Portfolio Assessment Tool (EPAT): Sustainable energy planning using the WEF nexus approach – Texas case', *Science of The Total Environment*, (648):1649–1664.

Muldoon, J.P. (2018). 'International Organizations and Governance in a Time of Transition', *Journal of International Organizations Studies*, 9(2):13–26.

Murphy, D.F. & Stott, L. (Eds.) (2021). *Partnerships for the Sustainable Development Goals (SDGs)*. Basel, Switzerland: MDPI.

Musgrave, R.A. (1959). 'Taxes and the Budget', *Challenge*, 8(2):18–22.

Nawaz, W. & Koç, M. (2019). 'Exploring Organizational Sustainability: Themes, Functional Areas, and Best Practices', *Sustainability*, 11(16):4307.

Nelson, J., Ishikawa, E. & Geaneotes, A. (2009). *Developing inclusive business models: a review of Coca-Cola's Manual Distribution Centers in Ethiopia and Tanzania*. Washington DC: World Bank Group.

Netherlands Environmental Planning Agency (2018). *Natural capital accounting for the sustainable development goals. Current and potential uses and steps forward*, policy study. The Hague: PBL.

Ney, S. & Verweij, M. (2015). 'Messy institutions for wicked problems: How to generate clumsy solutions?', *Environment and Planning C: Politics and Space*, 33(6):1679–1696.

Nickerson, J. & Sanders, R. (Eds.) (2014). *Tackling Wicked Government Problems. A Practical Guide for Developing Enterprise Leaders*. Revised Edition. Brookings Institution Press.

Nidumolu, R., Prahalad, C.K. & Rangaswami, M.R. (2009). 'Why Sustainability Is Now the Key Driver of Innovation', *Harvard Business Review*, September.

Nie, M. (2003). 'Drivers of natural resource-based political conflict', *Policy Sciences*, 36(3/4):307–341.

Nie, P., Wang, C. & Cui, T. (2019). 'Players acting as leaders in turn improve cooperation', *Royal Society Open Science*, 6(7):190251.

Nielsen, A.E. & Thomsen, C. (2018). 'Reviewing corporate social responsibility communication: a legitimacy perspective', *Corporate Communications: An International Journal*, 23(4):492–511.

Nilsson, M., Chisholm, E., Griggs, D., Howden-Chapman, P., McCollum, D., Messerli, P., Neumann, B., Stevance, A., Visbeck, M. & Stafford-Smith, M. (2018). 'Mapping interactions between the sustainable development goals: lessons learned and ways forward', *Sustainability Science*, 13(6):1489–1503.

Nilsson, M., Griggs, D. & Visbeck, M. (2016). 'Map the interactions between Sustainable Development Goals', *Nature*, 534(7607):320–322.

North, D.C. (1990). *Institutions, Institutional Change and Economic Performance*. Cambridge: Cambridge University Press.

Nosratabadi, S., Mosavi, A., Shamshirband, S., Zavadskas, E.K., Rakotonirainy, A. & Chau, K.W. (2019). 'Sustainable Business Models: A Review', *Sustainability*, 11(6):1663.

Nunhes, T., Bernardo, M. & Oliveira, O. (2019). 'Guiding principles of integrated management systems: Toward unifying a starting point for researchers and practitioners', *Journal of Cleaner Production*, (210):977–993.

Nuttavuthisit, K. & Thogersen, J. (2017). 'The Importance of Consumer Trust for the Emergence of a Market for Green Products: The Case of Organic Food', *Journal of Business Ethics*, (140):323–337.

Nye, J.S. Jr. (2004). *Soft Power: The Means to Success in World Politics*. Public Affairs.

OECD (2020). *OECD Business and Finance Outlook 2020: Sustainable and Resilient Finance*, OECD Publishing, Paris.

OECD (2019). *Measuring distance to the SDG Targets 2019. An Assessment of Where OECD Countries Stand*. Paris: OECD Publishing.

OECD (2019a). *Governance as an SDG Accelerator. Country Experiences and Tools*. Paris: OECD Publishing.

OECD (2019b). *Policy Coherence for Sustainable Development 2019: Empowering People and Ensuring Inclusiveness and Equality*. Paris: OECD Publishing.

OECD (2018). *OECD Due Diligence Guidance for Responsible Business Conduct*, 31 May.

OECD (2017). *How's Life? 2017: Measuring Well-being*. Paris: OECD Publishing.

OECD (2016). *Better Policies for Sustainable Development 2016: A New Framework for Policy Coherence*. Paris: OECD Publishing.

OECD (2016a). *Development Co-operation Report 2016: The Sustainable Development Goals as Business Opportunities – Highlights*. The Development Assistance Committee, 18 July.

OECD (2015). *Better Policies for Development 2015: Policy Coherence and Green Growth*, Paris: OECD Publishing.

OECD (2014). *OECD Guidelines for Multinational Enterprise. Responsible Business Conduct Matters*.

OECD (2014a). *All On Board. Making Inclusive Growth Happen*. OECD Initiative on Inclusive Growth. Paris: OECD Publishing.

OECD (2011). *OECD Guidelines for Multinational Enterprises*. OECD Publishing.

Olson, M. (1982). *The Rise and Decline of Nations: Economic Growth, Stagflation, and Social Rigidities*. Yale University Press.

Olsson, A., Wadell, C., Odenrick, P. & Bergendahl, M.N. (2010). 'An action learning method for increased innovation capacity in organisations,' *Action Learning: Research and Practice* 7(2):167–179.

Ordaz, E. (2019). 'The SDGs Indicators: A Challenging Task for the International Statistical Community', *Global Policy*, 10(s1):141–143.

Orlitzky, M. (2009). 'Corporate Social Performance and Financial Performance: A Research Synthesis'. In: Crane, A., Matten, D., McWilliams, A., Moon, J. & Siegel, D.S. (Eds.). *The Oxford Handbook of Corporate Social Responsibility*. Oxford: Oxford University Press.

Orlitzky, M., Schmidt, F.L. & Rynes, S.L. (2003). 'Corporate Social and Financial Performance: A Meta-Analysis', *Organization Studies*, 24(3):403–441.

Osterwalder, A. & Pigneur, Y. (2010). *Business Model Generation: A Handbook for Visionaries, Game Changers, and Challengers*. John Wiley & Sons.

Ostrom, E. (2015). *Governing The Commons. The Evolution of Institutions for Collective Action*. Cambridge: Cambridge University Press.

Oxfam International (2020). *Time to care. Unpaid and underpaid care work and the global inequality crisis*, Oxfam Briefing Paper, 20 January.

Oxfam International (2018). *Reward Work, Not Wealth.* Oxfam Briefing Paper, January.

Oxfam (2017). *Raising The Bar: Rethinking the role of business in the Sustainable Development Goals*, Oxfam Discussion Papers, February.

Paauwe, J. & Farndale, E. (2017). *Strategy, HRM, and Performance: A Contextual Approach* (second edition). Oxford: Oxford University Press.

Panigrahi, S.S., Bahinipati, B. & Jain, V. (2019). 'Sustainable supply chain management: A review of literature and implications for future research', *Management of Environmental Quality: An International Journal*, 30(5):1001–1049.

Parkhurst, J. (2017). *The Politics of Evidence: From evidence-based policy to the good governance of evidence.* Routledge Studies in Governance and Public Policy. London: Routledge.

Parkhust, J. (2016). 'Appeals to evidence for the resolution of wicked problems: the origins and mechanisms of evidentiary bias", *Policy Sciences*, (49):373–393.

Parmigiani, A. & Rivera-Santos, M. (2011). 'Clearing a Path Through the Forest: A Meta-Review of Interorganizational Relationships', *Journal of Management*, 37(4):1108–1136.

Partos (2016). *Ready for Change? Global Goals at home and abroad*, 19 May. The Hague: Partos.

Pattberg, P. & Widerberg, O. (2016). 'Transnational multistakeholder partnerships for sustainable development: Conditions for success', *Ambio*, (45):42–51.

Pattberg, P., Biermann, F., Chan, S. & Mert, A. (Eds.) (2012). *Public-Private Partnerships for Sustainable Development. Emergence, Influence and Legitimacy.* Cheltenham: Edward Elgar.

Patton, M.Q., McKegg, K. & Wehipeihana, N. (Eds.) (2016). *Developmental Evaluation Exemplars. Principles in Practice.* New York: The Guilford Press.

Peeters, D. (2019). *Moving from 'Wanting' to 'Doing': The Intention-Realization Gap of Sustainable Business Model Innovation – a systemic literature review.* Excerpt from Master Thesis, October. Rotterdam School of Management (RSM), Erasmus University.

Pellegrini, C., Annunziata, E., Rizzi, F. & Frey, M. (2019). 'The role of networks and sustainable intrapreneurship as interactive drives catalyzing the adoption of sustainable innovation', *Corporate Social Responsibility and Environmental Management*, 26(5): 1026–1048.

Perez, C. (2002). *Technological Revolutions and Financial Capital. The Dynamics of Bubbles and Golden Ages.* Cheltenham: Edward Elgar.

Peterson, J.B. (2018). *12 Rules for Life. An Antidote to Chaos.* Random House Canada.

Pfeffer, J. (1993). *Managing with Power. Politics and Influence in Organizations.* Harvard Business Review Press.

Pfefferbaum, B.J., Reissman, D.B., Pfefferbaum, R.L., Klomp, R.W. & Gurwitch, R.H. (2005). 'Building Resilience to Mass Trauma Events'. In: Doll, L., Bonzo, S., Mercy, J. & Sleet, D. (Eds.) *Handbook on Injury and Violence Prevention Interventions.* New York: Kluwer Academic Publishers.

Pfisterer, S. & Van Tulder, R. (2020). 'Navigating the governance tension to enhance the impact of Public-Private Partnerships for the SDGs', *Sustainability,* 13(1):111.

Pinker, S. (2018). *Enlightment Now. The Case for Reason, Science, Humanism and Progress.* Allan Lane.

Podgorodnichenko, N., Edgar, F. & McAndrew, I. (2020). 'The role of HRM in developing sustainable organizations: Contemporary challenges and contradictions', *Human Resource Management Review*, (30):100685.

Pogge, T. & Sengupta, M. (2015). 'The Sustainable Development Goals (SDGs) as Drafted: Nice Idea, Poor Execution', *Washington International Law Journal*, 24(3):571–587.

Polman, P. & Winston, A. (2021). *Net Positive. How courageous companies thrive by giving more then they take.* Harvard Business Review Press.

Ponte, S. (2020). 'The hidden costs of environmental upgrading in global value chains', *Review of International Political Economy*, DOI: 10.1080/09692290.2020.1816199.

Ponte, S., Sturgeon, T.J. & Dallas, M.P. (2019). 'Governance and power in global value chains'. In: Ponte, S., Gereffi, G. & Raj-Reichert, G. (Eds.) *Handbook on Global Value Chains*, (pp. 120–137). Edward Elgar Publishing.

Porter, M.E. (2003). 'CSR: a religion with too many priests?', *European Business Forum*, issue 15, Autumn.

Porter, M.E. (1985). *Competitive Advantage: creating and sustaining superior performance.* New York: The Free Press.

Porter, M.E. & Kramer, M.R. (2011). 'Creating Shared Value: How to Reinvent Capitalism and Unleash a Wave of Innovation and Growth', *Harvard Business Review*, January/February.

Porter, M.E. & Kramer, M.R. (2006). 'Strategy and Society: The Link Between Competitive Advantage and Corporate Social Responsibility', *Harvard Business Review*, December.

Porter, M.E. & Kramer, M.R. (2002). 'The Competitive Advantage of Corporate Philanthropy', *Harvard Business Review*, December.

Powell, W. (1990). 'Neither Markets Nor Hierarchy: Network Forms of Organization', *Research in Organizational Behavior*, (12):295–336.

Prahalad, C.K. (2011). 'Bottom of the Pyramid as a Source of Breakthrough Innovations', *Journal of Product Innovation Management*, 29(1):6–12.

Prahalad, C.K. (2004). *The Fortune at the Bottom of the Pyramid. Eradicating Poverty through Profits.* Wharton, PA: Wharton School Publishing.

Prahalad, C.K., & Hart, S.L. (2002). 'The fortune at the bottom of the pyramid', *Strategy + Business*, (26):2–14.

PrC (2015). *The State of Partnerships Report – 2015. Civil Society Organisations (CSOs) Under Siege – can partnerships provide new venues?* Rotterdam: Partnerships Resource Centre at RSM-Erasmus University.

PrC (2011). *The State of Partnerships Report – 2011. Dutch Development NGOs facing the Partnering Challenge.* Rotterdam: Partnerships Resource Centre at RSM-Erasmus University.

PRI (2019). *Principles for Responsible Investment. An investor initiative in partnership with UNEP Finance Initiative and the UN Global Compact.*

Probst, G. & Bassi, A.M. (2014). *Tackling Complexity: A Systemic Approach for Decision-Makers.* Sheffield: Greenleaf Publishing.

Putnam, R.D. (2000). *Bowling Alone: The Collapse and Revival of American Community.* New York: Simon & Schuster.

PwC (2016). *Navigating the SDGs: a business guide to engaging with the UN Global Goals.*

PwC (2015). *Make it your business: Engaging with the Sustainable Development Goals.*

PwC (2013). *Supplier Relationship Management. How key suppliers drive your company's competitive advantage.*

Quinn, R.E. (1988). *Beyond rational management: Mastering the paradoxes and competing demands of high performance.* San Francisco, CA: Jossey-Bass.

Quinn, R.E. & Rohrbaugh, J. (1983). 'A spatial model of effectiveness criteria: towards a competing values approach to organizational analysis', *Management Science*, (29):363–377.

Rahwan, I., Pasquier, P., Sonenberg, L. & Dignum, F. (2009). 'A formal analysis of interest-based negotiation', *Annals of Mathematics and Artificial Intelligence*, 55(3):253–276.

Raith, M.G. & Siebold, N. (2018). 'Building Business Models around Sustainable Development Goals', *Journal of Business Models*, 6(2):71–77.

Rajan, R.G. (2019). *The Third Pillar: How Markets and the State Leave the Community Behind.* Penguin Press.

Ramalingam, B., Laric, M. & Primrose, J. (2014). *From best practice to best fit: Understanding and navigating wicked problems in international development.* ODI Working Paper. London: Overseas Development Institute.

Ran, B. & Qi, H. (2018). 'Contingencies of Power Sharing in Collaborative Governance', *American Review of Public Administration*, 48(8):836–851.

Rasche, A. & Waddock, S. (2014). 'Global Sustainability Governance and the UN Global Compact: A Rejoinder to Critics', *Journal of Business Ethics*, 122(2):209–216.

Rasche, A., Waddock, S. & McIntosh, M. (2013). 'The United Nations Global Compact: Retrospect and Prospect', *Business and Society*, 52(1):6–30.

Raven, B.H. (1965). 'Social influence and power'. In: Steiner, I.D. & Fishbein, M. (Eds.), *Current studies in social psychology*, (pp. 371–382). New York: Holt, Rinehart, Winston.

Rawls, J. (1971). *A Theory of Justice.* Cambridge, MA: Harvard University Press.

Raworth, K. (2017). *Doughnut Economics. Seven Ways to Think Like a 21st-Century Economist.* Cornerstone.

Reed, I.A. (2013). 'Power: Relational, Discursive, and Performative Dimensions', *Sociological Theory*, 31(3):193–218.

Reich, R.B. (2020). *The System. Who Rigged It, How We Fix It.* London: Picador.

Reich, R.B. (2018). *The Common Good.* New York: Vintage Books.

Reinalda, B. (Ed.) (2013). *Routledge Handbook of International Organization.* London and New York: Routledge.

Reinecke, J. & Ansari, A. (2016). 'Taming wicked problems: The role of framing in the construction of corporate social responsibility', *Journal of Management Studies*, 53(3):299–329.

Reinert, E. (2007). *How Rich Countries Got Rich and Why Poor Countries Stay Poor.* Little, Brown Book Group.

Remington-Doucette, S. (2013). *Sustainable World: Approaches to Analyzing and Resolving Wicked Problems.* Kendall Hunt Publishing.

Rennings, K. (2000). 'Redefining innovation – eco-innovation research and the contribution from ecological economics', *Ecological Economics,* 32(2):319–332.

Riccaboni, A. & Leone, E.L. (2010). 'Implementing strategies through management control systems: the case of sustainability', *International Journal of Productivity and Performance Management*, 59(2):130–144.

Rifkin, J. (2011). *The Third Industrial Revolution. How Lateral Power is Transforming Energy, the Economy, and the World.* New York: Palgrave Macmillan.

Rittel, H.W.J. & Webber, M.M. (1973). 'Dilemmas in a general theory of planning', *Policy Sciences*, 4(2):155–169.

Ritzer, G.D. (1993). *The McDonaldization of Society. An Investigation into the Changing Character of Contemporary Social Life.* Pine Forge Press.

Rivera-Santos, M., Rufin, C. & Kolk, A. (2012). 'Bridging the institutional divide: Partnerships in subsistence markets', *Journal of Business Research*, 65(12):1721–1727.

Roberts, N.C. (2000). 'Wicked Problems and Network Approaches to Resolution', *The International Public Management Review*, 1(1):1–19.

Rodrik, D. (2011). *The Globalization Paradox: Democracy and the Future of the World Economy.* New York and London: W.W. Norton.

Rodrik, D., Subramanian, A. & Trebbi, F. (2004). 'Institutions Rule: The Primacy of Institutions Over Geography and Integration in Economic Development', *Journal of Economic Growth*, 9(2):131–165.

Rogers, P. (2009). 'Matching impact evaluation design to the nature of the intervention and the purpose of the evaluation', *Journal of Development Effectiveness*, (1):217–226.

Rogerson, A., with Calleja, R. (2019). *Mobilising Data for the SDGs: How could Data Acceleration Facility help, and how might it work?* Paris 21 Discussion Paper N°. 15, January.

Rosling, H., with Rosling, O. & Rosling Rönnlund, A. (2018). *Factfulness: Ten Reasons We're Wrong About the World – and Why Things Are Better Than You Think.* Flariton Books.

Rotmans, J. (2017). *Change of Era. Our world in transition.* Amsterdam: Boom Uitgevers.

Ruigrok, W. & Van Tulder, R. (1995). *The Logic of International Restructuring.* London: Routledge.

Sachs, J.D. (2015). *The Age of Sustainable Development.* New York: Columbia University Press.

Sachs, J.D, Kroll, C., Lafortune, G., Fuller, G. & Woelm, F. (2021). *Sustainable Development Report 2021. The Decade of Action for the Sustainable Development Goals.* Cambridge: Cambridge University Press. DOI 10.1017/9781009106559.

Sachs, J.D., Schmidt-Traub, G., Kroll, C., Lafortune, G. & Fuller, G. (2019). *Sustainable Development Report 2019.* New York: Bertelsmann Stiftung and Sustainable Development Solutions Network (SDSN), June.

Sachs, J.D., Schmidt-Traub, G., Mazzucato, M., Messner, D., Nakicenovic, N. & Rockström, J. (2019a). 'Six Transformations to Achieve the Sustainable Development Goals', *Nature Sustainability*, 2(9):805–814.

Salancik, G.R. & Pfeffer, J. (1977). 'Who Gets Power – And How They Hold on to It: A Strategic-Contingency Model of Power', *Organizational Dynamics*, Winter 77, 5(3):3–21.

Salwasser, H. (2004). 'Confronting the implications of wicked problems: changes needed in Sierra Nevada National Forest planning and problem solving. In: Murphy, D.D. & Stine, P.A. (Eds.), *Proceedings of the Sierra Nevada Science Symposium 2002*; General technical report PSW-GTR-193, USDA Forest Service, Kings Beach, CA: 7–22.

Samuelson, P.A. (1954). 'The Pure Theory of Public Expenditure', *The Review of Economics and Statistics*, 36(4):387–389.

SASB (2020). 'Exposure draft of the SASB Conceptual Framework', August 28, Sustainability Accounting Standards Board.

Schaltegger, S., Hansen, E.G. & Lüdeke-Freund, F. (2016). 'Business Models for Sustainability: Origins, Present Research, and Future Avenues', *Organization & Environment* 29(1):3–10.

Schaltegger, S., Harms, D., Windolph, S.E. & Hörisch, J. (2014). 'Involving Corporate Functions: Who contributes to Sustainable Development?', *Sustainability,* 6(5):3064–3085.

Schaltegger, S., Lüdeke-Freund, F. & Hansen, E.G. (2012). 'Business Cases for Sustainability: The Role of Business Model Innovation for Corporate Sustainability', *International Journal of Innovation and Sustainable Development*, 6(2):95–119.

Scharlemann, J., Brock, R., Balfour, N., Brown, C., Burgess, N., Guth, M., Ingram, D., Lane, R., Martin, J., Wicander, S. & Kapos, V. (2020). 'Towards understanding interactions between Sustainable Development Goals: the role of environment-human linkages', *Sustainability Science* (15):1573–1584.

Schenk, H. (2005). 'Organisational Economics in an Age of Restructuring, or: How Corporate Strategies Can Harm Your Economy'. In: De Gijsel, P. & Schenk, H. (Eds.) *Multidisciplinary Economics*, (pp. 333–365). Kluwer Academic Publishers.

Schlosser, E. (2005). *Fast Food Nation. The Dark Side of the All-American Meal.* Harper Perennial.

Schneider, A., Wickert, C. & Marti, E. (2017). 'Reducing Complexity by Creating Complexity: A Systems Theory Perspective on How Organizations Respond to Their Environments', *Journal of Management Studies*, 54(2):182–208.

Schoeneborn, D., Morsing, M. & Crane, A. (2020). 'Formative Perspectives on the Relation Between CSR Communication and CSR Practices: Pathways for Walking, Talking, and T(w)alking', *Business & Society*, 59(1):5–33.

Schoenherr, T. (2012). 'The role of environmental management in sustainable business development: A multi-country investigation', *International Journal of Production Economics*, 140(1):114–128.

Schoenmaker, D. & Schramade, W. (2019). *Principles of Sustainable Finance*. Oxford: Oxford University Press.

Schönherr, N., Findler, F. & Marinuzzi, A. (2017). 'Exploring the Interface of CSR and the Sustainable Development Goals', *Transnational Corporations*, 24(3):33–47.

Schroeder, P., Anggraeni, K. & Weber, U. (2018). 'The Relevance of Circular Economy Practices to the Sustainable Development Goals', *Journal of Industrial Ecology*, 23(1):77–95.

Schultz, M., Hatch, M.J. & Holten Larsen, M. (Eds.) (2000). *The Expressive Organization. Linking Identity, Reputation and the Corporate Brand*. Oxford: Oxford University Press.

Schwab, K. (2016). *The Fourth Industrial Revolution*. New York: Crown Business.

Schwartz, B. (2004). *The Paradox of Choice. Why More is Less*. HarperCollins Publishers.

SDSN-TReNDS (2019). *Counting on The World to Act. A Roadmap for Governments to Achieve Modern Data Systems for Sustainable Development*. Report by the Sustainable Development Solutions Network's Thematic Research Network on Data and Statistics (SDSN TReNDS).

Seitanidi, M., & Crane, A. (Eds.) (2014). *Social Partnerships and Responsible Business. A research handbook*. London: Routledge.

Sekerka, L. (2020). 'A strength-based approach to responsible management: professional moral courage and moral competency'. In: Laasch, O, Suddaby, R. Freeman, R.E. & Jamali, D. (Eds.), *Research Handbook of Responsible Management*, (pp. 549–565). Cheltenham: Edward Elgar.

Seuring, S. & Müller, M. (2008). 'From a literature review to a conceptual framework for sustainable supply chain management', *Journal of Cleaner Production,* 16(15):1699–1710.

Sharma, R. (2016). *The Rise and Fall of Nations. Forces of Change in the Post-Crisis World*. W. W. Norton & Company.

Shaxson, N. (2019). 'Tackling Tax Havens. The billions attracted by tax havens do harm to sending and receiving nations alike', *Finance & Development*, 56(3):7–10.

Sheth, J. & Parvatiyar, A. (2021). 'Sustainable Marketing: Market-Driving, Not Market-Driven', *Journal of Macromarketing*, 41(1):150–165.

Shift & WBCSD (2018). *The Human Rights Opportunity. 15 real-life cases of how business is contributing to the Sustainable Development Goals by putting people first*. New York: Shift.

Siegrist, M., Bowman, G., Mervine, E & Southam, C. (2020). 'Embedding environmental and sustainability into corporate financial decision-making', *Accounting & Finance*, (60):129–147.

Simon, D.H. & Prince, J.T. (2016). 'The effect of competition on toxic pollution releases', *Journal of Environmental Economics and Management*, (79):40–54.

Simons, L. & Nijhof, A. (2021). *Changing the game. Sustainable Market Transformation Strategies to Understand and Tackle the Big and Complex Sustainability Challenges of our Generation*. London and New York: Routledge.

Singh, K. & Ilge, B. (Eds.) (2016). *Rethinking Bilateral Investment Treaties: Critical Issues and Policy Choices*. Both Ends, Madyam, and Centre for Research on Multinational Corporations (SOMO). New Delhi: KS Designers.

Sinkovics, N., Sinkovics, R.R. & Archie-Acheampong, J. (2021). 'The business responsibility matrix: a diagnostic tool to aid the design of better interventions for achieving the SDGs', *Multinational Business Review*, 29(1):1–20.

Slawinski, N. & Bansal, P. (2012). 'A Matter of Time: The Temporal Perspectives of Organizational Responses to Climate Change', *Organization Studies*, 33(11):1537–1563.

Smith N.C. & Jarisch, D. (2019). 'GSK: Profits, Patents and Patients: Access to Medicines'. In: Lenssen G., Smith N. (Eds.) *Managing Sustainable Business*. Dordrecht: Springer.

Smith, W.K., Gonin, M. & Besharov, M.L. (2013). 'Managing Social-Business Tensions: A Review and Research Agenda for Social Enterprise', *Business Ethics Quarterly* 23(3):407–442.

Soper, K. (2008). 'Alternative Hedonism, cultural theory and the role of aesthetic revisioning', *Cultural Studies*, 22(5):567–587.

Soppe, A. (2004). 'Sustainable Corporate Finance', *Journal of Business Ethics*, 53(1):213–224.

Spencer, F. (2013). 'Turning Wicked Problems into Wicked Opportunities', *Futurist Forum*, 15 May.

Stacey, R.D. & Mowles, C. (2015). *Strategic Management and Organisational Dynamic. The challenge of complexity to ways of thinking about Organisations* (7th edition). Essex: Pearson.

Stadtler, L. & Probst, G. (2011). 'How broker organizations can facilitate public–private partnerships for development', *European Management Journal*, 30(1):32–46.

Stafford-Smith, M., Griggs, D., Gaffney, O., Ullah, F., Reyers, B., Kanie, N., Stigson, B., Shrivastava, P., Leach, M. & O'Connell, D. (2017). 'Integration: the key to implementing the Sustainable Development Goals', *Sustainability Science*, 12(6):911–919.

Stahl, G.K., Brewster, C.J., Collings, D.G. & Hajro, A. (2020). 'Enhancing the role of human resource management in corporate sustainability and social responsibility: A multi-stakeholder, multidimensional approach to HRM', *Human Resource Management Review*, (30):100708.

Steiner, G.A. & Steiner, J.F. (2000). *Business, Government and Society*, 9th edition. New York: McGraw Hill.

Stiglitz, J.E. (2019). *People, Power, and Profits: Progressive Capitalism for an Age of Discontent*. New York: Allen Lane.

Stiglitz, J.E. (2018). *Globalization and its Discontents Revisited – Anti-Globalization in the Era of Trump*. New York: Norton.

Stiglitz, J.E., Sen, A. & Fitoussi J.P. (2009). *Mismeasuring Our Lives: Why GDP Doesn't Add Up*. The report by the commission on the measurement of economic performance and social progress. New York: The New York Press.

Stigson, B. (2002). *WBCSD Sector Projects*. Geneva: WBCSD.

Stott, L. (Ed.) (2019). *Shaping Sustainable Change. The Role of Partnership Brokering in Optimising Collaborative Action*. London: Routledge.

Streeten, P.P. (2001). 'Comment'. In: Meier, G.M. & Stiglitz, J.E. (Eds.). *Frontiers of Development Economics. The Future in Perspective*, (pp. 87–93). New York: World Bank and Oxford University Press.

Strijker-van Asperen, Z.M. & Van Tulder, R. (2016). *Wicked Problems Plaza. Principles and Practices for Effective Multi-Stakeholder Dialogue*. Rotterdam: The Partnerships Resource Centre (PrC), RSM-Erasmus University.

Suchman, M.C. (1995). 'Managing legitimacy: strategic and institutional approaches', *Academy of Management Review*, 20(3):571–610.

Sukhdev, P. (2012). *Corporation 2020. Transforming Business for Tomorrow's World*. Washington: Island Press.

Surasky, J. (2019). 'Towards Second-Generation Voluntary National Reviews', IISD SDG Knowledge Hub, 17 October. Retrieved from: http://sdg.iisd.org/commentary/guest-articles/towards-second-generation-voluntary-national-reports/.

Teece, D. (2007). 'Explicating dynamic capabilities. The nature and microfoundations of (sustainable) enterprise performance', *Strategic Management Journal*, 28(13): 1319–1350.

Tennyson, R. (2019). 'What do partnership brokers do'. In: Stott, L. (ed.). *Shaping Sustainable Change. The Role of Partnership Brokering in Optimising Collaborative Action*, pp.20–34. London: Routledge/Greenleaf Publishing.

Tennyson, R. (2003). *The Partnering Toolkit.* Bangladesh: The Partnering Initiative.

Tennyson, R. & Mundy, J. (2019). *Brokering Better Partnerships Handbook.* London: Partnership Brokers Association.

Termeer, C.J.A.M., Dewulf, A. & Biesbroek, R. (2019). 'A critical assessment of the wicked problem concept: relevance and usefulness for policy science and practice', *Policy and Society*, 38(2):167–179.

Thaler, R.H. (2016). *Behavioral Economics. Past, Present and Future.* Chicago: University of Chicago Press.

Thaler, R.H. & Sunstein, C.R. (2008). *Nudge: Improving decisions about health, wealth and happiness.* New Haven, CT: Yale University Press.

The Economist (2018). 'The missing 235m. Why India needs women to work', 7 July.

The Economist (2018). 'Economists understand little about the causes of growth', 14 April.

Thornton, P.H., Ocasio, W. & Lounsbury, M. (2013). *The Institutional Logics Perspective: A New Approach to Culture, Structure, and Process*, Oxford University Press.

Tidd, J. (2021). 'A review and critical assessment of the ISO56002 innovation management systems standard: evidence and limitations', *International Journal of Innovation Management*, 25(1).

Tidd, J. & Bessant, J. (2021*). Managing innovation. Integrating technological, market and organizational change,* 7th edition, Wiley.

Tirole, J. (2017). *Economics for the Common Good.* Princeton, NJ: Princeton University Press.

Trevor, J. & Varcoe, B. (2017). 'How Aligned Is Your Organization?', *Harvard Business Review Digital Articles*, February.

True Price, Deloitte, EY & PwC (2017). *The Business Case for True Pricing; Why you will benefit from measuring, monetizing and improving your impact,* second edition.

TWI2050 (2019). *The Digital Revolution and Sustainable Development: Opportunities and Challenges.* Report prepared by The World In 2050 Initiative. Laxenburg, Austria: International Institute for Applied Systems Analysis (IIASA).

TWI2050 (2018). *Transformations to Achieve the Sustainable Development Goals.* Report prepared by The World In 2050 Initiative. Laxenburg, Austria: International Institute for Applied Systems Analysis (IIASA).

UN (2020). *Shared Responsibility, Global Solidarity: Responding to the socio-economic impacts of COVID-19*, March. New York: United Nations.

UN (2019). *The Report of the Secretary General: The Special Edition of the Sustainable Development Goals Progress Report.* New York: United Nations.

UN (2019a). *United Nations Secretary-General's Roadmap for Financing the 2030 Agenda for Sustainable Development 2019–2021*, July. New York: United Nations.

UN (2018). *The Sustainable Development Goals Report 2018.* New York: United Nations.

UN (2015). *Transforming Our World: The 2050 Agenda for Sustainable Development.* New York: United Nations.

UN (2012). *The Future We Want.* Outcome document of the United Nations Conference on Sustainable Development, Rio de Janeiro, Brazil, 20–22 June 2012. A/RES/66/288. New York: United Nations.

UN (2008). *Clarifying the concepts of 'sphere of influence' and 'complicity'*, Report of the Special Representative of the Secretary-General on the Issue of Human Rights and Transnational Corporations and Other Business Enterprises, A/HRC/8/16.

UN (2003). *Draft Norms on Responsibilities of Transnational Corporations and Other Business Enterprises with Regard to Human Rights.* Geneva: United Nations, 30 May.

UN (1995). *Report of the World Summit for Social Development, Copenhagen, 6–12 March 1995.* A/Conf.166/9, 19 April 1995. New York: United Nations.

UN (1992). *Convention on Biological Diversity*, New York: United Nations. Retrieved from: https://www.cbd.int/doc/legal/cbd-en.pdf.

UNCTAD (2019). 'Taking Stock of IIA Reform: Recent Developments', *International Investment Agreements (IIA) Issues Note*, Issue 3, June 2019.

UNCTAD (2015). *Investment Policy Framework for Sustainable Development*. New York and Geneva: United Nations Conference on Trade and Development.

UNCTAD (2014). *World Investment Report 2014. Investing in the SDGs: An Action Plan*. Geneva: United Nations Conference on Trade and Development.

UNCTAD (2002). 'Are some TNCs bigger than countries?', *World Investment Report 2002. Transnational Corporations and Export Competitiveness* (pp. 90–91). Geneva: United Nations Conference on Trade and Development.

UN DESA (2020). *World Economic Situation and Prospects 2020*. New York: United Nations.

UN DESA (2020a). *World Social Report 2020. Inequality In A Rapidly Changing World*. New York: United Nations.

UN DESA (2019). *The Sustainable Development Goals Report 2019*. New York: United Nations.

UN DESA (2019a). *Sustainable Development Outlook 2019. Gathering storms and silver linings. An overview of SDG challenges*. United Nations Department of Economic and Social Affairs.

UN DESA (2019b). *Handbook for the preparation of Voluntary National Reviews. The 2019 Edition*. United Nations Department of Economic and Social Affairs.

UN DESA (2019c). *2030 Agenda Partnership Accelerator*, United Nations Department of Economic and Social Affairs. New York.

UNDP (2021). *SDG Impact Standards Enterprises. Integrating impact management into Enterprises' decision-making to optimize their contributions to sustainable development and the SDGs*. Second public consultation draft, March.

UNDP (2017). *Institutional and Coordination Mechanisms. Guidance Note on Facilitating Integration and Coherence for SDG Implementation*. New York: United Nations Development Programme.

UNDP (2008). *Creating Value for All: Strategies for Doing Business with the Poor*. New York: United Nations Development Programme.

UN ECOSOC (2019). *Report of the Inter-Agency and Expert Group on Sustainable Development Goal Indicators*, UN Statistical Commission 51st Session, E/CN.3/2020/2, 20 December 2019.

UNEP (2019). *Measuring Progress: Towards Achieving the Environmental Dimension of the SDGs*. Nairobi: United Nations Environment Programme.

UNFSS (2020). *Scaling up Voluntary Sustainability Standards through Sustainable Public Procurement and Trade Policy*. 4th Flagship Report of the United Nations Forum on Sustainability Standards (UNFSS/4/2020).

UNGA (2018). *Repositioning the United Nations development system in the context of the quadrennial comprehensive policy review of operational activities for development of the United Nations system*, Seventy-second session, A/RES/72/279, 1 June 2018.

UNGA (2016). *Critical milestones towards coherent, efficient and inclusive follow-up and review at the global level – Report of the Secretary-General*, seventieth session, A/70/684, 15 January 2016.

UNGA (2016a). *Follow-up and review of the 2030 Agenda for Sustainable Development at the global level*, seventieth session, A/RES/70/299, 18 August 2016.

UN Global Compact (2020). 'UN Global Compact defines new level of ambition for corporate sustainability', 9 June 2020. https://www.unglobalcompact.org/news/4575-06-09-2020.

UN Global Compact & DNV GL (2020). *Uniting Business in the Decade of Action. Building on 20 Years of Progress*. UN Global Compact 20th Anniversary Progress Report.

UN Global Compact & Russell Reynolds Associates (2020). *Leadership for the Decade of Action*, New York.

UN Global Compact & Accenture Strategy (2019). *The Decade to Deliver. A Call to Business Action. The United Nations Global Compact – Accenture Strategy CEO Study on Sustainability 2019*, September.

UN Global Compact & Accenture Strategy (2016). *The United Nations Global Compact – Accenture Strategy CEO Study 2016. Agenda 2030: A Window of Opportunity*, June.

UN Global Compact & Accenture Strategy (2013). *The UN Global Compact – Accenture CEO Study on Sustainability 2013. Architects of a Better World*. September.

UNHCR (2020). *Global Trends Forced Displacement in 2019*. Copenhagen: United Nations High Commissioner for Refugees.

UN Independent Group of Scientists (2019). *Global Sustainable Development Report 2019: The Future is Now – Science for Achieving Sustainable Development*. New York: United Nations.

UN Inter-agency Task Force on Financing for Development (2020). *Financing for Sustainable Development Report 2020*. New York: United Nations.

UN Inter-agency Task Force on Financing for Development (2019). *Financing for Sustainable Development Report 2019*. New York: United Nations.

UN World Commission on Environment and Development (1987). *Our Common Future: Report of the World Commission on Environment and Development*. Oxford: Oxford University Press.

Unerman, J., Bebbington, J. & O'Dwyer, B. (2018). 'Corporate reporting and accounting for externalities', *Accounting and Business Research*, 48(5):497–522.

Utting, P. & Zammit, A. (2009). 'United Nations-Business Partnerships: Good Intentions and Contradictory Agendas', *Journal of Business Ethics*, 90(1):39–56.

Uzsoki, D. (2020). *Sustainable Investing: Shaping the future of finance*. Winnipeg, Manitoba CA: International Institute for Sustainable Development (IISD), February.

Vachani, S. & Smith, N.C. (2004). 'Socially Responsible Pricing: Lessons from the Pricing of AIDS Drugs in Developing Countries', *California Management Review*, 47(1):117–144.

Valente, M. (2012). 'Theorizing Firm Adoption of Sustaincentrism', *Organization Studies*, 33(4):563–591.

Van Dijk, S., Hillen, M., Panhuijsen, S. & Sprong, N. (2020) *Social Enterprises as Influencers of the Broader Business Community. A scoping study*. Amsterdam: Social Enterprise NL.

Van Egmond, K. (2014). *Sustainable Civilization*. London: Palgrave Macmillan.

Vangen, S. (2017). 'Developing Practice-Oriented Theory on Collaboration: A Paradox Lens', *Public Administration Review*, 77(2):263–272.

Vangen, S. & Huxham, C. (2012). 'The tangled web: unravelling the principle of common goals in collaborations', *Journal of Public Administration Research and Theory*, (22):731–760.

Van Huijstee, M. & Glasbergen, P. (2010). 'Business–NGO interactions in a multi-stakeholder context', *Business and Society Review*, 115(3):249–284.

Van Oorschot, M.M.P., Kok, M.T.J. & Van Tulder, R. (2020). *Business for biodiversity. Mobilising business towards net positive impact*. PBL Netherlands Environmental Assessment Agency, The Hague.

Van Riel, C. & Fombrun, C. (2007). *Essentials of Corporate Communication: Implementing Practices for Effective Reputation Management*. London: Routledge.

Van Riel, C. & Blackburn, C. (1995). *Principles of Corporate Communication*. Prentice Hall.

Van Staveren, I. (2014). *Economics After the Crisis. An Introduction to Economics from a Pluralist and Global Perspective*. London: Routledge.

Van Tulder, R. (2020). 'In search of an integrative approach to managing distance', *EIBAzine*, Spring-Summer, 26:8–16.

Van Tulder, R. (2020a). 'The multinational perspective on responsible management: managing risk-responsibility trade-offs across borders'. In: Laasch, O., Suddaby, R., Freeman, R.E. & Jamali, D. (Eds.), *Research Handbook of Responsible Management*, (pp. 242–259). Cheltenham: Edward Elgar Publishing.

Van Tulder, R. (2018). *Business & The Sustainable Development Goals: A Framework for Effective Corporate Involvement*. Rotterdam: Rotterdam School of Management, Erasmus University.

Van Tulder, R. (2018a). *Getting all the Motives Right. Driving International Corporate Responsibility (ICR) to the Next Level*. Rotterdam: SMO.

Van Tulder, R. (2018b) *Skill Sheets. An Integrated Approach to Research, Study and Management*. Third Edition. Amsterdam: Pearson Education.

Van Tulder, R. (2017). 'Rescuing the Collaborative Paradigm from its supporters?', *Annual Review of Social Partnerships*, (12):27–31.

Van Tulder, R. (2015). 'Getting all motives right: a holistic approach to internalization motives of companies', *Multinational Business Review*, 23(1):36–56.

Van Tulder, R. (2011). 'Crisis . . . what crisis? (revisited): Exploring multinational enterprises' responsiveness to the financial crisis'. In: Claes, D.H. & Knutsen, C.H. (Eds.), *Governing the Global Economy: Politics, Institutions and Economic Development*, (pp. 247–276). London: Routledge.

Van Tulder, R., Rodrigues, S.B., Mirza, H. & Sexsmith, K. (2021). 'The UN's Sustainable Development Goals: Can multinational enterprises lead the Decade of Action?', *Journal of International Business Policy*, 4(1):1–21.

Van Tulder, R. & Van Mil, E. (2020). 'Responsible governance: broadening the corporate governance discourse to include positive duties and collective action'. In: Laasch, O., Suddaby, R., Freeman, R.E. & Jamali, D. (Eds.), *Research Handbook of Responsible Management* (pp. 175–194). Cheltenham: Edward Elgar Publishing.

Van Tulder, R., Verbeke, A. & Jancowska, B. (Eds.) (2020). *International Business in a VUCA World. The Changing Role of States and Firms*. Progress in International Business Research, Volume 14. Bingley: Emerald.

Van Tulder, R, & Kahlen, T. (2019). 'Creating a better fit: a scoping role for partnership brokers'. In: Stott, L. (ed.). *Shaping Sustainable Change. The Role of Partnership Brokering in Optimising Collaborative Action* (pp. 35–50). London: Routledge.

Van Tulder, R. & Lucht, L. (2019). 'Reversing materiality: From a Reactive Matrix to a Proactive SDG Agenda'. In: Bocken, N., Ritala, P., Albareda, L. & Verburg, R. (Eds.), *Innovation for Sustainability: Business Transformations Towards a Better World* (pp. 271–289). Cham: Palgrave Macmillan.

Van Tulder, R. & Roman, M. (2019). 'Re-assessing risk in international markets: a strategic, operational, and sustainability taxonomy'. In: Leonidou, L.C., Katsikeas, C.S., Samiee, S. & Leonidou, C.N. (Eds.), *Socially Responsible International Business: Critical Issues and the Way Forward* (pp. 158–183). Cheltenham UK: Edward Elgar.

Van Tulder, R. & Keen, N. (2018). 'Capturing Collaborative Challenges: Designing Complexity-Sensitive Theories of Change for Cross-Sector Partnerships', *Journal of Business Ethics*, 150(2):315–332.

Van Tulder, R., Seitanidi, M.M., Crane, A., & Brammer, S. (2016). 'Enhancing the Impact of Cross-Sector Partnerships. Four Impact Loops for Channeling Partnership Studies', *Journal of Business Ethics*, 135(1):1–17.

Van Tulder, R. & Pfisterer, S. (2014). 'Creating partnering space: exploring the right fit for sustainable development partnerships'. In: Seitanidi, M.M. & Crane, A. (Eds.), *Social Partnerships and Responsible Business. A research handbook*, (pp. 105–125). London: Routledge.

Van Tulder, R., Van Tilburg, R., Francken, M. & Da Rosa, A. (2014). *Managing the Transition to a Sustainable Enterprise. Lessons from Frontrunner Companies*. London: Routledge.

Van Tulder, R., Verbeke, A. & Strange, R. (Eds.) (2013). *International Business and Sustainable Development.* Progress in International Business Research, Volume 8. Bingley: Emerald.

Van Tulder, R. & Maas, K. (2012). *The partnerships effectiveness model.* Rotterdam: Partnerships Resource Centre.

Van Tulder, R., Van Wijk, J. & Kolk, A. (2009). 'From Chain Liability to Chain Responsibility: MNE Approaches to Implement Safety and Health Codes in International Supply Chains', *Journal of Business Ethics,* (85):399–412.

Van Tulder, R. with Van der Zwart, A. (2006). *International Business-Society Management. Linking Corporate Responsibility and Globalization.* London: Routledge.

Van Tulder, R., Kaptein, M., Van Mil, E.M. & Schilpzand, R. (2004). *De Strategische Stakeholderdialoog. Opkomst, succesfactoren, toekomst.* Erasmus University Rotterdam, Schuttelaar & Partners.

Van Vuuren, D., Kriegler, E., Riahi, K., Zimm, C., Creutzig, F., et al. (2018). 'Sustainable Development Pathways'. In: TWI2050 (2018). *Transformations to Achieve the Sustainable Development Goals.* Report prepared by The World in 2050 initiative, (pp. 69–105). Laxenburg, Austria: International Institute for Applied Systems Analysis (IIASA).

Van Zanten, J.A. & Van Tulder, R. (2021). 'Analyzing Companies' Interactions with the SDGs through Network Analysis: Four Corporate Sustainability Imperatives', *Business Strategy and the Environment,* 30(5):2396–2420.

Van Zanten, J.A. & Van Tulder, R. (2020). 'Towards nexus-based governance: defining interactions between economic activities and Sustainable Development Goals (SDGs)', *International Journal of Sustainable Development & World Ecology,* 28(3):210–226.

Van Zanten, J.A. & Van Tulder, R. (2020a). 'Beyond COVID-19: Applying "SDG logics" for resilient transformations', *Journal of International Business Policy,* (3):451–464.

Van Zanten, J.A. & Van Tulder, R. (2018). 'Multinational enterprises and the Sustainable Development Goals: An institutional approach to corporate engagement', *Journal of International Business Policy,* (1):208–233.

Varey, R.J. & Pirson, M. (2014). *Humanistic Marketing.* London: Palgrave Macmillan.

Vellema, S., Schouten, G. & Van Tulder, R. (2019). 'Four capacities configuring the transformative power of partnering for inclusive development', *Development Policy Review,* 38(6):710–727.

Vernon, R. (1971). *Sovereignty at Bay: The Multinational Spread of US Enterprises.* New York: Basic Books.

Verweij, M., Ney, S. & Thompson, M. (2011). 'Clumsy solutions for a wicked world'. In: Verweij, M. (2011). *Clumsy Solutions for a Wicked World: How to Improve Global Governance.* Basingstoke: Palgrave Macmillan.

Verweij, M., Douglas, M., Ellis, R., Engel, C., Hendriks, F., Lohmann, S. Ney, S. Rayner, S. & Thompson, M. (2006). 'Clumsy Solutions for a Complex World: The Case of Climate Change', *Public Administration,* 84(4):817–843.

Visser, W. (Ed.) (2016). *The World Guide to Sustainable Enterprise. Four Volume Set.* London: Routledge.

Visser, W. & Tolhurst, N. (Eds.) (2010). *The World Guide to CSR. A Country-by-Country Analysis of Corporate Sustainability and Responsibility.* London: Routledge.

Voorn, B., Van Genugten, M. & Van Thiel, S. (2019). 'Multiple principals, multiple problems: Implications for effective governance and a research agenda for joint service delivery', *Public Administration,* 97(3):671–685.

Vurro, C., Dacin, M.T. & Perrini, F. (2010). 'Institutional Antecedents of Partnering for Social Change: How Institutional Logics Shape Cross-Sector Social Partnerships', *Journal of Business Ethics,* 94(1):39–53.

Waddell, S. (2011). *Global Action Networks. Creating our Future Together.* Milan: Bocconi University Press, Palgrave MacMillan.

Waddell, S. (2000). 'New institutions for the practice of corporate citizenship: historical, inter-sectoral, and developmental perspectives', *Business and Society Review*, 105(1)107–126.

Waddock, S., Meszoely, G.M., Waddell, S. & Dentoni, D. (2015). 'The complexity of wicked problems in large scale change', *Journal of Organizational Change Management*, 28(6):993–1012.

Walls, J.L., Phan, P.H. & Berrone, P. (2011). 'Measuring Environmental Strategy: Construct Development, Reliability, and Validity', *Business & Society*, 50(1):71–115.

Wang, S., Su, D., Ma, M. & Kuang, W. (2021). 'Sustainable product development and service approach for application in industrial lightning products', *Sustainable Production and Consumption,* (27):1808–1821.

Wartick, S. & Wood, D. (1999). *International Business and Society.* Oxford: Blackwell Publishers.

Wassmer, U. (2010). 'Alliance Portfolios: A Review and Research Agenda', *Journal of Management*, 36(1):141–171.

Watkins, A. & Stratenus, I. (2016). *Crowdocracy: The End of Politics?* Wicked & Wise Series. Kent: Urbane Publications.

WBCSD (2021). *Vision 2050. Time to Transform. How business can lead the transformations the world needs.* Geneva: World Business Council for Sustainable Development.

WBCSD (2020). *The consequences of COVID-19 for the decade ahead. Vision 2050 issue brief.* World Business Council for Sustainable Development, May.

WBCSD (2019). *Reporting matters. Navigating the landscape: a path forward for sustainability reporting. WBCSD 2019 Report.* Geneva: World Business Council for Sustainable Development.

WBCSD (2015). *Reporting matters. Redefining performance and disclosure. WBCSD 2015 Report.* Geneva: World Business Council for Sustainable Development.

WBCSD (2002) *Stakeholder dialogue: the WBCSD approach to engagement,* Switzerland.

WBCSD & DNV GL (2018). *Business and the SDGs: A survey of WBCSD members and Global Network partners.* World Business Council for Sustainable Development, July.

Weaver, G.R., Trevino, L.K. & Cochran, P.L. (1999). 'Integrated and decoupled corporate social performance: Management commitments, external pressures, and corporate ethics prac-tices', *Academy of Management Journal*, 42(5):539–552.

WEF (2020). *Measuring Stakeholder Capitalism: Towards Common Metrics and Consistent Reporting of Sustainable Value Creation*, White Paper. World Economic Forum, September.

WEF (2020a). *The Global Risks Report 2020.* Insight Report, 15th Edition. Geneva: World Economic Forum.

WEF (2020b). *Taking the Pulse of the New Economy. Chief Economists Outlook*, REF 080120. Geneva: World Economic Forum, January.

WEF (2020c). *The Future of Jobs Report 2020.* Geneva: World Economic Forum.

WEF (2016). *The Global Risks Report 2016.* Insight Report, 11th Edition, REF: 080116. Geneva: World Economic Forum.

Weiss, T.G. & Wilkinson, R. (Eds.) (2014). *International Organizations and Global Governance.* Abingdon: Routledge.

Weitz, N., Carlsen, H. & Trimmer, C. (2019). 'SDG Synergies: An approach for coherent 2030 Agenda implementation', May. Stockholm: Stockholm Environment Institute (SEI).

Weitz, N., Carlsen, H., Nilsson, M. & Skånberg, K. (2018). 'Towards systemic and contextual priority setting for implementing the 2030 Agenda', *Sustainability Science*, 13(2):531–48.

Weitz, N., Persson, Å., Nilsson, M. & Tenggren, S. (2015). *Sustainable Development Goals for Sweden: Insights on Setting a National Agenda.* SEI Working Paper No. 2015–10.

Weitz, N., Nilsson, M. & Davis, M. (2014). 'A Nexus Approach to the Post-2015 Agenda: Formulating Integrated Water, Energy, and Food SDGs', *SAIS Review of International Affairs*, 34(2):37–50.

Whetten, D.A. & Cameron, K.S. (2008). *Developing Management Skills*, 7th Edition. Upper Saddle River: Prentice Hall.

Whetten, D.A., Cameron, K.S. & Woods, M. (2000). *Developing Management Skills for Europe*, Second Edition. Pearson Education.

White, K., Habib, R. & Hardisty, D.J. (2019). 'How to SHIFT Consumer Behaviors to be More Sustainable: A Literature Review and Guiding Framework', *Journal of Marketing*, 83(3):22–49.

White, K. & Habib, R. (2018). *SHIFT. A review and framework for encouraging environmentally sustainable consumer behaviour*, Sitra Studies 132. Erweko, Helsinki.

Whitelock, V.G. (2019). 'Multidimensional environmental social governance sustainability framework: Integration, using a purchasing, operations, and supply chain management context', *Sustainable Development*, (27):923–931.

Whiteman, G. & Mamen, K. (2002). 'Examining justice and conflict between mining companies and indigenous peoples: Cerro Colorado and the Ngäbe-Buglé', *Journal of Business and Management*, 8(3):293–310.

Whitley, R. (1999). *Divergent Capitalisms. The Social Structuring and change of Business Systems*. Oxford: Oxford University Press.

Wildavsky, A. (1979). *Speaking Truth to Power. The Art and Craft of Policy Analysis*. New Brunswick: Transaction.

Wilkinson, R. (Ed.) (2005). *The Global Governance Reader*. London: Routledge.

Williams, A., Kennedy, S., Philipp, F. & Whiteman, G. (2017). 'Systems thinking: A review of sustainability management research', *Journal of Cleaner Production*, (148):866–881.

Williamson, O.E. (2008). 'Outsourcing: Transaction Cost Economics and Supply Chain Management', *Journal of Supply Chain Management*, 44(2):5–16.

Wilson-Grau, R., Kosterink, P. & Scheers, G. (2016). 'Outcome Harvesting: a developmental evaluation inquiry framework supporting the development of an international social change network'. In: Patton, M.Q., McKegg, K. & Wehipeihana, N. (Eds.), *Developmental Evaluation Exemplars. Principles in Practice* (pp. 192_216). New York: The Guilford Press.

Witt, M.A. & Jackson, G. (2016). 'Varieties of Capitalism and institutional comparative advantage: A test and reinterpretation', *Journal of International Business Studies*, 47(7):778–806.

Womack, J.P., Jones, D.T. & Roos, D. (1990). *The Machine that Changed the World*. New York: Rawson Associates.

Wood, D. (1991). 'Corporate Social Responsibility Revisited', *Academy of Management Review*, 16(4):691–718.

Wood, S. (2011). 'The Meaning of 'Sphere of Influence'. In: Henriques, A. (Ed.), *Understanding ISO 26000: A Practical Approach to Social Responsibility* (pp. 115–130). London, UK: British Standards Institution.

World Bank (2020). *Poverty and Shared Prosperity 2020. Reversals of Fortune*. Washington, DC: World Bank.

World Bank Group (2019). *Implementing the 2030 Agenda. 2018 Update*. Washington, DC: World Bank Group.

World Bank (2018). *Poverty and Shared Prosperity 2018: Piecing Together the Poverty Puzzle*. Washington, DC: World Bank Group.

World Bank (2012). *Inclusive Green Growth: The Pathway to Sustainable Development*. Washington, DC: World Bank Group.

World Bank (2008). *The Growth Report: Strategies for Sustained Growth and Inclusive Development*, Commission on Growth and Development. Washington, DC: World Bank.

World Bank (1997). *World Development Report 1997. The state in a changing world.* Oxford: Oxford University Press.

World Cooperative Monitor (2019). *Exploring The Cooperative Economy Report 2019.* International Cooperative Alliance (ICA) and the European Research Institute on Cooperative and Social Enterprises (Euricse), December.

World Food Programme (2020). *Global Report on Food Crises 2020*, April. Food Security Information Network (FSIN) and Global Network Against Food Crises.

Xiang, W.N. (2013). 'Working with wicked problems in socio-ecological systems: Awareness, acceptance, and adaptation', *Landscape and Urban Planning*, 110(1):1–4.

Ye, K. & Zhang, R. (2011). 'Do Lenders Value Corporate Social Responsibility? Evidence from China', *Journal of Business Ethics*, 104(2):1–10.

Young, D. & Reeves, M. (2020). 'The Quest for Sustainable Business Model Innovation', *BCG Henderson Institute Newsletter*, March 10.

Young, I.M. (2006). 'Responsibility and global justice: A social connection model', *Social Philosophy and Policy*, 23(1):102–130.

Young, O.R. (2017). 'Conceptualization: Goal Setting as a Strategy for Earth System Governance'. In: Kanie, N. & Biermann, F. (Eds.), *Governing through Goals: Sustainable Development Goals as Governance Innovation*, (pp. 31–52). Cambridge, Massachusetts: The MIT Press.

Yunus, M. (2007). *Creating a World Without Poverty: Social Business and the Future of Capitalism.* New York: Public Affairs.

Zadek, S. (2004). 'The Path to Corporate Responsibility', *Harvard Business Review*, 82(12):125–132+150.

Zhang, T., Fletcher, P.O, Gino, F. & Bazerman, M.H. (2015). 'Reducing Bounded Ethicality: How to Help Individuals Notice and Avoid Unethical Behavior'. *Organizational Dynamics* 44(4):310–317.

Zink, T. & Geyer, R. (2017). 'Circular Economy Rebound', *Journal of Industrial Ecology*, 21(3):593–602.

Zuboff, S. (2019). *The Age of Surveillance Capitalism: The Fight for a Human Future at the New Frontier of Power.* London: Profile Books.

INDEX

Please note that page references to Figures and Tables will be in *italics*, while references to Principles and explanatory content of the individual SDGs will be in **bold**. Footnotes are denoted by the letter 'n' and Note number following the page number.

scarcity/depletion 2, 24, 29, 37, 414, 693, 694, 704; strategic resource-seeking 413–414

responsibilities: impact-based 542, 544; influence-based 542; joint/shared 26, 144, 214, 217, 247–248, 355, *376*, 377, 528, 777; leverage-based 542, 544, 879; partial 216–217; primary/core 210–*211*, 315, 878; societal roles and responsibilities 209–224; *see also* duties; fiduciary duties; sphere of influence

responsibility: assign 213, 272–273; denying *see* denial; having *218–220*; having and taking 214–224; sharing *216, 222* –224 *see* collective action, joint/shared responsibilities; taking 220–221; orientation 275, 613, *614*, 621, 625, 626, 634 *see* avoiding harm; doing good; duties

responsibility matrix 615

responsible agency challenges 281, *282–284*

Responsible Business Conduct (RBC), OECD guidelines for multinational enterprises **388**, 411–413, 451; *see also* due diligence

responsible governance 269–273; 577–578, four levels of *315*; principles of **528**

responsible organizing *431*; principles **388**, 446–448; *see* ISO 26000 Social Responsibility

responsiveness: corporate 345; corporate social responsiveness 351, *352, 403*, 411, *507, 628, 784 see* CSR 2.0; integration-responsiveness grid 604; international corporate responsiveness (ICR 2.0) *605*; local 604, *605–606*, 608–609, 630; responsive capabilities 609; responsive route 666

rethinking: the business model 478–480, *498*, 574–575 *see* business model innovation; CSR 343–353; capitalism

496–497, 504; economics 32–33; management 29–30; the partnership portfolio 874–875, *886–887*; societal resilience 376–378

return: on investment (ROI) 392, 398, 404, 413, 434, 438, *486, 489*, 727; on sustainability investment (ROSI) 737, 747, 766; social return on investment (SROI) 39, 85, *486, 736*; societal return *736*; see *also* investment principle; integrated value

reversing materiality 477–480, 507, *508*, 514; outside-in perspective 333, 477; principle **458**; *see also* materiality

rewards; employee 722–724, *725*; financial reward for risk-taking 398; reward systems/policies 646, 706, 710, 712, 723; sharing 829; socialization of 223, 223n3; *see also* incentives

rights: collective bargaining 388, **395**, 635, 645, 719, **721**; EU Charter of Fundamental Rights 308n19; of freely-chosen employment 721; of Indigenous Peoples 266, 302; LGBTQ 702n23; to remedy 528, 542; and responsibilities 603; no right to be wrong 172; right to disagree 854, right-to-repair legislation 594n16; workers' right to organize 721; *see also* human rights

risk: aversion 282, *498*; avoidance xxxii; orientation *36, 51*, 574, 680–681, *689*, 769; reduction 412–413; risk-sharing 223, *279, 281, 284*, 388, 829, 837; risk-taking 223–224, 239, *279, 282*, 480, *498*

risk management: 292–294, 407, 475, 565, 680 –681; CSR 388; CSR Risk Barometer 292, 321, 633; Equator Principles 312, 734; financial 728, 738; *see also* due diligence

risk mitigation: 407, *571*, 621, *629*, 691, *693*, 696; *see also* externalities; risks

Tripartite Declaration of Principles concerning Multinational Enterprises and Social Policy **644, 722**

triple bottom line 39; Triple-P 70, 338, 348

Triumph 406

true: costs 220, 555, 704–705, *746*; cost accounting 644, 705n26, 739; price *489*, 592, 707; true price gap 704; true value accounting 739, 740, *746*; *see also* Capitals Coalition; monetization; protocols; value accounting

True Price 704, 705n25

trust: dividend 871–872; Edelman Trust Barometer 220n2, 225, 348, 352; high-trust society *36*, 225; low-trust society *36*, 769; OECD Trust in Business Initiative 322; restoring 238, 359, 364, 848; stakeholder 775, 776, 777, 782–783, *785*

trust-building 228, 247, 253, 338, 782–783, 829, 848–*849*

trust gap 224–228, 461, 464–467; overcoming 225–228; in selected countries *226–227*; societal *212*; *see also* institutional void

Twitter 13

Uber 12, *498*, 501, 502, 607n23

uncertainty 194–195, 196: analytical 23, 135, *158*, 163; creating 368; decision-making under 172–173, 572–573, 646; embracing 513; geopolitical 18, 19, 173; growing 9–13, 16–19, 117; institutional 12, *158*; managing 181, 756; phases of uncertainty reduction 757–760; regulatory 12; *see also* complexity dimensions; VUCA (Volatile, Uncertain, Complex, Ambiguous); wicked problems

UN Conference on Sustainable Development 39–40

UNCTAD (UN Conference on Trade and Development) 115n1, 121, *127*, 139,

305–306; International Investment Navigators 321; UNCTAD Investment Policy Framework for Sustainable Development 306, 321

UN Declaration on the Rights of Indigenous Peoples **266, 302**

UNDESA (UN Department of Economic and Social Affairs) 120, *127*, 235n7, *375–376*, 737, 827, 898; 2030 Agenda Partnership Accelerator 901; SDG Knowledge Platform 120, 147, 197

UNDP (UN Development Programme) 121, *127*, 643 Business Call to Action Impact Lab 813; SDG Impact Standards 662–663, *662*, 811; Mainstreaming, Acceleration, and Policy Support (MAPS) 121; SDG Investor Platform 797n62

unemployment *46*, 120, 372: protection against *726*; rates of 85; youth 792; *see also* employment, flexibilization of workforce; jobs; SDG8 (decent work and economic growth)

UNEP (UN Environment Programme) *127*; UNEP-FI Principles for Positive Impact Finance **644**, 733; UNEP-FI Principles for Responsible Banking (PRB) **644**, *731*, 733; UNEP-FI Principles for Sustainable Insurance (PSI) **644**, 733–734

UNESCO (UN Educational, Scientific and Cultural Organization) *127*, 128–129, 894n15

UNFSS (UN Forum on Sustainability Standards) 559, 564

UN Global Compact *see* Global Compact

UN Global Humanitarian Platform (GHP) 853; GHP Principles of Partnership (PoP) 853

UN Guiding Principles on Business and Human Rights **388**, 793

UNICEF (UN International Children's Emergency Fund) *127*, 721, 844n3

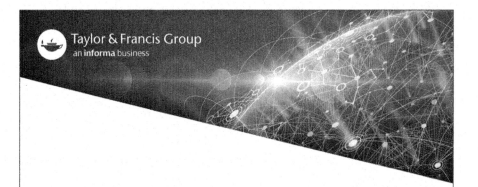